Collins
FRENCH
DICTIONARY

Published by Collins
An imprint of HarperCollins Publishers
Westerhill Road
Bishopbriggs
Glasgow G64 2QT

This Edition 2017

10 9 8 7 6 5 4 3 2 1

© HarperCollins Publishers 2017

ISBN 978-0-00-824116-2

Collins® is a registered trademark of
HarperCollins Publishers Limited

collinsdictionary.com

Typeset by Davidson Publishing
Solutions, Glasgow

Printed and bound in Great Britain by
Clays Ltd, St Ives plc

A catalogue record for this book is
available from the British Library.

If you would like to comment on any
aspect of this book, please contact us
at the given address or online.
E-mail: dictionaries@harpercollins.co.uk
 facebook.com/collinsdictionary
 @collinsdict

Acknowledgements

We would like to thank those authors
and publishers who kindly gave
permission for copyright material to
be used in the Collins Corpus. We
would also like to thank Times
Newspapers Ltd for providing
valuable data.

TABLE DES MATIÈRES   CONTENTS

PROJECT MANAGEMENT
Carol McCann

CONTRIBUTORS
Teresa Álvarez García
Gaëlle Amiot-Cadey
Sabine Citron
Cordelia Lilly
Val McNulty
Complexli
Jean-François Allan

COMPUTING
Thomas Callan

FOR THE PUBLISHER
Lucy Cooper
Kerry Ferguson
Ruth O'Donovan
Elaine Higgleton

SERIES EDITOR
Rob Scriven

Based on the first edition of
the Collins Gem French
Dictionary under the
direction of Pierre-Henri
Cousin.

INTRODUCTION

Nous sommes très heureux que vous ayez choisi ce dictionnaire
et espérons que vous aimerez l'utiliser et que vous en tirerez
profit au lycée, à la maison, en vacances ou au travail.

Cette introduction a pour but de vous donner quelques conseils
sur la façon d'utiliser au mieux votre dictionnaire, en vous
référant non seulement à son importante nomenclature
mais aussi aux informations contenues dans chaque
entrée. Ceci vous aidera à lire et à comprendre, mais aussi à
communiquer et à vous exprimer en anglais contemporain.

Au début du dictionnaire, vous trouverez la liste des
abréviations utilisées dans le texte et celle de la
transcription des sons par des symboles phonétiques.
Vous y trouverez également la liste des verbes irréguliers
en anglais, suivis d'une section finale sur les nombres
et sur les expressions de temps.

COMMENT UTILISER VOTRE DICTIONNAIRE
Ce dictionnaire offre une richesse d'informations et
utilise diverses formes et tailles de caractères, symboles,
abréviations, parenthèses et crochets. Les conventions et
symboles utilisés sont expliqués dans les sections qui suivent.

ENTRÉES
Les mots que vous cherchez dans le dictionnaire – les entrées
– sont classés par ordre alphabétique. Ils sont imprimés en
gras pour pouvoir être repérés rapidement. Les entrées
figurant en haut de page indiquent le premier (sur la page
de gauche) et le dernier mot (sur la page de droite) des deux
pages en question.

Des informations sur l'usage ou sur la forme de certaines
entrées sont données entre parenthèses, après la
transcription phonétique. Ces indications apparaissent sous
forme abrégée et en italiques (par ex. (*fam*), (*Comm*)).

Pour plus de facilité, les mots de la même famille sont regroupés sous la même entrée (**ronger, rongeur; accept, acceptance**) et apparaissent également en **gras**.

Les expressions courantes dans lesquelles apparaît l'entrée sont indiquées par des caractères romains gras différents (par exemple **retard** : [...] **avoir du ~**).

TRANSCRIPTION PHONÉTIQUE

La transcription phonétique de chaque entrée (indiquant sa prononciation) est indiquée entre crochets immédiatement après l'entrée (par ex. **fumer** [fyme]; **knee** [ni:]). La liste des symboles phonétiques figure page xiii.

TRADUCTIONS

Les traductions des entrées apparaissent en caractères ordinaires ; lorsque plusieurs sens ou usages coexistent, ces traductions sont séparées par un point-virgule. Vous trouverez des synonymes de l'entrée en italiques entre parenthèses avant les traductions (par ex. **poser** (*installer : moquette, carrelage*)) ou des mots qui fournissent le contexte dans lequel l'entrée est susceptible d'être utilisée (par ex. **poser** (*question*)).

MOTS-CLÉS

Une importance particulière est accordée à certains mots français et anglais qui sont considérés comme des « mots-clés » dans chacune des langues. Cela peut être dû à leur utilisation très fréquente ou au fait qu'ils ont divers types d'usage (par ex. **vouloir**, **plus**; **get**, **that**). L'utilisation de triangles et de chiffres aide à distinguer différentes catégories grammaticales et différents sens. D'autres renseignements utiles apparaissent en italiques et entre parenthèses dans la langue de l'utilisateur.

DONNÉES GRAMMATICALES

Les catégories grammaticales sont données sous forme abrégée et en italiques après la transcription phonétique (par ex. *vt*, *adv*, *conj*). Les genres des noms français sont indiqués de la manière suivante : *nm* pour un nom masculin et *nf* pour un nom féminin. Le féminin et le pluriel irréguliers de certains noms sont également indiqués (par ex. **directeur, -trice** ; **cheval, -aux**).

Le masculin et le féminin des adjectifs sont indiqués lorsque ces deux formes sont différentes (par ex. **noir, e**). Lorsque l'adjectif a un féminin ou un pluriel irrégulier, ces formes sont clairement indiquées (par ex. **net, nette**). Les pluriels irréguliers des noms, et les formes irrégulières des verbes anglais sont indiqués entre parenthèses, avant la catégorie grammaticale (par ex. **man** [...] (*pl* **men**) *n* ; **give** (*pt* **gave**; *pp* **~n**) *vt*).

INTRODUCTION

We are delighted that you have decided to buy this
dictionary and hope you will enjoy and benefit from
using it at school, at home, on holiday or at work.

This introduction gives you a few tips on how to get the most
out of your dictionary – not simply from its comprehensive
wordlist but also from the information provided in each entry.
This will help you to read and understand modern French,
as well as communicate and express yourself in the
language. This dictionary begins by listing the abbreviations
used in the text and illustrating the sounds shown by the
phonetic symbols. You will also find French verb forms,
followed by a final section on numbers and time expressions.

USING YOUR DICTIONARY
A wealth of information is presented in the dictionary,
using various typefaces, sizes of type, symbols, abbreviations and
brackets. The various conventions and symbols used are
explained in the following sections.

HEADWORDS
The words you look up in a dictionary – 'headwords' – are
listed alphabetically. They are printed in **bold** for rapid
identification. The headwords appearing at the top of each
page indicate the first (if it appears on a left-hand page) and
last word (if it appears on a right-hand page) dealt with on
the page in question.

Information about the usage or form of certain headwords is
given in brackets after the phonetic spelling. This usually
appears in abbreviated form and in italics (e.g. (*fam*), (*Comm*)).

Where appropriate, words related to headwords are grouped in
the same entry (**ronger, rongeur; accept, acceptance**) and are also
in **bold**. Common expressions in which the headword appears
are shown in a bold roman type (e.g. **retard:** [...] **avoir du ~**).

PHONETIC SPELLINGS

The phonetic spelling of each headword (indicating its pronunciation) is given in square brackets immediately after the headword (e.g. **fumer** [fyme]; **knee** [niː]). A list of these symbols is given on page xiii.

TRANSLATIONS

Headword translations are given in ordinary type and, where more than one meaning or usage exists, these are separated by a semi-colon. You will often find other words in italics in brackets before the translations. These offer suggested contexts in which the headword might appear (e.g. **rough** (*voice*), [...] (*weather*)) or provide synonyms (e.g. **rough** (*violent*)). The gender of the translation also appears in italics immediately following the key element of the translation.

KEY WORDS

Special status is given to certain French and English words which are considered as 'key' words in each language. They may, for example, occur very frequently or have several types of usage (e.g. **vouloir, plus; get, that**). A combination of triangles and numbers helps you to distinguish different parts of speech and different meanings. Further helpful information is provided in brackets and italics.

GRAMMATICAL INFORMATION

Parts of speech are given in abbreviated form in italics after the phonetic spellings of headwords (e.g. *vt, adv, conj*). Genders of French nouns are indicated as follows: *nm* for a masculine and *nf* for a feminine noun. Feminine and irregular plural forms of nouns are also shown (**directeur, -trice**; **cheval, -aux**).

Adjectives are given in both masculine and feminine forms where these forms are different (e.g. **noir, e**). Clear information is provided where adjectives have an irregular feminine or plural form (e.g. **net, nette**).

ABRÉVIATIONS

ABBREVIATIONS

abréviation	ab(b)r	abbreviation
adjectif, locution adjectivale	adj	adjective, adjectival phrase
administration	Admin	administration
adverbe, locution adverbiale	adv	adverb, adverbial phrase
agriculture	Agr	agriculture
anatomie	Anat	anatomy
architecture	Archit	architecture
article défini	art déf	definite article
article indéfini	art indéf	indefinite article
automobile	Aut(o)	the motor car and motoring
aviation, voyages aériens	Aviat	flying, air travel
biologie	Bio(l)	biology
botanique	Bot	botany
anglais britannique	BRIT	British English
chimie	Chem	chemistry
commerce, finance, banque	Comm	commerce, finance, banking
informatique	Comput	computing
conjonction	conj	conjunction
construction	Constr	building
nom utilisé comme adjectif	cpd	compound element
cuisine	Culin	cookery
article défini	def art	definite article
déterminant: article; adjectif démonstratif ou indéfini etc	dét	determiner: article, demonstrative etc
économie	Écon, Econ	economics
électricité, électronique	Élec, Elec	electricity, electronics
en particulier	esp	especially
exclamation, interjection	excl	exclamation, interjection
féminin	f	feminine
langue familière (! emploi vulgaire)	fam(!)	colloquial usage (! particularly offensive)
emploi figuré	fig	figurative use
(verbe anglais) dont la particule est inséparable	fus	(phrasal verb) where the particle is inseparable
généralement	gén, gen	generally
géographie, géologie	Géo, Geo	geography, geology
géométrie	Géom, Geom	geometry
langue familière (! emploi vulgaire)	inf(!)	colloquial usage (! particularly offensive)
infinitif	infin	infinitive
informatique	Inform	computing
invariable	inv	invariable
irrégulier	irreg	irregular
domaine juridique	Jur	law

ABRÉVIATIONS

ABBREVIATIONS

grammaire, linguistique	*Ling*	grammar, linguistics
masculin	*m*	masculine
mathématiques, algèbre	*Math*	mathematics, calculus
médecine	*Méd, Med*	medical term, medicine
masculin ou féminin	*m/f*	masculine or feminine
domaine militaire, armée	*Mil*	military matters
musique	*Mus*	music
nom	*n*	noun
navigation, nautisme	*Navig, Naut*	sailing, navigation
nom ou adjectif numéral	*num*	numeral noun or adjective
	o.s.	oneself
péjoratif	*péj, pej*	derogatory, pejorative
photographie	*Phot(o)*	photography
physiologie	*Physiol*	physiology
pluriel	*pl*	plural
politique	*Pol*	politics
participe passé	*pp*	past participle
préposition	*prép, prep*	preposition
pronom	*pron*	pronoun
psychologie, psychiatrie	*Psych*	psychology, psychiatry
temps du passé	*pt*	past tense
quelque chose	*qch*	
quelqu'un	*qn*	
religion, domaine ecclésiastique	*Rel*	religion
	sb	somebody
enseignement, système scolaire et universitaire	*Scol*	schooling, schools and universities
singulier	*sg*	singular
	sth	something
subjonctif	*sub*	subjunctive
sujet (grammatical)	*su(b)j*	(grammatical) subject
superlatif	*superl*	superlative
techniques, technologie	*Tech*	technical term, technology
télécommunications	*Tél, Tel*	telecommunications
télévision	*TV*	television
typographie	*Typ(o)*	typography, printing
anglais des USA	*US*	American English
verbe (auxiliaire)	*vb (aux)*	(auxiliary) verb
verbe intransitif	*vi*	intransitive verb
verbe transitif	*vt*	transitive verb
zoologie	*Zool*	zoology
marque déposée	®	registered trademark
indique une équivalence culturelle	≈	introduces a cultural equivalent

TRANSCRIPTION PHONÉTIQUE

CONSONNES | CONSONANTS

NB. **p, b, t, d, k, g** sont suivis d'une aspiration en anglais.

NB. **p, b, t, d, k, g** are not aspirated in French.

Français	Symbole	English
pou**p**ée	p	**p**u**pp**y
bom**b**e	b	**b**a**b**y
ten**t**e **th**ermal	t	**t**en**t**
din**d**e	d	**d**a**dd**y
co**q** **qu**i **k**épi	k	**c**ork **k**iss **ch**ord
ga**g**e ba**gu**e	g	**g**a**g** **g**uess
sale **c**e na**t**ion	s	**s**o ri**c**e ki**ss**
zéro ro**s**e	z	cou**s**in bu**zz**
ta**ch**e **ch**at	ʃ	**sh**eep **s**ugar
gilet **j**uge	ʒ	plea**s**ure bei**g**e
	tʃ	**ch**urch
	dʒ	**j**udge **g**eneral
fer **ph**are	f	**f**arm ra**ff**le
ver**v**eine	v	**v**ery re**v**el
	θ	**th**in ma**th**s
	ð	**th**at o**th**er
lent sa**ll**e	l	**l**ittle ba**ll**
rare **r**ent**r**er	R	
	r	**r**at **r**are
ma**m**an fe**mm**e	m	**m**u**mm**y co**mb**
non bo**nn**e	n	**n**o ra**n**
a**gn**eau vi**gn**e	ɲ	
	ŋ	si**ng**ing ba**n**k
	h	**h**at re**h**earse
yeux pa**ill**e p**i**ed	j	**y**et
n**ou**er **ou**i	w	**w**all **w**ail
h**ui**le l**ui**	ɥ	
	x	lo**ch**

DIVERS | MISCELLANEOUS

pour l'anglais: le r final se prononce en liaison devant une voyelle — ʳ — in English transcription: final r can be pronounced before a vowel

pour l'anglais: précède la syllabe accentuée — ' — in French wordlist: no liaison before aspirate h

En règle générale, la prononciation est donnée entre crochets après chaque entrée. Toutefois, du côté anglais-français et dans le cas des expressions composées de deux ou plusieurs mots non réunis par un trait d'union et faisant l'objet d'une entrée séparée, la prononciation doit être cherchée sous chacun des mots constitutifs de l'expression en question.

PHONETIC TRANSCRIPTION

VOYELLES		VOWELS
NB. La mise en équivalence de certains sons n'indique qu'une ressemblance approximative.		NB. The pairing of some vowel sounds only indicates approximate equivalence.

ici vie lyrique	i i:	heel bead
	ɪ	hit pity
jouer été	e	
lait jouet merci	ɛ	set tent
plat amour	a æ	bat apple
bas pâte	ɑ ɑ:	after car calm
	ʌ	fun cousin
le premier	ə	over above
beurre peur	œ	
peu deux	ø ə:	urgent fern work
or homme	ɔ	wash pot
mot eau gauche	o ɔ:	born cork
genou roue	u	full hook
	u:	boom shoe
rue urne	y	

DIPHTONGUES		DIPHTHONGS
	ɪə	beer tier
	ɛə	tear fair there
	eɪ	date plaice day
	aɪ	life buy cry
	aʊ	owl foul now
	əʊ	low no
	ɔɪ	boil boy oily
	ʊə	poor tour

NASALES		NASAL VOWELS
matin plein	ɛ̃	
brun	œ̃	
sang an dans	ɑ̃	
non pont	ɔ̃	

In general, we give the pronunciation of each entry in square brackets after the word in question. However, on the English-French side, where the entry is composed of two or more unhyphenated words, each of which is given elsewhere in this dictionary, you will find the pronunciation of each word in its alphabetical position.

FRENCH VERB TABLES

a Present participle **b** Past participle **c** Present **d** Imperfect **e** Future
f Conditional **g** Present subjunctive

1 **ARRIVER a** arrivant **b** arrivé **c** arrive, arrives, arrive, arrivons, arrivez, arrivent **d** arrivais **e** arriverai **f** arriverais **g** arrive

2 **FINIR a** finissant **b** fini **c** finis, finit, finissons, finissez, finissent **d** finissais **e** finirai **f** finirais **g** finisse

3 **PLACER a** plaçant **b** placé **c** place, places, place, plaçons, placez, placent **d** plaçais, plaçais, plaçait, placions, placiez, plaçaient **e** placerai, placeras, placera, placerons, placerez, placeront **f** placerais, placerais, placerait, placerions, placeriez, placeraient **g** place

3 **BOUGER a** bougeant **b** bougé **c** bouge, bougeons **d** bougeais, bougions **e** bougerai **f** bougerais **g** bouge

4 **appeler a** appelant **b** appelé **c** appelle, appelons **d** appelais **e** appellerai **f** appellerais **g** appelle

4 **jeter a** jetant **b** jeté **c** jette, jetons **d** jetais **e** jetterai **f** jetterais **g** jette

5 **geler a** gelant **b** gelé **c** gèle, gelons **d** gelais **e** gèlerai **f** gèlerais **g** gèle

6 **CÉDER a** cédant **b** cédé **c** cède, cèdes, cède, cédons, cédez, cèdent **d** cédais, cédais, cédait, cédions, cédiez, cédaient **e** céderai, céderas, cédera, céderons, céderez, céderont **f** céderais, céderais, céderait, céderions, céderiez, céderaient **g** cède

7 **épier a** épiant **b** épié **c** épie, épions **d** épiais **e** épierai **f** épierais **g** épie

8 **noyer a** noyant **b** noyé **c** noie, noyons **d** noyais **e** noierai **f** noierais **g** noie

9 **ALLER a** allant **b** allé **c** vais, vas, va, allons, allez, vont **d** allais **e** irai **f** irais **g** aille

10 **HAÏR a** haïssant **b** haï **c** hais, hais, hait, haïssons, haïssez, haïssent **d** haïssais, haïssais, haïssait, haïssions, haïssiez, haïssaient **e** haïrai, haïras, haïra, haïrons, haïrez, haïront **f** haïrais, haïrais, haïrait, haïrions, haïriez, haïraient **g** haïsse

11 **courir a** courant **b** couru **c** cours, courons **d** courais **e** courrai **g** coure

12 **cueillir a** cueillant **b** cueilli **c** cueille, cueillons **d** cueillais **e** cueillerai **g** cueille

13 **assaillir – a** assaillant **b** assailli **c** assaille, assaillons **d** assaillais **e** assaillirai **g** assaille

14 **servir a** servant **b** servi **c** sers, servons **d** servais **g** serve

15 **bouillir a** bouillant **b** bouilli **c** bous, bouillons **d** bouillais **g** bouille

16 **partir a** partant **b** parti **c** pars, partons **d** partais **g** parte

17 **fuir a** fuyant **b** fui **c** fuis, fuyons, fuient **d** fuyais **g** fuie

18 **couvrir a** couvrant **b** couvert **c** couvre, couvrons **d** couvrais **g** couvre

19 **mourir a** mourant **b** mort **c** meurs, mourons, meurent **d** mourais **e** mourrai **g** meure

20 **vêtir a** vêtant **b** vêtu **c** vêts, vêtons **d** vêtais **e** vêtirai **g** vête

21 **acquérir a** acquérant **b** acquis **c** acquiers, acquérons, acquièrent **d** acquérais **e** acquerrai **g** acquière

22 venir a venant b venu c viens, venons, viennent d venais e viendrai g vienne

23 pleuvoir a pleuvant b plu c pleut, pleuvent d pleuvait e pleuvra g pleuve

24 prévoir *like* voir e prévoirai

25 pourvoir a pourvoyant b pourvu c pourvois, pourvoyons, pourvoient d pourvoyais g pourvoie

26 asseoir a asseyant b assis c assieds, asseyons, asseyez, asseyent d asseyais e assiérai g asseye

28 RECEVOIR a recevant b reçu c reçois, reçois, reçoit, recevons, recevez, reçoivent d recevais e recevrai f recevrais g reçoive

29 valoir a valant b valu c vaux, vaut, valons d valais e vaudrai g vaille

30 voir a voyant b vu c vois, voyons, voient d voyais e verrai g voie

31 vouloir a voulant b voulu c veux, veut, voulons, veulent d voulais e voudrai g veuille; *impératif* veuillez!

32 savoir a sachant b su c sais, savons, savent d savais e saurai g sache *impératif* sache! sachons! sachez!

33 pouvoir a pouvant b pu c peux, peut, pouvons, peuvent d pouvais e pourrai g puisse

34 AVOIR a ayant b eu c ai, as, a, avons, avez, ont d avais e aurai f aurais g aie, aies, ait, ayons, ayez, aient

35 conclure a concluant b conclu c conclus, concluons d concluais g conclue

36 rire a riant b ri c ris, rions d riais g rie

37 dire a disant b dit c dis, disons, dites, disent d disais g dise

38 nuire a nuisant b nui c nuis, nuisons d nuisais e nuirai f nuirais g nuise

39 écrire a écrivant b écrit c écris, écrivons d écrivais g écrive

40 suivre a suivant b suivi c suis, suivons d suivais g suive

41 RENDRE a rendant b rendu c rends, rends, rend, rendons, rendez, rendent d rendais e rendrai f rendrais g rende

42 vaincre a vainquant b vaincu c vaincs, vainc, vainquons d vainquais g vainque

43 lire a lisant b lu c lis, lisons d lisais g lise

44 croire a croyant b cru c crois, croyons, croient d croyais g croie

45 CLORE a closant b clos c clos, clos, clôt, closent e clorai, cloras, clora, clorons, clorez, cloront f clorais, clorais, clorait, clorions, cloriez, cloraient

46 vivre a vivant b vécu c vis, vivons d vivais g vive

47 MOUDRE a moulant b moulu c mouds, mouds, moud, moulons, moulez, moulent d moulais, moulais, moulait, moulions, mouliez, moulaient e moudrai, moudras, moudra, moudrons, moudrez, moudront f moudrais, moudrais, moudrait, moudrions, moudriez, moudraient g moule

48 coudre a cousant b cousu c couds, cousons, cousez, cousent d cousais g couse

49 joindre a joignant b joint c joins, joignons d joignais g joigne

50 TRAIRE a trayant b trait c trais, trais, trait, trayons, trayez, traient d trayais, trayais, trayait, trayions, trayiez, trayaient e trairai, trairas, traira, trairons, trairez, trairont f trairais, trairais, trairait, trairions, trairiez, trairaient g traie

51 ABSOUDRE a absolvant b absous c absous, absous, absout, absolvons, absolvez, absolvent

d absolvais, absolvais, absolvait, absolvions, absolviez, absolvaient **e** absoudrai, absoudras, absoudra, absoudrons, absoudrez, absoudront **f** absoudrais, absoudrais, absoudrait, absoudrions, absoudriez, absoudraient **g** absolve

52 craindre a craignant **b** craint **c** crains, craignons **d** craignais **g** craigne

53 boire a buvant **b** bu **c** bois, buvons, boivent **d** buvais **g** boive

54 plaire a plaisant **b** plu **c** plais, plaît, plaisons **d** plaisais **g** plaise

55 croître a croissant **b** crû, crue, crus, crues **c** croîs, croissons **d** croissais **g** croisse

56 mettre a mettant **b** mis **c** mets, mettons **d** mettais **g** mette

57 connaître a connaissant **b** connu **c** connais, connaît, connaissons **d** connaissais **g** connaisse

58 prendre a prenant **b** pris **c** prends, prenons, prennent **d** prenais **g** prenne

59 naître a naissant **b** né **c** nais, naît, naissons **d** naissais **g** naisse

60 FAIRE a faisant **b** fait **c** fais, fait, faisons, faites, font **d** faisais **e** ferai **f** ferais **g** fasse

61 ÊTRE a étant **b** été **c** suis, es, est, sommes, êtes, sont **d** étais **e** serai **f** serais **g** sois, sois, soit, soyons, soyez, soient

VERBES IRRÉGULIERS ANGLAIS

PRÉSENT	PASSÉ	PARTICIPE	PRÉSENT	PASSÉ	PARTICIPE
arise	arose	arisen	**fall**	fell	fallen
awake	awoke	awoken	**feed**	fed	fed
be	was, were	been	**feel**	felt	felt
(am, is,			**fight**	fought	fought
are; being)			**find**	found	found
bear	bore	born(e)	**flee**	fled	fled
beat	beat	beaten	**fling**	flung	flung
become	became	become	**fly**	flew	flown
begin	began	begun	**forbid**	forbad(e)	forbidden
bend	bent	bent	**forecast**	forecast	forecast
bet	bet,	bet,	**forget**	forgot	forgotten
	betted	betted	**forgive**	forgave	forgiven
bid (*at auction,*	bid	bid	**forsake**	forsook	forsaken
cards)			**freeze**	froze	frozen
bid (*say*)	bade	bidden	**get**	got	got,
bind	bound	bound			(*us*) gotten
bite	bit	bitten	**give**	gave	given
bleed	bled	bled	**go** (goes)	went	gone
blow	blew	blown	**grind**	ground	ground
break	broke	broken	**grow**	grew	grown
breed	bred	bred	**hang**	hung	hung
bring	brought	brought	**hang** (*execute*)	hanged	hanged
build	built	built	**have**	had	had
burn	burnt,	burnt,	**hear**	heard	heard
	burned	burned	**hide**	hid	hidden
burst	burst	burst	**hit**	hit	hit
buy	bought	bought	**hold**	held	held
can	could	(*been able*)	**hurt**	hurt	hurt
cast	cast	cast	**keep**	kept	kept
catch	caught	caught	**kneel**	knelt,	knelt,
choose	chose	chosen		kneeled	kneeled
cling	clung	clung	**know**	knew	known
come	came	come	**lay**	laid	laid
cost	cost	cost	**lead**	led	led
cost (*work*	costed	costed	**lean**	leant,	leant,
out price of)				leaned	leaned
creep	crept	crept	**leap**	leapt,	leapt,
cut	cut	cut		leaped	leaped
deal	dealt	dealt	**learn**	learnt,	learnt,
dig	dug	dug		learned	learned
do (does)	did	done	**leave**	left	left
draw	drew	drawn	**lend**	lent	lent
dream	dreamed,	dreamed,	**let**	let	let
	dreamt	dreamt	**lie** (lying)	lay	lain
drink	drank	drunk	**light**	lit,	lit,
drive	drove	driven		lighted	lighted
dwell	dwelt	dwelt	**lose**	lost	lost
eat	ate	eaten	**make**	made	made

PRÉSENT	PASSÉ	PARTICIPE	PRÉSENT	PASSÉ	PARTICIPE
may	might	–	speed	sped,	sped,
mean	meant	meant		speeded	speeded
meet	met	met	spell	spelt,	spelt,
mistake	mistook	mistaken		spelled	spelled
mow	mowed	mown,	spend	spent	spent
		mowed	spill	spilt,	spilt,
must	(had to)	(had to)		spilled	spilled
pay	paid	paid	spin	spun	spun
put	put	put	spit	spat	spat
quit	quit,	quit,	spoil	spoiled,	spoiled,
	quitted	quitted		spoilt	spoilt
read	read	read	spread	spread	spread
rid	rid	rid	spring	sprang	sprung
ride	rode	ridden	stand	stood	stood
ring	rang	rung	steal	stole	stolen
rise	rose	risen	stick	stuck	stuck
run	ran	run	sting	stung	stung
saw	sawed	sawed,	stink	stank	stunk
		sawn	stride	strode	stridden
say	said	said	strike	struck	struck
see	saw	seen	strive	strove	striven
seek	sought	sought	swear	swore	sworn
sell	sold	sold	sweep	swept	swept
send	sent	sent	swell	swelled	swollen,
set	set	set			swelled
sew	sewed	sewn	swim	swam	swum
shake	shook	shaken	swing	swung	swung
shear	sheared	shorn,	take	took	taken
		sheared	teach	taught	taught
shed	shed	shed	tear	tore	torn
shine	shone	shone	tell	told	told
shoot	shot	shot	think	thought	thought
show	showed	shown	throw	threw	thrown
shrink	shrank	shrunk	thrust	thrust	thrust
shut	shut	shut	tread	trod	trodden
sing	sang	sung	wake	woke,	woken,
sink	sank	sunk		waked	waked
sit	sat	sat	wear	wore	worn
slay	slew	slain	weave	wove	woven
sleep	slept	slept	weave (wind)	weaved	weaved
slide	slid	slid	wed	wedded,	wedded,
sling	slung	slung		wed	wed
slit	slit	slit	weep	wept	wept
smell	smelt,	smelt,	win	won	won
	smelled	smelled	wind	wound	wound
sow	sowed	sown,	wring	wrung	wrung
		sowed	write	wrote	written
speak	spoke	spoken			

LES NOMBRES

un (une)	1	one
deux	2	two
trois	3	three
quatre	4	four
cinq	5	five
six	6	six
sept	7	seven
huit	8	eight
neuf	9	nine
dix	10	ten
onze	11	eleven
douze	12	twelve
treize	13	thirteen
quatorze	14	fourteen
quinze	15	fifteen
seize	16	sixteen
dix-sept	17	seventeen
dix-huit	18	eighteen
dix-neuf	19	nineteen
vingt	20	twenty
vingt et un (une)	21	twenty-one
vingt-deux	22	twenty-two
trente	30	thirty
quarante	40	forty
cinquante	50	fifty
soixante	60	sixty
soixante-dix	70	seventy
soixante-et-onze	71	seventy-one
soixante-douze	72	seventy-two
quatre-vingts	80	eighty
quatre-vingt-un (-une)	81	eighty-one
quatre-vingt-dix	90	ninety
cent	100	a hundred, one hundred
cent un (une)	101	a hundred and one
deux cents	200	two hundred
deux cent un (une)	201	two hundred and one
quatre cents	400	four hundred
mille	1000	a thousand
cinq mille	5000	five thousand
un million	1000000	a million

LES NOMBRES

premier (première), 1ᵉʳ (1ʳᵉ)
deuxième, 2ᵉ or 2ᵉᵐᵉ
troisième, 3ᵉ or 3ᵉᵐᵉ
quatrième, 4ᵉ or 4ᵉᵐᵉ
cinquième, 5ᵉ or 5ᵉᵐᵉ
sixième, 6ᵉ or 6ᵉᵐᵉ
septième
huitième
neuvième
dixième
onzième
douzième
treizième
quartorzième
quinzième
seizième
dix-septième
dix-huitième
dix-neuvième
vingtième
vingt-et-unième
vingt-deuxième
trentième
centième
cent-unième
millième

LES FRACTIONS ETC

un demi
un tiers
un quart
un cinquième
zéro virgule cinq, 0,5
trois virgule quatre, 3,4
dix pour cent
cent pour cent

EXEMPLES

elle habite au septième (étage)
il habite au sept
au chapitre/à la page sept
il est arrivé (le) septième

NUMBERS

first, 1st
second, 2nd
third, 3rd
fourth, 4th
fifth, 5th
sixth, 6th
seventh
eighth
ninth
tenth
eleventh
twelfth
thirteenth
fourteenth
fifteenth
sixteenth
seventeenth
eighteenth
nineteenth
twentieth
twenty-first
twenty-second
thirtieth
hundredth
hundred-and-first
thousandth

FRACTIONS ETC

a half
a third
a quarter
a fifth
(nought) point five, 0.5
three point four, 3.4
ten per cent
a hundred per cent

EXAMPLES

she lives on the 7th floor
he lives at number 7
chapter/page 7
he came in 7th

L'HEURE

quelle heure est-il?

il est ...

minuit
une heure (du matin)

une heure cinq
une heure dix
une heure et quart

une heure vingt-cinq

une heure et demie, une heure trente
deux heures moins vingt-cinq, une
 heure trente-cinq
deux heures moins vingt, une heure
 quarante
deux heures moins le quart, une heure
 quarante-cinq
deux heures moins dix, une heure
 cinquante
midi

deux heures (de l'après-midi),
 quatorze heures
sept heures (du soir), dix-sept heures

à quelle heure?

à minuit
à sept heures

dans vingt minutes
il y a un quart d'heure

THE TIME

what time is it?

it's ou it is ...

midnight, twelve p.m.
one o'clock (in the
 morning), one (a.m.)

five past one
ten past one
a quarter past one,
 one fifteen
twenty-five past one,
 one twenty-five
half-past one, one thirty
twenty-five to two,
 one thirty-five
twenty to two, one forty

a quarter to two,
 one forty-five
ten to two, one fifty

twelve o'clock, midday,
 noon
two o'clock (in the
 afternoon), two (p.m.)
seven o'clock (in the
 evening), seven (p.m.)

(at) what time?

at midnight
at seven o'clock

in twenty minutes
fifteen minutes ago

a

4 (*attribution, appartenance*) to; **le livre est à Paul/à lui/à nous** this book is Paul's/his/ours; **donner qch à qn** to give sth to sb; **un ami à moi** a friend of mine

5 (*moyen*) with; **se chauffer au gaz** to have gas heating; **à bicyclette** on *ou* by bicycle; **à pied** on foot; **à la main/machine** by hand/machine

6 (*provenance*) from; **boire à la bouteille** to drink from the bottle

7 (*caractérisation, manière*): **l'homme aux yeux bleus** the man with the blue eyes; **à la russe** the Russian way

8 (*but, destination*): **tasse à café** coffee cup; **maison à vendre** house for sale; **je n'ai rien à lire** I don't have anything to read; **à bien réfléchir …** thinking about it …, on reflection …

9 (*rapport, évaluation, distribution*): **100 km/unités à l'heure** 100 km/ units per *ou* an hour; **payé à l'heure** paid by the hour; **cinq à six** five to six o.s.

10 (*conséquence, résultat*): **à ce qu'il prétend** according to him; **à leur grande surprise** much to their surprise; **à nous trois nous n'avons pas su le faire** we couldn't do it even between the three of us; **ils sont arrivés à quatre** four of them arrived (together)

abaisser [abese] /1/ *vt* to lower, bring down; (*manette*) to pull down; **s'abaisser** *vi* to go down; (*fig*) to demean o.s.

abandon [abɑ̃dɔ̃] *nm* abandoning; giving up; withdrawal; **être à l'~** to be in a state of neglect; **laisser à l'~** to abandon

abandonner [abɑ̃dɔne] /1/ *vt* (*personne*) to leave, abandon, desert; (*projet, activité*) to abandon, give up; (*Sport*) to retire *ou* withdraw from; (*céder*) to surrender; **s'~ à** (*paresse, plaisirs*) to give o.s. up to

abat-jour [abaʒuʀ] *nm inv* lampshade

---

a [a] *vb voir* **avoir**

 MOT-CLÉ

à [a] (*à + le* = **au**, *à + les* = **aux**) *prép* **1** (*endroit, situation*) at, in; **être à Paris/ au Portugal** to be in Paris/Portugal; **être à la maison/à l'école** to be at home/at school; **à la campagne** in the country; **c'est à 10 m/km/à 20 minutes (d'ici)** it's 10 m/km/20 minutes away

2 (*direction*) to; **aller à Paris/au Portugal** to go to Paris/Portugal; **aller à la maison/à l'école** to go home/to school; **à la campagne** to the country

3 (*temps*): **à 3 heures/minuit** at 3 o'clock/midnight; **au printemps** in the spring; **au mois de juin** in June; **à Noël/Pâques** at Christmas/Easter; **à demain/la semaine prochaine!** see you tomorrow/next week!

abats [aba] *nmpl (de bœuf, porc)* offal *sg; (de volaille)* giblets

abattement [abatmɑ̃] *nm:* **~ fiscal** ≈ tax allowance

abattoir [abatwaʀ] *nm* slaughterhouse

abattre [abatʀ] /41/ *vt (arbre)* to cut down, fell; *(mur, maison)* to pull down; *(avion, personne)* to shoot down; *(animal)* to shoot, kill; *(fig)* to wear out, tire out; to demoralize; **s'abattre** *vi* to crash down; **ne pas se laisser ~** to keep one's spirits up, not to let things get one down; **s'~ sur** to beat down on; *(coups, injures)* to rain down on; **~ du travail** *ou* **de la besogne** to get through a lot of work

abbaye [abei] *nf* abbey

abbé [abe] *nm* priest; *(d'abbaye)* abbot

abcès [apsɛ] *nm* abscess

abdiquer [abdike] /1/ *vi* to abdicate

abdominal, e, -aux [abdɔminal, -o] *adj* abdominal; **abdominaux** *nmpl:* **faire des abdominaux** to do sit-ups

abeille [abɛj] *nf* bee

aberrant, e [abeʀɑ̃, -ɑ̃t] *adj* absurd

aberration [abeʀasjɔ̃] *nf* aberration

abîme [abim] *nm* abyss, gulf

abîmer [abime] /1/ *vt* to spoil, damage; **s'abîmer** *vi* to get spoilt *ou* damaged

aboiement [abwamɑ̃] *nm* bark, barking *no pl*

abolir [abɔliʀ] /2/ *vt* to abolish

abominable [abɔminabl] *adj* abominable

abondance [abɔ̃dɑ̃s] *nf* abundance

abondant, e [abɔ̃dɑ̃, -ɑ̃t] *adj* plentiful, abundant, copious; **abonder** /1/ *vi* to abound, be plentiful; **abonder dans le sens de qn** to concur with sb

abonné, e [abɔne] *nm/f* subscriber; season ticket holder

abonnement [abɔnmɑ̃] *nm* subscription; *(pour transports en commun, concerts)* season ticket

abonner [abɔne] /1/ *vt:* **s'abonner à** to subscribe to, take out a subscription to ; **s'~ aux tweets de qn sur Twitter** to follow sb on Twitter

abord [abɔʀ] *nm:* **abords** *nmpl (environs)* surroundings; **d'~** first; **au premier ~** at first sight, initially

abordable [abɔʀdabl] *adj (personne)* approachable; *(prix)* reasonable

aborder [abɔʀde] /1/ *vi* to land ▷ *vt (sujet, difficulté)* to tackle; *(personne)* to approach; *(rivage etc)* to reach

aboutir [abutiʀ] /2/ *vi (négociations etc)* to succeed; **~ à/dans/sur** to end up at/in/on; **n'~ à rien** to come to nothing

aboyer [abwaje] /8/ *vi* to bark

abréger [abʀeʒe] /3, 6/ *vt* to shorten

abreuver [abʀœve] /1/: **s'abreuver** *vi* to drink; **abreuvoir** *nm* watering place

abréviation [abʀevjasjɔ̃] *nf* abbreviation

abri [abʀi] *nm* shelter; **être à l'~** to be under cover; **se mettre à l'~** to shelter; **à l'~ de** sheltered from; *(danger)* safe from

abricot [abʀiko] *nm* apricot

abriter [abʀite] /1/ *vt* to shelter; **s'abriter** *vi* to shelter, take cover

abrupt, e [abʀypt] *adj* sheer, steep; *(ton)* abrupt

abruti, e [abʀyti] *adj* stunned, dazed ▷ *nm/f (fam)* idiot; **~ de travail** overworked

absence [apsɑ̃s] *nf* absence; *(Méd)* blackout; **en l'~ de** in the absence of; **avoir des ~s** to have mental blanks

absent, e [apsɑ̃, -ɑ̃t] *adj* absent ▷ *nm/f* absentee; **absenter** /1/: **s'absenter** *vi* to take time off work; *(sortir)* to leave, go out

absolu, e [apsɔly] *adj* absolute; **absolument** *adv* absolutely

absorbant, e [apsɔʀbɑ̃, -ɑ̃t] *adj* absorbent

absorber [apsɔrbe] /1/ vt to absorb; (gén, Méd: manger, boire) to take

abstenir [apstənir] /22/: **s'abstenir** vi: **s'~ de qch/de faire** to refrain from sth/from doing

abstrait, e [apstrɛ, -ɛt] adj abstract

absurde [apsyrd] adj absurd

abus [aby] nm abuse; **~ de confiance** breach of trust; **il y a de l'~!** (fam) that's a bit much!; **abuser** /1/ vi to go too far, overstep the mark; **s'abuser** vi (se méprendre) to be mistaken; **abuser de** (violer, duper) to take advantage of; **abusif, -ive** adj exorbitant; (punition) excessive

académie [akademi] nf academy; (Scol: circonscription) ≈ regional education authority; see note "Académie française"

● **ACADÉMIE FRANÇAISE**
●
● The Académie française was founded
● by Cardinal Richelieu in 1635,
● during the reign of Louis XIII. It is
● made up of forty elected scholars
● and writers who are known as 'les
● Quarante' or 'les Immortels'. One
● of the Académie's functions is to
● keep an eye on the development
● of the French language, and its
● recommendations are frequently
● the subject of lively public debate.
● It has produced several editions
● of its famous dictionary and also
● awards various literary prizes.

acajou [akaʒu] nm mahogany

acariâtre [akarjɑtr] adj cantankerous

accablant, e [akablɑ̃, -ɑ̃t] adj (chaleur) oppressive; (témoignage, preuve) overwhelming

accabler [akable] /1/ vt to overwhelm, overcome; **~ qn d'injures** to heap ou shower abuse on sb; **~ qn de travail** to overwork sb

accalmie [akalmi] nf lull

accaparer [akapare] /1/ vt to monopolize; (travail etc) to take up (all) the time ou attention of

accéder [aksede] /6/: **~ à** vt (lieu) to reach; (accorder: requête) to grant, accede to

accélérateur [akseleratœr] nm accelerator

accélérer [akselere] /6/ vt to speed up ▷ vi to accelerate

accent [aksɑ̃] nm accent; (Phonétique, fig) stress; **mettre l'~ sur** (fig) to stress; **~ aigu/grave/circonflexe** acute/grave/circumflex accent; **accentuer** /1/ vt (Ling) to accent; (fig) to accentuate, emphasize; **s'accentuer** vi to become more marked ou pronounced

acceptation [aksɛptasjɔ̃] nf acceptance

accepter [aksɛpte] /1/ vt to accept; **~ de faire** to agree to do

accès [aksɛ] nm (à un lieu) access; (Méd: de toux) fit; (: de fièvre) bout; **d'~ facile/malaisé** easily/not easily accessible; **facile d'~** easy to get to; **~ de colère** fit of anger; **accessible** adj accessible; (livre, sujet): **accessible à qn** within the reach of sb

accessoire [akseswar] adj secondary; (frais) incidental ▷ nm accessory; (Théât) prop

accident [aksidɑ̃] nm accident; **par ~** by chance; **~ de la route** road accident; **accidenté, e** adj damaged ou injured (in an accident); (relief, terrain) uneven; hilly; **accidentel, le** adj accidental

acclamer [aklame] /1/ vt to cheer, acclaim

acclimater [aklimate] /1/: **s'acclimater** vi to become acclimatized

accolade [akɔlad] nf (amicale) embrace; (signe) brace

accommoder [akɔmɔde] /1/ vt (Culin) to prepare; **s'accommoder**

de to put up with; *(se contenter de)* to make do with

accompagnateur, -trice [akɔ̃paɲatœʀ, -tʀis] *nm/f (Mus)* accompanist; *(de voyage)* guide; *(de voyage organisé)* courier

accompagner [akɔ̃paɲe] /1/ *vt* to accompany, be ou go ou come with; *(Mus)* to accompany

accompli, e [akɔ̃pli] *adj* accomplished

accomplir [akɔ̃pliʀ] /2/ *vt (tâche, projet)* to carry out; *(souhait)* to fulfil; **s'accomplir** *vi* to be fulfilled

accord [akɔʀ] *nm* agreement; *(entre des styles, tons etc)* harmony; *(Mus)* chord; **se mettre d'~** to come to an agreement (with each other); **être d'~** to agree; **d'~!** OK!

accordéon [akɔʀdeɔ̃] *nm (Mus)* accordion

accorder [akɔʀde] /1/ *vt (faveur, délai)* to grant; **~ de l'importance/de la valeur à qch** to attach importance/ value to sth; *(harmoniser)* to match; *(Mus)* to tune

accoster [akɔste] /1/ *vt (Navig)* to draw alongside ▷ *vi* to berth

accouchement [akuʃmɑ̃] *nm* delivery, (child)birth; labour

accoucher [akuʃe] /1/ *vi* to give birth, have a baby; **~ d'un garçon** to give birth to a boy

accouder [akude] /1/: **s'accouder** *vi*: **s'~ à/contre/sur** to rest one's elbows on/against/on; **accoudoir** *nm* armrest

accoupler [akuple] /1/ *vt* to couple; *(pour la reproduction)* to mate; **s'accoupler** *vi* to mate

accourir [akuʀiʀ] /11/ *vi* to rush ou run up

accoutumance [akutymɑ̃s] *nf (gén)* adaptation; *(Méd)* addiction

accoutumé, e [akutyme] *adj (habituel)* customary, usual

accoutumer [akutyme] /1/ *vt*: **s'accoutumer à** to get accustomed ou used to

accroc [akʀo] *nm (déchirure)* tear; *(fig)* hitch, snag

accrochage [akʀoʃaʒ] *nm (Auto)* (minor) collision; *(dispute)* clash, brush

accrocher [akʀoʃe] /1/ *vt (suspendre)* to hang; *(fig)* to catch, attract; **s'accrocher** *(se disputer)* to have a clash ou brush; **~ qch à** *(suspendre)* to hang sth (up) on; *(attacher: remorque)* to hitch sth (up) to; *(déchirer)* to catch sth (on); **il a accroché ma voiture** he bumped into my car; **s'~ à** *(rester pris à)* to catch on; *(agripper, fig)* to hang on ou cling to

accroissement [akʀwasmɑ̃] *nm* increase

accroître [akʀwatʀ] /55/ *vt*: **s'accroître** *vi* to increase

accroupir [akʀupiʀ] /2/: **s'accroupir** *vi* to squat, crouch (down)

accru, e [akʀy] *pp de* **accroître**

accueil [akœj] *nm* welcome; **comité/centre d'~** reception committee/centre; **accueillir** /12/ *vt* to welcome; *(aller chercher)* to meet, collect

accumuler [akymyle] /1/ *vt* to accumulate, amass; **s'accumuler** *vi* to accumulate; to pile up

accusation [akyzasjɔ̃] *nf (gén)* accusation; *(Jur)* charge; *(partie)*: **l'~** the prosecution

accusé, e [akyze] *nm/f* accused; *(prévenu(e))* defendant ▷ *nm*: **~ de réception** acknowledgement of receipt

accuser [akyze] /1/ *vt* to accuse; *(fig)* to emphasize, bring out; (: *montrer*) to show; **~ qn de** to accuse sb of; *(Jur)* to charge sb with; **~ réception de** to acknowledge receipt of

acéré, e [asere] *adj* sharp

acharné, e [aʃaʀne] *adj (lutte, adversaire)* fierce, bitter; *(travail)* relentless

acharner [aʃaʀne] /1/: **s'acharner** *vi*: **s'~ sur** to go at fiercely; **s'~ contre**

to set o.s. against; *(malchance)* to hound; **s'~ à faire** to try doggedly to do; to persist in doing

achat [aʃa] *nm* purchase; **faire l'~ de** to buy; **faire des ~s** to do some shopping

acheter [aʃte] /5/ *vt* to buy, purchase; *(soudoyer)* to buy; **~ qch à** *(marchand)* to buy *ou* purchase sth from; *(ami etc: offrir)* to buy sth for; **acheteur, -euse** *nm/f* buyer; shopper; *(Comm)* buyer

achever [aʃ(ə)ve] /5/ *vt* to complete, finish; *(blessé)* to finish off; **s'achever** *vi* to end

acide [asid] *adj* sour, sharp; *(Chimie)* acid(ic) ▷ *nm* acid; **acidulé, e** *adj* slightly acid; **bonbons acidulés** acid drops

acier [asje] *nm* steel; **aciérie** *nf* steelworks *sg*

acné [akne] *nf* acne

acompte [akɔ̃t] *nm* deposit

à-côté [akote] *nm* side-issue; *(argent)* extra

à-coup [aku] *nm*: **par ~s** by fits and starts

acoustique [akustik] *nf (d'une salle)* acoustics *pl*

acquéreur [akerœr] *nm* buyer, purchaser

acquérir [akerir] /21/ *vt* to acquire

acquis, e [aki, -iz] *pp de* **acquérir** ▷ *nm* (accumulated) experience; **son aide nous est ~e** we can count on *ou* be sure of his help

acquitter [akite] /1/ *vt (Jur)* to acquit; *(facture)* to pay, settle; **s'~ de** to discharge; *(promesse, tâche)* to fulfil

âcre [ɑkr] *adj* acrid, pungent

acrobate [akrɔbat] *nm/f* acrobat; **acrobatie** *nf* acrobatics *sg*

acte [akt] *nm* act, action; *(Théât)* act; **prendre ~ de** to note, take note of; **faire ~ de présence** to put in an appearance; **faire ~ de candidature** to submit an application; **~ de**

mariage/naissance marriage/birth certificate

acteur [aktœr] *nm* actor

actif, -ive [aktif, -iv] *adj* active ▷ *nm* *(Comm)* assets *pl*; *(fig)*: **avoir à son ~** to have to one's credit; **population active** working population

action [aksjɔ̃] *nf (gén)* action; *(Comm)* share; **une bonne/mauvaise ~** a good/an unkind deed; **actionnaire** *nm/f* shareholder; **actionner** /1/ *vt* *(mécanisme)* to activate; *(machine)* to operate

activer [aktive] /1/ *vt* to speed up; **s'activer** *vi* to bustle about; *(se hâter)* to hurry up

activité [aktivite] *nf* activity; **en ~** *(volcan)* active; *(fonctionnaire)* in active life

actrice [aktris] *nf* actress

actualité [aktyalite] *nf (d'un problème)* topicality; *(événements)*: **l'~** current events; **les ~s** *(Ciné, TV)* the news; **d'~** topical

actuel, le [aktyɛl] *adj (présent)* present; *(d'actualité)* topical; **à l'heure ~le** at this moment in time; **actuellement** [aktyɛlmɑ̃] *adv* at present, at the present time

▌ Attention à ne pas traduire *actuellement* par *actually*.

acuponcture [akypɔ̃ktyr] *nf* acupuncture

adaptateur, -trice [adaptatœr, -tris] *nm/f* adapter

adapter [adapte] /1/ *vt* to adapt; **s'~ (à)** *(personne)* to adapt (to); **~ qch à** *(approprier)* to adapt sth to (fit); **~ qch sur/dans/à** *(fixer)* to fit sth on/into/to

addition [adisjɔ̃] *nf* addition; *(au café)* bill; **additionner** /1/ *vt* to add (up)

adepte [adɛpt] *nm/f* follower

adéquat, e [adekwa(t), -at] *adj* appropriate, suitable

adhérent, e [aderɑ̃, -ɑ̃t] *nm/f* member

adhérer [adeʀe] /6/: **~ à** (coller) to adhere ou stick to; (se rallier à: parti, club) to join; **adhésif, -ive** adj adhesive, sticky; **ruban adhésif** sticky ou adhesive tape

adieu, x [adjø] excl goodbye ▷ nm farewell

adjectif [adʒɛktif] nm adjective

adjoint, e [adʒwɛ̃, -wɛ̃t] nm/f assistant; **~ au maire** deputy mayor; **directeur ~** assistant manager

admettre [admɛtʀ] /56/ vt (visiteur) to admit; (candidat: Scol) to pass; (tolérer) to allow, accept; (reconnaître) to admit, acknowledge

administrateur, -trice [administʀatœʀ, -tʀis] nm/f (Comm) director; (Admin) administrator

administration [administʀasjɔ̃] nf administration; **l'A~** ≈ the Civil Service

administrer [administʀe] /1/ vt (firme) to manage, run; (biens, remède, sacrement etc) to administer

admirable [admiʀabl] adj admirable, wonderful

admirateur, -trice [admiʀatœʀ, -tʀis] nm/f admirer

admiration [admiʀasjɔ̃] nf admiration

admirer [admiʀe] /1/ vt to admire

admis, e [admi, -iz] pp de **admettre**

admissible [admisibl] adj (candidat) eligible; (comportement) admissible, acceptable

ADN sigle m (= acide désoxyribonucléique) DNA

ado [ado] (fam) nm/f teen

adolescence [adɔlesɑ̃s] nf adolescence

adolescent, e [adɔlesɑ̃, -ɑ̃t] nm/f adolescent, teenager

adopter [adɔpte] /1/ vt to adopt; **adoptif, -ive** adj (parents) adoptive; (fils, patrie) adopted

adorable [adɔʀabl] adj adorable

adorer [adɔʀe] /1/ vt to adore; (Rel) to worship

adosser [adose] /1/ vt: **~ qch à** ou **contre** to stand sth against; **s'~ à** ou **contre** to lean with one's back against

adoucir [adusiʀ] /2/ vt (goût, température) to make milder; (avec du sucre) to sweeten; (peau, voix, eau) to soften; **s'adoucir** vi (caractère) to mellow

adresse [adʀɛs] nf skill, dexterity; (domicile) address; **~ électronique** email address

adresser [adʀese] /1/ vt (lettre: expédier) to send; (: écrire l'adresse sur) to address; (injure, compliments) to address; **s'adresser à** (parler à) to speak to, address; (s'informer auprès de) to go and see (: bureau) to enquire at; (livre, conseil) to be aimed at; **~ la parole à qn** to speak to ou address sb

adroit, e [adʀwa, -wat] adj skilled

ADSL sigle m (= asymmetrical digital subscriber line) ADSL, broadband

adulte [adylt] nm/f adult, grown-up ▷ adj (personne, attitude) adult, grown-up; (chien, arbre) fully-grown, mature

adverbe [advɛʀb] nm adverb

adversaire [advɛʀsɛʀ] nm/f (Sport, gén) opponent, adversary

aération [aeʀasjɔ̃] nf airing; (circulation de l'air) ventilation

aérer [aeʀe] /6/ vt to air; (fig) to lighten

aérien, ne [aeʀjɛ̃, -ɛn] adj (Aviat) air cpd, aerial; (câble, métro) overhead; (fig) light; **compagnie ~ne** airline (company)

aéro: aérobic nf aerobics sg; **aérogare** nf airport (buildings); (en ville) air terminal; **aéroglisseur** nm hovercraft; **aérophagie** nf (Méd) wind, aerophagia (Méd); **aéroport** nm airport; **aérosol** nm aerosol

affaiblir [afebliʀ] /2/: **s'affaiblir** vi to weaken

affaire [afɛʀ] nf (problème, question) matter; (criminelle, judiciaire) case; (scandaleuse etc) affair; (entreprise) business; (*marché, transaction*) (business) deal, (piece of) business no pl; (*occasion intéressante*) good deal; **affaires** nfpl affairs; (*activité commerciale*) business sg; (*effets personnels*) things, belongings; **~s de sport** sports gear; **tirer qn/se tirer d'~** to get sb/o.s. out of trouble; **ceci fera l'~** this will do (nicely); **avoir ~ à** (*en contact*) to be dealing with; **ce sont mes ~s** (*cela me concerne*) that's my business; **occupe-toi de tes ~s!** mind your own business!; **les ~s étrangères** (*Pol*) foreign affairs; **affairer** /1/: **s'affairer** vi to busy o.s., bustle about

affamé, e [afame] *adj* starving

affecter [afɛkte] /1/ *vt* to affect; **~ qch à** to allocate *ou* allot sth to; **~ qn à** to appoint sb to; (*diplomate*) to post sb to

affectif, -ive [afɛktif, -iv] *adj* emotional

affection [afɛksjɔ̃] *nf* affection; (*mal*) ailment; **affectionner** /1/ *vt* to be fond of; **affectueux, -euse** *adj* affectionate

affichage [afiʃaʒ] *nm* billposting; (*électronique*) display; **"~ interdit"** "stick no bills"; **~ à cristaux liquides** liquid crystal display, LCD

affiche [afiʃ] *nf* poster; (*officielle*) (public) notice; (*Théât*) bill; **être à l'~** to be on

afficher [afiʃe] /1/ *vt* (*affiche*) to put up; (*réunion*) to put up a notice about; (*électroniquement*) to display; (*fig*) to exhibit, display; **s'afficher** vi (*péj*) to flaunt o.s.; (*électroniquement*) to be displayed; **"défense d'~"** "no bill posters"

affilée [afile]: **d'~** *adv* at a stretch

affirmatif, -ive [afiʀmatif, -iv] *adj* affirmative

affirmer [afiʀme] /1/ *vt* to assert

affligé, e [afliʒe] *adj* distressed, grieved; **~ de** (*maladie, tare*) afflicted with

affliger [afliʒe] /3/ *vt* (*peiner*) to distress, grieve

affluence [aflyɑ̃s] *nf* crowds *pl*; **heures d'~** rush hour *sg*; **jours d'~** busiest days

affluent [aflyɑ̃] *nm* tributary

affolement [afɔlmɑ̃] *nm* panic

affoler [afɔle] /1/ *vt* to throw into a panic; **s'affoler** vi to panic

affranchir [afʀɑ̃ʃiʀ] /2/ *vt* to put a stamp *ou* stamps on; (*à la machine*) to frank (*BRIT*), meter (*US*); (*fig*) to free, liberate; **affranchissement** *nm* postage

affreux, -euse [afʀø, -øz] *adj* dreadful, awful

affront [afʀɔ̃] *nm* affront; **affrontement** *nm* clash, confrontation

affronter [afʀɔ̃te] /1/ *vt* to confront, face

affût [afy] *nm*: **à l'~ (de)** (*gibier*) lying in wait (for); (*fig*) on the look-out (for)

Afghanistan [afganistɑ̃] *nm*: **l'~** Afghanistan

afin [afɛ̃]: **~ que** *conj* so that, in order that; **~ de faire** in order to do, so as to do

africain, e [afʀikɛ̃, -ɛn] *adj* African ▷ *nm/f*: **A~, e** African

Afrique [afʀik] *nf*: **l'~** Africa; **l'~ australe/du Nord/du Sud** southern/North/South Africa

agacer [agase] /3/ *vt* to irritate

âge [aʒ] *nm* age; **quel ~ as-tu?** how old are you?; **prendre de l'~** to be getting on (in years); **le troisième ~** (*personnes âgées*) senior citizens; (*période*) retirement; **âgé, e** *adj* old, elderly; **âgé de 10 ans** 10 years old

agence [aʒɑ̃s] *nf* agency, office; (*succursale*) branch; **~ immobilière** estate agent's (office) (*BRIT*), real estate office (*US*); **~ de voyages** travel agency

agenda [aʒɛ̃da] *nm* diary; **~ électronique** PDA

Attention à ne pas traduire *agenda* par le mot anglais *agenda*.

agenouiller [aʒ(ə)nuje] /1/: **s'agenouiller** *vi* to kneel (down)

agent, e [aʒɑ̃, -ɑ̃t] *nm/f (aussi:* **~(e) de police)** policeman (policewoman); *(Admin)* official, officer; **~ immobilier** estate agent *(BRIT)*, realtor *(US)*

agglomération [aglɔmeʀasjɔ̃] *nf* town; *(Auto)* built-up area; **l'~ parisienne** the urban area of Paris

aggraver [agʀave] /1/: **s'aggraver** *vi* to worsen

agile [aʒil] *adj* agile, nimble

agir [aʒiʀ] /2/ *vi* to act; **il s'agit de** it's a matter *ou* question of; *(ça traite de)* it is about; **il s'agit de faire** we *(ou you etc)* must do; **de quoi s'agit-il?** what is it about?

agitation [aʒitasjɔ̃] *nf* (hustle and) bustle; *(trouble)* agitation, excitement; *(politique)* unrest, agitation

agité, e [aʒite] *adj* fidgety, restless; *(troublé)* agitated, perturbed; *(mer)* rough

agiter [aʒite] /1/ *vt (bouteille, chiffon)* to shake; *(bras, mains)* to wave; *(préoccuper, exciter)* to trouble

agneau, x [aɲo] *nm* lamb

agonie [agɔni] *nf* mortal agony, death pangs *pl; (fig)* death throes *pl*

agrafe [agʀaf] *nf (de vêtement)* hook, fastener; *(de bureau)* staple; **agrafer** /1/ *vt* to fasten; to staple; **agrafeuse** [agʀaføz] *nf* stapler

agrandir [agʀɑ̃diʀ] /2/ *vt* to extend; **s'agrandir** *vi (ville, famille)* to grow, expand; *(trou, écart)* to get bigger; **agrandissement** *nm (photographie)* enlargement

agréable [agʀeabl] *adj* pleasant, nice

agréé, e [agʀee] *adj:* **concessionnaire ~** registered dealer

agréer [agʀee] /1/ *vt (requête)* to accept; **~ à** to please, suit; **veuillez ~, Monsieur/Madame,**

mes salutations distinguées *(personne nommée)* yours sincerely; *(personne non nommée)* yours faithfully

agrégation [agʀegasjɔ̃] *nf* highest teaching diploma in France; **agrégé, e** *nm/f* holder of the *agrégation*

agrément [agʀemɑ̃] *nm (accord)* consent, approval; *(attraits)* charm, attractiveness; *(plaisir)* pleasure

agresser [agʀese] /1/ *vt* to attack; **agresseur** *nm* aggressor, attacker; *(Pol, Mil)* aggressor; **agressif, -ive** *adj* aggressive

agricole [agʀikɔl] *adj* agricultural; **agriculteur, -trice** *nm/f* farmer; **agriculture** *nf* agriculture; farming

agripper [agʀipe] /1/ *vt* to grab, clutch; **s'~ à** to cling (on) to, clutch, grip

agroalimentaire [agʀɔalimɑ̃tɛʀ] *nm* farm-produce industry

agrumes [agʀym] *nmpl* citrus fruit(s)

aguets [agɛ]: **aux ~** *adv*: **être aux ~** to be on the look-out

ai [e] *vb voir* **avoir**

aide [ɛd] *nm/f* assistant ▷ *nf* assistance, help; *(secours financier)* aid; **à l'~ de** with the help *ou* aid of; **appeler (qn) à l'~** to call for help (from sb); **à l'~!** help!; **~ judiciaire** legal aid; **~ ménagère** *nf* ≈ home help *(BRIT) ou* helper *(US)*; **aide-mémoire** *nm inv* memoranda pages *pl;* (key facts) handbook

aider [ede] /1/ *vt* to help; **~ à qch** to help (towards) sth; **~ qn à faire qch** to help sb to do sth; **s'~ de** *(se servir de)* to use, make use of

aide-soignant, e [ɛdswaɲɑ̃, -ɑ̃t] *nm/f* auxiliary nurse

aie *etc* [ɛ] *vb voir* **avoir**

aïe [aj] *excl* ouch!

aigle [ɛgl] *nm* eagle

aigre [ɛgʀ] *adj* sour, sharp; *(fig)* sharp, cutting; **aigre-doux, -douce** *adj (sauce)* sweet and sour; **aigreur** *nf* sourness; sharpness

aigu, ë [egy] *adj* (*objet, arête*) sharp; (*son, voix*) high-pitched, shrill; (*note*) high(-pitched)

aiguille [eguij] *nf* needle; (*de montre*) hand; **~ à tricoter** knitting needle

aiguiser [egize] /1/ *vt* to sharpen; (*fig*) to stimulate (: *sens*) to excite

ail [aj] *nm* garlic

aile [ɛl] *nf* wing; **aileron** *nm* (*de requin*) fin; **ailier** *nm* winger

aille *etc* [aj] *vb voir* **aller**

ailleurs [ajœʁ] *adv* elsewhere, somewhere else; **partout/nulle part ~** everywhere/nowhere else; **d'~** (*du reste*) moreover, besides; **par ~** (*d'autre part*) moreover, furthermore

aimable [ɛmabl] *adj* kind, nice

aimant [ɛmɑ̃] *nm* magnet

aimer [eme] /1/ *vt* to love; (*d'amitié, affection, par goût*) to like; **j'aimerais ...** (*souhait*) I would like ...; **j'aime faire du ski** I like skiing; **je t'aime** I love you; **bien ~ qn/qch** to like sb/sth; **j'aime mieux Paul (que Pierre)** I prefer Paul (to Pierre); **j'aimerais autant** *ou* **mieux y aller maintenant** I'd sooner *ou* rather go now

aine [ɛn] *nf* groin

aîné, e [ene] *adj* elder, older; (*le plus âgé*) eldest, oldest ▷ *nm/f* oldest child *ou* one, oldest boy *ou* son/girl *ou* daughter

ainsi [ɛ̃si] *adv* (*de cette façon*) like this, in this way, thus; (*ce faisant*) thus ▷ *conj* thus, so; **~ que** (*comme*) (just) as; (*et aussi*) as well as; **pour ~ dire** so to speak; **et ~ de suite** and so on (and so forth)

air [ɛʁ] *nm* air; (*mélodie*) tune; (*expression*) look, air; **paroles/menaces en l'~** empty words/threats; **prendre l'~** to get some (fresh) air; **avoir l'~** to look, appear; **avoir l'~ triste** to look *ou* seem sad; **avoir l'~ de qch** to look like sth; **avoir l'~ de faire** to look as though one is doing

airbag [ɛʁbag] *nm* airbag

aisance [ɛzɑ̃s] *nf* ease; (*richesse*) affluence

aise [ɛz] *nf* comfort; **être à l'~** *ou* **à son ~** to be comfortable; (*pas embarrassé*) to be at ease; (*financièrement*) to be comfortably off; **se mettre à l'~** to make o.s. comfortable; **être mal à l'~** *ou* **à son ~** to be uncomfortable; (*gêné*) to be ill at ease; **en faire à son ~** to do as one likes; **aisé, e** *adj* easy; (*assez riche*) well-to-do, well-off

aisselle [ɛsɛl] *nf* armpit

ait [ɛ] *vb voir* **avoir**

ajonc [aʒɔ̃] *nm* gorse *no pl*

ajourner [aʒuʁne] /1/ *vt* (*réunion*) to adjourn; (*décision*) to defer, postpone

ajouter [aʒute] /1/ *vt* to add

alarme [alaʁm] *nf* alarm; **donner l'~** to give *ou* raise the alarm; **alarmer** /1/ *vt* to alarm; **s'alarmer** *vi* to become alarmed

Albanie [albani] *nf*: **l'~** Albania

album [albɔm] *nm* album

alcool [alkɔl] *nm*: **l'~** alcohol; **un ~** a spirit, a brandy; **bière sans ~** non-alcoholic *ou* alcohol-free beer; **~ à brûler** methylated spirits (*BRIT*), wood alcohol (*US*); **~ à 90°** surgical spirit; **alcoolique** *adj, nm/f* alcoholic; **alcoolisé, e** *adj* alcoholic; **une boisson non alcoolisée** a soft drink; **alcoolisme** *nm* alcoholism; **alco(o)test®** *nm* Breathalyser® (*test*) breath-test

aléatoire [aleatwaʁ] *adj* uncertain; (*Inform, Statistique*) random

alentour [alɑ̃tuʁ] *adv* around (about); **alentours** *nmpl* surroundings; **aux ~s de** in the vicinity *ou* neighbourhood of, around about; (*temps*) around about

alerte [alɛʁt] *adj* agile, nimble; (*style*) brisk, lively ▷ *nf* alert; warning; **~ à la bombe** bomb scare; **alerter** /1/ *vt* to alert

algèbre [alʒɛbʁ] *nf* algebra

Alger [alʒe] *n* Algiers
Algérie [alʒeʀi] *nf*: **l'~** Algeria;
algérien, ne *adj* Algerian ▷ *nm/f*:
Algérien, ne Algerian
algue [alg] *nf* seaweed *no pl*;
(*Bot*) alga
alibi [alibi] *nm* alibi
aligner [aliɲe] /1/ *vt* to align, line
up; (*idées, chiffres*) to string together;
(*adapter*): **~ qch sur** to bring sth into
alignment with; **s'aligner** /1/ *vt* to align;
(*soldats
etc*) to line up; **s'~ sur** (*Pol*) to align
o.s. with
aliment [alimã] *nm* food;
alimentation *nf* (*en eau etc, de
moteur*) supplying; (*commerce*) food
trade; (*régime*) diet; (*Inform*) feed;
alimentation (générale) (general)
grocer's; **alimenter** /1/ *vt* to feed;
(*Tech*): **alimenter (en)** to supply
(with), feed (with); (*fig*) to sustain,
keep going
allaiter [alete] /1/ *vt* to (breast-)feed,
nurse; (*animal*) to suckle
allécher [aleʃe] /6/ *vt*: **~ qn** to make
sb's mouth water; to tempt sb,
entice sb
allée [ale] *nf* (*de jardin*) path; (*en ville*)
avenue, drive; **~s et venues** comings
and goings
allégé, e [aleʒe] *adj* (*yaourt etc*)
low-fat
alléger [aleʒe] /6, 3/ *vt* (*voiture*) to
make lighter; (*chargement*) to lighten;
(*souffrance*) to alleviate, soothe
Allemagne [almaɲ] *nf*: **l'~**
Germany; **allemand, e** *adj* German
▷ *nm* (*Ling*) German ▷ *nm/f*:
Allemand, e German
aller [ale] /9/ *nm* (*trajet*) outward
journey; (*billet*) single (*BRIT*) *ou*
one-way ticket (*US*) ▷ *vi* (*gén*) to
go; **~ simple** (*billet*) single (*BRIT*) *ou*
one-way ticket (*US*); **~ (et) retour (AR)**
return trip *ou* journey (*BRIT*), round
trip (*US*); (*billet*) return (*BRIT*) *ou*
round-trip (*US*) ticket; **~ à** (*convenir*)
to suit; (*forme, pointure etc*) to fit;

~ avec (*couleurs, style etc*) to go (well)
with; **je vais le faire/me fâcher** I'm
going to do it/to get angry; **~ voir/
chercher qn** to go and see/look for
sb; **comment allez-vous?** how are
you?; **comment ça va?** how are
you?; (*affaires etc*) how are things?;
il va bien/mal he's well/not well,
he's fine/ill; **ça va bien/mal** (*affaires
etc*) it's going well/not going well;
~ mieux to be better; **allez!** come
on!; **allons!** come now!
allergie [alɛʀʒi] *nf* allergy
allergique [alɛʀʒik] *adj*: **~ à**
allergic to
alliance [aljãs] *nf* (*Mil, Pol*) alliance;
(*bague*) wedding ring
allier [alje] /7/ *vt* (*Pol, gén*) to ally; (*fig*)
to combine; **s'allier** to become allies;
(*éléments, caractéristiques*) to combine
allô [alo] *excl* hullo, hallo
allocation [alɔkasjõ] *nf* allowance;
~ (de) chômage unemployment
benefit; **~s familiales** ≈ child benefit
allonger [alõʒe] /3/ *vt* to lengthen,
make longer; (*étendre: bras, jambe*)
to stretch (out); **s'allonger** *vi* to
get longer; (*se coucher*) to lie down,
stretch out; **~ le pas** to hasten one's
step(s)
allumage [alymaʒ] *nm* (*Auto*)
ignition
allume-cigare [alymsigaʀ] *nm inv*
cigar lighter
allumer [alyme] /1/ *vt* (*lampe, phare,
radio*) to put *ou* switch on; (*pièce*)
to put *ou* switch the light(s) on in;
(*feu, bougie, cigare, pipe, gaz*) to light;
s'allumer *vi* (*lumière, lampe*) to come
ou go on
allumette [alymɛt] *nf* match
allure [alyʀ] *nf* (*vitesse*) speed; (: *à
pied*) pace; (*démarche*) walk; (*aspect,
air*) look; **avoir de l'~** to have style; **à
toute ~** at full speed
allusion [a(l)lyzjõ] *nf* allusion; (*sous-
entendu*) hint; **faire ~ à** to allude *ou*
refer to; to hint at

MOT-CLÉ

alors [alɔʀ] *adv* **1** (*à ce moment-là*) then, at that time; **il habitait alors à Paris** he lived in Paris at that time **2** (*par conséquent*) then; **tu as fini? alors je m'en vais** have you finished? I'm going then **3**: **et alors?** so (what)? ▶ *conj*: **alors que** (*au moment où*) when, as; **il est arrivé alors que je partais** he arrived as I was leaving; (*tandis que*) whereas, while; **alors que son frère travaillait dur, lui se reposait** while his brother was working hard, HE would rest; (*bien que*) even though; **il a été puni alors qu'il n'a rien fait** he was punished, even though he had done nothing

alourdir [aluʀdiʀ] /2/ *vt* to weigh down, make heavy
Alpes [alp] *nfpl*: **les ~** the Alps
alphabet [alfabɛ] *nm* alphabet; (*livre*) ABC (book)
alpinisme [alpinism] *nm* mountaineering, climbing
Alsace [alzas] *nf* Alsace; **alsacien, ne** *adj* Alsatian ▷ *nm/f*: **Alsacien, ne** Alsatian
altermondialisme [altɛʀmɔ̃djalism] *nm* anti-globalism; **altermondialiste** *adj, nm/f* anti-globalist
alternatif, -ive [altɛʀnatif, -iv] *adj* alternating ▷ *nf* alternative; **alternative** *nf* (*choix*) alternative; **alterner** /1/ *vt* to alternate
altitude [altityd] *nf* altitude, height
alto [alto] *nm* (*instrument*) viola
aluminium [alyminjɔm] *nm* aluminium (BRIT), aluminum (US)
amabilité [amabilite] *nf* kindness
amaigrissant, e [amegʀisɑ̃, -ɑ̃t] *adj*: **régime ~** slimming (BRIT) *ou* weight-reduction (US) diet
amande [amɑ̃d] *nf* (*de l'amandier*) almond; **amandier** *nm* almond (tree)

amant [amɑ̃] *nm* lover
amas [amɑ] *nm* heap, pile; **amasser** /1/ *vt* to amass
amateur [amatœʀ] *nm* amateur; **en ~** (*péj*) amateurishly; **~ de musique/ sport** *etc* music/sport *etc* lover
ambassade [ɑ̃basad] *nf* embassy; **l'~ de France** the French Embassy; **ambassadeur, -drice** *nm/f* ambassador/ambassadress
ambiance [ɑ̃bjɑ̃s] *nf* atmosphere; **il y a de l'~** everyone's having a good time
ambigu, ë [ɑ̃bigy] *adj* ambiguous
ambitieux, -euse [ɑ̃bisjø, -jøz] *adj* ambitious
ambition [ɑ̃bisjɔ̃] *nf* ambition
ambulance [ɑ̃bylɑ̃s] *nf* ambulance; **ambulancier, -ière** *nm/f* ambulanceman/woman (BRIT), paramedic (US)
âme [ɑm] *nf* soul; **~ sœur** kindred spirit
amélioration [ameljɔʀasjɔ̃] *nf* improvement
améliorer [ameljɔʀe] /1/ *vt* to improve; **s'améliorer** *vi* to improve, get better
aménager [amenaʒe] /3/ *vt* (*agencer*) to fit out; (: *terrain*) to lay out; (: *quartier, territoire*) to develop; (*installer*) to fix up, put in; **ferme aménagée** converted farmhouse
amende [amɑ̃d] *nf* fine; **faire ~ honorable** to make amends
amener [am(ə)ne] /5/ *vt* to bring; (*causer*) to bring about; **s'amener** *vi* (*fam*) to show up, turn up; **~ qn à qch/à faire** to lead sb to sth/to do
amer, amère [amɛʀ] *adj* bitter
américain, e [ameʀikɛ̃, -ɛn] *adj* American ▷ *nm/f*: **A~, e** American
Amérique [ameʀik] *nf* America; **l'~ centrale** Central America; **l'~ latine** Latin America; **l'~ du Nord** North America; **l'~ du Sud** South America
amertume [amɛʀtym] *nf* bitterness

ameublement [amœbləmã] nm furnishing; (meubles) furniture

ami, e [ami] nm/f friend; (amant/maîtresse) boyfriend/girlfriend ▷ adj: **pays/groupe ~** friendly country/group; **petit ~/petite ~e** boyfriend/girlfriend

amiable [amjabl]: **à l'~** adv (Jur) out of court; (gén) amicably

amiante [amjãt] nm asbestos

amical, e, -aux [amikal, -o] adj friendly; **amicalement** adv in a friendly way; (formule épistolaire) regards

amincir [amɛ̃siʀ] /2/ vt: **~ qn** to make sb thinner ou slimmer; (vêtement) to make sb look slimmer

amincissant, e [amɛ̃sisã, -ãt] adj slimming; **régime ~** diet; **crème ~e** slimming cream

amiral, -aux [amiʀal, -o] nm admiral

amitié [amitje] nf friendship; **prendre en ~** to take a liking to; **faire** ou **présenter ses ~s à qn** to send sb one's best wishes; **~s** (formule épistolaire) (with) best wishes

amonceler [amɔ̃s(ə)le] /4/ vt to pile ou heap up; **s'amonceler** to pile ou heap up; (fig) to accumulate

amont [amɔ̃]: **en ~** adv upstream

amorce [amɔʀs] nf (sur un hameçon) bait; (explosif) cap; (tube) primer; (: contenu) priming; (fig: début) beginning(s), start

amortir [amɔʀtiʀ] /2/ vt (atténuer: choc) to absorb, cushion; (: bruit, douleur) to deaden; (Comm: dette) to pay off; **~ un abonnement** to make a season ticket pay (for itself); **amortisseur** nm shock absorber

amour [amuʀ] nm love; **faire l'~** to make love; **amoureux, -euse** adj (regard, tempérament) amorous; (vie, problèmes) love cpd; (personne): **être amoureux (de qn)** to be in love (with sb) ▷ nmpl courting couple(s); **amour-propre** nm self-esteem, pride

ampère [ãpɛʀ] nm amp(ere)

amphithéâtre [ãfiteatʀ] nm amphitheatre; (d'université) lecture hall ou theatre

ample [ãpl] adj (vêtement) roomy, ample; (gestes, mouvement) broad; (ressources) ample; **amplement** adv: **amplement suffisant** more than enough; **ampleur** nf (de dégâts, problème) extent

amplificateur [ãplifikatœʀ] nm amplifier

amplifier [ãplifje] /7/ vt (fig) to expand, increase

ampoule [ãpul] nf (électrique) bulb; (de médicament) phial; (aux mains, pieds) blister

amusant, e [amyzã, -ãt] adj (divertissant, spirituel) entertaining, amusing; (comique) funny, amusing

amuse-gueule [amyzgœl] nm inv appetizer, snack

amusement [amyzmã] nm (voir amusé) amusement; (jeu etc) pastime, diversion

amuser [amyze] /1/ vt (divertir) to entertain, amuse; (égayer, faire rire) to amuse; **s'amuser** vi (jouer) to amuse o.s.; (se divertir) to enjoy o.s., have fun; (fig) to mess around

amygdale [amidal] nf tonsil

an [ã] nm year; **être âgé de** ou **avoir 3 ans** to be 3 (years old); **le jour de l'an, le premier de l'an, le nouvel an** New Year's Day

analphabète [analfabɛt] nm/f illiterate

analyse [analiz] nf analysis; (Méd) test; **analyser** /1/ vt to analyse; (Méd) to test

ananas [anana(s)] nm pineapple

anatomie [anatɔmi] nf anatomy

ancêtre [ãsɛtʀ] nm/f ancestor

anchois [ãʃwa] nm anchovy

ancien, ne [ãsjɛ̃, -jɛn] adj old; (de jadis, de l'antiquité) ancient; (précédent, ex-) former, old; (par l'expérience) senior ▷ nm/f (dans une tribu etc) elder;

ancienneté nf (Admin) (length of) service; (privilèges obtenus) seniority

ancre [ākʀ] nf anchor; **jeter/lever l'~** to cast/weigh anchor; **ancrer** /1/ vt (Constr: câble etc) to anchor; (fig) to fix firmly

Andorre [ādɔʀ] nf Andorra

andouille [āduj] nf (Culin) sausage made of chitterlings; (fam) clot, nit

âne [ɑn] nm donkey, ass; (péj) dunce

anéantir [aneātiʀ] /2/ vt to annihilate, wipe out; (fig) to obliterate, destroy

anémie [anemi] nf anaemia; **anémique** adj anaemic

anesthésie [anɛstezi] nf anaesthesia; **~ générale/locale** general/local anaesthetic; **faire une ~ locale à qn** to give sb a local anaesthetic

ange [āʒ] nm angel; **être aux ~s** to be over the moon

angine [āʒin] nf throat infection; **~ de poitrine** angina (pectoris)

anglais, e [āglɛ, -ɛz] adj English ▷ nm (Ling) English ▷ nm/f: **A~, e** Englishman/woman; **les A~** the English; **filer à l'~e** to take French leave

angle [āgl] nm angle; (coin) corner

Angleterre [āglətɛʀ] nf: **l'~** England

anglo... [āglɔ] préfixe Anglo-, anglo(-); **anglophone** adj English-speaking

angoisse [āgwas] nf: **l'~** anguish no pl; **angoissé, e** adj (personne) distressed

anguille [āgij] nf eel

animal, e, -aux [animal, -o] adj, nm animal

animateur, -trice [animatœʀ, -tʀis] nm/f (de télévision) host; (de groupe) leader, organizer

animation [animasjɔ̃] nf (voir animé) busyness; liveliness; (Ciné: technique) animation

animé, e [anime] adj (rue, lieu) busy, lively; (conversation, réunion) lively, animated

animer [anime] /1/ vt (ville, soirée) to liven up; (mettre en mouvement) to drive

anis [ani(s)] nm (Culin) aniseed; (Bot) anise

ankyloser [ākiloze] /1/: **s'ankyloser** vi to get stiff

anneau, x [ano] nm (de rideau, bague) ring; (de chaîne) link

année [ane] nf year

annexe [anɛks] adj (problème) related; (document) appended; (salle) adjoining ▷ nf (bâtiment) annex(e); (jointe à une lettre, un dossier) enclosure

anniversaire [anivɛʀsɛʀ] nm birthday; (d'un événement, bâtiment) anniversary

annonce [anɔ̃s] nf announcement; (signe, indice) sign; (aussi: **~ publicitaire**) advertisement; **les petites ~s** the small ou classified ads

annoncer [anɔ̃se] /3/ vt to announce; (être le signe de) to herald; **s'annoncer bien/difficile** to look promising/difficult

annuaire [anɥɛʀ] nm yearbook, annual; **~ téléphonique** (telephone) directory, phone book

annuel, le [anɥɛl] adj annual, yearly

annulation [anylasjɔ̃] nf cancellation

annuler [anyle] /1/ vt (rendez-vous, voyage) to cancel, call off; (jugement) to quash (BRIT), repeal (US); (Math, Physique) to cancel out

anonymat [anɔnima] nm anonymity; **garder l'~** to remain anonymous

anonyme [anɔnim] adj anonymous; (fig) impersonal

anorak [anɔʀak] nm anorak

anorexie [anɔʀɛksi] nf anorexia

anormal, e, -aux [anɔʀmal, -o] adj abnormal

ANPE sigle f (= Agence nationale pour l'emploi) national employment agency (functions include job creation)

antarctique [ɑ̃taʀktik] *adj* Antarctic
▷ *nm*: **l'A~** the Antarctic

antenne [ɑ̃tɛn] *nf* (*de radio, télévision*)
aerial; (*d'insecte*) antenna, feeler;
(*poste avancé*) outpost; (*petite
succursale*) sub-branch; **passer
à/avoir l'~** to go/be on the air;
~ parabolique satellite dish

antérieur, e [ɑ̃teʀjœʀ] *adj* (*d'avant*)
previous, earlier; (*de devant*) front

anti... [ɑ̃ti] *préfixe* anti...;
antialcoolique *adj* anti-alcohol;
antibiotique *nm* antibiotic;
antibrouillard *adj*: **phare
antibrouillard** fog lamp

anticipation [ɑ̃tisipasjɔ̃] *nf*: **livre/
film d'~** science fiction book/film

anticipé, e [ɑ̃tisipe] *adj*: **avec mes
remerciements ~s** thanking you in
advance *ou* anticipation

anticiper [ɑ̃tisipe] /1/ *vt* (*événement,
coup*) to anticipate, foresee

anti: anticorps *nm* antibody;
antidote *nm* antidote; **antigel** *nm*
antifreeze; **antihistaminique** *nm*
antihistamine

antillais, e [ɑ̃tijɛ, -ɛz] *adj* West
Indian, Caribbean ▷ *nm/f*: **A~, e** West
Indian, Caribbean

Antilles [ɑ̃tij] *nfpl*: **les ~** the West
Indies; **les Grandes/Petites ~** the
Greater/Lesser Antilles

antilope [ɑ̃tilɔp] *nf* antelope

anti: antimite(s) *adj, nm*: **(produit)
antimite(s)** mothproofer, moth
repellent; **antimondialisation** *nf*
anti-globalization; **antipathique**
adj unpleasant, disagreeable;
antipelliculaire *adj* anti-dandruff

antiquaire [ɑ̃tikɛʀ] *nm/f* antique
dealer

antique [ɑ̃tik] *adj* antique; (*très
vieux*) ancient, antiquated; **antiquité**
nf (*objet*) antique; **l'Antiquité**
Antiquity; **magasin/marchand
d'antiquités** antique shop/dealer

anti: antirabique *adj* rabies *cpd*;
antirouille *adj inv* anti-rust *cpd*;

antisémite *adj* anti-Semitic;
antiseptique *adj, nm* antiseptic;
antivirus *nm* (*Inform*) antivirus
(program); **antivol** *adj, nm*:
(dispositif) antivol antitheft device

anxieux, -euse [ɑ̃ksjø, -jøz] *adj*
anxious, worried

AOC *sigle f* (= *Appellation d'origine
contrôlée*) *guarantee of quality of wine*

août [u(t)] *nm* August

apaiser [apeze] /1/ *vt* (*colère*) to calm;
(*douleur*) to soothe; (*personne*) to calm
(down), pacify; **s'apaiser** *vi* (*tempête,
bruit*) to die down, subside; (*personne*)
to calm down

apercevoir [apɛʀsəvwaʀ] /28/ *vt* to
see; **s'apercevoir de** *vt* to notice; **s'~
que** to notice that

aperçu [apɛʀsy] *nm* (*vue d'ensemble*)
general survey

apéritif, -ive [apeʀitif, -iv] *adj*
which stimulates the appetite ▷ *nm*
(*boisson*) aperitif; (*réunion*) (pre-lunch
ou -dinner) drinks *pl*

à-peu-près [apøpʀɛ] *nm inv* (*péj*)
vague approximation

apeuré, e [apœʀe] *adj* frightened,
scared

aphte [aft] *nm* mouth ulcer

apitoyer [apitwaje] /8/ *vt* to move
to pity; **s'~ (sur qn/qch)** to feel pity
ou compassion (for sb/over sth)

aplatir [aplatiʀ] /2/ *vt* to flatten;
s'aplatir *vi* to become flatter; (*écrasé*)
to be flattened

aplomb [aplɔ̃] *nm* (*équilibre*) balance,
equilibrium; (*fig*) self-assurance
nerve; **d'~** steady

apostrophe [apɔstʀɔf] *nf* (*signe*)
apostrophe

apparaître [apaʀɛtʀ] /57/ *vi* to
appear

appareil [apaʀɛj] *nm* (*outil, machine*)
piece of apparatus, device; (*électrique
etc*) appliance; (*avion*) (aero)plane ,
aircraft *inv*; (*téléphonique*) telephone;
(*dentier*) brace (BRIT), braces (US); **qui
est à l'~?** who's speaking?; **dans le**

plus simple ~ in one's birthday suit; **~ (photo)** camera; **~ numérique** digital camera; **appareiller** /1/ vi (Navig) to cast off, get under way ▷ vt (assortir) to match up

apparemment [aparamɑ̃] adv apparently

apparence [aparɑ̃s] nf appearance; **en ~** apparently

apparent, e [aparɑ̃, -ɑ̃t] adj visible; (évident) obvious; (superficiel) apparent

apparenté, e [aparɑ̃te] adj: **~ à** related to; (fig) similar to

apparition [aparisjɔ̃] nf appearance; (surnaturelle) apparition

appartement [apartəmɑ̃] nm flat (BRIT), apartment (US)

appartenir [apartəniʀ] /22/: **~ à** vt to belong to; **il lui appartient de** it is up to him to

apparu, e [apary] pp de **apparaître**

appât [apɑ] nm (Pêche) bait; (fig) lure, bait

appel [apɛl] nm call; (nominal) roll call (: Scol) register; (Mil: recrutement) call-up; **faire ~ à** (invoquer) to appeal to; (avoir recours à) to call on; (nécessiter) to call for, require; **faire ou interjeter ~** (Jur) to appeal; **faire l'~** to call the roll; (Scol) to call the register; **sans ~** (fig) final, irrevocable; **~ d'offres** (Comm) invitation to tender; **faire un ~ de phares** to flash one's headlights; **~ (téléphonique)** (tele) phone call

appelé [ap(ə)le] nm (Mil) conscript

appeler [ap(ə)le] /4/ vt to call; (faire venir: médecin etc) to call, send for; **s'appeler** vi: **elle s'appelle Gabrielle** her name is Gabrielle, she's called Gabrielle; **comment vous appelez-vous?** what's your name?; **comment ça s'appelle?** what is it ou that called?

appendicite [apɑ̃disit] nf appendicitis

appesantir [apəzɑ̃tiʀ] /2/: **s'appesantir** vi to grow heavier; **s'~ sur** (fig) to dwell at length on

appétissant, e [apetisɑ̃, -ɑ̃t] adj appetizing, mouth-watering

appétit [apeti] nm appetite; **bon ~!** enjoy your meal!

applaudir [aplodiʀ] /2/ vt to applaud ▷ vi to applaud, clap; **applaudissements** nmpl applause sg, clapping sg

appli [apli] nf app

application [aplikasjɔ̃] nf application

appliquer [aplike] /1/ vt to apply; (loi) to enforce; **s'appliquer** vi (élève etc) to apply o.s.; **s'~ à** to apply to

appoint [apwɛ̃] nm (extra) contribution ou help; **avoir/faire l'~** to have/give the right change ou money; **chauffage d'~** extra heating

apporter [aporte] /1/ vt to bring

appréciable [apresjabl] adj appreciable

apprécier [apresje] /7/ vt to appreciate; (évaluer) to estimate, assess

appréhender [apreɑ̃de] /1/ vt (craindre) to dread; (arrêter) to apprehend

apprendre [aprɑ̃dʀ] /58/ vt to learn; (événement, résultats) to learn of, hear of; **~ qch à qn** (informer) to tell sb (of) sth; (enseigner) to teach sb sth; **~ à faire qch** to learn to do sth; **~ à qn à faire qch** to teach sb to do sth; **apprenti, e** nm/f apprentice; **apprentissage** nm learning; (Comm, Scol: période) apprenticeship

apprêter [aprete] /1/: **s'apprêter** vi: **s'~ à qch/à faire qch** to prepare for sth/for doing sth

appris, e [apri, -iz] pp de **apprendre**

apprivoiser [aprivwaze] /1/ vt to tame

approbation [aprobasjɔ̃] nf approval

approcher [aproʃe] /1/ vi to approach, come near ▷ vt to approach; (rapprocher): **~ qch (de qch)** to bring ou put ou move sth near (to sth); **s'approcher de** to approach, go ou come ou move near to; **~ de** (lieu, but) to draw near to; (quantité, moment) to approach

approfondir [apʀɔfɔ̃diʀ] /2/ vt to deepen; (question) to go further into

approprié, e [apʀɔpʀije] adj: **~ (à)** appropriate (to), suited (to)

approprier [apʀɔpʀije] /7/: **s'approprier** vt to appropriate, take over; **s'~ en** to stock up with

approuver [apʀuve] /1/ vt to agree with; (trouver louable) to approve of

approvisionner [apʀɔvizjɔne] /1/ vt to supply; (compte bancaire) to pay funds into; **s'~ en** to stock up with

approximatif, -ive [apʀɔksimatif, -iv] adj approximate, rough; (imprécis) vague

appt abr = **appartement**

appui [apɥi] nm support; **prendre ~ sur** to lean on; (objet) to rest on; **l'~ de la fenêtre** the windowsill, the window ledge

appuyer [apɥije] /8/ vt (poser, soutenir: personne, demande) to support; (com   ) to lean on; (comptersur) to rely on; **~ qch sur/contre/à** to lean ou rest sth on/against/on; **~ sur le frein** to brake, to apply the brakes

après [apʀɛ] prép after ▷ adv afterwards; **deux heures ~** two hours later; **~ qu'il est parti/avoir fait** after he left/having done; **courir ~ qn** to run after sb; **crier ~ qn** to shout at sb; **être toujours ~ qn** (critiquer etc) to be always on at sb; **~ quoi** after which; **d'~** (selon) according to; **~ coup** after the event, afterwards; **~ tout** (au fond) after all; **et (puis) ~?** so what?; **après-demain** adv the day after tomorrow; **après-midi** [apʀɛmidi] nm ou f inv afternoon; **après-rasage** nm inv after-shave; **après-shampooing**

nm inv conditioner; **après-ski** nm inv snow boot

après-soleil [apʀɛsɔlɛj] adj inv after-sun cpd ▷ nm after-sun cream ou lotion

apte [apt] adj: **~ à qch/faire qch** capable of sth/doing sth; **~ (au service)** (Mil) fit (for service)

aquarelle [akwaʀɛl] nf watercolour

aquarium [akwaʀjɔm] nm aquarium

arabe [aʀab] adj Arabic; (désert, cheval) Arabian; (nation, peuple) Arab ▷ nm (Ling) Arabic ▷ nm/f: **A~** Arab

Arabie [aʀabi] nf: **l'~ Saoudite** ou **Séoudite** Saudi Arabia

arachide [aʀaʃid] nf groundnut (plant); (graine) peanut, groundnut

araignée [aʀɛɲe] nf spider

arbitraire [aʀbitʀɛʀ] adj arbitrary

arbitre [aʀbitʀ] nm (Sport) referee (: Tennis, Cricket) umpire; (fig) arbiter, judge; (Jur) arbitrator; **arbitrer** /1/ vt to referee; to umpire; to arbitrate

arbre [aʀbʀ] nm tree; (Tech) shaft

arbuste [aʀbyst] nm small shrub

arc [aʀk] nm (arme) bow; (Géom) arc; (Archit) arch; **en ~ de cercle** semi-circular

arcade [aʀkad] nf arch(way); **~s** arcade sg, arches

arc-en-ciel [aʀkɑ̃sjɛl] nm rainbow

arche [aʀʃ] nf arch; **~ de Noé** Noah's Ark

archéologie [aʀkeɔlɔʒi] nf arch(a)eology; **archéologue** nm/f arch(a)eologist

archet [aʀʃɛ] nm bow

archipel [aʀʃipɛl] nm archipelago

architecte [aʀʃitɛkt] nm architect

architecture [aʀʃitɛktyʀ] nf architecture

archives [aʀʃiv] nfpl (collection) archives

arctique [aʀktik] adj Arctic ▷ nm: **l'A~** the Arctic

ardent, e [aʀdɑ̃, -ɑ̃t] adj (soleil) blazing; (amour) ardent, passionate; (prière) fervent

ardoise [aʀdwaz] nf slate
ardu, e [aʀdy] adj (travail) arduous; (problème) difficult
arène [aʀɛn] nf arena; **arènes** nfpl bull-ring sg
arête [aʀɛt] nf (de poisson) bone; (d'une montagne) ridge
argent [aʀʒɑ̃] nm (métal) silver; (monnaie) money; **~ de poche** pocket money; **~ liquide** ready money, (ready) cash; **argenterie** nf silverware
argentin, e [aʀʒɑ̃tɛ̃, -in] adj Argentinian ▷ nm/f: **A~, e** Argentinian
Argentine [aʀʒɑ̃tin] nf: **l'~** Argentina
argentique [aʀʒɑ̃tik] adj (appareil photo) film cpd
argile [aʀʒil] nf clay
argot [aʀgo] nm slang; **argotique** adj slang cpd; (très familier) slangy
argument [aʀgymɑ̃] nm argument
argumenter [aʀgymɑ̃te] /1/ vi to argue
aride [aʀid] adj arid
aristocratie [aʀistɔkʀasi] nf aristocracy; **aristocratique** adj aristocratic
arithmétique [aʀitmetik] adj arithmetic(al) ▷ nf arithmetic
arme [aʀm] nf weapon; **armes** nfpl weapons, arms; (blason) (coat of) arms; **~ à feu** firearm; **~s de destruction massive** weapons of mass destruction
armée [aʀme] nf army; **~ de l'air** Air Force; **~ de terre** Army
armer [aʀme] /1/ vt to arm; (arme à feu) to cock; (appareil photo) to wind on; **s'armer** vi: **s'~ de** to arm o.s. with; **~ qch de** to reinforce sth with
armistice [aʀmistis] nm armistice; **l'A~** ≈ Remembrance (BRIT) ou Veterans (US) Day
armoire [aʀmwaʀ] nf (tall) cupboard; (penderie) wardrobe (BRIT), closet (US)

armure [aʀmyʀ] nf armour no pl, suit of armour; **armurier** nm gunsmith
arnaque [aʀnak] (fam) nf swindling; **c'est de l'~** it's daylight robbery; **arnaquer** /1/ (fam) vt to do (fam)
arobase [aʀobaz] nf (Inform) 'at' symbol; **"paul ~ société point fr"** "paul at société dot fr"
aromates [aʀɔmat] nmpl seasoning sg, herbs (and spices)
aromathérapie [aʀɔmateʀapi] nf aromatherapy
aromatisé, e [aʀɔmatize] adj flavoured
arôme [aʀom] nm aroma
arracher [aʀaʃe] /1/ vt to pull out; (page etc) to tear off, tear out; (légume, herbe, souche) to pull up; (bras etc) to tear off; **s'arracher** vt (article très recherché) to fight over; **~ qch à qn** to snatch sth from sb; (fig) to wring sth out of sb
arrangement [aʀɑ̃ʒmɑ̃] nm arrangement
arranger [aʀɑ̃ʒe] /3/ vt to arrange; (réparer) to fix, put right; (régler) to settle, sort out; (convenir à) to suit, be convenient for; **cela m'arrange** that suits me (fine); **s'arranger** vi (se mettre d'accord) to come to an agreement ou arrangement; **je vais m'~** I'll manage; **ça va s'~** it'll sort itself out
arrestation [aʀɛstasjɔ̃] nf arrest
arrêt [aʀɛ] nm stopping; (de bus etc) stop; (Jur) judgment, decision; **être à l'~** to be stopped; **rester ou tomber en ~ devant** to stop short in front of; **sans ~** non-stop; (fréquemment) continually; **~ de travail** stoppage (of work)
arrêter [aʀete] /1/ vt to stop; (chauffage etc) to turn off, switch off; (fixer: date etc) to appoint, decide on; (criminel, suspect) to arrest; **s'arrêter** vi to stop; **~ de faire** to stop doing
arrhes [aʀ] nfpl deposit sg
arrière [aʀjɛʀ] nm back; (Sport) fullback ▷ adj inv: **siège/roue**

~ back ou rear seat/wheel; **à l'~** behind, at the back; **en ~** behind; (regarder) backwards; **arrière-goût** nm aftertaste; **arrière-grand-mère** nf great-grandmother; **arrière-grand-père** nm great-grandfather; **arrière-pays** nm inv hinterland; **arrière-pensée** nf ulterior motive; (doute) mental reservation; **arrière-plan** nm background; **à l'arrière-plan** in the background; **arrière-saison** nf late autumn

arrimer [aʀime] /1/ vt (cargaison) to stow; (fixer) to secure

arrivage [aʀivaʒ] nm consignment

arrivée [aʀive] nf arrival; (ligne d'arrivée) finish

arriver [aʀive] /1/ vi to arrive; (survenir) to happen, occur; **il arrive à Paris à 8 h** he gets to ou arrives in Paris at 8; **~ à** (atteindre) to reach; **~ à (faire) qch** to manage (to do) sth; **en ~ à faire ...** to end up doing ...; **il arrive que ...** it happens that ...; **il lui arrive de faire ...** he sometimes does ...

arrobase [aʀɔbaz] nf (Inform) 'at' symbol

arrogance [aʀɔgɑ̃s] nf arrogance

arrogant, e [aʀɔgɑ̃, -ɑ̃t] adj arrogant

arrondissement [aʀɔ̃dismɑ̃] nm (Admin) ≈ district

arroser [aʀoze] /1/ vt to water; (victoire etc) to celebrate (over a drink); (Culin) to baste; **arrosoir** nm watering can

arsenal, -aux [aʀsənal, -o] nm (Navig) naval dockyard; (Mil) arsenal; (fig) gear, paraphernalia

art [aʀ] nm art

artère [aʀtɛʀ] nf (Anat) artery; (rue) main road

arthrite [aʀtʀit] nf arthritis

artichaut [aʀtiʃo] nm artichoke

article [aʀtikl] nm article; (Comm) item, article; **à l'~ de la mort** at the point of death

articulation [aʀtikylasjɔ̃] nf articulation; (Anat) joint

articuler [aʀtikyle] /1/ vt to articulate

artificiel, le [aʀtifisjɛl] adj artificial

artisan [aʀtizɑ̃] nm artisan, (self-employed) craftsman; **artisanal, e, -aux** [aʀtizanal, -o] adj of ou made by craftsmen; (péj) cottage industry cpd; **de fabrication artisanale** home-made; **artisanat** [aʀtizana] nm arts and crafts pl

artiste [aʀtist] nm/f artist; (Théât, Mus) performer; (de variétés) entertainer; **artistique** adj artistic

as vb [a]; voir **avoir** ▷ nm [ɑs] ace

ascenseur [asɑ̃sœʀ] nm lift (BRIT), elevator (US)

ascension [asɑ̃sjɔ̃] nf ascent; (de montagne) climb; **l'A~** (Rel) the Ascension

● **L'ASCENSION**
●
● The fête de l'Ascension is a public
● holiday in France. It always falls on
● a Thursday, usually in May. Many
● French people take the following
● Friday off work and enjoy a long
● weekend.

asiatique [azjatik] adj Asian, Asiatic ▷ nm/f: **A~** Asian

Asie [azi] nf: **l'~** Asia

asile [azil] nm (refuge) refuge, sanctuary; **droit d'~** (Pol) (political) asylum

aspect [aspɛ] nm appearance, look; (fig) aspect, side; **à l'~ de** at the sight of

asperge [aspɛʀʒ] nf asparagus no pl

asperger [aspɛʀʒe] /3/ vt to spray, sprinkle

asphalte [asfalt] nm asphalt

asphyxier [asfiksje] /7/ vt to suffocate, asphyxiate; (fig) to stifle

aspirateur [aspiʀatœʀ] nm vacuum cleaner; **passer l'~** to vacuum

aspirer [aspiʀe] /1/ vt (air) to inhale; (liquide) to suck (up); (appareil) to suck ou draw up; **~ à** to aspire to

aspirine [aspiʀin] nf aspirin

assagir [asaʒiʀ] /2/ vt, **s'assagir** vi to quieten down, settle down

assaillir [asajiʀ] /13/ vt to assail, attack

assaisonnement [asɛzɔnmɑ̃] nm seasoning

assaisonner [asɛzɔne] /1/ vt to season

assassin [asasɛ̃] nm murderer; assassin; **assassiner** /1/ vt to murder; (Pol) to assassinate

assaut [aso] nm assault, attack; **prendre d'~** to (take by) storm, assault; **donner l'~ (à)** to attack

assécher [aseʃe] /6/ vt to drain

assemblage [asɑ̃blaʒ] nm (action) assembling; **un ~ de** (fig) a collection of

assemblée [asɑ̃ble] nf (réunion) meeting; (public, assistance) gathering; (Pol) assembly; **l'A~ nationale (AN)** the (French) National Assembly

assembler [asɑ̃ble] /1/ vt (joindre, monter) to assemble, put together; (amasser) to gather (together), collect (together); **s'assembler** vi to gather

asseoir [aswaʀ] /26/ vt (malade, bébé) to sit up; (personne debout) to sit down; (autorité, réputation) to establish; **s'asseoir** vi to sit (o.s.) down

assez [ase] adv (suffisamment) enough, sufficiently; (passablement) rather, quite, fairly; **~ de pain/livres** enough ou sufficient bread/books; **vous en avez ~?** have you got enough?; **j'en ai ~!** I've had enough!

assidu, e [asidy] adj assiduous, painstaking; (régulier) regular

assied etc [asje] vb voir asseoir

assiérai etc [asjeʀe] vb voir asseoir

assiette [asjɛt] nf plate; (contenu) plate(ful); **il n'est pas dans son ~** he's not feeling quite himself; **~ à dessert** dessert ou side plate; **~ anglaise** assorted cold meats; **~ creuse** (soup) dish, soup plate; **~ plate** (dinner) plate

assimiler [asimile] /1/ vt to assimilate, absorb; (comparer): **~ qch/qn à** to liken ou compare sth/sb to; **s'assimiler** vi (s'intégrer) to be assimilated ou absorbed

assis, e [asi, -iz] pp de asseoir ▷ adj sitting (down), seated

assistance [asistɑ̃s] nf (public) audience; (aide) assistance; **enfant de l'A~ (publique)** child in care

assistant, e [asistɑ̃, -ɑ̃t] nm/f assistant; (d'université) probationary lecturer; **~e sociale** social worker

assisté, e [asiste] adj (Auto) power-assisted; **~ par ordinateur** computer-assisted; **direction ~e** power steering

assister [asiste] /1/ vt to assist; **~ à** (scène, événement) to witness; (conférence) to attend, be (present) at; (spectacle, match) to be at, see

association [asɔsjasjɔ̃] nf association

associé, e [asɔsje] nm/f associate; (Comm) partner

associer [asɔsje] /7/ vt to associate; **~ qn à** (profits) to give sb a share of; (affaire) to make sb a partner in; (joie, triomphe) to include sb in; **~ qch à** (joindre, allier) to combine sth with; **s'associer** vi to join together; **s'~ à** (couleurs, qualités) to be combined with; (opinions, joie de qn) to share in; **s'~ à** ou **avec qn pour faire** to join (forces) ou join together with sb to do

assoiffé, e [aswafe] adj thirsty

assommer [asɔme] /1/ vt (étourdir, abrutir) to knock out, stun

Assomption [asɔ̃psjɔ̃] nf: **l'~** the Assumption

● **L'ASSOMPTION**
●
● The *fête de l'Assomption*, more
● commonly known as "le 15 août"
● is a national holiday in France.
● Traditionally, large numbers of
● holidaymakers leave home on
● 15 August, frequently causing
● chaos on the roads.

assorti, e [asɔʀti] *adj* matched, matching; **fromages/légumes ~s** assorted cheeses/vegetables; **~ à** matching; **assortiment** *nm* assortment, selection

assortir [asɔʀtiʀ] /2/ *vt* to match; **~ qch à** to match sth with; **~ qch de** to accompany sth with

assouplir [asupliʀ] /2/ *vt* to make supple; (*fig*) to relax; **assouplissant** *nm* (fabric) softener

assumer [asyme] /1/ *vt* (*fonction, emploi*) to assume, take on

assurance [asyʀɑ̃s] *nf* (*certitude*) assurance; (*confiance en soi*) (self-) confidence; (*contrat*) insurance (policy); (*secteur commercial*) insurance; **~ au tiers** third party insurance; **~ maladie (AM)** health insurance; **~ tous risques** (*Auto*) comprehensive insurance; **~s sociales (AS)** ≈ National Insurance (*BRIT*), ≈ Social Security (*US*); **assurance-vie** *nf* life assurance *ou* insurance

assuré, e [asyʀe] *adj* (*réussite, échec, victoire etc*) certain, sure; (*démarche, voix*) assured; (*pas*) steady ▷ *nm/f* insured (person); **assurément** *adv* assuredly, most certainly

assurer [asyʀe] /1/ *vt* (*Comm*) to insure; (*victoire etc*) to ensure; (*frontières, pouvoir*) to make secure; (*service, garde*) to provide, operate; **s'assurer (contre)** (*Comm*) to insure o.s. (against); **~ à qn que** to assure sb that; **~ qn de** to assure sb of; **s'~ de/ que** (*vérifier*) to make sure of/that; **s'~ (de)** (*aide de qn*) to secure

asthmatique [asmatik] *adj*, *nm/f* asthmatic

asthme [asm] *nm* asthma

asticot [astiko] *nm* maggot

astre [astʀ] *nm* star

astrologie [astʀɔlɔʒi] *nf* astrology

astronaute [astʀɔnot] *nm/f* astronaut

astronomie [astʀɔnɔmi] *nf* astronomy

astuce [astys] *nf* shrewdness, astuteness; (*truc*) trick, clever way; **astucieux, -euse** *adj* clever

atelier [atəlje] *nm* workshop; (*de peintre*) studio

athée [ate] *adj* atheistic ▷ *nm/f* atheist

Athènes [atɛn] *n* Athens

athlète [atlɛt] *nm/f* (*Sport*) athlete; **athlétisme** *nm* athletics *sg*

atlantique [atlɑ̃tik] *adj* Atlantic ▷ *nm*: **l'(océan) A~** the Atlantic (Ocean)

atlas [atlɑs] *nm* atlas

atmosphère [atmɔsfɛʀ] *nf* atmosphere

atome [atom] *nm* atom; **atomique** *adj* atomic; nuclear

atomiseur [atɔmizœʀ] *nm* atomizer

atout [atu] *nm* trump; (*fig*) asset

atroce [atʀɔs] *adj* atrocious

attachant, e [ataʃɑ̃, -ɑ̃t] *adj* engaging, likeable

attache [ataʃ] *nf* clip, fastener; (*fig*) tie

attacher [ataʃe] /1/ *vt* to tie up; (*étiquette*) to attach, tie on; (*ceinture*) to fasten; (*souliers*) to do up ▷ *vi* (*poêle, riz*) to stick; **s'~ à** (*par affection*) to become attached to; **~ qch à** to tie *ou* fasten *ou* attach sth to

attaque [atak] *nf* attack; (*cérébrale*) stroke; (*d'épilepsie*) fit

attaquer [atake] /1/ *vt* to attack; (*en justice*) to sue ▷ *vt* to attack; **s'attaquer à** *vt* (*personne*) to attack; (*épidémie, misère*) to tackle

attarder [ataʀde] /1/: **s'attarder** *vi* to linger

atteindre [atɛ̃dʀ] /49/ vt to reach;
(blesser) to hit; (émouvoir) to affect;
atteint, e adj (Méd): **être atteint
de** to be suffering from ▷ nf attack;
hors d'atteinte out of reach; **porter
atteinte à** to strike a blow at

attendant [atɑ̃dɑ̃]: **en ~** adv
meanwhile, in the meantime

attendre [atɑ̃dʀ] /41/ vt to wait for;
(être destiné ou réservé à) to await,
be in store for ▷ vi to wait; **s'~ à (ce
que)** to expect (that); **attendez-
moi, s'il vous plaît** wait for me,
please; **~ un enfant** to be expecting
a baby; **~ de faire/d'être** to wait
until one does/is; **attendez qu'il
vienne** wait until he comes; **~ qch
de** to expect sth of;

> Attention à ne pas traduire
> *attendre* par *to attend*.

attendrir [atɑ̃dʀiʀ] /2/ vt to move
(to pity); (viande) to tenderize

attendu, e [atɑ̃dy] adj (événement)
long-awaited; (prévu) expected;
~ que considering that, since

attentat [atɑ̃ta] nm assassination
attempt; **~ à la pudeur** indecent
assault no pl; **~ suicide** suicide
bombing

attente [atɑ̃t] nf wait; (espérance)
expectation

attenter [atɑ̃te] /1/: **~ à** vt (liberté) to
violate, **~ à la vie de qn** to make an
attempt on sb's life

attentif, -ive [atɑ̃tif, -iv] adj
(auditeur) attentive; (travail) careful;
~ à paying attention to

attention [atɑ̃sjɔ̃] nf attention;
(prévenance) attention,
thoughtfulness no pl; **à l'~ de** for the
attention of; **faire ~ (à)** to be careful
(of); **faire ~ (à ce) que** to be ou make
sure that; **~!** careful!, watch out!;
~ à la voiture! watch out for that
car!; **attentionné, e** [atɑ̃sjɔne] adj
thoughtful, considerate

atténuer [atenɥe] /1/ vt (douleur) to
alleviate, ease; (couleurs) to soften;
s'atténuer vi to ease; (violence etc)
to abate

atterrir [ateʀiʀ] /2/ vi to land;
atterrissage nm landing

attestation nf certificate

attirant, e [atiʀɑ̃, -ɑ̃t] adj attractive,
appealing

attirer [atiʀe] /1/ vt to attract;
(appâter) to lure, entice; **~ qn dans
un coin/vers soi** to draw sb into a
corner/towards one; **~ l'attention
de qn** to attract sb's attention;
~ l'attention de qn sur qch to draw
sb's attention to sth; **s'~ des ennuis**
to bring trouble upon o.s., get into
trouble

attitude [atityd] nf attitude;
(position du corps) bearing

attraction [atʀaksjɔ̃] nf attraction;
(de cabaret, cirque) number

attrait [atʀɛ] nm appeal, attraction

attraper [atʀape] /1/ vt to catch;
(habitude, amende) to get, pick up;
(fam: duper) to con; **se faire ~** (fam)
to be told off

attrayant, e [atʀɛjɑ̃, -ɑ̃t] adj
attractive

attribuer [atʀibɥe] /1/ vt (prix) to
award; (rôle, tâche) to allocate, assign;
(imputer): **~ qch à** to attribute sth
to; **s'attribuer** vt (s'approprier) to
claim for o.s.

attrister [atʀiste] /1/ vt to sadden

attroupement [atʀupmɑ̃] nm
crowd

attrouper [atʀupe] /1/: **s'attrouper**
vi to gather

au [o] prép voir **à**

aubaine [obɛn] nf godsend

aube [ob] nf dawn, daybreak; **à l'~** at
dawn ou daybreak

aubépine [obepin] nf hawthorn

auberge [obɛʀʒ] nf inn; **~ de
jeunesse** youth hostel

aubergine [obɛʀʒin] nf aubergine

aucun, e [okœ̃, -yn] adj, pron no;
(positif) any ▷ pron none; (positif)
any(one); **sans ~ doute** without any

doubt; **plus qu'~ autre** more than any other; **il le fera mieux qu'~ de nous** he'll do it better than any of us; **~ des deux** neither of the two; **~ d'entre eux** none of them

audace [odas] *nf* daring, boldness; (*péj*) audacity; **audacieux, -euse** *adj* daring, bold

au-delà [od(ə)la] *adv* beyond ▷ *nm*: **l'~** the hereafter; **~ de** beyond

au-dessous [odsu] *adv* underneath; below; **~ de** under(neath), below; (*limite, somme etc*) below, under; (*dignité, condition*) below

au-dessus [odsy] *adv* above; **~ de** above

au-devant [od(ə)vã] *prép*: **aller ~ de** (*personne, danger*) to go (out) and meet; (*souhaits de qn*) to anticipate

audience [odjãs] *nf* audience; (*Jur: séance*) hearing

audio-visuel, le [odjovizyɛl] *adj* audio-visual

audition [odisjõ] *nf* (*ouïe, écoute*) hearing; (*Jur: de témoins*) examination; (*Mus, Théât: épreuve*) audition

auditoire [oditwaʀ] *nm* audience

augmentation [ogmãtasjõ] *nf* increase; **~ (de salaire)** rise (in salary) (BRIT), (pay) raise (US)

augmenter [ogmãte] /1/ *vt* to increase; (*salaire, prix*) to increase, raise, put up; (*employé*) to increase the salary of ▷ *vi* to increase

augure [ogyʀ] *nm*: **de bon/mauvais ~** of good/ill omen

aujourd'hui [oʒuʀdɥi] *adv* today

aumône [omon] *nf* alms *sg* (*pl inv*); **aumônier** *nm* chaplain

auparavant [opaʀavã] *adv* before(hand)

auprès [opʀɛ]: **~ de** *prép* next to, close to; (*recourir, s'adresser*) to; (*en comparaison de*) compared with

auquel [okɛl] *pron voir* **lequel**

aurai *etc* [ɔʀe] *vb voir* **avoir**

aurons *etc* [oʀõ] *vb voir* **avoir**

aurore [ɔʀɔʀ] *nf* dawn, daybreak

ausculter [ɔskylte] /1/ *vt* to sound

aussi [osi] *adv* (*également*) also, too; (*de comparaison*) as ▷ *conj* therefore, consequently; **~ fort que** as strong as; **moi ~** me too

aussitôt [osito] *adv* straight away, immediately; **~ que** as soon as

austère [ɔstɛʀ] *adj* austere

austral, e [ɔstʀal] *adj* southern

Australie [ɔstʀali] *nf*: **l'~** Australia; **australien, ne** *adj* Australian ▷ *nm/f*: **Australien, ne** Australian

autant [otã] *adv* so much; **je ne savais pas que tu la détestais ~** I didn't know you hated her so much; (*comparatif*): **~ (que)** as much (as); (*nombre*) as many (as); **~ (de)** so much (ou many); as much (ou many); **~ partir** we (ou you etc) may as well leave; **~ dire que ...** one might as well say that ...; **pour ~** for all that; **d'~ plus/mieux (que)** all the more/ the better (since)

autel [otɛl] *nm* altar

auteur [otœʀ] *nm* author

authentique [otãtik] *adj* authentic, genuine

auto [oto] *nf* car; **autobiographie** *nf* autobiography; **autobronzant** *nm* self-tanning cream (*or* lotion *etc*); **autobus** *nm* bus; **autocar** *nm* coach

autochtone [otokton] *nm/f* native

auto: autocollant, e *adj* self-adhesive; (*enveloppe*) self-seal ▷ *nm* sticker; **autocuiseur** *nm* pressure cooker; **autodéfense** *nf* self-defence; **autodidacte** *nm/f* self-taught person; **auto-école** *nf* driving school; **autographe** *nm* autograph

automate [otomat] *nm* (*machine*) (automatic) machine

automatique [otomatik] *adj* automatic ▷ *nm*: **l'~** ≈ direct dialling

automne [oton] *nm* autumn (BRIT), fall (US)

automobile [otomobil] *adj* motor *cpd* ▷ *nf* (motor) car; **automobiliste** *nm/f* motorist

automutiler [otomytile] /1/:
s'automutiler vr to self-harm
autonome [ɔtɔnɔm] adj
autonomous; **autonomie** nf
autonomy; (Pol) self-government
autopsie [ɔtɔpsi] nf post-mortem
(examination), autopsy
autoradio [otoradjo] nf car radio
autorisation [ɔtɔRizasjɔ̃] nf
authorization; (papiers) permit
autorisé, e [ɔtɔRize] adj (opinion,
sources) authoritative
autoriser [ɔtɔRize] /1/ vt to give
permission for, authorize; (fig) to
allow (of)
autoritaire [ɔtɔRitɛR] adj
authoritarian
autorité [ɔtɔRite] nf authority; **faire
~** to be authoritative
autoroute [otoRut] nf motorway
(BRIT), expressway (US); **~ de
l'information** (Inform) information
superhighway

○ **AUTOROUTE**

- Motorways in France, indicated
- by blue road signs with the letter
- A followed by a number, are toll
- roads. The speed limit is 130 km/h
- (110 km/h when it is raining). At the
- tollgate, the lanes marked 'réservé'
- and with an orange 't' are reserved
- for people who subscribe to
- 'télépéage', an electronic payment
- system.

auto-stop [otostɔp] nm: **faire de
l'~** to hitch-hike; **prendre qn en ~** to
give sb a lift; **auto-stoppeur, -euse**
nm/f hitch-hiker
autour [otuR] adv around; **~ de**
around; **tout ~** all around

 MOT-CLÉ

autre [otR] adj **1** (différent) other,
different; **je préférerais un**

autre verre I'd prefer another ou a
different glass
2 (supplémentaire) other; **je
voudrais un autre verre d'eau** I'd
like another glass of water
3: **autre chose** something else;
autre part somewhere else;
d'autre part on the other hand
▶ pron: **un autre** another (one);
nous/vous autres us/you;
d'autres others; **l'autre** the other
(one); **les autres** the others; (autrui)
others; **l'un et l'autre** both of
them; **se détester l'un l'autre/les
uns les autres** to hate each other
ou one another; **d'une semaine/
minute à l'autre** from one week/
minute ou moment to the next;
(incessamment) any week/minute
ou moment now; **entre autres**
(personnes) among others; (choses)
among other things

autrefois [otRəfwa] adv in the past
autrement [otRəmɑ̃] adv differently;
(d'une manière différente) in another
way; (sinon) otherwise; **~ dit** in
other words
Autriche [otRiʃ] nf: **l'~** Austria;
autrichien, ne adj Austrian ▷ nm/f:
Autrichien, ne Austrian
autruche [otRyʃ] nf ostrich
aux [o] prép voir **à**
auxiliaire [ɔksiljɛR] adj, nm/f
auxiliary
auxquels, auxquelles [okɛl] pron
voir **lequel**
avalanche [avalɑ̃ʃ] nf avalanche
avaler [avale] /1/ vt to swallow
avance [avɑ̃s] nf (de troupes etc)
advance; (progrès) progress; (d'argent)
advance; (opposé à retard) lead;
avances nfpl (amoureuses) advances;
(être) en ~ (to be) early; (sur un
programme) (to be) ahead of schedule;
d'~, à l'~ in advance
avancé, e [avɑ̃se] adj advanced;
(travail etc) well on, well under way

avancement [avɑ̃smɑ̃] *nm*
(*professionnel*) promotion

avancer [avɑ̃se] /3/ *vi* to move
forward, advance; (*projet, travail*) to
make progress; (*montre, réveil*) to be
fast ▷ *vt* to move forward,
advance; (*argent*) to advance; (*montre,
pendule*) to put forward; **s'avancer**
vi to move forward, advance; (*fig*) to
commit o.s.

avant [avɑ̃] *prép* before ▷ *adj inv*:
siège/roue ~ front seat/wheel
▷ *nm* (*d'un véhicule, bâtiment*) front;
(*Sport: joueur*) forward; **~ qu'il
parte/de partir** before he leaves/
leaving; **~ tout** (*surtout*) above all;
à l'~ (*dans un véhicule*) in (the) front;
en ~ (*se pencher, tomber*) forward(s);
partir en ~ to go on ahead; **en ~ de**
in front of

avantage [avɑ̃taʒ] *nm* advantage;
~s sociaux fringe benefits;
avantager /3/ *vt* (*favoriser*) to favour;
(*embellir*) to flatter; **avantageux,
-euse** *adj* (*prix*) attractive

avant: avant-bras *nm inv* forearm;
avant-coureur *adj inv*: **signe
avant-coureur** advance indication
ou sign; **avant-dernier, -ière** *adj,
nm/f* next to last, last but one;
avant-goût *nm* foretaste; **avant-
hier** *adv* the day before yesterday;
avant-première *nf* (*de film*) preview;
avant-veille *nf*: **l'avant-veille** two
days before

avare [avaR] *adj* miserly, avaricious
▷ *nm/f* miser; **~ de compliments**
stingy *ou* sparing with one's
compliments

avec [avɛk] *prép* with; (*à l'égard de*)
to(wards), with; **et ~ ça?** (*dans un
magasin*) anything *ou* something else?

avenir [avniʀ] *nm*: **l'~** the future; **à
l'~** in future; **carrière/politicien
d'~** career/politician with prospects
ou a future

aventure [avɑ̃tyʀ] *nf*: **l'~** adventure;
une ~ (*amoureuse*) an affair;

aventureux, -euse *adj* adventurous,
venturesome; (*projet*) risky, chancy

avenue [avny] *nf* avenue

avérer [aveʀe] /6/: **s'avérer** *vr*:
s'~ faux/coûteux to prove (to be)
wrong/expensive

averse [avɛʀs] *nf* shower

averti, e [avɛʀti] *adj* (well-)
informed

avertir [avɛʀtiʀ] /2/ *vt*: **~ qn (de
qch/que)** to warn sb (of sth/that);
(*renseigner*) to inform sb (of sth/
that); **avertissement** *nm* warning;
avertisseur *nm* horn, siren

aveu, x [avø] *nm* confession

aveugle [avœgl] *adj* blind ▷ *nm/f*
blind person

aviation [avjasjɔ̃] *nf* aviation; (*sport,
métier de pilote*) flying; (*Mil*) air force

avide [avid] *adj* eager; (*péj*) greedy,
grasping

avion [avjɔ̃] *nm* (aero)plane (*BRIT*),
(air)plane (*US*); **aller (quelque part)
en ~** to go (somewhere) by plane, fly
(somewhere); **par ~** by airmail; **~ à
réaction** jet (plane)

aviron [aviʀɔ̃] *nm* oar; (*sport*): **l'~**
rowing

avis [avi] *nm* opinion; (*notification*)
notice; **à mon ~** in my opinion;
changer d'~ to change one's mind;
jusqu'à nouvel ~ until further notice

aviser [avize] /1/ *vt* (*informer*): **~ qn
de/que** to advise *ou* inform *ou* notify
sb of/that ▷ *vi* to think about things,
assess the situation; **nous aviserons
sur place** we'll work something out
once we're there; **s'~ de qch/que**
to become suddenly aware of sth/
that; **s'~ de faire** to take it into one's
head to do

avocat, e [avɔka, -at] *nm/f* (*Jur*)
≈ barrister (*BRIT*), lawyer ▷ *nm*
(*Culin*) avocado (pear); **l'~ de la
défense/partie civile** the counsel
for the defence/plaintiff; **~ général**
assistant public prosecutor

avoine [avwan] *nf* oats *pl*

a

MOT-CLÉ

avoir [avwaʀ] /34/ vt **1** (*posséder*) to have; **elle a deux enfants/une belle maison** she has (got) two children/a lovely house; **il a les yeux bleus** he has (got) blue eyes; **vous avez du sel?** do you have any salt?; **avoir du courage/de la patience** to be brave/patient
2 (*éprouver*): **avoir de la peine** to be *ou* feel sad; *voir aussi* **faim, peur**
3 (*âge, dimensions*) to be; **il a 3 ans** he is 3 (years old); **le mur a 3 mètres de haut** the wall is 3 metres high
4 (*fam: duper*) to do, have; **on vous a eu!** you've been done *ou* had!; (*fait une plaisanterie*) we *ou* they had you there
5: **en avoir contre qn** to have a grudge against sb; **en avoir assez** to be fed up; **j'en ai pour une demi-heure** it'll take me half an hour
6 (*obtenir, attraper*) to get; **j'ai réussi à avoir mon train** I managed to get *ou* catch my train; **j'ai réussi à avoir le renseignement qu'il me fallait** I managed to get (hold of) the information I needed
▶ *vb aux* **1** to have; **avoir mangé/dormi** to have eaten/slept
2 (*avoir + à + infinitif*): **avoir à faire qch** to have to do sth; **vous n'avez qu'à lui demander** you only have to ask him
▶ *vb impers* **1**: **il y a** (+ *singulier*) there is; (+ *pluriel*) there are; **il y avait du café/des gâteaux** there was coffee/there were cakes; **qu'y a-t-il?, qu'est-ce qu'il y a?** what's the matter?, what is it?; **il doit y avoir une explication** there must be an explanation; **il n'y a qu'à ...** we (*ou* you *etc*) will just have to ...; **il ne peut y en avoir qu'un** there can only be one
2: **il y a** (*temporel*): **il y a 10 ans** 10 years ago; **il y a 10 ans/ longtemps que je le connais** I've

known him for 10 years/a long time; **il y a 10 ans qu'il est arrivé** it's 10 years since he arrived
▶ *nm* assets *pl*, resources *pl*; (*Comm*) credit

avortement [avɔʀtəmɑ̃] *nm* abortion
avouer [avwe] /1/ *vt* (*crime, défaut*) to confess (to); **~ avoir fait/que** to admit *ou* confess to having done/that
avril [avʀil] *nm* April
axe [aks] *nm* axis (*pl* axes); (*de roue etc*) axle; (*fig*) main line; **~ routier** trunk road (BRIT), main road, highway (US)
ayons *etc* [ɛjɔ̃] *vb voir* **avoir**

bâbord [bɑbɔʀ] *nm*: **à** *ou* **par ~** to port, on the port side

baby-foot [babifut] *nm inv* table football

baby-sitting [babisitiŋ] *nm* baby-sitting; **faire du ~** to baby-sit

bac [bak] *nm* (*récipient*) tub

baccalauréat [bakalɔʀea] *nm* ≈ high school diploma

bâcler [bɑkle] /1/ *vt* to botch (up)

baffe [baf] *nf* (*fam*) slap, clout

bafouiller [bafuje] /1/ *vi, vt* to stammer

bagage [bagaʒ] *nm*: **~s** luggage *sg*; (*connaissances*) background, knowledge; **~s à main** hand-luggage

bagarre [bagaʀ] *nf* fight, brawl; **bagarrer** /1/: **se bagarrer** *vi* to (have a) fight

bagnole [baɲɔl] *nf* (*fam*) car

bague [bag] *nf* ring; **~ de fiançailles** engagement ring

baguette [bagɛt] *nf* stick; (*cuisine chinoise*) chopstick; (*de chef d'orchestre*) baton; (*pain*) stick of (French) bread; **~ magique** magic wand

baie [bɛ] *nf* (*Géo*) bay; (*fruit*) berry; **~ (vitrée)** picture window

baignade [bɛɲad] *nf* bathing; **"~ interdite"** "no bathing"

baigner [beɲe] /1/ *vt* (*bébé*) to bath; **se baigner** *vi* to go swimming *ou* bathing; **baignoire** *nf* bath(tub)

bail (*pl* **baux**) [baj, bo] *nm* lease

bâiller [bɑje] /1/ *vi* to yawn; (*être ouvert*) to gape

bain [bɛ̃] *nm* bath; **prendre un ~** to have a bath; **se mettre dans le ~** (*fig*) to get into (the way of) it *ou* things; **~ de bouche** mouthwash; **~ moussant** bubble bath; **~ de soleil**; **prendre un ~ de soleil** to sunbathe; **bain-marie** *nm*: **faire chauffer au bain-marie** (*boîte etc*) to immerse in boiling water

baiser [beze] /1/ *nm* kiss ▷ *vt* (*main, front*) to kiss; (*fam!*) to screw (!)

baisse [bɛs] *nf* fall, drop; **en ~** falling

baisser [bese] /1/ *vt* to lower; (*radio, chauffage*) to turn down ▷ *vi* to fall, drop, go down; (*vue, santé*) to fail, dwindle; **se baisser** *vi* to bend down

bal [bal] *nm* dance; (*grande soirée*) ball; **~ costumé/masqué** fancy-dress/masked ball

balade [balad] (*fam*) *nf* (*à pied*) walk, stroll; (*en voiture*) drive; **balader** /1/ (*fam*): **se balader** *vi* to go for a walk *ou* stroll; to go for a drive; **baladeur** [baladœʀ] *nm* personal stereo, Walkman®

balai [balɛ] *nm* broom, brush

balance [balɑ̃s] *nf* scales *pl*; (*signe*): **la B~** Libra; **~ commerciale** balance of trade

balancer [balɑ̃se] /3/ *vt* to swing; (*lancer*) to fling, chuck; (*renvoyer, jeter*) to chuck out; **se balancer** *vi* to swing; to rock; **se ~ de qch** (*fam*) not to

give a toss about sth; **balançoire** nf
swing; (sur pivot) seesaw
balayer [baleje] /8/ vt (feuilles etc)
to sweep up, brush up; (pièce, cour)
to sweep; (chasser) to sweep away
ou aside; (radar) to scan; **balayeur,
-euse** [balejœr, -øz] nm/f road
sweeper ▷ nf (engin) road sweeper
balbutier [balbysje] /7/ vi, vt to
stammer
balcon [balkɔ̃] nm balcony; (Théât)
dress circle
Bâle [bɑl] n Basle ou Basel
Baléares [baleɑr] nfpl: **les ~** the
Balearic Islands, the Balearics
baleine [balɛn] nf whale
balise [baliz] nf (Navig) beacon,
(marker) buoy; (Aviat) runway light,
beacon; (Auto, Ski) sign, marker;
baliser /1/ vt to mark out (with
beacons ou lights etc)
balle [bal] nf (de fusil) bullet; (de sport)
ball; (fam: franc) franc
ballerine [bal(ə)rin] nf (danseuse)
ballet dancer; (chaussure) pump,
ballet shoe
ballet [balɛ] nm ballet
ballon [balɔ̃] nm (de sport) ball; (jouet,
Aviat) balloon; **~ de football** football;
~ d'oxygène oxygen bottle
balnéaire [balneɛr] adj seaside cpd;
station ~ seaside resort
balustrade [balystrad] nf railings
pl, handrail
bambin [bɑ̃bɛ̃] nm little child
bambou [bɑ̃bu] nm bamboo
banal, e [banal] adj banal,
commonplace; (péj) trite; **banalité**
nf banality
banane [banan] nf banana; (sac)
waist-bag, bum-bag
banc [bɑ̃] nm seat, bench; (de
poissons) shoal; **~ d'essai** (fig) testing
ground
bancaire [bɑ̃kɛr] adj banking;
(chèque, carte) bank cpd
bancal, e [bɑ̃kal] adj wobbly
bandage [bɑ̃daʒ] nm bandage

bande [bɑ̃d] nf (de tissu etc) strip;
(Méd) bandage; (motif, dessin) stripe;
(groupe) band; (péj): **une ~ de** a bunch
ou crowd of; **faire ~ à part** to keep
to o.s.; **~ dessinée (BD)** comic strip;
~ magnétique magnetic tape;
~ sonore sound track
bande-annonce [bɑ̃danɔ̃s] nf
trailer
bandeau, x [bɑ̃do] nm headband;
(sur les yeux) blindfold
bander [bɑ̃de] /1/ vt (blessure)
to bandage; **~ les yeux à qn** to
blindfold sb
bandit [bɑ̃di] nm bandit
bandoulière [bɑ̃duljɛr] nf: **en ~**
(slung ou worn) across the shoulder
Bangladesh [bɑ̃gladɛʃ] nm: **le ~**
Bangladesh
banlieue [bɑ̃ljø] nf suburbs pl;
quartiers de ~ suburban areas;
trains de ~ commuter trains
bannir [banir] /2/ vt to banish
banque [bɑ̃k] nf bank; (activités)
banking; **~ de données** data bank
banquet [bɑ̃kɛ] nm dinner;
(d'apparat) banquet
banquette [bɑ̃kɛt] nf seat
banquier [bɑ̃kje] nm banker
banquise [bɑ̃kiz] nf ice field
baptême [batɛm] nm christening;
baptism; **~ de l'air** first flight
baptiser [batize] /1/ vt to christen;
to baptize
bar [bar] nm bar
baraque [barak] nf shed; (fam)
house; **~ foraine** fairground stand;
baraqué, e (fam) adj well-built, hefty
barbant, e [barbɑ̃, -ɑ̃t] adj (fam)
deadly (boring)
barbare [barbar] adj barbaric
barbe [barb] nf beard; **(au nez et)
à la ~ de qn** (fig) under sb's very
nose; **la ~!** (fam) damn it!; **quelle ~!**
(fam) what a drag ou bore!; **~ à papa**
candy-floss (BRIT), cotton candy (US)
barbelé [barbəle] adj, nm: **(fil de fer)
~** barbed wire no pl

barbiturique [baʀbityʀik] nm barbiturate

barbouiller [baʀbuje] /1/ vt to daub; **avoir l'estomac barbouillé** to feel queasy ou sick

barbu, e [baʀby] adj bearded

barder [baʀde] /1/ vi (fam): **ça va ~** sparks will fly

barème [baʀɛm] nm (Scol) scale; (liste) table

baril [baʀi(l)] nm barrel; (de poudre) keg

bariolé, e [baʀjɔle] adj many-coloured, rainbow-coloured

baromètre [baʀɔmɛtʀ] nm barometer

baron [baʀɔ̃] nm baron

baronne [baʀɔn] nf baroness

baroque [baʀɔk] adj (Art) baroque; (fig) weird

barque [baʀk] nf small boat

barquette [baʀkɛt] nf small boat-shaped tart; (récipient: en aluminium) tub; (: en bois) basket; (pour repas) tray; (pour fruits) punnet

barrage [baʀaʒ] nm dam; (sur route) roadblock, barricade

barre [baʀ] nf (de fer etc) rod; (Navig) helm; (écrite) line, stroke

barreau, x [baʀo] nm bar; (Jur): **le ~ the Bar**

barrer [baʀe] /1/ vt (route etc) to block; (mot) to cross out; (chèque) to cross (BRIT); (Navig) to steer; **se barrer** vi (fam) to clear off

barrette [baʀɛt] nf (pour cheveux) (hair) slide (BRIT) ou clip (US)

barricader [baʀikade] /1/: **se barricader** vi: **se ~ chez soi** to lock o.s. in

barrière [baʀjɛʀ] nf fence; (obstacle) barrier; (porte) gate

barrique [baʀik] nf barrel, cask

bar-tabac [baʀtaba] nm bar (which sells tobacco and stamps)

bas, basse [ba, bas] adj low ▷ nm (vêtement) stocking; (partie inférieure): **le ~ de** the lower part ou foot ou bottom of ▷ adv low; (parler) softly;

au ~ mot at the lowest estimate; **enfant en ~ âge** young child; **en ~** down below; (d'une liste, d'un mur etc) at (ou to) the bottom; (dans une maison) downstairs; **en ~ de** at the bottom of; **à ~ la dictature!** down with dictatorship!

bas-côté [bakote] nm (de route) verge (BRIT), shoulder (US)

basculer [baskyle] /1/ vi to fall over, topple (over); (benne) to tip up ▷ vt (contenu) to tip out; (benne) tip up

base [baz] nf base; (fondement, principe) basis (pl bases); **la ~** (Pol) the rank and file; **de ~** basic; **à ~ de café etc** coffee etc -based; **~ de données** database; **baser** /1/ vt: **baser qch sur** to base sth on; **se baser sur** (données, preuves) to base one's argument on

bas-fond [bafɔ̃] nm (Navig) shallow; **bas-fonds** nmpl (fig) dregs

basilic [bazilik] nm (Culin) basil

basket [baskɛt] nm basketball

baskets [baskɛt] nfpl trainers (BRIT), sneakers (US)

basque [bask] adj Basque ▷ nm/f: **B~** Basque; **le Pays ~** the Basque country

basse [bas] adj voir **bas** ▷ nf (Mus) bass; **basse-cour** nf farmyard

bassin [basɛ̃] nm (pièce d'eau) pond, pool; (de fontaine, Géo) basin; (Anat) pelvis; (portuaire) dock

bassine [basin] nf basin; (contenu) bowl, bowlful

basson [basɔ̃] nm bassoon

bat [ba] vb voir **battre**

bataille [bataj] nf battle; (rixe) fight; **elle avait les cheveux en ~** her hair was a mess

bateau, x [bato] nm boat; ship; **bateau-mouche** nm (passenger) pleasure boat (on the Seine)

bâti, e [bati] adj (terrain) developed; **bien ~** well-built

bâtiment [batimɑ̃] nm building; (Navig) ship, vessel; (industrie): **le ~** the building trade

bâtir [bɑtiʀ] /2/ *vt* to build
bâtisse [bɑtis] *nf* building
bâton [bɑtɔ̃] *nm* stick; **parler à ~s rompus** to chat about this and that
bats [ba] *vb voir* **battre**
battement [batmɑ̃] *nm* (*de cœur*) beat; (*intervalle*) interval (*between classes, trains etc*); **10 minutes de ~** 10 minutes to spare
batterie [batʀi] *nf* (*Mil, Élec*) battery; (*Mus*) drums *pl*, drum kit; **~ de cuisine** kitchen utensils *pl*; (*casseroles etc*) pots and pans *pl*
batteur [batœʀ] *nm* (*Mus*) drummer; (*appareil*) whisk
battre [batʀ] /41/ *vt* to beat; (*blé*) to thresh; (*cartes*) to shuffle; (*passer au peigne fin*) to scour ▷ *vi* (*cœur*) to beat; (*volets etc*) to bang, rattle; **se battre** *vi* to fight; **~ la mesure** to beat time; **~ son plein** to be at its height, be going full swing; **~ des mains** to clap one's hands
baume [bom] *nm* balm
bavard, e [bavaʀ, -aʀd] *adj* (very) talkative; gossipy; **bavarder** /1/ *vi* to chatter; (*indiscrètement*) to gossip; (*révéler un secret*) to blab
baver [bave] /1/ *vi* to dribble; (*chien*) to slobber, slaver; **en ~** (*fam*) to have a hard time (of it)
bavoir [bavwaʀ] *nm* bib
bavure [bavyʀ] *nf* smudge; (*fig*) hitch; (*policière etc*) blunder
bazar [bazaʀ] *nm* general store; (*fam*) jumble; **bazarder** /1/ *vt* (*fam*) to chuck out
BCBG *sigle adj* (= *bon chic bon genre*) smart and trendy, ≈ preppy
BD *sigle f* = **bande dessinée**
bd *abr* = **boulevard**
béant, e [beɑ̃, -ɑ̃t] *adj* gaping
beau (bel), belle, beaux [bo, bɛl] *adj* beautiful, lovely; (*homme*) handsome ▷ *adv*: **il fait ~** the weather's fine ▷ *nm*: **un ~ jour** one (fine) day; **de plus belle** more than ever, even more; **bel et bien** well

and truly; **le plus ~ c'est que ...** the best of it is that ...; **on a ~ essayer** however hard *ou* no matter how hard we try; **faire le ~** (*chien*) to sit up and beg

 MOT-CLÉ

beaucoup [boku] *adv* **1** a lot; **il boit beaucoup** he drinks a lot; **il ne boit pas beaucoup** he doesn't drink much *ou* a lot
2 (*suivi de plus, trop etc*) much, a lot; **il est beaucoup plus grand** he is much *ou* a lot *ou* far taller; **c'est beaucoup plus cher** it's a lot *ou* much more expensive; **il a beaucoup plus de temps que moi** he has much *ou* a lot more time than me; **il y a beaucoup plus de touristes ici** there are a lot *ou* many more tourists here; **beaucoup trop vite** much too fast; **il fume beaucoup trop** he smokes far too much
3: **beaucoup de** (*nombre*) many, a lot of; (*quantité*) a lot of; **beaucoup d'étudiants/de touristes** a lot of *ou* many students/tourists; **beaucoup de courage** a lot of courage; **il n'a pas beaucoup d'argent** he hasn't got much *ou* a lot of money
4: **de beaucoup** by far

beau: beau-fils *nm* son-in-law; (*remariage*) stepson; **beau-frère** *nm* brother-in-law; **beau-père** *nm* father-in-law; (*remariage*) stepfather
beauté [bote] *nf* beauty; **de toute ~** beautiful; **finir qch en ~** to complete sth brilliantly
beaux-arts [bozaʀ] *nmpl* fine arts
beaux-parents [bopaʀɑ̃] *nmpl* wife's/husband's family, in-laws
bébé [bebe] *nm* baby
bec [bɛk] *nm* beak, bill; (*de cafetière etc*) spout; (*de casserole etc*) lip; (*fam*) mouth; **~ de gaz** (street) gaslamp

bêche [bɛʃ] *nf* spade; **bêcher** /1/ *vt* to dig

bedaine [bədɛn] *nf* paunch

bedonnant, e [bədɔnɑ̃, -ɑ̃t] *adj* potbellied

bée [be] *adj*: **bouche ~** gaping

bégayer [begeje] /8/ *vt, vi* to stammer

beige [bɛʒ] *adj* beige

beignet [bɛɲɛ] *nm* fritter

bel [bɛl] *adj m voir* **beau**

bêler [bele] /1/ *vi* to bleat

belette [bəlɛt] *nf* weasel

belge [bɛlʒ] *adj* Belgian ▷ *nm/f*: **B~** Belgian

Belgique [bɛlʒik] *nf*: **la ~** Belgium

bélier [belje] *nm* ram; (*signe*): **le B~** Aries

belle [bɛl] *adj voir* **beau** ▷ *nf* (*Sport*): **la ~** the decider; **belle-fille** *nf* daughter-in-law; (*remariage*) stepdaughter; **belle-mère** *nf* mother-in-law; (*remariage*) stepmother; **belle-sœur** *nf* sister-in-law

belvédère [bɛlvedɛR] *nm* panoramic viewpoint (*or small building there*)

bémol [bemɔl] *nm* (*Mus*) flat

bénédiction [benediksjɔ̃] *nf* blessing

bénéfice [benefis] *nm* (*Comm*) profit; (*avantage*) benefit; **bénéficier de** /7/ *vi*: **bénéficier de** to enjoy; (*profiter*) to benefit by *ou* from; **bénéfique** *adj* beneficial

Benelux [benelyks] *nm*: **le ~** Benelux, the Benelux countries

bénévole [benevɔl] *adj* voluntary, unpaid

bénin, -igne [benɛ̃, -iɲ] *adj* minor, mild; (*tumeur*) benign

bénir [beniR] /2/ *vt* to bless; **bénit, e** *adj* consecrated; **eau bénite** holy water

benne [bɛn] *nf* skip; (*de téléphérique*) (cable) car; **~ à ordures** (*amovible*) skip

béquille [bekij] *nf* crutch; (*de bicyclette*) stand

berceau, x [bɛRso] *nm* cradle, crib

bercer [bɛRse] /3/ *vt* to rock, cradle; (*musique etc*) to lull; **~ qn de** (*promesses etc*) to delude sb with; **berceuse** *nf* lullaby

béret [beRɛ] *nm* (*aussi*: **~ basque**) beret

berge [bɛRʒ] *nf* bank

berger, -ère [bɛRʒe, -ɛR] *nm/f* shepherd/shepherdess; **~ allemand** alsatian (dog) (*BRIT*), German shepherd (dog) (*US*)

Berlin [bɛRlɛ̃] *n* Berlin

Bermudes [bɛRmyd] *nfpl*: **les (îles) ~** Bermuda

Berne [bɛRn] *n* Bern

berner [bɛRne] /1/ *vt* to fool

besogne [bəzɔɲ] *nf* work *no pl*, job

besoin [bəzwɛ̃] *nm* need; (*pauvreté*): **le ~** need, want; **faire ses ~s** to relieve o.s.; **avoir ~ de qch/faire qch** to need sth/to do sth; **au ~** if need be; **être dans le ~** to be in need *ou* want

bestiole [bɛstjɔl] *nf* (tiny) creature

bétail [betaj] *nm* livestock, cattle *pl*

bête [bɛt] *nf* animal; (*bestiole*) insect, creature ▷ *adj* stupid, silly; **chercher la petite ~** to nit-pick; **~ noire** pet hate; **~ sauvage** wild beast

bêtise [betiz] *nf* stupidity; (*action, remarque*) stupid thing (to say *ou* do)

béton [betɔ̃] *nm* concrete; **(en) ~** (*fig: alibi, argument*) cast iron; **~ armé** reinforced concrete

betterave [bɛtRav] *nf* beetroot (*BRIT*), beet (*US*); **~ sucrière** sugar beet

Beur [bœR] *nm/f see note* **"Beur"**

- **BEUR**
-
- *Beur* is a term used to refer to a
- person born in France of North
- African immigrant parents. It is
- not racist and is often used by the
- media, anti-racist groups and
- second-generation North Africans
- themselves. The word itself comes
- from back slang or 'verlan'.

beurre [bœʀ] *nm* butter; **beurrer** /ʎ/ *vt* to butter; **beurrier** *nm* butter dish

biais [bjɛ] *nm* (*moyen*) device, expedient; (*aspect*) angle; **en ~, de ~** (*obliquement*) at an angle; **par le ~ de** by means of

bibelot [biblo] *nm* trinket, curio

biberon [bibʀɔ̃] *nm* (feeding) bottle; **nourrir au ~** to bottle-feed

bible [bibl] *nf* bible

bibliobus [biblijɔbys] *nm* mobile library van

bibliothécaire *nm/f* librarian

bibliothèque *nf* library; (*meuble*) bookcase

bic® [bik] *nm* Biro®

bicarbonate [bikaʀbɔnat] *nm*: **~ (de soude)** bicarbonate of soda

biceps [bisɛps] *nm* biceps

biche [biʃ] *nf* doe

bicolore [bikɔlɔʀ] *adj* two-coloured

bicoque [bikɔk] *nf* (*péj*) shack

bicyclette [bisiklɛt] *nf* bicycle

bidet [bidɛ] *nm* bidet

bidon [bidɔ̃] *nm* can ▷ *adj inv* (*fam*) phoney

bidonville [bidɔ̃vil] *nm* shanty town

bidule [bidyl] *nm* (*fam*) thingamajig

○ **MOT-CLÉ**

bien [bjɛ̃] *nm* **1** (*avantage, profit*): **faire du bien à qn** to do sb good; **dire du bien de** to speak well of; **c'est pour son bien** it's for his own good

2 (*possession, patrimoine*) possession, property; **son bien le plus précieux** his most treasured possession; **avoir du bien** to have property; **biens (de consommation** *etc*) (consumer *etc*) goods

3 (*moral*): **le bien** good; **distinguer le bien du mal** to tell good from evil

▷ *adv* **1** (*de façon satisfaisante*) well; **elle travaille/mange bien** she works/eats well; **croyant bien faire, je/il ...** thinking I/he was doing the right thing, I/he ...; **tiens-toi bien!** (*assieds-toi correctement*)

sit up straight!; (*debout*) stand up straight!; (*sois sage*) behave yourself!; (*prépare-toi*) wait for it!

2 (*valeur intensive*) quite; **bien jeune** quite young; **bien assez** quite enough; **bien mieux** (very) much better; **bien du temps/des gens** quite a time/a number of people; **j'espère bien y aller** I do hope to go; **je veux bien le faire** (*concession*) I'm quite willing to do it; **il faut bien le faire** it has to be done; **cela fait bien deux ans que je ne l'ai pas vu** I haven't seen him for at least *ou* a good two years; **Paul est bien venu, n'est-ce pas?** Paul HAS come, hasn't he?; **où peut-il bien être passé?** where on earth can he have got to?

▶ *excl* right!, OK!, fine!; **(c'est) bien fait!** it serves you (*ou* him *etc*) right!; **bien sûr!** certainly!

▶ *adj inv* **1** (*en bonne forme, à l'aise*): **je me sens bien** I feel fine; **je ne me sens pas bien** I don't feel well; **on est bien dans ce fauteuil** this chair is very comfortable

2 (*joli, beau*) good-looking; **tu es bien dans cette robe** you look good in that dress

3 (*satisfaisant*) good; **elle est bien, cette maison/secrétaire** it's a good house/she's a good secretary; **c'est très bien (comme ça)** it's fine (like that); **c'est bien?** is that all right?

4 (*moralement*) right; (: *personne*) good, nice; (*respectable*) respectable; **ce n'est pas bien de ...** it's not right to ...; **elle est bien, cette femme** she's a nice woman, she's a good sort; **des gens bien** respectable people

5 (*en bons termes*): **être bien avec qn** to be on good terms with sb; **bien-aimé, e** *adj, nm/f* beloved; **bien-être** *nm* well-being; **bienfaisance** *nf* charity; **bienfait** *nm* act of generosity, benefaction; (*de la science etc*) benefit; **bienfaiteur, -trice**

nm/f benefactor/benefactress;
bien-fondé *nm* soundness; **bien que**
conj although

bientôt [bjɛ̃to] *adv* soon; **à ~** see
you soon
bienveillant, e [bjɛ̃vɛjɑ̃, -ɑ̃t] *adj*
kindly
bienvenu, e [bjɛ̃vny] *adj* welcome
▷ *nf*: **souhaiter la ~e à** to welcome;
~e à welcome to
bière [bjɛʀ] *nf* (*boisson*) beer; (*cercueil*)
bier; **~ blonde** lager; **~ brune** brown
ale (*BRIT*), dark beer (*US*); **~ (à la)
pression** draught beer
bifteck [biftɛk] *nm* steak
bigoudi [bigudi] *nm* curler
bijou, x [biʒu] *nm* jewel; **bijouterie**
nf jeweller's (shop); **bijoutier, -ière**
nm/f jeweller
bikini [bikini] *nm* bikini
bilan [bilɑ̃] *nm* (*Comm*) balance
sheet(s); (*fig*) (net) outcome (: *de
victimes*) toll; **faire le ~ de** to assess;
to review; **déposer son ~** to file a
bankruptcy statement; **~ de santé**
check-up
bile [bil] *nf* bile; **se faire de la ~** (*fam*)
to worry o.s. sick
bilieux, -euse [biljø, -øz] *adj* bilious;
(*fig: colérique*) testy
bilingue [bilɛ̃g] *adj* bilingual
billard [bijaʀ] *nm* billiards *sg*; (*table*)
billiard table
bille [bij] *nf* ball; (*du jeu de billes*)
marble
billet [bijɛ] *nm* (*aussi*: **~ de banque**)
(bank)note; (*de cinéma, de bus
etc*) ticket; (*courte lettre*) note;
~ électronique e-ticket; **billetterie**
nf ticket office; (*distributeur*) ticket
dispenser; (*Banque*) cash dispenser
billion [biljɔ̃] *nm* billion (*BRIT*),
trillion (*US*)
bimensuel, le [bimɑ̃sɥɛl] *adj*
bimonthly
bio [bjo] *adj* organic
bio... [bjɔ] *préfixe* bio...;

biocarburant [bjokaʀbyʀɑ̃] *nm*
biofuel; **biochimie** *nf* biochemistry;
biodiesel *nm* biodiesel; **biogazole** *nm*
biodiesel; **biographie** *nf* biography;
biologie *nf* biology; **biologique** *adj*
biological; **biométrie** *nf* biometrics;
biotechnologie *nf* biotechnology;
bioterrorisme *nm* bioterrorism
bipolaire [bipɔlɛʀ] *adj* bipolar
Birmanie [biʀmani] *nf* Burma
bis¹, e [bi, biz] *adj* (*couleur*) greyish
brown ▷ *nf* (*baiser*) kiss; (*vent*) North
wind; **faire une** *ou* **la ~e à qn** to kiss
sb; **grosses ~es (de)** (*sur lettre*) love
and kisses (from)
bis² [bis] *adv*: **12 ~** 12a *ou* A ▷ *excl*,
nm encore
biscotte [biskɔt] *nf* toasted bread
(*sold in packets*)
biscuit [biskɥi] *nm* biscuit (*BRIT*),
cookie (*US*)
bise [biz] *nf voir* **bis²**
bisexuel, le [bisɛksɥɛl] *adj* bisexual
bisou [bizu] *nm* (*fam*) kiss
bissextile [bisɛkstil] *adj*: **année ~**
leap year
bistro(t) [bistʀo] *nm* bistro, café
bitume [bitym] *nm* asphalt
bizarre [bizaʀ] *adj* strange, odd
blague [blag] *nf* (*propos*) joke; (*farce*)
trick; **sans ~!** no kidding!; **blaguer**
/1/ *vi* to joke
blaireau, x [blɛʀo] *nm* (*Zool*) badger;
(*brosse*) shaving brush
blâme [blɑm] *nm* blame; (*sanction*)
reprimand; **blâmer** /1/ *vt* to blame
blanc, blanche [blɑ̃, blɑ̃ʃ] *adj* white;
(*non imprimé*) blank ▷ *nm/f* white,
white man/woman ▷ *nm* (*couleur*)
white; (*espace non écrit*) blank; (*aussi*:
~ d'œuf) (egg-)white; (*aussi*: **~ de
poulet**) breast, white meat; (*aussi*:
vin ~) white wine ▷ *nf* (*Mus*) minim
(*BRIT*), half-note (*US*); **chèque
en ~** blank cheque; **à ~** (*chauffer*)
white-hot; (*tirer, charger*) with blanks;
~ cassé off-white; **blancheur** *nf*
whiteness

blanchir [blɑ̃ʃiʀ] /2/ vt (gén) to whiten; (linge) to launder; (Culin) to blanch; (fig: disculper) to clear ▷ vi (cheveux) to go white; **blanchisserie** nf laundry

blason [blɑzɔ̃] nm coat of arms

blasphème [blasfɛm] nm blasphemy

blazer [blazɛʀ] nm blazer

blé [ble] nm wheat

bled [blɛd] nm (péj) hole

blême [blɛm] adj pale

blessé, e [blese] adj injured ▷ nm/f injured person, casualty

blesser [blese] /1/ vt to injure; (délibérément) to wound; (offenser) to hurt; **se blesser** to injure o.s.; **se ~ au pied** etc to injure one's foot etc; **blessure** nf (accidentelle) injury; (intentionnelle) wound

bleu, e [blø] adj blue; (bifteck) very rare ▷ nm (couleur) blue; (contusion) bruise; (vêtement: aussi: **~s**) overalls pl; **fromage ~** blue cheese; **~ marine/nuit/roi** navy/midnight/royal blue; **bleuet** nm cornflower

bloc [blɔk] nm (de pierre etc) block; (de papier à lettres) pad; (ensemble) group, block; **serré à ~** tightened right down; **en ~** as a whole; **~ opératoire** operating ou theatre block; **blocage** nm (des prix) freezing; (Psych) hang-up; **bloc-notes** nm note pad

blog [blɔg] nm blog; **blogosphère** nf blogosphere; **bloguer** /1/ vi to blog

blond, e [blɔ̃, -ɔ̃d] adj fair; blond; (sable, blés) golden

bloquer [blɔke] /1/ vt (passage) to block; (pièce mobile) to jam; (crédits, compte) to freeze

blottir [blɔtiʀ] /2/: **se blottir** vi to huddle up

blouse [bluz] nf overall

blouson [bluzɔ̃] nm blouson (jacket); **~ noir** (fig) ≈ rocker

bluff [blœf] nm bluff

bobine [bɔbin] nf reel; (Élec) coil

bobo [bobo] sigle m/f (= bourgeois bohème) boho

bocal, -aux [bɔkal, -o] nm jar

bock [bɔk] nm glass of beer

bœuf [pl **bœufs**) [bœf, bø] nm ox; (Culin) beef

bof [bɔf] excl (fam: indifférence) don't care!; (pas terrible) nothing special

bohémien, ne [bɔemjɛ̃, -ɛn] nm/f gipsy

boire [bwaʀ] /53/ vt to drink; (s'imprégner de) to soak up; **~ un coup** to have a drink

bois [bwa] nm wood; **de ~, en ~** wooden; **boisé, e** adj woody, wooded

boisson [bwasɔ̃] nf drink

boîte [bwat] nf box; (fam: entreprise) firm; **aliments en ~** canned ou tinned (BRIT) foods; **~ à gants** glove compartment; **~ à ordures** dustbin (BRIT), trash can (US); **~ aux lettres** letter box; **~ d'allumettes** box of matches; (vide) matchbox; **~ de conserves** can ou tin (BRIT) (of food); **~ de nuit** night club; **~ de vitesses** gear box; **~ postale (BP)** PO box; **~ vocale** voice mail

boiter [bwate] /1/ vi to limp; (fig: raisonnement) to be shaky

boîtier [bwatje] nm case

boive etc [bwav] vb voir **boire**

bol [bɔl] nm bowl; **un ~ d'air** a breath of fresh air; **en avoir ras le ~** (fam) to have had a bellyful; **avoir du ~** (fam) to be lucky

bombarder [bɔ̃baʀde] /1/ vt to bomb; **~ qn de** (cailloux, lettres) to bombard sb with

bombe [bɔ̃b] nf bomb; (atomiseur) (aerosol) spray

 MOT-CLÉ

bon, bonne [bɔ̃, bɔn] adj **1** (agréable, satisfaisant) good; **un bon repas/restaurant** a good meal/restaurant; **être bon en maths** to be good at maths

2 (*charitable*): **être bon (envers)** to be good (to)
3 (*correct*) right; **le bon numéro/moment** the right number/moment
4 (*souhaits*): **bon anniversaire!** happy birthday!; **bon courage!** good luck!; **bon séjour!** enjoy your stay!; **bon voyage!** have a good trip!; **bonne année!** happy New Year!; **bonne chance!** good luck!; **bonne fête!** happy holiday!; **bonne nuit!** good night!
5 (*approprié*): **bon à/pour** fit to/for; **à quoi bon (…)?** what's the point *ou* use (of …)?
6: **bon enfant** *adj inv* accommodating, easy-going; **bonne femme** (*péj*) woman; **de bonne heure** early; **bon marché** cheap; **bon mot** witticism; **bon sens** common sense; **bon vivant** jovial chap; **bonnes œuvres** charitable works, charities
▶ *nm* **1** (*billet*) voucher; (*aussi*: **bon cadeau**) gift voucher; **bon d'essence** petrol coupon; **bon du Trésor** Treasury bond
2: **avoir du bon** to have its good points; **pour de bon** for good
▶ *adv*: **il fait bon** it's *ou* the weather is fine; **sentir bon** to smell good; **tenir bon** to stand firm
▶ *excl* good!; **ah bon?** really?; **bon, je reste** right, I'll stay; *voir aussi* **bonne**

bonbon [bɔ̃bɔ̃] *nm* (boiled) sweet
bond [bɔ̃] *nm* leap; **faire un ~** to leap in the air
bondé, e [bɔ̃de] *adj* packed (full)
bondir [bɔ̃diR] /2/ *vi* to leap
bonheur [bɔnœʀ] *nm* happiness; **porter ~ (à qn)** to bring (sb) luck; **au petit ~** haphazardly; **par ~** fortunately
bonhomme [bɔnɔm] (*pl* **bonshommes**) *nm* fellow; **~ de neige** snowman

bonjour [bɔ̃ʒuʀ] *excl, nm* hello; (*selon l'heure*) good morning (*ou* afternoon); **c'est simple comme ~!** it's easy as pie!
bonne [bɔn] *adj f voir* **bon** ▷ *nf* (*domestique*) maid
bonnet [bɔnɛ] *nm* hat; (*de soutien-gorge*) cup; **~ de bain** bathing cap
bonsoir [bɔ̃swaʀ] *excl* good evening
bonté [bɔ̃te] *nf* kindness *no pl*
bonus [bɔnys] *nm* (*Assurances*) no-claims bonus; (*de DVD*) extras *pl*
bord [bɔʀ] *nm* (*de table, verre, falaise*) edge; (*de rivière, lac*) bank; (*de route*) side; (*monter*) **à ~** (to go) on board; **jeter par-dessus ~** to throw overboard; **le commandant de ~/les hommes du ~** the ship's master/crew; **au ~ de la mer/route** at the seaside/roadside; **être au ~ des larmes** to be on the verge of tears
bordeaux [bɔʀdo] *nm* Bordeaux ▷ *adj inv* maroon
bordel [bɔʀdɛl] *nm* brothel; (*fam!*) bloody (BRIT) *ou* goddamn (US) mess (!)
border [bɔʀde] /1/ *vt* (*être le long de*) to line, border; (*qn dans son lit*) to tuck up; **~ qch de** (*garnir*) to trim sth with
bordure [bɔʀdyʀ] *nf* border; **en ~ de** on the edge of
borne [bɔʀn] *nf* boundary stone; (*aussi*: **~ kilométrique**) kilometre-marker, ≈ milestone; **bornes** *nfpl* (*fig*) limits; **dépasser les ~s** to go too far
borné, e [bɔʀne] *adj* (*personne*) narrow-minded
borner [bɔʀne] /1/ *vt*: **se ~ à faire** (*se contenter de*) to content o.s. with doing; (*se limiter à*) to limit o.s. to doing
bosniaque [bɔznjak] *adj* Bosnian ▷ *nm/f*: **B~** Bosnian
Bosnie-Herzégovine [bɔsniɛʀzegɔvin] *nf* Bosnia-Herzegovina
bosquet [bɔskɛ] *nm* grove

bosse [bɔs] nf (de terrain etc) bump; (enflure) lump; (du bossu, du chameau) hump; **avoir la ~ des maths** etc (fam) to have a gift for maths etc; **il a roulé sa ~** (fam) he's been around

bosser [bɔse] /1/ vi (fam) to work; (: dur) to slave (away)

bossu, e [bɔsy] nm/f hunchback

botanique [bɔtanik] nf botany ▷ adj botanic(al)

botte [bɔt] nf (soulier) (high) boot; (gerbe): **~ de paille** bundle of straw; **~ de radis/d'asperges** bunch of radishes/asparagus; **~s de caoutchouc** wellington boots

bottine [bɔtin] nf ankle boot

bouc [buk] nm goat; (barbe) goatee; **~ émissaire** scapegoat

boucan [bukã] nm din, racket

bouche [buʃ] nf mouth; **faire du ~ à ~ à qn** to give sb the kiss of life (BRIT), give sb mouth-to-mouth resuscitation; **rester ~ bée** to stand open-mouthed; **~ d'égout** manhole; **~ d'incendie** fire hydrant; **~ de métro** métro entrance

bouché, e [buʃe] adj (flacon etc) stoppered; (temps, ciel) overcast; (péj: personne) thick; **avoir le nez ~** to have a blocked(-up) nose; **c'est un secteur ~** there's no future in that area; **l'évier est ~** the sink's blocked

bouchée [buʃe] nf mouthful; **~s à la reine** chicken vol-au-vents

boucher [buʃe] /1/ nm butcher ▷ vt (pour colmater) to stop up; (trou) to fill up; (obstruer) to block (up); **se boucher** vi (tuyau etc) to block up, get blocked up; **j'ai le nez bouché** my nose is blocked; **se ~ le nez** to hold one's nose

bouchère [buʃɛʁ] nf butcher

boucherie nf butcher's (shop); (fig) slaughter

bouchon [buʃɔ̃] nm (en liège) cork; (autre matière) stopper; (de tube) top; (fig: embouteillage) holdup; (Pêche) float

boucle [bukl] nf (forme, figure) loop; (objet) buckle; **~ (de cheveux)** curl; **~ d'oreille** earring

bouclé, e [bukle] adj (cheveux) curly

boucler [bukle] /1/ vt (fermer: ceinture etc) to fasten; (terminer) to finish off; (enfermer) to shut away; (quartier) to seal off ▷ vi to curl

bouder [bude] /1/ vi to sulk ▷ vt (personne) to refuse to have anything to do with

boudin [budɛ̃] nm: **~ (noir)** black pudding; **~ blanc** white pudding

boue [bu] nf mud

bouée [bwe] nf buoy; **~ (de sauvetage)** lifebuoy

boueux, -euse [bwø, -øz] adj muddy

bouffe [buf] nf (fam) grub, food

bouffée [bufe] nf (de cigarette) puff; **une ~ d'air pur** a breath of fresh air; **~ de chaleur** hot flush (BRIT) ou flash (US)

bouffer [bufe] /1/ vi (fam) to eat

bouffi, e [bufi] adj swollen

bouger [buʒe] /3/ vi to move; (dent etc) to be loose; (s'activer) to get moving ▷ vt to move; **les prix/les couleurs n'ont pas bougé** prices/ colours haven't changed

bougie [buʒi] nf candle; (Auto) spark(ing) plug

bouillabaisse [bujabɛs] nf type of fish soup

bouillant, e [bujã, -ãt] adj (qui bout) boiling; (très chaud) boiling (hot)

bouillie [buji] nf (de bébé) cereal; **en ~** (fig) crushed

bouillir [bujiʁ] /15/ vi to boil ▷ vt to boil; **~ de colère** etc to seethe with anger etc

bouilloire [bujwaʁ] nf kettle

bouillon [bujɔ̃] nm (Culin) stock no pl; **bouillonner** /1/ vi to bubble; (fig: idées) to bubble up

bouillotte [bujɔt] nf hot-water bottle

boulanger, -ère [bulãʒe, -ɛʁ] nm/f baker; **boulangerie** nf bakery

boule [bul] *nf* (*gén*) ball; (*de pétanque*) bowl; **~ de neige** snowball

boulette [bulɛt] *nf* (*de viande*) meatball

boulevard [bulvaʀ] *nm* boulevard

bouleversement [bulvɛʀsəmɑ̃] *nm* upheaval

bouleverser [bulvɛʀse] /1/ *vt* (*émouvoir*) to overwhelm; (*causer du chagrin à*) to distress; (*pays, vie*) to disrupt; (*papiers, objets*) to turn upside down

boulimie [bulimi] *nf* bulimia

boulimique [bulimik] *adj* bulimic

boulon [bulɔ̃] *nm* bolt

boulot¹ [bulo] *nm* (*fam: travail*) work

boulot², te [bulo, -ɔt] *adj* plump, tubby

boum [bum] *nm* bang ▷ *nf* (*fam*) party

bouquet [bukɛ] *nm* (*de fleurs*) bunch (of flowers), bouquet; (*de persil etc*) bunch; **c'est le ~!** that's the last straw!

bouquin [bukɛ̃] *nm* (*fam*) book; **bouquiner** /1/ *vi* (*fam*) to read

bourdon [buʀdɔ̃] *nm* bumblebee

bourg [buʀ] *nm* small market town (*ou* village)

bourgeois, e [buʀʒwa, -waz] *adj* ≈ (upper) middle class; **bourgeoisie** *nf* ≈ upper middle classes *pl*

bourgeon [buʀʒɔ̃] *nm* bud

Bourgogne [buʀgɔɲ] *nf*: **la ~** Burgundy ▷ *nm*: **b~** Burgundy (wine)

bourguignon, ne [buʀgiɲɔ̃, -ɔn] *adj* of *ou* from Burgundy, Burgundian

bourrasque [buʀask] *nf* squall

bourratif, -ive [buʀatif, -iv] (*fam*) *adj* filling, stodgy

bourré, e [buʀe] *adj* (*rempli*): **~ de** crammed full of; (*fam: ivre*) pickled, plastered

bourrer [buʀe] /1/ *vt* (*pipe*) to fill; (*poêle*) to pack; (*valise*) to cram (full)

bourru, e [buʀy] *adj* surly, gruff

bourse [buʀs] *nf* (*subvention*) grant; (*porte-monnaie*) purse; **la B~** the Stock Exchange

bous [bu] *vb voir* **bouillir**

bousculade [buskylad] *nf* (*hâte*) rush; (*poussée*) crush; **bousculer** /1/ *vt* (*heurter*) to knock into; (*fig*) to push, rush

boussole [busɔl] *nf* compass

bout [bu] *vb voir* **bouillir** ▷ *nm* bit; (*d'un bâton etc*) tip; (*d'une ficelle, table, rue, période*) end; **au ~ de** at the end of, after; **pousser qn à ~** to push sb to the limit (of his patience); **venir à ~ de** to manage to finish (off) *ou* overcome; **à ~ portant** at point-blank range

bouteille [butɛj] *nf* bottle; (*de gaz butane*) cylinder

boutique [butik] *nf* shop

bouton [butɔ̃] *nm* button; (*Bot*) bud; (*sur la peau*) spot; **boutonner** /1/ *vt* to button up; **boutonnière** *nf* buttonhole; **bouton-pression** *nm* press stud

bovin, e [bɔvɛ̃, -in] *adj* bovine ▷ *nm*: **~s** cattle *pl*

bowling [bolɪŋ] *nm* (tenpin) bowling; (*salle*) bowling alley

boxe [bɔks] *nf* boxing

BP *sigle f* = **boîte postale**

bracelet [bʀaslɛ] *nm* bracelet

braconnier [bʀakɔnje] *nm* poacher

brader [bʀade] /1/ *vt* to sell off; **braderie** *nf* cut-price (*BRIT*) *ou* cut-rate (*US*) stall

braguette [bʀagɛt] *nf* fly, flies *pl* (*BRIT*), zipper (*US*)

braise [bʀɛz] *nf* embers *pl*

brancard [bʀɑ̃kaʀ] *nm* (*civière*) stretcher; **brancardier** *nm* stretcher-bearer

branche [bʀɑ̃ʃ] *nf* branch

branché, e [bʀɑ̃ʃe] *adj* (*fam*) trendy

brancher [bʀɑ̃ʃe] /1/ *vt* to connect (up); (*en mettant la prise*) to plug in

brandir [bʀɑ̃diʀ] /2/ *vt* to brandish

braquer [bʀake] /1/ *vi* (*Auto*) to turn (the wheel) ▷ *vt* (*revolver etc*): **~ qch sur** to aim sth at, point sth at; (*mettre en colère*): **~ qn** to antagonize sb

bras [bʀɑ] nm arm; **~ dessus ~ dessous** arm in arm; **se retrouver avec qch sur les ~** (fam) to be landed with sth; **~ droit** (fig) right hand man

brassard [bʀasaʀ] nm armband

brasse [bʀas] nf (nage) breast-stroke; **~ papillon** butterfly(-stroke)

brassée [bʀase] nf armful

brasser [bʀase] /1/ vt to mix; **~ l'argent/les affaires** to handle a lot of money/business

brasserie [bʀasʀi] nf (restaurant) bar (selling food); (usine) brewery

brave [bʀav] adj (courageux) brave; (bon, gentil) good, kind

braver [bʀave] /1/ vt to defy

bravo [bʀavo] excl bravo! ▷ nm cheer

bravoure [bʀavuʀ] nf bravery

break [bʀɛk] nm (Auto) estate car

brebis [bʀəbi] nf ewe; **~ galeuse** black sheep

bredouiller [bʀəduje] /1/ vi, vt to mumble, stammer

bref, brève [bʀɛf, bʀɛv] adj short, brief ▷ adv in short; **d'un ton ~** sharply, curtly; **en ~** in short, in brief

Brésil [bʀezil] nm: **le ~** Brazil

Bretagne [bʀətaɲ] nf: **la ~** Brittany

bretelle [bʀətɛl] nf (de vêtement) strap; (d'autoroute) slip road (BRIT), entrance ou exit ramp (US); **bretelles** nfpl (pour pantalon) braces (BRIT), suspenders (US)

breton, ne [bʀətɔ̃, -ɔn] adj Breton ▷ nm/f: **B~, ne** Breton

brève [bʀɛv] adj f voir **bref**

brevet [bʀəvɛ] nm diploma, certificate; **~ (des collèges)** school certificate, taken at approx. 16 years; **~ (d'invention)** patent; **breveté, e** adj patented

bricolage [bʀikɔlaʒ] nm: **le ~** do-it-yourself (jobs)

bricoler [bʀikɔle] /1/ vi (en amateur) to do DIY jobs; (passe-temps) to potter about ▷ vt (réparer) to fix up; **bricoleur, -euse** nm/f handyman/woman, DIY enthusiast

bridge [bʀidʒ] nm (Cartes) bridge

brièvement [bʀijɛvmɑ̃] adv briefly

brigade [bʀigad] nf (Police) squad; (Mil) brigade; **brigadier** nm ≈ sergeant

brillamment [bʀijamɑ̃] adv brilliantly

brillant, e [bʀijɑ̃, -ɑ̃t] adj (remarquable) bright; (luisant) shiny, shining

briller [bʀije] /1/ vi to shine

brin [bʀɛ̃] nm (de laine, ficelle etc) strand; (fig): **un ~ de** a bit of

brindille [bʀɛ̃dij] nf twig

brioche [bʀijɔʃ] nf brioche (bun); (fam: ventre) paunch

brique [bʀik] nf brick; (de lait) carton

briquet [bʀikɛ] nm (cigarette) lighter

brise [bʀiz] nf breeze

briser [bʀize] /1/ vt to break; **se briser** vi to break

britannique [bʀitanik] adj British ▷ nm/f: **B~** Briton, British person; **les B~s** the British

brocante [bʀɔkɑ̃t] nf (objets) secondhand goods pl, junk; **brocanteur, -euse** nm/f junk shop owner; junk dealer

broche [bʀɔʃ] nf brooch; (Culin) spit; (Méd) pin; **à la ~** spit-roasted

broché, e [bʀɔʃe] adj (livre) paperbacked

brochet [bʀɔʃɛ] nm pike inv

brochette [bʀɔʃɛt] nf (ustensile) skewer; (plat) kebab

brochure [bʀɔʃyʀ] nf pamphlet, brochure, booklet

broder [bʀɔde] /1/ vt to embroider ▷ vi: **~ (sur des faits ou une histoire)** to embroider the facts; **broderie** nf embroidery

bronches [bʀɔ̃ʃ] nfpl bronchial tubes; **bronchite** nf bronchitis

bronze [bʀɔ̃z] nm bronze

bronzer [bʀɔ̃ze] /1/ vi to get a tan; **se bronzer** to sunbathe

brosse [bʀɔs] nf brush; **coiffé en ~** with a crewcut; **~ à cheveux**

hairbrush; **~ à dents** toothbrush; **~ à habits** clothesbrush; **brosser** /1/ vt (nettoyer) to brush; (fig: tableau etc) to paint; **se brosser les dents** to brush one's teeth

brouette [bʀuɛt] nf wheelbarrow

brouillard [bʀujaʀ] nm fog

brouiller [bʀuje] /1/ vt (œufs, message) to scramble; (idées) to mix up; (rendre trouble) to cloud; (désunir: amis) to set at odds; **se brouiller** vi (ciel, vue) to cloud over; **se ~ (avec)** to fall out (with)

brouillon, ne [bʀujɔ̃, -ɔn] adj (sans soin) untidy; (qui manque d'organisation) disorganized ▷ nm (first) draft; **(papier) ~** rough paper

broussailles [bʀusaj] nfpl undergrowth sg; **broussailleux, -euse** adj bushy

brousse [bʀus] nf: **la ~** the bush

brouter [bʀute] /1/ vi to graze

brugnon [bʀynɔ̃] nm nectarine

bruiner [bʀɥine] /1/ vb impers: **il bruine** it's drizzling, there's a drizzle

bruit [bʀɥi] nm: **un ~** a noise, a sound; (fig: rumeur) a rumour; **le ~** noise; **sans ~** without a sound, noiselessly; **~ de fond** background noise

brûlant, e [bʀylɑ̃, -ɑ̃t] adj burning (hot); (liquide) boiling (hot)

brûlé, e [bʀyle] adj (fig: démasqué) blown ▷ nm: **odeur de ~** smell of burning

brûler [bʀyle] /1/ vt to burn; (eau bouillante) to scald; (consommer: électricité, essence) to use; (: feu rouge, signal) to go through (without stopping) ▷ vi to burn; **se brûler** to burn o.s.; (s'ébouillanter) to scald o.s.; **tu brûles** (jeu) you're getting warm ou hot

brûlure [bʀylyʀ] nf (lésion) burn; **~s d'estomac** heartburn sg

brume [bʀym] nf mist

brumeux, -euse [bʀymø, -øz] adj misty

brun, e [bʀœ̃, -yn] adj (gén, bière) brown; (cheveux, personne, tabac) dark; **elle est ~e** she's got dark hair

brunch [bʀœ̃tʃ] nm brunch

brushing [bʀœʃiŋ] nm blow-dry

brusque [bʀysk] adj abrupt

brut, e [bʀyt] adj (diamant) uncut; (soie, minéral) raw; (Comm) gross; **(pétrole) ~** crude (oil)

brutal, e, -aux [bʀytal, -o] adj brutal

Bruxelles [bʀysɛl] n Brussels

bruyamment [bʀɥijamɑ̃] adv noisily

bruyant, e [bʀɥijɑ̃, -ɑ̃t] adj noisy

bruyère [bʀyjɛʀ] nf heather

BTS sigle m (= Brevet de technicien supérieur) vocational training certificate taken at end of two-year higher education course

bu, e [by] pp de **boire**

buccal, e, -aux [bykal, -o] adj: **par voie ~e** orally

bûche [byʃ] nf log; **prendre une ~** (fig) to come a cropper (BRIT), fall flat on one's face; **~ de Noël** Yule log

bûcher [byʃe] /1/ nm (funéraire) pyre; (supplice) stake ▷ vi (fam) to swot, slave (away) ▷ vt to swot up, slave away at

budget [bydʒɛ] nm budget

buée [bɥe] nf (sur une vitre) mist

buffet [byfɛ] nm (meuble) sideboard; (de réception) buffet; **~ (de gare)** (station) buffet, snack bar

buis [bɥi] nm box tree; (bois) box(wood)

buisson [bɥisɔ̃] nm bush

bulbe [bylb] nm (Bot, Anat) bulb

Bulgarie [bylgaʀi] nf: **la ~** Bulgaria

bulle [byl] nf bubble

bulletin [byltɛ̃] nm (communiqué, journal) bulletin; (Scol) report; **~ d'informations** news bulletin; **~ (de vote)** ballot paper; **~ météorologique** weather report

bureau, x [byʀo] nm (meuble) desk; (pièce, service) office; (Inform) desktop; **~ de change** (foreign) exchange office ou bureau; **~ de poste** post office; **~ de tabac** tobacconist's (shop); **bureaucratie** [byʀɔkʀasi] *nf* bureaucracy

bus¹ *vb* [by] *voir* **boire**

bus² *nm* [bys] (*véhicule*) bus

buste [byst] *nm* (*Anat*) chest (: *de femme*) bust

but [by] *vb voir* **boire** ▷ *nm* (*cible*) target; (*fig*) goal, aim; (*Football etc*) goal; **de ~ en blanc** point-blank; **avoir pour ~ de faire** to aim to do; **dans le ~ de** with the intention of

butane [bytan] *nm* butane; (*domestique*) calor gas® (BRIT), butane

butiner [bytine] /1/ *vi* (*abeilles*) to gather nectar

buvais *etc* [byvɛ] *vb voir* **boire**

buvard [byvaʀ] *nm* blotter

buvette [byvɛt] *nf* bar

c' [s] *pron voir* **ce**

ça [sa] *pron* (*pour désigner*) this (: *plus loin*) that; (*comme sujet indéfini*) it; **ça m'étonne que** it surprises me that; **ça va?** how are you?; how are things?; (*d'accord?*) OK?, all right?; **où ça?** where's that?; **pourquoi ça?** why's that?; **qui ça?** who's that?; **ça alors!** (*désapprobation*) well!, really!; **c'est ça** that's right; **ça y est** that's it

cabane [kaban] *nf* hut, cabin

cabaret [kabaʀɛ] *nm* night club

cabillaud [kabijo] *nm* cod *inv*

cabine [kabin] *nf* (*de bateau*) cabin; (*de piscine etc*) cubicle; (*de camion, train*) cab; (*d'avion*) cockpit; **~ d'essayage** fitting room; **~ (téléphonique)** call ou (tele) phone box

cabinet [kabinɛ] *nm* (*petite pièce*) closet; (*de médecin*) surgery (BRIT), office (US); (*de notaire etc*) office (: *clientèle*) practice; (*Pol*) cabinet;

cabinets *nmpl* (*w.-c.*) toilet *sg*; **~ de toilette** toilet

câble [kabl] *nm* cable; **le ~** (*TV*) cable television, cablevision (*us*)

cacahuète [kakaɥɛt] *nf* peanut

cacao [kakao] *nm* cocoa

cache [kaʃ] *nm* mask, card (*for masking*)

cache-cache [kaʃkaʃ] *nm*: **jouer à ~** to play hide-and-seek

cachemire [kaʃmiʀ] *nm* cashmere

cacher [kaʃe] /1/ *vt* to hide, conceal; **~ qch à qn** to hide *ou* conceal sth from sb; **se cacher** *vi* (*volontairement*) to hide; (*être caché*) to be hidden *ou* concealed

cachet [kaʃɛ] *nm* (*comprimé*) tablet; (*de la poste*) postmark; (*rétribution*) fee; (*fig*) style, character

cachette [kaʃɛt] *nf* hiding place; **en ~** on the sly, secretly

cactus [kaktys] *nm* cactus

cadavre [kadavʀ] *nm* corpse, (dead) body

Caddie® [kadi] *nm* (supermarket) trolley (*BRIT*), (grocery) cart (*us*)

cadeau, x [kado] *nm* present, gift; **faire un ~ à qn** to give sb a present *ou* gift; **faire ~ de qch à qn** to make a present of sth to sb, give sb sth as a present

cadenas [kadna] *nm* padlock

cadet, te [kadɛ, -ɛt] *adj* younger; (*le plus jeune*) youngest ▷ *nm/f* youngest child *ou* one

cadran [kadʀɑ̃] *nm* dial; **~ solaire** sundial

cadre [kadʀ] *nm* frame; (*environnement*) surroundings *pl* ▷ *nm/f* (*Admin*) managerial employee, executive; **dans le ~ de** (*fig*) within the framework *ou* context of

cafard [kafaʀ] *nm* cockroach; **avoir le ~** to be down in the dumps

café [kafe] *nm* coffee; (*bistro*) café ▷ *adj inv* coffee *cpd*; **~ au lait** white coffee; **~ noir** black coffee; **café-tabac** *nm* tobacconist's or newsagent's

also serving coffee and spirits; **cafétéria** [kafeteʀja] *nf* cafeteria; **cafetière** *nf* (*pot*) coffee-pot

cage [kaʒ] *nf* cage; **~ d'escalier** (stair) well; **~ thoracique** rib cage

cageot [kaʒo] *nm* crate

cagoule [kagul] *nf* (*passe-montagne*) balaclava

cahier [kaje] *nm* notebook; **~ de brouillons** rough book, jotter; **~ d'exercices** exercise book

caille [kaj] *nf* quail

caillou, x [kaju] *nm* (little) stone; **caillouteux, -euse** *adj* stony

Caire [kɛʀ] *nm*: **le ~** Cairo

caisse [kɛs] *nf* box; (*où l'on met la recette*) till; (*où l'on paye*) cash desk (*BRIT*), checkout counter; (: *au supermarché*) checkout; (*de banque*) cashier's desk; **~ enregistreuse** cash register; **~ d'épargne (CE)** savings bank; **~ de retraite** pension fund; **caissier, -ière** *nm/f* cashier

cake [kɛk] *nm* fruit cake

calandre [kalɑ̃dʀ] *nf* radiator grill

calcaire [kalkɛʀ] *nm* limestone ▷ *adj* (*eau*) hard; (*Géo*) limestone *cpd*

calcul [kalkyl] *nm* calculation; **le ~** (*Scol*) arithmetic; **~ (biliaire)** (gall) stone; **calculateur** *nm*, **calculatrice** *nf* calculator; **calculer** /1/ *vt* to calculate, work out; **calculette** *nf* (pocket) calculator

cale [kal] *nf* (*de bateau*) hold; (*en bois*) wedge

calé, e [kale] *adj* (*fam*) clever, bright

caleçon [kalsɔ̃] *nm* (*d'homme*) boxer shorts; (*de femme*) leggings

calendrier [kalɑ̃dʀije] *nm* calendar; (*fig*) timetable

calepin [kalpɛ̃] *nm* notebook

caler [kale] /1/ *vt* to wedge ▷ *vi* (*moteur, véhicule*) to stall

calibre [kalibʀ] *nm* calibre

câlin, e [kalɛ̃, -in] *adj* cuddly, cuddlesome; (*regard, voix*) tender

calmant [kalmɑ̃] *nm* tranquillizer, sedative; (*contre la douleur*) painkiller

calme [kalm] *adj* calm, quiet ▷ *nm*
calm(ness), quietness; **sans perdre
son ~** without losing one's cool *ou*
calmness; **calmer** /1/ *vt* to calm
(down); (*douleur, inquiétude*) to ease,
soothe; **se calmer** *vi* to calm down

calorie [kalɔʀi] *nf* calorie

camarade [kamaʀad] *nm/f* friend,
pal; (*Pol*) comrade

Cambodge [kɑ̃bɔdʒ] *nm*: **le ~**
Cambodia

cambriolage [kɑ̃bʀijɔlaʒ] *nm*
burglary; **cambrioler** /1/ *vt* to burgle
(*BRIT*), burglarize (*US*); **cambrioleur,
-euse** *nm/f* burglar

camelote [kamlɔt] (*fam*) *nf* rubbish,
trash, junk

caméra [kameʀa] *nf* (*Ciné, TV*)
camera; (*d'amateur*) cine-camera

Cameroun [kamʀun] *nm*: **le ~**
Cameroon

caméscope® [kameskɔp] *nm*
camcorder

camion [kamjɔ̃] *nm* lorry (*BRIT*),
truck; **~ de dépannage** breakdown
(*BRIT*) *ou* tow (*US*) truck; **camionnette**
nf (small) van; **camionneur** *nm*
(*entrepreneur*) haulage contractor
(*BRIT*), trucker (*US*); (*chauffeur*) lorry
(*BRIT*) *ou* truck driver

camomille [kamɔmij] *nf* camomile;
(*boisson*) camomile tea

camp [kɑ̃] *nm* camp; (*fig*) side

campagnard, e [kɑ̃paɲaʀ, -aʀd] *adj*
country *cpd*

campagne [kɑ̃paɲ] *nf* country,
countryside; (*Mil, Pol, Comm*)
campaign; **à la ~** in/to the country

camper [kɑ̃pe] /1/ *vi* to camp ▷ *vt*
to sketch; **se ~ devant** to plant o.s.
in front of; **campeur, -euse** *nm/f*
camper

camping [kɑ̃piŋ] *nm* camping;
(terrain de) ~ campsite, camping
site; **faire du ~** to go camping;
camping-car *nm* camper,
motorhome (*US*); **camping-gaz®**
nm inv camp(ing) stove

Canada [kanada] *nm*: **le ~** Canada;
canadien, ne *adj* Canadian ▷ *nm/f*:
Canadien, ne Canadian ▷ *nf* (*veste*)
fur-lined jacket

canal, -aux [kanal, -o] *nm* canal;
(*naturel, TV*) channel; **canalisation**
nf (*tuyau*) pipe

canapé [kanape] *nm* settee, sofa

canard [kanaʀ] *nm* duck; (*fam:
journal*) rag

cancer [kɑ̃sɛʀ] *nm* cancer; (*signe*):
le C~ Cancer

cancre [kɑ̃kʀ] *nm* dunce

candidat, e [kɑ̃dida, -at] *nm/f*
candidate; (*à un poste*) applicant,
candidate; **candidature** *nf* (*Pol*)
candidature; (*à poste*) application;
poser sa candidature à un poste to
apply for a job

cane [kan] *nf* (female) duck

canette [kanɛt] *nf* (*de bière*) (flip-top)
bottle

canevas [kanva] *nm* (*Couture*) canvas
(for tapestry work)

caniche [kaniʃ] *nm* poodle

canicule [kanikyl] *nf* scorching heat

canif [kanif] *nm* penknife, pocket
knife

canne [kan] *nf* (walking) stick; **~ à
pêche** fishing rod; **~ à sucre** sugar
cane

cannelle [kanɛl] *nf* cinnamon

canoë [kanɔe] *nm* canoe; (*sport*)
canoeing; **~ (kayak)** kayak

canot [kano] *nm* ding(h)y; **~
pneumatique** rubber *ou* inflatable
ding(h)y; **~ de sauvetage** lifeboat

cantatrice [kɑ̃tatʀis] *nf* (opera) singer

cantine [kɑ̃tin] *nf* canteen

canton [kɑ̃tɔ̃] *nm* district (*consisting
of several communes*); (*en Suisse*)
canton

caoutchouc [kautʃu] *nm* rubber;
~ mousse foam rubber; **en ~**
rubber *cpd*

CAP *sigle m* (= *Certificat d'aptitude
professionnelle*) vocational training
certificate taken at secondary school

cap [kap] nm (Géo) cape; (promontoire) headland; (fig: tournant) watershed; (Navig): **changer de ~** to change course; **mettre le ~ sur** to head for

capable [kapabl] adj able, capable; **~ de qch/faire** capable of sth/doing

capacité [kapasite] nf ability; (Jur, Inform, d'un récipient) capacity

cape [kap] nf cape, cloak; **rire sous ~** to laugh up one's sleeve

CAPES [kapɛs] sigle m (= Certificat d'aptitude au professorat de l'enseignement du second degré) secondary teaching diploma

capitaine [kapitɛn] nm captain

capital, e, -aux [kapital, -o] adj (œuvre) major; (question, rôle) fundamental ▷ nm capital; (fig) stock ▷ nf (ville) capital; (lettre) capital (letter); **d'une importance ~e** of capital importance; **capitaux** nmpl (fonds) capital sg; **~ (social)** authorized capital; **~ d'exploitation** working capital; **capitalisme** nm capitalism; **capitaliste** adj, nm/f capitalist

caporal, -aux [kapɔral, -o] nm lance corporal

capot [kapo] nm (Auto) bonnet (BRIT), hood (US)

câpre [kɑpʀ] nf caper

caprice [kapʀis] nm whim, caprice; **faire des ~s** to be temperamental; **capricieux, -euse** adj (fantasque) capricious; whimsical; (enfant) temperamental

Capricorne [kapʀikɔʀn] nm: **le ~** Capricorn

capsule [kapsyl] nf (de bouteille) cap; cap; (Bot etc, spatiale) capsule

capter [kapte] /1/ vt (ondes radio) to pick up; (fig) to win, capture

captivant, e [kaptivã, -ãt] adj captivating

capture [kaptyʀ] nf (action) capture; **~ d'écran** (Inform) screenshot

capturer [kaptyʀe] /1/ vt to capture

capuche [kapyʃ] nf hood

capuchon [kapyʃɔ̃] nm hood; (de stylo) cap, top

car [kaʀ] nm coach (BRIT), bus ▷ conj because, for

carabine [kaʀabin] nf rifle

caractère [kaʀaktɛʀ] nm (gén) character; **en ~s gras** in bold type; **en petits ~s** in small print; **en ~s d'imprimerie** in block capitals; **avoir bon/mauvais ~** to be good-/ ill-natured ou tempered

caractériser [kaʀakteʀize] /1/ vt to characterize; **se ~ par** to be characterized ou distinguished by

caractéristique [kaʀakteʀistik] adj, nf characteristic

carafe [kaʀaf] nf decanter; (pour eau, vin ordinaire) carafe

caraïbe [kaʀaib] adj Caribbean; **les Caraïbes** nfpl the Caribbean (Islands)

carambolage [kaʀɑ̃bɔlaʒ] nm multiple crash, pileup

caramel [kaʀamɛl] nm (bonbon) caramel, toffee; (substance) caramel

caravane [kaʀavan] nf caravan; **caravaning** nm caravanning

carbone [kaʀbɔn] nm carbon; (double) carbon (copy)

carbonique [kaʀbɔnik] adj: **gaz ~** carbon dioxide; **neige ~** dry ice

carbonisé, e [kaʀbɔnize] adj charred

carburant [kaʀbyʀɑ̃] nm (motor) fuel

carburateur [kaʀbyʀatœʀ] nm carburettor

cardiaque [kaʀdjak] adj cardiac, heart cpd ▷ nm/f heart patient; **être ~** to have a heart condition

cardigan [kaʀdigɑ̃] nm cardigan

cardiologue [kaʀdjɔlɔg] nm/f cardiologist, heart specialist

Carême [kaʀɛm] nm: **le ~** Lent

carence [kaʀɑ̃s] nf (manque) deficiency

caresse [kaʀɛs] nf caress

caresser [kaʀese] /1/ vt to caress; (animal) to stroke

cargaison [kaʀɡɛzɔ̃] nf cargo, freight

cargo [kaʀɡo] nm freighter

caricature [kaʀikatyʀ] nf caricature

carie [kaʀi] nf: **la ~ (dentaire)** tooth decay; **une ~** a bad tooth

carnaval [kaʀnaval] nm carnival

carnet [kaʀnɛ] nm (calepin) notebook; (de tickets, timbres etc) book; **~ de chèques** cheque book

carotte [kaʀɔt] nf carrot

carré, e [kaʀe] adj square; (fig: franc) straightforward ▷ nm (Math) square; **kilomètre ~** square kilometre

carreau, x [kaʀo] nm (en faïence etc) (floor) tile; (au mur) (wall) tile; (de fenêtre) (window) pane; (motif) check, square; (Cartes: couleur) diamonds pl; **tissu à ~x** checked fabric

carrefour [kaʀfuʀ] nm crossroads sg

carrelage [kaʀlaʒ] nm (sol) (tiled) floor

carrelet [kaʀlɛ] nm (poisson) plaice

carrément [kaʀemɑ̃] adv (franchement) straight out, bluntly; (sans détours, sans hésiter) straight; (intensif) completely; **c'est ~ impossible** it's completely impossible

carrière [kaʀjɛʀ] nf (de roches) quarry; (métier) career; **militaire de ~** professional soldier

carrosserie [kaʀɔsʀi] nf body, bodywork no pl (BRIT)

carrure [kaʀyʀ] nf build; (fig) calibre

cartable [kaʀtabl] nm satchel, (school)bag

carte [kaʀt] nf (de géographie) map; (marine, du ciel) chart; (de fichier, d'abonnement etc, à jouer) card; (au restaurant) menu; (aussi: ~ postale) (post)card; (aussi: ~ de visite) (visiting) card; **avoir/donner ~ blanche** to have/give carte blanche ou a free hand; **à la ~** (au restaurant) à la carte; **~ à puce** smartcard; **~ bancaire** cash card; **C~ Bleue®** debit card; **~ de crédit** credit card; **~ de fidélité** loyalty card; **~ d'identité** identity card; **la**

~ grise (Auto) ≈ the (car) registration document; **~ mémoire** (d'appareil photo numérique) memory card; **~ routière** road map; **~ de séjour** residence permit; **~ SIM** SIM card; **~ téléphonique** phonecard

carter [kaʀtɛʀ] nm sump

carton [kaʀtɔ̃] nm (matériau) cardboard; (boîte) (cardboard) box; **faire un ~** to score a hit; **~ (à dessin)** portfolio

cartouche [kaʀtuʃ] nf cartridge; (de cigarettes) carton

cas [kɑ] nm case; **ne faire aucun ~ de** to take no notice of; **en aucun ~** on no account; **au ~ où** in case; **en ~ de** in case of, in the event of; **en ~ de besoin** if need be; **en tout ~** in any case, at any rate

cascade [kaskad] nf waterfall, cascade

case [kɑz] nf (hutte) hut; (compartiment) compartment; (sur un formulaire, de mots croisés) box

caser [kaze] /1/ (fam) vt (mettre) to put; (loger) to put up; **se caser** vi (se marier) to settle down; (trouver un emploi) to find a (steady) job

caserne [kazɛʀn] nf barracks

casier [kazje] nm (case) compartment; (pour courrier) pigeonhole (: à clef) locker; **~ judiciaire** police record

casino [kazino] nm casino

casque [kask] nm helmet; (chez le coiffeur) (hair-)dryer; (pour audition) (head-)phones pl, headset

casquette [kaskɛt] nf cap

casse-croûte nm inv snack

casse-noisettes, casse-noix nm inv nutcrackers pl

casse-pieds nm/f inv (fam): **il est ~, c'est un ~** he's a pain (in the neck)

casser [kase] /1/ vt to break; (Jur) to quash; **se casser** vi, vt to break; **~ les pieds à qn** (fam: irriter) to get on sb's nerves; **se ~ la tête** (fam) to go to a lot of trouble

casserole [kasʀɔl] nf saucepan

casse-tête [kɑstɛt] nm inv
(difficultés) headache (fig)
cassette [kasɛt] nf (bande
magnétique) cassette; (coffret) casket
cassis [kasis] nm blackcurrant
cassoulet [kasulɛ] nm sausage and
bean hotpot
catalogue [katalɔg] nm catalogue
catalytique [katalitik] adj: pot ~
catalytic converter
catastrophe [katastʀɔf] nf
catastrophe, disaster
catéchisme [kateʃism] nm catechism
catégorie [kategɔʀi] nf category;
catégorique adj categorical
cathédrale [katedʀal] nf cathedral
catholique [katɔlik] adj, nm/f
(Roman) Catholic; **pas très ~** a bit
shady ou fishy
cauchemar [koʃmaʀ] nm nightmare
cause [koz] nf cause; (Jur) lawsuit,
case; **à ~ de** because of, owing to;
pour ~ de on account of; **(et) pour ~**
and for (a very) good reason; **être en
~** (intérêts) to be at stake; **remettre
en ~** to challenge; **causer** /1/ vt to
cause ▷ vi to chat, talk
caution [kosjɔ̃] nf guarantee, security;
(Jur) bail (bond); (fig) backing, support;
libéré sous ~ released on bail
cavalier, -ière [kavalje, -jɛʀ] adj
(désinvolte) offhand ▷ nm/f rider; (au
bal) partner ▷ nm (Échecs) knight
cave [kav] nf cellar
caverne [kavɛʀn] nf cave
CD sigle m (= compact disc) CD
CDD sigle m (= contrat à durée
déterminée) fixed-term contract
CDI sigle m (= centre de documentation et
d'information) school library; (= contrat
à durée indéterminée) permanent ou
open-ended contract
CD-ROM [sedeʀɔm] nm inv CD-Rom

 MOT-CLÉ

ce, cette [sə, sɛt] (devant nm **cet**
+ voyelle ou h aspiré; pl **ces**) adj dém

(proximité) this; these pl; (non-
proximité) that; those pl; **cette
maison(-ci/là)** this/that house;
cette nuit (qui vient) tonight; (passée)
last night
▶ pron 1: **c'est** it's, it is; **c'est un
peintre** he's ou he is a painter; **ce
sont des peintres** they're ou they
are painters; **c'est le facteur** etc (à
la porte) it's the postman etc; **qui est-
ce?** who is it?; (en désignant) who is
he/she?; **qu'est-ce?** what is it?; **c'est
toi qui lui as parlé** it was you who
spoke to him
2: **c'est ça** (correct) that's right
3: **ce qui, ce que** what; **ce qui me
plaît, c'est sa franchise** what I
like about him ou her is his ou her
frankness; **il est bête, ce qui me
chagrine** he's stupid, which saddens
me; **tout ce qui bouge** everything
that ou which moves; **tout ce que
je sais** all I know; **ce dont j'ai parlé**
what I talked about; **ce que c'est
grand!** it's so big!; voir aussi **c'est-à-
dire; -ci; est-ce que; n'est-ce pas**

ceci [səsi] pron this
céder [sede] /6/ vt to give up ▷ vi
(pont, barrage) to give way; (personne)
to give in; **~ à** to yield to, give in to
cédérom [sedeʀɔm] nm CD-ROM
CEDEX [sedɛks] sigle m (= courrier
d'entreprise à distribution exceptionnelle)
accelerated postal service for bulk users
cédille [sedij] nf cedilla
ceinture [sɛ̃tyʀ] nf belt; (taille) waist;
~ de sécurité safety ou seat belt
cela [s(ə)la] pron that; (comme sujet
indéfini) it; **~ m'étonne que** it
surprises me that; **quand/où ~?**
when/where (was that)?
célèbre [selɛbʀ] adj famous;
célébrer /6/ vt to celebrate
céleri [sɛlʀi] nm: **~(-rave)** celeriac;
~ (en branche) celery
célibataire [selibatɛʀ] adj single,
unmarried ▷ nm/f bachelor/

unmarried *ou* single woman; **mère ~** single *ou* unmarried mother

celle, celles [sɛl] *pron voir* **celui**

cellule [selyl] *nf* (*gén*) cell; **~ souche** stem cell

cellulite [selylit] *nf* cellulite

MOT-CLÉ

celui, celle (*mpl* **ceux**, *fpl* **celles**) [səlɥi, sɛl] *pron* 1: **celui-ci/là, celle-ci/là** this one/that one; **ceux-ci, celles-ci** these (ones); **ceux-là, celles-là** those (ones); **celui de mon frère** my brother's; **celui du salon/du dessous** the one in (*ou* from) the lounge/below

2 (+ *relatif*): **celui qui bouge** the one which *ou* that moves; (*personne*) the one who moves; **celui que je vois** the one (which *ou* that) I see; (*personne*) the one (whom) I see; **celui dont je parle** the one I'm talking about

3 (*valeur indéfinie*): **celui qui veut** whoever wants

cendre [sɑ̃dʀ] *nf* ash; **~s** (*d'un défunt*) ashes; **sous la ~** (*Culin*) in (the) embers; **cendrier** *nm* ashtray

censé, e [sɑ̃se] *adj*: **être ~ faire** to be supposed to do

censeur [sɑ̃sœʀ] *nm* (*Scol*) deputy head (*BRIT*), vice-principal (*US*)

censure [sɑ̃syʀ] *nf* censorship; **censurer** /1/ *vt* (*Ciné, Presse*) to censor; (*Pol*) to censure

cent [sɑ̃] *num* a hundred, one hundred ▷ *nm* (*US, Canada, partie de l'euro etc*) cent; **centaine** *nf*: **une centaine (de)** about a hundred, a hundred or so; **des centaines (de)** hundreds (of); **centenaire** *adj* hundred-year-old ▷ *nm* (*anniversaire*) centenary; (*monnaie*) cent; **centième** *num* hundredth; **centigrade** *nm* centigrade; **centilitre** *nm* centilitre; **centime** *nm* centime; **centime**

d'euro euro cent; **centimètre** *nm* centimetre; (*ruban*) tape measure, measuring tape

central, e, -aux [sɑ̃tʀal, -o] *adj* central ▷ *nm*: **~ (téléphonique)** (telephone) exchange ▷ *nf* power station; **~e électrique/nucléaire** electric/nuclear power station

centre [sɑ̃tʀ] *nm* centre; **~ commercial/sportif/culturel** shopping/sports/arts centre; **~ d'appels** call centre; **centre-ville** *nm* town centre (*BRIT*) *ou* center (*US*)

cèpe [sɛp] *nm* (edible) boletus

cependant [s(ə)pɑ̃dɑ̃] *adv* however, nevertheless

céramique [seʀamik] *nf* ceramics *sg*

cercle [sɛʀkl] *nm* circle; **~ vicieux** vicious circle

cercueil [sɛʀkœj] *nm* coffin

céréale [seʀeal] *nf* cereal

cérémonie [seʀemɔni] *nf* ceremony; **sans ~** (*inviter, manger*) informally

cerf [sɛʀ] *nm* stag

cerf-volant [sɛʀvɔlɑ̃] *nm* kite

cerise [səʀiz] *nf* cherry; **cerisier** *nm* cherry (tree)

cerner [sɛʀne] /1/ *vt* (*Mil etc*) to surround; (*fig: problème*) to delimit, define

certain, e [sɛʀtɛ̃, -ɛn] *adj* certain; **~ (de/que)** certain *ou* sure (of/that); **d'un ~ âge** past one's prime, not so young; **un ~ temps** (quite) some time; **sûr et ~** absolutely certain; **un ~ Georges** someone called Georges; **~s** *pron* some; **certainement** *adv* (*probablement*) most probably *ou* likely; (*bien sûr*) certainly, of course

certes [sɛʀt] *adv* (*sans doute*) admittedly; (*bien sûr*) of course; indeed (yes)

certificat [sɛʀtifika] *nm* certificate

certifier [sɛʀtifje] /7/ *vt*: **~ qch à qn** to guarantee sth to sb

certitude [sɛʀtityd] *nf* certainty

cerveau, x [sɛʀvo] *nm* brain

cervelas [sɛʀvəla] *nm* saveloy

cervelle [sɛrvɛl] nf (Anat) brain; (Culin) brain(s)

CES sigle m (= Collège d'enseignement secondaire) ≈ (junior) secondary school

ces [se] adj dém voir **ce**

cesse [sɛs]: **sans ~** adv (tout le temps) continually, constantly; (sans interruption) continuously; **il n'avait de ~ que** he would not rest until; **cesser** /1/ vt to stop ▷ vi to stop, cease; **cesser de faire** to stop doing; **cessez-le-feu** nm inv ceasefire

c'est-à-dire [sɛtadir] adv that is (to say)

cet [sɛt] adj dém voir **ce**

ceux [sø] pron voir **celui**

chacun, e [ʃakœ̃, -yn] pron each; (indéfini) everyone, everybody

chagrin, e [ʃagrɛ̃, -in] adj morose ▷ nm grief, sorrow; **avoir du ~** to be grieved ou sorrowful

chahut [ʃay] nm uproar; **chahuter** /1/ vt to rag, bait ▷ vi to make an uproar

chaîne [ʃɛn] nf chain; (Radio, TV: stations) channel; **travail à la ~** production line work; **réactions en ~** chain reactions; **~ (haute-fidélité ou hi-fi)** hi-fi system; **~ (de montagnes)** (mountain) range

chair [ʃɛr] nf flesh; **avoir la ~ de poule** to have goose pimples ou gooseflesh; **bien en ~** plump, well-padded; **en ~ et en os** in the flesh; **~ à saucisse** sausage meat

chaise [ʃɛz] nf chair; **~ longue** deckchair

châle [ʃal] nm shawl

chaleur [ʃalœr] nf heat; (fig: d'accueil) warmth; **chaleureux, -euse** adj warm

chamailler [ʃamaje] /1/: **se chamailler** vi to squabble, bicker

chambre [ʃɑ̃br] nf bedroom; (Pol) chamber; (Comm) chamber; **faire ~ à part** to sleep in separate rooms; **~ à un lit/deux lits** single/twin-bedded room; **~ à air** (de pneu) (inner) tube; **~ d'amis** spare ou guest room; **~ à**

coucher bedroom; **~ d'hôte** ≈ bed and breakfast (in private home); **~ meublée** bedsit(ter) (BRIT), furnished room; **~ noire** (Photo) dark room

chameau, x [ʃamo] nm camel

chamois [ʃamwa] nm chamois

champ [ʃɑ̃] nm field; **~ de bataille** battlefield; **~ de courses** racecourse

champagne [ʃɑ̃paɲ] nm champagne

champignon [ʃɑ̃piɲɔ̃] nm mushroom; (terme générique) fungus; **~ de couche** ou **de Paris** button mushroom

champion, ne [ʃɑ̃pjɔ̃, -ɔn] adj, nm/f champion; **championnat** nm championship

chance [ʃɑ̃s] nf: **la ~** luck; **chances** nfpl (probabilités) chances; **avoir de la ~** to be lucky; **il a des ~s de gagner** he has a chance of winning; **bonne ~!** good luck!

change [ʃɑ̃ʒ] nm (Comm) exchange

changement [ʃɑ̃ʒmɑ̃] nm change; **~ climatique** climate change; **~ de vitesse** gears pl; (action) gear change

changer [ʃɑ̃ʒe] /3/ vt (modifier) to change, alter; (remplacer, Comm) to change ▷ vi to change, alter; **se changer** vi to change (o.s.); **~ de** (remplacer: adresse, nom, voiture etc) to change one's; **~ de train** to change trains; **~ d'avis, ~ d'idée** to change one's mind; **~ de vitesse** to change gear; **~ qn/qch de place** to move sb/sth to another place

chanson [ʃɑ̃sɔ̃] nf song

chant [ʃɑ̃] nm song; (art vocal) singing; (d'église) hymn

chantage [ʃɑ̃taʒ] nm blackmail; **faire du ~** to use blackmail

chanter [ʃɑ̃te] /1/ vt, vi to sing; **si cela lui chante** (fam) if he feels like it ou fancies it; **chanteur, -euse** nm/f singer

chantier [ʃɑ̃tje] nm (building) site; (sur une route) roadworks pl; **mettre en ~** to start work on; **~ naval** shipyard

chantilly [ʃɑ̃tiji] *nf voir* **crème**

chantonner [ʃɑ̃tɔne] /1/ *vi, vt* to sing to oneself, hum

chapeau, x [ʃapo] *nm* hat; **~!** well done!

chapelle [ʃapɛl] *nf* chapel

chapitre [ʃapitr] *nm* chapter

chaque [ʃak] *adj* each, every; (*indéfini*) every

char [ʃaʀ] *nm*: **~ (d'assaut)** tank; **~ à voile** sand yacht

charbon [ʃaʀbɔ̃] *nm* coal; **~ de bois** charcoal

charcuterie [ʃaʀkytʀi] *nf* (*magasin*) pork butcher's shop and delicatessen; (*produits*) cooked pork meats *pl*; **charcutier, -ière** *nm/f* pork butcher

chardon [ʃaʀdɔ̃] *nm* thistle

charge [ʃaʀʒ] *nf* (*fardeau*) load; (*Élec, Mil, Jur*) charge; (*rôle, mission*) responsibility; **charges** *nfpl* (*du loyer*) service charges; **à la ~ de** (*dépendant de*) dependent upon; (*aux frais de*) chargeable to; **prendre en ~** to take charge of; (*véhicule*) to take on; (*dépenses*) to take care of; **~s sociales** social security contributions

chargement [ʃaʀʒəmɑ̃] *nm* (*objets*) load

charger [ʃaʀʒe] /3/ *vt* (*voiture, fusil, caméra*) to load; (*batterie*) to charge ▷ *vi* (*Mil etc*) to charge; **se ~ de** to see to, take care of

chargeur [ʃaʀʒœʀ] *nm* (*de batterie*) charger

chariot [ʃaʀjo] *nm* trolley; (*charrette*) waggon

charité [ʃaʀite] *nf* charity; **faire la ~ à** to give (something) to

charmant, e [ʃaʀmɑ̃, -ɑ̃t] *adj* charming

charme [ʃaʀm] *nm* charm; **charmer** /1/ *vt* to charm

charpente [ʃaʀpɑ̃t] *nf* frame(work); **charpentier** *nm* carpenter

charrette [ʃaʀɛt] *nf* cart

charter [tʃaʀtœʀ] *nm* (*vol*) charter flight

chasse [ʃas] *nf* hunting; (*au fusil*) shooting; (*poursuite*) chase; (*aussi*: **~ d'eau**) flush; **prendre en ~** to give chase to; **tirer la ~ (d'eau)** to flush the toilet, pull the chain; **~ à courre** hunting; **chasse-neige** *nm inv* snowplough (BRIT), snowplow (US), **chasser** /1/ *vt* to hunt; (*expulser*) to chase away *ou* out, drive away *ou* out; **chasseur, -euse** *nm/f* hunter ▷ *nm* (*avion*) fighter

chat[1] [ʃa] *nm* cat

chat[2] [tʃat] *nm* (*Internet: salon*) chat room; (*: conversation*) chat

châtaigne [ʃatɛɲ] *nf* chestnut

châtain [ʃatɛ̃] *adj inv* chestnut (brown); (*personne*) chestnut-haired

château, x [ʃato] *nm* (*forteresse*) castle; (*résidence royale*) palace; (*manoir*) mansion; **~ d'eau** water tower; **~ fort** stronghold, fortified castle

châtiment [ʃatimɑ̃] *nm* punishment

chaton [ʃatɔ̃] *nm* (*Zool*) kitten

chatouiller [ʃatuje] /1/ *vt* to tickle; **chatouilleux, -euse** [ʃatujø, -øz] *adj* ticklish; (*fig*) touchy, over-sensitive

chatte [ʃat] *nf* (she-)cat

chatter [tʃate] /1/ *vi* (*Internet*) to chat

chaud, e [ʃo, -od] *adj* (*gén*) warm; (*très chaud*) hot ▷ *nm*: **il fait ~** it's warm; it's hot; **avoir ~** to be warm; to be hot; **ça me tient ~** it keeps me warm; **rester au ~** to stay in the warm

chaudière [ʃodjɛʀ] *nf* boiler

chauffage [ʃofaʒ] *nm* heating; **~ central** central heating

chauffe-eau [ʃofo] *nm inv* water heater

chauffer [ʃofe] /1/ *vt* to heat ▷ *vi* to heat up, warm up; (*trop chauffer: moteur*) to overheat; **se chauffer** *vi* (*au soleil*) to warm o.s.

chauffeur [ʃofœʀ] *nm* driver; (*privé*) chauffeur

chaumière [ʃomjɛʀ] *nf* (thatched) cottage

chaussée [ʃose] *nf* road(way)

chausser [ʃose] /1/ vt (bottes, skis) to put on; (enfant) to put shoes on; **~ du 38/42** to take size 38/42

chaussette [ʃosɛt] nf sock

chausson [ʃosɔ̃] nm slipper; (de bébé) bootee; **~ (aux pommes)** (apple) turnover

chaussure [ʃosyʀ] nf shoe; **~s basses** flat shoes; **~s montantes** ankle boots; **~s de ski** ski boots

chauve [ʃov] adj bald; **chauve-souris** nf bat

chauvin, e [ʃovɛ̃, -in] adj chauvinistic

chaux [ʃo] nf lime; **blanchi à la ~** whitewashed

chef [ʃɛf] nm head, leader; (de cuisine) chef; **général-/commandant en ~** general-/commander-in-chief; **~ d'accusation** charge; **~ d'entreprise** company head; **~ d'état** head of state; **~ de famille** head of the family; **~ de file** (de parti etc) leader; **~ de gare** station master; **~ d'orchestre** conductor; **chef-d'œuvre** nm masterpiece; **chef-lieu** nm county town

chelou, e [ʃəlu] (fam) adj sketchy, dodgy

chemin [ʃəmɛ̃] nm path; (itinéraire, direction, trajet) way; **en ~** on the way; **~ de fer** railway (BRIT), railroad (US)

cheminée [ʃəmine] nf chimney; (à l'intérieur) chimney piece, fireplace; (de bateau) funnel

chemise [ʃəmiz] nf shirt; (dossier) folder; **~ de nuit** nightdress

chemisier [ʃəmizje] nm blouse

chêne [ʃɛn] nm oak (tree); (bois) oak

chenil [ʃənil] nm kennels pl

chenille [ʃənij] nf (Zool) caterpillar

chèque [ʃɛk] nm cheque (BRIT), check (US); **faire/toucher un ~** to write/cash a cheque; **par ~** by cheque; **~ barré/sans provision** crossed (BRIT)/bad cheque; **~ de voyage** traveller's cheque; **chéquier** [ʃekje] nm cheque book

cher, -ère [ʃɛʀ] adj (aimé) dear; (coûteux) expensive, dear ▷ adv: **cela coûte ~** it's expensive

chercher [ʃɛʀʃe] /1/ vt to look for; (gloire etc) to seek; **aller ~** to go for, go and fetch; **~ à faire** to try to do; **chercheur, -euse** nm/f researcher

chéri, e [ʃeri] adj beloved, dear; **(mon) ~** darling

cheval, -aux [ʃəval, -o] nm horse; (Auto): **~ (vapeur)** horsepower no pl; **faire du ~** to ride; **à ~** on horseback; **à ~ sur** astride; (fig) overlapping; **~ de course** race horse

chevalier [ʃəvalje] nm knight

chevaux [ʃəvo] nmpl voir **cheval**

chevet [ʃəvɛ] nm: **au ~ de qn** at sb's bedside; **lampe de ~** bedside lamp

cheveu, x [ʃəvø] nm hair ▷ nmpl (chevelure) hair sg; **avoir les ~x courts/en brosse** to have short hair/a crew cut

cheville [ʃəvij] nf (Anat) ankle; (de bois) peg; (pour enfoncer une vis) plug

chèvre [ʃɛvʀ] nf (she-)goat

chèvrefeuille [ʃɛvʀəfœj] nm honeysuckle

chevreuil [ʃəvʀœj] nm roe deer inv; (Culin) venison

 MOT-CLÉ

chez [ʃe] prép **1** (à la demeure de) at; (: direction) to; **chez qn** at/to sb's house ou place; **je suis chez moi** I'm at home; **je rentre chez moi** I'm going home; **allons chez Nathalie** let's go to Nathalie's

2 (+profession) at; (: direction) to; **chez le boulanger/dentiste** at ou to the baker's/dentist's

3 (dans le caractère, l'œuvre de) in; **chez ce poète** in this poet's work; **c'est ce que je préfère chez lui** that's what I like best about him

chic [ʃik] adj inv chic, smart; (généreux) nice, decent ▷ nm stylishness; **avoir**

le **~ de** ou **pour** to have the knack of ou for; **~!** great!

chicorée [ʃikɔʀe] nf (café) chicory; (salade) endive

chien [ʃjɛ̃] nm dog; (de pistolet) hammer; **~ d'aveugle** guide dog; **~ de garde** guard dog

chienne [ʃjɛn] nf (she-)dog, bitch

chiffon [ʃifɔ̃] nm (piece of) rag; **chiffonner** /1/ vt to crumple; (tracasser) to concern

chiffre [ʃifʀ] nm (représentant un nombre) figure; numeral; (montant, total) total, sum; **en ~s ronds** in round figures; **~ d'affaires (CA)** turnover; **chiffrer** /1/ vt (dépense) to put a figure to, assess; (message) to (en)code, cipher ▷ vi: **chiffrer à, se chiffrer à** to add up to

chignon [ʃiɲɔ̃] nm chignon, bun

Chili [ʃili] nm: **le ~** Chile; **chilien, ne** adj Chilean ▷ nm/f: **Chilien, ne** Chilean

chimie [ʃimi] nf chemistry; **chimiothérapie** [ʃimjɔteʀapi] nf chemotherapy; **chimique** adj chemical; **produits chimiques** chemicals

chimpanzé [ʃɛ̃pɑ̃ze] nm chimpanzee

Chine [ʃin] nf: **la ~** China; **chinois, e** adj Chinese ▷ nm (Ling) Chinese ▷ nm/f: **Chinois, e** Chinese

chiot [ʃjo] nm pup(py)

chips [ʃips] nfpl crisps (BRIT), (potato) chips (US)

chirurgie [ʃiʀyʀʒi] nf surgery; **~ esthétique** cosmetic ou plastic surgery; **chirurgien, ne** nm/f surgeon

chlore [klɔʀ] nm chlorine

choc [ʃɔk] nm (heurt) impact; shock; (collision) crash; (moral) shock; (affrontement) clash

chocolat [ʃɔkɔla] nm chocolate; **~ au lait** milk chocolate

chœur [kœʀ] nm (chorale) choir; (Opéra, Théât) chorus; **en ~** in chorus

choisir [ʃwaziʀ] /2/ vt to choose, select

choix [ʃwa] nm choice; selection; **avoir le ~** to have the choice; **de premier ~** (Comm) class ou grade one; **de ~** choice cpd, selected; **au ~** as you wish ou prefer

chômage [ʃomaʒ] nm unemployment; **mettre au ~** to make redundant, put out of work; **être au ~** to be unemployed ou out of work; **chômeur, -euse** nm/f unemployed person

chope [ʃɔp] nf tankard

choquer [ʃɔke] /1/ vt (offenser) to shock; (commotionner) to shake (up)

chorale [kɔʀal] nf choir

chose [ʃoz] nf thing; **c'est peu de ~** it's nothing much

chou, x [ʃu] nm cabbage; **mon petit ~** (my) sweetheart; **~ à la crème** cream bun (made of choux pastry); **~ de Bruxelles** Brussels sprout; **choucroute** nf sauerkraut

chouette [ʃwɛt] nf owl ▷ adj (fam) great, smashing

chou-fleur [ʃuflœʀ] nm cauliflower

chrétien, ne [kʀetjɛ̃, -ɛn] adj, nm/f Christian

Christ [kʀist] nm: **le ~** Christ; **christianisme** nm Christianity

chronique [kʀɔnik] adj chronic ▷ nf (de journal) column, page; (historique) chronicle; (Radio, TV): **la ~ sportive/théâtrale** the sports/theatre review

chronologique [kʀɔnɔlɔʒik] adj chronological

chronomètre [kʀɔnɔmɛtʀ] nm stopwatch; **chronométrer** /6/ vt to time

chrysanthème [kʀizɑ̃tɛm] nm chrysanthemum

● **CHRYSANTHÈME**
●
● Chrysanthemums are strongly
● associated with funerals in France,
● and therefore should not be given
● as gifts.

chuchotement [ʃyʃɔtmɑ̃] nm whisper

chuchoter [ʃyʃɔte] /1/ vt, vi to whisper

chut excl [ʃyt] sh!

chute [ʃyt] nf fall; (déchet) scrap; **faire une ~ (de 10 m)** to fall (10 m); **~s de pluie/neige** rain/snowfalls; **~ (d'eau)** waterfall; **~ libre** free fall

Chypre [ʃipʀ] nm/f Cyprus

-ci [si] adv voir **par** ▷ adj dém: **ce garçon~/-là** this/that boy; **ces femmes~/-là** these/those women

cible [sibl] nf target

cicatrice [sikatʀis] nf scar; **cicatriser** /1/ vt to heal

ci-contre [sikɔ̃tʀ] adv opposite

ci-dessous [sidəsu] adv below

ci-dessus [sidəsy] adv above

cidre [sidʀ] nm cider

Cie abr (= compagnie) Co

ciel [sjɛl] nm sky; (Rel) heaven

cieux [sjø] nmpl voir **ciel**

cigale [sigal] nf cicada

cigare [sigaʀ] nm cigar

cigarette [sigaʀɛt] nf cigarette; **~ électronique** e-cigarette

ci-inclus, e [siɛ̃kly, -yz] adj, adv enclosed

ci-joint, e [siʒwɛ̃, -ɛ̃t] adj, adv enclosed

cil [sil] nm (eye)lash

cime [sim] nf top; (montagne) peak

ciment [simɑ̃] nm cement

cimetière [simtjɛʀ] nm cemetery; (d'église) churchyard

cinéaste [sineast] nm/f film-maker

cinéma [sinema] nm cinema

cinq [sɛ̃k] num five; **cinquantaine** nf: **une cinquantaine (de)** about fifty; **avoir la cinquantaine** (âge) to be around fifty; **cinquante** num fifty; **cinquantenaire** adj, nm/f fifty-year-old; **cinquième** num fifth ▷ nf (Scol) year 8 (BRIT), seventh grade (US)

cintre [sɛ̃tʀ] nm coat-hanger

cintré, e [sɛ̃tʀe] adj (chemise) fitted

cirage [siʀaʒ] nm (shoe) polish

circonflexe [siʀkɔ̃flɛks] adj: **accent ~** circumflex accent

circonstance [siʀkɔ̃stɑ̃s] nf circumstance; (occasion) occasion; **~s atténuantes** mitigating circumstances

circuit [siʀkɥi] nm (trajet) tour, (round) trip; (Élec, Tech) circuit

circulaire [siʀkylɛʀ] adj, nf circular

circulation [siʀkylasjɔ̃] nf circulation; (Auto): **la ~** (the) traffic

circuler [siʀkyle] /1/ vi (véhicules) to drive (along); (passants) to walk along; (train etc) to run; (sang, devises) to circulate; **faire ~** (nouvelle) to spread (about), circulate; (badauds) to move on

cire [siʀ] nf wax; **ciré** nm oilskin; **cirer** [siʀe] /1/ vt to wax, polish

cirque [siʀk] nm circus; (fig) chaos, bedlam; **quel ~!** what a carry-on!

ciseau, x [sizo] nm: **~ (à bois)** chisel ▷ nmpl (paire de ciseaux) (pair of) scissors

citadin, e [sitadɛ̃, -in] nm/f city dweller

citation [sitasjɔ̃] nf (d'auteur) quotation; (Jur) summons sg

cité [site] nf town; (plus grande) city; **~ universitaire** students' residences pl

citer [site] /1/ vt (un auteur) to quote (from); (nommer) to name; (Jur) to summon

citoyen, ne [sitwajɛ̃, -ɛn] nm/f citizen

citron [sitʀɔ̃] nm lemon; **~ pressé** (fresh) lemon juice; **~ vert** lime; **citronnade** nf still lemonade

citrouille [sitʀuj] nf pumpkin

civet [sive] nm: **~ de lapin** rabbit stew

civière [sivjɛʀ] nf stretcher

civil, e [sivil] adj (Jur, Admin, poli) civil; (non militaire) civilian; **en ~** in civilian clothes; **dans le ~** in civilian life

civilisation [sivilizasjɔ̃] nf civilization

clair, e [klɛʀ] adj light; (chambre) light, bright; (eau, son, fig) clear ▷ adv: **voir ~** to see clearly ▷ nm: **mettre au ~**

(*notes etc*) to tidy up; **tirer qch au ~** to clear sth up, clarify sth; **~ de lune** moonlight; **clairement** *adv* clearly
clairière [klɛrjɛr] *nf* clearing
clandestin, e [klɑ̃dɛstɛ̃, -in] *adj* clandestine, covert; (*Pol*) underground, clandestine; (*travailleur, immigration*) illegal; **passager ~** stowaway
claque [klak] *nf* (*gifle*) slap; **claquer** /1/ *vi* (*porte*) to bang, slam; (*fam: mourir*) to snuff it ▷ *vt* (*porte*) to slam, bang; (*doigts*) to snap; (*fam: dépenser*) to blow; **elle claquait des dents** her teeth were chattering; **être claqué** (*fam*) to be dead tired; **se claquer un muscle** to pull *ou* strain a muscle; **claquettes** *nfpl* tap-dancing *sg*; (*chaussures*) flip-flops
clarinette [klarinɛt] *nf* clarinet
classe [klas] *nf* class; (*Scol: local*) class(room); (: *leçon*) class; (: *élèves*) class; **aller en ~** to go to school; **classement** *nm* (*rang: Scol*) place; (: *Sport*) placing; (*liste: Scol*) class list (in order of merit); (: *Sport*) placings *pl*
classer [klase] /1/ *vt* (*idées, livres*) to classify; (*papiers*) to file; (*candidat, concurrent*) to grade; (*Jur: affaire*) to close; **se ~ premier/dernier** to come first/last; (*Sport*) to finish first/last; **classeur** *nm* (*cahier*) file
classique [klasik] *adj* (*sobre, coupe etc*) classic(al), classical; (*habituel*) standard, classic
clavicule [klavikyl] *nf* collarbone
clavier [klavje] *nm* keyboard; (*de portable*) keypad
clé [kle] *nf* key; (*Mus*) clef; (*de mécanicien*) spanner (BRIT), wrench (US); **prix ~s en main** (*d'une voiture*) on-the-road price; ; **~ de contact** ignition key; **~ USB** USB key
clergé [klɛrʒe] *nm* clergy
clic [klik] *nm* (*Inform*) click
cliché [kliʃe] *nm* (*fig*) cliché; (*Photo*) negative; print; (*Typo*) (printing) plate; (*Ling*) cliché

client, e [klijɑ̃, -ɑ̃t] *nm/f* (*acheteur*) customer, client; (*d'hôtel*) guest, patron; (*du docteur*) patient; (*de l'avocat*) client; **clientèle** *nf* (*du magasin*) customers *pl*, clientèle; (*du docteur, de l'avocat*) practice
cligner [kliɲe] /1/ *vi*: **~ des yeux** to blink (one's eyes); **~ de l'œil** to wink; **clignotant** *nm* (*Auto*) indicator; **clignoter** /1/ *vi* (*étoiles etc*) to twinkle; (*lumière*) to flicker
climat [klima] *nm* climate
climatisation [klimatizasjɔ̃] *nf* air conditioning; **climatisé, e** *adj* air-conditioned
clin d'œil [klɛ̃dœj] *nm* wink; **en un ~** in a flash
clinique [klinik] *nf* (private) clinic
clip [klip] *nm* (*pince*) clip; (*boucle d'oreille*) clip-on; **(vidéo) ~** pop (*ou* promotional) video
cliquer [klike] /1/ *vi* (*Inform*) to click; **~ deux fois** to double-click ▷ *vt* to click; **~ sur** to click on
clochard, e [klɔʃar, -ard] *nm/f* tramp
cloche [klɔʃ] *nf* (*d'église*) bell; (*fam*) clot; **clocher** /1/ *nm* church tower; (*en pointe*) steeple ▷ *vi* (*fam*) to be *ou* go wrong; **de clocher** (*péj*) parochial
cloison [klwazɔ̃] *nf* partition (wall)
clonage [klɔnaʒ] *nm* cloning
cloner [klɔne] /1/ *vt* to clone
cloque [klɔk] *nf* blister
clore [klɔr] /45/ *vt* to close
clôture [klotyr] *nf* closure; (*barrière*) enclosure
clou [klu] *nm* nail; **clous** *nmpl* = **passage clouté**; **pneus à ~s** studded tyres; **le ~ du spectacle** the highlight of the show; **~ de girofle** clove
clown [klun] *nm* clown
club [klœb] *nm* club
CNRS *sigle m* (= *Centre national de la recherche scientifique*) ≈ SERC (BRIT), ≈ NSF (US)

coaguler [kɔagyle] /1/ vi, vt, **se coaguler** vi (sang) to coagulate

cobaye [kɔbaj] nm guinea-pig

coca® [kɔka] nm Coke®

cocaïne [kɔkain] nf cocaine

coccinelle [kɔksinɛl] nf ladybird (BRIT), ladybug (US)

cocher [kɔʃe] /1/ vt to tick off

cochon, ne [kɔʃɔ̃, -ɔn] nm pig ▷ adj (fam) dirty, smutty; **~ d'Inde** guinea-pig; **cochonnerie** nf (fam: saleté) filth; (marchandises) rubbish, trash

cocktail [kɔktɛl] nm cocktail; (réception) cocktail party

cocorico [kɔkɔriko] excl, nm cock-a-doodle-do

cocotte [kɔkɔt] nf (en fonte) casserole; **ma ~** (fam) sweetie (pie); **~ (minute)®** pressure cooker

code [kɔd] nm code ▷ adj: **phares ~s** dipped lights; **se mettre en ~(s)** to dip (BRIT) ou dim (US) one's (head) lights; **~ à barres** bar code; **~ civil** Common Law; **~ pénal** penal code; **~ postal** (numéro) postcode (BRIT), zip code (US); **~ de la route** highway code; **~ secret** cipher

cœur [kœr] nm heart; (Cartes: couleur) hearts pl; (: carte) heart; **avoir bon ~** to be kind-hearted; **avoir mal au ~** to feel sick; **par ~** by heart; **de bon ~** willingly; **cela lui tient à ~** that's (very) close to his heart

coffre [kɔfr] nm (meuble) chest; (d'auto) boot (BRIT), trunk (US); **coffre-fort** nm safe; **coffret** nm casket

cognac [kɔɲak] nm brandy, cognac

cogner [kɔɲe] /1/ vi to knock; **se ~ contre** to knock ou bump into; **se ~ la tête** to bang one's head

cohérent, e [kɔerɑ̃, -ɑ̃t] adj coherent, consistent

coiffé, e [kwafe] adj: **bien/mal ~** with tidy/untidy hair; **~ d'un béret** wearing a beret

coiffer [kwafe] /1/ vt (fig: surmonter) to cover, top; **~ qn** to do sb's hair; **se**

coiffer vi to do one's hair; **coiffeur, -euse** nm/f hairdresser ▷ nf (table) dressing table; **coiffure** nf (cheveux) hairstyle, hairdo; (art): **la coiffure** hairdressing

coin [kwɛ̃] nm corner; (pour coincer) wedge; **l'épicerie du ~** the local grocer; **dans le ~** (aux alentours) in the area, around about; (habiter) locally; **je ne suis pas du ~** I'm not from here; **au ~ du feu** by the fireside; **regard en ~** side(ways) glance

coincé, e [kwɛ̃se] adj stuck, jammed; (fig: inhibé) inhibited, with hang-ups

coïncidence [kɔɛ̃sidɑ̃s] nf coincidence

coing [kwɛ̃] nm quince

col [kɔl] nm (de chemise) collar; (encolure, cou) neck; (de montagne) pass; **~ roulé** polo-neck; **~ de l'utérus** cervix

colère [kɔlɛr] nf anger; **une ~** a fit of anger; **être en ~ (contre qn)** to be angry (with sb); **mettre qn en ~** to make sb angry; **se mettre en ~ contre qn** to get angry with sb; **se mettre en ~** to get angry; **coléreux, -euse, colérique** adj quick-tempered, irascible

colin [kɔlɛ̃] nm hake

colique [kɔlik] nf diarrhoea

colis [kɔli] nm parcel

collaborer [kɔ(l)labɔre] /1/ vi to collaborate; **~ à** to collaborate on; (revue) to contribute to

collant, e [kɔlɑ̃, -ɑ̃t] adj sticky; (robe etc) clinging, skintight; (péj) clinging ▷ nm (bas) tights pl; (de danseur) leotard

colle [kɔl] nf glue; (à papiers peints) (wallpaper) paste; (devinette) teaser, riddle; (Scol: fam) detention

collecte [kɔlɛkt] nf collection; **collectif, -ive** adj collective; (visite, billet etc) group cpd

collection [kɔlɛksjɔ̃] nf collection; (Édition) series; **collectionner** /1/ vt (tableaux, timbres) to

collect; **collectionneur, -euse**
[kɔlɛksjɔnœr, -øz] *nm/f* collector
collectivité [kɔlɛktivite] *nf* group;
les ~s locales local authorities
collège [kɔlɛʒ] *nm* (*école*) (secondary)
school; (*assemblée*) body; **collégien,**
ne *nm/f* secondary school pupil
(BRIT), high school student (US)
collègue [kɔ(l)lɛg] *nm/f* colleague
coller [kɔle] /1/ *vt* (*papier, timbre*)
to stick (on); (*affiche*) to stick up;
(*enveloppe*) to stick down; (*morceaux*)
to stick *ou* glue together; (*Inform*) to
paste; (*fam: mettre, fourrer*) to stick,
shove; (*Scol: fam*) to keep in ▷ *vi*
(*être collant*) to be sticky; (*adhérer*) to
stick; **~ à** to stick to; **être collé à un**
examen (*fam*) to fail an exam
collier [kɔlje] *nm* (*bijou*) necklace; (*de*
chien, Tech) collar
colline [kɔlin] *nf* hill
collision [kɔlizjɔ̃] *nf* collision, crash;
entrer en ~ (avec) to collide (with)
collyre [kɔlir] *nm* eye lotion
colombe [kɔlɔ̃b] *nf* dove
Colombie [kɔlɔ̃bi] *nf*: **la ~** Colombia
colonie [kɔlɔni] *nf* colony; **~ (de**
vacances) holiday camp (*for children*)
colonne [kɔlɔn] *nf* column; **se**
mettre en ~ par deux/quatre to
get into twos/fours; **~ (vertébrale)**
spine, spinal column
colorant [kɔlɔrɑ̃] *nm* colouring
colorer [kɔlɔre] /1/ *vt* to colour
colorier [kɔlɔrje] /7/ *vt* to colour (in)
coloris [kɔlɔri] *nm* colour, shade
colza [kɔlza] *nm* rape(seed)
coma [kɔma] *nm* coma; **être dans le**
~ to be in a coma
combat [kɔ̃ba] *nm* fight; fighting
no pl; **~ de boxe** boxing match;
combattant *nm*: **ancien**
combattant war veteran;
combattre /41/ *vt* to fight; (*épidémie,*
ignorance) to combat, fight against
combien [kɔ̃bjɛ̃] *adv* (*quantité*) how
much; (*nombre*) how many; **~ de**
how much; (*nombre*) how many; **~**

~ de temps how long; **~ coûte/**
pèse ceci? how much does this cost/
weigh?; **on est le ~ aujourd'hui?**
(*fam*) what's the date today?
combinaison [kɔ̃binɛzɔ̃] *nf*
combination; (*astuce*) scheme; (*de*
femme) slip; (*de plongée*) wetsuit; (*bleu*
de travail) boilersuit (BRIT), coveralls
pl (US)
combiné [kɔ̃bine] *nm* (*aussi:*
~ téléphonique) receiver
comble [kɔ̃bl] *adj* (*salle*) packed
(full) ▷ *nm* (*du bonheur, plaisir*) height;
combles *nmpl* (*Constr*) attic *sg*, loft *sg*;
c'est le ~! that beats everything!
combler [kɔ̃ble] /1/ *vt* (*trou*) to fill in;
(*besoin, lacune*) to fill; (*déficit*) to make
good; (*satisfaire*) fulfil
comédie [kɔmedi] *nf* comedy; (*fig*)
playacting *no pl*; **faire une ~** (*fig*) to
make a fuss; **~ musicale** musical;
comédien, ne *nm/f* actor/actress
comestible [kɔmɛstibl] *adj* edible
comique [kɔmik] *adj* (*drôle*) comical;
(*Théât*) comic ▷ *nm* (*artiste*) comic,
comedian
commandant [kɔmɑ̃dɑ̃] *nm* (*gén*)
commander, commandant; (*Navig*)
captain
commande [kɔmɑ̃d] *nf* (*Comm*)
order; **commandes** *nfpl* (*Aviat etc*)
controls; **sur ~** to order; **commander**
/1/ *vt* (*Comm*) to order; (*diriger,*
ordonner) to command; **commander**
à qn de faire to command *ou* order
sb to do

 MOT-CLÉ

comme [kɔm] *prép* **1** (*comparaison*)
like; **tout comme son père** just like
his father; **fort comme un bœuf** as
strong as an ox; **joli comme tout**
ever so pretty
2 (*manière*) like; **faites-le comme ça**
do it like this, do it this way; **comme**
ci, comme ça so-so, middling
3 (*en tant que*) as a; **donner comme**

prix to give as a prize; **travailler comme secrétaire** to work as a secretary

4: **comme il faut** adv properly

▶ conj 1 (ainsi que) as; **elle écrit comme elle parle** she writes as she talks; **comme si** as if

2 (au moment où, alors que) as; **il est parti comme j'arrivais** he left as I arrived

3 (parce que, puisque) as; **comme il était en retard, il …** as he was late, he …

▶ adv: **comme il est fort/c'est bon!** he's so strong/it's so good!

commencement [kɔmãsmã] nm beginning, start

commencer [kɔmãse] /3/ vt, vi to begin, start; **~ à** ou **de faire** to begin ou start doing

comment [kɔmã] adv how; **~?** (que dites-vous) (I beg your) pardon?; **et ~!** and how!

commentaire [kɔmãtɛʀ] nm comment; remark; **~ (de texte)** commentary

commerçant, e [kɔmɛʀsã, -ãt] nm/f shopkeeper, trader

commerce [kɔmɛʀs] nm (activité) trade, commerce; (boutique) business; **~ électronique** e-commerce; **~ équitable** fair trade; **commercial, e, -aux** adj commercial, trading; (péj) commercial; **commercialiser** /1/ vt to market

commettre [kɔmɛtʀ] /56/ vt to commit

commissaire [kɔmisɛʀ] nm (de police) ≈ (police) superintendent; **~ aux comptes** (Admin) auditor; **commissariat** nm police station

commission [kɔmisjɔ̃] nf (comité, pourcentage) commission; (message) message; (course) errand; **commissions** nfpl (achats) shopping sg

commode [kɔmɔd] adj (pratique) convenient, handy; (facile) easy; (personne): **pas ~** awkward (to deal with) ▷ nf chest of drawers

commun, e [kɔmœ̃, -yn] adj common; (pièce) communal, shared; (réunion, effort) joint ▷ nf (Admin) commune, ≈ district (: urbaine) ≈ borough; **communs** nmpl (bâtiments) outbuildings; **cela sort du ~** it's out of the ordinary; **le ~ des mortels** the common run of people; **en ~ (faire)** jointly; **mettre en ~** to pool, share; **d'un ~ accord** of one accord

communauté [kɔmynote] nf community

commune [kɔmyn] adj f, nf voir **commun**

communication [kɔmynikasjɔ̃] nf communication

communier [kɔmynje] /7/ vi (Rel) to receive communion

communion [kɔmynjɔ̃] nf communion

communiquer [kɔmynike] /1/ vt (nouvelle, dossier) to pass on, convey; (peur etc) to communicate ▷ vi to communicate; **se ~ à** (se propager) to spread to

communisme [kɔmynism] nm communism; **communiste** adj, nm/f communist

commutateur [kɔmytatœʀ] nm (Élec) (change-over) switch, commutator

compact, e [kɔ̃pakt] adj (dense) dense; (appareil) compact

compagne [kɔ̃paɲ] nf companion

compagnie [kɔ̃paɲi] nf (firme, Mil) company; **tenir ~ à qn** to keep sb company; **fausser ~ à qn** to give sb the slip, slip ou sneak away from sb; **~ aérienne** airline (company)

compagnon [kɔ̃paɲɔ̃] nm companion

comparable [kɔ̃paʀabl] adj: **~ (à)** comparable (to)

comparaison [kɔ̃paʀɛzɔ̃] nf
comparison

comparer [kɔ̃paʀe] /1/ vt to
compare; **~ qch/qn à** ou **et** (pour
choisir) to compare sth/sb with ou
and; (pour établir une similitude) to
compare sth/sb to ou and

compartiment [kɔ̃paʀtimã] nm
compartment

compas [kɔ̃pɑ] nm (Géom) (pair of)
compasses pl; (Navig) compass

compatible [kɔ̃patibl] adj
compatible

compatriote [kɔ̃patʀijɔt] nm/f
compatriot

compensation [kɔ̃pãsasjɔ̃] nf
compensation

compenser [kɔ̃pãse] /1/ vt to
compensate for, make up for

compétence [kɔ̃petãs] nf
competence

compétent, e [kɔ̃petã, -ãt] adj (apte)
competent, capable

compétition [kɔ̃petisjɔ̃] nf (gén)
competition; (Sport: épreuve) event; **la
~ automobile** motor racing

complément [kɔ̃plemã] nm
complement; (reste) remainder;
~ d'information (Admin)
supplementary ou further
information; **complémentaire**
adj complementary; (additionnel)
supplementary

complet, -ète [kɔ̃plɛ, -ɛt] adj
complete; (plein: hôtel etc) full ▷ nm
(aussi: **~-veston**) suit; **pain ~**
wholemeal bread; **complètement**
adv completely; **compléter** /6/
vt (porter à la quantité voulue) to
complete; (augmenter: connaissances,
études) to complement, supplement;
(: garde-robe) to add to

complexe [kɔ̃plɛks] adj complex
▷ nm: **~ hospitalier/industriel**
hospital/industrial complex;
complexé, e adj mixed-up, hung-up

complication [kɔ̃plikasjɔ̃] nf
complexity, intricacy; (difficulté, ennui)
complication; **complications** nfpl
(Méd) complications

complice [kɔ̃plis] nm accomplice

compliment [kɔ̃plimã]
nm (louange) compliment;
compliments nmpl (félicitations)
congratulations

compliqué, e [kɔ̃plike] adj
complicated, complex; (personne)
complicated

comportement [kɔ̃pɔʀtəmã] nm
behaviour

comporter [kɔ̃pɔʀte] /1/ vt (consister
en) to consist of, comprise; (être
équipé de) to have; **se comporter** vi
to behave

composer [kɔ̃poze] /1/ vt (musique,
texte) to compose; (mélange, équipe) to
make up; (faire partie de) to make up,
form ▷ vi (transiger) to come to terms;
se ~ de to be composed of, be made
up of; **~ un numéro** (au téléphone) to
dial a number; **compositeur, -trice**
nm/f (Mus) composer; **composition**
nf composition; (Scol) test

composter [kɔ̃pɔste] /1/ vt (billet)
to punch

> **● COMPOSTER**
> ●
> ● In France you have to punch your
> ● ticket on the platform to validate it
> ● before getting onto the train.

compote [kɔ̃pɔt] nf stewed fruit no
pl; **~ de pommes** stewed apples

compréhensible [kɔ̃pʀeãsibl]
adj comprehensible; (attitude)
understandable

compréhensif, -ive [kɔ̃pʀeãsif, -iv]
adj understanding

■ Attention à ne pas traduire
  compréhensif par comprehensive.

comprendre [kɔ̃pʀãdʀ] /58/ vt
to understand; (se composer de) to
comprise, consist of

compresse [kɔ̃pʀɛs] nf compress

comprimé [kɔ̃pʀime] nm tablet

compris, e [kɔ̃pri, -iz] *pp de*
comprendre ▷ *adj (inclus)* included;
~ entre *(situé)* contained between;
**la maison ~e/non ~e, y/non ~ la
maison** including/excluding the
house; **100 euros tout ~** 100 euros
all inclusive *ou* all-in

comptabilité [kɔ̃tabilite] *nf*
(activité, technique) accounting,
accountancy; accounts *pl*, books
pl; *(service)* accounts office *ou*
department

comptable [kɔ̃tabl] *nm/f*
accountant

comptant [kɔ̃tɑ̃] *adv*: **payer ~** to pay
cash; **acheter ~** to buy for cash

compte [kɔ̃t] *nm* count; *(total,
montant)* count, (right) number; *
(bancaire, facture)* account; **comptes**
nmpl accounts, books; *(fig)*
explanation *sg*; **en fin de ~** all things
considered; **s'en tirer à bon ~** to get
off lightly; **pour le ~ de** on behalf
of; **pour son propre ~** for one's own
benefit; **travailler à son ~** to work
for oneself; **régler un ~** *(s'acquitter de
qch)* to settle an account; *(se venger)* to
get one's own back; **rendre des ~s à
qn** *(fig)* to be answerable to sb; **tenir
~ de qch** to take sth into account;
~ courant (CC) current account;
~ à rebours countdown; **~ rendu**
account, report; *(de film, livre)* review;
voir aussi **rendre; compte-gouttes**
nm inv dropper

compter [kɔ̃te] /1/ *vt* to count;
(facturer) to charge for; *(avoir à son
actif, comporter)* to have; *(prévoir)*
to allow, reckon; *(penser, espérer)*:
~ réussir/revenir to expect to
succeed/return ▷ *vi* to count; *(être
économe)* to economize; *(figurer)*:
~ parmi to be *ou* rank among; **~ sur**
to count (up)on; **~ avec qch/qn** to
reckon with *ou* take account of sth/
sb; **sans ~ que** besides which

compteur [kɔ̃tœr] *nm* meter; **~ de
vitesse** speedometer

comptine [kɔ̃tin] *nf* nursery rhyme

comptoir [kɔ̃twar] *nm (de magasin)*
counter; *(de café)* counter, bar

con, ne [kɔ̃, kɔn] *adj (fam!)* bloody
(BRIT!) *ou* damned stupid

concentrer [kɔ̃sɑ̃tre] /1/ *vt* to
concentrate; **se concentrer** *vi* to
concentrate

concerner [kɔ̃serne] /1/ *vt* to
concern; **en ce qui me concerne** as
far as I am concerned

concert [kɔ̃ser] *nm* concert; **de ~**
(décider) unanimously

concessionnaire [kɔ̃sesjɔner]
nm/f agent, dealer

concevoir [kɔ̃s(ə)vwar] /28/ *vt (idée,
projet)* to conceive (of); *(comprendre)*
to understand; *(enfant)* to conceive;
maison bien/mal conçue well-/
badly-designed *ou* -planned house

concierge [kɔ̃sjerʒ] *nm/f* caretaker

concis, e [kɔ̃si, -iz] *adj* concise

conclure [kɔ̃klyr] /35/ *vt* to
conclude; **conclusion** *nf* conclusion

conçois [kɔ̃swa] *vb voir* **concevoir**

concombre [kɔ̃kɔ̃br] *nm* cucumber

concours [kɔ̃kur] *nm* competition;
(Scol) competitive examination;
(assistance) aid, help; **~ de
circonstances** combination of
circumstances; **~ hippique** horse
show; *voir* **'hors-concours**

concret, -ète [kɔ̃kre, -et] *adj*
concrete

conçu, e [kɔ̃sy] *pp de* **concevoir**

concubinage [kɔ̃kybinaʒ] *nm (Jur)*
cohabitation

concurrence [kɔ̃kyrɑ̃s] *nf*
competition; **jusqu'à ~ de** up to;
faire ~ à to be in competition with

concurrent, e [kɔ̃kyrɑ̃, -ɑ̃t] *nm/f*
(Sport, Écon etc) competitor; *(Scol)*
candidate

condamner [kɔ̃dane] /1/ *vt (blâmer)*
to condemn; *(Jur)* to sentence; *(porte,
ouverture)* to fill in, block up; **~ qn à
deux ans de prison** to sentence sb to
two years' imprisonment

condensation [kɔ̃dɑ̃sasjɔ̃] nf
condensation

condition [kɔ̃disjɔ̃] nf condition;
conditions nfpl (tarif, prix) terms;
(circonstances) conditions; **sans
~** unconditionally; **à ~ de** ou **que**
provided that; **conditionnel, le** nm
conditional (tense)

conditionnement [kɔ̃disjɔnmɑ̃]
nm (emballage) packaging

condoléances [kɔ̃dɔleɑ̃s] nfpl
condolences

conducteur, -trice [kɔ̃dyktœr,
-tris] nm/f driver ▷ nm (Élec etc)
conductor

conduire [kɔ̃dɥir] /38/ vt to drive;
(délégation, troupeau) to lead; **se
conduire** vi to behave; **~ vers/à** to
lead towards/to; **~ qn quelque part**
to take sb somewhere; to drive sb
somewhere

conduite [kɔ̃dɥit] nf (comportement)
behaviour; (d'eau, de gaz) pipe; **sous
la ~ de** led by

confection [kɔ̃fɛksjɔ̃] nf (fabrication)
making; (Couture) **la ~** the clothing
industry

conférence [kɔ̃ferɑ̃s] nf (exposé)
lecture; (pourparlers) conference; **~ de
presse** press conference

confesser [kɔ̃fese] /1/ vt to confess;
confession nf confession; (culte:
catholique etc) denomination

confetti [kɔ̃feti] nm confetti no pl

confiance [kɔ̃fjɑ̃s] nf (en l'honnêteté de
qn) confidence, trust; (en la valeur de qch)
faith; **avoir ~ en** to have confidence
ou faith in, trust; **faire ~ à** to trust;
mettre qn en ~ to win sb's trust; **~ en
soi** self-confidence; voir **question**

confiant, e [kɔ̃fjɑ̃, -ɑ̃t] adj confident;
trusting

confidence [kɔ̃fidɑ̃s] nf confidence;
confidentiel, le adj confidential

confier [kɔ̃fje] /7/ vt: **~ à qn** (objet
en dépôt, travail etc) to entrust to sb;
(secret, pensée) to confide to sb; **se ~ à
qn** to confide in sb

confirmation [kɔ̃firmasjɔ̃] nf
confirmation

confirmer [kɔ̃firme] /1/ vt to
confirm

confiserie [kɔ̃fizri] nf (magasin)
confectioner's ou sweet shop;
confiseries nfpl (bonbons)
confectionery sg

confisquer [kɔ̃fiske] /1/ vt to
confiscate

confit, e [kɔ̃fi, -it] adj: **fruits ~s**
crystallized fruits ▷ nm: **~ d'oie**
potted goose

confiture [kɔ̃fityr] nf jam

conflit [kɔ̃fli] nm conflict

confondre [kɔ̃fɔ̃dr] /41/ vt (jumeaux,
faits) to confuse, mix up; (témoin,
menteur) to confound; **se confondre**
vi to merge; **se ~ en excuses** to offer
profuse apologies

conforme [kɔ̃fɔrm] adj: **~ à** (en
accord avec: loi, règle) in accordance
with; **conformément** adv:
conformément à in accordance
with; **conformer** /1/ vt: **se
conformer à** to conform to

confort [kɔ̃fɔr] nm comfort; **tout ~**
(Comm) with all mod cons (BRIT) ou
modern conveniences; **confortable**
adj comfortable

confronter [kɔ̃frɔ̃te] /1/ vt to
confront

confus, e [kɔ̃fy, -yz] adj (vague)
confused; (embarrassé) embarrassed;
confusion nf (voir confus) confusion;
embarrassment; (voir confondre)
confusion; mixing up

congé [kɔ̃ʒe] nm (vacances) holiday;
en ~ on holiday; **semaine/jour de
~** week/day off; **prendre ~ de qn** to
take one's leave of sb; **donner son
~ à** to hand ou give in one's notice
to; **~ de maladie** sick leave; **~ de
maternité** maternity leave; **~s
payés** paid holiday ou leave

congédier [kɔ̃ʒedje] /7/ vt to dismiss

congélateur [kɔ̃ʒelatœr] nm
freezer

congeler [kɔ̃ʒ(ə)le] /5/ vt to freeze;
les produits congelés frozen foods;
se congeler vi to freeze

congestion [kɔ̃ʒɛstjɔ̃] nf congestion

Congo [kɔ̃ɡo] nm: **le ~** the Congo

congrès [kɔ̃ɡʀɛ] nm congress

conifère [kɔnifɛʀ] nm conifer

conjoint, e [kɔ̃ʒwɛ̃, -wɛ̃t] adj joint
▷ nm/f spouse

conjonctivite [kɔ̃ʒɔ̃ktivit] nf
conjunctivitis

conjoncture [kɔ̃ʒɔ̃ktyʀ]
nf circumstances pl; **la ~
(économique)** the economic
climate ou situation

conjugaison [kɔ̃ʒyɡɛzɔ̃] nf (Ling)
conjugation

connaissance [kɔnɛsɑ̃s] nf (savoir)
knowledge no pl; (personne connue)
acquaintance; **être sans ~** to be
unconscious; **perdre/reprendre
~** to lose/regain consciousness; **à
ma/sa ~** to (the best of) my/his
knowledge; **faire ~ avec qn** ou **la ~
de qn** to meet sb

connaisseur, -euse [kɔnɛsœʀ, -øz]
nm/f connoisseur

connaître [kɔnɛtʀ] /57/ vt to know;
(éprouver) to experience; (avoir: succès)
to have; to enjoy; **~ de nom/vue** to
know by name/sight; **ils se sont
connus à Genève** they (first) met
in Geneva; **s'y ~ en qch** to know
about sth

connecter [kɔnɛkte] /1/ vt to
connect; **se ~ à Internet** to log onto
the Internet

connerie [kɔnʀi] nf (fam) (bloody)
stupid (BRIT) ou damn-fool (US) thing
to do ou say

connexion [kɔnɛksjɔ̃] nf connection

connu, e [kɔny] adj (célèbre) well-
known

conquérir [kɔ̃keʀiʀ] /21/ vt to
conquer; **conquête** nf conquest

consacrer [kɔ̃sakʀe] /1/ vt (Rel) to
consecrate; **~ qch à** (employer) to
devote ou dedicate sth to; **se ~ à**

qch/faire to dedicate ou devote o.s.
to sth/to doing

conscience [kɔ̃sjɑ̃s] nf conscience;
avoir/prendre ~ de to be/become
aware of; **perdre/reprendre ~** to
lose/regain consciousness; **avoir
bonne/mauvaise ~** to have a clear/
guilty conscience; **consciencieux,
-euse** adj conscientious; **conscient, e**
adj conscious

consécutif, -ive [kɔ̃sekytif, -iv] adj
consecutive; **~ à** following upon

conseil [kɔ̃sɛj] nm (avis) piece of
advice; (assemblée) council; **donner
un ~** ou **des ~s à qn** to give sb (a
piece of) advice; **prendre ~ (auprès
de qn)** to take advice (from sb);
~ d'administration (CA) board
(of directors); **~ général** regional
council; **le ~ des ministres** ≈ the
Cabinet; **~ municipal (CM)** town
council

conseiller¹ [kɔ̃seje] vt (personne)
to advise; (méthode, action) to
recommend, advise; **~ à qn de faire
qch** to advise sb to do sth

conseiller², -ière [kɔ̃seje, -ɛʀ]
nm/f adviser; **~ d'orientation** (Scol)
careers adviser (BRIT), (school)
counselor (US)

consentement [kɔ̃sɑ̃tmɑ̃] nm
consent

consentir [kɔ̃sɑ̃tiʀ] /16/ vt: **~ (à
qch/faire)** to agree ou consent (to
sth/to doing)

conséquence [kɔ̃sekɑ̃s] nf
consequence; **en ~** (donc)
consequently; (de façon appropriée)
accordingly; **conséquent, e** adj
logical, rational; (fam: important)
substantial; **par conséquent**
consequently

conservateur, -trice [kɔ̃sɛʀvatœʀ,
-tʀis] nm/f (Pol) conservative; (de
musée) curator ▷ nm (pour aliments)
preservative

conservatoire [kɔ̃sɛʀvatwaʀ] nm
academy

conserve [kɔ̃sɛʀv] nf (gén pl) canned ou tinned (BRIT) food; **en ~** canned, tinned (BRIT)

conserver [kɔ̃sɛʀve] /1/ vt (faculté) to retain, keep; (amis, livres) to keep; (préserver, Culin) to preserve

considérable [kɔ̃siderabl] adj considerable, significant, extensive

considération [kɔ̃siderasjɔ̃] nf consideration; (estime) esteem

considérer [kɔ̃sidere] /6/ vt to consider; **~ qch comme** to regard sth as

consigne [kɔ̃siɲ] nf (de gare) left luggage (office) (BRIT), checkroom (US); (ordre, instruction) instructions pl; **~ automatique** left-luggage locker

consister [kɔ̃siste] /1/ vi: **~ en/dans/à faire** to consist of/in/in doing

consoler [kɔ̃sɔle] /1/ vt to console

consommateur, -trice [kɔ̃sɔmatœʀ, -tʀis] nm/f (Écon) consumer; (dans un café) customer

consommation [kɔ̃sɔmasjɔ̃] nf (Écon) consumption; (boisson) drink; **de ~** (biens, société) consumer cpd

consommer [kɔ̃sɔme] /1/ vt (personne) to eat ou drink, consume; (voiture, usine, poêle) to use, consume; (Jur: mariage) to consummate ▷ vi (dans un café) to (have a) drink

consonne [kɔ̃sɔn] nf consonant

constamment [kɔ̃stamɑ̃] adv constantly

constant, e [kɔ̃stɑ̃, -ɑ̃t] adj constant; (personne) steadfast

constat [kɔ̃sta] nm (de police) report; **~ (à l'amiable)** (jointly agreed) statement for insurance purposes; **~ d'échec** acknowledgement of failure

constatation [kɔ̃statasjɔ̃] nf (remarque) observation

constater [kɔ̃state] /1/ vt (remarquer) to note; (Admin, Jur: attester) to certify

consterner [kɔ̃stɛʀne] /1/ vt to dismay

constipé, e [kɔ̃stipe] adj constipated

constitué, e [kɔ̃stitɥe] adj: **~ de** made up ou composed of

constituer [kɔ̃stitɥe] /1/ vt (comité, équipe) to set up; (dossier, collection) to put together; (éléments, parties: composer) to make up, constitute; (: représenter, être) to constitute; **se ~ prisonnier** to give o.s. up

constructeur [kɔ̃stʀyktœʀ] nm/f manufacturer, builder

constructif, -ive [kɔ̃stʀyktif, -iv] adj constructive

construction [kɔ̃stʀyksjɔ̃] nf construction, building

construire [kɔ̃stʀɥiʀ] /38/ vt to build, construct

consul [kɔ̃syl] nm consul; **consulat** nm consulate

consultant, e adj, nm consultant

consultation [kɔ̃syltasjɔ̃] nf consultation; **heures de ~** (Méd) surgery (BRIT) ou office (US) hours

consulter [kɔ̃sylte] /1/ vt to consult ▷ vi (médecin) to hold surgery (BRIT), be in (the office) (US)

contact [kɔ̃takt] nm contact; **au ~ de** (air, peau) on contact with; (gens) through contact with; **mettre/couper le ~** (Auto) to switch on/off the ignition; **entrer en ~** to come into contact; **prendre ~ avec** to get in touch ou contact with; **contacter** /1/ vt to contact, get in touch with

contagieux, -euse [kɔ̃taʒjø, -øz] adj infectious; (par le contact) contagious

contaminer [kɔ̃tamine] /1/ vt to contaminate

conte [kɔ̃t] nm tale; **~ de fées** fairy tale

contempler [kɔ̃tɑ̃ple] /1/ vt to contemplate, gaze at

contemporain, e [kɔ̃tɑ̃pɔʀɛ̃, -ɛn] adj, nm/f contemporary

contenir [kɔ̃t(ə)niʀ] /22/ vt to contain; (avoir une capacité de) to hold

content, e [kɔ̃tɑ̃, -ɑ̃t] *adj* pleased, glad; **~ de** pleased with; **contenter** /1/ *vt* to satisfy, please; **se contenter de** to content o.s. with

contenu, e [kɔ̃t(ə)ny] *nm* (*d'un bol*) contents *pl*; (*d'un texte*) content

conter [kɔ̃te] /1/ *vt* to recount, relate

conteste [kɔ̃tɛst]: **sans ~** *adv* unquestionably, indisputably; **contester** /1/ *vt* to question ▷ *vi* (*Pol*, *gén*) to rebel (against established authority)

contexte [kɔ̃tɛkst] *nm* context

continent [kɔ̃tinɑ̃] *nm* continent

continu, e [kɔ̃tiny] *adj* continuous; **faire la journée ~e** to work without taking a full lunch break; **(courant) ~** direct current, DC

continuel, le [kɔ̃tinɥɛl] *adj* (*qui se répète*) constant, continual; (*continu*) continuous

continuer [kɔ̃tinɥe] /1/ *vt* (*travail, voyage etc*) to continue (with), carry on (with), go on with; (*prolonger: alignement, rue*) to continue ▷ *vi* (*pluie, vie, bruit*) to continue, go on; **~ à** *ou* **de faire** to go on *ou* continue doing

contourner [kɔ̃turne] /1/ *vt* to bypass, walk *ou* drive round; (*difficulté*) to get round

contraceptif, -ive [kɔ̃trasɛptif, -iv] *adj, nm* contraceptive; **contraception** *nf* contraception

contracté, e [kɔ̃trakte] *adj* tense

contracter [kɔ̃trakte] /1/ *vt* (*muscle etc*) to tense, contract; (*maladie, dette, obligation*) to contract; (*assurance*) to take out; **se contracter** *vi* (*métal, muscles*) to contract

contractuel, le [kɔ̃traktɥɛl] *nm/f* (*agent*) traffic warden

contradiction [kɔ̃tradiksjɔ̃] *nf* contradiction; **contradictoire** *adj* contradictory, conflicting

contraignant, e [kɔ̃trɛɲɑ̃, -ɑ̃t] *adj* restricting

contraindre [kɔ̃trɛ̃dr] /52/ *vt*: **~ qn à faire** to force *ou* compel sb to do

contraint, e [kɔ̃trɛ̃, ɛ̃t] *pp de* **contraindre** ▷ *nf* constraint

contraire [kɔ̃trɛr] *adj, nm* opposite; **~ à** contrary to; **au ~** on the contrary

contrarier [kɔ̃trarje] /1/ *vt* (*personne*) to annoy; (*projets*) to thwart, frustrate; **contrariété** [kɔ̃trarjete] *nf* annoyance

contraste [kɔ̃trast] *nm* contrast

contrat [kɔ̃tra] *nm* contract

contravention [kɔ̃travɑ̃sjɔ̃] *nf* parking ticket

contre [kɔ̃tr] *prép* against; (*en échange*) (in exchange) for; **par ~** on the other hand

contrebande [kɔ̃trəbɑ̃d] *nf* (*trafic*) contraband, smuggling; (*marchandise*) contraband, smuggled goods *pl*; **faire la ~ de** to smuggle

contrebas [kɔ̃trəba]: **en ~** *adv* (down) below

contrebasse [kɔ̃trəbas] *nf* (double) bass

contre: contrecoup *nm* repercussions *pl*; **contredire** /37/ *vt* (*personne*) to contradict; (*témoignage, assertion, faits*) to refute

contrefaçon [kɔ̃trəfasɔ̃] *nf* forgery

contre: contre-indication (*pl* **contre-indications**) *nf* (*Méd*) contra-indication; **"contre-indication en cas d'eczéma"** "should not be used by people with eczema"; **contre-indiqué, e** *adj* (*Méd*) contraindicated; (*déconseillé*) unadvisable, ill-advised

contremaître [kɔ̃trəmɛtr] *nm* foreman

contre-plaqué [kɔ̃trəplake] *nm* plywood

contresens [kɔ̃trəsɑ̃s] *nm* (*erreur*) misinterpretation; (*mauvaise traduction*) mistranslation; **à ~** the wrong way

contretemps [kɔ̃trətɑ̃] *nm* hitch; **à ~** (*fig*) at an inopportune moment

contribuer [kɔ̃tribɥe] /1/: **~ à** *vt* to contribute towards; **contribution** *nf* contribution;

mettre à contribution to call upon; **contributions directes/indirectes** direct/indirect taxation

contrôle [kɔ̃tʀol] *nm* checking *no pl*, check; monitoring; (*test*) test, examination; **perdre le ~ de son véhicule** to lose control of one's vehicle; **~ continu** (*Scol*) continuous assessment; **~ d'identité** identity check

contrôler [kɔ̃tʀole] /1/ *vt* (*vérifier*) to check; (*surveiller: opérations*) to supervise; (: *prix*) to monitor, control; (*maîtriser*, *Comm: firme*) to control; **contrôleur, -euse** *nm/f* (*de train*) (ticket) inspector; (*de bus*) (bus) conductor/tress

controversé, e [kɔ̃tʀɔvɛʀse] *adj* (*personnage, question*) controversial

contusion [kɔ̃tyzjɔ̃] *nf* bruise, contusion

convaincre [kɔ̃vɛ̃kʀ] /42/ *vt*: **~ qn (de qch)** to convince sb (of sth); **~ qn (de faire)** to persuade sb (to do)

convalescence [kɔ̃valesɑ̃s] *nf* convalescence

convenable [kɔ̃vnabl] *adj* suitable; (*assez bon*) decent

convenir [kɔ̃vniʀ] /22/ *vi* to be suitable; **~ à** to suit; **~ de** (*bien-fondé de qch*) to admit (to), acknowledge; (*date, somme etc*) to agree upon; **~ que** (*admettre*) to admit that; **~ de faire qch** to agree to do sth

convention [kɔ̃vɑ̃sjɔ̃] *nf* convention; **conventions** *nfpl* (*convenances*) convention *sg*; **~ collective** (*Écon*) collective agreement; **conventionné, e** *adj* (*Admin*) applying charges laid down by the state

convenu, e [kɔ̃vny] *pp de* **convenir** ▷ *adj* agreed

conversation [kɔ̃vɛʀsasjɔ̃] *nf* conversation

convertir [kɔ̃vɛʀtiʀ] /2/ *vt*: **~ qn (à)** to convert sb (to); **~ qch en** to convert sth into; **se ~ (à)** to be converted (to)

conviction [kɔ̃viksjɔ̃] *nf* conviction

convienne *etc* [kɔ̃vjɛn] *vb voir* **convenir**

convivial, e [kɔ̃vivjal] *adj* (*Inform*) user-friendly

convocation [kɔ̃vɔkasjɔ̃] *nf* (*document*) notification to attend; (*Jur*) summons *sg*

convoquer [kɔ̃vɔke] /1/ *vt* (*assemblée*) to convene; (*subordonné, témoin*) to summon; (*candidat*) to ask to attend

coopération [kɔɔpeʀasjɔ̃] *nf* co-operation; (*Admin*): **la C~** ≈ Voluntary Service Overseas (*BRIT*) *ou the* Peace Corps (*US: done as alternative to military service*)

coopérer [kɔɔpeʀe] /6/ *vi*: **~ (à)** to co-operate (in)

coordonné, e [kɔɔʀdɔne] *adj* coordinated; **coordonnées** *nfpl* (*détails personnels*) address, phone number, schedule *etc*

coordonner [kɔɔʀdɔne] /1/ *vt* to coordinate

copain, copine *nm/f* pal; (*petit ami*) boyfriend; (*petite amie*) girlfriend

copie [kɔpi] *nf* copy; (*Scol*) script, paper; **copier** /7/ *vt*, *vi* to copy; **copier coller** (*Inform*) copy and paste; **copier sur** to copy from; **copieur** *nm* (photo)copier

copieux, -euse [kɔpjø, -øz] *adj* copious

copine [kɔpin] *nf voir* **copain**

coq [kɔk] *nm* cockerel

coque [kɔk] *nf* (*de noix, mollusque*) shell; (*de bateau*) hull; **à la ~** (*Culin*) (soft-)boiled

coquelicot [kɔkliko] *nm* poppy

coqueluche [kɔklyʃ] *nf* whooping-cough

coquet, te [kɔkɛ, -ɛt] *adj* appearance-conscious; (*logement*) smart, charming

coquetier [kɔk(ə)tje] *nm* egg-cup

coquillage [kɔkijaʒ] *nm* (*mollusque*) shellfish *inv*; (*coquille*) shell

coquille [kɔkij] nf shell; (Typo) misprint; ~ **St Jacques** scallop

coquin, e [kɔkɛ̃, -in] adj mischievous, roguish; (polisson) naughty

cor [kɔʀ] nm (Mus) horn; (Méd) ~ **(au pied)** corn

corail, -aux [kɔʀaj, -o] nm coral no pl

Coran [kɔʀɑ̃] nm: **le** ~ the Koran

corbeau, x [kɔʀbo] nm crow

corbeille [kɔʀbɛj] nf basket; (Inform) recycle bin; ~ **à papier** waste paper basket ou bin

corde [kɔʀd] nf rope; (de violon, raquette, d'arc) string; **usé jusqu'à la** ~ threadbare; ~ **à linge** washing ou clothes line; ~ **à sauter** skipping rope; ~**s vocales** vocal cords

cordée [kɔʀde] nf (d'alpinistes) rope, roped party

cordialement [kɔʀdjalmɑ̃] adv (formule épistolaire) (kind) regards

cordon [kɔʀdɔ̃] nm cord, string; ~ **sanitaire/de police** sanitary/ police cordon; ~ **ombilical** umbilical cord

cordonnerie [kɔʀdɔnʀi] nf shoe repairer's ou mender's (shop); **cordonnier** nm shoe repairer ou mender

Corée [kɔʀe] nf: **la** ~ **du Sud/du Nord** South/North Korea

coriace [kɔʀjas] adj tough

corne [kɔʀn] nf horn; (de cerf) antler

cornée [kɔʀne] nf cornea

corneille [kɔʀnɛj] nf crow

cornemuse [kɔʀnəmyz] nf bagpipes pl

cornet [kɔʀnɛ] nm (paper) cone; (de glace) cornet, cone

corniche [kɔʀniʃ] nf (route) coast road

cornichon [kɔʀniʃɔ̃] nm gherkin

Cornouailles [kɔʀnwaj] fpl Cornwall

corporel, le [kɔʀpɔʀɛl] adj bodily; (punition) corporal

corps [kɔʀ] nm body; **à** ~ **perdu** headless; **prendre** ~ to take shape; **le** ~ **électoral** the electorate; **le** ~ **enseignant** the teaching profession

correct, e [kɔʀɛkt] adj correct; **correcteur, -trice** nm/f (Scol) examiner; **correction** nf (voir corriger) correction; (voir correct) correctness; (coups) thrashing

correspondance [kɔʀɛspɔ̃dɑ̃s] nf correspondence; (de train, d'avion) connection; **cours par** ~ correspondence course; **vente par** ~ mail-order business

correspondant, e [kɔʀɛspɔ̃dɑ̃, -ɑ̃t] nm/f correspondent; (Tél) person phoning (ou being phoned)

correspondre [kɔʀɛspɔ̃dʀ] /41/ vi to correspond, tally; ~ **à** to correspond to; ~ **avec qn** to correspond with sb

corrida [kɔʀida] nf bullfight

corridor [kɔʀidɔʀ] nm corridor

corrigé [kɔʀiʒe] nm (Scol: d'exercice) correct version

corriger [kɔʀiʒe] /3/ vt (devoir) to correct; (punir) to thrash; ~ **qn de** (défaut) to cure sb of

corrompre [kɔʀɔ̃pʀ] /41/ vt to corrupt; (acheter: témoin etc) to bribe

corruption [kɔʀypsjɔ̃] nf corruption; (de témoins) bribery

corse [kɔʀs] adj Corsican ▷ nm/f: **C~** Corsican ▷ nf: **la C~** Corsica

corsé, e [kɔʀse] adj (café etc) full-flavoured (BRIT) ou -flavored (US); (sauce) spicy; (problème) tough

cortège [kɔʀtɛʒ] nm procession

cortisone [kɔʀtizɔn] nf cortisone

corvée [kɔʀve] nf chore, drudgery no pl

cosmétique [kɔsmetik] nm beauty care product

cosmopolite [kɔsmɔpɔlit] adj cosmopolitan

costaud, e [kɔsto, -od] adj strong, sturdy

costume [kɔstym] nm (d'homme) suit; (de théâtre) costume; **costumé, e** adj dressed up

cote [kɔt] nf (en Bourse etc) quotation; ~ **d'alerte** danger ou flood level; ~ **de popularité** popularity rating

côte [kot] nf (rivage) coast(line); (pente) hill; (Anat) rib; (d'un tricot, tissu) rib, ribbing no pl; **~ à ~** side by side; **la C~ (d'Azur)** the (French) Riviera

côté [kote] nm (gén) side; (direction) way, direction; **de chaque ~ (de)** on each side of; **de tous les ~s** from all directions; **de quel ~ est-il parti?** which way ou in which direction did he go?; **de ce/de l'autre ~** this/ the other way; **du ~ de** (provenance) from; (direction) towards; **du ~ de Lyon** (proximité) near Lyons; **de ~** (regarder) sideways; **mettre de ~** to put aside, put on one side; **mettre de l'argent de ~** to save some money; **à ~** (right) nearby; (voisins) next door; **à ~ de** beside; next to; (fig) in comparison to; **être aux ~s de** to be by the side of

Côte d'Ivoire [kotdivwaʀ] nf: **la ~** Côte d'Ivoire, the Ivory Coast

côtelette [kotlɛt] nf chop

côtier, -ière [kotje, -jɛʀ] adj coastal

cotisation [kɔtizasjɔ̃] nf subscription, dues pl; (pour une pension) contributions pl

cotiser [kɔtize] /1/ vi: **~ (à)** to pay contributions (to); **se cotiser** vi to club together

coton [kɔtɔ̃] nm cotton; **~ hydrophile** cotton wool (BRIT), absorbent cotton (US)

Coton-Tige® nm cotton bud

cou [ku] nm neck

couchant [kuʃɑ̃] adj: **soleil ~** setting sun

couche [kuʃ] nf layer; (de peinture, vernis) coat; (de bébé) nappy (BRIT), diaper (US); **~s sociales** social levels ou strata

couché, e [kuʃe] adj lying down; (au lit) in bed

coucher [kuʃe] /1/ vt (personne) to put to bed (: loger) to put up; (objet) to lay on its side ▷ vi to sleep; **~ avec qn** to sleep with sb; **se coucher** vi (pour dormir) to go to bed; (pour se reposer)

to lie down; (soleil) to set; **~ de soleil** sunset

couchette [kuʃɛt] nf couchette; (pour voyageur, sur bateau) berth

coucou [kuku] nm cuckoo

coude [kud] nm (Anat) elbow; (de tuyau, de la route) bend; **~ à ~** shoulder to shoulder, side by side

coudre [kudʀ] /48/ vt (bouton) to sew on ▷ vi to sew

couette [kwɛt] nf duvet; **couettes** nfpl (cheveux) bunches

couffin [kufɛ̃] nm Moses basket

couler [kule] /1/ vi to flow, run; (fuir: stylo, récipient) to leak; (: nez) to run; (sombrer: bateau) to sink ▷ vt (cloche, sculpture) to cast; (bateau) to sink; (faire échouer: personne) to bring down, ruin

couleur [kulœʀ] nf colour (BRIT), color (US); (Cartes) suit; **en ~s** (film) in colo(u)r; **télévision en ~s** colo(u)r television; **de ~** (homme, femme: vieilli) colo(u)red

couleuvre [kulœvʀ] nf grass snake

coulisse [kulis] nf (Tech) runner; **coulisses** nfpl (Théât) wings; (fig): **dans les ~s** behind the scenes

couloir [kulwaʀ] nm corridor, passage; (d'avion) aisle; (de bus) gangway; **~ aérien** air corridor ou lane; **~ de navigation** shipping lane

coup [ku] nm (heurt, choc) knock; (affectif) blow, shock; (agressif) blow; (avec arme à feu) shot; (de l'horloge) stroke; (Sport: golf) stroke; (: tennis) shot; (fam: fois) time; **~ de coude/ genou** nudge (with the elbow)/with the knee; **donner un ~ de balai** to give the floor a sweep; **être dans le/ hors du ~** to be/not to be in on it; (à la page) to be hip ou trendy; **du ~** as a result; **d'un seul ~** (subitement) suddenly; (à la fois) at one go; **du premier ~** first time ou go; **du même ~** at the same time; **à ~ sûr** definitely, without fail; **après ~** afterwards; **~ sur ~** in quick succession; **sur le ~**

outright; **sous le ~ de** (*surprise etc*) under the influence of; **à tous les ~s** every time; **tenir le ~** to hold out; **~ de chance** stroke of luck; **~ de couteau** stab (of a knife); **~ d'envoi** kick-off; **~ d'essai** first attempt; **~ d'état** coup d'état; **~ de feu** shot; **~ de filet** (*Police*) haul; **~ de foudre** (*fig*) love at first sight; **~ franc** free kick; **~ de frein** (*sharp*) braking *no pl*; **~ de grâce** coup de grâce; **~ de main: donner un ~ de main à qn** to give sb a (helping) hand; **~ d'œil** glance; **~ de pied** kick; **~ de poing** punch; **~ de soleil** sunburn *no pl*; **~ de sonnette** ring of the bell; **~ de téléphone** phone call; **~ de tête** (*fig*) (*sudden*) impulse; **~ de théâtre** (*fig*) dramatic turn of events; **~ de tonnerre** clap of thunder; **~ de vent** gust of wind; **en ~ de vent** (*rapidement*) in a tearing hurry

coupable [kupabl] *adj* guilty ▷ *nm/f* (*gén*) culprit; (*Jur*) guilty party

coupe [kup] *nf* (*verre*) goblet; (*à fruits*) dish; (*Sport*) cup; (*de cheveux, de vêtement*) cut; (*graphique, plan*) (cross) section

couper [kupe] /1/ *vt* to cut; (*retrancher*) to cut (out); (*route, courant*) to cut off; (*appétit*) to take away; (*vin, cidre: à table*) to dilute (with water) ▷ *vi* to cut; (*prendre un raccourci*) to take a short-cut; **se couper** *vi* (*se blesser*) to cut o.s.; **~ la parole à qn** to cut sb short; **nous avons été coupés** we've been cut off

couple [kupl] *nm* couple

couplet [kuplɛ] *nm* verse

coupole [kupɔl] *nf* dome

coupon [kupɔ̃] *nm* (*ticket*) coupon; (*de tissu*) remnant

coupure [kupyʀ] *nf* cut; (*billet de banque*) note; (*de journal*) cutting; **~ de courant** power cut

cour [kuʀ] *nf* (*de ferme, jardin*) (court) yard; (*d'immeuble*) back yard; (*Jur,*

royale) court; **faire la ~ à qn** to court sb; **~ d'assises** court of assizes; **~ de récréation** playground

courage [kuʀaʒ] *nm* courage, bravery; **courageux, -euse** *adj* brave, courageous

couramment [kuʀamɑ̃] *adv* commonly; (*parler*) fluently

courant, e [kuʀɑ̃, -ɑ̃t] *adj* (*fréquent*) common; (*Comm, gén: normal*) standard; (*en cours*) current ▷ *nm* current; (*fig*) movement; (: *d'opinion*) trend; **être au ~ (de)** (*fait, nouvelle*) to know (about); **mettre qn au ~ (de)** to tell sb (about); (*nouveau travail etc*) to teach sb the basics (of); **se tenir au ~ (de)** (*techniques etc*) to keep o.s. up-to-date (on); **dans le ~ de** (*pendant*) in the course of; **le 10 ~** (*Comm*) the 10th inst.; **~ d'air** draught; **~ électrique** (electric) current, power

courbature [kuʀbatyʀ] *nf* ache

courbe [kuʀb] *adj* curved ▷ *nf* curve

coureur, -euse [kuʀœʀ, -øz] *nm/f* (*Sport*) runner (*ou* driver); (*péj*) womanizer/manhunter

courge [kuʀʒ] *nf* (*Culin*) marrow; **courgette** *nf* courgette (BRIT), zucchini (US)

courir [kuʀiʀ] /11/ *vi* to run ▷ *vt* (*Sport: épreuve*) to compete in; (: *risque*) to run; (: *danger*) to face; **~ les cafés/bals** to do the rounds of the cafés/dances; **le bruit court que** the rumour is going round that

couronne [kuʀɔn] *nf* crown; (*de fleurs*) wreath, circlet

courons [kuʀɔ̃] *vb voir* **courir**

courriel [kuʀjɛl] *nm* email

courrier [kuʀje] *nm* mail, post; (*lettres à écrire*) letters *pl*; **est-ce que j'ai du ~?** are there any letters for me?; **~ électronique** email

▎ Attention à ne pas traduire *courrier* par le mot anglais *courier*.

courroie [kuʀwa] *nf* strap; (*Tech*) belt

courrons *etc* [kuʀɔ̃] *vb voir* **courir**

cours [kur] *nm* (*leçon*) class (: *particulier*) lesson; (*série de leçons*) course; (*écoulement*) flow; (*Comm*: *de devises*) rate; (: *de denrées*) price; **donner libre ~ à** to give free expression to; **avoir ~** (*Scol*) to have a class *ou* lecture; **en ~** (*année*) current; (*travaux*) in progress; **en ~ de route** on the way; **au ~ de** in the course of, during; **le ~ du change** the exchange rate; **~ d'eau** waterway; **~ du soir** night school

course [kurs] *nf* running; (*Sport*: *épreuve*) race; (*d'un taxi, autocar*) journey, trip; (*petite mission*) errand; **courses** *nfpl* (*achats*) shopping *sg*; **faire les** *ou* **ses ~s** to go shopping

court, e [kur, kurt] *adj* short ▷ *adv* short; **~ (de tennis)** (tennis) court; **à ~ de** short of; **prendre qn de ~** to catch sb unawares; **court-circuit** *nm* short-circuit

courtoisie [kurtwazi] *nf* courtesy

couru, e [kury] *pp de* **courir**

cousais *etc* [kuze] *vb voir* **coudre**

couscous [kuskus] *nm* couscous

cousin, e [kuzɛ̃, -in] *nm/f* cousin

coussin [kusɛ̃] *nm* cushion

cousu, e [kuzy] *pp de* **coudre**

coût [ku] *nm* cost; **le ~ de la vie** the cost of living

couteau, x [kuto] *nm* knife

coûter [kute] /1/ *vt* to cost ▷ *vi* to cost; **~ cher** to be expensive; **combien ça coûte?** how much is it?, what does it cost?; **coûte que coûte** at all costs; **coûteux, -euse** *adj* costly, expensive

coutume [kutym] *nf* custom

couture [kutyr] *nf* sewing; (*profession*) dress-making; (*points*) seam; **couturier** *nm* fashion designer; **couturière** *nf* dressmaker

couvent [kuvɑ̃] *nm* (*de sœurs*) convent; (*de frères*) monastery

couver [kuve] /1/ *vt* to hatch; (*maladie*) to be sickening for ▷ *vi* (*feu*) to smoulder; (*révolte*) to be brewing

couvercle [kuvɛrkl] *nm* lid; (*de bombe aérosol etc, qui se visse*) cap, top

couvert, e [kuvɛr, -ɛrt] *pp de* **couvrir** ▷ *adj* (*ciel*) overcast ▷ *nm* place setting; (*place à table*) place; **couverts** *nmpl* (*ustensiles*) cutlery *sg*; **~ de** covered with *ou* in; **mettre le ~** to lay the table

couverture [kuvɛrtyr] *nf* blanket; (*de livre, fig, Assurances*) cover; (*Presse*) coverage

couvre-lit [kuvrəli] *nm* bedspread

couvrir [kuvrir] /18/ *vt* to cover; **se couvrir** *vi* (*ciel*) to cloud over; (*s'habiller*) to cover up; (*se coiffer*) to put on one's hat

cow-boy [koboj] *nm* cowboy

crabe [krab] *nm* crab

cracher [kraʃe] /1/ *vi* to spit ▷ *vt* to spit out

crachin [kraʃɛ̃] *nm* drizzle

craie [krɛ] *nf* chalk

craindre [krɛ̃dr] /52/ *vt* to fear, be afraid of; (*être sensible à: chaleur, froid*) to be easily damaged by

crainte [krɛ̃t] *nf* fear; **de ~ de/ que** for fear of/that; **craintif, -ive** *adj* timid

crampe [krɑ̃p] *nf* cramp; **j'ai une ~ à la jambe** I've got cramp in my leg

cramponner [krɑ̃pɔne] /1/: **se cramponner** *vi*: **se ~ (à)** to hang *ou* cling on (to)

cran [krɑ̃] *nm* (*entaille*) notch; (*de courroie*) hole; (*courage*) guts *pl*

crâne [krɑn] *nm* skull

crapaud [krapo] *nm* toad

craquement [krakmɑ̃] *nm* crack, snap; (*du plancher*) creak, creaking *no pl*

craquer [krake] /1/ *vi* (*bois, plancher*) to creak; (*fil, branche*) to snap; (*couture*) to come apart; (*fig: accusé*) to break down, fall apart ▷ *vt*: **~ une allumette** to strike a match; **j'ai craqué** (*fam*) I couldn't resist it

crasse [kras] *nf* grime, filth; **crasseux, -euse** *adj* filthy

cravache [kʀavaʃ] nf (riding) crop
cravate [kʀavat] nf tie
crawl [kʀol] nm crawl; **dos ~é**
backstroke
crayon [kʀɛjɔ̃] nm pencil; **~ à bille**
ball-point pen; **~ de couleur** crayon;
crayon-feutre (pl **crayons-feutres**)
nm felt(-tip) pen
création [kʀeasjɔ̃] nf creation
crèche [kʀɛʃ] nf (de Noël) crib;
(garderie) crèche, day nursery
crédit [kʀedi] nm (gén) credit; **crédits**
nmpl funds; **acheter à ~** to buy on
credit ou on easy terms; **faire ~ à**
qn to give sb credit; **créditer** /1/ vt:
créditer un compte (de) to credit an
account (with)
créer [kʀee] /1/ vt to create
crémaillère [kʀemajɛʀ] nf: **pendre**
la ~ to have a house-warming party
crème [kʀɛm] nf cream; (entremets)
cream dessert ▷ adj inv cream; **un**
(café) ~ ≈ a white coffee; **~ anglaise**
(egg) custard; **~ chantilly** whipped
cream; **~ à raser** shaving cream;
~ solaire sun cream
créneau, x [kʀeno] nm (de
fortification) crenel(le); (fig, aussi
Comm) gap, slot; (Auto): **faire un ~** to
reverse into a parking space (between
cars alongside the kerb)
crêpe [kʀɛp] nf (galette) pancake
▷ nm (tissu) crêpe; **crêperie** nf
pancake shop ou restaurant
crépuscule [kʀepyskyl] nm twilight,
dusk
cresson [kʀesɔ̃] nm watercress
creuser [kʀøze] /1/ vt (trou, tunnel)
to dig; (sol) to dig a hole in; (fig) to go
(deeply) into; **ça creuse** that gives
you a real appetite; **se ~ (la cervelle)**
to rack one's brains
creux, -euse [kʀø, -øz] adj hollow
▷ nm hollow; **heures creuses**
slack periods; (électricité, téléphone)
off-peak periods; **avoir un ~** (fam)
to be hungry
crevaison [kʀəvɛzɔ̃] nf puncture

crevé, e [kʀəve] adj (fam: fatigué)
shattered (BRIT), exhausted
crever [kʀəve] /5/ vt (tambour,
ballon) to burst ▷ vi (pneu) to burst;
(automobiliste) to have a puncture
(BRIT) ou a flat (tire) (US); (fam) to die
crevette [kʀəvɛt] nf: **~ (rose)**
prawn; **~ grise** shrimp
cri [kʀi] nm cry, shout; (d'animal:
spécifique) cry, call; **c'est le dernier ~**
(fig) it's the latest fashion
criard, e [kʀijaʀ, -aʀd] adj (couleur)
garish, loud; (voix) yelling
cric [kʀik] nm (Auto) jack
crier [kʀije] /7/ vi (pour appeler) to
shout, cry (out); (de peur, de douleur
etc) to scream, yell ▷ vt (ordre, injure)
to shout (out), yell (out)
crime [kʀim] nm crime; (meurtre)
murder; **criminel, le** nm/f criminal;
murderer
crin [kʀɛ̃] nm (de cheval) hair no pl
crinière [kʀinjɛʀ] nf mane
crique [kʀik] nf creek, inlet
criquet [kʀike] nm grasshopper
crise [kʀiz] nf crisis (pl crises); (Méd)
attack (: d'épilepsie) fit; **~ cardiaque**
heart attack; **avoir une ~ de foie** to
have really bad indigestion; **piquer**
une ~ de nerfs to go hysterical
cristal, -aux [kʀistal, -o] nm crystal
critère [kʀitɛʀ] nm criterion (pl criteria)
critiquable [kʀitikabl] adj open
to criticism
critique [kʀitik] adj critical ▷ nm/f
(de théâtre, musique) critic ▷ nf
criticism; (Théât etc article) review
critiquer [kʀitike] /1/ vt (dénigrer)
to criticize; (évaluer, juger) to assess,
examine (critically)
croate [kʀɔat] adj Croatian ▷ nm
(Ling) Croat, Croatian ▷ nm/f: **C~**
Croat, Croatian
Croatie [kʀɔasi] nf: **la ~** Croatia
crochet [kʀɔʃɛ] nm hook; (détour)
detour; (Tricot: aiguille) crochet hook;
(: technique) crochet; **vivre aux ~s de**
qn to live ou sponge off sb

crocodile [kʀɔkɔdil] *nm* crocodile

croire [kʀwaʀ] /44/ *vt* to believe; **se ~ fort** to think one is strong; **~ que** to believe *ou* think that; **~ à, ~ en** to believe in

croisade [kʀwazad] *nf* crusade

croisement [kʀwazmɑ̃] *nm* (*carrefour*) crossroads *sg*; (*Bio*) crossing (: *résultat*) crossbreed

croiser [kʀwaze] /1/ *vt* (*personne, voiture*) to pass; (*route*) to cross, cut across; (*Bio*) to cross; **se croiser** (*personnes, véhicules*) to pass each other; (*routes*) to cross; (*regards*) to meet; **se ~ les bras** (*fig*) to fold one's arms, to twiddle one's thumbs

croisière [kʀwazjeʀ] *nf* cruise

croissance [kʀwasɑ̃s] *nf* growth

croissant, e [kʀwasɑ̃, -ɑ̃t] *adj* growing ▷ *nm* (*à manger*) croissant; (*motif*) crescent

croître [kʀwatʀ] /55/ *vi* to grow

croix [kʀwa] *nf* cross; **la C~ Rouge** the Red Cross

croque-madame [kʀɔkmadam] *nm inv* toasted cheese sandwich with a fried egg on top

croque-monsieur [kʀɔkməsjø] *nm inv* toasted ham and cheese sandwich

croquer [kʀɔke] /1/ *vt* (*manger*) to crunch (: *fruit*) to munch; (*dessiner*) to sketch; **chocolat à ~** plain dessert chocolate

croquis [kʀɔki] *nm* sketch

crotte [kʀɔt] *nf* droppings *pl*; **crottin** [kʀɔtɛ̃] *nm* dung, manure; (*fromage*) (small round) cheese (*made of goat's milk*)

croustillant, e [kʀustijɑ̃, -ɑ̃t] *adj* crisp

croûte [kʀut] *nf* crust; (*du fromage*) rind; (*Méd*) scab; **en ~** (*Culin*) in pastry

croûton [kʀutɔ̃] *nm* (*Culin*) crouton; (*bout du pain*) crust, heel

croyant, e [kʀwajɑ̃, -ɑ̃t] *nm/f* believer

CRS *sigle fpl* (= *Compagnies républicaines de sécurité*) state security police force ▷ *sigle m* member of the CRS

cru, e [kʀy] *pp de* **croire** ▷ *adj* (*non cuit*) raw; (*lumière, couleur*) harsh; (*paroles, langage*) crude ▷ *nm* (*vignoble*) vineyard; (*vin*) wine; **un grand ~** a great vintage; **jambon ~** Parma ham

crû [kʀy] *pp de* **croître**

cruauté [kʀyote] *nf* cruelty

cruche [kʀyʃ] *nf* pitcher, (earthenware) jug

crucifix [kʀysifi] *nm* crucifix

crudité [kʀydite] *nf* crudeness *no pl*; **crudités** *nfpl* (*Culin*) selection of raw vegetables

crue [kʀy] *nf* (*inondation*) flood; *voir aussi* **cru**

cruel, le [kʀyɛl] *adj* cruel

crus, crûs *etc* [kʀy] *vb voir* **croire**; **croître**

crustacés [kʀystase] *nmpl* shellfish

Cuba [kyba] *nm* Cuba; **cubain, e** *adj* Cuban ▷ *nm/f*: **Cubain, e** Cuban

cube [kyb] *nm* cube; (*jouet*) brick; **mètre ~** cubic metre; **2 au ~ = 8** 2 cubed is 8

cueillette [kœjɛt] *nf* picking; (*quantité*) crop, harvest

cueillir [kœjiʀ] /12/ *vt* (*fruits, fleurs*) to pick, gather; (*fig*) to catch

cuiller, cuillère [kɥijeʀ] *nf* spoon; **~ à café** coffee spoon; (*Culin*) ≈ teaspoonful; **~ à soupe** soup spoon; (*Culin*) ≈ tablespoonful; **cuillerée** *nf* spoonful

cuir [kɥiʀ] *nm* leather; (*avant tannage*) hide; **~ chevelu** scalp

cuire [kɥiʀ] /38/ *vt*: (*aliments*) to cook; (*au four*) to bake ▷ *vi* to cook; **bien cuit** (*viande*) well done; **trop cuit** overdone

cuisine [kɥizin] *nf* (*pièce*) kitchen; (*art culinaire*) cookery, cooking; (*nourriture*) cooking, food; **faire la ~** to cook; **cuisiné, e** *adj*: **plat cuisiné** ready-made meal *ou* dish; **cuisiner** /1/ *vt* to cook; (*fam*) to grill ▷ *vi* to cook; **cuisinier, -ière** *nm/f* cook ▷ *nf* (*poêle*) cooker

cuisse [kɥis] *nf* thigh; (*Culin*) leg

cuisson [kɥisɔ̃] nf cooking
cuit, e [kɥi, -it] pp de **cuire**
cuivre [kɥivʀ] nm copper; **les ~s**
(Mus) the brass
cul [ky] nm (fam!) arse (!)
culminant, e [kylminɑ̃, -ɑ̃t] adj:
point ~ highest point
culot [kylo] (fam) nm (effronterie) cheek
culotte [kylɔt] nf (de femme) panties
pl, knickers pl (BRIT)
culte [kylt] nm (religion) religion;
(hommage, vénération) worship;
(protestant) service
cultivateur, -trice [kyltivatœʀ,
-tʀis] nm/f farmer
cultivé, e [kyltive] adj (personne)
cultured, cultivated
cultiver [kyltive] /1/ vt to cultivate;
(légumes) to grow, cultivate
culture [kyltyʀ] nf cultivation;
(connaissances etc) culture; **les ~s
intensives** intensive farming;
~ OGM GM crop; **~ physique** physical
training; **culturel, le** adj cultural
cumin [kymɛ̃] nm cumin
cure [kyʀ] nf (Méd) course of
treatment; **~ d'amaigrissement**
slimming course; **~ de repos** rest
cure
curé [kyʀe] nm parish priest
cure-dent [kyʀdɑ̃] nm toothpick
curieux, -euse [kyʀjø, -øz] adj
(étrange) strange, curious; (indiscret)
curious, inquisitive ▷ nmpl (badauds)
onlookers; **curiosité** nf curiosity;
(site) unusual feature ou sight
curriculum vitae [kyʀikylɔmvite]
nm inv curriculum vitae
curseur [kyʀsœʀ] nm (Inform) cursor;
(de règle) slide; (de fermeture-éclair)
slider
cutané, e [kytane] adj skin cpd
cuve [kyv] nf vat; (à mazout etc) tank
cuvée [kyve] nf vintage
cuvette [kyvɛt] nf (récipient) bowl,
basin; (Géo) basin
CV sigle m (Auto); = **cheval (vapeur)**;
(Admin) = **curriculum vitae**

cybercafé [siberkafe] nm Internet
café
cyberespace [siberɛspas] nm
cyberspace
cybernaute [sibernot] nm/f
Internet user
cyclable [siklabl] adj: **piste ~**
cycle track
cycle [sikl] nm cycle; **cyclisme**
[siklism] nm cycling; **cycliste**
[siklist] nm/f cyclist ▷ adj cycle cpd;
coureur cycliste racing cyclist
cyclomoteur [siklomotœʀ] nm
moped
cyclone [siklon] nm hurricane
cygne [siɲ] nm swan
cylindre [silɛ̃dʀ] nm cylinder;
cylindrée nf (Auto) (cubic) capacity;
une (voiture de) grosse cylindrée a
big-engined car
cymbale [sɛ̃bal] nf cymbal
cynique [sinik] adj cynical
cystite [sistit] nf cystitis

d

d' *prép, art voir* **de**

dactylo [daktilo] *nf* (*aussi:* **~graphe**) typist; (*aussi:* **~graphie**) typing

dada [dada] *nm* hobby-horse

daim [dɛ̃] *nm* (fallow) deer *inv*; (*cuir suédé*) suede

daltonien, ne [daltɔnjɛ̃, -ɛn] *adj* colour-blind

dame [dam] *nf* lady; (*Cartes, Échecs*) queen; **dames** *nfpl* (*jeu*) draughts *sg* (BRIT), checkers *sg* (US)

Danemark [danmark] *nm*: **le ~** Denmark

danger [dɑ̃ʒe] *nm* danger; **mettre en ~** (*personne*) to put in danger; (*projet, carrière*) to jeopardize; **être en ~** (*personne*) to be in danger; **être en ~ de mort** to be in peril of one's life; **être hors de ~** to be out of danger; **dangereux, -euse** *adj* dangerous

danois, e [danwa, -waz] *adj* Danish ▷ *nm* (*Ling*) Danish ▷ *nm/f*: **D~, e** Dane

---

dans [dɑ̃] *prép* **1** (*position*) in; (: *à l'intérieur de*) inside; **c'est dans le tiroir/le salon** it's in the drawer/lounge; **dans la boîte** in *ou* inside the box; **marcher dans la ville/la rue** to walk about the town/along the street; **je l'ai lu dans le journal** I read it in the newspaper

2 (*direction*) into; **elle a couru dans le salon** she ran into the lounge; **monter dans une voiture/le bus** to get into a car/on to the bus

3 (*provenance*) out of, from; **je l'ai pris dans le tiroir/salon** I took it out of *ou* from the drawer/lounge; **boire dans un verre** to drink out of *ou* from a glass

4 (*temps*) in; **dans deux mois** in two months, in two months' time

5 (*approximation*) about; **dans les 20 euros** about 20 euros

---

danse [dɑ̃s] *nf*: **la ~** dancing; (*classique*) (ballet) dancing; **une ~** a dance; **danser** /1/ *vi, vt* to dance; **danseur, -euse** *nm/f* ballet dancer; (*au bal etc*) dancer (: *cavalier*) partner

date [dat] *nf* date; **de longue ~** longstanding; **~ de naissance** date of birth; **~ limite** deadline; **dater** /1/ *vt, vi* to date; **dater de** to date from; **à dater de** (as) from

datte [dat] *nf* date

dauphin [dofɛ̃] *nm* (*Zool*) dolphin

davantage [davɑ̃taʒ] *adv* more; (*plus longtemps*) longer; **~ de** more

---

de, d' [də, d] (*de + le = du, de + les = des*) *prép* **1** (*appartenance*) of; **le toit de la maison** the roof of the house; **la voiture d'Elisabeth/de mes parents** Elisabeth's/my parents' car

2 (*provenance*) from; **il vient de Londres** he comes from London; **elle**

est sortie du cinéma she came out of the cinema
3 (*moyen*) with; **je l'ai fait de mes propres mains** I did it with my own two hands
4 (*caractérisation, mesure*): **un mur de brique/bureau d'acajou** a brick wall/mahogany desk; **un billet de 10 euros** a 10 euro note; **une pièce de 2 m de large** *ou* **large de 2 m** a room 2 m wide, a 2m-wide room; **un bébé de 10 mois** a 10-month-old baby; **12 mois de crédit/travail** 12 months' credit/work; **elle est payée 20 euros de l'heure** she's paid 20 euros an hour *ou* per hour; **augmenter de 10 euros** to increase by 10 euros
5 (*rapport*) from; **de quatre à six** from four to six
6 (*cause*): **mourir de faim** to die of hunger; **rouge de colère** red with fury
7 (*vb +de +infin*) to; **il m'a dit de rester** he told me to stay
▶ **art 1** (*phrases affirmatives*) some (*souvent omis*); **du vin, de l'eau, des pommes** (some) wine, (some) water, (some) apples; **des enfants sont venus** some children came; **pendant des mois** for months
2 (*phrases interrogatives et négatives*) any; **a-t-il du vin?** has he got any wine?; **il n'a pas de pommes/d'enfants** he hasn't (got) any apples/children, he has no apples/children

dé [de] *nm* (*à jouer*) die *ou* dice; (*aussi*: **dé à coudre**) thimble
déballer [debale] /1/ *vt* to unpack
débarcadère [debaʁkadɛʁ] *nm* wharf
débardeur [debaʁdœʁ] *nm* (*pour femme*) vest top; (*pour homme*) sleeveless top
débarquer [debaʁke] /1/ *vt* to unload, land ▷ *vi* to disembark; (*fig*) to turn up
débarras [debaʁa] *nm* (*pièce*) lumber room; (*placard*) junk cupboard; **bon ~!** good riddance!; **débarrasser** /1/ *vt*

to clear ▷ *vi* (*enlever le couvert*) to clear away; **se débarrasser de** *vt* to get rid of; **débarrasser qn de** (*vêtements, paquets*) to relieve sb of
débat [deba] *nm* discussion, debate; **débattre** /41/ *vt* to discuss, debate; **se débattre** *vi* to struggle
débit [debi] *nm* (*d'un liquide, fleuve*) (rate of) flow; (*d'un magasin*) turnover (of goods); (*élocution*) delivery; (*bancaire*) debit; **~ de boissons** drinking establishment; **~ de tabac** tobacconist's (shop)
déblayer [debleje] /8/ *vt* to clear
débloquer [debloke] /1/ *vt* (*frein, fonds*) to release; (*prix, crédits*) to free ▷ *vi* (*fam*) to talk rubbish
déboîter [debwate] /1/ *vt* (*Auto*) to pull out; **se ~ le genou** *etc* to dislocate one's knee *etc*
débordé, e [debɔʁde] *adj*: **être ~ de** (*travail, demandes*) to be snowed under with
déborder [debɔʁde] /1/ *vi* to overflow; (*lait etc*) to boil over; **~ (de) qch** (*dépasser*) to extend beyond sth; **~ de** (*joie, zèle*) to be brimming over with *ou* bursting with
débouché [debuʃe] *nm* (*pour vendre*) outlet; (*perspective d'emploi*) opening
déboucher [debuʃe] /1/ *vt* (*évier, tuyau etc*) to unblock; (*bouteille*) to uncork ▷ *vi*: **~ de** to emerge from; **~ sur** (*études*) to lead on to
debout [dəbu] *adv*: **être ~** (*personne*) to be standing, stand; (*levé, éveillé*) to be up (and about); **se mettre ~** to get up (on one's feet); **se tenir ~** to stand; **~!** stand up!; (*du lit*) get up!; **cette histoire ne tient pas ~** this story doesn't hold water
déboutonner [debutɔne] /1/ *vt* to undo, unbutton
débraillé, e [debʁaje] *adj* slovenly, untidy
débrancher [debʁɑ̃ʃe] /1/ *vt* (*appareil électrique*) to unplug; (*téléphone, courant électrique*) to disconnect

débrayage [debʀɛjaʒ] nm (Auto) clutch; **débrayer** /8/ vi (Auto) to declutch; (cesser le travail) to stop work

débris [debʀi] nm fragment ▷ nmpl: **des ~ de verre** bits of glass

débrouillard, e [debʀujaʀ, -aʀd] adj smart, resourceful

débrouiller [debʀuje] /1/ vt to disentangle, untangle; **se débrouiller** vi to manage; **débrouillez-vous** you'll have to sort things out yourself

début [deby] nm beginning, start; **débuts** nmpl (de carrière) début sg; **~ juin** in early June; **débutant, e** nm/f beginner, novice; **débuter** /1/ vi to begin, start; (faire ses débuts) to start out

décaféiné, e [dekafeine] adj decaffeinated

décalage [dekalaʒ] nm gap; **~ horaire** time difference (between time zones), time-lag

décaler [dekale] /1/ vt to shift forward ou back

décapotable [dekapɔtabl] adj convertible

décapsuleur [dekapsylœʀ] nm bottle-opener

décédé, e [desede] adj deceased

décéder [desede] /6/ vi to die

décembre [desɑ̃bʀ] nm December

décennie [deseni] nf decade

décent, e [desɑ̃, -ɑ̃t] adj decent

déception [desɛpsjɔ̃] nf disappointment

décès [desɛ] nm death

décevoir [des(ə)vwaʀ] /28/ vt to disappoint

décharge [deʃaʀʒ] nf (dépôt d'ordures) rubbish tip ou dump; (électrique) electrical discharge; **décharger** /3/ vt (marchandise, véhicule) to unload; (faire feu) to discharge, fire; **décharger qn de** (responsabilité) to relieve sb of, release sb from

déchausser [deʃose] /1/ vt (skis) to take off; **se déchausser** vi to take off one's shoes; (dent) to come ou work loose

déchet [deʃɛ] nm (de bois, tissu etc) scrap; **déchets** nmpl (ordures) refuse sg, rubbish sg; **~s nucléaires** nuclear waste

déchiffrer [deʃifʀe] /1/ vt to decipher

déchirant, e [deʃiʀɑ̃, -ɑ̃t] adj heart-rending

déchirement [deʃiʀmɑ̃] nm (chagrin) wrench, heartbreak; (gén pl: conflit) rift, split

déchirer [deʃiʀe] /1/ vt to tear; (mettre en morceaux) to tear up; (arracher) to tear out; (fig) to tear apart; **se déchirer** vi to tear, rip; **se ~ un muscle/tendon** to tear a muscle/tendon

déchirure [deʃiʀyʀ] nf (accroc) tear, rip; **~ musculaire** torn muscle

décidé, e [deside] adj (personne, air) determined; **c'est ~** it's decided; **décidément** adv really

décider [deside] /1/ vt: **~ qch** to decide on sth; **~ de faire/que** to decide to do/that; **~ qn (à faire qch)** to persuade ou induce sb (to do sth); **se ~ à faire** to decide ou make up one's mind to do; **se ~ pour qch** to decide on ou in favour of sth

décimal, e, -aux [desimal, -o] adj decimal

décimètre [desimɛtʀ] nm decimetre

décisif, -ive [desizif, -iv] adj decisive

décision [desizjɔ̃] nf decision

déclaration [deklaʀasjɔ̃] nf declaration; (discours: Pol etc) statement; **~ (d'impôts)** ≈ tax return; **~ de revenus** statement of income; **faire une ~ de vol** to report a theft

déclarer [deklaʀe] /1/ vt to declare; (décès, naissance) to register; **se déclarer** vi (feu, maladie) to break out

déclencher [deklɑ̃ʃe] /1/ vt (mécanisme etc) to release; (sonnerie) to set off; (attaque, grève) to launch; (provoquer) to trigger off; **se déclencher** vi (sonnerie) to go off

décliner [dekline] /1/ *vi* to decline ▷ *vt* (*invitation*) to decline; (*nom, adresse*) to state

décoiffer [dekwafe] /1/ *vt*: ~ **qn** to mess up sb's hair; **je suis toute décoiffée** my hair is in a real mess

déçois *etc* [deswa] *vb voir* **décevoir**

décollage [dekɔlaʒ] *nm* (*Aviat, Écon*) takeoff

décoller [dekɔle] /1/ *vt* to unstick ▷ *vi* (*avion*) to take off; **se décoller** *vi* to come unstuck

décolleté, e [dekɔlte] *adj* low-cut ▷ *nm* low neck(line); (*plongeant*) cleavage

décolorer [dekɔlɔʀe] /1/: **se décolorer** *vi* to fade; **se faire ~ les cheveux** to have one's hair bleached

décommander [dekɔmɑ̃de] /1/ *vt* to cancel; **se décommander** *vi* to cancel

déconcerter [dekɔ̃sɛʀte] /1/ *vt* to disconcert, confound

décongeler [dekɔ̃ʒ(ə)le] /5/ *vt* to thaw (out)

déconner [dekɔne] /1/ *vi* (*fam!*) to talk (a load of) rubbish (BRIT) *ou* garbage (US)

déconseiller [dekɔ̃seje] /1/ *vt*: ~ **qch (à qn)** to advise (sb) against sth; **c'est déconseillé** it's not advised *ou* advisable

décontracté, e [dekɔ̃tʀakte] *adj* relaxed, laid-back (*fam*)

décontracter [dekɔ̃tʀakte] /1/: **se décontracter** *vi* to relax

décor [dekɔʀ] *nm* décor; (*paysage*) scenery; **décorateur, -trice** *nm/f* (*interior*) decorator; **décoration** *nf* decoration; **décorer** /1/ *vt* to decorate

décortiquer [dekɔʀtike] /1/ *vt* to shell; (*fig: texte*) to dissect

découdre /48/: **se découdre** *vi* to come unstitched

découper [dekupe] /1/ *vt* (*papier, tissu etc*) to cut up; (*volaille, viande*) to carve; (*manche, article*) to cut out

décourager [dekuʀaʒe] /3/ *vt* to discourage; **se décourager** *vi* to lose heart, become discouraged

décousu, e [dekuzy] *adj* unstitched; (*fig*) disjointed, disconnected

découvert, e [dekuvɛʀ, -ɛʀt] *adj* (*tête*) bare, uncovered; (*lieu*) open, exposed ▷ *nm* (*bancaire*) overdraft ▷ *nf* discovery; **faire la ~e de** to discover

découvrir [dekuvʀiʀ] /18/ *vt* to discover; (*enlever ce qui couvre ou protège*) to uncover; (*montrer, dévoiler*) to reveal; **se découvrir** *vi* (*chapeau*) to take off one's hat; (*se déshabiller*) to take something off; (*ciel*) to clear

décrire [dekʀiʀ] /39/ *vt* to describe

décrocher [dekʀɔʃe] /1/ *vt* (*dépendre*) to take down; (*téléphone*) to take off the hook; (: *pour répondre*): ~ **(le téléphone)** to pick up *ou* lift the receiver; (*fig: contrat etc*) to get, land ▷ *vi* (: *abandonner*) to drop out; (: *cesser d'écouter*) to switch off

déçu, e [desy] *pp de* **décevoir**

dédaigner [dedeɲe] /1/ *vt* to despise, scorn; (*négliger*) to disregard, spurn; **dédaigneux, -euse** *adj* scornful, disdainful; **dédain** *nm* scorn, disdain

dedans [dədɑ̃] *adv* inside; (*pas en plein air*) indoors, inside ▷ *nm* inside; **au ~** inside

dédicacer [dedikase] /3/ *vt*: ~ **(à qn)** to sign (for sb), autograph (for sb)

dédier [dedje] /7/ *vt*: ~ **à** to dedicate to

dédommagement [dedɔmaʒmɑ̃] *nm* compensation

dédommager [dedɔmaʒe] /3/ *vt*: ~ **qn (de)** to compensate sb (for)

dédouaner [dedwane] /1/ *vt* to clear through customs

déduire [dedɥiʀ] /38/ *vt*: ~ **qch (de)** (*ôter*) to deduct sth (from); (*conclure*) to deduce *ou* infer sth (from)

défaillance [defajɑ̃s] *nf* (*syncope*) blackout; (*fatigue*) (sudden) weakness

no pl; (*technique*) fault, failure;
~ cardiaque heart failure
défaire [defɛʀ] /60/ *vt* (*installation*,
échafaudage) to take down,
dismantle; (*paquet etc*, *nœud*,
vêtement) to undo; **se défaire** *vi* to
come undone; **se ~ de** to get rid of
défait, e [defɛ, -ɛt] *adj* (*visage*)
haggard, ravaged ▷ *nf* defeat
défaut [defo] *nm* (*moral*) fault, failing,
defect; (*d'étoffe*, *métal*) fault, flaw;
(*manque*, *carence*) **~ de** shortage of;
prendre qn en ~ to catch sb out;
faire ~ (*manquer*) to be lacking; **à ~ de**
for lack *ou* want of
défavorable [defavɔʀabl] *adj*
unfavourable (BRIT), unfavorable (US)
défavoriser [defavɔʀize] /1/ *vt* to
put at a disadvantage
défectueux, -euse [defɛktɥø, -øz]
adj faulty, defective
défendre [defɑ̃dʀ] /41/ *vt* to defend;
(*interdire*) to forbid; **se défendre** *vi*
to defend o.s.; **~ à qn qch/de faire**
to forbid sb sth/to do; **il se défend**
(*fig*) he can hold his own; **se ~ de/
contre** (*se protéger*) to protect o.s.
from/against; **se ~ de** (*se garder de*) to
refrain from
défense [defɑ̃s] *nf* defence;
(*d'éléphant etc*) tusk; **ministre de la ~**
Minister of Defence (BRIT), Defence
Secretary; **"~ de fumer/cracher"**
"no smoking/spitting"
défi [defi] *nm* challenge; **lancer un ~
à qn** to challenge sb; **sur un ton de
~** defiantly
déficit [defisit] *nm* (*Comm*) deficit
défier [defje] /7/ *vt* (*provoquer*) to
challenge; (*fig*) to defy; **~ qn de faire**
to challenge *ou* defy sb to do
défigurer [defiguʀe] /1/ *vt* to
disfigure
défilé [defile] *nm* (*Géo*) (narrow)
gorge *ou* pass; (*soldats*) parade;
(*manifestants*) procession, march
défiler [defile] /1/ *vi* (*troupes*) to
march past; (*sportifs*) to parade;

(*manifestants*) to march; (*visiteurs*) to
pour, stream; **faire ~ un document**
(*Inform*) to scroll a document; **se
défiler** *vi*: **il s'est défilé** (*fam*) he
wriggled out of it
définir [definiʀ] /2/ *vt* to define
définitif, -ive [definitif, -iv] *adj*
(*final*) final, definitive; (*pour
longtemps*) permanent, definitive;
(*sans appel*) definite ▷ *nf*: **en
définitive** eventually; (*somme
toute*) when all is said and done;
définitivement *adv* permanently
déformer [defɔʀme] /1/ *vt* to put out
of shape; (*pensée*, *fait*) to distort; **se
déformer** *vi* to lose its shape
défouler [defule] /1/: **se défouler** *vi*
to unwind, let off steam
défunt, e [defœ̃, -œ̃t] *adj*: **son ~ père**
his late father ▷ *nm/f* deceased
dégagé, e [degaʒe] *adj* (*route*, *ciel*)
clear; **sur un ton ~** casually
dégager [degaʒe] /3/ *vt* (*exhaler*) to
give off; (*délivrer*) to free, extricate;
(*désencombrer*) to clear; (*isoler*, *mettre
en valeur*) to bring out; **se dégager**
vi (*passage*, *ciel*) to clear; **~ qn de**
(*engagement*, *parole etc*) to release *ou*
free sb from
dégâts [dega] *nmpl* damage *sg*; **faire
des ~** to damage
dégel [deʒɛl] *nm* thaw; **dégeler** /5/ *vt*
to thaw (out)
dégivrer [deʒivʀe] /1/ *vt* (*frigo*) to
defrost; (*vitres*) to de-ice
dégonflé, e [degɔ̃fle] *adj* (*pneu*) flat
dégonfler [degɔ̃fle] /1/ *vt* (*pneu*,
ballon) to let down, deflate; **se
dégonfler** *vi* (*fam*) to chicken out
dégouliner [deguline] /1/ *vi* to
trickle, drip
dégourdi, e [deguʀdi] *adj* smart,
resourceful
dégourdir [deguʀdiʀ] /2/ *vt*: **se ~
(les jambes)** to stretch one's legs
dégoût [degu] *nm* disgust, distaste;
dégoûtant, e *adj* disgusting;
dégoûté, e *adj* disgusted; **dégoûté**

de sick of; **dégoûter** /1/ vt to disgust; **dégoûter qn de qch** to put sb off sth

dégrader [degʀade] /1/ vt (Mil: officier) to degrade; (abîmer) to damage, deface; **se dégrader** vi (relations, situation) to deteriorate

degré [dəgʀe] nm degree

dégressif, -ive [degʀesif, -iv] adj on a decreasing scale

dégringoler [degʀɛ̃gɔle] /1/ vi to tumble (down)

déguisement [degizmɑ̃] nm (pour s'amuser) fancy dress

déguiser [degize] /1/: **se déguiser (en)** vi (se costumer) to dress up (as); (pour tromper) to disguise o.s. (as)

dégustation [degystasjɔ̃] nf (de fromages etc) sampling; **~ de vin(s)** wine-tasting

déguster [degyste] /1/ vt (vins) to taste; (fromages etc) to sample; (savourer) to enjoy

dehors [dəɔʀ] adv outside; (en plein air) outdoors ▷ nm outside ▷ nmpl (apparences) appearances; **mettre** ou **jeter ~** to throw out; **au ~** outside; **au ~ de** outside; **en ~ de** apart from

déjà [deʒa] adv already; (auparavant) before, already

déjeuner [deʒœne] /1/ vi to (have) lunch; (le matin) to have breakfast ▷ nm lunch

delà [dəla] adv: **en ~ (de), au ~ (de)** beyond

délacer [delase] /3/ vt (chaussures) to undo, unlace

délai [delɛ] nm (attente) waiting period; (sursis) extension (of time); (temps accordé) time limit; **sans ~** without delay; **dans les ~s** within the time limit

délaisser [delese] /1/ vt to abandon, desert

délasser [delɑse] /1/ vt to relax; **se délasser** vi to relax

délavé, e [delave] adj faded

délayer [deleje] /8/ vt (Culin) to mix (with water etc); (peinture) to thin down

delco® [dɛlko] nm (Auto) distributor

délégué, e [delege] nm/f representative

déléguer [delege] /6/ vt to delegate

délibéré, e [delibeʀe] adj (conscient) deliberate

délicat, e [delika, -at] adj delicate; (plein de tact) tactful; (attentionné) thoughtful; **délicatement** adv delicately; (avec douceur) gently

délice [delis] nm delight

délicieux, -euse [delisjø, -øz] adj (au goût) delicious; (sensation, impression) delightful

délimiter [delimite] /1/ vt (terrain) to delimit, demarcate

délinquant, e [delɛ̃kɑ̃, -ɑ̃t] adj, nm/f delinquent

délirer [deliʀe] /1/ vi to be delirious; **tu délires!** (fam) you're crazy!

délit [deli] nm (criminal) offence

délivrer [delivʀe] /1/ vt (prisonnier) to (set) free, release; (passeport, certificat) to issue

deltaplane® [dɛltaplan] nm hang-glider

déluge [delyʒ] nm (biblique) Flood; (grosse pluie) downpour

demain [d(ə)mɛ̃] adv tomorrow; **~ matin/soir** tomorrow morning/ evening

demande [d(ə)mɑ̃d] nf (requête) request; (revendication) demand; (formulaire) application; (Écon): **la ~** demand; **"~s d'emploi"** "situations wanted"

demandé, e [d(ə)mɑ̃de] adj (article etc): **très ~** (very) much in demand

demander [d(ə)mɑ̃de] /1/ vt to ask for; (date, heure, chemin) to ask; (requérir, nécessiter) to require, demand; **~ qch à qn** to ask sb for sth; **~ à qn de faire** to ask sb to do; **se ~ si/pourquoi** etc to wonder if/why etc; **je ne demande pas mieux** I'm asking nothing more; **demandeur, -euse** nm/f: **demandeur d'asile**

asylum-seeker; **demandeur d'emploi** job-seeker

démangeaison [demɑ̃ʒɛzɔ̃] nf itching; **avoir des ~s** to be itching

démanger [demɑ̃ʒe] /3/ vi to itch

démaquillant [demakijɑ̃] nm make-up remover

démaquiller [demakije] /1/ vt: **se démaquiller** to remove one's make-up

démarche [demaʀʃ] nf (allure) gait, walk; (intervention) step; (fig: intellectuelle) thought processes pl; **faire les ~s nécessaires (pour obtenir qch)** to take the necessary steps (to obtain sth)

démarrage [demaʀaʒ] nm start

démarrer [demaʀe] /1/ vi (conducteur) to start (up); (véhicule) to move off; (travaux, affaire) to get moving; **démarreur** nm (Auto) starter

démêlant, e [demelɑ̃, -ɑ̃t] adj: **crème ~e** (hair) conditioner ▷ nm conditioner

démêler [demele] /1/ vt to untangle; **démêlés** nmpl problems

déménagement [demenaʒmɑ̃] nm move; **entreprise/camion de ~** removal (BRIT) ou moving (US) firm/van

déménager [demenaʒe] /3/ vt (meubles) to (re)move ▷ vi to move (house); **déménageur** nm removal man

démerder [demɛʀde] /1/: **se démerder** vi (fam!) to bloody well manage for o.s.

démettre [demɛtʀ] /56/ vt: **~ qn de** (fonction, poste) to dismiss sb from; **se ~ l'épaule** etc to dislocate one's shoulder etc

demeurer [d(ə)mœʀe] /1/ vi (habiter) to live; (rester) to remain

demi, e [dəmi] adj half; **et ~: trois heures/bouteilles et ~es** three and a half hours/bottles ▷ nm (bière: = 0.25 litre) ≈ half-pint; **il est 2 heures et ~e** it's half past 2; **il est midi et ~** it's

half past 12; **à ~** half-; **à la ~e** (heure) on the half-hour; **demi-douzaine** nf half-dozen, half a dozen; **demi-finale** nf semifinal; **demi-frère** nm half-brother; **demi-heure** nf: **une demi-heure** a half-hour, half an hour; **demi-journée** nf half-day, half a day; **demi-litre** nm half-litre (BRIT), half-liter (US), half a litre ou liter; **demi-livre** nf half-pound, half a pound; **demi-pension** nf half-board; **demi-pensionnaire** nm/f: **être demi-pensionnaire** to take school lunches

démis, e [demi] adj (épaule etc) dislocated

demi-sœur [dəmisœʀ] nf half-sister

démission [demisjɔ̃] nf resignation; **donner sa ~** to give ou hand in one's notice; **démissionner** /1/ vi to resign

demi-tarif [dəmitaʀif] nm half-price; (Transports) half-fare; **voyager à ~** to travel half-fare

demi-tour [dəmituʀ] nm about-turn; **faire ~** to turn (and go) back

démocratie [demɔkʀasi] nf democracy; **démocratique** adj democratic

démodé, e [demɔde] adj old-fashioned

demoiselle [d(ə)mwazɛl] nf (jeune fille) young lady; (célibataire) single lady, maiden lady; **~ d'honneur** bridesmaid

démolir [demɔliʀ] /2/ vt to demolish

démon [demɔ̃] nm (enfant turbulent) devil, demon; **le D~** the Devil

démonstration [demɔ̃stʀasjɔ̃] nf demonstration

démonter [demɔ̃te] /1/ vt (machine etc) to take down, dismantle; **se démonter** vi (meuble) to be dismantled, be taken to pieces; (personne) to lose countenance

démontrer [demɔ̃tʀe] /1/ vt to demonstrate

démouler [demule] /1/ vt to turn out

démuni, e [demyni] adj (sans argent) impoverished; **~ de** without

dénicher [denife] /1/ vt (fam: objet) to unearth; (: restaurant etc) to discover

dénier [denje] /7/ vt to deny

dénivellation [denivelasjɔ̃] nf (pente) ramp

dénombrer [denɔ̃bʀe] /1/ vt to count

dénomination [denɔminasjɔ̃] nf designation, appellation

dénoncer [denɔ̃se] /3/ vt to denounce; **se dénoncer** to give o.s. up, come forward

dénouement [denumɑ̃] nm outcome

dénouer [denwe] /1/ vt to unknot, undo

denrée [dɑ̃ʀe] nf (aussi: ~ **alimentaire**) food(stuff)

dense [dɑ̃s] adj dense; **densité** nf density

dent [dɑ̃] nf tooth; ~ **de lait/sagesse** milk/wisdom tooth; **dentaire** adj dental; **cabinet dentaire** dental surgery

dentelle [dɑ̃tɛl] nf lace no pl

dentier [dɑ̃tje] nm denture

dentifrice [dɑ̃tifʀis] nm: **(pâte)** ~ toothpaste

dentiste nm/f dentist

dentition [dɑ̃tisjɔ̃] nf teeth pl

dénué, e [denɥe] adj: ~ **de** devoid of

déodorant [deɔdɔʀɑ̃] nm deodorant

déontologie [deɔ̃tɔlɔʒi] nf (professional) code of practice

dépannage [depanaʒ] nm: **service/ camion de ~** (Auto) breakdown service/truck

dépanner [depane] /1/ vt (voiture, télévision) to fix, repair; (fig) to bail out, help out; **dépanneuse** nf breakdown lorry (BRIT), tow truck (US)

dépareillé, e [depaʀeje] adj (collection, service) incomplete; (gant, volume, objet) odd

départ [depaʀ] nm departure; (Sport) start; **au ~** at the start; **la veille de son ~** the day before he leaves/left

département [depaʀtəmɑ̃] nm department

● **DÉPARTEMENTS**
●
● France is divided into 96
● administrative units called
● départements. These local
● government divisions are headed
● by a state-appointed 'préfet',
● and administered by an elected
● 'Conseil général'. Départements are
● usually named after prominent
● geographical features such as
● rivers or mountain ranges.

dépassé, e [depase] adj superseded, outmoded; (fig) out of one's depth

dépasser [depase] /1/ vt (véhicule, concurrent) to overtake; (endroit) to pass, go past; (somme, limite) to exceed; (fig: en beauté etc) to surpass, outshine ▷ vi (jupon) to show; **se dépasser** to excel o.s.

dépaysé, e [depeize] adj disoriented

dépaysement [depeizmɑ̃] nm change of scenery

dépêcher [depeʃe] /1/: **se dépêcher** vi to hurry

dépendance [depɑ̃dɑ̃s] nf dependence no pl; (bâtiment) outbuilding

dépendre [depɑ̃dʀ] /41/ vt: ~ **de** vt to depend on, to be dependent on; **ça dépend** it depends

dépens [depɑ̃] nmpl: **aux ~ de** at the expense of

dépense [depɑ̃s] nf spending no pl, expense, expenditure no pl; **dépenser** /1/ vt to spend; (fig) to expend, use up; **se dépenser** vi to exert o.s.

dépeupler [depœple] /1/: **se dépeupler** vi to become depopulated

dépilatoire [depilatwaʀ] adj: **crème ~** hair-removing ou depilatory cream

dépister [depiste] /1/ vt to detect; (voleur) to track down

dépit [depi] nm vexation, frustration; **en ~ de** in spite of; **en ~ du bon sens** contrary to all good sense; **dépité, e** adj vexed, frustrated

déplacé, e [deplase] adj (propos) out of place, uncalled-for

déplacement [deplasmɑ̃] nm (voyage) trip, travelling no pl; **en ~** away (on a trip)

déplacer [deplase] /3/ vt (table, voiture) to move, shift; **se déplacer** vi to move; (voyager) to travel; **se ~ une vertèbre** to slip a disc

déplaire [deplɛʀ] /54/ vi: **ceci me déplaît** I don't like this, I dislike this; **se ~ quelque part** to dislike or be unhappy somewhere; **déplaisant, e** adj disagreeable

dépliant [deplijɑ̃] nm leaflet

déplier [deplije] /7/ vt to unfold

déposer [depoze] /1/ vt (gén: mettre, poser) to lay down, put down; (à la banque, à la consigne) to deposit; (passager) to drop (off), set down; (roi) to depose; (marque) to register; (plainte) to lodge; **se déposer** vi to settle; **dépositaire** nm/f (Comm) agent; **déposition** nf statement

dépôt [depo] nm (à la banque, sédiment) deposit; (entrepôt, réserve) warehouse, store

dépourvu, e [depuʀvy] adj: **~ de** lacking in, without; **prendre qn au ~** to catch sb unawares

dépression nf depression; **~ (nerveuse)** (nervous) breakdown

déprimant, e [depʀimɑ̃, -ɑ̃t] adj depressing

déprimer [depʀime] /1/ vt to depress

MOT-CLÉ

depuis [dəpɥi] prép **1** (point de départ dans le temps) since; **il habite Paris depuis 1983/l'an dernier** he has been living in Paris since 1983/last year; **depuis quand?** since when?;

depuis quand le connaissez-vous? how long have you known him?

2 (temps écoulé) for; **il habite Paris depuis cinq ans** he has been living in Paris for five years; **je le connais depuis trois ans** I've known him for three years

3 (lieu) **il a plu depuis Metz** it's been raining since Metz; **elle a téléphoné depuis Valence** she rang from Valence

4 (quantité, rang) from; **depuis les plus petits jusqu'aux plus grands** from the youngest to the oldest

▶ adv (temps) since (then); **je ne lui ai pas parlé depuis** I haven't spoken to him since (then); **depuis que** conj (ever) since; **depuis qu'il m'a dit ça** (ever) since he said that to me

député, e [depyte] nm/f (Pol) ≈ Member of Parliament (BRIT), ≈ Congressman/woman (US)

dérangement [deʀɑ̃ʒmɑ̃] nm (gêne, déplacement) trouble; (gastrique etc) disorder; **en ~** (téléphone) out of order

déranger [deʀɑ̃ʒe] /3/ vt (personne) to trouble, bother; (projets) to disrupt, upset; (objets, vêtements) to disarrange; **se déranger;** vi: **surtout ne vous dérangez pas pour moi** please don't put yourself out on my account; **est-ce que cela vous dérange si ...?** do you mind if ...?

déraper [deʀape] /1/ vi (voiture) to skid; (personne, semelles, couteau) to slip

dérégler [deʀegle] /6/ vt (mécanisme) to put out of order; (estomac) to upset

dérisoire [deʀizwaʀ] adj derisory

dérive [deʀiv] nf: **aller à la ~** (Navig, fig) to drift

dérivé, e [deʀive] nm (Tech) by-product

dermatologue [dɛʀmatɔlɔg] nm/f dermatologist

dernier, -ière [dɛʀnje, -jɛʀ] adj last; (le plus récent: gén avant n) latest, last; **lundi/le mois ~** last Monday/month; **le ~ cri** the last word (in fashion); **en ~** last; **ce ~, cette dernière** the latter; **dernièrement** adv recently

dérogation [deʀɔgasjɔ̃] nf (special) dispensation

dérouiller [deʀuje] /1/ vt: **se ~ les jambes** to stretch one's legs (fig)

déroulement [deʀulmɑ̃] nm (d'une opération etc) progress

dérouler [deʀule] /1/ vt (ficelle) to unwind; **se dérouler** vi (avoir lieu) to take place; (se passer) to go; **tout s'est déroulé comme prévu** everything went as planned

dérouter [deʀute] /1/ vt (avion, train) to reroute, divert; (étonner) to disconcert, throw (out)

derrière [dɛʀjɛʀ] adv, prép behind ▷ nm (d'une maison) back; (postérieur) behind, bottom; **les pattes de ~** the back legs, the hind legs; **par ~** from behind; (fig) behind one's back

des [de] art voir **de**

dès [dɛ] prép from; **~ que** as soon as; **~ son retour** as soon as he was (ou is) back

désaccord [dezakɔʀ] nm disagreement

désagréable [dezagʀeabl] adj unpleasant

désagrément [dezagʀemɑ̃] nm annoyance, trouble no pl

désaltérer [dezalteʀe] /6/ vt: **se désaltérer** to quench one's thirst

désapprobateur, -trice [dezapʀɔbatœʀ, -tʀis] adj disapproving

désapprouver [dezapʀuve] /1/ vt to disapprove of

désarmant, e [dezaʀmɑ̃, -ɑ̃t] adj disarming

désastre [dezastʀ] nm disaster; **désastreux, -euse** adj disastrous

désavantage [dezavɑ̃taʒ] nm disadvantage; **désavantager** /3/ vt to put at a disadvantage

descendre [desɑ̃dʀ] /41/ vt (escalier, montagne) to go (ou come) down; (valise, paquet) to take ou get down; (étagère etc) to lower; (fam: abattre) to shoot down ▷ vi to go (ou come) down; (passager: s'arrêter) to get out, alight; **~ à pied/en voiture** to walk/drive down; **~ de** (famille) to be descended from; **~ du train** to get out of ou off the train; **~ d'un arbre** to climb down from a tree; **~ de cheval** to dismount; **~ à l'hôtel** to stay at a hotel

descente [desɑ̃t] nf descent, going down; (chemin) way down; (Ski) downhill (race); **au milieu de la ~** halfway down; **~ de lit** bedside rug; **~ (de police)** (police) raid

description [dɛskʀipsjɔ̃] nf description

déséquilibre [dezekilibʀ] nm (position): **être en ~** to be unsteady; (fig: des forces, du budget) imbalance

désert, e [dezɛʀ, -ɛʀt] adj deserted ▷ nm desert; **désertique** adj desert cpd

désespéré, e [dezɛspeʀe] adj desperate

désespérer [dezɛspeʀe] /6/ vi: **~ de** to despair of; **désespoir** nm despair; **en désespoir de cause** in desperation

déshabiller [dezabije] /1/ vt to undress; **se déshabiller** vi to undress (o.s.)

déshydraté, e [dezidʀate] adj dehydrated

désigner [dezine] /1/ vt (montrer) to point out, indicate; (dénommer) to denote; (candidat etc) to name

désinfectant, e [dezɛ̃fɛktɑ̃, -ɑ̃t] adj, nm disinfectant

désinfecter [dezɛ̃fɛkte] /1/ vt to disinfect

désintéressé, e [dezɛ̃teʀese] adj disinterested, unselfish

désintéresser [dezɛ̃teʀese] /1/ vt: **se désintéresser (de)** to lose interest (in)

désintoxication [dezɛ̃tɔksikasjɔ̃] nf: **faire une cure de ~** to have ou undergo treatment for alcoholism (ou drug addiction)

désinvolte [dezɛ̃vɔlt] adj casual, off-hand

désir [deziʀ] nm wish; (fort, sensuel) desire; **désirer** /1/ vt to want, wish for; (sexuellement) to desire; **je désire ...** (formule de politesse) I would like ...

désister [deziste]: **se désister** vi to stand down, withdraw

désobéir [dezɔbeiʀ] /2/ vi: **~ (à qn/qch)** to disobey (sb/sth); **désobéissant, e** adj disobedient

désodorisant [dezɔdɔʀizɑ̃] nm air freshener, deodorizer

désolé, e [dezɔle] adj (paysage) desolate; **je suis ~** I'm sorry

désordonné, e [dezɔʀdɔne] adj untidy

désordre [dezɔʀdʀ] nm disorder(liness), untidiness; (anarchie) disorder; **en ~** in a mess, untidy

désormais [dezɔʀmɛ] adv from now on

desquels, desquelles [dekɛl] voir **lequel**

dessécher [deseʃe] /6/: **se dessécher** vi to dry out

desserrer [deseʀe] /1/ vt to loosen; (frein) to release

dessert [desɛʀ] nm dessert, pudding

desservir [desɛʀviʀ] /14/ vt (ville, quartier) to serve; (débarrasser): **~ (la table)** to clear the table

dessin [desɛ̃] nm (œuvre, art) drawing; (motif) pattern, design; **~ animé** cartoon (film); **~ humoristique** cartoon; **dessinateur, -trice** nm/f drawer; (de bandes dessinées) cartoonist; (industriel) draughtsman (BRIT), draftsman (US); **dessiner** /1/ vt to draw; (concevoir) to design; **se dessiner** vi (forme) to be outlined; (fig: solution) to emerge

dessous [d(ə)su] adv underneath, beneath ▷ nm underside; **les voisins du ~** the downstairs neighbours ▷ nmpl (sous-vêtements) underwear sg; **en ~** underneath; below; **par ~** underneath; below; **avoir le ~** to get the worst of it; **dessous-de-plat** nm inv tablemat

dessus [d(ə)sy] adv on top; (collé, écrit) on it ▷ nm top; **les voisins/l'appartement du ~** the upstairs neighbours/flat; **en ~** above; **par ~** adv over it; prép over; **au-~** above; **avoir/prendre le ~** to have/get the upper hand; **sens ~ dessous** upside down; **dessus-de-lit** nm inv bedspread

destin [dɛstɛ̃] nm fate; (avenir) destiny

destinataire [dɛstinatɛʀ] nm/f (Postes) addressee; (d'un colis) consignee

destination [dɛstinasjɔ̃] nf (lieu) destination; (usage) purpose; **à ~ de** bound for; travelling to

destiner [dɛstine] /1/ vt: **~ qch à qn** (envisager de donner) to intend sb to have sth; (adresser) to intend sth for sb; **se ~ à l'enseignement** to intend to become a teacher; **être destiné à** (usage) to be intended ou meant for

détachant [detaʃɑ̃] nm stain remover

détacher [detaʃe] /1/ vt (enlever) to detach, remove; (délier) to untie; (Admin): **~ qn (auprès de ou à)** to post sb (to); **se détacher** vi (se séparer) to come off; (page) to come out; (se défaire) to come undone; **se ~ sur** to stand out against; **se ~ de** (se désintéresser) to grow away from

détail [detaj] nm detail; (Comm): **le ~** retail; **au ~** (Comm) retail; **en ~** in detail; **détaillant, e** nm/f retailer; **détaillé, e** adj (récit, plan, explications) detailed; (facture) itemized; **détailler** /1/ vt (expliquer) to explain in detail

détecter [detɛkte] /1/ vt to detect

détective [detɛktiv] nm detective; **~ (privé)** private detective ou investigator

déteindre [detɛ̃dʀ] /52/ vi to fade; (au lavage) to run; **~ sur** (vêtement) to run into; (fig) to rub off on

détendre [detɑ̃dʀ] /41/ vt (personne, atmosphère, corps, esprit) to relax; **se détendre** vi (ressort) to lose its tension; (personne) to relax

détenir [det(ə)niʀ] /22/ vt (fortune, objet, secret) to be in possession of; (prisonnier) to detain; (record) to hold; **~ le pouvoir** to be in power

détente [detɑ̃t] nf relaxation

détention [detɑ̃sjɔ̃] nf (de fortune, objet, secret) possession; (captivité) detention; **~ préventive** (pre-trial) custody

détenu, e [det(ə)ny] pp de **détenir** ▷ nm/f prisoner

détergent [detɛʀʒɑ̃] nm detergent

détériorer [deteʀjɔʀe] /1/ vt to damage; **se détériorer** vi to deteriorate

déterminé, e [detɛʀmine] adj (résolu) determined; (précis) specific, definite

déterminer [detɛʀmine] /1/ vt (fixer) to determine; **~ qn à faire** to decide sb to do; **se ~ à faire** to make up one's mind to do

détester [detɛste] /1/ vt to hate, detest

détour [detuʀ] nm detour; (tournant) bend, curve; **ça vaut le ~** it's worth the trip; **sans ~** (fig) plainly

détourné, e [detuʀne] adj (sentier, chemin, moyen) roundabout

détourner [detuʀne] /1/ vt to divert; (par la force) to hijack; (yeux, tête) to turn away; (de l'argent) to embezzle; **se détourner** vi to turn away

détraquer [detʀake] /1/ vt to put out of order; (estomac) to upset; **se détraquer** vi to go wrong

détriment [detʀimɑ̃] nm: **au ~ de** to the detriment of

détroit [detʀwa] nm strait

détruire [detʀɥiʀ] /38/ vt to destroy

dette [dɛt] nf debt

DEUG [dœg] sigle m = **Diplôme d'études universitaires générales**

- ● **DEUG**
- ●
- ● French students sit their DEUG
- ● ('diplôme d'études universitaires
- ● générales') after two years at
- ● university. They can then choose to
- ● leave university altogether, or go
- ● on to study for their 'licence'. The
- ● certificate specifies the student's
- ● major subject and may be awarded
- ● with distinction.

deuil [dœj] nm (perte) bereavement; (période) mourning; **prendre le/être en ~** to go into/be in mourning

deux [dø] num two; **les ~** both; **ses ~ mains** both his hands, his two hands; **~ fois** twice; **deuxième** num second; **deuxièmement** adv secondly; **deux-pièces** nm inv (tailleur) two-piece (suit); (de bain) two-piece (swimsuit); (appartement) two-roomed flat (BRIT) ou apartment (US); **deux-points** nm inv colon sg; **deux-roues** nm inv two-wheeled vehicle

devais etc [dəvɛ] vb voir **devoir**

dévaluation [devalɥasjɔ̃] nf devaluation

devancer [d(ə)vɑ̃se] /3/ vt to get ahead of; (arriver avant) to arrive before; (prévenir) to anticipate

devant [d(ə)vɑ̃] adv in front; (à distance: en avant) ahead ▷ prép in front of; (en avant) ahead of; (avec mouvement: passer) past; (fig) before, in front of (: vu) in view of ▷ nm front; **prendre les ~s** to make the first move; **les pattes de ~** the front legs, the forelegs; **par ~** (boutonner) at the front; (entrer) the front way; **aller au-~ de qn** to go out to meet sb; **aller au-~ de** (désirs de qn) to anticipate

devanture [d(ə)vɑ̃tyʀ] nf (étalage) display; (vitrine) (shop) window

développement [dev(ə)lɔpmɑ̃]
nm development; **pays en voie de
~** developing countries; **~ durable**
sustainable development

développer [dev(ə)lɔpe] /1/ *vt* to
develop; **se développer** *vi* to develop

devenir [dəv(ə)niʀ] /22/ *vi* to
become; **que sont-ils devenus?**
what has become of them?

devez [dəve] *vb voir* **devoir**

déviation [devjasjɔ̃] *nf* (*Auto*)
diversion (*BRIT*), detour (*US*)

devienne *etc* [dəvjɛn] *vb voir* **devenir**

deviner [d(ə)vine] /1/ *vt* to guess;
(*apercevoir*) to distinguish; **devinette**
nf riddle

devis [d(ə)vi] *nm* estimate, quotation

devise [dəviz] *nf* (*formule*) motto,
watchword; **devises** *nfpl* (*argent*)
currency *sg*

dévisser [devise] /1/ *vt* to unscrew,
undo; **se dévisser** *vi* to come
unscrewed

devoir [d(ə)vwaʀ] /28/ *nm* duty;
(*Scol*) homework *no pl* (: *en classe*)
exercise ▷ *vt* (*argent, respect*): **~ qch
(à qn)** to owe (sb) sth; **combien
est-ce que je vous dois?** how
much do I owe you?; **il doit le faire**
(*obligation*) he has to do it, he must
do it; **cela devait arriver un jour**
it was bound to happen; **il doit
partir demain** (*intention*) he is due
to leave tomorrow; **il doit être tard**
(*probabilité*) it must be late

dévorer [devɔʀe] /1/ *vt* to devour;
(*feu, soucis*) to consume; **~ qn/qch
des yeux** *ou* **du regard** (*convoitise*) to
eye sb/sth greedily

dévoué, e [devwe] *adj* devoted

dévouer [devwe] /1/: **se dévouer** *vi*
(*se sacrifier*): **se ~ (pour)** to sacrifice
o.s. (for); (*se consacrer*): **se ~ à** to
devote *ou* dedicate o.s. to

devrai *etc* [dəvʀe] *vb voir* **devoir**

dézipper [dezipe] /1/ *vt* to unzip

diabète [djabɛt] *nm* diabetes *sg*;
diabétique *nm/f* diabetic

diable [djɑbl] *nm* devil

diabolo [djabɔlo] *nm* (*boisson*)
lemonade and fruit cordial

diagnostic [djagnɔstik] *nm*
diagnosis *sg*; **diagnostiquer** /1/ *vt*
to diagnose

diagonal, e, -aux [djagɔnal, -o]
adj, nf diagonal; **en ~e** diagonally

diagramme [djagʀam] *nm* chart,
graph

dialecte [djalɛkt] *nm* dialect

dialogue [djalɔg] *nm* dialogue

diamant [djamɑ̃] *nm* diamond

diamètre [djamɛtʀ] *nm* diameter

diapo [djapo], **diapositive**
[djapozitiv] *nf* transparency, slide

diarrhée [djaʀe] *nf* diarrhoea

dictateur [diktatœʀ] *nm* dictator;
dictature [diktatyʀ] *nf* dictatorship

dictée [dikte] *nf* dictation

dicter [dikte] /1/ *vt* to dictate

dictionnaire [diksjɔnɛʀ] *nm*
dictionary

dièse [djɛz] *nm* sharp

diesel [djezɛl] *nm, adj inv* diesel

diète [djɛt] *nf* (*jeûne*) starvation
diet; (*régime*) diet; **diététique** *adj*:
magasin diététique health food
shop (*BRIT*) *ou* store (*US*)

dieu, x [djø] *nm* god; **D~** God; **mon
D~!** good heavens!

différemment [difeʀamɑ̃] *adv*
differently

différence [difeʀɑ̃s] *nf* difference; **à
la ~ de** unlike; **différencier** /7/ *vt* to
differentiate

différent, e [difeʀɑ̃, -ɑ̃t] *adj*
(*dissemblable*) different; **~ de** different
from; **~s objets** different *ou* various
objects

différer [difeʀe] /6/ *vt* to postpone,
put off ▷ *vi*: **~ (de)** to differ (from)

difficile [difisil] *adj* difficult;
(*exigeant*) hard to please;
difficilement *adv* with difficulty

difficulté [difikylte] *nf* difficulty;
en ~ (*bateau, alpiniste*) in trouble *ou*
difficulties

diffuser [difyze] /1/ vt (chaleur, bruit, lumière) to diffuse; (émission, musique) to broadcast; (nouvelle, idée) to circulate; (Comm) to distribute

digérer [diʒeʀe] /6/ vt to digest; (fig: accepter) to stomach, put up with; **digestif, -ive** nm (after-dinner) liqueur; **digestion** nf digestion

digne [diɲ] adj dignified; ~ **de** worthy of; ~ **de foi** trustworthy; **dignité** nf dignity

digue [dig] nf dike, dyke

dilemme [dilɛm] nm dilemma

diligence [diliʒɑ̃s] nf stagecoach

diluer [dilɥe] /1/ vt to dilute

dimanche [dimɑ̃ʃ] nm Sunday

dimension [dimɑ̃sjɔ̃] nf (grandeur) size; (dimensions) dimensions

diminuer [diminɥe] /1/ vt to reduce, decrease; (ardeur etc) to lessen; (dénigrer) to belittle ▷ vi to decrease, diminish; **diminutif** nm (surnom) pet name

dinde [dɛ̃d] nf turkey

dindon [dɛ̃dɔ̃] nm turkey

dîner [dine] /1/ nm dinner ▷ vi to have dinner

dingue [dɛ̃g] adj (fam) crazy

dinosaure [dinɔzɔʀ] nm dinosaur

diplomate [diplɔmat] adj diplomatic ▷ nm diplomat; (fig) diplomatist; **diplomatie** nf diplomacy

diplôme [diplom] nm diploma certificate; **avoir des ~s** to have qualifications; **diplômé, e** adj qualified

dire [diʀ] /37/ vt to say; (secret, mensonge) to tell; **se dire** (à soi-même) to say to oneself ▷ nm: **au ~ de** according to; ~ **qch à qn** to tell sb sth; ~ **à qn qu'il fasse** ou **de faire** to tell sb to do; **on dit que** they say that; **on dirait que** it looks (ou sounds etc) as though; **que dites-vous de** (penser) what do you think of; **si cela lui dit** if he fancies it; **dis donc!, dites donc!** (pour attirer l'attention)

hey!; (au fait) by the way; **ceci** ou **cela dit** that being said; **ça ne se dit pas** (impoli) you shouldn't say that; (pas en usage) you don't say that

direct, e [diʀɛkt] adj direct ▷ nm: **en ~** (émission) live; **directement** adv directly

directeur, -trice [diʀɛktœʀ, -tʀis] nm/f (d'entreprise) director; (de service) manager/eress; (d'école) head(teacher) (BRIT), principal (US)

direction [diʀɛksjɔ̃] nf (d'entreprise) management; (Auto) steering; (sens) direction; **"toutes ~s"** "all routes"

dirent [diʀ] vb voir **dire**

dirigeant, e [diʀiʒɑ̃, -ɑ̃t] adj (classes) ruling ▷ nm/f (d'un parti etc) leader

diriger [diʀiʒe] /3/ vt (entreprise) to manage, run; (véhicule) to steer; (orchestre) to conduct; (recherches, travaux) to supervise; (arme): ~ **sur** to point ou level ou aim at; **se diriger** vi (s'orienter) to find one's way; ~ **son regard sur** to look in the direction of; **se ~ vers** ou **sur** to make ou head for

dis [di] vb voir **dire**

discerner [disɛʀne] /1/ vt to discern, make out

discipline [disiplin] nf discipline; **discipliner** /1/ vt to discipline

discontinu, e [diskɔ̃tiny] adj intermittent

discontinuer [diskɔ̃tinɥe] /1/ vi: **sans ~** without stopping, without a break

discothèque [diskɔtɛk] nf (boîte de nuit) disco(thèque)

discours [diskuʀ] nm speech

discret, -ète [diskʀɛ, -ɛt] adj discreet; (fig: musique, style, maquillage) unobtrusive; **discrétion** nf discretion; **à discrétion** as much as one wants

discrimination nf discrimination; **sans ~** indiscriminately

discussion [diskysjɔ̃] nf discussion

discutable [diskytabl] adj debatable

discuter [diskyte] /1/ vt (contester)
to question, dispute; (débattre: prix)
to discuss ▷ vi to talk; (protester) to
argue; **~ de** to discuss

dise etc [diz] vb voir **dire**

disjoncteur [disjɔ̃ktœʀ] nm (Élec)
circuit breaker

disloquer [dislɔke] /1/: **se disloquer**
vi (parti, empire) to break up; (meuble)
to come apart; **se ~ l'épaule** to
dislocate one's shoulder

disons etc [dizɔ̃] vb voir **dire**

disparaître [dispaʀɛtʀ] /57/ vi to
disappear; (se perdre: traditions etc)
to die out; (personne: mourir) to die;
faire ~ (objet, tache, trace) to remove;
(personne, douleur) to get rid of

disparition [dispaʀisjɔ̃] nf
disappearance; **espèce en voie de ~**
endangered species

disparu, e [dispaʀy] nm/f missing
person; **être porté ~** to be reported
missing

dispensaire [dispɑ̃sɛʀ] nm
community clinic

dispenser [dispɑ̃se] /1/ vt: **~ qn de**
to exempt sb from

disperser [dispɛʀse] /1/ vt to
scatter; **se disperser** vi to scatter

disponible [dispɔnibl] adj available

disposé, e [dispoze] adj: **bien/mal
~** (humeur) in a good/bad mood; **~ à**
(prêt à) willing ou prepared to

disposer [dispoze] /1/ vt to arrange
▷ vi: **vous pouvez ~** you may leave;
~ de to have (at one's disposal);
se ~ à faire to prepare to do, be
about to do

dispositif [dispozitif] nm device;
(fig) system, plan of action

disposition [dispozisjɔ̃] nf
(arrangement) arrangement, layout;
(humeur) mood; **prendre ses ~s** to
make arrangements; **avoir des ~s
pour la musique** etc to have a special
aptitude for music etc; **à la ~ de qn** at
sb's disposal; **je suis à votre ~** I am at
your service

disproportionné, e
[dispʀopɔʀsjɔne] adj disproportionate,
out of all proportion

dispute [dispyt] nf quarrel,
argument; **disputer** /1/ vt (match) to
play; (combat) to fight; **se disputer**
vi to quarrel

disqualifier [diskalifje] /7/ vt to
disqualify

disque [disk] nm (Mus) record; (forme,
pièce) disc; (Sport) discus; **~ compact**
compact disc; **~ dur** hard disk;
disquette nf floppy (disk), diskette

dissertation [disɛʀtasjɔ̃] nf (Scol)
essay

dissimuler [disimyle] /1/ vt to
conceal

dissipé, e [disipe] adj (indiscipliné)
unruly

dissolvant [disɔlvɑ̃] nm nail polish
remover

dissuader [disɥade] /1/ vt: **~ qn de
faire/de qch** to dissuade sb from
doing/from sth

distance [distɑ̃s] nf distance; (fig:
écart) gap; **à ~** at ou from a distance;
distancer /3/ vt to outdistance

distant, e [distɑ̃, -ɑ̃t] adj (réservé)
distant; **~ de** (lieu) far away ou a long
way from

distillerie [distilʀi] nf distillery

distinct, e [distɛ̃(kt), distɛ̃kt]
adj distinct; **distinctement**
[distɛ̃ktəmɑ̃] adv distinctly;
distinctif, -ive adj distinctive

distingué, e [distɛ̃ge] adj
distinguished

distinguer [distɛ̃ge] /1/ vt to
distinguish; **se distinguer** vi: **se
~ (de)** to distinguish o.s. ou be
distinguished (from)

distraction [distʀaksjɔ̃] nf (manque
d'attention) absent-mindedness;
(passe-temps) distraction,
entertainment

distraire [distʀɛʀ] /50/ vt (déranger)
to distract; (divertir) to entertain,
divert; **se distraire** vi to amuse ou

enjoy o.s.; **distrait, e** [distʀɛ, -ɛt] *pp de* **distraire** ▷ *adj* absent-minded
distrayant, e [distʀɛjɑ̃, -ɑ̃t] *adj* entertaining
distribuer [distʀibɥe] /1/ *vt* to distribute; to hand out; (*Cartes*) to deal (out); (*courrier*) to deliver; **distributeur** *nm* (*Auto, Comm*) distributor; (*automatique*) (vending) machine; **distributeur de billets** cash dispenser
dit, e [di, dit] *pp de* **dire** ▷ *adj* (*fixé*): **le jour ~** the arranged day; (*surnommé*): **X, ~ Pierrot** X, known as *ou* called Pierrot
dites [dit] *vb voir* **dire**
divan [divɑ̃] *nm* divan
divers, e [divɛʀ, -ɛʀs] *adj* (*varié*) diverse, varied; (*différent*) different, various; **~es personnes** various *ou* several people
diversité [divɛʀsite] *nf* diversity, variety
divertir [divɛʀtiʀ] /2/: **se divertir** *vi* to amuse *ou* enjoy o.s.; **divertissement** *nm* entertainment
diviser [divize] /1/ *vt* to divide; **division** *nf* division
divorce [divɔʀs] *nm* divorce; **divorcé, e** *nm/f* divorcee; **divorcer** /3/ *vi* to get a divorce, get divorced; **divorcer de** *ou* **d'avec qn** to divorce sb
divulguer [divylge] /1/ *vt* to disclose
dix [di, dis, diz] *num* ten; **dix-huit** *num* eighteen; **dix-huitième** *num* eighteenth; **dixième** *num* tenth; **dix-neuf** *num* nineteen; **dix-neuvième** *num* nineteenth; **dix-sept** *num* seventeen; **dix-septième** *num* seventeenth
dizaine [dizɛn] *nf*: **une ~ (de)** about ten, ten or so
do [do] *nm* (*note*) C; (*en chantant la gamme*) do(h)
docile [dɔsil] *adj* docile
dock [dɔk] *nm* dock; **docker** *nm* docker

docteur, e [dɔktœʀ] *nm/f* doctor; **doctorat** *nm*: **doctorat (d'Université)** ≈ doctorate
doctrine [dɔktʀin] *nf* doctrine
document [dɔkymɑ̃] *nm* document; **documentaire** *adj, nm* documentary; **documentation** *nf* documentation, literature; **documenter** /1/ *vt*: **se documenter (sur)** to gather information *ou* material (on *ou* about)
dodo [dodo] *nm*: **aller faire ~** to go to beddy-byes
dogue [dɔg] *nm* mastiff
doigt [dwa] *nm* finger; **à deux ~s de** within an ace (BRIT) *ou* an inch of; **un ~ de lait/whisky** a drop of milk/ whisky; **~ de pied** toe
doit *etc* [dwa] *vb voir* **devoir**
dollar [dɔlaʀ] *nm* dollar
domaine [dɔmɛn] *nm* estate, property; (*fig*) domain, field
domestique [dɔmɛstik] *adj* domestic ▷ *nm/f* servant, domestic
domicile [dɔmisil] *nm* home, place of residence; **à ~** at home; **livrer à ~** to deliver; **domicilié, e** *adj*: **être domicilié à** to have one's home in *ou* at
dominant, e [dɔminɑ̃, -ɑ̃t] *adj* (*opinion*) predominant
dominer [dɔmine] /1/ *vt* to dominate; (*sujet*) to master; (*surpasser*) to outclass, surpass; (*surplomber*) to tower above, dominate ▷ *vi* to be in the dominant position; **se dominer** *vi* to control o.s.
domino [dɔmino] *nm* domino; **dominos** *nmpl* (*jeu*) dominoes *sg*
dommage [dɔmaʒ] *nm*: **~s** (*dégâts, pertes*) damage *no pl*; **c'est ~ de faire/que** it's a shame *ou* pity to do/ that; **quel ~!, c'est ~!** what a pity *ou* shame!
dompter [dɔ̃(p)te] /1/ *vt* to tame; **dompteur, -euse** *nm/f* trainer
DOM-ROM [dɔmʀɔm] *sigle m(pl)* (= *Département(s) et Régions/*

Territoire(s) d'outre-mer) French overseas departments and regions

don [dɔ̃] *nm* gift; (*charité*) donation; **avoir des ~s pour** to have a gift *ou* talent for; **elle a le ~ de m'énerver** she's got a knack of getting on my nerves

donc [dɔ̃k] *conj* therefore, so; (*après une digression*) so, then

dongle [dɔ̃gl] *nm* dongle

donné, e [dɔne] *adj* (*convenu: lieu, heure*) given; (*pas cher*) very cheap; **données** *nfpl* data; **c'est ~** it's a gift; **étant ~ que ...** given that ...

donner [dɔne] /1/ *vt* to give; (*vieux habits etc*) to give away; (*spectacle*) to put on; **~ qch à qn** to give sb sth, give sth to sb; **~ sur** (*fenêtre, chambre*) to look (out) onto; **ça donne soif/faim** it makes you (feel) thirsty/hungry; **se ~ à fond (à son travail)** to give one's all (to one's work); **se ~ du mal** *ou* **de la peine (pour faire qch)** to go to a lot of trouble (to do sth); **s'en ~ à cœur joie** (*fam*) to have a great time (of it)

○ **MOT-CLÉ**

dont [dɔ̃] *pron relatif* **1** (*appartenance: objets*) whose, of which; (*: êtres animés*) whose; **la maison dont le toit est rouge** the house the roof of which is red, the house whose roof is red; **l'homme dont je connais la sœur** the man whose sister I know **2** (*parmi lesquel(le)s*): **deux livres, dont l'un est ...** two books, one of which is ...; **il y avait plusieurs personnes, dont Gabrielle** there were several people, among them Gabrielle; **10 blessés, dont 2 grièvement** 10 injured, 2 of them seriously **3** (*complément d'adjectif, de verbe*): **le fils dont il est si fier** the son he's so proud of; **le pays dont il est originaire** the country he's from; **ce**

dont je parle what I'm talking about; **la façon dont il l'a fait** the way (in which) he did it

dopage [dɔpaʒ] *nm* (*Sport*) drug use; (*de cheval*) doping

doré, e [dɔʀe] *adj* golden; (*avec dorure*) gilt, gilded

dorénavant [dɔʀenavɑ̃] *adv* henceforth

dorer [dɔʀe] /1/ *vt* to gild; **(faire) ~** (*Culin*) to brown

dorloter [dɔʀlɔte] /1/ *vt* to pamper

dormir [dɔʀmiʀ] /16/ *vi* to sleep; (*être endormi*) to be asleep

dortoir [dɔʀtwaʀ] *nm* dormitory

dos [do] *nm* back; (*de livre*) spine; **"voir au ~"** "see over"; **de ~** from the back

dosage [dozaʒ] *nm* mixture

dose [doz] *nf* dose; **doser** /1/ *vt* to measure out; **il faut savoir doser ses efforts** you have to be able to pace yourself

dossier [dosje] *nm* (*renseignements, fichier*) file; (*de chaise*) back; (*Presse*) feature; (*Inform*) folder; **un ~ scolaire** a school report

douane [dwan] *nf* customs *pl*; **douanier, -ière** *adj* customs *cpd* ▷ *nm* customs officer

double [dubl] *adj, adv* double ▷ *nm* (*autre exemplaire*) duplicate, copy; (*sosie*) double; (*Tennis*) doubles *sg*; (*2 fois plus*): **le ~ (de)** twice as much (*ou* many) (as); **en ~ (exemplaire)** in duplicate; **faire ~ emploi** to be redundant; **double-cliquer** /1/ *vi* (*Inform*) to double-click

doubler [duble] /1/ *vt* (*multiplier par 2*) to double; (*vêtement*) to line; (*dépasser*) to overtake, pass; (*film*) to dub; (*acteur*) to stand in for ▷ *vi* to double

doublure [dublyʀ] *nf* lining; (*Ciné*) stand-in

douce [dus] *adj f voir* **doux**; **douceâtre** *adj* sickly sweet;

doucement adv gently; (lentement) slowly; **douceur** nf softness; (de climat) mildness; (de quelqu'un) gentleness

douche [duʃ] nf shower; **prendre une ~** to have ou take a shower; **doucher** /1/: **se doucher** vi to have ou take a shower

doué, e [dwe] adj gifted, talented; **être ~ pour** to have a gift for

douille [duj] nf (Élec) socket

douillet, te [dujɛ, -ɛt] adj cosy; (péj: à la douleur) soft

douleur [dulœʀ] nf pain; (chagrin) grief, distress; **douloureux, -euse** adj painful

doute [dut] nm doubt; **sans ~** no doubt; (probablement) probably; **sans nul** ou **aucun ~** without (a) doubt; **douter** /1/ vt to doubt; **douter de** (allié, sincérité de qn) to have (one's) doubts about, doubt; (résultat, réussite) to be doubtful of; **douter que** to doubt whether ou if; **se douter de qch/que** to suspect sth/that; **je m'en doutais** I suspected as much; **douteux, -euse** adj (incertain) doubtful; (péj) dubious-looking

Douvres [duvʀ] n Dover

doux, douce [du, dus] adj soft; (sucré, agréable) sweet; (peu fort: moutarde etc, clément: climat) mild; (pas brusque) gentle

douzaine [duzɛn] nf (12) dozen; (environ 12): **une ~ (de)** a dozen or so

douze [duz] num twelve; **douzième** num twelfth

dragée [dʀaʒe] nf sugared almond

draguer [dʀage] /1/ vt (rivière) to dredge; (fam) to try and pick up

dramatique [dʀamatik] adj dramatic; (tragique) tragic ▷ nf (TV) (television) drama

drame [dʀam] nm drama

drap [dʀa] nm (de lit) sheet; (tissu) woollen fabric

drapeau, x [dʀapo] nm flag

drap-housse [dʀaus] nm fitted sheet

dresser [dʀese] /1/ vt (mettre vertical, monter) to put up, erect; (liste, bilan, contrat) to draw up; (animal) to train; **se dresser** vi (falaise, obstacle) to stand; (personne) to draw o.s. up; **~ l'oreille** to prick up one's ears; **~ qn contre qn d'autre** to set sb against sb else

drogue [dʀɔg] nf drug; **la ~** drugs pl; **drogué, e** nm/f drug addict; **droguer** /1/ vt (victime) to drug; **se droguer** vi (aux stupéfiants) to take drugs; (péj: de médicaments) to dose o.s. up; **droguerie** nf ≈ hardware shop (BRIT) ou store (US); **droguiste** nm ≈ keeper (ou owner) of a hardware shop ou store

droit, e [dʀwa, dʀwat] adj (non courbe) straight; (vertical) upright, straight; (fig: loyal, franc) upright, straight(forward); (opposé à gauche) right, right-hand ▷ adv straight ▷ nm (prérogative) right; (taxe) duty, tax; (: d'inscription) fee; (lois, branche): **le ~** law ▷ nf (Pol) right (wing); **avoir le ~ de** to be allowed to; **avoir ~ à** to be entitled to; **être dans son ~** to be within one's rights; **à ~e** on the right; (direction) (to the) right; **~s d'auteur** royalties; **~s d'inscription** enrolment ou registration fees; **droitier, -ière** adj right-handed

drôle [dʀol] adj (amusant) funny, amusing; (bizarre) funny, peculiar; **un ~ de ...** (bizarre) a strange ou funny ...; (intensif) an incredible ..., a terrific ...

dromadaire [dʀɔmadɛʀ] nm dromedary

du [dy] art voir **de**

dû, due [dy] pp de **devoir** ▷ adj (somme) owing, owed; (causé par): **dû à** due to ▷ nm due

dune [dyn] nf dune

duplex [dyplɛks] nm (appartement) split-level apartment, duplex

duquel [dykɛl] voir **lequel**

dur, e [dyʀ] *adj* (*pierre, siège, travail, problème*) hard; (*lumière, voix, climat*) harsh; (*sévère*) hard, harsh; (*cruel*) hard(-hearted); (*porte, col*) stiff; (*viande*) tough ▷ *adv* hard ▷ *nm* (*fam: meneur*) tough nut; **~ d'oreille** hard of hearing

durant [dyʀɑ̃] *prép* (*au cours de*) during; (*pendant*) for; **des mois ~** for months

durcir [dyʀsiʀ] /2/ *vt, vi* to harden; **se durcir** *vi* to harden

durée [dyʀe] *nf* length; (*d'une pile etc*) life; **de courte ~** (*séjour, répit*) brief

durement [dyʀmɑ̃] *adv* harshly

durer [dyʀe] /1/ *vi* to last

dureté [dyʀte] *nf* hardness; harshness; stiffness; toughness

durit® [dyʀit] *nf* (*car radiator*) hose

duvet [dyvɛ] *nm* down

DVD *sigle m* (= *digital versatile disc*) DVD

dynamique [dinamik] *adj* dynamic; **dynamisme** *nm* dynamism

dynamo [dinamo] *nf* dynamo

dyslexie [dislɛksi] *nf* dyslexia, word blindness

eau, x [o] *nf* water ▷ *nfpl* (*Méd*) waters; **prendre l'~** to leak, let in water; **tomber à l'~** (*fig*) to fall through; **~ de Cologne** eau de Cologne; **~ courante** running water; **~ douce** fresh water; **~ gazeuse** sparkling (mineral) water; **~ de Javel** bleach; **~ minérale** mineral water; **~ plate** still water; **~ salée** salt water; **~ de toilette** toilet water; **eau-de-vie** *nf* brandy

ébène [ebɛn] *nf* ebony; **ébéniste** [ebenist] *nm* cabinetmaker

éblouir [ebluiʀ] /2/ *vt* to dazzle

éboueur [ebwœʀ] *nm* dustman (*BRIT*), garbage man (*US*)

ébouillanter [ebujɑ̃te] /1/ *vt* to scald; (*Culin*) to blanch

éboulement [ebulmɑ̃] *nm* rock fall

ébranler [ebʀɑ̃le] /1/ *vt* to shake; (*rendre instable*) to weaken; **s'ébranler** *vi* (*partir*) to move off

ébullition [ebylisjɔ̃] *nf* boiling point; **en ~** boiling

écaille [ekɑj] nf (de poisson) scale; (matière) tortoiseshell; **écailler** /1/ vt (poisson) to scale; **s'écailler** vi to flake ou peel (off)

écart [ekaʀ] nm gap; **à l'~** out of the way; **à l'~ de** away from; **faire un ~** (voiture) to swerve

écarté, e [ekaʀte] adj (lieu) out-of-the-way, remote; (ouvert): **les jambes ~es** legs apart; **les bras ~s** arms outstretched

écarter [ekaʀte] /1/ vt (séparer) to move apart, separate; (éloigner) to push back, move away; (ouvrir: bras, jambes) to spread, open; (: rideau) to draw (back); (éliminer: candidat, possibilité) to dismiss; **s'écarter** vi to part; (personne) to move away; **s'~ de** to wander from

échafaudage [eʃafodaʒ] nm scaffolding

échalote [eʃalɔt] nf shallot

échange [eʃɑ̃ʒ] nm exchange; **en ~ de** in exchange ou return for; **échanger** /3/ vt: **échanger qch (contre)** to exchange sth (for)

échantillon [eʃɑ̃tijɔ̃] nm sample

échapper [eʃape] /1/: **~ à** vt (gardien) to escape (from); (punition, péril) to escape; **~ à qn** (détail, sens) to escape sb; (objet qu'on tient) to slip out of sb's hands; **laisser ~** (cri etc) to let out; **l'~ belle** to have a narrow escape

écharde [eʃaʀd] nf splinter (of wood)

écharpe [eʃaʀp] nf scarf; **avoir le bras en ~** to have one's arm in a sling

échauffer [eʃofe] /1/ vt (métal, moteur) to overheat; **s'échauffer** vi (Sport) to warm up; (discussion) to become heated

échéance [eʃeɑ̃s] nf (d'un paiement: date) settlement date; (fig) deadline; **à brève/longue ~** in the short/long term

échéant [eʃeɑ̃]: **le cas ~** adv if the case arises

échec [eʃɛk] nm failure; (Échecs): **~ et mat/au roi** checkmate/check;

échecs nmpl (jeu) chess sg; **tenir en ~** to hold in check

échelle [eʃɛl] nf ladder; (fig, d'une carte) scale

échelon [eʃ(ə)lɔ̃] nm (d'échelle) rung; (Admin) grade; **échelonner** /1/ vt to space out, spread out

échiquier [eʃikje] nm chessboard

écho [eko] nm echo; **échographie** nf: **passer une échographie** to have a scan

échouer [eʃwe] /1/ vi to fail; **s'échouer** vi to run aground

éclabousser [eklabuse] /1/ vt to splash

éclair [eklɛʀ] nm (d'orage) flash of lightning, lightning no pl; (gâteau) éclair

éclairage [eklɛʀaʒ] nm lighting

éclaircie [eklɛʀsi] nf bright ou sunny interval

éclaircir [eklɛʀsiʀ] /2/ vt to lighten; (fig: mystère) to clear up; (point) to clarify; **s'éclaircir** vi (ciel) to brighten up; **s'~ la voix** to clear one's throat; **éclaircissement** nm clarification

éclairer [eklɛʀe] /1/ vt (lieu) to light (up); (personne: avec une lampe de poche etc) to light the way for; (fig: rendre compréhensible) to shed light on ▷ vi: **~ mal/bien** to give a poor/good light; **s'~ à la bougie/l'électricité** to use candlelight/have electric lighting

éclat [ekla] nm (de bombe, de verre) fragment; (du soleil, d'une couleur etc) brightness, brilliance; (d'une cérémonie) splendour; (scandale): **faire un ~** to cause a commotion; **~ de rire** burst ou roar of laughter; **~ de voix** shout

éclatant, e [eklatɑ̃, -ɑ̃t] adj brilliant

éclater [eklate] /1/ vi (pneu) to burst; (bombe) to explode; (guerre, épidémie) to break out; (groupe, parti) to break up; **~ de rire/en sanglots** to burst out laughing/sobbing

écluse [eklyz] nf lock

écœurant, e [ekœʀɑ̃, -ɑ̃t] adj sickening; (gâteau etc) sickly

écœurer [ekœʀe] vt: **~ qn** (nourriture) to make sb feel sick; (fig: conduite, personne) to disgust sb

école [ekɔl] nf school; **aller à l'~** to go to school; **~ maternelle** nursery school; **~ primaire** primary (BRIT) ou grade (US) school; **~ secondaire** secondary (BRIT) ou high (US) school; **écolier, -ière** nm/f schoolboy/girl

écologie [ekɔlɔʒi] nf ecology; **écologique** adj environment-friendly; **écologiste** nm/f ecologist

économe [ekɔnɔm] adj thrifty ▷ nm/f (de lycée etc) bursar (BRIT), treasurer (US)

économie [ekɔnɔmi] nf economy; (gain: d'argent, de temps etc) saving; (science) economics sg; **économies** nfpl (pécule) savings; **économique** adj (avantageux) economical; (Écon) economic; **économiser** /1/ vt, vi to save

écorce [ekɔʀs] nf bark; (de fruit) peel

écorcher [ekɔʀʃe] /1/ vt: **s'~ le genou** etc to scrape ou graze one's knee etc; **écorchure** nf graze

écossais, e [ekɔsɛ, -ɛz] adj Scottish ▷ nm/f: **É~, e** Scot

Écosse [ekɔs] nf: **l'~** Scotland

écotaxe [ekɔtaks] nf green tax

écouter [ekute] /1/ vt to listen to; **s'écouter** vi (malade) to be a bit of a hypochondriac; **si je m'écoutais** if I followed my instincts; **écouteur** nm (Tél) receiver; **écouteurs** nmpl (casque) headphones, headset sg

écran [ekʀɑ̃] nm screen; **le petit ~** television; **~ tactile** touchscreen; **~ total** sunblock

écrasant, e [ekʀɑzɑ̃, -ɑ̃t] adj overwhelming

écraser [ekʀɑze] /1/ vt to crush; (piéton) to run over; **s'~ (au sol)** vi to crash; **s'~ contre** to crash into

écrémé, e [ekʀeme] adj (lait) skimmed

écrevisse [ekʀəvis] nf crayfish inv

écrire [ekʀiʀ] /39/ vt, vi to write; **s'écrire** vi to write to one another;

ça s'écrit comment? how is it spelt?; **écrit** nm (examen) written paper; **par écrit** in writing

écriteau, x [ekʀito] nm notice, sign

écriture [ekʀityʀ] nf writing; **écritures** nfpl (Comm) accounts, books; **l'É~ (sainte)** the É~s the Scriptures

écrivain [ekʀivɛ̃] nm the writer

écrou [ekʀu] nm nut

écrouler [ekʀule] /1/: **s'écrouler** vi to collapse

écru, e [ekʀy] adj off-white, écru

écume [ekym] nf foam

écureuil [ekyʀœj] nm squirrel

écurie [ekyʀi] nf stable

eczéma [ɛgzema] nm eczema

EDF sigle f (= Électricité de France) national electricity company

Édimbourg [edɛ̃buʀ] n Edinburgh

éditer [edite] /1/ vt (publier) to publish; (annoter) to edit; **éditeur, -trice** nm/f publisher; **édition** nf edition; **l'édition** publishing

édredon [edʀədɔ̃] nm eiderdown

éducateur, -trice [edykatœʀ, -tʀis] nm/f teacher; (en école spécialisée) instructor

éducatif, -ive [edykatif, -iv] adj educational

éducation [edykasjɔ̃] nf education; (familiale) upbringing; (manières) (good) manners pl

édulcorant [edylkɔʀɑ̃] nm sweetener

éduquer [edyke] /1/ vt to educate; (élever) to bring up

effacer [efase] /3/ vt to erase, rub out; **s'effacer** vi (inscription etc) to wear off; (pour laisser passer) to step aside

effarant, e [efaʀɑ̃, -ɑ̃t] adj alarming

effectif, -ive [efɛktif, -iv] adj real ▷ nm (Scol) total number of pupils; (Comm) manpower sg; **effectivement** adv (réellement) actually, really; (en effet) indeed

effectuer [efɛktɥe] /1/ vt (opération, mission) to carry out; (déplacement, trajet) to make

effervescent, e [efɛʀvesã, -ãt] *adj*
effervescent

effet [efɛ] *nm* effect; (*impression*)
impression; **effets** *nmpl* (*vêtements
etc*) things; **faire ~** (*médicament*) to
take effect; **faire de l'~** (*impressionner*)
to make an impression; **faire bon/
mauvais ~ sur qn** to make a good/
bad impression on sb; **en ~** indeed;
~ de serre greenhouse effect

efficace [efikas] *adj* (*personne*)
efficient; (*action, médicament*)
effective; **efficacité** *nf* efficiency;
effectiveness

effondrer [efɔ̃dʀe] /1/: **s'effondrer**
vi to collapse

efforcer [efɔʀse] /3/: **s'efforcer de**
vt: **s'~ de faire** to try hard to do

effort [efɔʀ] *nm* effort

effrayant, e [efʀejã, -ãt] *adj*
frightening

effrayer [efʀeje] /8/ *vt* to frighten,
scare; **s'effrayer (de)** to be
frightened *ou* scared (by)

effréné, e [efʀene] *adj* wild

effronté, e [efʀɔ̃te] *adj* insolent

effroyable [efʀwajabl] *adj*
horrifying, appalling

égal, e, -aux [egal, -o] *adj* equal;
(*constant: vitesse*) steady ▷ *nm/f*
equal; **être ~ à** (*prix, nombre*) to
be equal to; **ça m'est ~** it's all the
same to me, I don't mind; **sans ~**
matchless, unequalled; **d'~ à ~** as
equals; **également** *adv* equally;
(*aussi*) too, as well; **égaler** /1/ *vt* to
equal; **égaliser** /1/ *vt* (*sol, salaires*)
to level (out); (*chances*) to equalize
▷ *vi* (*Sport*) to equalize; **égalité** *nf*
equality; **être à égalité (de points)**
to be level

égard [egaʀ] *nm*: **égards** *nmpl*
consideration *sg*; **à cet ~** in
this respect; **par ~ pour** out of
consideration for; **à l'~ de** towards

égarer [egaʀe] /1/ *vt* to mislay;
s'égarer *vi* to get lost, lose one's way;
(*objet*) to go astray

églefin [egləfɛ̃] *nm* haddock

église [egliz] *nf* church; **aller à l'~** to
go to church

égoïsme [egɔism] *nm* selfishness;
égoïste *adj* selfish

égout [egu] *nm* sewer

égoutter [egute] /1/ *vi* to drip;
s'égoutter *vi* to drip; **égouttoir** *nm*
draining board; (*mobile*) draining
rack

égratignure [egʀatiɲyʀ] *nf* scratch

Égypte [eʒipt] *nf*: **l'~** Egypt;
égyptien, ne *adj* Egyptian ▷ *nm/f*:
Égyptien, ne Egyptian

eh [e] *excl* hey!; **eh bien** well

élaborer [elabɔʀe] /1/ *vt* to
elaborate; (*projet, stratégie*) to work
out; (*rapport*) to draft

élan [elã] *nm* (*Zool*) elk, moose; (*Sport*)
run up; (*fig: de tendresse etc*) surge;
prendre son ~/de l'~ to take a run
up/gather speed

élancer [elãse] /3/: **s'élancer** *vi* to
dash, hurl o.s.

élargir [elaʀʒiʀ] /2/ *vt* to widen;
s'élargir *vi* to widen; (*vêtement*) to
stretch

élastique [elastik] *adj* elastic ▷ *nm*
(*de bureau*) rubber band; (*pour la
couture*) elastic *no pl*

élection [elɛksjɔ̃] *nf* election

électricien, ne [elɛktʀisjɛ̃, -ɛn]
nm/f electrician

électricité [elɛktʀisite] *nf*
electricity; **allumer/éteindre l'~** to
put on/off the light

électrique [elɛktʀik] *adj*
electric(al)

électrocuter [elɛktʀɔkyte] /1/ *vt* to
electrocute

électroménager [elɛktʀomenaʒe]
adj: **appareils ~s** domestic
(electrical) appliances ▷ *nm*: **l'~**
household appliances

électronique [elɛktʀɔnik] *adj*
electronic ▷ *nf* electronics *sg*

élégance [elegãs] *nf* elegance

élégant, e [elegã, -ãt] *adj* elegant

élément [elemɑ̃] nm element; (pièce) component, part; **élémentaire** adj elementary

éléphant [elefɑ̃] nm elephant

élevage [el(ə)vaʒ] nm breeding; (de bovins) cattle breeding ou rearing; **truite d'~** farmed trout

élevé, e [el(ə)ve] adj high; **bien/mal ~** well-/ill-mannered

élève [elɛv] nm/f pupil

élever [el(ə)ve] /5/ vt (enfant) to bring up, raise; (bétail, volaille) to breed; (hausser: taux, niveau) to raise; (édifier: monument) to put up, erect; **s'élever** vi (avion, alpiniste) to go up; (niveau, température, aussi) to rise; **s'~ à** (frais, dégâts) to amount to, add up to; **s'~ contre** to rise up against; **~ la voix** to raise one's voice; **éleveur, -euse** nm/f stock breeder

éliminatoire [eliminatwaʀ] nf (Sport) heat

éliminer [elimine] /1/ vt to eliminate

élire [eliʀ] /43/ vt to elect

elle [ɛl] pron (sujet) she; (: chose) it; (complément) her; it; **~s** (sujet) they; (complément) them; **~-même** herself; itself; **~s-mêmes** themselves; voir **il**

éloigné, e [elwaɲe] adj distant, far-off; (parent) distant

éloigner [elwaɲe] /1/ vt (échéance) to put off, postpone; (soupçons, danger) to ward off; **~ qch (de)** to move ou take sth away (from); **s'éloigner (de)** (personne) to go away (from); (véhicule) to move away (from); (affectivement) to become estranged (from); **~ qn (de)** to take sb away ou remove sb (from)

élu, e [ely] pp de **élire** ▷ nm/f (Pol) elected representative

Élysée [elize] nm: **(le palais de) l'~** the Élysée palace

émail, -aux [emaj, -o] nm enamel

e-mail [imɛl] nm email; **envoyer qch par ~** to email sth

émanciper [emɑ̃sipe] /1/: **s'émanciper** vi (fig) to become emancipated ou liberated

emballage [ɑ̃balaʒ] nm (papier) wrapping; (carton) packaging

emballer [ɑ̃bale] /1/ vt to wrap (up); (dans un carton) to pack (up); (fig: fam) to thrill (to bits); **s'emballer** vi (moteur) to race; (cheval) to bolt; (fig: personne) to get carried away

embarcadère [ɑ̃baʀkadɛʀ] nm landing stage (BRIT), pier

embarquement [ɑ̃baʀkəmɑ̃] nm embarkation; (de marchandises) loading; (de passagers) boarding

embarquer [ɑ̃baʀke] /1/ vt (personne) to embark; (marchandise) to load; (fam) to cart off ▷ vi (passager) to board; **s'embarquer** vi to board; **s'~ dans** (affaire, aventure) to embark upon

embarras [ɑ̃baʀa] nm (confusion) embarrassment; **être dans l'~** to be in a predicament ou an awkward position; **vous n'avez que l'~ du choix** the only problem is choosing

embarrassant, e [ɑ̃baʀasɑ̃, -ɑ̃t] adj embarrassing

embarrasser [ɑ̃baʀase] /1/ vt (encombrer) to clutter (up); (gêner) to hinder, hamper; to put in an awkward position; **s'embarrasser de** to burden o.s. with

embaucher [ɑ̃boʃe] /1/ vt to take on, hire

embêtant, e [ɑ̃bɛtɑ̃, -ɑ̃t] adj annoying

embêter [ɑ̃bɛte] /1/ vt to bother; **s'embêter** vi (s'ennuyer) to be bored

emblée [ɑ̃ble]: **d'~** adv straightaway

embouchure [ɑ̃buʃyʀ] nf (Géo) mouth

embourber [ɑ̃buʀbe] /1/: **s'embourber** vi to get stuck in the mud

embouteillage [ɑ̃butɛjaʒ] nm traffic jam, (traffic) holdup (BRIT)

embranchement [ɑ̃bʀɑ̃ʃmɑ̃] nm
(routier) junction

embrasser [ɑ̃bʀase] /1/ vt to kiss;
(sujet, période) to embrace, encompass

embrayage [ɑ̃bʀejaʒ] nm clutch

embrouiller [ɑ̃bʀuje] /1/ vt (fils) to
tangle (up); (fiches, idées, personne) to
muddle up; **s'embrouiller** vi to get
in a muddle

embruns [ɑ̃bʀœ̃] nmpl sea spray sg

embué, e [ɑ̃bɥe] adj misted up

émeraude [em(ə)ʀod] nf emerald

émerger [emɛʀʒe] /3/ vi to emerge;
(faire saillie, aussi fig) to stand out

émeri [em(ə)ʀi] nm: **toile** ou **papier**
~ emery paper

émerveiller [emɛʀveje] /1/ vt to
fill with wonder; **s'émerveiller de**
to marvel at

émettre [emɛtʀ] /56/ vt (son, lumière)
to give out, emit; (message etc: Radio)
to transmit; (billet, timbre, emprunt,
chèque) to issue; (hypothèse, avis) to
voice, put forward ▷ vi to broadcast

émeus etc [emø] vb voir **émouvoir**

émeute [emøt] nf riot

émigrer [emigʀe] /1/ vi to emigrate

émincer [emɛ̃se] /3/ vt to slice thinly

émission [emisjɔ̃] nf (voir
émettre) emission; (d'un message)
transmission; (de billet, timbre,
emprunt, chèque) issue; (Radio, TV)
programme, broadcast

emmêler [ɑ̃mele] /1/ vt to tangle
(up); (fig) to muddle up; **s'emmêler** vi
to get into a tangle

emménager [ɑ̃menaʒe] /3/ vi to
move in; **~ dans** to move into

emmener [ɑ̃m(ə)ne] /5/ vt to take
(with one); (comme otage, capture) to
take away; **~ qn au cinéma** to take
sb to the cinema

emmerder [ɑ̃mɛʀde] /1/ (!) vt to
bug, bother; **s'emmerder** vi to be
bored stiff

émoticone [emɔticon] nm smiley

émotif, -ive [emɔtif, -iv] adj emotional

émotion [emosjɔ̃] nf emotion

émouvoir [emuvwaʀ] /27/ vt to
move; **s'émouvoir** vi to be moved;
to be roused

empaqueter [ɑ̃pakte] /4/ vt to
pack up

emparer [ɑ̃paʀe] /1/: **s'emparer de**
vt (objet) to seize, grab; (comme otage,
Mil) to seize; (peur etc) to take hold of

empêchement [ɑ̃pɛʃmɑ̃] nm
(unexpected) obstacle, hitch

empêcher [ɑ̃peʃe] /1/ vt to prevent;
~ qn de faire to prevent ou stop sb
(from) doing; **il n'empêche que**
nevertheless; **il n'a pas pu s'~ de rire**
he couldn't help laughing

empereur [ɑ̃pʀœʀ] nm emperor

empiffrer [ɑ̃pifʀe] /1/: **s'empiffrer** vi
(péj) to stuff o.s.

empiler [ɑ̃pile] /1/ vt to pile (up)

empire [ɑ̃piʀ] nm empire; (fig)
influence

empirer [ɑ̃piʀe] /1/ vi to worsen,
deteriorate

emplacement [ɑ̃plasmɑ̃] nm site

emploi [ɑ̃plwa] nm use; (poste) job,
situation; (Comm, Écon) employment;
mode d'~ directions for use; **~ du**
temps timetable, schedule

employé, e [ɑ̃plwaje] nm/f
employee; **~ de bureau/banque**
office/bank employee ou clerk

employer [ɑ̃plwaje] /8/ vt to use;
(ouvrier, main-d'œuvre) to employ; **s'~**
à qch/à faire to apply ou devote o.s.
to sth/to doing; **employeur, -euse**
nm/f employer

empoigner [ɑ̃pwaɲe] /1/ vt to grab

empoisonner [ɑ̃pwazɔne] /1/ vt to
poison; (empester: air, pièce) to stink
out; (fam): **~ qn** to drive sb mad

emporter [ɑ̃pɔʀte] /1/ vt to take
(with one); (en dérobant ou enlevant,
emmener: blessés, voyageurs) to take
away; (entraîner) to carry away ou
along; (rivière, vent) to carry away;
s'emporter vi (de colère) to fly into a
rage; **l'~ (sur)** to get the upper hand
(of); **plats à ~** take-away meals

empreint, e [ɑ̃pRɛ̃, -ɛ̃t] *adj*: **~ de** marked with ▷ *nf* (*de pied, main*) print; **~e (digitale)** fingerprint; **~e écologique** carbon footprint

empressé, e [ɑ̃prese] *adj* attentive

empresser [ɑ̃prese] /1/: **s'empresser** *vi*: **s'~ auprès de qn** to surround sb with attentions; **s'~ de faire** to hasten to do

emprisonner [ɑ̃prizɔne] /1/ *vt* to imprison

emprunt [ɑ̃prœ̃] *nm* loan (*from debtor's point of view*)

emprunter [ɑ̃prœ̃te] /1/ *vt* to borrow; (*itinéraire*) to take, follow

ému, e [emy] *pp de* **émouvoir** ▷ *adj* (*gratitude*) touched; (*compassion*) moved

○ MOT-CLÉ

en [ɑ̃] *prép* **1** (*endroit, pays*) in; (: *direction*) to; **habiter en France/ ville** to live in France/town; **aller en France/ville** to go to France/town
2 (*moment, temps*) in; **en été/juin** in summer/June; **en 3 jours/20 ans** in 3 days/20 years
3 (*moyen*) by; **en avion/taxi** by plane/taxi
4 (*composition*) made of; **c'est en verre/coton/laine** it's (made of) glass/cotton/wool; **un collier en argent** a silver necklace
5 (*description, état*): **une femme (habillée) en rouge** a woman (dressed) in red; **peindre qch en rouge** to paint sth red; **en T/étoile** T-/star-shaped; **en chemise/chaussettes** in one's shirt sleeves/socks; **en soldat** as a soldier; **cassé en plusieurs morceaux** broken into several pieces; **en réparation** being repaired, under repair; **en vacances** on holiday; **en deuil** in mourning; **le même en plus grand** the same but *ou* only bigger
6 (*avec gérondif*) while; on; **en dormant** while sleeping, as one

sleeps; **en sortant** on going out, as he *etc* went out; **sortir en courant** to run out
7: **en tant que** as; **je te parle en ami** I'm talking to you as a friend
▶ *pron* **1** (*indéfini*): **j'en ai/veux** I have/want some; **en as-tu?** have you got any?; **je n'en veux pas** I don't want any; **j'en ai deux** I've got two; **combien y en a-t-il?** how many (of them) are there?; **j'en ai assez** I've got enough (of it *ou* them); (*j'en ai marre*) I've had enough
2 (*provenance*) from there; **j'en viens** I've come from there
3 (*cause*): **il en est malade/perd le sommeil** he is ill/can't sleep because of it
4 (*complément de nom, d'adjectif, de verbe*): **j'en connais les dangers** I know its *ou* the dangers; **j'en suis fier/ai besoin** I am proud of it/need it

encadrer [ɑ̃kɑdRe] /1/ *vt* (*tableau, image*) to frame; (*fig: entourer*) to surround; (*personnel, soldats etc*) to train

encaisser [ɑ̃kese] /1/ *vt* (*chèque*) to cash; (*argent*) to collect; (*fig: coup, défaite*) to take

en-cas [ɑ̃ka] *nm inv* snack

enceinte [ɑ̃sɛ̃t] *adj f*: **~ (de six mois)** (six months) pregnant ▷ *nf* (*mur*) wall; (*espace*) enclosure; **~ (acoustique)** speaker

encens [ɑ̃sɑ̃] *nm* incense

encercler [ɑ̃sɛRkle] /1/ *vt* to surround

enchaîner [ɑ̃ʃene] /1/ *vt* to chain up; (*mouvements, séquences*) to link (together) ▷ *vi* to carry on

enchanté, e [ɑ̃ʃɑ̃te] *adj* (*ravi*) delighted; (*ensorcelé*) enchanted; **~ (de faire votre connaissance)** pleased to meet you

enchère [ɑ̃ʃɛR] *nf* bid; **mettre/ vendre aux ~s** to put up for (sale by)/ sell by auction

enclencher [āklāʒe] /1/ vt
(*mécanisme*) to engage; **s'enclencher**
vi to engage

encombrant, e [ākɔ̄brā, -āt] adj
cumbersome, bulky

encombrement [ākɔ̄brəmā] nm:
être pris dans un ~ to be stuck in a
traffic jam

encombrer [ākɔ̄bre] /1/ vt to clutter
(up); (*gêner*) to hamper; **s'encombrer
de** (*bagages etc*) to load ou burden
o.s. with

 MOT-CLÉ

encore [ākɔʀ] adv **1** (*continuation*)
still; **il y travaille encore** he's still
working on it; **pas encore** not yet
2 (*de nouveau*) again; **j'irai encore
demain** I'll go again tomorrow;
encore une fois (once) again
3 (*en plus*) more; **encore un peu de
viande?** a little more meat?; **encore
deux jours** two more days
4 (*intensif*) even, still; **encore plus
fort/mieux** even louder/better,
louder/better still; **quoi encore?**
what now?
5 (*restriction*) even so ou then, only;
encore pourrais-je le faire si …
even so, I might be able to do it if …; **si
encore** if only

encourager [ākuraʒe] /3/ vt to
encourage; **~ qn à faire qch** to
encourage sb to do sth

encourir [ākuriʀ] /11/ vt to incur

encre [ākʀ] nf ink; **~ de Chine**
Indian ink

encyclopédie [āsiklɔpedi] nf
encyclopaedia

endetter [ādete] /1/: **s'endetter** vi to
get into debt

endive [ādiv] nf chicory no pl

endormi, e [ādɔʀmi] adj asleep

endormir [ādɔʀmiʀ] /16/ vt to put
to sleep; (*chaleur etc*) to send to sleep;
(*Méd: dent, nerf*) to anaesthetize; (*fig:

soupçons*) to allay; **s'endormir** vi to
fall asleep, go to sleep

endroit [ādʀwa] nm place; (*opposé à
l'envers*) right side; **à l'~** (*vêtement*) the
right way out; (*objet posé*) the right
way round

endurance [ādyrās] nf endurance

endurant, e [ādyrā, -āt] adj tough,
hardy

endurcir [ādyrsiʀ] /2/: **s'endurcir**
vi (*physiquement*) to become tougher;
(*moralement*) to become hardened

endurer [ādyre] /1/ vt to endure,
bear

énergétique [enɛʀʒetik] adj
(*aliment*) energizing

énergie [enɛʀʒi] nf (*Physique*) energy;
(*Tech*) power; (*morale*) vigour, spirit;
énergique adj energetic; vigorous;
(*mesures*) drastic, stringent

énervant, e [enɛʀvā, -āt] adj
irritating, annoying

énerver [enɛʀve] /1/ vt to irritate,
annoy; **s'énerver** vi to get excited,
get worked up

enfance [āfās] nf childhood

enfant [āfā] nm/f child; **enfantin, e**
adj childlike; (*langage*) children's cpd

enfer [āfɛʀ] nm hell

enfermer [āfɛʀme] /1/ vt to shut up;
(*à clef, interner*) to lock up; **s'enfermer**
to shut o.s. away

enfiler [āfile] /1/ vt (*vêtement*) to
slip on; (*perles*) to string; (*aiguille*) to
thread; **~ un tee-shirt** to slip into
a T-shirt

enfin [āfɛ̄] adv at last; (*en énumérant*)
lastly; (*de restriction, résignation*) still;
(*pour conclure*) in a word; (*somme
toute*) after all

enflammer [āflame] /1/:
s'enflammer vi to catch fire; (*Méd*) to
become inflamed

enflé, e [āfle] adj swollen

enfler [āfle] /1/ vi to swell (up)

enfoncer [āfɔ̄se] /3/ vt (*clou*) to drive
in; (*faire pénétrer*) **~ qch dans** to push
(*ou* drive) sth into; (*forcer: porte*) to

break open; **s'enfoncer** vi to sink; **s'~ dans** to sink into; (forêt, ville) to disappear into

enfouir [ɑ̃fwiʀ] /2/ vt (dans le sol) to bury; (dans un tiroir etc) to tuck away

enfuir [ɑ̃fɥiʀ] /17/: **s'enfuir** vi to run away ou off

engagement [ɑ̃gaʒmɑ̃] nm commitment; **sans ~** without obligation

engager [ɑ̃gaʒe] /3/ vt (embaucher) to take on; (: artiste) to engage; (commencer) to start; (lier) to bind, commit; (impliquer, entraîner) to involve; (investir) to invest, lay out; (introduire, clé) to insert; (inciter): **~ qn à faire** to urge sb to do; **s'engager** vi (Mil) to enlist; (promettre) to commit o.s.; (débuter: conversation etc) to start (up); **s'~ à faire** to undertake to do; **s'~ dans** (rue, passage) to turn into; (fig: affaire, discussion) to enter into, embark on

engelures [ɑ̃ʒlyʀ] nfpl chilblains

engin [ɑ̃ʒɛ̃] nm machine; (outil) instrument; (Auto) vehicle; (Aviat) aircraft inv

⬛ Attention à ne pas traduire engin par le mot anglais engine.

engloutir [ɑ̃glutiʀ] /2/ vt to swallow up

engouement [ɑ̃gumɑ̃] nm (sudden) passion

engouffrer [ɑ̃gufʀe] /1/ vt to swallow up, devour; **s'engouffrer dans** to rush into

engourdir [ɑ̃guʀdiʀ] /2/ vt to numb; (fig) to dull, blunt; **s'engourdir** vi to go numb

engrais [ɑ̃gʀɛ] nm manure; **~ (chimique)** (chemical) fertilizer

engraisser [ɑ̃gʀese] /1/ vt to fatten (up)

engrenage [ɑ̃gʀənaʒ] nm gears pl, gearing; (fig) chain

engueuler [ɑ̃gœle] /1/ vt (fam) to bawl at ou out

enhardir [ɑ̃aʀdiʀ] /2/: **s'enhardir** vi to grow bolder

énigme [enigm] nf riddle

enivrer [ɑ̃nivʀe] /1/ vt: **s'enivrer** to get drunk

enjamber [ɑ̃ʒɑ̃be] /1/ vt to stride over

enjeu, x [ɑ̃ʒø] nm stakes pl

enjoué, e [ɑ̃ʒwe] adj playful

enlaidir [ɑ̃lediʀ] /2/ vt to make ugly ▷ vi to become ugly

enlèvement [ɑ̃lɛvmɑ̃] nm (rapt) abduction, kidnapping

enlever [ɑ̃l(ə)ve] /5/ vt (ôter: gén) to remove; (: vêtement, lunettes) to take off; (emporter: ordures etc) to collect; (kidnapper) to abduct, kidnap; (obtenir: prix, contrat) to win; (prendre): **~ qch à qn** to take sth (away) from sb

enliser [ɑ̃lize] /1/: **s'enliser** vi to sink, get stuck

enneigé, e [ɑ̃neʒe] adj snowy

ennemi, e [ɛnmi] adj hostile; (Mil) enemy cpd ▷ nm/f enemy

ennui [ɑ̃nɥi] nm (lassitude) boredom; (difficulté) trouble no pl; **avoir des ~s** to have problems; **ennuyer** /8/ vt to bother; (lasser) to bore; **s'ennuyer** vi to be bored; **si cela ne vous ennuie pas** if it's no trouble to you; **ennuyeux, -euse** adj boring, tedious; (agaçant) annoying

énorme [enɔʀm] adj enormous, huge; **énormément** adv enormously; **énormément de neige/gens** an enormous amount of snow/number of people

enquête [ɑ̃kɛt] nf (de journaliste, de police) investigation; (judiciaire, administrative) inquiry; (sondage d'opinion) survey; **enquêter** /1/ vi to investigate; **enquêter (sur)** to do a survey (on)

enragé, e [ɑ̃ʀaʒe] adj (Méd) rabid, with rabies; (fig) fanatical

enrageant, e [ɑ̃ʀaʒɑ̃, -ɑ̃t] adj infuriating

enrager [ɑ̃ʀaʒe] /3/ vi to be furious

enregistrement [ɑ̃ʀ(ə)ʒistʀəmɑ̃] nm recording; **~ des bagages** baggage check-in

e

enregistrer [ãʀ(ə)ʒistʀe] /1/ vt (Mus) to record; (fig: mémoriser) to make a mental note of; (bagages: à l'aéroport) to check in

enrhumer [ãʀyme] /1/: **s'enrhumer** vi to catch a cold

enrichir [ãʀiʃiʀ] /2/ vt to make rich(er); (fig) to enrich; **s'enrichir** vi to get rich(er)

enrouer [ãʀwe] /1/: **s'enrouer** vi to go hoarse

enrouler [ãʀule] /1/ vt (fil, corde) to wind (up); **s'enrouler** to coil up; **~ qch autour de** to wind sth (a)round

enseignant, e [ãsɛɲã, -ãt] nm/f teacher

enseignement [ãsɛɲ(ə)mã] nm teaching; (Admin) education

enseigner [ãseɲe] /1/ vt, vi to teach; **~ qch à qn/à qn que** to teach sb sth/sb that

ensemble [ãsãbl] adv together ▷ nm (assemblage) set; (vêtements) outfit; (unité, harmonie) unity; **l'~ du/de la** (totalité) the whole ou entire; **impression/idée d'~** overall ou general impression/idea; **dans l'~** (en gros) on the whole

ensoleillé, e [ãsɔleje] adj sunny

ensuite [ãsɥit] adv then, next; (plus tard) afterwards, later

entamer [ãtame] /1/ vt (pain, bouteille) to start; (hostilités, pourparlers) to open

entasser [ãtase] /1/ vt (empiler) to pile up, heap up; **s'entasser** vi (s'amonceler) to pile up; **s'~ dans** to cram into

entendre [ãtãdʀ] /41/ vt to hear; (comprendre) to understand; (vouloir dire) to mean; **s'entendre** vi (sympathiser) to get on; (se mettre d'accord) to agree; **j'ai entendu dire que** I've heard (it said) that; **~ parler de** to hear of

entendu, e [ãtãdy] adj (réglé) agreed; (au courant: air) knowing; **(c'est) ~** all right, agreed; **bien ~** of course

entente [ãtãt] nf understanding; (accord, traité) agreement; **à double ~** (sens) with a double meaning

enterrement [ãtɛʀmã] nm (cérémonie) funeral, burial

enterrer [ãteʀe] /1/ vt to bury

entêtant, e [ãtɛtã, -ãt] adj heady

en-tête [ãtɛt] nm heading; **papier à ~** headed notepaper

entêté, e [ãtete] adj stubborn

entêter [ãtete] /1/: **s'~ (à faire)** to persist (in doing)

enthousiasme [ãtuzjasm] nm enthusiasm; **enthousiasmer** /1/ vt to fill with enthusiasm; **s'enthousiasmer (pour qch)** to get enthusiastic (about sth); **enthousiaste** adj enthusiastic

entier, -ière [ãtje, -jɛʀ] adj whole; (total, complet: satisfaction etc) complete; (fig: caractère) unbending ▷ nm (Math) whole; **en ~** totally; **lait ~** full-cream milk; **entièrement** adv entirely, wholly

entonnoir [ãtɔnwaʀ] nm funnel

entorse [ãtɔʀs] nf (Méd) sprain; (fig): **~ à la loi/au règlement** infringement of the law/rule

entourage [ãtuʀaʒ] nm circle; (famille) family (circle); (ce qui enclôt) surround

entourer [ãtuʀe] /1/ vt to surround; (apporter son soutien à) to rally round; **~ de** to surround with; **s'entourer de** to surround o.s. with

entracte [ãtʀakt] nm interval

entraide [ãtʀɛd] nf mutual aid ou assistance

entrain [ãtʀɛ̃] nm spirit; **avec ~** energetically; **faire qch sans ~** to do sth half-heartedly ou without enthusiasm

entraînement [ãtʀɛnmã] nm training

entraîner [ãtʀene] /1/ vt (charrier) to carry ou drag along; (Tech) to drive; (emmener: personne) to take (off); (mener à l'assaut, influencer) to lead;

(*Sport*) to train; (*impliquer*) to entail; **~ qn à faire** (*inciter*) to lead sb to do; **s'entraîner** *vi* (*Sport*) to train; **s'~ à qch/à faire** to train o.s. for sth/to do; **entraîneur** *nm/f* (*Sport*) coach, trainer ▷ *nm* (*Hippisme*) trainer

entre [ɑ̃tʀ] *prép* between; (*parmi*) among(st); **l'un d'~ eux/nous** one of them/us; **~ autres (choses)** among other things; **ils se battent ~ eux** they are fighting among(st) themselves; **entrecôte** *nf* entrecôte *ou* rib steak

entrée [ɑ̃tʀe] *nf* entrance; (*accès: au cinéma etc*) admission; (*billet*) (admission) ticket; (*Culin*) first course

entre: entrefilet *nm* (*article*) paragraph, short report; **entremets** *nm* (cream) dessert

entrepôt [ɑ̃tʀəpo] *nm* warehouse

entreprendre [ɑ̃tʀəpʀɑ̃dʀ] /58/ *vt* (*se lancer dans*) to undertake; (*commencer*) to begin *ou* start (upon)

entrepreneur, -euse [ɑ̃tʀəpʀənœʀ, -øz] *nm/f*: **~ (en bâtiment)** (building) contractor

entrepris, e [ɑ̃tʀəpʀi, -iz] *pp de* **entreprendre** ▷ *nf* (*société*) firm, business; (*action*) undertaking, venture

entrer [ɑ̃tʀe] /1/ *vi* to go (*ou* come) in, enter ▷ *vt* (*Inform*) to input, enter; **~ dans** (*gén*) to enter; (*pièce*) to go (*ou* come) into, enter; (*club*) to join; (*heurter*) to run into; **(faire) ~ qch dans** to get sth into; **~ à l'hôpital** to go into hospital; **faire ~** (*visiteur*) to show in

entre-temps [ɑ̃tʀətɑ̃] *adv* meanwhile

entretenir [ɑ̃tʀət(ə)niʀ] /22/ *vt* to maintain; (*famille, maîtresse*) to support, keep; **~ qn (de)** to speak to sb (about)

entretien [ɑ̃tʀətjɛ̃] *nm* maintenance; (*discussion*) discussion, talk; (*pour un emploi*) interview

entrevoir [ɑ̃tʀəvwaʀ] /30/ *vt* (*à peine*) to make out; (*brièvement*) to catch a glimpse of

entrevu, e [ɑ̃tʀəvy] *pp de* **entrevoir** ▷ *nf* (*audience*) interview

entrouvert, e [ɑ̃tʀuvɛʀ, -ɛʀt] *adj* half-open

énumérer [enymeʀe] /6/ *vt* to list

envahir [ɑ̃vaiʀ] /2/ *vt* to invade; (*inquiétude, peur*) to come over; **envahissant, e** *adj* (*péj: personne*) intrusive

enveloppe [ɑ̃v(ə)lɔp] *nf* (*de lettre*) envelope; (*crédits*) budget; **envelopper** /1/ *vt* to wrap; (*fig*) to envelop, shroud

enverrai *etc* [ɑ̃veʀe] *vb voir* **envoyer**

envers [ɑ̃vɛʀ] *prép* towards, to ▷ *nm* other side; (*d'une étoffe*) wrong side; **à l'~** (*verticalement*) upside down; (*pull*) back to front; (*vêtement*) inside out

envie [ɑ̃vi] *nf* (*sentiment*) envy; (*souhait*) desire, wish; **avoir ~ de** to feel like; (*désir plus fort*) to want; **avoir ~ de faire** to feel like doing; to want to do; **avoir ~ que** to wish that; **cette glace me fait ~** I fancy some of that ice cream; **envier** /7/ *vt* to envy; **envieux, -euse** *adj* envious

environ [ɑ̃viʀɔ̃] *adv*: **~ 3 h/2 km** (around) about 3 o'clock/2 km; *voir aussi* **environs**

environnant, e [ɑ̃viʀɔnɑ̃, -ɑ̃t] *adj* surrounding

environnement [ɑ̃viʀɔnmɑ̃] *nm* environment

environs [ɑ̃viʀɔ̃] *nmpl* surroundings; **aux ~ de** around

envisager [ɑ̃vizaʒe] /3/ *vt* to contemplate; (*avoir en vue*) to envisage; **~ de faire** to consider doing

envoler [ɑ̃vɔle] /1/: **s'envoler** *vi* (*oiseau*) to fly away *ou* off; (*avion*) to take off; (*papier, feuille*) to blow away; (*fig*) to vanish (into thin air)

envoyé, e [ɑ̃vwaje] *nm/f* (*Pol*) envoy; (*Presse*) correspondent; **~ spécial** special correspondent

envoyer [ɑ̃vwaje] /8/ *vt* to send; (*lancer*) to hurl, throw; **~ chercher**

to send for; **~ promener qn** (fam) to send sb packing

éolien, ne [eɔljɛ̃, -ɛn] adj wind ▷ nf wind turbine

épagneul, e [epaɲœl] nm/f spaniel

épais, se [epɛ, -ɛs] adj thick; **épaisseur** nf thickness

épanouir [epanwiʀ] /2/: **s'épanouir** vi (fleur) to bloom, open out; (visage) to light up; (se développer) to blossom (out)

épargne [epaʀɲ] nf saving

épargner [epaʀɲe] /1/ vt to save; (ne pas tuer ou endommager) to spare ▷ vi to save; **~ qch à qn** to spare sb sth

éparpiller [epaʀpije] /1/ vt to scatter; **s'éparpiller** vi to scatter; (fig) to dissipate one's efforts

épatant, e [epatɑ̃, -ɑ̃t] adj (fam) super

épater [epate] /1/ vt (fam) to amaze; (: impressionner) to impress

épaule [epol] nf shoulder

épave [epav] nf wreck

épée [epe] nf sword

épeler [ep(ə)le] /4/ vt to spell

éperon [epʀɔ̃] nm spur

épervier [epɛʀvje] nm sparrowhawk

épi [epi] nm (de blé, d'orge) ear; (de maïs) cob

épice [epis] nf spice

épicé, e [epise] adj spicy

épicer [epise] /3/ vt to spice

épicerie [episʀi] nf grocer's shop; (denrées) groceries pl; **~ fine** delicatessen (shop); **épicier, -ière** nm/f grocer

épidémie [epidemi] nf epidemic

épiderme [epidɛʀm] nm skin

épier [epje] /7/ vt to spy on, watch closely

épilepsie [epilɛpsi] nf epilepsy

épiler [epile] /1/ vt (jambes) to remove the hair from; (sourcils) to pluck

épinards [epinaʀ] nmpl spinach sg

épine [epin] nf thorn, prickle; (d'oursin etc) spine

épingle [epɛ̃gl] nf pin; **~ de nourrice** ou **de sûreté** ou **double** safety pin

épisode [epizɔd] nm episode; **film/ roman à ~s** serial; **épisodique** adj occasional

épluche-légumes [eplyʃlegym] nm inv potato peeler

éplucher [eplyʃe] /1/ vt (fruit, légumes) to peel; (comptes, dossier) to go over with a fine-tooth comb; **épluchures** nfpl peelings

éponge [epɔ̃ʒ] nf sponge; **éponger** /3/ vt (liquide) to mop ou sponge up; (surface) to sponge; (fig: déficit) to soak up

époque [epɔk] nf (de l'histoire) age, era; (de l'année, la vie) time; **d'~** (meuble) period cpd

épouse [epuz] nf wife; **épouser** /1/ vt to marry

épousseter [epuste] /4/ vt to dust

épouvantable [epuvɑ̃tabl] adj appalling, dreadful

épouvantail [epuvɑ̃taj] nm scarecrow

épouvante [epuvɑ̃t] nf terror; **film d'~** horror film; **épouvanter** /1/ vt to terrify

époux [epu] nm husband ▷ nmpl: **les ~** the (married) couple

épreuve [epʀœv] nf (d'examen) test; (malheur, difficulté) trial, ordeal; (Photo) print; (Typo) proof; (Sport) event; **à toute ~** unfailing; **mettre à l'~** to put to the test

éprouver [epʀuve] /1/ vt (tester) to test; to afflict, distress; (ressentir) to experience

EPS sigle f (= Éducation physique et sportive) ≈ PE

épuisé, e [epɥize] adj exhausted; (livre) out of print; **épuisement** nm exhaustion

épuiser [epɥize] /1/ vt (fatiguer) to exhaust, wear ou tire out; (stock, sujet) to exhaust; **s'épuiser** vi to wear ou tire o.s. out, exhaust o.s.

épuisette [epɥizɛt] nf shrimping net

équateur [ekwatœʀ] nm equator; **(la république de) l'É~** Ecuador

équation [ekwasjɔ̃] nf equation

équerre [ekɛʀ] nf (à dessin) (set) square

équilibre [ekilibʀ] nm balance;
garder/perdre l'~ to keep/lose one's
balance; **être en ~** to be balanced;
équilibré, e adj well-balanced;
équilibrer /1/ vt to balance;
s'équilibrer vi to balance

équipage [ekipaʒ] nm crew

équipe [ekip] nf team; **travailler en
~** to work as a team

équipé, e [ekipe] adj: **bien/mal ~**
well-/poorly-equipped

équipement [ekipmɑ̃] nm
equipment

équiper [ekipe] /1/ vt to equip; **~ qn/
qch de** to equip sb/sth with

équipier, -ière [ekipje, -jɛʀ] nm/f
team member

équitation [ekitasjɔ̃] nf (horse-)
riding; **faire de l'~** to go (horse-)riding

équivalent, e [ekivalɑ̃, -ɑ̃t] adj, nm
equivalent

équivaloir [ekivalwaʀ] /29/: **~ à** vt
to be equivalent to

érable [eʀabl] nm maple

érafler [eʀafle] /1/ vt to scratch;
éraflure nf scratch

ère [ɛʀ] nf era; **en l'an 1050 de notre
~** in the year 1050 A.D.

érection [eʀɛksjɔ̃] nf erection

éroder [eʀɔde] /1/ vt to erode

érotique [eʀɔtik] adj erotic

errer [eʀe] /1/ vi to wander

erreur [eʀœʀ] nf mistake, error; **par
~** by mistake; **faire ~** to be mistaken

éruption [eʀypsjɔ̃] nf eruption;
(boutons) rash

es [ɛ] vb voir **être**

ès [ɛs] prép: **licencié ès lettres/
sciences** ≈ Bachelor of Arts/Science

ESB sigle f (= encéphalopathie
spongiforme bovine) BSE

escabeau, x [ɛskabo] nm (tabouret)
stool; (échelle) stepladder

escalade [ɛskalad] nf climbing no
pl; (Pol etc) escalation; **escalader** /1/
vt to climb

escale [ɛskal] nf (Navig: durée) call;
(: port) port of call; (Aviat) stop(over);
faire ~ à (Navig) to put in at; (Aviat)
to stop over at; **vol sans ~** nonstop
flight

escalier [ɛskalje] nm stairs pl;
dans l'~ ou **les ~s** on the stairs;
~ mécanique ou **roulant** escalator

escapade [ɛskapad] nf: **faire une
~** to go on a jaunt; (s'enfuir) to run
away ou off

escargot [ɛskaʀɡo] nm snail

escarpé, e [ɛskaʀpe] adj steep

esclavage [ɛsklavaʒ] nm slavery

esclave [ɛsklav] nm/f slave

escompte [ɛskɔ̃t] nm discount

escrime [ɛskʀim] nf fencing

escroc [ɛskʀo] nm swindler, con-
man; **escroquer** /1/ vt: **escroquer
qn (de qch)/qch à qn** to swindle
sb (out of sth)/sth out of sb;
escroquerie
[ɛskʀɔkʀi] nf swindle

espace [ɛspas] nm space; **espacer**
/3/ vt to space out; **s'espacer** vi
(visites etc) to become less frequent

espadon [ɛspadɔ̃] nm swordfish inv

espadrille [ɛspadʀij] nf rope-soled
sandal

Espagne [ɛspaɲ] nf: **l'~** Spain;
espagnol, e adj Spanish ▷ nm
(Ling) Spanish ▷ nm/f: **Espagnol, e**
Spaniard

espèce [ɛspɛs] nf (Bio, Bot, Zool)
species inv; (gén: sorte) sort, kind,
type; (péj): **~ de maladroit/de
brute!** you clumsy oaf/you brute!;
espèces nfpl (Comm) cash sg; **payer
en ~s** to pay (in) cash

espérance [ɛspeʀɑ̃s] nf hope; **~ de
vie** life expectancy

espérer [ɛspeʀe] /6/ vt to hope for;
j'espère (bien) I hope so; **~ que/
faire** to hope that/to do

espiègle [ɛspjɛɡl] adj mischievous

espion, ne [ɛspjɔ̃, -ɔn] nm/f spy;
espionnage nm espionage, spying;
espionner /1/ vt to spy (up)on

espoir [ɛspwaʀ] *nm* hope; **dans l'~ de/que** in the hope of/that; **reprendre ~** not to lose hope

esprit [ɛspʀi] *nm* (*pensée, intellect*) mind; (*humour, ironie*) wit; (*mentalité, d'une loi etc, fantôme etc*) spirit; **faire de l'~** to try to be witty; **reprendre ses ~s** to come to; **perdre l'~** to lose one's mind

esquimau, de, x [ɛskimo, -od] *adj* Eskimo ▷ *nm*: **E~®** ice lolly (*BRIT*), popsicle (*US*) ▷ *nm/f*: **E~, de** Eskimo

essai [esɛ] *nm* (*tentative*) attempt, try; (*de produit*) testing; (*Rugby*) try; (*Littérature*) essay; **à l'~** on a trial basis; **mettre à l'~** to put to the test

essaim [esɛ̃] *nm* swarm

essayer [eseje] /8/ *vt* to try; (*vêtement, chaussures*) to try (on); (*restaurant, méthode, voiture*) to try (out) ▷ *vi* to try; **~ de faire** to try *ou* attempt to do

essence [esɑ̃s] *nf* (*de voiture*) petrol (*BRIT*), gas(oline) (*US*); (*extrait de plante*) essence; (*espèce: d'arbre*) species *inv*

essentiel, le [esɑ̃sjɛl] *adj* essential; **c'est l'~** (*ce qui importe*) that's the main thing; **l'~ de** the main part of

essieu, x [esjø] *nm* axle

essor [esɔʀ] *nm* (*de l'économie etc*) rapid expansion

essorer [esɔʀe] /1/ *vt* (*en tordant*) to wring (out); (*par la force centrifuge*) to spin-dry; **essoreuse** *nf* spin-dryer

essouffler [esufle] /1/: **s'essouffler** *vi* to get out of breath

essuie-glace [esɥiglas] *nm* windscreen (*BRIT*) *ou* windshield (*US*) wiper

essuyer [esɥije] /8/ *vt* to wipe; (*fig: subir*) to suffer; **s'essuyer** (*après le bain*) to dry o.s.; **~ la vaisselle** to dry up

est *vb* [ɛ] *voir* **être** ▷ *nm* [ɛst]: **l'~** the east ▷ *adj inv* [ɛst] east; (*région*) east(ern); **à l'~** in the east; (*direction*) to the east, east(wards); **à l'~ de** (to the) east of

est-ce que [ɛskə] *adv*: **~ c'est cher/c'était bon?** is it expensive/was it good?; **quand est-ce qu'il part?** when does he leave?, when is he leaving?; *voir aussi* **que**

esthéticienne [ɛstetisjɛn] *nf* beautician

esthétique [ɛstetik] *adj* attractive

estimation [ɛstimasjɔ̃] *nf* valuation; (*chiffre*) estimate

estime [ɛstim] *nf* esteem, regard; **estimer** /1/ *vt* (*respecter*) to esteem; (*expertiser: bijou*) to value; (*évaluer: coût etc*) to assess, estimate; (*penser*) **estimer que/être** to consider that/o.s. to be

estival, e, -aux [ɛstival, -o] *adj* summer *cpd*

estivant, e [ɛstivɑ̃, -ɑ̃t] *nm/f* (summer) holiday-maker

estomac [ɛstɔma] *nm* stomach

estragon [ɛstʀagɔ̃] *nm* tarragon

estuaire [ɛstɥɛʀ] *nm* estuary

et [e] *conj* and; **et lui?** what about him?; **et alors?** so what?

étable [etabl] *nf* cowshed

établi, e [etabli] *nm* (work)bench

établir [etabliʀ] /2/ *vt* (*papiers d'identité, facture*) to make out; (*liste, programme*) to draw up; (*gouvernement, artisan etc*) to set up; (*réputation, usage, fait, culpabilité, relations*) to establish; **s'établir** *vi* to be established; **s'~ (à son compte)** to set up in business; **s'~ à/près de** to settle in/near

établissement [etablismɑ̃] *nm* (*entreprise, institution*) establishment; **~ scolaire** school, educational establishment

étage [etaʒ] *nm* (*d'immeuble*) storey, floor; **au 2ème ~** on the 2nd (*BRIT*) *ou* 3rd (*US*) floor; **à l'~** upstairs; **c'est à quel ~?** what floor is it on?

étagère [etaʒɛʀ] *nf* (*rayon*) shelf; (*meuble*) shelves *pl*

étai [etɛ] *nm* stay, prop

étain [etɛ̃] *nm* pewter *no pl*

étais etc [etɛ] vb voir **être**

étaler [etale] /1/ vt (carte, nappe) to spread (out); (peinture, liquide) to spread; (échelonner: paiements, dates, vacances) to spread, stagger; (marchandises) to display; (richesses, connaissances) to parade; **s'étaler** vi (liquide) to spread out; (fam) to fall flat on one's face; **s'~ sur** (paiements etc) to be spread over

étalon [etalɔ̃] nm (cheval) stallion

étanche [etɑ̃ʃ] adj (récipient) watertight; (montre, vêtement) waterproof

étang [etɑ̃] nm pond

étant [etɑ̃] vb voir **être**; **donné**

étape [etap] nf stage; (lieu d'arrivée) stopping place; (: Cyclisme) staging point

état [eta] nm (Pol, condition) state; **en bon/mauvais ~** in good/poor condition; **en ~ (de marche)** in (working) order; **remettre en ~** to repair; **hors d'~** out of order; **être en ~/hors d'~ de faire** to be in a state/in no fit state to do; **être dans tous ses ~s** to be in a state; **faire ~ de** (alléguer) to put forward; **l'É~** the State; **~ civil** civil status; **~ des lieux** inventory of fixtures; **États-Unis** nmpl: **les États-Unis (d'Amérique)** the United States (of America)

et cætera, et cetera, etc. [ɛtseteʀa] adv etc

été [ete] pp de **être** ▷ nm summer

éteindre [etɛ̃dʀ] /52/ vt (lampe, lumière, radio, chauffage) to turn ou switch off; (cigarette, incendie, bougie) to put out, extinguish; **s'éteindre** vi (feu, lumière) to go out; (mourir) to pass away; **éteint, e** adj (fig) lacklustre, dull; (volcan) extinct

étendre [etɑ̃dʀ] /41/ vt (pâte, liquide) to spread; (carte etc) to spread out; (lessive, linge) to hang up ou out; (bras, jambes) to stretch out; (fig: agrandir) to extend; **s'étendre** vi (augmenter, se propager) to spread; (terrain, forêt

etc): **s'~ jusqu'à/de ... à** to stretch as far as/from ... to; **s'~ sur** (se coucher) to lie down (on); (fig: expliquer) to elaborate ou enlarge (upon)

étendu, e [etɑ̃dy] adj extensive

éternel, le [etɛʀnɛl] adj eternal

éternité [etɛʀnite] nf eternity; **ça a duré une ~** it lasted for ages

éternuement [etɛʀnymɑ̃] nm sneeze

éternuer [etɛʀnɥe] /1/ vi to sneeze

êtes [ɛt(z)] vb voir **être**

Éthiopie [etjɔpi] nf: **l'~** Ethiopia

étiez [etje] vb voir **être**

étinceler [etɛ̃s(ə)le] /4/ vi to sparkle

étincelle [etɛ̃sɛl] nf spark

étiquette [etikɛt] nf label; (protocole): **l'~** etiquette

étirer [etiʀe] /1/ vt to stretch out; **s'étirer** vi (personne) to stretch; (convoi, route): **s'~ sur** to stretch out over

étoile [etwal] nf star; **à la belle ~** (out) in the open; **~ filante** shooting star; **~ de mer** starfish; **étoilé, e** adj starry

étonnant, e [etɔnɑ̃, -ɑ̃t] adj surprising

étonnement [etɔnmɑ̃] nm surprise, amazing

étonner [etɔne] /1/ vt to surprise, amaze; **s'étonner que/de** to be surprised that/at; **cela m'~ait (que)** (j'en doute) I'd be (very) surprised (if)

étouffer [etufe] /1/ vt to suffocate; (bruit) to muffle; (scandale) to hush up ▷ vi to suffocate; **s'étouffer** vi (en mangeant etc) to choke; **on étouffe** it's stifling

étourderie [etuʀdəʀi] nf (caractère) absent-mindedness no pl; (faute) thoughtless blunder

étourdi, e [etuʀdi] adj (distrait) scatterbrained, heedless

étourdir [etuʀdiʀ] /2/ vt (assommer) to stun, daze; (griser) to make dizzy ou giddy; **étourdissement** nm dizzy spell

étrange [etʀɑ̃ʒ] *adj* strange

étranger, -ère [etʀɑ̃ʒe, -ɛʀ] *adj* foreign; (*pas de la famille, non familier*) strange ▷ *nm/f* foreigner; stranger ▷ *nm*: **à l'~** abroad

étrangler [etʀɑ̃gle] /1/ *vt* to strangle; **s'étrangler** *vi* (*en mangeant etc*) to choke

 MOT-CLÉ

être [ɛtʀ] /61/ *nm* being; **être humain** human being
▶ *vb copule* **1** (*état, description*) to be; **il est instituteur** he is *ou* he's a teacher; **vous êtes grand/intelligent/fatigué** you are *ou* you're tall/clever/tired
2 (+*à: appartenir*) to be; **le livre est à Paul** the book is Paul's *ou* belongs to Paul; **c'est à moi/eux** it is *ou* it's mine/theirs
3 (+*de: provenance*): **il est de Paris** he is from Paris; (: *appartenance*): **il est des nôtres** he is one of us
4 (*date*): **nous sommes le 10 janvier** it's the 10th of January (today)
▶ *vi* to be; **je ne serai pas ici demain** I won't be here tomorrow
▶ *vb aux* **1** to have; to be; **être arrivé/allé** to have arrived/gone; **il est parti** he has left, he has gone
2 (*forme passive*) to be; **être fait par** to be made by; **il a été promu** he has been promoted
3 (+*à* +*inf, obligation, but*): **c'est à réparer** it needs repairing; **c'est à essayer** it should be tried; **il est à espérer que ...** it is *ou* it's to be hoped that ...
▶ *vb impers* **1**: **il est** (+ *adj*) it is; **il est impossible de le faire** it's impossible to do it
2: **il est** (*heure, date*): **il est 10 heures** it is *ou* it's 10 o'clock
3 (*emphatique*): **c'est moi** it's me; **c'est à lui de le faire** it's up to him to do it

étrennes [etʀɛn] *nfpl* ≈ Christmas box *sg*

étrier [etʀije] *nm* stirrup

étroit, e [etʀwa, -wat] *adj* narrow; (*vêtement*) tight; (*fig: liens, collaboration*) close; **à l'~** cramped; **~ d'esprit** narrow-minded

étude [etyd] *nf* studying; (*ouvrage, rapport*) study; (*Scol: salle de travail*) study room; **études** *nfpl* (*Scol*) studies; **être à l'~** (*projet etc*) to be under consideration; **faire des ~s (de droit/médecine)** to study (law/medicine)

étudiant, e [etydjɑ̃, -ɑ̃t] *nm/f* student

étudier [etydje] /7/ *vt, vi* to study

étui [etɥi] *nm* case

eu, eue [y] *pp de* **avoir**

euh [ø] *excl* er

euro [øʀo] *nm* euro

Europe [øʀɔp] *nf*: **l'~** Europe; **européen, ne** *adj* European ▷ *nm/f*: **Européen, ne** European

eus *etc* [y] *vb voir* **avoir**

eux [ø] *pron* (*sujet*) they; (*objet*) them

évacuer [evakɥe] /1/ *vt* to evacuate

évader [evade] /1/: **s'évader** *vi* to escape

évaluer [evalɥe] /1/ *vt* (*expertiser*) to assess, evaluate; (*juger approximativement*) to estimate

évangile [evɑ̃ʒil] *nm* gospel; **É~** Gospel

évanouir [evanwiʀ] /2/: **s'évanouir** *vi* to faint; (*disparaître*) to vanish, disappear; **évanouissement** *nm* (*syncope*) fainting fit

évaporer [evapɔʀe] /1/: **s'évaporer** *vi* to evaporate

évasion [evazjɔ̃] *nf* escape

éveillé, e [eveje] *adj* awake; (*vif*) alert, sharp; **éveiller** /1/ *vt* to (a)waken; (*soupçons etc*) to arouse; **s'éveiller** *vi* to (a)waken; (*fig*) to be aroused

événement [evɛnmɑ̃] *nm* event

éventail [evɑ̃taj] *nm* fan; (*choix*) range

éventualité [evãtɥalite] nf
eventuality; possibility; **dans l'~ de**
in the event of

éventuel, le [evãtɥɛl] adj possible
Attention à ne pas traduire
éventuel par *eventual*.

éventuellement [evãtɥɛlmã] adv
possibly
Attention à ne pas traduire
éventuellement par *eventually*.

évêque [evɛk] nm bishop

évidemment [evidamã] adv
(*bien sûr*) of course; (*certainement*)
obviously

évidence [evidãs] nf obviousness;
(*fait*) obvious fact; **de toute ~** quite
obviously *ou* evidently; **être en ~** to
be clearly visible; **mettre en ~** (*fait*)
to highlight; **évident, e** adj obvious,
evident; **ce n'est pas évident** it's not
as simple as all that

évier [evje] nm (kitchen) sink

éviter [evite] /1/ vt to avoid; **~ de
faire/que qch ne se passe** to avoid
doing/sth happening; **~ qch à qn** to
spare sb sth

évoluer [evɔlɥe] /1/ vi (*enfant,
maladie*) to develop; (*situation,
moralement*) to evolve, develop; (*aller
et venir*) to move about; **évolution** nf
development; evolution

évoquer [evɔke] /1/ vt to call to
mind, evoke; (*mentionner*) to mention

ex- [ɛks] préfixe ex-; **son ~mari** her ex-
husband; **son ~femme** his ex-wife

exact, e [ɛgza(kt), ɛgzakt] adj exact;
(*correct*) correct; (*ponctuel*) punctual;
l'heure ~e the right *ou* exact time;
exactement adv exactly

ex aequo [ɛgzeko] adj equally placed;
arriver ~ to finish neck and neck

exagéré, e [ɛgzaʒere] adj (*prix etc*)
excessive

exagérer [ɛgzaʒere] /6/ vt to
exaggerate ▷ vi (*abuser*) to go too far;
(*déformer les faits*) to exaggerate

examen [ɛgzamɛ̃] nm examination;
(*Scol*) exam, examination; **à l'~** under

consideration; **~ médical** (medical)
examination; (*analyse*) test

examinateur, -trice
[ɛgzaminatœr, -tris] nm/f examiner

examiner [ɛgzamine] /1/ vt to
examine

exaspérant, e [ɛgzasperã, -ãt] adj
exasperating

exaspérer [ɛgzaspere] /6/ vt to
exasperate

exaucer [ɛgzose] /3/ vt (*vœu*) to grant

excéder [ɛksede] /6/ vt (*dépasser*) to
exceed; (*agacer*) to exasperate

excellent, e [ɛkselã, -ãt] adj
excellent

excentrique [ɛksãtrik] adj
eccentric

excepté, e [ɛksɛpte] adj, prép: **les
élèves ~s, ~ les élèves** except for *ou*
apart from the pupils

exception [ɛksɛpsjõ] nf exception;
à l'~ de except for, with the
exception of; **d'~** (*mesure, loi*) special,
exceptional; **exceptionnel, le** adj
exceptional; **exceptionnellement**
adv exceptionally

excès [ɛksɛ] nm surplus ▷ nmpl
excesses; **faire des ~** to overindulge;
~ de vitesse speeding no pl; **excessif,
-ive** adj excessive

excitant, e [ɛksitã, -ãt] adj exciting
▷ nm stimulant; **excitation** nf (*état*)
excitement

exciter [ɛksite] /1/ vt to excite; (*café
etc*) to stimulate; **s'exciter** vi to get
excited

exclamer [ɛksklame] /1/:
s'exclamer vi to exclaim

exclu, e [ɛskly] adj: **il est/n'est pas
~ que …** it's out of the question/not
impossible that …

exclure [ɛsklyr] /35/ vt (*faire sortir*)
to expel; (*ne pas compter*) to exclude,
leave out; (*rendre impossible*) to
exclude, rule out; **exclusif, -ive** adj
exclusive; **exclusion** nf expulsion; **à
l'exclusion de** with the exclusion *ou*
exception of; **exclusivité** nf (*Comm*)

exclusive rights *pl*; **film passant en exclusivité** à film showing only at

excursion [ɛkskyʀsjɔ̃] *nf* (*en autocar*) excursion, trip; (*à pied*) walk, hike

excuse [ɛkskyz] *nf* excuse; **excuses** *nfpl* (*regret*) apology *sg*, apologies; **excuser** /1/ *vt* to excuse; **s'excuser (de)** to apologize (for); **"excusez-moi"** "I'm sorry"; (*pour attirer l'attention*) "excuse me"

exécuter [ɛgzekyte] /1/ *vt* (*prisonnier*) to execute; (*tâche etc*) to execute, carry out; (*Mus: jouer*) to perform, execute; **s'exécuter** *vi* to comply

exemplaire [ɛgzɑ̃plɛʀ] *nm* copy

exemple [ɛgzɑ̃pl] *nm* example; **par ~** for instance, for example; **donner l'~** to set an example

exercer [ɛgzɛʀse] /3/ *vt* (*pratiquer*) to exercise, practise; (*influence, contrôle, pression*) to exert; (*former*) to exercise, train; **s'exercer** *vi* (*médecin*) to be in practice; (*sportif, musicien*) to practise

exercice [ɛgzɛʀsis] *nm* exercise

exhiber [ɛgzibe] /1/ *vt* (*montrer: papiers, certificat*) to present, produce; (*péj*) to display, flaunt; **s'exhiber** *vi* to parade; (*exhibitionniste*) to expose o.s.; **exhibitionniste** *nm/f* exhibitionist

exigeant, e [ɛgziʒɑ̃, -ɑ̃t] *adj* demanding; (*péj*) hard to please

exiger [ɛgziʒe] /3/ *vt* to demand, require

exil [ɛgzil] *nm* exile; **exiler** /1/ *vt* to exile; **s'exiler** *vi* to go into exile

existence [ɛgzistɑ̃s] *nf* existence

exister [ɛgziste] /1/ *vi* to exist; **il existe un/des** there is a/are (some)

exorbitant, e [ɛgzɔʀbitɑ̃, -ɑ̃t] *adj* exorbitant

exotique [ɛgzɔtik] *adj* exotic; **yaourt aux fruits ~s** tropical fruit yoghurt

expédier [ɛkspedje] /7/ *vt* (*lettre, paquet*) to send; (*troupes, renfort*) to dispatch; (*péj: travail etc*) to dispose of, dispatch; **expéditeur, -trice** *nm/f* sender; **expédition** *nf* sending; (*scientifique, sportive, Mil*) expedition

expérience [ɛksperjɑ̃s] *nf* (*de la vie, des choses*) experience; (*scientifique*) experiment

expérimenté, e [ɛksperimɑ̃te] *adj* experienced

expérimenter [ɛksperimɑ̃te] /1/ *vt* to test out, experiment with

expert, e [ɛkspɛʀ, -ɛʀt] *adj* ▷ *nm* expert; **~ en assurances** insurance valuer; **expert-comptable** *nm* ≈ chartered (BRIT) *ou* certified public (US) accountant

expirer [ɛkspire] /1/ *vi* (*prendre fin, lit: mourir*) to expire; (*respirer*) to breathe out

explication [ɛksplikasjɔ̃] *nf* explanation; (*discussion*) discussion; (*dispute*) argument

explicite [ɛksplisit] *adj* explicit

expliquer [ɛksplike] /1/ *vt* to explain; **s'expliquer** to explain o.s.; **s'~ avec qn** (*discuter*) to explain o.s. to sb

exploit [ɛksplwa] *nm* exploit, feat; **exploitant** *nm/f*: **exploitant (agricole)** farmer; **exploitation** *nf* exploitation; (*d'une entreprise*) running;

exploitation agricole farming concern; **exploiter** /1/ *vt* (*personne, don*) to exploit; (*entreprise, ferme*) to run, operate; (*mine*) to exploit, work

explorer [ɛksplɔʀe] /1/ *vt* to explore

exploser [ɛksploze] /1/ *vi* to explode, blow up; (*engin explosif*) to go off; (*personne: de colère*) to explode; **explosif, -ive** *adj, nm* explosive; **explosion** *nf* explosion; **explosion de joie/colère** outburst of joy/rage

exportateur, -trice [ɛkspɔʀtatœʀ, -tʀis] *adj* export *cpd*, exporting ▷ *nm* exporter

exportation [ɛkspɔʀtasjɔ̃] *nf* (*action*) exportation; (*produit*) export

exporter [ɛkspɔʀte] /1/ *vt* to export

exposant [ɛkspozɑ̃] *nm* exhibitor

exposé, e [ɛkspoze] nm talk ▷ adj:
~ **au sud** facing south

exposer [ɛkspoze] /1/ vt
(marchandise) to display; (peinture) to
exhibit, show; (parler de) to explain,
set out; (mettre en danger, orienter,
Photo) to expose; **s'exposer à** (soleil,
danger) to expose o.s. to; **exposition**
nf (manifestation) exhibition; (Photo)
exposure

exprès¹ [ɛksprɛ] adv (délibérément)
on purpose; (spécialement) specially;
faire ~ de faire qch to do sth on
purpose

exprès², -esse [ɛksprɛs] adj inv
(Postes: lettre, colis) express

express [ɛksprɛs] adj, nm: **(café) ~**
espresso; **(train) ~** fast train

expressif, -ive [ɛksprɛsif, -iv] adj
expressive

expression [ɛksprɛsjɔ̃] nf
expression

exprimer [ɛksprime] /1/ vt
(sentiment, idée) to express; (jus,
liquide) to press out; **s'exprimer** vi
(personne) to express o.s.

expulser [ɛkspylse] /1/ vt to expel;
(locataire) to evict; (Football) to
send off

exquis, e [ɛkski, -iz] adj exquisite

extasier [ɛkstazje] /7/: **s'extasier** vi:
s'~ sur to go into raptures over

exténuer [ɛkstenɥe] /1/ vt to
exhaust

extérieur, e [ɛksterjœr] adj (porte,
mur etc) outer, outside; (commerce,
politique) foreign; (influences, pressions)
external; (apparent: calme, gaieté etc)
outer ▷ nm (d'une maison, d'un récipient
etc) outside, exterior; (apparence)
exterior; **à l'~** outside; (à l'étranger)
abroad

externat [ɛksterna] nm day school

externe [ɛkstern] adj external, outer
▷ nm/f (Méd) non-resident medical
student, extern (US); (Scol) day pupil

extincteur [ɛkstɛ̃ktœr] nm (fire)
extinguisher

extinction [ɛkstɛ̃ksjɔ̃] nf: ~ **de voix**
loss of voice

extra [ɛkstra] adj inv first-rate; (fam)
fantastic ▷ nm inv extra help

extraire [ɛkstrɛr] /50/ vt to extract;
~ **qch de** to extract sth from; **extrait**
nm extract; **extrait de naissance**
birth certificate

extraordinaire [ɛkstraɔrdinɛr]
adj extraordinary; (Pol, Admin:
mesures etc) special

extravagant, e [ɛkstravagɑ̃, -ɑ̃t]
adj extravagant

extraverti, e [ɛkstraverti] adj
extrovert

extrême [ɛkstrɛm] adj, nm extreme;
d'un ~ à l'autre from one extreme
to another; **extrêmement** adv
extremely; **Extrême-Orient** nm:
l'Extrême-Orient the Far East

extrémité [ɛkstremite] nf
end; (situation) straits pl, plight;
(geste désespéré) extreme action;
extrémités nfpl (pieds et mains)
extremities

exubérant, e [ɛgzyberɑ̃, -ɑ̃t] adj
exuberant

f

F *abr* (= *franc*) fr.; (*appartement*): **un F2/F3** a 2-/3-roomed flat (BRIT) *ou* apartment (US)

fa [fa] *nm inv* (*Mus*) F; (*en chantant la gamme*) fa

fabricant, e [fabʀikɑ̃, -ɑ̃t] *nm/f* manufacturer

fabrication [fabʀikasjɔ̃] *nf* manufacture

fabrique [fabʀik] *nf* factory; **fabriquer** [fabʀike] /1/ *vt* to make; (*industriellement*) to manufacture; (*fam*): **qu'est-ce qu'il fabrique?** what is he up to?

fac [fak] *nf* (*fam*: *Scol*) (= *faculté*) Uni (BRIT *fam*), ≈ college (US)

façade [fasad] *nf* front, façade

face [fas] *nf* face; (*fig*: *aspect*) side ▷ *adj*: **le côté ~** heads; **en ~ de** opposite; (*fig*) in front of; **de ~** face on; **~ à** facing; (*fig*) faced with, in the face of; **faire ~ à** to face; **~ à ~** *adv* facing each other; **face-à-face** *nm inv* encounter

fâché, e [faʃe] *adj* angry; (*désolé*) sorry

fâcher [faʃe] /1/ *vt* to anger; **se fâcher** *vi* to get angry; **se ~ avec** (*se brouiller*) to fall out with

facile [fasil] *adj* easy; (*caractère*) easy-going; **facilement** *adv* easily; **facilité** *nf* easiness; (*disposition, don*) aptitude; **facilités** *nfpl* (*possibilités*) facilities; (*Comm*) terms; **faciliter** /1/ *vt* to make easier

façon [fasɔ̃] *nf* (*manière*) way; (*d'une robe etc*) making-up; cut; **façons** *nfpl* (*péj*) fuss *sg*; **sans ~** *adv* without fuss; **non merci, sans ~** no thanks, honestly; **de ~ à** so as to; **de ~ à ce que** so that; **de toute ~** anyway, in any case

facteur, -trice [faktœʀ, -tʀis] *nm/f* postman/woman (BRIT), mailman/woman (US) ▷ *nm* (*Math, gén: élément*) factor

facture [faktyʀ] *nf* (*à payer: gén*) bill; (: *Comm*) invoice

facultatif, -ive [fakyltatif, -iv] *adj* optional

faculté [fakylte] *nf* (*intellectuelle, d'université*) faculty; (*pouvoir, possibilité*) power

fade [fad] *adj* insipid

faible [fɛbl] *adj* weak; (*voix, lumière, vent*) faint; (*rendement, intensité, revenu etc*) low ▷ *nm* (*pour quelqu'un*) weakness, soft spot; **faiblesse** *nf* weakness; **faiblir** [feblir] /2/ *vi* to weaken; (*lumière*) to dim; (*vent*) to drop

faïence [fajɑ̃s] *nf* earthenware *no pl*

faillir [fajiʀ] /2/ *vi*: **j'ai failli tomber/lui dire** I almost *ou* nearly fell/told him

faillite [fajit] *nf* bankruptcy; **faire ~** to go bankrupt

faim [fɛ̃] *nf* hunger; **avoir ~** to be hungry; **rester sur sa ~** (*aussi fig*) to be left wanting more

fainéant, e [fɛneɑ̃, -ɑ̃t] *nm/f* idler, loafer

○ **MOT-CLÉ**

faire [fɛr] /60/ *vt* **1** (*fabriquer, être l'auteur de*) to make; **faire du vin/ une offre/un film** to make wine/ an offer/a film; **faire du bruit** to make a noise

2 (*effectuer: travail, opération*) to do; **que faites-vous?** (*quel métier etc*) what do you do?; (*quelle activité: au moment de la question*) what are you doing?; **faire la lessive/le ménage** to do the washing/the housework

3 (*études*) to do; (*sport, musique*) to play; **faire du droit/du français** to do law/French; **faire du rugby/ piano** to play rugby/the piano

4 (*visiter*): **faire les magasins** to go shopping; **faire l'Europe** to tour *ou* do Europe

5 (*distance*): **faire du 50 (à l'heure)** to do 50 (km an hour); **nous avons fait 1000 km en 2 jours** we did *ou* covered 1000 km in 2 days

6 (*simuler*): **faire le malade/ l'ignorant** to act the invalid/the fool

7 (*transformer, avoir un effet sur*): **faire de qn un frustré/avocat** to make sb frustrated/a lawyer; **ça ne me fait rien** (*m'est égal*) I don't care *ou* mind; (*me laisse froid*) it has no effect on me; **ça ne fait rien** it doesn't matter; **faire que** (*impliquer*) to mean that

8 (*calculs, prix, mesures*): **deux et deux font quatre** two and two are *ou* make four; **ça fait 10 m/15 euros** it's 10 m/15 euros; **je vous le fais 10 euros** I'll let you have it for 10 euros; **je fais du 40** I take a size 40

9: **qu'a-t-il fait de sa valise/de sa sœur?** what has he done with his case/his sister?

10: **ne faire que: il ne fait que critiquer** (*sans cesse*) all he (ever) does is criticize; (*seulement*) he's only criticizing

11 (*dire*) to say; **vraiment? fit-il** really? he said

12 (*maladie*) to have; **faire du diabète/de la tension** to have diabetes *sg*/high blood pressure

▶ *vi* **1** (*agir, s'y prendre*) to act, do; **il faut faire vite** we (*ou* you *etc*) must act quickly; **comment a-t-il fait pour?** how did he manage to?; **faites comme chez vous** make yourself at home

2 (*paraître*) to look; **faire vieux/ démodé** to look old/old-fashioned; **ça fait bien** it looks good

3 (*remplaçant un autre verbe*) to do; **ne le casse pas comme je l'ai fait** don't break it as I did; **je peux le voir? — faites!** can I see it? — please do!

▶ *vb impers* **1**: **il fait beau** *etc* the weather is fine *etc*; *voir aussi* **froid; jour** *etc*

2 (*temps écoulé, durée*): **ça fait deux ans qu'il est parti** it's two years since he left; **ça fait deux ans qu'il y est** he's been there for two years

▶ *vb aux* **1**: **faire** (+*infinitif: action directe*) to make; **faire tomber/ bouger qch** to make sth fall/ move; **faire démarrer un moteur/ chauffer de l'eau** to start up an engine/heat some water; **cela fait dormir** it makes you sleep; **faire travailler les enfants** to make the children work *ou* get the children to work; **il m'a fait traverser la rue** he helped me to cross the road

2: **faire** (+*infinitif: indirectement, par un intermédiaire*): **faire réparer qch** to get *ou* have sth repaired; **faire punir les enfants** to have the children punished

se faire *vr* **1** (*vin, fromage*) to mature

2 (*être convenable*): **cela se fait beaucoup/ne se fait pas** it's done a lot/not done

3 (+*nom ou pron*): **se faire une jupe** to make o.s. a skirt; **se faire des amis** to make friends; **se faire du souci** to worry; **il ne s'en fait pas** he doesn't worry

4 (+adj: devenir): **se faire vieux** to be getting old; (: délibérément): **se faire beau** to do o.s. up
5: **se faire à** (s'habituer) to get used to; **je n'arrive pas à me faire à la nourriture/au climat** I can't get used to the food/climate
6 (: +infinitif): **se faire examiner la vue/opérer** to have one's eyes tested/have an operation; **se faire couper les cheveux** to get one's hair cut; **il va se faire tuer/punir** he's going to get himself killed/get (himself) punished; **il s'est fait aider** he got somebody to help him; **il s'est fait aider par Simon** he got Simon to help him; **se faire faire un vêtement** to get a garment made for o.s.
7 (impersonnel): **comment se fait-il/faisait-il que?** how is it/was it that?

faire-part [fɛʀpaʀ] nm inv announcement (of birth, marriage etc)
faisan, e [fəzɑ̃, -an] nm/f pheasant
faisons etc [fəzɔ̃] vb voir **faire**
fait¹ [fɛ] nm (événement) event, occurrence; (réalité, donnée) fact; **être au ~ (de)** to be informed (of); **au ~** (à propos) by the way; **en venir au ~** to get to the point; **du ~ de ceci/qu'il a menti** because of ou on account of this/his having lied; **de ce ~** for this reason; **en ~** in fact; **prendre qn sur le ~** to catch sb in the act; **~ divers** (short) news item
fait², e [fɛ, fɛt] adj (mûr: fromage, melon) ripe; **c'est bien ~ (pour lui** ou **eux** etc**)** it serves him (ou them etc) right
faites [fɛt] vb voir **faire**
falaise [falɛz] nf cliff
falloir [falwaʀ] /29/ vb impers: **il faut faire les lits** we (ou you etc) have to ou must make the beds; **il faut que je fasse les lits** I have to ou must make the beds; **il a fallu qu'il parte** he had to leave; **il faudrait**

qu'elle rentre she should come ou go back, she ought to come ou go back; **il faut faire attention** you have to be careful; **il me faudrait 100 euros** I would need 100 euros; **il vous faut tourner à gauche après l'église** you have to turn left past the church; **nous avons ce qu'il (nous) faut** we have what we need; **il ne fallait pas** you shouldn't have (done); **s'en falloir** vi: **il s'en est fallu de 10 euros/5 minutes** we (ou they etc) were 10 euros short/5 minutes late (ou early); **il s'en faut de beaucoup qu'il soit …** he is far from being …; **il s'en est fallu de peu que cela n'arrive** it very nearly happened; **comme il faut** adj proper; adv properly
famé, e [fame] adj: **mal ~** disreputable, of ill repute
fameux, -euse [famø, -øz] adj (illustre) famous; (bon: repas, plat etc) first-rate, first-class; (intensif): **un ~ problème** etc a real problem etc
familial, e, -aux [familjal, -o] adj family cpd
familiarité [familjaʀite] nf familiarity
familier, -ière [familje, -jɛʀ] adj (connu, impertinent) familiar; (atmosphère) informal, friendly; (Ling) informal, colloquial ▷ nm regular (visitor)
famille [famij] nf family; **il a de la ~ à Paris** he has relatives in Paris
famine [famin] nf famine
fana [fana] adj, nm/f (fam) = **fanatique**
fanatique [fanatik] adj: **~ (de)** fanatical (about) ▷ nm/f fanatic
faner [fane] /1/: **se faner** vi to fade
fanfare [fɑ̃faʀ] nf (orchestre) brass band; (musique) fanfare
fantaisie [fɑ̃tezi] nf (spontanéité) fancy, imagination; (caprice) whim ▷ adj: **bijou (de) ~** (piece of) costume jewellery (BRIT) ou jewelry (US)

fantasme [fɑ̃tasm] nm fantasy
fantastique [fɑ̃tastik] adj fantastic
fantôme [fɑ̃tom] nm ghost, phantom
faon [fɑ̃] nm fawn (deer)
FAQ sigle f (= foire aux questions) FAQ pl
farce [faʀs] nf (viande) stuffing; (blague) (practical) joke; (Théât) farce; **farcir** /2/ vt (viande) to stuff
farder [faʀde] /1/: **se farder** vi to make o.s. up
farine [faʀin] nf flour
farouche [faʀuʃ] adj shy, timid
fart [faʀt] nm (ski) wax
fascination [fasinasjɔ̃] nf fascination
fasciner [fasine] /1/ vt to fascinate
fascisme [faʃism] nm fascism
fasse etc [fas] vb voir **faire**
fastidieux, -euse [fastidjø, -øz] adj tedious, tiresome
fatal, e [fatal] adj fatal; (inévitable) inevitable; **fatalité** nf (destin) fate; (coïncidence) fateful coincidence
fatidique [fatidik] adj fateful
fatigant, e [fatigɑ̃, -ɑ̃t] adj tiring; (agaçant) tiresome
fatigue [fatig] nf tiredness, fatigue; **fatigué, e** adj tired; **fatiguer** /1/ vt to tire, make tired; (fig: agacer) to annoy ▷ vi (moteur) to labour, strain; **se fatiguer** to get tired
fauché, e [foʃe] adj (fam) broke
faucher [foʃe] /1/ vt (herbe) to cut; (champs, blés) to reap; (véhicule) to mow down; (fam: voler) to pinch
faucon [fokɔ̃] nm falcon, hawk
faudra etc [fodʀa] vb voir **falloir**
faufiler [fofile] /1/: **se faufiler** vi: **se ~ dans** to edge one's way into; **se ~ parmi/entre** to thread one's way among/between
faune [fon] nf (Zool) wildlife, fauna
fausse [fos] adj f voir **faux²**; **faussement** adv (accuser) wrongly, wrongfully; (croire) falsely
fausser [fose] /1/ vt (objet) to bend, buckle; (fig) to distort; **~ compagnie à qn** to give sb the slip

faut [fo] vb voir **falloir**
faute [fot] nf (erreur) mistake, error; (péché, manquement) misdemeanour; (Football etc) offence; (Tennis) fault; **c'est de sa/ma ~** it's his/my fault; **être en ~** to be in the wrong; **~ de** (temps, argent) for ou through lack of; **sans ~** without fail; **~ de frappe** typing error; **~ professionnelle** professional misconduct no pl
fauteuil [fotœj] nm armchair; **~ d'orchestre** seat in the front stalls (BRIT) ou the orchestra (US); **~ roulant** wheelchair
fautif, -ive [fotif, -iv] adj (incorrect) incorrect, inaccurate; (responsable) at fault, in the wrong; **il se sentait ~** he felt guilty
fauve [fov] nm wildcat ▷ adj (couleur) fawn
faux¹ [fo] nf scythe
faux², fausse [fo, fos] adj (inexact) wrong; (piano, voix) out of tune; (billet) fake, forged; (sournois, postiche) false ▷ adv (Mus) out of tune ▷ nm (copie) fake, forgery; **faire ~ bond à qn** to let sb down; **~ frais** nm pl extras, incidental expenses; **~ mouvement** awkward movement; **faire un ~ pas** to trip; (fig) to make a faux pas; **~ témoignage** (délit) perjury; **fausse alerte** false alarm; **fausse couche** miscarriage; **fausse note** wrong note; **faux-filet** nm sirloin
faveur [favœʀ] nf favour; **traitement de ~** preferential treatment; **en ~ de** in favo(u)r of
favorable [favoʀabl] adj favo(u)rable
favori, te [favoʀi, -it] adj, nm/f favo(u)rite
favoriser [favoʀize] /1/ vt to favour
fax [faks] nm fax
fécond, e [fekɔ̃, -ɔ̃d] adj fertile; **féconder** /1/ vt to fertilize
féculent [fekylɑ̃] nm starchy food
fédéral, e, -aux [federal, -o] adj federal

fée [fe] *nf* fairy

feignant, e [fɛɲɑ̃, -ɑ̃t] *nm/f*
= **fainéant**

feindre [fɛ̃dʀ] /52/ *vt* to feign; ~ **de
faire** to pretend to do

fêler [fele] /1/ *vt* to crack

félicitations [felisitasjɔ̃] *nfpl*
congratulations

féliciter [felisite] /1/ *vt*: ~ **qn (de)** to
congratulate sb (on)

félin, e [felɛ̃, -in] *nm* (big) cat

femelle [fəmɛl] *adj, nf* female

féminin, e [feminɛ̃, -in] *adj*
feminine; (*sexe*) female; (*équipe,
vêtements etc*) women's ▷ *nm* (Ling)
feminine; **féministe** *adj* feminist

femme [fam] *nf* woman; (*épouse*)
wife; ~ **de chambre** chambermaid;
~ **au foyer** housewife; ~ **de ménage**
cleaning lady

fémur [femyʀ] *nm* femur, thighbone

fendre [fɑ̃dʀ] /41/ *vt* (*couper en deux*)
to split; (*fissurer*) to crack; (*traverser*)
to cut through; **se fendre** *vi* to crack

fenêtre [f(ə)nɛtʀ] *nf* window

fenouil [fənuj] *nm* fennel

fente [fɑ̃t] *nf* (*fissure*) crack; (*de boîte à
lettres etc*) slit

fer [fɛʀ] *nm* iron; ~ **à cheval** horseshoe;
~ **forgé** wrought iron; ~ **à friser**
curling tongs; ~ **(à repasser)** iron

ferai *etc* [fəʀe] *vb voir* **faire**

fer-blanc [fɛʀblɑ̃] *nm* tin(plate)

férié, e [feʀje] *adj*: **jour** ~ public
holiday

ferions *etc* [fəʀjɔ̃] *vb voir* **faire**

ferme [fɛʀm] *adj* firm ▷ *adv* (*travailler
etc*) hard ▷ *nf* (*exploitation*) farm;
(*maison*) farmhouse

fermé, e [fɛʀme] *adj* closed, shut;
(*gaz, eau etc*) off; (*fig: milieu*) exclusive

fermenter [fɛʀmɑ̃te] /1/ *vi* to ferment

fermer [fɛʀme] /1/ *vt* to close, shut;
(*cesser l'exploitation de*) to close down,
shut down; (*eau, lumière, électricité,
robinet*) to turn off; (*aéroport, route*)
to close ▷ *vi* to close, shut; (*magasin:
définitivement*) to close down, shut

down; **se fermer** *vi* to close, shut; ~
à clef to lock

fermeté [fɛʀməte] *nf* firmness

fermeture [fɛʀmətyʀ] *nf* closing;
(*dispositif*) catch; **heure de** ~ closing
time; ~ **éclair**® *ou* **à glissière** zip
(fastener) (BRIT), zipper (US)

fermier, -ière [fɛʀmje, -jɛʀ] *nm/f*
farmer

féroce [feʀɔs] *adj* ferocious, fierce

ferons *etc* [fəʀɔ̃] *vb voir* **faire**

ferrer [feʀe] /1/ *vt* (*cheval*) to shoe

ferroviaire [feʀɔvjɛʀ] *adj* rail *cpd*,
railway *cpd* (BRIT), railroad *cpd* (US)

ferry(-boat) [feʀe(bot)] *nm* ferry

fertile [fɛʀtil] *adj* fertile; ~ **en
incidents** eventful, packed with
incidents

fervent, e [fɛʀvɑ̃, -ɑ̃t] *adj* fervent

fesse [fɛs] *nf* buttock; **fessée** *nf*
spanking

festin [fɛstɛ̃] *nm* feast

festival [fɛstival] *nm* festival

festivités [fɛstivite] *nfpl* festivities

fêtard, e [fɛtaʀ, -aʀd] (*fam*) *nm/f* (*péj*)
high liver, merrymaker

fête [fɛt] *nf* (*religieuse*) feast; (*publique*)
holiday; (*réception*) party; (*kermesse*)
fête, fair; (*du nom*) feast day, name
day; **faire la** ~ to live it up; **faire** ~
à qn to give sb a warm welcome;
les ~**s (de fin d'année)** the festive
season; **la salle/le comité des** ~**s**
the village hall/festival committee;
la ~ **des Mères/Pères** Mother's/
Father's Day; ~ **foraine** (fun)fair; **la
~ de la musique**; *see note* "**fête de la
musique**"; **fêter** /1/ *vt* to celebrate;
(*personne*) to have a celebration for

⊙ FÊTE DE LA MUSIQUE

- The *Fête de la Musique* is a music
- festival which has taken place
- every year since 1981. On 21 June
- throughout France local musicians
- perform free of charge in parks,
- streets and squares.

feu, x [fø] *nm* (*gén*) fire; (*signal lumineux*) light; (*de cuisinière*) ring; **feux** *nmpl* (*Auto*) (traffic) lights; **au ~!** (*incendie*) fire!; **à ~ doux/vif** over a slow/brisk heat; **à petit ~** (*Culin*) over a gentle heat; (*fig*) slowly; **faire ~** to fire; **ne pas faire long ~** not to last long; **prendre ~** to catch fire; **mettre le ~ à** to set fire to; **faire du ~** to make a fire; **avez-vous du ~?** (*pour cigarette*) have you (got) a light?; **~ rouge/vert/orange** red/green/amber (*BRIT*) *ou* yellow (*US*) light; **~ arrière** rear light; **~ d'artifice** firework; (*spectacle*) fireworks *pl*; **~ de joie** bonfire; **~x de brouillard** fog lights *ou* lamps; **~x de croisement** dipped (*BRIT*) *ou* dimmed (*US*) headlights; **~x de position** sidelights; **~x de route** (*Auto*) headlights (on full (*BRIT*) *ou* high (*US*) beam)

feuillage [fœjaʒ] *nm* foliage, leaves *pl*

feuille [fœj] *nf* (*d'arbre*) leaf; **~ (de papier)** sheet (of paper); **~ de calcul** spreadsheet; **~ d'impôts** tax form; **~ de maladie** medical expenses claim form; **~ de paye** pay slip

feuillet [fœjɛ] *nm* leaf

feuilleté, e [fœjte] *adj*: **pâte ~** flaky pastry

feuilleter [fœjte] /4/ *vt* (*livre*) to leaf through

feuilleton [fœjtɔ̃] *nm* serial

feutre [føtʀ] *nm* felt; (*chapeau*) felt hat; (*stylo*) felt-tip(ped pen); **feutré, e** *adj* (*pas, voix, atmosphère*) muffled

fève [fɛv] *nf* broad bean

février [fevʀije] *nm* February

fiable [fjabl] *adj* reliable

fiançailles [fjɑ̃saj] *nfpl* engagement *sg*

fiancé, e [fjɑ̃se] *nm/f* fiancé (fiancée) ▷ *adj*: **être ~ (à)** to be engaged (to)

fibre [fibʀ] *nf* fibre; **~ de verre** fibreglass

ficeler [fis(ə)le] /4/ *vt* to tie up

ficelle [fisɛl] *nf* string *no pl*; (*morceau*) piece *ou* length of string

fiche [fiʃ] *nf* (*carte*) (index) card; (*formulaire*) form; (*Élec*) plug; **~ de paye** pay slip

ficher [fiʃe] /1/ *vt* (*dans un fichier*) to file; (: *Police*) to put on file; (*fam*: *faire*) to do; (: *donner*) to give; (: *mettre*) to stick *ou* shove; **fiche(-moi) le camp** (*fam*) clear off; **fiche-moi la paix** (*fam*) leave me alone; **se ~ de** (*fam*: *rire de*) to make fun of; (: *être indifférent à*) not to care about

fichier [fiʃje] *nm* file; **~ joint** (*Inform*) attachment

fichu, e [fiʃy] *pp de* **ficher** ▷ *adj* (*fam*: *fini, inutilisable*) bust, done for; (: *intensif*) wretched, darned ▷ *nm* (*foulard*) (head)scarf; **mal ~** feeling lousy

fictif, -ive [fiktif, -iv] *adj* fictitious

fiction [fiksjɔ̃] *nf* fiction; (*fait imaginé*) invention

fidèle [fidɛl] *adj*: **~ (à)** faithful (to) ▷ *nm/f* (*Rel*): **les ~s** (*à l'église*) the congregation; **fidélité** *nf* (*d'un conjoint*) fidelity, faithfulness; (*d'un ami, client*) loyalty

fier¹ [fje]: **se ~ à** *vt* to trust

fier², fière [fjɛʀ] *adj* proud; **~ de** proud of; **fierté** *nf* pride

fièvre [fjɛvʀ] *nf* fever; **avoir de la ~/39 de ~** to have a high temperature/a temperature of 39°C; **fiévreux, -euse** *adj* feverish

figer [fiʒe] /3/: **se figer** *vi* to congeal, (*personne*) to freeze

fignoler [fiɲɔle] /1/ *vt* to put the finishing touches to

figue [fig] *nf* fig; **figuier** *nm* fig tree

figurant, e [figyʀɑ̃, -ɑ̃t] *nm/f* (*Théât*) walk-on; (*Ciné*) extra

figure [figyʀ] *nf* (*visage*) face; (*image, tracé, forme, personnage*) figure; (*illustration*) picture, diagram

figuré, e [figyʀe] *adj* (*sens*) figurative

figurer [figyʀe] /1/ *vi* to appear ▷ *vt* to represent; **se ~ que** to imagine that

fil [fil] *nm* (*brin, fig*: *d'une histoire*) thread; (*d'un couteau*) edge; **au ~ des**

années with the passing of the years; **au ~ de l'eau** with the stream *ou* current; **coup de ~** (*fam*) phone call; **donner/recevoir un coup de ~** to make/get a phone call; **~ électrique** electric wire; **~ de fer** wire; **~ de fer barbelé** barbed wire

file [fil] *nf* line; (*Auto*) lane; **~ (d'attente)** queue (*BRIT*), line (*US*); **à la ~** (*d'affilée*) in succession; **à la** *ou* **en ~ indienne** in single file

filer [file] /1/ *vt* (*tissu, toile, verre*) to spin; (*prendre en filature*) to shadow, tail; (*fam: donner*) **~ qch à qn** to slip sb sth ▷ *vi* (*bas, maille, liquide, pâte*) to run; (*aller vite*) to fly past *ou* by; (*fam: partir*) to make off; **~ doux** to behave o.s.

filet [file] *nm* net; (*Culin*) fillet; (*d'eau, de sang*) trickle; **~ (à provisions)** string bag

filial, e, -aux [filjal, -o] *adj* filial ▷ *nf* (*Comm*) subsidiary

filière [filjɛʀ] *nf* (*carrière*) path; **suivre la ~** to work one's way up (through the hierarchy)

fille [fij] *nf* girl; (*opposé à fils*) daughter; **vieille ~** old maid; **fillette** *nf* (little) girl

filleul, e [fijœl] *nm/f* godchild, godson (goddaughter)

film [film] *nm* (*pour photo*) (roll of) film; (*œuvre*) film, picture, movie

fils [fis] *nm* son; **~ à papa** (*péj*) daddy's boy

filtre [filtʀ] *nm* filter; **filtrer** /1/ *vt* to filter; (*fig: candidats, visiteurs*) to screen

fin¹ [fɛ̃] *nf* end; **fins** *nfpl* (*but*) ends; **~ mai** at the end of May; **prendre ~** to come to an end; **mettre ~ à** to put an end to; **à la ~** in the end, eventually; **en ~ de compte** in the end; **sans ~** endless

fin², e [fɛ̃, fin] *adj* (*papier, couche, fil*) thin; (*cheveux, poudre, pointe, visage*) fine; (*taille*) neat, slim; (*esprit, remarque*) subtle ▷ *adv* (*moudre,*

couper) finely; **~ prêt/soûl** quite ready/drunk; **avoir la vue/l'ouïe ~e** to have keen eyesight/hearing; **or/ linge/vin ~** fine gold/linen/wine; **~es herbes** mixed herbs

final, e [final] *adj, nf* final ▷ *nm* (*Mus*) finale; **quarts de ~e** quarter finals; **finalement** *adv* finally, in the end; (*après tout*) after all

finance [finɑ̃s] *nf* finance; **finances** *nfpl* (*situation financière*) finances; (*activités financières*) finance *sg*; **moyennant ~** for a fee *ou* consideration; **financer** /3/ *vt* to finance; **financier, -ière** *adj* financial

finesse [finɛs] *nf* thinness; (*raffinement*) fineness; (*subtilité*) subtlety

fini, e [fini] *adj* finished; (*Math*) finite ▷ *nm* (*d'un objet manufacturé*) finish

finir [finiʀ] /2/ *vt* to finish ▷ *vi* to finish, end; **~ de faire** to finish doing; (*cesser*) to stop doing; **~ par faire** to end *ou* finish up doing; **il finit par m'agacer** he's beginning to get on my nerves; **en ~ avec** to be *ou* have done with; **il va mal ~** he will come to a bad end

finition [finisjɔ̃] *nf* (*résultat*) finish

finlandais, e [fɛ̃lɑ̃dɛ, -ɛz] *adj* Finnish ▷ *nm/f*: **F~, e** Finn

Finlande [fɛ̃lɑ̃d] *nf*: **la ~** Finland

finnois, e [finwa, -waz] *adj* Finnish ▷ *nm* (*Ling*) Finnish

fioul [fjul] *nm* fuel oil

firme [fiʀm] *nf* firm

fis [fi] *vb voir* **faire**

fisc [fisk] *nm* tax authorities *pl*; **fiscal, e, -aux** *adj* tax *cpd*, fiscal; **fiscalité** *nf* tax system

fissure [fisyʀ] *nf* crack; **fissurer** /1/ *vt* to crack; **se fissurer** *vi* to crack

fit [fi] *vb voir* **faire**

fixation [fiksasjɔ̃] *nf* (*attache*) fastening; (*Psych*) fixation

fixe [fiks] *adj* fixed; (*emploi*) steady, regular ▷ *nm* (*salaire*) basic salary; (*téléphone*) landline; **à heure ~** at a set time; **menu à prix ~** set menu

fixé, e [fikse] *adj*: **être ~ (sur)** (*savoir à quoi s'en tenir*) to have made up one's mind (about)

fixer [fikse] /1/ *vt* (*attacher*): **~ qch (à/sur)** to fix *ou* fasten sth (to/onto); (*déterminer*) to fix, set; (*poser son regard sur*) to stare at; **se fixer** (*s'établir*) to settle down; **se ~ sur** (*attention*) to focus on

flacon [flakɔ̃] *nm* bottle

flageolet [flaʒɔlɛ] *nm* (*Culin*) dwarf kidney bean

flagrant, e [flagrɑ̃, -ɑ̃t] *adj* flagrant, blatant; **en ~ délit** in the act

flair [flɛʀ] *nm* sense of smell; (*fig*) intuition; **flairer** /1/ *vt* (*humer*) to sniff (at); (*détecter*) to scent

flamand, e [flamɑ̃, -ɑ̃d] *adj* Flemish ▷ *nm* (*Ling*) Flemish ▷ *nm/f*: **F~, e** Fleming

flamant [flamɑ̃] *nm* flamingo

flambant [flɑ̃bɑ̃] *adv*: **~ neuf** brand new

flambé, e [flɑ̃be] *adj* (*Culin*) flambé

flambée [flɑ̃be] *nf* blaze; **~ des prix** (sudden) shooting up of prices

flamber [flɑ̃be] /1/ *vi* to blaze (up)

flamboyer [flɑ̃bwaje] /8/ *vi* to blaze (up)

flamme [flam] *nf* flame; (*fig*) fire, fervour; **en ~s** on fire, ablaze

flan [flɑ̃] *nm* (*Culin*) custard tart *ou* pie

flanc [flɑ̃] *nm* side; (*Mil*) flank

flancher [flɑ̃ʃe] /1/ *vi* to fail, pack up

flanelle [flanɛl] *nf* flannel

flâner [flɑne] /1/ *vi* to stroll

flanquer [flɑ̃ke] /1/ *vt* to flank; (*fam: mettre*) to chuck, shove; **~ par terre/à la porte** (*jeter*) to fling to the ground/chuck out

flaque [flak] *nf* (*d'eau*) puddle; (*d'huile, de sang etc*) pool

flash [flaʃ] (*pl* **flashes**) *nm* (*Photo*) flash; **~ (d'information)** newsflash

flatter [flate] /1/ *vt* to flatter; **se ~ de qch** to pride o.s. on sth; **flatteur, -euse** *adj* flattering

flèche [flɛʃ] *nf* arrow; (*de clocher*) spire; **monter en ~** (*fig*) to soar, rocket; **partir en ~** to be off like a shot; **fléchette** *nf* dart

flétrir [fletʀiʀ] /2/: **se flétrir** *vi* to wither

fleur [flœʀ] *nf* flower; (*d'un arbre*) blossom; **être en ~** (*arbre*) to be in blossom; **tissu à ~s** flowered *ou* flowery fabric

fleuri, e [flœʀi] *adj* (*jardin*) in flower *ou* bloom; (*style, tissu, papier*) flowery; (*teint*) glowing

fleurir [flœʀiʀ] /2/ *vi* (*rose*) to flower; (*arbre*) to blossom; (*fig*) to flourish ▷ *vt* (*tombe*) to put flowers on; (*chambre*) to decorate with flowers

fleuriste [flœʀist] *nm/f* florist

fleuve [flœv] *nm* river

flexible [flɛksibl] *adj* flexible

flic [flik] *nm* (*fam: péj*) cop

flipper [flipœʀ] *nm* pinball (machine)

flirter [flœʀte] /1/ *vi* to flirt

flocon [flɔkɔ̃] *nm* flake

flore [flɔʀ] *nf* flora

florissant, e [flɔʀisɑ̃, -ɑ̃t] *adj* (*économie*) flourishing

flot [flo] *nm* flood, stream; **flots** *nmpl* (*de la mer*) waves; **être à ~** (*Navig*) to be afloat; **entrer à ~s** to stream *ou* pour in

flottant, e [flɔtɑ̃, -ɑ̃t] *adj* (*vêtement*) loose(-fitting)

flotte [flɔt] *nf* (*Navig*) fleet; (*fam: eau*) water; (*: pluie*) rain

flotter [flɔte] /1/ *vi* to float; (*nuage, odeur*) to drift; (*drapeau*) to fly; (*vêtements*) to hang loose ▷ *vb impers* (*fam: pleuvoir*): **il flotte** it's raining; **faire ~** to float; **flotteur** *nm* float

flou, e [flu] *adj* fuzzy, blurred; (*fig*) woolly (BRIT), vague

fluide [flyid] *adj* fluid; (*circulation etc*) flowing freely ▷ *nm* fluid

fluor [flyɔʀ] *nm*: **dentifrice au ~** fluoride toothpaste

fluorescent, e [flyɔʀesɑ̃, -ɑ̃t] *adj* fluorescent

flûte [flyt] nf (aussi: **~ traversière**) flute; (verre) flute glass; (pain) (thin) baguette; **~!** drat it!; **~ (à bec)** recorder

flux [fly] nm incoming tide; (écoulement) flow; **le ~ et le re~** the ebb and flow

foc [fɔk] nm jib

foi [fwa] nf faith; **digne de ~** reliable; **être de bonne/mauvaise ~** to be in good faith/not to be in good faith

foie [fwa] nm liver; **crise de ~** stomach upset

foin [fwɛ̃] nm hay; **faire du ~** (fam) to kick up a row

foire [fwaʀ] nf fair; (fête foraine) (fun)fair; **~ aux questions** (Internet) frequently asked questions; **faire la ~** to whoop it up; **~ (exposition)** trade fair

fois [fwa] nf time; **une/deux ~** once/twice; **deux ~ deux** twice two; **une ~ (passé)** once; (futur) sometime; **une (bonne) ~ pour toutes** once and for all; **une ~ que c'est fait** once it's done; **des ~ (parfois)** sometimes; **à la ~ (ensemble)** (all) at once

fol [fɔl] adj m voir **fou**

folie [fɔli] nf (d'une décision, d'un acte) madness, folly; (état) madness, insanity; **la ~ des grandeurs** delusions of grandeur; **faire des ~s** (en dépenses) to be extravagant

folklorique [fɔlklɔʀik] adj folk cpd; (fam) weird

folle [fɔl] adj f, nf voir **fou**; **follement** adv (très) madly, wildly

foncé, e [fɔ̃se] adj dark

foncer [fɔ̃se] /3/ vi to go darker; (fam: aller vite) to tear ou belt along; **~ sur** to charge at

fonction [fɔ̃ksjɔ̃] nf function; (emploi, poste) post, position; **fonctions** nfpl (professionnelles) duties; **voiture de ~** company car; **en ~ de** (par rapport à) according to; **faire ~ de** to serve as; **la ~ publique** the state ou civil (BRIT) service; **fonctionnaire** nm/f

state employee ou official; (dans l'administration) ≈ civil servant; **fonctionner** /1/ vi to work, function

fond [fɔ̃] nm voir aussi **fonds**; (d'un récipient, trou) bottom; (d'une salle, scène) back; (d'un tableau, décor) background; (opposé à la forme) content; (Sport): **le ~** long distance (running); **au ~ de** at the bottom of; at the back of; **à ~ (connaître, soutenir)** thoroughly; (appuyer, visser) right down ou home; **à ~ (de train)** (fam) full tilt; **dans le ~, au ~** (en somme) basically, really; **de ~ en comble** from top to bottom; **~ de teint** foundation

fondamental, e, -aux [fɔ̃damɑ̃tal, -o] adj fundamental

fondant, e [fɔ̃dɑ̃, -ɑ̃t] adj (neige) melting; (poire) that melts in the mouth

fondation [fɔ̃dasjɔ̃] nf founding; (établissement) foundation; **fondations** nfpl (d'une maison) foundations

fondé, e [fɔ̃de] adj (accusation etc) well-founded; **être ~ à croire** to have grounds for believing ou good reason to believe

fondement [fɔ̃dmɑ̃] nm: **sans ~** (rumeur etc) groundless, unfounded

fonder [fɔ̃de] /1/ vt to found; (fig): **~ qch sur** to base sth on; **se ~ sur** (personne) to base o.s. on

fonderie [fɔ̃dʀi] nf smelting works sg

fondre [fɔ̃dʀ] /41/ vt (aussi: **faire ~**) to melt; (dans l'eau) to dissolve; (fig: mélanger) to merge, blend ▷ vi (à la chaleur) to melt; to dissolve; (fig) to melt away; (se précipiter): **~ sur** to swoop down on; **~ en larmes** to dissolve into tears

fonds [fɔ̃] nm (Comm): **~ (de commerce)** business ▷ nmpl (argent) funds

fondu, e [fɔ̃dy] adj (beurre, neige) melted; (métal) molten ▷ nf (Culin) fondue

font [fɔ̃] *vb voir* **faire**

fontaine [fɔ̃tɛn] *nf* fountain; (*source*) spring

fonte [fɔ̃t] *nf* melting; (*métal*) cast iron; **la ~ des neiges** the (spring) thaw

foot [fut], **football** [futbol] *nm* football, soccer; **footballeur, -euse** *nm/f* footballer, (BRIT), football *ou* soccer player

footing [futiŋ] *nm* jogging; **faire du ~** to go jogging

forain, e [fɔʀɛ̃, -ɛn] *adj* fairground *cpd* ▷ *nm* (*marchand*) stallholder; (*acteur etc*) fairground entertainer

forçat [fɔʀsa] *nm* convict

force [fɔʀs] *nf* strength; (*Physique, Mécanique*) force; **forces** *nfpl* (*physiques*) strength *sg*; (*Mil*) forces; **à ~ de faire** by dint of doing; **de ~** forcibly, by force; **dans la ~ de l'âge** in the prime of life; **les ~s de l'ordre** the police

forcé, e [fɔʀse] *adj* forced; **c'est ~!** it's inevitable!; **forcément** *adv* inevitably; **pas forcément** not necessarily

forcer [fɔʀse] /3/ *vt* to force; (*moteur, voix*) to strain ▷ *vi* (*Sport*) to overtax o.s.; **se ~ à faire qch** to force o.s. to do sth; **~ la dose/l'allure** to overdo it/increase the pace

forestier, -ière [fɔʀɛstje, -jɛʀ] *adj* forest *cpd*

forêt [fɔʀɛ] *nf* forest

forfait [fɔʀfɛ] *nm* (*Comm*) all-in deal *ou* price; **déclarer ~** to withdraw; **forfaitaire** *adj* inclusive

forge [fɔʀʒ] *nf* forge, smithy; **forgeron** *nm* (black)smith

formaliser [fɔʀmalize] /1/: **se formaliser** *vi*: **se ~ (de)** to take offence (at)

formalité [fɔʀmalite] *nf* formality; **simple ~** mere formality

format [fɔʀma] *nm* size; **formater** /1/ *vt* (*disque*) to format

formation [fɔʀmasjɔ̃] *nf* forming; training; **la ~ permanente** *ou*

continue continuing education; **la ~ professionnelle** vocational training

forme [fɔʀm] *nf* (*gén*) form; (*d'un objet*) shape, form; **formes** *nfpl* (*bonnes manières*) proprieties; (*d'une femme*) figure *sg*; **en ~ de poire** pear-shaped, in the shape of a pear; **être en (bonne ou pleine) ~** (*Sport etc*) to be on form; **en bonne et due ~** in due form

formel, le [fɔʀmɛl] *adj* (*preuve, décision*) definite, positive; **formellement** *adv* (*interdit*) strictly; (*absolument*) positively

former [fɔʀme] /1/ *vt* to form; (*éduquer*) to train; **se former** *vi* to form

formidable [fɔʀmidabl] *adj* tremendous

formulaire [fɔʀmylɛʀ] *nm* form

formule [fɔʀmyl] *nf* (*gén*) formula; (*expression*) phrase; **~ de politesse** polite phrase; (*en fin de lettre*) letter ending

fort, e [fɔʀ, fɔʀt] *adj* strong; (*intensité, rendement*) high, great; (*corpulent*) large; (*doué*): **être ~ (en)** to be good (at) ▷ *adv* (*serrer, frapper*) hard; (*sonner*) loud(ly); (*beaucoup*) greatly, very much; (*très*) very ▷ *nm* (*édifice*) fort; (*point fort*) strong point, forte; **~e tête** rebel; **forteresse** *nf* fortress

fortifiant [fɔʀtifjɑ̃] *nm* tonic

fortune [fɔʀtyn] *nf* fortune; **faire ~** to make one's fortune; **de ~** makeshift; **fortuné, e** *adj* wealthy

forum [fɔʀɔm] *nm* forum; **~ de discussion** (*Internet*) message board

fosse [fos] *nf* (*grand trou*) pit; (*tombe*) grave

fossé [fose] *nm* ditch; (*fig*) gulf, gap

fossette [fosɛt] *nf* dimple

fossile [fosil] *nm* fossil ▷ *adj* fossilized, fossil *cpd*

fou (fol), folle [fu, fɔl] *adj* mad; (*déréglé etc*) wild, erratic; (*fam: extrême, très grand*) terrific, tremendous ▷ *nm/f* madman/woman ▷ *nm* (*du* *roi*) jester; **être ~ de** to be mad *ou* crazy about; **avoir le ~ rire** to have the giggles

foudre [fudʀ] *nf*: **la ~** lightning

foudroyant, e [fudʀwajɑ̃, -ɑ̃t] *adj* (*progrès*) lightning *cpd*; (*succès*) stunning; (*maladie, poison*) violent

fouet [fwɛ] *nm* whip; (*Culin*) whisk; **de plein ~** *adv* (*se heurter*) head on; **fouetter** /1/ *vt* to whip; (*crème*) to whisk

fougère [fuʒɛʀ] *nf* fern

fougue [fug] *nf* ardour, spirit; **fougueux, -euse** *adj* fiery

fouille [fuj] *nf* search; **fouilles** *nfpl* (*archéologiques*) excavations; **fouiller** /1/ *vt* to search; (*creuser*) to dig ▷ *vi*: **fouiller dans/parmi** to rummage in/among; **fouillis** *nm* jumble, muddle

foulard [fulaʀ] *nm* scarf

foule [ful] *nf* crowd; **la ~** crowds *pl*; **une ~ de** masses of

foulée [fule] *nf* stride

fouler [fule] /1/ *vt* to press; (*sol*) to tread upon; **se ~ la cheville** to sprain one's ankle; **ne pas se ~** not to overexert o.s.; **il ne se foule pas** he doesn't put himself out; **foulure** *nf* sprain

four [fuʀ] *nm* oven; (*de potier*) kiln; (*Théât: échec*) flop

fourche [fuʀʃ] *nf* pitchfork

fourchette [fuʀʃɛt] *nf* fork; (*Statistique*) bracket, margin

fourgon [fuʀgɔ̃] *nm* van; (*Rail*) wag(g)on; **fourgonnette** *nf* (delivery) van

fourmi [fuʀmi] *nf* ant; **avoir des ~s dans les jambes/mains** to have pins and needles in one's legs/hands; **fourmilière** *nf* ant-hill; **fourmiller** /1/ *vi* to swarm

fourneau, x [fuʀno] *nm* stove

fourni, e [fuʀni] *adj* (*barbe, cheveux*) thick; (*magasin*): **bien ~ (en)** well stocked (with)

fournir [fuʀniʀ] /2/ *vt* to supply; (*preuve, exemple*) to provide, supply; (*effort*) to put in; **~ qch à qn** to

supply sth to sb, supply *ou* provide sb with sth; **fournisseur, -euse** *nm/f* supplier; **fournisseur d'accès à Internet** (Internet) service provider, ISP; **fourniture** *nf* supply(ing); **fournitures scolaires** school stationery

fourrage [fuʀaʒ] *nm* fodder

fourré, e [fuʀe] *adj* (*bonbon, chocolat*) filled; (*manteau, botte*) fur-lined ▷ *nm* thicket

fourrer [fuʀe] /1/ *vt* (*fam*) to stick, shove; **se ~ dans/sous** to get into/under

fourrière [fuʀjɛʀ] *nf* pound

fourrure [fuʀyʀ] *nf* fur; (*pelage*) coat

foutre [futʀ] *vt* (*fam!*) = **ficher**; **foutu, e** *adj* (*fam!*) = **fichu**

foyer [fwaje] *nm* (*de cheminée*) hearth; (*famille*) family; (*domicile*) home; (*local de réunion*) (social) club; (*résidence*) hostel; (*salon*) foyer; **lunettes à double ~** bi-focal glasses

fracassant, e [fʀakasɑ̃, -ɑ̃t] *adj* (*succès*) staggering

fraction [fʀaksjɔ̃] *nf* fraction

fracturation [fʀaktyʀasjɔ̃] *nf*: **~ hydraulique** fracking

fracture [fʀaktyʀ] *nf* fracture; **~ du crâne** fractured skull; **fracturer** /1/ *vt* (*coffre, serrure*) to break open; (*os, membre*) to fracture; **se fracturer le crâne** to fracture one's skull

fragile [fʀaʒil] *adj* fragile, delicate; (*fig*) frail; **fragilité** *nf* fragility

fragment [fʀagmɑ̃] *nm* (*d'un objet*) fragment, piece

fraîche [fʀɛʃ] *adj f voir* **frais**; **fraîcheur** *nf* coolness; (*d'un aliment*) freshness; *voir* **frais**; **fraîchir** /2/ *vi* to get cooler; (*vent*) to freshen

frais, fraîche [fʀɛ, fʀɛʃ] *adj* (*air, eau, accueil*) cool; (*petit pois, œufs, nouvelles, couleur, troupes*) fresh ▷ *adv* (*récemment*) newly, fresh(ly) ▷ *nm*: **mettre au ~** to put in a cool place; **prendre le ~** to take a breath of cool air ▷ *nmpl* (*débours*) expenses; (*Comm*) costs; **il fait ~** it's cool; **servir ~** serve chilled; **faire des ~** to go to a lot of expense; **~ généraux** overheads; **~ de scolarité** school fees (BRIT), tuition (US)

fraise [fʀɛz] nf strawberry; **~ des bois** wild strawberry

framboise [fʀãbwaz] nf raspberry

franc, franche [fʀã, fʀãʃ] adj (personne) frank, straightforward; (visage) open; (net: refus, couleur) clear; (: coupure) clean; (intensif) downright ▷ nm franc

français, e [fʀãsɛ, -ɛz] adj French ▷ nm (Ling) French ▷ nm/f: **F~, e** Frenchman/woman

France [fʀãs] nf: **la ~** France; **~ 2, ~ 3** public-sector television channels

> ○ **FRANCE TÉLÉVISION**
> ○
> ○ France 2 and France 3 are public-
> ○ sector television channels. France
> ○ 2 is a national general interest and
> ○ entertainment channel; France
> ○ 3 provides regional news and
> ○ information as well as programmes
> ○ for the national network.

franche [fʀãʃ] adj f voir **franc**; **franchement** adv frankly; clearly; (nettement) definitely; (tout à fait) downright

franchir [fʀãʃiʀ] /2/ vt (obstacle) to clear, get over; (seuil, ligne, rivière) to cross; (distance) to cover

franchise [fʀãʃiz] nf frankness; (douanière) exemption; (Assurances) excess

franc-maçon [fʀãmasõ] nm Freemason

franco [fʀãko] adv (Comm): **~ (de port)** postage paid

francophone [fʀãkɔfɔn] adj French-speaking

franc-parler [fʀãpaʀle] nm inv outspokenness; **avoir son ~** to speak one's mind

frange [fʀãʒ] nf fringe

frangipane [fʀãʒipan] nf almond paste

frappant, e [fʀapã, -ãt] adj striking

frappé, e [fʀape] adj iced

frapper [fʀape] /1/ vt to hit, strike; (étonner) to strike; **~ dans ses mains** to clap one's hands; **frappé de stupeur** dumbfounded

fraternel, le [fʀatɛʀnɛl] adj brotherly, fraternal; **fraternité** nf brotherhood

fraude [fʀod] nf fraud; (Scol) cheating; **passer qch en ~** to smuggle sth in (ou out); **~ fiscale** tax evasion

frayeur [fʀɛjœʀ] nf fright

fredonner [fʀədɔne] /1/ vt to hum

freezer [fʀizœʀ] nm freezing compartment

frein [fʀɛ̃] nm brake; **mettre un ~ à** (fig) to put a brake on, check; **~ à main** handbrake; **freiner** /1/ vi to brake ▷ vt (progrès etc) to check

frêle [fʀɛl] adj frail, fragile

frelon [fʀəlõ] nm hornet

frémir [fʀemiʀ] /2/ vi (de froid, de peur) to shudder; (de colère) to shake; (de joie, feuillage) to quiver

frêne [fʀɛn] nm ash (tree)

fréquemment [fʀekamã] adv frequently

fréquent, e [fʀekã, -ãt] adj frequent

fréquentation [fʀekãtasjõ] nf frequenting; **fréquentations** nfpl (relations) company sg; **avoir de mauvaises ~s** to be in with the wrong crowd, keep bad company

fréquenté, e [fʀekãte] adj: **très ~** (very) busy; **mal ~** patronized by disreputable elements

fréquenter [fʀekãte] /1/ vt (lieu) to frequent; (personne) to see; **se fréquenter** to see a lot of each other

frère [fʀɛʀ] nm brother

fresque [fʀɛsk] nf (Art) fresco

fret [fʀɛ(t)] nm freight

friand, e [fʀijɑ̃, -ɑ̃d] adj: **~ de** very fond of ▷ nm: **~ au fromage** cheese puff

friandise [fʀijɑ̃diz] nf sweet

fric [fʀik] nm (fam) cash, bread

friche [fʀiʃ]: **en ~** adj, adv (lying) fallow

friction [fʀiksjɔ̃] nf (massage) rub, rub-down; (Tech, fig) friction

frigidaire® [fʀiʒidɛʀ] nm refrigerator

frigo [fʀigo] nm fridge

frigorifique [fʀigoʀifik] adj refrigerating

frileux, -euse [fʀilø, -øz] adj sensitive to (the) cold

frimer [fʀime] /1/ vi (fam) to show off

fringale [fʀɛ̃gal] nf (fam): **avoir la ~** to be ravenous

fringues [fʀɛ̃g] nfpl (fam) clothes

fripé, e [fʀipe] adj crumpled

frire [fʀiʀ] vt to fry ▷ vi to fry

frisé, e [fʀize] adj (cheveux) curly; (personne) curly-haired

frisson [fʀisɔ̃] nm (de froid) shiver; (de peur) shudder; **frissonner** /1/ vi (de fièvre, froid) to shiver; (d'horreur) to shudder

frit, e [fʀi, fʀit] pp de **frire** ▷ nf: **(pommes) ~es** chips (BRIT), French fries; **friteuse** nf deep fryer, chip pan (BRIT); **friture** nf (huile) (deep) fat; (plat): **friture (de poissons)** fried fish

froid, e [fʀwa, fʀwad] adj ▷ nm cold; **il fait ~** it's cold; **avoir ~** to be cold; **prendre ~** to catch a chill ou cold; **être en ~ avec** to be on bad terms with; **froidement** adv (accueillir) coldly; (décider) coolly

froisser [fʀwase] /1/ vt to crumple (up), crease; (fig) to hurt, offend; **se froisser** vi to crumple, crease; (personne) to take offence (BRIT) ou offense (US); **se ~ un muscle** to strain a muscle

frôler [fʀole] /1/ vt to brush against; (projectile) to skim past; (fig) to come

very close to, come within a hair's breadth of

fromage [fʀɔmaʒ] nm cheese; **~ blanc** soft white cheese

froment [fʀɔmɑ̃] nm wheat

froncer [fʀɔ̃se] /3/ vt to gather; **~ les sourcils** to frown

front [fʀɔ̃] nm forehead, brow; (Mil, Météorologie, Pol) front; **de ~** (se heurter) head-on; (rouler) together (2 or 3 abreast); (simultanément) at once; **faire ~ à** to face up to

frontalier, -ière [fʀɔ̃talje, -jɛʀ] adj border cpd, frontier cpd ▷ **(travailleurs) ~s** commuters from across the border

frontière [fʀɔ̃tjɛʀ] nf frontier, border

frotter [fʀɔte] /1/ vi to rub, scrape ▷ vt to rub; (pommes de terre, plancher) to scrub; **~ une allumette** to strike a match

fruit [fʀɥi] nm fruit no pl; **~s de mer** seafood(s); **~s secs** dried fruit sg; **fruité, e** [fʀɥite] adj fruity; **fruitier, -ière** adj: **arbre fruitier** fruit tree

frustrer [fʀystʀe] /1/ vt to frustrate

fuel(-oil) [fjul(ɔjl)] nm fuel oil; (pour chauffer) heating oil

fugace [fygas] adj fleeting

fugitif, -ive [fyʒitif, -iv] adj (lueur, amour) fleeting ▷ nm/f fugitive

fugue [fyg] nf: **faire une ~** to run away, abscond

fuir [fɥiʀ] /17/ vt to flee from; (éviter) to shun ▷ vi to run away; (gaz, robinet) to leak

fuite [fɥit] nf flight; (divulgation) leak; **être en ~** to be on the run; **mettre en ~** to put to flight

fulgurant, e [fylgyʀɑ̃, -ɑ̃t] adj lightning cpd, dazzling

fumé, e [fyme] adj (Culin) smoked; (verre) tinted ▷ nf smoke

fumer [fyme] /1/ vi to smoke; (liquide) to steam ▷ vt to smoke

fûmes [fym] vb voir **être**

fumeur, -euse [fymœʀ, -øz] nm/f smoker

fumier [fymje] *nm* manure

funérailles [fyneʀɑj] *nfpl* funeral *sg*

fur [fyʀ]: **au ~ et à mesure** *adv* as one goes along; **au ~ et à mesure que** as

furet [fyʀɛ] *nm* ferret

fureter [fyʀ(ə)te] /5/ *vi* (*péj*) to nose about

fureur [fyʀœʀ] *nf* fury; **être en ~** to be infuriated; **faire ~** to be all the rage

furie [fyʀi] *nf* fury; (*femme*) shrew, vixen; **en ~** (*mer*) raging; **furieux, -euse** *adj* furious

furoncle [fyʀɔ̃kl] *nm* boil

furtif, -ive [fyʀtif, -iv] *adj* furtive

fus [fy] *vb voir* **être**

fusain [fyzɛ̃] *nm* (*Art*) charcoal

fuseau, x [fyzo] *nm* (*pantalon*) (ski-)pants *pl*; (*pour filer*) spindle; **~ horaire** time zone

fusée [fyze] *nf* rocket

fusible [fyzibl] *nm* (*Élec: fil*) fuse wire; (: *fiche*) fuse

fusil [fyzi] *nm* (*de guerre, à canon rayé*) rifle, gun; (*de chasse, à canon lisse*) shotgun, gun; **fusillade** *nf* gunfire *no pl*, shooting *no pl*; **fusiller** /1/ *vt* to shoot; **fusiller qn du regard** to look daggers at sb

fusionner [fyzjɔne] /1/ *vi* to merge

fût [fy] *vb voir* **être** ▷ *nm* (*tonneau*) barrel, cask

futé, e [fyte] *adj* crafty; **Bison ~®** TV and radio traffic monitoring service

futile [fytil] *adj* futile; (*frivole*) frivolous

futur, e [fytyʀ] *adj, nm* future

fuyard, e [fɥijaʀ, -aʀd] *nm/f* runaway

g

Gabon [gabɔ̃] *nm*: **le ~** Gabon

gâcher [gɑʃe] /1/ *vt* (*gâter*) to spoil; (*gaspiller*) to waste; **gâchis** *nm* waste *no pl*

gaffe [gaf] *nf* blunder; **faire ~** (*fam*) to watch out

gage [gaʒ] *nm* (*dans un jeu*) forfeit; (*fig: de fidélité*) token; **gages** *nmpl* (*salaire*) wages; **mettre en ~** to pawn

gagnant, e [gaɲɑ̃, -ɑ̃t] *adj*: **billet/ numéro ~** winning ticket/number ▷ *nm/f* winner

gagne-pain [gaɲpɛ̃] *nm inv* job

gagner [gaɲe] /1/ *vt* to win; (*somme d'argent, revenu*) to earn; (*aller vers, atteindre*) to reach; (*s'emparer de*) to overcome; (*envahir*) to spread to ▷ *vi* to win; (*fig*) to gain; **~ du temps/ de la place** to gain time/save space; **~ sa vie** to earn one's living

gai, e [ge] *adj* cheerful; (*un peu ivre*) merry; **gaiement** *adv* cheerfully;

gaieté nf cheerfulness; **de gaieté de cœur** with a light heart

gain [gɛ̃] nm (revenu) earnings pl; (bénéfice: gén pl) profits pl

gala [gala] nm official reception; **soirée de ~** gala evening

galant, e [galɑ̃, -ɑ̃t] adj (courtois) courteous, gentlemanly; (entreprenant) flirtatious, gallant; (scène, rendez-vous) romantic

galerie [galʀi] nf gallery; (Théât) circle; (de voiture) roof rack; (fig: spectateurs) audience; **~ marchande** shopping mall; **~ de peinture** (private) art gallery

galet [galɛ] nm pebble

galette [galɛt] nf flat pastry cake; **la ~ des Rois** cake traditionally eaten on Twelfth Night

---

● **GALETTE DES ROIS**
●
● A galette des Rois is a cake eaten
● on Twelfth Night containing a
● figurine. The person who finds it
● is the king (or queen) and gets a
● paper crown. They then choose
● someone else to be their queen
● (or king).

---

galipette [galipɛt] nf somersault

Galles [gal] nfpl: **le pays de ~** Wales; **gallois, e** adj Welsh ▷ nm (Ling) Welsh ▷ nm/f: **Gallois, e** Welshman(-woman)

galocher [galɔʃe] (fam) vt to French kiss

galon [galɔ̃] nm (Mil) stripe; (décoratif) piece of braid

galop [galo] nm gallop; **galoper** /1/ vi to gallop

gambader [gɑ̃bade] /1/ vi (animal, enfant) to leap about

gamin, e [gamɛ̃, -in] nm/f kid ▷ adj mischievous

gamme [gam] nf (Mus) scale; (fig) range

gang [gɑ̃g] nm (de criminels) gang

gant [gɑ̃] nm glove; **~ de toilette** (face) flannel (BRIT), face cloth

garage [gaʀaʒ] nm garage; **garagiste** nm/f garage owner; (mécanicien) garage mechanic

garantie [gaʀɑ̃ti] nf guarantee; **(bon de) ~** guarantee ou warranty slip

garantir [gaʀɑ̃tiʀ] /2/ vt to guarantee; **je vous garantis que** I can assure you that

garçon [gaʀsɔ̃] nm boy; (aussi: **~ de café**) waiter; **vieux ~** (célibataire) bachelor; **~ de courses** messenger

garde [gaʀd] nm (de prisonnier) guard; (de domaine etc) warden; (soldat, sentinelle) guardsman ▷ nf (soldats) guard; **de ~** on duty; **monter la ~** to stand guard; **mettre en ~** to warn; **prendre ~ (à)** to be careful (of); **~ champêtre** nm rural policeman; **~ du corps** nm bodyguard; **~ à vue** nf (Jur) ≈ police custody; **garde-boue** nm inv mudguard; **garde-chasse** nm gamekeeper

garder [gaʀde] /1/ vt (conserver) to keep; (surveiller: enfants) to look after; (: immeuble, lieu, prisonnier) to guard; **se garder** vi (aliment: se conserver) to keep; **se ~ de faire** to be careful not to do; **~ le lit/la chambre** to stay in bed/indoors; **pêche/chasse gardée** private fishing/hunting (ground)

garderie [gaʀdəʀi] nf day nursery, crèche

garde-robe [gaʀdəʀɔb] nf wardrobe

gardien, ne [gaʀdjɛ̃, -ɛn] nm/f (garde) guard; (de prison) warder; (de domaine, réserve) warden; (de musée etc) attendant; (de phare, cimetière) keeper; (d'immeuble) caretaker; (fig) guardian; **~ de but** goalkeeper; **~ de nuit** night watchman; **~ de la paix** policeman

gare [gaʀ] nf (railway) station ▷ excl: **~ à ...** mind ...!; **~ à toi!** watch out!; **~ routière** bus station

garer [gaʀe] /1/ vt to park; **se garer** vi to park

garni, e [gaʀni] adj (plat) served with vegetables (and chips, pasta or rice)

garniture [gaʀnityʀ] nf(Culin)
vegetables pl; **~ de frein** brake lining

gars [ga] nm guy

Gascogne [gaskɔɲ] nf: **la ~** Gascony;
le golfe de ~ the Bay of Biscay

gas-oil [gazɔjl] nm diesel oil

gaspiller [gaspije] /1/ vt to waste

gastronome [gastʀɔnɔm] nm/f
gourmet; **gastronomique** adj
gastronomic

gâteau, x [gato] nm cake; **~ sec**
biscuit

gâter [gate] /1/ vt to spoil; **se gâter**
vi (dent, fruit) to go bad; (temps,
situation) to change for the worse

gâteux, -euse [gatø, -øz] adj senile

gauche [goʃ] adj left, left-hand;
(maladroit) awkward, clumsy ▷ nf
(Pol) left (wing); **le bras ~** the left
arm; **le côté ~** the left-hand side;
à ~ on the left; (direction) (to the)
left; **gaucher, -ère** adj left-handed;
gauchiste nm/f leftist

gaufre [gofʀ] nf waffle

gaufrette [gofʀɛt] nf wafer

gaulois, e [golwa, -waz] adj Gallic
▷ nm/f: **G~,-e** Gaul

gaz [gaz] nm inv gas; **ça sent le ~** I can
smell gas, there's a smell of gas

gaze [gaz] nf gauze

gazette [gazɛt] nf news sheet

gazeux, -euse [gazø, -øz] adj (eau)
sparkling; (boisson) fizzy

gazoduc [gazodyk] nm gas pipeline

gazon [gazɔ̃] nm (herbe) grass;
(pelouse) lawn

géant, e [ʒeɑ̃, -ɑ̃t] adj gigantic;
(Comm) giant-size ▷ nm/f giant

geindre [ʒɛ̃dʀ] /52/ vi to groan, moan

gel [ʒɛl] nm frost; **~ douche** shower
gel

gélatine [ʒelatin] nf gelatine

gelé, e [ʒəle] adj frozen ▷ nf jelly;
(gel) frost

geler [ʒ(ə)le] /5/ vt, vi to freeze; **il
gèle** it's freezing

gélule [ʒelyl] nf (Méd) capsule

Gémeaux [ʒemo] nmpl: **les ~** Gemini

gémir [ʒemiʀ] /2/ vi to groan, moan

gênant, e [ʒɛnɑ̃, -ɑ̃t] adj (objet) in the
way; (histoire, personne) embarrassing

gencive [ʒɑ̃siv] nf gum

gendarme [ʒɑ̃daʀm] nm gendarme;
gendarmerie nf military police force in
countryside and small towns; their police
station or barracks

gendre [ʒɑ̃dʀ] nm son-in-law

gêné, e [ʒene] adj embarrassed

gêner [ʒene] /1/ vt (incommoder) to
bother; (encombrer) to be in the way
of; (embarrasser): **~ qn** to make sb feel
ill-at-ease; **se gêner** to put o.s. out;
ne vous gênez pas! don't mind me!

général, e, -aux [ʒeneʀal, -o] adj,
nm general; **en ~** usually, in general;
généralement adv generally;
généraliser /1/ vt, vi to generalize;
se généraliser vi to become
widespread; **généraliste** nm/f
general practitioner, GP

génération [ʒeneʀasjɔ̃] nf generation

généreux, -euse [ʒeneʀø, -øz] adj
generous

générique [ʒeneʀik] nm (Ciné, TV)
credits pl

générosité [ʒeneʀozite] nf
generosity

genêt [ʒ(ə)nɛ] nm (Bot) broom no pl

génétique [ʒenetik] adj genetic

Genève [ʒ(ə)nɛv] n Geneva

génial, e, -aux [ʒenjal, -o] adj of
genius; (fam: formidable) fantastic,
brilliant

génie [ʒeni] nm genius; (Mil): **le
~** ≈ the Engineers pl; **~ civil** civil
engineering

genièvre [ʒ(ə)njɛvʀ] nm juniper (tree)

génisse [ʒenis] nf heifer

génital, e, -aux [ʒenital, -o] adj
genital; **les parties ~es** the genitals

génois, e [ʒenwa, -waz] adj Genoese
▷ nf (gâteau) ≈ sponge cake

génome [ʒenom] nm genome

genou, x [ʒ(ə)nu] nm knee; **à ~x**
on one's knees; **se mettre à ~x** to
kneel down

g

genre [ʒɑ̃R] *nm* kind, type, sort; (*Ling*) gender; **avoir bon ~** to look a nice sort; **avoir mauvais ~** to be coarse-looking; **ce n'est pas son ~** it's not like him

gens [ʒɑ̃] *nmpl* (*f in some phrases*) people *pl*

gentil, le [ʒɑ̃ti, -ij] *adj* kind; (*enfant: sage*) good; (*sympathique: endroit etc*) nice; **gentillesse** *nf* kindness; **gentiment** *adv* kindly

géographie [ʒeɔgRafi] *nf* geography

géologie [ʒeɔlɔʒi] *nf* geology

géomètre [ʒeɔmɛtR] *nm*: **(arpenteur-)~** (land) surveyor

géométrie [ʒeɔmetRi] *nf* geometry; **géométrique** *adj* geometric

géranium [ʒeRanjɔm] *nm* geranium

gérant, e [ʒeRɑ̃, -ɑ̃t] *nm/f* manager/manageress; **~ d'immeuble** managing agent

gerbe [ʒɛRb] *nf* (*de fleurs, d'eau*) spray; (*de blé*) sheaf

gercé, e [ʒɛRse] *adj* chapped

gerçure [ʒɛRsyR] *nf* crack

gérer [ʒeRe] /6/ *vt* to manage

germain, e [ʒɛRmɛ̃, -ɛn] *adj*: **cousin ~** first cousin

germe [ʒɛRm] *nm* germ; **germer** /1/ *vi* to sprout; (*semence*) to germinate

geste [ʒɛst] *nm* gesture

gestion [ʒɛstjɔ̃] *nf* management

Ghana [gana] *nm*: **le ~** Ghana

gibier [ʒibje] *nm* (*animaux*) game

gicler [ʒikle] /1/ *vi* to spurt, squirt

gifle [ʒifl] *nf* slap (in the face); **gifler** /1/ *vt* to slap (in the face)

gigantesque [ʒigɑ̃tɛsk] *adj* gigantic

gigot [ʒigo] *nm* leg (of mutton *ou* lamb)

gigoter [ʒigɔte] /1/ *vi* to wriggle (about)

gilet [ʒilɛ] *nm* waistcoat; (*pull*) cardigan; **~ de sauvetage** life jacket

gin [dʒin] *nm* gin; **~-tonic** gin and tonic

gingembre [ʒɛ̃ʒɑ̃bR] *nm* ginger

girafe [ʒiRaf] *nf* giraffe

giratoire [ʒiRatwaR] *adj*: **sens ~** roundabout

girofle [ʒiRɔfl] *nm*: **clou de ~** clove

girouette [ʒiRwɛt] *nf* weather vane *ou* cock

gitan, e [ʒitɑ̃, -an] *nm/f* gipsy

gîte [ʒit] *nm* (*maison*) home; (*abri*) shelter; **~ (rural)** (country) holiday cottage *ou* apartment, gîte (*self-catering accommodation in the country*)

givre [ʒivR] *nm* (hoar) frost; **givré, e** *adj* covered in frost; (*fam: fou*) nuts; **citron givré/orange givrée** lemon/orange sorbet (*served in fruit skin*)

glace [glas] *nf* ice; (*crème glacée*) ice cream; (*miroir*) mirror; (*de voiture*) window

glacé, e [glase] *adj* (*mains, vent, pluie*) freezing; (*lac*) frozen; (*boisson*) iced

glacer [glase] /3/ *vt* to freeze; (*gâteau*) to ice; **~ qn** (*intimider*) to chill sb; (*fig*) to make sb's blood run cold

glacial, e [glasjal] *adj* icy

glacier [glasje] *nm* (*Géo*) glacier; (*marchand*) ice-cream maker

glacière [glasjɛR] *nf* icebox

glaçon [glasɔ̃] *nm* icicle; (*pour boisson*) ice cube

glaïeul [glajœl] *nm* gladiola

glaise [glɛz] *nf* clay

gland [glɑ̃] *nm* acorn; (*décoration*) tassel

glande [glɑ̃d] *nf* gland

glissade [glisad] *nf* (*par jeu*) slide; (*chute*) slip; **faire des ~s** to slide

glissant, e [glisɑ̃, -ɑ̃t] *adj* slippery

glissement [glismɑ̃] *nm*: **~ de terrain** landslide

glisser [glise] /1/ *vi* (*avancer*) to glide *ou* slide along; (*coulisser, tomber*) to slide; (*déraper*) to slip; (*être glissant*) to be slippery ▷ *vt* to slip; **se ~ dans/entre** to slip into/between

global, e, -aux [glɔbal, -o] *adj* overall

globe [glɔb] *nm* globe

globule [glɔbyl] *nm* (*du sang*): **~ blanc/rouge** white/red corpuscle

gloire [glwaʀ] nf glory
glousser [gluse] /1/ vi to cluck; (rire) to chuckle
glouton, ne [glutɔ̃, -ɔn] adj gluttonous
gluant, e [glyɑ̃, -ɑ̃t] adj sticky, gummy
glucose [glykoz] nm glucose
glycine [glisin] nf wisteria
GO sigle fpl (= grandes ondes) LW
goal [gol] nm goalkeeper
gobelet [gɔblɛ] nm (en métal) tumbler; (en plastique) beaker; (à dés) cup
goéland [gɔelɑ̃] nm (sea)gull
goélette [gɔelɛt] nf schooner
goinfre [gwɛ̃fʀ] nm glutton
golf [gɔlf] nm golf; (terrain) golf course; ~ **miniature** crazy ou miniature golf
golfe [gɔlf] nm gulf; (petit) bay
gomme [gɔm] nf (à effacer) rubber (BRIT), eraser; **gommer** /1/ vt to rub out (BRIT), erase
gonflé, e [gɔ̃fle] adj swollen; **il est ~** (fam: courageux) he's got some nerve; (: impertinent) he's got a nerve
gonfler [gɔ̃fle] /1/ vt (pneu, ballon) to inflate, blow up; (nombre, importance) to inflate ▷ vi to swell (up); (Culin: pâte) to rise
gonzesse [gɔ̃zɛs] nf (fam) chick, bird (BRIT)
googler [gugle] /1/ vt to google
gorge [gɔʀʒ] nf (Anat) throat; (Géo) gorge
gorgé, e [gɔʀʒe] adj: ~ **de** filled with ▷ nf (petite) sip; (grande) gulp
gorille [gɔʀij] nm gorilla; (fam) bodyguard
gosse [gɔs] nm/f kid
goudron [gudʀɔ̃] nm tar; **goudronner** /1/ vt to tar(mac) (BRIT), asphalt (US)
gouffre [gufʀ] nm abyss, gulf
goulot [gulo] nm neck; **boire au ~** to drink from the bottle
goulu, e [guly] adj greedy

gourde [guʀd] nf (récipient) flask; (fam) (clumsy) clot ou oaf ▷ adj oafish
gourdin [guʀdɛ̃] nm club, bludgeon
gourmand, e [guʀmɑ̃, -ɑ̃d] adj greedy; **gourmandise** nf greed; (bonbon) sweet
gousse [gus] nf: ~ **d'ail** clove of garlic
goût [gu] nm taste; **de bon ~** tasteful; **de mauvais ~** tasteless; **avoir bon/ mauvais ~** to taste nice/ nasty; **prendre ~ à** to develop a taste ou a liking for
goûter [gute] /1/ vt (essayer) to taste; (apprécier) to enjoy ▷ vi to have (afternoon) tea ▷ nm (afternoon) tea; **je peux ~?** can I have a taste?
goutte [gut] nf drop; (Méd) gout; (alcool) nip (BRIT), drop (US); **tomber ~ à ~** to drip; **goutte-à-goutte** nm inv (Méd) drip
gouttière [gutjɛʀ] nf gutter
gouvernail [guvɛʀnaj] nm rudder; (barre) helm, tiller
gouvernement [guvɛʀnəmɑ̃] nm government
gouverner [guvɛʀne] /1/ vt to govern
grâce [gʀɑs] nf (charme, Rel) grace; (faveur) favour; (Jur) pardon; **faire ~ à qn de qch** to spare sb sth; **demander ~** to beg for mercy; ~ **à** thanks to; **gracieux, -euse** adj graceful
grade [gʀad] nm rank; **monter en ~** to be promoted
gradin [gʀadɛ̃] nm tier; (de stade) step; **gradins** nmpl (de stade) terracing no pl
gradué, e [gʀadɥe] adj: **verre ~** measuring jug
graduel, le [gʀadɥɛl] adj gradual
graduer [gʀadɥe] /1/ vt (effort etc) to increase gradually; (règle, verre) to graduate
graffiti [gʀafiti] nmpl graffiti
grain [gʀɛ̃] nm (gén) grain; (Navig) squall; ~ **de beauté** beauty spot; ~ **de café** coffee bean; ~ **de poivre** peppercorn

graine [gʀɛn] nf seed

graissage [gʀɛsaʒ] nm lubrication, greasing

graisse [gʀɛs] nf fat; (*lubrifiant*) grease; **graisser** /1/ vt to lubricate, grease; (*tacher*) to make greasy; **graisseux, -euse** adj greasy

grammaire [gʀamɛʀ] nf grammar

gramme [gʀam] nm gramme

grand, e [gʀɑ̃, gʀɑ̃d] adj (*haut*) tall; (*gros, vaste, large*) big, large; (*long*) long; (*plus âgé*) big; (*adulte*) grown-up; (*important, brillant*) great ▷ adv: **~ ouvert** wide open; **au ~ air** in the open (air); **les ~s blessés/brûlés** the severely injured/burned; **~ ensemble** housing scheme; **~ magasin** department store; **~e personne** grown-up; **~e surface** hypermarket; **~es écoles** prestige university-level colleges with competitive entrance examinations; **~es lignes** (*Rail*) main lines; **~es vacances** summer holidays (BRIT) ou vacation (US); **grand-chose** nm/f inv: **pas grand-chose** not much; **Grande-Bretagne** nf: **la Grande-Bretagne** (Great) Britain; **grandeur** nf (*dimension*) size; **grandeur nature** life-size; **grandiose** adj imposing; **grandir** /2/ vi to grow; grow ▷ vt: **grandir qn** (*vêtement, chaussure*) to make sb look taller; **grand-mère** nf grandmother; **grand-peine: à grand-peine** adv with (great) difficulty; **grand-père** nm grandfather; **grands-parents** nmpl grandparents

grange [gʀɑ̃ʒ] nf barn

granit [gʀanit] nm granite

graphique [gʀafik] adj graphic ▷ nm graph

grappe [gʀap] nf cluster; **~ de raisin** bunch of grapes

gras, se [gʀɑ, gʀɑs] adj (*viande, soupe*) fatty; (*personne*) fat; (*surface, main, cheveux*) greasy; (*plaisanterie*) coarse; (*Typo*) bold ▷ nm (*Culin*) fat; **faire la ~se matinée** to have a lie-in

(BRIT), sleep late; **grassement** adv: **grassement payé** handsomely paid

gratifiant, e [gʀatifjɑ̃, -ɑ̃t] adj gratifying, rewarding

gratin [gʀatɛ̃] nm (*Culin*) cheese- (*ou* crumb-)topped dish (: *croûte*) topping; **tout le ~ parisien** all the best people of Paris; **gratiné** adj (*Culin*) au gratin

gratis [gʀatis] adv free

gratitude [gʀatityd] nf gratitude

gratte-ciel [gʀatsjɛl] nm inv skyscraper

gratter [gʀate] /1/ vt (*frotter*) to scrape; (*avec un ongle*) to scratch; (*enlever: avec un outil*) to scrape off; (: *avec un ongle*) to scratch off ▷ vi (*irriter*) to be scratchy; (*démanger*) to itch; **se gratter** to scratch o.s.

gratuit, e [gʀatɥi, -ɥit] adj (*entrée*) free; (*fig*) gratuitous

grave [gʀav] adj (*maladie, accident*) serious, bad; (*sujet, problème*) serious, grave; (*personne, air*) grave, solemn; (*voix, son*) deep, low-pitched; **gravement** adv seriously; (*parler, regarder*) gravely

graver [gʀave] /1/ vt (*plaque, nom*) to engrave; (*CD, DVD*) to burn

graveur [gʀavœʀ] nm engraver; **~ de CD/DVD** CD/DVD burner or writer

gravier [gʀavje] nm (loose) gravel no pl; **gravillons** nmpl gravel sg

gravir [gʀaviʀ] /2/ vt to climb (up)

gravité [gʀavite] nf (*de maladie, d'accident*) seriousness; (*de sujet, problème*) gravity

graviter [gʀavite] /1/ vi to revolve

gravure [gʀavyʀ] nf engraving; (*reproduction*) print

gré [gʀe] nm: **à son ~** to his liking; **contre le ~ de qn** against sb's will; **de son (plein) ~** of one's own free will; **de ~ ou de force** whether one likes it or not; **de bon ~** willingly; **bon ~ mal ~** like it or not; **savoir (bien) ~ à qn de qch** to be (most) grateful to sb for sth

grec, grecque [gʀɛk] adj Greek; (classique: vase etc) Grecian ▷ nm (Ling) Greek ▷ nm/f: **Grec, Grecque** Greek
Grèce [gʀɛs] nf: **la ~** Greece
greffe [gʀɛf] nf (Bot, Méd: de tissu) graft; (Méd: d'organe) transplant; **greffer** /1/ vt (Bot, Méd: tissu) to graft; (Méd: organe) to transplant
grêle [gʀɛl] adj (very) thin ▷ nf hail; **grêler** /1/ vb impers: **il grêle** it's hailing; **grêlon** nm hailstone
grelot [gʀəlo] nm little bell
grelotter /1/ vi to shiver
grenade [gʀənad] nf (explosive) grenade; (Bot) pomegranate; **grenadine** nf grenadine
grenier [gʀənje] nm attic; (de ferme) loft
grenouille [gʀənuj] nf frog
grès [gʀɛ] nm sandstone; (poterie) stoneware
grève [gʀɛv] nf (d'ouvriers) strike; (plage) shore; **se mettre en/faire ~** to go on/be on strike; **~ de la faim** hunger strike; **~ sauvage** wildcat strike
gréviste [gʀevist] nm/f striker
grièvement [gʀijɛvmɑ̃] adv seriously
griffe [gʀif] nf claw; (d'un couturier, parfumeur) label; **griffer** /1/ vt to scratch
grignoter [gʀiɲɔte] /1/ vt (personne) to nibble at; (souris) to gnaw at ▷ vi to nibble
gril [gʀil] nm steak ou grill pan; **grillade** nf grill
grillage [gʀijaʒ] nm (treillis) wire netting; (clôture) wire fencing
grille [gʀij] nf (portail) (metal) gate; (clôture) railings pl; (d'égout) (metal) grate; grid
grille-pain [gʀijpɛ̃] nm inv toaster
griller [gʀije] /1/ vt (aussi: **faire ~**) (pain) to toast; (viande) to grill; (châtaignes) to roast; (fig: ampoule etc) to burn out; **~ un feu rouge** to jump the lights

grillon [gʀijɔ̃] nm cricket
grimace [gʀimas] nf grimace; (pour faire rire): **faire des ~s** to pull ou make faces
grimper [gʀɛ̃pe] /1/ vi, vt to climb
grincer [gʀɛ̃se] /3/ vi (porte, roue) to grate; (plancher) to creak; **~ des dents** to grind one's teeth
grincheux, -euse [gʀɛ̃ʃø, -øz] adj grumpy
grippe [gʀip] nf flu, influenza; **~ A** swine flu; **~ aviaire** bird flu; **grippé, e** adj: **être grippé** to have (the) flu
gris, e [gʀi, gʀiz] adj grey; (ivre) tipsy
grisaille [gʀizaj] nf greyness, dullness
griser [gʀize] /1/ vt to intoxicate
grive [gʀiv] nf thrush
Groenland [gʀɔɛnlɑ̃d] nm: **le ~** Greenland
grogner [gʀɔɲe] /1/ vi to growl; (fig) to grumble; **grognon, ne** adj grumpy
grommeler [gʀɔmle] /4/ vi to mutter to o.s.
gronder [gʀɔ̃de] /1/ vi to rumble; (fig: révolte) to be brewing ▷ vt to scold; **se faire ~** to get a telling-off
gros, se [gʀo, gʀos] adj big, large; (obèse) fat; (travaux, dégâts) extensive; (large) thick; (rhume, averse) heavy ▷ adv: **risquer/gagner ~** to risk/win a lot ▷ nm/f fat man/woman ▷ nm (Comm): **le ~** the wholesale business; **prix de ~** wholesale price; **par ~ temps/~se mer** in rough weather/ heavy seas; **le ~ de** the bulk of; **en ~** roughly; (Comm) wholesale; **~ lot** jackpot; **~ mot** swearword; **~ plan** (Photo) close-up; **~ sel** cooking salt; **~ titre** headline; **~se caisse** big drum
groseille [gʀozɛj] nf: **~ (rouge)/ (blanche)** red/white currant; **~ à maquereau** gooseberry
grosse [gʀos] adj f voir **gros**; **grossesse** nf pregnancy; **grosseur** nf size; (tumeur) lump
grossier, -ière [gʀosje, -jɛʀ] adj coarse; (insolent) rude; (dessin)

g

rough; (*travail*) roughly done; (*imitation, instrument*) crude; (*évident: erreur*) gross; **grossièrement** *adv* (*vulgairement*) coarsely; (*sommairement*) roughly; crudely; (*en gros*) roughly; (*mot*): **grossièreté** *nf* rudeness; (*mot*): **dire des grossièretés** to use coarse language

grossir [gʀosiʀ] /2/ *vi* (*personne*) to put on weight ▷ *vt* (*exagérer*) to exaggerate; (*au microscope*) to magnify; (*vêtement*): **~ qn** to make sb look fatter

grossiste [gʀosist] *nm/f* wholesaler

grotesque [gʀotɛsk] *adj* (*extravagant*) grotesque; (*ridicule*) ludicrous

grotte [gʀot] *nf* cave

groupe [gʀup] *nm* group; **~ de parole** support group; **~ sanguin** blood group; **~ scolaire** school complex; **grouper** /1/ *vt* to group; **se grouper** *vi* to get together

grue [gʀy] *nf* crane

GSM [ʒeɛsɛm] *nm, adj* GSM

guenon [gənɔ̃] *nf* female monkey

guépard [gepaʀ] *nm* cheetah

guêpe [gɛp] *nf* wasp

guère [gɛʀ] *adv* (*avec adjectif, adverbe*): **ne ... ~** hardly; (*avec verbe: pas beaucoup*): **ne ... ~** (*tournure négative*) much; (*pas souvent*) hardly ever; (*tournure négative*) (*very*) long; **il n'y a ~ que/de** there's hardly anybody (*ou* anything) but/hardly any; **ce n'est ~ difficile** it's hardly difficult; **nous n'avons ~ de temps** we have hardly any time

guérilla [geʀija] *nf* guerrilla warfare

guérillero [geʀijeʀo] *nm* guerrilla

guérir [geʀiʀ] /2/ *vt* (*personne, maladie*) to cure; (*membre, plaie*) to heal ▷ *vi* (*personne, malade*) to recover, be cured; (*maladie*) to be cured; (*plaie, chagrin, blessure*) to heal; **guérison** *nf* (*de maladie*) curing; (*de membre, plaie*) healing; (*de malade*) recovery; **guérisseur, -euse** *nm/f* healer

guerre [gɛʀ] *nf* war; **en ~** at war; **faire la ~ à** to wage war against; **~ civile/mondiale** civil/world war; **guerrier, -ière** *adj* warlike ▷ *nm/f* warrior

guet [gɛ] *nm*: **faire le ~** to be on the watch *ou* look-out; **guet-apens** [gɛtapɑ̃] *nm* ambush; **guetter** /1/ *vt* (*épier*) to watch (intently); (*attendre*) to watch (out) for; (: *pour surprendre*) to be lying in wait for

gueule [gœl] *nf* (*d'animal*) mouth; (*fam: visage*) mug; (: *bouche*) gob (!), mouth; **ta ~!** (*fam*) shut up!; **avoir la ~ de bois** (*fam*) to have a hangover, be hung over; **gueuler** /1/ *vi* to bawl

gui [gi] *nm* mistletoe

guichet [giʃɛ] *nm* (*de bureau, banque*) counter; **les ~s** (*à la gare, au théâtre*) the ticket office

guide [gid] *nm* (*personne*) guide; (*livre*) guide (book) ▷ *nf* (*fille scout*) (girl) guide; **guider** /1/ *vt* to guide

guidon [gidɔ̃] *nm* handlebars *pl*

guignol [giɲɔl] *nm* ≈ Punch and Judy show; (*fig*) clown

guillemets [gijmɛ] *nmpl*: **entre ~** in inverted commas *ou* quotation marks

guindé, e [gɛ̃de] *adj* (*personne, air*) stiff, starchy; (*style*) stilted

Guinée [gine] *nf*: **la (République de) ~** (the Republic of) Guinea

guirlande [giʀlɑ̃d] *nf* (*fleurs*) garland; **~ de Noël** tinsel *no pl*

guise [giz] *nf*: **à votre ~** as you wish *ou* please; **en ~ de** by way of

guitare [gitaʀ] *nf* guitar

Guyane [gɥijan] *nf*: **la ~ (française)** (French) Guiana

gym [ʒim] *nf* (*exercices*) gym; **gymnase** *nm* gym(nasium); **gymnaste** *nm/f* gymnast; **gymnastique** *nf* gymnastics *sg*; (*au réveil etc*) keep-fit exercises *pl*

gynécologie [ʒinekolɔʒi] *nf* gynaecology; **gynécologique** *adj* gynaecological; **gynécologue** *nm/f* gynaecologist

h

habile [abil] *adj* skilful; (*malin*) clever; **habileté** [abilte] *nf* skill, skilfulness; cleverness

habillé, e [abije] *adj* dressed; (*chic*) dressy

habiller [abije] /1/ *vt* to dress; (*fournir en vêtements*) to clothe; (*couvrir*) to cover; **s'habiller** *vi* to dress (o.s.); (*se déguiser, mettre des vêtements chic*) to dress up

habit [abi] *nm* outfit; **habits** *nmpl* (*vêtements*) clothes; **~ (de soirée)** evening dress; (*pour homme*) tails *pl*

habitant, e [abitã, -ãt] *nm/f* inhabitant; (*d'une maison*) occupant; **loger chez l'~** to stay with the locals

habitation [abitasjɔ̃] *nf* house; **~s à loyer modéré (HLM)** ≈ council flats

habiter [abite] /1/ *vt* to live in ▷ *vi*: **~ à/dans** to live in *ou* at/in

habitude [abityd] *nf* habit; **avoir l'~ de faire** to be in the habit of doing; (*expérience*) to be used to doing;

avoir l'~ **des enfants** to be used to children; **d'~** usually; **comme d'~** as usual

habitué, e [abitɥe] *nm/f* (*de maison*) regular visitor; (*client*) regular (customer)

habituel, le [abitɥɛl] *adj* usual

habituer [abitɥe] /1/ *vt*: **~ qn à** to get sb used to; **s'habituer à** to get used to

'**hache** ['aʃ] *nf* axe

'**hacher** ['aʃe] /1/ *vt* (*viande*) to mince ; (*persil*) to chop; '**hachis** *nm* mince *no pl*; '**hachis Parmentier** ≈ shepherd's pie

'**haie** ['ɛ] *nf* hedge; (*Sport*) hurdle

'**haillons** ['ɑjɔ̃] *nmpl* rags

'**haine** ['ɛn] *nf* hatred

'**haïr** ['aiʀ] /10/ *vt* to detest, hate

'**hâlé, e** ['ɑle] *adj* (sun)tanned, sunburnt

haleine [alɛn] *nf* breath; **hors d'~** out of breath; **tenir en ~** (*attention*) to hold spellbound; (*en attente*) to keep in suspense; **de longue ~** long-term

'**haleter** ['alte] /5/ *vi* to pant

'**hall** ['ol] *nm* hall

'**halle** ['al] *nf* (covered) market; '**halles** *nfpl* (*d'une grande ville*) central food market *sg*

hallucination [alysinasjɔ̃] *nf* hallucination

'**halte** ['alt] *nf* stop, break; (*escale*) stopping place ▷ *excl* stop!; **faire ~** to stop

haltère [altɛʀ] *nm* dumbbell, barbell; (**poids et**) **~s** (*activité*) weightlifting *sg*; **haltérophilie** *nf* weightlifting

'**hamac** ['amak] *nm* hammock

'**hamburger** ['ɑ̃buʀɡœʀ] *nm* hamburger

'**hameau, x** ['amo] *nm* hamlet

hameçon [amsɔ̃] *nm* (fish) hook

'**hamster** ['amstɛʀ] *nm* hamster

'**hanche** ['ɑ̃ʃ] *nf* hip

'**hand-ball** ['ɑ̃dbal] *nm* handball

'handicapé, e ['ɑ̃dikape] adj
disabled ▷ nm/f person with a
disability; **~ mental/physique**
person with learning difficulties/
a disability; **~ moteur** person with
a movement disorder
'hangar ['ɑ̃gaʀ] nm shed; (Aviat)
hangar
'hanneton ['antɔ̃] nm cockchafer
'hanter ['ɑ̃te] /1/ vt to haunt
'hantise ['ɑ̃tiz] nf obsessive fear
'harceler ['aʀsəle] /5/ vt to harass;
~ qn de questions to plague sb with
questions
'hardi, e ['aʀdi] adj bold, daring
'hareng ['aʀɑ̃] nm herring; **~ saur**
kipper, smoked herring
'hargne ['aʀɲ] nf aggressivity,
aggressiveness; **'hargneux, -euse**
adj aggressive
'haricot ['aʀiko] nm bean; **~ blanc/
rouge** haricot/kidney bean; **~ vert**
French (BRIT) ou green bean
harmonica [aʀmɔnika] nm mouth
organ
harmonie [aʀmɔni] nf harmony;
harmonieux, -euse adj harmonious;
(couleurs, couple) well-matched
'harpe ['aʀp] nf harp
'hasard ['azaʀ] nm: **le ~** chance, fate;
un ~ a coincidence; **au ~** (sans but)
aimlessly; (à l'aveuglette) at random;
par ~ by chance; **à tout ~** (en espérant
trouver ce qu'on cherche) on the off
chance; (en cas de besoin) just in case
'hâte ['ɑt] nf haste; **à la ~** hurriedly,
hastily; **en ~** posthaste, with all
possible speed; **avoir ~ de** to be
eager ou anxious to; **'hâter** /1/ vt to
hasten; **se 'hâter** to hurry; **'hâtif,
-ive** adj (travail) hurried; (décision)
hasty
'hausse ['os] nf rise, increase; **être en
~** to be going up; **'hausser** /1/ vt to
raise; **hausser les épaules** to shrug
(one's shoulders)
'haut, e ['o, 'ot] adj high; (grand) tall
▷ adv high ▷ nm top (part); **de 3 m de ~**

3 m high, 3 m in height; **en ~ lieu**
in high places; **à ~e voix, (tout) ~**
aloud, out loud; **des ~s et des bas**
ups and downs; **du ~ de** from the top
of; **de ~ en bas** from top to bottom;
plus ~ higher up, further up; (dans un
texte) above; (parler) louder; **en ~**
(être/aller) at (ou to) the top; (dans une
maison) upstairs; **en ~ de** at the top
of; **~ débit** broadband
'hautain, e ['otɛ̃, -ɛn] adj haughty
'hautbois ['obwɑ] nm oboe
'hauteur ['otœʀ] nf height; **à la ~
de** (sur la même ligne) level with; (fig:
tâche, situation) equal to; **à la ~** (fig)
up to it
'haut-parleur ['opaʀlœʀ] nm (loud)
speaker
Hawaï [awai] n Hawaii; **les îles ~** the
Hawaiian Islands
'Haye ['ɛ] n: **la '~** the Hague
hebdomadaire [ɛbdɔmadɛʀ] adj,
nm weekly
hébergement [ebɛʀʒəmɑ̃] nm
accommodation
héberger [ebɛʀʒe] /3/ vt (touristes) to
accommodate, lodge; (amis) to put
up; (réfugiés) to take in
hébergeur [ebɛʀʒœʀ] nm (Internet)
host
hébreu, x [ebʀø] adj m, nm Hebrew
Hébrides [ebʀid] nf: **les ~** the
Hebrides
hectare [ɛktaʀ] nm hectare
'hein ['ɛ̃] excl eh?
'hélas ['elas] excl alas! ▷ adv
unfortunately
'héler ['ele] /6/ vt to hail
hélice [elis] nf propeller
hélicoptère [elikɔptɛʀ] nm
helicopter
helvétique [ɛlvetik] adj Swiss
hématome [ematom] nm
haematoma
hémisphère [emisfɛʀ] nm: **~ nord/
sud** northern/southern hemisphere
hémorragie [emɔʀaʒi] nf bleeding
no pl, haemorrhage

hémorroïdes [emɔʀɔid] *nfpl* piles, haemorrhoids

'**hennir** ['eniʀ] /2/ *vi* to neigh, whinny

hépatite [epatit] *nf* hepatitis

herbe [ɛʀb] *nf* grass; (*Culin*, *Méd*) herb; **~s de Provence** mixed herbs; **en ~** unripe; (*fig*) budding; **herbicide** *nm* weed-killer; **herboriste** *nm/f* herbalist

héréditaire [eʀeditɛʀ] *adj* hereditary

'**hérisson** ['eʀisɔ̃] *nm* hedgehog

héritage [eʀitaʒ] *nm* inheritance; (*coutumes*, *système*) heritage; legacy

hériter [eʀite] /1/ *vi*: **~ de qch (de qn)** to inherit sth (from sb); **héritier, -ière** *nm/f* heir/heiress

hermétique [ɛʀmetik] *adj* airtight; (*à l'eau*) watertight; (*fig*: *écrivain*, *style*) abstruse; (: *visage*) impenetrable

hermine [ɛʀmin] *nf* ermine

'**hernie** ['ɛʀni] *nf* hernia

héroïne [eʀɔin] *nf* heroine; (*drogue*) heroin

héroïque [eʀɔik] *adj* heroic

'**héron** ['eʀɔ̃] *nm* heron

'**héros** ['eʀo] *nm* hero

hésitant, e [ezitã, -ãt] *adj* hesitant

hésitation [ezitasjɔ̃] *nf* hesitation

hésiter [ezite] /1/ *vi*: **~ (à faire)** to hesitate (to do)

hétérosexuel, le [eteʀɔsɛkɥɛl] *adj* heterosexual

'**hêtre** ['ɛtʀ] *nm* beech

heure [œʀ] *nf* hour; (*Scol*) period; (*moment*, *moment fixé*) time; **c'est l'~** it's time; **quelle ~ est-il?** what time is it?; **2 ~s (du matin)** 2 o'clock (in the morning); **être à l'~** to be on time; (*montre*) to be right; **mettre à l'~** to set right; **à toute ~** at any time; **24 ~s sur 24** round the clock, 24 hours a day; **à l'~** qu'il est at this time (of day); (*fig*) now; **à l'~ actuelle** at the present time; **sur l'~** at once; **à une ~ avancée (de la nuit)** at a late hour (of the night); **de bonne ~** early; **~ de pointe** rush hour; (*téléphone*) peak period; **~s de bureau** office hours; **~s supplémentaires** overtime *sg*

heureusement [œʀøzmã] *adv* (*par bonheur*) fortunately, luckily

heureux, -euse [œʀø, -øz] *adj* happy; (*chanceux*) lucky, fortunate

'**heurt** ['œʀ] *nm* (*choc*) collision

'**heurter** ['œʀte] /1/ *vt* (*mur*) to strike, hit; (*personne*) to collide with

hexagone [ɛgzagɔn] *nm* hexagon; **l'H~** (*la France*) France (*because of its roughly hexagonal shape*)

hiberner [ibɛʀne] /1/ *vi* to hibernate

'**hibou, x** ['ibu] *nm* owl

'**hideux, -euse** ['idø, -øz] *adj* hideous

hier [jɛʀ] *adv* yesterday; **~ matin/soir/midi** yesterday morning/evening/lunchtime; **toute la journée d'~** all day yesterday; **toute la matinée d'~** all yesterday morning

'**hiérarchie** ['jeʀaʀʃi] *nf* hierarchy

hindou, e [ɛ̃du] *adj* Hindu ▷ *nm/f*: **H~, e** Hindu; (*Indien*) Indian

hippique [ipik] *adj* equestrian, horse *cpd*; **un club ~** a riding centre; **un concours ~** a horse show; **hippisme** [ipism] *nm* (horse-)riding

hippodrome [ipɔdʀom] *nm* racecourse

hippopotame [ipɔpɔtam] *nm* hippopotamus

hirondelle [iʀɔ̃dɛl] *nf* swallow

'**hisser** ['ise] /1/ *vt* to hoist, haul up

histoire [istwaʀ] *nf* (*science*, *événements*) history; (*anecdote*, *récit*, *mensonge*) story; (*affaire*) business *no pl*; (*chichis*: *gén pl*) fuss *no pl*; **histoires** *nfpl* (*ennuis*) trouble *sg*; **~ géo** humanities *pl*; **historique** *adj* historical; (*important*) historic ▷ *nm*: **faire l'historique de** to give the background to

'**hit-parade** ['itpaʀad] *nm*: **le ~** the charts

hiver [ivɛʀ] *nm* winter; **hivernal, e, -aux** *adj* winter *cpd*; (*comme en hiver*) wintry; **hiverner** /1/ *vi* to winter

h

HLM *sigle m ou f* (= *habitations à loyer modéré*) low-rent, state-owned housing; **un(e) ~** ≈ a council flat (*ou* house)

'**hobby** ['ɔbi] *nm* hobby

'**hocher** ['ɔʃe] /1/ *vt*: **~ la tête** to nod; (*signe négatif ou dubitatif*) to shake one's head

'**hockey** ['ɔkɛ] *nm*: **~ (sur glace/gazon)** (ice/field) hockey

'**hold-up** ['ɔldœp] *nm inv* hold-up

'**hollandais, e** ['ɔlɑ̃dɛ, -ɛz] *adj* Dutch ▷ *nm* (*Ling*) Dutch ▷ *nm/f*: **H~, e** Dutchman/woman

'**Hollande** ['ɔlɑ̃d] *nf*: **la ~** Holland

'**homard** ['ɔmaʀ] *nm* lobster

homéopathique [ɔmeɔpatik] *adj* homoeopathic

homicide [ɔmisid] *nm* murder; **~ involontaire** manslaughter

hommage [ɔmaʒ] *nm* tribute; **rendre ~ à** to pay tribute to

homme [ɔm] *nm* man; **~ d'affaires** businessman; **~ d'État** statesman; **~ de main** hired man; **~ de paille** stooge; **~ politique** politician; **l'~ de la rue** the man in the street

homogène *adj* homogeneous

homologue *nm/f* counterpart

homologué, e *adj* (*Sport*) ratified; (*tarif*) authorized

homonyme *nm* (*Ling*) homonym; (*d'une personne*) namesake

homoparental, e, -aux [ɔmɔpaʀɑ̃tal, o] *adj* (*famille*) same-sex

homosexuel, le *adj* homosexual

'**Hong-Kong** ['ɔ̃gkɔ̃g] *n* Hong Kong

'**Hongrie** ['ɔ̃gʀi] *nf*: **la ~** Hungary; '**hongrois, e** *adj* Hungarian ▷ *nm* (*Ling*) Hungarian ▷ *nm/f*: **Hongrois, e** Hungarian

honnête [ɔnɛt] *adj* (*intègre*) honest; (*juste, satisfaisant*) fair; **honnêtement** *adv* honestly; **honnêteté** *nf* honesty

honneur [ɔnœʀ] *nm* honour; (*mérite*): **l'~ lui revient** the credit is his; **en l'~ de** (*personne*) in honour of;

(*événement*) on the occasion of; **faire ~ à** (*engagements*) to honour; (*famille, professeur*) to be a credit to; (*fig: repas etc*) to do justice to

honorable [ɔnɔʀabl] *adj* worthy, honourable; (*suffisant*) decent

honoraire [ɔnɔʀɛʀ] *adj* honorary; **honoraires** *nmpl* fees; **professeur ~** professor emeritus

honorer [ɔnɔʀe] /1/ *vt* to honour; (*estimer*) to hold in high regard; (*faire honneur à*) to do credit to

'**honte** ['ɔ̃t] *nf* shame; **avoir ~ de** to be ashamed of; **faire ~ à qn** to make sb (feel) ashamed; '**honteux, -euse** *adj* ashamed; (*conduite, acte*) shameful, disgraceful

hôpital, -aux [ɔpital, -o] *nm* hospital; **où est l'~ le plus proche?** where is the nearest hospital?

'**hoquet** ['ɔkɛ] *nm*: **avoir le ~** to have (the) hiccups

horaire [ɔʀɛʀ] *adj* hourly ▷ *nm* timetable, schedule; **horaires** *nmpl* (*heures de travail*) hours; **~ flexible** *ou* **mobile** *ou* **à la carte** *ou* **souple** flex(i)time

horizon [ɔʀizɔ̃] *nm* horizon

horizontal, e, -aux *adj* horizontal

horloge [ɔʀlɔʒ] *nf* clock; **l'~ parlante** the speaking clock; **horloger, -ère** *nm/f* watchmaker; clockmaker

'**hormis** ['ɔʀmi] *prép* save

horoscope [ɔʀɔskɔp] *nm* horoscope

horreur [ɔʀœʀ] *nf* horror; **quelle ~!** how awful!; **avoir ~ de** to loathe *ou* detest; **horrible** *adj* horrible; **horrifier** /7/ *vt* to horrify

'**hors** ['ɔʀ] *prép*: **~ de** out of; **~ pair** outstanding; **~ de propos** inopportune; **~ service (HS), ~ d'usage** out of service; **être ~ de soi** to be beside o.s.; '**hors-bord** *nm inv* speedboat (with outboard motor); '**hors-d'œuvre** *nm inv* hors d'œuvre; '**hors-la-loi** *nm inv* outlaw; '**horstaxe** *adj* duty-free

hortensia [ɔʀtɑ̃sja] *nm* hydrangea

hospice [ɔspis] *nm* (*de vieillards*) home

hospitalier, -ière [ɔspitalje, -jɛʀ] *adj* (*accueillant*) hospitable; (*Méd: service, centre*) hospital *cpd*

hospitaliser [ɔspitalize] /1/ *vt* to take (*ou* send) to hospital, hospitalize

hospitalité [ɔspitalite] *nf* hospitality

hostie [ɔsti] *nf* host

hostile [ɔstil] *adj* hostile; **hostilité** *nf* hostility

hôte [ot] *nm* (*maître de maison*) host ▷ *nm/f* (*invité*) guest

hôtel [otɛl] *nm* hotel; **aller à l'~** to stay in a hotel; **~ (particulier)** (private) mansion; **~ de ville** town hall; *see note* **"hôtels"**; **hôtellerie** [otɛlʀi] *nf* hotel business

● **HÔTELS**
●
● There are six categories of hotel
● in France, from zero ('non classé')
● to four stars and luxury four
● stars ('quatre étoiles luxe'). Prices
● include VAT but not breakfast. In
● some towns, guests pay a small
● additional tourist tax, the 'taxe
● de séjour'.

hôtesse [otɛs] *nf* hostess; **~ de l'air** flight attendant

'houblon [ublɔ̃] *nm* (*Bot*) hop; (*pour la bière*) hops *pl*

'houille [uj] *nf* coal; **~ blanche** hydroelectric power

'houle [ul] *nf* swell; **'houleux, -euse** *adj* stormy

'hourra [uʀa] *excl* hurrah!

'housse [us] *nf* cover

'houx [u] *nm* holly

hovercraft [ovœʀkʀaft] *nm* hovercraft

'hublot [yblo] *nm* porthole

'huche [yʃ] *nf:* **huche à pain** bread bin

'huer [ɥe] /1/ *vt* to boo

huile [ɥil] *nf* oil

huissier [ɥisje] *nm* usher; (*Jur*) ≈ bailiff

'huit ['ɥi(t)] *num* eight; **samedi en ~** a week on Saturday; **dans ~ jours** in a week('s time); **'huitaine** ['ɥitɛn] *nf:* **une huitaine de jours** a week or so; **'huitième** *num* eighth

huître [ɥitʀ] *nf* oyster

humain, e [ymɛ̃, -ɛn] *adj* human; (*compatissant*) humane ▷ *nm* human (being); **humanitaire** *adj* humanitarian; **humanité** *nf* humanity

humble [œ̃bl] *adj* humble

'humer ['yme] /1/ *vt* (*parfum*) to inhale; (*pour sentir*) to smell

humeur [ymœʀ] *nf* mood; **de bonne/mauvaise ~** in a good/ bad mood

humide [ymid] *adj* damp; (*main, yeux*) moist; (*climat, chaleur*) humid; (*saison, route*) wet

humilier [ymilje] /7/ *vt* to humiliate

humilité [ymilite] *nf* humility, humbleness

humoristique [ymɔʀistik] *adj* humorous

humour [ymuʀ] *nm* humour; **avoir de l'~** to have a sense of humour; **~ noir** sick humour

'huppé, e ['ype] *adj* (*fam*) posh

'hurlement ['yʀləmɑ̃] *nm* howling *no pl*, howl; yelling *no pl*, yell

'hurler ['yʀle] /1/ *vi* to howl, yell

'hutte ['yt] *nf* hut

hydratant, e [idʀatɑ̃, -ɑ̃t] *adj* (*crème*) moisturizing

hydraulique [idʀolik] *adj* hydraulic

hydravion [idʀavjɔ̃] *nm* seaplane

hydrogène [idʀɔʒɛn] *nm* hydrogen

hydroglisseur [idʀɔglisœʀ] *nm* hydroplane

hyène [jɛn] *nf* hyena

hygiène [iʒjɛn] *nf* hygiene

hygiénique [iʒenik] *adj* hygienic

hymne [imn] *nm* hymn

hyperlien [ipɛʀljɛ̃] *nm* hyperlink

hypermarché [ipɛrmarʃe] *nm*
   hypermarket
hypermétrope [ipɛrmetrɔp] *adj*
   long-sighted
hypertension [ipɛrtɑ̃sjɔ̃] *nf* high
   blood pressure
hypnose [ipnoz] *nf* hypnosis;
   hypnotiser /1/ *vt* to hypnotize
hypocrisie [ipɔkrizi] *nf* hypocrisy;
   hypocrite *adj* hypocritical
hypothèque [ipɔtɛk] *nf* mortgage
hypothèse [ipɔtɛz] *nf* hypothesis
hystérique [isterik] *adj* hysterical

iceberg [isbɛrg] *nm* iceberg
ici [isi] *adv* here; **jusqu'~** as far as this;
   (*temporel*) until now; **d'~ là** by then;
   d'~ demain by tomorrow; in the
   meantime; **d'~ peu** before long
icône [ikon] *nf* icon
idéal, e, -aux [ideal, -o] *adj* ideal
   ▷ *nm* ideal; **idéaliste** *adj* idealistic
   ▷ *nm/f* idealist
idée [ide] *nf* idea; **se faire des ~s** to
   imagine things, get ideas into one's
   head; **avoir dans l'~ que** to have an
   idea that; **~s noires** black *ou* dark
   thoughts; **~s reçues** accepted ideas
   ou wisdom
identifier [idɑ̃tifje] /7/ *vt* to identify;
   s'identifier *vi*: **s'~ avec** *ou* **à qn/qch**
   (*héros etc*) to identify with sb/sth
identique [idɑ̃tik] *adj*: **~ (à)**
   identical (to)
identité [idɑ̃tite] *nf* identity
idiot, e [idjo, idjɔt] *adj* idiotic
   ▷ *nm/f* idiot

idole [idɔl] nf idol
if [if] nm yew
ignoble [iɲɔbl] adj vile
ignorant, e [iɲɔʀɑ̃, -ɑ̃t] adj ignorant;
~ **de** ignorant of, not aware of
ignorer [iɲɔʀe] /1/ vt not to know;
(personne) to ignore
il [il] pron he; (animal, chose, en tournure
impersonnelle) it; **il neige** it's snowing;
Pierre est-il arrivé? has Pierre
arrived?; **il a gagné** he won; voir
aussi **avoir**
île [il] nf island; **l'~ Maurice**
Mauritius; **les ~s anglo-normandes**
the Channel Islands; **les ~s
Britanniques** the British Isles
illégal, e, -aux [ilegal, -o] adj illegal
illimité, e [ilimite] adj unlimited
illisible [ilizibl] adj illegible; (roman)
unreadable
illogique [ilɔʒik] adj illogical
illuminer [ilymine] /1/ vt to light
up; (monument, rue: pour une fête) to
illuminate; (: au moyen de projecteurs)
floodlight
illusion [ilyzjɔ̃] nf illusion; **se faire
des ~s** to delude o.s.; **faire ~** to
delude ou fool people
illustration [ilystʀasjɔ̃] nf
illustration
illustré, e [ilystʀe] adj illustrated
▷ nm comic
illustrer [ilystʀe] /1/ vt to illustrate;
s'illustrer to become famous,
win fame
ils [il] pron they
image [imaʒ] nf (gén) picture;
(comparaison, ressemblance) image;
~ **de marque** brand image; (d'une
personne) (public) image; **imagé, e**
adj (texte) full of imagery; (langage)
colourful
imaginaire [imaʒinɛʀ] adj imaginary
imagination [imaʒinasjɔ̃] nf
imagination; **avoir de l'~** to be
imaginative
imaginer [imaʒine] /1/ vt to
imagine; (inventer: expédient, mesure)

to devise, think up; **s'imaginer** vt (se
figurer: scène etc) to imagine, picture;
s'~ que to imagine that
imam [imam] nm imam
imbécile [ɛ̃besil] adj idiotic ▷ nm/f
idiot
imbu, e [ɛ̃by] adj: ~ **de** full of
imitateur, -trice [imitatœʀ, -tʀis]
nm/f (gén) imitator; (Music-Hall)
impersonator
imitation [imitasjɔ̃] nf imitation; (de
personalité) impersonation
imiter [imite] /1/ vt to imitate;
(contrefaire) to forge; (ressembler à)
to look like
immangeable [ɛ̃mɑ̃ʒabl] adj
inedible
immatriculation [imatʀikylasjɔ̃]
nf registration

immatriculer [imatʀikyle] /1/ vt to
register; **faire/se faire ~** to register
immédiat, e [imedja, -at] adj
immediate ▷ nm: **dans l'~** for the
time being; **immédiatement** adv
immediately
immense [imɑ̃s] adj immense
immerger [imɛʀʒe] /3/ vt to
immerse, submerge
immeuble [imœbl] nm building;
~ **locatif** block of rented flats
immigration [imigʀasjɔ̃] nf
immigration

immigré, e [imigʀe] nm/f
immigrant

imminent, e [iminã, -ãt] adj
imminent

immobile [imɔbil] adj still,
motionless

immobilier, -ière [imɔbilje,
-jɛʀ] adj property cpd ▷ nm: **l'~** the
property ou the real estate business

immobiliser [imɔbilize] /1/ vt (gén)
to immobilize; (circulation, véhicule,
affaires) to bring to a standstill;
s'immobiliser (personne) to stand
still; (machine, véhicule) to come to a
halt ou a standstill

immoral, e, -aux [imɔʀal, -o] adj
immoral

immortel, le [imɔʀtɛl] adj immortal

immunisé, e [im(m)ynize] adj: **~
contre** immune to

immunité [imynite] nf immunity

impact [ɛ̃pakt] nm impact

impair, e [ɛ̃pɛʀ] adj odd ▷ nm faux
pas, blunder

impardonnable [ɛ̃paʀdɔnabl] adj
unpardonable, unforgivable

imparfait, e [ɛ̃paʀfɛ, -ɛt] adj
imperfect

impartial, e, -aux [ɛ̃paʀsjal, -o] adj
impartial, unbiased

impasse [ɛ̃pas] nf dead-end, cul-de-
sac; (fig) deadlock

impassible [ɛ̃pasibl] adj impassive

impatience [ɛ̃pasjɑ̃s] nf impatience

impatient, e [ɛ̃pasjɑ̃, -ɑ̃t] adj
impatient; **impatienter** /1/:
s'impatienter vi to get impatient

impeccable [ɛ̃pekabl] adj faultless;
(propre) spotlessly clean; (fam)
smashing

impensable [ɛ̃pɑ̃sabl] adj (événement
hypothétique) unthinkable; (événement
qui a eu lieu) unbelievable

impératif, -ive [ɛ̃peʀatif, -iv] adj
imperative ▷ nm (Ling) imperative;
impératifs nmpl (exigences: d'une
fonction, d'une charge) requirements;
(: de la mode) demands

impératrice [ɛ̃peʀatʀis] nf empress

imperceptible [ɛ̃pɛʀsɛptibl] adj
imperceptible

impérial, e, -aux [ɛ̃peʀjal, -o] adj
imperial

impérieux, -euse [ɛ̃peʀjø, -øz] adj
(caractère, ton) imperious; (obligation,
besoin) pressing, urgent

impérissable [ɛ̃peʀisabl] adj
undying

imperméable [ɛ̃pɛʀmeabl] adj
waterproof; (fig): **~ à** impervious to
▷ nm raincoat

impertinent, e [ɛ̃pɛʀtinã, -ãt] adj
impertinent

impitoyable [ɛ̃pitwajabl] adj
pitiless, merciless

implanter [ɛ̃plɑ̃te] /1/: **s'implanter
dans** vi to be established in

impliquer [ɛ̃plike] /1/ vt to imply;
~ qn (dans) to implicate sb (in)

impoli, e [ɛ̃pɔli] adj impolite, rude

impopulaire [ɛ̃pɔpylɛʀ] adj
unpopular

importance [ɛ̃pɔʀtɑ̃s] nf
importance; (de somme) size; **sans ~**
unimportant

important, e [ɛ̃pɔʀtɑ̃, -ɑ̃t] adj
important; (en quantité: somme,
retard) considerable, sizeable;
(: gamme, dégâts) extensive; (péj: airs,
ton) self-important ▷ nm: **l'~** the
important thing

importateur, -trice [ɛ̃pɔʀtatœʀ,
-tʀis] nm/f importer

importation [ɛ̃pɔʀtasjɔ̃] nf (produit)
import

importer [ɛ̃pɔʀte] /1/ vt (Comm)
to import; (maladies, plantes) to
introduce ▷ vi (être important) to
matter; **il importe qu'il fasse** it is
important that he should do; **peu
m'importe** (je n'ai pas de préférence)
I don't mind; (je m'en moque) I don't
care; **peu importe (que)** it doesn't
matter (if); voir aussi **n'importe**

importun, e [ɛ̃pɔʀtœ̃, -yn] adj
irksome, importunate; (arrivée, visite)

inopportune, ill-timed ▷ *nm* intruder;
importuner /1/ *vt* to bother

imposant, e [ɛ̃pozɑ̃, -ɑ̃t] *adj*
imposing

imposer [ɛ̃poze] /1/ *vt* (*taxer*) to
tax; **~ qch à qn** to impose sth on
sb; **s'imposer** (*être nécessaire*) to be
imperative; **en ~ à** to impress; **s'~
comme** to emerge as; **s'~ par** to win
recognition through

impossible [ɛ̃pɔsibl] *adj* impossible;
il m'est ~ de le faire it is impossible
for me to do it, I can't possibly do
it; **faire l'~ (pour que)** to do one's
utmost (so that)

imposteur [ɛ̃pɔstœʀ] *nm* impostor

impôt [ɛ̃po] *nm* tax; **~ sur le chiffre
d'affaires** corporation (BRIT) *ou*
corporate (US) tax; **~ foncier** land
tax; **~ sur le revenu** income tax;
~s locaux rates, local taxes (US), ≈
council tax (BRIT)

impotent, e [ɛ̃pɔtɑ̃, -ɑ̃t] *adj*
disabled

impraticable [ɛ̃pratikabl] *adj*
(*projet*) impracticable, unworkable;
(*piste*) impassable

imprécis, e [ɛ̃presi, -iz] *adj*
imprecise

imprégner [ɛ̃preɲe] /6/ *vt*: **~ (de)**
(*tissu, tampon*) to soak *ou* impregnate
(with); (*lieu, air*) to fill (with);
s'imprégner de (*fig*) to absorb

imprenable [ɛ̃prənabl] *adj*
(*forteresse*) impregnable; **vue ~**
unimpeded outlook

impression [ɛ̃presjɔ̃] *nf*
impression; (*d'un ouvrage, tissu*)
printing; **faire bonne/mauvaise
~** to make a good/bad impression;
impressionnant, e *adj* (*imposant*)
impressive; (*bouleversant*) upsetting;
impressionner /1/ *vt* (*frapper*) to
impress; (*troubler*) to upset

imprévisible [ɛ̃previzibl] *adj*
unforeseeable

imprévu, e [ɛ̃prevy] *adj* unforeseen,
unexpected ▷ *nm* (*incident*)

unexpected incident; **des vacances
pleines d'~** holidays full of surprises;
en cas d'~ if anything unexpected
happens; **sauf ~** unless anything
unexpected crops up

imprimante [ɛ̃primɑ̃t] *nf* printer;
~ à laser laser printer

imprimé [ɛ̃prime] *nm* (*formulaire*)
printed form; (*Postes*) printed matter
no pl; (*tissu*) printed fabric; **un ~ à
fleurs/pois** (*tissu*) a floral/polka-
dot print

imprimer [ɛ̃prime] /1/ *vt* to print;
(*publier*) to publish; **imprimerie** *nf*
printing; (*établissement*) printing
works *sg*; **imprimeur** *nm* printer

impropre [ɛ̃prɔpr] *adj*
inappropriate; **~ à** unsuitable for

improviser [ɛ̃prɔvize] /1/ *vt, vi* to
improvize

improviste [ɛ̃prɔvist]: **à l'~** *adv*
unexpectedly, without warning

imprudence [ɛ̃prydɑ̃s] *nf* (*d'une
personne, d'une action*) carelessness *no
pl*; (*d'une remarque*) imprudence *no pl*;
commettre une ~ to do something
foolish

imprudent, e [ɛ̃prydɑ̃, -ɑ̃t] *adj*
(*conducteur, geste, action*) careless;
(*remarque*) unwise, imprudent;
(*projet*) foolhardy

impuissant, e [ɛ̃pɥisɑ̃, -ɑ̃t] *adj*
helpless; (*sans effet*) ineffectual;
(*sexuellement*) impotent

impulsif, -ive [ɛ̃pylsif, -iv] *adj*
impulsive

impulsion [ɛ̃pylsjɔ̃] *nf* (*Élec, instinct*)
impulse; (*élan, influence*) impetus

inabordable [inabɔrdabl] *adj* (*cher*)
prohibitive

inacceptable [inakseptabl] *adj*
unacceptable

inaccessible [inaksesibl] *adj*
inaccessible; **~ à** impervious to

inachevé, e [inaʃve] *adj* unfinished

inactif, -ive [inaktif, -iv] *adj*
inactive; (*remède*) ineffective; (*Bourse:
marché*) slack

inadapté, e [inadapte] *adj (Psych)*
maladjusted; **~ à** not adapted to,
unsuited to
inadéquat, e [inadekwa, -wat] *adj*
inadequate
inadmissible [inadmisibl] *adj*
inadmissible
inadvertance [inadvɛrtãs]: **par ~**
adv inadvertently
inanimé, e [inanime] *adj (matière)*
inanimate; *(évanoui)* unconscious;
(sans vie) lifeless
inanition [inanisjɔ̃] *nf*: **tomber d'~**
to faint with hunger (and exhaustion)
inaperçu, e [inapɛrsy] *adj*: **passer
~** to go unnoticed
inapte [inapt] *adj*: **~ à** incapable of;
(Mil) unfit for
inattendu, e [inatãdy] *adj*
unexpected
inattentif, -ive [inatãtif, -iv] *adj*
inattentive; **~ à** *(dangers, détails)*
heedless of; **inattention** *nf*
inattention; **faute d'inattention**
careless mistake
inaugurer [inɔgyre] /1/ *vt*
(monument) to unveil; *(exposition,
usine)* to open; *(fig)* to inaugurate
inavouable [inavwabl] *adj*
(bénéfices) undisclosable; *(honteux)*
shameful
incalculable [ɛ̃kalkylabl] *adj*
incalculable
incapable [ɛ̃kapabl] *adj* incapable;
~ de faire incapable of doing;
(empêché) unable to do
incapacité [ɛ̃kapasite] *nf*
(incompétence) incapability;
(impossibilité) incapacity; **être dans
l'~ de faire** to be unable to do
incarcérer [ɛ̃karsere] /6/ *vt* to
incarcerate, imprison
incassable [ɛ̃kasabl] *adj* unbreakable
incendie [ɛ̃sãdi] *nm* fire; **~ criminel**
arson *no pl*; **~ de forêt** forest fire;
incendier /7/ *vt (mettre le feu à)*
to set fire to, set alight; *(brûler
complètement)* to burn down

incertain, e [ɛ̃sɛrtɛ̃, -ɛn] *adj*
uncertain; *(temps)* unsettled;
(imprécis: contours) indistinct, blurred;
incertitude *nf* uncertainty
incessamment [ɛ̃sesamã] *adv*
very shortly
incident [ɛ̃sidã] *nm* incident; **~ de
parcours** minor hitch *ou* setback;
~ technique technical difficulties *pl*
incinérer [ɛ̃sinere] /6/ *vt (ordures)* to
incinerate; *(mort)* to cremate
incisif, -ive [ɛ̃sizif, -iv] *adj* incisive
▷ *nf* incisor
inciter [ɛ̃site] /1/ *vt*: **~ qn à (faire)
qch** to prompt *ou* encourage sb to
do sth; *(à la révolte etc)* to incite sb
to do sth
incivilité [ɛ̃sivilite] *nf (grossièreté)*
incivility; **incivilités** *nfpl* antisocial
behaviour *sg*
inclinable [ɛ̃klinabl] *adj*: **siège à
dossier ~** reclining seat
inclination [ɛ̃klinasjɔ̃] *nf (penchant)*
inclination
incliner [ɛ̃kline] /1/ *vt (bouteille)* to
tilt ▷ *vi*: **~ à qch/à faire** to incline
towards sth/doing; **s'incliner** *vi*
(route) to slope; **s'~ (devant)** to bow
(before)
inclure [ɛ̃klyr] /35/ *vt* to include;
(joindre à un envoi) to enclose
inclus, e [ɛ̃kly, -yz] *pp de* **inclure**
▷ *adj* included; *(joint à un envoi)*
enclosed; *(compris: frais, dépense)*
included; **jusqu'au 10 mars** = until
10th March inclusive
incognito [ɛ̃kɔnito] *adv* incognito
▷ *nm*: **garder l'~** to remain incognito
incohérent, e [ɛ̃kɔerã, -ãt] *adj*
(comportement) inconsistent; *(geste,
langage, texte)* incoherent
incollable [ɛ̃kɔlabl] *adj (riz)* that
does not stick; *(fam)*: **il est ~** he's got
all the answers
incolore [ɛ̃kɔlɔr] *adj* colourless
incommoder [ɛ̃kɔmɔde] /1/ *vt*:
~ qn *(chaleur, odeur)* to bother *ou*
inconvenience sb

incomparable [ɛ̃kɔ̃paʀabl] *adj*
incomparable

incompatible [ɛ̃kɔ̃patibl] *adj*
incompatible

incompétent, e [ɛ̃kɔ̃petã, -ãt] *adj*
incompetent

incomplet, -ète [ɛ̃kɔ̃plɛ, -ɛt] *adj*
incomplete

incompréhensible [ɛ̃kɔ̃pʀeãsibl]
adj incomprehensible

incompris, e [ɛ̃kɔ̃pʀi, -iz] *adj*
misunderstood

inconcevable [ɛ̃kɔ̃svabl] *adj*
inconceivable

inconfortable [ɛ̃kɔ̃fɔʀtabl] *adj*
uncomfortable

incongru, e [ɛ̃kɔ̃gʀy] *adj* unseemly

inconnu, e [ɛ̃kɔny] *adj* unknown
▷ *nm/f* stranger ▷ *nm*: **l'~** the
unknown ▷ *nf* unknown factor

inconsciemment [ɛ̃kɔ̃sjamã] *adv*
unconsciously

inconscient, e [ɛ̃kɔ̃sjã, -ãt] *adj*
unconscious; (*irréfléchi*) thoughtless,
reckless; (*sentiment*) subconscious
▷ *nm* (*Psych*): **l'~** the unconscious;
~ de unaware of

inconsidéré, e [ɛ̃kɔ̃sideʀe] *adj*
ill-considered

inconsistant, e [ɛ̃kɔ̃sistã, -ãt] *adj*
flimsy, weak

inconsolable [ɛ̃kɔ̃sɔlabl] *adj*
inconsolable

incontestable [ɛ̃kɔ̃tɛstabl] *adj*
indisputable

incontinent, e [ɛ̃kɔ̃tinã, -ãt] *adj*
incontinent

incontournable [ɛ̃kɔ̃tuʀnabl] *adj*
unavoidable

incontrôlable [ɛ̃kɔ̃tʀolabl]
adj unverifiable; (*irrépressible*)
uncontrollable

inconvénient [ɛ̃kɔ̃venjã] *nm*
disadvantage, drawback; **si vous
n'y voyez pas d'~** if you have no
objections

incorporer [ɛ̃kɔʀpɔʀe] /1/ *vt*: **~ (à)**
to mix in (with); **~ (dans)** (*paragraphe*

etc) to incorporate (in); (*Mil: appeler*)
to recruit (into); **il a très bien su s'~
à notre groupe** he was very easily
incorporated into our group

incorrect, e [ɛ̃kɔʀɛkt] *adj* (*impropre,
inconvenant*) improper; (*défectueux*)
faulty; (*inexact*) incorrect; (*impoli*)
impolite; (*déloyal*) underhand

incorrigible [ɛ̃kɔʀiʒibl] *adj*
incorrigible

incrédule [ɛ̃kʀedyl] *adj* incredulous;
(*Rel*) unbelieving

incroyable [ɛ̃kʀwajabl] *adj* incredible

incruster [ɛ̃kʀyste] /1/ *vt*;
s'incruster *vi* (*invité*) to take root;
~ qch dans/qch de (*Art*) to inlay sth
into/sth with

inculpé, e [ɛ̃kylpe] *nm/f* accused

inculper [ɛ̃kylpe] /1/ *vt*: **~ (de)** to
charge (with)

inculquer [ɛ̃kylke] /1/ *vt*: **~ qch à** to
inculcate sth in, instil sth into

Inde [ɛ̃d] *nf*: **l'~** India

indécent, e [ɛ̃desã, -ãt] *adj* indecent

indécis, e [ɛ̃desi, -iz] *adj* (*par nature*)
indecisive; (*perplexe*) undecided

indéfendable [ɛ̃defãdabl] *adj*
indefensible

indéfini, e [ɛ̃defini] *adj* (*imprécis,
incertain*) undefined; (*illimité, Ling*)
indefinite; **indéfiniment** *adv*
indefinitely; **indéfinissable** *adj*
indefinable

indélébile [ɛ̃delebil] *adj* indelible

indélicat, e [ɛ̃delika, -at] *adj* tactless

indemne [ɛ̃demn] *adj* unharmed;
indemniser /1/ *vt*: **indemniser qn
(de)** to compensate sb (for)

indemnité [ɛ̃demnite] *nf*
(*dédommagement*) compensation
no pl; (*allocation*) allowance; **~ de
licenciement** redundancy payment

indépendamment [ɛ̃depãdamã]
adv independently; **~ de** (*abstraction
faite de*) irrespective of; (*en plus de*)
over and above

indépendance [ɛ̃depãdãs] *nf*
independence

indépendant, e [ɛ̃depɑ̃dɑ̃, -ɑ̃t] *adj*
independent; **~ de** independent of;
travailleur ~ self-employed worker

indescriptible [ɛ̃dɛskʀiptibl] *adj*
indescribable

indésirable [ɛ̃deziʀabl] *adj*
undesirable

indestructible [ɛ̃dɛstʀyktibl] *adj*
indestructible

indéterminé, e [ɛ̃detɛʀmine] *adj*
(*date, cause, nature*) unspecified;
(*forme, longueur, quantité*)
indeterminate

index [ɛ̃dɛks] *nm* (*doigt*) index finger;
(*d'un livre etc*) index; **mettre à l'~** to
blacklist

indicateur [ɛ̃dikatœʀ] *nm* (*Police*)
informer; (*Tech*) gauge; indicator
▷ *adj*: **poteau ~** signpost; **~ des
chemins de fer** railway timetable;
~ de rues street directory

indicatif, -ive [ɛ̃dikatif, -iv] *adj*: **à
titre ~** for (your) information ▷ *nm*
(*Ling*) indicative; (*d'une émission*)
theme *ou* signature tune; (*Tél*) dialling
code (BRIT), area code (US); **quel est
l'~ de …** what's the code for …?

indication [ɛ̃dikasjɔ̃] *nf* indication;
(*renseignement*) information *no
pl*; **indications** *nfpl* (*directives*)
instructions

indice [ɛ̃dis] *nm* (*marque, signe*)
indication, sign; (*Police: lors d'une
enquête*) clue; (*Jur: présomption*)
piece of evidence; (*Science, Écon,
Tech*) index; **~ de protection** (sun
protection) factor

indicible [ɛ̃disibl] *adj* inexpressible

indien, ne [ɛ̃djɛ̃, -ɛn] *adj* Indian
▷ *nm/f*: **I~, ne** Indian

indifféremment [ɛ̃difeʀamɑ̃] *adv*
(*sans distinction*) equally

indifférence [ɛ̃difeʀɑ̃s] *nf* indifference

indifférent, e [ɛ̃difeʀɑ̃, -ɑ̃t] *adj*
(*peu intéressé*) indifferent; **ça m'est
~ (que …)** it doesn't matter to me
(whether …); **elle m'est ~e** I am
indifferent to her

indigène [ɛ̃diʒɛn] *adj* native,
indigenous; (*de la région*) local ▷ *nm/f*
native

indigeste [ɛ̃diʒɛst] *adj* indigestible

indigestion [ɛ̃diʒɛstjɔ̃] *nf*
indigestion *no pl*; **avoir une ~** to have
indigestion

indigne [ɛ̃diɲ] *adj*: **~ (de)** unworthy
(of)

indigner [ɛ̃diɲe] /1/ *vt*; **s'indigner
(de/contre)** to be (*ou* become)
indignant (at)

indiqué, e [ɛ̃dike] *adj* (*date, lieu*)
given; (*adéquat*) appropriate;
(*conseillé*) advisable

indiquer [ɛ̃dike] /1/ *vt*: **~ qch/qn
à qn** to point sth/sb out to sb; (*faire
connaître: médecin, lieu, restaurant*)
to tell sb of sth/sb; (*pendule, aiguille*)
to show; (*étiquette, plan*) to show,
indicate; (*renseigner sur*) to point
out, tell; (*déterminer: date, lieu*) to
give, state; (*dénoter*) to indicate,
point to; **pourriez-vous m'~ les
toilettes/l'heure?** could you direct
me to the toilets/tell me the time?

indiscipliné, e [ɛ̃disipline] *adj*
undisciplined

indiscret, -ète [ɛ̃diskʀɛ, -ɛt] *adj*
indiscreet

indiscutable [ɛ̃diskytabl] *adj*
indisputable

indispensable [ɛ̃dispɑ̃sabl] *adj*
indispensable, essential

indisposé, e [ɛ̃dispoze] *adj*
indisposed

indistinct, e [ɛ̃distɛ̃, -ɛ̃kt] *adj*
indistinct; **indistinctement** *adv*
(*voir, prononcer*) indistinctly; (*sans
distinction*) indiscriminately

individu [ɛ̃dividy] *nm* individual;
individuel, le *adj* (*gén*) individual;
(*opinion, livret, contrôle, avantages*)
personal; **chambre individuelle**
single room; **maison individuelle**
detached house; **propriété
individuelle** personal *ou* private
property

indolore [ɛ̃dɔlɔʀ] *adj* painless

Indonésie [ɛ̃dɔnezi] *nf*: **l'~** Indonesia

indu, e [ɛ̃dy] *adj*: **à une heure ~e** at some ungodly hour

indulgent, e [ɛ̃dylʒɑ̃, -ɑ̃t] *adj* (*parent, regard*) indulgent; (*juge, examinateur*) lenient

industrialisé, e [ɛ̃dystʀijalize] *adj* industrialized

industrie [ɛ̃dystʀi] *nf* industry; **industriel, le** *adj* industrial ▷ *nm* industrialist

inébranlable [inebʀɑ̃labl] *adj* (*masse, colonne*) solid; (*personne, certitude, foi*) unwavering

inédit, e [inedi, -it] *adj* (*correspondance etc*) (hitherto) unpublished; (*spectacle, moyen*) novel, original; (*film*) unreleased

inefficace [inefikas] *adj* (*remède, moyen*) ineffective; (*machine, employé*) inefficient

inégal, e, -aux [inegal, -o] *adj* unequal; (*irrégulier*) uneven; **inégalable** *adj* matchless; **inégalé, e** *adj* (*record*) unequalled; (*beauté*) unrivalled; **inégalité** *nf* inequality

inépuisable [inepɥizabl] *adj* inexhaustible

inerte [inɛʀt] *adj* (*immobile*) lifeless; (*apathique*) passive

inespéré, e [inɛspeʀe] *adj* unhoped-for, unexpected

inestimable [inɛstimabl] *adj* priceless; (*fig: bienfait*) invaluable

inévitable [inevitabl] *adj* unavoidable; (*fatal, habituel*) inevitable

inexact, e [inɛgzakt] *adj* inaccurate

inexcusable [inɛkskyzabl] *adj* unforgivable

inexplicable [inɛksplikabl] *adj* inexplicable

in extremis [inɛkstʀemis] *adv* at the last minute ▷ *adj* last-minute

infaillible [ɛ̃fajibl] *adj* infallible

infarctus [ɛ̃faʀktys] *nm*: **~ (du myocarde)** coronary (thrombosis)

infatigable [ɛ̃fatigabl] *adj* tireless

infect, e [ɛ̃fɛkt] *adj* revolting; (*repas, vin*) revolting, foul; (*personne*) obnoxious; (*temps*) foul

infecter [ɛ̃fɛkte] /1/ *vt* (*atmosphère, eau*) to contaminate; (*Méd*) to infect; **s'infecter** to become infected *ou* septic; **infection** *nf* infection; (*puanteur*) stench

inférieur, e [ɛ̃feʀjœʀ] *adj* lower; (*en qualité, intelligence*) inferior ▷ *nm/f* inferior; **~ à** (*somme, quantité*) less *ou* smaller than; (*moins bon que*) inferior to

infernal, e, -aux [ɛ̃fɛʀnal, -o] *adj* (*insupportable: chaleur, rythme*) infernal; (*: enfant*) horrid; (*méchanceté, complot*) diabolical

infidèle [ɛ̃fidɛl] *adj* unfaithful

infiltrer [ɛ̃filtʀe] /1/: **s'infiltrer** *vi*: **s'~ dans** to penetrate into; (*liquide*) to seep into; (*fig: noyauter*) to infiltrate

infime [ɛ̃fim] *adj* minute, tiny

infini, e [ɛ̃fini] *adj* infinite ▷ *nm* infinity; **à l'~** endlessly; **infiniment** *adv* infinitely; **infinité** *nf*: **une infinité de** an infinite number of

infinitif, -ive [ɛ̃finitif, -iv] *nm* infinitive

infirme [ɛ̃fiʀm] *adj* disabled ▷ *nm/f* person with a disability

infirmerie [ɛ̃fiʀməʀi] *nf* sick bay

infirmier, -ière [ɛ̃fiʀmje, -jɛʀ] *nm/f* nurse; **infirmière chef** sister

infirmité [ɛ̃fiʀmite] *nf* disability

inflammable [ɛ̃flamabl] *adj* (in)flammable

inflation [ɛ̃flasjɔ̃] *nf* inflation

influençable [ɛ̃flyɑ̃sabl] *adj* easily influenced

influence [ɛ̃flyɑ̃s] *nf* influence; **influencer** /3/ *vt* to influence; **influent, e** *adj* influential

informaticien, ne [ɛ̃fɔʀmatisjɛ̃, -ɛn] *nm/f* computer scientist

information [ɛ̃fɔʀmasjɔ̃] *nf* (*renseignement*) piece of information; (*Presse, TV: nouvelle*) item of

i

news; (*diffusion de renseignements*, *Inform*) information; (*Jur*) inquiry, investigation; **informations** *nfpl* (*TV*) news *sg*

informatique [ɛ̃fɔʀmatik] *nf* (*technique*) data processing; (*science*) computer science ▷ *adj* computer *cpd*; **informatiser** /1/ *vt* to computerize

informer [ɛ̃fɔʀme] /1/ *vt*: **~ qn (de)** to inform sb (of); **s'informer (sur)** to inform o.s. (about); **s'~ (de qch/ si)** to inquire *ou* find out (about sth/ whether *ou* if)

infos [ɛ̃fo] *nfpl* (= *informations*) news

infraction [ɛ̃fʀaksjɔ̃] *nf* offence; **~ à** violation *ou* breach of; **être en ~** to be in breach of the law

infranchissable [ɛ̃fʀɑ̃ʃisabl] *adj* impassable; (*fig*) insuperable

infrarouge [ɛ̃fʀaʀuʒ] *adj* infrared

infrastructure [ɛ̃fʀastʀyktyʀ] *nf* (*Aviat*, *Mil*) ground installations *pl*; (*Écon*: *touristique etc*) facilities *pl*

infuser [ɛ̃fyze] /1/ *vt* (*thé*) to brew; (*tisane*) to infuse ▷ *vi* to brew; to infuse; **infusion** *nf* (*tisane*) herb tea

ingénier [ɛ̃ʒenje] /7/: **s'ingénier** *vi*: **s'~ à faire** to strive to do

ingénierie [ɛ̃ʒeniʀi] *nf* engineering

ingénieur [ɛ̃ʒenjœʀ] *nm* engineer; **~ du son** sound engineer

ingénieux, -euse [ɛ̃ʒenjø, -øz] *adj* ingenious, clever

ingrat, e [ɛ̃gʀa, -at] *adj* (*personne*) ungrateful; (*travail*, *sujet*) thankless; (*visage*) unprepossessing

ingrédient [ɛ̃gʀedjɑ̃] *nm* ingredient

inhabité, e [inabite] *adj* uninhabited

inhabituel, le [inabitɥel] *adj* unusual

inhibition [inibisjɔ̃] *nf* inhibition

inhumain, e [inymɛ̃, -ɛn] *adj* inhuman

inimaginable [inimaʒinabl] *adj* unimaginable

ininterrompu, e [inɛ̃teʀɔ̃py] *adj* (*file*, *série*) unbroken; (*flot*, *vacarme*)

uninterrupted, non-stop; (*effort*) unremitting, continuous; (*suite*, *ligne*) unbroken

initial, e, -aux [inisjal, -o] *adj* initial; **initiales** *nfpl* initials

initiation [inisjasjɔ̃] *nf*: **~ à** introduction to

initiative [inisjativ] *nf* initiative

initier [inisje] /7/ *vt*: **~ qn à** to initiate sb into; (*faire découvrir*: *art*, *jeu*) to introduce sb to

injecter [ɛ̃ʒɛkte] /1/ *vt* to inject; **injection** *nf* injection; **à injection** (*Auto*) fuel injection *cpd*

injure [ɛ̃ʒyʀ] *nf* insult, abuse *no pl*; **injurier** /7/ *vt* to insult, abuse; **injurieux, -euse** *adj* abusive, insulting

injuste [ɛ̃ʒyst] *adj* unjust, unfair; **injustice** [ɛ̃ʒystis] *nf* injustice

inlassable [ɛ̃lasabl] *adj* tireless

inné, e [ine] *adj* innate, inborn

innocent, e [inɔsɑ̃, -ɑ̃t] *adj* innocent; **innocenter** /1/ *vt* to clear, prove innocent

innombrable [inɔ̃bʀabl] *adj* innumerable

innover [inɔve] /1/ *vi*: **~ en matière d'art** to break new ground in the field of art

inoccupé, e [inɔkype] *adj* unoccupied

inodore [inɔdɔʀ] *adj* (*gaz*) odourless; (*fleur*) scentless

inoffensif, -ive [inɔfɑ̃sif, -iv] *adj* harmless, innocuous

inondation [inɔ̃dasjɔ̃] *nf* flood

inonder [inɔ̃de] /1/ *vt* to flood; **~ de** to flood *ou* swamp with

inopportun, e [inɔpɔʀtœ̃, -yn] *adj* ill-timed, untimely

inoubliable [inublijabl] *adj* unforgettable

inouï, e [inwi] *adj* unheard-of, extraordinary

inox [inɔks] *nm* stainless (steel)

inquiet, -ète [ɛ̃kjɛ, -ɛt] *adj* anxious; **inquiétant, e** *adj* worrying, disturbing; **inquiéter** /6/ vt to worry; **s'inquiéter** to worry; **s'inquiéter de** to worry about; (s'enquérir de) to inquire about; **inquiétude** nf anxiety

insaisissable [ɛ̃sezizabl] adj (fugitif, ennemi) elusive; (différence, nuance) imperceptible

insalubre [ɛ̃salybʀ] adj insalubrious

insatisfait, e [ɛ̃satisfɛ, -ɛt] adj (non comblé) unsatisfied; (mécontent) dissatisfied

inscription [ɛ̃skʀipsjɔ̃] nf inscription; (à une institution) enrolment

inscrire [ɛ̃skʀiʀ] /39/ vt (marquer: sur son calepin etc) to note ou write down; (: sur un mur, une affiche etc) to write; (: dans la pierre, le métal) to inscribe; (mettre: sur une liste, un budget etc) to put down; **~ qn à** (club, école etc) to enrol sb at; **s'inscrire** (pour une excursion etc) to put one's name down; **s'~ (à)** (club, parti) to join; (université) to register ou enrol (at); (examen, concours) to register ou enter (for)

insecte [ɛ̃sɛkt] nm insect; **insecticide** nm insecticide

insensé, e [ɛ̃sɑ̃se] adj mad

insensible [ɛ̃sɑ̃sibl] adj (nerf, membre) numb; (dur, indifférent) insensitive

inséparable [ɛ̃sepaʀabl] adj: **~ (de)** inseparable (from) ▷ nmpl: **~s** (oiseaux) lovebirds

insigne [ɛ̃siɲ] nm (d'un parti, club) badge ▷ adj distinguished; **insignes** nmpl (d'une fonction) insignia pl

insignifiant, e [ɛ̃siɲifjɑ̃, -ɑ̃t] adj insignificant; trivial

insinuer [ɛ̃sinɥe] /1/ vt to insinuate; **s'insinuer dans** (fig) to worm one's way into

insipide [ɛ̃sipid] adj insipid

insister [ɛ̃siste] /1/ vi to insist; (s'obstiner) to keep on; **~ sur** (détail, note) to stress

insolation [ɛ̃sɔlasjɔ̃] nf (Méd) sunstroke no pl

insolent, e [ɛ̃sɔlɑ̃, -ɑ̃t] adj insolent

insolite [ɛ̃sɔlit] adj strange, unusual

insomnie [ɛ̃sɔmni] nf insomnia no pl; **avoir des ~s** to sleep badly

insouciant, e [ɛ̃susjɑ̃, -ɑ̃t] adj carefree; **~ du danger** heedless of (the) danger

insoupçonnable [ɛ̃supsɔnabl] adj unsuspected; (personne) above suspicion

insoupçonné, e [ɛ̃supsɔne] adj unsuspected

insoutenable [ɛ̃sutnabl] adj (argument) untenable; (chaleur) unbearable

inspecter [ɛ̃spɛkte] /1/ vt to inspect; **inspecteur, -trice** nm/f inspector; **inspecteur d'Académie** (regional) director of education; **inspecteur des finances** ≈ tax inspector (BRIT), ≈ Internal Revenue Service agent (US); **inspecteur (de police)** (police) inspector; **inspection** nf inspection

inspirer [ɛ̃spiʀe] /1/ vt (gén) to inspire ▷ vi (aspirer) to breathe in; **s'inspirer de** to be inspired by

instable [ɛ̃stabl] adj (meuble, équilibre) unsteady; (population, temps) unsettled; (paix, régime, caractère) unstable

installation [ɛ̃stalasjɔ̃] nf (mise en place) installation; **installations** nfpl installations; (industrielles) plant sg; (de sport, dans un camping) facilities; **l'~ électrique** wiring

installer [ɛ̃stale] /1/ vt to put; (meuble) to put in; (rideau, étagère, tente) to put up; (appartement) to fit out; **s'installer** (s'établir: artisan, dentiste etc) to set o.s. up; (emménager) to settle in; (sur un siège, à un emplacement) to settle (down); (fig: maladie, grève) to take a firm hold ou grip; **s'~ à l'hôtel/chez qn** to move into a hotel/in with sb

instance [ɛ̃stɑ̃s] nf (Admin: autorité) authority; **affaire en ~** matter pending; **être en ~ de divorce** to be awaiting a divorce

instant [ɛ̃stɑ̃] nm moment, instant; **dans un ~** in a moment; **à l'~** this instant; **je l'ai vu à l'~** I've just this minute seen him, I saw him a moment ago; **pour l'~** for the moment, for the time being

instantané, e [ɛ̃stɑ̃tane] adj (lait, café) instant; (explosion, mort) instantaneous ▷ nm snapshot

instar [ɛ̃staʀ]: **à l'~ de** prép following the example of, like

instaurer [ɛ̃stɔʀe] /1/ vt to institute; (couvre-feu) to impose; **s'instaurer** vi (collaboration, paix etc) to be established; (doute) to set in

instinct [ɛ̃stɛ̃] nm instinct; **instinctivement** adv instinctively

instituer [ɛ̃stitɥe] /1/ vt to establish

institut [ɛ̃stity] nm institute; **~ de beauté** beauty salon; **I~ universitaire de technologie (IUT)** ≈ Institute of technology

instituteur, -trice [ɛ̃stitytœʀ, -tʀis] nm/f (primary (BRIT) ou grade (US) school) teacher

institution [ɛ̃stitysjɔ̃] nf institution; (collège) private school; **institutions** nfpl (structures politiques et sociales) institutions

instructif, -ive [ɛ̃stʀyktif, -iv] adj instructive

instruction [ɛ̃stʀyksjɔ̃] nf (enseignement, savoir) education; (Jur) (preliminary) investigation and hearing; **instructions** nfpl (mode d'emploi) instructions; **~ civique** civics sg

instruire [ɛ̃stʀɥiʀ] /38/ vt (élèves) to teach; (recrues) to train; (Jur: affaire) to conduct the investigation for; **s'instruire** to educate o.s.; **instruit, e** adj educated

instrument [ɛ̃stʀymɑ̃] nm instrument; **~ à cordes/vent** stringed/wind instrument; **~ de mesure** measuring instrument; **~ de musique** musical instrument; **~ de travail** (working) tool

insu [ɛ̃sy] nm: **à l'~ de qn** without sb knowing

insuffisant, e [ɛ̃syfizɑ̃, -ɑ̃t] adj (en quantité) insufficient; (en qualité) inadequate; (sur une copie) poor

insulaire [ɛ̃sylɛʀ] adj island cpd; (attitude) insular

insuline [ɛ̃sylin] nf insulin

insulte [ɛ̃sylt] nf insult; **insulter** /1/ vt to insult

insupportable [ɛ̃sypɔʀtabl] adj unbearable

insurmontable [ɛ̃syʀmɔ̃tabl] adj (difficulté) insuperable; (aversion) unconquerable

intact, e [ɛ̃takt] adj intact

intarissable [ɛ̃taʀisabl] adj inexhaustible

intégral, e, -aux [ɛ̃tegʀal, -o] adj complete; **texte ~** unabridged version; **bronzage ~** all-over suntan; **intégralement** adv in full; **intégralité** nf whole (ou full) amount; **dans son intégralité** in its entirety; **intégrant, e** adj: **faire partie intégrante de** to be an integral part of

intègre [ɛ̃tegʀ] adj upright

intégrer [ɛ̃tegʀe] /6/: **s'intégrer** vr: **s'~ à** ou **dans** to become integrated into; **bien s'~** to fit in

intégrisme [ɛ̃tegʀism] nm fundamentalism

intellectuel, le [ɛ̃telɛktɥel] adj, nm/f intellectual; (péj) highbrow

intelligence [ɛ̃teliʒɑ̃s] nf intelligence; (compréhension): **l'~ de** the understanding of; (complicité): **regard d'~** glance of complicity; (accord): **vivre en bonne ~ avec qn** to be on good terms with sb

intelligent, e [ɛ̃teliʒɑ̃, -ɑ̃t] adj intelligent

intelligible [ɛ̃teliʒibl] adj intelligible

intempéries [ɛ̃tɑ̃peʀi] nfpl bad weather sg

intenable [ɛ̃tnabl] adj unbearable

intendant, e [ɛ̃tɑ̃dɑ̃, -ɑ̃t] nm/f (Mil) quartermaster; (Scol) bursar

intense [ε̃tɑ̃s] adj intense; **intensif, -ive** adj intensive; **cours intensif** crash course

intenter [ε̃tɑ̃te] /1/ vt: **~ un procès contre** ou **à qn** to start proceedings against sb

intention [ε̃tɑ̃sjɔ̃] nf intention; (Jur) intent; **avoir l'~ de faire** to intend to do; **à l'~ de** for; (renseignement) for the benefit ou information of; (film, ouvrage) aimed at; **à cette ~** with this aim in view; **intentionné, e** adj: **bien intentionné** well-meaning ou -intentioned; **mal intentionné** ill-intentioned

interactif, -ive [ε̃tεraktif, -iv] adj (aussi Inform) interactive

intercepter [ε̃tεrsεpte] /1/ vt to intercept; (lumière, chaleur) to cut off

interchangeable [ε̃tεrʃɑ̃ʒabl] adj interchangeable

interdiction [ε̃tεrdiksjɔ̃] nf ban; **~ de fumer** no smoking

interdire [ε̃tεrdir] /37/ vt to forbid; (Admin) to ban, prohibit; (: journal, livre) to ban; **~ à qn de faire** to forbid sb to do; (empêchement) to prevent ou preclude sb from doing

interdit, e [ε̃tεrdi, -it] pp de **interdire** ▷ adj (stupéfait) taken aback; **film ~ aux moins de 18/12 ans** ≈ 18-/12A-rated film; **stationnement ~** no parking

intéressant, e [ε̃teresɑ̃, -ɑ̃t] adj interesting; (avantageux) attractive

intéressé, e [ε̃terese] adj (parties) involved, concerned; (amitié, motifs) self-interested

intéresser [ε̃terese] /1/ vt (captiver) to interest; (toucher) to be of interest ou concern to; (Admin: concerner) to affect, concern; **s'intéresser à** vi to take an interest in

intérêt [ε̃terε] nm interest; (égoïsme) self-interest; **tu as ~ à accepter** it's in your interest to accept; **tu as ~ à te dépêcher** you'd better hurry

intérieur, e [ε̃terjœr] adj (mur, escalier, poche) inside; (commerce, politique) domestic; (cour, calme, vie) inner; (navigation) inland ▷ nm (d'une maison, d'un récipient etc) inside; (d'un pays, aussi décor, mobilier) interior; **l'I~** (the Department of) the Interior, ≈ the Home Office (BRIT); **à l'~ (de)** inside; **intérieurement** adv inwardly

intérim [ε̃terim] nm interim period; **assurer l'~ (de)** to deputize (for); **président par ~** interim president; **faire de l'~** to temp

intérimaire [ε̃terimεr] adj (directeur, ministre) acting; (secrétaire, personnel) temporary ▷ nm/f (secrétaire etc) temporary, temp (BRIT)

interlocuteur, -trice [ε̃tεrlɔkytœr, -tris] nm/f speaker; **son ~** the person he ou she was speaking to

intermédiaire [ε̃tεrmedjεr] adj intermediate; (solution) temporary ▷ nm/f intermediary; (Comm) middleman; **sans ~** directly; **par l'~ de** through

interminable [ε̃tεrminabl] adj never-ending

intermittence [ε̃tεrmitɑ̃s] nf: **par ~** intermittently, sporadically

internat [ε̃tεrna] nm boarding school

international, e, -aux [ε̃tεrnasjɔnal, -o] adj, nm/f international

internaute [ε̃tεrnot] nm/f Internet user

interne [ε̃tεrn] adj internal ▷ nm/f (Scol) boarder; (Méd) houseman

Internet [ε̃tεrnεt] nm: **l'~** the Internet

interpeller [ε̃tεrpele] /1/ vt (appeler) to call out to; (apostropher) to shout at; (Police) to take in for questioning; (Pol) to question; (concerner) to concern

interphone [ε̃tεrfɔn] nm intercom; (d'immeuble) entry phone

interposer [ɛ̃tɛʀpoze] /1/ vt;
s'interposer to intervene; **par
personnes interposées** through a
third party

interprète [ɛ̃tɛʀpʀɛt] nm/f
interpreter; (porte-parole) spokesman

interpréter [ɛ̃tɛʀpʀete] /6/ vt to
interpret; (jouer) to play; (chanter)
to sing

interrogatif, -ive [ɛ̃teʀɔgatif, -iv]
adj (Ling) interrogative

interrogation [ɛ̃teʀɔgasjɔ̃] nf
question; (Scol) (written ou oral) test

interrogatoire [ɛ̃teʀɔgatwaʀ] nm
(Police) questioning no pl; (Jur, aussi fig)
cross-examination

interroger [ɛ̃teʀɔʒe] /3/ vt to
question; (Inform) to search; (Scol)
to test

interrompre [ɛ̃teʀɔ̃pʀ] /41/ vt (gén)
to interrupt; (négociations) to break
off; (match) to stop; **s'interrompre** to
break off; **interrupteur** nm switch;
interruption nf interruption; (pause)
break; **sans interruption** without a
break; **interruption volontaire de
grossesse** abortion

intersection [ɛ̃tɛʀsɛksjɔ̃] nf
intersection

intervalle [ɛ̃tɛʀval] nm (espace)
space; (de temps) interval; **dans l'~** in
the meantime; **à deux jours d'~** two
days apart

intervenir [ɛ̃tɛʀvəniʀ] /22/ vi (gén)
to intervene; **~ auprès de/en faveur
de qn** to intervene with/on behalf
of sb; **intervention** nf intervention;
(discours) speech; **intervention
(chirurgicale)** operation

interview [ɛ̃tɛʀvju] nf interview

intestin, e [ɛ̃tɛstɛ̃, -in] adj internal
▷ nm intestine

intime [ɛ̃tim] adj intimate; (vie,
journal) private; (convictions) inmost;
(dîner, cérémonie) quiet ▷ nm/f close
friend; **un journal ~** a diary

intimider [ɛ̃timide] /1/ vt to
intimidate

intimité [ɛ̃timite] nf: **dans l'~** in
private; (sans formalités) with only a
few friends, quietly

intolérable [ɛ̃tɔleʀabl] adj
intolerable

intox [ɛ̃tɔks] (fam) nf brainwashing

intoxication [ɛ̃tɔksikasjɔ̃] nf: **~
alimentaire** food poisoning

intoxiquer [ɛ̃tɔksike] /1/ vt to
poison; (fig) to brainwash

intraitable [ɛ̃tʀɛtabl] adj inflexible,
uncompromising

intransigeant, e [ɛ̃tʀɑ̃ziʒɑ̃, -ɑ̃t] adj
intransigent

intrépide [ɛ̃tʀepid] adj dauntless

intrigue [ɛ̃tʀig] nf (scénario) plot;
intriguer /1/ vt to puzzle, intrigue

introduction [ɛ̃tʀɔdyksjɔ̃] nf
introduction

introduire [ɛ̃tʀɔdɥiʀ] /38/ vt to
introduce; (visiteur) to show in;
(aiguille, clef); **~ qch dans** to insert
ou introduce sth into; **s'introduire** vi
(techniques, usages) to be introduced;
s'~ dans to gain entry into; (dans un
groupe) to get o.s. accepted into

introuvable [ɛ̃tʀuvabl] adj
which cannot be found; (Comm)
unobtainable

intrus, e [ɛ̃tʀy, -yz] nm/f intruder

intuition [ɛ̃tɥisjɔ̃] nf intuition

inusable [inyzabl] adj hard-wearing

inutile [inytil] adj useless; (superflu)
unnecessary; **inutilement** adv
needlessly; **inutilisable** adj unusable

invalide [ɛ̃valid] adj disabled ▷ nm/f:
~ de guerre disabled ex-serviceman

invariable [ɛ̃vaʀjabl] adj invariable

invasion [ɛ̃vazjɔ̃] nf invasion

inventaire [ɛ̃vɑ̃tɛʀ] nm inventory;
(Comm: liste) stocklist; (: opération)
stocktaking no pl

inventer [ɛ̃vɑ̃te] /1/ vt to invent;
(subterfuge) to devise, invent;
(histoire, excuse) to make up, invent;
inventeur, -trice nm/f inventor;
inventif, -ive adj inventive;
invention nf invention

inverse [ɛ̃vɛʀs] *adj* opposite ▷ *nm* inverse; **l'~** the opposite; **dans l'ordre ~** in the reverse order; **dans le sens ~ des aiguilles d'une montre** anti-clockwise; **en sens ~** in (*ou* from) the opposite direction; **inversement** *adv* conversely; **inverser** /1/ *vt* to reverse, invert; (*Élec*) to reverse

investir [ɛ̃vɛstiʀ] /2/ *vt* to invest; **~ qn de** (*d'une fonction, d'un pouvoir*) to vest *ou* invest sb with sth; **s'investir** *vi* (*Psych*) to involve o.s.; **s'~ dans** to put a lot into; **investissement** *nm* investment

invisible [ɛ̃vizibl] *adj* invisible

invitation [ɛ̃vitasjɔ̃] *nf* invitation

invité, e [ɛ̃vite] *nm/f* guest

inviter [ɛ̃vite] /1/ *vt* to invite; **~ qn à faire qch** to invite sb to do sth

invivable [ɛ̃vivabl] *adj* unbearable

involontaire [ɛ̃vɔlɔ̃tɛʀ] *adj* (*mouvement*) involuntary; (*insulte*) unintentional; (*complice*) unwitting

invoquer [ɛ̃vɔke] /1/ *vt* (*Dieu, muse*) to call upon, invoke; (*prétexte*) to put forward (as an excuse); (*loi, texte*) to refer to

invraisemblable [ɛ̃vʀɛsɑ̃blabl] *adj* (*fait, nouvelle*) unlikely, improbable; (*bizarre*) incredible

iode [jɔd] *nm* iodine

irai *etc* [iʀe] *vb voir* **aller**

Irak [iʀak] *nm*: **l'~** Iraq *ou* Irak; **irakien, ne** *adj* Iraqi ▷ *nm/f*: **Irakien, ne** Iraqi

Iran [iʀɑ̃] *nm*: **l'~** Iran; **iranien, ne** *adj* Iranian ▷ *nm/f*: **Iranien, ne** Iranian

irions *etc* [iʀjɔ̃] *vb voir* **aller**

iris [iʀis] *nm* iris

irlandais, e [iʀlɑ̃dɛ, -ɛz] *adj* Irish ▷ *nm/f*: **I~, e** Irishman/woman

Irlande [iʀlɑ̃d] *nf*: **l'~** Ireland; **la République d'~** the Irish Republic; **~ du Nord** Northern Ireland; **la mer d'~** the Irish Sea

ironie [iʀɔni] *nf* irony; **ironique** *adj* ironical; **ironiser** /1/ *vi* to be ironical

irons *etc* [iʀɔ̃] *vb voir* **aller**

irradier [iʀadje] /7/ *vt* to irradiate

irraisonné, e [iʀɛzɔne] *adj* irrational

irrationnel, le [iʀasjɔnɛl] *adj* irrational

irréalisable [iʀealizabl] *adj* unrealizable; (*projet*) impracticable

irrécupérable [iʀekypeʀabl] *adj* beyond repair; (*personne*) beyond redemption *ou* recall

irréel, le [iʀeɛl] *adj* unreal

irréfléchi, e [iʀefleʃi] *adj* thoughtless

irrégularité [iʀegylaʀite] *nf* irregularity; (*de travail, d'effort, de qualité*) unevenness *no pl*

irrégulier, -ière [iʀegylje, -jɛʀ] *adj* irregular; (*travail, effort, qualité*) uneven; (*élève, athlète*) erratic

irrémédiable [iʀemedjabl] *adj* irreparable

irremplaçable [iʀɑ̃plasabl] *adj* irreplaceable

irréparable [iʀepaʀabl] *adj* beyond repair; (*fig*) irreparable

irréprochable [iʀepʀɔʃabl] *adj* irreproachable, beyond reproach; (*tenue, toilette*) impeccable

irrésistible [iʀezistibl] *adj* irresistible; (*preuve, logique*) compelling; (*amusant*) hilarious

irrésolu, e [iʀezɔly] *adj* irresolute

irrespectueux, -euse [iʀɛspɛktɥø, -øz] *adj* disrespectful

irresponsable [iʀɛspɔ̃sabl] *adj* irresponsible

irriguer [iʀige] /1/ *vt* to irrigate

irritable [iʀitabl] *adj* irritable

irriter [iʀite] /1/ *vt* to irritate

irruption [iʀypsjɔ̃] *nf*: **faire ~ chez qn** to burst in on sb

Islam [islam] *nm*: **l'~** Islam; **islamique** *adj* Islamic; **islamophobie** *nf* Islamophobia

Islande [islɑ̃d] *nf*: **l'~** Iceland

isolant, e [izɔlɑ̃, -ɑ̃t] *adj* insulating; (*insonorisant*) soundproofing

isolation [izɔlasjɔ̃] *nf* insulation; **~ acoustique** soundproofing

isolé, e [izɔle] *adj* isolated; (*contre le froid*) insulated

isoler [izɔle] /1/ *vt* to isolate; (*prisonnier*) to put in solitary confinement; (*ville*) to cut off, isolate; (*contre le froid*) to insulate; **s'isoler** *vi* to isolate o.s.

Israël [israɛl] *nm*: **l'~** Israel; **israélien, ne** *adj* Israeli ▷ *nm/f*: **Israélien, ne** Israeli; **israélite** *adj* Jewish ▷ *nm/f*: **Israélite** Jew/Jewess

issu, e [isy] *adj*: **~ de** (*né de*) descended from; (*résultant de*) stemming from ▷ *nf* (*ouverture, sortie*) exit; (*solution*) way out, solution; (*dénouement*) outcome; **à l'~e de** at the conclusion *ou* close of; **voie sans ~e** dead end; **~e de secours** emergency exit

Italie [itali] *nf*: **l'~** Italy; **italien, ne** *adj* Italian ▷ *nm* (*Ling*) Italian ▷ *nm/f*: **Italien, ne** Italian

italique [italik] *nm*: **en ~(s)** in italics

itinéraire [itinerɛʀ] *nm* itinerary, route; **~ bis** alternative route

IUT *sigle m* = **Institut universitaire de technologie**

IVG *sigle f* (= *interruption volontaire de grossesse*) abortion

ivoire [ivwaʀ] *nm* ivory

ivre [ivʀ] *adj* drunk; **~ de** (*colère*) wild with; **ivrogne** *nm/f* drunkard

J

j' [ʒ] *pron voir* **je**

jacinthe [ʒasɛ̃t] *nf* hyacinth

jadis [ʒɑdis] *adv* formerly

jaillir [ʒajiʀ] /2/ *vi* (*liquide*) to spurt out; (*cris, réponses*) to burst out

jais [ʒɛ] *nm* jet; **(d'un noir) de ~** jet-black

jalousie [ʒaluzi] *nf* jealousy; (*store*) (venetian) blind

jaloux, -ouse [ʒalu, -uz] *adj* jealous; **être ~ de qn/qch** to be jealous of sb/sth

jamaïquain, e [ʒamaikɛ̃, -ɛn] *adj* Jamaican ▷ *nm/f*: **J~, e** Jamaican

Jamaïque [ʒamaik] *nf*: **la ~** Jamaica

jamais [ʒamɛ] *adv* never; (*sans négation*) ever; **ne ... ~** never; **si ~ ...** if ever ...; **je ne suis ~ allé en Espagne** I've never been to Spain

jambe [ʒɑ̃b] *nf* leg

jambon [ʒɑ̃bɔ̃] *nm* ham

jante [ʒɑ̃t] *nf* (*wheel*) rim

janvier [ʒɑ̃vje] *nm* January

Japon [ʒapɔ̃] *nm*: **le ~** Japan;
  japonais, e *adj* Japanese ▷ *nm* (*Ling*)
  Japanese ▷ *nm/f*: **Japonais, e** Japanese
jardin [ʒaʀdɛ̃] *nm* garden; **~
  d'enfants** nursery school; **jardinage**
  nm gardening; **jardiner** /1/ *vi*
  to garden; **jardinier, -ière** *nm/f*
  gardener ▷ *nf* (*de fenêtre*) window
  box; **jardinière (de légumes)** (*Culin*)
  mixed vegetables
jargon [ʒaʀgɔ̃] *nm* (*charabia*)
  gibberish; (*publicitaire, scientifique
  etc*) jargon
jarret [ʒaʀɛ] *nm* back of knee; (*Culin*)
  knuckle, shin
jauge [ʒoʒ] *nf* (*instrument*) gauge;
  ~ (de niveau) d'huile (*Auto*) dipstick
jaune [ʒon] *adj, nm* yellow ▷ *adv*
  (*fam*): **rire ~** to laugh on the other
  side of one's face; **~ d'œuf** (egg)
  yolk; **jaunir** /2/ *vi, vt* to turn yellow;
  jaunisse *nf* jaundice
Javel [ʒavɛl] *nf voir* **eau**
javelot [ʒavlo] *nm* javelin
J.-C. *sigle m* = **Jésus-Christ**
je, j' [ʒə, ʒ] *pron* I
jean [dʒin] *nm* jeans *pl*
Jésus-Christ [ʒezykʀi(st)] *n* Jesus
  Christ; **600 avant/après ~** 600
  B.C./A.D.
jet [ʒɛ] *nm* (*lancer: action*) throwing
  no pl; (: *résultat*) throw; (*jaillissement:
  d'eaux*) jet; (: *de sang*) spurt; **~ d'eau**
  spray
jetable [ʒətabl] *adj* disposable
jetée [ʒəte] *nf* jetty; (*grande*) pier
jeter [ʒəte] /4/ *vt* (*gén*) to throw;
  (*se défaire de*) to throw away *ou* out;
  ~ qch à qn to throw sth to sb; (*de
  façon agressive*) to throw sth at sb;
  ~ un coup d'œil (à) to take a look
  (at); **~ un sort à qn** to cast a spell on
  sb; **se ~ sur** to throw o.s. onto; **se ~
  dans** (*fleuve*) to flow into
jeton [ʒətɔ̃] *nm* (*au jeu*) counter
jette *etc* [ʒɛt] *vb voir* **jeter**
jeu, x [ʒø] *nm* (*divertissement, Tech:
  d'une pièce*) play; (*Tennis: partie,*

Football etc: façon de jouer) game;
  (*Théât etc*) acting; (*série d'objets, jouet*)
  set; (*Cartes*) hand; (*au casino*) **le ~**
  gambling; **en ~** at stake; **remettre
  en ~** to throw in; **entrer/mettre en ~**
  to come/bring into play; **~ de cartes**
  pack of cards; **~ d'échecs** chess set;
  ~ de hasard game of chance; **~ de
  mots** pun; **~ de société** board game;
  ~ télévisé television quiz; **~ vidéo**
  video game
jeudi [ʒødi] *nm* Thursday
jeun [ʒœ̃]: **à ~** *adv* on an empty
  stomach; **être à ~** to have eaten
  nothing; **rester à ~** not to eat
  anything
jeune [ʒœn] *adj* young; **les ~s** young
  people; **~ fille** girl; **~ homme** young
  man; **~s gens** young people
jeûne [ʒøn] *nm* fast
jeunesse [ʒœnɛs] *nf* youth; (*aspect*)
  youthfulness
joaillier, -ière [ʒoaje, -jɛʀ] *nm/f*
  jeweller
jogging [dʒɔgiŋ] *nm* jogging;
  (*survêtement*) tracksuit; **faire du ~**
  to go jogging
joie [ʒwa] *nf* joy
joindre [ʒwɛ̃dʀ] /49/ *vt* to join;
  (*contacter*) to contact, get in touch
  with; **~ qch à** (*à une lettre*) to enclose
  sth with; **~ un fichier à un mail**
  (*Inform*) to attach a file to an email;
  se ~ à qn to join sb; **se ~ à qch** to
  join in sth
joint, e [ʒwɛ̃, -ɛ̃t] *adj*: **~ (à)** (*lettre,
  paquet*) attached (to), enclosed
  (with) ▷ *nm* joint; (*ligne*) join; **pièce
  ~e** (*de lettre*) enclosure; (*de mail*)
  attachment; **~ de culasse** cylinder
  head gasket
joli, e [ʒɔli] *adj* pretty, attractive; **une
  ~e somme/situation** a nice little
  sum/situation; **c'est du ~!** (*ironique*)
  that's very nice!; **tout ça, c'est bien
  ~ mais ...** that's all very well but ...
jonc [ʒɔ̃] *nm* (*bul*)rush
jonction [ʒɔ̃ksjɔ̃] *nf* junction

jongleur, -euse [ʒɔ̃glœʀ, -øz] *nm/f*
juggler

jonquille [ʒɔ̃kij] *nf* daffodil

Jordanie [ʒɔʀdani] *nf*: **la ~** Jordan

joue [ʒu] *nf* cheek

jouer [ʒwe] /1/ *vt* to play; (*somme
d'argent, réputation*) to stake, wager;
(*simuler: sentiment*) to affect, feign
▷ *vi* to play; (*Théât, Ciné*) to act; (*au
casino*) to gamble; (*bois, porte: se
voiler*) to warp; (*clef, pièce: avoir du jeu*)
to be loose; **~ sur** (*miser*) to gamble
on; **~ de** (*Mus*) to play; **~ à** (*jeu, sport,
roulette*) to play; **~ un tour à qn** to
play a trick on sb; **~ la comédie** to
put on an act; **~ serré** to play a close
game; **à toi/nous de ~** it's your/our
go *ou* turn; **bien joué!** well done!; **on
joue Hamlet au théâtre X** Hamlet is
on at the X theatre

jouet [ʒwe] *nm* toy; **être le ~ de**
(*illusion etc*) to be the victim of

joueur, -euse [ʒwœʀ, -øz] *nm/f*
player; **être beau/mauvais ~** to be a
good/bad loser

jouir [ʒwiʀ] /2/ *vi* (*sexe: fam*) to come
▷ *vt*: **~ de** to enjoy

jour [ʒuʀ] *nm* day; (*opposé à la nuit*)
day, daytime; (*clarté*) daylight; (*fig:
aspect, ouverture*) opening; **sous un ~
favorable/nouveau** in a favourable/
new light; **de ~** (*crème, service*) day *cpd*;
travailler de ~ to work during the
day; **voyager de ~** to travel by day; **au
~ le ~** from day to day; **de nos ~s** these
days; **du ~ au lendemain** overnight;
il fait ~ it's daylight; **au grand ~** (*fig*)
in the open; **mettre au ~** to disclose;
mettre à ~ to bring up to date;
donner le ~ à to give birth to; **voir le
~** to be born; **~ férié** public holiday; **le
~ J** D-day; **~ ouvrable** working day

journal, -aux [ʒuʀnal, -o] *nm*
(*news*)paper; (*personnel*) journal;
(*intime*) diary; **~ de bord** log; **~ parlé/
télévisé** radio/television news *sg*

journalier, -ière [ʒuʀnalje, -jɛʀ] *adj*
daily; (*banal*) everyday

journalisme [ʒuʀnalism] *nm*
journalism; **journaliste** *nm/f*
journalist

journée [ʒuʀne] *nf* day; **la ~
continue** the 9 to 5 working day
(*with short lunch break*)

joyau, x [ʒwajo] *nm* gem, jewel

joyeux, -euse [ʒwajø, -øz] *adj* joyful,
merry; **~ Noël!** Merry *ou* Happy
Christmas!; **~ anniversaire!** many
happy returns!

jubiler [ʒybile] /1/ *vi* to be jubilant,
exult

judas [ʒyda] *nm* (*trou*) spy-hole

judiciaire [ʒydisjɛʀ] *adj* judicial

judicieux, -euse [ʒydisjø, -øz] *adj*
judicious

judo [ʒydo] *nm* judo

juge [ʒyʒ] *nm* judge; **~ d'instruction**
examining (*BRIT*) *ou* committing
(*US*) magistrate; **~ de paix** justice
of the peace

jugé [ʒyʒe]: **au ~** *adv* by guesswork

jugement [ʒyʒmɑ̃] *nm* judgment;
(*Jur: au pénal*) sentence; (: *au civil*)
decision

juger [ʒyʒe] /3/ *vt* to judge;
(*estimer*) to consider; **~ qn/qch
satisfaisant** to consider sb/sth (to
be) satisfactory; **~ bon de faire** to
consider it a good idea to do

juif, -ive [ʒɥif, -iv] *adj* Jewish
▷ *nm/f*: **J~, -ive** Jew/Jewess *ou* Jewish
woman

juillet [ʒɥijɛ] *nm* July

juin [ʒɥɛ̃] *nm* June
jumeau, -elle, x [ʒymo, -ɛl] *adj,
nm/f* twin
jumeler [ʒymle] /4/ *vt* to twin
jumelle [ʒymɛl] *adj f, nf voir* **jumeau**
jument [ʒymã] *nf* mare
jungle [ʒɔ̃gl] *nf* jungle
jupe [ʒyp] *nf* skirt
jupon [ʒypɔ̃] *nm* waist slip *ou* petticoat
juré, e [ʒyʀe] *nm/f* juror ▷ *adj*:
ennemi ~ sworn *ou* avowed enemy
jurer [ʒyʀe] /1/ *vt* (*obéissance etc*) to
swear, vow ▷ *vi* (*dire des jurons*) to
swear, curse; (*dissoner*): **~ (avec)** to
clash (with); **~ de faire/que** to swear
ou vow to do/that; **~ de qch** (*s'en
porter garant*) to swear to sth
juridique [ʒyʀidik] *adj* legal
juron [ʒyʀɔ̃] *nm* curse, swearword
jury [ʒyʀi] *nm* jury; (*Art, Sport*) panel
of judges; (*Scol*) board (of examiners),
jury
jus [ʒy] *nm* juice; (*de viande*) gravy,
(meat) juice; **~ de fruits** fruit juice
jusque [ʒysk]: **jusqu'à** *prép* (*endroit*)
as far as, (up) to; (*moment*) until,
till; (*limite*) up to; **~ sur/dans** up
to; (*y compris*) even on/in; **jusqu'à
ce que** until; **jusqu'à présent** *ou*
maintenant so far; **jusqu'où?**
how far?
justaucorps [ʒystokɔʀ] *nm inv*
leotard
juste [ʒyst] *adj* (*équitable*) just,
fair; (*légitime*) just; (*exact, vrai*)
right; (*pertinent*) apt; (*étroit*) tight;
(*insuffisant*) on the short side ▷ *adv*
right; (*chanter*) in tune; (*seulement*)
just; **~ assez/au-dessus** just
enough/above; **pouvoir tout ~
faire** to be only just able to do; **au
~** exactly; **le ~ milieu** the happy
medium; **c'était ~** it was a close
thing; **justement** *adv* justly;
(*précisément*) just, precisely; **justesse**
nf (*précision*) accuracy; (*d'une
remarque*) aptness; (*d'une opinion*)
soundness; **de justesse** only just

justice [ʒystis] *nf* (*équité*) fairness,
justice; (*Admin*) justice; **rendre ~ à qn**
to do sb justice
justificatif, -ive [ʒystifikatif, -iv]
adj (*document etc*) supporting; **pièce
justificative** written proof
justifier [ʒystifje] /7/ *vt* to justify;
~ de to prove
juteux, -euse [ʒytø, -øz] *adj* juicy
juvénile [ʒyvenil] *adj* youthful

k

kit [kit] *nm* kit; **~ piéton** *ou* **mains libres** hands-free kit; **en ~** in kit form
kiwi [kiwi] *nm* kiwi
klaxon [klaksɔn] *nm* horn; **klaxonner** /1/ *vi, vt* to hoot (*BRIT*), honk (one's horn) (*US*)
km *abr* (= *kilomètre*) km
km/h *abr* (= *kilomètres/heure*) km/h, kph
K.-O. *adj inv* shattered, knackered
Kosovo [kɔsɔvo] *nm*: **le ~** Kosovo
Koweit, Kuweit [kɔwɛt] *nm*: **le ~** Kuwait
k-way® [kawɛ] *nm* (lightweight nylon) cagoule
kyste [kist] *nm* cyst

K [ka] *nm inv* K
kaki [kaki] *adj inv* khaki
kangourou [kɑ̃guʁu] *nm* kangaroo
karaté [kaʁate] *nm* karate
kascher [kaʃɛʁ] *adj inv* kosher
kayak [kajak] *nm* kayak; **faire du ~** to go kayaking
képi [kepi] *nm* kepi
kermesse [kɛʁmɛs] *nf* bazaar, (charity) fête; village fair
kidnapper [kidnape] /1/ *vt* to kidnap
kilo [kilo] *nm* kilo; **kilogramme** *nm* kilogramme; **kilométrage** *nm* number of kilometres travelled, ≈ mileage; **kilomètre** *nm* kilometre; **kilométrique** *adj* (*distance*) in kilometres
kinésithérapeute [kineziteʁapøt] *nm/f* physiotherapist
kiosque [kjɔsk] *nm* kiosk, stall
kir [kiʁ] *nm* kir (*white wine with blackcurrant liqueur*)

l' [l] *art déf voir* **le**

la [la] *art déf voir* **le** ▷ *nm* (*Mus*) A; (*en chantant la gamme*) la

là [la] *adv* there; (*ici*) here; (*dans le temps*) then; **elle n'est pas là** she isn't here; **c'est là que** this is where; **là où** where; **de là** (*fig*) hence; **par là** (*fig*) by that; *voir aussi* **-ci; celui; là-bas** *adv* there

labo [labo] *nm* (= *laboratoire*) lab

laboratoire [labɔʀatwaʀ] *nm* laboratory; **~ de langues/ d'analyses** language/(medical) analysis laboratory

laborieux, -euse [labɔʀjø, -øz] *adj* (*tâche*) laborious

labourer /1/ *vt* to plough

labyrinthe [labiʀɛ̃t] *nm* labyrinth, maze

lac [lak] *nm* lake

lacet [lasɛ] *nm* (*de chaussure*) lace; (*de route*) sharp bend; (*piège*) snare

lâche [lɑʃ] *adj* (*poltron*) cowardly; (*desserré*) loose, slack ▷ *nm/f* coward

lâcher [lɑʃe] /1/ *vt* to let go of; (*ce qui tombe, abandonner*) to drop; (*oiseau, animal: libérer*) to release, set free; (*fig: mot, remarque*) to let slip, come out with ▷ *vi* (*freins*) to fail; **~ les amarres** (*Navig*) to cast off (the moorings); **~ prise** to let go

lacrymogène [lakʀimɔʒɛn] *adj*: **grenade/gaz ~** tear gas grenade/ tear gas

lacune [lakyn] *nf* gap

là-dedans [ladədɑ̃] *adv* inside (there), in it; (*fig*) in that

là-dessous [ladsu] *adv* underneath, under there; (*fig*) behind that

là-dessus [ladsy] *adv* on there; (*fig: sur ces mots*) at that point; (: *à ce sujet*) about that

ladite [ladit] *adj f voir* **ledit**

lagune [lagyn] *nf* lagoon

là-haut [lao] *adv* up there

laid, e [lɛ, lɛd] *adj* ugly; **laideur** *nf* ugliness *no pl*

lainage [lɛnaʒ] *nm* (*vêtement*) woollen garment; (*étoffe*) woollen material

laine [lɛn] *nf* wool

laïque [laik] *adj* lay, civil; (*Scol*) state *cpd* (as opposed to private and Roman Catholic) ▷ *nm/f* layman(-woman)

laisse [lɛs] *nf* (*de chien*) lead, leash; **tenir en ~** to keep on a lead *ou* leash

laisser [lese] /1/ *vt* to leave ▷ *vb aux*: **~ qn faire** to let sb do; **se ~ aller** to let o.s. go; **laisse-toi faire** let me (*ou* him) do it; **laisser-aller** *nm* carelessness, slovenliness; **laissez-passer** *nm inv* pass

lait [lɛ] *nm* milk; **frère/sœur de ~** foster brother/sister; **~ écrémé/ entier/concentré/condensé** skimmed/full-fat/condensed/ evaporated milk; **laitage** *nm* dairy product; **laiterie** *nf* dairy; **laitier, -ière** *adj* dairy *cpd* ▷ *nm/f* milkman (dairywoman)

laiton [lɛtɔ̃] *nm* brass

laitue [lety] *nf* lettuce

lambeau, x [lɑ̃bo] *nm* scrap; **en ~x** in tatters, tattered

lame [lam] *nf* blade; (*vague*) wave; (*lamelle*) strip; **~ de fond** ground swell *no pl*; **~ de rasoir** razor blade; **lamelle** *nf* small blade

lamentable [lamɑ̃tabl] *adj* appalling

lamenter [lamɑ̃te] /1/: **se lamenter** *vi*: **se ~ (sur)** to moan (over)

lampadaire [lɑ̃padɛʀ] *nm* (*de salon*) standard lamp; (*dans la rue*) street lamp

lampe [lɑ̃p] *nf* lamp; (*Tech*) valve; **~ à pétrole** oil lamp; **~ à bronzer** sunlamp; **~ de poche** torch (BRIT), flashlight (US); **~ halogène** halogen lamp

lance [lɑ̃s] *nf* spear; **~ d'incendie** fire hose

lancée [lɑ̃se] *nf*: **être/continuer sur sa ~** to be under way/keep going

lancement [lɑ̃smɑ̃] *nm* launching *no pl*

lance-pierres [lɑ̃spjɛʀ] *nm inv* catapult

lancer [lɑ̃se] /3/ *nm* (*Sport*) throwing *no pl*, throw ▷ *vt* to throw; (*émettre, projeter*) to throw out, send out; (*produit, fusée, bateau, artiste*) to launch; (*injure*) to hurl, fling; **se lancer** *vi* (*prendre de l'élan*) to build up speed; (*se précipiter*): **se ~ sur** *ou* **contre** to rush at; **~ du poids** putting the shot; **~ qch à qn** to throw sth to sb; (*de façon agressive*) to throw sth at sb; **~ un cri** *ou* **un appel** to shout *ou* call out; **se ~ dans** (*discussion*) to launch into; (*aventure*) to embark on

landau [lɑ̃do] *nm* pram (BRIT), baby carriage (US)

lande [lɑ̃d] *nf* moor

langage [lɑ̃gaʒ] *nm* language

langouste [lɑ̃gust] *nf* crayfish *inv*; **langoustine** *nf* Dublin Bay prawn

langue [lɑ̃g] *nf* (*Anat, Culin*) tongue; (*Ling*) language; **tirer la ~ (à)** to stick out one's tongue (at); **de ~ française** French-speaking; **~ maternelle** native language, mother tongue; **~s vivantes** modern languages

langueur [lɑ̃gœʀ] *nf* languidness

languir [lɑ̃giʀ] /2/ *vi* to languish; (*conversation*) to flag; **faire ~ qn** to keep sb waiting

lanière [lanjɛʀ] *nf* (*de fouet*) lash; (*de valise, bretelle*) strap

lanterne [lɑ̃tɛʀn] *nf* (*portable*) lantern; (*électrique*) light, lamp; (*de voiture*) (side)light

laper [lape] /1/ *vt* to lap up

lapidaire [lapidɛʀ] *adj* (*fig*) terse

lapin [lapɛ̃] *nm* rabbit; (*peau*) rabbitskin; (*fourrure*) cony; **poser un ~ à qn** to stand sb up

Laponie [laponi] *nf*: **la ~** Lapland

laps [laps] *nm*: **~ de temps** space of time, time *no pl*

laque [lak] *nf* (*vernis*) lacquer; (*pour cheveux*) hair spray

laquelle [lakɛl] *pron voir* **lequel**

larcin [laʀsɛ̃] *nm* theft

lard [laʀ] *nm* (*graisse*) fat; (*bacon*) (streaky) bacon

lardon [laʀdɔ̃] *nm* piece of chopped bacon

large [laʀʒ] *adj* wide; broad; (*fig*) generous ▷ *adv*: **calculer/voir ~** to allow extra/think big ▷ *nm* (*largeur*): **5 m de ~** 5 m wide *ou* in width; (*mer*): **le ~** the open sea; **au ~ de** off; **~ d'esprit** broad-minded; **largement** *adv* widely; (*de loin*) greatly; (*amplement, au minimum*) easily; (*donner etc*) generously; **c'est largement suffisant** that's ample; **largesse** *nf* generosity; **largesses** *nfpl* (*dons*) liberalities; **largeur** *nf* (*qu'on mesure*) width; (*impression visuelle*) wideness, width; (*d'esprit*) broadness

larguer [laʀge] /1/ *vt* to drop; **~ les amarres** to cast off (the moorings)

larme [laʀm] *nf* tear; (*fig*): **une ~ de** a drop of; **en ~s** in tears; **larmoyer** /8/ *vi* (*yeux*) to water; (*se plaindre*) to whimper

larvé, e [larve] *adj (fig)* latent
laryngite [larɛ̃ʒit] *nf* laryngitis
las, lasse [lɑ, lɑs] *adj* weary
laser [lazɛr] *nm:* **(rayon) ~** laser
(beam); **chaîne** *ou* **platine ~**
compact disc (player); **disque ~**
compact disc
lasse [lɑs] *adj f voir* **las**
lasser [lɑse] /1/ *vt* to weary, tire
latéral, e, -aux [lateral, -o] *adj* side
cpd, lateral
latin, e [latɛ̃, -in] *adj* Latin ▷ *nm (Ling)*
Latin ▷ *nm/f:* **L~, e** Latin
latitude [latityd] *nf* latitude
lauréat, e [lɔrea, -at] *nm/f* winner
laurier [lɔrje] *nm (Bot)* laurel; *(Culin)*
bay leaves *pl*
lavable [lavabl] *adj* washable
lavabo [lavabo] *nm* washbasin;
lavabos *nmpl* toilet *sg*
lavage [lavaʒ] *nm* washing *no pl*,
wash; **~ de cerveau** brainwashing
no pl
lavande [lavɑ̃d] *nf* lavender
lave [lav] *nf* lava *no pl*
lave-linge [lavlɛ̃ʒ] *nm inv* washing
machine
laver [lave] /1/ *vt* to wash; *(tache)* to
wash off; **se laver** *vi* to have a wash,
wash; **se ~ les mains/dents** to
wash one's hands/clean one's teeth;
~ la vaisselle/le linge to wash the
dishes/clothes; **~ qn de** *(accusation)*
to clear sb of; **laverie** *nf:* **laverie**
(automatique) Launderette®
(brit), Laundromat® (us); **lavette** *nf*
dish cloth; *(fam)* drip; **laveur, -euse**
nm/f cleaner; **lave-vaisselle** *nm inv*
dishwasher; **lavoir** *nm* wash house;
(évier) sink
laxatif, -ive [laksatif, -iv] *adj, nm*
laxative
layette [lɛjɛt] *nf* layette

MOT-CLÉ

le, la, l' [lə, la, l] *(pl* **les**) *art déf* **1**
the; **le livre/la pomme/l'arbre**
the book/the apple/the tree; **les**
étudiants the students
2 *(noms abstraits):* **le courage/**
l'amour/la jeunesse courage/
love/youth
3 *(indiquant la possession):* **se casser**
la jambe *etc* to break one's leg *etc*;
levez la main put your hand up;
avoir les yeux gris/le nez rouge to
have grey eyes/a red nose
4 *(temps):* **le matin/soir** in the
morning/evening; mornings/
evenings; **le jeudi** *etc (d'habitude)* on
Thursdays *etc*; *(ce jeudi-là etc)* on (the)
Thursday
5 *(distribution, évaluation)* a, an; **trois**
euros le mètre/kilo three euros a *ou*
per metre/kilo; **le tiers/quart de** a
third/quarter of
▷ *pron* **1** *(personne: mâle)* him;
(: femelle) her; *(: pluriel)* them; **je le/**
la/les vois I can see him/her/them
2 *(animal, chose: singulier)* it; *(: pluriel)*
them; **je le (ou la) vois** I can see it; **je**
les vois I can see them
3 *(remplaçant une phrase):* **je ne le**
savais pas I didn't know (about it);
il était riche et ne l'est plus he was
once rich but no longer is

lécher [leʃe] /6/ *vt* to lick; *(laper:*
lait, eau) to lick *ou* lap up; **se ~ les**
doigts/lèvres to lick one's fingers/
lips; **lèche-vitrines** *nm inv:* **faire**
du lèche-vitrines to go window-
shopping
leçon [ləsɔ̃] *nf* lesson; **faire la ~ à** *(fig)*
to give a lecture to; **~s de conduite**
driving lessons; **~s particulières**
private lessons *ou* tuition *sg* (brit)
lecteur, -trice [lɛktœr, -tris]
nm/f reader; *(d'université)* (foreign
language) assistant ▷ *nm (Tech):*
~ de cassettes cassette player;
~ de disquette(s) disk drive; **~ de**
CD/DVD CD/DVD player; **~ MP3**
MP3 player
lecture [lɛktyr] *nf* reading

Attention à ne pas traduire *lecture* par *le* mot anglais *lecture*.

ledit, ladite [ləðit, ladit] (*mpl* **lesdits**, *fpl* **lesdites**) *adj* the aforesaid

légal, e, -aux [legal, -o] *adj* legal; **légaliser** /1/ *vt* to legalize; **légalité** *nf* legality

légendaire [leʒɑ̃dɛʀ] *adj* legendary

légende [leʒɑ̃d] *nf* (*mythe*) legend; (*de carte, plan*) key; (*de dessin*) caption

léger, -ère [leʒe, -ɛʀ] *adj* light; (*bruit, retard*) slight; (*superficiel*) thoughtless; (*volage*) free and easy; **à la légère** (*parler, agir*) rashly, thoughtlessly; **légèrement** *adv* (*s'habiller, bouger*) lightly; **légèrement plus grand** slightly bigger; **manger légèrement** to eat a light meal; **légèreté** *nf* lightness; (*d'une remarque*) flippancy

législatif, -ive [leʒislatif, -iv] *adj* legislative; **législatives** *nfpl* general election *sg*

légitime [leʒitim] *adj* (*Jur*) lawful, legitimate; (*fig*) rightful, legitimate; **en état de ~ défense** in self-defence

legs [lɛg] *nm* legacy

léguer [lege] /6/ *vt*: **~ qch à qn** (*Jur*) to bequeath sth to sb

légume [legym] *nm* vegetable; **~s verts** green vegetables; **~s secs** pulses

lendemain [lɑ̃dmɛ̃] *nm*: **le ~** the next *ou* following day; **le ~ matin/ soir** the next *ou* following morning/ evening; **le ~ de** the day after

lent, e [lɑ̃, lɑ̃t] *adj* slow; **lentement** *adv* slowly; **lenteur** *nf* slowness *no pl*

lentille [lɑ̃tij] *nf* (*Optique*) lens *sg*; (*Bot*) lentil; **~s de contact** contact lenses

léopard [leɔpaʀ] *nm* leopard

lèpre [lɛpʀ] *nf* leprosy

MOT-CLÉ

lequel, laquelle [ləkɛl, lakɛl] (*mpl* **lesquels**, *fpl* **lesquelles**) (*à + lequel* = **auquel**, *de + lequel* = **duquel** *etc*)

pron **1** (*interrogatif*) which, which one; **lequel des deux?** which one?

2 (*relatif: personne: sujet*) who; (: *objet, après préposition*) whom; (: *chose*) which

▶ *adj*: **auquel cas** in which case

les [le] *art déf, pron voir* **le**

lesbienne [lɛsbjɛn] *nf* lesbian

lesdits, lesdites [ledi, ledit] *adj pl voir* **ledit**

léser [leze] /6/ *vt* to wrong

lésiner [lezine] /1/ *vi*: **ne pas ~ sur les moyens** (*pour mariage etc*) to push the boat out

lésion [lezjɔ̃] *nf* lesion, damage *no pl*

lessive [lesiv] *nf* (*poudre*) washing powder; (*linge*) washing *no pl*, wash; **lessiver** /1/ *vt* to wash; (*fam: fatiguer*) to tire out, exhaust

lest [lɛst] *nm* ballast

leste [lɛst] *adj* sprightly, nimble

lettre [lɛtʀ] *nf* letter; **lettres** *nfpl* (*étude, culture*) literature *sg*; (*Scol*) arts (subjects); **à la ~** literally; **en toutes ~s** in full; **~ piégée** letter bomb

leucémie [løsemi] *nf* leukaemia

MOT-CLÉ

leur [lœʀ] *adj poss* their; **leur maison** their house; **leurs amis** their friends

▶ *pron* **1** (*objet indirect*) (to) them; **je leur ai dit la vérité** I told them the truth; **je le leur ai donné** I gave it to them, I gave them it

2 (*possessif*): **le (la) leur, les leurs** theirs

levain [ləvɛ̃] *nm* leaven

levé, e [ləve] *adj*: **être ~** to be up; **levée** *nf* (*Postes*) collection

lever [ləve] /5/ *vt* (*vitre, bras etc*) to raise; (*soulever de terre, supprimer: interdiction, siège*) to lift; (*impôts, armée*) to levy ▷ *vi* to rise ▷ *nm*: **au ~** on getting up; **se lever** *vi* to get up; (*soleil*) to rise; (*jour*) to break;

(*brouillard*) to lift; **ça va se ~** (*temps*) it's going to clear up; **~ du jour** daybreak; **~ de soleil** sunrise

levier [ləvje] *nm* lever

lèvre [levʀ] *nf* lip

lévrier [levʀije] *nm* greyhound

levure [ləvyʀ] *nf* yeast; **~ chimique** baking powder

lexique [lɛksik] *nm* vocabulary, lexicon; (*glossaire*) vocabulary

lézard [lezaʀ] *nm* lizard

lézarde [lezaʀd] *nf* crack

liaison [ljezɔ̃] *nf* (*rapport*) connection; (*Rail, Aviat etc*) link; (*amoureuse*) affair; (*Culin, Phonétique*) liaison; **entrer/être en ~ avec** to get/be in contact with

liane [ljan] *nf* creeper

liasse [ljas] *nf* wad, bundle

Liban [libã] *nm*: **le ~** (the) Lebanon

libeller [libele] /1/ *vt* (*chèque, mandat*): **~ (au nom de)** to make out (to); (*lettre*) to word

libellule [libelyl] *nf* dragonfly

libéral, e, -aux [liberal, -o] *adj, nm/f* liberal; **les professions ~es** liberal professions

libérer [libere] /6/ *vt* (*délivrer*) to free, liberate; (*Psych*) to liberate; (*relâcher: prisonnier*) to discharge, release; (*gaz, cran d'arrêt*) to release; **se libérer** *vi* (*de rendez-vous*) to get out of previous engagements

liberté [libɛʀte] *nf* freedom; (*loisir*) free time; **libertés** *nfpl* (*privautés*) liberties; **mettre/être en ~** to set/be free; **en ~ provisoire/surveillée/conditionnelle** on bail/probation/parole

libraire [libʀɛʀ] *nm/f* bookseller

librairie [libʀeʀi] *nf* bookshop

Attention à ne pas traduire *librairie* par library.

libre [libʀ] *adj* free; (*route*) clear; (*place etc*) free; (*ligne*) not engaged; (*Scol*) non-state; **~ de qch/de faire** free from sth/to do; **~ arbitre** free will; **libre-échange** *nm* free trade; **libre-service** *nm inv* self-service store

Libye [libi] *nf*: **la ~** Libya

licence [lisãs] *nf* (*permis*) permit; (*diplôme*) (first) degree; (*liberté*) liberty; **licencié, e** *nm/f* (*Scol*): **licencié ès lettres/en droit** ≈ Bachelor of Arts/Law

licenciement [lisãsimã] *nm* redundancy

licencier [lisãsje] /7/ *vt* (*renvoyer*) to dismiss; (*débaucher*) to make redundant

licite [lisit] *adj* lawful

lie [li] *nf* dregs *pl*, sediment

lié, e [lje] *adj*: **très ~ avec** very friendly with *ou* close to

Liechtenstein [liʃtɛnʃtajn] *nm*: **le ~** Liechtenstein

liège [ljɛʒ] *nm* cork

lien [ljɛ̃] *nm* (*corde, fig: affectif, culturel*) bond; (*rapport*) link, connection; **~ de parenté** family tie; **~ hypertexte** hyperlink

lier [lje] /7/ *vt* (*attacher*) to tie up; (*joindre*) to link up; (*fig: unir, engager*) to bind; **~ conversation (avec)** to strike up a conversation (with); **~ connaissance avec** to get to know

lierre [ljɛʀ] *nm* ivy

lieu, x [ljø] *nm* place; **lieux** *nmpl* (*locaux*) premises; (*endroit: d'un accident etc*) scene *sg*; **arriver/être sur les ~x** to arrive/be on the scene; **en premier ~** in the first place; **en dernier ~** lastly; **avoir ~** to take place; **tenir ~ de** to serve as; **donner ~ à** to give rise to; **au ~ de** instead of; **~ commun** commonplace; **lieu-dit** (*pl* **lieux-dits**) *nm* locality

lieutenant [ljøtnã] *nm* lieutenant

lièvre [ljɛvʀ] *nm* hare

ligament [ligamã] *nm* ligament

ligne [liɲ] *nf* (*gén*) line; (*Transports: liaison*) service; (: *trajet*) route; (*silhouette*) figure; **garder la ~** to keep one's figure; **en ~** (*Inform*) online; **entrer en ~ de compte** to be taken into account; **~ fixe** (*Tél*) landline

ligné, e [liɲe] *adj*: **papier ~** ruled paper ▷ *nf* line, lineage

ligoter [ligɔte] /1/ *vt* to tie up

ligue [lig] *nf* league

lilas [lila] *nm* lilac

limace [limas] *nf* slug

limande [limãd] *nf* dab

lime [lim] *nf* file; **~ à ongles** nail file; **limer** /1/ *vt* to file

limitation [limitasjɔ̃] *nf*: **~ de vitesse** speed limit

limite [limit] *nf* (*de terrain*) boundary; (*partie ou point extrême*) limit; **à la ~** (*au pire*) if the worst comes (*ou* came) to the worst; **vitesse/charge ~** maximum speed/load; **cas ~** borderline case; **date ~** deadline; **date ~ de vente/consommation** sell-by/best-before date; **limiter** /1/ *vt* (*restreindre*) to limit, restrict; (*délimiter*) to border; **limitrophe** *adj* border *cpd*

limoger [limɔʒe] /3/ *vt* to dismiss

limon [limɔ̃] *nm* silt

limonade [limɔnad] *nf* lemonade

lin [lɛ̃] *nm* (*tissu, toile*) linen

linceul [lɛ̃sœl] *nm* shroud

linge [lɛ̃ʒ] *nm* (*serviettes etc*) linen; (*aussi*: **~ de corps**) underwear; (*lessive*) washing; **lingerie** *nf* lingerie, underwear

lingot [lɛ̃go] *nm* ingot

linguistique [lɛ̃gɥistik] *adj* linguistic ▷ *nf* linguistics *sg*

lion, ne [ljɔ̃, ljɔn] *nm/f* lion (lioness); (*signe*): **le L~** Leo; **lionceau, x** *nm* lion cub

liqueur [likœr] *nf* liqueur

liquidation [likidasjɔ̃] *nf* (*vente*) sale, liquidation; (*Comm*) clearance (sale)

liquide [likid] *adj* liquid ▷ *nm* liquid; (*Comm*): **en ~** in ready money *ou* cash; **je n'ai pas de ~** I haven't got any cash; **liquider** /1/ *vt* to liquidate; (*Comm: articles*) to clear, sell off

lire [liʀ] /43/ *nf* (*monnaie*) lira ▷ *vt*, *vi* to read

lis *vb* [li] *voir* **lire** ▷ *nm* [lis] = **lys**

Lisbonne [lizbɔn] *n* Lisbon

liseuse [lizøz] *nf* e-reader

lisible [lizibl] *adj* legible

lisière [lizjɛʀ] *nf* (*de forêt*) edge

lisons [lizɔ̃] *vb voir* **lire**

lisse [lis] *adj* smooth

lisseur [liːsœʀ] *nm* straighteners

liste [list] *nf* list; **faire la ~ de** to list; **~ électorale** electoral roll; **~ de mariage** wedding (present) list; **listing** *nm* (*Inform*) printout

lit [li] *nm* bed; **petit ~, ~ à une place** single bed; **grand ~, ~ à deux places** double bed; **faire son ~** to make one's bed; **aller/se mettre au ~** to go to/get into bed; **~ de camp** camp bed; **~ d'enfant** cot (*BRIT*), crib (*US*)

literie [litʀi] *nf* bedding, bedclothes *pl*

litige [litiʒ] *nm* dispute

litre [litʀ] *nm* litre

littéraire [literɛʀ] *adj* literary ▷ *nm/f* arts student; **elle est très ~** she's very literary

littéral, e, -aux [literal, -o] *adj* literal

littérature [literatyʀ] *nf* literature

littoral, e, -aux [litɔral, -o] *nm* coast

livide [livid] *adj* livid, pallid

livraison [livʀɛzɔ̃] *nf* delivery

livre [livʀ] *nm* book ▷ *nf* (*poids, monnaie*) pound; **~ numérique** e-book; **~ de poche** paperback

livré, e [livʀe] *adj*: **~ à soi-même** left to oneself *ou* one's own devices

livrer [livʀe] /1/ *vt* (*Comm*) to deliver; (*otage, coupable*) to hand over; (*secret, information*) to give away; **se ~ à** (*se rendre*) to give o.s. up to; (*faire: pratiques, actes*) to indulge in; (*enquête*) to carry out

livret [livʀɛ] *nm* booklet; (*d'opéra*) libretto; **~ de caisse d'épargne** (savings) bank-book; **~ de famille** (official) family record book; **~ scolaire** (school) report book

livreur, -euse [livrœr, -øz] nm/f
delivery boy ou man/girl ou woman
local, e, -aux [lɔkal, -o] adj local
▷ nm (salle) premises pl ▷ nmpl
premises; **localité** nf locality
locataire [lɔkatɛr] nm/f tenant; (de
chambre) lodger
location [lɔkasjɔ̃] nf (par le locataire)
renting; (par le propriétaire) renting
out, letting; (bureau) booking office;
"~ de voitures" "car hire (BRIT) ou
rental (US)"; **habiter en ~** to live in
rented accommodation; **prendre
une ~ (pour les vacances)** to rent a
house etc (for the holidays)
█ Attention à ne pas traduire
location par le mot anglais location.
locomotive [lɔkɔmɔtiv] nf
locomotive, engine
locution [lɔkysjɔ̃] nf phrase
loge [lɔʒ] nf (Théât: d'artiste) dressing
room; (: de spectateurs) box; (de
concierge, franc-maçon) lodge
logement [lɔʒmɑ̃] nm flat (BRIT),
apartment (US); accommodation no
pl (BRIT), accommodations pl (US);
(Pol, Admin): **le ~** housing
loger [lɔʒe] /3/ vt to accommodate
▷ vi to live; **se loger** vr: **trouver à
se ~** to find accommodation; **se ~
dans** (balle, flèche) to lodge itself in;
être logé, nourri to have board and
lodging; **logeur, -euse** nm/f
landlord (landlady)
logiciel [lɔʒisjɛl] nm piece of
software
logique [lɔʒik] adj logical ▷ nf logic
logo [lɔgo] nm logo
loi [lwa] nf law; **faire la ~** to lay down
the law
loin [lwɛ̃] adv far; (dans le temps: futur)
a long way off; (: passé) a long time
ago; **plus ~** further; **~ de** far from;
~ d'ici a long way from here; **au ~**
far off; **de ~** from a distance; (fig: de
beaucoup) by far
lointain, e [lwɛ̃tɛ̃, -ɛn] adj faraway,
distant; (dans le futur, passé) distant;

(cause, parent) remote, distant ▷ nm:
dans le ~ in the distance
loir [lwar] nm dormouse
Loire [lwar] nf: **la ~** the Loire
loisir [lwazir] nm: **heures de ~**
spare time; **loisirs** nmpl (temps libre)
leisure sg; (activités) leisure activities;
avoir le ~ de faire to have the time
ou opportunity to do; **(tout) à ~**
at leisure
londonien, ne [lɔ̃dɔnjɛ̃, -ɛn] adj
London cpd, of London ▷ nm/f: **L~,
ne** Londoner
Londres [lɔ̃dr] n London
long, longue [lɔ̃, lɔ̃g] adj long ▷ adv:
en savoir ~ to know a great deal
▷ nm: **de 3 m de ~** 3 m long, 3 m in
length; **ne pas faire ~ feu** not to last
long; **(tout) le ~ de** (all) along; **tout
au ~ de** (année, vie) throughout; **de
~ en large** (marcher) to and fro, up
and down
longer [lɔ̃ʒe] /3/ vt to go (ou walk
ou drive) along(side); (mur, route)
to border
longiligne [lɔ̃ʒiliɲ] adj long-limbed
longitude [lɔ̃ʒityd] nf longitude
longtemps [lɔ̃tɑ̃] adv (for) a long
time, (for) long; **avant ~** before
long; **pour/pendant ~** for a long
time; **mettre ~ à faire** to take a long
time to do; **il en a pour ~** he'll be a
long time
longue [lɔ̃g] adj f voir **long** ▷ nf: **à
la ~** in the end; **longuement** adv
(longtemps) for a long time; (en détail)
at length
longueur [lɔ̃gœr] nf length;
longueurs nfpl (fig: d'un film etc)
tedious parts; **en ~** lengthwise; **tirer
en ~** to drag on; **à ~ de journée** all
day long
loquet [lɔkɛ] nm latch
lorgner [lɔrɲe] /1/ vt to eye; (fig) to
have one's eye on
lors [lɔr] **~ de** prép (au moment de)
at the time of; (pendant) during;
~ même que even though

lorsque [lɔʀsk] *conj* when, as

losange [lozɑ̃ʒ] *nm* diamond

lot [lo] *nm* (*part*) share; (*de loterie*) prize; (*fig: destin*) fate, lot; (*Comm, Inform*) batch; **le gros ~** the jackpot

loterie [lɔtʀi] *nf* lottery

lotion [losjɔ̃] *nf* lotion; **~ après rasage** after-shave (lotion)

lotissement [lɔtismɑ̃] *nm* housing development; (*parcelle*) (building) plot, lot

loto [lɔto] *nm* lotto

lotte [lɔt] *nf* monkfish

louange [lwɑ̃ʒ] *nf*: **à la ~ de** in praise of; **louanges** *nfpl* praise *sg*

loubar(d) [lubaʀ] *nm* (*fam*) lout

louche [luʃ] *adj* shady, fishy, dubious ▷ *nf* ladle; **loucher** /1/ *vi* to squint

louer [lwe] /1/ *vt* (*maison: propriétaire*) to let, rent (out); (: *locataire*) to rent; (*voiture etc: entreprise*) to hire out (*BRIT*), rent (out); (: *locataire*) to hire (*BRIT*), rent; (*réserver*) to book; (*faire l'éloge de*) to praise; **"à ~"** "to let" (*BRIT*), "for rent" (*US*)

loup [lu] *nm* wolf; **jeune ~** young go-getter

loupe [lup] *nf* magnifying glass; **à la ~** in minute detail

louper [lupe] /1/ *vt* (*fam: manquer*) to miss; (*examen*) to flunk

lourd, e [luʀ, luʀd] *adj* heavy; (*chaleur, temps*) sultry; **~ de** (*menaces*) charged with; (*conséquences*) fraught with; **lourdaud, e** *adj* clumsy; **lourdement** *adv* heavily

loutre [lutʀ] *nf* otter

louveteau, x [luvto] *nm* wolf-cub; (*scout*) cub (scout)

louvoyer [luvwaje] /8/ *vi* (*fig*) to hedge, evade the issue

loyal, e, -aux [lwajal, -o] *adj* (*fidèle*) loyal, faithful; (*fair-play*) fair; **loyauté** *nf* loyalty, faithfulness; fairness

loyer [lwaje] *nm* rent

lu, e [ly] *pp de* **lire**

lubie [lybi] *nf* whim, craze

lubrifiant [lybʀifjɑ̃] *nm* lubricant

lubrifier [lybʀifje] /7/ *vt* to lubricate

lubrique [lybʀik] *adj* lecherous

lucarne [lykaʀn] *nf* skylight

lucide [lysid] *adj* lucid; (*accidenté*) conscious

lucratif, -ive [lykʀatif, -iv] *adj* lucrative; profitable; **à but non ~** non profit-making

lueur [lɥœʀ] *nf* (*chatoyante*) glimmer *no pl*; (*pâle*) (faint) light; (*fig*) glimmer, gleam

luge [lyʒ] *nf* sledge (*BRIT*), sled (*US*)

lugubre [lygybʀ] *adj* gloomy; dismal

MOT-CLÉ

lui [lɥi] *pron* **1** (*objet indirect: mâle*) (to) him; (: *femelle*) (to) her; (: *chose, animal*) (to) it; **je lui ai parlé** I have spoken to him (*ou* to her); **il lui a offert un cadeau** he gave him (*ou* her) a present

2 (*après préposition, comparatif: personne*) him; (: *chose, animal*) it; **elle est contente de lui** she is pleased with him; **je la connais mieux que lui** I know her better than he does; I know her better than him; **cette voiture est à lui** this car belongs to him, this is HIS car; **c'est à lui de jouer** it's his turn *ou* go

3 (*sujet, forme emphatique*) he; **lui, il est à Paris** HE is in Paris; **c'est lui qui l'a fait** HE did it

4 (*objet, forme emphatique*) him; **c'est lui que j'attends** I'm waiting for HIM

5: lui-même himself; itself

luire [lɥiʀ] /38/ *vi* to shine; (*reflets chauds, cuivrés*) to glow

lumière [lymjɛʀ] *nf* light; **mettre en ~** (*fig*) to highlight; **~ du jour/soleil** day/sunlight

luminaire [lyminɛʀ] *nm* lamp, light

lumineux, -euse [lyminø, -øz] *adj* luminous; (*éclairé*) illuminated; (*ciel, journée, couleur*) bright; (*rayon etc*) of light, light *cpd*; (*fig: regard*) radiant

lunatique [lynatik] *adj* whimsical, temperamental

lundi [lœdi] *nm* Monday; **on est ~** it's Monday; **le(s) ~(s)** on Mondays; **à ~!** see you (on) Monday!; **~ de Pâques** Easter Monday

lune [lyn] *nf* moon; **~ de miel** honeymoon

lunette [lynɛt] *nf*: **~s** glasses, spectacles; (*protectrices*) goggles; **~ arrière** (*Auto*) rear window; **~s noires** dark glasses; **~s de soleil** sunglasses

lustre [lystʀ] *nm* (*de plafond*) chandelier; (*fig: éclat*) lustre; **lustrer** /1/ *vt*: **lustrer qch** to make sth shine

luth [lyt] *nm* lute

lutin [lytɛ̃] *nm* imp, goblin

lutte [lyt] *nf* (*conflit*) struggle; (*Sport*): **la ~** wrestling; **lutter** /1/ *vi* to fight, struggle

luxe [lyks] *nm* luxury; **de ~** luxury *cpd*

Luxembourg [lyksɑ̃buʀ] *nm*: **le ~** Luxembourg

luxer [lykse] /1/ *vt*: **se ~ l'épaule** to dislocate one's shoulder

luxueux, -euse [lyksɥø, -øz] *adj* luxurious

lycée [lise] *nm* (state) secondary (*BRIT*) *ou* high (*US*) school; **lycéen, ne** *nm/f* secondary school pupil

Lyon [ljɔ̃] *n* Lyons

lyophilisé, e [ljɔfilize] *adj* (*café*) freeze-dried

lyrique [liʀik] *adj* lyrical; (*Opéra*) lyric; **artiste ~** opera singer

lys [lis] *nm* lily

M *abr* = **Monsieur**

m' [m] *pron voir* **me**

ma [ma] *adj poss voir* **mon**

macaron [makaʀɔ̃] *nm* (*gâteau*) macaroon; (*insigne*) (round) badge

macaroni(s) [makaʀɔni] *nm* (*pl*) macaroni *sg*; **~ au gratin** macaroni cheese (*BRIT*), macaroni and cheese (*US*)

Macédoine [masedwan] *nf* Macedonia

macédoine [masedwan] *nf*: **~ de fruits** fruit salad; **~ de légumes** mixed vegetables *pl*

macérer [masere] /6/ *vi, vt* to macerate; (*dans du vinaigre*) to pickle

mâcher [mɑʃe] /1/ *vt* to chew; **ne pas ~ ses mots** not to mince one's words

machin [maʃɛ̃] *nm* (*fam*) thingamajig; (*personne*): **M~(e)** what's-his(*ou* her)-name

machinal, e, -aux [maʃinal, -o] *adj*
mechanical, automatic

machination [maʃinasjɔ̃] *nf*
frame-up

machine [maʃin] *nf* machine;
(*locomotive*) engine; **~ à laver/
coudre/tricoter** washing/sewing/
knitting machine; **~ à sous** fruit
machine

mâchoire [maʃwaʀ] *nf* jaw

mâchonner [maʃɔne] /1/ *vt* to
chew (at)

maçon [masɔ̃] *nm* bricklayer;
(*constructeur*) builder; **maçonnerie**
nf (*murs*) brickwork; (: *de pierre*)
masonry, stonework

Madagascar [madagaskaʀ] *nf*
Madagascar

Madame [madam] (*pl* **Mesdames**)
nf: **~ X** Mrs X; **occupez-vous de
~/Monsieur/Mademoiselle**
please serve this lady/gentleman/
(young) lady; **bonjour ~/
Monsieur/Mademoiselle** good
morning; (*ton déférent*) good
morning Madam/Sir/Madam; (*le
nom est connu*) good morning Mrs
X/Mr X/Miss X; **~/Monsieur/
Mademoiselle!** (*pour appeler*)
excuse me!; **~/Monsieur/
Mademoiselle** (*sur lettre*) Dear
Madam/Sir/Madam; **chère ~/cher
Monsieur/chère Mademoiselle**
Dear Mrs X/Mr X/Miss X;
Mesdames Ladies; **mesdames,
mesdemoiselles, messieurs** ladies
and gentlemen

madeleine [madlɛn] *nf* madeleine,
≈ sponge finger cake

Mademoiselle [madmwazɛl] (*pl*
Mesdemoiselles) *nf* Miss; *voir aussi*
Madame

Madère [madɛʀ] *nf* Madeira ▷ *nm*:
madère Madeira (wine)

Madrid [madʀid] *n* Madrid

magasin [magazɛ̃] *nm* (*boutique*)
shop; (*entrepôt*) warehouse; **en ~**
(*Comm*) in stock

magazine [magazin] *nm* magazine

Maghreb [magʀɛb] *nm*: **le ~**
North(-West) Africa; **maghrébin,
e** *adj* North African ▷ *nm/f*:
Maghrébin, e North African

magicien, ne [maʒisjɛ̃, -ɛn] *nm/f*
magician

magie [maʒi] *nf* magic; **magique** *adj*
magic; (*fig*) magical

magistral, e, -aux [maʒistʀal, -o]
adj (*œuvre, adresse*) masterly; (*ton*)
authoritative; **cours ~** lecture

magistrat [maʒistʀa] *nm*
magistrate

magnétique [maɲetik] *adj*
magnetic

magnétophone [maɲetɔfɔn] *nm*
tape recorder; **~ à cassettes** cassette
recorder

magnétoscope [maɲetɔskɔp] *nm*:
~ (à cassette) video (recorder)

magnifique [maɲifik] *adj*
magnificent

magret [magʀɛ] *nm*: **~ de canard**
duck breast

mai [mɛ] *nm* May; *voir aussi* **juillet**

commemorates the surrender of
the German army to Eisenhower
on 7 May, 1945. It is marked by
parades of ex-servicemen and
ex-servicewomen in most towns.
The social upheavals of May and
June 1968, with their student
demonstrations, workers' strikes
and general rioting, are usually
referred to as 'les événements de
mai 68'. De Gaulle's Government
survived, but reforms in
education and a move towards
decentralization ensued.

maigre [mɛgʀ] *adj* (very) thin,
skinny; (*viande*) lean; (*fromage*)
low-fat; (*végétation*) thin, sparse; (*fig*)
poor, meagre, skimpy; **jours ~s** days
of abstinence, fish days; **maigreur**
nf thinness; **maigrir** /2/ *vi* to get
thinner, lose weight; **maigrir de 2
kilos** to lose 2 kilos

mail [mɛl] *nm* email

maille [maj] *nf* stitch; **~ à
l'endroit/à l'envers** plain/purl stitch

maillet [majɛ] *nm* mallet

maillon [majɔ̃] *nm* link

maillot [majo] *nm* (*aussi:* **~ de
corps**) vest; (*de sportif*) jersey; **~ de
bain** swimming (BRIT)
costume, swimsuit; (*d'homme*)
(swimming *ou* bathing (BRIT))
trunks *pl*

main [mɛ̃] *nf* hand; **à la ~** (*tenir, avoir*)
in one's hand; (*faire, tricoter etc*) by
hand; **se donner la ~** to hold hands;
donner *ou* **tendre la ~ à qn** to hold
out one's hand to sb; **se serrer la
~** to shake hands; **serrer la ~ à qn**
to shake hands with sb; **sous la ~**
to *ou* at hand; **haut les ~s!** hands
up!; **attaque à ~ armée** armed
attack; **à remettre en ~s propres**
to be delivered personally; **mettre
la dernière ~ à** to put the finishing
touches to; **se faire/perdre la ~** to
get one's hand in/lose one's touch;

avoir qch bien en ~ to have got
the hang of sth; **main-d'œuvre** *nf*
manpower, labour; **mainmise** *nf*
(*fig*): **avoir la mainmise sur** to have a
grip *ou* stranglehold on

mains-libres [mɛ̃libʀ] *adj inv*
(*téléphone, kit*) hands-free

maint, e [mɛ̃, mɛ̃t] *adj* many a; **~s**
many; **à ~es reprises** time and
(time) again

maintenant [mɛ̃tnɑ̃] *adv* now;
(*actuellement*) nowadays

maintenir [mɛ̃tniʀ] /22/ *vt* (*retenir,
soutenir*) to support; (*contenir: foule
etc*) to keep in check; (*conserver*) to
maintain; **se maintenir** *vi* (*prix*) to
keep steady; (*préjugé*) to persist

maintien [mɛ̃tjɛ̃] *nm* maintaining;
(*attitude*) bearing

maire [mɛʀ] *nm* mayor; **mairie** *nf*
(*bâtiment*) town hall; (*administration*)
town council

mais [mɛ] *conj* but; **~ non!** of
course not!; **~ enfin** but after all;
(*indignation*) look here!

maïs [mais] *nm* maize (BRIT),
corn (US)

maison [mɛzɔ̃] *nf* house; (*chez-soi*)
home; (*Comm*) firm ▷ *adj inv* (*Culin*)
home-made; (*Comm*) in-house, own;
à la ~ at home; (*direction*) home;
~ close brothel; **~ des jeunes** ≈ youth
club; **~ mère** parent company; **~ de
passe** = **maison close**; **~ de repos**
convalescent home; **~ de retraite**
old people's home; **~ de santé**
psychiatric facility

maître, -esse [mɛtʀ, mɛtʀɛs] *nm/f*
master (mistress); (*Scol*) teacher,
schoolmaster/-mistress ▷ *nm* (*peintre
etc*) master; (*titre*): **M~ (Mᵉ)** Maître
(*term of address for lawyers etc*) ▷ *adj*
(*principal, essentiel*) main; **être ~
de** (*soi-même, situation*) to be in
control of; **une maîtresse femme**
a forceful woman; **~ chanteur**
blackmailer; **~/maîtresse d'école**
schoolmaster/-mistress; **~ d'hôtel**

m

(*domestique*) butler; (*d'hôtel*) head waiter; **~ nageur** lifeguard; **maîtresse de maison** hostess; (*ménagère*) housewife

maîtrise [metʀiz] *nf* (*aussi:* **~ de soi**) self-control, self-possession; (*habileté*) skill, mastery; (*suprématie*) mastery, command; (*diplôme*) ≈ master's degree; **maîtriser** /1/ *vt* (*cheval, incendie*) to (bring under) control; (*sujet*) to master; (*émotion*) to control, master; **se maîtriser** to control o.s.

majestueux, -euse [maʒɛstɥø, -øz] *adj* majestic

majeur, e [maʒœʀ] *adj* (*important*) major; (*Jur*) of age ▷ *nm* (*doigt*) middle finger; **en ~e partie** for the most part; **la ~e partie de** most of

majorer [maʒɔʀe] /1/ *vt* to increase

majoritaire [maʒɔʀitɛʀ] *adj* majority *cpd*

majorité [maʒɔʀite] *nf* (*gén*) majority; (*parti*) party in power; **en ~** (*composé etc*) mainly; **avoir la ~** to have the majority

majuscule [maʒyskyl] *adj, nf*: **(lettre) ~** capital (letter)

mal (*pl* **maux**) [mal, mo] *nm* (*opposé au bien*) evil; (*tort, dommage*) harm; (*douleur physique*) pain, ache; (*maladie*) illness, sickness *no pl* ▷ *adv* badly ▷ *adj*: **être ~ (à l'aise)** to be uncomfortable; **être ~ avec qn** to be on bad terms with sb; **il a ~ compris** he misunderstood; **se sentir** *ou* **se trouver ~** to feel ill *ou* unwell; **dire/penser du ~ de** to speak/think ill of; **avoir du ~ à faire qch** to have trouble doing sth; **se donner du ~ pour faire qch** to go to a lot of trouble to do sth; **ne voir aucun ~ à** to see no harm in, see nothing wrong in; **faire du ~ à qn** to hurt sb; **se faire ~** to hurt o.s.; **ça fait ~** it hurts; **j'ai ~ au dos** my back aches; **avoir ~ à la tête/à la gorge** to have a headache/a sore throat; **avoir ~ aux**

dents/à l'oreille to have toothache/earache; **avoir le ~ du pays** to be homesick; **~ de mer** seasickness; **~ en point** in a bad state; *voir aussi* **cœur**

malade [malad] *adj* ill, sick; (*poitrine, jambe*) bad; (*plante*) diseased ▷ *nm/f* invalid, sick person; (*à l'hôpital etc*) patient; **tomber ~** to fall ill; **être ~ du cœur** to have heart trouble *ou* a bad heart; **~ mental** mentally ill person; **maladie** *nf* (*spécifique*) disease, illness; (*mauvaise santé*) illness, sickness; **maladif, -ive** *adj* sickly; (*curiosité, besoin*) pathological

maladresse [maladʀɛs] *nf* clumsiness *no pl*; (*gaffe*) blunder

maladroit, e [maladʀwa, -wat] *adj* clumsy

malaise [malɛz] *nm* (*Méd*) feeling of faintness; (*fig*) uneasiness, malaise; **avoir un ~** to feel faint *ou* dizzy

Malaisie [malɛzi] *nf*: **la ~** Malaysia

malaria [malaʀja] *nf* malaria

malaxer [malakse] /1/ *vt* (*pétrir*) to knead; (*mêler*) to mix

malbouffe [malbuf] *nf* (*fam*): **la ~** junk food

malchance [malʃɑ̃s] *nf* misfortune, ill luck *no pl*; **par ~** unfortunately; **malchanceux, -euse** *adj* unlucky

mâle [mal] *adj* (*Élec, Tech*) male; (*viril: voix, traits*) manly ▷ *nm* male

malédiction [malediksjɔ̃] *nf* curse

mal: **malentendant, e** *adj, nm/f*: **les malentendants** the hard of hearing; **malentendu** *nm* misunderstanding; **il y a eu un malentendu** there's been a misunderstanding; **malfaçon** *nf* fault; **malfaisant, e** *adj* evil, harmful; **malfaiteur** *nm* lawbreaker, criminal; (*voleur*) burglar, thief; **malfamé, e** *adj* disreputable

malgache [malgaʃ] *adj* Malagasy, Madagascan ▷ *nm* (*Ling*) Malagasy ▷ *nm/f*: **M~** Malagasy, Madagascan

malgré [malgʀe] *prép* in spite of, despite; **~ tout** in spite of everything

malheur [malœʀ] nm (situation)
adversity, misfortune; (événement)
misfortune (: plus fort) disaster,
tragedy; **faire un ~** to be a smash
hit; **malheureusement** adv
unfortunately; **malheureux, -euse**
adj (triste) unhappy, miserable;
(infortuné, regrettable) unfortunate;
(malchanceux) unlucky; (insignifiant)
wretched ▷ nm/f poor soul

malhonnête [malɔnɛt] adj
dishonest; **malhonnêteté** nf
dishonesty

malice [malis] nf mischievousness;
(méchanceté): **par ~** out of malice ou
spite; **sans ~** guileless; **malicieux,
-euse** adj mischievous

⬛ Attention à ne pas traduire
malicieux par malicious.

malin, -igne [malɛ̃, -iɲ] adj (futé)
(f gén **maline**) smart, shrewd; (Méd)
malignant

malingre [malɛ̃gʀ] adj puny

malle [mal] nf trunk; **mallette** nf
(small) suitcase; (pour documents)
attaché case

malmener [malməne] /5/ vt to
manhandle; (fig) to give a rough ride to

malodorant, e [malɔdɔʀɑ̃, -ɑ̃t] adj
foul-smelling

malpoli, e [malpɔli] adj impolite

malsain, e [malsɛ̃, -ɛn] adj
unhealthy

malt [malt] nm malt

Malte [malt] nf Malta

maltraiter [maltʀete] /1/ vt to
manhandle, ill-treat

malveillance [malvejɑ̃s] nf
(animosité) ill will; (intention de nuire)
malevolence

malversation [malvɛʀsasjɔ̃] nf
embezzlement

maman [mamɑ̃] nf mum(my)

mamelle [mamɛl] nf teat

mamelon [mamlɔ̃] nm (Anat) nipple

mamie [mami] nf (fam) granny

mammifère [mamifɛʀ] nm
mammal

mammouth [mamut] nm
mammoth

manche [mɑ̃ʃ] nf (de vêtement)
sleeve; (d'un jeu, tournoi) round; (Géo):
la M~ the (English) Channel ▷ nm
(d'outil, casserole) handle; (de pelle,
pioche etc) shaft; **à ~s courtes/
longues** short-/long-sleeved; **~
à balai** broomstick; (Aviat, Inform)
joystick nm inv

manchette [mɑ̃ʃɛt] nf (de chemise)
cuff; (coup) forearm blow; (titre)
headline

manchot [mɑ̃ʃo] nm one-armed
man; armless man; (Zool) penguin

mandarine [mɑ̃daʀin] nf mandarin
(orange), tangerine

mandat [mɑ̃da] nm (postal) postal
ou money order; (d'un député etc)
mandate; (procuration) power of
attorney, proxy; (Police) warrant;
~ d'arrêt warrant for arrest;
~ de perquisition search warrant;
mandataire nm/f (représentant,
délégué) representative; (Jur) proxy

manège [manɛʒ] nm riding school;
(à la foire) roundabout (BRIT), merry-
go-round; (fig) game, ploy

manette [manɛt] nf lever, tap; **~ de
jeu** joystick

mangeable [mɑ̃ʒabl] adj edible,
eatable

mangeoire [mɑ̃ʒwaʀ] nf trough,
manger

manger [mɑ̃ʒe] /3/ vt to eat; (ronger:
rouille etc) to eat into ou away ▷ vi to
eat; **donner à ~** (enfant) to feed

mangue [mɑ̃g] nf mango

maniable [manjabl] adj (outil)
handy; (voiture, voilier) easy to handle

maniaque [manjak] adj finicky,
fussy ▷ nm/f (méticuleux) fusspot;
(fou) maniac

manie [mani] nf mania; (tic) odd
habit; **avoir la ~ de** to be obsessive
about

manier [manje] /7/ vt to handle

maniéré, e [manjeʀe] adj affected

manière [manjɛʀ] nf (façon) way, manner; **manières** nfpl (attitude) manners; (chichis) fuss sg; **de ~ à** so as to; **de cette ~** in this way ou manner; **d'une ~ générale** generally speaking, as a general rule; **de toute ~** in any case; **d'une certaine ~** in a (certain) way

manifestant, e [manifɛstɑ̃, -ɑ̃t] nm/f demonstrator

manifestation [manifɛstasjɔ̃] nf (de joie, mécontentement) expression, demonstration; (symptôme) outward sign; (fête etc) event; (Pol) demonstration

manifeste [manifɛst] adj obvious, evident ▷ nm manifesto; **manifester** /1/ vt (volonté, intentions) to show, indicate; (joie, peur) to express, show ▷ vi to demonstrate; **se manifester** vi (émotion) to show ou express itself; (difficultés) to arise; (symptômes) to appear

manigancer [manigɑ̃se] /3/ vt to plot

manipulation [manipylasjɔ̃] nf handling; (Pol, génétique) manipulation

manipuler [manipyle] /1/ vt to handle; (fig) to manipulate

manivelle [manivɛl] nf crank

mannequin [mankɛ̃] nm (Couture) dummy; (Mode) model

manœuvre [manœvʀ] nf (gén) manoeuvre (BRIT), maneuver (US) ▷ nm labourer; **manœuvrer** /1/ vt to manoeuvre (BRIT), maneuver (US); (levier, machine) to operate ▷ vi to manoeuvre ou maneuver

manoir [manwaʀ] nm manor ou country house

manque [mɑ̃k] nm (insuffisance, vide) emptiness, gap; (Méd) withdrawal; **~ de** lack of; **être en état de ~** to suffer withdrawal symptoms

manqué [mɑ̃ke] adj failed; **garçon ~** tomboy

manquer [mɑ̃ke] /1/ vi (faire défaut) to be lacking; (être absent) to be missing; (échouer) to fail ▷ vt to miss ▷ vb impers: **il (nous) manque encore 10 euros** we are still 10 euros short; **il manque des pages (au livre)** there are some pages missing ou some pages are missing (from the book); **~ à qn** (absent etc): **il/cela me manque** I miss him/that; **~ à** (règles etc) to be in breach of, fail to observe; **~ de** to lack; **ne pas ~ de faire: je ne manquerai pas de lui dire** I'll be sure to tell him; **il a manqué (de) se tuer** he very nearly got killed

mansarde [mɑ̃saʀd] nf attic; **mansardé, e** adj: **chambre mansardée** attic room

manteau, x [mɑ̃to] nm coat

manucure [manykyʀ] nf manicurist

manuel, le [manɥɛl] adj manual ▷ nm (ouvrage) manual, handbook

manufacture [manyfaktyʀ] nf factory; **manufacturé, e** adj manufactured

manuscrit, e [manyskʀi, -it] adj handwritten ▷ nm manuscript

manutention [manytɑ̃sjɔ̃] nf (Comm) handling

mappemonde [mapmɔ̃d] nf (plane) map of the world; (sphère) globe

maquereau, x [makʀo] nm (Zool) mackerel inv; (fam) pimp

maquette [makɛt] nf (d'un décor, bâtiment, véhicule) (scale) model

maquillage [makijaʒ] nm making up; (produits) make-up

maquiller [makije] /1/ vt (personne, visage) to make up; (truquer: passeport, statistique) to fake; (: voiture volée) to do over (respray etc); **se maquiller** vi to make o.s. up

maquis [maki] nm (Géo) scrub; (Mil) maquis, underground fighting no pl

maraîcher, -ère [maʀeʃe, maʀeʃɛʀ] adj: **cultures maraîchères** market gardening sg ▷ nm/f market gardener

marais [maʀɛ] nm marsh, swamp

marasme [maʀasm] nm stagnation, sluggishness

marathon [maratɔ̃] nm marathon

marbre [maʀbʀ] nm marble

marc [maʀ] nm (de raisin, pommes) marc

marchand, e [maʀʃɑ̃, -ɑ̃d] nm/f shopkeeper, tradesman/-woman; (au marché) stallholder; **~ de charbon/vins** coal/wine merchant ▷ adj: **prix/valeur ~(e)** market price/value; **~/e de fruits** fruiterer (BRIT), fruit seller (US); **~/e de journaux** newsagent; **~/e de légumes** greengrocer (BRIT), produce dealer (US); **~/e de poisson** fishmonger (BRIT), fish seller (US); **marchander** /1/ vi to bargain, haggle; **marchandise** nf goods pl, merchandise no pl

marche [maʀʃ] nf (d'escalier) step; (activité) walking; (promenade, trajet, allure) walk; (démarche) walk, gait; (Mil, Mus) march; (fonctionnement) running; (des événements) course; **dans le sens de la ~** (Rail) facing the engine; **en ~** (monter etc) while the vehicle is moving ou in motion; **mettre en ~** to start; **se mettre en ~** (personne) to get moving; (machine) to start; **être en état de ~** to be in working order; **~ arrière** reverse (gear); **faire ~ arrière** to reverse; (fig) to backtrack, back-pedal; **~ à suivre** (correct) procedure

marché [maʀʃe] nm market; (transaction) bargain, deal; **faire du ~ noir** to buy and sell on the black market; **~ aux puces** flea market

marcher [maʀʃe] /1/ vi to walk; (Mil) to march; (aller: voiture, train, affaires) to go; (prospérer) to go well; (fonctionner) to work, run; (fam: consentir) to go along, agree; (: croire naïvement) to be taken in; **faire ~ qn** (pour rire) to pull sb's leg; (pour tromper) to lead sb up the garden path; **marcheur, -euse** nm/f walker

mardi [maʀdi] nm Tuesday; **M~ gras** Shrove Tuesday

mare [maʀ] nf pond; (flaque) pool

marécage [maʀekaʒ] nm marsh, swamp; **marécageux, -euse** adj marshy

maréchal, -aux [maʀeʃal, -o] nm marshal

marée [maʀe] nf tide; (poissons) fresh (sea) fish; **~ haute/basse** high/low tide; **~ noire** oil slick

marelle [maʀɛl] nf: **(jouer à) la ~** (to play) hopscotch

margarine [maʀgaʀin] nf margarine

marge [maʀʒ] nf margin; **en ~ de** (fig) on the fringe of; **~ bénéficiaire** profit margin

marginal, e, -aux [maʀʒinal, -o] nm/f (original) eccentric; (déshérité) dropout

marguerite [maʀgəʀit] nf marguerite, (oxeye) daisy; (d'imprimante) daisy-wheel

mari [maʀi] nm husband

mariage [maʀjaʒ] nm marriage; (noce) wedding; **~ civil/religieux** registry office (BRIT) ou civil/church wedding

marié, e [maʀje] adj married ▷ nm/f (bride)groom/bride; **les ~s** the bride and groom; **les (jeunes) ~s** the newly-weds

marier [maʀje] /7/ vt to marry; (fig) to blend; **se ~ (avec)** to marry, get married (to)

marin, e [maʀɛ̃, -in] adj sea cpd, marine ▷ nm sailor ▷ nf navy; **~e marchande** merchant navy

marine [maʀin] adj f voir **marin** ▷ adj inv navy (blue) ▷ nm (Mil) marine

mariner [maʀine] /1/ vt to marinate

marionnette [maʀjɔnɛt] nf puppet

maritalement [maʀitalmɑ̃] adv: **vivre ~** to live together (as husband and wife)

maritime [maʀitim] adj sea cpd, maritime

mark [maʀk] nm mark

marmelade [maʀməlad] *nf* stewed fruit, compote; **~ d'oranges** (orange) marmalade

marmite [maʀmit] *nf* (cooking-) pot

marmonner [maʀmɔne] /1/ *vt, vi* to mumble, mutter

marmotter [maʀmɔte] /1/ *vt* to mumble

Maroc [maʀɔk] *nm*: **le ~** Morocco; **marocain, e** [maʀɔkɛ̃, -ɛn] *adj* Moroccan ▷ *nm/f*: **Marocain, e** Moroccan

maroquinerie [maʀɔkinʀi] *nf* (commerce) leather shop; (articles) fine leather goods *pl*

marquant, e [maʀkɑ̃, -ɑ̃t] *adj* outstanding

marque [maʀk] *nf* mark; (Comm: de nourriture) brand; (: de voiture, produits manufacturés) make; (: de disques) label; **de ~** high-class; (personnage, hôte) distinguished; **~ déposée** registered trademark; **~ de fabrique** trademark; **une grande ~ de vin** a well-known brand of wine

marquer [maʀke] /1/ *vt* to mark; (inscrire) to write down; (bétail) to brand; (Sport: but etc) to score; (: joueur) to mark; (accentuer: taille etc) to emphasize; (manifester: refus, intérêt) to show ▷ *vi* (événement, personnalité) to stand out, be outstanding; (Sport) to score; **~ les points** to keep the score

marqueterie [maʀkɛtʀi] *nf* inlaid work, marquetry

marquis, e [maʀki, -iz] *nm/f* marquis *ou* marquess (marchioness)

marraine [maʀɛn] *nf* godmother

marrant, e [maʀɑ̃, -ɑ̃t] *adj* (fam) funny

marre [maʀ] *adv* (fam): **en avoir ~ de** to be fed up with

marrer [maʀe] /1/: **se marrer** *vi* (fam) to have a (good) laugh

marron, ne [maʀɔ̃, -ɔn] *nm* (fruit) chestnut ▷ *adj inv* brown ▷ *adj* (péj)

crooked; **~s glacés** marrons glacés; **marronnier** *nm* chestnut (tree)

mars [maʀs] *nm* March

Marseille [maʀsɛj] *n* Marseilles

marteau, x [maʀto] *nm* hammer; **être ~** (fam) to be nuts; **marteau-piqueur** *nm* pneumatic drill

marteler [maʀtəle] /5/ *vt* to hammer

martien, ne [maʀsjɛ̃, -ɛn] *adj* Martian, of *ou* from Mars

martyr, e [maʀtiʀ] *nm/f* martyr ▷ *adj* martyred; **enfants ~s** battered children; **martyre** *nm* martyrdom; (fig: sens affaibli) agony, torture; **martyriser** /1/ *vt* (Rel) to martyr; (fig) to bully (: enfant) to batter

marxiste [maʀksist] *adj, nm/f* Marxist

mascara [maskaʀa] *nm* mascara

masculin, e [maskylɛ̃, -in] *adj* masculine; (sexe, population) male; (équipe, vêtements) men's; (viril) manly ▷ *nm* masculine

masochiste [mazɔfist] *adj* masochistic

masque [mask] *nm* mask; **~ de beauté** face pack; **~ de plongée** diving mask; **masquer** /1/ *vt* (cacher: porte, goût) to hide, conceal; (dissimuler: vérité, projet) to mask, obscure

massacre [masakʀ] *nm* massacre, slaughter; **massacrer** /1/ *vt* to massacre, slaughter; (texte etc) to murder

massage [masaʒ] *nm* massage

masse [mas] *nf* mass; (Élec) earth; (maillet) sledgehammer; **une ~ de** (fam) masses *ou* loads of; **la ~** (péj) the masses *pl*; **en ~** (adv: en bloc) in bulk; (en foule) en masse; *adj*: exécutions, production) mass *cpd*

masser [mase] /1/ *vt* (assembler: gens) to gather; (pétrir) to massage; **se masser** *vi* (foule) to gather; **masseur, -euse** *nm/f* masseur(-euse)

massif, -ive [masif, -iv] *adj* (porte) solid, massive; (visage) heavy, large;

(*bois, or*) solid; (*dose*) massive; (*déportations etc*) mass *cpd* ▷ *nm* (*montagneux*) massif; (*de fleurs*) clump, bank; **le M~ Central** the Massif Central

massue [masy] *nf* club, bludgeon

mastic [mastik] *nm* (*pour vitres*) putty; (*pour fentes*) filler

mastiquer [mastike] /1/ *vt* (*aliment*) to chew, masticate

mat, e [mat] *adj* (*couleur, métal*) mat(t); (*bruit, son*) dull ▷ *adj inv* (*Échecs*): **être ~** to be checkmate

mât [mɑ] *nm* (*Navig*) mast; (*poteau*) pole, post

match [matʃ] *nm* match; **faire ~ nul** to draw ; **~ aller** first leg; **~ retour** second leg, return match

matelas [matla] *nm* mattress; **~ pneumatique** air bed *ou* mattress

matelot [matlo] *nm* sailor, seaman

mater [mate] /1/ *vt* (*personne*) to bring to heel, subdue; (*révolte*) to put down

matérialiser [materjalize] /1/: **se matérialiser** *vi* to materialize

matérialiste [materjalist] *adj* materialistic

matériau, x [materjo] *nm* material; **matériaux** *nmpl* material(s)

matériel, le [materjɛl] *adj* material ▷ *nm* equipment *no pl*; (*de camping etc*) gear *no pl*; (*Inform*) hardware

maternel, le [matɛrnɛl] *adj* (*amour, geste*) motherly, maternal; (*grand-père, oncle*) maternal ▷ *nf* (*aussi*: **école maternelle**) (state) nursery school

maternité [matɛrnite] *nf* (*établissement*) maternity hospital; (*état de mère*) motherhood, maternity; (*grossesse*) pregnancy; **congé de ~** maternity leave

mathématique [matematik] *adj* mathematical; **mathématiques** *nfpl* mathematics *sg*

maths [mat] *nfpl* maths

matière [matjɛr] *nf* matter; (*Comm, Tech*) material; matter *no pl*; (*fig: d'un* *livre etc*) subject matter, material; (*Scol*) subject; **en ~ de** as regards; **~s grasses** fat (content) *sg*; **~s premières** raw materials

Matignon [matiɲɔ̃] *nm*: **(l'hôtel) ~** *the French Prime Minister's residence*

matin [matɛ̃] *nm, adv* morning; **le ~** (*pendant le matin*) in the morning; **demain/hier/dimanche ~** tomorrow/yesterday/Sunday morning; **tous les ~s** every morning; **du ~ au soir** from morning till night; **une heure du ~** one o'clock in the morning; **de grand** *ou* **bon ~** early in the morning; **matinal, e, -aux** [matinal, -o] *adj* (*toilette, gymnastique*) morning *cpd*; **être matinal** (*personne*) to be up early; (*habituellement*) to be an early riser; **matinée** *nf* morning; (*spectacle*) matinée

matou [matu] *nm* tom(cat)

matraque [matrak] *nf* (*de policier*) truncheon (BRIT), billy (US)

matricule [matrikyl] *nm* (*Mil*) regimental number; (*Admin*) reference number

matrimonial, e, -aux [matrimɔnjal, -o] *adj* marital, marriage *cpd*

maudit, e [modi, -it] *adj* (*fam: satané*) blasted, confounded

maugréer [mogree] /1/ *vi* to grumble

maussade [mosad] *adj* sullen; (*ciel, temps*) gloomy

mauvais, e [mɔvɛ, -ɛz] *adj* bad; (*méchant, malveillant*) malicious, spiteful; (*faux*): **le ~ numéro** the wrong number ▷ *adv*: **il fait ~** the weather is bad; **sentir ~** to have a nasty smell, smell bad *ou* nasty; **la mer est ~e** the sea is rough; **~e plaisanterie** nasty trick; **~ joueur** bad loser; **~e herbe** weed; **~e langue** gossip, scandalmonger (BRIT)

mauve [mov] *adj* mauve

maux [mo] *nmpl voir* **mal**

m

maximum [maksimɔm] *adj, nm*
maximum; **au ~** (*le plus possible*) as
much as one can; (*tout au plus*) at the
(very) most *ou* maximum; **faire le ~**
to do one's level best

mayonnaise [majɔnɛz] *nf*
mayonnaise

mazout [mazut] *nm* (fuel) oil

me, m' [mə, m] *pron* (*direct: téléphoner,
attendre etc*) me; (*indirect: parler, donner
etc*) (to) me; (*réfléchi*) myself

mec [mɛk] *nm* (*fam*) guy, bloke (BRIT)

mécanicien, ne [mekanisjɛ̃,
-ɛn] *nm/f* mechanic; (*Rail*) (train *ou*
engine) driver

mécanique [mekanik] *adj*
mechanical ▷ *nf* (*science*) mechanics
sg; (*mécanisme*) mechanism; **ennui ~**
engine trouble *no pl*

mécanisme [mekanism] *nm*
mechanism

méchamment [meʃamɑ̃] *adv*
nastily, maliciously; spitefully

méchanceté [meʃɑste] *nf* nastiness,
maliciousness; **dire des ~s à qn** to
say spiteful things to sb

méchant, e [meʃɑ̃, -ɑ̃t] *adj* nasty,
malicious, spiteful; (*enfant: pas sage*)
naughty; (*animal*) vicious

mèche [mɛʃ] *nf* (*de lampe, bougie*)
wick; (*d'un explosif*) fuse; (*de cheveux*)
lock; **se faire faire des ~s** to have
highlights put in one's hair; **de ~ avec**
in league with

méchoui [meʃwi] *nm whole sheep
barbecue*

méconnaissable [mekɔnɛsabl] *adj*
unrecognizable

méconnaître [mekɔnɛtR] /57/
vt (*ignorer*) to be unaware of;
(*mésestimer*) to misjudge

mécontent, e [mekɔtɑ̃, -ɑ̃t]
adj: **~ (de)** discontented *ou*
dissatisfied *ou* displeased
(with); (*contrarié*) annoyed
(at); **mécontentement** *nm*
dissatisfaction, discontent,
displeasure; (*irritation*) annoyance

Mecque [mɛk] *nf*: **la ~** Mecca

médaille [medaj] *nf* medal

médaillon [medajɔ̃] *nm* (*bijou*) locket

médecin [medsɛ̃] *nm* doctor

médecine [medsin] *nf* medicine

média [medja] *nmpl*: **les ~** the
media; **médiatique** *adj* media *cpd*

médical, e, -aux [medikal, -o] *adj*
medical; **passer une visite ~e** to
have a medical

médicament [medikamɑ̃] *nm*
medicine, drug

médiéval, e, -aux [medjeval, -o]
adj medieval

médiocre [medjɔkR] *adj* mediocre,
poor

méditer [medite] /1/ *vi* to meditate

Méditerranée [mediteRane]
nf: **la (mer) ~** the Mediterranean
(Sea); **méditerranéen, ne**
adj Mediterranean ▷ *nm/f*:
Méditerranéen, ne Mediterranean

méduse [medyz] *nf* jellyfish

méfait [mefɛ] *nm* (*faute*)
misdemeanour, wrongdoing;
méfaits *nmpl* (*ravages*) ravages,
damage *sg*

méfiance [mefjɑs] *nf* mistrust,
distrust

méfiant, e [mefjɑ̃, -ɑ̃t] *adj*
mistrustful, distrustful

méfier [mefje] /7/: **se méfier** *vi* to be
wary; (*faire attention*) to be careful; **se
~ de** to mistrust, distrust, be wary of

méga-octet [megaɔktɛ] *nm*
megabyte

mégarde [megaRd] *nf*: **par ~**
(*accidentellement*) accidentally; (*par
erreur*) by mistake

mégère [meʒɛR] *nf* shrew

mégot [mego] *nm* cigarette end
ou butt

meilleur, e [mɛjœR] *adj, adv* better
▷ *nm*: **le ~** the best; **le ~ des deux** the
better of the two; **il fait ~ qu'hier**
it's better weather than yesterday;
~ marché cheaper

mél [mɛl] *nm* email

mélancolie [melãkɔli] nf melancholy, gloom; **mélancolique** adj melancholy

mélange [melãʒ] nm mixture; **mélanger** /3/ vt to mix; (vins, couleurs) to blend; (mettre en désordre, confondre) to muddle (up)

mêlée [mele] nf mêlée, scramble; (Rugby) scrum(mage)

mêler [mele] /1/ vt (substances, odeurs, races) to mix; (embrouiller) to muddle (up), mix up; **se mêler** vi to mix; **se ~ à** (personne) to join; (s'associer à) to mix with; **se ~ de** (personne) to meddle with, interfere in; **mêle-toi de tes affaires!** mind your own business!

mélodie [melɔdi] nf melody; **mélodieux, -euse** adj melodious

melon [məlɔ̃] nm (Bot) (honeydew) melon; (aussi: **chapeau ~**) bowler (hat)

membre [mãbʀ] nm (Anat) limb; (personne, pays, élément) member ▷ adj member cpd

mémé [meme] nf (fam) granny

MOT-CLÉ

même [mɛm] adj **1** (avant le nom) same; **en même temps** at the same time; **ils ont les mêmes goûts** they have the same ou similar tastes
2 (après le nom, renforcement): **il est la loyauté même** he is loyalty itself; **ce sont ses paroles/celles-là même** they are his very words/the very ones
▶ pron: **le (la) même** the same one
▶ adv **1** (renforcement): **il n'a même pas pleuré** he didn't even cry; **même lui l'a dit** even HE said it; **ici même** at this very place; **même si** even if
2: **à même: à même la bouteille** straight from the bottle; **à même la peau** next to the skin; **être à même de faire** to be in a position to do, be able to do
3: **de même** likewise; **faire de même** to do likewise ou the same; **lui de**

même so does (ou did ou is) he; **de même que** just as; **il en va de même pour** the same goes for

mémoire [memwaʀ] nf memory ▷ nm (Scol) dissertation, paper; **à la ~ de** to the ou in memory of; **de ~** from memory; **~ morte** read-only memory, ROM; **~ vive** random access memory, RAM

mémoires [memwaʀ] nmpl memoirs

mémorable [memɔʀabl] adj memorable

menace [mənas] nf threat; **menacer** /3/ vt to threaten

ménage [menaʒ] nm (travail) housework; (couple) (married) couple; (famille, Admin) household; **faire le ~** to do the housework; **ménagement** nm care and attention

ménager¹ [menaʒe] vt (traiter avec mesure) to handle with tact; (utiliser) to use sparingly; (prendre soin de) to take (great) care of, look after; (organiser) to arrange

ménager², -ère [menaʒe, -ɛʀ] adj household cpd, domestic ▷ nf housewife

mendiant, e [mãdjã, -ãt] nm/f beggar

mendier [mãdje] /7/ vi to beg ▷ vt to beg (for)

mener [məne] /5/ vt to lead; (enquête) to conduct; (affaires) to manage ▷ vi: **~ à/dans** (emmener) to take to/into; **~ qch à bonne fin** ou **à terme** ou **à bien** to see sth through (to a successful conclusion), complete sth successfully

meneur, -euse [mənœʀ, -øz] nm/f leader; (péj) ringleader

méningite [menẽʒit] nf meningitis no pl

ménopause [menopoz] nf menopause

menotte [mənɔt] nf (langage enfantin) handie; **menottes** nfpl handcuffs

m

mensonge [mɑ̃sɔ̃ʒ] nm: **le ~** lying no pl; **un ~** a lie; **mensonger, -ère** adj false

mensualité [mɑ̃sɥalite] nf (somme payée) monthly payment

mensuel, le [mɑ̃sɥɛl] adj monthly

mensurations [mɑ̃syRasjɔ̃] nfpl measurements

mental, e, -aux [mɑ̃tal, -o] adj mental; **mentalité** nf mentality

menteur, -euse [mɑ̃tœR, -øz] nm/f liar

menthe [mɑ̃t] nf mint

mention [mɑ̃sjɔ̃] nf (note) note, comment; (Scol): **~ (très) bien/passable** (very) good/satisfactory pass; **"rayer la ~ inutile"** "delete as appropriate"; **mentionner** /1/ vt to mention

mentir [mɑ̃tiR] /16/ vi to lie

menton [mɑ̃tɔ̃] nm chin

menu, e [məny] adj (mince) slim, slight; (frais, difficulté) minor ▷ adv (couper, hacher) very fine ▷ nm menu; **~ touristique** popular ou tourist menu

menuiserie [mənɥizRi] nf (travail) joinery, carpentry; (d'amateur) woodwork; **menuisier** nm joiner, carpenter

méprendre [mepRɑ̃dR] /58/: **se méprendre** vi: **se ~ sur** to be mistaken about

mépris, e [mepRi, -iz] pp de **méprendre** ▷ nm (dédain) contempt, scorn; **au ~ de** regardless of, in defiance of; **méprisable** adj contemptible, despicable; **méprisant, e** adj scornful; **méprise** nf mistake, error; **mépriser** /1/ vt to scorn, despise; (gloire, danger) to scorn, spurn

mer [mɛR] nf sea; (marée) tide; **en ~** at sea; **en haute** ou **pleine ~** off shore, on the open sea; **la ~ Morte** the Dead Sea; **la ~ Noire** the Black Sea; **la ~ du Nord** the North Sea; **la ~ Rouge** the Red Sea

mercenaire [mɛRsənɛR] nm mercenary, hired soldier

mercerie [mɛRsəRi] nf (boutique) haberdasher's (shop) (BRIT), notions store (US)

merci [mɛRsi] excl thank you ▷ nf: **à la ~ de qn/qch** at sb's mercy/the mercy of sth; **~ beaucoup** thank you very much; **~ de** ou **pour** thank you for; **sans ~** merciless; mercilessly

mercredi [mɛRkRədi] nm Wednesday; **~ des Cendres** Ash Wednesday; voir aussi **lundi**

mercure [mɛRkyR] nm mercury

merde [mɛRd] (!) nf shit (!) ▷ excl (bloody) hell (!)

mère [mɛR] nf mother ▷ adj inv mother cpd; **~ célibataire** single parent, unmarried mother; **~ de famille** housewife, mother

merguez [mɛRgɛz] nf spicy North African sausage

méridional, e, -aux [meRidjɔnal, -o] adj southern ▷ nm/f Southerner

meringue [məRɛ̃g] nf meringue

mérite [meRit] nm merit; **avoir du ~ (à faire qch)** to deserve credit (for doing sth); **mériter** /1/ vt to deserve

merle [mɛRl] nm blackbird

merveille [mɛRvɛj] nf marvel, wonder; **faire ~** ou **des ~s** to work wonders; **à ~** perfectly, wonderfully; **merveilleux, -euse** adj marvellous, wonderful

mes [me] adj poss voir **mon**

mésange [mezɑ̃ʒ] nf tit (mouse)

mésaventure [mezavɑ̃tyR] nf misadventure, misfortune

Mesdames [medam] nfpl voir **Madame**

Mesdemoiselles [medmwazɛl] nfpl voir **Mademoiselle**

mesquin, e [mɛskɛ̃, -in] adj mean, petty; **mesquinerie** nf meanness no pl; (procédé) mean trick

message [mesaʒ] nm message; **~ SMS** text message; **messager, -ère** nm/f messenger; **messagerie** nf

(*Internet*): **messagerie électronique** email; **messagerie instantanée** instant messenger; **messagerie vocale** voice mail

messe [mɛs] *nf* mass; **aller à la ~** to go to mass

Messieurs [mesjø] *nmpl voir* **Monsieur**

mesure [məzyʀ] *nf* (*évaluation, dimension*) measurement; (*étalon, récipient, contenu*) measure; (*Mus: cadence*) time, tempo; (: *division*) bar; (*retenue*) moderation; (*disposition*) measure, step; **sur ~** (*costume*) made-to-measure; **dans la ~ où** insofar as, inasmuch as; **dans une certaine ~** to some *ou* a certain extent; **à ~ que** as; **être en ~ de** to be in a position to

mesurer [məzyʀe] /1/ *vt* to measure; (*juger*) to weigh up, assess; (*modérer: ses paroles etc*) to moderate

métal, -aux [metal, -o] *nm* metal; **métallique** *adj* metallic

météo [meteo] *nf* (*bulletin*) (weather) forecast

météorologie [meteɔʀɔlɔʒi] *nf* meteorology

méthode [metɔd] *nf* method; (*livre, ouvrage*) manual, tutor

méticuleux, -euse [metikylø, -øz] *adj* meticulous

métier [metje] *nm* (*profession: gén*) job; (: *manuel*) trade; (: *artisanal*) craft; (*technique, expérience*) (acquired) skill *ou* technique; (*aussi: ~ à tisser*) (weaving) loom

métrage [metʀaʒ] *nm*: **long/moyen/court ~** feature *ou* full-length/medium-length/short film

mètre [mɛtʀ] *nm* metre; (*règle*) metre rule; (*ruban*) tape measure; **métrique** *adj* metric

métro [metʀo] *nm* underground (BRIT), subway (US)

métropole [metʀɔpɔl] *nf* (*capitale*) metropolis; (*pays*) home country

mets [mɛ] *nm* dish

metteur [metœʀ] *nm*: **~ en scène** (*Théât*) producer; (*Ciné*) director

MOT-CLÉ

mettre [mɛtʀ] /56/ *vt* **1** (*placer*) to put; **mettre en bouteille/en sac** to bottle/put in bags *ou* sacks

2 (*vêtements: revêtir*) to put on; (: *porter*) to wear; **mets ton gilet** put your cardigan on; **je ne mets plus mon manteau** I no longer wear my coat

3 (*faire fonctionner: chauffage, électricité*) to put on; (: *réveil, minuteur*) to set; (*installer: gaz, eau*) to put in, lay on; **mettre en marche** to start up

4 (*consacrer*): **mettre du temps/deux heures à faire qch** to take time/two hours to do sth; **y mettre du sien** to pull one's weight

5 (*noter, écrire*) to say, put (down); **qu'est-ce qu'il a mis sur la carte?** what did he say *ou* write on the card?; **mettez au pluriel ...** put ... into the plural

6 (*supposer*): **mettons que ...** let's suppose *ou* say that ...

se mettre *vr* **1** (*se placer*): **vous pouvez vous mettre là** you can sit (*ou* stand) there; **où ça se met?** where does it go?; **se mettre au lit** to get into bed; **se mettre au piano** to sit down at the piano; **se mettre de l'encre sur les doigts** to get ink on one's fingers

2 (*s'habiller*): **se mettre en maillot de bain** to get into *ou* put on a swimsuit; **n'avoir rien à se mettre** to have nothing to wear

3: **se mettre à** to begin, start; **se mettre à faire** to begin *ou* start doing *ou* to do; **se mettre au piano** to start learning the piano; **se mettre au régime** to go on a diet; **se mettre au travail/à l'étude** to get down to work/one's studies

m

meuble [mœbl] *nm* piece of furniture; (*ameublement*) furniture *no pl*; **meublé** *nm* furnished flat (BRIT) *ou* apartment (US); **meubler** /1/ *vt* to furnish; **se meubler** to furnish one's house

meuf [mœf] *nf* (*fam*) woman

meugler [møgle] /1/ *vi* to low, moo

meule [møl] *nf* (*à broyer*) millstone; (*de foin, blé*) stack; (*de fromage*) round

meunier, -ière [mønje, -jɛR] *nm* miller ▷ *nf* miller's wife

meurs *etc* [mœR] *vb voir* **mourir**

meurtre [mœRtR] *nm* murder; **meurtrier, -ière** *adj* (*arme, épidémie, combat*) deadly; (*fureur, instincts*) murderous ▷ *nm/f* murderer(-ess)

meurtrir [mœRtRiR] /2/ *vt* to bruise; (*fig*) to wound

meus *etc* [mœ] *vb voir* **mouvoir**

meute [møt] *nf* pack

mexicain, e [mɛksikɛ̃, -ɛn] *adj* Mexican ▷ *nm/f*: **M~, e** Mexican

Mexico [mɛksiko] *n* Mexico City

Mexique [mɛksik] *nm*: **le ~** Mexico

mi [mi] *nm* (*Mus*) E; (*en chantant la gamme*) mi

mi... [mi] *préfixe* half(-), mid-; **à la mi-janvier** in mid-January; **à mi-jambes/-corps** (up *ou* down) to the knees/waist; **à mi-hauteur/-pente** halfway up (*ou* down)/up (*ou* down) the hill

miauler [mjole] /1/ *vi* to miaow

miche [miʃ] *nf* round *ou* cob loaf

mi-chemin [miʃmɛ̃]: **à ~** *adv* halfway, midway

mi-clos, e [miklo, -kloz] *adj* half-closed

micro [mikRo] *nm* mike, microphone; (*Inform*) micro

microbe [mikRɔb] *nm* germ, microbe

micro: micro-onde *nf*: **four à micro-ondes** microwave oven; **micro-ordinateur** *nm* microcomputer; **microscope** *nm* microscope; **microscopique** *adj* microscopic

midi [midi] *nm* midday, noon; (*moment du déjeuner*) lunchtime; (*sud*) south; **le M~** the South (of France), the Midi; **à ~** at 12 (o'clock) *ou* midday *ou* noon

mie [mi] *nf* inside (of the loaf)

miel [mjɛl] *nm* honey; **mielleux, -euse** *adj* (*personne*) sugary, syrupy

mien, ne [mjɛ̃, mjɛn] *pron*: **le (la) ~(ne), les ~s** mine; **les ~s** my family

miette [mjɛt] *nf* (*de pain, gâteau*) crumb; (*fig: de la conversation etc*) scrap; **en ~s** in pieces *ou* bits

 MOT-CLÉ

mieux [mjø] *adv* **1** (*d'une meilleure façon*): **mieux (que)** better (than); **elle travaille/mange mieux** she works/eats better; **aimer mieux** to prefer; **elle va mieux** she is better; **de mieux en mieux** better and better
2 (*de la meilleure façon*) best; **ce que je sais le mieux** what I know best; **les livres les mieux faits** the best made books
▶ *adj inv* **1** (*plus à l'aise, en meilleure forme*) better; **se sentir mieux** to feel better
2 (*plus satisfaisant*) better; **c'est mieux ainsi** it's better like this; **c'est le mieux des deux** it's the better of the two; **le/la mieux, les mieux** the best; **demandez-lui, c'est le mieux** ask him, it's the best thing
3 (*plus joli*) better-looking; **il est mieux que son frère** (*plus beau*) he's better-looking than his brother; (*plus gentil*) he's nicer than his brother; **il est mieux sans moustache** he looks better without a moustache
4: **au mieux** at best; **au mieux avec** on the best of terms with; **pour le mieux** for the best
▶ *nm* **1** (*progrès*) improvement
2: **de mon/ton mieux** as best I/you can (*ou* could); **faire de son mieux** to do one's best

mignon, ne [miɲɔ̃, -ɔn] adj sweet, cute

migraine [migʀɛn] nf headache; (Méd) migraine

mijoter [miʒɔte] /1/ vt to simmer; (préparer avec soin) to cook lovingly; (affaire, projet) to plot, cook up ▷ vi to simmer

milieu, x [miljø] nm (centre) middle; (aussi: **juste ~**) happy medium; (Bio, Géo) environment; (entourage social) milieu; (familial) background; (pègre): **le ~** the underworld; **au ~ de** in the middle of; **au beau ou en plein ~ (de)** right in the middle (of)

militaire [militɛʀ] adj military, army cpd ▷ nm serviceman

militant, e [militɑ̃, -ɑ̃t] adj, nm/f militant

militer [milite] /1/ vi to be a militant

mille [mil] num a ou one thousand ▷ nm (mesure): **~ (marin)** nautical mile; **mettre dans le ~ (fig)** to be bang on (target); **millefeuille** nm cream ou vanilla slice; **millénaire** nm millennium ▷ adj thousand-year-old; (fig) ancient; **mille-pattes** nm inv centipede

millet [mijɛ] nm millet

milliard [miljaʀ] nm milliard, thousand million (BRIT), billion (US); **milliardaire** nm/f multimillionaire (BRIT), billionaire (US)

millier [milje] nm thousand; **un ~ (de)** a thousand or so, about a thousand; **par ~s** in (their) thousands, by the thousand

milligramme [miligʀam] nm milligramme

millimètre [milimɛtʀ] nm millimetre

million [miljɔ̃] nm million; **deux ~s de** two million; **millionnaire** nm/f millionaire

mime [mim] nm/f (acteur) mime(r) ▷ nm (art) mime, miming; **mimer** /1/ vt to mime; (singer) to mimic, take off

minable [minabl] adj (personne) shabby(-looking); (travail) pathetic

mince [mɛ̃s] adj thin; (personne, taille) slim, slender; (fig: profit, connaissances) slight, small; (: prétexte) weak ▷ excl: **~ (alors)!** darn it!; **minceur** nf thinness; (d'une personne) slimness, slenderness; **mincir** /2/ vi to get slimmer ou thinner

mine [min] nf (physionomie) expression, look; (extérieur) exterior, appearance; (de crayon) lead; (gisement, exploitation, explosif) mine; **avoir bonne ~** (personne) to look well; (ironique) to look an utter idiot; **avoir mauvaise ~** to look unwell; **faire ~ de faire** to make a pretence of doing; **~ de rien** although you wouldn't think so

miner [mine] /1/ vt (saper) to undermine, erode; (Mil) to mine

minerai [minʀɛ] nm ore

minéral, e, -aux [mineʀal, -o] adj mineral

minéralogique [mineʀalɔʒik] adj: **plaque ~** number (BRIT) ou license (US) plate; **numéro ~** registration (BRIT) ou license (US) number

minet, te [minɛ, -ɛt] nm/f (chat) pussy-cat; (péj) young trendy

mineur, e [minœʀ] adj minor ▷ nm/f (Jur) minor ▷ nm (travailleur) miner

miniature [minjatyʀ] adj, nf miniature

minibus [minibys] nm minibus

minier, -ière [minje, -jɛʀ] adj mining

mini-jupe [miniʒyp] nf mini-skirt

minime [minim] adj minor, minimal

minimiser [minimize] /1/ vt to minimize; (fig) to play down

minimum [minimɔm] adj, nm minimum; **au ~** at the very least

ministère [ministɛʀ] nm (cabinet) government; (département) ministry; (Rel) ministry

ministre [ministʀ] nm minister (BRIT), secretary; (Rel) minister; **~ d'État** senior minister ou secretary

m

Minitel® [minitɛl] *nm* (*former*) videotext terminal and service

minoritaire [minɔritɛr] *adj* minority *cpd*

minorité [minɔrite] *nf* minority; **être en ~** to be in the *ou* a minority

minuit [minɥi] *nm* midnight

minuscule [minyskyl] *adj* minute, tiny ▷ *nf*: **(lettre) ~** small letter

minute [minyt] *nf* minute; **à la ~** (*just*) this instant; (*passé*) there and then; **minuter** /1/ *vt* to time; **minuterie** *nf* time switch

minutieux, -euse [minysjø, -øz] *adj* (*personne*) meticulous; (*travail*) requiring painstaking attention to detail

mirabelle [mirabɛl] *nf* (cherry) plum

miracle [mirakl] *nm* miracle

mirage [miraʒ] *nm* mirage

mire [mir] *nf*: **point de ~** (*fig*) focal point

miroir [mirwar] *nm* mirror

miroiter [mirwate] /1/ *vi* to sparkle, shimmer; **faire ~ qch à qn** to paint sth in glowing colours for sb, dangle sth in front of sb's eyes

mis, e [mi, miz] *pp de* **mettre** ▷ *adj*: **bien ~** well dressed ▷ *nf* (*argent: au jeu*) stake; (*tenue*) clothing; attire; **être de ~e** to be acceptable *ou* in season; **~e de fonds** capital outlay; **~e à jour** update; **~e en plis** set; **~e au point** (*fig*) clarification; **~e en scène** production

miser [mize] /1/ *vt* (*enjeu*) to stake, bet; **~ sur** (*cheval, numéro*) to bet on; (*fig*) to bank *ou* count on

misérable [mizerabl] *adj* (*lamentable, malheureux*) pitiful, wretched; (*pauvre*) poverty-stricken; (*insignifiant, mesquin*) miserable ▷ *nm/f* wretch

misère [mizɛr] *nf* (extreme) poverty, destitution; **misères** *nfpl* (*malheurs*) woes, miseries; (*ennuis*) little troubles; **salaire de ~** starvation wage

missile [misil] *nm* missile

mission [misjɔ̃] *nf* mission; **partir en ~** (*Admin, Pol*) to go on an assignment; **missionnaire** *nm/f* missionary

mité, e [mite] *adj* moth-eaten

mi-temps [mitɑ̃] *nf inv* (*Sport: période*) half; (*: pause*) half-time; **à ~** part-time

miteux, -euse [mitø, -øz] *adj* seedy

mitigé, e [mitiʒe] *adj* (*sentiments*) mixed

mitoyen, ne [mitwajɛ̃, -ɛn] *adj* (*mur*) common, party *cpd*; **maisons ~nes** semi-detached houses; (*plus de deux*) terraced (BRIT) *ou* row (US) houses

mitrailler [mitraje] /1/ *vt* to machine-gun; (*fig: photographier*) to snap away at; **~ qn de** to pelt *ou* bombard sb with; **mitraillette** *nf* submachine gun; **mitrailleuse** *nf* machine gun

mi-voix [mivwa]: **à ~** *adv* in a low *ou* hushed voice

mixage [miksaʒ] *nm* (*Ciné*) (sound) mixing

mixer [miksœr] *nm* (food) mixer

mixte [mikst] *adj* (*gén*) mixed; (*Scol*) mixed, coeducational; **cuisinière ~** combined gas and electric cooker

mixture [mikstyr] *nf* mixture; (*fig*) concoction

Mlle (*pl* **Mlles**) *abr* = **Mademoiselle**

MM *abr* = **Messieurs**

Mme (*pl* **Mmes**) *abr* = **Madame**

mobile [mɔbil] *adj* mobile; (*pièce de machine*) moving ▷ *nm* (*motif*) motive; (*œuvre d'art*) mobile; **(téléphone) ~** mobile (phone)

mobilier, -ière [mɔbilje, -jɛr] *nm* furniture

mobiliser [mɔbilize] /1/ *vt* to mobilize

mobylette® [mɔbilɛt] *nf* moped

mocassin [mɔkasɛ̃] *nm* moccasin

moche [mɔʃ] *adj* (*fam: laid*) ugly; (*mauvais, méprisable*) rotten

modalité [mɔdalite] *nf* form, mode

mode [mɔd] *nf* fashion ▷ *nm* (*manière*) form, mode; (*Ling*) mood; (*Inform,*

Mus) mode; **à la ~** fashionable, in
fashion; **~ d'emploi** directions pl
(for use); **~ de paiement** method of
payment; **~ de vie** way of life
modèle [mɔdɛl] *adj* ▷ *nm* model;
(*qui pose: de peintre*) sitter; **~ déposé**
registered design; **~ réduit** small-
scale model; **modeler** /5/ *vt* to model
modem [mɔdɛm] *nm* modem
modéré, e [mɔdeʀe] *adj*, *nm/f*
moderate
modérer [mɔdeʀe] /6/ *vt* to
moderate; **se modérer** *vi* to restrain
o.s
moderne [mɔdɛʀn] *adj*
modern ▷ *nm* (*Art*) modern style;
(*ameublement*) modern furniture;
moderniser /1/ *vt* to modernize
modeste [mɔdɛst] *adj* modest;
modestie *nf* modesty
modifier [mɔdifje] /7/ *vt* to modify,
alter; **se modifier** *vi* to alter
modique [mɔdik] *adj* modest
module [mɔdyl] *nm* module
moelle [mwal] *nf* marrow
moelleux, -euse [mwalø, -øz] *adj*
soft; (*gâteau*) light and moist
mœurs [mœʀ] *nfpl* (*conduite*) morals;
(*manières*) manners; (*pratiques
sociales*) habits
moi [mwa] *pron* me; (*emphatique*):
~, je ... for my part, I ..., I myself ...;
c'est ~ qui l'ai fait I did it, it was me
who did it; **apporte-le-~** bring it to
me; **à ~** mine; (*dans un jeu*) my turn;
moi-même *pron* myself; (*emphatique*)
I myself
moindre [mwɛ̃dʀ] *adj* lesser;
lower; **le (la) ~, les ~s** the least; the
slightest; **c'est la ~ des choses** it's
nothing at all
moine [mwan] *nm* monk, friar
moineau, x [mwano] *nm* sparrow

 MOT-CLÉ

moins [mwɛ̃] *adv* **1** (*comparatif*):
moins (que) less (than); **moins**

grand que less tall than, not as tall
as; **il a trois ans de moins que
moi** he's three years younger than
me; **moins je travaille, mieux
je me porte** the less I work, the
better I feel
2 (*superlatif*): **le moins** (the) least;
c'est ce que j'aime le moins it's
what I like (the) least; **le (la) moins
doué(e)** the least gifted; **au moins,
du moins** at least; **pour le moins** at
the very least
3: **moins de** (*quantité*) less (than);
(*nombre*) fewer (than); **moins de
sable/d'eau** less sand/water;
moins de livres/gens fewer books/
people; **moins de deux ans** less
than two years; **moins de midi** not
yet midday
4: **de moins, en moins**: 100 euros/
3 jours de moins 100 euros/3 days
less; **trois livres en moins** three
books fewer; three books too few;
de l'argent en moins less money;
le soleil en moins but for the sun,
minus the sun; **de moins en moins**
less and less
5: **à moins de, à moins que** unless;
à moins de faire unless we do (*ou*
he does *etc*); **à moins que tu ne
fasses** unless you do; **à moins d'un
accident** barring any accident
▶ *prép*: **quatre moins deux** four
minus two; **dix heures moins cinq**
five to ten; **il fait moins cinq** it's five
(degrees) below (freezing), it's minus
five; **il est moins cinq** it's five to

mois [mwa] *nm* month
moisi [mwazi] *nm* mould, mildew;
odeur de ~ musty smell; **moisir**
/2/ *vi* to go mouldy; **moisissure** *nf*
mould *no pl*
moisson [mwasɔ̃] *nf* harvest;
moissonner /1/ *vt* to harvest,
reap; **moissonneuse** *nf* (*machine*)
harvester
moite [mwat] *adj* sweaty, sticky

moitié [mwatje] *nf* half; **la ~** half; **la ~ de** half (of); **la ~ du temps/des gens** half the time/the people; **à la ~ de** halfway through; **à ~** half (*avant le verbe*), half- (*avant l'adjectif*); **à ~ prix** (at) half price

molaire [mɔlɛʀ] *nf* molar

molester [mɔlɛste] /1/ *vt* to manhandle, maul (about)

molle [mɔl] *adj f voir* **mou**; **mollement** *adv* (*péj: travailler*) sluggishly; (*protester*) feebly

mollet [mɔlɛ] *nm* calf ▷ *adj m*: **œuf ~** soft-boiled egg

molletonné, e [mɔltɔne] *adj* fleece-lined

mollir [mɔliʀ] /2/ *vi* (*personne*) to relent; (*substance*) to go soft

mollusque [mɔlysk] *nm* mollusc

môme [mom] *nm/f* (*fam: enfant*) brat

moment [mɔmɑ̃] *nm* moment; **ce n'est pas le ~** this is not the right time; **au même ~** at the same time; (*instant*) at the same moment; **pour un bon ~** for a good while; **pour le ~** for the moment, for the time being; **au ~ de** at the time of; **au ~ où** as; **à tout ~** at any time *ou* moment; (*continuellement*) constantly, continually; **en ce ~** at the moment; (*aujourd'hui*) at present; **sur le ~** at the time; **par ~s** now and then, at times; **d'un ~ à l'autre** any time (now); **du ~ où** *ou* **que** seeing that, since; **momentané, e** *adj* temporary, momentary; **momentanément** *adv* for a while

momie [mɔmi] *nf* mummy

mon, ma (*pl* **mes**) [mɔ̃, ma, me] *adj poss* my

Monaco [mɔnako] *nm*: **le ~** Monaco

monarchie [mɔnaʀʃi] *nf* monarchy

monastère [mɔnastɛʀ] *nm* monastery

mondain, e [mɔ̃dɛ̃, -ɛn] *adj* (*soirée, vie*) society *cpd*

monde [mɔ̃d] *nm* world; **le ~** (*personnes mondaines*) (high) society; **il y a du ~** (*beaucoup de gens*) there are a lot of people; (*quelques personnes*) there are some people; **beaucoup/peu de ~** many/few people; **mettre au ~** to bring into the world; **pas le moins du ~** not in the least; **mondial, e, -aux** *adj* (*population*) world *cpd*; (*influence*) world-wide; **mondialement** *adv* throughout the world; **mondialisation** *nf* globalization

monégasque [mɔnegask] *adj* Monegasque, of *ou* from Monaco ▷ *nm/f*: **M~** Monegasque

monétaire [mɔnetɛʀ] *adj* monetary

moniteur, -trice [mɔnitœʀ, -tʀis] *nm/f* (*Sport*) instructor (instructress); (*de colonie de vacances*) supervisor ▷ *nm* (*écran*) monitor

monnaie [mɔnɛ] *nf* (*Écon: moyen d'échange*) currency; (*petites pièces*): **avoir de la ~** to have (some) change; **faire de la ~** to get (some) change; **avoir/faire la ~ de 20 euros** to have change of/get change for 20 euros; **rendre à qn la ~ (sur 20 euros)** to give sb the change (from *ou* out of 20 euros)

monologue [mɔnɔlɔg] *nm* monologue, soliloquy; **monologuer** /1/ *vi* to soliloquize

monopole [mɔnɔpɔl] *nm* monopoly

monotone [mɔnɔtɔn] *adj* monotonous

Monsieur (*pl* **Messieurs**) [məsjø, mesjø] *nm* (*titre*) Mr; **un/le monsieur** (*homme quelconque*) a/the gentleman; **~, ...** (*en tête de lettre*) Dear Sir, ...; *voir aussi* **Madame**

monstre [mɔ̃stʀ] *nm* monster ▷ *adj* (*fam: effet, publicité*) massive; **un travail ~** a fantastic amount of work; **monstrueux, -euse** *adj* monstrous

mont [mɔ̃] *nm*: **par ~s et par vaux** up hill and down dale; **le M~ Blanc** Mont Blanc

montage [mɔ̃taʒ] *nm* (*d'une machine etc*) assembly; (*Photo*) photomontage; (*Ciné*) editing

montagnard, e [mɔ̃taɲaʀ, -aʀd]
adj mountain *cpd* ▷ *nm/f* mountain-
dweller

montagne [mɔ̃taɲ] *nf* (*cime*)
mountain; (*région*): **la ~** the
mountains *pl*; **~s russes** big dipper
sg, switchback *sg*; **montagneux,**
-euse *adj* mountainous; (*basse*
montagne) hilly

montant, e [mɔ̃tɑ̃, -ɑ̃t] *adj* rising;
(*robe, corsage*) high-necked ▷ *nm*
(*somme, total*) (sum) total, (total)
amount; (*de fenêtre*) upright; (*de*
lit) post

monte-charge [mɔ̃tʃaʀʒ] *nm inv*
goods lift, hoist

montée [mɔ̃te] *nf* rise; (*escalade*)
climb; (*côte*) hill; **au milieu de la ~**
halfway up

monter [mɔ̃te] /1/ *vt* (*escalier, côte*)
to go (*ou* come) up; (*valise, paquet*)
to take (*ou* bring) up; (*étagère*) to
raise; (*tente, échafaudage*) to put up;
(*machine*) to assemble; (*Ciné*) to edit;
(*Théât*) to put on, stage; (*société, coup*
etc) to set up ▷ *vi* to go (*ou* come) up;
(*chemin, niveau, température, voix, prix*)
to go up, rise; (*passager*) to get on;
~ à cheval (*faire du cheval*) to ride (a
horse); **~ sur** to climb up onto; **~ sur**
ou **à un arbre/une échelle** to climb
(up) a tree/ladder; **se ~ à** (*frais etc*) to
add up to, come to

montgolfière [mɔ̃gɔlfjɛʀ] *nf* hot-air
balloon

montre [mɔ̃tʀ] *nf* watch; **contre la ~**
(*Sport*) against the clock

Montréal [mɔ̃real] *n* Montreal

montrer [mɔ̃tʀe] /1/ *vt* to show;
~ qch à qn to show sb sth

monture [mɔ̃tyʀ] *nf* (*bête*) mount;
(*d'une bague*) setting; (*de lunettes*)
frame

monument [mɔnymɑ̃] *nm*
monument; **~ aux morts** war
memorial

moquer [mɔke] /1/: **se ~ de** *vt*
to make fun of, laugh at; (*fam: se*

désintéresser de) not to care about;
(*tromper*): **se ~ de qn** to take sb
for a ride

moquette [mɔkɛt] *nf* fitted carpet

moqueur, -euse [mɔkœʀ, -øz] *adj*
mocking

moral, e, -aux [mɔral, -o] *adj* moral
▷ *nm* morale ▷ *nf* (*conduite*) morals
pl (*règles*); (*valeurs*) moral standards
pl, morality; (*d'une fable etc*) moral;
faire la ~e à to lecture, preach at;
moralité *nf* morality; (*conclusion,*
enseignement) moral

morceau, x [mɔrso] *nm* piece, bit;
(*d'une œuvre*) passage, extract; (*Mus*)
piece; (*Culin: de viande*) cut; (: *de sucre*)
lump; **mettre en ~x** to pull to pieces
ou bits; **manger un ~** to have a bite
(to eat)

morceler [mɔrsəle] /4/ *vt* to break
up, divide up

mordant, e [mɔrdɑ̃, -ɑ̃t] *adj* (*ton,*
remarque) scathing, cutting; (*froid*)
biting ▷ *nm* (*fougue*) bite, punch

mordiller [mɔrdije] /1/ *vt* to nibble
at, chew at

mordre [mɔrdr] /41/ *vt* to bite ▷ *vi*
(*poisson*) to bite; **~ sur** (*fig*) to go over
into, overlap into; **~ à l'hameçon** to
bite, rise to the bait

mordu, e [mɔrdy] *nm/f* enthusiast;
un ~ du jazz/de la voile a jazz/
sailing fanatic *ou* buff

morfondre [mɔrfɔ̃dr] /41/: **se**
morfondre *vi* to mope

morgue [mɔrg] *nf* (*arrogance*)
haughtiness; (*lieu: de la police*)
morgue; (: *à l'hôpital*) mortuary

morne [mɔrn] *adj* dismal, dreary

morose [mɔroz] *adj* sullen, morose

mors [mɔr] *nm* bit

morse [mɔrs] *nm* (*Zool*) walrus; (*Tél*)
Morse (code)

morsure [mɔrsyr] *nf* bite

mort[1] [mɔr] *nf* death

mort[2]**, e** [mɔr, mɔrt] *pp de* **mourir**
▷ *adj* dead ▷ *nm/f* (*défunt*) dead man/
woman; (*victime*): **il y a eu plusieurs**

~s several people were killed; **~ de peur/fatigue** frightened to death/dead tired

mortalité [mɔrtalite] *nf* mortality, death rate

mortel, le [mɔrtɛl] *adj* (*poison etc*) deadly, lethal; (*accident, blessure*) fatal; (*silence, ennemi*) deadly; (*danger, frayeur, péché*) mortal; (*ennui, soirée*) deadly (boring)

mort-né, e [mɔrne] *adj* (*enfant*) stillborn

mortuaire [mɔrtɥɛr] *adj*: **avis ~s** death announcements

morue [mɔry] *nf* (*Zool*) cod *inv*

mosaïque [mɔzaik] *nf* mosaic

Moscou [mɔsku] *n* Moscow

mosquée [mɔske] *nf* mosque

mot [mo] *nm* word; (*message*) line, note; **~ à ~** word for word; **~ de passe** password; **~s croisés** crossword (puzzle) *sg*

motard [mɔtar] *nm* biker; (*policier*) motorcycle cop

mot-dièse *nm* (*Inform: Twitter*) hashtag

motel [mɔtɛl] *nm* motel

moteur, -trice [mɔtœr, -tris] *adj* (*Anat, Physiol*) motor; (*Tech*) driving; (*Auto*): **à 4 roues motrices** 4-wheel drive ▷ *nm* engine, motor; **à ~** power-driven, motor *cpd*; **~ de recherche** search engine

motif [mɔtif] *nm* (*cause*) motive; (*décoratif*) design, pattern, motif; **sans ~** groundless

motivation [mɔtivasjɔ̃] *nf* motivation

motiver [mɔtive] /1/ *vt* (*justifier*) to justify, account for; (*Admin, Jur, Psych*) to motivate

moto [mɔto] *nf* (motor)bike; **motocycliste** *nm/f* motorcyclist

motorisé, e [mɔtɔrize] *adj* (*personne*) having one's own transport

motrice [mɔtris] *adj f voir* **moteur**

motte [mɔt] *nf*: **~ de terre** lump of earth, clod (of earth); **~ de beurre** lump of butter

mou (mol), molle [mu, mɔl] *adj* soft; (*personne*) sluggish; (*résistance, protestations*) feeble ▷ *nm*: **avoir du ~** to be slack

mouche [muʃ] *nf* fly

moucher [muʃe] /1/: **se moucher** *vi* to blow one's nose

moucheron [muʃrɔ̃] *nm* midge

mouchoir [muʃwar] *nm* handkerchief, hanky; **~ en papier** tissue, paper hanky

moudre [mudr] /47/ *vt* to grind

moue [mu] *nf* pout; **faire la ~** to pout; (*fig*) to pull a face

mouette [mwɛt] *nf* (sea)gull

moufle [mufl] *nf* (*gant*) mitt(en)

mouillé, e [muje] *adj* wet

mouiller [muje] /1/ *vt* (*humecter*) to wet, moisten; (*tremper*): **~ qn/qch** to make sb/sth wet ▷ *vi* (*Navig*) to lie *ou* be at anchor; **se mouiller** to get wet; (*fam: prendre des risques*) to commit o.s

moulant, e [mulɑ̃, -ɑ̃t] *adj* figure-hugging

moule [mul] *nf* mussel ▷ *nm* (*Culin*) mould; **~ à gâteau** *nm* cake tin (BRIT) *ou* pan (US)

mouler [mule] /1/ *vt* (*vêtement*) to hug, fit closely round

moulin [mulɛ̃] *nm* mill; **~ à café** coffee mill; **~ à eau** watermill; **~ à légumes** (vegetable) shredder; **~ à paroles** (*fig*) chatterbox; **~ à poivre** pepper mill; **~ à vent** windmill

moulinet [mulinɛ] *nm* (*de canne à pêche*) reel; (*mouvement*): **faire des ~s avec qch** to whirl sth around

moulinette® [mulinɛt] *nf* (vegetable) shredder

moulu, e [muly] *pp de* **moudre**

mourant, e [murɑ̃, -ɑ̃t] *adj* dying

mourir [murir] /1/ *vi* to die; (*civilisation*) to die out; **~ de froid/faim/vieillesse** to die of exposure/hunger/old age; **~ de faim/d'ennui** (*fig*) to be starving/be bored to death; **~ d'envie de faire** to be dying to do

mousse [mus] *nf* (*Bot*) moss; (*de savon*) lather; (*écume: sur eau, bière*) froth, foam; (*Culin*) mousse ▷ *nm* (*Navig*) ship's boy; **~ à raser** shaving foam

mousseline [muslin] *nf* muslin; **pommes ~** creamed potatoes

mousser [muse] /1/ *vi* (*bière, détergent*) to foam; (*savon*) to lather; **mousseux, -euse** *adj* frothy ▷ *nm*: **(vin) mousseux** sparkling wine

mousson [musɔ̃] *nf* monsoon

moustache [mustaʃ] *nf* moustache; **moustaches** *nfpl* (*d'animal*) whiskers *pl*; **moustachu, e** *adj* with a moustache

moustiquaire [mustikɛʀ] *nf* mosquito net

moustique [mustik] *nm* mosquito

moutarde [mutaʀd] *nf* mustard

mouton [mutɔ̃] *nm* sheep *inv*; (*peau*) sheepskin; (*Culin*) mutton

mouvement [muvmɑ̃] *nm* movement; (*geste*) gesture; **avoir un bon ~** to make a nice gesture; **en ~** in motion; on the move; **mouvementé, e** *adj* (*vie, poursuite*) eventful; (*réunion*) turbulent

mouvoir [muvwaʀ] /27/: **se mouvoir** *vi* to move

moyen, ne [mwajɛ̃, -ɛn] *adj* average; (*tailles, prix*) medium; (*de grandeur moyenne*) medium-sized ▷ *nm* (*façon*) means *sg*, way ▷ *nf* average; (*Statistique*) mean; (*Scol: à l'examen*) pass mark; **moyens** *nmpl* (*capacités*) means; **très ~** (*résultats*) pretty poor; **je n'en ai pas les ~s** I can't afford it; **au ~ de** by means of; **par tous les ~s** by every possible means, every possible way; **par ses propres ~s** all by oneself; **~ âge** Middle Ages; **~ de transport** means of transport; **~ne d'âge** average age; **~ne entreprise** (*Comm*) medium-sized firm

moyennant [mwajɛnɑ̃] *prép* (*somme*) for; (*service, conditions*) in return for; (*travail, effort*) with

Moyen-Orient [mwajɛnɔʀjɑ̃] *nm*: **le ~** the Middle East

moyeu, x [mwajø] *nm* hub

MST *sigle f* (= *maladie sexuellement transmissible*) STD

mû, mue [my] *pp de* **mouvoir**

muer [mɥe] /1/ *vi* (*oiseau, mammifère*) to moult; (*serpent*) to slough (its skin); (*jeune garçon*): **il mue** his voice is breaking

muet, te [mɥɛ, -ɛt] *adj* (*fig*): **~ d'admiration** *etc* speechless with admiration *etc*; (*Ciné*) silent

mufle [myfl] *nm* muzzle; (*goujat*) boor

mugir [myʒiʀ] /2/ *vi* (*bœuf*) to bellow; (*vache*) to low; (*fig*) to howl

muguet [mygɛ] *nm* lily of the valley

mule [myl] *nf* (*Zool*) (she-)mule

mulet [mylɛ] *nm* (*Zool*) (he-)mule; (*poisson*) mullet

multinational, e, -aux [myltinasjɔnal, -o] *adj, nf* multinational

multiple [myltipl] *adj* multiple, numerous; (*varié*) many, manifold; **multiplication** *nf* multiplication; **multiplier** /7/ *vt* to multiply; **se multiplier** *vi* to multiply

municipal, e, -aux [mynisipal, -o] *adj* (*élections, stade*) municipal; (*conseil*) town *cpd*; **piscine/ bibliothèque ~e** public swimming pool/library; **municipalité** *nf* (*corps municipal*) town council; (*commune*) municipality

munir [myniʀ] /2/ *vt*: **~ qn/qch de** to equip sb/sth with; **se ~ de** to provide o.s. with

munitions [mynisjɔ̃] *nfpl* ammunition *sg*

mur [myʀ] *nm* wall; **~ (payant)** (*Inform*) paywall; **~ du son** sound barrier

mûr, e [myʀ] *adj* ripe; (*personne*) mature

muraille [myʀaj] *nf* (high) wall

mural, e, -aux [myʀal, -o] *adj* wall *cpd* ▷ *nm* (*Art*) mural

m

mûre [myʀ] nf blackberry

muret [myʀɛ] nm low wall

mûrir [myʀiʀ] /2/ vi (fruit, blé) to ripen; (abcès, furoncle) to come to a head; (fig: idée, personne) to mature ▷ vt (personne) to (make) mature; (pensée, projet) to nurture

murmure [myʀmyʀ] nm murmur; **murmurer** /1/ vi to murmur

muscade [myskad] nf (aussi: **noix (de) ~**) nutmeg

muscat [myska] nm (raisin) muscat grape; (vin) muscatel (wine)

muscle [myskl] nm muscle; **musclé, e** adj muscular; (fig) strong-arm cpd

museau, x [myzo] nm muzzle; (Culin) brawn

musée [myze] nm museum; (de peinture) art gallery

museler [myzle] /4/ vt to muzzle; **muselière** nf muzzle

musette [myzɛt] nf (sac) lunch bag

musical, e, -aux [myzikal, -o] adj musical

music-hall [myzikol] nm (salle) variety theatre; (genre) variety

musicien, ne [myzisjɛ̃, -ɛn] adj musical ▷ nm/f musician

musique [myzik] nf music

musulman, e [myzylmɑ̃, -an] adj, nm/f Moslem, Muslim

mutation [mytasjɔ̃] nf (Admin) transfer

muter [myte] /1/ vt to transfer, move

mutilé, e [mytile] nm/f person with a disability (through loss of limbs)

mutiler [mytile] /1/ vt to mutilate, maim

mutin, e [mytɛ̃, -in] adj (enfant, air, ton) mischievous, impish ▷ nm/f (Mil, Navig) mutineer; **mutinerie** nf mutiny

mutisme [mytism] nm silence

mutuel, le [mytɥɛl] adj mutual ▷ nf mutual benefit society

myope [mjɔp] adj short-sighted

myosotis [mjɔzɔtis] nm forget-me-not

myrtille [miʀtij] nf blueberry

mystère [mistɛʀ] nm mystery; **mystérieux, -euse** adj mysterious

mystifier [mistifje] /7/ vt to fool

mythe [mit] nm myth

mythologie [mitɔlɔʒi] nf mythology

n

n' [n] *adv voir* **ne**

nacre [nakʀ] *nf* mother-of-pearl

nage [naʒ] *nf* swimming; (*manière*) style of swimming, stroke; **traverser/s'éloigner à la ~** to swim across/away; **en ~** bathed in sweat; **nageoire** *nf* fin; **nager** /3/ *vi* to swim; **nageur, -euse** *nm/f* swimmer

naïf, -ïve [naif, naiv] *adj* naïve

nain, e [nɛ̃, nɛn] *nm/f* (*péj*) dwarf (!)

naissance [nɛsɑ̃s] *nf* birth; **donner ~ à** to give birth to; (*fig*) to give rise to; **lieu de ~** place of birth

naître [nɛtʀ] /59/ *vi* to be born; (*conflit, complications*): **~ de** to arise from, be born out of; **je suis né en 1960** I was born in 1960; **faire ~** (*fig*) to give rise to, arouse

naïveté [naivte] *nf* naivety

nana [nana] *nf* (*fam: fille*) bird (*BRIT*), chick

nappe [nap] *nf* tablecloth; (*de pétrole, gaz*) layer; **napperon** *nm* table-mat

narguer [naʀge] /1/ *vt* to taunt

narine [naʀin] *nf* nostril

natal, e [natal] *adj* native; **natalité** *nf* birth rate

natation [natasjɔ̃] *nf* swimming

natif, -ive [natif, -iv] *adj* native

nation [nasjɔ̃] *nf* nation; **national, e, -aux** *adj* national ▷ *nf*: (**route**) **nationale** ≈ A road (*BRIT*), ≈ state highway (*US*); **nationaliser** /1/ *vt* to nationalize; **nationalisme** *nm* nationalism; **nationalité** *nf* nationality

natte [nat] *nf* (*tapis*) mat; (*cheveux*) plait

naturaliser [natyʀalize] /1/ *vt* to naturalize

nature [natyʀ] *nf* nature ▷ *adj, adv* (*Culin*) plain, without seasoning or sweetening; (*café, thé*) black; without sugar; (*yaourt*) natural; **payer en ~** to pay in kind; **~ morte** still-life; **naturel, le** *adj* natural ▷ *nm* naturalness; (*caractère*) disposition, nature; **naturellement** *adv* naturally; (*bien sûr*) of course

naufrage [nofʀaʒ] *nm* (ship)wreck; **faire ~** to be shipwrecked

nausée [noze] *nf* nausea; **avoir la ~** to feel sick

nautique [notik] *adj* nautical, water *cpd*; **sports ~s** water sports

naval, e [naval] *adj* naval; (*industrie*) shipbuilding

navet [navɛ] *nm* turnip; (*péj: film*) third-rate film

navette [navɛt] *nf* shuttle; **faire la ~ (entre)** to go to and fro (between)

navigateur [navigatœʀ] *nm* (*Navig*) seafarer; (*Inform*) browser

navigation [navigasjɔ̃] *nf* navigation, sailing

naviguer [navige] /1/ *vi* to navigate, sail; **~ sur Internet** to browse the Internet

navire [naviʀ] *nm* ship

navrer [navʀe] /1/ *vt* to upset, distress; **je suis navré (de/de faire/que)** I'm so sorry (for/for doing/that)

ne, n' [nə, n] *adv voir* **pas¹**; **plus²**;
jamais *etc*; (*sans valeur négative, non
traduit*): **c'est plus loin que je ne le
croyais** it's further than I thought

né, e [ne] *pp de* **naître**; **né en 1960**
born in 1960; **née Scott** née Scott

néanmoins [neɑ̃mwɛ̃] *adv*
nevertheless

néant [neɑ̃] *nm* nothingness;
réduire à ~ to bring to nought;
(*espoir*) to dash

nécessaire [neseseʀ] *adj* necessary
▷ *nm* necessary; (*sac*) kit; **faire le ~**
to do the necessary; **~ de couture**
sewing kit; **~ de toilette** toilet bag;
nécessité *nf* necessity; **nécessiter**
/1/ *vt* to require

nectar [nɛktaʀ] *nm* nectar

néerlandais, e [neɛʀlɑ̃dɛ, -ɛz]
adj Dutch

nef [nɛf] *nf* (*d'église*) nave

néfaste [nefast] *adj* (*nuisible*)
harmful; (*funeste*) ill-fated

négatif, -ive [negatif, -iv] *adj*
negative ▷ *nm* (*Photo*) negative

négligé, e [negliʒe] *adj* (*en désordre*)
slovenly ▷ *nm* (*tenue*) negligee

négligeable [negliʒabl] *adj*
negligible

négligent, e [negliʒɑ̃, -ɑ̃t] *adj*
careless; negligent

négliger [negliʒe] /3/ *vt* (*épouse,
jardin*) to neglect; (*tenue*) to be
careless about; (*avis, précautions*) to
disregard; **~ de faire** to fail to do, not
bother to do

négociant, e [negɔsjɑ̃, -jɑ̃t] *nm/f*
merchant

négociation [negɔsjasjɔ̃] *nf*
negotiation

négocier [negɔsje] /7/ *vi, vt* to
negotiate

nègre [nɛgʀ] *nm* (*péj*) Negro (!);
(*écrivain*) ghost writer

neige [nɛʒ] *nf* snow; **neiger** /3/ *vi*
to snow

nénuphar [nenyfaʀ] *nm* water-lily

néon [neɔ̃] *nm* neon

néo-zélandais, e [neɔzelɑ̃dɛ, -ɛz]
adj New Zealand *cpd* ▷ *nm/f*: **N~, e**
New Zealander

Népal [nepal] *nm*: **le ~** Nepal

nerf [nɛʀ] *nm* nerve; **être** *ou* **vivre
sur les ~s** to live on one's nerves;
nerveux, -euse *adj* nervous;
(*irritable*) touchy, nervy; (*voiture*)
nippy, responsive; **nervosité** *nf*
excitability, tenseness

n'est-ce pas [nɛspɑ] *adv* isn't it?,
won't you? *etc* (*selon le verbe qui
précède*)

net, nette [nɛt] *adj* (*sans équivoque,
distinct*) clear; (*amélioration, différence*)
marked, distinct; (*propre*) neat,
clean; (*Comm: prix, salaire, poids*) net
▷ *adv* (*refuser*) flatly ▷ *nm*: **mettre
au ~** to copy out; **s'arrêter ~** to
stop dead; **nettement** *adv* clearly;
(*incontestablement*) decidedly;
netteté *nf* clearness

nettoyage [netwajaʒ] *nm* cleaning;
~ à sec dry cleaning

nettoyer [netwaje] /8/ *vt* to clean

neuf¹ [nœf] *num* nine

neuf², neuve [nœf, nœv] *adj* new;
remettre à ~ to do up (as good as
new), refurbish; **quoi de ~?** what's
new?

neutre [nøtʀ] *adj* (*Ling*) neuter

neuve [nœv] *adj f voir* **neuf²**

neuvième [nœvjɛm] *num* ninth

neveu, x [nəvø] *nm* nephew

New York [njujɔʀk] *n* New York

nez [ne] *nm* nose; **avoir du ~** to have
flair; **~ à ~ avec** face to face with

ni [ni] *conj*: **ni ... ni** neither ... nor;
**je n'aime ni les lentilles ni les
épinards** I like neither lentils nor
spinach; **il n'a dit ni oui ni non** he
didn't say either yes or no; **elles ne
sont venues ni l'une ni l'autre**
neither of them came; **il n'a rien
vu ni entendu** he didn't see or hear
anything

niche [niʃ] *nf* (*du chien*) kennel; (*de mur*)
recess, niche; **nicher** /1/ *vi* to nest

nid [ni] *nm* nest; **~ de poule** pothole
nièce [njɛs] *nf* niece
nier [nje] /7/ *vt* to deny
Nil [nil] *nm*: **le ~** the Nile
n'importe [nɛ̃pɔʀt] *adv*: **~ qui/ quoi/où** anybody/anything/ anywhere; **~ quand** any time; **~ quel/quelle** any; **~ lequel/laquelle** any (one); **~ comment** (*sans soin*) carelessly
niveau, x [nivo] *nm* level; (*des élèves, études*) standard; **~ de vie** standard of living
niveler [nivle] /4/ *vt* to level
noble [nɔbl] *adj* noble; **noblesse** *nf* nobility; (*d'une action etc*) nobleness
noce [nɔs] *nf* wedding; (*gens*) wedding party (*ou* guests *pl*); **faire la ~** (*fam*) to go on a binge; **~s d'or/d'argent/de diamant** golden/ silver/diamond wedding
nocif, -ive [nɔsif, -iv] *adj* harmful
nocturne [nɔktyʀn] *adj* nocturnal ▷ *nf* late opening
Noël [nɔɛl] *nm* Christmas
nœud [nø] *nm* knot; (*ruban*) bow; **~ papillon** bow tie
noir, e [nwaʀ] *adj* black; (*obscur, sombre*) dark ▷ *nm/f* black man/ woman ▷ *nm*: **dans le ~** in the dark ▷ *nf* (*Mus*) crotchet (*BRIT*), quarter note (*US*); **travailler au ~** to work on the side; **noircir** /2/ *vt, vi* to blacken
noisette [nwazɛt] *nf* hazelnut
noix [nwa] *nf* walnut; (*Culin*): **une ~ de beurre** a knob of butter; **à la ~** (*fam*) worthless; **~ de cajou** cashew nut; **~ de coco** coconut; **~ muscade** nutmeg
nom [nɔ̃] *nm* name; (*Ling*) noun; **~ de famille** surname; **~ de jeune fille** maiden name; **~ d'utilisateur** username
nomade [nɔmad] *nm/f* nomad
nombre [nɔ̃bʀ] *nm* number; **venir en ~** to come in large numbers; **depuis ~ d'années** for many years; **au ~ de mes amis** among

my friends; **nombreux, -euse** *adj* many, numerous; (*avec nom sg*: **foule** *etc*) large; **peu nombreux** few; **de nombreux cas** many cases
nombril [nɔ̃bʀi(l)] *nm* navel
nommer [nɔme] /1/ *vt* to name; (*élire*) to appoint, nominate; **se nommer** *vr*: **il se nomme Pascal** his name's Pascal, he's called Pascal
non [nɔ̃] *adv* (*réponse*) no; (*suivi d'un adjectif, adverbe*) not; **Paul est venu, ~?** Paul came, didn't he?; **~ pas que** not that; **moi ~ plus** neither do I, I don't either; **je pense que ~** I don't think so; **~ alcoolisé** non-alcoholic
nonchalant, e [nɔ̃ʃalɑ̃, -ɑ̃t] *adj* nonchalant
non-fumeur, -euse [nɔ̃fymœʀ, -øz] *nm/f* non-smoker
non-sens [nɔ̃sɑ̃s] *nm* absurdity
nord [nɔʀ] *nm* North ▷ *adj* northern; north; **au ~** (*situation*) in the north; (*direction*) to the north; **au ~ de** to the north of; **nord-africain, e** *adj* North-African ▷ *nm/f*: **Nord-Africain, e** North African; **nord-est** *nm* North-East; **nord-ouest** *nm* North-West
normal, e, -aux [nɔʀmal, -o] *adj* normal ▷ *nf*: **la ~e** the norm, the average; **c'est tout à fait ~** it's perfectly natural; **vous trouvez ça ~?** does it seem right to you?; **normalement** *adv* (*en général*) normally
normand, e [nɔʀmɑ̃, -ɑ̃d] *adj* Norman ▷ *nm/f*: **N~, e** (*de Normandie*) Norman
Normandie [nɔʀmɑ̃di] *nf*: **la ~** Normandy
norme [nɔʀm] *nf* norm; (*Tech*) standard
Norvège [nɔʀvɛʒ] *nf*: **la ~** Norway; **norvégien, ne** *adj* Norwegian ▷ *nm* (*Ling*) Norwegian ▷ *nm/f*: **Norvégien, ne** Norwegian
nos [no] *adj poss voir* **notre**
nostalgie [nɔstalʒi] *nf* nostalgia; **nostalgique** *adj* nostalgic

notable [nɔtabl] *adj* notable, noteworthy; (*marqué*) noticeable, marked ▷ *nm* prominent citizen

notaire [nɔtɛʀ] *nm* solicitor

notamment [nɔtamɑ̃] *adv* in particular, among others

note [nɔt] *nf* (*écrite, Mus*) note; (*Scol*) mark (BRIT), grade; (*facture*) bill; **~ de service** memorandum

noter [nɔte] /1/ *vt* (*écrire*) to write down; (*remarquer*) to note, notice; (*devoir*) to mark, give a grade to

notice [nɔtis] *nf* summary, short article; (*brochure*): **~ explicative** explanatory leaflet, instruction booklet

notifier [nɔtifje] /7/ *vt*: **~ qch à qn** to notify sb of sth, notify sth to sb

notion [nɔsjɔ̃] *nf* notion, idea

notoire [nɔtwaʀ] *adj* widely known; (*en mal*) notorious

notre (*pl* **nos**) [nɔtʀ(ə), no] *adj poss* our

nôtre [notʀ] *adj* ours ▷ *pron*: **le/la ~** ours; **les ~s** ours; (*alliés etc*) our own people; **soyez des ~s** join us

nouer [nwe] /1/ *vt* to tie, knot; (*fig: alliance etc*) to strike up

noueux, -euse [nwø, -øz] *adj* gnarled

nourrice [nuʀis] *nf* ≈ child-minder

nourrir [nuʀiʀ] /2/ *vt* to feed; (*fig: espoir*) to harbour, nurse; **nourrissant, e** *adj* nutritious; **nourrisson** *nm* (unweaned) infant; **nourriture** *nf* food

nous [nu] *pron* (*sujet*) we; (*objet*) us; **nous-mêmes** *pron* ourselves

nouveau (nouvel), -elle, x [nuvo, -ɛl] *adj* new ▷ *nm/f* new pupil (*ou* employee) ▷ *nm*: **il y a du ~** there's something new ▷ *nf* (piece of) news *sg*; (*Littérature*) short story; **nouvelles** *nfpl* (*Presse, TV*) news; **de ~ à ~** again; **je suis sans nouvelles de lui** I haven't heard from him; **Nouvel An** New Year; **~ venu, nouvelle venue** newcomer; **~x mariés** newly-weds; **nouveau-né, e** *nm/f* newborn

(baby); **nouveauté** *nf* novelty; (*chose nouvelle*) something new

nouvelle: Nouvelle-Calédonie [nuvɛlkaledɔni] *nf*: **la Nouvelle-Calédonie** New Caledonia; **Nouvelle-Zélande** [nuvɛlzelɑ̃d] *nf*: **la Nouvelle-Zélande** New Zealand

novembre [nɔvɑ̃bʀ] *nm* November; *voir aussi* **juillet**

- **LE 11 NOVEMBRE**
-
- *Le 11 novembre* is a public holiday
- in France and commemorates
- the signing of the armistice, near
- Compiègne, at the end of the First
- World War.

noyade [nwajad] *nf* drowning *no pl*

noyau, x [nwajo] *nm* (*de fruit*) stone; (*Bio, Physique*) nucleus; (*fig: centre*) core

noyer [nwaje] /8/ *nm* walnut (tree); (*bois*) walnut ▷ *vt* to drown; (*moteur*) to flood; **se noyer** to be drowned, drown; (*suicide*) to drown o.s.

nu, e [ny] *adj* naked; (*membres*) naked, bare; (*chambre, fil, plaine*) bare ▷ *nm* (*Art*) nude; **tout nu** stark naked; **se mettre nu** to strip

nuage [nɥaʒ] *nm* (*aussi Inform*) cloud; **informatique en ~** cloud computing; **nuageux, -euse** *adj* cloudy

nuance [nɥɑ̃s] *nf* (*de couleur, sens*) shade; **il y a une ~ (entre)** there's a slight difference (between); **nuancer** /3/ *vt* (*pensée, opinion*) to qualify

nucléaire [nykleɛʀ] *adj* nuclear ▷ *nm*: **le ~** nuclear power

nudiste [nydist] *nm/f* nudist

nuée [nɥe] *nf*: **une ~ de** a cloud *ou* host *ou* swarm of

nuire [nɥiʀ] /38/ *vi* to be harmful; **~ à** to harm, do damage to; **nuisible** [nɥizibl] *adj* harmful; **(animal) nuisible** pest

nuit [nɥi] *nf* night; **il fait ~** it's dark; **cette ~** (*hier*) last night; (*aujourd'hui*)

tonight; **de ~** (*vol, service*) night *cpd*;
~ blanche sleepless night
nul, nulle [nyl] *adj* (*aucun*) no;
(*minime*) nil, non-existent; (*non
valable*) null; (*péj*) useless, hopeless
▷ *pron* none, no one; **résultat ~,
match ~** draw; **nulle part** nowhere;
nullement *adv* by no means
numérique [nymeʀik] *adj*
numerical; (*affichage, son, télévision*)
digital
numéro [nymeʀo] *nm* number;
(*spectacle*) act, turn; (*Presse*) issue,
number; **~ de téléphone** (tele)phone
number; **~ vert** ≈ Freefone® number
(*BRIT*), ≈ toll-free number (*US*);
numéroter /1/ *vt* to number
nuque [nyk] *nf* nape of the neck
nu-tête [nytɛt] *adj inv* bareheaded
nutritif, -ive [nytʀitif, -iv] *adj*
(*besoins, valeur*) nutritional; (*aliment*)
nutritious, nourishing
nylon [nilɔ̃] *nm* nylon

oasis [ɔazis] *nm ou f* oasis
obéir [ɔbeiʀ] /2/ *vi* to obey; **~ à** to
obey; **obéissance** *nf* obedience;
obéissant, e *adj* obedient
obèse [ɔbɛz] *adj* obese; **obésité** *nf*
obesity
objecter [ɔbʒɛkte] /1/ *vt*: **~ (à qn)
que** to object (to sb) that; **objecteur**
nm: **objecteur de conscience**
conscientious objector
objectif, -ive [ɔbʒɛktif, -iv] *adj*
objective ▷ *nm* (*Optique, Photo*) lens
sg; (*Mil, fig*) objective
objection [ɔbʒɛksjɔ̃] *nf* objection
objectivité [ɔbʒɛktivite] *nf*
objectivity
objet [ɔbʒɛ] *nm* object; (*d'une
discussion, recherche*) subject; **être
ou faire l'~ de** (*discussion*) to be the
subject of; (*soins*) to be given *ou*
shown; **sans ~** purposeless; (*sans
fondement*) groundless; **~ d'art** objet
d'art; **~s personnels** personal items;

~s trouvés lost property sg (BRIT), lost-and-found sg (US); **~s de valeur** valuables

obligation [ɔbligasjɔ̃] nf obligation; (Comm) bond, debenture; **obligatoire** adj compulsory, obligatory; **obligatoirement** adv necessarily; (fam: sans aucun doute) inevitably

obliger [ɔbliʒe] /3/ vt (contraindre): **~ qn à faire** to force ou oblige sb to do; **je suis bien obligé (de le faire)** I have to (do it)

oblique [ɔblik] adj oblique; **en ~** diagonally

oblitérer [ɔblitere] /6/ vt (timbreposte) to cancel

obnubiler [ɔbnybile] /1/ vt to obsess

obscène [ɔpsɛn] adj obscene

obscur, e [ɔpskyr] adj dark; (raisons) obscure; **obscurcir** /2/ vt to darken; (fig) to obscure; **s'obscurcir** vi to grow dark; **obscurité** nf darkness; **dans l'obscurité** in the dark, in darkness

obsédé, e [ɔpsede] nm/f fanatic; **~(e) sexuel(le)** sex maniac

obséder [ɔpsede] /6/ vt to obsess, haunt

obsèques [ɔpsɛk] nfpl funeral sg

observateur, -trice [ɔpsɛrvatœr, -tris] adj observant, perceptive ▷ nm/f observer

observation [ɔpsɛrvasjɔ̃] nf observation; (d'un règlement etc) observance; (reproche) reproof; **en ~** (Méd) under observation

observatoire [ɔpsɛrvatwar] nm observatory

observer [ɔpsɛrve] /1/ vt (regarder) to observe, watch; (scientifiquement, aussi: règlement, jeûne etc) to observe; (surveiller) to watch; (remarquer) to observe, notice; **faire ~ qch à qn** (dire) to point out sth to sb

obsession [ɔpsesjɔ̃] nf obsession

obstacle [ɔpstakl] nm obstacle; (Équitation) jump, hurdle; **faire ~ à** (projet) to hinder, put obstacles in the path of

obstiné, e [ɔpstine] adj obstinate

obstiner [ɔpstine] /1/: **s'obstiner** vi to insist, dig one's heels in; **s'~ à faire** to persist (obstinately) in doing

obstruer [ɔpstrye] /1/ vt to block, obstruct

obtenir [ɔptənir] /22/ vt to obtain, get; (résultat) to achieve, obtain; **~ de pouvoir faire** to obtain permission to do

obturateur [ɔptyratœr] nm (Photo) shutter

obus [ɔby] nm shell

occasion [ɔkazjɔ̃] nf (aubaine, possibilité) opportunity; (circonstance) occasion; (Comm: article non neuf) secondhand buy; (: acquisition avantageuse) bargain; **à plusieurs ~s** on several occasions; **à l'~** sometimes, on occasions; **d'~** secondhand; **occasionnel, le** adj occasional

occasionner [ɔkazjɔne] /1/ vt to cause

occident [ɔksidɑ̃] nm: **l'O~** the West; **occidental, e, -aux** adj western; (Pol) Western ▷ nm/f Westerner

occupation [ɔkypasjɔ̃] nf occupation

occupé, e [ɔkype] adj (Mil, Pol) occupied; (personne) busy; (place, sièges) taken; (toilettes) engaged; **la ligne est ~e** the line's engaged (BRIT) ou busy (US)

occuper [ɔkype] /1/ vt to occupy; (poste, fonction) to hold; **s'~ (à qch)** to occupy o.s ou keep o.s. busy (with sth); **s'~ de** (être responsable de) to be in charge of; (se charger de: affaire) to take charge of, deal with; (: clients etc) to attend to

occurrence [ɔkyrɑ̃s] nf: **en l'~** in this case

océan [ɔseɑ̃] nm ocean

octet [ɔktɛ] nm byte

octobre [ɔktɔbr] nm October

oculiste [ɔkylist] *nm/f* eye specialist

odeur [ɔdœʀ] *nf* smell

odieux, -euse [ɔdjø, -øz] *adj* hateful

odorant, e [ɔdɔʀɑ̃, -ɑ̃t] *adj* sweet-smelling, fragrant

odorat [ɔdɔʀa] *nm* (sense of) smell

œil [œj] (*pl* **yeux**) *nm* eye; **avoir un ~ poché** *ou* **au beurre noir** to have a black eye; **à l'~** (*fam*) for free; **à l'~ nu** with the naked eye; **fermer les yeux (sur)** (*fig*) to turn a blind eye (to); **les yeux fermés** (*aussi fig*) with one's eyes shut; **ouvrir l'~** (*fig*) to keep one's eyes open *ou* an eye out

œillères [œjɛʀ] *nfpl* blinkers (BRIT), blinders (US)

œillet [œjɛ] *nm* (*Bot*) carnation

œuf [œf] *nm* egg; **~ à la coque/dur/ mollet** boiled/hard-boiled/soft-boiled egg; **~ au plat/poché** fried/ poached egg; **~s brouillés** scrambled eggs; **~ de Pâques** Easter egg

œuvre [œvʀ] *nf* (*tâche*) task, undertaking; (*ouvrage achevé, livre, tableau etc*) work; (*ensemble de la production artistique*) works *pl* ▷ *nm* (*Constr*): **le gros ~** the shell; **mettre en ~** (*moyens*) to make use of; **~ d'art** work of art; **~s de bienfaisance** charitable works

offense [ɔfɑ̃s] *nf* insult; **offenser** /1/ *vt* to offend, hurt; **s'offenser de** *vi* to take offence (BRIT) *ou* offense (US) at

offert, e [ɔfɛʀ, -ɛʀt] *pp de* **offrir**

office [ɔfis] *nm* (*agence*) bureau, agency; (*Rel*) service ▷ *nm ou f* (*pièce*) pantry; **faire ~ de** to act as; **d'~** automatically; **~ du tourisme** tourist office

officiel, le [ɔfisjɛl] *adj, nm/f* official

officier [ɔfisje] /7/ *nm* officer

officieux, -euse [ɔfisjø, -øz] *adj* unofficial

offrande [ɔfʀɑ̃d] *nf* offering

offre [ɔfʀ] *nf* offer; (*aux enchères*) bid; (*Admin: soumission*) tender; (*Écon*): **l'~ et la demande** supply and demand; **~ d'emploi** job advertised;

"~s d'emploi" "situations vacant"; **~ publique d'achat (OPA)** takeover bid

offrir [ɔfʀiʀ] /18/ *vt*: **~ (à qn)** to offer (to sb); (*faire cadeau*) to give to (sb); **s'offrir,** *vt* (*vacances, voiture*) to treat o.s. to; **~ (à qn) de faire qch** to offer to do sth (for sb); **~ à boire à qn** (*chez soi*) to offer sb a drink; **je vous offre un verre** I'll buy you a drink

OGM *sigle m* (= *organisme génétiquement modifié*) GMO

oie [wa] *nf* (*Zool*) goose

oignon [ɔɲɔ̃] *nm* onion; (*de tulipe etc*) bulb

oiseau, x [wazo] *nm* bird; **~ de proie** bird of prey

oisif, -ive [wazif, -iv] *adj* idle

oléoduc [ɔleɔdyk] *nm* (oil) pipeline

olive [ɔliv] *nf* (*Bot*) olive; **olivier** *nm* olive (tree)

OLP *sigle f* (= *Organisation de libération de la Palestine*) PLO

olympique [ɔlɛ̃pik] *adj* Olympic

ombragé, e [ɔ̃bʀaʒe] *adj* shaded, shady

ombre [ɔ̃bʀ] *nf* (*espace non ensoleillé*) shade; (*ombre portée, tache*) shadow; **à l'~** in the shade; **dans l'~** (*fig*) in the dark; **~ à paupières** eye shadow

omelette [ɔmlɛt] *nf* omelette; **~ norvégienne** baked Alaska

omettre [ɔmɛtʀ] /56/ *vt* to omit, leave out

omoplate [ɔmɔplat] *nf* shoulder blade

MOT-CLÉ

on [ɔ̃] *pron* **1** (*indéterminé*) you, one; **on peut le faire ainsi** you *ou* one can do it like this, it can be done like this **2** (*quelqu'un*): **on les a attaqués** they were attacked; **on vous demande au téléphone** there's a phone call for you, you're wanted on the phone **3** (*nous*) we; **on va y aller demain** we're going tomorrow

4 (*les gens*) they; **autrefois, on croyait ...** they used to believe ..
5: **on ne peut plus** *adv*: **on ne peut plus stupide** as stupid as can be

oncle [ɔ̃kl] *nm* uncle
onctueux, -euse [ɔ̃ktɥø, -øz] *adj* creamy; smooth
onde [ɔ̃d] *nf* wave; **~s courtes (OC)** short wave *sg*; **~s moyennes (OM)** medium wave *sg*; **grandes ~s (GO)**, **~s longues (OL)** long wave *sg*
ondée [ɔ̃de] *nf* shower
on-dit [ɔ̃di] *nm inv* rumour
onduler [ɔ̃dyle] /1/ *vi* to undulate; (*cheveux*) to wave
onéreux, -euse [ɔnerø, -øz] *adj* costly
ongle [ɔ̃gl] *nm* nail
ont [ɔ̃] *vb voir* **avoir**
ONU *sigle f* (= *Organisation des Nations unies*) UN(O)
onze ['ɔ̃z] *num* eleven; **onzième** *num* eleventh
OPA *sigle f* = **offre publique d'achat**
opaque [ɔpak] *adj* opaque
opéra [ɔpera] *nm* opera; (*édifice*) opera house
opérateur, -trice [ɔperatœr, -tris] *nm/f* operator; **~ (de prise de vues)** cameraman
opération [ɔperasjɔ̃] *nf* operation; (*Comm*) dealing
opératoire [ɔperatwar] *adj* (*choc etc*) post-operative
opérer [ɔpere] /6/ *vt* (*Méd*) to operate on; (*faire, exécuter*) to carry out, make ▷ *vi* (*remède: faire effet*) to act, work; (*Méd*) to operate; **s'opérer** *vi* (*avoir lieu*) to occur, take place; **se faire ~** to have an operation
opérette [ɔperɛt] *nf* operetta, light opera
opinion [ɔpinjɔ̃] *nf* opinion; **l'~ (publique)** public opinion
opportun, e [ɔpɔrtœ̃, -yn] *adj* timely, opportune; **opportuniste** [ɔpɔrtynist] *nm/f* opportunist

opposant, e [ɔpozɑ̃, -ɑ̃t] *nm/f* opponent
opposé, e [ɔpoze] *adj* (*direction, rive*) opposite; (*faction*) opposing; (*opinions, intérêts*) conflicting; (*contre*) **~ à** opposed to, against ▷ *nm*: **l'~** the other *ou* opposite side (*ou* direction); (*contraire*) the opposite; **à l'~** (*fig*) on the other hand; **à l'~ de** (*fig*) contrary to, unlike
opposer [ɔpoze] /1/ *vt* (*personnes, armées, équipes*) to oppose; (*couleurs, termes, tons*) to contrast; **~ qch à** (*comme obstacle, défense*) to set sth against; (*comme objection*) to put sth forward against; **s'opposer** *vi* (*équipes*) to confront each other; (*opinions*) to conflict; (*couleurs, styles*) to contrast; **s'~ à** (*interdire, empêcher*) to oppose
opposition [ɔpozisjɔ̃] *nf* opposition; **par ~ à** as opposed to; **entrer en ~ avec** to come into conflict with; **faire ~ à un chèque** to stop a cheque
oppressant, e [ɔpresɑ̃, -ɑ̃t] *adj* oppressive
oppresser [ɔprese] /1/ *vt* to oppress; **oppression** *nf* oppression
opprimer [ɔprime] /1/ *vt* to oppress
opter [ɔpte] /1/ *vi*: **~ pour** to opt for; **~ entre** to choose between
opticien, ne [ɔptisjɛ̃, -ɛn] *nm/f* optician
optimisme [ɔptimism] *nm* optimism; **optimiste** [ɔptimist] *adj* optimistic ▷ *nm/f* optimist
option [ɔpsjɔ̃] *nf* option; **matière à ~** (*Scol*) optional subject
optique [ɔptik] *adj* (*nerf*) optic; (*verres*) optical ▷ *nf* (*fig: manière de voir*) perspective
or [ɔr] *nm* gold ▷ *conj* now, but; **en or** gold *cpd*; **une affaire en or** a real bargain; **il croyait gagner or il a perdu** he was sure he would win and yet he lost
orage [ɔraʒ] *nm* (thunder)storm; **orageux, -euse** *adj* stormy

oral, e, -aux [ɔʀal, -o] *adj* oral; (*Méd*): **par voie ~e** orally ▷ *nm* oral

orange [ɔʀɑ̃ʒ] *adj inv, nf* orange; **orangé, e** *adj* orangey, orange-coloured; **orangeade** *nf* orangeade; **oranger** *nm* orange tree

orateur [ɔʀatœʀ] *nm* speaker

orbite [ɔʀbit] *nf* (*Anat*) (eye-)socket; (*Physique*) orbit

Orcades [ɔʀkad] *nfpl*: **les ~** the Orkneys, the Orkney Islands

orchestre [ɔʀkɛstʀ] *nm* orchestra; (*de jazz, danse*) band; (*places*) stalls *pl* (BRIT), orchestra (US)

orchidée [ɔʀkide] *nf* orchid

ordinaire [ɔʀdinɛʀ] *adj* ordinary; (*modèle, qualité*) standard; (*péj: commun*) common ▷ *nm* ordinary; (*menus*) everyday fare ▷ *nf* (*essence*) ≈ two-star (petrol) (BRIT), ≈ regular (gas) (US); **d'~** usually, normally; **comme à l'~** as usual

ordinateur [ɔʀdinatœʀ] *nm* computer; **~ individuel** *ou* **personnel** personal computer; **~ portable** laptop (computer)

ordonnance [ɔʀdɔnɑ̃s] *nf* (*Méd*) prescription; (*Mil*) orderly, batman (BRIT)

ordonné, e [ɔʀdɔne] *adj* tidy, orderly

ordonner [ɔʀdɔne] /1/ *vt* (*agencer*) to organize, arrange; (*donner un ordre*): **~ à qn de faire** to order sb to do; (*Rel*) to ordain; (*Méd*) to prescribe

ordre [ɔʀdʀ] *nm* order; (*propreté et soin*) orderliness, tidiness; **à l'~ de** payable to; (*nature*): **d'~ pratique** of a practical nature; **ordres** *nmpl* (*Rel*) holy orders; **mettre en ~** to tidy (up), put in order; **par ~ alphabétique/ d'importance** in alphabetical order/ in order of importance; **être aux ~s de qn/sous les ~s de qn** to be at sb's disposal/under sb's command; **jusqu'à nouvel ~** until further notice; **de premier ~** first-rate; **~ du jour** (*d'une réunion*) agenda; **à l'~ du jour** (*fig*) topical; **~ public** law and order

ordure [ɔʀdyʀ] *nf* filth *no pl*; **ordures** *nfpl* (*balayures, déchets*) rubbish *sg*, refuse *sg*; **~s ménagères** household refuse

oreille [ɔʀɛj] *nf* ear; **avoir de l'~** to have a good ear (for music)

oreiller [ɔʀeje] *nm* pillow

oreillons [ɔʀɛjɔ̃] *nmpl* mumps *sg*

ores [ɔʀ]: **d'~ et déjà** *adv* already

orfèvrerie [ɔʀfɛvʀəʀi] *nf* goldsmith's (*ou* silversmith's) trade; (*ouvrage*) (silver *ou* gold) plate

organe [ɔʀgan] *nm* organ; (*porte-parole*) representative, mouthpiece

organigramme [ɔʀganigʀam] *nm* (*hiérarchique, structure*) organization chart; (*des opérations*) flow chart

organique [ɔʀganik] *adj* organic

organisateur, -trice [ɔʀganizatœʀ, -tʀis] *nm/f* organizer

organisation [ɔʀganizasjɔ̃] *nf* organization; **O~ des Nations unies (ONU)** United Nations (Organization) (UN(O))

organiser [ɔʀganize] /1/ *vt* to organize; (*mettre sur pied: service etc*) to set up; **s'organiser** to get organized

organisme [ɔʀganism] *nm* (*Bio*) organism; (*corps humain*) body; (*Admin, Pol etc*) body

organiste [ɔʀganist] *nm/f* organist

orgasme [ɔʀgasm] *nm* orgasm, climax

orge [ɔʀʒ] *nf* barley

orgue [ɔʀg] *nm* organ

orgueil [ɔʀgœj] *nm* pride; **orgueilleux, -euse** *adj* proud

oriental, e, -aux [ɔʀjɑ̃tal, -o] *adj* (*langue, produit*) oriental; (*frontière*) eastern

orientation [ɔʀjɑ̃tasjɔ̃] *nf* (*de recherches*) orientation; (*d'une maison etc*) aspect; (*d'un journal*) leanings *pl*; **avoir le sens de l'~** to have a (good) sense of direction; **~ professionnelle** careers advisory service

orienté, e [ɔʀjɑ̃te] *adj* (*fig: article, journal*) slanted; **bien/mal ~**

(appartement) well/badly positioned; **~ au sud** facing south, with a southern aspect

orienter [ɔʀjɑ̃te] /1/ vt (tourner: antenne) to direct, turn; (: voyageur, touriste, recherches) to direct; (fig: élève) to orientate; **s'orienter** (se repérer) to find one's bearings; **s'~ vers** (fig) to turn towards

origan [ɔʀigɑ̃] nm oregano

originaire [ɔʀiʒinɛʀ] adj: **être ~ de** to be a native of

original, e, -aux [ɔʀiʒinal, -o] adj original; (bizarre) eccentric ▷ nm/f eccentric ▷ nm (document etc, Art) original

origine [ɔʀiʒin] nf origin; **origines** nfpl (d'une personne) origins; **d'~** (pays) of origin; (pneus etc) original; **d'~ française** of French origin; **à l'~** originally; **originel, le** adj original

orme [ɔʀm] nm elm

ornement [ɔʀnəmɑ̃] nm ornament

orner [ɔʀne] /1/ vt to decorate, adorn

ornière [ɔʀnjɛʀ] nf rut

orphelin, e [ɔʀfəlɛ̃, -in] adj orphan(ed) ▷ nm/f orphan; **~ de père/mère** fatherless/motherless; **orphelinat** nm orphanage

orteil [ɔʀtɛj] nm toe; **gros ~** big toe

orthographe [ɔʀtɔgʀaf] nf spelling

ortie [ɔʀti] nf (stinging) nettle

os [ɔs] nm bone; **os à moelle** marrowbone

osciller [ɔsile] /1/ vi (au vent etc) to rock; (fig): **~ entre** to waver ou fluctuate between

osé, e [oze] adj daring, bold

oseille [ozɛj] nf sorrel

oser [oze] /1/ vi, vt to dare; **~ faire** to dare (to) do

osier [ozje] nm willow; **d'~, en ~** wicker(work) cpd

osseux, -euse [ɔsø, -øz] adj bony; (tissu, maladie, greffe) bone cpd

otage [ɔtaʒ] nm hostage; **prendre qn comme ~** to take sb hostage

OTAN sigle f (= Organisation du traité de l'Atlantique Nord) NATO

otarie [ɔtaʀi] nf sea-lion

ôter [ote] /1/ vt to remove; (soustraire) to take away; **~ qch à qn** to take sth (away) from sb; **~ qch de** to remove sth from

otite [ɔtit] nf ear infection

ou [u] conj or; **ou ... ou** either ... or; **ou bien** or (else)

⬤ MOT-CLÉ

où [u] pron relatif **1** (position, situation) where, that (souvent omis); **la chambre où il était** the room (that) he was in, the room where he was; **la ville où je l'ai rencontré** the town where I met him; **la pièce d'où il est sorti** the room he came out of; **le village d'où je viens** the village I come from; **les villes par où il est passé** the towns he was through **2** (temps, état) that (souvent omis); **le jour où il est parti** the day (that) he left; **au prix où c'est** at the price it is ▷ adv **1** (interrogation) where; **où est-il/va-t-il?** where is he/is he going?; **par où?** which way?; **d'où vient que ...?** how come ...?

2 (position) where; **je sais où il est** I know where he is; **où que l'on aille** wherever you go

ouate [wat] nf cotton wool (BRIT), cotton (US)

oubli [ubli] nm (acte): **l'~ de** forgetting; (trou de mémoire) lapse of memory; (négligence) omission, oversight; **tomber dans l'~** to sink into oblivion

oublier [ublije] /7/ vt to forget; (ne pas voir: erreurs etc) to miss; (laisser quelque part: chapeau etc) to leave behind

ouest [wɛst] nm west ▷ adj inv west; (région) western; **à l'~** in the west; (direction) (to the) west, westwards; **à l'~ de** (to the) west of

ouf [uf] *excl* phew!

oui [wi] *adv* yes

ouï-dire ['widiʀ]: **par ~** *adv* by hearsay

ouïe [wi] *nf* hearing; **ouïes** *nfpl* (*de poisson*) gills

ouragan [uʀagɑ̃] *nm* hurricane

ourlet [uʀlɛ] *nm* hem

ours [uʀs] *nm* bear; **~ brun/blanc** brown/polar bear; **~ (en peluche)** teddy (bear)

oursin [uʀsɛ̃] *nm* sea urchin

ourson [uʀsɔ̃] *nm* (bear-)cub

ouste [ust] *excl* hop it!

outil [uti] *nm* tool; **outiller** /1/ *vt* to equip

outrage [utʀaʒ] *nm* insult; **~ à la pudeur** indecent behaviour *no pl*

outrance [utʀɑ̃s]: **à ~** *adv* excessively, to excess

outre [utʀ] *prép* besides ▷ *adv*: **passer ~ à** to disregard, take no notice of; **en ~** besides, moreover; **~ mesure** to excess; (*manger, boire*) immoderately; **outre-Atlantique** *adv* across the Atlantic; **outre-mer** *adv* overseas

ouvert, e [uvɛʀ, -ɛʀt] *pp de* **ouvrir** ▷ *adj* open; (*robinet, gaz etc*) on; **ouvertement** *adv* openly; **ouverture** *nf* opening; (*Mus*) overture; **ouverture d'esprit** open-mindedness; **heures d'ouverture** (*Comm*) opening hours

ouvrable [uvʀabl] *adj*: **jour ~** working day, weekday

ouvrage [uvʀaʒ] *nm* (*tâche, de tricot etc*) work *no pl*; (*texte, livre*) work

ouvre-boîte(s) [uvʀəbwat] *nm inv* tin (BRIT) *ou* can opener

ouvre-bouteille(s) [uvʀəbutɛj] *nm inv* bottle-opener

ouvreuse [uvʀøz] *nf* usherette

ouvrier, -ière [uvʀije, -jɛʀ] *nm/f* worker ▷ *adj* working-class; (*problèmes, conflit*) industrial; (*mouvement*) labour *cpd*; **classe ouvrière** working class

ouvrir [uvʀiʀ] /18/ *vt* (*gén*) to open; (*brèche, passage*) to open up; (*commencer l'exploitation de, créer*) to open (up); (*eau, électricité, chauffage, robinet*) to turn on; (*Méd: abcès*) to open up, cut open ▷ *vi* to open; to open up; **s'ouvrir** *vi* to open; **s'~ à qn (de qch)** to open one's heart to sb (about sth); **~ l'appétit à qn** to whet sb's appetite

ovaire [ɔvɛʀ] *nm* ovary

ovale [ɔval] *adj* oval

OVNI [ɔvni] *sigle m* (= *objet volant non identifié*) UFO

oxyder [ɔkside] /1/: **s'oxyder** *vi* to become oxidized

oxygéné, e [ɔksiʒene] *adj*: **eau ~e** hydrogen peroxide

oxygène [ɔksiʒɛn] *nm* oxygen

ozone [ozon] *nm* ozone; **trou dans la couche d'~** hole in the ozone layer

O

P

mie sandwich loaf; **~ au chocolat** pain au chocolat; **~ aux raisins** currant pastry

pair, e [pɛʀ] *adj (nombre)* even ▷ *nm* peer; **aller de ~ (avec)** to go hand in hand *ou* together (with); **jeune fille au ~** au pair; **paire** *nf* pair

paisible [pezibl] *adj* peaceful, quiet

paix [pɛ] *nf* peace; **faire la ~ avec** to make peace with; **fiche-lui la ~!** *(fam)* leave him alone!

Pakistan [pakistɑ̃] *nm*: **le ~** Pakistan

palais [palɛ] *nm* palace; *(Anat)* palate

pâle [pɑl] *adj* pale; **bleu ~** pale blue

Palestine [palɛstin] *nf*: **la ~** Palestine

palette [palɛt] *nf (de peintre)* palette; *(de produits)* range

pâleur [pɑlœʀ] *nf* paleness

palier [palje] *nm (d'escalier)* landing; *(fig)* level, plateau; **par ~s** in stages

pâlir [pɑliʀ] */2/ vi* to turn *ou* go pale; *(couleur)* to fade

pallier [palje] */7/ vt*: **~ à** to offset, make up for

palme [palm] *nf (de plongeur)* flipper; **palmé, e** [palme] *adj (pattes)* webbed

palmier [palmje] *nm* palm tree; *(gâteau)* heart-shaped biscuit made of flaky pastry

pâlot, te [pɑlo, -ɔt] *adj* pale, peaky

palourde [paluʀd] *nf* clam

palper [palpe] */1/ vt* to feel, finger

palpitant, e [palpitɑ̃, -ɑ̃t] *adj* thrilling

palpiter [palpite] */1/ vi (cœur, pouls)* to beat (: *plus fort*) to pound, throb

paludisme [palydism] *nm* malaria

pamphlet [pɑ̃flɛ] *nm* lampoon, satirical tract

pamplemousse [pɑ̃pləmus] *nm* grapefruit

pan [pɑ̃] *nm* section, piece ▷ *excl* bang!

panache [panaʃ] *nm* plume; *(fig)* spirit, panache

panaché, e [panaʃe] *nm (bière)* shandy; **glace ~e** mixed ice cream

pacifique [pasifik] *adj* peaceful ▷ *nm*: **le P~, l'océan P~** the Pacific (Ocean)

pack [pak] *nm* pack

pacotille [pakɔtij] *nf* cheap junk *pl*

PACS *sigle m* (= *pacte civil de solidarité*) ≈ civil partnership; **pacser** /1/: **se pacser** *vi* ≈ to form a civil partnership

pacte [pakt] *nm* pact, treaty

pagaille [pagaj] *nf* mess, shambles *sg*

page [paʒ] *nf* page ▷ *nm* page (boy); **à la ~** *(fig)* up-to-date; **~ d'accueil** *(Inform)* home page; **~ Web** *(Inform)* web page

païen, ne [pajɛ̃, -ɛn] *adj, nm/f* pagan, heathen

paillasson [pajasɔ̃] *nm* doormat

paille [pɑj] *nf* straw

pain [pɛ̃] *nm (substance)* bread; *(unité)* loaf (of bread); *(morceau)*: **~ de cire** *etc* bar of wax *etc*; **~ bis/ complet** brown/wholemeal *(BRIT)* *ou* wholewheat *(US)* bread; **~ d'épice** ≈ gingerbread; **~ grillé** toast; **~ de**

pancarte [pɑ̃kaʀt] nf sign, notice

pancréas [pɑ̃kʀeɑs] nm pancreas

pandémie [pɑ̃demi] nf pandemic

pané, e [pane] adj fried in breadcrumbs

panier [panje] nm basket; **mettre au ~** to chuck away; **~ à provisions** shopping basket; **panier-repas** nm packed lunch

panique [panik] adj panicky ▷ nf panic; **paniquer** /1/ vi to panic

panne [pan] nf breakdown; **être/ tomber en ~** to have broken down/ break down; **être en ~ d'essence** ou **en ~ sèche** to have run out of petrol (BRIT) ou gas (US); **~ d'électricité** ou **de courant** power ou electrical failure

panneau, x [pano] nm (écriteau) sign, notice; **~ d'affichage** notice (BRIT) ou bulletin (US) board; **~ indicateur** signpost; **~ de signalisation** roadsign

panoplie [panɔpli] nf (jouet) outfit; (d'armes) display; (fig) array

panorama [panɔʀama] nm panorama

panse [pɑ̃s] nf paunch

pansement [pɑ̃smɑ̃] nm dressing, bandage; **~ adhésif** sticking plaster

pantacourt [pɑ̃takuʀ] nm cropped trousers pl

pantalon [pɑ̃talɔ̃] nm trousers pl (BRIT), pants pl (US), pair of trousers ou pants; **~ de ski** ski pants pl

panthère [pɑ̃tɛʀ] nf panther

pantin [pɑ̃tɛ̃] nm puppet

pantoufle [pɑ̃tufl] nf slipper

paon [pɑ̃] nm peacock

papa [papa] nm dad(dy)

pape [pap] nm pope

paperasse [papʀas] nf (péj) bumf no pl, papers pl; **paperasserie** nf (péj) red tape no pl; paperwork no pl

papeterie [papɛtʀi] nf (magasin) stationer's (shop) (BRIT)

papi [papi] nm (fam) granddad

papier [papje] nm paper; (article) article; **papiers** nmpl (aussi: **~s**)

d'identité) (identity) papers; **~ (d') aluminium** aluminium (BRIT) ou aluminum (US) foil, tinfoil; **~ calque** tracing paper; **~ hygiénique** ou **(de) toilette** toilet paper; **~ journal** newspaper; **~ à lettres** writing paper, notepaper; **~ peint** wallpaper; **~ de verre** sandpaper

papillon [papijɔ̃] nm butterfly; (fam: contravention) (parking) ticket; **~ de nuit** moth

papillote [papijɔt] nf: **en ~** cooked in tinfoil

papoter [papɔte] /1/ vi to chatter

paquebot [pakbo] nm liner

pâquerette [pakʀɛt] nf daisy

Pâques [pɑk] nm, nfpl Easter

- **PÂQUES**
-
-
- In France, Easter eggs are said to
- be brought by the Easter bells or
- cloches de Pâques which fly from
- Rome and drop them in people's
- gardens.

paquet [pakɛ] nm packet; (colis) parcel; (fig: tas): **~ de** pile ou heap of; **paquet-cadeau** nm gift-wrapped parcel

par [paʀ] prép by; **finir** etc **~** to end etc with; **~ amour** out of love; **passer ~** Lyon/la côte to go via ou through Lyons/along by the coast; **~ la fenêtre** (jeter, regarder) out of the window; **trois ~ jour/personne** three a ou per day/head; **deux ~ deux** in twos; **~ ici** this way; (dans le coin) round here; **~-ci, ~-là** here and there; **~ temps de pluie** in wet weather

parabolique [paʀabɔlik] adj: **antenne ~** satellite dish

parachute [paʀaʃyt] nm parachute; **parachutiste** [paʀaʃytist] nm/f parachutist; (Mil) paratrooper

parade [paʀad] nf (spectacle, défilé) parade; (Escrime, Boxe) parry

paradis [paʀadi] nm heaven, paradise

paradoxe [paʀadɔks] nm paradox

paraffine [paʀafin] nf paraffin

parages [paʀaʒ] nmpl: **dans les ~ (de)** in the area ou vicinity (of)

paragraphe [paʀagʀaf] nm paragraph

paraître [paʀɛtʀ] /57/ vb copule to seem, look, appear ▷ vi to appear; (être visible) to show; (Presse, Édition) to be published, come out, appear ▷ vb impers: **il paraît que** it seems ou appears that

parallèle [paʀalɛl] adj parallel; (police, marché) unofficial ▷ nm (comparaison): **faire un ~ entre** to draw a parallel between ▷ nf parallel (line)

paralyser [paʀalize] /1/ vt to paralyze

paramédical, e, -aux [paʀamedikal, -o] adj: **personnel ~** paramedics pl, paramedical workers pl

paraphrase [paʀafʀaz] nf paraphrase

parapluie [paʀaplɥi] nm umbrella

parasite [paʀazit] nm parasite; **parasites** nmpl (Tél) interference sg

parasol [paʀasɔl] nm parasol, sunshade

paratonnerre [paʀatɔnɛʀ] nm lightning conductor

parc [paʀk] nm (public) park, gardens pl; (de château etc) grounds pl; (d'enfant) playpen; **~ d'attractions** amusement park; **~ éolien** wind farm; **~ de stationnement** car park; **~ à thème** theme park

parcelle [paʀsɛl] nf fragment, scrap; (de terrain) plot, parcel

parce que [paʀsk] conj because

parchemin [paʀʃəmɛ̃] nm parchment

parc(o)mètre [paʀk(ɔ)mɛtʀ] nm parking meter

parcourir [paʀkuʀiʀ] /11/ vt (trajet, distance) to cover; (article, livre) to skim ou glance through; (lieu) to go all over, travel up and down; (frisson, vibration) to run through

parcours [paʀkuʀ] nm (trajet) journey; (itinéraire) route

par-dessous [paʀdəsu] prép, adv under(neath)

pardessus [paʀdəsy] nm overcoat

par-dessus [paʀdəsy] prép over (the top of) ▷ adv over (the top); **~ le marché** on top of it all; **~ tout** above all; **en avoir ~ la tête** to have had enough

par-devant [paʀdəvɑ̃] adv (passer) round the front

pardon [paʀdɔ̃] nm forgiveness no pl ▷ excl (I'm) sorry; (pour interpeller etc) excuse me; **demander ~ à qn (de)** to apologize to sb (for); **je vous demande ~** I'm sorry; (pour interpeller) excuse me; **pardonner** /1/ vt to forgive; **pardonner qch à qn** to forgive sb for sth

pare: pare-brise nm inv windscreen (BRIT), windshield (US); **pare-chocs** nm inv bumper ; **pare-feu** nm inv (de foyer) fireguard; (Inform) firewall ▷ adj inv

pareil, le [paʀɛj] adj (identique) the same, alike; (similaire) similar; (tel): **un courage/livre ~** such courage/a book, courage/a book like this; **de ~s livres** such books; **faire ~** to do the same (thing); **~ à** the same as; similar to; **sans ~** unparalleled, unequalled

parent, e [paʀɑ̃, -ɑ̃t] nm/f: **un/une ~/e** a relative ou relation; **parents** nmpl (père et mère) parents; **parenté** nf (lien) relationship

parenthèse [paʀɑ̃tɛz] nf (ponctuation) bracket, parenthesis; (digression) parenthesis, digression; **entre ~s** in brackets; (fig) incidentally

paresse [paʀɛs] nf laziness; **paresseux, -euse** adj lazy

parfait, e [paʀfɛ, -ɛt] adj perfect ▷ nm (Ling) perfect (tense); **parfaitement** adv perfectly ▷ excl (most) certainly

parfois [paʀfwa] *adv* sometimes
parfum [paʀfœ̃] *nm* (*produit*) perfume, scent; (*odeur: de fleur*) scent, fragrance; (*goût*) flavour ; **parfumé, e** *adj* (*fleur, fruit*) fragrant; (*femme*) perfumed; **parfumé au café** coffee-flavoured (BRIT) ou -flavored (US); **parfumer** /1/ *vt* (*odeur, bouquet*) to perfume; (*crème, gâteau*) to flavour ; **parfumerie** *nf* (*produits*) perfumes; (*boutique*) perfume shop (BRIT) ou store (US)
pari [paʀi] *nm* bet; **parier** /7/ *vt* to bet
Paris [paʀi] *n* Paris; **parisien, ne** *adj* Parisian; (*Géo, Admin*) Paris *cpd* ▷ *nm/f*: **Parisien, ne** Parisian
parité [paʀite] *nf*: **~ hommes-femmes** (*Pol*) balanced representation of men and women
parjure [paʀʒyʀ] *nm* perjury
parking [paʀkiŋ] *nm* (*lieu*) car park (BRIT), parking lot (US)

> Attention à ne pas traduire *parking* par le mot anglais *parking*.

parlant, e [paʀlɑ̃, -ɑ̃t] *adj* (*comparaison, preuve*) eloquent; (*Ciné*) talking
parlement [paʀləmɑ̃] *nm* parliament; **parlementaire** *adj* parliamentary ▷ *nm/f* ≈ Member of Parliament (BRIT) ou Congress (US)
parler [paʀle] /1/ *vi* to speak, talk; (*avouer*) to talk; **~ (à qn) de** to talk ou speak (to sb) about; **~ le/en français** to speak French/in French; **~ affaires** to talk business; **sans ~ de** (*fig*) not to mention, to say nothing of; **tu parles!** (*bien sûr*) you bet!
parloir [paʀlwaʀ] *nm* (*d'une prison, d'un hôpital*) visiting room
parmi [paʀmi] *prép* among(st)
paroi [paʀwa] *nf* wall; (*cloison*) partition
paroisse [paʀwas] *nf* parish
parole [paʀɔl] *nf* (*mot, promesse*) word; (*faculté*): **la ~** speech; **paroles** *nfpl* (*Mus*) words, lyrics; **tenir ~** to

keep one's word; **prendre la ~** to speak; **demander la ~** to ask for permission to speak; **je le crois sur ~** I'll take his word for it
parquet [paʀkɛ] *nm* (*parquet*) floor; (*Jur*) public prosecutor's office; **le ~ (général)** ≈ the Bench
parrain [paʀɛ̃] *nm* godfather; **parrainer** /1/ *vt* (*nouvel adhérent*) to sponsor
pars [paʀ] *vb voir* **partir**
parsemer [paʀsəme] /5/ *vt* (*feuilles, papiers*) to be scattered over; **~ qch de** to scatter sth with
part [paʀ] *nf* (*qui revient à qn*) share; (*fraction, partie*) part; **prendre ~ à** (*débat etc*) to take part in; (*soucis, douleur de qn*) to share in; **faire ~ de qch à qn** to announce sth to sb, inform sb of sth; **pour ma ~** as for me, as far as I'm concerned; **à ~ entière** full; **de la ~ de** (*au nom de*) on behalf of; (*donné par*) from; **de toute(s) ~(s)** from all sides ou quarters; **de ~ et d'autre** on both sides, on either side; **d'une ~ ... d'autre ~** on the one hand ... on the other hand; **d'autre ~** (*de plus*) moreover; **à ~** *adv* separately; (*de côté*) aside; *prép* apart from, except for; **faire la ~ des choses** to make allowances
partage [paʀtaʒ] *nm* sharing (out) *no pl*, share-out; dividing up
partager [paʀtaʒe] /3/ *vt* to share; (*distribuer, répartir*) to share (out); (*morceler, diviser*) to divide (up); **se partager** *vt* (*héritage etc*) to share between themselves (*ou ourselves etc*)
partenaire [paʀtənɛʀ] *nm/f* partner
parterre [paʀtɛʀ] *nm* (*de fleurs*) (flower) bed; (*Théât*) stalls *pl*
parti [paʀti] *nm* (*Pol*) party; (*décision*) course of action; (*personne à marier*) match; **tirer ~ de** to take advantage of, turn to good account; **prendre ~ (pour/contre)** to take sides ou a stand (for/against); **~ pris** bias

partial, e, -aux [paʀsjal, -o] adj
biased, partial

participant, e [paʀtisipɑ̃, -ɑ̃t] nm/f
participant; (à un concours) entrant

participation [paʀtisipasjɔ̃]
nf participation; (financière)
contribution

participer [paʀtisipe] /1/: ~ **à** vt
(course, réunion) to take part in; (frais
etc) to contribute to; (chagrin, succès
de qn) to share (in)

particularité [paʀtikylaʀite] nf
(distinctive) characteristic

particulier, -ière [paʀtikylje, -jɛʀ]
adj (personnel, privé) private; (étrange)
peculiar, odd; (spécial) special,
particular; (spécifique) particular ▷ nm
(individu: Admin) private individual;
~ **à** peculiar to; **en** ~ (surtout) in
particular, particularly; (en privé)
in private; **particulièrement** adv
particularly

partie [paʀti] nf (gén) part; (Jur etc:
protagonistes) party; (de cartes, tennis
etc) game; **une** ~ **de campagne/de
pêche** an outing in the country/a
fishing party ou trip; **en** ~ partly, in
part; **faire** ~ **de** (chose) to be part of;
prendre qn à ~ to take sb to task;
en grande ~ largely, in the main;
~ **civile** (Jur) party claiming damages in
a criminal case

partiel, le [paʀsjɛl] adj partial ▷ nm
(Scol) class exam

partir [paʀtiʀ] /16/ vi (gén) to go;
(quitter) to go, leave; (tache) to go,
come out; ~ **de** (lieu) (quitter) to leave;
(commencer à) to start from; ~ **pour/à**
(lieu, pays etc) to leave for/go off to;
à ~ **de** from

partisan, e [paʀtizɑ̃, -an] nm/f
partisan; **être** ~ **de qch/faire** to
be in favour (BRIT) ou favor (US) of
sth/doing

partition [paʀtisjɔ̃] nf (Mus) score

partout [paʀtu] adv everywhere;
~ **où il allait** everywhere ou wherever
he went

paru [paʀy] pp de **paraître**

parution [paʀysjɔ̃] nf publication

parvenir [paʀvəniʀ] /22/: ~ **à** vt
(atteindre) to reach; (réussir): ~ **à faire**
to manage to do, succeed in doing;
faire ~ **qch à qn** to have sth sent to sb

○ **MOT-CLÉ**

pas¹ [pɑ] adv **1** (en corrélation avec
ne, non etc) not; **il ne pleure pas**
(habituellement) he does not ou
doesn't cry; (maintenant) he's not ou
isn't crying; **il n'a pas pleuré/ne
pleurera pas** he did not ou didn't/
will not ou won't cry; **ils n'ont pas de
voiture/d'enfants** they haven't got
a car/any children; **il m'a dit de ne
pas le faire** he told me not to do it;
non pas que ... not that ..
2 (employé sans ne etc): **pas moi**
not me, I don't (ou can't etc); **elle
travaille, (mais) lui pas** ou **pas lui**
she works but he doesn't ou does
not; **une pomme pas mûre** an
apple which isn't ripe; **pas du tout**
not at all; **pas de sucre, merci** no
sugar, thanks; **ceci est à vous ou
pas?** is this yours or not?, is this yours
or isn't it?
3: **pas mal** (joli: personne, maison) not
bad; **pas mal fait** not badly done ou
made; **comment ça va? — pas mal**
how are things? — not bad; **pas mal
de** quite a lot of

pas² [pɑ] nm (enjambée, Danse) step;
(bruit) (foot)step; (trace) footprint;
(allure, mesure) pace; ~ **à** ~ step
by step; **au** ~ at a walking pace;
marcher à grands ~ to stride along;
à ~ **de loup** stealthily; **faire les cent**
~ to pace up and down; **faire les
premiers** ~ to make the first move;
sur le ~ **de la porte** on the doorstep

passage [pɑsaʒ] nm (fait de passer);
voir **passer**; (lieu, prix de la traversée,
extrait de livre etc) passage; (chemin)

way; **de ~** (touristes) passing through; **~ clouté** pedestrian crossing; **"~ interdit"** "no entry"; **~ à niveau** level (BRIT) ou grade (US) crossing; **~ souterrain** subway (BRIT), underpass

passager, -ère [pasaʒe, -ɛʁ] adj passing ▷ nm/f passenger

passant, e [pasɑ̃, -ɑ̃t] adj (rue, endroit) busy ▷ nm/f passer-by; **remarquer qch en ~** to notice sth in passing

passe [pas] nf (Sport) pass; (Navig) channel; **être en ~ de faire** to be on the way to doing; **être dans une mauvaise ~** to be going through a bad patch

passé, e [pase] adj (événement, temps) past; (dernier: semaine etc) last; (couleur, tapisserie) faded ▷ prép after ▷ nm past; (Ling) past (tense); **~ de mode** out of fashion; **~ composé** perfect (tense); **~ simple** past historic

passe-partout [paspaʁtu] nm inv master ou skeleton key ▷ adj inv all-purpose

passeport [paspɔʁ] nm passport

passer [pase] /1/ vi (se rendre, aller) to go; (voiture, piétons: défiler) to pass (by), go by; (facteur, laitier etc) to come, call; (pour rendre visite) to call ou drop in; (film, émission) to be on; (temps, jours) to pass, go by; (couleur, papier) to fade; (mode) to die out; (douleur) to pass, go away; (Scol): **~ dans la classe supérieure** to go up (to the next class) ▷ vt (frontière, rivière etc) to cross; (douane) to go through; (examen) to sit, take; (visite médicale etc) to have; (journée, temps) to spend; **~ qch à qn** (sel etc) to pass sth to sb; (prêter) to lend sb sth; (lettre, message) to pass sth on to sb; (tolérer) to let sb get away with sth; (enfiler: vêtement) to slip on; (film, pièce) to show, put on; (disque) to play, put on; (commande) to place; (marché,

accord) to agree on; **se passer** vi (avoir lieu: scène, action) to take place; (se dérouler: entretien etc) to go; (arriver) **que s'est-il passé?** what happened?; (s'écouler: semaine etc) to pass, go by; **se ~ de** to go ou do without; **se ~ par** to go through; **~ avant qch/qn** (fig) to come before sth/sb; **~ un coup de fil à qn** (fam) to give sb a ring; **laisser ~** (air, lumière, personne) to let through; (occasion) to let slip, miss; (erreur) to overlook; **~ à la radio/télévision** to be on the radio/on television; **~ à table** to sit down to eat; **~ au salon** to go through to ou into the sitting room; **~ son tour** to miss one's turn; **~ la seconde** (Auto) to change into second; **~ le balai/l'aspirateur** to sweep up/hoover; **je vous passe M. Dupont** (je vous mets en communication avec lui) I'm putting you through to Mr Dupont; (je lui passe l'appareil) here is Mr Dupont, I'll hand you over to Mr Dupont

passerelle [pasʁɛl] nf footbridge; (de navire, avion) gangway

passe-temps [pastɑ̃] nm inv pastime

passif, -ive [pasif, -iv] adj passive

passion [pasjɔ̃] nf passion; **passionnant, e** adj fascinating; **passionné, e** adj (personne, tempérament) passionate; (description, récit) impassioned; **être passionné de** ou **pour qch** to have a passion for sth; **passionner** /1/ vt (personne) to fascinate, grip

passoire [paswaʁ] nf sieve; (à légumes) colander; (à thé) strainer

pastèque [pastɛk] nf watermelon

pasteur [pastœʁ] nm (protestant) minister, pastor

pastille [pastij] nf (à sucer) lozenge, pastille

patate [patat] nf spud; **~ douce** sweet potato

patauger [patoʒe] /3/ vi to splash about

p

pâte [pɑt] nf (à tarte) pastry; (à pain)
dough; (à frire) batter; **pâtes** nfpl
(macaroni etc) pasta sg; **~ d'amandes**
almond paste, marzipan; **~ brisée**
shortcrust (BRIT) ou pie crust (US)
pastry; **~ à choux/feuilletée** choux/
puff ou flaky (BRIT) pastry; **~ de
fruits** crystallized fruit no pl; **~ à
modeler** modelling clay, Plasticine®
(BRIT)
pâté [pate] nm (charcuterie) pâté;
(tache) ink blot; (de sable) sandpie;
~ (en croûte) ≈ meat pie; **~ de
maisons** block of houses)
pâtée [pate] nf mash, feed
patente [patɑ̃t] nf (Comm) trading
licence (BRIT) ou license (US)
paternel, le [patɛʀnɛl] adj (amour,
soins) fatherly; (ligne, autorité)
paternal
pâteux, -euse [patø, -øz] adj pasty;
avoir la bouche ou **langue pâteuse**
to have a furred (BRIT) ou coated
tongue
pathétique [patetik] adj moving
patience [pasjɑ̃s] nf patience
patient, e [pasjɑ̃, -ɑ̃t] adj, nm/f
patient; **patienter** /1/ vi to wait
patin [patɛ̃] nm skate; (sport) skating;
~s (à glace) (ice) skates; **~s à
roulettes** roller skates
patinage [patinaʒ] nm skating
patiner [patine] /1/ vi to skate; (roue,
voiture) to spin; **se patiner** vi (meuble,
cuir) to acquire a sheen; **patineur,
-euse** nm/f skater; **patinoire** nf
skating rink, (ice) rink
pâtir [patiʀ] /2/: **~ de** vt to suffer
because of
pâtisserie [patisʀi] nf (boutique)
cake shop; (à la maison) pastry- ou
cake-making, baking; **pâtisseries**
nfpl (gâteaux) pastries, cakes;
pâtissier, -ière nm/f pastrycook
patois [patwa] nm dialect, patois
patrie [patʀi] nf homeland
patrimoine [patʀimwan] nm
(culture) heritage

patriotique [patʀijɔtik] adj
patriotic
patron, ne [patʀɔ̃, -ɔn] nm/f boss;
(Rel) patron saint ▷ nm (Couture)
pattern; **patronat** nm employers pl;
patronner /1/ vt to sponsor, support
patrouille [patʀuj] nf patrol
patte [pat] nf (jambe) leg; (pied: de
chien, chat) paw; (: d'oiseau) foot
pâturage [patyʀaʒ] nm pasture
paume [pom] nf palm
paumé, e [pome] nm/f (fam)
drop-out
paupière [popjɛʀ] nf eyelid
pause [poz] nf (arrêt) break; (en
parlant, Mus) pause; **~ de midi** lunch
break
pauvre [povʀ] adj poor; **les ~s** the
poor; **pauvreté** nf (état) poverty
pavé, e [pave] adj (cour) paved; (rue)
cobbled ▷ nm (bloc) paving stone;
cobblestone; **~ numérique** keypad
pavillon [pavijɔ̃] nm (de banlieue)
small (detached) house; pavilion;
(Navig) flag
payant, e [pɛjɑ̃, -ɑ̃t] adj (spectateurs
etc) paying; (fig: entreprise) profitable;
(effort) which pays off; **c'est ~** you
have to pay, there is a charge
paye [pɛj] nf pay, wages pl
payer [peje] /8/ vt (créancier, employé,
loyer) to pay; (achat, réparations, faute)
to pay for ▷ vi to pay; (métier) to be
well-paid; (effort, tactique etc) to
pay off; **il me l'a fait ~ 10 euros** he
charged me 10 euros for it; **~ qch à
qn** to buy sth for sb, buy sb sth; **se ~
la tête de qn** to take the mickey out
of sb (BRIT)

pays [pei] *nm* country; (*région*) region; **du ~** local

paysage [peizaʒ] *nm* landscape

paysan, ne [peizɑ̃, -an] *nm/f* farmer; (*péj*) peasant ▷ *adj* (*rural*) country *cpd*; (*agricole*) farming

Pays-Bas [peiba] *nmpl:* **les ~** the Netherlands

PC *sigle m* (*Inform:* = *personal computer*) PC; = **permis de construire**; (= *prêt conventionné*) *type of loan for house purchase*

PDA *sigle m* (= *personal digital assistant*) PDA

PDG *sigle m* = **président directeur général**

péage [peaʒ] *nm* toll; (*endroit*) tollgate

peau, x [po] *nf* skin; **gants de ~** leather gloves; **être bien/mal dans sa ~** to be at ease/ill-at-ease; **~ de chamois** (*chiffon*) chamois leather, shammy

péché [peʃe] *nm* sin

pêche [pɛʃ] *nf* (*sport, activité*) fishing; (*poissons pêchés*) catch; (*fruit*) peach; **~ à la ligne** (*en rivière*) angling

pécher [peʃe] /6/ *vi* (*Rel*) to sin

pêcher [peʃe] /1/ *vi* to go fishing ▷ *vt* (*attraper*) to catch; (*chercher*) to fish for ▷ *nm* peach tree

pécheur, -eresse [peʃœʀ, peʃʀɛs] *nm/f* sinner

pêcheur [peʃœʀ] *nm voir* **pêcher** fisherman; (*à la ligne*) angler

pédagogie [pedagoʒi] *nf* educational methods *pl*, pedagogy; **pédagogique** *adj* educational

pédale [pedal] *nf* pedal

pédalo [pedalo] *nm* pedal-boat

pédant, e [pedɑ̃, -ɑ̃t] *adj* (*péj*) pedantic ▷ *nm/f* pedant

pédestre [pedɛstʀ] *adj:* **randonnée ~** ramble; **sentier ~** pedestrian footpath

pédiatre [pedjatʀ] *nm/f* paediatrician , child specialist

pédicure [pedikyʀ] *nm/f* chiropodist

pègre [pɛgʀ] *nf* underworld

peigne [pɛɲ] *nm* comb; **peigner** /1/ *vt* to comb (the hair of); **se peigner** *vi* to comb one's hair; **peignoir** *nm* dressing gown; **peignoir de bain** bathrobe

peindre [pɛ̃dʀ] /52/ *vt* to paint; (*fig*) to portray, depict

peine [pɛn] *nf* (*affliction*) sorrow, sadness *no pl*; (*mal, effort*) trouble *no pl*, effort; (*difficulté*) difficulty; (*Jur*) sentence; **faire de la ~ à qn** to distress *ou* upset sb; **prendre la ~ de faire** to go to the trouble of doing; **se donner de la ~** to make an effort; **ce n'est pas la ~ de faire** there's no point in doing, it's not worth doing; **avoir de la ~** to be sad; **à ~** scarcely, barely; **à ~ ... que** hardly ... than, no sooner ... than; **~ capitale** capital punishment; **~ de mort** death sentence *ou* penalty; **peiner** [pene] /1/ *vi* to work hard; to struggle; (*moteur, voiture*) to labour (BRIT), labor (US) ▷ *vt* to grieve, sadden

peintre [pɛ̃tʀ] *nm* painter; **~ en bâtiment** painter and decorator

peinture [pɛ̃tyʀ] *nf* painting; (*couche de couleur, couleur*) paint; (*surfaces peintes: aussi:* **~s**) paintwork; **"~ fraîche"** "wet paint"

péjoratif, -ive [peʒɔʀatif, -iv] *adj* pejorative, derogatory

Pékin [pekɛ̃] *n* Beijing

pêle-mêle [pɛlmɛl] *adv* higgledy-piggledy

peler [pəle] /5/ *vt, vi* to peel

pèlerin [pɛlʀɛ̃] *nm* pilgrim

pèlerinage [pɛlʀinaʒ] *nm* pilgrimage

pelle [pɛl] *nf* shovel; (*d'enfant, de terrassier*) spade

pellicule [pelikyl] *nf* film; **pellicules** *nfpl* (*Méd*) dandruff *sg*

pelote [pəlɔt] *nf* (*de fil, laine*) ball; **~ basque** pelota

peloton [pəlɔtɔ̃] *nm* group; squad; (*Sport*) pack

pelotonner [pəlɔtɔne] /1/: **se pelotonner** *vi* to curl (o.s.) up

P

pelouse [pəluz] nf lawn

peluche [pəlyʃ] nf: **animal en ~** soft toy, fluffy animal; **chien/lapin en ~** fluffy dog/rabbit

pelure [pəlyʀ] nf peeling, peel no pl

pénal, e, -aux [penal, -o] adj penal; **pénalité** nf penalty

penchant [pɑ̃ʃɑ̃] nm: **un ~ à faire/à qch** a tendency to do/to sth; **un ~ pour qch** a liking ou fondness for sth

pencher [pɑ̃ʃe] /1/ vi to tilt, lean over ▷ vt to tilt; **se pencher** vi to lean over; (se baisser) to bend down; **se ~ sur** (fig: problème) to look into; **~ pour** to be inclined to favour (BRIT) ou favor (US)

pendant, e [pɑ̃dɑ̃, -ɑ̃t] adj hanging (out) ▷ prép (au cours de) during; (indiquant la durée) for; **~ que** while

pendentif [pɑ̃dɑ̃tif] nm pendant

penderie [pɑ̃dʀi] nf wardrobe

pendre [pɑ̃dʀ] /41/ vt, vi to hang; **se ~ (à)** (se suicider) to hang o.s. (on); **~ qch à** (mur) to hang sth (up) on; (plafond) to hang sth (up) from

pendule [pɑ̃dyl] nf clock ▷ nm pendulum

pénétrer [penetʀe] /6/ vi to come ou get in ▷ vt to penetrate; **~ dans** to enter

pénible [penibl] adj (astreignant) hard; (affligeant) painful; (personne, caractère) tiresome; **péniblement** adv with difficulty

péniche [peniʃ] nf barge

pénicilline [penisilin] nf penicillin

péninsule [penɛ̃syl] nf peninsula

pénis [penis] nm penis

pénitence [penitɑ̃s] nf (repentir) penitence; (peine) penance; **pénitencier** nm penitentiary (US)

pénombre [penɔ̃bʀ] nf (faible clarté) half-light; (obscurité) darkness

pensée [pɑ̃se] nf thought; (démarche, doctrine) thinking no pl; (Bot) pansy; **en ~** in one's mind

penser [pɑ̃se] /1/ vi to think ▷ vt to think; **~ à** (prévoir) to think of; (ami, vacances) to think of ou about; **~ faire qch** to be thinking of doing sth, intend to do sth; **faire ~ à** to remind one of; **pensif, -ive** adj pensive, thoughtful

pension [pɑ̃sjɔ̃] nf (allocation) pension; (prix du logement) board and lodging, bed and board; (école) boarding school; **~ alimentaire** (de divorcée) maintenance allowance; alimony; **~ complète** full board; **~ de famille** boarding house, guesthouse; **pensionnaire** nm/f (Scol) boarder; **pensionnat** nm boarding school

pente [pɑ̃t] nf slope; **en ~** sloping

Pentecôte [pɑ̃tkot] nf: **la ~** Whitsun (BRIT), Pentecost

pénurie [penyʀi] nf shortage

pépé [pepe] nm (fam) grandad

pépin [pepɛ̃] nm (Bot: graine) pip; (fam: ennui) snag, hitch

pépinière [pepinjɛʀ] nf nursery

perçant, e [pɛʀsɑ̃, -ɑ̃t] adj (vue, regard, yeux) sharp; (cri, voix) piercing, shrill

perce-neige [pɛʀsənɛʒ] nm ou f inv snowdrop

percepteur, -trice [pɛʀsɛptœʀ, -tʀis] nm/f tax collector

perception [pɛʀsɛpsjɔ̃] nf perception; (bureau) tax (collector's) office

percer [pɛʀse] /3/ vt to pierce; (ouverture etc) to make; (mystère, énigme) to penetrate ▷ vi to break through; **perceuse** nf drill

percevoir [pɛʀsəvwaʀ] /28/ vt (distinguer) to perceive, detect; (taxe, impôt) to collect; (revenu, indemnité) to receive

perche [pɛʀʃ] nf (bâton) pole

percher [pɛʀʃe] /1/ vt to perch; **se percher** vi to perch; **perchoir** nm perch

perçois etc [pɛʀswa] vb voir **percevoir**

perçu, e [pɛʀsy] pp de **percevoir**

percussion [pɛʀkysjɔ̃] nf percussion

percuter [pɛrkyte] /1/ vt to strike; (véhicule) to crash into

perdant, e [pɛrdã, -ãt] nm/f loser

perdre [pɛrdʀ] /41/ vt to lose; (gaspiller: temps, argent) to waste; (personne: moralement etc) to ruin ▷ vi to lose; (sur une vente etc) to lose out; **se perdre** vi (s'égarer) to get lost, lose one's way; (se gâter) to go to waste; **je me suis perdu** (et je le suis encore) I'm lost; (et je ne le suis plus) I got lost

perdrix [pɛrdʀi] nf partridge

perdu, e [pɛrdy] pp de **perdre** ▷ adj (isolé) out-of-the-way; (Comm: emballage) non-returnable; (malade): **il est ~** there's no hope left for him; **à vos moments ~s** in your spare time

père [pɛr] nm father; **~ de famille** father; **le ~ Noël** Father Christmas

perfection [pɛrfɛksjɔ̃] nf perfection; **à la ~** to perfection; **perfectionné, e** adj sophisticated; **perfectionner** /1/ vt to improve, perfect; **se perfectionner en anglais** to improve one's English

perforer [pɛrfɔre] /1/ vt (ticket, bande, carte) to punch

performant, e [pɛrfɔrmã, -ãt] adj: **très ~** high-performance cpd

perfusion [pɛrfyzjɔ̃] nf: **faire une ~ à qn** to put sb on a drip

péril [peril] nm peril

périmé, e [perime] adj (Admin) out-of-date, expired

périmètre [perimɛtʀ] nm perimeter

période [perjɔd] nf period; **périodique** adj periodic ▷ nm periodical; **garniture** ou **serviette périodique** sanitary towel (BRIT) ou napkin (US)

périphérique [periferik] adj (quartiers) outlying ▷ nm (Auto): **(boulevard) ~** ring road (BRIT), beltway (US)

périr [perir] /2/ vi to die, perish

périssable [perisabl] adj perishable

perle [pɛrl] nf pearl; (de plastique, métal, sueur) bead

permanence [pɛrmanãs] nf permanence; (local) (duty) office; **assurer une ~** (service public, bureaux) to operate ou maintain a basic service; **être de ~** to be on call ou duty; **en ~** continuously

permanent, e [pɛrmanã, -ãt] adj permanent; (spectacle) continuous ▷ nf perm

perméable [pɛrmeabl] adj (terrain) permeable; **~ à** (fig) receptive ou open to

permettre [pɛrmɛtʀ] /56/ vt to allow, permit; **~ à qn de faire/qch** to allow sb to do/sth; **se ~ de faire qch** to take the liberty of doing sth

permis [pɛrmi] nm permit, licence; **~ (de conduire)** (driving) licence (BRIT), (driver's) license (US); **~ construire** planning permission (BRIT), building permit (US); **~ de séjour** residence permit; **~ de travail** work permit

permission [pɛrmisjɔ̃] nf permission; (Mil) leave; **en ~** on leave; **avoir la ~ de faire** to have permission to do

Pérou [peru] nm: **le ~** Peru

perpétuel, le [pɛrpetɥɛl] adj perpetual; **perpétuité** nf: **à perpétuité** for life; **être condamné à perpétuité** to be sentenced to life imprisonment

perplexe [pɛrplɛks] adj perplexed, puzzled

perquisitionner [pɛrkizisjɔne] /1/ vi to carry out a search

perron [perɔ̃] nm steps pl (in front of mansion etc)

perroquet [perɔkɛ] nm parrot

perruche [peryʃ] nf budgerigar (BRIT), budgie (BRIT), parakeet (US)

perruque [peryk] nf wig

persécuter [pɛrsekyte] /1/ vt to persecute

persévérer [pɛrsevere] /6/ vi to persevere

persil [pɛrsi] nm parsley

P

Persique [pɛRsik] *adj*: **le golfe ~** the (Persian) Gulf

persistant, e [pɛRsistɑ̃, -ɑ̃t] *adj* persistent

persister [pɛRsiste] /1/ *vi* to persist; **~ à faire qch** to persist in doing sth

personnage [pɛRsɔnaʒ] *nm* (*notable*) personality; (*individu*) character, individual; (*de roman, film*) character; (*Peinture*) figure

personnalité [pɛRsɔnalite] *nf* personality; (*personnage*) prominent figure

personne [pɛRsɔn] *nf* person ▷ *pron* nobody, no one; (*avec négation en anglais*) anybody, anyone; **~ âgée** elderly person; **personnel, le** *adj* personal; (*égoïste*) selfish ▷ *nm* personnel; **personnellement** *adv* personally

perspective [pɛRspɛktiv] *nf* (*Art*) perspective; (*vue, coup d'œil*) view; (*point de vue*) viewpoint, angle; (*chose escomptée, envisagée*) prospect; **en ~** in prospect

perspicace [pɛRspikas] *adj* clear-sighted, gifted with (*ou* showing) insight; **perspicacité** *nf* insight

persuader [pɛRsɥade] /1/ *vt*: **~ qn (de/de faire)** to persuade sb (of/to do); **persuasif, -ive** *adj* persuasive

perte [pɛRt] *nf* loss; (*de temps*) waste; (*fig: morale*) ruin; **à ~ de vue** as far as the eye can (*ou* could) see; **~s blanches** (vaginal) discharge *sg*

pertinent, e [pɛRtinɑ̃, -ɑ̃t] *adj* apt, relevant

perturbation [pɛRtyRbasjɔ̃] *nf*: **~ (atmosphérique)** atmospheric disturbance

perturber [pɛRtyRbe] /1/ *vt* to disrupt; (*Psych*) to perturb, disturb

pervers, e [pɛRvɛR, -ɛRs] *adj* perverted

pervertir [pɛRvɛRtiR] /2/ *vt* to pervert

pesant, e [pəzɑ̃, -ɑ̃t] *adj* heavy; (*fig: présence*) burdensome

pèse-personne [pɛzpɛRsɔn] *nm* (bathroom) scales *pl*

peser [pəze] /5/ *vt* to weigh ▷ *vi* to be heavy; (*fig: avoir de l'importance*) to carry weight

pessimiste [pesimist] *adj* pessimistic ▷ *nm/f* pessimist

peste [pɛst] *nf* plague

pétale [petal] *nm* petal

pétanque [petɑ̃k] *nf* type of bowls

● **PÉTANQUE**
●
● *Pétanque* is a version of the game
● of 'boules', played on a variety of
● hard surfaces. Standing with their
● feet together, players throw steel
● bowls at a wooden jack. *Pétanque*
● originated in the South of France
● and is still very much associated
● with that area.

pétard [petaR] *nm* banger (BRIT), firecracker

péter [pete] /6/ *vi* (*fam: casser, sauter*) to bust; (*fam!*) to fart (!)

pétillant, e [petijɑ̃, -ɑ̃t] *adj* (*eau*) sparkling

pétiller [petije] /1/ *vi* (*flamme, bois*) to crackle; (*mousse, champagne*) to bubble; (*yeux*) to sparkle

petit, e [pəti, -it] *adj* small; (*avec nuance affective*) little; (*voyage*) short, little; (*bruit etc*) faint, slight ▷ *nm/f* (*petit enfant*) little one, child; **petits** *nmpl* (*d'un animal*) young *pl*; **faire des ~s** to have kittens (*ou* puppies *etc*); **la classe des ~s** the infant class; **les tout-~s** toddlers; **~ à ~** bit by bit, gradually; **~(e) ami(e)** boyfriend/girlfriend; **les ~es annonces** the small ads; **~ déjeuner** breakfast; **~ four** petit four; **~ pain** (bread) roll; **~s pois** garden peas; **petite-fille** *nf* granddaughter; **petit-fils** *nm* grandson

pétition [petisjɔ̃] *nf* petition

petits-enfants [pətizɑ̃fɑ̃] *nmpl* grandchildren

pétrin [petʀɛ̃] nm (fig): **dans le ~** in
a jam ou fix
pétrir [petʀiʀ] /2/ vt to knead
pétrole [petʀɔl] nm oil; (pour lampe,
réchaud etc) paraffin; **pétrolier, -ière**
nm oil tanker

> Attention à ne pas traduire *pétrole*
par le mot anglais *petrol*.

MOT-CLÉ

peu [pø] adv **1** (modifiant verbe, adjectif,
adverbe): **il boit peu** he doesn't drink
(very) much; **il est peu bavard** he's
not very talkative; **peu avant/après**
shortly before/afterwards
2 (modifiant nom): **peu de: peu de
gens/d'arbres** few ou not (very)
many people/trees; **il a peu d'espoir**
he hasn't (got) much hope, he has
little hope; **pour peu de temps** for
(only) a short while
3: **peu à peu** little by little; **à peu
près** just about, more or less; **à peu
près 10 kg/10 euros** approximately
10 kg/10 euros
▶ nm **1**: **le peu de gens qui** the few
people who; **le peu de sable qui**
what little sand, the little sand which
2: **un peu** a little; **un petit peu** a
little bit; **un peu d'espoir** a little
hope; **elle est un peu bavarde** she's
rather talkative; **un peu plus de**
slightly more than; **un peu moins de**
slightly less than; (avec pluriel) slightly
fewer than
▶ pron: **peu le savent** few know (it);
de peu (only) just

peuple [pœpl] nm people; **peupler**
/1/ vt (pays, région) to populate;
(étang) to stock; (hommes, poissons)
to inhabit
peuplier [pøplije] nm poplar (tree)
peur [pœʀ] nf fear; **avoir ~ (de/
de faire/que)** to be frightened ou
afraid (of/of doing/that); **faire ~ à**
to frighten; **de ~ de/que** for fear of/

that; **peureux, -euse** adj fearful,
timorous
peut [pø] vb voir **pouvoir**
peut-être [pøtɛtʀ] adv perhaps,
maybe; **~ que** perhaps, maybe; **~
bien qu'il fera/est** he may well do/be
phare [faʀ] nm (en mer) lighthouse;
(de véhicule) headlight
pharmacie [faʀmasi] nf (magasin)
chemist's (BRIT), pharmacy; (armoire)
medicine chest ou cupboard;
pharmacien, ne nm/f pharmacist,
chemist (BRIT)
phénomène [fenɔmɛn] nm
phenomenon
philosophe [filɔzɔf] nm/f
philosopher ▷ adj philosophical
philosophie [filɔzɔfi] nf philosophy
phobie [fɔbi] nf phobia
phoque [fɔk] nm seal
phosphorescent, e [fɔsfɔʀesɑ̃, -ɑ̃t]
adj luminous
photo [foto] nf photo; **prendre
en ~** to take a photo of; **aimer la/
faire de la ~** to like taking/take
photos; **~ d'identité** passport
photo; **photocopie** nf photocopy;
photocopier /7/ vt to photocopy
photocopieur [fotɔkɔpjœʀ] nm,
photocopieuse [fotɔkɔpjøz] nf
(photo)copier
photo: photographe nm/f
photographer; **photographie** nf
(procédé, technique) photography;
(cliché) photograph; **photographier**
/7/ vt to photograph
phrase [fʀɑz] nf sentence
physicien, ne [fizisjɛ̃, -ɛn] nm/f
physicist
physique [fizik] adj physical ▷ nm
physique ▷ nf physics sg; **au ~**
physically; **physiquement** adv
physically
pianiste [pjanist] nm/f pianist
piano [pjano] nm piano; **pianoter** /1/
vi to tinkle away (at the piano)
pic [pik] nm (instrument) pick(axe);
(montagne) peak; (Zool) woodpecker;

à ~ vertically; (*fig: tomber, arriver*) just at the right time

pichet [piʃɛ] *nm* jug

picorer [pikɔʀe] /1/ *vt* to peck

pie [pi] *nf* magpie

pièce [pjɛs] *nf* (*d'un logement*) room; (*Théât*) play; (*de mécanisme, machine*) part; (*de monnaie*) coin; (*document*) document; (*de drap, fragment, d'une collection*) piece; **deux euros ~** two euros each; **vendre à la ~** to sell separately *ou* individually; **travailler/payer à la ~** to do piecework/pay piece rate; **un maillot une ~** a one-piece swimsuit; **un deux-~s cuisine** a two-room(ed) flat (BRIT) *ou* apartment (US) with kitchen; **~ à conviction** exhibit; **~ d'eau** ornamental lake *ou* pond; **~ d'identité: avez-vous une ~ d'identité?** have you got any (means of) identification?; **~ jointe** (*Inform*) attachment; **~ montée** tiered cake; **~ de rechange** spare (part); **~s détachées** spares, (spare) parts; **~s justificatives** supporting documents

pied [pje] *nm* foot; (*de table*) leg; (*de lampe*) base; **~s nus** barefoot; **à ~** on foot; **au ~ de la lettre** literally; **avoir ~** to be able to touch the bottom, not to be out of one's depth; **avoir le ~ marin** to be a good sailor; **sur ~** (*debout, rétabli*) up and about; **mettre sur ~** (*entreprise*) to set up; **c'est le ~!** (*fam*) it's brilliant!; **mettre les ~s dans le plat** (*fam*) to put one's foot in it; **il se débrouille comme un ~** (*fam*) he's completely useless; **pied-noir** *nm* Algerian-born Frenchman

piège [pjɛʒ] *nm* trap; **prendre au ~** to trap; **piéger** /3, 6/ *vt* (*avec une bombe*) to booby-trap; **lettre/voiture piégée** letter-/car-bomb

piercing [pjɛʀsiŋ] *nm* piercing

pierre [pjɛʀ] *nf* stone; **~ tombale** tombstone; **pierreries** *nfpl* gems, precious stones

piétiner [pjetine] /1/ *vi* (*trépigner*) to stamp (one's foot); (*fig*) to be at a standstill ▷ *vt* to trample on

piéton, ne [pjetɔ̃, -ɔn] *nm/f* pedestrian; **piétonnier, -ière** *adj* pedestrian *cpd*

pieu, x [pjø] *nm* post; (*pointu*) stake

pieuvre [pjœvʀ] *nf* octopus

pieux, -euse [pjø, -øz] *adj* pious

pigeon [piʒɔ̃] *nm* pigeon

piger [piʒe] /3/ *vi* (*fam*) to get it ▷ *vt* (*fam*) to get

pigiste [piʒist] *nm/f* freelance journalist (*paid by the line*)

pignon [piɲɔ̃] *nm* (*de mur*) gable

pile [pil] *nf* (*tas, pilier*) pile; (*Élec*) battery ▷ *adv* (*net, brusquement*) dead; **à deux heures ~** at two on the dot; **jouer à ~ ou face** to toss up (for it); **~ ou face?** heads or tails?

piler [pile] /1/ *vt* to crush, pound

pilier [pilje] *nm* pillar

piller [pije] /1/ *vt* to pillage, plunder, loot

pilote [pilɔt] *nm* pilot; (*de char, voiture*) driver ▷ *adj* pilot *cpd*; **~ de chasse/d'essai/de ligne** fighter/test/airline pilot; **~ de course** racing driver; **piloter** /1/ *vt* (*navire*) to pilot; (*avion*) to fly; (*automobile*) to drive

pilule [pilyl] *nf* pill; **prendre la ~** to be on the pill

piment [pimɑ̃] *nm* (*Bot*) pepper, capsicum; (*fig*) spice, piquancy; **~ rouge** (*Culin*) chilli; **pimenté, e** *adj* (*plat*) hot and spicy

pin [pɛ̃] *nm* pine (tree)

pinard [pinaʀ] *nm* (*fam*) (cheap) wine, plonk (BRIT)

pince [pɛ̃s] *nf* (*outil*) pliers *pl*; (*de homard, crabe*) pincer, claw; (*Couture: pli*) dart; **~ à épiler** tweezers *pl*; **~ à linge** clothes peg (BRIT) *ou* pin (US)

pincé, e [pɛ̃se] *adj* (*air*) stiff

pinceau, x [pɛ̃so] *nm* (paint)brush

pincer [pɛ̃se] /3/ *vt* to pinch; (*fam*) to nab

pinède [pinɛd] nf pinewood, pine forest

pingouin [pɛ̃gwɛ̃] nm penguin

ping-pong [piŋpɔ̃g] nm table tennis

pinson [pɛ̃sɔ̃] nm chaffinch

pintade [pɛ̃tad] nf guinea-fowl

pion, ne [pjɔ̃, pjɔn] nm/f (Scol: péj) student paid to supervise schoolchildren ▷ nm (Échecs) pawn; (Dames) piece

pionnier [pjɔnje] nm pioneer

pipe [pip] nf pipe; **fumer la** ou **une ~** to smoke a pipe

piquant, e [pikɑ̃, -ɑ̃t] adj (barbe, rosier etc) prickly; (saveur, sauce) hot, pungent; (fig: détail) titillating; (: mordant, caustique) biting ▷ nm (épine) thorn, prickle; (fig) spiciness, spice

pique [pik] nf pike; (fig): **envoyer** ou **lancer des ~s à qn** to make cutting remarks to sb ▷ nm (Cartes) spades pl

pique-nique [piknik] nm picnic; **pique-niquer** /1/ vi to (have a) picnic

piquer [pike] /1/ vt (percer) to prick; (Méd) to give an injection to; (: animal blessé etc) to put to sleep; (insecte, fumée, ortie) to sting; (moustique) to bite; (froid) to bite; (intérêt etc) to arouse; (fam: voler) to pinch ▷ vi (oiseau, avion) to go into a dive

piquet [pikɛ] nm (pieu) post, stake; (de tente) peg

piqûre [pikyʀ] nf (d'épingle) prick; (d'ortie) sting; (de moustique) bite; (Méd) injection, shot (US); **faire une ~ à qn** to give sb an injection

pirate [piʀat] adj ▷ nm pirate; **~ de l'air** hijacker

pire [piʀ] adj worse; (superlatif): **le (la) ~ ...** the worst ... ▷ nm: **le ~ (de)** the worst (of); **au ~** at (the very) worst

pis [pi] nm (de vache) udder ▷ adj, adv worse; **de mal en ~** from bad to worse

piscine [pisin] nf (swimming) pool; **~ couverte** indoor (swimming) pool

pissenlit [pisɑ̃li] nm dandelion

pistache [pistaʃ] nf pistachio (nut)

piste [pist] nf (d'un animal, sentier) track, trail; (indice) lead; (de stade, de magnétophone) track; (de cirque) ring; (de danse) floor; (de patinage) rink; (de ski) run; (Aviat) runway; **~ cyclable** cycle track

pistolet [pistɔlɛ] nm (arme) pistol, gun; (à peinture) spray gun; **pistolet-mitrailleur** nm submachine gun

piston [pistɔ̃] nm (Tech) piston; **avoir du ~** (fam) to have friends in the right places; **pistonner** /1/ vt (candidat) to pull strings for

piteux, -euse [pitø, -øz] adj pitiful, sorry (avant le nom); **en ~ état** in a sorry state

pitié [pitje] nf pity; **il me fait ~** I feel sorry for him; **avoir ~ de** (compassion) to pity, feel sorry for; (merci) to have pity ou mercy on

pitoyable [pitwajabl] adj pitiful

pittoresque [pitɔʀɛsk] adj picturesque

pizza [pidza] nf pizza

PJ sigle f (= police judiciaire) ≈ CID (BRIT), ≈ FBI (US)

placard [plakaʀ] nm (armoire) cupboard; (affiche) poster, notice

place [plas] nf (emplacement, situation, classement) place; (de ville, village) square; (espace libre) room, space; (de parking) space; (siège: de train, cinéma, voiture) seat; (emploi) job; **en ~** (mettre) in its place; **sur ~** on the spot; **faire ~ à** to give way to; **ça prend de la ~** it takes up a lot of room ou space; **à la ~ de** in place of, instead of; **à votre ~ ...** if I were you ...; **se mettre à la ~ de qn** to put o.s. in sb's place ou in sb's shoes

placé, e [plase] adj: **haut ~** (fig) high-ranking; **être bien/mal ~** to be well/badly placed; (spectateur) to have a good/bad seat; **il est bien ~ pour le savoir** he is in a position to know

placement [plasmɑ̃] nm (Finance) investment; **agence** ou **bureau de ~** employment agency

p

placer [plase] /3/ vt to place; (convive, spectateur) to seat; (capital, argent) to place, invest; **se ~ au premier rang** to go and stand (ou sit) in the first row

plafond [plafɔ̃] nm ceiling

plage [plaʒ] nf beach; **~ arrière** (Auto) parcel ou back shelf

plaider [plede] /1/ vi (avocat) to plead ▷ vt to plead; **~ pour** (fig) to speak for; **plaidoyer** nm (Jur) speech for the defence (BRIT) ou defense (US); (fig) plea

plaie [plɛ] nf wound

plaignant, e [plɛɲɑ̃, -ɑ̃t] nm/f plaintiff

plaindre [plɛ̃dʀ] /52/ vt to pity, feel sorry for; **se plaindre** vi (gémir) to moan; (protester, rouspéter): **se ~ (à qn) (de)** to complain (to sb) (about); **se ~ de** (souffrir) to complain of (as)

plaine [plɛn] nf plain

plain-pied [plɛ̃pje] adv: **de ~ (avec)** on the same level (as)

plaint, e [plɛ̃, -ɛ̃t] pp de **plaindre** ▷ nf (gémissement) moan, groan; (doléance) complaint; **porter ~e** to lodge a complaint

plaire [plɛʀ] /54/ vi to be a success, be successful; **cela me plaît** I like it; **ça plaît beaucoup aux jeunes** it's very popular with young people; **se ~ quelque part** to like being somewhere; **s'il vous plaît, s'il te plaît** please

plaisance [plɛzɑ̃s] nf (aussi: **navigation de ~**) (pleasure) sailing, yachting

plaisant, e [plɛzɑ̃, -ɑ̃t] adj pleasant; (histoire, anecdote) amusing

plaisanter [plɛzɑ̃te] /1/ vi to joke; **plaisanterie** nf joke

plaisir [plɛziʀ] nm pleasure; **faire ~ à qn** (délibérément) to be nice to sb, please sb; **ça me fait ~** I'm delighted ou very pleased with this; **j'espère que ça te fera ~** I hope you'll like it; **pour le** ou **pour son** ou **par ~** for pleasure

plaît [plɛ] vb voir **plaire**

plan, e [plɑ̃, -an] adj flat ▷ nm plan; (fig) level, plane; (Ciné) shot; **au premier/second ~** in the foreground/middle distance; **à l'arrière ~** in the background; **~ d'eau** lake

planche [plɑ̃ʃ] nf (pièce de bois) plank, (wooden) board; (illustration) plate; **~ à repasser** ironing board; **~ (à roulettes)** skateboard; **~ à voile** (sport) windsurfing

plancher [plɑ̃ʃe] /1/ nm floor; (planches) floorboards pl ▷ vi to work hard

planer [plane] /1/ vi to glide; (fam: rêveur) to have one's head in the clouds; **~ sur** (danger) to hang over

planète [planɛt] nf planet

planeur [planœʀ] nm glider

planifier [planifje] /7/ vt to plan

planning [planiŋ] nm programme, schedule; **~ familial** family planning

plant [plɑ̃] nm seedling, young plant

plante [plɑ̃t] nf plant; **~ d'appartement** house ou pot plant; **~ du pied** sole (of the foot); **~ verte** house plant

planter [plɑ̃te] /1/ vt (plante) to plant; (enfoncer) to hammer ou drive in; (tente) to put up, pitch; (fam: mettre) to dump; **se planter** vi (fam: se tromper) to get it wrong; (: ordinateur) to crash

plaque [plak] nf plate; (de verglas, d'eczéma) patch; (avec inscription) plaque; **~ chauffante** hotplate; **~ de chocolat** bar of chocolate; **~ tournante** (fig) centre

plaqué, e [plake] adj: **~ or/argent** gold-/silver-plated

plaquer [plake] /1/ vt (Rugby) to bring down; (fam: laisser tomber) to drop

plaquette [plakɛt] nf (de chocolat) bar; (de beurre) packet; **~ de frein** brake pad

plastique [plastik] adj ▷ nm plastic ▷ nf plastic arts pl; (d'une statue) modelling; **plastiquer** /1/ vt to blow up

plat, e [pla, -at] adj flat; (style) flat, dull ▷ nm (récipient, Culin) dish; (d'un repas) course; **à ~ ventre** face down; **à ~** (pneu, batterie) flat; (fam: fatigué) dead beat; **~ cuisiné** pre-cooked meal (ou dish); **~ du jour** dish of the day; **~ principal** ou **de résistance** main course

platane [platan] nm plane tree

plateau, x [plato] nm (support) tray; (Géo) plateau; (Ciné) set; **~ à fromages** cheeseboard

plate-bande [platbɑ̃d] nf flower bed

plate-forme [platfɔʀm] nf platform; **~ de forage/pétrolière** drilling/oil rig

platine [platin] nm platinum ▷ nf (d'un tourne-disque) turntable; **~ laser** ou **compact-disc** compact disc (player)

plâtre [plɑtʀ] nm (matériau) plaster; (statue) plaster statue; (Méd) (plaster) cast; **avoir un bras dans le ~** to have an arm in plaster

plein, e [plɛ̃, -ɛn] adj full ▷ nm: **faire le ~ (d'essence)** to fill up (with petrol (BRIT) ou gas (US)); **à ~es mains** (ramasser) in handfuls; **à ~ temps** full-time; **en ~ air** in the open air; **en ~ soleil** in direct sunlight; **en ~e nuit/ rue** in the middle of the night/street; **en ~ jour** in broad daylight

pleurer [plœʀe] /1/ vi to cry; (yeux) to water ▷ vt to mourn (for); **~ sur** lament (over), bemoan

pleurnicher [plœʀniʃe] /1/ vi to snivel, whine

pleurs [plœʀ] nmpl: **en ~** in tears

pleut [plø] vb voir **pleuvoir**

pleuvoir [pløvwaʀ] /23/ vb impers to rain ▷ vi (coups) to rain down; (critiques, invitations) to shower down; **il pleut** it's raining; **il pleut des cordes** ou **à verse** ou **à torrents** it's pouring (down), it's raining cats and dogs

pli [pli] nm fold; (de jupe) pleat; (de pantalon) crease

pliant, e [plijɑ̃, -ɑ̃t] adj folding

plier [plije] /7/ vt to fold; (pour ranger) to fold up; (genou, bras) to bend ▷ vi to bend; (fig) to yield; **se ~ à** to submit to

plisser [plise] /1/ vt (yeux) to screw up; (front) to furrow; (jupe) to put pleats in

plomb [plɔ̃] nm (métal) lead; (d'une cartouche) (lead) shot; (Pêche) sinker; (Élec) fuse; **sans ~** (essence) unleaded

plomberie [plɔ̃bʀi] nf plumbing

plombier [plɔ̃bje] nm plumber

plonge [plɔ̃ʒ] nf: **faire la ~** to be a washer-up (BRIT) ou dishwasher (person)

plongeant, e [plɔ̃ʒɑ̃, -ɑ̃t] adj (vue) from above; (tir, décolleté) plunging

plongée [plɔ̃ʒe] nf (Sport) diving no pl; (: sans scaphandre) skin diving; **~ sous-marine** diving

plongeoir [plɔ̃ʒwaʀ] nm diving board

plongeon [plɔ̃ʒɔ̃] nm dive

plonger [plɔ̃ʒe] /3/ vi to dive ▷ vt: **~ qch dans** to plunge sth into; **se ~ dans** (études, lecture) to bury ou immerse o.s. in; **plongeur, -euse** [plɔ̃ʒœʀ, -øz] nm/f diver

plu [ply] pp de **plaire; pleuvoir**

pluie [plɥi] nf rain

plume [plym] nf feather; (pour écrire) (pen) nib; (fig) pen

plupart [plypaʀ]: **la ~** pron the majority, most (of them); **la ~ des** most, the majority of; **la ~ du temps/d'entre nous** most of the time/of us; **pour la ~** for the most part, mostly

pluriel [plyʀjɛl] nm plural

plus¹ [ply] vb voir **plaire**

MOT-CLÉ

plus² [ply] adv **1** (forme négative): **ne ... plus** no more, no longer; **je n'ai plus d'argent** I've got no more money ou

P

no money left; **il ne travaille plus** he's no longer working, he doesn't work any more
2 [ply, plyz + *voyelle*] (*comparatif*) more, ...+er; (*superlatif*): **le plus** the most, the ...+est; **plus grand/ intelligent (que)** bigger/more intelligent (than); **le plus grand/ intelligent** the biggest/most intelligent; **tout au plus** at the very most
3 [plys, plyz + *voyelle*] (*davantage*) more; **il travaille plus (que)** he works more (than); **plus il travaille, plus il est heureux** the more he works, the happier he is; **plus de 10 personnes/trois heures/quatre kilos** more than *ou* over 10 people/ three hours/four kilos; **trois heures de plus que** three hours more than; **de plus** what's more, moreover; **il a trois ans de plus que moi** he's three years older than me; **trois kilos en plus** three kilos more; **en plus de** in addition to; **de plus en plus** more and more; **plus ou moins** more or less; **ni plus ni moins** no more, no less
▶ *prép* [plys]: **quatre plus deux** four plus two

plusieurs [plyzjœʀ] *adj, pron* several; **ils sont ~** there are several of them
plus-value [plyvaly] *nf* (*bénéfice*) capital gain
plutôt [plyto] *adv* rather; **je ferais ~ ceci** I'd rather *ou* sooner do this; **~ que (de) faire** rather than *ou* instead of doing
pluvieux, -euse [plyvjø, -øz] *adj* rainy, wet
PME *sigle fpl* (= *petites et moyennes entreprises*) small businesses
PMU *sigle m* (= *pari mutuel urbain*) (*dans un café*) betting agency
PNB *sigle m* (= *produit national brut*) GNP
pneu [pnø] *nm* tyre (BRIT), tire (US)

pneumonie [pnømɔni] *nf* pneumonia
poche [pɔʃ] *nf* pocket; (*sous les yeux*) bag, pouch; **argent de ~** pocket money
pochette [pɔʃɛt] *nf* (*d'aiguilles etc*) case; (*de femme*) clutch bag; (*mouchoir*) breast pocket handkerchief; **~ de disque** record sleeve
podcast [pɔdkast] *nm* podcast; **podcaster** /1/ *vi* to podcast
poêle [pwal] *nm* stove ▷ *nf*: **~ (à frire)** frying pan
poème [pɔɛm] *nm* poem
poésie [pɔezi] *nf* (*poème*) poem; (*art*): **la ~** poetry
poète [pɔɛt] *nm* poet
poids [pwa] *nm* weight; (*Sport*) shot; **vendre au ~** to sell by weight; **perdre/prendre du ~** to lose/put on weight; **~ lourd** (*camion*) (big) lorry (BRIT), truck (US)
poignant, e [pwaɲã, -ãt] *adj* poignant
poignard [pwaɲaʀ] *nm* dagger; **poignarder** /1/ *vt* to stab, knife
poigne [pwaɲ] *nf* grip; **avoir de la ~** (*fig*) to rule with a firm hand
poignée [pwaɲe] *nf* (*de sel etc, fig*) handful; (*de couvercle, porte*) handle; **~ de main** handshake
poignet [pwaɲɛ] *nm* (*Anat*) wrist; (*de chemise*) cuff
poil [pwal] *nm* (*Anat*) hair; (*de pinceau, brosse*) bristle; (*de tapis, tissu*) strand; (*pelage*) coat; **à ~** (*fam*) starkers; **au ~** (*fam*) hunky-dory; **poilu, e** *adj* hairy
poinçonner [pwɛ̃sɔne] /1/ *vt* (*bijou etc*) to hallmark; (*billet, ticket*) to punch
poing [pwɛ̃] *nm* fist; **coup de ~** punch
point [pwɛ̃] *nm* dot; (*de ponctuation*) full stop, period (US); (*Couture, Tricot*) stitch ▷ *adv* = **pas¹**; **faire le ~** (*fig*) to take stock (of the situation); **sur le ~ de faire** (just) about to do; **à tel ~ que** so much so that; **mettre au ~** (*mécanisme, procédé*) to develop;

(*affaire*) to settle; **à ~** (*Culin: viande*) medium; **à ~ (nommé)** just at the right time; **deux ~s** colon; **~ (de côté)** stitch (*pain*); **~ d'exclamation** exclamation mark; **~ faible** weak spot; **~ final** full stop, period (*us*); **~ d'interrogation** question mark; **~ mort**; **au ~ mort** (*Auto*) in neutral; **~ de repère** landmark; (*dans le temps*) point of reference; **~ de vente** retail outlet; **~ de vue** viewpoint; (*fig: opinion*) point of view; **~s cardinaux** cardinal points; **~s de suspension** suspension points

pointe [pwɛ̃t] *nf* point; (*clou*) tack; **une ~ d'ail/d'accent** a touch *ou* hint of garlic/of an accent; **être à la ~ de** (*fig*) to be in the forefront of; **sur la ~ des pieds** on tiptoe; **en ~** *adj* pointed, tapered; **de ~** (*technique etc*) leading; **heures/jours de ~** peak hours/days

pointer [pwɛ̃te] /1/ *vt* (*diriger: canon, longue-vue, doigt*): **~ vers qch**, **~ sur qch** to point at sth ▷ *vi* (*employé*) to clock in *ou* on

pointeur, -euse [pwɛ̃tœʀ, -øz] *nf* timeclock ▷ *nm* (*Inform*) cursor

pointillé [pwɛ̃tije] *nm* (*trait*) dotted line

pointilleux, -euse [pwɛ̃tijø, -øz] *adj* particular, pernickety

pointu, e [pwɛ̃ty] *adj* pointed; (*voix*) shrill; (*analyse*) precise

pointure [pwɛ̃tyʀ] *nf* size

point-virgule [pwɛ̃viʀgyl] *nm* semi-colon

poire [pwaʀ] *nf* pear; (*fam, péj*) mug

poireau, x [pwaʀo] *nm* leek

poirier [pwaʀje] *nm* pear tree

pois [pwa] *nm* (*Bot*) pea; (*sur une étoffe*) dot, spot; **à ~** (*cravate etc*) spotted, polka-dot *cpd*; **~ chiche** chickpea

poison [pwazɔ̃] *nm* poison

poisseux, -euse [pwasø, -øz] *adj* sticky

poisson [pwasɔ̃] *nm* fish *gén inv*; **les P~s** (*Astrologie: signe*) Pisces; **~ d'avril**

April fool; (*blague*) April fool's day trick; *see note* **"poisson d'avril"**; **~ rouge** goldfish; **poissonnerie** *nf* fishmonger's; **poissonnier, -ière** *nm/f* fishmonger (*BRIT*), fish merchant (*us*)

● **POISSON D'AVRIL**
●
● The traditional April Fools'
● Day prank in France involves
● attaching a cut-out paper fish,
● known as a 'poisson d'avril', to the
● back of one's victim, without being
● caught.

poitrine [pwatʀin] *nf* chest; (*seins*) bust, bosom; (*Culin*) breast

poivre [pwavʀ] *nm* pepper

poivron [pwavʀɔ̃] *nm* pepper, capsicum

polaire [pɔlɛʀ] *adj* polar

pôle [pol] *nm* (*Géo, Élec*) pole; **le ~ Nord/Sud** the North/South Pole

poli, e [pɔli] *adj* polite; (*lisse*) smooth

police [pɔlis] *nf* police; **~ judiciaire (PJ)** ≈ Criminal Investigation Department (CID) (*BRIT*), ≈ Federal Bureau of Investigation (FBI) (*us*); **~ secours** ≈ emergency services *pl* (*BRIT*), ≈ paramedics *pl* (*us*); **policier, -ière** *adj* police *cpd* ▷ *nm* policeman; (*aussi:* **roman policier**) detective novel

polir [pɔliʀ] /2/ *vt* to polish

politesse [pɔlitɛs] *nf* politeness

politicien, ne [pɔlitisjɛ̃, -ɛn] *nm/f* (*péj*) politician

politique [pɔlitik] *adj* political ▷ *nf* politics *sg*; (*principes, tactique*) policies *pl*

politiquement [pɔlitikmɑ̃] *adv* politically; **~ correct** politically correct

pollen [pɔlɛn] *nm* pollen

polluant, e [pɔlɥɑ̃, -ɑ̃t] *adj* polluting ▷ *nm* pollutant; **non ~** non-polluting

polluer [pɔlɥe] /1/ vt to pollute;
pollution nf pollution
polo [pɔlo] nm (tricot) polo shirt
Pologne [pɔlɔɲ] nf: **la ~** Poland;
polonais, e adj Polish ▷ nm (Ling)
Polish ▷ nm/f: **Polonais, e** Pole
poltron, ne [pɔltRɔ̃, -ɔn] adj
cowardly
polycopier [pɔlikɔpje] /7/ vt to
duplicate
Polynésie [pɔlinezi] nf: **la ~** Polynesia;
la ~ française French Polynesia
polyvalent, e [pɔlivalɑ̃, -ɑ̃t] adj
(rôle) varied; (salle) multi-purpose
pommade [pɔmad] nf ointment,
cream
pomme [pɔm] nf apple; **tomber
dans les ~s** (fam) to pass out;
~ d'Adam Adam's apple; **~ de pin**
pine ou fir cone; **~ de terre** potato; **~s
vapeur** boiled potatoes
pommette [pɔmɛt] nf cheekbone
pommier [pɔmje] nm apple tree
pompe [pɔ̃p] nf pump; (faste)
pomp (and ceremony); **~ à eau/
essence** water/petrol pump; **~s
funèbres** undertaker's sg, funeral
parlour sg; **pomper** /1/ vt to pump;
(aspirer) to pump up; (absorber) to
soak up
pompeux, -euse [pɔ̃pø, -øz] adj
pompous
pompier [pɔ̃pje] nm fireman
pompiste [pɔ̃pist] nm/f petrol (BRIT)
ou gas (US) pump attendant
poncer [pɔ̃se] /3/ vt to sand (down)
ponctuation [pɔ̃ktɥasjɔ̃] nf
punctuation
ponctuel, le [pɔ̃ktɥɛl] adj punctual
pondéré, e [pɔ̃deRe] adj level-
headed, composed
pondre [pɔ̃dR] /41/ vt to lay
poney [pɔnɛ] nm pony
pont [pɔ̃] nm bridge; (Navig) deck;
faire le ~ to take the extra day off;
see note **"faire le pont"**; **~ suspendu**
suspension bridge; **pont-levis** nm
drawbridge

● **FAIRE LE PONT**
●
● The expression 'faire le pont' refers
● to the practice of taking a Monday
● or Friday off to make a long
● weekend if a public holiday falls on
● a Tuesday or Thursday. The French
● commonly take an extra day off
● work to give four consecutive days'
● holiday at 'l'Ascension', 'le 14 juillet'
● and le '15 août'.

pop [pɔp] adj inv pop
populaire [pɔpylɛR] adj popular;
(manifestation) mass cpd; (milieux,
clientèle) working-class; (mot etc) used
by the lower classes (of society)
popularité [pɔpylaRite] nf
popularity
population [pɔpylasjɔ̃] nf population
populeux, -euse [pɔpylø, -øz] adj
densely populated
porc [pɔR] nm pig; (Culin) pork
porcelaine [pɔRsəlɛn] nf porcelain,
china; (objet) piece of china(ware)
porc-épic [pɔRkepik] nm porcupine
porche [pɔRʃ] nm porch
porcherie [pɔRʃəRi] nf pigsty
pore [pɔR] nm pore
porno [pɔRno] adj porno ▷ nm porn
port [pɔR] nm harbour, port; (ville)
port; (de l'uniforme etc) wearing;
(pour lettre) postage; (pour colis,
aussi: posture) carriage; **~ d'arme**
(Jur) carrying of a firearm; **~ payé**
postage paid
portable [pɔRtabl] adj (portatif)
portable; (téléphone) mobile
▷ nm (Inform) laptop (computer);
(téléphone) mobile (phone)
portail [pɔRtaj] nm gate
portant, e [pɔRtɑ̃, -ɑ̃t] adj: **bien/
mal ~** in good/poor health
portatif, -ive [pɔRtatif, -iv] adj
portable
porte [pɔRt] nf door; (de ville,
forteresse) gate; **mettre à la ~** to
throw out; **~ d'entrée** front door

porté, e [pɔʀte] adj: **être ~ à faire qch** to be apt to do sth; **être ~ sur qch** to be partial to sth

porte: porte-avions nm inv aircraft carrier; **porte-bagages** nm inv luggage rack (ou basket etc); **porte-bonheur** nm inv lucky charm; **porte-clefs** nm inv key ring; **porte-documents** nm inv attaché ou document case

portée [pɔʀte] nf (d'une arme) range; (fig: importance) impact, import; (: capacités) scope, capability; (de chatte etc) litter; (Mus) stave, staff; **à/ hors de ~ (de)** within/out of reach (of); **à ~ de (la) main** within (arm's) reach; **à la ~ de qn** (fig) at sb's level, within sb's capabilities

porte: portefeuille nm wallet; **portemanteau, x** nm coat rack; (cintre) coat hanger; **porte-monnaie** nm inv purse; **porte-parole** nm inv spokesperson

porter [pɔʀte] /1/ vt to carry; (sur soi: vêtement, barbe, bague) to wear; (fig: responsabilité etc) to bear, carry; (inscription, marque, titre, patronyme, fruits, fleurs) to bear; (coup) to deal; (attention) to turn; (apporter): **~ qch quelque part/à qn** to take sth somewhere/to sb ▷ vi to carry; (coup, argument) to hit home; **se porter** vi (se sentir): **se ~ bien/mal** to be well/unwell; **~ sur** (conférence etc) to concern; **se faire ~ malade** to report sick

porteur, -euse [pɔʀtœʀ, -øz] nm/f ▷ nm (de bagages) porter; (de chèque) bearer

porte-voix [pɔʀtəvwa] nm inv megaphone

portier [pɔʀtje] nm doorman

portière [pɔʀtjɛʀ] nf door

portion [pɔʀsjɔ̃] nf (part) portion, share; (partie) portion, section

porto [pɔʀto] nm port (wine)

portrait [pɔʀtʀɛ] nm portrait; (photographie) photograph; **portrait-robot** nm Identikit® ou Photo-fit® (BRIT) picture

portuaire [pɔʀtɥɛʀ] adj port cpd, harbour cpd

portugais, e [pɔʀtygɛ, -ɛz] adj Portuguese ▷ nm (Ling) Portuguese ▷ nm/f: **P~, e** Portuguese

Portugal [pɔʀtygal] nm: **le ~** Portugal

pose [poz] nf (de moquette) laying; (attitude, d'un modèle) pose; (Photo) exposure

posé, e [poze] adj calm

poser [poze] /1/ vt (place) to put down, to put; (déposer, installer: moquette, carrelage) to lay; (rideaux, papier peint) to hang; (question) to ask; (principe, conditions) to lay ou set down; (problème) to formulate; (difficulté) to pose ▷ vi (modèle) to pose; **se poser** vi (oiseau, avion) to land; (question) to arise; **~ qch (sur)** to put sth down (on); **~ qn à** to drop sb at; **~ qch sur qch/quelque part** to put sth on sth/somewhere; **~ sa candidature à un poste** to apply for a post

positif, -ive [pozitif, -iv] adj positive

position [pozisjɔ̃] nf position; **prendre ~** (fig) to take a stand

posologie [pozɔlɔʒi] nf dosage

posséder [pɔsede] /6/ vt to own, possess; (qualité, talent) to have, possess; (sexuellement) to possess; **possession** nf ownership no pl; possession; **être en possession de qch** to be in possession of sth; **prendre possession de qch** to take possession of sth

possibilité [pɔsibilite] nf possibility; **possibilités** nfpl potential sg

possible [pɔsibl] adj possible; (projet, entreprise) feasible ▷ nm: **faire son ~** to do all one can, do one's utmost; **le plus/moins de livres ~** as many/ few books as possible; **le plus vite ~** as quickly as possible; **dès que ~** as soon as possible

p

postal, e, -aux [pɔstal, -o] *adj* postal

poste¹ [pɔst] *nf* (*service*) post, postal service; (*administration, bureau*) post office; **mettre à la ~** to post; **~ restante (PR)** poste restante (BRIT), general delivery (US)

poste² [pɔst] *nm* (*fonction, Mil*) post; (*Tél*) extension; (*de radio etc*) set; **~ d'essence** filling station; **~ d'incendie** fire point; **~ de pilotage** cockpit, flight deck; **~ (de police)** police station; **~ de secours** first-aid post

poster /1/ *vt* [pɔste] to post ▷ *nm* [pɔstɛʀ] poster

postérieur, e [pɔsteʀjœʀ] *adj* (*date*) later; (*partie*) back ▷ *nm* (*fam*) behind

postuler [pɔstyle] /1/ *vi*: **~ à** *ou* **pour un emploi** to apply for a job

pot [po] *nm* (*en verre*) jar; (*en terre*) pot; (*en plastique, carton*) carton; (*en métal*) tin; (*fam: chance*) luck; **avoir du ~** to be lucky; **boire** *ou* **prendre un ~** (*fam*) to have a drink; **petit ~ (pour bébé)** (jar of) baby food; **~ catalytique** catalytic converter; **~ d'échappement** exhaust pipe

potable [pɔtabl] *adj*: **eau (non) ~** (not) drinking water

potage [pɔtaʒ] *nm* soup; **potager, -ère** *adj*: (**jardin**) **potager** kitchen *ou* vegetable garden

pot-au-feu [pɔtofø] *nm inv* (beef) stew

pot-de-vin [podvɛ̃] *nm* bribe

pote [pɔt] *nm* (*fam*) pal

poteau, x [pɔto] *nm* post; **~ indicateur** signpost

potelé, e [pɔtle] *adj* plump, chubby

potentiel, le [pɔtɑ̃sjɛl] *adj, nm* potential

poterie [pɔtʀi] *nf* pottery; (*objet*) piece of pottery

potier, -ière [pɔtje, -jɛʀ] *nm/f* potter

potiron [pɔtiʀɔ̃] *nm* pumpkin

pou, x [pu] *nm* louse

poubelle [pubɛl] *nf* (dust)bin

pouce [pus] *nm* thumb

poudre [pudʀ] *nf* powder; (*fard*) (face) powder; (*explosif*) gunpowder; **en ~**: **café en ~** instant coffee; **lait en ~** dried *ou* powdered milk

poudreux, -euse [pudʀø, -øz] *adj* dusty; (*neige*) powder *cpd*

poudre: poudrier [pudʀije] *nm* (powder) compact

pouffer [pufe] /1/ *vi*: **~ (de rire)** to burst out laughing

poulailler [pulaje] *nm* henhouse

poulain [pulɛ̃] *nm* foal; (*fig*) protégé

poule [pul] *nf* hen; (*Culin*) (boiling) fowl; **~ mouillée** coward

poulet [pulɛ] *nm* chicken; (*fam*) cop

poulie [puli] *nf* pulley

pouls [pu] *nm* pulse; **prendre le ~ de qn** to take sb's pulse

poumon [pumɔ̃] *nm* lung

poupée [pupe] *nf* doll

pour [puʀ] *prép* for ▷ *nm*: **le ~ et le contre** the pros and cons; **~ faire** (so as) to do, in order to do; **~ avoir fait** for having done; **~ que** so that, in order that; **fermé ~ (cause de) travaux** closed for refurbishment *ou* alterations; **c'est ~ ça que ...** that's why ...; **~ quoi faire?** what for?; **~ 20 euros d'essence** 20 euros' worth of petrol; **~ cent** per cent; **~ ce qui est de** as for

pourboire [puʀbwaʀ] *nm* tip

pourcentage [puʀsɑ̃taʒ] *nm* percentage

pourchasser [puʀʃase] /1/ *vt* to pursue

pourparlers [puʀpaʀle] *nmpl* talks, negotiations

pourpre [puʀpʀ] *adj* crimson

pourquoi [puʀkwa] *adv, conj* why ▷ *nm inv*: **le ~ (de)** the reason (for)

pourrai *etc* [puʀe] *vb voir* **pouvoir**

pourri, e [puʀi] *adj* rotten

pourrir [puʀiʀ] /2/ *vi* to rot; (*fruit*) to go rotten *ou* bad ▷ *vt* to rot; (*fig*) to spoil thoroughly; **pourriture** *nf* rot

poursuite [puʀsɥit] nf pursuit, chase; **poursuites** nfpl (Jur) legal proceedings
poursuivre [puʀsɥivʀ] /40/ vt to pursue, chase (after); (obséder) to haunt; (Jur) to bring proceedings against, prosecute (: au civil) to sue; (but) to strive towards; (voyage, études) to carry on with, continue; **se poursuivre** vi to go on, continue
pourtant [puʀtã] adv yet; **c'est ~ facile** (and) yet it's easy
pourtour [puʀtuʀ] nm perimeter
pourvoir [puʀvwaʀ] /25/ vt: **~ qch/ qn de** to equip sth/sb with ▷ vi: **~ à** to provide for; **pourvu, e** adj: **pourvu de** equipped with; **pourvu que** (si) provided that, so long as; (espérons que) let's hope (that)
pousse [pus] nf growth; (bourgeon) shoot
poussée [puse] nf thrust; (d'acné) eruption; (fig: prix) upsurge
pousser [puse] /1/ vt to push; (émettre: cri etc) to give; (stimuler: élève) to urge on; (poursuivre: études, discussion) to carry on ▷ vi to push; (croître) to grow; **se pousser** vi to move over; **~ qn à faire qch** (inciter) to urge ou press sb to do sth; **faire ~** (plante) to grow
poussette [puset] nf pushchair (BRIT), stroller (US)
poussière [pusjɛʀ] nf dust; **poussiéreux, -euse** adj dusty
poussin [pusɛ̃] nm chick
poutre [putʀ] nf beam

MOT-CLÉ

pouvoir [puvwaʀ] /33/ nm power; (dirigeants): **le pouvoir** those in power; **les pouvoirs publics** the authorities; **pouvoir d'achat** purchasing power
▶ vb aux **1** (être en état de) can, be able to; **je ne peux pas le réparer** I can't ou I am not able to repair it; **déçu de ne pas pouvoir le faire** disappointed not to be able to do it
2 (avoir la permission) can, may, be allowed to; **vous pouvez aller au cinéma** you can ou may go to the pictures
3 (probabilité, hypothèse) may, might, could; **il a pu avoir un accident** he may ou might ou could have had an accident; **il aurait pu le dire!** he might ou could have said (so)!
▶ vb impers may, might, could; **il peut arriver que** it may ou might ou could happen that; **il pourrait pleuvoir** it might rain
▶ vt can, be able to; **j'ai fait tout ce que j'ai pu** I did all I could; **je n'en peux plus** (épuisé) I'm exhausted; (à bout) I can't take any more
se pouvoir vi: **il se peut que** it may ou might be that; **cela se pourrait** that's quite possible

prairie [pʀeʀi] nf meadow
praline [pʀalin] nf sugared almond
praticable [pʀatikabl] adj passable; practicable
pratiquant, e [pʀatikã, -ãt] nm/f (regular) churchgoer
pratique [pʀatik] nf practice ▷ adj practical; **pratiquement** adv (pour ainsi dire) practically, virtually; **pratiquer** /1/ vt to practise; (l'équitation, la pêche) to go in for; (le golf, football) to play; (intervention, opération) to carry out
pré [pʀe] nm meadow
préalable [pʀealabl] adj preliminary; **au ~** beforehand
préambule [pʀeãbyl] nm preamble; (fig) prelude; **sans ~** straight away
préau, x [pʀeo] nm (d'une cour d'école) covered playground
préavis [pʀeavi] nm notice
précaution [pʀekosjɔ̃] nf precaution; **avec ~** cautiously; **par ~** as a precaution
précédemment [pʀesedamã] adv before, previously

P

précédent, e [pʀesedɑ̃, -ɑ̃t] adj
previous ▷ nm precedent; **sans ~**
unprecedented; **le jour ~** the day
before, the previous day

précéder [pʀesede] /6/ vt to precede

prêcher [pʀeʃe] /1/ vt to preach

précieux, -euse [pʀesjø, -øz] adj
precious; (collaborateur, conseils)
invaluable

précipice [pʀesipis] nm drop, chasm

précipitamment [pʀesipitamɑ̃]
adv hurriedly, hastily

précipitation [pʀesipitasjɔ̃] nf
(hâte) haste

précipité, e [pʀesipite] adj hurried;
hasty

précipiter [pʀesipite] /1/ vt (hâter:
départ) to hasten; **se précipiter** vi
to speed up; **~ qn/qch du haut de**
(faire tomber) to throw ou hurl sb/sth
off ou from; **se ~ sur/vers** to rush
at/towards

précis, e [pʀesi, -iz] adj precise;
(tir, mesures) accurate, precise; **à
4 heures ~es** at 4 o'clock sharp;
précisément adv precisely; **préciser**
/1/ vt (expliquer) to be more specific
about, clarify; (spécifier) to state,
specify; **se préciser** vi to become
clear(er); **précision** nf precision;
(détail) point ou detail (made clear or
to be clarified)

précoce [pʀekɔs] adj early; (enfant)
precocious

préconçu, e [pʀekɔ̃sy] adj
preconceived

préconiser [pʀekɔnize] /1/ vt to
advocate

prédécesseur [pʀedesesœʀ] nm
predecessor

prédilection [pʀedilɛksjɔ̃] nf: **avoir
une ~ pour** to be partial to

prédire [pʀediʀ] /37/ vt to predict

prédominer [pʀedɔmine] /1/ vi to
predominate

préface [pʀefas] nf preface

préfecture [pʀefɛktyʀ] nf prefecture;
~ de police police headquarters

préférable [pʀefeʀabl] adj
preferable

préféré, e [pʀefeʀe] adj, nm/f
favourite

préférence [pʀefeʀɑ̃s] nf
preference; **de ~** preferably

préférer [pʀefeʀe] /6/ vt: **~ qn/qch
(à)** to prefer sb/sth (to), like sb/sth
better (than); **~ faire** to prefer to do;
je préférerais du thé I would rather
have tea, I'd prefer tea

préfet [pʀefɛ] nm prefect

préhistorique [pʀeistɔʀik] adj
prehistoric

préjudice [pʀeʒydis] nm (matériel)
loss; (moral) harm no pl; **porter ~ à** to
harm, be detrimental to; **au ~ de** at
the expense of

préjugé [pʀeʒyʒe] nm prejudice;
avoir un ~ contre to be prejudiced
against

prélasser [pʀelɑse] /1/: **se prélasser**
vi to lounge

prélèvement [pʀelɛvmɑ̃] nm
(montant) deduction; **faire un ~ de
sang** to take a blood sample

prélever [pʀelve] /5/ vt (échantillon)
to take; **~ (sur)** (argent) to deduct
(from); (sur son compte) to withdraw
(from)

prématuré, e [pʀematyʀe] adj
premature ▷ nm premature baby

premier, -ière [pʀəmje, -jɛʀ] adj
first; (rang) front; (fig: fondamental)
basic ▷ nf (Rail, Aviat etc) first
class; (Scol) year 12 (BRIT), eleventh
grade (US); **de ~ ordre** first-rate;
le ~ venu the first person to come
along; **P~ Ministre** Prime Minister;
premièrement adv firstly

prémonition [pʀemɔnisjɔ̃] nf
premonition

prenant, e [pʀənɑ̃, -ɑ̃t] adj
absorbing, engrossing

prénatal, e [pʀenatal] adj (Méd)
antenatal

prendre [pʀɑ̃dʀ] /58/ vt to take;
(repas) to have; (aller chercher) to

get; (*malfaiteur, poisson*) to catch; (*passager*) to pick up; (*personnel*) to take on; (*traiter: enfant, problème*) to handle; (*voix, ton*) to put on; (*ôter*): **~ qch à** to take sth from; (*coincer*): **se ~ les doigts dans** to get one's fingers caught in ▷ *vi* (*liquide, ciment*) to set; (*greffe, vaccin*) to take; (*feu: foyer*) to go; (*se diriger*): **~ à gauche** to turn (to the) left; **~ froid** to catch cold; **se ~ pour** to think one is; **s'en ~ à** to attack; **se ~ d'amitié/d'affection pour** to befriend/become fond of; **s'y ~** (*procéder*) to set about it

preneur [pʀənœʀ] *nm*: **être ~** to be willing to buy; **trouver ~** to find a buyer

prénom [pʀenɔ̃] *nm* first name

préoccupation [pʀeɔkypasjɔ̃] *nf* (*souci*) concern; (*idée fixe*) preoccupation

préoccuper [pʀeɔkype] /1/ *vt* (*tourmenter, tracasser*) to concern; (*absorber, obséder*) to preoccupy; **se ~ de qch** to be concerned about sth

préparatifs [pʀepaʀatif] *nmpl* preparations

préparation [pʀepaʀasjɔ̃] *nf* preparation

préparer [pʀepaʀe] /1/ *vt* to prepare; (*café, repas*) to make; (*examen*) to prepare for; (*voyage, entreprise*) to plan; **se préparer** *vi* (*orage, tragédie*) to brew, be in the air; **se ~ (à qch/à faire)** to prepare (o.s.) *ou* get ready (for sth/to do); **~ qch à qn** (*surprise etc*) to have sth in store for sb

prépondérant, e [pʀepɔ̃deʀɑ̃, -ɑ̃t] *adj* major, dominating

préposé, e [pʀepoze] *nm/f* employee; (*facteur*) postman/woman

préposition [pʀepozisjɔ̃] *nf* preposition

près [pʀɛ] *adv* near, close; **~ de** near (to), close to; (*environ*) nearly, almost; **de ~** closely; **à cinq kg ~** to within about five kg; **il n'est pas à 10 minutes ~** he can spare 10 minutes

présage [pʀezaʒ] *nm* omen

presbyte [pʀɛsbit] *adj* long-sighted

presbytère [pʀɛsbiteʀ] *nm* presbytery

prescription [pʀɛskʀipsjɔ̃] *nf* prescription

prescrire [pʀɛskʀiʀ] /39/ *vt* to prescribe

présence [pʀezɑ̃s] *nf* presence; (*au bureau etc*) attendance

présent, e [pʀezɑ̃, -ɑ̃t] *adj, nm* present; **à ~ que** now that

présentation [pʀezɑ̃tasjɔ̃] *nf* presentation; (*de nouveau venu*) introduction; (*allure*) appearance; **faire les ~s** to do the introductions

présenter [pʀezɑ̃te] /1/ *vt* to present; (*invité, candidat*) to introduce; (*félicitations, condoléances*) to offer; **~ qn à** to introduce sb to ▷ *vi*: **~ mal/bien** to have an unattractive/a pleasing appearance; **se présenter** *vi* (*à une élection*) to stand; (*occasion*) to arise; **se ~ à un examen** to sit an exam; **je vous présente Nadine** this is Nadine

préservatif [pʀezeʀvatif] *nm* condom, sheath

préserver [pʀezeʀve] /1/ *vt*: **~ de** (*protéger*) to protect from

président [pʀezidɑ̃] *nm* (*Pol*) president; (*d'une assemblée, Comm*) chairman; **~ directeur général** chairman and managing director

présidentiel, le [pʀezidɑ̃sjɛl] *adj* presidential; **présidentielles** *nfpl* presidential election(s)

présider [pʀezide] /1/ *vt* to preside over; (*dîner*) to be the guest of honour (BRIT) *ou* honor (US) at

presque [pʀɛsk] *adv* almost, nearly; **~ rien** hardly anything; **~ pas** hardly (at all); **~ pas de** hardly any; **personne, ou ~** next to nobody, hardly anyone

presqu'île [pʀɛskil] *nf* peninsula

pressant, e [pʀesɑ̃, -ɑ̃t] *adj* urgent

presse [pʀɛs] *nf* press; (*affluence*): **heures de ~** busy times

P

pressé, e [pʀese] *adj* in a hurry;
(*besogne*) urgent; **orange ~e** freshly
squeezed orange juice
pressentiment [pʀesɑ̃timɑ̃] *nm*
foreboding, premonition
pressentir [pʀesɑ̃tiʀ] /16/ *vt* to
sense
presse-papiers [pʀɛspapje] *nm inv*
paperweight
presser [pʀese] /1/ *vt* (*fruit, éponge*)
to squeeze; (*interrupteur, bouton*) to
press; (*allure, affaire*) to speed up;
(*inciter*): **~ qn de faire** to urge *ou* press
sb to do ▷ *vi* to be urgent; **se presser**
vi (*se hâter*) to hurry (up); **rien ne
presse** there's no hurry; **se ~ contre
qn** to squeeze up against sb; **le
temps presse** there's not much time
pressing [pʀesiŋ] *nm* (*magasin*)
dry-cleaner's
pression [pʀesjɔ̃] *nf* pressure;
(*bouton*) press stud (BRIT), snap
fastener (US); (*fam: bière*) draught
beer; **faire ~ sur** to put pressure on;
sous ~ pressurized, under pressure;
(*fig*) keyed up; **~ artérielle** blood
pressure
prestataire [pʀɛstateʀ] *nm/f* person
receiving benefits; **~ de services**
provider of services
prestation [pʀɛstasjɔ̃] *nf* (*allocation*)
benefit; (*d'une entreprise*) service
provided; (*d'un joueur, artiste*)
performance
prestidigitateur, -trice
[pʀɛstidiʒitatœʀ, -tʀis] *nm/f*
conjurer
prestige [pʀɛstiʒ] *nm* prestige;
prestigieux, -euse *adj* prestigious
présumer [pʀezyme] /1/ *vt*: **~ que** to
presume *ou* assume that
prêt, e [pʀɛ, pʀɛt] *adj* ready ▷ *nm*
(*somme prêtée*) loan; **prêt-à-porter**
nm ready-to-wear *ou* off-the-peg
(BRIT) clothes *pl*
prétendre [pʀetɑ̃dʀ] /41/ *vt*
(*affirmer*): **~ que** to claim that; **~ faire
qch** (*avoir l'intention de*) to mean *ou*

intend to do sth; **prétendu, e** *adj*
(*supposé*) so-called

> Attention à ne pas traduire
> *prétendre* par *to pretend*.

prétentieux, -euse [pʀetɑ̃sjø, -øz]
adj pretentious
prétention [pʀetɑ̃sjɔ̃] *nf*
pretentiousness; (*exigence, ambition*)
claim
prêter [pʀete] /1/ *vt*: **~ qch à qn**
(*livres, argent*) to lend sth to sb;
(*caractère, propos*) to attribute sth
to sb
prétexte [pʀetɛkst] *nm* pretext,
excuse; **sous aucun ~** on no account;
prétexter [pʀetɛkste] /1/ *vt* to give
as a pretext *ou* an excuse
prêtre [pʀɛtʀ] *nm* priest
preuve [pʀœv] *nf* proof; (*indice*)
proof, evidence *no pl*; **faire ~ de**
to show; **faire ses ~s** to prove o.s.
(*ou* itself)
prévaloir [pʀevalwaʀ] /29/ *vi* to
prevail
prévenant, e [pʀevnɑ̃, -ɑ̃t] *adj*
thoughtful, kind
prévenir [pʀevniʀ] /22/ *vt* (*éviter:
catastrophe etc*) to avoid, prevent;
(*anticiper: désirs, besoins*) to
anticipate; **~ qn (de)** (*avertir*) to warn
sb (about); (*informer*) to tell *ou* inform
sb (about)
préventif, -ive [pʀevɑ̃tif, -iv] *adj*
preventive
prévention [pʀevɑ̃sjɔ̃] *nf*
prevention; **~ routière** road safety
prévenu, e [pʀevny] *nm/f* (*Jur*)
defendant, accused
prévision [pʀevizjɔ̃] *nf*: **~s**
predictions; (*météorologiques,
économiques*) forecast *sg*; **en
~ de** in anticipation of; **~s
météorologiques** *ou* **du temps**
weather forecast *sg*
prévoir [pʀevwaʀ] /24/ *vt* (*deviner*)
to foresee; (*s'attendre à*) to expect,
reckon on; (*organiser: voyage etc*)
to plan; (*préparer, réserver*) to

allow; **comme prévu** as planned; **prévoyant, e** adj gifted with (ou showing) foresight; **prévu, e** pp de **prévoir**

prier [pʀije] /7/ vi to pray ▷ vt (Dieu) to pray to; (implorer) to beg; (demander): **~ qn de faire** to ask sb to do; **se faire ~** to need coaxing ou persuading; **je vous en prie** (allez-y) please do; (de rien) don't mention it; **prière** nf prayer; **"prière de faire ..."** "please do ..."

primaire [pʀimɛʀ] adj primary ▷ nm (Scol) primary education

prime [pʀim] nf (bonification) bonus; (subside) allowance; (Comm: cadeau) free gift; (Assurances, Bourse) premium ▷ adj: **de ~ abord** at first glance; **primer** /1/ vt (récompenser) to award a prize to ▷ vi to dominate

primevère [pʀimvɛʀ] nf primrose

primitif, -ive [pʀimitif, -iv] adj primitive; (originel) original

prince [pʀɛ̃s] nm prince; **princesse** nf princess

principal, e, -aux [pʀɛ̃sipal, -o] adj principal, main ▷ nm (Scol) head (teacher) (BRIT), principal (US); (essentiel) main thing

principe [pʀɛ̃sip] nm principle; **par ~** on principle; **en ~** (habituellement) as a rule; (théoriquement) in principle

printemps [pʀɛ̃tɑ̃] nm spring

priorité [pʀijɔʀite] nf priority; (Auto)**~ à droite** right of way to vehicles coming from the right

pris, e [pʀi, pʀiz] pp de **prendre** ▷ adj (place) taken; (journée, mains) full; (personne) busy; **avoir le nez/ la gorge ~(e)** to have a stuffy nose/a bad throat; **être ~ de peur/de fatigue/de panique** to be stricken with fear/overcome with fatigue/ panic-stricken

prise [pʀiz] nf (d'une ville) capture; (Pêche, Chasse) catch; (point d'appui ou pour empoigner) hold; (Élec: fiche) plug; (: femelle) socket; **être aux ~s avec** to be grappling with; **~ de courant** power point; **~ multiple** adaptor; **~ de sang** blood test

priser [pʀize] /1/ vt (estimer) to prize, value

prison [pʀizɔ̃] nf prison; **aller/être en ~** to go to/be in prison ou jail; **prisonnier, -ière** nm/f prisoner ▷ adj captive

privé, e [pʀive] adj private; (en punition): **tu es ~ de télé!** no TV for you! ▷ nm (Comm) private sector; **en ~** in private

priver [pʀive] /1/ vt: **~ qn de** to deprive sb of; **se ~ de** to go ou do without

privilège [pʀivilɛʒ] nm privilege

prix [pʀi] nm price; (récompense, Scol) prize; **hors de ~** exorbitantly priced; **à aucun ~** not at any price; **à tout ~** at all costs

probable [pʀɔbabl] adj likely, probable; **probablement** adv probably

problème [pʀɔblɛm] nm problem

procédé [pʀɔsede] nm (méthode) process; (comportement) behaviour no pl

procéder [pʀɔsede] /6/ vi to proceed; (moralement) to behave; **~ à** to carry out

procès [pʀɔsɛ] nm trial (poursuites) proceedings pl; **être en ~ avec** to be involved in a lawsuit with

processus [pʀɔsesys] nm process

procès-verbal, -aux [pʀɔsɛvɛʀbal, -o] nm (de réunion) minutes pl; (aussi: **PV**): **avoir un ~** to get a parking ticket

prochain, e [pʀɔʃɛ̃, -ɛn] adj next; (proche: départ, arrivée) impending ▷ nm fellow man; **la ~e fois/semaine ~e** next time/week; **prochainement** adv soon, shortly

proche [pʀɔʃ] adj nearby; (dans le temps) imminent; (parent, ami) close; **proches** nmpl (parents) close relatives; **être ~ (de)** to be near, be close (to)

proclamer [pʀɔklame] /1/ vt to proclaim

procuration [pʀɔkyʀasjɔ̃] nf proxy

procurer [pʀɔkyʀe] /1/ vt (fournir): ~ **qch à qn** (obtenir) to get ou obtain sth for sb; (plaisir etc) to bring ou give sb sth; **se procurer** vt to get; **procureur** nm public prosecutor

prodige [pʀɔdiʒ] nm marvel, wonder; (personne) prodigy; **prodiguer** /1/ vt (soins, attentions): **prodiguer qch à qn** to lavish sth on sb

producteur, -trice [pʀɔdyktœʀ, -tʀis] nm/f producer

productif, -ive [pʀɔdyktif, -iv] adj productive

production [pʀɔdyksjɔ̃] nf production; (rendement) output

productivité [pʀɔdyktivite] nf productivity

produire [pʀɔdɥiʀ] /38/ vt to produce; **se produire** vi (acteur) to perform, appear; (événement) to happen, occur

produit, e [pʀɔdɥi, -it] nm product; ~ **chimique** chemical; ~ **d'entretien** cleaning product; ~**s agricoles** farm produce sg; ~**s de beauté** beauty products, cosmetics

prof [pʀɔf] nm (fam) teacher

proférer [pʀɔfeʀe] /6/ vt to utter

professeur, e [pʀɔfesœʀ] nm/f teacher; (titulaire d'une chaire) professor; ~ **(de faculté)** (university) lecturer

profession [pʀɔfesjɔ̃] nf (libérale) profession; (gén) occupation; **"sans ~"** "unemployed"; **professionnel, le** adj, nm/f professional

profil [pʀɔfil] nm profile; **de ~** in profile

profit [pʀɔfi] nm (avantage) benefit, advantage; (Comm, Finance) profit; **au ~ de** in aid of; **tirer** ou **retirer ~ de** to profit from; **profitable** adj (utile) beneficial; (lucratif) profitable; **profiter** /1/ vi: **profiter de** (situation, occasion) to take advantage of; (vacances, jeunesse etc) to make the most of

profond, e [pʀɔfɔ̃, -ɔ̃d] adj deep; (méditation, mépris) profound; **profondément** adv deeply; **il dort profondément** he is sound asleep; **profondeur** nf depth; **l'eau a quelle profondeur?** how deep is the water?

programme [pʀɔgʀam] nm programme; (Scol) syllabus, curriculum; (Inform) program; **programmer** /1/ vt (organiser, prévoir: émission) to schedule; (Inform) to program; **programmeur, -euse** nm/f (computer) programmer

progrès [pʀɔgʀɛ] nm progress no pl; **faire des/être en ~** to make/ be making progress; **progresser** /1/ vi to progress; **progressif, -ive** adj progressive

proie [pʀwa] nf prey no pl

projecteur [pʀɔʒɛktœʀ] nm projector; (de théâtre, cirque) spotlight

projectile [pʀɔʒɛktil] nm missile

projection [pʀɔʒɛksjɔ̃] nf projection; (séance) showing

projet [pʀɔʒɛ] nm plan; (ébauche) draft; ~ **de loi** bill; **projeter** /4/ vt (envisager) to plan; (film, photos) to project; (ombre, lueur) to throw, cast; (jeter) to throw up (ou off ou out)

prolétaire [pʀɔletɛʀ] adj, nm/f proletarian

prolongement [pʀɔlɔ̃ʒmɑ̃] nm extension; **dans le ~ de** running on from

prolonger [pʀɔlɔ̃ʒe] /3/ vt (débat, séjour) to prolong; (délai, billet, rue) to extend; **se prolonger** vi to go on

promenade [pʀɔmnad] nf walk (ou drive ou ride); **faire une ~** to go for a walk; **une ~ (à pied)/en voiture/à vélo** a walk/drive/(bicycle) ride

promener [pʀɔmne] /5/ vt (personne, chien) to take out for a walk; (doigts, regard): ~ **qch sur** to run sth over; **se promener** vi to go for (ou be out for) a walk

promesse [pʀɔmɛs] nf promise

promettre [pʀɔmɛtʀ] /56/ vt to promise ▷ vi to look promising; **~ à qn de faire** to promise sb that one will do

promiscuité [pʀɔmiskɥite] nf lack of privacy

promontoire [pʀɔmɔ̃twaʀ] nm headland

promoteur, -trice [pʀɔmɔtœʀ, -tʀis] nm/f: **~ (immobilier)** property developer (BRIT), real estate promoter (US)

promotion [pʀɔmosjɔ̃] nf promotion; **en ~** on (special) offer

promouvoir [pʀɔmuvwaʀ] /27/ vt to promote

prompt, e [pʀɔ̃, pʀɔ̃t] adj swift, rapid

prôner [pʀone] /1/ vt (préconiser) to advocate

pronom [pʀɔnɔ̃] nm pronoun

prononcer [pʀɔnɔ̃se] /3/ vt to pronounce; (dire) to utter; (discours) to deliver; **se prononcer** vi to be pronounced; **se ~ (sur)** (se décider) to reach a decision (on ou about), give a verdict (on); **ça se prononce comment?** how do you pronounce this?; **prononciation** nf pronunciation

pronostic [pʀɔnɔstik] nm (Méd) prognosis; (fig: aussi: **~s**) forecast

propagande [pʀɔpagɑ̃d] nf propaganda

propager [pʀɔpaʒe] /3/ vt to spread; **se propager** vi to spread

prophète, prophétesse [pʀɔfɛt, pʀɔfetɛs] nm/f prophet(ess)

prophétie [pʀɔfesi] nf prophecy

propice [pʀɔpis] adj favourable

proportion [pʀɔpɔʀsjɔ̃] nf proportion; **toute(s) ~(s) gardée(s)** making due allowance(s)

propos [pʀɔpo] nm (paroles) talk no pl, remark; (intention, but) intention, aim; (sujet): **à quel ~?** what about?; **à ~ de** about, regarding; **à tout ~** for no reason at all; **à ~** by the way; (opportunément) (just) at the right moment

proposer [pʀɔpoze] /1/ vt to propose; **~ qch (à qn)/de faire** (suggérer) to suggest sth (to sb)/ doing, propose sth (to sb)/(to) do; (offrir) to offer (sb) sth/to do; **se ~ (pour faire)** to offer one's services (to do); **proposition** nf suggestion; proposal; (Ling) clause

propre [pʀɔpʀ] adj clean; (net) neat, tidy; (possessif) own; (sens) literal; (particulier): **~ à** peculiar to; (approprié): **~ à** suitable ou appropriate for ▷ nm: **recopier au ~** to make a fair copy of; **proprement** adv (avec propreté) cleanly; **à proprement parler** strictly speaking; **le village proprement dit** the village itself; **propreté** nf cleanliness

propriétaire [pʀɔpʀijetɛʀ] nm/f owner; (pour le locataire) landlord(-lady)

propriété [pʀɔpʀijete] nf (droit) ownership; (objet, immeuble etc) property

propulser [pʀɔpylse] /1/ vt to propel

prose [pʀoz] nf prose (style)

prospecter [pʀɔspɛkte] /1/ vt to prospect; (Comm) to canvass

prospectus [pʀɔspɛktys] nm leaflet

prospère [pʀɔspɛʀ] adj prosperous; **prospérer** /6/ vi to thrive

prosterner [pʀɔstɛʀne] /1/: **se prosterner** vi to bow low, prostrate o.s.

prostituée [pʀɔstitɥe] nf prostitute

prostitution [pʀɔstitysjɔ̃] nf prostitution

protecteur, -trice [pʀɔtɛktœʀ, -tʀis] adj protective; (air, ton: péj) patronizing ▷ nm/f protector

protection [pʀɔtɛksjɔ̃] nf protection; (d'un personnage influent: aide) patronage

protéger [pʀɔteʒe] /6, 3/ vt to protect; **se ~ de/contre** to protect o.s. from

protège-slip [pʀɔtɛʒslip] nm panty liner

P

protéine [pʀɔtein] nf protein

protestant, e [pʀɔtɛstɑ̃, -ɑ̃t] adj, nm/f Protestant

protestation [pʀɔtɛstasjɔ̃] nf (plainte) protest

protester [pʀɔteste] /1/ vi: **~ (contre)** to protest (against ou about); **~ de** (son innocence, sa loyauté) to protest

prothèse [pʀɔtɛz] nf: **~ dentaire** denture

protocole [pʀɔtɔkɔl] nm (fig) etiquette

proue [pʀu] nf bow(s pl), prow

prouesse [pʀuɛs] nf feat

prouver [pʀuve] /1/ vt to prove

provenance [pʀɔvnɑ̃s] nf origin; **avion en ~ de** plane (arriving) from

provenir [pʀɔvniʀ] /22/: **~ de** vt to come from

proverbe [pʀɔvɛʀb] nm proverb

province [pʀɔvɛ̃s] nf province

proviseur [pʀɔvizœʀ] nm ≈ head (teacher) (BRIT), ≈ principal (US)

provision [pʀɔvizjɔ̃] nf (réserve) stock, supply; **provisions** nfpl (vivres) provisions, food no pl

provisoire [pʀɔvizwaʀ] adj temporary; **provisoirement** adv temporarily

provocant, e [pʀɔvɔkɑ̃, -ɑ̃t] adj provocative

provoquer [pʀɔvɔke] /1/ vt (défier) to provoke; (causer) to cause, bring about; (inciter): **~ qn à** to incite sb to

proxénète [pʀɔksenɛt] nm procurer

proximité [pʀɔksimite] nf nearness, closeness; (dans le temps) imminence, closeness; **à ~** near ou close by; **à ~ de** near (to), close to

prudemment [pʀydamɑ̃] adv carefully; wisely, sensibly

prudence [pʀydɑ̃s] nf carefulness; **avec ~** carefully; **par (mesure de) ~** as a precaution

prudent, e [pʀydɑ̃, -ɑ̃t] adj (pas téméraire) careful (: en général) safety-conscious; (sage, conseillé) wise, sensible; **c'est plus ~.** it's wiser

prune [pʀyn] nf plum

pruneau, x [pʀyno] nm prune

prunier [pʀynje] nm plum tree

PS sigle m = **parti socialiste**; (= post-scriptum) PS

pseudonyme [psødɔnim] nm (gén) fictitious name; (d'écrivain) pseudonym, pen name

psychanalyse [psikanaliz] nf psychoanalysis

psychiatre [psikjatʀ] nm/f psychiatrist; **psychiatrique** adj psychiatric

psychique [psiʃik] adj psychological

psychologie [psikɔlɔʒi] nf psychology; **psychologique** adj psychological; **psychologue** nm/f psychologist

pu [py] pp de **pouvoir**

puanteur [pɥɑ̃tœʀ] nf stink, stench

pub [pyb] nf (fam) = **publicité**; **la ~** advertising

public, -ique [pyblik] adj public; (école, instruction) state cpd ▷ nm public; (assistance) audience; **en ~** in public

publicitaire [pyblisitɛʀ] adj advertising cpd; (film, voiture) publicity cpd

publicité [pyblisite] nf (méthode, profession) advertising; (annonce) advertisement; (révélations) publicity

publier [pyblije] /7/ vt to publish

publipostage [pyblipɔstaʒ] nm (mass) mailing

publique [pyblik] adj f voir **public**

puce [pys] nf flea; (Inform) chip; **carte à ~** smart card; **(marché aux) ~s** flea market sg

pudeur [pydœʀ] nf modesty; **pudique** adj (chaste) modest; (discret) discreet

puer [pɥe] /1/ (péj) vi to stink

puéricultrice [pɥeʀikyltʀis] nf ≈ paediatric nurse

puéril, e [pɥeʀil] adj childish

puis [pɥi] vb voir **pouvoir** ▷ adv then

puiser [pɥize] /1/ vt: ~ **(dans)** to draw (from)

puisque [pɥisk] conj since

puissance [pɥisɑ̃s] nf power; **en ~** adj potential

puissant, e [pɥisɑ̃, -ɑ̃t] adj powerful

puits [pɥi] nm well

pull(-over) [pyl(ɔvœʀ)] nm sweater

pulluler [pylyle] /1/ vi to swarm

pulpe [pylp] nf pulp

pulvériser [pylveʀize] /1/ vt to pulverize; (liquide) to spray

punaise [pynɛz] nf (Zool) bug; (clou) drawing pin (BRIT), thumb tack (US)

punch [pɔ̃ʃ] nm (boisson) punch

punir [pyniʀ] /2/ vt to punish; **punition** nf punishment

pupille [pypij] nf (Anat) pupil ▷ nm/f (enfant) ward

pupitre [pypitʀ] nm (Scol) desk

pur, e [pyʀ] adj pure; (vin) undiluted; (whisky) neat; **en ~e perte** to no avail; **c'est de la folie ~e** it's sheer madness

purée [pyʀe] nf: ~ **(de pommes de terre)** ≈ mashed potatoes pl; ~ **de marrons** chestnut purée

purement [pyʀmɑ̃] adv purely

purgatoire [pyʀgatwaʀ] nm purgatory

purger [pyʀʒe] /3/ vt (Méd, Pol) to purge; (Jur: peine) to serve

pur-sang [pyʀsɑ̃] nm inv thoroughbred

pus [py] nm pus

putain [pytɛ̃] nf (!) whore (!)

puzzle [pœzl] nm jigsaw (puzzle)

PV sigle m = **procès-verbal**

pyjama [piʒama] nm pyjamas pl (BRIT), pajamas pl (US)

pyramide [piʀamid] nf pyramid

Pyrénées [piʀene] nfpl: **les ~** the Pyrenees

QI sigle m (= quotient intellectuel) IQ

quadragénaire [kadʀaʒenɛʀ] nm/f man/woman in his/her forties

quadruple [k(w)adʀypl] nm: **le ~ de** four times as much as

quai [ke] nm (de port) quay; (de gare) platform; **être à ~** (navire) to be alongside

qualification [kalifikasjɔ̃] nf qualification

qualifier [kalifje] /7/ vt to qualify; ~ **qch/qn de** to describe sth/sb as; **se qualifier** vi to qualify

qualité [kalite] nf quality

quand [kɑ̃] conj, adv when; ~ **je serai riche** when I'm rich; ~ **même** all the same; ~ **même, il exagère!** really, he overdoes it!; ~ **bien même** even though

quant [kɑ̃]: ~ **à** prép (pour ce qui est de) as for, as to; (au sujet de) regarding

quantité [kɑ̃tite] nf quantity, amount; **une** ou **des ~(s) de** (grand nombre) a great deal of

q

quarantaine [kaʀɑ̃tɛn] *nf*
(*isolement*) quarantine; **une ~ (de)**
forty or so, about forty; **avoir la ~**
(*âge*) to be around forty

quarante [kaʀɑ̃t] *num* forty

quart [kaʀ] *nm* (*fraction*) quarter;
(*surveillance*) watch; **un ~ de vin** a
quarter litre of wine; **le ~ de** a quarter
of; **~ d'heure** quarter of an hour; **~s
de finale** quarter finals

quartier [kaʀtje] *nm* (*de ville*) district,
area; (*de bœuf, de la lune*) quarter;
(*de fruit, fromage*) piece; **cinéma/
salle de ~** local cinema/hall; **avoir
~ libre** to be free; **~ général (QG)**
headquarters (HQ)

quartz [kwaʀts] *nm* quartz

quasi [kazi] *adv* almost, nearly;
quasiment *adv* almost, (very) nearly;
quasiment jamais hardly ever

quatorze [katɔʀz] *num* fourteen

quatorzième [katɔʀzjɛm] *num*
fourteenth

quatre [katʀ] *num* four; **à ~ pattes**
on all fours; **se mettre en ~ pour
qn** to go out of one's way for sb;
~ à ~ (*monter, descendre*) four at
a time; **quatre-vingt-dix** *num*
ninety; **quatre-vingts** *num* eighty;
quatrième *num* fourth ▷ *nf* (*Scol*)
year 9 (BRIT), eighth grade (US)

quatuor [kwatyɔʀ] *nm* quartet(te)

MOT-CLÉ

que [kə] *conj* **1** (*introduisant complétive*)
that; **il sait que tu es là** he knows
(that) you're here; **je veux que tu
acceptes** I want you to accept; **il
a dit que oui** he said he would (*ou*
it was *etc*)
2 (*reprise d'autres conjonctions*): **quand
il rentrera et qu'il aura mangé**
when he gets back and (when) he has
eaten; **si vous y allez ou que vous
...** if you go there or if you ...
3 (*en tête de phrase, hypothèse, souhait
etc*): **qu'il le veuille ou non** whether

he likes it or not; **qu'il fasse ce qu'il
voudra!** let him do as he pleases!
4 (*but*): **tenez-le qu'il ne tombe pas**
hold it so (that) it doesn't fall
5 (*après comparatif*) than, as; *voir aussi*
plus², **aussi**, **autant** *etc*
6 (*seulement*): **ne ... que** only; **il ne
boit que de l'eau** he only drinks
water
7 (*temps*): **il y a quatre ans qu'il est
parti** it is four years since he left, he
left four years ago
▷ *adv* (*exclamation*): **qu'il ou qu'est-ce
qu'il est bête/court vite!** he's so
silly!/he runs so fast!; **que de livres!**
what a lot of books!
▷ *pron* **1** (*relatif: personne*) whom;
(: *chose*) that, which; **l'homme que
je vois** the man (whom) I see; **le livre
que tu vois** the book (that *ou* which)
you see; **un jour que j'étais ...** a day
when I was ...
2 (*interrogatif*) what; **que fais-tu?**,
qu'est-ce que tu fais? what are you
doing?; **qu'est-ce que c'est?** what
is it?, what's that?; **que faire?** what
can one do?

Québec [kebɛk] *nm*: **le ~** Quebec
(Province)

québécois, e *adj* Quebec *cpd* ▷ *nm*
(*Ling*) Quebec French ▷ *nm/f*: **Q~, e**
Quebecois, Quebec(k)er

MOT-CLÉ

quel, quelle [kɛl] *adj* **1** (*interrogatif:
personne*) who; (: *chose*) what; **quel
est cet homme?** who is this man?;
quel est ce livre? what is this
book?; **quel livre/homme?** what
book/man?; (*parmi un certain choix*)
which book/man?; **quels acteurs
préférez-vous?** which actors do you
prefer?; **dans quels pays êtes-vous
allé?** which *ou* what countries did
you go to?
2 (*exclamatif*): **quelle surprise/**

coïncidence! what a surprise/
coincidence!
3: **quel que soit le coupable**
whoever is guilty; **quel que soit
votre avis** whatever your opinion
(may be)

quelconque [kɛlkɔ̃k] *adj* (*médiocre*:
repas) indifferent, poor; (*sans attrait*)
ordinary, plain; (*indéfini*): **un ami/
prétexte ~** some friend/pretext
or other

MOT-CLÉ

quelque [kɛlk] *adj* **1** (*au singulier*)
some; (*au pluriel*) a few, some;
(*tournure interrogative*) any; **quelque
espoir** some hope; **il a quelques
amis** he has a few *ou* some friends;
a-t-il quelques amis? does he have
any friends?; **les quelques livres
qui** the few books which; **20 kg et
quelque(s)** a bit over 20 kg
2: **quelque ... que: quelque
livre qu'il choisisse** whatever (*ou*
whichever) book he chooses
3: **quelque chose** something;
(*tournure interrogative*) anything;
quelque chose d'autre something
else; anything else; **quelque part**
somewhere; anywhere; **en quelque
sorte** as it were
▶ *adv* **1** (*environ*): **quelque 100
mètres** some 100 metres
2: **quelque peu** rather, somewhat

quelquefois [kɛlkəfwa] *adv*
sometimes
quelques-uns, -unes [kɛlkəzœ̃,
-yn] *pron* some, a few
quelqu'un [kɛlkœ̃] *pron* someone,
somebody; (*+ tournure interrogative
ou négative*) anyone, anybody; **~
d'autre** someone *ou* somebody else;
anybody else
qu'en dira-t-on [kɑ̃diʀatɔ̃] *nm inv*:
le ~ gossip, what people say

querelle [kəʀɛl] *nf* quarrel; **quereller
/1/: **se quereller *vi* to quarrel
qu'est-ce que [kɛskə] *voir* que
qu'est-ce qui [kɛski] *voir* qui
question [kɛstjɔ̃] *nf* question;
(*fig*) matter; issue; **il a été ~ de** we
(*ou* they) spoke about; **de quoi
est-il ~?** what is it about?; **il n'en
est pas ~** there's no question of
it; **en ~** in question; **hors de ~** out
of the question; **(re)mettre en ~**
to question; **questionnaire** *nm*
questionnaire; **questionner** /1/ *vt*
to question
quête [kɛt] *nf* collection; (*recherche*)
quest, search; **faire la ~** (*à l'église*) to
take the collection; (*artiste*) to pass
the hat round
quetsche [kwɛtʃ] *nf* damson
queue [kø] *nf* tail; (*fig: du classement*)
bottom; (: *de poêle*) handle; (: *de fruit,
feuille*) stalk; (: *de train, colonne, file*)
rear; **faire la ~** to queue (up) (*BRIT*),
line up (*US*); **~ de cheval** ponytail; **~
de poisson: faire une ~ de poisson
à qn** (*Auto*) to cut in front of sb

MOT-CLÉ

q

qui [ki] *pron* **1** (*interrogatif: personne*)
who; (: *chose*): **qu'est-ce qui est
sur la table?** what is on the table?;
qui est-ce qui? who?; **qui est-ce
que?** who?; **à qui est ce sac?** whose
bag is this?; **à qui parlais-tu?** who
were you talking to?, to whom were
you talking?; **chez qui allez-vous?**
whose house are you going to?
2 (*relatif: personne*) whom; **l'ami de qui je vous ai parlé**
the friend I told you about; **la dame
chez qui je suis allé** the lady whose
house I went to
3 (*sans antécédent*): **amenez qui vous
voulez** bring who you like; **qui que
ce soit** whoever it may be

quiche [kiʃ] *nf* quiche

quiconque [kikɔ̃k] *pron* (*celui qui*) whoever, anyone who; (*n'importe qui, personne*) anyone, anybody

quille [kij] *nf*: **(jeu de) ~s** skittles *sg* (BRIT), bowling (US)

quincaillerie [kɛ̃kɑjʀi] *nf* (*ustensiles*) hardware; (*magasin*) hardware shop *ou* store (US)

quinquagénaire [kɛ̃kazenɛʀ] *nm/f* man/woman in his/her fifties

quinquennat [kɛ̃kena] *nm* five year term of office (of French President)

quinte [kɛ̃t] *nf*: **~ (de toux)** coughing fit

quintuple [kɛ̃typl] *nm*: **le ~ de** five times as much as

quinzaine [kɛ̃zɛn] *nf*: **une ~ (de)** about fifteen, fifteen or so; **une ~ (de jours)** a fortnight (BRIT), two weeks

quinze [kɛ̃z] *num* fifteen; **dans ~ jours** in a fortnight('s time) (BRIT), in two weeks(' time)

quinzième [kɛ̃zjɛm] *num* fifteenth

quittance [kitɑ̃s] *nf* (*reçu*) receipt

quitte [kit] *adj*: **être ~ envers qn** to be no longer in sb's debt; (*fig*) to be quits with sb; **~ à faire** even if it means doing

quitter [kite] /1/ *vt* to leave; (*vêtement*) to take off; **se quitter** *vi* (*couples, interlocuteurs*) to part; **ne quittez pas** (*au téléphone*) hold the line

qui-vive [kiviv] *nm inv*: **être sur le ~** to be on the alert

 MOT-CLÉ

quoi [kwa] *pron interrog* **1** what; **~ de neuf?** what's new?; **~?** (*qu'est-ce que tu dis?*) what?
2 (*avec prép*): **à ~ tu penses?** what are you thinking about?; **de ~ parlez-vous?** what are you talking about?; **à ~ bon?** what's the use?
▶ *pron relatif*: **as-tu de ~ écrire?** do you have anything to write with?; **il n'y a pas de ~** (please) don't mention it; **il n'y a pas de ~ rire** there's nothing to laugh about
▶ *pron* (*locutions*): **~ qu'il arrive** whatever happens; **~ qu'il en soit** be that as it may; **~ que ce soit** anything at all
▶ *excl* what!

quoique [kwak] *conj* (al)though

quotidien, ne [kɔtidjɛ̃, -ɛn] *adj* daily; (*banal*) everyday ▷ *nm* (*journal*) daily (paper); **quotidiennement** *adv* daily, every day

r

R, r *abr* = route; rue

rab [Rab] *nm (fam: nourriture)* extra; **est-ce qu'il y a du ~?** are there any seconds?

rabâcher [Rabaʃe] /1/ *vt* to keep on repeating

rabais [Rabɛ] *nm* reduction, discount; **rabaisser** /1/ *vt (rabattre: prix)* to reduce; *(dénigrer)* to belittle

Rabat [Raba(t)] *n* Rabat

rabattre [Rabatʀ] /41/ *vt (couvercle, siège)* to pull down; *(déduire)* to reduce; **se rabattre** *vi (bords, couvercle)* to fall shut; *(véhicule, coureur)* to cut in; **se ~ sur** to fall back on

rabbin [Rabɛ̃] *nm* rabbi

rabougri, e [Rabugʀi] *adj* stunted

raccommoder [Rakɔmɔde] /1/ *vt* to mend, repair

raccompagner [Rakɔ̃paɲe] /1/ *vt* to take *ou* see back

raccord [RakɔR] *nm* link; *(retouche)* touch-up; **raccorder** /1/ *vt* to join (up), link up; *(pont etc)* to connect, link

raccourci [RakuRsi] *nm* short cut

raccourcir [RakuRsiR] /2/ *vt* to shorten ▷ *vi (jours)* to grow shorter, draw in

raccrocher [RakRɔʃe] /1/ *vt (tableau, vêtement)* to hang back up; *(récepteur)* to put down ▷ *vi (Tél)* to hang up, ring off

race [Ras] *nf* race; *(d'animaux, fig)* breed; **de ~** purebred, pedigree

rachat [Raʃa] *nm* buying; *(du même objet)* buying back

racheter [Raʃte] /5/ *vt (article perdu)* to buy another; *(davantage)* to buy more; *(après avoir vendu)* to buy back; *(d'occasion)* to buy; *(Comm: part, firme)* to buy up; **se racheter** *(gén)* to make amends; **~ du lait/trois œufs** to buy more milk/another three eggs

racial, e, -aux [Rasjal, -o] *adj* racial

racine [Rasin] *nf* root; **~ carrée/ cubique** square/cube root

racisme [Rasism] *nm* racism

raciste [Rasist] *adj, nm/f* racist

racket [Rakɛt] *nm* racketeering *no pl*

raclée [Rakle] *nf (fam)* hiding, thrashing

racler [Rakle] /1/ *vt (os, plat)* to scrape; **se ~ la gorge** to clear one's throat

racontars [Rakɔ̃taR] *nmpl* stories, gossip *sg*

raconter [Rakɔ̃te] /1/ *vt*: **~ (à qn)** *(décrire)* to relate (to sb), tell (sb) about; *(dire)* to tell (sb); **~ une histoire** to tell a story

radar [RadaR] *nm* radar; **~ (automatique)** *(Auto)* speed camera

rade [Rad] *nf (natural)* harbour; **rester en ~** *(fig)* to be left stranded

radeau, x [Rado] *nm* raft

radiateur [RadjatœR] *nm* radiator, heater; *(Auto)* radiator; **~ électrique/à gaz** electric/gas heater *ou* fire

radiation [Radjasjɔ̃] *nf (Physique)* radiation

radical, e, -aux [Radikal, -o] *adj* radical

radieux, -euse [ʀadjø, -øz] adj
radiant

radin, e [ʀadɛ̃, -in] adj (fam) stingy

radio [ʀadjo] nf radio; (Méd) X-ray
▷ nm radio operator; **à la ~** on
the radio; **radioactif, -ive** adj
radioactive; **radiocassette** nf
cassette radio; **radiographie**
nf radiography; (photo) X-ray
photograph; **radiophonique** adj
radio cpd; **radio-réveil** (pl **radios-
réveils**) nm radio alarm (clock)

radis [ʀadi] nm radish

radoter [ʀadɔte] /1/ vi to ramble on

radoucir [ʀadusiʀ] /2/: **se radoucir**
vi (se réchauffer) to become milder; (se
calmer) to calm down

rafale [ʀafal] nf (vent) gust (of wind);
(de balles, d'applaudissements) burst

raffermir [ʀafɛʀmiʀ] /2/ vt, **se
raffermir** vi to firm up

raffiner [ʀafine] /1/ vt to refine;
raffinerie nf refinery

raffoler [ʀafɔle] /1/: **~ de** vt to be
very keen on

rafle [ʀafl] nf (de police) raid; **rafler** /1/
vt (fam) to swipe, nick

rafraîchir [ʀafʀeʃiʀ] /2/ vt
(atmosphère, température) to cool
(down); (boisson) to chill; (fig: rénover)
to brighten up; **se rafraîchir** vi to
grow cooler; (en se lavant) to freshen
up; (en buvant etc) to refresh o.s.;
rafraîchissant, e adj refreshing;
rafraîchissement nm (boisson)
cool drink; **rafraîchissements** nmpl
(boissons, fruits etc) refreshments

rage [ʀaʒ] nf (Méd): **la ~** rabies; (fureur)
rage, fury; **faire ~** to rage; **~ de dents**
(raging) toothache

ragot [ʀago] nm (fam) malicious
gossip no pl

ragoût [ʀagu] nm stew

raide [ʀɛd] adj (tendu) taut, tight;
(escarpé) steep; (droit: cheveux)
straight; (ankylosé, dur, guindé) stiff;
(fam: sans argent) flat broke; (osé,
licencieux) daring ▷ adv (en pente)

steeply; **~ mort** stone dead; **raideur**
nf (rigidité) stiffness; **avec raideur**
(répondre) stiffly, abruptly; **raidir** /2/
vt (muscles) to stiffen; **se raidir** vi to
stiffen; (personne) to tense up; (: se
préparer moralement) to brace o.s.; (fig:
devenir intransigeant) to harden

raie [ʀɛ] nf (Zool) skate, ray; (rayure)
stripe; (des cheveux) parting

raifort [ʀɛfɔʀ] nm horseradish

rail [ʀaj] nm rail; (chemins de fer)
railways pl; **par ~** by rail

railler [ʀaje] /1/ vt to scoff at, jeer at

rainure [ʀenyʀ] nf groove

raisin [ʀezɛ̃] nm (aussi: **~s**) grapes pl;
~s secs raisins

raison [ʀezɔ̃] nf reason; **avoir ~** to be
right; **donner ~ à qn** to agree with
sb; (fait) to prove sb right; **se faire
une ~** to learn to live with it; **perdre
la ~** to become insane; **~ de plus** all
the more reason; **à plus forte ~** all
the more so; **sans ~** for no reason;
en ~ de because of; **à ~ de** at the
rate of; **~ sociale** corporate name;
raisonnable adj reasonable, sensible

raisonnement [ʀezɔnmɑ̃] nm
reasoning; argument

raisonner [ʀezɔne] /1/ vi (penser) to
reason; (argumenter, discuter) to argue
▷ vt (personne) to reason with

rajeunir [ʀaʒœniʀ] /2/ vt (en
recrutant) to inject new blood into
▷ vi to become (ou look) younger; **~
qn** (coiffure, robe) to make sb look
younger

rajouter [ʀaʒute] /1/ vt to add

rajuster [ʀaʒyste] /1/ vt (vêtement) to
straighten, tidy; (salaires) to adjust

ralenti [ʀalɑ̃ti] nm: **au ~** (fig) at a
slower pace; **tourner au ~** (Auto) to
tick over, idle

ralentir [ʀalɑ̃tiʀ] /2/ vt, vi, **se
ralentir** vi to slow down

râler [ʀɑle] /1/ vi to groan; (fam) to
grouse, moan (and groan)

rallier [ʀalje] /7/ vt (rejoindre) to
rejoin; (gagner à sa cause) to win over

rallonge [Ralɔ̃ʒ] nf (de table) (extra) leaf

rallonger [Ralɔ̃ʒe] /3/ vt to lengthen

rallye [Rali] nm rally; (Pol) march

ramassage [Ramɑsaʒ] nm: ~ **scolaire** school bus service

ramasser [Ramɑse] /1/ vt (objet tombé ou par terre) to pick up; (recueillir: copies, ordures) to collect; (récolter) to gather; **ramassis** nm (péj: de voyous) bunch; (de choses) jumble

rambarde [Rɑ̃baRd] nf guardrail

rame [Ram] nf (aviron) oar; (de métro) train; (de papier) ream

rameau, x [Ramo] nm (small) branch; **les R~x** (Rel) Palm Sunday sg

ramener [Ramne] /5/ vt to bring back; (reconduire) to take back; **~ qch à** (réduire à) to reduce sth to

ramer [Rame] /1/ vi to row

ramollir [RamɔliR] /2/ vt to soften; **se ramollir** vi to get (ou go) soft

rampe [Rɑ̃p] nf (d'escalier) banister(s pl); (dans un garage, d'un terrain) ramp; **la ~** (Théât) the footlights pl; **~ de lancement** launching pad

ramper [Rɑ̃pe] /1/ vi to crawl

rancard [RɑkaR] nm (fam) date

rancart [RɑkaR] nm: **mettre au ~** to scrap

rance [Rɑ̃s] adj rancid

rancœur [RɑkœR] nf rancour

rançon [Rɑ̃sɔ̃] nf ransom

rancune [Rɑ̃kyn] nf grudge, rancour; **garder ~ à qn (de qch)** to bear sb a grudge (for sth); **sans ~!** no hard feelings!; **rancunier, -ière** adj vindictive, spiteful

randonnée [Rɑ̃dɔne] nf ride; (à pied) walk, ramble; (en montagne) hike, hiking no pl; **la ~** (activité) hiking, walking; **une ~ à cheval** a pony trek

rang [Rɑ̃] nm (rangée) row; (grade, condition sociale, classement) rank; **rangs** nmpl (Mil) ranks; **se mettre en ~s/sur un ~** to get into ou form rows/a line; **au premier ~** in the first row; (fig) ranking first

rangé, e [Rɑ̃ʒe] adj (vie) well-ordered; (sérieux: personne) steady

rangée [Rɑ̃ʒe] nf row

ranger [Rɑ̃ʒe] /3/ vt (classer, grouper) to order, arrange; (mettre à sa place) to put away; (mettre de l'ordre dans) to tidy up; (fig: classer) **~ qn/qch parmi** to rank sb/sth among; **se ranger** vi (véhicule, conducteur) to pull over or in; (piéton) to step aside; (s'assagir) to settle down; **se ~ à** (avis) to come round to

ranimer [Ranime] /1/ vt (personne évanouie) to bring round; (douleur, souvenir) to revive; (feu) to rekindle

rapace [Rapas] nm bird of prey

râpe [Rɑp] nf (Culin) grater; **râper** /1/ vt (Culin) to grate

rapide [Rapid] adj fast; (prompt: intelligence, coup d'œil, mouvement) quick ▷ nm express (train); (de cours d'eau) rapid; **rapidement** adv fast; quickly

rapiécer [Rapjese] /3, 6/ vt to patch

rappel [Rapɛl] nm (Théât) curtain call; (Méd: vaccination) booster; (d'une aventure, d'un nom) reminder; **rappeler** /4/ vt to call back; (ambassadeur, Mil) to recall; (faire se souvenir): **rappeler qch à qn** to remind sb of sth; **se rappeler** vt (se souvenir de) to remember, recall

rapport [RapɔR] nm (compte rendu) report; (profit) yield, return; (lien, analogie) relationship; (corrélation) connection; **rapports** nmpl (entre personnes, pays) relations; **avoir ~ à** to have something to do with; **être/ se mettre en ~ avec qn** to be/get in touch with sb; **par ~ à** in relation to; **~s (sexuels)** (sexual) intercourse sg; **~ qualité-prix** value (for money)

rapporter [RapɔRte] /1/ vt (rendre, ramener) to bring back; (investissement) to yield; (relater) to report ▷ vi (investissement) to give a good return ou yield; (activité) to be very profitable; **se ~ à** to relate to

rapprochement [ʀapʀɔʃmɑ̃] nm (de nations, familles) reconciliation; (analogie, rapport) parallel

rapprocher [ʀapʀɔʃe] /1/ vt (deux objets) to bring closer together; (ennemis, partis etc) to bring together; (comparer) to establish a parallel between; (chaise d'une table): ~ **qch (de)** to bring sth closer (to); **se rapprocher** vi to draw closer ou nearer; **se ~ de** to come closer to; (présenter une analogie avec) to be close to

raquette [ʀakɛt] nf (de tennis) racket; (de ping-pong) bat

rare [ʀɑʀ] adj rare; **se faire ~** to become scarce; **rarement** adv rarely, seldom

ras, e [ʀɑ, ʀɑz] adj (tête, cheveux) close-cropped; (poil, herbe) short ▷ adv short; **en ~e campagne** in open country; **à ~ bords** to the brim; **en avoir ~ le bol** (fam) to be fed up

raser [ʀɑze] /1/ vt (barbe, cheveux) to shave off; (menton, personne) to shave; (fam: ennuyer) to bore; (démolir) to raze (to the ground); (frôler) to graze, skim; **se raser** vi to shave; (fam) to be bored (to tears); **rasoir** nm razor

rassasier [ʀasazje] /7/ vt: **être rassasié** to be sated

rassemblement [ʀasɑ̃bləmɑ̃] nm (groupe) gathering; (Pol) union

rassembler [ʀasɑ̃ble] /1/ vt (réunir) to assemble, gather; (documents, notes) to gather together, collect; **se rassembler** vi to gather

rassurer [ʀasyʀe] /1/ vt to reassure; **se rassurer** vi to be reassured; **rassure-toi** don't worry

rat [ʀa] nm rat

rate [ʀat] nf spleen

raté, e [ʀate] adj (tentative) unsuccessful, failed ▷ nm/f (fam: personne) failure

râteau, x [ʀɑto] nm rake

rater [ʀate] /1/ vi (affaire, projet etc) to go wrong, fail ▷ vt (cible, train, occasion) to miss; (démonstration, plat) to spoil; (examen) to fail

ration [ʀasjɔ̃] nf ration

RATP sigle f (= Régie autonome des transports parisiens) Paris transport authority

rattacher [ʀataʃe] /1/ vt (animal, cheveux) to tie up again; **~ qch à** (relier) to link sth with

rattraper [ʀatʀape] /1/ vt (fugitif) to recapture; (retenir, empêcher de tomber) to catch (hold of); (atteindre, rejoindre) to catch up with; (réparer: erreur) to make up for; **se rattraper** vi to make up for it; **se ~ (à)** (se raccrocher) to stop o.s. falling (by catching hold of)

rature [ʀatyʀ] nf deletion, erasure

rauque [ʀok] adj (voix) hoarse

ravages [ʀavaʒ] nmpl: **faire des ~** to wreak havoc

ravi, e [ʀavi] adj: **être ~ de/que** to be delighted with/that

ravin [ʀavɛ̃] nm gully, ravine

ravir [ʀaviʀ] /2/ vt (enchanter) to delight; **à ~** adv beautifully

raviser [ʀavize] /1/: **se raviser** vi to change one's mind

ravissant, e [ʀavisɑ̃, -ɑ̃t] adj delightful

ravisseur, -euse [ʀavisœʀ, -øz] nm/f abductor, kidnapper

ravitailler [ʀavitaje] /1/ vt (en vivres, munitions) to provide with fresh supplies; (véhicule) to refuel; **se ravitailler** vi to get fresh supplies

raviver [ʀavive] /1/ vt (feu) to rekindle; (douleur) to revive; (couleurs) to brighten up

rayé, e [ʀeje] adj (à rayures) striped

rayer [ʀeje] /8/ vt (érafler) to scratch; (barrer) to cross ou score out; (d'une liste) to cross ou strike off

rayon [ʀejɔ̃] nm (de soleil etc) ray; (Géom) radius; (de roue) spoke; (étagère) shelf; (de grand magasin) department; **dans un ~ de** within a radius of; **~ de soleil** sunbeam; **~s X** X-rays

rayonnement [ʀɛjɔnmɑ̃] nm (d'une culture) influence

rayonner [ʀɛjɔne] /1/ vi (fig) to shine forth; (: visage, personne) to be radiant; (touriste) to go touring (from one base)

rayure [ʀɛjyʀ] nf (motif) stripe; (éraflure) scratch; **à ~s** striped

raz-de-marée [ʀɑdmaʀe] nm inv tidal wave

ré [ʀe] nm (Mus) D; (en chantant la gamme) re

réaction [ʀeaksjɔ̃] nf reaction

réadapter [ʀeadapte] /1/: **se ~ (à)** vi to readjust (to)

réagir [ʀeaʒiʀ] /2/ vi to react

réalisateur, -trice [ʀealizatœʀ, -tʀis] nm/f (TV, Ciné) director

réalisation [ʀealizasjɔ̃] nf realization; (Ciné) production; **en cours de ~** under way

réaliser [ʀealize] /1/ vt (projet, opération) to carry out, realize; (rêve, souhait) to realize, fulfil; (exploit) to achieve; (film) to produce; (se rendre compte de) to realize; **se réaliser** vi to be realized

réaliste [ʀealist] adj realistic

réalité [ʀealite] nf reality; **en ~** in (actual) fact; **dans la ~** in reality

réanimation [ʀeanimasjɔ̃] nf resuscitation; **service de ~** intensive care unit

rébarbatif, -ive [ʀebaʀbatif, -iv] adj forbidding

rebattu, e [ʀəbaty] adj hackneyed

rebelle [ʀəbɛl] nm/f rebel ▷ adj (troupes) rebel; (enfant) rebellious; (mèche etc) unruly

rebeller [ʀəbele] /1/: **se rebeller** vi to rebel

rebondir [ʀəbɔ̃diʀ] /2/ vi (ballon: au sol) to bounce; (: contre un mur) to rebound; (fig) to get moving again

rebord [ʀəbɔʀ] nm edge; **le ~ de la fenêtre** the windowsill

rebours [ʀəbuʀ]: **à ~** adv the wrong way

rebrousser [ʀəbʀuse] /1/ vt: **~ chemin** to turn back

rebuter [ʀəbyte] /1/ vt to put off

récalcitrant, e [ʀekalsitʀɑ̃, -ɑ̃t] adj refractory

récapituler [ʀekapityle] /1/ vt to recapitulate; to sum up

receler [ʀəsəle] /5/ vt (produit d'un vol) to receive; (fig) to conceal; **receleur, -euse** nm/f receiver

récemment [ʀesamɑ̃] adv recently

recensement [ʀəsɑ̃smɑ̃] nm census

recenser [ʀəsɑ̃se] /1/ vt (population) to take a census of; (dénombrer) to list

récent, e [ʀesɑ̃, -ɑ̃t] adj recent

récépissé [ʀesepise] nm receipt

récepteur, -trice [ʀesɛptœʀ, -tʀis] adj receiving ▷ nm receiver

réception [ʀesɛpsjɔ̃] nf receiving no pl; (accueil) reception, welcome; (bureau) reception (desk); (réunion mondaine) reception, party; **réceptionniste** nm/f receptionist

recette [ʀəsɛt] nf recipe; (Comm) takings pl; **recettes** nfpl (Comm: rentrées) receipts; **faire ~** (spectacle, exposition) to be a winner

recevoir [ʀəsvwaʀ] /28/ vt to receive; (client, patient, représentant) to see; **être reçu** (à un examen) to pass

rechange [ʀəʃɑ̃ʒ]: **de ~** adj (pièces, roue) spare; (fig: solution) alternative; **des vêtements de ~** a change of clothes

recharge [ʀəʃaʀʒ] nf refill; **rechargeable** adj (stylo etc) refillable; **recharger** /3/ vt (briquet, stylo) to refill; (batterie) to recharge

réchaud [ʀeʃo] nm (portable) stove

réchauffement [ʀeʃofmɑ̃] nm warming (up); **le ~ de la planète** global warming

réchauffer [ʀeʃofe] /1/ vt (plat) to reheat; (mains, personne) to warm; **se réchauffer** vi (température) to get warmer; (personne) to warm o.s. (up)

rêche [ʀɛʃ] adj rough

recherche [ʀəʃɛʀʃ] nf (action): **la ~ de** the search for; (raffinement) studied elegance; (*scientifique etc*): **la ~** research; **recherches** *nfpl* (*de la police*) investigations; (*scientifiques*): research *sg*; **être/se mettre à la ~ de** to be/go in search of

recherché, e [RəʃɛRʃe] *adj* (*rare, demandé*) much sought-after; (*raffiné*) affected; (*tenue*) elegant

rechercher [RəʃɛRʃe] /1/ *vt* (*objet égaré, personne*) to look for; (*causes d'un phénomène, nouveau procédé*) to try to find; (*bonheur etc, l'amitié de qn*) to seek

rechute [Rəʃyt] *nf* (*Méd*) relapse

récidiver [Residive] /1/ *vi* to commit a second (*ou* subsequent) offence; (*fig*) to do it again

récif [Resif] *nm* reef

récipient [Resipjɑ̃] *nm* container

réciproque [Resiprɔk] *adj* reciprocal

récit [Resi] *nm* story; **récital** *nm* recital; **réciter** /1/ *vt* to recite

réclamation [Reklamasjɔ̃] *nf* complaint; **réclamations** *nfpl* complaints department *sg*

réclame [Reklɑm] *nf*: **une ~** an ad(vertisement), an advert (*BRIT*); **article en ~** special offer; **réclamer** /1/ *vt* to ask for; (*revendiquer*) to claim, demand ▷ *vi* to complain

réclusion [Reklyzjɔ̃] *nf* imprisonment

recoin [Rəkwɛ̃] *nm* nook, corner

reçois *etc* [Rəswa] *vb voir* **recevoir**

récolte [Rekɔlt] *nf* harvesting, gathering; (*produits*) harvest, crop; **récolter** /1/ *vt* to harvest, gather (in); (*fig*) to get

recommandé [Rəkɔmɑ̃de] *nm* (*Postes*): **en ~** by registered mail

recommander [Rəkɔmɑ̃de] /1/ *vt* to recommend; (*Postes*) to register

recommencer [Rəkɔmɑ̃se] /3/ *vt* (*reprendre: lutte, séance*) to resume, start again; (*refaire: travail, explications*) to start afresh, start (over) again ▷ *vi* to start again; (*récidiver*) to do it again

récompense [Rekɔ̃pɑ̃s] *nf* reward; (*prix*) award; **récompenser** /1/ *vt*: **récompenser qn (de** *ou* **pour)** to reward sb (for)

réconcilier [Rekɔ̃silje] /7/ *vt* to reconcile; **se réconcilier (avec)** to be reconciled (with)

reconduire [Rəkɔ̃dɥiR] /38/ *vt* (*raccompagner*) to take *ou* see back; (*renouveler*) to renew

réconfort [Rekɔ̃fɔR] *nm* comfort; **réconforter** /1/ *vt* (*consoler*) to comfort

reconnaissance [Rəkɔnɛsɑ̃s] *nf* (*action de reconnaître*) recognition; (*gratitude*) gratitude, gratefulness; (*Mil*) reconnaissance, recce; **reconnaissant, e** *adj* grateful; **je vous serais reconnaissant de bien vouloir** I should be most grateful if you would (kindly)

reconnaître [RəkɔnɛtR] /57/ *vt* to recognize; (*Mil: lieu*) to reconnoitre; (*Jur: enfant, dette, droit*) to acknowledge; **~ que** to admit *ou* acknowledge that; **~ qn/qch à** (*l'identifier grâce à*) to recognize sb/sth by; **reconnu, e** *adj* (*indiscuté, connu*) recognized

reconstituer [Rəkɔ̃stitɥe] /1/ *vt* (*fresque, vase brisé*) to piece together, reconstitute; (*événement, accident*) to reconstruct

reconstruire [Rəkɔ̃stRɥiR] /38/ *vt* to rebuild

reconvertir [Rəkɔ̃vɛRtiR] /2/ *vt* to reconvert; **se ~ dans** (*un métier, une branche*) to move into

record [RəkɔR] *nm, adj* record

recoupement [Rəkupmɑ̃] *nm*: **par ~** by cross-checking

recouper [Rəkupe] /1/: **se recouper** *vi* (*témoignages*) to tie ou match up

recourber [RəkuRbe] /1/: **se recourber** *vi* to curve (up), bend (up)

recourir [RəkuRiR] /11/: **~ à** *vt* (*ami, agence*) to turn *ou* appeal to; (*force, ruse, emprunt*) to resort to

recours [Rəkur] *nm*: **avoir ~ à** = **recourir à**; **en dernier ~** as a last resort

recouvrer [Rəkuvre] /1/ *vt* (*vue, santé etc*) to recover, regain

recouvrir [Rəkuvrir] /18/ *vt* (*couvrir à nouveau*) to re-cover; (*couvrir entièrement, aussi fig*) to cover

récréation [Rekreasjɔ̃] *nf* (*Scol*) break

recroqueviller [Rəkrɔkvije] /1/: **se recroqueviller** *vi* (*personne*) to huddle up

recrudescence [Rəkrydesɑ̃s] *nf* fresh outbreak

recruter [Rəkryte] /1/ *vt* to recruit

rectangle [Rɛktɑ̃gl] *nm* rectangle; **rectangulaire** *adj* rectangular

rectificatif, -ive [Rɛktifikatif, -iv] *adj* corrected ▷ *nm* correction

rectifier [Rɛktifje] /7/ *vt* (*calcul, adresse*) to correct; (*erreur, faute*) to rectify

rectiligne [Rɛktiliɲ] *adj* straight

recto [Rɛkto] *nm* front (*of a sheet of paper*); **~ verso** on both sides (of the page)

reçu, e [Rəsy] *pp de* **recevoir** ▷ *adj* (*candidat*) successful; (*admis, consacré*) accepted ▷ *nm* (*Comm*) receipt

recueil [Rəkœj] *nm* collection; **recueillir** /12/ *vt* to collect; (*voix, suffrages*) to win; (*accueillir: réfugiés, chat*) to take in; **se recueillir** *vi* to gather one's thoughts; to meditate

recul [Rəkyl] *nm* (*déclin*) decline; (*éloignement*) distance; **avoir un mouvement de ~** to recoil; **prendre du ~** to stand back; (*fig*) to be on the decline; **être en ~** to be on the decline; **avec le ~** in retrospect; **reculé, e** *adj* remote; **reculer** /1/ *vi* to move back, back away; (*Auto*) to reverse, back (up); (*fig*) to (be on the) decline ▷ *vt* to move back; (*véhicule*) to reverse, back (up); (*date, décision*) to postpone; **reculer devant** (*danger, difficulté*) to shrink from; **reculons**: **à reculons** *adv* backwards

récupérer [Rekypere] /6/ *vt* to recover, get back; (*déchets etc*) to salvage (for reprocessing); (*journée, heures de travail*) to make up ▷ *vi* to recover

récurer [Rekyre] /1/ *vt* to scour; **poudre à ~** scouring powder

reçus *etc* [Rəsy] *vb voir* **recevoir**

recycler [Rəsikle] /1/ *vt* (*matériau*) to recycle; **se recycler** *vi* to retrain

rédacteur, -trice [Redaktœr, -tris] *nm/f* (*journaliste*) writer; subeditor; (*d'ouvrage de référence*) editor, compiler

rédaction [Redaksjɔ̃] *nf* writing; (*rédacteurs*) editorial staff; (*Scol: devoir*) essay, composition

redescendre [Rədesɑ̃dr] /41/ *vi* to go back down ▷ *vt* (*pente etc*) to go down

rédiger [Rediʒe] /3/ *vt* to write; (*contrat*) to draw up

redire [Rədir] /37/ *vt* to repeat; **trouver à ~ à** to find fault with

redoubler [Rəduble] /1/ *vi* (*tempête, violence*) to intensify; (*Scol*) to repeat a year; **~ de patience/prudence** to be doubly patient/careful

redoutable [Rədutabl] *adj* formidable, fearsome

redouter [Rədute] /1/ *vt* to dread

redressement [Rədrɛsmɑ̃] *nm* (*économique*) recovery

redresser [Rədrese] /1/ *vt* (*arbre, mât*) to set upright; (*pièce tordue*) to straighten out; (*situation, économie*) to put right; **se redresser** *vi* (*personne*) to sit (*ou* stand) up; (*pays, situation*) to recover

réduction [Redyksjɔ̃] *nf* reduction

réduire [Reduir] /38/ *vt* to reduce; (*prix, dépenses*) to cut; reduce; **réduit** *nm* tiny room

rééducation [Reedykasjɔ̃] *nf* (*d'un membre*) re-education; (*de délinquants, d'un blessé*) rehabilitation

réel, le [Reɛl] *adj* real; **réellement** *adv* really

r

réexpédier [ʀeɛkspedje] /7/ vt
(à l'envoyeur) to return, send back;
(au destinataire) to send on, forward
refaire [ʀəfɛʀ] /60/ vt to do again;
(sport) to take up again; (réparer,
restaurer) to do up
réfectoire [ʀefɛktwaʀ] nm refectory
référence [ʀefeʀɑ̃s] nf reference;
références nfpl (recommandations)
reference sg
référer [ʀefeʀe] /6/: **se ~ à** vt to
refer to
refermer [ʀəfɛʀme] /1/ vt to close
again, shut again; **se refermer** vi
(porte) to close ou shut (again)
refiler [ʀəfile] /1/ vt (fam): **~ qch à qn**
to palm (BRIT) ou fob sth off on sb
réfléchi, e [ʀefleʃi] adj (caractère)
thoughtful; (action) well-thought-
out; (Ling) reflexive; **c'est tout ~** my
mind's made up
réfléchir [ʀefleʃiʀ] /2/ vt to reflect
▷ vi to think; **~ à** ou **sur** to think about
reflet [ʀəflɛ] nm reflection; (sur
l'eau etc) sheen no pl, glint; **refléter**
/6/ vt to reflect; **se refléter** vi to be
reflected
réflexe [ʀeflɛks] adj, nm reflex
réflexion [ʀeflɛksjɔ̃] nf (de la
lumière etc) reflection; (fait de penser)
thought; (remarque) remark; **~ faite,
à la ~** on reflection; **délai de ~**
cooling-off period; **groupe de ~**
think tank
réflexologie [ʀeflɛksɔlɔʒi] nf
reflexology
réforme [ʀefɔʀm] nf reform; (Rel):
la R~ the Reformation; **réformer**
/1/ vt to reform; (Mil) to declare unfit
for service
refouler [ʀəfule] /1/ vt (envahisseurs)
to drive back; (liquide, larmes) to force
back; (désir, colère) to repress
refrain [ʀəfʀɛ̃] nm refrain, chorus
refréner /6/, **réfréner** [ʀəfʀene,
ʀefʀene] vt to curb, check
réfrigérateur [ʀefʀiʒeʀatœʀ] nm
refrigerator

refroidir [ʀəfʀwadiʀ] /2/ vt to
cool; (personne) to put off ▷ vi to cool
(down); **se refroidir** vi (temps) to get
cooler ou colder; (fig: ardeur) to cool
(off); **refroidissement** nm (grippe
etc) chill
refuge [ʀəfyʒ] nm refuge; **réfugié,
e** adj, nm/f refugee; **réfugier** /7/: **se
réfugier** vi to take refuge
refus [ʀəfy] nm refusal; **ce n'est pas
de ~** I won't say no, it's very welcome;
refuser /1/ vt to refuse; (Scol:
candidat) to fail; **refuser qch à qn/de
faire** to refuse sb sth/to do; **refuser
du monde** to have to turn people
away; **se refuser à qch** ou **à faire
qch** to refuse to do sth
regagner [ʀəgaɲe] /1/ vt (argent,
faveur) to win back; (lieu) to get back to
régal [ʀegal] nm treat; **régaler** /1/
vt: **régaler qn de** to treat sb to; **se
régaler** vi to have a delicious meal;
(fig) to enjoy o.s.
regard [ʀəgaʀ] nm (coup d'œil) look,
glance; (expression) look (in one's eye);
au ~ de (loi, morale) from the point of
view of; **en ~ de** in comparison with
regardant, e [ʀəgaʀdɑ̃, -ɑ̃t] adj:
très/peu ~ (sur) quite fussy/very
free (about); (économe) very tight-
fisted/quite generous (with)
regarder [ʀəgaʀde] /1/ vt to look
at; (film, télévision, match) to watch;
(concerner) to concern ▷ vi to look;
ne pas ~ à la dépense to spare no
expense; **~ qn/qch comme** to regard
sb/sth as
régie [ʀeʒi] nf (Comm, Industrie)
state-owned company; (Théât, Ciné)
production; (Radio, TV) control room
régime [ʀeʒim] nm (Pol) régime;
(Admin: carcéral, fiscal etc) system;
(Méd) diet; (de bananes, dattes) bunch;
se mettre au/suivre un ~ to go on/
be on a diet
régiment [ʀeʒimɑ̃] nm regiment
région [ʀeʒjɔ̃] nf region; **régional, e,
-aux** adj regional

régir [ʀeʒiʀ] /2/ vt to govern

régisseur [ʀeʒisœʀ] nm (d'un domaine) steward; (Ciné, TV) assistant director; (Théât) stage manager

registre [ʀaʒistʀ] nm register

réglage [ʀeglaʒ] nm adjustment

réglé, e [ʀegle] adj well-ordered; (arrangé) settled

règle [ʀɛgl] nf (instrument) ruler; (loi, prescription) rule; **règles** nfpl (Physiol) period sg; **en ~** (papiers d'identité) in order; **en ~ générale** as a (general) rule

règlement [ʀɛglǝmɑ̃] nm (paiement) settlement; (arrêté) regulation; (règles, statuts) regulations pl, rules pl; **réglementaire** adj conforming to the regulations; (tenue, uniforme) regulation cpd; **réglementation** nf (règlements) regulations pl; **réglementer** /1/ vt to regulate

régler [ʀegle] /6/ vt (mécanisme, machine) to regulate, adjust; (thermostat etc) to set, adjust; (question, conflit, facture, dette) to settle; (fournisseur) to settle up with

réglisse [ʀeglis] nm ou f liquorice

règne [ʀɛɲ] nm (d'un roi etc, fig) reign; **le ~ végétal/animal** the vegetable/animal kingdom; **régner** /6/ vi (roi) to rule, reign; (fig) to reign

regorger [ʀǝgɔʀʒe] /3/ vi: **~ de** to overflow with, be bursting with

regret [ʀǝgʀɛ] nm regret; **à ~** with regret; **sans ~** with no regrets; **regrettable** adj regrettable; **regretter** /1/ vt to regret; (personne) to miss; **non, je regrette** no, I'm sorry

regrouper [ʀǝgʀupe] /1/ vt (grouper) to group together; (contenir) to include, comprise; **se regrouper** vi to gather (together)

régulier, -ière [ʀegylje, -jɛʀ] adj (gén) regular; (vitesse, qualité) steady; (répartition, pression) even; (Transports: ligne, service) scheduled, regular; (légal, réglementaire) lawful,

in order; (fam: correct) straight, on the level; **régulièrement** adv regularly; evenly

rehausser [ʀǝose] /1/ vt (relever) to heighten, raise; (fig: souligner) to set off, enhance

rein [ʀɛ̃] nm kidney; **reins** nmpl (dos) back sg

reine [ʀɛn] nf queen

reine-claude [ʀɛnklod] nf greengage

réinscriptible [ʀeɛ̃skʀiptibl] adj (CD, DVD) rewritable

réinsertion [ʀeɛ̃sɛʀsjɔ̃] nf (de délinquant) reintegration, rehabilitation

réintégrer [ʀeɛ̃tegʀe] /6/ vt (lieu) to return to; (fonctionnaire) to reinstate

rejaillir [ʀǝʒajiʀ] /2/ vi to splash up; **~ sur** (fig) (scandale) to rebound on; (gloire) to be reflected on

rejet [ʀǝʒɛ] nm rejection; **rejeter** /4/ vt (relancer) to throw back; (vomir) to bring ou throw up; (écarter) to reject; (déverser) to throw out, discharge; **rejeter la responsabilité de qch sur qn** to lay the responsibility for sth at sb's door

rejoindre [ʀǝʒwɛ̃dʀ] /49/ vt (famille, régiment) to rejoin, return to; (lieu) to get (back) to; (route etc) to meet, join; (rattraper) to catch up (with); **se rejoindre** vi to meet; **je te rejoins au café** I'll see ou meet you at the café

réjouir [ʀeʒwiʀ] /2/ vt to delight; **se ~ de qch/de faire** to be delighted about sth/to do; **réjouissances** nfpl (fête) festivities

relâche [ʀǝlɑʃ] nm (Sport): **(course de) ~** relay (race); **prendre le ~ (de)** to take

relâche: **sans ~** adv without respite ou a break; **relâché, e** adj loose, lax; **relâcher** /1/ vt (ressort, prisonnier) to release; (étreinte, cordes) to loosen; **se relâcher** vi (discipline) to become slack ou lax; (élève etc) to slacken off

relais [ʀǝlɛ] nm (Sport): **(course de) ~** relay (race); **prendre le ~ (de)** to take over (from); **~ routier** ≈ transport café (BRIT); ≈ truck stop (US)

relancer [Rəlɑ̃se] /3/ vt (balle) to throw back (again); (moteur) to restart; (fig) to boost, revive; (personne): **~ qn** to pester sb

relatif, -ive [Rəlatif, -iv] adj relative

relation [Rəlasjɔ̃] nf (rapport) relation(ship); (connaissance) acquaintance; **relations** nfpl (rapports) relations; (connaissances) connections; **être/entrer en ~(s) avec** to be in contact ou be dealing/ get in contact with

relaxer [Rəlakse] /1/: **se relaxer** vi to relax

relayer [Rəleje] /8/ vt (collaborateur, coureur etc) to relieve; **se relayer** vi (dans une activité) to take it in turns

reléguer [Rəlege] /6/ vt to relegate

relevé, e [Rəlve] adj (manches) rolled-up; (sauce) highly-seasoned ▷ nm (lecture) reading; **~ bancaire** ou **de compte** bank statement

relève [Rəlɛv] nf (personne) relief; **prendre la ~** to take over

relever [Rəlve] /5/ vt (statue, meuble) to stand up again; (personne tombée) to help up; (vitre, plafond, niveau de vie) to raise; (col) to turn up; (style, conversation) to elevate; (plat, sauce) to season; (sentinelle, équipe) to relieve; (fautes, points) to pick out; (défi) to accept, take up; (noter: adresse etc) to take down, note; (: plan) to sketch; (compteur) to read; (ramasser: cahiers, copies) to collect, take in ▷ vi: **~ de** (maladie) to be recovering from; (être du ressort de) to be a matter for; (fig) to pertain to; **se relever** vi (se remettre debout) to get up; **~ qn de** (fonctions) to relieve sb of; **~ la tête** to look up

relief [Rəljɛf] nm relief; **mettre en ~** (fig) to bring out, highlight

relier [Rəlje] /7/ vt to link up; (livre) to bind; **~ qch à** to link sth to

religieux, -euse [Rəliʒjø, -øz] adj religious ▷ nm monk

religion [Rəliʒjɔ̃] nf religion

relire [RəliR] /43/ vt (à nouveau) to reread, read again; (vérifier) to read over

reluire [RəlɥiR] /38/ vi to gleam

remanier [Rəmanje] /7/ vt to reshape, recast; (Pol) to reshuffle

remarquable [Rəmarkabl] adj remarkable

remarque [Rəmark] nf remark; (écrite) note

remarquer [Rəmarke] /1/ vt (voir) to notice; **se remarquer** vi to be noticeable; **se faire ~** to draw attention to o.s.; **faire ~ (à qn) que** to point out (to sb) that; **faire ~ qch (à qn)** to point sth out (to sb); **remarquez, ...** mind you, ...

rembourrer [RɑbuRe] /1/ vt to stuff

remboursement [RɑbuRsəmɑ̃] nm (de dette, d'emprunt) repayment; (de frais) refund; **rembourser** /1/ vt to pay back, repay; (frais, billet etc) to refund; **se faire rembourser** to get a refund

remède [Rəmɛd] nm (médicament) medicine; (traitement, fig) remedy, cure

remémorer [RəmemɔRe] /1/: **se remémorer** vt to recall, recollect

remerciements [Rəmɛrsimɑ̃] nmpl thanks; **(avec) tous mes ~** (with) grateful ou many thanks

remercier [Rəmɛrsje] /7/ vt to thank; (congédier) to dismiss; **~ qn de/d'avoir fait** to thank sb for/for having done

remettre [RəmɛtR] /56/ vt (vêtement): **~ qch** to put sth back on; (replacer): **~ qch quelque part** to put sth back somewhere; (ajouter): **~ du sel/un sucre** to add more salt/ another lump of sugar; (ajourner): **~ qch (à)** to postpone sth ou put sth off (until); **se remettre** vi to get better; **~ qch à qn** (donner) to hand over sth to sb; (prix, décoration) to present sb with sth; **se ~ de** to recover from;

s'en ~ à to leave it (up) to; **se ~ à faire/qch** to start doing/sth again

remis, e [Rəmi, -iz] *pp de* **remettre** ▷ *nf* (*rabais*) discount; (*local*) shed; **~e en cause/question** calling into question/challenging; **~e en jeu** (*Football*) throw-in; **~e de peine** remission of sentence; **~e des prix** prize-giving

remontant [Rəmɔ̃tɑ̃] *nm* tonic, pick-me-up

remonte-pente [Rəmɔ̃tpɑ̃t] *nm* ski lift

remonter [Rəmɔ̃te] /1/ *vi* to go back up; (*prix, température*) to go up again; (*en voiture*) to get back in ▷ *vt* (*pente*) to go up; (*fleuve*) to sail (*ou* swim *etc*) up; (*manches, pantalon*) to roll up; (*fam*) to turn up; (*niveau, limite*) to raise; (*fig: personne*) to buck up; (*moteur, meuble*) to put back together, reassemble; (*montre, mécanisme*) to wind up; **~ le moral à qn** to raise sb's spirits; **~ à** (*dater de*) to date *ou* go back to

remords [Rəmɔr] *nm* remorse *no pl*; **avoir des ~** to feel remorse

remorque [Rəmɔrk] *nf* trailer; **remorquer** /1/ *vt* to tow; **remorqueur** *nm* tug(boat)

remous [Rəmu] *nm* (*d'un navire*) (back)wash *no pl*; (*de rivière*) swirl, eddy *pl*; (*fig*) stir *sg*

remparts [Rɑ̃par] *nmpl* walls, ramparts

remplaçant, e [Rɑ̃plasɑ̃, -ɑ̃t] *nm/f* replacement, stand-in; (*Scol*) supply (BRIT) *ou* substitute (US) teacher

remplacement [Rɑ̃plasmɑ̃] *nm* replacement; **faire des ~s** (*professeur*) to do supply *ou* substitute teaching; (*secrétaire*) to temp

remplacer [Rɑ̃plase] /3/ *vt* to replace; **~ qch/qn par** to replace sth/sb with

rempli, e [Rɑ̃pli] *adj* (*emploi du temps*) full, busy; **~ de** full of, filled with

remplir [Rɑ̃plir] /2/ *vt* to fill (up); (*questionnaire*) to fill out *ou* up; (*obligations, fonction, condition*) to fulfil; **se remplir** *vi* to fill up

remporter [Rɑ̃pɔrte] /1/ *vt* (*marchandise*) to take away; (*fig*) to win, achieve

remuant, e [Rəmɥɑ̃, -ɑ̃t] *adj* restless

remue-ménage [Rəmymenaʒ] *nm inv* commotion

remuer [Rəmɥe] /1/ *vt* to move; (*café, sauce*) to stir ▷ *vi* to move; **se remuer** *vi* to move; (*fam: s'activer*) to get a move on

rémunérer [Remynere] /6/ *vt* to remunerate

renard [Rənar] *nm* fox

renchérir [Rɑ̃ʃerir] /2/ *vi* (*fig*): **~ (sur)** (*en paroles*) to add something (to)

rencontre [Rɑ̃kɔ̃tr] *nf* meeting; (*imprévue*) encounter; **aller à la ~ de qn** to go and meet sb; **rencontrer** /1/ *vt* to meet; (*mot, expression*) to come across; (*difficultés*) to meet with; **se rencontrer** *vi* to meet

rendement [Rɑ̃dmɑ̃] *nm* (*d'un travailleur, d'une machine*) output; (*d'une culture, d'un champ*) yield

rendez-vous [Rɑ̃devu] *nm* appointment; (*d'amoureux*) date; (*lieu*) meeting place; **donner ~ à qn** to arrange to meet sb; **avoir/prendre ~ (avec)** to have/make an appointment (with)

rendre [Rɑ̃dr] /41/ *vt* (*livre, argent etc*) to give back, return; (*otages, visite, politesse, invitation*) to return; (*sang, aliments*) to bring up; (*exprimer, traduire*) to render; (*faire devenir*): **~ qn célèbre/qch possible** to make sb famous/sth possible; **se rendre** *vi* (*capituler*) to surrender, give o.s. up; (*aller*): **se ~ quelque part** to go somewhere; **se ~ compte de qch** to realize sth; **~ la monnaie** to give change

rênes [Rɛn] *nfpl* reins

renfermé, e [ʀɑ̃fɛʀme] adj (fig)
withdrawn ▷ nm: **sentir le ~** to
smell stuffy
renfermer [ʀɑ̃fɛʀme] /1/ vt to contain
renforcer [ʀɑ̃fɔʀse] /3/ vt to
reinforce; **renfort** nm: **renforts** nmpl
reinforcements; **à grand renfort de**
with a great deal of
renfrogné, e [ʀɑ̃fʀɔɲe] adj sullen,
scowling
renier [ʀənje] /7/ vt (parents) to
disown, repudiate; (foi) to renounce
renifler [ʀənifle] /1/ vi to sniff ▷ vt
(odeur) to sniff
renne [ʀɛn] nm reindeer inv
renom [ʀənɔ̃] nm reputation;
(célébrité) renown; **renommé, e** adj
celebrated, renowned ▷ nf fame
renoncer [ʀənɔ̃se] /3/: **~ à** vt to
give up; **~ à faire** to give up the idea
of doing
renouer [ʀənwe] /1/ vt: **~ avec**
(habitude) to take up again
renouvelable [ʀ(ə)nuvlabl] adj
(contrat, bail, énergie) renewable
renouveler [ʀənuvle] /4/ vt to
renew; (exploit, méfait) to repeat;
se renouveler vi (incident) to recur,
happen again; **renouvellement** nm
renewal
rénover [ʀenɔve] /1/ vt (immeuble)
to renovate, do up; (quartier) to
redevelop
renseignement [ʀɑ̃sɛɲmɑ̃]
nm information no pl, piece of
information; **(guichet des) ~s**
information desk; **(service des)**
~s (Tél) directory inquiries (BRIT),
information (US)
renseigner [ʀɑ̃sɛɲe] /1/ vt: **~ qn**
(sur) to give information to sb
(about); **se renseigner** vi to ask for
information, make inquiries
rentabilité [ʀɑ̃tabilite] nf
profitability
rentable [ʀɑ̃tabl] adj profitable
rente [ʀɑ̃t] nf income; (pension)
pension

rentrée [ʀɑ̃tʀe] nf: **~ (d'argent)** cash
no pl coming in; **la ~ (des classes**
ou scolaire) the start of the new
school year
rentrer [ʀɑ̃tʀe] /1/ vi (entrer de
nouveau) to go (ou come) back in;
(entrer) to go (ou come) in; (revenir chez
soi) to go (ou come) (back) home; (air,
clou: pénétrer) to go in; (revenu, argent)
to come in ▷ vt to bring in; (véhicule)
to put away; (chemise dans pantalon
etc) to tuck in; (griffes) to draw in;
~ le ventre to pull in one's stomach;
~ dans (heurter) to crash into; **~ dans**
l'ordre to get back to normal; **~ dans**
ses frais to recover one's expenses
(ou initial outlay)
renverse [ʀɑ̃vɛʀs]: **à la ~** adv
backwards
renverser [ʀɑ̃vɛʀse] /1/ vt (faire
tomber: chaise, verre) to knock over,
overturn; (: piéton) to knock down;
(: liquide, contenu) to spill, upset;
(retourner) to turn upside down;
(: ordre des mots etc) to reverse; (fig:
gouvernement etc) to overthrow;
(stupéfier) to bowl over; **se renverser**
vi (verre, vase) to fall over; (contenu)
to spill
renvoi [ʀɑ̃vwa] nm (d'employé)
dismissal; (d'élève) expulsion;
(référence) cross-reference;
(éructation) belch; **renvoyer** /8/
vt to send back; (congédier) to
dismiss; (élève: définitivement) to
expel; (lumière) to reflect; (ajourner):
renvoyer qch (à) to postpone sth
(until)
repaire [ʀəpɛʀ] nm den
répandre [ʀepɑ̃dʀ] /41/ vt
(renverser) to spill; (étaler, diffuser) to
spread; (chaleur, odeur) to give off;
se répandre vi to spill; to spread;
répandu, e adj (opinion, usage)
widespread
réparateur, -trice [ʀepaʀatœʀ,
-tʀis] nm/f repairer
réparation [ʀepaʀasjɔ̃] nf repair

réparer [ʀepaʀe] /1/ vt to repair; (fig: offense) to make up for, atone for; (: oubli, erreur) to put right

repartie [ʀepaʀti] nf retort; **avoir de la ~** to be quick at repartee

repartir [ʀəpaʀtiʀ] /16/ vi to set off again; (voyageur) to leave again; (fig) to get going again; **~ à zéro** to start from scratch (again)

répartir [ʀepaʀtiʀ] /2/ vt (pour attribuer) to share out; (pour disperser, disposer) to divide up; (poids, chaleur) to distribute; **se répartir** vt (travail, rôles) to share out between themselves; **répartition** nf (des richesses etc) distribution

repas [ʀəpɑ] nm meal

repassage [ʀəpasaʒ] nm ironing

repasser [ʀəpase] /1/ vi to come (ou go) back ▷ vt (vêtement, tissu) to iron; (examen) to retake, resit; (film) to show again; (leçon, rôle: revoir) to go over (again)

repentir [ʀəpɑ̃tiʀ] /16/ nm repentance; **se repentir** vi to repent; **se ~ d'avoir fait qch** (regretter) to regret having done sth

répercussions [ʀepɛʀkysjɔ̃] nfpl repercussions

répercuter [ʀepɛʀkyte] /1/: **se répercuter** vi (bruit) to reverberate; (fig): **se ~ sur** to have repercussions on

repère [ʀəpɛʀ] nm mark; (monument etc) landmark

repérer [ʀəpeʀe] /6/ vt (erreur, connaissance) to spot; (abri, ennemi) to locate; **se repérer** vi to get one's bearings

répertoire [ʀepɛʀtwaʀ] nm (liste) (alphabetical) list; (carnet) index notebook; (Inform) directory; (d'un théâtre, artiste) repertoire

répéter [ʀepete] /6/ vt to repeat; (préparer: leçon) to learn, go over; (Théât) to rehearse; **se répéter** (redire) to repeat o.s.; (se reproduire) to be repeated, recur

répétition [ʀepetisjɔ̃] nf repetition; (Théât) rehearsal; **~ générale** final dress rehearsal

répit [ʀepi] nm respite; **sans ~** without letting up

replier [ʀəplije] /7/ vt (rabattre) to fold down ou over; **se replier** vi (armée) to withdraw, fall back; **se ~ sur soi-même** to withdraw into oneself

réplique [ʀeplik] nf (repartie, fig) reply; (Théât) line; (copie) replica; **répliquer** /1/ vi to reply; (riposter) to retaliate

répondeur [ʀepɔ̃dœʀ] nm: **~ (automatique)** (Tél) answering machine

répondre [ʀepɔ̃dʀ] /41/ vi to answer, reply; (freins, mécanisme) to respond; **~ à** to reply to, answer; (affection, salut) to return; (provocation) to respond to; (correspondre à) (besoin) to answer; (conditions) to meet; (description) to match; **~ à qn** (avec impertinence) to answer sb back; **~ de** to answer for

réponse [ʀepɔ̃s] nf answer, reply; **en ~ à** in reply to

reportage [ʀəpɔʀtaʒ] nm report

reporter¹ [ʀəpɔʀtɛʀ] nm reporter

reporter² [ʀəpɔʀte] vt (ajourner): **~ qch (à)** to postpone sth (until); (transférer): **~ qch sur** to transfer sth to; **se ~ à** (époque) to think back to; (document) to refer to

repos [ʀəpo] nm rest; (fig) peace (and quiet); (Mil): **~!** (stand) at ease!; **ce n'est pas de tout ~!** it's no picnic!

reposant, e [ʀ(ə)pozɑ̃, -ɑ̃t] adj restful

reposer [ʀəpoze] /1/ vt (verre, livre) to put down; (délasser) to rest ▷ vi: **laisser ~** (pâte) to leave to stand

repoussant, e [ʀəpusɑ̃, -ɑ̃t] adj repulsive

repousser [ʀəpuse] /1/ vi to grow again ▷ vt to repel, repulse; (offre) to turn down, reject; (*tiroir, personne*) to push back; (*différer*) to put back

reprendre [ʀəpʀɑ̃dʀ] /58/ vt (*prisonnier, ville*) to recapture; (*firme, entreprise*) to take over; (*emprunter: argument, idée*) to take up, use; (*refaire: article etc*) to go over again; (*jupe etc*) to alter; (*réprimander*) to tell off; (*corriger*) to correct; (*travail, promenade*) to resume; (*chercher*): **je viendrai te ~ à 4 h** I'll come and fetch you *ou* I'll come back for you at 4; (*se resservir de*): **~ du pain/un œuf** to take (*ou eat*) more bread/ another egg ▷ vi (*classes, pluie*) to start (up) again; (*activités, travaux, combats*) to resume, start (up) again; (*affaires, industrie*) to pick up; (*dire*): **reprit-il** he went on; **~ des forces** to recover one's strength; **~ courage** to take new heart; **~ la route** to resume one's journey, set off again; **~ haleine** *ou* **son souffle** to get one's breath back

représentant, e [ʀəpʀezɑ̃tɑ̃, -ɑ̃t] nm/f representative

représentation [ʀəpʀezɑ̃tasjɔ̃] nf representation; (*spectacle*) performance

représenter [ʀəpʀezɑ̃te] /1/ vt to represent; (*donner: pièce, opéra*) to perform; **se représenter** vt (*se figurer*) to imagine

répression [ʀepʀesjɔ̃] nf repression

réprimer [ʀepʀime] /1/ vt (*émotions*) to suppress; (*peuple etc*) repress

repris, e [ʀəpʀi, -iz] pp de **reprendre** ▷ nm: **~ de justice** ex-prisoner, ex-convict

reprise [ʀəpʀiz] nf (*recommencement*) resumption; (*économique*) recovery; (*TV*) repeat; (*Comm*) trade-in, part exchange; (*raccommodage*) mend; **à plusieurs ~s** on several occasions

repriser [ʀəpʀize] /1/ vt (*chaussette, lainage*) to darn; (*tissu*) to mend

reproche [ʀəpʀɔʃ] nm (*remontrance*) reproach; **faire des ~s à qn** to

reproach sb; **sans ~(s)** beyond *ou* above reproach; **reprocher** /1/ vt: **reprocher qch à qn** to reproach *ou* blame sb for sth; **reprocher qch à** (*machine, théorie*) to have sth against

reproduction [ʀəpʀɔdyksjɔ̃] nf reproduction

reproduire [ʀəpʀɔdɥiʀ] /38/ vt to reproduce; **se reproduire** vi (*Bio*) to reproduce; (*recommencer*) to recur, re-occur

reptile [ʀɛptil] nm reptile

république [ʀepyblik] nf republic

répugnant, e [ʀepyɲɑ̃, -ɑ̃t] adj repulsive

répugner [ʀepyɲe] /1/: **~ à** vt: **~ à qn** to repel *ou* disgust sb; **~ à faire** to be loath *ou* reluctant to do

réputation [ʀepytasjɔ̃] nf reputation; **réputé, e** adj renowned

requérir [ʀəkeʀiʀ] /21/ vt (*nécessiter*) to require, call for

requête [ʀəkɛt] nf request

requin [ʀəkɛ̃] nm shark

requis, e [ʀəki, -iz] adj required

RER sigle m (= *Réseau express régional*) Greater Paris high-speed train service

rescapé, e [ʀɛskape] nm/f survivor

rescousse [ʀɛskus] nf: **aller à la ~ de qn** to go to sb's aid *ou* rescue

réseau, x [ʀezo] nm network; **~ social** social network

réseautage [ʀezotaʒ] nm social networking

réservation [ʀezɛʀvasjɔ̃] nf reservation; booking

réserve [ʀezɛʀv] nf (*retenue*) reserve; (*entrepôt*) storeroom; (*restriction, aussi: d'Indiens*) reservation; (*de pêche, chasse*) preserve; **de ~** (*provisions etc*) in reserve

réservé, e [ʀezɛʀve] adj reserved; (*chasse, pêche*) private

réserver [ʀezɛʀve] /1/ vt to reserve; (*chambre, billet etc*) to book, reserve; (*mettre de côté, garder*): **~ qch pour** *ou* **à** to keep *ou* save sth for

réservoir [ʀezɛʀvwaʀ] nm tank

résidence [ʀezidãs] *nf* residence;
~ principale/secondaire main/
second home; **~ universitaire**
hall of residence (BRIT), dormitory
(US); **résidentiel, le** *adj* residential;
résider /1/ *vi*: **résider à** *ou* **dans** *ou*
en to reside in; **résider dans** (*fig*)
to lie in

résidu [ʀezidy] *nm* residue *no pl*

résigner [ʀeziɲe] /1/: **se résigner** *vi*:
se ~ (à qch/à faire) to resign o.s. (to
sth/to doing)

résilier [ʀezilje] /7/ *vt* to terminate

résistance [ʀezistãs] *nf* resistance;
(*de réchaud, bouilloire*: *fil*) element

résistant, e [ʀezistã, -ãt] *adj*
(*personne*) robust, tough; (*matériau*)
strong, hard-wearing

résister [ʀeziste] /1/ *vi* to resist; **~ à**
(*assaut, tentation*) to resist; (*matériau,
plante*) to withstand; (*désobéir à*) to
stand up to, oppose

résolu, e [ʀezɔly] *pp de* **résoudre**
▷ *adj*: **être ~ à qch/faire** to be set
upon sth/doing

résolution [ʀezɔlysjɔ̃] *nf* (*fermeté,
décision*) resolution; (*d'un problème*)
solution

résolvais *etc* [ʀezɔlvɛ] *vb voir*
résoudre

résonner [ʀezɔne] /1/ *vi* (*cloche, pas*)
to reverberate, resound; (*salle*) to be
resonant

résorber [ʀezɔʀbe] /1/: **se résorber**
vi (*Méd*) to be resorbed; (*fig*) to be
absorbed

résoudre [ʀezudʀ] /51/ *vt* to solve;
se ~ à faire to bring o.s. to do

respect [ʀɛspɛ] *nm* respect; **tenir
en ~** to keep at bay; **présenter
ses ~s à qn** to pay one's respects
to sb; **respecter** /1/ *vt* to respect;
respectueux, -euse *adj* respectful

respiration [ʀɛspiʀasjɔ̃] *nf*
breathing *no pl*

respirer [ʀɛspiʀe] /1/ *vi* to breathe;
(*fig*: *se reposer*) to get one's breath;
(: *être soulagé*) to breathe again ▷ *vt* to
breathe (in), inhale; (*manifester*: *santé,
calme etc*) to exude

resplendir [ʀɛsplãdiʀ] /2/ *vi* to
shine; (*fig*): **~ (de)** to be radiant (with)

responsabilité [ʀɛspɔ̃sabilite] *nf*
responsibility; (*légale*) liability

responsable [ʀɛspɔ̃sabl] *adj*
responsible ▷ *nm/f* (*personne
coupable*) person responsible; (*du
ravitaillement etc*) person in charge;
(*de parti, syndicat*) official; **~ de**
responsible for

ressaisir [ʀəseziʀ] /2/: **se ressaisir**
vi to regain one's self-control

ressasser [ʀəsase] /1/ *vt* to keep
turning over

ressemblance [ʀəsãblãs] *nf*
resemblance, similarity, likeness

ressemblant, e [ʀəsãblã, -ãt] *adj*
(*portrait*) lifelike, true to life

ressembler [ʀəsãble] /1/: **~ à** *vt* to
be like, resemble; (*visuellement*) to
look like; **se ressembler** *vi* to be (*ou*
look) alike

ressentiment [ʀəsãtimã] *nm*
resentment

ressentir [ʀəsãtiʀ] /16/ *vt* to feel; **se
~ de** to feel (*ou* show) the effects of

resserrer [ʀəseʀe] /1/ *vt* (*nœud,
boulon*) to tighten (up); (*fig*: *liens*) to
strengthen

resservir [ʀəseʀviʀ] /14/ *vi* to do *ou*
serve again; **~ qn (d'un plat)** to give
sb a second helping (of a dish); **se ~
de** (*plat*) to take a second helping of;
(*outil etc*) to use again

ressort [ʀəsɔʀ] *nm* (*pièce*) spring;
(*force morale*) spirit; **en dernier ~** as a
last resort; **être du ~ de** to fall within
the competence of

ressortir [ʀəsɔʀtiʀ] /16/ *vi* to go
(*ou* come) out (again); (*contraster*) to
stand out; **~ de**: **il ressort de ceci
que** it emerges from this that; **faire ~**
(*fig*: *souligner*) to bring out

ressortissant, e [ʀəsɔʀtisã, -ãt]
nm/f national

ressources [ʀəsuʀs] *nfpl* resources

r

ressusciter [resysite] /1/ vt (fig) to revive, bring back ▷ vi to rise (from the dead)

restant, e [restã, -ãt] adj remaining ▷ nm: **le ~ (de)** the remainder (of); **un ~ de** (de trop) some leftover

restaurant [restorã] nm restaurant

restauration [restorasjɔ̃] nf restoration; (hôtellerie) catering; **~ rapide** fast food

restaurer [restore] /1/ vt to restore; **se restaurer** vi to have something to eat

reste [rest] nm (restant): **le ~ (de)** the rest (of); (de trop): **un ~ (de)** some leftover; **restes** nmpl leftovers; (d'une cité etc, dépouille mortelle) remains; **du ~, au ~** besides, moreover

rester [reste] /1/ vi to stay, remain; (subsister) to remain, be left; (durer) to last, live on ▷ vb impers: **il reste du pain/deux œufs** there's some bread/there are two eggs left (over); **il me reste assez de temps** I have enough time left; **il ne me reste plus qu'à ...** I've just got to ...; **restons-en là** let's leave it at that

restituer [restitɥe] /1/ vt (objet, somme): **~ qch (à qn)** to return ou restore sth (to sb)

restreindre [restrɛ̃dr] /52/ vt to restrict, limit

restriction [restriksjɔ̃] nf restriction

résultat [rezylta] nm result; (d'élection etc) results pl; **résultats** nmpl (d'une enquête) findings

résulter [rezylte] /1/: **~ de** vt to result from, be the result of

résumé [rezyme] nm summary, résumé; **en ~** in brief; (pour conclure) to sum up

résumer [rezyme] /1/ vt (texte) to summarize; (récapituler) to sum up
> Attention à ne pas traduire résumer par to resume.

résurrection [rezyreksjɔ̃] nf resurrection

rétablir [retablir] /2/ vt to restore, re-establish; **se rétablir** vi (guérir) to recover; (silence, calme) to return, be restored; **rétablissement** nm restoring; (guérison) recovery

retaper [rətape] /1/ vt (maison, voiture etc) to do up; (fam: revigorer) to buck up

retard [rətar] nm (d'une personne attendue) lateness no pl; (sur l'horaire, un programme, une échéance) delay; (fig: scolaire, mental etc) backwardness; **en ~ (de deux heures)** (two hours) late; **désolé d'être en ~** sorry I'm late; **avoir du ~** to be late; (sur un programme) to be behind (schedule); **prendre du ~** (train, avion) to be delayed; **sans ~** without delay

retardataire [rətardater] nm/f latecomer

retardement [rətardəmã]: **à ~** adj delayed action cpd; **bombe à ~** time bomb

retarder [rətarde] /1/ vt to delay; (horloge) to put back; **~ qn (d'une heure)** to delay sb (an hour); (départ, date): **~ qch (de deux jours)** to put sth back (two days) ▷ vi (montre) to be slow

retenir [rətnir] /22/ vt (garder, retarder) to keep, detain; (maintenir: objet qui glisse, colère, larmes, rire) to hold back; (se rappeler) to retain; (accepter) to accept; (fig: empêcher d'agir): **~ qn (de faire)** to hold sb back (from doing); (prélever): **~ qch (sur)** to deduct sth (from); **se retenir** vi (se raccrocher): **se ~ à** to hold onto; (se contenir): **se ~ de faire** to restrain o.s. from doing; **~ son souffle** ou **haleine** to hold one's breath

retentir [rətãtir] /2/ vi to ring out; **retentissant, e** adj resounding

retenu, e [rətny] adj (place) reserved ▷ nf (prélèvement) deduction; (Scol) detention; (modération) (self-)restraint

réticence [ʀetisɑ̃s] *nf* reticence *no pl*, reluctance *no pl*; **réticent, e** *adj* reticent, reluctant

rétine [ʀetin] *nf* retina

retiré, e [ʀətiʀe] *adj* (*solitaire*) secluded; (*éloigné*) remote

retirer [ʀətiʀe] /1/ *vt* (*argent, plainte*) to withdraw; (*vêtement*) to take off, remove; (*reprendre: billets*) to collect, pick up; **~ qn/qch de** to take sb away from/sth out of, remove sb/ sth from

retomber [ʀətɔ̃be] /1/ *vi* (*à nouveau*) to fall again; (*atterrir: après un saut etc*) to land; (*échoir*): **~ sur qn** to fall on sb

rétorquer [ʀetɔʀke] /1/ *vt*: **~ (à qn) que** to retort (to sb) that

retouche [ʀətuʃ] *nf* (*sur vêtement*) alteration; **retoucher** /1/ *vt* (*photographie, tableau*) to touch up; (*texte, vêtement*) to alter

retour [ʀətuʀ] *nm* return; **au ~** (*en route*) on the way back; **à mon/ton ~** on my/your return; **être de ~ (de)** to be back (from); **quand serons-nous de ~?** when do we get back?; **par ~ du courrier** by return of post

retourner [ʀətuʀne] /1/ *vt* (*dans l'autre sens: matelas, crêpe*) to turn (over); (*sac, vêtement*) to turn inside out; (*émouvoir*) to shake; (*renvoyer, restituer*): **~ qch à qn** to return sth to sb ▷ *vi* (*aller, revenir*): **~ quelque part/à** to go back ou return somewhere/to; **~ à** (*état, activité*) to return to, go back to; **se retourner** *vi* (*tourner la tête*) to turn round; **se ~ contre** (*fig*) to turn against

retrait [ʀətʀɛ] *nm* (*d'argent*) withdrawal; **en ~** set back; **~ du permis (de conduire)** disqualification from driving (BRIT), revocation of driver's license (US)

retraite [ʀətʀɛt] *nf* (*d'une armée, Rel*) retreat; (*d'un employé*) retirement; (*revenu*) (retirement) pension; **prendre sa ~** to retire; **~ anticipée** early retirement; **retraité, e** *adj* retired ▷ *nm/f* (old age) pensioner

retrancher [ʀətʀɑ̃ʃe] /1/ *vt*: **~ qch de** (*nombre, somme*) to take ou deduct sth from; **se ~ derrière/dans** to take refuge behind/in

rétrécir [ʀetʀesiʀ] /2/ *vt* (*vêtement*) to take in ▷ *vi* to shrink; **se rétrécir** (*route, vallée*) to narrow

rétro [ʀetʀo] *adj inv*: **la mode ~** the nostalgia vogue

rétrospectif, -ive [ʀetʀɔspɛktif, -iv] *adj* retrospective ▷ *nf* (*Art*) retrospective; (*Ciné*) season, retrospective; **rétrospectivement** *adv* in retrospect

retrousser [ʀətʀuse] /1/ *vt* to roll up

retrouvailles [ʀətʀuvaj] *nfpl* reunion *sg*

retrouver [ʀətʀuve] /1/ *vt* (*fugitif, objet perdu*) to find; (*calme, santé*) to regain; (*revoir*) to see again; (*rejoindre*) to meet (again), join; **se retrouver** *vi* to meet; (*s'orienter*) to find one's way; **se ~ quelque part** to find o.s. somewhere; **s'y ~** (*y voir clair*) to make sense of it; (*rentrer dans ses frais*) to break even

rétroviseur [ʀetʀɔvizœʀ] *nm* (rear-view) mirror

retweeter [ʀətwite] /1/ *vt* (*Inform: Twitter*) to retweet

réunion [ʀeynjɔ̃] *nf* (*séance*) meeting

réunir [ʀeyniʀ] /2/ *vt* (*rassembler*) to gather together; (*inviter: amis, famille*) to have round, have in; (*cumuler: qualités etc*) to combine; (*rapprocher: ennemis*) to bring together (again), reunite; (*rattacher: parties*) to join (together); **se réunir** *vi* (*se rencontrer*) to meet

réussi, e [ʀeysi] *adj* successful

réussir [ʀeysiʀ] /2/ *vi* to succeed, be successful; (*à un examen*) to pass ▷ *vt* to make a success of; **~ à faire** to succeed in doing; **~ à qn** (*être bénéfique à*) to agree with sb; **réussite** *nf* success; (*Cartes*) patience

revaloir [RəvalwaR] /29/ vt: **je vous revaudrai cela** I'll repay you some day; (en mal) I'll pay you back for this

revanche [Rəvɑ̃ʃ] nf revenge; (sport) revenge match; **en ~** on the other hand

rêve [REv] nm dream; **de ~** dream cpd; **faire un ~** to have a dream

réveil [Revɛj] nm waking up no pl; (fig) awakening; (pendule) alarm (clock); **au ~** on waking (up); **réveiller** /1/ vt (personne) to wake up; (fig) to awaken, revive; **se réveiller** vi to wake up

réveillon [Revɛjɔ̃] nm Christmas Eve; (de la Saint-Sylvestre) New Year's Eve; **réveillonner** /1/ vi to celebrate Christmas Eve (ou New Year's Eve)

révélateur, -trice [RevelatœR, -tRis] adj: **~ (de qch)** revealing (sth)

révéler [Revele] /6/ vt to reveal; **se révéler** vi to be revealed, reveal itself; **se ~ facile/faux** to prove (to be) easy/false

revenant, e [Rəvnɑ̃, -ɑ̃t] nm/f ghost

revendeur, -euse [Rəvɑ̃dœR, -øz] nm/f (détaillant) retailer; (de drogue) (drug-)dealer

revendication [Rəvɑ̃dikasjɔ̃] nf claim, demand

revendiquer [Rəvɑ̃dike] /1/ vt to claim, demand; (responsabilité) to claim

revendre [Rəvɑ̃dR] /41/ vt (d'occasion) to resell; (détailler) to sell; **à ~** (en abondance) to spare

revenir [RəvniR] /22/ vi to come back; **faire ~** (Culin) to brown; **~ cher/à 100 euros (à qn)** to cost (sb) a lot/100 euros; **~ à** (reprendre: études, projet) to return to, go back to; (équivaloir à) to amount to; **~ à qn** (part, honneur) to go to sb, be sb's; (souvenir, nom) to come back to sb; **~ sur** (question, sujet) to go back over; (engagement) to go back on; **~ à soi** to come round; **je n'en**

reviens pas I can't get over it; **~ sur ses pas** to retrace one's steps; **cela revient à dire que/au même** it amounts to saying that/to the same thing

revenu [Rəvny] nm income; **revenus** nmpl income sg

rêver [Reve] /1/ vi, vt to dream; **~ de qch/de faire** to dream of sth/of doing; **~ à** to dream of

réverbère [RevɛRbɛR] nm street lamp ou light; **réverbérer** /6/ vt to reflect

revers [RəvɛR] nm (de feuille, main) back; (d'étoffe) wrong side; (de pièce, médaille) back, reverse; (Tennis, Ping-Pong) backhand; (de veston) lapel; (fig: échec) setback

revêtement [Rəvɛtmɑ̃] nm (des sols) flooring; (de chaussée) surface

revêtir [RəvɛtiR] /20/ vt (habit) to don, put on; (prendre: importance, apparence) to take on; **~ qch de** to cover sth with

rêveur, -euse [RevœR, -øz] adj dreamy ▷ nm/f dreamer

revient [Rəvjɛ̃] vb voir **revenir**

revigorer [RəvigɔRe] /1/ vt (air frais) to invigorate, brace up; (repas, boisson) to revive, buck up

revirement [RəviRmɑ̃] nm change of mind; (d'une situation) reversal

réviser [Revize] /1/ vt to revise; (machine, installation, moteur) to overhaul, service

révision [Revizjɔ̃] nf revision; (de voiture) servicing no pl

revivre [RəvivR] /46/ vi (reprendre des forces) to come alive again ▷ vt (épreuve, moment) to relive

revoir [RəvwaR] /30/ vt to see again ▷ nm: **au ~** goodbye

révoltant, e [Revɔltɑ̃, -ɑ̃t] adj revolting, appalling

révolte [Revɔlt] nf rebellion, revolt

révolter [Revɔlte] /1/ vt to revolt; **se révolter** vi: **se ~ (contre)** to rebel (against)

révolu, e [Revɔly] *adj* past;
(*Admin*): **âgé de 18 ans ~s** over 18
years of age

révolution [Revɔlysjɔ̃] *nf* revolution;
révolutionnaire *adj*, *nm/f*
revolutionary

revolver [RevɔlvɛR] *nm* gun; (*à
barillet*) revolver

révoquer [Revɔke] /1/ *vt*
(*fonctionnaire*) to dismiss; (*arrêt,
contrat*) to revoke

revu, e [Rəvy] *pp de* **revoir** ▷ *nf*
review; (*périodique*) review, magazine;
(*de music-hall*) variety show; **passer
en ~** (*mentalement*) to go through

rez-de-chaussée [Redʃose] *nm inv*
ground floor

RF *sigle f* = **République française**

Rhin [Rɛ̃] *nm*: **le ~** the Rhine

rhinocéros [RinɔseRɔs] *nm*
rhinoceros

Rhône [Ron] *nm*: **le ~** the Rhone

rhubarbe [Rybarb] *nf* rhubarb

rhum [Rɔm] *nm* rum

rhumatisme [Rymatism] *nm*
rheumatism *no pl*

rhume [Rym] *nm* cold; **~ de cerveau**
head cold; **le ~ des foins** hay fever

ricaner [Rikane] /1/ *vi* (*avec
méchanceté*) to snigger; (*bêtement,
avec gêne*) to giggle

riche [Riʃ] *adj* rich; (*personne, pays*)
rich, wealthy; **~ en** rich in; **richesse**
nf wealth; (*fig: de sol, musée etc*)
richness; **richesses** *nfpl* (*ressources,
argent*) wealth *sg*; (*fig: trésors*)
treasures

ricochet [Rikɔʃɛ] *nm*: **faire des ~s** to
skip stones

ride [Rid] *nf* wrinkle

rideau, x [Rido] *nm* curtain; **~ de fer**
(*lit*) metal shutter

rider [Ride] /1/ *vt* to wrinkle; **se rider**
vi to become wrinkled

ridicule [Ridikyl] *adj* ridiculous
▷ *nm*: **le ~** ridicule; **ridiculiser** /1/ *vt*
to ridicule; **se ridiculiser** *vi* to make
a fool of o.s.

MOT-CLÉ

rien [Rjɛ̃] *pron* **1**: **(ne) ... rien**
nothing; (*tournure négative*) anything;
qu'est-ce que vous avez? — rien
what have you got? — nothing; **il n'a
rien dit/fait** he said/did nothing,
he hasn't said/done anything;
n'avoir peur de rien to be afraid
ou frightened of nothing, not to be
afraid *ou* frightened of anything; **il
n'a rien** (*n'est pas blessé*) he's all right;
ça ne fait rien it doesn't matter
2 (*quelque chose*): **a-t-il jamais rien
fait pour nous?** has he ever done
anything for us?
3: **rien de**: **rien d'intéressant**
nothing interesting; **rien d'autre**
nothing else; **rien du tout** nothing
at all
4: **rien que** just, only; nothing but;
rien que pour lui faire plaisir only
ou just to please him; **rien que la
vérité** nothing but the truth; **rien
que cela** that alone
▶ *excl*: **de rien!** not at all!
▶ *nm*: **un petit rien** (*cadeau*) a little
something; **des riens** trivia *pl*; **un
rien de** a hint of; **en un rien de
temps** in no time at all

rieur, -euse [Rjœr, -øz] *adj* cheerful

rigide [Riʒid] *adj* stiff; (*fig*) rigid;
(*moralement*) strict

rigoler [Rigɔle] /1/ *vi* (*rire*) to laugh;
(*s'amuser*) to have (some) fun;
(*plaisanter*) to be joking *ou* kidding;
rigolo, rigolote *adj* funny ▷ *nm/f*
comic; (*péj*) fraud, phoney

rigoureusement [Rigurøzmɑ̃] *adv*
rigorously

rigoureux, -euse [Riguro, -øz] *adj*
rigorous; (*climat, châtiment*) harsh,
severe

rigueur [Rigœr] *nf* rigour; **"tenue
de soirée de ~"** "evening dress (to be
worn)"; **à la ~** at a pinch; **tenir ~ à qn
de qch** to hold sth against sb

r

rillettes [ʀijɛt] *nfpl* ≈ potted meat *sg* (*made from pork or goose*)

rime [ʀim] *nf* rhyme

rinçage [ʀɛ̃saʒ] *nm* rinsing (out); (*opération*) rinse

rincer [ʀɛ̃se] /3/ *vt* to rinse; (*récipient*) to rinse out

ringard, e [ʀɛ̃gaʀ, -aʀd] *adj* old-fashioned

riposter [ʀipɔste] /1/ *vi* to retaliate ▷ *vt*: **~ que** to retort that

rire [ʀiʀ] /36/ *vi* to laugh; (*se divertir*) to have fun ▷ *nm* laugh; **le ~** laughter; **~ de** to laugh at; **pour ~** (*pas sérieusement*) for a joke *ou* a laugh

risible [ʀizibl] *adj* laughable

risque [ʀisk] *nm* risk; **le ~** danger; **à ses ~s et périls** at his own risk; **risqué, e** *adj* risky; (*plaisanterie*) risqué, daring; **risquer** /1/ *vt* to risk; (*allusion, question*) to venture, hazard; **se risquer** *vi*: **ça ne risque rien** it's quite safe; **il risque de se tuer** he could get *ou* risks getting himself killed; **ce qui risque de se produire** what might *ou* could well happen; **il ne risque pas de recommencer** there's no chance of him doing that again; **se risquer à faire** (*tenter*) to dare to do

rissoler [ʀisɔle] /1/ *vi, vt*: **(faire) ~** to brown

ristourne [ʀistuʀn] *nf* discount

rite [ʀit] *nm* rite; (*fig*) ritual

rivage [ʀivaʒ] *nm* shore

rival, e, -aux [ʀival, -o] *adj, nm/f* rival; **rivaliser** /1/ *vi*: **rivaliser avec** to rival, vie with; **rivalité** *nf* rivalry

rive [ʀiv] *nf* shore; (*de fleuve*) bank; **riverain, e** *nm/f* riverside (*ou* lakeside) resident; (*d'une route*) local *ou* roadside resident

rivière [ʀivjɛʀ] *nf* river

riz [ʀi] *nm* rice; **rizière** *nf* paddy field

RMI *sigle m* (= *revenu minimum d'insertion*) ≈ income support (BRIT), ≈ welfare (US)

RN *sigle f* = **route nationale**

robe [ʀɔb] *nf* dress; (*de juge, d'ecclésiastique*) robe; (*pelage*) coat; **~ de soirée/de mariée** evening/wedding dress; **~ de chambre** dressing gown

robinet [ʀɔbinɛ] *nm* tap (BRIT), faucet (US)

robot [ʀɔbo] *nm* robot; **~ de cuisine** food processor

robuste [ʀɔbyst] *adj* robust, sturdy; **robustesse** *nf* robustness, sturdiness

roc [ʀɔk] *nm* rock

rocade [ʀɔkad] *nf* bypass

rocaille [ʀɔkaj] *nf* loose stones *pl*; (*jardin*) rockery, rock garden

roche [ʀɔʃ] *nf* rock

rocher [ʀɔʃe] *nm* rock

rocheux, -euse [ʀɔʃø, -øz] *adj* rocky

rodage [ʀɔdaʒ] *nm*: **en ~** running *ou* breaking in

rôder [ʀode] /1/ *vi* to roam *ou* wander about; (*de façon suspecte*) to lurk (about *ou* around); **rôdeur, -euse** *nm/f* prowler

rogne [ʀɔɲ] *nf*: **être en ~** to be mad *ou* in a temper

rogner [ʀɔɲe] /1/ *vt* to trim; **~ sur** (*fig*) to cut down *ou* back on

rognons [ʀɔɲɔ̃] *nmpl* kidneys

roi [ʀwa] *nm* king; **le jour** *ou* **la fête des R~s** Twelfth Night

rôle [ʀol] *nm* role; part

rollers [ʀɔlœʀ] *nmpl* Rollerblades®

romain, e [ʀɔmɛ̃, -ɛn] *adj* Roman ▷ *nm/f*: **R~, e** Roman

roman, e [ʀɔmɑ̃, -an] *adj* (*Archit*) Romanesque ▷ *nm* novel; **~ policier** detective novel

romancer [ʀɔmɑ̃se] /3/ *vt* to romanticize; **romancier, -ière** *nm/f* novelist; **romanesque** *adj* (*amours, aventures*) storybook *cpd*; (*sentimental: personne*) romantic

roman-feuilleton [ʀɔmɑ̃fœjtɔ̃] *nm* serialized novel

romanichel, le [ʀɔmaniʃɛl] *nm/f* gipsy

romantique [ʀɔmɑ̃tik] *adj* romantic

romarin [ʀɔmaʀɛ̃] nm rosemary

Rome [ʀɔm] n Rome

rompre [ʀɔ̃pʀ] /41/ vt to break; (entretien, fiançailles) to break off ▷ vi (fiancés) to break it off; **se rompre** vi to break; **rompu, e** adj (fourbu) exhausted

ronce [ʀɔ̃s] nf bramble branch; **ronces** nfpl brambles

ronchonner [ʀɔ̃ʃɔne] /1/ vi (fam) to grouse, grouch

rond, e [ʀɔ̃, ʀɔ̃d] adj round; (joues, mollets) well-rounded; (fam: ivre) tight ▷ nm (cercle) ring; (fam: sou): **je n'ai plus un ~** I haven't a penny left ▷ nf (gén: de surveillance) rounds pl, patrol; (danse) round (dance); (Mus) semibreve (BRIT), whole note (US); **en ~** (s'asseoir, danser) in a ring; **à la ~e** (alentour): **à 10 km à la ~e** for 10 km round; **rondelet, te** adj plump

rondelle [ʀɔ̃dɛl] nf (Tech) washer; (tranche) slice, round

rond-point [ʀɔ̃pwɛ̃] nm roundabout

ronflement [ʀɔ̃fləmɑ̃] nm snore

ronfler [ʀɔ̃fle] /1/ vi to snore; (moteur, poêle) to hum

ronger [ʀɔ̃ʒe] /3/ vt to gnaw (at); (vers, rouille) to eat into; **se ~ les sangs** to worry o.s. sick; **se ~ les ongles** to bite one's nails; **rongeur, -euse** [ʀɔ̃ʒœʀ, -øz] nm/f rodent

ronronner [ʀɔ̃ʀɔne] /1/ vi to purr

rosbif [ʀɔsbif] nm: **du ~** roasting beef; (cuit) roast beef

rose [ʀoz] nf rose ▷ adj pink; **~ bonbon** adj inv candy pink

rosé, e [ʀoze] adj pinkish; **(vin) ~** rosé (wine)

roseau, x [ʀozo] nm reed

rosée [ʀoze] nf dew

rosier [ʀozje] nm rosebush, rose tree

rossignol [ʀɔsiɲɔl] nm (Zool) nightingale

rotation [ʀɔtasjɔ̃] nf rotation

roter [ʀɔte] /1/ vi (fam) to burp, belch

rôti [ʀoti] nm: **du ~** roasting meat; (cuit) roast meat; **un ~ de bœuf/porc** a joint of beef/pork

rotin [ʀɔtɛ̃] nm rattan (cane); **fauteuil en ~** cane (arm)chair

rôtir [ʀotiʀ] /2/ vt (aussi: **faire ~**) to roast ▷ vi to roast; **rôtisserie** nf (restaurant) steakhouse; (traiteur) roast meat shop; **rôtissoire** nf (roasting) spit

rotule [ʀɔtyl] nf kneecap

rouage [ʀwaʒ] nm cog(wheel), gearwheel; **les ~s de l'État** the wheels of State

roue [ʀu] nf wheel; **~ de secours** spare wheel

rouer [ʀwe] /1/ vt: **~ qn de coups** to give sb a thrashing

rouge [ʀuʒ] adj, nm/f red ▷ nm red; **(vin) ~** red wine; **passer au ~** (signal) to go red; (automobiliste) to go through a red light; **sur la liste ~** ex-directory (BRIT), unlisted (US); **~ à joue** blusher; **~ (à lèvres)** lipstick; **rouge-gorge** nm robin (redbreast)

rougeole [ʀuʒɔl] nf measles sg

rougeoyer [ʀuʒwaje] /8/ vi to glow red

rouget [ʀuʒɛ] nm mullet

rougeur [ʀuʒœʀ] nf redness; **rougeurs** nfpl (Méd) red blotches

rougir [ʀuʒiʀ] /2/ vi to turn red; (de honte, timidité) to blush, flush; (de plaisir, colère) to flush

rouille [ʀuj] nf rust; **rouillé, e** adj rusty; **rouiller** /1/ vt to rust ▷ vi to rust, go rusty

roulant, e [ʀulɑ̃, -ɑ̃t] adj (meuble) on wheels; (surface, trottoir, tapis) moving; **escalier ~** escalator

rouleau, x [ʀulo] nm roll; (à mise en plis, à peinture, vague) roller; **~ à pâtisserie** rolling pin

roulement [ʀulmɑ̃] nm (bruit) rumbling no pl, rumble; (rotation) rotation; **par ~** on a rota (BRIT) ou rotation (US) basis; **~ (à billes)** ball bearings pl; **~ de tambour** drum roll

r

rouler [ʀule] /1/ vt to roll; (papier, tapis) to roll up; (Culin: pâte) to roll out; (fam: duper) to do, con ▷ vi (bille, boule) to roll; (voiture, train) to go, run; (automobiliste) to drive; (cycliste) to ride; (bateau) to roll; **se ~ dans** (boue) to roll in; (couverture) to roll o.s. (up) in

roulette [ʀulɛt] nf (de table, fauteuil) castor; (de dentiste) drill; (jeu): **la ~** roulette; **à ~s** on castors; **ça a marché comme sur des ~s** (fam) it went off very smoothly

roulotte [ʀulɔt] nf caravan

roumain, e [ʀumɛ̃, -ɛn] adj Rumanian ▷ nm/f: **R~, e** Rumanian

Roumanie [ʀumani] nf: **la ~** Rumania

rouquin, e [ʀukɛ̃, -in] nm/f (péj) redhead

rouspéter [ʀuspete] /6/ vi (fam) to moan

rousse [ʀus] adj f voir **roux**

roussir [ʀusiʀ] /2/ vt to scorch ▷ vi (Culin): **faire ~** to brown

route [ʀut] nf road; (fig: chemin) way; (itinéraire, parcours) route; (fig: voie) road, path; **il y a trois heures de ~** it's a three-hour ride ou journey; **en ~** on the way; **en ~!** let's go!; **mettre en ~** to start up; **se mettre en ~** to set off; **~ nationale** ≈ A-road (BRIT), ≈ state highway (US)

routeur [ʀutœʀ] nm (Inform) router

routier, -ière [ʀutje, -jɛʀ] adj road cpd ▷ nm (camionneur) (long-distance) lorry (BRIT) ou truck (US) driver; (restaurant) ≈ transport café (BRIT), ≈ truck stop (US)

routine [ʀutin] nf routine; **routinier, -ière** [ʀutinje, -jɛʀ] adj (péj: travail) humdrum; (: personne) addicted to routine

rouvrir [ʀuvʀiʀ] /18/ vt, vi to reopen, open again; **se rouvrir** vi to open up again

roux, rousse [ʀu, ʀus] adj red; (personne) red-haired ▷ nm/f redhead

royal, e, -aux [ʀwajal, -o] adj royal; (fig) fit for a king

royaume [ʀwajom] nm kingdom; (fig) realm

Royaume-Uni [ʀwajomyni] nm: **le ~** the United Kingdom

royauté [ʀwajote] nf (régime) monarchy

ruban [ʀybɑ̃] nm ribbon; **~ adhésif** adhesive tape

rubéole [ʀybeɔl] nf German measles sg, rubella

rubis [ʀybi] nm ruby

rubrique [ʀybʀik] nf (titre, catégorie) heading; (Presse: article) column

ruche [ʀyʃ] nf hive

rude [ʀyd] adj (barbe, toile) rough; (métier, tâche) hard, tough; (climat) severe, harsh; (bourru) harsh, rough; (fruste: manières) rugged, tough; (fam: fameux) jolly good; **rudement** adv (très) terribly

rudimentaire [ʀydimɑ̃tɛʀ] adj rudimentary, basic

rudiments [ʀydimɑ̃] nmpl: **avoir des ~ d'anglais** to have a smattering of English

rue [ʀy] nf street

ruée [ʀɥe] nf rush

ruelle [ʀɥɛl] nf alley(way)

ruer [ʀɥe] /1/ vi (cheval) to kick out; **se ruer** vi: **se ~ sur** to pounce on; **se ~ vers/dans/hors de** to rush ou dash towards/into/out of

rugby [ʀygbi] nm rugby (football)

rugir [ʀyʒiʀ] /2/ vi to roar

rugueux, -euse [ʀygø, -øz] adj rough

ruine [ʀɥin] nf ruin; **ruiner** /1/ vt to ruin; **ruineux, -euse** adj ruinous

ruisseau, x [ʀɥiso] nm stream, brook

ruisseler [ʀɥisle] /4/ vi to stream

rumeur [ʀymœʀ] nf (bruit confus) rumbling; (nouvelle) rumour

ruminer [ʀymine] /1/ vt (herbe) to ruminate; (fig) to ruminate on ou over, chew over

rupture [ʀyptyʀ] nf (de négociations etc) breakdown; (de contrat) breach;

(*dans continuité*) break; (*séparation, désunion*) break-up, split

rural, e, -aux [ʀyʀal, -o] *adj* rural, country *cpd*

ruse [ʀyz] *nf*: **la ~** cunning, craftiness; (*pour tromper*) trickery; **une ~** a trick, a ruse; **rusé, e** *adj* cunning, crafty

russe [ʀys] *adj* Russian ▷ *nm* (*Ling*) Russian ▷ *nm/f*: **R~** Russian

Russie [ʀysi] *nf*: **la ~** Russia

rustine [ʀystin] *nf* repair patch (*for bicycle inner tube*)

rustique [ʀystik] *adj* rustic

rythme [ʀitm] *nm* rhythm; (*vitesse*) rate (: *de la vie*) pace, tempo; **rythmé, e** *adj* rhythmic(al)

S

s' [s] *pron voir* **se**

sa [sa] *adj poss voir* **son**[1]

sable [sabl] *nm* sand

sablé [sable] *nm* shortbread biscuit

sabler [sable] /1/ *vt* (*contre le verglas*) to grit; **~ le champagne** to drink champagne

sabot [sabo] *nm* clog; (*de cheval, bœuf*) hoof; **~ de frein** brake shoe

saboter [sabɔte] /1/ *vt* (*travail, morceau de musique*) to botch, make a mess of; (*machine, installation, négociation etc*) to sabotage

sac [sak] *nm* bag; (*à charbon etc*) sack; **mettre à ~** to sack; **~ à provisions/ de voyage** shopping/travelling bag; **~ de couchage** sleeping bag; **~ à dos** rucksack; **~ à main** handbag

saccadé, e [sakade] *adj* jerky; (*respiration*) spasmodic

saccager [sakaʒe] /3/ *vt* (*piller*) to sack; (*dévaster*) to create havoc in

saccharine [sakaʀin] *nf* saccharin(e)

sachet [saʃɛ] nm (small) bag; (de lavande, poudre, shampooing) sachet; **~ de thé** tea bag; **du potage en ~** packet soup

sacoche [sakɔʃ] nf (gén) bag; (de bicyclette) saddlebag

sacré, e [sakre] adj sacred; (fam: satané) blasted; (: fameux): **un ~ ...** a heck of a ...

sacrement [sakrəmã] nm sacrament

sacrifice [sakrifis] nm sacrifice; **sacrifier** /7/ vt to sacrifice

sacristie [sakristi] nf sacristy; (culte protestant) vestry

sadique [sadik] adj sadistic

safran [safrã] nm saffron

sage [saʒ] adj wise; (enfant) good

sage-femme [saʒfam] nf midwife

sagesse [saʒɛs] nf wisdom

Sagittaire [saʒitɛr] nm: **le ~** Sagittarius

Sahara [saara] nm: **le ~** the Sahara (Desert)

saignant, e [sɛɲã, -ãt] adj (viande) rare

saigner [seɲe] /1/ vi to bleed ▷ vt to bleed; (animal) to bleed to death; **~ du nez** to have a nosebleed

saillir [sajir] /13/ vi to project, stick out; (veine, muscle) to bulge

sain, e [sɛ̃, sɛn] adj healthy; **~ et sauf** safe and sound, unharmed; **~ d'esprit** sound in mind, sane

saindoux [sɛ̃du] nm lard

saint, e [sɛ̃, sɛ̃t] adj holy ▷ nm/f saint; **la S~e Vierge** the Blessed Virgin

Saint-Esprit [sɛ̃tɛspri] nm: **le ~** the Holy Spirit ou Ghost

sainteté [sɛ̃tǝte] nf holiness

Saint-Sylvestre [sɛ̃silvɛstr] nf: **la ~** New Year's Eve

sais etc [sɛ] vb voir **savoir**

saisie [sezi] nf seizure; **~ (de données)** (data) capture

saisir [sezir] /2/ vt to take hold of, grab; (fig: occasion) to seize; (comprendre) to grasp; (entendre) to get, catch; (Inform) to capture; (Culin) to fry quickly; (Jur: biens, publication) to seize; **saisissant, e** adj startling, striking

saison [sezõ] nf season; **haute/ basse/morte ~** high/low/slack season; **saisonnier, -ière** adj seasonal

salade [salad] nf (Bot) lettuce etc (generic term); (Culin) (green) salad; (fam: confusion) tangle, muddle; **~ composée** mixed salad; **~ de fruits** fruit salad; **~ verte** green salad; **saladier** nm (salad) bowl

salaire [salɛr] nm (annuel, mensuel) salary; (hebdomadaire, journalier) pay, wages pl; **~ minimum interprofessionnel de croissance** index-linked guaranteed minimum wage

salarié, e [salarje] nm/f salaried employee; wage-earner

salaud [salo] nm (fam!) sod (!), bastard (!)

sale [sal] adj dirty, filthy; (fig: mauvais) nasty

salé, e [sale] adj (liquide, saveur, mer, goût) salty; (Culin: amandes, beurre etc) salted; (: gâteaux) savoury; (fig: grivois) spicy; (: note, facture) steep

saler [sale] /1/ vt to salt

saleté [salte] nf (état) dirtiness; (crasse) dirt, filth; (tache etc) dirt no pl; (fig: tour) filthy trick; (: chose sans valeur) rubbish no pl; (: obscénité) filth no pl

salière [saljɛr] nf saltcellar

salir [salir] /2/ vt to (make) dirty; (fig) to soil the reputation of; **se salir** vi to get dirty; **salissant, e** adj (tissu) which shows the dirt; (métier) dirty, messy

salle [sal] nf room; (d'hôpital) ward; (de restaurant) dining room; (d'un cinéma) auditorium (: public) audience; **~ d'attente** waiting room; **~ de bain(s)** bathroom; **~ de classe** classroom; **~ de concert** concert hall; **~ d'eau** shower-room;

~ d'embarquement (*à l'aéroport*) departure lounge; **~ de jeux** (*pour enfants*) playroom; **~ à manger** dining room; **~ des professeurs** staffroom; **~ de séjour** living room; **~ des ventes** saleroom

salon [salɔ̃] *nm* lounge, sitting room; (*mobilier*) lounge suite; (*exposition*) exhibition, show; **~ de coiffure** hairdressing salon; **~ de thé** tearoom

salope [salɔp] *nf* (*fam!*) bitch (*!*); **saloperie** *nf* (*fam!: action*) dirty trick; (*: chose sans valeur*) rubbish *no pl*

salopette [salɔpɛt] *nf* dungarees *pl*; (*d'ouvrier*) overall(s)

salsifis [salsifi] *nm* salsify

salubre [salybʀ] *adj* healthy, salubrious

saluer [salɥe] /1/ *vt* (*pour dire bonjour, fig*) to greet; (*pour dire au revoir*) to take one's leave; (*Mil*) to salute

salut [saly] *nm* (*sauvegarde*) safety; (*Rel*) salvation; (*geste*) wave; (*parole*) greeting; (*Mil*) salute ▷ *excl* (*fam: pour dire bonjour*) hi (there); (*: pour dire au revoir*) see you!, bye!

salutations [salytasjɔ̃] *nfpl* greetings; **recevez mes ~ distinguées** ou **respectueuses** yours faithfully

samedi [samdi] *nm* Saturday

SAMU [samy] *sigle m* (= *service d'assistance médicale d'urgence*) ≈ ambulance (service) (*BRIT*), ≈ paramedics (*US*)

sanction [sɑ̃ksjɔ̃] *nf* sanction; **sanctionner** /1/ *vt* (*loi, usage*) to sanction; (*punir*) to punish

sandale [sɑ̃dal] *nf* sandal

sandwich [sɑ̃dwitʃ] *nm* sandwich

sang [sɑ̃] *nm* blood; **en ~** covered in blood; **se faire du mauvais ~** to fret, get in a state; **sang-froid** *nm* calm, sangfroid; **de sang-froid** in cold blood; **sanglant, e** *adj* bloody

sangle [sɑ̃gl] *nf* strap

sanglier [sɑ̃glije] *nm* (wild) boar

sanglot [sɑ̃glo] *nm* sob; **sangloter** /1/ *vi* to sob

sangsue [sɑ̃sy] *nf* leech

sanguin, e [sɑ̃gɛ̃, -in] *adj* blood *cpd*

sanitaire [sanitɛʀ] *adj* health *cpd*; **sanitaires** *nmpl* (*salle de bain et w.-c.*) bathroom *sg*

sans [sɑ̃] *prép* without; **~ qu'il s'en aperçoive** without him ou his noticing; **un pull ~ manches** a sleeveless jumper; **~ faute** without fail; **~ arrêt** without a break; **~ ça** (*fam*) otherwise; **sans-abri** *nmpl* homeless; **sans-emploi** *nm/f inv* unemployed person; **les sans-emploi** the unemployed; **sans-gêne** *adj inv* inconsiderate

santé [sɑ̃te] *nf* health; **être en bonne ~** to be in good health; **boire à la ~ de qn** to drink (to) sb's health; **à ta** ou **votre ~!** cheers!

saoudien, ne [saudjɛ̃, -ɛn] *adj* Saudi (Arabian) ▷ *nm/f*: **S~, ne** Saudi (Arabian)

saoul, e [su, sul] *adj* = **soûl**

saper [sape] /1/ *vt* to undermine, sap

sapeur-pompier [sapœʀpɔ̃pje] *nm* fireman

saphir [safiʀ] *nm* sapphire

sapin [sapɛ̃] *nm* fir (tree); (*bois*) fir; **~ de Noël** Christmas tree

sarcastique [saʀkastik] *adj* sarcastic

Sardaigne [saʀdɛɲ] *nf*: **la ~** Sardinia

sardine [saʀdin] *nf* sardine

SARL [saʀl] *sigle f* (= *société à responsabilité limitée*) ≈ plc (*BRIT*), ≈ Inc. (*US*)

sarrasin [saʀazɛ̃] *nm* buckwheat

satané, e [satane] *adj* (*fam*) confounded

satellite [satelit] *nm* satellite

satin [satɛ̃] *nm* satin

satire [satiʀ] *nf* satire; **satirique** *adj* satirical

satisfaction [satisfaksjɔ̃] *nf* satisfaction

satisfaire [satisfɛʀ] /60/ *vt* to satisfy; **~ à** (*revendications, conditions*)

to meet; **satisfaisant, e** adj
(acceptable) satisfactory; **satisfait,
e** adj satisfied; **satisfait de** happy ou
satisfied with

saturer [satyʀe] /1/ vt to saturate

sauce [sos] nf sauce; (avec un rôti)
gravy; **~ tomate** tomato sauce;
saucière nf sauceboat

saucisse [sosis] nf sausage

saucisson [sosisɔ̃] nm (slicing)
sausage

sauf¹ [sof] prép except; **~ si** (à moins
que) unless; **~ avis contraire** unless
you hear to the contrary; **~ erreur** if
I'm not mistaken

sauf², sauve [sof, sov] adj
unharmed, unhurt; (fig: honneur)
intact, saved; **laisser la vie sauve à
qn** to spare sb's life

sauge [soʒ] nf sage

saugrenu, e [sogʀəny] adj
preposterous

saule [sol] nm willow (tree)

saumon [somɔ̃] nm salmon inv

saupoudrer [sopudʀe] /1/ vt: **~ qch
de** to sprinkle sth with

saur [sɔʀ] adj m: **hareng ~** smoked ou
red herring, kipper

saut [so] nm jump; (discipline sportive)
jumping; **faire un ~ chez qn** to pop
over to sb's (place); **~ en hauteur/
longueur** high/long jump; **~ à la
perche** pole vaulting; **~ à l'élastique**
bungee jumping; **~ périlleux**
somersault

sauter [sote] /1/ vi to jump, leap;
(exploser) to blow up, explode;
(: fusibles) to blow; (se détacher) to
pop out (ou off) ▷ vt to jump (over),
leap (over); (fig: omettre) to skip, miss
(out); **faire ~** to blow up; (Culin) to
sauté; **~ à la corde** to skip; **~ au cou
de qn** to fly into sb's arms; **~ sur une
occasion** to jump at an opportunity;
~ aux yeux to be quite obvious

sauterelle [sotʀɛl] nf grasshopper

sautiller [sotije] /1/ vi (oiseau) to hop;
(enfant) to skip

sauvage [sovaʒ] adj (gén) wild;
(peuplade) savage; (farouche)
unsociable; (barbare) wild, savage;
(non officiel) unauthorized, unofficial;
faire du camping ~ to camp in
the wild ▷ nm/f savage; (timide)
unsociable type

sauve [sov] adj f voir **sauf²**

sauvegarde [sovgaʀd] nf
safeguard; (Inform) backup;
sauvegarder /1/ vt to safeguard;
(Inform: enregistrer) to save; (: copier)
to back up

sauve-qui-peut [sovkipø] excl run
for your life!

sauver [sove] /1/ vt to save; (porter
secours à) to rescue; (récupérer) to
salvage, rescue; **se sauver** vi (s'enfuir)
to run away; (fam: partir) to be off;
sauvetage nm rescue; **sauveteur**
nm rescuer; **sauvette: à la sauvette**
adv (se marier etc) hastily, hurriedly;
sauveur nm saviour (BRIT), savior
(US)

savant, e [savɑ̃, -ɑ̃t] adj scholarly,
learned ▷ nm scientist

saveur [savœʀ] nf flavour; (fig)
savour

savoir [savwaʀ] /32/ vt to know; (être
capable de): **il sait nager** he can swim
▷ nm knowledge; **se savoir** vi (être
connu) to be known; **je n'en sais rien**
I (really) don't know; **à ~ (que)** that
is, namely; **faire ~ qch à qn** to let sb
know sth; **pas que je sache** not as
far as I know

savon [savɔ̃] nm (produit) soap;
(morceau) bar ou tablet of soap; (fam):
passer un ~ à qn to give sb a good
dressing-down; **savonner** /1/ vt to
soap; **savonnette** nf bar of soap

savourer [savuʀe] /1/ vt to savour;
savoureux, -euse adj tasty; (fig:
anecdote) spicy, juicy

saxo(phone) [saksɔ(fɔn)] nm
sax(ophone)

scabreux, -euse [skabʀø, -øz] adj
risky; (indécent) improper, shocking

scandale [skãdal] *nm* scandal;
faire un ~ (*scène*) to make a scene;
(*Jur*) create a disturbance; **faire ~**
to scandalize people; **scandaleux,
-euse** *adj* scandalous, outrageous

scandinave [skãdinav] *adj*
Scandinavian ▷ *nm/f*: **S~**
Scandinavian

Scandinavie [skãdinavi] *nf*: **la ~**
Scandinavia

scarabée [skaRabe] *nm* beetle

scarlatine [skaRlatin] *nf* scarlet
fever

scarole [skaRɔl] *nf* endive

sceau, x [so] *nm* seal

sceller [sele] /1/ *vt* to seal

scénario [senaRjo] *nm* scenario

scène [sɛn] *nf* (*gén*) scene; (*estrade,
fig: théâtre*) stage; **entrer en ~** to
come on stage; **mettre en ~** (*Théât*)
to stage; (*Ciné*) to direct; **faire une ~
(à qn)** to make a scene (with sb); **~ de
ménage** domestic fight *ou* scene

sceptique [sɛptik] *adj* sceptical

schéma [ʃema] *nm* (*diagramme*)
diagram, sketch; **schématique** *adj*
diagrammatic(al), schematic; (*fig*)
oversimplified

sciatique [sjatik] *nf* sciatica

scie [si] *nf* saw

sciemment [sjamã] *adv* knowingly

science [sjãs] *nf* science; (*savoir*)
knowledge; **~s humaines/sociales**
social sciences; **~s naturelles** (*Scol*)
natural science *sg*, biology *sg*; **~s
po** political science *ou* studies *pl*;
science-fiction *nf* science fiction;
scientifique *adj* scientific ▷ *nm/f*
scientist; (*étudiant*) science student

scier [sje] /7/ *vt* to saw; (*retrancher*) to
saw off; **scierie** *nf* sawmill

scintiller [sẽtije] /1/ *vi* to sparkle;
(*étoile*) to twinkle

sciure [sjyR] *nf*: **~ (de bois)** sawdust

sclérose [skleRoz] *nf*: **~ en plaques
(SEP)** multiple sclerosis (MS)

scolaire [skɔlɛR] *adj* school *cpd*;
scolariser /1/ *vt* to provide with

schooling (*ou* schools); **scolarité** *nf*
schooling

scooter [skutœR] *nm* (motor) scooter

score [skɔR] *nm* score

scorpion [skɔRpjõ] *nm* (*signe*): **le
S~** Scorpio

scotch [skɔtʃ] *nm* (*whisky*) scotch,
whisky; **Scotch®** (*adhésif*)
Sellotape® (BRIT), Scotch tape® (US)

scout, e [skut] *adj, nm* scout

script [skRipt] *nm* (*écriture*) printing;
(*Ciné*) (shooting) script

scrupule [skRypyl] *nm* scruple

scruter [skRyte] /1/ *vt* to scrutinize;
(*l'obscurité*) to peer into

scrutin [skRytẽ] *nm* (*vote*) ballot;
(*ensemble des opérations*) poll

sculpter [skylte] /1/ *vt* to sculpt;
(*érosion*) to carve; **sculpteur** *nm*
sculptor; **sculpture** *nf* sculpture

SDF *sigle m* (= *sans domicile fixe*)
homeless person; **les ~** the homeless

○ **MOT-CLÉ**

se, s' [sə, s] *pron* **1** (*emploi réfléchi*)
oneself; (: *masc*) himself; (: *fém*)
herself; (: *sujet non humain*) itself;
(: *pl*) themselves; **se savonner** to
soap o.s.

2 (*réciproque*) one another, each
other; **ils s'aiment** they love one
another *ou* each other

3 (*passif*): **cela se répare facilement**
it is easily repaired

4 (*possessif*): **se casser la jambe/se
laver les mains** to break one's leg/
wash one's hands

séance [seãs] *nf* (*d'assemblée*)
meeting, session; (*de tribunal*) sitting,
session; (*musicale, Ciné, Théât*)
performance

seau, x [so] *nm* bucket, pail

sec, sèche [sɛk, sɛʃ] *adj* dry; (*raisins,
figues*) dried; (*insensible: cœur,
personne*) hard, cold ▷ *nm*: **tenir au ~**
to keep in a dry place ▷ *adv* hard; **je le**

bois ~ I drink it straight *ou* neat; **à ~** (*puits*) dried up
sécateur [sekatœʀ] *nm* secateurs *pl* (BRIT), shears *pl*
sèche [sɛʃ] *adj f voir* sec; **sèche-cheveux** *nm inv* hair-drier; **sèche-linge** *nm inv* tumble dryer; **sèchement** *adv* (*répliquer etc*) drily
sécher [seʃe] /6/ *vt* to dry; (*dessécher: peau, blé*) to dry (out); (: *étang*) to dry up; (*fam: classe, cours*) to skip ▷ *vi* to dry; to dry out; to dry up; (*fam: candidat*) to be stumped; **se sécher** *vi* (*après le bain*) to dry o.s.; **sécheresse** *nf* dryness; (*absence de pluie*) drought; **séchoir** *nm* drier
second, e [səgɔ̃, -ɔ̃d] *adj* second ▷ *nm* (*assistant*) second in command; (*Navig*) first mate ▷ *nf* second; (*Scol*) ≈ year 11 (BRIT), ≈ tenth grade (US); (*Aviat, Rail etc*) second class; **voyager en ~e** to travel second-class; **secondaire** *adj* secondary; **seconder** /1/ *vt* to assist
secouer [səkwe] /1/ *vt* to shake; (*passagers*) to rock; (*traumatiser*) to shake (up)
secourir [səkuʀiʀ] /11/ *vt* (*venir en aide à*) to assist, aid; **secourisme** *nm* first aid; **secouriste** *nm/f* first-aid worker
secours *nm* help, aid, assistance ▷ *nmpl* aid *sg*; **au ~!** help!; **appeler au ~** to shout *ou* call for help; **porter ~ à qn** to give sb assistance, help sb; **les premiers ~** first aid *sg*

- **ÉQUIPES DE SECOURS**
-
- Emergency phone numbers can
- be dialled free from public phones.
- For the police ('la police') dial 17; for
- medical services ('le SAMU') dial 15;
- for the fire brigade ('les sapeurs—
- pompiers') dial 18.

secousse [səkus] *nf* jolt, bump; (*électrique*) shock; (*fig: psychologique*) jolt, shock

secret, -ète [səkʀɛ, -ɛt] *adj* secret; (*fig: renfermé*) reticent, reserved ▷ *nm* secret; (*discrétion absolue*): **le ~** secrecy; **en ~** in secret, secretly; **~ professionnel** professional secrecy
secrétaire [səkʀetɛʀ] *nm/f* secretary ▷ *nm* (*meuble*) writing desk; **~ de direction** private *ou* personal secretary; **~ d'État** ≈ junior minister; **secrétariat** *nm* (*profession*) secretarial work; (*bureau*) (secretary's) office; (: *d'organisation internationale*) secretariat
secteur [sɛktœʀ] *nm* sector; (*Admin*) district; (*Élec*): **branché sur le ~** plugged into the mains (supply)
section [sɛksjɔ̃] *nf* section; (*de parcours d'autobus*) fare stage; (*Mil: unité*) platoon; **sectionner** /1/ *vt* to sever
sécu [seky] *nf* = **sécurité sociale**
sécurité [sekyʀite] *nf* (*absence de troubles*) security; (*absence de danger*) safety; **système de ~** security (*ou* safety) system; **être en ~** to be safe; **la ~ routière** road safety; **la ~ sociale** ≈ (the) Social Security (BRIT), ≈ (the) Welfare (US)
sédentaire [sedɑ̃tɛʀ] *adj* sedentary
séduction [sedyksjɔ̃] *nf* seduction; (*charme, attrait*) appeal, charm
séduire [seduiʀ] /38/ *vt* to charm; (*femme: abuser de*) to seduce; **séduisant, e** *adj* (*femme*) seductive; (*homme, offre*) very attractive
ségrégation [segʀegasjɔ̃] *nf* segregation
seigle [sɛgl] *nm* rye
seigneur [sɛɲœʀ] *nm* lord
sein [sɛ̃] *nm* breast; (*entrailles*) womb; **au ~ de** (*équipe, institution*) within
séisme [seism] *nm* earthquake
seize [sɛz] *num* sixteen; **seizième** *num* sixteenth
séjour [seʒuʀ] *nm* stay; (*pièce*) living room; **séjourner** /1/ *vi* to stay
sel [sɛl] *nm* salt; (*fig: piquant*) spice
sélection [selɛksjɔ̃] *nf* selection; **sélectionner** /1/ *vt* to select

self [sɛlf] nm (fam) self-service

selfie [sɛlfi] nm selfie

self-service [sɛlfsɛʀvis] adj self-service ▷ nm self-service (restaurant)

selle [sɛl] nf saddle; **selles** nfpl (Méd) stools; **seller** /1/ vt to saddle

selon [səlɔ̃] prép according to; (en se conformant à) in accordance with; **~ moi** as I see it; **~ que** according to

semaine [səmɛn] nf week; **en ~** during the week, on weekdays

semblable [sɑ̃blabl] adj similar; (de ce genre): **de ~s mésaventures** such mishaps ▷ nm fellow creature ou man; **~ à** similar to, like

semblant [sɑ̃blɑ̃] nm: **un ~ de vérité** a semblance of truth; **faire ~ (de faire)** to pretend (to do)

sembler [sɑ̃ble] /1/ vb copule to seem ▷ vb impers: **il semble (bien) que/ inutile de** it (really) seems ou appears that/useless to; **il me semble (bien) que** it (really) seems to me that; **comme bon lui semble** as he sees fit

semelle [səmɛl] nf sole; (intérieure) insole, inner sole

semer [səme] /5/ vt to sow; (fig: éparpiller) to scatter; (: confusion) to spread; (fam: poursuivants) to lose, shake off; **semé de** (difficultés) riddled with

semestre [səmɛstʀ] nm half-year; (Scol) semester

séminaire [seminɛʀ] nm seminar; **~ en ligne** webinar

semi-remorque [səmiʀəmɔʀk] nm articulated lorry (BRIT), semi(trailer) (US)

semoule [səmul] nf semolina

sénat [sena] nm senate; **sénateur** nm senator

Sénégal [senegal] nm: **le ~** Senegal

sens [sɑ̃s] nm (Physiol) sense; (signification) meaning, sense; (direction) direction; **à mon ~** to my mind; **dans le ~ des aiguilles d'une montre** clockwise; **dans le ~ contraire des aiguilles d'une**

montre anticlockwise; **dans le mauvais ~** (aller) the wrong way; in the wrong direction; **bon ~** good sense; **~ dessus dessous** upside down; **~ interdit, ~ unique** one-way street

sensation [sɑ̃sasjɔ̃] nf sensation; **faire ~** to cause a sensation, create a stir; **à ~** (péj) sensational; **sensationnel, le** adj sensational, fantastic

sensé, e [sɑ̃se] adj sensible

sensibiliser [sɑ̃sibilize] /1/ vt: **~ qn (à)** to make sb sensitive (to)

sensibilité [sɑ̃sibilite] nf sensitivity

sensible [sɑ̃sibl] adj sensitive; (aux sens) perceptible; (appréciable: différence, progrès) appreciable, noticeable; **~ à** sensitive to; **sensiblement** adv (à peu près): **ils ont sensiblement le même poids** they weigh approximately the same; **sensiblerie** nf sentimentality

> Attention à ne pas traduire sensible par le mot anglais sensible.

sensuel, le [sɑ̃sɥɛl] adj (personne) sensual; (musique) sensuous

sentence [sɑ̃tɑ̃s] nf (Jur) sentence

sentier [sɑ̃tje] nm path

sentiment [sɑ̃timɑ̃] nm feeling; **recevez mes ~s respectueux** (personne nommée) yours sincerely; (personne non nommée) yours faithfully; **sentimental, e, -aux** adj sentimental; (vie, aventure) love cpd

sentinelle [sɑ̃tinɛl] nf sentry

sentir [sɑ̃tiʀ] /16/ vt (par l'odorat) to smell; (par le goût) to taste; (au toucher, fig) to feel; (répandre une odeur de) to smell of (: ressemblance) to smell like ▷ vi to smell; **~ mauvais** to smell bad; **se ~ bien** to feel good; **se ~ mal** (être indisposé) to feel unwell ou ill; **se ~ le courage/la force de faire** to feel brave/strong enough to do; **il ne peut pas le ~** (fam) he can't stand him; **je ne me sens pas bien** I don't feel well

S

séparation [sepaʀasjɔ̃] nf
separation; (cloison) division,
partition

séparé, e [sepaʀe] adj (appartements,
pouvoirs) separate; (époux) separated;
séparément adv separately

séparer [sepaʀe] /1/ vt to separate;
(désunir) to drive apart; (détacher):
~ **qch de** to pull sth (off) from; **se
séparer** vi (époux) to separate, part;
(prendre congé: amis etc) to part; (se
diviser: route, tige etc) to divide; **se ~
de** (époux) to separate ou part from;
(employé, objet personnel) to part with

sept [sɛt] num seven; **septante** num
(BELGIQUE, SUISSE) seventy

septembre [sɛptɑ̃bʀ] nm
September

septicémie [sɛptisemi] nf blood
poisoning, septicaemia

septième [sɛtjɛm] num seventh

séquelles [sekɛl] nfpl after-effects;
(fig) aftermath sg

serbe [sɛʀb] adj Serbian

Serbie [sɛʀbi] nf: **la ~** Serbia

serein, e [sǝʀɛ̃, -ɛn] adj serene

sergent [sɛʀʒɑ̃] nm sergeant

série [seʀi] nf series inv; (de clés,
casseroles, outils) set; (catégorie:
Sport) rank; **en ~** in quick succession;
(Comm) mass cpd; **de ~** (voiture)
standard; **hors ~** (Comm) custom-
built; **~ noire** (crime) thriller

sérieusement [seʀjøzmɑ̃] adv
seriously

sérieux, -euse [seʀjø, -øz] adj
serious; (élève, employé) reliable,
responsible; (client, maison) reliable,
dependable ▷ nm seriousness; (d'une
entreprise etc) reliability; **garder son ~**
to keep a straight face; **prendre qch/
qn au ~** to take sth/sb seriously

serin [sǝʀɛ̃] nm canary

seringue [sǝʀɛ̃g] nf syringe

serment [sɛʀmɑ̃] nm (juré) oath;
(promesse) pledge, vow

sermon [sɛʀmɔ̃] nm sermon

séropositif, -ive [seʀopozitif, -iv]
adj HIV positive

serpent [sɛʀpɑ̃] nm snake;
serpenter /1/ vi to wind

serpillière [sɛʀpijɛʀ] nf floorcloth

serre [sɛʀ] nf (Agr) greenhouse;
serres nfpl (griffes) claws, talons

serré, e [seʀe] adj (réseau) dense;
(habits) tight; (fig: lutte, match) tight,
close-fought; (passagers etc) (tightly)
packed; **avoir le cœur ~** to have a
heavy heart

serrer [seʀe] /1/ vt (tenir) to grip
ou hold tight; (comprimer, coincer)
to squeeze; (poings, mâchoires) to
clench; (vêtement) to be too tight for;
(ceinture, nœud, frein, vis) to tighten
▷ vi: **~ à droite** to keep to the right

serrure [seʀyʀ] nf lock; **serrurier** nm
locksmith

sers, sert [sɛʀ] vb voir **servir**

servante [sɛʀvɑ̃t] nf (maid) servant

serveur, -euse [sɛʀvœʀ, -øz] nm/f
waiter (waitress)

serviable [sɛʀvjabl] adj obliging,
willing to help

service [sɛʀvis] nm service; (série
de repas): **premier ~** first sitting;
(assortiment de vaisselle) set, service;
(bureau: de la vente etc) department,
section; **faire le ~** to serve; **rendre
~ à qn** to help sb; **rendre un ~ à qn**
to do sb a favour; **être de ~** to be on
duty; **être/mettre en ~** to be in/put
into service ou operation; **~ compris/
non compris** service included/
not included; **hors ~** out of order;
~ après-vente after-sales service;
~ militaire military service; see
note **"service militaire"**; **~ d'ordre**
police (ou stewards) in charge of
maintaining order; **~s secrets** secret
service sg

● **SERVICE MILITAIRE**
●
● Until 1997, French men over
● the age of 18 who were passed
● as fit, and who were not in

full-time higher education,
were required to do ten months'
'service militaire'. Conscientious
objectors were required to do two
years' community service. Since
1997, military service has been
suspended in France. However, all
sixteen-year-olds, both male and
female, are required to register
for a compulsory one-day training
course, the 'JDC' ('journée défense
et citoyenneté'), which covers
basic information on the principles
and organization of defence in
France, and also advises on career
opportunities in the military and in
the voluntary sector. Young people
must attend the training day
before their eighteenth birthday.

serviette [sɛʀvjɛt] *nf* (*de table*)
(table) napkin, serviette; (*de toilette*)
towel; (*porte-documents*) briefcase; **~
hygiénique** sanitary towel
servir [sɛʀviʀ] /14/ *vt* to serve; (*au
restaurant*) to wait on; (*au magasin*)
to serve, attend to ▷ *vi* (*Tennis*) to
serve; (*Cartes*) to deal; **se servir** *vi*
(*prendre d'un plat*) to help o.s.; **vous
êtes servi?** are you being served?;
sers-toi! help yourself!; **se ~ de** (*plat*)
to help o.s. to; (*voiture, outil, relations*)
to use; **~ à qn** (*diplôme, livre*) to be of
use to sb; **~ à qch/à faire** (*outil etc*) to
be used for sth/for doing; **ça ne sert
à rien** it's no use; **~ (à qn) de ...** to
serve as ... (for sb)
serviteur [sɛʀvitœʀ] *nm* servant
ses [se] *adj poss voir* **son¹**
seuil [sœj] *nm* doorstep; (*fig*)
threshold
seul, e [sœl] *adj* (*sans compagnie*)
alone; (*unique*): **un ~ livre** only one
book, a single book; **le ~ livre** the
only book ▷ *adv* (*vivre*) alone, on one's
own; **faire qch (tout) ~** to do sth
(all) on one's own *ou* (all) by oneself
▷ *nm/f*: **il en reste un(e) ~(e)** there's

only one left; **à lui (tout) ~** single-
handed, on his own; **se sentir ~** to
feel lonely; **parler tout ~** to talk to
oneself; **seulement** *adv* only; **non
seulement ... mais aussi** *ou* **encore**
not only ... but also
sève [sɛv] *nf* sap
sévère [seveʀ] *adj* severe
sexe [sɛks] *nm* sex; (*organe mâle*)
member; **sexuel, le** *adj* sexual
shampooing [ʃɑ̃pwɛ̃] *nm* shampoo
Shetland [ʃɛtlɑ̃d] *n*: **les îles ~** the
Shetland Islands, Shetland
shopping [ʃɔpiŋ] *nm*: **faire du ~** to
go shopping
short [ʃɔʀt] *nm* (pair of) shorts *pl*

 MOT-CLÉ

si [si] *adv* **1** (*oui*) yes; **"Paul n'est pas
venu" — "si!"** "Paul hasn't come" —
"Yes he has!"; **je vous assure que si**
I assure you he did/she is *etc*
2 (*tellement*) so; **si gentil/
rapidement** so kind/fast; **(tant
et) si bien que** so much so that; **si
rapide qu'il soit** however fast he
may be
▶ *conj* if; **si tu veux** if you want;
je me demande si I wonder if *ou*
whether; **si seulement** if only
▶ *nm* (*Mus*) B; (: *en chantant la
gamme*) ti

Sicile [sisil] *nf*: **la ~** Sicily
sida [sida] *nm* (= *syndrome immuno-
déficitaire acquis*) AIDS *sg*
sidéré, e [sideʀe] *adj* staggered
sidérurgie [sideʀyʀʒi] *nf* steel
industry
siècle [sjɛkl] *nm* century
siège [sjɛʒ] *nm* seat; (*d'entreprise*)
head office; (*d'organisation*)
headquarters *pl*; (*Mil*) siege; **~ social**
registered office; **siéger** /3, 6/ *vi* to sit
sien, ne [sjɛ̃, sjɛn] *pron*: **le (la)
~(ne), les ~(ne)s** (*d'un homme*) his;
(*d'une femme*) hers; (*d'une chose*) its

sieste [sjɛst] nf (afternoon) snooze ou nap; **faire la ~** to have a snooze ou nap
sifflement [sifləmã] nm whistle
siffler [sifle] /1/ vi (gén) to whistle; (en respirant) to wheeze; (serpent, vapeur) to hiss ▷ vt (chanson) to whistle; (chien etc) to whistle for; (fille) to whistle at; (pièce, orateur) to hiss, boo; (fin du match, départ) to blow one's whistle for; (fam: verre, bouteille) to guzzle
sifflet [siflɛ] nm whistle; **coup de ~** whistle
siffloter [siflɔte] /1/ vi, vt to whistle
sigle [sigl] nm acronym
signal, -aux [siɲal, -o] nm signal; (indice, écriteau) sign; **donner le ~ de** to give the signal for; **~ d'alarme** alarm signal; **signalement** nm description, particulars pl
signaler [siɲale] /1/ vt to indicate; (vol, perte) to report; (personne, faire un signe) to signal; **~ qch à qn/à qn que** to point out sth to sb/to sb that
signature [siɲatyʀ] nf signature; (action) signing
signe [siɲ] nm sign; (Typo) mark; **faire un ~ de la main/tête** to give a sign with one's hand/shake one's head; **faire ~ à qn** (fig: contacter) to get in touch with sb; **faire ~ à qn d'entrer** to motion (to) sb to come in; **signer** /1/ vt to sign; **se signer** vi to cross o.s.
significatif, -ive [siɲifikatif, -iv] adj significant
signification [siɲifikasjɔ̃] nf meaning
signifier [siɲifje] /7/ vt (vouloir dire) to mean; (faire connaître): **~ qch (à qn)** to make sth known (to sb)
silence [silãs] nm silence; (Mus) rest; **garder le ~ (sur qch)** to keep silent (about sth), say nothing (about sth); **silencieux, -euse** adj quiet, silent ▷ nm silencer
silhouette [silwɛt] nf outline, silhouette; (figure) figure

sillage [sijaʒ] nm wake
sillon [sijɔ̃] nm furrow; (de disque) groove; **sillonner** /1/ vt to criss-cross
simagrées [simagʀe] nfpl fuss sg
similaire [similɛʀ] adj similar; **similicuir** nm imitation leather; **similitude** nf similarity
simple [sɛ̃pl] adj simple; (non multiple) single; **~ messieurs/dames** nm (Tennis) men's/ladies' singles sg; **~ d'esprit** nm/f simpleton; **~ soldat** private
simplicité [sɛ̃plisite] nf simplicity; **en toute ~** quite simply
simplifier [sɛ̃plifje] /7/ vt to simplify
simuler [simyle] /1/ vt to sham, simulate
simultané, e [simyltane] adj simultaneous
sincère [sɛ̃sɛʀ] adj sincere; **sincèrement** adv sincerely; genuinely; **sincérité** nf sincerity
Singapour [sɛ̃gapuʀ] nm: Singapore
singe [sɛ̃ʒ] nm monkey; (de grande taille) ape; **singer** /3/ vt to ape, mimic; **singeries** nfpl antics
singulariser [sɛ̃gylaʀize] /1/: **se singulariser** vi to call attention to o.s.
singularité [sɛ̃gylaʀite] nf peculiarity
singulier, -ière [sɛ̃gylje, -jɛʀ] adj remarkable, singular ▷ nm singular
sinistre [sinistʀ] adj sinister ▷ nm (incendie) blaze; (catastrophe) disaster; (Assurances) damage (giving rise to a claim); **sinistré, e** adj disaster-stricken ▷ nm/f disaster victim
sinon [sinɔ̃] conj (autrement, sans quoi) otherwise, or else; (sauf) except, other than; (si ce n'est) if not
sinueux, -euse [sinɥø, -øz] adj winding
sinus [sinys] nm (Anat) sinus; (Géom) sine; **sinusite** nf sinusitis
sirène [siʀɛn] nf siren; **~ d'alarme** fire alarm; (pendant la guerre) air-raid siren

sirop [siʀo] nm (à diluer: de fruit etc) syrup; (pharmaceutique) syrup, mixture; **~ contre la toux** cough syrup ou mixture

siroter [siʀɔte] /1/ vt to sip

sismique [sismik] adj seismic

site [sit] nm (paysage, environnement) setting; (d'une ville etc: emplacement) site; **~ (pittoresque)** beauty spot; **~s touristiques** places of interest; **~ web** (Inform) website

sitôt [sito] adv: **~ parti** as soon as he etc had left; **pas de ~** not for a long time; **~ (après) que** as soon as

situation [sitɥasjɔ̃] nf situation; (d'un édifice, d'une ville) position; location; **~ de famille** marital status

situé, e [sitɥe] adj: **bien ~** well situated

situer [sitɥe] /1/ vt to site, situate; (en pensée) to set, place; **se situer** vi: **se ~ à/près de** to be situated at/near

six [sis] num six; **sixième** num sixth ▷ nf (Scol) year 7

skaï® [skaj] nm ≈ Leatherette®

skate [sket], **skate-board** [sketbɔʀd] nm (sport) skateboarding; (planche) skateboard

ski [ski] nm (objet) ski; (sport) skiing; **faire du ~** to ski; **~ de fond** cross-country skiing; **~ nautique** water-skiing; **~ de piste** downhill skiing; **~ de randonnée** cross-country skiing; **skier** /7/ vi to ski; **skieur, -euse** nm/f skier

slip [slip] nm (sous-vêtement) pants pl (BRIT), briefs pl; (de bain: d'homme) trunks pl; (: du bikini) (bikini) briefs pl

slogan [slɔgɑ̃] nm slogan

Slovaquie [slɔvaki] nf: **la ~** Slovakia

SMIC [smik] sigle m = **salaire minimum interprofessionnel de croissance**

smoking [smɔkiŋ] nm dinner ou evening suit

SMS sigle m (= short message service) (service) SMS; (message) text (message)

SNCF sigle f (= Société nationale des chemins de fer français) French railways

snob [snɔb] adj snobbish ▷ nm/f snob; **snobisme** nm snobbery, snobbishness

sobre [sɔbʀ] adj (personne) temperate, abstemious; (élégance, style) sober

sobriquet [sɔbʀike] nm nickname

social, e, -aux [sɔsjal, -o] adj social

socialisme [sɔsjalism] nm socialism; **socialiste** nm/f socialist

société [sɔsjete] nf society; (sportive) club; (Comm) company; **la ~ d'abondance/de consommation** the affluent/consumer society; **~ anonyme** ≈ limited company (BRIT), ≈ incorporated company (US)

sociologie [sɔsjɔlɔʒi] nf sociology

socle [sɔkl] nm (de colonne, statue) plinth, pedestal; (de lampe) base

socquette [sɔket] nf ankle sock

sœur [sœʀ] nf sister; (religieuse) nun, sister

soi [swa] pron oneself; **en ~** (intrinsèquement) in itself; **cela va de ~** that ou it goes without saying; **soi-disant** adj inv so-called ▷ adv supposedly

soie [swa] nf silk; **soierie** nf (tissu) silk

soif [swaf] nf thirst; **avoir ~** to be thirsty; **donner ~ à qn** to make sb thirsty

soigné, e [swaɲe] adj (tenue) well-groomed, neat; (travail) careful, meticulous

soigner [swaɲe] /1/ vt (malade, maladie: docteur) to treat; (: infirmière, mère) to nurse, look after; (travail, détails) to take care over; (jardin, chevelure, invités) to look after; **soigneux, -euse** adj tidy, neat; (méticuleux) painstaking, careful

soi-même [swamɛm] pron oneself

soin [swɛ̃] nm (application) care; (propreté, ordre) tidiness, neatness; **soins** nmpl (à un malade, blessé) treatment sg, medical attention sg; (hygiène) care sg; **avoir** ou **prendre ~**

S

de to take care of, look after; **avoir** ou **prendre ~ de faire** to take care to do; **les premiers ~s** first aid sg

soir [swaʀ] nm evening; **ce ~** this evening, tonight; **à ce ~!** see you this evening (ou tonight)!; **sept/dix heures du ~** seven in the evening/ten at night; **demain ~** tomorrow evening, tomorrow night; **soirée** nf evening; (réception) party

soit [swa] vb voir **être** ▷ conj (à savoir) namely; (ou): **~ ... ~** either ... or ▷ adv so be it, very well; **~ que ... ~ que** ou **ou que** whether ... or whether

soixantaine [swasɑ̃tɛn] nf: **une ~ (de)** sixty or so, about sixty; **avoir la ~** (âge) to be around sixty

soixante [swasɑ̃t] num sixty; **soixante-dix** num seventy

soja [sɔʒa] nm soya; (graines) soya beans pl; **germes de ~** beansprouts

sol [sɔl] nm ground; (de logement) floor; (Agr, Géo) soil; (Mus) G (: en chantant la gamme) so(h)

solaire [sɔlɛʀ] adj (énergie etc) solar; (crème etc) sun cpd

soldat [sɔlda] nm soldier

solde [sɔld] nf pay ▷ nm (Comm) balance; **soldes** nmpl ou nfpl (Comm) sales; **en ~** at sale price; **solder** /1/ vt (marchandise) to sell at sale price, sell off

sole [sɔl] nf sole inv (fish)

soleil [sɔlɛj] nm sun; (lumière) sun(light); (temps ensoleillé) sun(shine); **il y a** ou **il fait du ~** it's sunny; **au ~** in the sun

solennel, le [sɔlanɛl] adj solemn

solfège [sɔlfɛʒ] nm rudiments pl of music

solidaire [sɔlidɛʀ] adj: **être ~s** (personnes) to show solidarity, stand ou stick together; **être ~ de** (collègues) to stand by; **solidarité** nf solidarity; **par solidarité (avec)** in sympathy (with)

solide [sɔlid] adj solid; (mur, maison, meuble) solid, sturdy; (connaissances, argument) sound; (personne) robust, sturdy ▷ nm solid

soliste [sɔlist] nm/f soloist

solitaire [sɔlitɛʀ] adj (sans compagnie) solitary, lonely; (lieu) lonely ▷ nm/f (ermite) recluse; (fig: ours) loner

solitude [sɔlityd] nf loneliness; (paix) solitude

solliciter [sɔlisite] /1/ vt (personne) to appeal to; (emploi, faveur) to seek

sollicitude [sɔlisityd] nf concern

soluble [sɔlybl] adj soluble

solution [sɔlysjɔ̃] nf solution; **~ de facilité** easy way out

solvable [sɔlvabl] adj solvent

sombre [sɔ̃bʀ] adj dark; (fig) gloomy; **sombrer** /1/ vi (bateau) to sink; **sombrer dans** (misère, désespoir) to sink into

sommaire [sɔmɛʀ] adj (simple) basic; (expéditif) summary ▷ nm summary

somme [sɔm] nf (Math) sum; (fig) amount; (argent) sum, amount ▷ nm: **faire un ~** to have a (short) nap; **en ~**, **~ toute** all in all

sommeil [sɔmɛj] nm sleep; **avoir ~** to be sleepy; **sommeiller** /1/ vi to doze

sommet [sɔmɛ] nm top; (d'une montagne) summit, top; (fig: de la perfection, gloire) height

sommier [sɔmje] nm bed base

somnambule [sɔmnɑ̃byl] nm/f sleepwalker

somnifère [sɔmnifɛʀ] nm sleeping drug; sleeping pill ou tablet

somnoler [sɔmnɔle] /1/ vi to doze

somptueux, -euse [sɔ̃ptɥø, -øz] adj sumptuous

son¹, sa (pl **ses**) [sɔ̃, sa, se] adj poss (antécédent humain: mâle) his (: femelle) her; (: valeur indéfinie) one's, his (her); (: non humain) its

son² [sɔ̃] nm sound; (de blé etc) bran

sondage [sɔ̃daʒ] nm: **~ (d'opinion)** (opinion) poll

sonde [sɔ̃d] nf (Navig) lead ou sounding line; (Méd) probe; (Tech: de forage, sondage) drill

sonder [sɔ̃de] /1/ vt (Navig) to sound; (Tech) to bore, drill; (fig: personne) to sound out; **~ le terrain** (fig) to see how the land lies

songe [sɔ̃ʒ] nm dream; **songer** /3/ vi: **songer à** (rêver à) to think over; (envisager) to contemplate, think of; **songer que** to think that; **songeur, -euse** adj pensive

sonnant, e [sɔnɑ̃, -ɑ̃t] adj: **à huit heures ~es** on the stroke of eight

sonné, e [sɔne] adj (fam) cracked; **il est midi ~** it's gone twelve

sonner [sɔne] /1/ vi to ring ⊳ vt (cloche) to ring; (glas, tocsin) to sound; (portier, infirmière) to ring for; **~ faux** (instrument) to sound out of tune; (rire) to ring false

sonnerie [sɔnri] nf (son) ringing; (sonnette) bell; (de portable) ringtone; **~ d'alarme** alarm bell

sonnette [sɔnɛt] nf bell; **~ d'alarme** alarm bell

sonore [sɔnɔʁ] adj (voix) sonorous, ringing; (salle, métal) resonant; (ondes, film, signal) sound cpd; **sonorisation** nf (équipement: de salle de conférences) public address system, P.A. system; (: de discothèque) sound system; **sonorité** nf (de piano, violon) tone; (d'une salle) acoustics pl

sophistiqué, e [sɔfistike] adj sophisticated

sorbet [sɔʁbɛ] nm water ice, sorbet

sorcier, -ière [sɔʁsje, -jɛʁ] nm/f sorcerer (witch ou sorceress)

sordide [sɔʁdid] adj (lieu) squalid; (action) sordid

sort [sɔʁ] nm (fortune, destinée) fate; (condition, situation) lot; (magique): **jeter un ~** to cast a spell; **tirer au ~** to draw lots

sorte [sɔʁt] nf sort, kind; **de la ~** in that way; **en quelque ~** in a way; **de**
(telle) **~ que** so that; **faire en ~ que** to see to it that

sortie [sɔʁti] nf (issue) way out, exit; (verbale) sally; (promenade) outing; (le soir, au restaurant etc) night out; (Comm: d'un disque) release; (: d'un livre) publication; (: d'un modèle) launching; **~ de bain** (vêtement) bathrobe; **~ de secours** emergency exit

sortilège [sɔʁtilɛʒ] nm (magic) spell

sortir [sɔʁtiʁ] /16/ vi (gén) to come out; (partir, se promener, aller au spectacle etc) to go out; (bourgeon, plante, numéro gagnant) to come up ⊳ vt (gén) to take out; (produit, ouvrage, modèle) to bring out; (fam: dire) to come out with; **~ avec qn** to be going out with sb; **~ de** (endroit) to go (ou come) out of, leave; (cadre, compétence) to be outside; (provenir de) to come from; **s'en ~** (malade) to pull through; (d'une difficulté etc) to get through

sosie [sɔzi] nm double

sot, sotte [so, sɔt] adj silly, foolish ⊳ nm/f fool; **sottise** nf silliness no pl; foolishness no pl; (propos, acte) silly ou foolish thing (to do ou say)

sou [su] nm: **près de ses ~s** tight-fisted; **sans le ~** penniless

soubresaut [subʁəso] nm start; (cahot) jolt

souche [suʃ] nf (d'arbre) stump; (de carnet) counterfoil (BRIT), stub

souci [susi] nm (inquiétude) worry; (préoccupation) concern; (Bot) marigold; **se faire du ~** to worry; **soucier** /7/: **se soucier de** vt to care about; **soucieux, -euse** adj concerned, worried

soucoupe [sukup] nf saucer; **~ volante** flying saucer

soudain, e [sudɛ̃, -ɛn] adj (douleur, mort) sudden ⊳ adv suddenly, all of a sudden

Soudan [sudɑ̃] nm: **le ~** Sudan

soude [sud] nf soda

souder [sude] /1/ *vt* (*avec fil à souder*) to solder; (*par soudure autogène*) to weld; (*fig*) to bind *ou* knit together

soudure [sudyʀ] *nf* soldering; welding; (*joint*) soldered joint; weld

souffle [sufl] *nm* (*en expirant*) breath; (*en soufflant*) puff, blow; (*respiration*) breathing; (*d'explosion, de ventilateur*) blast; (*du vent*) blowing; **être à bout de ~** to be out of breath; **un ~ d'air** *ou* **de vent** a breath of air

soufflé, e [sufle] *adj* (*fam: ahuri, stupéfié*) staggered ▷ *nm* (*Culin*) soufflé

souffler [sufle] /1/ *vi* (*gén*) to blow; (*haleter*) to puff (and blow) ▷ *vt* (*feu, bougie*) to blow out; (*chasser: poussière etc*) to blow; (*Tech: verre*) to blow; (*dire*): **~ qch à qn** to whisper sth to sb

souffrance [sufʀɑ̃s] *nf* suffering; **en ~** (*affaire*) pending

souffrant, e [sufʀɑ̃, -ɑ̃t] *adj* unwell

souffre-douleur [sufʀədulœʀ] *nm inv* butt, underdog

souffrir [sufʀiʀ] /18/ *vi* to suffer; (*éprouver des douleurs*) to be in pain ▷ *vt* to suffer, endure; (*supporter*) to bear, stand; **~ de** (*maladie, froid*) to suffer from; **elle ne peut pas le ~** she can't stand *ou* bear him

soufre [sufʀ] *nm* sulphur

souhait [swɛ] *nm* wish; **tous nos ~s pour la nouvelle année** (our) best wishes for the New Year; **souhaitable** *adj* desirable

souhaiter [swete] /1/ *vt* to wish for; **~ la bonne année à qn** to wish sb a happy New Year; **~ que** to hope that

soûl, e [su, sul] *adj* drunk ▷ *nm*: **tout son ~** to one's heart's content

soulagement [sulaʒmɑ̃] *nm* relief

soulager [sulaʒe] /3/ *vt* to relieve

soûler [sule] /1/ *vt*: **~ qn** to get sb drunk; (*boisson*) to make sb drunk; (*fig*) to make sb's head spin *ou* reel; **se soûler** *vi* to get drunk

soulever [sulve] /5/ *vt* to lift; (*vagues, poussière*) to send up; (*enthousiasme*) to arouse; (*question, débat, protestations, difficultés*) to raise; **se soulever** *vi* (*peuple*) to rise up; (*personne couchée*) to lift o.s. up

soulier [sulje] *nm* shoe

souligner [suliɲe] /1/ *vt* to underline; (*fig*) to emphasize, stress

soumettre [sumɛtʀ] /56/ *vt* (*pays*) to subject, subjugate; (*rebelles*) to put down, subdue; **~ qch à qn** (*projet etc*) to submit sth to sb; **se ~ (à)** to submit (to)

soumis, e [sumi, -iz] *adj* submissive; **soumission** *nf* submission

soupçon [supsɔ̃] *nm* suspicion; (*petite quantité*): **un ~ de** a hint *ou* touch of; **soupçonner** /1/ *vt* to suspect; **soupçonneux, -euse** *adj* suspicious

soupe [sup] *nf* soup

souper [supe] /1/ *vi* to have supper ▷ *nm* supper

soupeser [supəze] /5/ *vt* to weigh in one's hand(s); (*fig*) to weigh up

soupière [supjɛʀ] *nf* (*soup*) tureen

soupir [supiʀ] *nm* sigh; **pousser un ~ de soulagement** to heave a sigh of relief

soupirer [supiʀe] /1/ *vi* to sigh

souple [supl] *adj* supple; (*fig: règlement, caractère*) flexible; (*: démarche, taille*) lithe, supple; **souplesse** *nf* suppleness; (*de caractère*) flexibility

source [suʀs] *nf* (*point d'eau*) spring; (*d'un cours d'eau, fig*) source; **tenir qch de bonne ~/de ~ sûre** to have sth on good authority/from a reliable source

sourcil [suʀsij] *nm* (eye)brow; **sourciller** /1/ *vi*: **sans sourciller** without turning a hair *ou* batting an eyelid

sourd, e [suʀ, suʀd] *adj* deaf; (*bruit, voix*) muffled; (*douleur*) dull ▷ *nm/f* deaf person; **faire la ~e oreille** to turn a deaf ear; **sourdine** *nf* (*Mus*) mute; **en sourdine** softly, quietly; **sourd-muet, sourde-muette** *adj* with a speech and hearing impairment

souriant, e [suʀjɑ̃, -ɑ̃t] *adj* cheerful

sourire [suʀiʀ] /36/ *nm* smile ▷ *vi* to smile; **~ à qn** to smile at sb; (*fig: plaire à*) to appeal to sb; (*chance*) to smile on sb; **garder le ~** to keep smiling

souris [suʀi] *nf* mouse

sournois, e [suʀnwa, -waz] *adj* deceitful, underhand

sous [su] *prép* under; **~ la pluie/le soleil** in the rain/sunshine; **~ terre** underground; **~ peu** shortly, before long; **sous-bois** *nm inv* undergrowth

souscrire [suskʀiʀ] /39/: **~ à** *vt* to subscribe to

sous: sous-directeur, -trice *nm/f* assistant manager/manageress; **sous-entendre** /41/ *vt* to imply, infer; **sous-entendu, e** *adj* implied ▷ *nm* innuendo, insinuation; **sous-estimer** /1/ *vt* to underestimate; **sous-jacent, e** *adj* underlying; **sous-louer** /1/ *vt* to sublet; **sous-marin, e** *adj* (*flore, volcan*) submarine; (*navigation, pêche, explosif*) underwater ▷ *nm* submarine; **sous-pull** *nm* thin poloneck sweater; **soussigné, e** *adj*: **je soussigné** I the undersigned; **sous-sol** *nm* basement; **sous-titre** [sutitʀ] *nm* subtitle

soustraction [sustʀaksjɔ̃] *nf* subtraction

soustraire [sustʀɛʀ] /50/ *vt* to subtract, take away; (*dérober*): **~ qch à qn** to remove sth from sb; **se ~ à** (*autorité, obligation, devoir*) to elude, escape from

sous: sous-traitant *nm* subcontractor; **sous-traiter** /1/ *vt, vi* to subcontract; **sous-vêtement** *nm* item of underwear; **sous-vêtements** *nmpl* underwear *sg*

soutane [sutan] *nf* cassock, soutane

soute [sut] *nf* hold

soutenir [sutniʀ] /22/ *vt* to support; (*assaut, choc, regard*) to stand up to, withstand; (*intérêt, effort*) to keep up; (*assurer*): **~ que** to maintain that;

soutenu, e *adj* (*efforts*) sustained, unflagging; (*style*) elevated

souterrain, e [sutɛʀɛ̃, -ɛn] *adj* underground ▷ *nm* underground passage

soutien [sutjɛ̃] *nm* support; **soutien-gorge** *nm* bra

soutirer [sutiʀe] /1/ *vt*: **~ qch à qn** to squeeze *ou* get sth out of sb

souvenir [suvniʀ] /22/ *nm* (*réminiscence*) memory; (*cadeau*) souvenir ▷ *vb*: **se ~ de** to remember; **se ~ que** to remember that; **en ~ de** in memory *ou* remembrance of; **avec mes affectueux/meilleurs ~s, ...** with love from, .../regards, ...

souvent [suvɑ̃] *adv* often; **peu ~** seldom, infrequently

souverain, e [suvʀɛ̃, -ɛn] *nm/f* sovereign, monarch

soyeux, -euse [swajø, -øz] *adj* silky

spacieux, -euse [spasjø, -øz] *adj* spacious; roomy

spaghettis [spageti] *nmpl* spaghetti *sg*

sparadrap [spaʀadʀa] *nm* adhesive *ou* sticking (BRIT) plaster, bandaid® (US)

spatial, e, -aux [spasjal, -o] *adj* (*Aviat*) space *cpd*

speaker, ine [spikœʀ, -kʀin] *nm/f* announcer

spécial, e, -aux [spesjal, -o] *adj* special; (*bizarre*) peculiar; **spécialement** *adv* especially, particularly; (*tout exprès*) specially; **spécialiser** /1/: **se spécialiser** *vi* to specialize; **spécialiste** *nm/f* specialist; **spécialité** *nf* speciality; (*Scol*) special field

spécifier [spesifje] /7/ *vt* to specify, state

spécimen [spesimɛn] *nm* specimen

spectacle [spɛktakl] *nm* (*tableau, scène*) sight; (*représentation*) show; (*industrie*) show business; **spectaculaire** *adj* spectacular

spectateur, -trice [spɛktatœʀ, -tʀis] *nm/f* (*Ciné etc*) member of the

S

audience; (*Sport*) spectator; (*d'un événement*) onlooker, witness
spéculer [spekyle] /1/ *vi* to speculate
spéléologie [speleɔlɔʒi] *nf* potholing
sperme [spɛʁm] *nm* semen, sperm
sphère [sfɛʁ] *nf* sphere
spirale [spiʁal] *nf* spiral
spirituel, le [spiʁituɛl] *adj* spiritual; (*fin, piquant*) witty
splendide [splɑ̃did] *adj* splendid
spontané, e [spɔ̃tane] *adj* spontaneous; **spontanéité** *nf* spontaneity
sport [spɔʁ] *nm* sport ▷ *adj inv* (*vêtement*) casual; **faire du ~** to do sport; **~s d'hiver** winter sports; **sportif, -ive** *adj* (*journal, association, épreuve*) sports *cpd*; (*allure, démarche*) athletic; (*attitude, esprit*) sporting
spot [spɔt] *nm* (*lampe*) spot(light); (*annonce*): **~ (publicitaire)** commercial (break)
square [skwaʁ] *nm* public garden(s)
squelette [skəlɛt] *nm* skeleton; **squelettique** *adj* scrawny
SRAS [sʁas] *sigle m* (= *syndrome respiratoire aigu sévère*) SARS
Sri Lanka [sʁilɑ̃ka] *nm*: **le ~** Sri Lanka
stabiliser [stabilize] /1/ *vt* to stabilize
stable [stabl] *adj* stable, steady
stade [stad] *nm* (*Sport*) stadium; (*phase, niveau*) stage
stage [staʒ] *nm* (*cours*) training course; **~ de formation (professionnelle)** vocational (training) course; **~ de perfectionnement** advanced training course; **stagiaire** [staʒjɛʁ] *nm/f, adj* trainee

Attention à ne pas traduire *stage* par le mot anglais *stage*.

stagner [stagne] /1/ *vi* to stagnate
stand [stɑ̃d] *nm* (*d'exposition*) stand; (*de foire*) stall; **~ de tir** (*à la foire, Sport*) shooting range

standard [stɑ̃daʁ] *adj inv* standard ▷ *nm* switchboard; **standardiste** *nm/f* switchboard operator
standing [stɑ̃diŋ] *nm* standing; **de grand ~** luxury
starter [staʁtɛʁ] *nm* (*Auto*) choke
station [stasjɔ̃] *nf* station; (*de bus*) stop; (*de villégiature*) resort; **~ de ski** ski resort; **~ de taxis** taxi rank (BRIT) *ou* stand (US); **stationnement** *nm* parking; **stationner** /1/ *vi* to park; **station-service** *nf* service station
statistique [statistik] *nf* (*science*) statistics *sg*; (*rapport, étude*) statistic ▷ *adj* statistical
statue [staty] *nf* statue
statu quo [statykwo] *nm* status quo
statut [staty] *nm* status; **statuts** *nmpl* (*Jur, Admin*) statutes; **statutaire** *adj* statutory
Sté *abr* (= *société*) soc
steak [stɛk] *nm* steak; **~ haché** hamburger
sténo [stenɔ] *nf* (*aussi*: **~graphie**) shorthand
stérile [steʁil] *adj* sterile
stérilet [steʁilɛ] *nm* coil, loop
stériliser [steʁilize] /1/ *vt* to sterilize
stimulant, e [stimylɑ̃, -ɑ̃t] *adj* stimulating ▷ *nm* (*Méd*) stimulant; (*fig*) stimulus, incentive
stimuler [stimyle] /1/ *vt* to stimulate
stipuler [stipyle] /1/ *vt* to stipulate
stock [stɔk] *nm* stock; **stocker** /1/ *vt* to stock
stop [stɔp] *nm* (*Auto: écriteau*) stop sign; (: *signal*) brake-light; **faire du ~** (*fam*) to hitch(hike); **stopper** /1/ *vt* to stop ▷ *vi* to stop, halt
store [stɔʁ] *nm* blind; (*de magasin*) shade, awning
strabisme [stʁabism] *nm* squint(ing)
strapontin [stʁapɔ̃tɛ̃] *nm* jump *ou* foldaway seat
stratégie [stʁateʒi] *nf* strategy; **stratégique** *adj* strategic

stress [strɛs] *nm inv* stress;
stressant, e *adj* stressful; **stresser**
/1/ *vt*: **stresser qn** to make sb (feel)
tense

strict, e [strikt] *adj* strict; (*tenue,*
décor) severe, plain; **le ~ nécessaire/**
minimum the bare essentials/
minimum

strident, e [stridã, -ãt] *adj* shrill,
strident

strophe [strɔf] *nf* verse, stanza

structure [stryktyr] *nf* structure; **~s**
d'accueil/touristiques reception/
tourist facilities

studieux, -euse [stydjø, -øz] *adj*
studious

studio [stydjo] *nm* (*logement*) studio
flat (BRIT) *ou* apartment (US);
(*d'artiste*, TV *etc*) studio

stupéfait, e [stypefɛ, -ɛt] *adj*
astonished

stupéfiant, e [stypefjã, -ãt] *adj*
(*étonnant*) stunning, astonishing
▷ *nm* (*Méd*) drug, narcotic

stupéfier [stypefje] /7/ *vt* (*étonner*)
to stun, astonish

stupeur [stypœr] *nf* astonishment

stupide [stypid] *adj* stupid;
stupidité *nf* stupidity *no pl*; (*parole,*
acte) stupid thing (to say *ou* do)

style [stil] *nm* style

stylé, e [stile] *adj* well-trained

styliste [stilist] *nm/f* designer

stylo [stilo] *nm*: **~ (à encre)**
(fountain) pen; **~ (à) bille** ballpoint
pen

su, e [sy] *pp de* **savoir** ▷ *nm*: **au su de**
with the knowledge of

suave [sɥav] *adj* sweet

subalterne [sybaltɛrn] *adj* (*employé,*
officier) junior; (*rôle*) subordinate,
subsidiary ▷ *nm/f* subordinate

subconscient [sypkɔ̃sjã] *nm*
subconscious

subir [sybir] /2/ *vt* (*affront, dégâts,*
mauvais traitements) to suffer;
(*traitement, opération, châtiment*) to
undergo

subit, e [sybi, -it] *adj* sudden;
subitement *adv* suddenly, all of a
sudden

subjectif, -ive [sybʒɛktif, -iv] *adj*
subjective

subjonctif [sybʒɔ̃ktif] *nm*
subjunctive

subjuguer [sybʒyge] /1/ *vt* to
subjugate

submerger [sybmɛrʒe] /3/ *vt* to
submerge; (*fig*) to overwhelm

subordonné, e [sybɔrdɔne] *adj,*
nm/f subordinate

subrepticement [sybrɛptismã]
adv surreptitiously

subside [sypsid] *nm* grant

subsidiaire [sypsidjɛr] *adj*:
question ~ deciding question

subsister [sybziste] /1/ *vi* (*rester*) to
remain, subsist; (*survivre*) to live on

substance [sypstãs] *nf* substance

substituer [sypstitɥe] /1/ *vt*: **~ qn/**
qch à to substitute sb/sth for; **se ~ à**
qn (*évincer*) to substitute o.s. for sb

substitut [sypstity] *nm* (*succédané*)
substitute

subterfuge [syptɛrfyʒ] *nm* subterfuge

subtil, e [syptil] *adj* subtle

subvenir [sybvənir] /22/: **~ à** *vt*
to meet

subvention [sybvãsjɔ̃] *nf* subsidy,
grant; **subventionner** /1/ *vt* to
subsidize

suc [syk] *nm* (*Bot*) sap; (*de viande,*
fruit) juice

succéder [syksede] /6/: **~ à** *vt* to
succeed; **se succéder** *vi* (*accidents,*
années) to follow one another

succès [syksɛ] *nm* success; **avoir du**
~ to be a success, be successful; **à ~**
successful; **~ de librairie** bestseller

successeur [syksesœr] *nm*
successor

successif, -ive [syksesif, -iv] *adj*
successive

succession [syksesjɔ̃] *nf* (*série, Pol*)
succession; (*Jur: patrimoine*) estate,
inheritance

S

succomber [sykɔ̃be] /1/ vi to die, succumb; (fig): **~ à** to succumb to

succulent, e [sykylɑ̃, -ɑ̃t] adj delicious

succursale [sykyʀsal] nf branch

sucer [syse] /3/ vt to suck; **sucette** nf (bonbon) lollipop; (de bébé) dummy (BRIT), pacifier (US)

sucre [sykʀ] nm (substance) sugar; (morceau) lump of sugar, sugar lump ou cube; **~ en morceaux/ cristallisé/en poudre** lump ou cube/ granulated/caster sugar; **~ glace** icing sugar (BRIT), confectioner's sugar (US); **~ d'orge** barley sugar; **sucré, e** adj (produit alimentaire) sweetened; (au goût) sweet; **sucrer** /1/ vt (thé, café) to sweeten, put sugar in; **sucrerie** nf sugar refinery; **sucreries** nfpl (bonbons) sweets, sweet things; **sucrier** nm (récipient) sugar bowl ou basin

sud [syd] nm: **le ~** the south ▷ adj inv south; (côte) south, southern; **au ~** (situation) in the south; (direction) to the south; **au ~ de** (to the) south of; **sud-africain, e** adj South African ▷ nm/f: **Sud-Africain, e** South African; **sud-américain, e** adj South American ▷ nm/f: **Sud-Américain, e** South American; **sud-est** nm, adj inv south-east; **sud-ouest** nm, adj inv south-west

Suède [sɥɛd] nf: **la ~** Sweden; **suédois, e** adj Swedish ▷ nm (Ling) Swedish ▷ nm/f: **Suédois, e** Swede

suer [sɥe] /1/ vi to sweat; (suinter) to ooze; **sueur** nf sweat; **en sueur** sweating, in a sweat; **avoir des sueurs froides** to be in a cold sweat

suffire [syfiʀ] /37/ vi (être assez): **~ (à qn/pour qch/pour faire)** to be enough ou sufficient (for sb/for sth/ to do); **il suffit d'une négligence/ qu'on oublie pour que ...** it only takes one act of carelessness/one only needs to forget for ...; **ça suffit!** that's enough!

suffisamment [syfizamɑ̃] adv sufficiently, enough; **~ de** sufficient, enough

suffisant, e [syfizɑ̃, -ɑ̃t] adj sufficient; (résultats) satisfactory; (vaniteux) self-important, bumptious

suffixe [syfiks] nm suffix

suffoquer [syfɔke] /1/ vt to choke, suffocate; (stupéfier) to astound ▷ vi to choke, suffocate

suffrage [syfʀaʒ] nm (Pol: voix) vote

suggérer [sygʒeʀe] /6/ vt to suggest; **suggestion** nf suggestion

suicide [sɥisid] nm suicide; **suicider** /1/: **se suicider** vi to commit suicide

suie [sɥi] nf soot

suisse [sɥis] adj Swiss ▷ nm/f: **S~** Swiss inv ▷ nf: **la S~** Switzerland; **la S~ romande/allemande** French-speaking/German-speaking Switzerland

suite [sɥit] nf (continuation: d'énumération etc) rest, remainder; (: de feuilleton) continuation; (: second film etc sur le même thème) sequel; (série) series, succession; (conséquence) result; (ordre, liaison logique) coherence; (appartement, Mus) suite; (escorte) retinue, suite; **suites** nfpl (d'une maladie etc) effects; **une ~ de** a series ou succession of; **prendre la ~ de** (directeur etc) to succeed, take over from; **donner ~ à** (requête, projet) to follow up; **faire ~ à** to follow; **(faisant) ~ à votre lettre du** further to your letter of the; **de ~** (d'affilée) in succession; (immédiatement) at once; **par la ~** afterwards, subsequently; **à la ~** one after the other; **à la ~ de** (derrière) behind; (en conséquence de) following

suivant, e [sɥivɑ̃, -ɑ̃t] adj next, following ▷ prép (selon) according to; **au ~!** next!

suivi, e [sɥivi] adj (effort, qualité) consistent; (cohérent) coherent; **très/ peu ~** (cours) well-/poorly-attended

suivre [sɥivʀ] /40/ vt (gén) to follow; (Scol: cours) to attend; (: programme) to keep up with; (Comm: article) to continue to stock ▷ vi to follow; (élève: assimiler le programme) to keep up; **se suivre** vi (accidents, personnes, voitures etc) to follow one after the other; **faire ~** (lettre) to forward; **"à ~"** "to be continued"

sujet, te [syʒɛ, -ɛt] adj: **être ~ à** (vertige etc) to be liable ou subject to ▷ nm/f (d'un souverain) subject ▷ nm subject; **au ~ de** about; **~ de conversation** topic ou subject of conversation; **~ d'examen** (Scol) examination question

super [sypɛʀ] adj inv great, fantastic

superbe [sypɛʀb] adj magnificent, superb

superficie [sypɛʀfisi] nf (surface) area

superficiel, le [sypɛʀfisjɛl] adj superficial

superflu, e [sypɛʀfly] adj superfluous

supérieur, e [sypeʀjœʀ] adj (lèvre, étages, classes) upper; **~ (à)** (plus élevé: température, niveau) higher (than); (meilleur: qualité, produit) superior (to); (excellent, hautain) superior ▷ nm/f superior; **supériorité** nf superiority

supermarché [sypɛʀmaʀʃe] nm supermarket

superposer [sypɛʀpoze] /1/ vt (faire chevaucher) to superimpose; **lits superposés** bunk beds

superpuissance [sypɛʀpɥisɑ̃s] nf superpower

superstitieux, -euse [sypɛʀstisjø, -øz] adj superstitious

superviser [sypɛʀvize] /1/ vt to supervise

supplanter [syplɑ̃te] /1/ vt to supplant

suppléant, e [sypleɑ̃, -ɑ̃t] adj (juge, fonctionnaire) deputy cpd; (professeur) supply cpd (BRIT), substitute cpd (US) ▷ nm/f (professeur) supply ou substitute teacher

suppléer [syplee] /1/ vt (ajouter: mot manquant etc) to supply, provide; (compenser: lacune) to fill in; **~ à** to make up for

supplément [syplemɑ̃] nm supplement; **un ~ de travail** extra ou additional work; **un ~ de frites** etc an extra portion of chips etc; **le vin est en ~** wine is extra; **payer un ~** to pay an additional charge; **supplémentaire** adj additional, further; (train, bus) relief cpd, extra

supplication [syplikasjɔ̃] nf supplication; **supplications** nfpl pleas, entreaties

supplice [syplis] nm torture no pl

supplier [syplije] /7/ vt to implore, beseech

support [sypɔʀ] nm support; **~ audio-visuel** audio-visual aid; **~ publicitaire** advertising medium

supportable [sypɔʀtabl] adj (douleur, température) bearable

supporter¹ [sypɔʀtɛʀ] nm supporter, fan

supporter² [sypɔʀte] vt (conséquences, épreuve) to bear, endure; (défauts, personne) to tolerate, put up with; (chose, chaleur etc) to withstand; (personne, chaleur, vin) to take

> Attention à ne pas traduire supporter par to support.

S

supposer [sypoze] /1/ vt to suppose; (impliquer) to presuppose; **en supposant** ou **à ~ que** supposing (that)

suppositoire [sypozitwaʀ] nm suppository

suppression [sypʀesjɔ̃] nf (voir supprimer) removal; deletion; cancellation

supprimer [sypʀime] /1/ vt (cloison, cause, anxiété) to remove; (clause, mot) to delete; (congés, service d'autobus etc) to cancel; (emplois, privilèges, témoin gênant) to do away with

suprême [sypʀɛm] adj supreme

○ **MOT-CLÉ**

sur [syʀ] *prép* **1** (*position*) on; (: *par-dessus*) over; (: *au-dessus*) above; **pose-le sur la table** put it on the table; **je n'ai pas d'argent sur moi** I haven't any money on me **2** (*direction*) towards; **en allant sur Paris** going towards Paris; **sur votre droite** on *ou* to your right **3** (*à propos de*) on, about; **un livre/ une conférence sur Balzac** a book/ lecture on *ou* about Balzac **4** (*proportion, mesures*) out of; **un sur 10** one in 10; (*Scol*) one out of 10; **4 m sur 2** 4 m by 2; **avoir accident sur accident** to have one accident after another

sûr, e [syʀ] *adj* sure, certain; (*digne de confiance*) reliable; (*sans danger*) safe; **~ de soi** self-assured, self-confident; **le plus ~ est de** the safest thing is to

surcharge [syʀʃaʀʒ] *nf* (*de passagers, marchandises*) excess load; **surcharger** /3/ *vt* to overload; (*décoration*) to overdo

surcroît [syʀkʀwa] *nm*: **~ de qch** additional sth; **par** *ou* **de ~** moreover; **en ~** in addition

surdité [syʀdite] *nf* deafness

sûrement [syʀmɑ̃] *adv* (*sans risques*) safely; (*certainement*) certainly

surenchère [syʀɑ̃ʃɛʀ] *nf* (*aux enchères*) higher bid; **surenchérir** /2/ *vi* to bid higher; (*fig*) to try and outbid each other

surestimer [syʀɛstime] /1/ *vt* to overestimate

sûreté [syʀte] *nf* (*exactitude: de renseignements etc*) reliability; (*sécurité*) safety; (*d'un geste*) steadiness; **mettre en ~** to put in a safe place; **pour plus de ~** as an extra precaution; to be on the safe side

surf [sœʀf] *nm* surfing

surface [syʀfas] *nf* surface; (*superficie*) surface area; **une grande ~** a supermarket; **faire ~** to surface; **en ~** near the surface; (*fig*) superficially

surfait, e [syʀfɛ, -ɛt] *adj* overrated

surfer [sœʀfe] /1/ *vi* to surf; **~ sur Internet** to surf *ou* browse the Internet

surgelé, e [syʀʒəle] *adj* (deep-)frozen ▷ *nm*: **les ~s** (deep-)frozen food

surgir [syʀʒiʀ] /2/ *vi* to appear suddenly; (*fig: problème, conflit*) to arise

sur: surhumain, e *adj* superhuman; **sur-le-champ** *adv* immediately; **surlendemain** *nm*: **le surlendemain (soir)** two days later (in the evening); **le surlendemain de** two days after; **surmenage** *nm* overwork; **surmener** /5/: **se surmener** *vi* to overwork

surmonter [syʀmɔ̃te] /1/ *vt* (*vaincre*) to overcome; (*être au-dessus de*) to top

surnaturel, le [syʀnatyʀɛl] *adj, nm* supernatural

surnom [syʀnɔ̃] *nm* nickname

surnombre [syʀnɔ̃bʀ] *nm*: **être en ~** to be too many (*ou* one too many)

surpeuplé, e [syʀpœple] *adj* overpopulated

surplace [syʀplas] *nm*: **faire du ~** to mark time

surplomber [syʀplɔ̃be] /1/ *vi* to be overhanging ▷ *vt* to overhang

surplus [syʀply] *nm* (*Comm*) surplus; (*reste*) **~ de bois** wood left over

surprenant, e [syʀpʀənɑ̃, -ɑ̃t] *adj* amazing

surprendre [syʀpʀɑ̃dʀ] /58/ *vt* (*étonner, prendre à l'improviste*) to amaze; (*tomber sur: intrus etc*) to catch; (*conversation*) to overhear

surpris, e [syʀpʀi, -iz] *adj*: **~ (de/ que)** amazed *ou* surprised (at/that); **surprise** *nf* surprise; **faire une surprise à qn** to give sb a surprise; **surprise-partie** *nf* party

sursaut [syʀso] *nm* start, jump; **~ de** (*énergie, indignation*) sudden fit *ou* burst of; **en ~** with a start; **sursauter** /1/ vi to (give a) start, jump

sursis [syʀsi] nm (Jur: gén) suspended sentence; (aussi fig) reprieve

surtout [syʀtu] adv (avant tout, d'abord) above all; (spécialement, particulièrement) especially; **~, ne dites rien!** whatever you do, don't say anything!; **~ pas!** certainly ou definitely not!; **~ que ...** especially as ...

surveillance [syʀvɛjãs] nf watch; (Police, Mil) surveillance; **sous ~ médicale** under medical supervision

surveillant, e [syʀvɛjã, -ãt] nm/f (de prison) warder; (Scol) monitor

surveiller [syʀveje] /1/ vt (enfant, élèves, bagages) to watch, keep an eye on; (prisonnier, suspect) to keep (a) watch on; (territoire, bâtiment) to (keep) watch over; (travaux, cuisson) to supervise; (Scol: examen) to invigilate; **~ son langage/sa ligne** to watch one's language/figure

survenir [syʀvǝniʀ] /22/ vi (incident, retards) to occur, arise; (événement) to take place

survêt [syʀvɛt], **survêtement** [syʀvɛtmã] nm tracksuit

survie [syʀvi] nf survival; **survivant, e** nm/f survivor; **survivre** /46/ vi to survive; **survivre à** (accident etc) to survive

survoler [syʀvɔle] /1/ vt to fly over; (fig: livre) to skim through

survolté, e [syʀvɔlte] adj (fig) worked up

sus [sy(s)]: **en ~ de** prép in addition to, over and above; **en ~** in addition

susceptible [sysɛptibl] adj touchy, sensitive; **~ de faire** (probabilité) liable to do

susciter [sysite] /1/ vt (admiration) to arouse; (obstacles, ennuis): **~ (à qn)** to create (for sb)

suspect, e [syspɛ(kt), -ɛkt] adj suspicious; (témoignage, opinions, vin etc) suspect ▷ nm/f suspect;

suspecter /1/ vt to suspect; (honnêteté de qn) to question, have one's suspicions about

suspendre [syspãdʀ] /41/ vt (interrompre, démettre) to suspend; (accrocher: vêtement): **~ qch (à)** to hang sth up (on)

suspendu, e [syspãdy] adj (accroché): **~ à** hanging on (ou from); (perché): **~ au-dessus de** suspended over

suspens [syspã]: **en ~** adv (affaire) in abeyance; **tenir en ~** to keep in suspense

suspense [syspãs] nm suspense

suspension [syspãsjõ] nf suspension; (lustre) pendant light fitting

suture [sytyʀ] nf: **point de ~** stitch

svelte [svɛlt] adj slender, svelte

SVP abr (= s'il vous plaît) please

sweat [swit] nm (fam) sweatshirt

sweat-shirt (pl **sweat-shirts**) [switʃœrt] nm sweatshirt

syllabe [silab] nf syllable

symbole [sɛ̃bɔl] nm symbol; **symbolique** adj symbolic; (geste, offrande) token cpd; **symboliser** /1/ vt to symbolize

symétrique [simetʀik] adj symmetrical

sympa [sɛ̃pa] adj inv (fam) nice; **sois ~, prête-le moi** be a pal and lend it to me

sympathie [sɛ̃pati] nf (inclination) liking; (affinité) fellow feeling; (condoléances) sympathy; **avoir de la ~ pour qn** to like sb; **sympathique** adj nice, friendly

Attention à ne pas traduire sympathique par sympathetic.

sympathisant, e [sɛ̃patizã, -ãt] nm/f sympathizer

sympathiser [sɛ̃patize] /1/ vi (voisins etc: s'entendre) to get on (BRIT) ou along (US) (well)

symphonie [sɛ̃fɔni] nf symphony

symptôme [sɛ̃ptom] nm symptom

S

synagogue [sinagɔg] *nf* synagogue
syncope [sɛ̃kɔp] *nf* (*Méd*) blackout;
tomber en ~ to faint, pass out
syndic [sɛ̃dik] *nm* managing agent
syndical, e, -aux [sɛ̃dikal, -o] *adj*
(trade-)union *cpd*; **syndicaliste** *nm/f*
trade unionist
syndicat [sɛ̃dika] *nm* (*d'ouvriers,
employés*) (trade(s)) union; **~
d'initiative** tourist office *ou* bureau;
syndiqué, e *adj* belonging to a
(trade) union; **syndiquer** /1/: **se
syndiquer** *vi* to form a trade union;
(*adhérer*) to join a trade union
synonyme [sinɔnim] *adj*
synonymous ▷ *nm* synonym; **~ de**
synonymous with
syntaxe [sɛ̃taks] *nf* syntax
synthèse [sɛ̃tɛz] *nf* synthesis
synthétique [sɛ̃tetik] *adj* synthetic
Syrie [siʀi] *nf*: **la ~** Syria
systématique [sistematik] *adj*
systematic
système [sistɛm] *nm* system; **le ~ D**
resourcefulness

t' [t] *pron voir* **te**
ta [ta] *adj poss voir* **ton¹**
tabac [taba] *nm* tobacco; (*aussi*: **débit**
ou **bureau de ~**) tobacconist's (shop)
tabagisme [tabaʒism] *nm*: **~ passif**
passive smoking
table [tabl] *nf* table; **à ~!** dinner
etc is ready!; **se mettre à ~** to sit
down to eat; **mettre** *ou* **dresser/
desservir la ~** to lay *ou* set/clear
the table; **~ à repasser** ironing
board; **~ de cuisson** hob; **~ des
matières** (table of) contents *pl*; **~
de nuit** *ou* **de chevet** bedside table;
~ d'orientation viewpoint indicator;
~ roulante (tea) trolley (*BRIT*), tea
wagon (*US*)
tableau, x [tablo] *nm* (*Art*) painting;
(*reproduction, fig*) picture; (*panneau*)
board; (*schéma*) table, chart;
~ d'affichage notice board; **~ de
bord** dashboard; (*Aviat*) instrument
panel; **~ noir** blackboard

tablette [tablɛt] nf (planche) shelf; **~ de chocolat** bar of chocolate; **~ tactile** (Inform) tablet

tablier [tablije] nm apron

tabou [tabu] nm taboo

tabouret [taburɛ] nm stool

tac [tak] nm: **du ~ au ~** tit for tat

tache [taʃ] nf (saleté) stain, mark; (Art, de couleur, lumière) spot; **~ de rousseur** ou **de son** freckle

tâche [taʃ] nf task

tacher [taʃe] /1/ vt to stain, mark

tâcher [taʃe] /1/ vi: **~ de faire** to try to do, endeavour (BRIT) ou endeavor (US) to do

tacheté, e [taʃte] adj: **~ de** speckled ou spotted with

tact [takt] nm tact; **avoir du ~** to be tactful

tactique [taktik] adj tactical ▷ nf (technique) tactics sg; (plan) tactic

taie [tɛ] nf: **~ (d'oreiller)** pillowslip, pillowcase

taille [taj] nf cutting; (d'arbre) pruning; (milieu du corps) waist; (hauteur) height; (grandeur) size; **de ~ à faire** capable of doing; **de ~** sizeable

taille-crayon(s) [tajkRɛjɔ̃] nm inv pencil sharpener

tailler [taje] /1/ vt (pierre, diamant) to cut; (arbre, plante) to prune; (vêtement) to cut out; (crayon) to sharpen

tailleur [tajœR] nm (couturier) tailor; (vêtement) suit; **en ~** (assis) cross-legged

taillis [taji] nm copse

taire [tɛR] /54/ vi: **faire ~ qn** to make sb be quiet; **se taire** vi to be silent ou quiet; **taisez-vous!** be quiet!

Taiwan [tajwan] nf Taiwan

talc [talk] nm talc, talcum powder

talent [talɑ̃] nm talent

talkie-walkie [tɔkiwɔki] nm walkie-talkie

talon [talɔ̃] nm heel; (de chèque, billet) stub, counterfoil (BRIT); **~s plats/ aiguilles** flat/stiletto heels

talus [taly] nm embankment

tambour [tɑ̃buR] nm (Mus, Tech) drum; (musicien) drummer; (porte) revolving door(s pl); **tambourin** nm tambourine

Tamise [tamiz] nf: **la ~** the Thames

tamisé, e [tamize] adj (fig) subdued, soft

tampon [tɑ̃pɔ̃] nm (de coton, d'ouate) pad; (aussi: **~ hygiénique** ou **périodique**) tampon; (amortisseur, Inform: aussi: **mémoire ~**) buffer; (bouchon) plug, stopper; (cachet, timbre) stamp; **tamponner** /1/ vt (timbres) to stamp; (heurter) to crash ou ram into; **tamponneuse** adj f: **autos tamponneuses** dodgems

tandem [tɑ̃dɛm] nm tandem

tandis [tɑ̃di]: **~ que** conj while

tanguer [tɑ̃ge] /1/ vi to pitch (and toss)

tant [tɑ̃] adv so much; **~ de** (sable, eau) so much; (gens, livres) so many; **~ que** as long as; **~ que** as much as; **~ mieux** that's great; (avec une certaine réserve) so much the better; **~ pis** too bad; (conciliant) never mind; **~ bien que mal** as well as can be expected

tante [tɑ̃t] nf aunt

tantôt [tɑ̃to] adv (parfois): **tantôt ... tantôt** now ... now; (cet après-midi) this afternoon

taon [tɑ̃] nm horsefly

tapage [tapaʒ] nm uproar, din

tapageur, -euse [tapaʒœR, -øz] adj noisy; (voyant) loud, flashy

tape [tap] nf slap

tape-à-l'œil [tapalœj] adj inv flashy, showy

taper [tape] /1/ vt (porte) to bang, slam; (enfant) to slap; (dactylographier) to type (out); (fam: emprunter): **~ qn de 10 euros** to touch sb for 10 euros ▷ vi (soleil) to beat down; **se taper** vt (fam: travail) to get landed with; (: boire, manger) to down; **~ sur qn** to thump sb; (fig) to run sb down; **~ sur qch** (clou etc) to hit sth; (table etc) to bang on sth; **~ à** (*porte etc*) to knock on; **~ dans** (*se servir*) to dig into; **~ des mains/pieds** to clap one's hands/ stamp one's feet; **~ (à la machine)** to type

tapi, e [tapi] *adj*: **~ dans/derrière** (*caché*) hidden away in/behind

tapis [tapi] *nm* carpet; (*petit*) rug; **~ roulant** (*pour piétons*) moving walkway; (*pour bagages*) carousel; **~ de sol** (*de tente*) groundsheet; **~ de souris** (*Inform*) mouse mat

tapisser [tapise] /1/ *vt* (*avec du papier peint*) to paper; (*recouvrir*): **~ qch (de)** to cover sth (with); **tapisserie** *nf* (*tenture, broderie*) tapestry; (*papier peint*) wallpaper

tapissier, -ière [tapisje, -jɛʀ] *nm/f*: **~-décorateur** interior decorator

tapoter [tapote] /1/ *vt* (*joue, main*) to pat; (*objet*) to tap

taquiner [takine] /1/ *vt* to tease

tard [taʀ] *adv* late ⊳ *nm*: **sur le ~** late in life; **plus ~** later (on); **au plus ~** at the latest; **il est trop ~** it's too late

tarder [taʀde] /1/ *vi* (*chose*) to be a long time coming; (*personne*): **~ à faire** to delay doing; **il me tarde d'être** I am longing to be; **sans (plus) ~** without (further) delay

tardif, -ive [taʀdif, -iv] *adj* late

tarif [taʀif] *nm*: **~ des consommations** price list; **~s postaux/douaniers** postal/ customs rates; **~ des taxis** taxi fares; **~ plein/réduit** (*train*) full/reduced fare; (*téléphone*) peak/off-peak rate

tarir [taʀiʀ] /2/ *vi* to dry up, run dry

tarte [taʀt] *nf* tart; **~ aux pommes/à la crème** apple/custard tart; **~ Tatin** ≈ apple upside-down tart

tartine [taʀtin] *nf* slice of bread (and butter (*ou* jam)); **~ de miel** slice of bread and honey; **tartiner** /1/ *vt* to spread; **fromage à tartiner** cheese spread

tartre [taʀtʀ] *nm* (*des dents*) tartar; (*de chaudière*) fur, scale

tas [tɑ] *nm* heap, pile; **un ~ de** (*fig*) heaps of, lots of; **en ~** in a heap *ou* pile; **formé sur le ~** trained on the job

tasse [tɑs] *nf* cup; **~ à café/thé** coffee/teacup

tassé, e [tɑse] *adj*: **bien ~** (*café etc*) strong

tasser [tɑse] /1/ *vt* (*terre, neige*) to pack down; (*entasser*): **~ qch dans** to cram sth into; **se tasser** *vi* (*se serrer*) to squeeze up; (*s'affaisser*) to settle; (*personne: avec l'âge*) to shrink; (*fig*) to sort itself out, settle down

tâter [tate] /1/ *vt* to feel; (*fig*) to try out; **~ de** (*prison etc*) to have a taste of; **se tâter** (*hésiter*) to be in two minds

tatillon, ne [tatijɔ̃, -ɔn] *adj* pernickety

tâtonnement [tatɔnmɑ̃] *nm*: **par ~s** (*fig*) by trial and error

tâtonner [tatɔne] /1/ *vi* to grope one's way along

tâtons [tatɔ̃]: **à ~** *adv*: **chercher/ avancer à ~** to grope around for/ grope one's way forward

tatouage [tatwaʒ] *nm* tattoo

tatouer [tatwe] /1/ *vt* to tattoo

taudis [todi] *nm* hovel, slum

taule [tol] *nf* (*fam*) nick (BRIT), jail

taupe [top] *nf* mole

taureau, x [tɔʀo] *nm* bull; (*signe*): **le T~** Taurus

taux [to] *nm* rate; (*d'alcool*) level; **~ d'intérêt** interest rate

taxe [taks] *nf* tax; (*douanière*) duty; **toutes ~s comprises** inclusive of tax; **la boutique hors ~s** the duty-free shop; **~ de séjour** tourist tax; **~ à** *ou* **sur la valeur ajoutée** value added tax

taxer [takse] /1/ *vt* (*personne*) to tax; (*produit*) to put a tax on, tax

taxi [taksi] *nm* taxi; (*chauffeur: fam*) taxi driver

Tchécoslovaquie [tʃekɔslɔvaki] *nf*: **la ~** Czechoslovakia; **tchèque** *adj* Czech ⊳ *nm* (*Ling*) Czech ⊳ *nm/f*:

Tchèque Czech; **la République tchèque** the Czech Republic
Tchétchénie [tʃetʃeni] nf: **la ~** Chechnya
te, t' [tə] pron you; (réfléchi) yourself
technicien, ne [tɛknisjɛ̃, -ɛn] nm/f technician
technico-commercial, e, -aux [tɛknikokɔmɛrsjal, -o] adj: **agent ~** sales technician
technique [tɛknik] adj technical ▷ nf technique; **techniquement** adv technically
techno [tɛkno] nf: **la (musique) ~** techno (music)
technologie [tɛknɔlɔʒi] nf technology; **technologique** adj technological
teck [tɛk] nm teak
tee-shirt [tiʃœrt] nm T-shirt, tee-shirt
teindre [tɛ̃dr] /52/ vt to dye; **se ~ (les cheveux)** to dye one's hair; **teint, e** adj dyed ▷ nm (du visage) complexion; (: momentané) colour ▷ nf shade; **grand teint** colourfast
teinté, e [tɛ̃te] adj: **~ de** (fig) tinged with
teinter [tɛ̃te] /1/ vt (verre) to tint; (bois) to stain
teinture [tɛ̃tyr] nf dye; **~ d'iode** tincture of iodine; **teinturerie** nf dry cleaner's; **teinturier, -ière** nm/f dry cleaner
tel, telle [tɛl] adj (pareil) such; (comme): **~ un/des ...** like a/like ...; (indéfini) such-and-such a; (intensif): **un ~/de ~s ...** such (a)/such ...; **venez ~ jour** come on such-and-such a day; **rien de ~** nothing like it; **~ que** like, such as; **~ quel** as it is ou stands (ou was etc)
télé [tele] nf (fam) TV; **à la ~** on TV ou telly; **télécabine** nf (benne) cable car; **télécarte** nf phonecard; **téléchargeable** adj downloadable; **téléchargement** nm (action) downloading; (fichier) download;

télécharger /3/ vt (recevoir) to download; (transmettre) to upload; **télécommande** nf remote control; **télécopieur** nm fax (machine); **télédistribution** nf cable TV; **télégramme** nm telegram; **télégraphier** /7/ vt to telegraph, cable; **téléguider** /1/ vt to operate by remote control; **télématique** nf telematics sg; **téléobjectif** nm telephoto lens sg; **télépathie** nf telepathy; **téléphérique** nm cable-car
téléphone [telefɔn] nm telephone; **avoir le ~** to be on the (tele)phone; **au ~** on the phone; **~ sans fil** cordless (tele)phone; **téléphoner** /1/ vi to make a phone call; **téléphoner à** to phone, call up; **téléphonique** adj (tele)phone cpd
téléréalité [telerealite] nf reality TV
télescope [teleskɔp] nm telescope
télescoper [teleskɔpe] /1/ vt to smash up; **se télescoper** (véhicules) to concertina
télé: téléscripteur nm teleprinter; **télésiège** nm chairlift; **téléski** nm ski-tow; **téléspectateur, -trice** nm/f (television) viewer; **télétravail** nm telecommuting; **télévente** nf telesales; **téléviseur** nm television set; **télévision** nf television; **à la télévision** on television; **télévision numérique** digital TV; **télévision par câble/satellite** cable/satellite television
télex [telɛks] nm telex
telle [tɛl] adj f voir **tel**; **tellement** adv (tant) so much; (si) so; **tellement de** (sable, eau) so much; (gens, livres) so many; **il s'est endormi tellement il était fatigué** he was so tired (that) he fell asleep; **pas tellement** not really; **pas tellement fort/lentement** not (all) that strong/slowly; **il ne mange pas tellement** he doesn't eat (all that) much
téméraire [temerɛr] adj reckless, rash

témoignage [temwaɲaʒ] nm (Jur: déclaration) testimony no pl, evidence no pl; (rapport, récit) account; (fig: d'affection etc) token, mark; (geste) expression

témoigner [temwaɲe] /1/ vt (intérêt, gratitude) to show ▷ vi (Jur) to testify, give evidence; **~ de** to bear witness to, testify to

témoin [temwɛ̃] nm witness ▷ adj: **appartement-~** show flat; **être ~ de** to witness; **~ oculaire** eyewitness

tempe [tɑ̃p] nf temple

tempérament [tɑ̃peramɑ̃] nm temperament, disposition; **à ~** (vente) on deferred (payment) terms; (achat) by instalments, hire purchase cpd

température [tɑ̃peratyR] nf temperature; **avoir** ou **faire de la ~** to be running ou have a temperature

tempête [tɑ̃pɛt] nf storm; **~ de sable/neige** sand/snowstorm

temple [tɑ̃pl] nm temple; (protestant) church

temporaire [tɑ̃pɔRɛR] adj temporary

temps [tɑ̃] nm (atmosphérique) weather; (durée) time; (époque) time, times pl; (Ling) tense; (Mus) beat; (Tech) stroke; **un ~ de chien** (fam) rotten weather; **quel ~ fait-il?** what's the weather like?; **il fait beau/ mauvais ~** the weather is fine/ bad; **avoir le ~/tout le ~/juste le ~** to have time/plenty of time/just enough time; **en ~ de paix/guerre** in peacetime/wartime; **en ~ utile** ou **voulu** in due time ou course; **ces derniers ~** lately; **dans quelque ~** in a (little) while; **de ~ en ~, de ~ à autre** from time to time; **à ~** (partir, arriver) in time; **à ~ complet, à plein ~** adv, adj full-time; **à ~ partiel, à mi-~** adv, adj part-time; **dans le ~** at one time; **~ d'arrêt** pause, halt; **~ libre** free ou spare time; **~ mort** (Comm) slack period

tenable [tənabl] adj bearable

tenace [tənas] adj persistent

tenant, e [tənɑ̃, -ɑ̃t] nm/f (Sport): **~ du titre** title-holder

tendance [tɑ̃dɑ̃s] nf (opinions) leanings pl, sympathies pl; (inclination) tendency; (évolution) trend ▷ adj inv trendy; **avoir ~ à** to have a tendency to, tend to

tendeur [tɑ̃dœR] nm (attache) elastic strap

tendre [tɑ̃dR] /41/ adj tender; (bois, roche, couleur) soft ▷ vt (élastique, peau) to stretch; (corde) to tighten; (muscle) to tense; (donner): **~ qch à qn** to hold sth out to sb; (offrir) to offer sb sth; (fig: piège) to set, lay; **se tendre** vi (corde) to tighten; (relations) to become strained; **~ à qch/à faire** to tend towards sth/to do; **~ l'oreille** to prick up one's ears; **~ la main/le bras** to hold out one's hand/stretch out one's arm; **tendrement** adv tenderly; **tendresse** nf tenderness

tendu, e [tɑ̃dy] pp de **tendre** ▷ adj (corde) tight; (muscles) tensed; (relations) strained

ténèbres [tenɛbR] nfpl darkness sg

teneur [tənœR] nf content; (d'une lettre) terms pl, content

tenir [təniR] /22/ vt to hold; (magasin, hôtel) to run; (promesse) to keep ▷ vi to hold; (neige, gel) to last; **se tenir** vi (avoir lieu) to be held, take place; (être: personne) to stand; **se ~ droit** to stand up (ou sit up) straight; **bien se ~** to behave well; **se ~ à qch** to hold on to sth; **s'en ~ à qch** to confine o.s. to sth; **~ à** (personne, objet) to be attached to, care about (ou for); (réputation) to care about; **~ à faire** to want to do; **~ de** (ressembler à) to take after; **ça ne tient qu'à lui** it is entirely up to him; **~ qn pour** to take sb for; **~ qch de qn** (histoire) to have heard ou learnt sth from sb; (qualité, défaut) to have inherited ou got sth from sb; **~ dans** to fit into; **~ compte de qch** to take sth into account; **~ les**

comptes to keep the books; **~ le coup** to hold out; **~ bon** to stand ou hold fast; **~ au chaud/à l'abri** to keep hot/under shelter ou cover; **un manteau qui tient chaud** a warm coat; **tiens** (ou **tenez**), **voilà le stylo** there's the pen!; **tiens, voilà Alain!** look, here's Alain!; **tiens?** (surprise) really?

tennis [tenis] nm tennis; (aussi: **court de ~**) tennis court ▷ nmpl, nfpl (aussi: **chaussures de ~**) tennis ou gym shoes; **~ de table** table tennis; **tennisman** nm tennis player

tension [tɑ̃sjɔ̃] nf tension; (Méd) blood pressure; **faire** ou **avoir de la ~** to have high blood pressure

tentation [tɑ̃tasjɔ̃] nf temptation

tentative [tɑ̃tativ] nf attempt

tente [tɑ̃t] nf tent

tenter [tɑ̃te] /1/ vt (éprouver, attirer) to tempt; (essayer): **~ qch/de faire** to attempt ou try sth/to do; **~ sa chance** to try one's luck

tenture [tɑ̃tyR] nf hanging

tenu, e [təny] pp de **tenir** ▷ adj: **bien ~** (maison, comptes) well-kept; **~ de faire** (obligé) under an obligation to do ▷ nf (vêtements) clothes pl; (comportement) manners pl, behaviour; (d'une maison) upkeep; **en petite ~e** scantily dressed ou clad

ter [tɛR] adj: **16 ~** 16b ou B

terme [tɛRm] nm term; (fin) end; **être en bons/mauvais ~s avec qn** to be on good/bad terms with sb; **à court/long ~** adj short-/long-term ou -range; adv in the short/long term; **avant ~** (Méd) prematurely; **mettre un ~ à** to put an end ou a stop to

terminaison [tɛRminɛzɔ̃] nf (Ling) ending

terminal, e, -aux [tɛRminal, -o] nm terminal ▷ nf (Scol) ≈ year 13 (BRIT), ≈ twelfth grade (US)

terminer [tɛRmine] /1/ vt to finish; **se terminer** vi to end

terne [tɛRn] adj dull

ternir [tɛRniR] /2/ vt to dull; (fig) to sully, tarnish; **se ternir** vi to become dull

terrain [teRɛ̃] nm (sol, fig) ground; (Comm: étendue de terre) land no pl; (: parcelle) plot (of land); (: à bâtir) site; **sur le ~** (fig) on the field; **~ de football/rugby** football/rugby pitch (BRIT) ou field (US); **~ d'aviation** airfield; **~ de camping** campsite; **~ de golf** golf course; **~ de jeu** (pour les petits) playground; (Sport) games field; **~ de sport** sports ground; **~ vague** waste ground no pl

terrasse [teRas] nf terrace; **à la ~** (café) outside; **terrasser** /1/ vt (adversaire) to floor; (maladie etc) to lay low

terre [tɛR] nf (gén, aussi Élec) earth; (substance) soil, earth; (opposé à mer) land no pl; (contrée) land; **terres** nfpl (terrains) lands, land sg; **en ~** (pipe, poterie) clay cpd; **à ou par ~** (mettre, être, s'asseoir) on the ground (ou floor); (jeter, tomber) to the ground, down; **~ à ~** adj inv down-to-earth; **~ cuite** terracotta; **la ~ ferme** dry land; **~ glaise** clay

terreau [teRo] nm compost

terre-plein [tɛRplɛ̃] nm platform; (sur chaussée) central reservation

terrestre [teRɛstR] adj (surface) earth's, of the earth; (Bot, Zool, Mil) land cpd; (Rel) earthly

terreur [teRœR] nf terror no pl

terrible [teRibl] adj terrible, dreadful; (fam) terrific; **pas ~** nothing special

terrien, ne [teRjɛ̃, -ɛn] adj: **propriétaire ~** landowner ▷ nm/f (non martien etc) earthling

terrier [teRje] nm burrow, hole; (chien) terrier

terrifier [teRifje] /7/ vt to terrify

terrine [teRin] nf (récipient) terrine; (Culin) pâté

territoire [teRitwaR] nm territory

terroriser [teRɔRize] /1/ vt to terrorize

t

terrorisme [terɔrism] nm terrorism; **terroriste** [terɔrist] nm/f terrorist

tertiaire [tersjer] adj tertiary ▷ nm (Écon) service industries pl

tes [te] adj poss voir **ton¹**

test [test] nm test

testament [testamɑ̃] nm (Jur) will; (fig) legacy; (Rel): **T~** Testament

tester [teste] /1/ vt to test

testicule [testikyl] nm testicle

tétanos [tetanos] nm tetanus

têtard [tetar] nm tadpole

tête [tet] nf head; (cheveux) hair no pl; (visage) face; **de ~** adj (wagon etc) front cpd ▷ adv (calculer) in one's head, mentally; **perdre la ~** (fig) (s'affoler) to lose one's head; (devenir fou) to go off one's head; **tenir ~ à qn** to stand up to ou defy sb; **la ~ en bas** with one's head down; **la ~ la première** (tomber) head-first; **faire une ~** (Football) to head the ball; **faire la ~** (fig) to sulk; **en ~** (Sport) in the lead; **à la ~ de** at the head of; **à ~ reposée** in a more leisurely moment; **n'en faire qu'à sa ~** to do as one pleases; **en avoir par-dessus la ~** to be fed up; **en ~ à ~** in private, alone together; **de la ~ aux pieds** from head to toe; **~ de lecture** (playback) head; **~ de liste** (Pol) chief candidate; **~ de mort** skull and crossbones; **~ de série** (Tennis) seeded player, seed; **~ de Turc** (fig) whipping boy (BRIT), butt; **tête-à-queue** nm inv: **faire un tête-à-queue** to spin round; **tête-à-tête** nm inv: **en tête-à-tête** in private, alone together

téter [tete] /6/ vt: **~ (sa mère)** to suck at one's mother's breast, feed

tétine [tetin] nf teat; (sucette) dummy (BRIT), pacifier (US)

têtu, e [tety] adj stubborn, pigheaded

texte [tekst] nm text; (morceau choisi) passage

texter [tekste] /1/ vi, vt to text

textile [tekstil] adj textile cpd ▷ nm textile; (industrie) textile industry

Texto [teksto] nm text (message)

textoter [tekstɔte] /1/ vi, vt to text

texture [tekstyr] nf texture

TGV sigle m = **train à grande vitesse**

thaïlandais, e [tailɑ̃dɛ, -ɛz] adj Thai ▷ nm/f: **T~, e** Thai

Thaïlande [tailɑ̃d] nf: **la ~** Thailand

thé [te] nm tea; **prendre le ~** to have tea; **~ au lait/citron** tea with milk/lemon; **faire le ~** to make the tea

théâtral, e, -aux [teatral, -o] adj theatrical

théâtre [teatr] nm theatre; (péj) playacting; (fig: lieu): **le ~ de** the scene of; **faire du ~** to act

théière [tejer] nf teapot

thème [tem] nm theme; (Scol: traduction) prose (composition)

théologie [teɔlɔʒi] nf theology

théorie [teɔri] nf theory; **théorique** adj theoretical

thérapie [terapi] nf therapy

thermal, e, -aux [termal, -o] adj: **station ~e** spa; **cure ~e** water cure

thermomètre [termɔmetr] nm thermometer

thermos® [termos] nm ou f: **(bouteille) ~** vacuum ou Thermos® flask: BRIT ou bottle (US)

thermostat [termɔsta] nm thermostat

thèse [tez] nf thesis

thon [tɔ̃] nm tuna (fish)

thym [tɛ̃] nm thyme

Tibet [tibe] nm: **le ~** Tibet

tibia [tibja] nm shin; shinbone, tibia

TIC sigle fpl (= technologies de l'information et de la communication) ICT sg

tic [tik] nm tic, (nervous) twitch; (de langage etc) mannerism

ticket [tike] nm ticket; **~ de caisse** till receipt

tiède [tjed] adj lukewarm; (vent, air) mild, warm; **tiédir** /2/ vi (se réchauffer) to grow warmer; (refroidir) to cool

tien, tienne [tjɛ̃, tjɛn] pron: **le (la) ~(ne)** yours; **les ~(ne)s** yours; **à la ~e!** cheers!

tiens [tjɛ̃] *vb, excl voir* **tenir**

tiercé [tjɛʀse] *nm system of forecast betting giving first three horses*

tiers, tierce [tjɛʀ, tjɛʀs] *adj* third ▷ *nm* (*Jur*) third party; (*fraction*) third; **le ~ monde** the third world

tige [tiʒ] *nf* stem; (*baguette*) rod

tignasse [tiɲas] *nf* (*péj*) shock *ou* mop of hair

tigre [tigʀ] *nm* tiger; **tigré, e** *adj* (*rayé*) striped; (*tacheté*) spotted; (*chat*) tabby; **tigresse** *nf* tigress

tilleul [tijœl] *nm* lime (tree), linden (tree); (*boisson*) lime(-blossom) tea

timbre [tɛ̃bʀ] *nm* (*tampon*) stamp; (*aussi*: **~-poste**) (*postage*) stamp; (*Mus: de voix, instrument*) timbre, tone

timbré, e [tɛ̃bʀe] *adj* (*fam*) cracked

timide [timid] *adj* shy; (*timoré*) timid; **timidement** *adv* shyly; timidly; **timidité** *nf* shyness; timidity

tintamarre [tɛ̃tamaʀ] *nm* din, uproar

tinter [tɛ̃te] /1/ *vi* to ring, chime; (*argent, clés*) to jingle

tique [tik] *nf* tick (*insect*)

tir [tiʀ] *nm* (*sport*) shooting; (*fait ou manière de tirer*) firing *no pl*; (*rafale*) fire; (*stand*) shooting gallery; **~ à l'arc** archery

tirage [tiʀaʒ] *nm* (*action*) printing; (*Photo*) print; (*de journal*) circulation; (*de livre*) (print-)run; edition; (*de loterie*) draw; **~ au sort** drawing lots

tire [tiʀ] *nf*: **vol à la ~** pickpocketing

tiré, e [tiʀe] *adj* (*visage, traits*) drawn; **~ par les cheveux** far-fetched

tire-bouchon [tiʀbuʃɔ̃] *nm* corkscrew

tirelire [tiʀliʀ] *nf* moneybox

tirer [tiʀe] /1/ *vt* (*gén*) to pull; (*ligne, trait*) to draw; (*rideau*) to draw; (*carte, conclusion, chèque*) to draw; (*en faisant feu: balle, coup*) to fire; (: *animal*) to shoot; (*journal, livre, photo*) to print; (*Football: corner etc*) to take ▷ *vi* (*faire feu*) to fire; (*faire du tir, Football*) to shoot; **se tirer** *vi* (*fam*) to push off;

(*aussi*: **s'en ~**) (*éviter le pire*) to get off; (*survivre*) to pull through; (*se débrouiller*) to manage; (*extraire*): **~ qch de** to take *ou* pull sth out of; **~ sur** (*corde, poignée*) to pull on *ou* at; (*faire feu sur*) to shoot *ou* fire at; (*pipe*) to draw on; (*fig: avoisiner*) to verge *ou* border on; **~ qn de** (*embarras etc*) to help *ou* get sb out of; **~ à sa fin** to be drawing to an end; **~ qch au clair** to clear sth up; **~ au sort** to draw lots; **~ parti de** to take advantage of; **~ profit de** to profit from; **~ les cartes** to read *ou* tell the cards

tiret [tiʀɛ] *nm* dash

tireur [tiʀœʀ] *nm* gunman; **~ d'élite** marksman

tiroir [tiʀwaʀ] *nm* drawer; **tiroir-caisse** *nm* till

tisane [tizan] *nf* herb tea

tisser [tise] /1/ *vt* to weave

tissu [tisy] *nm* fabric, material, cloth *no pl*; (*Anat, Bio*) tissue; **tissu-éponge** *nm* (terry) towelling *no pl*

titre [titʀ] *nm* (*gén*) title; (*de journal*) headline; (*diplôme*) qualification; (*Comm*) security; **en ~** (*champion, responsable*) official; **à juste ~** rightly; **à quel ~?** on what grounds?; **à aucun ~** on no account; **au même ~ (que)** in the same way (as); **à ~ d'information** for (your) information; **à ~ gracieux** free of charge; **à ~ d'essai** on a trial basis; **à ~ privé** in a private capacity; **~ de propriété** title deed; **~ de transport** ticket

tituber [titybe] /1/ *vi* to stagger *ou* reel (along)

titulaire [titylɛʀ] *adj* (*Admin*) with tenure ▷ *nm/f* (*de permis*) holder; **être ~ de** (*diplôme, permis*) to hold

toast [tost] *nm* slice *ou* piece of toast; (*de bienvenue*) (welcoming) toast; **porter un ~ à qn** to propose *ou* drink a toast to sb

toboggan [tɔbɔgɑ̃] nm slide; (Auto) flyover

toc [tɔk] nm: **en toc** imitation cpd
▷ excl: **toc, toc** knock knock

tocsin [tɔksɛ̃] nm alarm (bell)

tohu-bohu [tɔybɔy] nm commotion

toi [twa] pron you

toile [twal] nf (tableau) canvas; **de** ou **en ~** (pantalon) cotton; (sac) canvas; **~ d'araignée** cobweb; **la T~** (Internet) the Web; **~ cirée** oilcloth; **~ de fond** (fig) backdrop

toilette [twalɛt] nf (habits) outfit; **toilettes** nfpl toilet sg; **faire sa ~** to have a wash, get washed; **articles de ~** toiletries

toi-même [twamɛm] pron yourself

toit [twa] nm roof; **~ ouvrant** sun roof

toiture [twatyʀ] nf roof

Tokyo [tɔkjo] n Tokyo

tôle [tol] nf (plaque) steel (ou iron) sheet; **~ ondulée** corrugated iron

tolérable [tɔleʀabl] adj tolerable

tolérant, e [tɔleʀɑ̃, -ɑ̃t] adj tolerant

tolérer [tɔleʀe] /6/ vt to tolerate; (Admin: hors taxe etc) to allow

tollé [tɔle] nm: **un ~ (de protestations)** a general outcry

tomate [tɔmat] nf tomato; **~s farcies** stuffed tomatoes

tombe [tɔ̃b] nf (sépulture) grave; (avec monument) tomb

tombeau, x [tɔ̃bo] nm tomb

tombée [tɔ̃be] nf: **à la ~ du jour** ou **de la nuit** at nightfall

tomber [tɔ̃be] /1/ vi to fall; (fièvre, vent) to drop ▷ vt: **laisser ~** (objet) to drop; (personne) to let down; (activité) to give up; **laisse ~!** forget it!; **faire ~** to knock over; **~ sur** (rencontrer) to come across; **~ de fatigue/sommeil** to drop from exhaustion/be falling asleep on one's feet; **~ à l'eau** (projet etc) to fall through; **~ en panne** to break down; **~ en ruine** to fall into ruins; **ça tombe bien/mal** (fig) that's come at the right/wrong time; **il**

est **bien/mal tombé** (fig) he's been lucky/unlucky

tombola [tɔ̃bɔla] nf raffle

tome [tɔm] nm volume

ton¹, ta (pl **tes**) [tɔ̃, ta, te] adj poss your

ton² [tɔ̃] nm (gén) tone; (couleur) shade, tone; **de bon ~** in good taste

tonalité [tɔnalite] nf (au téléphone) dialling tone

tondeuse [tɔ̃døz] nf (à gazon) (lawn) mower; (du coiffeur) clippers pl; (pour la tonte) shears pl

tondre [tɔ̃dʀ] /41/ vt (pelouse, herbe) to mow; (haie) to cut, clip; (mouton, toison) to shear; (cheveux) to crop

tongs [tɔ̃g] nfpl flip-flops

tonifier [tɔnifje] /7/ vt (peau, organisme) to tone up

tonique [tɔnik] adj fortifying ▷ nm tonic

tonne [tɔn] nf metric ton, tonne

tonneau, x [tɔno] nm (à vin, cidre) barrel; **faire des ~x** (voiture, avion) to roll over

tonnelle [tɔnɛl] nf bower, arbour

tonner [tɔne] /1/ vi to thunder; **il tonne** it is thundering, there's some thunder

tonnerre [tɔnɛʀ] nm thunder

tonus [tɔnys] nm energy

top [tɔp] nm: **au troisième ~** at the third stroke ▷ adj: **~ secret** top secret

topinambour [tɔpinɑ̃buʀ] nm Jerusalem artichoke

torche [tɔʀʃ] nf torch

torchon [tɔʀʃɔ̃] nm cloth; (à vaisselle) tea towel ou cloth

tordre [tɔʀdʀ] /41/ vt (chiffon) to wring; (barre, fig: visage) to twist; **se tordre** vi; **se ~ le poignet/la cheville** to twist one's wrist/ankle; **se ~ de douleur/rire** to writhe in pain/be doubled up with laughter; **tordu, e** adj (fig) twisted; (fig) crazy

tornade [tɔʀnad] nf tornado

torrent [tɔʀɑ̃] nm mountain stream

torsade [tɔʀsad] *nf*: **un pull à ~s** a cable sweater

torse [tɔʀs] *nm* chest; (*Anat*, *Sculpture*) torso; **~ nu** stripped to the waist

tort [tɔʀ] *nm* (*défaut*) fault; **torts** *nmpl* (*Jur*) fault *sg*; **avoir ~** to be wrong; **être dans son ~** to be in the wrong; **donner ~ à qn** to lay the blame on sb; **causer du ~ à** to harm; **à ~** wrongly; **à ~ et à travers** wildly

torticolis [tɔʀtikɔli] *nm* stiff neck

tortiller [tɔʀtije] /1/ *vt* to twist; (*moustache*) to twirl; **se tortiller** *vi* to wriggle; (*en dansant*) to wiggle

tortionnaire [tɔʀsjɔnɛʀ] *nm* torturer

tortue [tɔʀty] *nf* tortoise; (*d'eau douce*) terrapin; (*d'eau de mer*) turtle

tortueux, -euse [tɔʀtɥø, -øz] *adj* (*rue*) twisting; (*fig*) tortuous

torture [tɔʀtyʀ] *nf* torture; **torturer** /1/ *vt* to torture; (*fig*) to torment

tôt [to] *adv* early; **~ ou tard** sooner or later; **si ~** so early; (*déjà*) so soon; **au plus ~** at the earliest; **plus ~** earlier

total, e, -aux [tɔtal, -o] *adj*, *nm* total; **au ~** in total *ou* all; (*fig*) on the whole; **faire le ~** to work out the total; **totalement** *adv* totally; **totaliser** /1/ *vt* to total (up); **totalitaire** *adj* totalitarian; **totalité** *nf*: **la totalité de: la totalité des élèves** all (of) the pupils; **la totalité de la population/classe** the whole population/class; **en totalité** entirely

toubib [tubib] *nm* (*fam*) doctor

touchant, e [tuʃɑ̃, -ɑ̃t] *adj* touching

touche [tuʃ] *nf* (*de piano, de machine à écrire*) key; (*de téléphone*) button; (*Peinture etc*) stroke, touch; (*fig: de couleur, nostalgie*) touch; (*Football: aussi*: **remise en ~**) throw-in; (*aussi*: **ligne de ~**) touch-line; (*Escrime*) hit; **~ dièse** (*de téléphone, clavier*) hash key

toucher [tuʃe] /1/ *nm* touch ▷ *vt* to touch; (*palper*) to feel; (*atteindre: d'un coup de feu etc*) to hit; (*concerner*) to concern, affect; (*contacter*) to reach, contact; (*recevoir: récompense*) to receive, get; (*: salaire*) to draw, get; (*chèque*) to cash; (*aborder: problème, sujet*) to touch on; **au ~** to the touch; **~ à** to touch; (*traiter de, concerner*) to have to do with, concern; **je vais lui en ~ un mot** I'll have a word with him about it; **~ au but** (*fig*) to near one's goal; **~ à sa fin** to be drawing to a close

touffe [tuf] *nf* tuft

touffu, e [tufy] *adj* thick, dense

toujours [tuʒuʀ] *adv* always; (*encore*) still; (*constamment*) forever; **essaie ~** (you can) try anyway; **pour ~** forever; **~ est-il que** the fact remains that; **~ plus** more and more

toupie [tupi] *nf* (spinning) top

tour [tuʀ] *nf* tower; (*immeuble*) high-rise block (BRIT) *ou* building (US); (*Échecs*) castle, rook ▷ *nm* (*excursion: à pied*) stroll, walk; (*: en voiture etc*) run, ride; (*: plus long*) trip; (*Sport: aussi*: **~ de piste**) lap; (*d'être servi ou de jouer etc*) turn; (*de roue etc*) revolution; (*Pol: aussi*: **~ de scrutin**) ballot; (*ruse, de prestidigitation, de cartes*) trick; (*de potier*) wheel; (*à bois, métaux*) lathe; (*circonférence*): **de 3 m de ~** 3 m round, with a circumference *ou* girth of 3 m; **faire le ~ de** to go (a)round; (*à pied*) to walk (a)round; **faire un ~** to go for a walk; **c'est au ~ de Renée** it's Renée's turn; **à ~ de rôle, ~ à ~** in turn; **~ de taille/tête** *nm* waist/head measurement; **~ de chant** *nm* song recital; **~ de contrôle** *nf* control tower; **la ~ Eiffel** the Eiffel Tower; **le T~ de France** the Tour de France; **~ de force** *nm* tour de force; **~ de garde** *nm* spell of duty; **un 33 ~s** an LP; **un 45 ~s** a single; **~ d'horizon** *nm* (*fig*) general survey

tourbe [tuʀb] *nf* peat

tourbillon [tuʀbijɔ̃] *nm* whirlwind; (*d'eau*) whirlpool; (*fig*) whirl, swirl;

tourbillonner /1/ *vi* to whirl *ou* twirl round

tourelle [tuʀɛl] *nf* turret

tourisme [tuʀism] *nm* tourism; **agence de ~** tourist agency; **faire du ~** to go touring; (*en ville*) to go sightseeing; **touriste** *nm/f* tourist; **touristique** *adj* tourist *cpd*; (*région*) touristic (*péj*)

tourment [tuʀmã] *nm* torment; **tourmenter** /1/ *vt* to torment; **se tourmenter** to fret, worry o.s.

tournage [tuʀnaʒ] *nm* (*d'un film*) shooting

tournant, e [tuʀnã, -ãt] *adj* (*feu, scène*) revolving ▷ *nm* (*de route*) bend; (*fig*) turning point

tournée [tuʀne] *nf* (*du facteur etc*) round; (*d'artiste, politicien*) tour; (*au café*) round (of drinks)

tourner /1/ *vt* to turn; (*sauce, mélange*) to stir; (*Ciné: faire les prises de vues*) to shoot; (*: produire*) to make ▷ *vi* to turn; (*moteur*) to run; (*compteur*) to tick away; (*lait etc*) to turn (sour); **se tourner** *vi* to turn (a)round; **se ~ vers** to turn to; to turn towards; **mal ~** to go wrong; **~ autour de** to go (a)round; (*péj*) to hang (a)round; **~ à/en** to turn into; **~ en ridicule** to ridicule; **~ le dos à** (*mouvement*) to turn one's back on; (*position*) to have one's back to; **se ~ les pouces** to twiddle one's thumbs; **~ de l'œil** to pass out

tournesol [tuʀnəsɔl] *nm* sunflower

tournevis [tuʀnəvis] *nm* screwdriver

tournoi [tuʀnwa] *nm* tournament

tournure [tuʀnyʀ] *nf* (*Ling*) turn of phrase; **la ~ de qch** (*évolution*) the way sth is developing; **~ d'esprit** turn *ou* cast of mind

tourte [tuʀt] *nf* pie

tourterelle [tuʀtəʀɛl] *nf* turtledove

tous [tu, tus] *adj, pron voir* **tout**

Toussaint [tusɛ̃] *nf*: **la ~** All Saints' Day

tousser [tuse] /1/ *vi* to cough

MOT-CLÉ

tout, e (*mpl* **tous**, *fpl* **toutes**) [tu, tut, tus, tut] *adj* **1** (*avec article singulier*) all; **tout le lait** all the milk; **toute la nuit** all night, the whole night; **tout le livre** the whole book; **tout un pain** a whole loaf; **tout le temps** all the time, the whole time; **c'est tout le contraire** it's quite the opposite **2** (*avec article pluriel*) every; all; **tous les livres** all the books; **toutes les nuits** every night; **toutes les fois** every time; **toutes les trois/deux semaines** every third/other *ou* second week, every three/two weeks; **tous les deux** both *ou* each of us (*ou* them *ou* you); **toutes les trois** all three of us (*ou* them *ou* you) **3** (*sans article*): **à tout âge** at any age; **pour toute nourriture, il avait ...** his only food was ...
▷ *pron* everything, all; **il a tout fait** he's done everything; **je les vois tous** I can see them all *ou* all of them; **nous y sommes tous allés** all of us went, we all went; **c'est tout** that's all; **en tout** in all; **tout ce qu'il sait** all he knows
▷ *nm* whole; **le tout** all of it (*ou* them); **le tout est de ...** the main thing is to ...; **pas du tout** not at all
▷ *adv* **1** (*très, complètement*) very; **tout près** *ou* **à côté** very near; **le tout premier** the very first; **tout seul** all alone; **le livre tout entier** the whole book; **tout en haut** right at the top; **tout droit** straight ahead

2: **tout en** while; **tout en travaillant** while working, as he *etc* works

3: **tout d'abord** first of all; **tout à coup** suddenly; **tout à fait** absolutely; **tout à l'heure** a short while ago; (*futur*) in a short while, shortly; **à tout à l'heure!** see you later!; **tout de même** all the same; **tout le monde** everybody; **tout simplement** quite simply; **tout de suite** immediately, straight away

toutefois [tutfwa] *adv* however
toutes [tut] *adj, pron voir* **tout**
tout-terrain [tuterɛ̃] *adj*: **vélo ~** mountain bike; **véhicule ~** four-wheel drive
toux [tu] *nf* cough
toxicomane [tɔksikɔman] *nm/f* drug addict
toxique [tɔksik] *adj* toxic
trac [tʀak] *nm* (*aux examens*) nerves *pl*; (*Théât*) stage fright; **avoir le ~** (*aux examens*) to get an attack of nerves; (*Théât*) to have stage fright
tracasser [tʀakase] /1/ *vt* to worry, bother; **se tracasser** to worry (o.s.)
trace [tʀas] *nf* (*empreintes*) tracks *pl*; (*marques, fig*) mark; (*restes, vestige*) trace; **~s de pas** footprints
tracer [tʀase] /3/ *vt* to draw; (*piste*) to open up
tract [tʀakt] *nm* tract, pamphlet
tracteur [tʀaktœʀ] *nm* tractor
traction [tʀaksjɔ̃] *nf*: **~ avant/arrière** front-wheel/rear-wheel drive
tradition [tʀadisjɔ̃] *nf* tradition; **traditionnel, le** *adj* traditional
traducteur, -trice [tʀadyktœʀ, -tʀis] *nm/f* translator
traduction [tʀadyksjɔ̃] *nf* translation
traduire [tʀaduiʀ] /38/ *vt* to translate; (*exprimer*) to convey; **~ en français** to translate into French; **~ en justice** to bring before the courts
trafic [tʀafik] *nm* traffic; **~ d'armes** arms dealing; **trafiquant, e** *nm/f*

trafficker; (*d'armes*) dealer; **trafiquer** /1/ *vt* (*péj: vin*) to doctor; (: *moteur, document*) to tamper with
tragédie [tʀaʒedi] *nf* tragedy; **tragique** *adj* tragic
trahir [tʀaiʀ] /2/ *vt* to betray; **trahison** *nf* betrayal; (*Jur*) treason
train [tʀɛ̃] *nm* (*Rail*) train; (*allure*) pace; **être en ~ de faire qch** to be doing sth; **~ à grande vitesse** high-speed train; **~ d'atterrissage** undercarriage; **~ électrique** (*jouet*) (electric) train set; **~ de vie** style of living
traîne [tʀɛn] *nf* (*de robe*) train; **être à la ~** to lag behind
traîneau, x [tʀɛno] *nm* sleigh, sledge
traîner [tʀene] /1/ *vt* (*remorque*) to pull; (*enfant, chien*) to drag *ou* trail along ▷ *vi* (*robe, manteau*) to trail; (*être en désordre*) to lie around; (*marcher lentement*) to dawdle (along); (*vagabonder*) to hang about; (*durer*) to drag on; **se traîner** *vi*: **se ~ par terre** to crawl (on the ground); **~ les pieds** to drag one's feet
train-train [tʀɛ̃tʀɛ̃] *nm* humdrum routine
traire [tʀɛʀ] /50/ *vt* to milk
trait, e [tʀɛ, -ɛt] *nm* (*ligne*) line; (*de dessin*) stroke; (*caractéristique*) feature, trait; **traits** *nmpl* (*du visage*) features; **d'un ~** (*boire*) in one gulp; **de ~** (*animal*) draught ; **avoir ~ à** to concern; **~ d'union** hyphen
traitant, e [tʀɛtɑ̃, -ɑ̃t] *adj*: **votre médecin ~** your usual *ou* family doctor; **shampooing ~** medicated shampoo
traite [tʀɛt] *nf* (*Comm*) draft; (*Agr*) milking; **d'une (seule) ~** without stopping (once)
traité [tʀete] *nm* treaty
traitement [tʀɛtmɑ̃] *nm* treatment; (*salaire*) salary; **~ de données** *ou* **de l'information** data processing; **~ de texte** word processing; (*logiciel*) word processing package

t

traiter [tʀete] /1/ vt to treat;
(qualifier): ~ **qn d'idiot** to call sb a fool
▷ vi to deal; ~ **de** to deal with
traiteur [tʀetœʀ] nm caterer
traître, -esse [tʀetʀ, -tʀes] adj
(dangereux) treacherous ▷ nm/f
traitor (traitress)
trajectoire [tʀaʒɛktwaʀ] nf path
trajet [tʀaʒɛ] nm (parcours, voyage)
journey; (itinéraire) route; (distance à
parcourir) distance; **il y a une heure
de** ~ the journey takes one hour
trampoline [tʀɑ̃pɔlin] nm
trampoline
tramway [tʀamwɛ] nm tram(way);
(voiture) tram(car) (BRIT), streetcar
(US)
tranchant, e [tʀɑ̃ʃɑ̃, -ɑ̃t] adj sharp;
(fig) peremptory ▷ nm (d'un couteau)
cutting edge; (de la main) edge; **à
double** ~ double-edged
tranche [tʀɑ̃ʃ] nf (morceau) slice;
(arête) edge; ~ **d'âge/de salaires**
age/wage bracket
tranché, e [tʀɑ̃ʃe] adj (couleurs)
distinct; (opinions) clear-cut
trancher [tʀɑ̃ʃe] /1/ vt to cut, sever
▷ vi to be decisive; ~ **avec** to contrast
sharply with
tranquille [tʀɑ̃kil] adj quiet; (rassuré)
easy in one's mind, with one's mind
at rest; **se tenir** ~ (enfant) to be
quiet; **avoir la conscience** ~ to have
an easy conscience; **laisse-moi/
laisse-ça** ~ leave me/it alone;
tranquillisant nm tranquillizer;
tranquillité nf peace (and quiet);
tranquillité d'esprit peace of mind
transférer [tʀɑ̃sfeʀe] /6/ vt to
transfer; **transfert** nm transfer
transformation [tʀɑ̃sfɔʀmasjɔ̃]
nf change, alteration; (radicale)
transformation; (Rugby) conversion;
transformations nfpl (travaux)
alterations
transformer [tʀɑ̃sfɔʀme] /1/ vt to
change; (radicalement) to transform;
(vêtement) alter; (matière première,

appartement, Rugby) to convert; ~ **en**
to turn into
transfusion [tʀɑ̃sfyzjɔ̃] nf:
~ **sanguine** blood transfusion
transgénique [tʀɑ̃sʒenik] adj
transgenic
transgresser [tʀɑ̃sgʀese] /1/ vt to
contravene
transi, e [tʀɑ̃zi] adj numb (with
cold), chilled to the bone
transiger [tʀɑ̃ziʒe] /3/ vi to
compromise
transit [tʀɑ̃zit] nm transit; **transiter**
/1/ vi to pass in transit
transition [tʀɑ̃zisjɔ̃] nf transition;
transitoire adj transitional
transmettre [tʀɑ̃smetʀ] /56/ vt
(passer): ~ **qch à qn** to pass sth on to
sb; (Tech, Tél, Méd) to transmit; (TV,
Radio: retransmettre) to broadcast;
transmission nf transmission
transparent, e [tʀɑ̃spaʀɑ̃, -ɑ̃t] adj
transparent
transpercer [tʀɑ̃speʀse] /3/ vt (froid,
pluie) to go through, pierce; (balle) to
go through
transpiration [tʀɑ̃spiʀasjɔ̃] nf
perspiration
transpirer [tʀɑ̃spiʀe] /1/ vi to
perspire
transplanter [tʀɑ̃splɑ̃te] /1/ vt
(Méd, Bot) to transplant
transport [tʀɑ̃spɔʀ] nm transport;
~**s en commun** public transport
sg; **transporter** /1/ vt to carry,
move; (Comm) to transport,
convey; **transporteur** nm haulage
contractor (BRIT), trucker (US)
transvaser [tʀɑ̃svaze] /1/ vt to
decant
transversal, e, -aux [tʀɑ̃sveʀsal,
-o] adj (mur, chemin, rue) running at
right angles; **coupe ~e** cross section
trapèze [tʀapɛz] nm (au cirque)
trapeze
trappe [tʀap] nf trap door
trapu, e [tʀapy] adj squat, stocky
traquenard [tʀaknaʀ] nm trap

traquer [tRake] /1/ vt to track down; (*harceler*) to hound

traumatiser [tRomatize] /1/ vt to traumatize

travail, -aux [tRavaj, -o] nm (*gén*) work; (*tâche, métier*) work no pl, job; (*Écon, Méd*) labour; **travaux** nmpl (*de réparation, agricoles etc*) work sg; (*sur route*) roadworks; (*de construction*) building (work) sg; **être sans ~** (*employé*) to be out of work; **~ (au) noir** moonlighting; **travaux des champs** farmwork sg; **travaux dirigés** (*Scol*) supervised practical work sg; **travaux forcés** hard labour sg; **travaux manuels** (*Scol*) handicrafts; **travaux ménagers** housework sg; **travaux pratiques** (*gén*) practical work sg; (*en laboratoire*) lab work sg

travailler [tRavaje] /1/ vi to work; (*bois*) to warp ▷ vt (*bois, métal*) to work; (*objet d'art, discipline*) to work on; **cela le travaille** it is on his mind; **travailleur, -euse** adj hard-working ▷ nm/f worker; **travailleur social** social worker; **travailliste** adj ≈ Labour cpd

travaux [tRavo] nmpl voir **travail**

travers [tRavER] nm fault, failing; **en ~ (de)** across; **au ~ (de)** through; **de ~** (*nez, bouche*) crooked; (*chapeau*) askew; **à ~** through; **regarder de ~** (*fig*) to look askance at; **comprendre de ~** to misunderstand

traverse [tRavERs] nf (*de voie ferrée*) sleeper; **chemin de ~** shortcut

traversée [tRavERse] nf crossing

traverser [tRavERse] /1/ vt (*gén*) to cross; (*ville, tunnel, aussi percer, fig*) to go through; (*ligne, trait*) to run across

traversin [tRavERsɛ̃] nm bolster

travesti [tRavesti] nm transvestite

trébucher [tRebyʃe] /1/ vi: **~ (sur)** to stumble (over), trip (over)

trèfle [tRɛfl] nm (*Bot*) clover; (*Cartes: couleur*) clubs pl; (*: carte*) club; **~ à quatre feuilles** four-leaf clover

treize [tRɛz] num thirteen; **treizième** num thirteenth

tréma [tRema] nm diaeresis

tremblement [tRɑ̃bləmɑ̃] nm: **~ de terre** earthquake

trembler [tRɑ̃ble] /1/ vi to tremble, shake; **~ de** (*froid, fièvre*) to shiver ou tremble with; (*peur*) to shake ou tremble with; **~ pour qn** to fear for sb

trémousser [tRemuse] /1/: **se trémousser** vi to jig about, wriggle about

trempé, e [tRɑ̃pe] adj soaking (wet), drenched; (*Tech*): **acier ~** tempered steel

tremper [tRɑ̃pe] /1/ vt to soak, drench; (*aussi*: **faire ~, mettre à ~**) to soak ▷ vi to soak; (*fig*): **~ dans** to be involved ou have a hand in; **se tremper** vi to have a quick dip

tremplin [tRɑ̃plɛ̃] nm springboard; (*Ski*) ski jump

trentaine [tRɑ̃tɛn] nf (*âge*): **avoir la ~** to be around thirty; **une ~ (de)** thirty or so, about thirty

trente [tRɑ̃t] num thirty; **être/ se mettre sur son ~ et un** to be wearing/put on one's Sunday best; **trentième** num thirtieth

trépidant, e [tRepidɑ̃, -ɑ̃t] adj (*fig: rythme*) pulsating; (*: vie*) hectic

trépigner [tRepiɲe] /1/ vi to stamp (one's feet)

très [tRɛ] adv very; **~ beau/bien** very beautiful/well; **~ critiqué** much criticized; **~ industrialisé** highly industrialized

trésor [tRezɔR] nm treasure; **~ (public)** public revenue; **trésorerie** nf (*gestion*) accounts pl; (*bureaux*) accounts department; **difficultés de trésorerie** cash problems, shortage of cash ou funds; **trésorier, -ière** nm/f treasurer

tressaillir [tResajiR] /13/ vi to shiver, shudder

t

tressauter [tʀesote] /1/ vi to start, jump

tresse [tʀɛs] nf braid, plait; **tresser** /1/ vt (cheveux) to braid, plait; (fil, jonc) to plait; (corbeille) to weave; (corde) to twist

trêve [tʀɛv] nf (Mil, Pol) truce; (fig) respite; **~ de ...** enough of this ...

tri [tʀi] nm: **faire le ~ (de)** to sort out; **le (bureau de) ~** (Postes) the sorting office

triangle [tʀijɑ̃gl] nm triangle; **triangulaire** adj triangular

tribord [tʀibɔʀ] nm: **à ~** to starboard, on the starboard side

tribu [tʀiby] nf tribe

tribunal, -aux [tʀibynal, -o] nm (Jur) court; (Mil) tribunal

tribune [tʀibyn] nf (estrade) platform, rostrum; (débat) forum; (d'église, de tribunal) gallery; (de stade) stand

tribut [tʀiby] nm tribute

tributaire [tʀibytɛʀ] adj: **être ~ de** to be dependent on

tricher [tʀiʃe] /1/ vi to cheat; **tricheur, -euse** nm/f cheat

tricolore [tʀikɔlɔʀ] adj three-coloured; (français) red, white and blue

tricot [tʀiko] nm (technique, ouvrage) knitting no pl; (vêtement) jersey, sweater; **~ de corps, ~ de peau** vest ; **tricoter** /1/ vt to knit

tricycle [tʀisikl] nm tricycle

trier [tʀije] /7/ vt to sort (out); (Postes, Inform, fruits) to sort

trimestre [tʀimɛstʀ] nm (Scol) term; (Comm) quarter; **trimestriel, le** adj quarterly; (Scol) end-of-term

trinquer [tʀɛ̃ke] /1/ vi to clink glasses

triomphe [tʀijɔ̃f] nm triumph; **triompher** /1/ vi to triumph, win; **triompher de** to triumph over, overcome

tripes [tʀip] nfpl (Culin) tripe sg

triple [tʀipl] adj triple ▷ nm: **le ~ (de)** (comparaison) three times as much

(as); **en ~ exemplaire** in triplicate; **tripler** /1/ vi, vt to triple, treble

triplés, -ées [tʀiple] nm/f pl triplets

tripoter [tʀipɔte] /1/ vt to fiddle with

triste [tʀist] adj sad; (couleur, temps, journée) dreary; (péj): **~ personnage/affaire** sorry individual/affair; **tristesse** nf sadness

trivial, e, -aux [tʀivjal, -o] adj coarse, crude; (commun) mundane

troc [tʀɔk] nm barter

trognon [tʀɔɲɔ̃] nm (de fruit) core; (de légume) stalk

trois [tʀwɑ] num three; **troisième** num third ▷ nf (Scol) year 10 (BRIT), ninth grade (US); **le troisième âge** (période de vie) one's retirement years; (personnes âgées) senior citizens pl

troll [tʀɔl] nm, **trolleur, -euse** [tʀɔlœʀ, -øz] nm/f (Inform) troll

trombe [tʀɔ̃b] nf: **des ~s d'eau** a downpour; **en ~** like a whirlwind

trombone [tʀɔ̃bɔn] nm (Mus) trombone; (de bureau) paper clip

trompe [tʀɔ̃p] nf (d'éléphant) trunk; (Mus) trumpet, horn

tromper [tʀɔ̃pe] /1/ vt to deceive; (vigilance, poursuivants) to elude; **se tromper** vi to make a mistake, be mistaken; **se ~ de voiture/jour** to take the wrong car/get the day wrong; **se ~ de 3 cm/20 euros** to be out by 3 cm/20 euros

trompette [tʀɔ̃pet] nf trumpet; **en ~** (nez) turned-up

trompeur, -euse [tʀɔ̃pœʀ, -øz] adj deceptive

tronc [tʀɔ̃] nm (Bot, Anat) trunk; (d'église) collection box

tronçon [tʀɔ̃sɔ̃] nm section; **tronçonner** /1/ vt to saw up; **tronçonneuse** nf chainsaw

trône [tʀon] nm throne

trop [tʀo] adv too; (avec verbe) too much; (aussi: **~ nombreux**) too many; (aussi: **~ souvent**) too often; **~ peu (nombreux)** too few; **~ longtemps** (for) too long; **~ de**

(*nombre*) too many; (*quantité*) too much; **de ~, en ~: des livres en ~** a few books too many; **du lait en ~** too much milk; **trois livres/cinq euros de ~** three books too many/five euros too much; **ça coûte ~ cher** it's too expensive

tropical, e, -aux [tʀɔpikal, -o] *adj* tropical

tropique [tʀɔpik] *nm* tropic

trop-plein [tʀɔplɛ̃] *nm* (*tuyau*) overflow *ou* outlet (pipe); (*liquide*) overflow

troquer [tʀɔke] /1/ *vt*: **~ qch contre** to barter *ou* trade sth for; (*fig*) to swap sth for

trot [tʀo] *nm* trot; **trotter** /1/ *vi* to trot

trottinette [tʀɔtinɛt] *nf* (child's) scooter

trottoir [tʀɔtwaʀ] *nm* pavement (BRIT), sidewalk (US); **faire le ~** (*péj*) to walk the streets; **~ roulant** moving walkway, travelator

trou [tʀu] *nm* hole; (*fig*) gap; (*Comm*) deficit; **~ d'air** air pocket; **~ de mémoire** blank, lapse of memory

troublant, e [tʀublɑ̃, -ɑ̃t] *adj* disturbing

trouble [tʀubl] *adj* (*liquide*) cloudy; (*image, photo*) blurred; (*affaire*) shady, murky ▷ *adv*: **voir ~** to have blurred vision ▷ *nm* agitation; **troubles** *nmpl* (*Pol*) disturbances, troubles, unrest *sg*; (*Méd*) trouble *sg*, disorders; **trouble-fête** *nm/f inv* spoilsport

troubler [tʀuble] /1/ *vt* to disturb; (*liquide*) to make cloudy; (*intriguer*) to bother; **se troubler** *vi* (*personne*) to become flustered *ou* confused

trouer [tʀue] /1/ *vt* to make a hole (*ou* holes) in

trouille [tʀuj] *nf* (*fam*): **avoir la ~** to be scared stiff

troupe [tʀup] *nf* troop; **~ (de théâtre)** (theatrical) company

troupeau, x [tʀupo] *nm* (*de moutons*) flock; (*de vaches*) herd

trousse [tʀus] *nf* case, kit; (*d'écolier*) pencil case; **aux ~s de** (*fig*) on the heels *ou* tail of; **~ à outils** toolkit; **~ de toilette** toilet bag

trousseau, x [tʀuso] *nm* (*de mariée*) trousseau; **~ de clefs** bunch of keys

trouvaille [tʀuvaj] *nf* find

trouver [tʀuve] /1/ *vt* to find; (*rendre visite*): **aller/venir ~ qn** to go/come and see sb; **se trouver** *vi* (*être*) to be; **je trouve que** I find *ou* think that; **~ à boire/critiquer** to find something to drink/criticize; **se ~ mal** to pass out

truand [tʀyɑ̃] *nm* villain; **truander** /1/ *vt*: **se faire truander** to be swindled

truc [tʀyk] *nm* (*astuce*) way; (*de cinéma, prestidigitateur*) trick effect; (*chose*) thing; thingumajig; **avoir le ~** to have the knack; **c'est pas son** (*ou* **mon** *etc*) **~** (*fam*) it's not really his (*ou* my *etc*) thing

truffe [tʀyf] *nf* truffle; (*nez*) nose

truffé, e [tʀyfe] *adj* (*Culin*) garnished with truffles

truie [tʀɥi] *nf* sow

truite [tʀɥit] *nf* trout *inv*

truquage [tʀykaʒ] *nm* special effects *pl*

truquer [tʀyke] /1/ *vt* (*élections, serrure, dés*) to fix

TSVP *abr* (= *tournez s'il vous plaît*) PTO

TTC *abr* (= *toutes taxes comprises*) inclusive of tax

tu[1] [ty] *pron* you ▷ *nm*: **employer le tu** to use the "tu" form

tu[2]**, e** [ty] *pp de* **taire**

tuba [tyba] *nm* (*Mus*) tuba; (*Sport*) snorkel

tube [tyb] *nm* tube; (*chanson, disque*) hit song *ou* record

tuberculose [tybɛʀkyloz] *nf* tuberculosis

tuer [tɥe] /1/ *vt* to kill; **se tuer** (*se suicider*) to kill o.s.; (*dans un accident*) to be killed; **se ~ au travail** (*fig*) to work o.s. to death; **tuerie** *nf* slaughter *no pl*

t

tue-tête [tytɛt]: **à ~** *adv* at the top of one's voice

tueur [tɥœʀ] *nm* killer; **~ à gages** hired killer

tuile [tɥil] *nf* tile; (*fam*) spot of bad luck, blow

tulipe [tylip] *nf* tulip

tuméfié, e [tymefje] *adj* puffy, swollen

tumeur [tymœʀ] *nf* growth, tumour

tumulte [tymylt] *nm* commotion; **tumultueux, -euse** *adj* stormy, turbulent

tunique [tynik] *nf* tunic

Tunis [tynis] *n* Tunis

Tunisie [tynizi] *nf*: **la ~** Tunisia; **tunisien, ne** *adj* Tunisian ▷ *nm/f*: **Tunisien, ne** Tunisian

tunnel [tynɛl] *nm* tunnel; **le ~ sous la Manche** the Channel Tunnel

turbulent, e [tyʀbylɑ̃, -ɑ̃t] *adj* boisterous, unruly

turc, turque [tyʀk] *adj* Turkish ▷ *nm* (*Ling*) Turkish ▷ *nm/f*: **Turc, Turque** Turk/Turkish woman

turf [tyʀf] *nm* racing; **turfiste** *nm/f* racegoer

Turquie [tyʀki] *nf*: **la ~** Turkey

turquoise [tyʀkwaz] *nf, adj inv* turquoise

tutelle [tytɛl] *nf* (*Jur*) guardianship; (*Pol*) trusteeship; **sous la ~ de** (*fig*) under the supervision of

tuteur, -trice [tytœʀ, -tʀis] *nm/f* (*Jur*) guardian; (*de plante*) stake, support

tutoyer [tytwaje] /8/ *vt*: **~ qn** to address sb as "tu"

tuyau, x [tɥijo] *nm* pipe; (*flexible*) tube; (*fam*) tip; **~ d'arrosage** hosepipe; **~ d'échappement** exhaust pipe; **tuyauterie** *nf* piping *no pl*

TVA *sigle f* (= *taxe à ou sur la valeur ajoutée*) VAT

tweet [twit] *nm* (*aussi Internet*: *Twitter*) tweet; **tweeter** /1/ *vi* (*Internet*: *Twitter*) to tweet

tympan [tɛ̃pɑ̃] *nm* (*Anat*) eardrum

type [tip] *nm* type; (*fam*) chap, guy ▷ *adj* typical, standard

typé, e [tipe] *adj* ethnic (*euphémisme*)

typique [tipik] *adj* typical

tyran [tiʀɑ̃] *nm* tyrant; **tyrannique** *adj* tyrannical

tzigane [dzigan] *adj* gipsy, tzigane

U

ulcère [ylsɛʀ] *nm* ulcer
ultérieur, e [ylteʀjœʀ] *adj* later, subsequent; **remis à une date ~e** postponed to a later date; **ultérieurement** *adv* later, subsequently
ultime [yltim] *adj* final

⬤ **MOT-CLÉ**

un, une [œ̃, yn] *art indéf* a; (*devant voyelle*) an; **un garçon/vieillard** a boy/an old man; **une fille** a girl
▶ *pron* one; **l'un des meilleurs** one of the best; **l'un ..., l'autre** (the) one ..., the other; **les uns ..., les autres** some ..., others; **l'un et l'autre** both (of them); **l'un ou l'autre** either (of them); **l'un l'autre, les uns les autres** each other, one another; **pas un seul** not a single one; **un par un** one by one
▶ *num* one; **une pomme seulement** one apple only, just one apple
▶ *nf*: **la une** (*Presse*) the front page

unanime [ynanim] *adj* unanimous; **unanimité** *nf*: **à l'unanimité** unanimously
uni, e [yni] *adj* (*ton, tissu*) plain; (*surface*) smooth, even; (*famille*) close(-knit); (*pays*) united
unifier [ynifje] /7/ *vt* to unite, unify
uniforme [ynifɔʀm] *adj* uniform; (*surface, ton*) even ▷ *nm* uniform; **uniformiser** /1/ *vt* (*systèmes*) to standardize
union [ynjɔ̃] *nf* union; **~ de consommateurs** consumers' association; **~ libre: vivre en ~ libre** (*en concubinage*) to cohabit; **l'U~ européenne** the European Union; **l'U~ soviétique** the Soviet Union
unique [ynik] *adj* (*seul*) only; (*exceptionnel*) unique; **un prix/ système ~** a single price/system; **fils/fille ~** only son/daughter, only child; **sens ~** one-way street; **uniquement** *adv* only, solely; (*juste*) only, merely
unir [yniʀ] /2/ *vt* (*nations*) to unite; (*en mariage*) to unite, join together; **s'unir** *vi* to unite; (*en mariage*) to be joined together
unitaire [ynitɛʀ] *adj*: **prix ~** unit price
unité [ynite] *nf* (*harmonie, cohésion*) unity; (*Math*) unit
univers [ynivɛʀ] *nm* universe; **universel, le** *adj* universal
universitaire [yniveʀsitɛʀ] *adj* university *cpd*; (*diplôme, études*) academic, university *cpd* ▷ *nm/f* academic
université [yniveʀsite] *nf* university
urbain, e [yʀbɛ̃, -ɛn] *adj* urban, city *cpd*, town *cpd*; **urbanisme** *nm* town planning
urgence [yʀʒɑ̃s] *nf* urgency; (*Méd etc*) emergency; **d'~** *adj* emergency *cpd* ▷ *adv* as a matter of urgency; **service des ~s** emergency service

u

urgent, e [yʀʒɑ̃, -ɑ̃t] *adj* urgent

urine [yʀin] *nf* urine; **urinoir** *nm* (public) urinal

urne [yʀn] *nf* (*électorale*) ballot box; (*vase*) urn

urticaire [yʀtikɛʀ] *nf* nettle rash

us [ys] *nmpl*: **us et coutumes** (habits and) customs

usage [yzaʒ] *nm* (*emploi, utilisation*) use; (*coutume*) custom; **à l'~** with use; **à l'~ de** (*pour*) for (use of); **en ~** in use; **hors d'~** out of service; **à ~ interne** (*Méd*) to be taken (internally); **à ~ externe** (*Méd*) for external use only; **usagé, e** *adj* (*usé*) worn; **usager, -ère** *nm/f* user

usé, e [yze] *adj* worn (down *ou* out *ou* away); (*banal: argument etc*) hackneyed

user [yze] /1/ *vt* (*outil*) to wear down; (*vêtement*) to wear out; (*matière*) to wear away; (*consommer: charbon etc*) to use; **s'user** *vi* (*tissu, vêtement*) to wear out; **~ de** (*moyen, procédé*) to use, employ; (*droit*) to exercise

usine [yzin] *nf* factory

usité, e [yzite] *adj* common

ustensile [ystɑ̃sil] *nm* implement; **~ de cuisine** kitchen utensil

usuel, le [yzɥɛl] *adj* everyday, common

usure [yzyʀ] *nf* wear

utérus [yteʀys] *nm* uterus, womb

utile [ytil] *adj* useful

utilisation [ytilizasjɔ̃] *nf* use

utiliser [ytilize] /1/ *vt* to use

utilitaire [ytilitɛʀ] *adj* utilitarian

utilité [ytilite] *nf* usefulness *no pl*; **de peu d'~** of little use *ou* help

utopie [ytɔpi] *nf* utopia

va [va] *vb voir* **aller**

vacance [vakɑ̃s] *nf* (*Admin*) vacancy; **vacances** *nfpl* holiday(s) *pl* (*BRIT*), vacation *sg* (*US*); **les grandes ~s** the summer holidays *ou* vacation; **prendre des/ses ~s** to take a holiday *ou* vacation/ one's holiday(s) *ou* vacation; **aller en ~s** to go on holiday *ou* vacation; **vacancier, -ière** *nm/f* holidaymaker

vacant, e [vakɑ̃, -ɑ̃t] *adj* vacant

vacarme [vakaʀm] *nm* row, din

vaccin [vaksɛ̃] *nm* vaccine; (*opération*) vaccination; **vaccination** *nf* vaccination; **vacciner** /1/ *vt* to vaccinate; **être vacciné** (*fig*) to be immune

vache [vaʃ] *nf* (*Zool*) cow; (*cuir*) cowhide ▷ *adj* (*fam*) rotten, mean; **vachement** *adv* (*fam*) really; **vacherie** *nf* (*action*) dirty trick; (*propos*) nasty remark

vaciller [vasije] /1/ *vi* to sway, wobble; (*bougie, lumière*) to flicker; (*fig*) to be failing, falter

VAE *sigle m* (= vélo (à assistance) électrique) e-bike

va-et-vient [vaevjɛ̃] *nm inv* comings and goings *pl*

vagabond, e [vagabɔ̃, -ɔ̃d] *adj* wandering ▷ *nm* (*rôdeur*) tramp, vagrant; (*voyageur*) wanderer; **vagabonder** /1/ *vi* to roam, wander

vagin [vaʒɛ̃] *nm* vagina

vague [vag] *nf* wave ▷ *adj* vague; (*regard*) faraway; (*manteau, robe*) loose(-fitting); (*quelconque*): **un ~ bureau/cousin** some office/cousin or other; **~ de fond** ground swell; **~ de froid** cold spell

vaillant, e [vajɑ̃, -ɑ̃t] *adj* (*courageux*) gallant; (*robuste*) hale and hearty

vain, e [vɛ̃, vɛn] *adj* vain; **en ~** in vain

vaincre [vɛ̃kʀ] /42/ *vt* to defeat; (*fig*) to conquer, overcome; **vaincu, e** *nm/f* defeated party; **vainqueur** *nm* victor; (*Sport*) winner

vaisseau, x [vɛso] *nm* (*Anat*) vessel; (*Navig*) ship, vessel; **~ spatial** spaceship

vaisselier [vɛsəlje] *nm* dresser

vaisselle [vɛsɛl] *nf* (*service*) crockery; (*plats etc à laver*) (dirty) dishes *pl*; **faire la ~** to do the dishes

valable [valabl] *adj* valid; (*acceptable*) decent, worthwhile

valet [valɛ] *nm* valet; (*Cartes*) jack

valeur [valœʀ] *nf* (*gén*) value; (*mérite*) worth, merit; (*Comm*: *titre*) security; **valeurs** *nfpl* (*morales*) values; **mettre en ~** (*fig*) to highlight; to show off to advantage; **avoir de la ~** to be valuable; **prendre de la ~** to go up *ou* gain in value; **sans ~** worthless

valide [valid] *adj* (*en bonne santé*) fit; (*valable*) valid; **valider** /1/ *vt* to validate

valise [valiz] *nf* (suit)case; **faire sa ~** to pack one's (suit)case

vallée [vale] *nf* valley

vallon [valɔ̃] *nm* small valley

valoir [valwaʀ] /29/ *vi* (*être valable*) to hold, apply ▷ *vt* (*prix, valeur, effort*) to be worth; (*causer*): **~ qch à qn** to earn sb sth; **se valoir** to be of equal merit; (*péj*) to be two of a kind; **faire ~** (*droits, prérogatives*) to assert; **se faire ~** to make the most of o.s.; **à ~ sur** to be deducted from; **vaille que vaille** somehow or other; **cela ne me dit rien qui vaille** I don't like the look of it at all; **ce climat ne me vaut rien** this climate doesn't suit me; **~ la peine** to be worth the trouble, be worth it; **~ mieux: il vaut mieux se taire** it's better to say nothing; **ça ne vaut rien** it's worthless; **que vaut ce candidat?** how good is this applicant?

valse [vals] *nf* waltz

vandalisme [vɑ̃dalism] *nm* vandalism

vanille [vanij] *nf* vanilla

vanité [vanite] *nf* vanity; **vaniteux, -euse** *adj* vain, conceited

vanne [van] *nf* gate; (*fam*) dig

vantard, e [vɑ̃taʀ, -aʀd] *adj* boastful

vanter [vɑ̃te] /1/ *vt* to speak highly of, praise; **se vanter** *vi* to boast, brag; **se ~ de** to pride o.s. on; (*péj*) to boast of

vapeur [vapœʀ] *nf* steam; (*émanation*) vapour, fumes *pl*; **vapeurs** *nfpl* (*bouffées*) vapours; **à ~** steam powered, steam *cpd*; **cuit à la ~** steamed; **vaporeux, -euse** *adj* (*flou*) hazy, misty; (*léger*) filmy; **vaporisateur** *nm* spray; **vaporiser** /1/ *vt* (*parfum etc*) to spray

vapoter [vapɔte] /1/ *vi* to smoke an e-cigarette

varappe [vaʀap] *nf* rock climbing

vareuse [vaʀøz] *nf* (*blouson*) pea jacket; (*d'uniforme*) tunic

variable [vaʀjabl] *adj* variable; (*temps, humeur*) changeable; (*divers*: *résultats*) varied, various

varice [vaʀis] *nf* varicose vein

varicelle [vaʀisɛl] *nf* chickenpox

V

varié, e [vaʀje] *adj* varied; (*divers*) various; **hors-d'œuvre ~s** selection of hors d'œuvres

varier [vaʀje] /7/ *vi* to vary; (*temps, humeur*) to change ▷ *vt* to vary; **variété** *nf* variety; **spectacle de variétés** variety show

variole [vaʀjɔl] *nf* smallpox

Varsovie [vaʀsɔvi] *n* Warsaw

vas [va] *vb voir* **aller**; **~-y!** go on!

vase [vɑz] *nm* vase ▷ *nf* silt, mud; **vaseux, -euse** *adj* silty, muddy; (*fig: confus*) woolly, hazy; (: *fatigué*) peaky

vasistas [vazistɑs] *nm* fanlight

vaste [vast] *adj* vast, immense

vautour [votuʀ] *nm* vulture

vautrer [votʀe] /1/: **se vautrer** *vi*: **se ~ dans** to wallow in; **se ~ sur** to sprawl on

va-vite [vavit]: **à la ~** *adv* in a rush

VDQS *sigle m* (= *vin délimité de qualité supérieure*) *label guaranteeing quality of wine*

veau, x [vo] *nm* (*Zool*) calf; (*Culin*) veal; (*peau*) calfskin

vécu, e [veky] *pp de* **vivre**

vedette [vədɛt] *nf* (*artiste etc*) star; (*canot*) patrol boat; (*police*) launch

végétal, e, -aux [veʒetal, -o] *adj* vegetable ▷ *nm* vegetable, plant; **végétalien, ne** *adj, nm/f* vegan

végétarien, ne [veʒetaʀjɛ̃, -ɛn] *adj, nm/f* vegetarian

végétation [veʒetasjɔ̃] *nf* vegetation; **végétations** *nfpl* (*Méd*) adenoids

véhicule [veikyl] *nm* vehicle; **~ utilitaire** commercial vehicle

veille [vɛj] *nf* (*Psych*) wakefulness; (*jour*): **la ~** the day before; **la ~ au soir** the previous evening; **la ~ de** the day before; **la ~ de Noël** Christmas Eve; **la ~ du jour de l'An** New Year's Eve; **à la ~ de** on the eve of

veillée [veje] *nf* (*soirée*) evening; (*réunion*) evening gathering; **~ (funèbre)** wake

veiller [veje] /1/ *vi* to stay *ou* sit up ▷ *vt* (*malade, mort*) to watch over, sit up with; **~ à** to attend to, see to; **~ à ce que** to make sure that; **~ sur** to keep a watch *ou* an eye on; **veilleur** *nm*: **veilleur de nuit** night watchman; **veilleuse** *nf* (*lampe*) night light; (*Auto*) sidelight; (*flamme*) pilot light

veinard, e [vɛnaʀ, -aʀd] *nm/f* lucky devil

veine [vɛn] *nf* (*Anat, du bois etc*) vein; (*filon*) vein, seam; **avoir de la ~** (*fam*) (*chance*) to be lucky

véliplanchiste [veliplɑ̃ʃist] *nm/f* windsurfer

vélo [velo] *nm* bike, cycle; **faire du ~** to go cycling; **vélomoteur** *nm* moped

velours [v(ə)luʀ] *nm* velvet; **~ côtelé** corduroy; **velouté, e** *adj* velvety ▷ *nm*: **velouté d'asperges/ de tomates** cream of asparagus/ tomato soup

velu, e [vəly] *adj* hairy

vendange [vɑ̃dɑ̃ʒ] *nf* (*aussi*: **~s**) grape harvest; **vendanger** /3/ *vi* to harvest the grapes

vendeur, -euse [vɑ̃dœʀ, -øz] *nm/f* shop *ou* sales assistant ▷ *nm* (*Jur*) vendor, seller

vendre [vɑ̃dʀ] /41/ *vt* to sell; **~ qch à qn** to sell sb sth; **"à ~"** "for sale"

vendredi [vɑ̃dʀədi] *nm* Friday; **V~ saint** Good Friday

vénéneux, -euse [venenø, -øz] *adj* poisonous

vénérien, ne [veneʀjɛ̃, -ɛn] *adj* venereal

vengeance [vɑ̃ʒɑ̃s] *nf* vengeance *no pl*, revenge *no pl*

venger [vɑ̃ʒe] /3/ *vt* to avenge; **se venger** *vi* to avenge o.s.; **se ~ de qch** to avenge o.s. for sth; to take one's revenge for sth; **se ~ de qn** to take revenge on sb; **se ~ sur** to take revenge on

venimeux, -euse [vənimø, -øz] *adj* poisonous, venomous; (*fig*: *haineux*) venomous, vicious

venin [vənɛ̃] *nm* venom, poison

venir [v(ə)niʀ] /22/ *vi* to come; **~ de** to come from; **~ de faire: je viens d'y aller/de le voir** I've just been there/seen him; **s'il vient à pleuvoir** if it should rain; **où veux-tu en ~?** what are you getting at?; **faire ~** (*docteur, plombier*) to call (out)

vent [vã] *nm* wind; **il y a du ~** it's windy; **c'est du ~** it's all hot air; **dans le ~** (*fam*) trendy

vente [vãt] *nf* sale; **la ~** (*activité*) selling; (*secteur*) sales *pl*; **mettre en ~** to put on sale; (*objets personnels*) to put up for sale; **~ aux enchères** auction sale; **~ de charité** jumble (BRIT) *ou* rummage (US) sale

venteux, -euse [vãtø, -øz] *adj* windy

ventilateur [vãtilatœʀ] *nm* fan

ventiler [vãtile] /1/ *vt* to ventilate

ventouse [vãtuz] *nf* (*de caoutchouc*) suction pad

ventre [vãtʀ] *nm* (*Anat*) stomach; (*fig*) belly; **avoir mal au ~** to have (a) stomach ache

venu, e [v(ə)ny] *pp de* **venir** ▷ *adj*: **être mal ~ à** *ou* **de faire** to have no grounds for doing, be in no position to do; **mal ~** ill-timed; **bien ~** timely

ver [vɛʀ] *nm* worm; (*des fruits etc*) maggot; (*du bois*) woodworm *no pl*; **~ luisant** glow-worm; **~ à soie** silkworm; **~ solitaire** tapeworm; **~ de terre** earthworm

verbe [vɛʀb] *nm* verb

verdâtre [vɛʀdɑtʀ] *adj* greenish

verdict [vɛʀdik(t)] *nm* verdict

verdir [vɛʀdiʀ] /2/ *vi, vt* to turn green; **verdure** *nf* greenery

véreux, -euse [veʀø, -øz] *adj* worm-eaten; (*malhonnête*) shady, corrupt

verge [vɛʀʒ] *nf* (*Anat*) penis

verger [vɛʀʒe] *nm* orchard

verglacé, e [vɛʀglase] *adj* icy, iced-over

verglas [vɛʀglɑ] *nm* (black) ice

véridique [veʀidik] *adj* truthful

vérification [veʀifikasjɔ̃] *nf* checking *no pl*, check

vérifier [veʀifje] /7/ *vt* to check; (*corroborer*) to confirm, bear out

véritable [veʀitabl] *adj* real; (*ami, amour*) true; **un ~ désastre** an absolute disaster

vérité [veʀite] *nf* truth; **en ~** to tell the truth

verlan [vɛʀlɑ̃] *nm* (back) slang

vermeil, le [vɛʀmɛj] *adj* ruby red

vermine [vɛʀmin] *nf* vermin *pl*

vermoulu, e [vɛʀmuly] *adj* worm-eaten

verni, e [vɛʀni] *adj* (*fam*) lucky; **cuir ~** patent leather

vernir [vɛʀniʀ] /2/ *vt* (*bois, tableau, ongles*) to varnish; (*poterie*) to glaze; **vernis** *nm* (*enduit*) varnish; glaze; (*fig*) veneer; **vernis à ongles** nail varnish (BRIT) *ou* polish; **vernissage** *nm* (*d'une exposition*) preview

vérole [veʀɔl] *nf* (*variole*) smallpox

verre [vɛʀ] *nm* glass; (*de lunettes*) lens *sg*; **boire** *ou* **prendre un ~** to have a drink; **~s de contact** contact lenses; **verrière** *nf* (*grand vitrage*) window; (*toit vitré*) glass roof

verrou [veʀu] *nm* (*targette*) bolt; **mettre qn sous les ~s** to put sb behind bars; **verrouillage** *nm* locking mechanism; **verrouillage central** *ou* **centralisé** central locking; **verrouiller** /1/ *vt* to bolt; to lock

verrue [veʀy] *nf* wart

vers [vɛʀ] *nm* line ▷ *nmpl* (*poésie*) verse *sg* ▷ *prép* (*en direction de*) toward(s); (*près de*) around (about); (*temporel*) about, around

versant [vɛʀsɑ̃] *nm* slopes *pl*, side

versatile [vɛʀsatil] *adj* fickle, changeable

verse [vɛʀs]: **à ~** *adv*: **il pleut à ~** it's pouring (with rain)

V

Verseau [vɛʀso] *nm*: **le ~** Aquarius
versement [vɛʀsəmɑ̃] *nm*
payment; **en trois ~s** in three
instalments
verser [vɛʀse] /1/ *vt* (*liquide, grains*) to
pour; (*larmes, sang*) to shed; (*argent*)
to pay; **~ sur un compte** to pay into
an account
version [vɛʀsjɔ̃] *nf* version; (*Scol*)
translation (*into the mother tongue*);
film en ~ originale film in the
original language
verso [vɛʀso] *nm* back; **voir au ~** see
over(leaf)
vert, e [vɛʀ, vɛʀt] *adj* green; (*vin*)
young; (*vigoureux*) sprightly ▷ *nm*
green; **les V~s** (*Pol*) the Greens
vertèbre [vɛʀtɛbʀ] *nf* vertebra
vertement [vɛʀtəmɑ̃] *adv*
(*réprimander*) sharply
vertical, e, -aux [vɛʀtikal, -o] *adj*
vertical; **verticale** *nf* vertical; **à la
verticale** vertically; **verticalement**
adv vertically
vertige [vɛʀtiʒ] *nm* (*peur du vide*)
vertigo; (*étourdissement*) dizzy spell;
(*fig*) fever; **vertigineux, -euse** *adj*
breathtaking
vertu [vɛʀty] *nf* virtue; **en ~ de** in
accordance with; **vertueux, -euse**
adj virtuous
verve [vɛʀv] *nf* witty eloquence; **être
en ~** to be in brilliant form
verveine [vɛʀvɛn] *nf* (*Bot*) verbena,
vervain; (*infusion*) verbena tea
vésicule [vezikyl] *nf* vesicle;
~ biliaire gall-bladder
vessie [vesi] *nf* bladder
veste [vɛst] *nf* jacket; **~ droite/
croisée** single-/double-breasted
jacket
vestiaire [vɛstjɛʀ] *nm* (*au théâtre
etc*) cloakroom; (*de stade etc*)
changing-room (BRIT), locker-room
(US)
vestibule [vɛstibyl] *nm* hall
vestige [vɛstiʒ] *nm* relic; (*fig*) vestige;
vestiges *nmpl* (*d'une ville*) remains

vestimentaire [vɛstimɑ̃tɛʀ] *adj*
(*détail*) of dress; (*élégance*) sartorial;
dépenses ~s clothing expenditure
veston [vɛstɔ̃] *nm* jacket
vêtement [vɛtmɑ̃] *nm* garment,
item of clothing; **vêtements** *nmpl*
clothes
vétérinaire [veteʀinɛʀ] *nm/f* vet,
veterinary surgeon
vêtir [vetiʀ] /20/ *vt* to clothe, dress
vêtu, e [vety] *pp de* **vêtir** ▷ *adj*: **~ de**
dressed in, wearing
vétuste [vetyst] *adj* ancient,
timeworn
veuf, veuve [vœf, vœv] *adj* widowed
▷ *nm* widower ▷ *nf* widow
vexant, e [vɛksɑ̃, -ɑ̃t] *adj*
(*contrariant*) annoying; (*blessant*)
upsetting
vexation [vɛksasjɔ̃] *nf* humiliation
vexer [vɛkse] /1/ *vt* to hurt; **se vexer**
vi to be offended
viable [vjabl] *adj* viable; (*économie,
industrie etc*) sustainable
viande [vjɑ̃d] *nf* meat; **je ne mange
pas de ~** I don't eat meat
vibrer [vibʀe] /1/ *vi* to vibrate; (*son,
voix*) to be vibrant; (*fig*) to be stirred;
faire ~ to (cause to) vibrate; to
stir, thrill
vice [vis] *nm* vice; (*défaut*) fault; **~ de
forme** legal flaw *ou* irregularity
vicié, e [visje] *adj* (*air*) polluted,
tainted; (*Jur*) invalidated
vicieux, -euse [visjø, -øz] *adj*
(*pervers*) dirty(-minded); (*méchant*)
nasty ▷ *nm/f* lecher
vicinal, e, -aux [visinal, -o] *adj*:
chemin ~ byroad, byway
victime [viktim] *nf* victim;
(*d'accident*) casualty
victoire [viktwaʀ] *nf* victory
victuailles [viktɥaj] *nfpl* provisions
vidange [vidɑ̃ʒ] *nf* (*d'un fossé,
réservoir*) emptying; (*Auto*) oil change;
(*de lavabo: bonde*) waste outlet;
vidanges *nfpl* (*matières*) sewage *sg*;
vidanger /3/ *vt* to empty

vide [vid] *adj* empty ▷ *nm* (*Physique*) vacuum; (*espace*) (empty) space, gap; (*futilité, néant*) void; **emballé sous ~** vacuum-packed; **avoir peur du ~** to be afraid of heights; **à ~** (*sans occupants*) empty; (*sans charge*) unladen

vidéo [video] *nf* video; **cassette ~** video cassette; **vidéoclip** *nm* music video; **vidéoconférence** *nf* videoconference

vide-ordures [vidɔʀdyʀ] *nm inv* (rubbish) chute

vider [vide] /1/ *vt* to empty; (*Culin: volaille, poisson*) to gut, clean out; **se vider** *vi* to empty; **~ les lieux** to quit *ou* vacate the premises; **videur** *nm* (*de boîte de nuit*) bouncer

vie [vi] *nf* life; **être en ~** to be alive; **sans ~** lifeless; **à ~** for life; **que faites-vous dans la ~?** what do you do?

vieil [vjɛj] *adj m voir* **vieux**; **vieillard** *nm* old man; **vieille** *adj f*, *nf voir* **vieux**; **vieilleries** *nfpl* old things *ou* stuff *sg*; **vieillesse** *nf* old age; **vieillir** /2/ *vi* (*prendre de l'âge*) to grow old; (*population, vin*) to age; (*doctrine, auteur*) to become dated ▷ *vt* to age; **se vieillir** to make o.s. older; **vieillissement** *nm* growing old; ageing

Vienne [vjɛn] *n* Vienna

viens [vjɛ̃] *vb voir* **venir**

vierge [vjɛʀʒ] *adj* virgin; (*page*) clean, blank ▷ *nf* virgin; (*signe*): **la V~** Virgo

Viêtnam, Vietnam [vjɛtnam] *nm*: **le ~** Vietnam; **vietnamien, ne** *adj* Vietnamese ▷ *nm/f*: **Vietnamien, ne** Vietnamese

vieux (vieil), vieille [vjø, vjɛj] *adj* old ▷ *nm/f* old man/woman ▷ *nmpl*: **les ~** (*pej*) old people; **un petit ~** a little old man; **mon ~/ ma vieille** (*fam*) old man/girl; **prendre un coup de ~** to put years on; **~ garçon** bachelor; **~ jeu** *adj inv* old-fashioned

vif, vive [vif, viv] *adj* (*animé*) lively; (*alerte*) sharp; (*lumière, couleur*) brilliant; (*air*) crisp; (*vent, émotion*) keen; (*fort: regret, déception*) great, deep; (*vivant*): **brûlé ~** burnt alive; **de vive voix** personally; **avoir l'esprit ~** to be quick-witted; **piquer qn au ~** to cut sb to the quick; **à ~** (*plaie*) open; **avoir les nerfs à ~** to be on edge

vigne [viɲ] *nf* (*plante*) vine; (*plantation*) vineyard; **vigneron** *nm* wine grower

vignette [viɲɛt] *nf* (*pour voiture*) ≈ (road) tax disc (BRIT), ≈ license plate sticker (US); (*sur médicament*) price label (*on medicines for reimbursement by Social Security*)

vignoble [viɲɔbl] *nm* (*plantation*) vineyard; (*vignes d'une région*) vineyards *pl*

vigoureux, -euse [viguʀø, -øz] *adj* vigorous, robust

vigueur [vigœʀ] *nf* vigour; **être/ entrer en ~** to be in/come into force; **en ~** current

vilain, e [vilɛ̃, -ɛn] *adj* (*laid*) ugly; (*affaire, blessure*) nasty; (*pas sage: enfant*) naughty; **~ mot** bad word

villa [vila] *nf* (detached) house; **~ en multipropriété** time-share villa

village [vilaʒ] *nm* village; **villageois, e** *adj* village *cpd* ▷ *nm/f* villager

ville [vil] *nf* town; (*importante*) city; (*administration*): **la ~** ≈ the (town) council; **~ d'eaux** spa; **~ nouvelle** new town

vin [vɛ̃] *nm* wine; **avoir le ~ gai/ triste** to get happy/miserable after a few drinks; **~ d'honneur** reception (*with wine and snacks*); **~ ordinaire** *ou* **de table** table wine; **~ de pays** local wine

vinaigre [vinɛgʀ] *nm* vinegar; **vinaigrette** *nf* vinaigrette, French dressing

vindicatif, -ive [vɛ̃dikatif, -iv] *adj* vindictive

V

vingt [vɛ̃, vɛ̃t] (2nd pron used when followed by a vowel) num twenty; **~-quatre heures sur ~-quatre** twenty-four hours a day, round the clock; **vingtaine** nf: **une vingtaine (de)** around twenty, twenty or so; **vingtième** num twentieth

vinicole [vinikɔl] adj wine cpd; wine-growing

vinyle [vinil] nm vinyl

viol [vjɔl] nm (d'une femme) rape; (d'un lieu sacré) violation

violacé, e [vjɔlase] adj purplish, mauvish

violemment [vjɔlamã] adv violently

violence [vjɔlãs] nf violence

violent, e [vjɔlã, -ãt] adj violent; (remède) drastic

violer [vjɔle] /1/ vt (femme) to rape; (sépulture) to desecrate; (loi, traité) to violate

violet, te [vjɔlɛ, -ɛt] adj, nm purple, mauve ▷ nf (fleur) violet

violon [vjɔlɔ̃] nm violin; (fam: prison) lock-up; **~ d'Ingres** (artistic) hobby; **violoncelle** nm cello; **violoniste** nm/f violinist

virage [viraʒ] nm (d'un véhicule) turn; (d'une route, piste) bend

viral, e, -aux [viral, -o] adj (aussi Inform) viral

virée [vire] nf run; (à pied) walk; (longue) hike

virement [virmã] nm (Comm) transfer

virer [vire] /1/ vt (Comm) to transfer; (fam: renvoyer) to sack ▷ vi to turn; (Chimie) to change colour (BRIT) ou color (US); **~ au bleu** to turn blue; **~ de bord** to tack

virevolter [virvɔlte] /1/ vi to twirl around

virgule [virgyl] nf comma; (Math) point

viril, e [viril] adj (propre à l'homme) masculine; (énergique, courageux) manly, virile

virtuel, le [virtɥɛl] adj potential; (théorique) virtual

virtuose [virtɥoz] nm/f (Mus) virtuoso; (gén) master

virus [virys] nm virus

vis vb [vi] voir **voir, vivre** ▷ nf [vis] screw

visa [viza] nm (sceau) stamp; (validation de passeport) visa

visage [vizaʒ] nm face

vis-à-vis [vizavi] **~ de** prép towards; **en ~** facing ou opposite each other

visée [vize] nf aiming; **visées** nfpl (intentions) designs

viser [vize] /1/ vi to aim ▷ vt to aim at; (concerner) to be aimed ou directed at; (apposer un visa sur) to stamp, visa; **~ à qch/faire** to aim at sth/at doing ou to do

visibilité [vizibilite] nf visibility

visible [vizibl] adj visible; (disponible): **est-il ~?** can he see me?, will he see visitors?

visière [vizjɛr] nf (de casquette) peak; (qui s'attache) eyeshade

vision [vizjɔ̃] nf vision; (sens) (eye)sight, vision; (fait de voir): **la ~ de** the sight of; **visionneuse** nf viewer

visiophone [vizjɔfɔn] nm videophone

visite [vizit] nf visit; **~ médicale** medical examination; **~ accompagnée** ou **guidée** guided tour; **faire une ~ à qn** to call on sb, pay sb a visit; **rendre ~ à qn** to visit sb, pay sb a visit; **être en ~ (chez qn)** to be visiting (sb); **avoir de la ~** to have visitors; **heures de ~** (hôpital, prison) visiting hours

visiter [vizite] /1/ vt to visit; **visiteur, -euse** nm/f visitor

vison [vizɔ̃] nm mink

visser [vise] /1/ vt: **~ qch** (fixer, serrer) to screw sth on

visuel, le [vizɥɛl] adj visual

vital, e, -aux [vital, -o] adj vital

vitamine [vitamin] nf vitamin

vite [vit] adv (rapidement) quickly, fast; (sans délai) quickly; soon; **~!** quick!; **faire ~** to be quick

vitesse [vitɛs] nf speed; (Auto: dispositif) gear; **prendre de la ~** to pick up ou gather speed; **à toute ~** at full ou top speed; **en ~** quickly

⬤ **LIMITE DE VITESSE**
⬤
⬤ The speed limit in France is 50
⬤ km/h in built-up areas, 90 km/h
⬤ on main roads, and 130 km/h on
⬤ motorways (110 km/h when it is
⬤ raining).

viticulteur [vitikyltœʀ] nm wine grower
vitrage [vitʀaʒ] nm: **double ~** double glazing
vitrail, -aux [vitʀaj, -o] nm stained-glass window
vitre [vitʀ] nf (window) pane; (de portière, voiture) window; **vitré, e** adj glass cpd
vitrine [vitʀin] nf (shop) window; (petite armoire) display cabinet; **en ~** in the window
vivable [vivabl] adj (personne) livable-with; (maison) fit to live in
vivace [vivas] adj (arbre, plante) hardy; (fig) enduring
vivacité [vivasite] nf liveliness, vivacity
vivant, e [vivã, -ãt] adj (qui vit) living, alive; (animé) lively; (preuve, exemple) living ▷ nm: **du ~ de qn** in sb's lifetime; **les ~s et les morts** the living and the dead
vive [viv] adj f voir **vif** ▷ vb voir **vivre** ▷ excl: **~ le roi!** long live the king!; **vivement** adv sharply ▷ excl: **vivement les vacances!** roll on the holidays!
vivier [vivje] nm (au restaurant etc) fish tank; (étang) fishpond
vivifiant, e [vivifjã, -ãt] adj invigorating
vivoter [vivɔte] /1/ vi (personne) to scrape a living, get by; (fig: affaire etc) to struggle along

vivre [vivʀ] /46/ vi, vt to live; **vivres** nmpl provisions, food supplies; **il vit encore** he is still alive; **se laisser ~** to take life as it comes; **ne plus ~** (être anxieux) to live on one's nerves; **il a vécu** (eu une vie aventureuse) he has seen life; **être facile à ~** to be easy to get on with; **faire ~ qn** (pourvoir à sa subsistance) to provide (a living) for sb; **~ de** to live on
vlan [vlã] excl wham!, bang!
VO sigle f = **version originale**; **voir un film en VO** to see a film in its original language
vocabulaire [vɔkabylɛʀ] nm vocabulary
vocation [vɔkasjɔ̃] nf vocation, calling
vœu, x [vø] nm wish; (à Dieu) vow; **faire ~ de** to take a vow of; **avec tous nos ~x** with every good wish ou our best wishes
vogue [vɔg] nf fashion, vogue; **en ~** in fashion, in vogue
voici [vwasi] prép (pour introduire, désigner) here is (+ sg); here are (+ pl); **et ~ que ...** and now it (ou he) ...; voir aussi **voilà**
voie [vwa] nf way; (Rail) track, line; (Auto) lane; **par ~ buccale** ou **orale** orally; **être en bonne ~** to be shaping ou going well; **mettre qn sur la ~** to put sb on the right track; **être en ~ d'achèvement/de rénovation** to be nearing completion/in the process of renovation; **à ~ unique** single-track; **route à deux/trois ~s** two-/three-lane road; **~ express** expressway; **~ ferrée** track; railway line (BRIT), railroad (US); **~ de garage** (Rail) siding; **la ~ lactée** the Milky Way; **la ~ publique** the public highway
voilà [vwala] prép (en désignant) there is (+ sg); there are (+ pl); **les ~** ou **voici** here ou there they are; **en ~** ou **voici un** here's one, there's one; **voici mon frère et ~ ma sœur** this is my brother

V

and that's my sister; **~ ou voici deux ans** two years ago; **~ ou voici deux ans que** it's two years since; **et ~!** there we are!; **~ tout** that's all; **"~ ou voici"** (en offrant etc) "there ou here you are"; **tiens! ~ Paul** look! there's Paul

voile [vwal] *nm* veil; (*tissu léger*) net ▷ *nf* sail; (*sport*) sailing; **voiler** /1/ *vt* to veil; (*fausser: roue*) to buckle; (*: bois*) to warp; **se voiler** *vi* (*lune, regard*) to mist over; (*voix*) to become husky; (*roue, disque*) to buckle; (*planche*) to warp; **voilier** *nm* sailing ship; (*de plaisance*) sailing boat; **voilure** *nf* (*de voilier*) sails *pl*

voir [vwaʀ] /30/ *vi, vt* to see; **se voir: cela se voit** (*c'est visible*) that's obvious, it shows; **faire ~ qch à qn** to show sb sth; **en faire ~ à qn** (*fig*) to give sb a hard time; **ne pas pouvoir ~ qn** not to be able to stand sb; **voyons!** let's see now; (*indignation etc*) come (along) now!; **ça n'a rien à ~ avec lui** that has nothing to do with him

voire [vwaʀ] *adv* or even

voisin, e [vwazɛ̃, -in] *adj* (*proche*) neighbouring; next; (*ressemblant*) connected ▷ *nm/f* neighbour; **voisinage** *nm* (*proximité*) proximity; (*environs*) vicinity; (*quartier, voisins*) neighbourhood

voiture [vwatyʀ] *nf* car; (*wagon*) coach, carriage; **~ de course** racing car; **~ de sport** sports car

voix [vwa] *nf* voice; (*Pol*) vote; **à haute ~** aloud; **à ~ basse** in a low voice; **à deux/quatre ~** (*Mus*) in two/four parts; **avoir ~ au chapitre** to have a say in the matter

vol [vɔl] *nm* (*trajet, voyage, groupe d'oiseaux*) flight; (*mode d'appropriation*) theft, stealing; (*larcin*) theft; **à ~ d'oiseau** as the crow flies; **au ~: attraper qch au ~** to catch sth as it flies past; **en ~** in flight; **~ libre** hang-gliding; **~ à main armée** armed

robbery; **~ régulier** scheduled flight; **~ à voile** gliding

volage [vɔlaʒ] *adj* fickle

volaille [vɔlaj] *nf* (*oiseaux*) poultry *pl*; (*viande*) poultry *no pl*; (*oiseau*) fowl

volant, e [vɔlɑ̃, -ɑ̃t] *adj* flying ▷ *nm* (*d'automobile*) (steering) wheel; (*de commande*) wheel; (*objet lancé*) shuttlecock; (*bande de tissu*) flounce

volcan [vɔlkɑ̃] *nm* volcano

volée [vɔle] *nf* (*Tennis*) volley; **à la ~: rattraper à la ~** to catch in midair; **à toute ~** (*sonner les cloches*) vigorously; (*lancer un projectile*) with full force

voler [vɔle] /1/ *vi* (*avion, oiseau, fig*) to fly; (*voleur*) to steal ▷ *vt* (*objet*) to steal; (*personne*) to rob; **~ qch à qn** to steal sth from sb; **on m'a volé mon portefeuille** my wallet (*BRIT*) *ou* billfold (*US*) has been stolen; **il ne l'a pas volé!** he asked for it!

volet [vɔlɛ] *nm* (*de fenêtre*) shutter; (*Aviat*) flap; (*de feuillet, document*) section; (*fig: d'un plan*) facet

voleur, -euse [vɔlœʀ, -øz] *nm/f* thief ▷ *adj* thieving; **"au ~!"** "stop thief!"

volley [vɔlɛ], **volley-ball** [vɔlɛbol] *nm* volleyball

volontaire [vɔlɔ̃tɛʀ] *adj* (*acte, activité*) voluntary; (*délibéré*) deliberate; (*caractère, personne: décidé*) self-willed ▷ *nm/f* volunteer

volonté [vɔlɔ̃te] *nf* (*faculté de vouloir*) will; (*énergie, fermeté*) will(power); (*souhait, désir*) wish; **se servir/boire à ~** to take/drink as much as one likes; **bonne ~** goodwill, willingness; **mauvaise ~** lack of goodwill, unwillingness

volontiers [vɔlɔ̃tje] *adv* (*avec plaisir*) willingly, gladly; (*habituellement, souvent*) readily, willingly; **"~"** "with pleasure"

volt [vɔlt] *nm* volt

volte-face [vɔltəfas] *nf inv*: **faire ~** to do an about-turn

voltige [vɔltiʒ] *nf* (*Équitation*) trick riding; (*au cirque*) acrobatics *sg*;

voltiger [vɔltiʒe] /3/ *vi* to flutter (about)

volubile [vɔlybil] *adj* voluble

volume [vɔlym] *nm* volume; (*Géom: solide*) solid; **volumineux, -euse** *adj* voluminous, bulky

volupté [vɔlypte] *nf* sensual delight *ou* pleasure

vomi [vɔmi] *nm* vomit; **vomir** /2/ *vi* to vomit, be sick ▷ *vt* to vomit, bring up; (*fig*) to belch out, spew out; (*exécrer*) to loathe, abhor

vorace [vɔʀas] *adj* voracious

vos [vo] *adj poss voir* **votre**

vote [vɔt] *nm* vote; **~ par correspondance/procuration** postal/proxy vote; **voter** [vɔte] /1/ *vi* to vote ▷ *vt* (*loi, décision*) to vote for

votre [vɔtʀ] (*pl* **vos**) *adj poss* your

vôtre [votʀ] *pron*: **le ~, la ~, les ~s** yours; **les ~s** (*fig*) your family *ou* folks; **à la ~** (*toast*) your (good) health!

vouer [vwe] /1/ *vt*: **~ sa vie/son temps à** (*étude, cause etc*) to devote one's life/time to; **~ une haine/ amitié éternelle à qn** to vow undying hatred/friendship to sb

○ **MOT-CLÉ**

vouloir [vulwaʀ] /31/ *vt* **1** (*exiger, désirer*) to want; **vouloir faire/ que qn fasse** to want to do/sb to do; **voulez-vous du thé?** would you like *ou* do you want some tea?; **que me veut-il?** what does he want with me?; **sans le vouloir** (*involontairement*) without meaning to, unintentionally; **je voudrais ceci/faire** I would *ou* I'd like this/to do; **le hasard a voulu que …** as fate would have it, …; **la tradition veut que …** tradition demands that … **2** (*consentir*): **je veux bien** (*bonne volonté*) I'll be happy to; (*concession*) fair enough, that's fine; **oui, si on veut** (*en quelque sorte*) yes, if you like; **veuillez attendre** please

wait; **veuillez agréer …** (*formule épistolaire*) yours faithfully

3: **en vouloir à qn** to bear sb a grudge; **s'en vouloir (de)** to be annoyed with o.s. (for); **il en veut à mon argent** he's after my money

4: **vouloir de: l'entreprise ne veut plus de lui** the firm doesn't want him any more; **elle ne veut pas de son aide** she doesn't want his help

5: **vouloir dire** to mean

▷ *nm*: **le bon vouloir de qn** sb's goodwill; sb's pleasure

voulu, e [vuly] *pp de* **vouloir** ▷ *adj* (*requis*) required, requisite; (*délibéré*) deliberate, intentional

vous [vu] *pron* you; (*objet indirect*) (to) you; (*réfléchi: sg*) yourself; (*: pl*) yourselves; (*réciproque*) each other ▷ *nm*: **employer le ~** (*vouvoyer*) to use the "vous" form; **~-même** yourself; **~-mêmes** yourselves

vouvoyer [vuvwaje] /8/ *vt*: **~ qn** to address sb as "vous"

voyage [vwajaʒ] *nm* journey, trip; (*fait de voyager*): **le ~** travel(ling); **partir/être en ~** to go off/be away on a journey *ou* trip; **faire bon ~** to have a good journey; **~ d'agrément/ d'affaires** pleasure/business trip; **~ de noces** honeymoon; **~ organisé** package tour

voyager [vwajaʒe] /3/ *vi* to travel; **voyageur, -euse** *nm/f* traveller; (*passager*) passenger; **voyageur (de commerce)** commercial traveller

voyant, e [vwajɑ̃, -ɑ̃t] *adj* (*couleur*) loud, gaudy ▷ *nm* (*signal*) (warning) light

voyelle [vwajɛl] *nf* vowel

voyou [vwaju] *nm* hoodlum

vrac [vʀak] : **en ~** *adv* loose; (*Comm*) in bulk

vrai, e [vʀɛ] *adj* (*véridique: récit, faits*) true; (*non factice, authentique*) real; **à ~ dire** to tell the truth; **vraiment** *adv* really;

vraisemblable adj likely; (excuse) plausible; **vraisemblablement** adv in all likelihood, very likely; **vraisemblance** nf likelihood; (romanesque) verisimilitude

vrombir [vʀɔ̃biʀ] /2/ vi to hum

VRP sigle m (= voyageur, représentant, placier) (sales) rep (fam)

VTT sigle m (= vélo tout-terrain) mountain bike

vu¹ [vy] prép (en raison de) in view of; **vu que** in view of the fact that

vu², e [vy] pp de **voir** ▷ adj: **bien/mal vu** (personne) well/poorly thought of

vue [vy] nf (sens, faculté) (eye)sight; (panorama, image, photo) view; **la ~ de** (spectacle) the sight of; **vues** nfpl (idées) views; (dessein) designs; **perdre la ~** to lose one's (eye)sight; **perdre de ~** to lose sight of; **hors de ~** out of sight; **à première ~** at first sight; **tirer à ~** to shoot on sight; **à ~ d'œil** visibly; **avoir ~ sur** to have a view of; **en ~** (visible) in sight; (célèbre) in the public eye; **en ~ de faire** with a view to doing; **~ d'ensemble** overall view

vulgaire [vylgɛʀ] adj (grossier) vulgar, coarse; (trivial) commonplace, mundane; (péj: quelconque): **de ~s touristes/chaises de cuisine** common tourists/kitchen chairs; (Bot, Zool: non latin) common; **vulgariser** /1/ vt to popularize

vulnérable [vylneʀabl] adj vulnerable

W

wagon [vagɔ̃] nm (de voyageurs) carriage; (de marchandises) truck, wagon; **wagon-lit** nm sleeper, sleeping car; **wagon-restaurant** nm restaurant ou dining car

wallon, ne [walɔ̃, -ɔn] adj Walloon ▷ nm (Ling) Walloon ▷ nm/f: **W~, ne** Walloon

watt [wat] nm watt

WC [vese] nmpl toilet sg

Web [wɛb] nm inv: **le ~** the (World Wide) Web; **webcam** nf webcam; **webmaster, webmestre** nm/f webmaster

week-end [wikɛnd] nm weekend

western [wɛstɛʀn] nm western

whisky [wiski] (pl **whiskies**) nm whisky

wifi [wifi] nm inv wifi

WWW sigle m (= World Wide Web) WWW

xénophobe [gzenɔfɔb] *adj*
xenophobic ▷ *nm/f* xenophobe
xérès [gzeʀɛs] *nm* sherry
xylophone [gzilɔfɔn] *nm* xylophone

y [i] *adv (à cet endroit)* there; *(dessus)* on
it *(ou them)*; *(dedans)* in it *(ou them)*
▷ *pron* (about *ou* on *ou* of) it *(vérifier la
syntaxe du verbe employé)*; **j'y pense**
I'm thinking about it; **ça y est!** that's
it!; *voir aussi* **aller, avoir**
yacht [jɔt] *nm* yacht
yaourt [jauʀt] *nm* yogurt; **~ nature/
aux fruits** plain/fruit yogurt
yeux [jø] *nmpl de* **œil**
yoga [jɔga] *nm* yoga
yoghourt [jɔguʀt] *nm* = **yaourt**
yougoslave [jugɔslav] *adj*
Yugoslav(ian) ▷ *nm/f*: **Y~**
Yugoslav(ian)
Yougoslavie [jugɔslavi] *nf*: **la
~** Yugoslavia; **l'ex-~** the former
Yugoslavia

Z

zone [zon] *nf* zone, area;
(*quartiers pauvres*): **la ~** the slums;
~ bleue ≈ restricted parking area;
~ industrielle (ZI) industrial estate
zoo [zoo] *nm* zoo
zoologie [zɔɔlɔʒi] *nf* zoology;
zoologique *adj* zoological
zut [zyt] *excl* dash (it)! (*BRIT*), nuts!
(*US*)

zapper [zape] /1/ *vi* to zap
zapping [zapiŋ] *nm*: **faire du ~** to
flick through the channels
zèbre [zɛbʀ] *nm* (*Zool*) zebra; **zébré, e**
adj striped, streaked
zèle [zɛl] *nm* zeal; **faire du ~** (*péj*) to
be over-zealous; **zélé, e** *adj* zealous
zéro [zeʀo] *nm* zero, nought (*BRIT*);
au-dessous de ~ below zero
(Centigrade), below freezing; **partir
de ~** to start from scratch; **trois
(buts) à ~** three (goals to) nil
zeste [zɛst] *nm* peel, zest
zézayer [zezeje] /8/ *vi* to have a lisp
zigzag [zigzag] *nm* zigzag; **zigzaguer**
/1/ *vi* to zigzag (along)
Zimbabwe [zimbabwe] *nm*: **le ~**
Zimbabwe
zinc [zɛ̃g] *nm* (*Chimie*) zinc
zipper [zipe] /1/ *vt* (*Inform*) to zip
zizi [zizi] *nm* (*fam*) willy
zodiaque [zɔdjak] *nm* zodiac
zona [zona] *nm* shingles *sg*

A [eɪ] n (Mus) la m

KEYWORD

a [eɪ, ə] (before vowel and silent h **an**)
indef art **1** un(e); **a book** un livre; **an
apple** une pomme; **she's a doctor**
elle est médecin
2 (instead of the number "one") un(e);
a year ago il y a un an; **a hundred/
thousand** etc **pounds** cent/mille
etc livres
3 (in expressing ratios, prices etc): **three
a day/week** trois par jour/semaine;
10 km an hour 10 km à l'heure; **£5 a
person** 5£ par personne; **30p a kilo**
30p le kilo

A2 n (BRIT Scol) deuxième partie de
l'examen équivalent au baccalauréat

A.A. n abbr (BRIT: = Automobile
Association) ≈ ACF m; (= Alcoholics
Anonymous) AA

A.A.A. n abbr (= American Automobile
Association) ≈ ACF m

aback [ə'bæk] adv: **to be taken ~**
être déconcertané(e)

abandon [ə'bændən] vt abandonner

abattoir ['æbətwɑː'] n (BRIT)
abattoir m

abbey ['æbɪ] n abbaye f

abbreviation [əbriːvɪ'eɪʃən] n
abréviation f

abdomen ['æbdəmən] n abdomen m

abduct [æb'dʌkt] vt enlever

abide [ə'baɪd] vt souffrir, supporter; **I
can't ~ it/him** je ne le supporte pas;
abide by vt fus observer, respecter

ability [ə'bɪlɪtɪ] n compétence f;
capacité f; (skill) talent m

able ['eɪbl] adj compétent(e); **to be
~ to do sth** pouvoir faire qch, être
capable de faire qch

abnormal [æb'nɔːməl] adj
anormal(e)

aboard [ə'bɔːd] adv à bord ▷ prep à
bord de; (train) dans

abolish [ə'bɔlɪʃ] vt abolir

abolition [æbə'lɪʃən] n abolition f

abort [ə'bɔːt] vt (Med) faire avorter;
(Comput, fig) abandonner; **abortion**
[ə'bɔːʃən] n avortement m; **to have
an abortion** se faire avorter

KEYWORD

about [ə'baut] adv **1** (approximately)
environ, à peu près; **about a
hundred/thousand** etc environ
cent/mille etc, une centaine (de)/
un millier (de) etc; **it takes about 10
hours** ça prend environ or à peu près
10 heures; **at about 2 o'clock** vers
2 heures; **I've just about finished** j'ai
presque fini
2 (referring to place) çà et là, de-ci
de-là; **to run about** courir çà et là;
to walk about se promener, aller
et venir; **they left all their things
lying about** ils ont laissé traîner
toutes leurs affaires

3: **to be about to do sth** être sur le
point de faire qch
▶ *prep* **1** (*relating to*) au sujet de, à
propos de; **a book about London** un
livre sur Londres; **what is it about?**
de quoi s'agit-il?; **we talked about
it** nous en avons parlé; **what** or
how about doing this? et si nous
faisions ceci?
2 (*referring to place*) dans; **to walk
about the town** se promener dans
la ville

above [ə'bʌv] *adv* au-dessus ▷ *prep*
au-dessus de; (*more than*) plus de;
mentioned ~ mentionné ci-dessus;
~ all par-dessus tout, surtout
abroad [ə'brɔːd] *adv* à l'étranger
abrupt [ə'brʌpt] *adj* (*steep, blunt*)
abrupt(e); (*sudden, gruff*) brusque
abscess ['æbsɪs] *n* abcès *m*
absence ['æbsəns] *n* absence *f*
absent ['æbsənt] *adj* absent(e);
absent-minded *adj* distrait(e)
absolute ['æbsəluːt] *adj* absolu(e);
absolutely [æbsə'luːtlɪ] *adv*
absolument
absorb [əb'zɔːb] *vt* absorber; **to be
~ed in a book** être plongé(e) dans
un livre; **absorbent cotton** *n* (*US*)
coton *m* hydrophile; **absorbing**
adj absorbant(e); (*book, film etc*)
captivant(e)
abstain [əb'steɪn] *vi*: **to ~ (from)**
s'abstenir (de)
abstract ['æbstrækt] *adj* abstrait(e)
absurd [əb'səːd] *adj* absurde
abundance [ə'bʌndəns] *n*
abondance *f*
abundant [ə'bʌndənt] *adj*
abondant(e)
abuse *n* [ə'bjuːs] (*insults*) insultes
fpl, injures *fpl*; (*ill-treatment*) mauvais
traitements *mpl*; (*of power etc*) abus
m ▷ *vt* [ə'bjuːz] (*insult*) insulter; (*ill-
treat*) malmener; (*power etc*) abuser
de; **abusive** *adj* grossier(-ière),
injurieux(-euse)

abysmal [ə'bɪzməl] *adj* exécrable;
(*ignorance etc*) sans bornes
academic [ækə'dɛmɪk] *adj*
universitaire; (*person: scholarly*)
intellectuel(le); (*pej: issue*)
oiseux(-euse), purement théorique
▷ *n* universitaire *m/f*; **academic year**
n (*University*) année *f* universitaire;
(*Scol*) année scolaire
academy [ə'kædəmɪ] *n* (*learned body*)
académie *f*; (*school*) collège *m*; **~ of
music** conservatoire *m*
accelerate [æk'sɛləreɪt] *vt*,
vi accélérer; **acceleration**
[æksɛlə'reɪʃən] *n* accélération *f*;
accelerator *n* (*BRIT*) accélérateur *m*
accent ['æksɛnt] *n* accent *m*
accept [ək'sɛpt] *vt* accepter;
acceptable *adj* acceptable;
acceptance *n* acceptation *f*
access ['æksɛs] *n* accès *m*; **to have
~ to** (*information, library etc*) avoir
accès à, pouvoir utiliser or consulter;
(*person*) avoir accès auprès de;
accessible [æk'sɛsəbl] *adj* accessible
accessory [æk'sɛsərɪ] *n* accessoire
m; **~ to** (*Law*) accessoire à
accident ['æksɪdənt] *n* accident
m; (*chance*) hasard *m*; **I've had
an ~** j'ai eu un accident; **by ~** (*by
chance*) par hasard; (*not deliberately*)
accidentellement; **accidental**
[æksɪ'dɛntl] *adj* accidentel(le);
accidentally [æksɪ'dɛntəlɪ] *adv*
accidentellement; **Accident and
Emergency Department** *n* (*BRIT*)
service *m* des urgences; **accident
insurance** *n* assurance *f* accident
acclaim [ə'kleɪm] *vt* acclamer ▷ *n*
acclamations *fpl*
accommodate [ə'kɔmədeɪt] *vt*
loger, recevoir; (*oblige, help*) obliger;
(*car etc*) contenir
accommodation,
(*US*) **accommodations**
[əkɔmə'deɪʃən(z)] *n*, *npl* logement *m*
accompaniment [ə'kʌmpənɪmənt]
n accompagnement *m*

accompany [ə'kʌmpənɪ] *vt*
accompagner

accomplice [ə'kʌmplɪs] *n* complice
m/f

accomplish [ə'kʌmplɪʃ] *vt* accomplir;
accomplishment *n* (*skill: gen pl*) talent
m; (*completion*) accomplissement *m*;
(*achievement*) réussite *f*

accord [ə'kɔːd] *n* accord *m* ▷ *vt*
accorder; **of his own ~** de son
plein gré; **accordance** *n*: **in
accordance with** conformément
à; **according: according to** *prep*
selon; **accordingly** *adv* (*appropriately*)
en conséquence; (*as a result*) par
conséquent

account [ə'kaunt] *n* (*Comm*)
compte *m*; (*report*) compte rendu,
récit *m*; (*completion*) accomplissement
records) comptabilité *f*, comptes;
of no ~ sans importance; **on ~** en
acompte; **to buy sth on ~** acheter
qch à crédit; **on no ~** en aucun cas;
on ~ of à cause de; **to take into ~,
take ~ of** tenir compte de; **account
for** *vt fus* (*explain*) expliquer, rendre
compte de; (*represent*) représenter;
accountable *adj*: **accountable
(for/to)** responsable (de/devant);
accountant *n* comptable *m/f*;
account number *n* numéro *m* de
compte

accumulate [ə'kjuːmjuleɪt] *vt*
accumuler, amasser ▷ *vi* s'accumuler,
s'amasser

accuracy ['ækjurəsɪ] *n* exactitude
f, précision *f*

accurate ['ækjurɪt] *adj* exact(e),
précis(e); (*device*) précis; **accurately**
adv avec précision

accusation [ækju'zeɪʃən] *n*
accusation *f*

accuse [ə'kjuːz] *vt*: **to ~ sb (of sth)**
accuser qn (de qch); **accused** *n* (*Law*)
accusé(e)

accustomed [ə'kʌstəmd] *adj*: **~ to**
habitué(e) *or* accoutumé(e) à

ace [eɪs] *n* as *m*

ache [eɪk] *n* mal *m*, douleur
f ▷ *vi* (*be sore*) faire mal, être
douloureux(-euse); **my head ~s**
j'ai mal à la tête

achieve [ə'tʃiːv] *vt* (*aim*) atteindre;
(*victory, success*) remporter, obtenir;
achievement *n* exploit *m*, réussite *f*;
(*of aims*) réalisation *f*

acid ['æsɪd] *adj*, *n* acide (*m*)

acknowledge [ək'nɔlɪdʒ] *vt*
(*also*: **~ receipt of**) accuser
réception de; (*fact*) reconnaître;
acknowledgement *n* (*of letter*)
accusé *m* de réception

acne ['æknɪ] *n* acné *m*

acorn ['eɪkɔːn] *n* gland *m*

acoustic [ə'kuːstɪk] *adj* acoustique

acquaintance [ə'kweɪntəns] *n*
connaissance *f*

acquire [ə'kwaɪər] *vt* acquérir;
acquisition [ækwɪ'zɪʃən] *n*
acquisition *f*

acquit [ə'kwɪt] *vt* acquitter; **to ~ o.s.
well** s'en tirer très honorablement

acre ['eɪkər] *n* acre *f* (= 4047 m²)

acronym ['ækrənɪm] *n* acronyme *m*

across [ə'krɔs] *prep* (*on the other
side*) de l'autre côté de; (*crosswise*) en
travers de ▷ *adv* de l'autre côté; en
travers; **to run/swim ~** traverser en
courant/à la nage; **~ from** en face de

acrylic [ə'krɪlɪk] *adj*, *n* acrylique (*m*)

act [ækt] *n* acte *m*, action *f*; (*Theat:
part of play*) acte; (: *of performer*)
numéro *m*; (*Law*) loi *f* ▷ *vi* agir; (*Theat*)
jouer; (*pretend*) jouer la comédie ▷ *vt*
(*role*) jouer, tenir; **to catch sb in the
~** prendre qn sur le fait *or* en flagrant
délit; **to ~ as** servir de qn; **act up** (*inf*) *vi*
(*person*) se conduire mal; (*knee, back,
injury*) jouer des tours; (*machine*)
être capricieux(-ieuse); **acting**
adj suppléant(e), par intérim ▷ *n*
(*activity*): **to do some acting** faire du
théâtre (*or* du cinéma)

action ['ækʃən] *n* action *f*; (*Mil*)
combat(s) *m(pl)*; (*Law*) procès *m*,
action en justice; **out of ~** hors de

combat; (*machine etc*) hors d'usage; **to take ~** agir, prendre des mesures; **action replay** *n* (BRIT TV) ralenti *m*

activate ['æktɪveɪt] *vt* (*mechanism*) actionner, faire fonctionner

active ['æktɪv] *adj* actif(-ive); (*volcano*) en activité; **actively** *adv* activement; (*discourage*) vivement

activist ['æktɪvɪst] *n* activiste *m/f*

activity [æk'tɪvɪtɪ] *n* activité *f*; **activity holiday** *n* vacances actives

actor ['æktər] *n* acteur *m*

actress ['æktrɪs] *n* actrice *f*

actual ['æktjʊəl] *adj* réel(le), véritable; (*emphatic use*) lui-même (elle-même)

> Be careful not to translate *actual* by the French word *actuel*.

actually ['æktjʊəlɪ] *adv* réellement, véritablement; (*in fact*) en fait

> Be careful not to translate *actually* by the French word *actuellement*.

acupuncture ['ækjupʌŋktʃər] *n* acuponcture *f*

acute [ə'kjuːt] *adj* aigu(ë); (*mind, observer*) pénétrant(e)

ad [æd] *n abbr* = **advertisement**

A.D. *adv abbr* (= *Anno Domini*) ap. J.-C.

adamant ['ædəmənt] *adj* inflexible

adapt [ə'dæpt] *vt* adapter ▷ *vi*: **to ~ (to)** s'adapter (à); **adapter, adaptor** *n* (*Elec*) adaptateur *m*; (*for several plugs*) prise *f* multiple

add [æd] *vt* ajouter; (*figures: also*: **to ~ up**) additionner; **it doesn't ~ up** (*fig*) cela ne rime à rien; **add up to** *vt fus* (*Math*) s'élever à; (*fig: mean*) signifier

addict ['ædɪkt] *n* toxicomane *m/f*; (*fig*) fanatique *m/f*; **addicted** [ə'dɪktɪd] *adj*: **to be addicted to** (*drink, drugs*) être adonné(e) à; (*fig: football etc*) être un(e) fanatique de; **addiction** [ə'dɪkʃən] *n* (*Med*) dépendance *f*; **addictive** [ə'dɪktɪv] *adj* qui crée une dépendance

addition [ə'dɪʃən] *n* (*adding up*) addition *f*; (*thing added*) ajout *m*; **in ~**

de plus, de surcroît; **in ~ to** en plus de; **additional** *adj* supplémentaire

additive ['ædɪtɪv] *n* additif *m*

address [ə'drɛs] *n* adresse *f*; (*talk*) discours *m*, allocution *f* ▷ *vt* adresser; (*speak to*) s'adresser à; **my ~ is ...** mon adresse, c'est ...; **address book** *n* carnet *m* d'adresses

adequate ['ædɪkwɪt] *adj* (*enough*) suffisant(e); (*satisfactory*) satisfaisant(e)

adhere [əd'hɪər] *vi*: **to ~ to** adhérer à; (*fig: rule, decision*) se tenir à

adhesive [əd'hiːzɪv] *n* adhésif *m*; **adhesive tape** *n* (BRIT) ruban *m* adhésif; (US Med) sparadrap *m*

adjacent [ə'dʒeɪsənt] *adj* adjacent(e), contigu(ë); **~ to** adjacent à

adjective ['ædʒɛktɪv] *n* adjectif *m*

adjoining [ə'dʒɔɪnɪŋ] *adj* voisin(e), adjacent(e), attenant(e)

adjourn [ə'dʒəːn] *vt* ajourner ▷ *vi* suspendre la séance; lever la séance; clore la session

adjust [ə'dʒʌst] *vt* (*machine*) ajuster, régler; (*prices, wages*) rajuster ▷ *vi*: **to ~ (to)** s'adapter (à); **adjustable** *adj* réglable; **adjustment** *n* (*of machine*) ajustage *m*, réglage *m*; (*of prices, wages*) rajustement *m*; (*of person*) adaptation *f*

administer [əd'mɪnɪstər] *vt* administrer; **administration** [ədmɪnɪs'treɪʃən] *n* (*management*) administration *f*; (*government*) gouvernement *m*; **administrative** [əd'mɪnɪstrətɪv] *adj* administratif(-ive)

administrator [əd'mɪnɪstreɪtər] *n* administrateur(-trice)

admiral ['ædmərəl] *n* amiral *m*

admiration [ædmə'reɪʃən] *n* admiration *f*

admire [əd'maɪər] *vt* admirer; **admirer** *n* (*fan*) admirateur(-trice)

admission [əd'mɪʃən] *n* admission *f*; (*to exhibition, night club etc*) entrée *f*; (*confession*) aveu *m*

admit [əd'mɪt] vt laisser entrer;
admettre; (agree) reconnaître,
admettre; (crime) reconnaître avoir
commis; **"children not ~ted"** "entrée
interdite aux enfants"; **admit to** vt
fus reconnaître, avouer; **admittance**
n admission f, (droit m d')entrée f;
admittedly adv il faut en convenir

adolescent [ædəu'lɛsnt] adj, n
adolescent(e)

adopt [ə'dɔpt] vt adopter; **adopted**
adj adoptif(-ive), adopté(e); **adoption**
[ə'dɔpʃən] n adoption f

adore [ə'dɔːʳ] vt adorer

adorn [ə'dɔːn] vt orner

Adriatic (Sea) [eɪdrɪ'ætɪk-] n: **the
Adriatic (Sea)** la mer Adriatique,
l'Adriatique f

adrift [ə'drɪft] adv à la dérive

ADSL n abbr (= asymmetric digital
subscriber line) ADSL m

adult ['ædʌlt] n adulte m/f ▷ adj
(grown-up) adulte; (for adults)
pour adultes; **adult education** n
éducation f des adultes

adultery [ə'dʌltərɪ] n adultère m

advance [əd'vɑːns] n avance f
▷ vt avancer ▷ vi s'avancer; **in ~** en
avance, d'avance; **to make ~s to
sb** (amorously) faire des avances à
qn; **~ booking** location f; **~ notice,
~ warning** préavis m; (verbal)
avertissement m; **do I need to
book in ~?** est-ce qu'il faut réserver à
l'avance?; **advanced** adj avancé(e);
(Scol: studies) supérieur(e)

advantage [əd'vɑːntɪdʒ] n (also
Tennis) avantage m; **to take ~ of**
(person) exploiter; (opportunity)
profiter de

advent ['ædvənt] n avènement m,
venue f; **A~** (Rel) avent m

adventure [əd'vɛntʃəʳ] n aventure
f; **adventurous** [əd'vɛntʃərəs] adj
aventureux(-euse)

adverb ['ædvəːb] n adverbe m

adversary ['ædvəsərɪ] n adversaire
m/f

adverse ['ædvəːs] adj adverse; (effect)
négatif(-ive); (weather, publicity)
mauvais(e); (wind) contraire

advert ['ædvəːt] n abbr (BRIT)
= **advertisement**

advertise ['ædvətaɪz] vi faire de la
publicité or de la réclame; (in classified
ads etc) mettre une annonce ▷ vt faire
de la publicité or de la réclame pour; (in
classified ads etc) mettre une annonce
pour vendre; **to ~ for** (staff) recruter
par (voie d')annonce; **advertisement**
[əd'vəːtɪsmənt] n publicité f, réclame
f; (in classified ads etc) annonce
f; **advertiser** n annonceur m;
advertising n publicité f

advice [əd'vaɪs] n conseils mpl;
(notification) avis m; **a piece of ~**
un conseil; **to take legal ~** consulter
un avocat

advisable [əd'vaɪzəbl] adj
recommandable, indiqué(e)

advise [əd'vaɪz] vt conseiller; **to
~ sb of sth** aviser or informer qn
de qch; **to ~ against sth/doing
sth** déconseiller qch/conseiller de
ne pas faire qch; **adviser, advisor**
n conseiller(-ère); **advisory** adj
consultatif(-ive)

advocate n ['ædvəkɪt] (lawyer)
avocat (plaidant); (upholder)
défenseur m, avocat(e) ▷ vt
['ædvəkeɪt] recommander, prôner;
to be an ~ of être partisan(e) de

Aegean [iː'dʒiːən] n, adj: **the ~ (Sea)**
la mer Égée, l'Égée f

aerial ['ɛərɪəl] n antenne f ▷ adj
aérien(ne)

aerobics [ɛə'rəubɪks] n aérobic m

aeroplane ['ɛərəpleɪn] n (BRIT)
avion m

aerosol ['ɛərəsɔl] n aérosol m

affair [ə'fɛəʳ] n affaire f; (also: **love ~**)
liaison f; aventure f

affect [ə'fɛkt] vt affecter; (subj:
disease) atteindre; **affected** adj
affecté(e); **affection** n affection f;
affectionate adj affectueux(-euse)

afflict [əˈflɪkt] vt affliger

affluent [ˈæfluənt] adj aisé(e), riche; **the ~ society** la société d'abondance

afford [əˈfɔːd] vt (behaviour) se permettre; (provide) fournir, procurer; **can we ~ a car?** avons-nous de quoi acheter or les moyens d'acheter une voiture?; **affordable** adj abordable

Afghanistan [æfˈgænɪstæn] n Afghanistan m

afraid [əˈfreɪd] adj effrayé(e); **to be ~ of or to** avoir peur de; **I am ~ that** je crains que + sub; **I'm ~ so/not** oui/non, malheureusement

Africa [ˈæfrɪkə] n Afrique f; **African** adj africain(e) ▷ n Africain(e); **African-American** adj afro-américain(e) ▷ n Afro-Américain(e)

after [ˈɑːftər] prep, adv après ▷ conj après que; **it's quarter ~ two** (us) il est deux heures et quart; **~ having done/~ he left** après avoir fait/après son départ; **to name sb ~ sb** donner à qn le nom de qn; **to ask ~ sb** demander des nouvelles de qn; **what/who are you ~?** que/qui cherchez-vous?; **~ you!** après vous!; **~ all** après tout; **after-effects** npl (of disaster, radiation, drink etc) répercussions fpl; (of illness) séquelles fpl, suites fpl; **aftermath** n conséquences fpl; **afternoon** n après-midi m/f; **after-shave (lotion)** n lotion f après-rasage; **aftersun (cream/lotion)** n après-soleil m inv; **afterwards**, (us) **afterward** [ˈɑːftəwəd(z)] adv après

again [əˈgɛn] adv de nouveau, encore (une fois); **to do sth ~** refaire qch; **~ and ~** à plusieurs reprises

against [əˈgɛnst] prep contre; (compared to) par rapport à

age [eɪdʒ] n âge m ▷ vt, vi vieillir; **he is 20 years of ~** il a 20 ans; **to come of ~** atteindre sa majorité; **it's been ~s since I saw you** ça fait une éternité que je ne t'ai pas vu

aged adj âgé(e); **~ 10** âgé de 10 ans

age: age group n tranche f d'âge; **age limit** n limite f d'âge

agency [ˈeɪdʒənsɪ] n agence f

agenda [əˈdʒɛndə] n ordre m du jour
▌Be careful not to translate agenda by the French word agenda.

agent [ˈeɪdʒənt] n agent m; (firm) concessionnaire m

aggravate [ˈægrəveɪt] vt (situation) aggraver; (annoy) exaspérer, agacer

aggression [əˈgrɛʃən] n agression f

aggressive [əˈgrɛsɪv] adj agressif(-ive)

agile [ˈædʒaɪl] adj agile

AGM n abbr (= annual general meeting) AG f

ago [əˈgəu] adv: **two days ~** il y a deux jours; **not long ~** il n'y a pas longtemps; **how long ~?** il y a combien de temps (de cela)?

agony [ˈægənɪ] n (pain) douleur f atroce; (distress) angoisse f; **to be in ~** souffrir le martyre

agree [əˈgriː] vt (price) convenir de ▷ vi: **to ~ with** (person) être d'accord avec; (statements etc) concorder avec; (Ling) s'accorder avec; **to ~ to do** accepter de or consentir à faire; **to ~ to sth** consentir à qch; **to ~ that** (admit) convenir or reconnaître que; **garlic doesn't ~ with me** je ne supporte pas l'ail; **agreeable** adj (pleasant) agréable; (willing) consentant(e), d'accord; **agreed** adj (time, place) convenu(e); **agreement** n accord m; **in agreement** d'accord

agricultural [ægrɪˈkʌltʃərəl] adj agricole

agriculture [ˈægrɪkʌltʃər] n agriculture f

ahead [əˈhɛd] adv en avant; devant; **go right or straight ~** (direction) allez tout droit; **go ~!** (permission) allez-y!; **~ of** devant; (fig: schedule etc) en avance sur; **~ of time** en avance

aid [eɪd] n aide f; (device) appareil m ▷ vt aider; **in ~ of** en faveur de

aide [eɪd] n (person) assistant(e)

AIDS [eɪdz] n abbr (= acquired immune (or immuno-)deficiency syndrome) SIDA m

ailing ['eɪlɪŋ] adj (person) souffreteux(euse); (economy) malade

ailment ['eɪlmənt] n affection f

aim [eɪm] n (objective) but m; (skill): **his ~ is bad** il vise mal ▷ vi (also: **to take ~**) viser ▷ vt: **to ~ sth (at)** (gun, camera) braquer or pointer qch (sur); (missile) lancer qch (à or contre or en direction de); (remark, blow) destiner or adresser qch (à); **to ~ at** viser; (fig) viser (à); **to ~ to do** avoir l'intention de faire

ain't [eɪnt] (inf) = **am not**; **aren't**; **isn't**

air [eəʳ] n air m ▷ vt aérer; (idea, grievance, views) mettre sur le tapis ▷ cpd (currents, attack etc) aérien(ne); **to throw sth into the ~** (ball etc) jeter qch en l'air; **by ~** par avion; **to be on the ~** (Radio, TV: programme) être diffusé(e); (: station) émettre; **airbag** n airbag m; **airbed** n (BRIT) matelas m pneumatique; **airborne** adj (plane) en vol; **as soon as the plane was airborne** dès que l'avion eut décollé; **air-conditioned** adj climatisé(e), à air conditionné; **air conditioning** n climatisation f; **aircraft** n inv avion m; **airfield** n terrain m d'aviation; **Air Force** n Armée f de l'air; **air hostess** n (BRIT) hôtesse f de l'air; **airing cupboard** n (BRIT) placard qui contient la chaudière et dans lequel on met le linge à sécher; **airlift** n pont aérien; **airline** n ligne aérienne, compagnie aérienne; **airliner** n avion m de ligne; **airmail** n: **by airmail** par avion; **airplane** n (US) avion m; **airport** n aéroport m; **air raid** n attaque aérienne; **airsick** adj: **to be airsick** avoir le mal de l'air; **airspace** n espace m aérien; **airstrip** n terrain m d'atterrissage; **air terminal** n aérogare f; **airtight** adj hermétique; **air-traffic controller** n aiguilleur m du ciel; **airy** adj bien aéré(e); (manners) dégagé(e)

aisle [aɪl] n (of church: central) allée f centrale; (: side) nef f latérale, bas-côté m; (in theatre, supermarket) allée; (on plane) couloir m; **aisle seat** n place f côté couloir

ajar [ə'dʒɑːʳ] adj entrouvert(e)

à la carte [ælæ'kɑːt] adv à la carte

alarm [ə'lɑːm] n alarme f ▷ vt alarmer; **alarm call** n coup m de fil pour réveiller; **could I have an alarm call at 7 am, please?** pouvez-vous me réveiller à 7 heures, s'il vous plaît?; **alarm clock** n réveille-matin m inv, réveil m; **alarmed** adj (frightened) alarmé(e); (protected by an alarm) protégé(e) par un système d'alarme; **alarming** adj alarmant(e)

Albania [æl'beɪnɪə] n Albanie f

albeit [ɔːl'biːɪt] conj bien que + sub, encore que + sub

album ['ælbəm] n album m

alcohol ['ælkəhɔl] n alcool m; **alcohol-free** adj sans alcool; **alcoholic** [ælkə'hɔlɪk] adj, n alcoolique (m/f)

alcove ['ælkəuv] n alcôve f

ale [eɪl] n bière f

alert [ə'ləːt] adj alerte, vif (vive); (watchful) vigilant(e) ▷ n alerte f ▷ vt alerter; **on the ~** sur le qui-vive; (Mil) en état d'alerte

algebra ['ældʒɪbrə] n algèbre m

Algeria [æl'dʒɪərɪə] n Algérie f

Algerian [æl'dʒɪərɪən] adj algérien(ne) ▷ n Algérien(ne)

Algiers [æl'dʒɪəz] n Alger

alias ['eɪlɪəs] adv alias ▷ n faux nom, nom d'emprunt

alibi ['ælɪbaɪ] n alibi m

alien ['eɪlɪən] n (from abroad) étranger(-ère); (from outer space) extraterrestre ▷ adj: **~ (to)** étranger(-ère) (à); **alienate** vt aliéner; (subj: person) s'aliéner

alight [ə'laɪt] adj en feu ▷ vi mettre pied à terre; (passenger) descendre; (bird) se poser

align [ə'laɪn] vt aligner

alike [ə'laɪk] *adj* semblable, pareil(le) ▷ *adv* de même; **to look ~** se ressembler

alive [ə'laɪv] *adj* vivant(e); (*active*) plein(e) de vie

 KEYWORD

all [ɔːl] *adj* (*singular*) tout(e); (*plural*) tous (toutes); **all day** toute la journée; **all night** toute la nuit; **all men** tous les hommes; **all five** tous les cinq; **all the books** tous les livres; **all his life** toute sa vie
▷ *pron* **1** tout; **I ate it all, I ate all of it** j'ai tout mangé; **all of us went** nous y sommes tous allés; **all of the boys went** tous les garçons y sont allés; **is that all?** c'est tout?; (*in shop*) ce sera tout?
2 (*in phrases*): **above all** surtout, par-dessus tout; **after all** après tout; **at all: not at all** (*in answer to question*) pas du tout; (*in answer to thanks*) je vous en prie!; **I'm not at all tired** je ne suis pas du tout fatigué(e); **anything at all will do** n'importe quoi fera l'affaire; **all in all** tout bien considéré, en fin de compte
▷ *adv*: seul(e); **it's not as hard as all that** ce n'est pas si difficile que ça; **all the more/ the better** d'autant plus/mieux; **all but** presque, pratiquement; **the score is 2 all** le score est de 2 partout

Allah ['ælə] *n* Allah *m*
allegation [ælɪ'ɡeɪʃən] *n* allégation *f*
alleged [ə'lɛdʒd] *adj* prétendu(e); **allegedly** *adv* à ce que l'on prétend, paraît-il
allegiance [ə'liːdʒəns] *n* fidélité *f*, obéissance *f*
allergic [ə'lə:dʒɪk] *adj*: **~ to** allergique à; **I'm ~ to penicillin** je suis allergique à la pénicilline
allergy ['ælədʒɪ] *n* allergie *f*

alleviate [ə'liːvɪeɪt] *vt* soulager, adoucir
alley ['ælɪ] *n* ruelle *f*
alliance [ə'laɪəns] *n* alliance *f*
allied ['ælaɪd] *adj* allié(e)
alligator ['ælɪɡeɪtəʳ] *n* alligator *m*
all-in ['ɔːlɪn] *adj*, *adv* (BRIT: *charge*) tout compris
allocate ['æləkeɪt] *vt* (*share out*) répartir, distribuer; **to ~ sth to** (*duties*) assigner or attribuer qch à; (*sum, time*) allouer qch à
allot [ə'lɔt] *vt* (*share out*) répartir, distribuer; **to ~ sth to** (*time*) allouer qch à; (*duties*) assigner qch à
all-out ['ɔːlaut] *adj* (*effort etc*) total(e)
allow [ə'lau] *vt* (*practice, behaviour*) permettre, autoriser; (*sum to spend etc*) accorder, allouer; (*sum, time estimated*) compter, prévoir; (*claim, goal*) admettre; (*concede*): **to ~ that** convenir que; **to ~ sb to do** permettre à qn de faire, autoriser qn à faire; **he is ~ed to ...** on lui permet de ...; **allow for** *vt fus* tenir compte de; **allowance** *n* (*money received*) allocation *f* (: *from parent etc*) subside *m*; (: *for expenses*) indemnité *f*; (US: *pocket money*) argent *m* de poche; (*Tax*) somme *f* déductible du revenu imposable, abattement *m*; **to make allowances for** (*person*) essayer de comprendre; (*thing*) tenir compte de
all right *adv* (*feel, work*) bien; (*as answer*) d'accord
ally ['ælaɪ] *n* allié *m* ▷ *vt* [ə'laɪ]: **to ~ o.s. with** s'allier avec
almighty [ɔːl'maɪtɪ] *adj* tout(e)-puissant(e); (*tremendous*) énorme
almond ['ɑːmənd] *n* amande *f*
almost ['ɔːlməust] *adv* presque
alone [ə'ləun] *adj*, *adv* seul(e); **to leave sb ~** laisser qn tranquille; **to leave sth ~** ne pas toucher à qch; **let ~ ...** sans parler de ...; encore moins ...
along [ə'lɔŋ] *prep* le long de ▷ *adv*: **is he coming ~ with us?** vient-il avec nous?; **he was hopping/limping ~**

il venait or avançait en sautillant/boitant; **~ with** avec, en plus de; (person) en compagnie de; **all ~** (all the time) depuis le début; **alongside** prep (along) le long de; (beside) à côté de ▷ adv bord à bord; côte à côte

aloof [ə'luːf] adj distant(e) ▷ adv: **to stand ~** se tenir à l'écart or à distance

aloud [ə'laud] adv à haute voix

alphabet ['ælfəbɛt] n alphabet m

Alps [ælps] npl; **the ~** les Alpes fpl

already [ɔːl'rɛdɪ] adv déjà

alright ['ɔːl'raɪt] adv (BRIT) = **all right**

also ['ɔːlsəu] adv aussi

altar ['ɔltər] n autel m

alter ['ɔltər] vt, vi changer; **alteration** [ɔltə'reɪʃən] n changement m, modification f; **alterations** npl (Sewing) retouches fpl; (Archit) modifications fpl

alternate adj [ɔl'təːnɪt] alterné(e), alternant(e), alternatif(-ive); (US) = **alternative** ▷ vi ['ɔltəːneɪt] alterner; **to ~ with** alterner avec; **on ~ days** un jour sur deux, tous les deux jours

alternative [ɔl'təːnətɪv] adj (solution, plan) autre, de remplacement; (lifestyle) parallèle ▷ n (choice) alternative f; (other possibility) autre possibilité f; **~ medicine** médecine alternative, médecine douce; **alternatively** adv: **alternatively one could ...** une autre or l'autre solution serait de ...

although [ɔːl'ðəu] conj bien que + sub

altitude ['æltɪtjuːd] n altitude f

altogether [ɔːltə'gɛðər] adv entièrement, tout à fait; (on the whole) tout compte fait; (in all) en tout

aluminium [ælju'mɪnɪəm], (US) **aluminum** [ə'luːmɪnəm] n aluminium m

always ['ɔːlweɪz] adv toujours

Alzheimer's (disease) ['æltshaɪməz-] n maladie f d'Alzheimer

am [æm] vb see **be**

a.m. adv abbr (= ante meridiem) du matin

amalgamate [ə'mælgəmeɪt] vt, vi fusionner

amass [ə'mæs] vt amasser

amateur ['æmətər] n amateur m

amaze [ə'meɪz] vt stupéfier; **to be ~d (at)** être stupéfait(e) (de); **amazed** adj stupéfait(e); **amazement** n surprise f, étonnement m; **amazing** adj étonnant(e), incroyable; (bargain, offer) exceptionnel(le)

Amazon ['æməzən] n (Geo) Amazone f

ambassador [æm'bæsədər] n ambassadeur m

amber ['æmbər] n ambre m; **at ~** (BRIT Aut) à l'orange

ambiguous [æm'bɪgjuəs] adj ambigu(ë)

ambition [æm'bɪʃən] n ambition f; **ambitious** [æm'bɪʃəs] adj ambitieux(-euse)

ambulance ['æmbjuləns] n ambulance f; **call an ~!** appelez une ambulance!

ambush ['æmbuʃ] n embuscade f ▷ vt tendre une embuscade à

amen ['ɑː'mɛn] excl amen

amend [ə'mɛnd] vt (law) amender; (text) corriger; **to make ~s** réparer ses torts, faire amende honorable; **amendment** n (to law) amendement m; (to text) correction f

amenities [ə'miːnɪtɪz] npl aménagements mpl, équipements mpl

America [ə'mɛrɪkə] n Amérique f; **American** adj américain(e) ▷ n Américain(e); **American football** n (BRIT) football m américain

amicable ['æmɪkəbl] adj amical(e); (Law) à l'amiable

amid(st) [ə'mɪd(st)] prep parmi, au milieu de

ammunition [æmju'nɪʃən] n munitions fpl

amnesty ['æmnɪstɪ] n amnistie f

among(st) [ə'mʌŋ(st)] *prep* parmi, entre

amount [ə'maunt] *n* (*sum of money*) somme *f*; (*total*) montant *m*; (*quantity*) quantité *f*; nombre *m* ▷ *vi*: **to ~ to** (*total*) s'élever à; (*be same as*) équivaloir à, revenir à

amp(ère) ['æmp(ɛəʳ)] *n* ampère *m*

ample ['æmpl] *adj* ample, spacieux(-euse); (*enough*): **this is ~** c'est largement suffisant; **to have ~ time/room** avoir bien assez de temps/place

amplifier ['æmplɪfaɪəʳ] *n* amplificateur *m*

amputate ['æmpjuteɪt] *vt* amputer

Amtrak ['æmtræk] (*US*) *n société mixte de transports ferroviaires interurbains pour voyageurs*

amuse [ə'mjuːz] *vt* amuser; **amusement** *n* amusement *m*; (*pastime*) distraction *f*; **amusement arcade** *n* salle *f* de jeu; **amusement park** *n* parc *m* d'attractions

amusing [ə'mjuːzɪŋ] *adj* amusant(e), divertissant(e)

an [æn, ən, n] *indef art see* **a**

anaemia, (*US*) **anemia** [ə'niːmɪə] *n* anémie *f*

anaemic, (*US*) **anemic** [ə'niːmɪk] *adj* anémique

anaesthetic, (*US*) **anesthetic** [ænɪs'θɛtɪk] *n* anesthésique *m*

analog(ue) ['ænəlɔg] *adj* (*watch, computer*) analogique

analogy [ə'nælədʒɪ] *n* analogie *f*

analyse, (*US*) **analyze** ['ænəlaɪz] *vt* analyser; **analysis** (*pl* **analyses**) [ə'næləsɪs, -siːz] *n* analyse *f*; **analyst** ['ænəlɪst] *n* (*political analyst etc*) analyste *m/f*; (*US*) psychanalyste *m/f*

analyze ['ænəlaɪz] *vt* (*US*) = **analyse**

anarchy ['ænəkɪ] *n* anarchie *f*

anatomy [ə'nætəmɪ] *n* anatomie *f*

ancestor ['ænsɪstəʳ] *n* ancêtre *m*, aïeul *m*

anchor ['æŋkəʳ] *n* ancre *f* ▷ *vi* (*also*: **to drop ~**) jeter l'ancre, mouiller ▷ *vt*

mettre à l'ancre; (*fig*): **to ~ sth to** fixer qch à

anchovy ['æntʃəvɪ] *n* anchois *m*

ancient ['eɪnʃənt] *adj* ancien(ne), antique; (*person*) d'un âge vénérable; (*car*) antédiluvien(ne)

and [ænd] *conj* et; **~ so on** et ainsi de suite; **try ~ come** tâchez de venir; **come ~ sit here** venez vous asseoir ici; **he talked ~ talked** il a parlé pendant des heures; **better ~ better** de mieux en mieux; **more ~ more** de plus en plus

Andorra [æn'dɔːrə] *n* (principauté *f* d')Andorre *f*

anemia *etc* [ə'niːmɪə] *n* (*US*) = **anaemia** *etc*

anesthetic [ænɪs'θɛtɪk] *n, adj* (*US*) = **anaesthetic**

angel ['eɪndʒəl] *n* ange *m*

anger ['æŋgəʳ] *n* colère *f*

angina [æn'dʒaɪnə] *n* angine *f* de poitrine

angle ['æŋgl] *n* angle *m*; **from their ~** de leur point de vue

angler ['æŋgləʳ] *n* pêcheur(-euse) à la ligne

Anglican ['æŋglɪkən] *adj, n* anglican(e)

angling ['æŋglɪŋ] *n* pêche *f* à la ligne

angrily ['æŋgrɪlɪ] *adv* avec colère

angry ['æŋgrɪ] *adj* en colère, furieux(-euse); (*wound*) enflammé(e); **to be ~ with sb/at sth** être furieux contre qn/de qch; **to get ~** se fâcher, se mettre en colère

anguish ['æŋgwɪʃ] *n* angoisse *f*

animal ['ænɪməl] *n* animal *m* ▷ *adj* animal(e)

animated ['ænɪmeɪtɪd] *adj* animé(e)

animation [ænɪ'meɪʃən] *n* (*of person*) entrain *m*; (*of street, Cine*) animation *f*

aniseed ['ænɪsiːd] *n* anis *m*

ankle ['æŋkl] *n* cheville *f*

annex ['ænɛks] *n* (*BRIT*: *also*: **~e**) annexe *f* ▷ *vt* [ə'nɛks] annexer

anniversary [ænɪ'vəːsərɪ] *n* anniversaire *m*

announce [ə'naʊns] vt annoncer;
(birth, death) faire part de;
announcement n annonce f; (for
births etc: in newspaper) avis m de
faire-part; (: letter, card) faire-part
m; **announcer** n (Radio, TV: between
programmes) speaker(ine); (: in a
programme) présentateur(-trice)

annoy [ə'nɔɪ] vt agacer, ennuyer,
contrarier; **don't get ~ed!** ne
vous fâchez pas!; **annoying** adj
agaçant(e), contrariant(e)

annual ['ænjuəl] adj annuel(le) ▷ n
(Bot) plante annuelle; (book) album m;
annually adv annuellement

annum ['ænəm] n see **per**

anonymous [ə'nɒnɪməs] adj
anonyme

anorak ['ænəræk] n anorak m

anorexia [ænə'rɛksɪə] n (also: ~
nervosa) anorexie f

anorexic [ænə'rɛksɪk] adj, n
anorexique (m/f)

another [ə'nʌðə°] adj: ~ **book**
(one more) un autre livre, encore un
livre, un livre de plus; (a different one)
un autre livre ▷ pron un(e) autre,
encore un(e), un(e) de plus; see
also **one**

answer ['ɑ:nsə°] n réponse f; (to
problem) solution f ▷ vi répondre
▷ vt (reply to) répondre à; (problem)
résoudre; (prayer) exaucer; **in ~ to
your letter** suite à or en réponse
à votre lettre; **to ~ the phone**
répondre (au téléphone); **to ~ the
bell** or **the door** aller or venir ouvrir
(la porte); **answer back** vi répondre,
répliquer; **answerphone** n (esp BRIT)
répondeur m (téléphonique)

ant [ænt] n fourmi f

Antarctic [ænt'ɑ:ktɪk] n: **the ~**
l'Antarctique m

antelope ['æntɪləʊp] n antilope f

antenatal ['æntɪ'neɪtl] adj
prénatal(e)

antenna (pl **antennae**) [æn'tɛnə,
-ni:] n antenne f

anthem ['ænθəm] n: **national ~**
hymne national

anthology [æn'θɒlədʒɪ] n
anthologie f

anthropology [ænθrə'pɒlədʒɪ] n
anthropologie f

anti ['æntɪ] prefix anti-; **antibiotic**
['æntɪbaɪ'ɒtɪk] n antibiotique m;
antibody ['æntɪbɒdɪ] n anticorps m

anticipate [æn'tɪsɪpeɪt] vt
s'attendre à, prévoir; (wishes,
request) aller au devant de, devancer;
anticipation [æntɪsɪ'peɪʃən] n
attente f

anticlimax ['æntɪ'klaɪmæks] n
déception f

anticlockwise ['æntɪ'klɒkwaɪz]
(BRIT) adv dans le sens inverse des
aiguilles d'une montre

antics ['æntɪks] npl singeries fpl

anti: antidote ['æntɪdəʊt] n antidote
m, contrepoison m; **antifreeze**
['æntɪfri:z] n antigel m; **anti-
globalization** n antimondialisation
f; **antihistamine** [æntɪ'hɪstəmɪn] n
antihistaminique m; **antiperspirant**
[æntɪ'pə:spɪrənt] n déodorant m

antique [æn'ti:k] n (ornament) objet
m d'art ancien; (furniture) meuble
ancien ▷ adj ancien(ne); **antique
shop** n magasin m d'antiquités

antiseptic [æntɪ'sɛptɪk] adj, n
antiseptique (m)

antisocial ['æntɪ'səʊʃəl] adj
(unfriendly) insociable; (against society)
antisocial(e)

antivirus [æntɪ'vaɪrəs] adj (Comput)
antivirus inv; **~ software** (logiciel
m) antivirus

antlers ['æntləz] npl bois mpl,
ramure f

anxiety [æŋ'zaɪətɪ] n anxiété f;
(keenness): **~ to do** grand désir or
impatience f de faire

anxious ['æŋkʃəs] adj (très)
inquiet(-ète); (always worried)
anxieux(-euse); (worrying)
angoissant(e); **~ to do/that** (keen)

qui tient beaucoup à faire/à ce que
+ *sub*; impatient(e) de faire/que + *sub*

○ **KEYWORD**

any ['enɪ] *adj* **1** (*in questions etc*:
singular) du, de l', de la; (: *plural*) des;
**do you have any butter/children/
ink?** avez-vous du beurre/des
enfants/de l'encre?
2 (*with negative*) de, d'; **I don't have
any money/books** je n'ai pas
d'argent/de livres
3 (*no matter which*) n'importe quel(le);
(*each and every*) tout(e), chaque;
choose any book you like vous
pouvez choisir n'importe quel livre;
any teacher you ask will tell you
n'importe quel professeur vous le dira
4 (*in phrases*): **in any case** de toute
façon; **any day now** d'un jour à
l'autre; **at any moment** à tout
moment, d'un instant à l'autre; **at
any rate** en tout cas; **any time**
n'importe quand; **he might come
(at) any time** il pourrait venir
n'importe quand; **come (at) any
time** venez quand vous voulez
▶ *pron* **1** (*in questions etc*) en; **have
you got any?** est-ce que vous en
avez?; **can any of you sing?** est-ce
que parmi vous il y en a qui savent
chanter?
2 (*with negative*) en; **I don't have
any (of them)** je n'en ai pas, je n'en
ai aucun
3 (*no matter which one(s)*) n'importe
lequel (*or* laquelle); (*anybody*)
n'importe qui; **take any of those
books (you like)** vous pouvez
prendre n'importe lequel de ces livres
▶ *adv* **1** (*in questions etc*): **do you
want any more soup/sandwiches?**
voulez-vous encore de la soupe/des
sandwichs?; **are you feeling any
better?** est-ce que vous vous sentez
mieux?
2 (*with negative*): **I can't hear him**

any more je ne l'entends plus;
don't wait any longer n'attendez
pas plus longtemps; **anybody**
pron n'importe qui; (*in interrogative
sentences*) quelqu'un; (*in negative
sentences*): **I don't see anybody** je ne
vois personne; **if anybody should
phone ...** si quelqu'un téléphone
...; **anyhow** *adv* quoi qu'il en soit;
(*haphazardly*) n'importe comment;
do it anyhow you like faites-le
comme vous voulez; **she leaves
things just anyhow** elle laisse
tout traîner; **I shall go anyhow**
j'irai de toute façon; **anyone** *pron*
= **anybody**; **anything** *pron* (*no matter
what*) n'importe quoi; (*in questions*)
quelque chose; (*with negative*) ne
... rien; **can you see anything?** tu
vois quelque chose?; **if anything
happens to me ...** s'il m'arrive quoi
que ce soit ...; **you can say anything
you like** vous pouvez dire ce que vous
voulez; **anything will do** n'importe
quoi fera l'affaire; **he'll eat anything**
il mange de tout; **anytime** *adv* (*at
any moment*) d'un moment à l'autre;
(*whenever*) n'importe quand; **anyway**
adv de toute façon; **anyway, I
couldn't come even if I wanted
to** de toute façon, je ne pouvais pas
venir même si je le voulais; **I shall
go anyway** j'irai quand même; **why
are you phoning, anyway?** au
fait, pourquoi tu me téléphones?;
anywhere *adv* n'importe où; (*in
interrogative sentences*) quelque part;
(*in negative sentences*): **I can't see him
anywhere** je ne le vois nulle part;
can you see him anywhere? tu le
vois quelque part?; **put the books
down anywhere** pose les livres
n'importe où; **anywhere in the
world** (*no matter where*) n'importe où
dans le monde

apart [ə'pɑːt] *adv* (*to one side*) à
part; de côté; à l'écart; (*separately*)

séparément; **to take/pull ~**
démonter; **10 miles/a long way ~** à
10 miles/très éloignés l'un de l'autre;
~ from prep à part, excepté

apartment [ə'pɑːtmənt] n (us)
appartement m, logement m; (room)
chambre f; **apartment building** n
(us) immeuble m; maison divisée en
appartements

apathy ['æpəθɪ] n apathie f,
indifférence f

ape [eɪp] n (grand) singe ▷ vt singer

aperitif [ə'perɪtɪf] n apéritif m

aperture ['æpətʃjuər] n orifice m,
ouverture f; (Phot) ouverture (du
diaphragme)

APEX ['eɪpɛks] n abbr (Aviat: = advance
purchase excursion) APEX m

apologize [ə'pɒlədʒaɪz] vi: **to ~ (for
sth to sb)** s'excuser (de qch auprès
de qn), présenter des excuses (à qn
pour qch)

apology [ə'pɒlədʒɪ] n excuses fpl

apostrophe [ə'pɒstrəfɪ] n
apostrophe f

app n abbr (inf: Comput: = application)
appli f

appal, (us) **appall** [ə'pɔːl] vt
consterner, atterrer; horrifier;
appalling adj épouvantable;
(stupidity) consternant(e)

apparatus [æpə'reɪtəs] n appareil m,
dispositif m; (in gymnasium) agrès mpl

apparent [ə'pærənt] adj
apparent(e); **apparently** adv
apparemment

appeal [ə'piːl] vi (Law) faire or
interjeter appel ▷ n (Law) appel m;
(request) appel; prière f; (charm) attrait
m, charme m; **to ~ for** demander
(instamment); implorer; **to ~ to** (beg)
faire appel à; (be attractive) plaire à;
it doesn't ~ to me cela ne m'attire
pas; **appealing** adj (attractive)
attrayant(e)

appear [ə'pɪər] vi apparaître,
se montrer; (Law) comparaître;
(publication) paraître, sortir, être

publié(e); (seem) paraître, sembler; **it
would ~ that** il semble que; **to ~ in
Hamlet** jouer dans Hamlet; **to ~ on
TV** passer à la télé; **appearance** n
apparition f; parution f; (look, aspect)
apparence f; aspect m

appendices [ə'pɛndɪsiːz] npl of
appendix

appendicitis [əpɛndɪ'saɪtɪs] n
appendicite f

appendix (pl **appendices**)
[ə'pɛndɪks, -siːz] n appendice m

appetite ['æpɪtaɪt] n appétit m

appetizer ['æpɪtaɪzər] n (food)
amuse-gueule m; (drink) apéritif m

applaud [ə'plɔːd] vt, vi applaudir

applause [ə'plɔːz] n
applaudissements mpl

apple ['æpl] n pomme f; **apple pie** n
tarte f aux pommes

appliance [ə'plaɪəns] n appareil m

applicable [ə'plɪkəbl] adj applicable;
to be ~ to (relevant) valoir pour

applicant ['æplɪkənt] n: **~ (for)**
candidat(e) (à)

application [æplɪ'keɪʃən] n (also
Comput) application f; (for a job, a
grant etc) demande f; candidature f;
application form n formulaire m de
demande

apply [ə'plaɪ] vt: **to ~ (to)** (paint,
ointment) appliquer (sur); (law, etc)
appliquer (à) ▷ vi: **to ~ to** (ask)
s'adresser à; (be suitable for, relevant
to) s'appliquer à; **to ~ (for)** (permit,
grant) faire une demande (en vue
d'obtenir); (job) poser sa candidature
(pour), faire une demande
d'emploi (concernant); **to ~ o.s. to**
s'appliquer à

appoint [ə'pɔɪnt] vt (to post)
nommer, engager; (date, place)
fixer, désigner; **appointment** n (to
post) nomination f; (job) poste m;
(arrangement to meet) rendez-vous
m; **to have an appointment**
avoir un rendez-vous; **to make
an appointment (with)** prendre

rendez-vous (avec); **I'd like to make an appointment** je voudrais prendre rendez-vous

appraisal [əˈpreɪzl] n évaluation f

appreciate [əˈpriːʃɪeɪt] vt (like) apprécier, faire cas de; (be grateful for) être reconnaissant(e) de; (be aware of) comprendre, se rendre compte de ▷ vi (Finance) prendre de la valeur; **appreciation** [əpriːʃɪˈeɪʃən] n appréciation f; (gratitude) reconnaissance f; (Finance) hausse f, valorisation f

apprehension [æprɪˈhɛnʃən] n appréhension f, inquiétude f

apprehensive [æprɪˈhɛnsɪv] adj inquiet(-ète), appréhensif(-ive)

apprentice [əˈprɛntɪs] n apprenti m

approach [əˈprəʊtʃ] vi approcher ▷ vt (come near) approcher de; (ask, apply to) s'adresser à; (subject, passer-by) aborder ▷ n approche f; accès m, abord m; (intellectual) démarche f

appropriate adj [əˈprəʊprɪɪt] (tool etc) qui convient, approprié(e); (moment, remark) opportun(e) ▷ vt [əˈprəʊprɪeɪt] (take) s'approprier

approval [əˈpruːvəl] n approbation f; **on ~** (Comm) à l'examen

approve [əˈpruːv] vt approuver; **approve of** vt fus (thing) approuver; (person): **they don't ~ of her** ils n'ont pas bonne opinion d'elle

approximate [əˈprɒksɪmɪt] adj approximatif(-ive); **approximately** adv approximativement

Apr. abbr = **April**

apricot [ˈeɪprɪkɔt] n abricot m

April [ˈeɪprəl] n avril m; **April Fools' Day** n le premier avril

● **APRIL FOOLS' DAY**
●
● April Fools' Day est le 1er avril, à
● l'occasion duquel on fait des farces
● de toutes sortes. Les victimes de
● ces farces sont les "April fools".

● Traditionnellement, on n'est censé
● faire des farces que jusqu'à midi.

apron [ˈeɪprən] n tablier m

apt [æpt] adj (suitable) approprié(e); **~ to do** (likely) susceptible de faire; ayant tendance à faire

aquarium [əˈkwɛərɪəm] n aquarium m

Aquarius [əˈkwɛərɪəs] n le Verseau

Arab [ˈærəb] n Arabe m/f ▷ adj arabe

Arabia [əˈreɪbɪə] n Arabie f; **Arabian** adj arabe; **Arabic** [ˈærəbɪk] adj, n arabe (m)

arbitrary [ˈɑːbɪtrərɪ] adj arbitraire

arbitration [ɑːbɪˈtreɪʃən] n arbitrage m

arc [ɑːk] n arc m

arcade [ɑːˈkeɪd] n arcade f; (passage with shops) passage m, galerie f; (with games) salle f de jeu

arch [ɑːtʃ] n arche f; (of foot) cambrure f, voûte f plantaire ▷ vt arquer, cambrer

archaeology, (us) **archeology** [ɑːkɪˈɔlədʒɪ] n archéologie f

archbishop [ɑːtʃˈbɪʃəp] n archevêque m

archeology [ɑːkɪˈɔlədʒɪ] (us) n = **archaeology**

architect [ˈɑːkɪtɛkt] n architecte m; **architectural** [ɑːkɪˈtɛktʃərəl] adj architectural(e); **architecture** n architecture f

archive [ˈɑːkaɪv] n (often pl) archives fpl

Arctic [ˈɑːktɪk] adj arctique ▷ n: **the ~** l'Arctique m

are [ɑːʳ] vb see **be**

area [ˈɛərɪə] n (Geom) superficie f; (zone) région f (: smaller) secteur m; (in room) coin m; (knowledge, research) domaine m; **area code** (us) n (Tel) indicatif m de zone

arena [əˈriːnə] n arène f

aren't [ɑːnt] = **are not**

Argentina [ɑːdʒənˈtiːnə] n Argentine f; **Argentinian**

[ɑːdʒən'tɪnɪən] *adj* argentin(e) ▷ *n* Argentin(e)

arguably ['ɑːgjuəblɪ] *adv*: **it is ~ ...** on peut soutenir que c'est ...

argue ['ɑːgjuː] *vi* (*quarrel*) se disputer; (*reason*) argumenter; **to ~ that** objecter *or* alléguer que, donner comme argument que

argument ['ɑːgjumənt] *n* (*quarrel*) dispute *f*, discussion *f*; (*reasons*) argument *m*

Aries ['ɛərɪz] *n* le Bélier

arise (*pt* **arose**, *pp* **arisen**) [ə'raɪz, ə'rəuz, ə'rɪzn] *vi* survenir, se présenter

arithmetic [ə'rɪθmətɪk] *n* arithmétique *f*

arm [ɑːm] *n* bras *m* ▷ *vt* armer; **arms** *npl* (*weapons*, *Heraldry*) armes *fpl*; **~ in ~** bras dessus bras dessous; **armchair** ['ɑːmtʃɛəʳ] *n* fauteuil *m*

armed [ɑːmd] *adj* armé(e); **armed forces** *npl*; **the armed forces** les forces armées; **armed robbery** *n* vol *m* à main armée

armour, (*US*) **armor** ['ɑːməʳ] *n* armure *f*; (*Mil*: *tanks*) blindés *mpl*

armpit ['ɑːmpɪt] *n* aisselle *f*

armrest ['ɑːmrɛst] *n* accoudoir *m*

army ['ɑːmɪ] *n* armée *f*

A road *n* (*BRIT*) ≈ route nationale

aroma [ə'rəumə] *n* arôme *m*; **aromatherapy** *n* aromathérapie *f*

arose [ə'rəuz] *pt of* **arise**

around [ə'raund] *adv* (*tout*) autour; (*nearby*) dans les parages ▷ *prep* autour de; (*near*) près de; (*fig*: *about*) environ; (: *date*, *time*) vers; **is he ~?** est-il dans les parages *or* là?

arouse [ə'rauz] *vt* (*sleeper*) éveiller; (*curiosity*, *passions*) éveiller, susciter; (*anger*) exciter

arrange [ə'reɪndʒ] *vt* arranger; **to ~ to do sth** prévoir de faire qch; **arrangement** *n* arrangement *m*; **arrangements** *npl* (*plans etc*) arrangements *mpl*, dispositions *fpl*

array [ə'reɪ] *n* (*of objects*) déploiement *m*, étalage *m*

arrears [ə'rɪəz] *npl* arriéré *m*; **to be in ~ with one's rent** devoir un arriéré de loyer

arrest [ə'rɛst] *vt* arrêter; (*sb's attention*) retenir, attirer ▷ *n* arrestation *f*; **under ~** en état d'arrestation

arrival [ə'raɪvl] *n* arrivée *f*; **new ~** nouveau venu/nouvelle venue; (*baby*) nouveau-né(e)

arrive [ə'raɪv] *vi* arriver; **arrive at** *vt fus* (*decision*, *solution*) parvenir à

arrogance ['ærəgəns] *n* arrogance *f*

arrogant ['ærəgənt] *adj* arrogant(e)

arrow ['ærəu] *n* flèche *f*

arse [ɑːs] *n* (*BRIT inf!*) cul *m* (!)

arson ['ɑːsn] *n* incendie criminel

art [ɑːt] *n* art *m*; **Arts** *npl* (*Scol*) les lettres *fpl*; **art college** *n* école *f* des beaux-arts

artery ['ɑːtərɪ] *n* artère *f*

art gallery *n* musée *m* d'art; (*saleroom*) galerie *f* de peinture

arthritis [ɑː'θraɪtɪs] *n* arthrite *f*

artichoke ['ɑːtɪtʃəuk] *n* artichaut *m*; **Jerusalem ~** topinambour *m*

article ['ɑːtɪkl] *n* article *m*

articulate *adj* [ɑː'tɪkjulɪt] (*person*) qui s'exprime clairement et aisément; (*speech*) bien articulé(e), prononcé(e) clairement ▷ *vi* [ɑː'tɪkjuleɪt] articuler, parler distinctement ▷ *vt* articuler

artificial [ɑːtɪ'fɪʃəl] *adj* artificiel(le)

artist ['ɑːtɪst] *n* artiste *m/f*; **artistic** [ɑː'tɪstɪk] *adj* artistique

art school *n* ≈ école *f* des beaux-arts

KEYWORD

as [æz] *conj* **1** (*time*: *moment*) comme, alors que; à mesure que; **he came in as I was leaving** il est arrivé comme je partais; **as the years went by** à mesure que les années passaient; **as from tomorrow** à partir de demain **2** (*because*) comme, puisque; **he left early as he had to be home by**

10 comme il *or* puisqu'il devait être de retour avant 10h, il est parti de bonne heure
3 (*referring to manner, way*) comme; **do as you wish** faites comme vous voudrez; **as she said** comme elle disait
▶ *adv* **1** (*in comparisons*): **as big as** aussi grand que; **twice as big as** deux fois plus grand que; **as much** *or* **many as** autant que; **as much money/many books as** autant d'argent/de livres que; **as soon as** dès que
2 (*concerning*): **as for** *or* **to that** quant à cela, pour ce qui est de cela
3: **as if** *or* **though** comme si; **he looked as if he was ill** il avait l'air d'être malade; *see also* **long; such; well**
▶ *prep* (*in the capacity of*) en tant que, en qualité de; **he works as a driver** il travaille comme chauffeur; **as chairman of the company, he ...** en tant que président de la société, il ...; **he gave me it as a present** il me l'a offert, il m'en a fait cadeau

a.s.a.p. *abbr* = **as soon as possible**
asbestos [æz'bɛstəs] *n* asbeste *m*, amiante *m*
ascent [ə'sɛnt] *n* (*climb*) ascension *f*
ash [æʃ] *n* (*dust*) cendre *f*; (*also:* ~ **tree**) frêne *m*
ashamed [ə'ʃeɪmd] *adj* honteux(-euse), confus(e); **to be ~ of** avoir honte de
ashore [ə'ʃɔːʳ] *adv* à terre
ashtray ['æʃtreɪ] *n* cendrier *m*
Ash Wednesday *n* mercredi *m* des Cendres
Asia ['eɪʃə] *n* Asie *f*; **Asian** *n* (*from Asia*) Asiatique *m/f*; (BRIT: *from Indian subcontinent*) Indo-Pakistanais(e)
▶ *adj* asiatique; indo-pakistanais(e)
aside [ə'saɪd] *adv* de côté; à l'écart
▶ *n* aparté *m*
ask [ɑːsk] *vt* demander; (*invite*) inviter; **to ~ sb sth/to do sth** demander à

qn qch/de faire qch; **to ~ sb about sth** questionner qn au sujet de qch; se renseigner auprès de qn au sujet de qch; **to ~ (sb) a question** poser une question (à qn); **to ~ sb out to dinner** inviter qn au restaurant; **ask for** *vt fus* demander; **it's just ~ing for trouble** *or* **for it** ce serait chercher des ennuis
asleep [ə'sliːp] *adj* endormi(e); **to fall ~** s'endormir
AS level *n abbr* (= *Advanced Subsidiary level*) première partie de l'examen équivalent au baccalauréat
asparagus [əs'pærəgəs] *n* asperges *fpl*
aspect ['æspɛkt] *n* aspect *m*; (*direction in which a building etc faces*) orientation *f*, exposition *f*
aspire [əs'paɪəʳ] *vi*: **to ~ to** aspirer à
aspirin ['æsprɪn] *n* aspirine *f*
ass [æs] *n* âne *m*; (*inf*) imbécile *m/f*; (*us inf!*) cul *m* (!)
assassin [ə'sæsɪn] *n* assassin *m*; **assassinate** *vt* assassiner
assault [ə'sɔːlt] *n* (*Mil*) assaut *m*; (*gen: attack*) agression *f* ▶ *vt* attaquer; (*sexually*) violenter
assemble [ə'sɛmbl] *vt* assembler ▶ *vi* s'assembler, se rassembler
assembly [ə'sɛmblɪ] *n* (*meeting*) rassemblement *m*; (*parliament*) assemblée *f*; (*construction*) assemblage *m*
assert [ə'səːt] *vt* affirmer, déclarer; (*authority*) faire valoir; (*innocence*) protester de; **assertion** [ə'səːʃən] *n* assertion *f*, affirmation *f*
assess [ə'sɛs] *vt* évaluer, estimer; (*tax, damages*) établir *or* fixer le montant de; (*person*) juger la valeur de; **assessment** *n* évaluation *f*, estimation *f*; (*of tax*) fixation *f*
asset ['æsɛt] *n* avantage *m*, atout *m*; (*person*) atout; **assets** *npl* (*Comm*) capital *m*; avoir(s) *m(pl)*; actif *m*
assign [ə'saɪn] *vt* (*date*) fixer, arrêter; **to ~ sth to** (*task*) assigner

qch à; (*resources*) affecter qch à;
assignment n (*task*) mission f;
(*homework*) devoir m
assist [əˈsɪst] vt aider, assister;
assistance n aide f, assistance f;
assistant n assistant(e), adjoint(e);
(BRIT: *also*: **shop assistant**)
vendeur(-euse)
associate adj, n [əˈsəuʃɪɪt]
associé(e) ▷ vt [əˈsəuʃɪeɪt] associer
▷ vi [əˈsəuʃɪeɪt]: **to ~ with sb**
fréquenter qn
association [əsəusɪˈeɪʃən] n
association f
assorted [əˈsɔːtɪd] adj assorti(e)
assortment [əˈsɔːtmənt] n
assortiment m; (*of people*) mélange m
assume [əˈsjuːm] vt supposer;
(*responsibilities etc*) assumer; (*attitude,
name*) prendre, adopter
assumption [əˈsʌmpʃən] n
supposition f, hypothèse f; (*of power*)
assomption f, prise f
assurance [əˈʃuərəns] n assurance f
assure [əˈʃuəʳ] vt assurer
asterisk [ˈæstərɪsk] n astérisque m
asthma [ˈæsmə] n asthme m
astonish [əˈstɒnɪʃ] vt étonner,
stupéfier; **astonished** adj
étonné(e); **to be astonished at**
être étonné(e) de; **astonishing**
adj étonnant(e), stupéfiant(e);
I find it astonishing that ...
je trouve incroyable que ... +
sub; **astonishment** n (grand)
étonnement, stupéfaction f
astound [əˈstaund] vt stupéfier,
sidérer
astray [əˈstreɪ] adv: **to go ~** s'égarer;
(*fig*) quitter le droit chemin; **to lead ~**
(*morally*) détourner du droit chemin
astrology [əsˈtrɒlədʒɪ] n astrologie f
astronaut [ˈæstrənɔːt] n
astronaute m/f
astronomer [əsˈtrɒnəməʳ] n
astronome m
astronomical [æstrəˈnɒmɪkl] adj
astronomique

astronomy [əsˈtrɒnəmɪ] n
astronomie f
astute [əsˈtjuːt] adj astucieux(-euse),
malin(-igne)
asylum [əˈsaɪləm] n asile m; **asylum
seeker** [-siːkəʳ] n demandeur(-euse)
d'asile

 KEYWORD

at [æt] prep **1** (*referring to position,
direction*) à; **at the top** au sommet;
at home/school à la maison *or* chez
soi/à l'école; **at the baker's** à la
boulangerie, chez le boulanger; **to
look at sth** regarder qch
2 (*referring to time*): **at 4 o'clock** à 4
heures; **at Christmas** à Noël; **at night**
la nuit; **at times** par moments, parfois
3 (*referring to rates, speed etc*) à; **at £1
a kilo** une livre le kilo; **two at a time**
deux à la fois; **at 50 km/h** à 50 km/h
4 (*referring to manner*): **at a stroke**
d'un seul coup; **at peace** en paix
5 (*referring to activity*): **to be at
work** (*in the office etc*) être au travail;
(*working*) travailler; **to play at
cowboys** jouer aux cowboys; **to be
good at sth** être bon en qch
6 (*referring to cause*): **shocked/
surprised/annoyed at sth** choqué
par/étonné de/agacé par qch; **I went
at his suggestion** j'y suis allé sur
son conseil
▶ n (@ *symbol*) arobase f

ate [eɪt] pt of **eat**
atheist [ˈeɪθɪɪst] n athée m/f
Athens [ˈæθɪnz] n Athènes
athlete [ˈæθliːt] n athlète m/f
athletic [æθˈlɛtɪk] adj athlétique;
athletics n athlétisme m
Atlantic [ətˈlæntɪk] adj atlantique
▷ n: **the ~ (Ocean)** l'(océan m)
Atlantique m
atlas [ˈætləs] n atlas m
A.T.M. n abbr (= *Automated Telling
Machine*) guichet m automatique

atmosphere ['ætməsfɪər] n (air)
atmosphère f; (fig: of place etc)
atmosphère, ambiance f

atom ['ætəm] n atome m; **atomic**
[ə'tɔmɪk] adj atomique; **atom(ic)
bomb** n bombe f atomique

atrocity [ə'trɔsɪtɪ] n atrocité f

attach [ə'tætʃ] vt (gen) attacher;
(document, letter) joindre; **to be ~ed
to sb/sth** (to like) être châtaié à qn/
qch; **to ~ a file to an email** joindre
un fichier à un e-mail; **attachment**
n (tool) accessoire m; (Comput) fichier
m joint; (love): **attachment (to)**
affection f (pour), attachement m (à)

attack [ə'tæk] vt attaquer; (task etc)
s'attaquer à ▷ n attaque f; **heart
~** crise f cardiaque; **attacker** n
attaquant m; agresseur m

attain [ə'teɪn] vt (also: **to ~ to**)
parvenir à, atteindre; (knowledge)
acquérir

attempt [ə'tɛmpt] n tentative f ▷ vt
essayer, tenter

attend [ə'tɛnd] vt (course) suivre;
(meeting, talk) assister à; (school,
church) aller à, fréquenter; (patient)
soigner, s'occuper de; **attend to**
vt fus (needs, affairs etc) s'occuper
de; (customer) s'occuper de, servir;
attendance n (being present)
présence f; (people present) assistance
f; **attendant** n employé(e);
gardien(ne) ▷ adj concomitant(e), qui
accompagne or s'ensuit

▌ Be careful not to translate attend
by the French word attendre.

attention [ə'tɛnʃən] n attention f
▷ excl (Mil) garde-à-vous!; **for the ~ of**
(Admin) à l'attention de

attic ['ætɪk] n grenier m, combles mpl

attitude ['ætɪtjuːd] n attitude f

attorney [ə'təːnɪ] n (US: lawyer)
avocat m; **Attorney General** n (BRIT)
≈ procureur général; (US) ≈ garde m
des Sceaux, ministre m de la Justice

attract [ə'trækt] vt attirer;
attraction [ə'trækʃən] n (gen pl:
pleasant things) attraction f, attrait
m; (Physics) attraction; (fig: towards
sb, sth) attirance f; **attractive** adj
séduisant(e), attrayant(e)

attribute n ['ætrɪbjuːt] attribut m
▷ vt [ə'trɪbjuːt]: **to ~ sth to** attribuer
qch à

aubergine ['əubəʒiːn] n aubergine f

auburn ['ɔːbən] adj auburn inv,
châtain roux inv

auction ['ɔːkʃən] n (also: **sale by ~**)
vente f aux enchères ▷ vt (also: **to sell
by ~**) vendre aux enchères

audible ['ɔːdɪbl] adj audible

audience ['ɔːdɪəns] n (people)
assistance f, public m; (on radio)
auditeurs mpl; (at theatre) spectateurs
mpl; (interview) audience f

audit ['ɔːdɪt] vt vérifier

audition [ɔː'dɪʃən] n audition f

auditor ['ɔːdɪtər] n vérificateur m
des comptes

auditorium [ɔːdɪ'tɔːrɪəm] n
auditorium m, salle f de concert or
de spectacle

Aug. abbr = **August**

August ['ɔːgəst] n août m

aunt [ɑːnt] n tante f; **auntie, aunty** n
diminutive of **aunt**

au pair ['əu'peər] n (also: **~ girl**) jeune
fille f au pair

aura ['ɔːrə] n atmosphère f; (of person)
aura f

austerity [ɔs'tɛrɪtɪ] n austérité f

Australia [ɔs'treɪlɪə] n Australie f;
Australian adj australien(ne) ▷ n
Australien(ne)

Austria ['ɔstrɪə] n Autriche f;
Austrian adj autrichien(ne) ▷ n
Autrichien(ne)

authentic [ɔː'θɛntɪk] adj
authentique

author ['ɔːθər] n auteur m

authority [ɔː'θɔrɪtɪ] n autorité f;
(permission) autorisation (formelle);
the authorities les autorités fpl,
l'administration f

authorize ['ɔːθəraɪz] vt autoriser

auto ['ɔːtəʊ] n (US) auto f, voiture f; **autobiography** [ɔːtəbaɪ'ɒgrəfɪ] n autobiographie f; **autograph** ['ɔːtəgrɑːf] n autographe m ▷ vt signer, dédicacer; **automatic** [ɔːtə'mætɪk] adj automatique ▷ n (gun) automatique m; (car) voiture f à transmission automatique; **automatically** adv automatiquement; **automobile** ['ɔːtəməbiːl] n (US) automobile f; **autonomous** [ɔː'tɒnəməs] adj autonome; **autonomy** [ɔː'tɒnəmɪ] n autonomie f

autumn ['ɔːtəm] n automne m

auxiliary [ɔːg'zɪlɪərɪ] adj, n auxiliaire (m/f)

avail [ə'veɪl] vt: **to ~ o.s. of** user de; profiter de ▷ n: **to no ~** sans résultat, en vain, en pure perte

availability [əveɪlə'bɪlɪtɪ] n disponibilité f

available [ə'veɪləbl] adj disponible

avalanche ['ævəlɑːnʃ] n avalanche f

Ave. abbr = **avenue**

avenue ['ævənjuː] n avenue f; (fig) moyen m

average ['ævərɪdʒ] n moyenne f ▷ adj moyen(ne) ▷ vt (a certain figure) atteindre or faire etc en moyenne; **on ~** en moyenne

avert [ə'vɜːt] vt (danger) prévenir, écarter; (one's eyes) détourner

avid ['ævɪd] adj avide

avocado [ævə'kɑːdəʊ] n (BRIT: also: ~ pear) avocat m

avoid [ə'vɔɪd] vt éviter

await [ə'weɪt] vt attendre

awake [ə'weɪk] (pt **awoke**, pp **awoken**) adj éveillé(e) ▷ vt éveiller ▷ vi s'éveiller; **to be ~** être réveillé(e)

award [ə'wɔːd] n (for bravery) récompense f; (prize) prix m; (Law: damages) dommages-intérêts mpl ▷ vt (prize) décerner; (Law: damages) accorder

aware [ə'wɛəʳ] adj: **~ of** (conscious) conscient(e) de; (informed) au courant de; **to become ~ of/that** prendre conscience de/que; se rendre compte de/que; **awareness** n conscience f, connaissance f

away [ə'weɪ] adv (au) loin; (movement): **she went ~** elle est partie ▷ adj (not in, not here) absent(e); **far ~** (au) loin; **two kilometres ~** à (une distance de) deux kilomètres, à deux kilomètres de distance; **two hours ~ by car** à deux heures de voiture or de route; **the holiday was two weeks ~** il restait deux semaines jusqu'aux vacances; **he's ~ for a week** il est parti (pour) une semaine; **to take sth ~ from sb** prendre qch à qn; **to take sth ~ from sth** (subtract) ôter qch de qch; **to work/pedal ~** travailler/pédaller à cœur joie; **to fade ~** (colour) s'estomper; (sound) s'affaiblir

awe [ɔː] n respect mêlé de crainte, effroi mêlé d'admiration; **awesome** ['ɔːsəm] (US) adj (inf: excellent) génial(e)

awful ['ɔːfəl] adj affreux(-euse); **an ~ lot of** énormément de; **awfully** adv (very) terriblement, vraiment

awkward ['ɔːkwəd] adj (clumsy) gauche, maladroit(e); (inconvenient) peu pratique; (embarrassing) gênant

awoke [ə'wəʊk] pt of **awake**

awoken [ə'wəʊkən] pp of **awake**

axe, (US) **ax** [æks] n hache f ▷ vt (project etc) abandonner; (jobs) supprimer

axle ['æksl] n essieu m

ay(e) [aɪ] excl (yes) oui

azalea [ə'zeɪlɪə] n azalée f

b

the people at the ~ **hear me properly?** est-ce que les gens du fond m'entendent?; ~ **to front** à l'envers; ~ **seat/wheel** (Aut) siège m/roue f arrière inv; ~ **payments/rent** arriéré m de paiements/loyer; ~ **garden/room** jardin/pièce sur l'arrière; **he ran** ~ il est revenu en courant; **throw the ball** ~ renvoie la balle; **can I have it** ~? puis-je le ravoir?, peux-tu me le rendre?; **he called** ~ (again) il a rappelé; **back down** vi rabattre de ses prétentions; **back out** vi (of promise) se dédire; **back up** vt (person) soutenir; (Comput) faire une copie de sauvegarde de; **backache** n mal m au dos; **backbencher** n (BRIT) membre du parlement sans portefeuille; **backbone** n colonne vertébrale, épine dorsale; **back door** n porte f de derrière; **backfire** vi (Aut) pétarader; (plans) mal tourner; **backgammon** n trictrac m; **background** n arrière-plan m; (of events) situation f, conjoncture f; (basic knowledge) éléments mpl de base; (experience) formation f; **family background** milieu familial; **backing** n (fig) soutien m, appui m; **backlog** n: **backlog of work** travail m en retard; **backpack** n sac m à dos; **backpacker** n randonneur(-euse); **backslash** n barre oblique inversée; **backstage** adv dans les coulisses; **backstroke** n dos crawlé; **backup** adj (train, plane) supplémentaire, de réserve; (Comput) de sauvegarde ▷ n (support) appui m, soutien m; (Comput: also: **backup file**) sauvegarde f; **backward** adj (movement) en arrière; (person, country) arriéré(e), attardé(e); **backwards** adv (move, go) en arrière; (read a list) à l'envers, à rebours; (fall) à la renverse; (walk) à reculons; **backyard** n arrière-cour f

B [biː] n (Mus) si m

B.A. abbr (Scol) = **Bachelor of Arts**

baby ['beɪbɪ] n bébé m; **baby carriage** n (US) voiture f d'enfant; **baby-sit** vi garder les enfants; **baby-sitter** n baby-sitter m/f; **baby wipe** n lingette f (pour bébé)

bachelor ['bætʃələʳ] n célibataire m; **B~ of Arts/Science (BA/BSc)** ≈ licencié(e) ès or en lettres/sciences

back [bæk] n (of person, horse) dos m; (of hand) dos, revers m; (of house) derrière m; (of car, train) arrière m; (of chair) dossier m; (of page) verso m; (Football) arrière m ▷ vt (financially) soutenir (financièrement); (candidate: also: ~ **up**) soutenir, appuyer; (horse: at races) parier or miser sur; (car) (faire) reculer ▷ vi reculer; (car etc) faire marche arrière ▷ adj (in compounds) de derrière, à l'arrière ▷ adv (not forward) en arrière; (returned): **he's** ~ il est rentré, il est de retour; **can**

bacon ['beɪkən] n bacon m, lard m

bacteria [bæk'tɪərɪə] npl bactéries fpl

bad [bæd] adj mauvais(e); (child) vilain(e); (mistake, accident) grave;

(*meat, food*) gâté(e), avarié(e); **his ~ leg** sa jambe malade; **to go ~** (*meat, food*) se gâter; (*milk*) tourner

bade [bæd] *pt of* **bid**

badge [bædʒ] *n* insigne *m*; (*of policeman*) plaque *f*; (*stick-on, sew-on*) badge *m*

badger ['bædʒər] *n* blaireau *m*

badly ['bædlɪ] *adv* (*work, dress etc*) mal; **to reflect ~ on sb** donner une mauvaise image de qn; **~ wounded** grièvement blessé; **he needs it ~** il en a absolument besoin; **~ off** *adj, adv* dans la gêne

bad-mannered ['bæd'mænəd] *adj* mal élevé(e)

badminton ['bædmɪntən] *n* badminton *m*

bad-tempered ['bæd'tɛmpəd] *adj* (*by nature*) ayant mauvais caractère; (*on one occasion*) de mauvaise humeur

bag [bæg] *n* sac *m*; **~s of** (*inf: lots of*) des tas de; **baggage** *n* bagages *mpl*; **baggage allowance** *n* franchise *f* de bagages; **baggage reclaim** *n* (*at airport*) livraison *f* des bagages; **baggy** *adj* avachi(e), qui fait des poches; **bagpipes** *npl* cornemuse *f*

bail [beɪl] *n* caution *f* ▷ *vt* (*prisoner: also:* **grant ~ to**) mettre en liberté sous caution; (*boat: also:* **~ out**) écoper; **to be released on ~** être libéré(e) sous caution; **bail out** *vt* (*prisoner*) payer la caution de

bait [beɪt] *n* appât *m* ▷ *vt* appâter; (*fig: tease*) tourmenter

bake [beɪk] *vt* (faire) cuire au four ▷ *vi* (*bread etc*) cuire (au four); (*make cakes etc*) faire de la pâtisserie; **baked beans** *npl* haricots blancs à la sauce tomate; **baked potato** *n* pomme *f* de terre en robe des champs; **baker** *n* boulanger *m*; **bakery** *n* boulangerie *f*; **baking** *n* (*process*) cuisson *f*; **baking powder** *n* levure *f* (chimique)

balance ['bæləns] *n* équilibre *m*; (*Comm: sum*) solde *m*; (*remainder*) reste

m; (*scales*) balance *f* ▷ *vt* mettre or faire tenir en équilibre; (*pros and cons*) peser; (*budget*) équilibrer; (*account*) balancer; (*compensate*) compenser, contrebalancer; **~ of trade/ payments** balance commerciale/ des comptes *or* paiements; **balanced** *adj* (*personality, diet*) équilibré(e); (*report*) objectif(-ive); **balance sheet** *n* bilan *m*

balcony ['bælkənɪ] *n* balcon *m*; **do you have a room with a ~?** avez-vous une chambre avec balcon?

bald [bɔːld] *adj* chauve; (*tyre*) lisse

ball [bɔːl] *n* boule *f*; (*football*) ballon *m*; (*for tennis, golf*) balle *f*; (*dance*) bal *m*; **to play ~** jouer au ballon (*or* à la balle); (*fig*) coopérer

ballerina [bælə'riːnə] *n* ballerine *f*

ballet ['bæleɪ] *n* ballet *m*; (*art*) danse *f* (classique); **ballet dancer** *n* danseur(-euse) de ballet

balloon [bə'luːn] *n* ballon *m*

ballot ['bælət] *n* scrutin *m*

ballpoint (pen) ['bɔːlpɔɪnt-] *n* stylo *m* à bille

ballroom ['bɔːlrum] *n* salle *f* de bal

Baltic [bɔːltɪk] *n*: **the ~ (Sea)** la (mer) Baltique

bamboo [bæm'buː] *n* bambou *m*

ban [bæn] *n* interdiction *f* ▷ *vt* interdire

banana [bə'nɑːnə] *n* banane *f*

band [bænd] *n* bande *f*; (*at a dance*) orchestre *m*; (*Mil*) musique *f*, fanfare *f*

bandage ['bændɪdʒ] *n* bandage *m*, pansement *m* ▷ *vt* (*wound, leg*) mettre un pansement *or* un bandage sur

Band-Aid® ['bændeɪd] *n* (*US*) pansement adhésif

B. & B. *n abbr* = **bed and breakfast**

bandit ['bændɪt] *n* bandit *m*

bang [bæŋ] *n* détonation *f*; (*of door*) claquement *m*; (*blow*) coup (violent) ▷ *vt* frapper (violemment); (*door*) claquer ▷ *vi* détoner, claquer

Bangladesh [bæŋglə'dɛʃ] *n* Bangladesh *m*

Bangladeshi [bæŋglə'deʃi] *adj* du Bangladesh ▷ *n* habitant(e) *m/f* du Bangladesh

bangle ['bæŋgl] *n* bracelet *m*

bangs [bæŋz] *npl* (*us*: *fringe*) frange *f*

banish ['bænɪʃ] *vt* bannir

banister(s) ['bænɪstə(z)] *n(pl)* rampe *f* (d'escalier)

banjo ['bændʒəʊ] (*pl* **banjoes** or **banjos**) *n* banjo *m*

bank [bæŋk] *n* banque *f*; (*of river, lake*) bord *m*, rive *f*; (*of earth*) talus *m*, remblai *m* ▷ *vi* (*Aviat*) virer sur l'aile; **bank on** *vt fus* miser on tabler sur; **bank account** *n* compte *m* en banque; **bank balance** *n* solde *m* bancaire; **bank card** (*BRIT*) *n* carte *f* d'identité bancaire; **bank charges** *npl* (*BRIT*) frais *mpl* de banque; **banker** *n* banquier *m*; **bank holiday** *n* (*BRIT*) jour férié (*où les banques sont fermées*); *voir article* **"bank holiday"**; **banking** *n* opérations *fpl* bancaires; profession *f* de banquier; **bank manager** *n* directeur *m* d'agence (bancaire); **banknote** *n* billet *m* de banque

○ **BANK HOLIDAY**
○
○ Le terme *bank holiday* s'applique
○ au Royaume-Uni aux jours fériés
○ pendant lesquels banques et
○ commerces sont fermés. Les
○ principaux *bank holidays* à part Noël
○ et Pâques se situent au mois de
○ mai et fin août, et contrairement
○ aux pays de tradition catholique,
○ ne coïncident pas nécessairement
○ avec une fête religieuse.

bankrupt ['bæŋkrʌpt] *adj* en faillite; **to go ~** faire faillite; **bankruptcy** *n* faillite *f*

bank statement *n* relevé *m* de compte

banner ['bænər] *n* bannière *f*

bannister(s) ['bænɪstə(z)] *n(pl)* = **banister(s)**

banquet ['bæŋkwɪt] *n* banquet *m*, festin *m*

baptism ['bæptɪzəm] *n* baptême *m*

baptize [bæp'taɪz] *vt* baptiser

bar [bɑːʳ] *n* (*pub*) bar *m*; (*counter*) comptoir *m*, bar; (*rod: of metal etc*) barre *f*; (: *of window etc*) barreau *m*; (*of chocolate*) tablette *f*, plaque *f*; (*fig: obstacle*) obstacle *m*; (*prohibition*) mesure *f* d'exclusion; (*Mus*) mesure *f* ▷ *vt* (*road*) barrer; (*person*) exclure; (*activity*) interdire; **~ of soap** savonnette *f*; **behind ~s** (*prisoner*) derrière les barreaux; **the B~** (*Law*) le barreau; **~ none** sans exception

barbaric [bɑː'bærɪk] *adj* barbare

barbecue ['bɑːbɪkjuː] *n* barbecue *m*

barbed wire ['bɑːbd-] *n* fil *m* de fer barbelé

barber ['bɑːbəʳ] *n* coiffeur *m* (pour hommes); **barber's (shop)**, (*us*) **barber shop** *n* salon *m* de coiffure (pour hommes)

bar code *n* code *m* à barres, code-barre *m*

bare [bɛəʳ] *adj* nu(e) ▷ *vt* mettre à nu, dénuder; (*teeth*) montrer; **barefoot** *adj, adv* nu-pieds, (les) pieds nus; **barely** *adv* à peine

bargain ['bɑːgɪn] *n* (*transaction*) marché *m*; (*good buy*) affaire *f*, occasion *f* ▷ *vi* (*haggle*) marchander; (*negotiate*) négocier, traiter; **into the ~** par-dessus le marché; **bargain for** *vt fus* (*inf*): **he got more than he ~ed for!** il en a eu pour son argent!

barge [bɑːdʒ] *n* péniche *f*; **barge in** *vi* (*walk in*) faire irruption; (*interrupt talk*) intervenir mal à propos

bark [bɑːk] *n* (*of tree*) écorce *f*; (*of dog*) aboiement *m* ▷ *vi* aboyer

barley ['bɑːlɪ] *n* orge *f*

barmaid ['bɑːmeɪd] *n* serveuse *f* (de bar), barmaid *f*

barman ['bɑːmən] (*irreg*) *n* serveur *m* (de bar), barman *m*

barn [bɑːn] *n* grange *f*

barometer [bə'rɒmɪtə^r] n
baromètre m

baron ['bærən] n baron m; **baroness**
n baronne f

barracks ['bærəks] npl caserne f

barrage ['bærɑ:ʒ] n (Mil) tir m de
barrage; (dam) barrage m; (of criticism)
feu m

barrel ['bærəl] n tonneau m; (of gun)
canon m

barren ['bærən] adj stérile

barrette [bə'rɛt] (US) n barrette f

barricade [bærɪ'keɪd] n barricade f

barrier ['bærɪə^r] n barrière f

barring ['bɑ:rɪŋ] prep sauf

barrister ['bærɪstə^r] n (BRIT) avocat
(plaidant)

barrow ['bærəu] n (cart) charrette
f à bras

bartender ['bɑ:tɛndə^r] n (US) serveur
m (de bar), barman m

base [beɪs] n base f ▷ vt (opinion,
belief): **to ~ sth on** baser or fonder qch
sur ▷ adj vil(e), bas(se)

baseball ['beɪsbɔ:l] n base-ball
m; **baseball cap** n casquette f de
base-ball

Basel [bɑ:l] n = **Basle**

basement ['beɪsmənt] n sous-sol m

bases ['beɪsi:z] npl of **basis**

bash [bæʃ] vt (inf) frapper, cogner

basic ['beɪsɪk] adj (precautions, rules)
élémentaire; (principles, research)
fondamental(e); (vocabulary, salary) de
base; (minimal) réduit(e) au minimum,
rudimentaire; **basically** adv (in fact) en
fait; (essentially) fondamentalement;
basics npl; **the basics** l'essentiel m

basil ['bæzl] n basilic m

basin ['beɪsn] n (vessel, also Geo)
cuvette f, bassin m; (BRIT: for food) bol
m; (also: **wash~**) lavabo m

basis (pl **bases**) ['beɪsɪs, -si:z] n base
f; **on a part-time/trial ~** à temps
partiel/à l'essai

basket ['bɑ:skɪt] n corbeille f; (with
handle) panier m; **basketball** n
basket-ball m

Basle [bɑ:l] n Bâle

Basque [bæsk] adj basque ▷ n
Basque m/f; **the ~ Country** le Pays
basque

bass [beɪs] n (Mus) basse f

bastard ['bɑ:stəd] n enfant
naturel(le), bâtard(e); (inf!) salaud m (!)

bat [bæt] n chauve-souris f; (for
baseball etc) batte f; (BRIT: for table
tennis) raquette f ▷ vt: **he didn't ~ an
eyelid** il n'a pas sourcillé or bronché

batch [bætʃ] n (of bread) fournée f; (of
papers) liasse f; (of applicants, letters)
paquet m

bath (pl **baths**) [bɑ:θ, bɑ:ðz] n bain
m; (bathtub) baignoire f ▷ vt baigner,
donner un bain à; **to have a ~**
prendre un bain; see also **baths**

bathe [beɪð] vi se baigner ▷ vt
baigner; (wound etc) laver

bathing ['beɪðɪŋ] n baignade f;
bathing costume, (US) **bathing suit**
n maillot m (de bain)

bath: bathrobe n peignoir m de bain;
bathroom n salle f de bains; **baths**
[bɑ:ðz] npl (BRIT: also: **swimming
baths**) piscine f; **bath towel** n
serviette f de bain; **bathtub** n
baignoire f

baton ['bætən] n bâton m; (Mus)
baguette f; (club) matraque f

batter ['bætə^r] vt battre ▷ n pâte
f à frire; **battered** adj (hat, pan)
cabossé(e); **battered wife/child**
épouse/enfant maltraité(e) or
martyr(e)

battery ['bætərɪ] n (for torch, radio)
pile f; (Aut, Mil) batterie f; **battery
farming** n élevage m en batterie

battle ['bætl] n bataille f, combat m
▷ vi se battre, lutter; **battlefield** n
champ m de bataille

bay [beɪ] n (of sea) baie f; (BRIT: for
parking) place f de stationnement;
(: for loading) aire f de chargement;
B~ of Biscay golfe m de Gascogne;
to hold sb at ~ tenir qn à distance
or en échec

bay leaf n laurier m
bazaar [bə'zɑ:ʳ] n (shop, market) bazar m; (sale) vente f de charité
BBC n abbr (= British Broadcasting Corporation) office de la radiodiffusion et télévision britannique
B.C. adv abbr (= before Christ) av. J.-C.

 KEYWORD

be [bi:] (pt **was, were**, pp **been**) aux vb **1** (with present participle, forming continuous tenses): **what are you doing?** que faites-vous?; **they're coming tomorrow** ils viennent demain; **I've been waiting for you for 2 hours** je t'attends depuis 2 heures
2 (with pp, forming passives) être; **to be killed** être tué(e); **the box had been opened** la boîte avait été ouverte; **he was nowhere to be seen** on ne le voyait nulle part
3 (in tag questions): **it was fun, wasn't it?** c'était drôle, n'est-ce pas?; **he's good-looking, isn't he?** il est beau, n'est-ce pas?; **she's back, is she?** elle est rentrée, n'est-ce pas or alors?
4 (+to +infinitive): **the house is to be sold** (necessity) la maison doit être vendue; (future) la maison va être vendue; **he's not to open it** il ne doit pas l'ouvrir
▶ vb + complement **1** (gen) être; **I'm English** je suis anglais(e); **I'm tired** je suis fatigué(e); **I'm hot/cold** j'ai chaud/froid; **he's a doctor** il est médecin; **be careful/good/quiet!** faites attention/soyez sages/taisez-vous!; **2 and 2 are 4** 2 et 2 font 4
2 (of health) aller; **how are you?** comment allez-vous?; **I'm better now** je vais mieux maintenant; **he's very ill** il est très malade
3 (of age) avoir; **how old are you?** quel âge avez-vous?; **I'm sixteen (years old)** j'ai seize ans
4 (cost) coûter; **how much was the meal?** combien a coûté le repas?; **that'll be £5, please** ça fera 5 livres, s'il vous plaît; **this shirt is £17** cette chemise coûte 17 livres
▶ vi **1** (exist, occur etc) être, exister; **the prettiest girl that ever was** la fille la plus jolie qui ait jamais existé; **is there a God?** y a-t-il un dieu?; **be that as it may** quoi qu'il en soit; **so be it** soit
2 (referring to place) être, se trouver; **I won't be here tomorrow** je ne serai pas là demain
3 (referring to movement) aller; **where have you been?** où êtes-vous allé(s)?
▶ impers vb **1** (referring to time) être; **it's 5 o'clock** il est 5 heures; **it's the 28th of April** c'est le 28 avril
2 (referring to distance): **it's 10 km to the village** le village est à 10 km
3 (referring to the weather) faire; **it's too hot/cold** il fait trop chaud/froid; **it's windy today** il y a du vent aujourd'hui
4 (emphatic): **it's me/the postman** c'est moi/le facteur; **it was Maria who paid the bill** c'est Maria qui a payé la note

beach [bi:tʃ] n plage f ▷ vt échouer
beacon ['bi:kən] n (lighthouse) fanal m; (marker) balise f
bead [bi:d] n perle f; (of dew, sweat) goutte f; **beads** npl (necklace) collier m
beak [bi:k] n bec m
beam [bi:m] n (Archit) poutre f; (of light) rayon m ▷ vi rayonner
bean [bi:n] n haricot m; (of coffee) grain m; **beansprouts** npl pousses fpl or germes mpl de soja
bear [bɛəʳ] n ours m ▷ vt (pt **bore**, pp **borne**) porter; (endure) supporter; (interest) rapporter ▷ vi: **to ~ right/left** obliquer à droite/gauche, se diriger vers la droite/gauche
beard [bɪəd] n barbe f

bearer ['bɛərəʳ] n porteur m; (of passport etc) titulaire m/f

bearing ['bɛərɪŋ] n maintien m, allure f; (connection) rapport m; **(ball) bearings** npl (Tech) roulement m (à billes)

beast [biːst] n bête f; (inf: person) brute f

beat [biːt] n battement m; (Mus) temps m, mesure f; (of policeman) ronde f ▷ vt, vi (pt **beat**, pp **beaten**) battre; **off the ~ en track** hors des chemins or sentiers battus; **to ~ it** (inf) ficher le camp; **beat up** vt (inf: person) tabasser; **beating** n raclée f

beautiful ['bjuːtɪful] adj beau (belle); **beautifully** adv admirablement

beauty ['bjuːtɪ] n beauté f; **beauty parlour**, (US) **beauty parlor** n institut m de beauté; **beauty salon** n institut m de beauté; **beauty spot** n (on skin) grain m de beauté; (BRIT Tourism) site naturel (d'une grande beauté)

beaver ['biːvəʳ] n castor m

became [bɪ'keɪm] pt of **become**

because [bɪ'kɔz] conj parce que; **~ of** prep à cause de

beckon ['bɛkən] vt (also: **~ to**) faire signe (de venir) à

become [bɪ'kʌm] vi devenir; **to ~ fat/thin** grossir/maigrir; **to ~ angry** se mettre en colère

bed [bɛd] n lit m; (of flowers) parterre m; (of coal, clay) couche f; (of sea, lake) fond m; **to go to ~** aller se coucher; **bed and breakfast** n (terms) chambre et petit déjeuner; (place) ≈ chambre f d'hôte; voir article **"bed and breakfast"**; **bedclothes** npl couvertures fpl et draps mpl; **bedding** n literie f; **bed linen** n draps mpl de lit (et taies fpl d'oreillers), literie f; **bedroom** n chambre f (à coucher); **bedside** n: **at sb's bedside** au chevet de qn; **bedside lamp** n lampe f de chevet; **bedside table** n table f de chevet; **bedsit(ter)** n (BRIT) chambre

meublée, studio m; **bedspread** n couvre-lit m, dessus-de-lit m; **bedtime** n: **it's bedtime** c'est l'heure de se coucher

b

● **BED AND BREAKFAST**
●
● Un *bed and breakfast* est une
● petite pension dans une maison
● particulière ou une ferme où l'on
● peut louer une chambre avec
● petit déjeuner compris pour
● un prix modique par rapport
● à ce que l'on paierait dans un
● hôtel. Ces établissements sont
● communément appelés "B & B",
● et sont signalés par une pancarte
● dans le jardin ou au-dessus de
● la porte.

bee [biː] n abeille f

beech [biːtʃ] n hêtre m

beef [biːf] n bœuf m; **roast ~** rosbif m; **beefburger** n hamburger m

been [biːn] pp of **be**

beer [bɪəʳ] n bière f; **beer garden** n (BRIT) jardin m d'un pub (où l'on peut emmener ses consommations)

beet [biːt] n (vegetable) betterave f; (US: also: **red ~**) betterave (potagère)

beetle ['biːtl] n scarabée m, coléoptère m

beetroot ['biːtruːt] n (BRIT) betterave f

before [bɪ'fɔːʳ] prep (of time) avant; (of space) devant ▷ conj avant que + sub; avant de ▷ adv avant; **~ going** avant de partir; **~ she goes** avant qu'elle (ne) parte; **the week ~** la semaine précédente or d'avant; **I've never seen it ~** c'est la première fois que je le vois; **beforehand** adv au préalable, à l'avance

beg [bɛg] vi mendier ▷ vt mendier; (forgiveness, mercy etc) demander; (entreat) supplier; **to ~ sb to do sth** supplier qn de faire qch; see also **pardon**

began [bɪ'gæn] pt of **begin**

beggar ['bɛgə'] n mendiant(e)

begin [bɪ'gɪn] (pt **began**, pp **begun**) vt, vi commencer; **to ~ doing** or **to do sth** commencer à faire qch; **beginner** n débutant(e); **beginning** n commencement m, début m

begun [bɪ'gʌn] pp of **begin**

behalf [bɪ'hɑːf] n **on ~ of**, (us) **in ~ of** (representing) de la part de; (for benefit of) pour le compte de; **on my/his ~** de ma/sa part

behave [bɪ'heɪv] vi se conduire, se comporter; (well: also: **~ o.s.**) se conduire bien or comme il faut; **behaviour**, (us) **behavior** n comportement m, conduite f

behind [bɪ'haɪnd] prep derrière; (time) en retard sur; (supporting) **to be ~ sb** soutenir qn ▷ adv derrière; en retard ▷ n derrière m; **~ the scenes** dans les coulisses; **to be ~ (schedule) with sth** être en retard dans qch

beige [beɪʒ] adj beige

Beijing ['beɪ'dʒɪŋ] n Pékin

being ['biːɪŋ] n être m; **to come into ~** prendre naissance

belated [bɪ'leɪtɪd] adj tardif(-ive)

belch [bɛltʃ] vi avoir un renvoi, roter ▷ vt (smoke etc: also: **~ out**) vomir, cracher

Belgian ['bɛldʒən] adj belge, de Belgique ▷ n Belge m/f

Belgium ['bɛldʒəm] n Belgique f

belief [bɪ'liːf] n (opinion) conviction f; (trust, faith) foi f

believe [bɪ'liːv] vt, vi croire, estimer; **to ~ in** (God) croire en; (ghosts, method) croire à; **believer** n (in idea, activity) partisan(e); (Rel) croyant(e)

bell [bɛl] n cloche f; (small) clochette f, grelot m; (on door) sonnette f; (electric) sonnerie f

bellboy ['bɛlbɔɪ], (us) **bellhop** ['bɛlhɔp] n groom m, chasseur m

bellow ['bɛləu] vi (bull) meugler; (person) brailler

bell pepper n (esp us) poivron m

belly ['bɛlɪ] n ventre m; **belly button** (inf) n nombril m

belong [bɪ'lɔŋ] vi: **to ~ to** appartenir à; (club etc) faire partie de; **this book ~s here** ce livre va ici, la place de ce livre est ici; **belongings** npl affaires fpl, possessions fpl

beloved [bɪ'lʌvɪd] adj (bien-)aimé(e), chéri(e)

below [bɪ'ləu] prep sous, au-dessous de ▷ adv en dessous; en contre-bas; **see ~** voir plus bas or plus loin or ci-dessous

belt [bɛlt] n ceinture f; (Tech) courroie f ▷ vt (thrash) donner une raclée à; **beltway** n (us Aut) route f de ceinture; (: motorway) périphérique m

bemused [bɪ'mjuːzd] adj médusé(e)

bench [bɛntʃ] n banc m; (in workshop) établi m; **the B~** (Law: judges) la magistrature, la Cour

bend [bɛnd] (pt, pp **bent**) vt courber; (leg, arm) plier ▷ vi se courber ▷ n (in road) virage m, tournant m; (in pipe, river) coude m; **bend down** vi se baisser; **bend over** vi se pencher

beneath [bɪ'niːθ] prep sous, au-dessous de; (unworthy of) indigne de ▷ adv dessous, au-dessous, en bas

beneficial [bɛnɪ'fɪʃəl] adj: **~ (to)** salutaire (pour), bénéfique (à)

benefit ['bɛnɪfɪt] n avantage m, profit m; (allowance of money) allocation f ▷ vt faire du bien à, profiter à ▷ vi: **he'll ~ from it** cela lui fera du bien, il y gagnera or s'en trouvera bien

Benelux ['bɛnɪlʌks] n Bénélux m

benign [bɪ'naɪn] adj (person, smile) bienveillant(e), affable; (Med) bénin(-igne)

bent [bɛnt] pt, pp of **bend** ▷ n inclination f, penchant m ▷ adj: **to be ~ on** être résolu(e) à

bereaved [bɪ'riːvd] n: **the ~** la famille du disparu

beret ['bɛreɪ] n béret m

Berlin [bə:'lɪn] n Berlin

Bermuda [bə'mjuːdə] *n* Bermudes *fpl*

Bern [bəːn] *n* Berne

berry ['bɛrɪ] *n* baie *f*

berth [bəːθ] *n* (*bed*) couchette *f*; (*for ship*) poste *m* d'amarrage, mouillage *m* ▷ *vi* (*in harbour*) venir à quai; (*at anchor*) mouiller

beside [bɪ'saɪd] *prep* à côté de; (*compared with*) par rapport à; **that's ~ the point** ça n'a rien à voir; **to be ~ o.s. (with anger)** être hors de soi; **besides** *adv* en outre, de plus ▷ *prep* en plus de; (*except*) excepté

best [bɛst] *adj* meilleur(e) ▷ *adv* le mieux; **the ~ part of** (*quantity*) le plus clair de, la plus grande partie de; **at ~** au mieux; **to make the ~ of sth** s'accommoder de qch (du mieux que l'on peut); **to do one's ~** faire de son mieux; **to the ~ of my knowledge** pour autant que je sache; **to the ~ of my ability** du mieux que je pourrai; **best-before date** *n* date *f* de limite d'utilisation *or* de consommation; **best man** (*irreg*) *n* garçon *m* d'honneur; **bestseller** *n* best-seller *m*, succès *m* de librairie

bet [bɛt] *n* pari *m* ▷ *vt*, *vi* (*pt* bet, *pp* betted) parier; **to ~ sb sth** parier qch à qn

betray [bɪ'treɪ] *vt* trahir

better ['bɛtə'] *adj* meilleur(e) ▷ *adv* mieux ▷ *vt* améliorer ▷ *n*: **to get the ~ of** triompher de, l'emporter sur; **you had ~ do it** vous feriez mieux de le faire; **he thought ~ of it** il s'est ravisé; **to get ~** (*Med*) aller mieux; (*improve*) s'améliorer

betting ['bɛtɪŋ] *n* paris *mpl*; **betting shop** *n* (BRIT) bureau *m* de paris

between [bɪ'twiːn] *prep* entre ▷ *adv* au milieu, dans l'intervalle

beverage ['bɛvərɪdʒ] *n* boisson *f* (*gén sans alcool*)

beware [bɪ'wɛə'] *vi*: **to ~ (of)** prendre garde (à); **"~ of the dog"** "(attention) chien méchant"

bewildered [bɪ'wɪldəd] *adj* dérouté(e), ahuri(e)

beyond [bɪ'jɔnd] *prep* (*in space, time*) au-delà de; (*exceeding*) au-dessus de ▷ *adv* au-delà; **~ doubt** hors de doute; **~ repair** irréparable

bias ['baɪəs] *n* (*prejudice*) préjugé *m*, parti pris; (*preference*) prévention *f*; **bias(s)ed** *adj* partial(e), montrant un parti pris

bib [bɪb] *n* bavoir *m*

Bible ['baɪbl] *n* Bible *f*

bicarbonate of soda [baɪ'kɑːbənɪt-] *n* bicarbonate *m* de soude

biceps ['baɪsɛps] *n* biceps *m*

bicycle ['baɪsɪkl] *n* bicyclette *f*; **bicycle pump** *n* pompe *f* à vélo

bid [bɪd] *n* offre *f*; (*at auction*) enchère *f*; (*attempt*) tentative *f* ▷ *vi* (*pt*, *pp* bid) faire une enchère *or* offre ▷ *vt* (*pt* **bade**, *pp* **bidden**) faire une enchère *or* offre de; **to ~ sb good day** souhaiter le bonjour à qn; **bidder** *n*: **the highest bidder** le plus offrant

bidet ['biːdeɪ] *n* bidet *m*

big [bɪg] *adj* (*in height: person, building, tree*) grand(e); (*in bulk, amount: person, parcel, book*) gros(se); **Big Apple** *n voir article* **"Big Apple"**; **bigheaded** *adj* prétentieux(-euse); **big toe** *n* gros orteil

---

● BIG APPLE
●
● Si l'on sait que "The Big Apple"
● désigne la ville de New York ("apple"
● est en réalité un terme d'argot
● signifiant "grande ville"), on connaît
● moins les surnoms donnés aux
● autres grandes villes américaines.
● Chicago est surnommée "Windy
● City" à cause des rafales soufflant
● du lac Michigan, La Nouvelle-
● Orléans doit son sobriquet
● de "Big Easy" à son style de
● vie décontracté, et l'industrie

- automobile a donné à Detroit son
- surnom de "Motown".

bike [baɪk] n vélo m; **bike lane** n piste
f cyclable

bikini [bɪˈkiːnɪ] n bikini m

bilateral [baɪˈlætərl] adj bilatéral(e)

bilingual [baɪˈlɪŋgwəl] adj bilingue

bill [bɪl] n note f, facture f; (in restaurant)
addition f, note f; (Pol) projet m de loi;
(US: banknote) billet m (de banque);
(notice) affiche f; (of bird) bec m; **put it
on my ~** mettez-le sur mon compte;
"post no ~s" "défense d'afficher"; **to fit
or fill the ~** (fig) faire l'affaire; **billboard**
n (US) panneau m d'affichage; **billfold**
[ˈbɪlfəuld] n (US) portefeuille m

billiards [ˈbɪljədz] n billard m

billion [ˈbɪljən] n (BRIT) billion m
(million de millions); (US) milliard m

bin [bɪn] n boîte f; (BRIT: also: **dust~,
litter ~**) poubelle f; (for coal) coffre m

bind (pt, pp bound) [baɪnd, baund] vt
attacher; (book) relier; (oblige) obliger,
contraindre ▷ n (inf: nuisance) scie f

binge [bɪndʒ] n (inf): **to go on a ~**
faire la bringue

bingo [ˈbɪŋgəu] n sorte de jeu de loto
pratiqué dans des établissements publics

binoculars [bɪˈnɔkjuləz] npl
jumelles fpl

bio...: **biochemistry** [baɪəˈkɛmɪstrɪ]
n biochimie f; **biodegradable**
[ˈbaɪəudɪˈɡreɪdəbl] adj biodégradable;
biodiesel [ˈbaɪəudiːzl] n biogazole m,
biodiesel m; **biofuel** [ˈbaɪəufjuəl] n
biocarburant m; **biography** [baɪˈɔɡrəfɪ]
n biographie f; **biological** adj
biologique; **biology** [baɪˈɔlədʒɪ] n
biologie f; **biometric** [baɪəˈmɛtrɪk]
adj biométrique

bipolar [baɪˈpəulər] adj bipolaire

birch [bəːtʃ] n bouleau m

bird [bəːd] n oiseau m; (BRIT inf: girl)
nana f; **bird flu** n grippe f aviaire;
bird of prey n oiseau m de proie;
birdwatching n ornithologie f
(d'amateur)

Biro® [ˈbaɪərəu] n stylo m à bille

birth [bəːθ] n naissance f; **to
give ~ to** donner naissance
à, mettre au monde; (animal)
mettre bas; **birth certificate**
n acte m de naissance; **birth
control** n (policy) limitation f des
naissances; (methods) méthode(s)
contraceptive(s); **birthday** n
anniversaire m ▷ cpd (cake, card etc)
d'anniversaire; **birthmark** n envie
f, tache f de vin; **birthplace** n lieu m
de naissance

biscuit [ˈbɪskɪt] n (BRIT) biscuit m; (US)
petit pain au lait

bishop [ˈbɪʃəp] n évêque m; (Chess)
fou m

bistro [ˈbiːstrəu] n petit restaurant
m, bistrot m

bit [bɪt] pt of **bite** ▷ n morceau m;
(Comput) bit m, élément m binaire; (of
tool) mèche f; (of horse) mors m; **a ~ of**
un peu de; **a ~ mad/dangerous** un
peu fou/risqué; **~ by ~** petit à petit

bitch [bɪtʃ] n (dog) chienne f; (offensive)
salope f (!), garce f

bite [baɪt] vt, vi (pt bit, pp bitten)
mordre; (insect) piquer ▷ n morsure
f; (insect bite) piqûre f; (mouthful)
bouchée f; **let's have a ~ (to eat)**
mangeons un morceau; **to ~ one's
nails** se ronger les ongles

bitten [ˈbɪtn] pp of **bite**

bitter [ˈbɪtər] adj amer(-ère);
(criticism) cinglant(e); (icy: weather,
wind) glacial(e) ▷ n (BRIT: beer) bière f
(à forte teneur en houblon)

bizarre [bɪˈzɑːr] adj bizarre

black [blæk] adj noir(e) ▷ n (colour)
noir m ▷ vt (BRIT Industry) boycotter;
to give sb a ~ eye pocher l'œil à qn,
faire un œil au beurre noir à qn; **to
be in the ~** (in credit) avoir un compte
créditeur; **~ and blue** (bruised)
couvert(e) de bleus; **black out** vi
(faint) s'évanouir; **blackberry** n mûre
f; **blackbird** n merle m; **blackboard**
n tableau noir; **black coffee** n café

noir; **blackcurrant** n cassis m;
black ice n verglas m; **blackmail**
n chantage m ▷ vt faire chanter,
soumettre au chantage; **black
market** n marché noir; **blackout**
n panne f d'électricité; (in wartime)
black-out m; (TV) interruption f
d'émission; (fainting) syncope f; **black
pepper** n poivre noir; **black pudding**
n boudin (noir); **Black Sea** n: **the
Black Sea** la mer Noire
bladder ['blædə'] n vessie f
blade [bleɪd] n lame f; (of propeller)
pale f; **a ~ of grass** un brin d'herbe
blame [bleɪm] n faute f, blâme m
▷ vt: **to ~ sb/sth for sth** attribuer
à qn/qch la responsabilité de qch;
reprocher qch à qn/qch; **I'm not to ~**
ce n'est pas ma faute
bland [blænd] adj (taste, food) doux
(douce), fade
blank [blæŋk] adj blanc (blanche);
(look) sans expression, dénué(e)
d'expression ▷ n espace m vide, blanc
m; (cartridge) cartouche f à blanc; **his
mind was a ~** il avait la tête vide
blanket ['blæŋkɪt] n couverture f; (of
snow, cloud) couche f
blast [blɑːst] n explosion f; (shock
wave) souffle m; (of air, steam) bouffée f
▷ vt faire sauter or exploser
blatant ['bleɪtənt] adj flagrant(e),
criant(e)
blaze [bleɪz] n (fire) incendie m; (fig)
flamboiement m ▷ vi (fire) flamber;
(fig) flamboyer, resplendir ▷ vt: **to ~
a trail** (fig) montrer la voie; **in a ~ of
publicity** à grand renfort de publicité
blazer ['bleɪzə'] n blazer m
bleach [bliːtʃ] n (also: **household ~**)
eau f de Javel ▷ vt (linen) blanchir;
bleachers npl (us Sport) gradins mpl
(en plein soleil)
bleak [bliːk] adj morne, désolé(e);
(weather) triste, maussade; (smile)
lugubre; (prospect, future) morose
bled [blɛd] pt, pp of **bleed**

bleed (pt, pp **bled**) [bliːd, blɛd] vt
saigner; (brakes, radiator) purger ▷ vi
saigner; **my nose is ~ing** je saigne
du nez
blemish ['blɛmɪʃ] n défaut m; (on
reputation) tache f
blend [blɛnd] n mélange m ▷ vt
mélanger ▷ vi (colours etc: also: ~ **in**)
se mélanger, se fondre, s'allier;
blender n (Culin) mixeur m
bless (pt, pp **blessed** or **blest**) [blɛs,
blɛst] vt bénir; ~ **you!** (after sneeze) à
tes souhaits!; **blessing** n bénédiction
f; (godsend) bienfait m
blew [bluː] pt of **blow**
blight [blaɪt] vt (hopes etc) anéantir,
briser
blind [blaɪnd] adj aveugle ▷ n (for
window) store m ▷ vt aveugler; ~
people les aveugles mpl; **blind alley**
n impasse f; **blindfold** n bandeau m
▷ adj, adv les yeux bandés ▷ vt bander
les yeux à
blink [blɪŋk] vi cligner des yeux; (light)
clignoter
bliss [blɪs] n félicité f, bonheur m sans
mélange
blister ['blɪstə'] n (on skin) ampoule f,
cloque f; (on paintwork) boursouflure f
▷ vi (paint) se boursoufler, se cloquer
blizzard ['blɪzəd] n blizzard m,
tempête f de neige
bloated ['bləʊtɪd] adj (face) bouffi(e);
(stomach, person) gonflé(e)
blob [blɒb] n (drop) goutte f; (stain,
spot) tache f
block [blɒk] n bloc m; (in pipes)
obstruction f; (toy) cube m; (of
buildings) pâté m (de maisons) ▷ vt
bloquer; (fig) faire obstacle à; **the
sink is ~ed** l'évier est bouché; ~
of flats (BRIT) immeuble (locatif);
mental ~ blocage m; **block up** vt
boucher; **blockade** [blɒˈkeɪd]
n blocus m ▷ vt faire le blocus
de; **blockage** n obstruction f;
blockbuster n (film, book) grand
succès; **block capitals** npl

majuscules *fpl* d'imprimerie; **block letters** *npl* majuscules *fpl*

blog [blɔg] *n* blog *m* ▷ *vi* bloguer

blogger ['blɔgəʳ] *n* blogueur(-euse)

blogosphere ['blɔgəsfɪəʳ] *n* blogosphère *f*

bloke [bləuk] *n* (BRIT inf) type *m*

blond(e) [blɔnd] *adj*, *n* blond(e)

blood [blʌd] *n* sang *m*; **blood donor** *n* donneur(-euse) de sang; **blood group** *n* groupe sanguin; **blood poisoning** *n* empoisonnement *m* du sang; **blood pressure** *n* tension (artérielle); **bloodshed** *n* effusion *f* de sang, carnage *m*; **bloodshot** *adj*: **bloodshot eyes** yeux injectés de sang; **bloodstream** *n* sang *m*, système sanguin; **blood test** *n* analyse *f* de sang; **blood transfusion** *n* transfusion *f* de sang; **blood type** *n* groupe sanguin; **blood vessel** *n* vaisseau sanguin; **bloody** *adj* sanglant(e); (BRIT inf!): **this bloody ...** ce foutu ..., ce putain de ... (!) ▷ *adv*: **bloody strong/good** (BRIT inf!) vachement *or* sacrément fort/bon

bloom [blu:m] *n* fleur *f* ▷ *vi* être en fleur

blossom ['blɔsəm] *n* fleur(s) *f(pl)* ▷ *vi* être en fleurs; (fig) s'épanouir

blot [blɔt] *n* tache *f* ▷ *vt* tacher; (ink) sécher

blouse [blauz] *n* (feminine garment) chemisier *m*, corsage *m*

blow [bləu] (*pt* **blew**, *pp* **blown**) *n* coup *m* ▷ *vi* souffler ▷ *vt* (instrument) jouer de; (fuse) faire sauter; **to ~ one's nose** se moucher; **blow away** *vi* s'envoler ▷ *vt* chasser, faire s'envoler; **blow out** *vi* (fire, flame) s'éteindre; (tyre) éclater; (fuse) sauter; **blow up** *vi* exploser, sauter ▷ *vt* faire sauter; (tyre) gonfler; (Phot) agrandir; **blow-dry** *n* (hairstyle) brushing *m*

blue [blu:] *adj* bleu(e); (depressed) triste; **~ film/joke** film *m*/histoire *f* pornographique; **out of the ~** (fig) à l'improviste, sans qu'on s'y attende; **bluebell** *n* jacinthe *f* des bois;

blueberry *n* myrtille *f*, airelle *f*; **blue cheese** *n* (fromage) bleu *m*; **blues** *npl*; **the blues** (Mus) le blues; **to have the blues** (inf: feeling) avoir le cafard

bluff [blʌf] *vi* bluffer ▷ *n* bluff *m*; **to call sb's ~** mettre qn au défi d'exécuter ses menaces

blunder ['blʌndəʳ] *n* gaffe *f*, bévue *f* ▷ *vi* faire une gaffe *or* une bévue

blunt [blʌnt] *adj* (knife) émoussé(e), peu tranchant(e); (pencil) mal taillé(e); (person) brusque, ne mâchant pas ses mots

blur [blɜːʳ] *n* (shape): **to become a ~** devenir flou ▷ *vt* brouiller, rendre flou(e); **blurred** *adj* flou(e)

blush [blʌʃ] *vi* rougir ▷ *n* rougeur *f*; **blusher** *n* rouge *m* à joues

board [bɔːd] *n* (wooden) planche *f*; (on wall) panneau *m*; (for chess etc) plateau *m*; (cardboard) carton *m*; (committee) conseil *m*, comité *m*; (in firm) conseil d'administration; (Naut, Aviat): **on ~** à bord ▷ *vt* (ship) monter à bord de; (train) monter dans; **full ~** (BRIT) pension complète; **half ~** (BRIT) demi-pension *f*; **~ and lodging** *n* chambre *f* avec pension; **to go by the ~** (hopes, principles) être abandonné(e); **board game** *n* jeu *m* de société; **boarding card** *n* (Aviat, Naut) carte *f* d'embarquement; **boarding pass** *n* (BRIT) = **boarding card**; **boarding school** *n* internat *m*, pensionnat *m*; **board room** *n* salle *f* du conseil d'administration

boast [bəust] *vi*: **to ~ (about** *or* **of)** se vanter (de)

boat [bəut] *n* bateau *m*; (small) canot *m*; barque *f*

bob [bɔb] *vi* (boat, cork on water: also: **~ up and down**) danser, se balancer

bobby pin ['bɔbɪ-] *n* (US) pince *f* à cheveux

body ['bɔdɪ] *n* corps *m*; (of car) carrosserie *f*; (fig: society) organe *m*, organisme *m*; **body-building** *n* body-building *m*, culturisme *m*; **bodyguard**

n garde *m* du corps; **bodywork** *n* carrosserie *f*

bog [bɔg] *n* tourbière *f* ⊳ *vt*: **to get ~ged down (in)** (*fig*) s'enliser (dans)

bogus ['bəugəs] *adj* bidon *inv*; fantôme

boil [bɔil] *vt* (faire) bouillir ⊳ *vi* bouillir ⊳ *n* (*Med*) furoncle *m*; **to come to the** *or* (*US*) **a ~** bouillir; **boil down** *vi* (*fig*): **to ~ down to** se réduire *or* ramener à; **boil over** *vi* déborder; **boiled egg** *n* œuf *m* à la coque; **boiler** *n* chaudière *f*; **boiling** ['bɔilɪŋ] *adj*: **I'm boiling (hot)** (*inf*) je crève de chaud; **boiling point** *n* point *m* d'ébullition

bold [bəuld] *adj* hardi(e), audacieux(-euse); (*pej*) effronté(e); (*outline, colour*) franc (franche), tranché(e), marqué(e)

bollard ['bɔləd] *n* (*BRIT Aut*) borne lumineuse *or* de signalisation

bolt [bəult] *n* verrou *m*; (*with nut*) boulon *m* ⊳ *adv*: **~ upright** droit(e) comme un piquet ⊳ *vt* (*door*) verrouiller; (*food*) engloutir ⊳ *vi* se sauver, filer (comme une flèche); (*horse*) s'emballer

bomb [bɔm] *n* bombe *f* ⊳ *vt* bombarder; **bombard** [bɔm'bɑːd] *vt* bombarder; **bomber** *n* (*Aviat*) bombardier *m*; (*terrorist*) poseur *m* de bombes; **bomb scare** *n* alerte *f* à la bombe

bond [bɔnd] *n* lien *m*; (*binding promise*) engagement *m*, obligation *f*; (*Finance*) obligation; **bonds** *npl* (*chains*) chaînes *fpl*; **in ~** (*of goods*) en entrepôt

bone [bəun] *n* os *m*; (*of fish*) arête *f* ⊳ *vt* désosser; ôter les arêtes de

bonfire ['bɔnfaiə*r*] *n* feu *m* (de joie); (*for rubbish*) feu

bonnet ['bɔnit] *n* bonnet *m*; (*BRIT: of car*) capot *m*

bonus ['bəunəs] *n* (*money*) prime *f*; (*advantage*) avantage *m*

boo [buː] *excl* hou!, peuh! ⊳ *vt* huer

book [buk] *n* livre *m*; (*of stamps, tickets etc*) carnet *m* ⊳ *vt* (*ticket*) prendre;

(*seat, room*) réserver; (*football player*) prendre le nom de, donner un carton à; **books** *npl* (*Comm*) comptes *mpl*, comptabilité *f*; **I ~ed a table in the name of ...** j'ai réservé une table au nom de ...; **book in** *vi* (*BRIT: at hotel*) prendre sa chambre; **book up** *vt* réserver; **the hotel is ~ed up** l'hôtel est complet; **bookcase** *n* bibliothèque *f* (*meuble*); **booking** *n* (*BRIT*) réservation *f*; **I confirmed my booking by fax/email** j'ai confirmé ma réservation par fax/e-mail; **booking office** *n* (*BRIT*) bureau *m* de location; **book-keeping** *n* comptabilité *f*; **booklet** *n* brochure *f*; **bookmaker** *n* bookmaker *m*; **bookmark** *n* (*for book*) marque-page *m*; (*Comput*) signet *m*; **bookseller** *n* libraire *m/f*; **bookshelf** *n* (*single*) étagère *f* (à livres); (*bookcase*) bibliothèque *f*; **bookshop, bookstore** *n* librairie *f*

boom [buːm] *n* (*noise*) grondement *m*; (*in prices, population*) forte augmentation; (*busy period*) boom *m*, vague *f* de prospérité ⊳ *vi* gronder; prospérer

boost [buːst] *n* stimulant *m*, remontant *m* ⊳ *vt* stimuler

boot [buːt] *n* botte *f*; (*for hiking*) chaussure *f* (de marche); (*ankle boot*) bottine *f*; (*BRIT: of car*) coffre *m* ⊳ *vt* (*Comput*) lancer, mettre en route; **to ~** (*in addition*) par-dessus le marché, en plus

booth [buːð] *n* (*at fair*) baraque (foraine); (*of telephone etc*) cabine *f*; (*also: **voting ~**) isoloir *m*

booze [buːz] (*inf*) *n* boissons *fpl* alcooliques, alcool *m*

border ['bɔːdə*r*] *n* bordure *f*; bord *m*; (*of a country*) frontière *f*; **borderline** *n* (*fig*) ligne *f* de démarcation

bore [bɔː*r*] *pt of* **bear** ⊳ *vt* (*person*) ennuyer, raser; (*hole*) percer; (*well, tunnel*) creuser ⊳ *n* (*person*) raseur(-euse); (*boring thing*) barbe *f*;

(of gun) calibre m; **bored** adj: **to be bored** s'ennuyer; **boredom** n ennui m

boring ['bɔːrɪŋ] adj ennuyeux(-euse)

born [bɔːn] adj: **to be ~** naître; **I was ~ in 1960** je suis né en 1960

borne [bɔːn] pp of **bear**

borough ['bʌrə] n municipalité f

borrow ['bɔrəu] vt: **to ~ sth (from sb)** emprunter qch (à qn)

Bosnian ['bɔznɪən] adj bosniaque, bosnien(ne) ▷ n Bosniaque m/f, Bosnien(ne)

bosom ['buzəm] n poitrine f; (fig) sein m

boss [bɔs] n patron(ne) ▷ vt (also: **~ about**, **~ around**) mener à la baguette; **bossy** adj autoritaire

both [bəuθ] adj les deux, l'un(e) et l'autre ▷ pron: **~ (of them)** les deux, tous (toutes) (les) deux, l'un(e) et l'autre; **~ of us went**, **we ~ went** nous y sommes allés tous les deux ▷ adv: **~ A and B** A et B

bother ['bɔðər] vt (worry) tracasser; (needle, bait) importuner, ennuyer; (disturb) déranger ▷ vi (also: **~ o.s.**) se tracasser, se faire du souci ▷ n (trouble) ennuis mpl; **to ~ doing** prendre la peine de faire; **don't ~** ce n'est pas la peine; **it's no ~** aucun problème

bottle ['bɔtl] n bouteille f; (baby's) biberon m; (of perfume, medicine) flacon m ▷ vt mettre en bouteille(s); **bottle bank** n conteneur m (de bouteilles); **bottle-opener** n ouvre-bouteille m

bottom ['bɔtəm] n (of container, sea etc) fond m; (buttocks) derrière m; (of page, list) bas m; (of mountain, tree, hill) pied m ▷ adj (shelf, step) du bas

bought [bɔːt] pt, pp of **buy**

boulder ['bəuldər] n gros rocher (gén lisse, arrondi)

bounce [bauns] vi (ball) rebondir; (cheque) être refusé (étant sans provision) ▷ vt faire rebondir ▷ n (rebound) rebond m; **bouncer** n (inf: at dance, club) videur m

bound [baund] pt, pp of **bind** ▷ n (gen pl) limite f; (leap) bond m ▷ vi (leap) bondir ▷ vt (limit) borner ▷ adj: **to be ~ to do sth** (obliged) être obligé(e) or avoir obligation de faire qch; **he's ~ to fail** (likely) il est sûr d'échouer, son échec est inévitable or assuré; **~ by** (law, regulation) engagé(e) par; **~ for** à destination de; **out of ~s** dont l'accès est interdit

boundary ['baundrɪ] n frontière f

bouquet ['bukeɪ] n bouquet m

bourbon ['buəbən] n (US: also: **~ whiskey**) bourbon m

bout [baut] n période f; (of malaria etc) accès m, crise f, attaque f; (Boxing etc) combat m, match m

boutique [buːˈtiːk] n boutique f

bow¹ [bəu] n nœud m; (weapon) arc m; (Mus) archet m

bow² [bau] n (with body) révérence f, inclination f (du buste or corps); (Naut: also: **~s**) proue f ▷ vi faire une révérence, s'incliner

bowels [bauəlz] npl intestins mpl; (fig) entrailles fpl

bowl [bəul] n (for eating) bol m; (for washing) cuvette f; (ball) boule f ▷ vi (Cricket) lancer (la balle); **bowler** n (Cricket) lanceur m (de la balle); (BRIT: also: **bowler hat**) (chapeau m) melon m; **bowling** n (game) jeu m de boules, jeu de quilles; **bowling alley** n bowling m; **bowling green** n terrain m de boules (gazonné et carré); **bowls** n (jeu m de) boules fpl

bow tie [bəu-] n nœud m papillon

box [bɔks] n boîte f; (also: **cardboard ~**) carton m; (Theat) loge f ▷ vt mettre en boîte ▷ vi boxer, faire de la boxe; **boxer** ['bɔksər] n (person) boxeur m; **boxer shorts** npl caleçon m; **boxing** ['bɔksɪŋ] n (sport) boxe f; **Boxing Day** n (BRIT) le lendemain de Noël; voir article **"Boxing Day"**; **boxing gloves** npl gants mpl de boxe; **boxing ring** n ring m; **box office** n bureau m de location

boy [bɔɪ] n garçon m; **boy band** n
boys band m
boycott ['bɔɪkɔt] n boycottage m ▷ vt
boycotter
boyfriend ['bɔɪfrɛnd] n (petit) ami
bra [brɑː] n soutien-gorge m
brace [breɪs] n (support) attache
f, agrafe f; (BRIT: also: **~s**: on
teeth) appareil m (dentaire);
(tool) vilebrequin m ▷ vt (support)
consolider, soutenir; **braces** npl (BRIT:
for trousers) bretelles fpl; **to ~ o.s.** (fig)
se préparer mentalement
bracelet ['breɪslɪt] n bracelet m
bracket ['brækɪt] n (Tech) tasseau
m, support m; (group) classe f,
tranche f; (also: **brace ~**) accolade f;
(also: **round ~**) parenthèse f; (also:
square ~) crochet m ▷ vt mettre entre
parenthèses; **in ~s** entre parenthèses
or crochets
brag [bræg] vi se vanter
braid [breɪd] n (trimming) galon m; (of
hair) tresse f, natte f
brain [breɪn] n cerveau m; **brains** npl
(intellect, food) cervelle f
braise [breɪz] vt braiser
brake [breɪk] n frein m ▷ vt, vi freiner;
brake light n feu m de stop
bran [bræn] n son m
branch [brɑːntʃ] n branche f; (Comm)
succursale f (: of bank) agence f;
branch off vi (road) bifurquer;
branch out vi diversifier ses activités
brand [brænd] n marque
(commerciale) ▷ vt (cattle) marquer
(au fer rouge); **brand name** n nom m
de marque; **brand-new** adj tout(e)
neuf (neuve), flambant neuf (neuve)

brandy ['brændɪ] n cognac m
brash [bræʃ] adj effronté(e)
brass [brɑːs] n cuivre m (jaune), laiton
m; **the ~** (Mus) les cuivres; **brass
band** n fanfare f
brat [bræt] n (pej) mioche m/f,
môme m/f
brave [breɪv] adj courageux(-euse),
brave ▷ vt braver, affronter; **bravery**
n bravoure f, courage m
brawl [brɔːl] n rixe f, bagarre f
Brazil [brə'zɪl] n Brésil m; **Brazilian**
adj brésilien(ne) ▷ n Brésilien(ne)
breach [briːtʃ] vt ouvrir une brèche
dans ▷ n (gap) brèche f; (breaking): **~
of contract** rupture f de contrat; **~ of
the peace** attentat m à l'ordre public
bread [brɛd] n pain m; **breadbin**
n (BRIT) boîte f or huche f à pain; **~
breadbox** n (US) boîte f or huche f à
pain; **breadcrumbs** npl miettes fpl de
pain; (Culin) chapelure f, panure f
breadth [brɛtθ] n largeur f
break [breɪk] (pt **broke**, pp **broken**)
vt casser, briser; (promise) rompre;
(law) violer ▷ vi se casser, se briser;
(weather) tourner; (storm) éclater;
(day) se lever ▷ n (gap) brèche f;
(fracture) cassure f; (rest) interruption
f, arrêt m (: short) pause f; (: at school)
récréation f; (chance) chance f,
occasion f favorable; **to ~ one's
leg** etc se casser la jambe etc; **to ~ a
record** battre un record; **to ~ the
news to sb** annoncer la nouvelle
à qn; **break down** vt (door etc)
enfoncer; (figures, data) décomposer,
analyser ▷ vi s'effondrer; (Med) faire
une dépression (nerveuse); (Aut)
tomber en panne; **my car has
broken down** ma voiture est en
panne; **break in** vt (horse etc) dresser
▷ vi (burglar) entrer par effraction;
(interrupt) interrompre; **break into**
vt fus (house) s'introduire or pénétrer
par effraction dans; **break off** vi
(speaker) s'interrompre; (branch)
se rompre ▷ vt (talks, engagement)

rompre; **break out** vi éclater, se déclarer; (*prisoner*) s'évader; **to ~ out in spots** se couvrir de boutons; **break up** vi (*partnership*) cesser, prendre fin; (*marriage*) se briser; (*crowd, meeting*) se séparer; (*ship*) se disloquer; (*Scol: pupils*) être en vacances; (*line*) couper ▷ vt fracasser, casser; (*fight etc*) interrompre, faire cesser; (*marriage*) désunir; **the line's** *or* **you're ~ing up** ça coupe; **breakdown** n (*Aut*) panne f; (*in communications, marriage*) rupture f; (*Med: also:* **nervous breakdown**) dépression (nerveuse); (*of figures*) ventilation f, répartition f; **breakdown van,** (*us*) **breakdown truck** n dépanneuse f

breakfast ['brɛkfəst] n petit déjeuner m; **what time is ~?** le petit déjeuner est à quelle heure?

break: break-in n cambriolage m; **breakthrough** n percée f

breast [brɛst] n (*of woman*) sein m; (*chest*) poitrine f; (*of chicken, turkey*) blanc m; **breast-feed** vt, vi (*irreg: like* **feed**) allaiter; **breast-stroke** n brasse f

breath [brɛθ] n haleine f, souffle m; **to take a deep ~** respirer à fond; **out of ~** à bout de souffle, essoufflé(e)

Breathalyser® ['brɛθəlaɪzəʳ] (*BRIT*) n alcootest m

breathe [bri:ð] vt, vi respirer; **breathe in** vi inspirer ▷ vt aspirer; **breathe out** vt, vi expirer; **breathing** n respiration f

breath: breathless adj essoufflé(e), haletant(e); **breathtaking** adj stupéfiant(e), à vous couper le souffle; **breath test** n alcootest m

bred [brɛd] pt, pp of **breed**

breed [bri:d] (*pt, pp* **bred**) vt élever, faire l'élevage de ▷ vi se reproduire ▷ n race f, variété f

breeze [bri:z] n brise f

breezy ['bri:zɪ] adj (*day, weather*) venteux(-euse); (*manner*) désinvolte; (*person*) jovial(e)

brew [bru:] vt (*tea*) faire infuser; (*beer*) brasser ▷ vi (*fig*) se préparer, couver; **brewery** n brasserie f (*fabrique*)

bribe [braɪb] n pot-de-vin m ▷ vt acheter; soudoyer; **bribery** n corruption f

bric-a-brac ['brɪkəbræk] n bric-à-brac m

brick [brɪk] n brique f; **bricklayer** n maçon m

bride [braɪd] n mariée f, épouse f; **bridegroom** n marié m, époux m; **bridesmaid** n demoiselle f d'honneur

bridge [brɪdʒ] n pont m; (*Naut*) passerelle f (de commandement); (*of nose*) arête f; (*Cards, Dentistry*) bridge m ▷ vt (*gap*) combler

bridle ['braɪdl] n bride f

brief [bri:f] adj bref (brève) ▷ n (*Law*) dossier m, cause f; (*gen*) tâche f ▷ vt mettre au courant; **briefs** npl slip m; **briefcase** n serviette f; porte-documents m inv; **briefing** n instructions fpl; (*Press*) briefing m; **briefly** adv brièvement

brigadier [brɪgə'dɪəʳ] n brigadier général

bright [braɪt] adj brillant(e); (*room, weather*) clair(e); (*person: clever*) intelligent(e), doué(e); (: *cheerful*) gai(e); (*idea*) génial(e); (*colour*) vif (vive)

brilliant ['brɪljənt] adj brillant(e); (*light, sunshine*) éclatant(e); (*inf: great*) super

brim [brɪm] n bord m

brine [braɪn] n (*Culin*) saumure f

bring (*pt, pp* **brought**) [brɪŋ, brɔ:t] vt (*thing*) apporter; (*person*) amener; **bring about** vt provoquer, entraîner; **bring back** vt rapporter; (*person*) ramener; **bring down** vt (*lower*) abaisser; (*shoot down*) abattre; (*government*) faire s'effondrer; **bring in** vt (*person*) faire entrer; (*object*) rentrer; (*Pol: legislation*) introduire; (*produce: income*) rapporter; **bring on** vt (*illness, attack*) provoquer;

(*player, substitute*) amener; **bring out**
vt sortir; (*meaning*) faire ressortir,
mettre en relief; **bring up** vt élever;
(*carry up*) monter; (*question*) soulever;
(*food: vomit*) vomir, rendre
brink [brɪŋk] n bord m
brisk [brɪsk] adj vif (vive); (*abrupt*)
brusque; (*trade etc*) actif(-ive)
bristle ['brɪsl] n poil m ▷ vi se hérisser
Brit [brɪt] n abbr (*inf: = British person*)
Britannique m/f
Britain ['brɪtən] n (*also:* **Great ~**) la
Grande-Bretagne
British ['brɪtɪʃ] adj britannique ▷ npl;
the ~ les Britanniques mpl; **British
Isles** npl; **the British Isles** les îles fpl
Britanniques
Briton ['brɪtən] n Britannique m/f
Brittany ['brɪtənɪ] n Bretagne f
brittle ['brɪtl] adj cassant(e), fragile
broad [brɔːd] adj large; (*distinction*)
général(e); (*accent*) prononcé(e); **in ~
daylight** en plein jour
B road n (BRIT) ≈ route
départementale
broad: broadband n transmission
f à haut débit; **broad bean** n fève
f; **broadcast** (*pt, pp* **broadcast**) n
émission f ▷ vt (*Radio*) radiodiffuser;
(*TV*) téléviser ▷ vi émettre; **broaden**
vt élargir; **to broaden one's mind**
élargir ses horizons ▷ vi s'élargir;
broadly adv en gros, généralement;
broad-minded adj large d'esprit
broccoli ['brɔkəlɪ] n brocoli m
brochure ['brəuʃjuər] n
prospectus m, dépliant m
broil [brɔil] vt (US) rôtir
broke [brəuk] pt of **break** ▷ adj (*inf*)
fauché(e)
broken ['brəukn] pp of **break** ▷ adj
(*stick, leg etc*) cassé(e); (*machine:
also:* **~ down**) fichu(e); **in ~ French/
English** dans un français/anglais
approximatif or hésitant
broker ['brəukər] n courtier m
bronchitis [brɔŋ'kaɪtɪs] n bronchite f
bronze [brɔnz] n bronze m

brooch [brəutʃ] n broche f
brood [bruːd] n couvée f ▷ vi (*person*)
méditer (sombrement), ruminer
broom [brum] n balai m; (*Bot*)
genêt m
Bros. abbr (*Comm: = brothers*) Frères
broth [brɔθ] n bouillon m de viande et
de légumes
brothel ['brɔθl] n maison close,
bordel m
brother ['brʌðər] n frère m; **brother-
in-law** n beau-frère m
brought [brɔːt] pt, pp of **bring**
brow [brau] n front m; (*eyebrow*)
sourcil m; (*of hill*) sommet m
brown [braun] adj brun(e), marron
inv; (*hair*) châtain inv; (*tanned*)
bronzé(e) ▷ n (*colour*) brun m, marron
m ▷ vt brunir; (*Culin*) faire dorer, faire
roussir; **brown bread** n pain m bis
Brownie ['braunɪ] n jeannette f
éclaireuse (cadette)
brown rice n riz m complet
brown sugar n cassonade f
browse [brauz] vi (*in shop*) regarder
(*sans acheter*); **to ~ through a
book** feuilleter un livre; **browser** n
(*Comput*) navigateur m
bruise [bruːz] n bleu m, ecchymose
f, contusion f ▷ vt contusionner,
meurtrir
brunette [bruː'nɛt] n (*femme*) brune
brush [brʌʃ] n brosse f; (*for painting*)
pinceau m; (*for shaving*) blaireau m;
(*quarrel*) accrochage m, prise f de bec
▷ vt brosser; (*also:* **~ past, ~ against**)
effleurer, frôler
Brussels ['brʌslz] n Bruxelles
Brussels sprout n chou m de
Bruxelles
brutal ['bruːtl] adj brutal(e)
B.Sc. n abbr = **Bachelor of Science**
BSE n abbr (= *bovine spongiform
encephalopathy*) ESB f, BSE f
bubble ['bʌbl] n bulle f ▷ vi
bouillonner, faire des bulles;
(*sparkle, fig*) pétiller; **bubble bath**
n bain moussant; **bubble gum** n

chewing-gum m; **bubblejet printer**
['bʌbldʒet-] n imprimante f à bulle
d'encre

buck [bʌk] n mâle m (d'un lapin, lièvre,
daim etc); (US inf) dollar m ▷ vi ruer,
lancer une ruade; **to pass the ~ (to
sb)** se décharger de la responsabilité
(sur qn)

bucket ['bʌkɪt] n seau m; **bucket list** n
liste f de choses à faire avant de mourir

buckle ['bʌkl] n boucle f ▷ vt (belt etc)
boucler, attacher ▷ vi (warp) tordre,
gauchir (: wheel) se voiler

bud [bʌd] n bourgeon m; (of flower)
bouton m ▷ vi bourgeonner; (flower)
éclore

Buddhism ['budɪzəm] n
bouddhisme m

Buddhist ['budɪst] adj bouddhiste
▷ n Bouddhiste m/f

buddy ['bʌdɪ] n (US) copain m

budge [bʌdʒ] vt faire bouger ▷ vi bouger

budgerigar ['bʌdʒərɪgɑːʳ] n
perruche f

budget ['bʌdʒɪt] n budget m ▷ vi: **to ~
for sth** inscrire qch au budget

budgie ['bʌdʒɪ] n = **budgerigar**

buff [bʌf] adj (couleur f) chamois m
▷ n (inf: enthusiast) mordu(e)

buffalo ['bʌfələu] (pl **buffalo** or
buffaloes) n (BRIT) buffle m; (US)
bison m

buffer ['bʌfəʳ] n tampon m; (Comput)
mémoire f tampon

buffet n ['bufeɪ] (food, BRIT: bar) buffet
m ▷ vt ['bʌfɪt] secouer, ébranler;
buffet car n (BRIT Rail) voiture-bar f

bug [bʌg] n (bedbug etc) punaise f;
(esp US: any insect) insecte m, bestiole
f; (fig: germ) virus m, microbe m;
(spy device) dispositif m d'écoute
(électronique), micro clandestin;
(Comput: of program) erreur f ▷ vt
(room) poser des micros dans; (inf:
annoy) embêter

buggy ['bʌgɪ] n poussette f

build [bɪld] n (of person) carrure
f, charpente f ▷ vt (pt, pp **built**)

construire, bâtir; **build up** vt
accumuler, amasser; (business)
développer; (reputation) bâtir; **builder**
n entrepreneur m; **building** n (trade)
construction f; (structure) bâtiment
m, construction f (: residential, offices)
immeuble m; **building site** n chantier
m (de construction); **building
society** n (BRIT) société f de crédit
immobilier

built [bɪlt] pt, pp of **build**; **built-in**
adj (cupboard) encastré(e); (device)
incorporé(e); intégré(e); **built-up** adj:
built-up area zone urbanisée

bulb [bʌlb] n (Bot) bulbe m, oignon m;
(Elec) ampoule f

Bulgaria [bʌl'gɛərɪə] n Bulgarie f;
Bulgarian adj bulgare ▷ n Bulgare
m/f

bulge [bʌldʒ] n renflement m,
gonflement m ▷ vi faire saillie;
présenter un renflement; (pocket,
file): **to be bulging with** être plein(e)
à craquer de

bulimia [bə'lɪmɪə] n boulimie f

bulimic [bju:'lɪmɪk] adj, n
boulimique m/f

bulk [bʌlk] n masse f, volume m; **in
~** (Comm) en gros, en vrac; **the ~
of** la plus grande or grosse partie
de; **bulky** adj volumineux(-euse),
encombrant(e)

bull [bul] n taureau m; (male elephant,
whale) mâle m

bulldozer ['buldəuzəʳ] n bulldozer m

bullet ['bulɪt] n balle f (de fusil etc)

bulletin ['bulɪtɪn] n bulletin m,
communiqué m; (also: **news ~**)
(bulletin d')informations fpl; **bulletin
board** n (Comput) messagerie f
(électronique)

bullfight ['bulfaɪt] n corrida f, course
f de taureaux; **bullfighter** n torero m;
bullfighting n tauromachie f

bully ['bulɪ] n brute f, tyran m ▷ vt
tyranniser, rudoyer

bum [bʌm] n (inf: BRIT: backside)
derrière m; (esp US: tramp)

vagabond(e), traîne-savates *m/f inv*; (*idler*) glandeur *m*

bumblebee ['bʌmblbiː] *n* bourdon *m*

bump [bʌmp] *n* (*blow*) coup *m*, choc *m*; (*jolt*) cahot *m*; (*on road etc, on head*) bosse *f* ▷ *vt* heurter, cogner; (*car*) emboutir; **bump into** *vt fus* rentrer dans, tamponner; (*inf: meet*) tomber sur; **bumper** *n* pare-chocs *m inv* ▷ *adj*: **bumper crop/harvest** récolte/moisson exceptionnelle; **bumpy** *adj* (*road*) cahoteux(-euse); **it was a bumpy flight/ride** on a été secoués dans l'avion/la voiture

bun [bʌn] *n* (*cake*) petit gâteau; (*bread*) petit pain au lait; (*of hair*) chignon *m*

bunch [bʌntʃ] *n* (*of flowers*) bouquet *m*; (*of keys*) trousseau *m*; (*of bananas*) régime *m*; (*of people*) groupe *m*; **bunches** *npl* (*in hair*) couettes *fpl*; **~ of grapes** grappe *f* de raisin

bundle ['bʌndl] *n* paquet *m* ▷ *vt* (*also*: **~ up**) faire un paquet de; (*put*): **to ~ sth/sb into** fourrer *or* enfourner qch/qn dans

bungalow ['bʌŋɡələu] *n* bungalow *m*

bungee jumping ['bʌndʒiːˈdʒʌmpɪŋ] *n* saut *m* à l'élastique

bunion ['bʌnjən] *n* oignon *m* (*au pied*)

bunk [bʌŋk] *n* couchette *f*; **bunk beds** *npl* lits superposés

bunker ['bʌŋkəʳ] *n* (*coal store*) soute *f* à charbon; (*Mil, Golf*) bunker *m*

bunny ['bʌnɪ] *n* (*also*: **~ rabbit**) lapin *m*

buoy [bɔɪ] *n* bouée *f*; **buoyant** *adj* (*ship*) flottable; (*carefree*) gai(e), plein(e) d'entrain; (*Comm: market, economy*) actif(-ive)

burden ['bəːdn] *n* fardeau *m*, charge *f* ▷ *vt* charger; (*oppress*) accabler, surcharger

bureau (*pl* **bureaux**) ['bjuərəu, -z] *n* (BRIT: *writing desk*) bureau *m*, secrétaire *m*; (US: *chest of drawers*) commode *f*; (*office*) bureau, office *m*

bureaucracy [bjuəˈrɔkrəsɪ] *n* bureaucratie *f*

bureaucrat ['bjuərəkræt] *n* bureaucrate *m/f*, rond-de-cuir *m*

bureau de change [-dəˈʃɑ̃ʒ] (*pl* **bureaux de change**) *n* bureau *m* de change

bureaux ['bjuərəuz] *npl of* **bureau**

burger ['bəːɡəʳ] *n* hamburger *m*

burglar ['bəːɡləʳ] *n* cambrioleur *m*; **burglar alarm** *n* sonnerie *f* d'alarme; **burglary** *n* cambriolage *m*

Burgundy ['bəːɡəndɪ] *n* Bourgogne *f*

burial ['berɪəl] *n* enterrement *m*

burn [bəːn] *vt, vi* (*pt* **burned**, *pp* **burnt**) brûler ▷ *n* brûlure *f*; **burn down** *vt* incendier, détruire par le feu; **burn out** *vt* (*writer etc*): **to ~ o.s. out** s'user (à force de travailler); **burning** *adj* (*building, forest*) en flammes; (*issue, question*) brûlant(e); (*ambition*) dévorant(e)

Burns' Night [bəːnz-] *n* fête écossaise à la mémoire du poète Robert Burns

---

○ **BURNS' NIGHT**
○
○ *Burns' Night* est une fête qui a lieu
○ le 25 janvier, à la mémoire du poète
○ écossais Robert Burns (1759–1796),
○ à l'occasion de laquelle les Écossais
○ partout dans le monde organisent
○ un souper, en général arrosé
○ de whisky. Le plat principal est
○ toujours le haggis, servi avec de la
○ purée de pommes de terre et de la
○ purée de rutabagas. On apporte
○ le haggis au son des cornemuses
○ et au cours du repas on lit des
○ poèmes de Burns et on chante ses
○ chansons.

---

burnt [bəːnt] *pt, pp of* **burn**

burp [bəːp] (*inf*) *n* rot *m* ▷ *vi* roter

burrow ['bʌrəu] *n* terrier *m* ▷ *vi* (*rabbit*) creuser un terrier; (*rummage*) fouiller

burst [bəːst] (*pt, pp* **burst**) *vt* faire éclater; (*river: banks etc*) rompre ▷ *vi* éclater; (tyre) crever ▷ n explosion f; (also: **~ pipe**) fuite f (due à une rupture); **a ~ of enthusiasm/energy** un accès d'enthousiasme/d'énergie; **to ~ into flames** s'enflammer soudainement; **to ~ out laughing** éclater de rire; **to ~ into tears** fondre en larmes; **to ~ open** vi s'ouvrir violemment or soudainement; **to be ~ing with** (container) être plein(e) (due à craquer) de, regorger de; (fig) être débordant(e) de; **burst into** vt fus (room etc) faire irruption dans

bury ['bɛrɪ] vt enterrer

bus (pl **buses**) [bʌs, 'bʌsɪz] n (auto)bus m; **bus conductor** n receveur(-euse) m/f de bus

bush [buʃ] n buisson m; (scrub land) brousse f; **to beat about the ~** tourner autour du pot

business ['bɪznɪs] n (matter, firm) affaire f; (trading) affaires fpl; (job, duty) travail m; **to be away on ~** être en déplacement d'affaires; **it's none of my ~** cela ne me regarde pas, ce ne sont pas mes affaires; **he means ~** il ne plaisante pas, il est sérieux; **business class** n (on plane) classe f affaires; **businesslike** adj sérieux(-euse), efficace; **businessman** (irreg) n homme m d'affaires; **business trip** n voyage m d'affaires; **businesswoman** (irreg) n femme f d'affaires

busker ['bʌskər] n (BRIT) artiste ambulant(e)

bus: bus pass n carte f de bus; **bus shelter** n abribus m; **bus station** n gare routière; **bus stop** n arrêt m d'autobus

bust [bʌst] n buste m; (measurement) tour m de poitrine ▷ adj (inf: broken) fichu(e), fini(e); **to go ~** (inf) faire faillite

bustling ['bʌslɪŋ] adj (town) très animé(e)

busy ['bɪzɪ] adj occupé(e); (shop, street) très fréquenté(e); (US:

telephone, line) occupé ▷ vt: **to ~ o.s.** s'occuper; **busy signal** n (US) tonalité f occupé inv

 KEYWORD

but [bʌt] conj mais; **I'd love to come, but I'm busy** j'aimerais venir mais je suis occupé; **he's not English but French** il n'est pas anglais mais français; **but that's far too expensive!** mais c'est bien trop cher! ▷ prep (apart from, except) sauf, excepté; **nothing but** rien d'autre que; **we've had nothing but trouble** nous n'avons eu que des ennuis; **no-one but him can do it** lui seul peut le faire; **who but a lunatic would do such a thing?** qui sinon un fou ferait une chose pareille?; **but for you/your help** sans toi/ton aide; **anything but that** tout sauf or excepté ça, tout mais pas ça ▷ adv (just, only) ne ... que; **she's but a child** elle n'est qu'une enfant; **had I but known** si seulement j'avais su; **I can but try** je peux toujours essayer; **all but finished** pratiquement terminé

butcher ['butʃər] n boucher m ▷ vt massacrer; (cattle etc for meat) tuer; **butcher's (shop)** n boucherie f

butler ['bʌtlər] n maître d'hôtel

butt [bʌt] n (cask) gros tonneau; (of gun) crosse f; (of cigarette) mégot m; (BRIT fig: target) cible f ▷ vt donner un coup de tête à

butter ['bʌtər] n beurre m ▷ vt beurrer; **buttercup** n bouton m d'or

butterfly ['bʌtəflaɪ] n papillon m; (Swimming: also: **~ stroke**) brasse f papillon

buttocks ['bʌtəks] npl fesses fpl

button ['bʌtn] n bouton m; (US: badge) pin m ▷ vt (also: **~ up**) boutonner ▷ vi se boutonner

buy [baɪ] (pt, pp **bought**) vt acheter
▷ n achat m; **to ~ sb sth/sth from
sb** acheter qch à qn; **to ~ sb a drink**
offrir un verre or à boire à qn; **can I ~
you a drink?** je vous offre un verre?;
where can I ~ some postcards?
où est-ce que je peux acheter des
cartes postales?; **buy out** vt (partner)
désintéresser; **buy up** vt acheter en
bloc, rafler; **buyer** n acheteur(-euse)
m/f

buzz [bʌz] n bourdonnement m; (inf:
phone call): **to give sb a ~** passer
un coup de fil à qn ▷ vi bourdonner;
buzzer n timbre m électrique

KEYWORD

by [baɪ] prep **1** (referring to cause, agent)
par, de; **killed by lightning** tué par
la foudre; **surrounded by a fence**
entouré d'une barrière; **a painting
by Picasso** un tableau de Picasso
2 (referring to method, manner, means):
by bus/car en autobus/voiture;
by train par le or en train; **to pay
by cheque** payer par chèque; **by
moonlight/candlelight** à la lueur
de la lune/d'une bougie; **by saving
hard, he …** à force d'économiser, il …
3 (via, through) par; **we came by
Dover** nous sommes venus par
Douvres
4 (close to, past) à côté de; **the house
by the school** la maison à côté de
l'école; **a holiday by the sea** des
vacances au bord de la mer; **she
went by me** elle est passée à côté de
moi; **I go by the post office every
day** je passe devant la poste tous
les jours
5 (with time: not later than) avant;
(: during): **by daylight** à la lumière du
jour; **by night** la nuit, de nuit; **by 4
o'clock** avant 4 heures; **by this time
tomorrow** d'ici demain à la même
heure; **by the time I got here it was
too late** lorsque je suis arrivé il était

déjà trop tard
6 (amount) à; **by the kilo/metre** au
kilo/au mètre; **paid by the hour**
payé à l'heure
7 (Math: measure): **to divide/
multiply by 3** diviser/multiplier par
3; **a room 3 metres by 4** une pièce
de 3 mètres sur 4; **it's broader by a
metre** c'est plus large d'un mètre
8 (according to) d'après, selon; **it's 3
o'clock by my watch** il est 3 heures
à ma montre; **it's all right by me** je
n'ai rien contre
9: **(all) by oneself** etc tout(e) seul(e)
▶ adv **1** see **go; pass** etc
2: **by and by** un peu plus tard,
bientôt; **by and large** dans
l'ensemble

bye(-bye) ['baɪ-] excl au revoir!, salut!
by-election ['baɪɪlɛkʃən] n (BRIT)
élection (législative) partielle
bypass ['baɪpɑːs] n rocade f; (Med)
pontage m ▷ vt éviter
byte [baɪt] n (Comput) octet m

b

C [si:] n (Mus) do m

cab [kæb] n taxi m; (of train, truck) cabine f

cabaret ['kæbəreɪ] n (show) spectacle m de cabaret

cabbage ['kæbɪdʒ] n chou m

cabin ['kæbɪn] n (house) cabane f, hutte f; (on ship) cabine f; (on plane) compartiment m; **cabin crew** n (Aviat) équipage m

cabinet ['kæbɪnɪt] n (Pol) cabinet m; (furniture) petit meuble à tiroirs et rayons; (also: **display ~**) vitrine f, petite armoire vitrée; **cabinet minister** n ministre m (membre du cabinet)

cable ['keɪbl] n câble m ▷ vt câbler, télégraphier; **cable car** n téléphérique m; **cable television** n télévision f par câble

cactus (pl **cacti**) ['kæktəs, -taɪ] n cactus m

café ['kæfeɪ] n ≈ café(-restaurant) m (sans alcool)

cafeteria [kæfɪ'tɪərɪə] n cafétéria f

caffeine ['kæfi:n] n caféine f

cage [keɪdʒ] n cage f

cagoule [kə'gu:l] n K-way® m

Cairo ['kaɪərəu] n Le Caire

cake [keɪk] n gâteau m; **~ of soap** savonnette f

calcium ['kælsɪəm] n calcium m

calculate ['kælkjuleɪt] vt calculer; (estimate: chances, effect) évaluer; **calculation** [kælkju'leɪʃən] n calcul m; **calculator** n calculatrice f

calendar ['kæləndə^r] n calendrier m

calf (pl **calves**) [kɑ:f, kɑ:vz] n (of cow) veau m; (of other animals) petit m; (also: **~skin**) veau m, vachette f; (Anat) mollet m

calibre, (US) **caliber** ['kælɪbə^r] n calibre m

call [kɔ:l] vt appeler; (meeting) convoquer ▷ vi appeler; (visit: also: **~ in, ~ round**) passer ▷ n (shout) appel m, cri m; (also: **telephone ~**) coup m de téléphone; **to be on ~** être de permanence; **to be ~ed** s'appeler; **can I make a ~ from here?** est-ce que je peux téléphoner d'ici?; **call back** vi (return) repasser; (Tel) rappeler ▷ vt (Tel) rappeler; **can you ~ back later?** pouvez-vous rappeler plus tard?; **call for** vt fus (demand) demander; (fetch) passer prendre; **call in** vt (doctor, expert, police) appeler, faire venir; **call off** vt annuler; **call on** vt fus (visit) rendre visite à, passer voir; (request): **to ~ on sb to do** inviter qn à faire; **call out** vi pousser un cri or des cris; **call up** vt (Mil) appeler, mobiliser; (Tel) appeler; **call box** n (BRIT) cabine f téléphonique; **call centre**, (US) **call center** n centre m d'appels; **caller** n (Tel) personne f qui appelle; (visitor) visiteur m

callous ['kæləs] adj dur(e), insensible

calm [kɑ:m] adj calme ▷ n calme m ▷ vt calmer, apaiser; **calm down** vi se calmer, s'apaiser ▷ vt calmer, apaiser; **calmly** ['kɑ:mlɪ] adv calmement, avec calme

Calor gas® ['kælə^r-] n (BRIT) butane m, butagaz® m

calorie ['kælərɪ] n calorie f

calves [kɑːvz] npl of **calf**

Cambodia [kæm'bəʊdɪə] n Cambodge m

camcorder ['kæmkɔːdə^r] n caméscope m

came [keɪm] pt of **come**

camel ['kæməl] n chameau m

camera ['kæmərə] n appareil photo m; (Cine, TV) caméra f; **in ~** à huis clos, en privé; **cameraman** (irreg) n caméraman m; **camera phone** n téléphone m avec appareil photo

camouflage ['kæməflɑːʒ] n camouflage m ▷ vt camoufler

camp [kæmp] n camp m ▷ vi camper ▷ adj (man) **1** (be able

campaign [kæm'peɪn] n (Mil, Pol) campagne f ▷ vi (also fig) faire campagne; **campaigner** n: **campaigner for** partisan(e) de; **campaigner against** opposant(e) à

camp: camp bed n (BRIT) lit m de camp; **camper** n campeur(-euse); (vehicle) camping-car m; **camping** n camping m; **to go camping** faire du camping; **campsite** n (terrain m de) camping m

campus ['kæmpəs] n campus m

can¹ [kæn] n (of milk, oil, water) bidon m; (tin) boîte f (de conserve) ▷ vt mettre en conserve

KEYWORD

can² [kæn] (negative **cannot** or **can't**, conditional, pt **could**) aux vb **1** (be able to) pouvoir; **you can do it if you try** vous pouvez le faire si vous essayez; **I can't hear you** je ne t'entends pas

2 (know how to) savoir; **I can swim/play tennis/drive** je sais nager/jouer au tennis/conduire; **can you speak French?** parlez-vous français?

3 (may) pouvoir; **can I use your phone?** puis-je me servir de votre téléphone?

4 (expressing disbelief, puzzlement etc): **it can't be true!** ce n'est pas possible!; **what can he want?** qu'est-ce qu'il peut bien vouloir?

5 (expressing possibility, suggestion etc): **he could be in the library** il est peut-être dans la bibliothèque; **she could have been delayed** il se peut qu'elle ait été retardée

Canada ['kænədə] n Canada m; **Canadian** [kə'neɪdɪən] adj canadien(ne) ▷ n Canadien(ne)

canal [kə'næl] n canal m

canary [kə'nɛərɪ] n canari m, serin m

cancel ['kænsəl] vt annuler; (train) supprimer; (party, appointment) décommander; (cross out) barrer, rayer; (cheque) faire opposition à; **I would like to ~ my booking** je voudrais annuler ma réservation; **cancellation** [kænsə'leɪʃən] n annulation f; suppression f

Cancer ['kænsə^r] n (Astrology) le Cancer

cancer ['kænsə^r] n cancer m

candidate ['kændɪdeɪt] n candidat(e)

candle ['kændl] n bougie f; (in church) cierge m; **candlestick** n (also: **candle holder**) bougeoir m; (bigger, ornate) chandelier m

candy ['kændɪ] n sucre candi; (US) bonbon m; **candy bar** (US) n barre f chocolatée; **candyfloss** n (BRIT) barbe f à papa

cane [keɪn] n canne f; (for baskets, chairs etc) rotin m ▷ vt (BRIT Scol) administrer des coups de bâton à

canister ['kænɪstə^r] n boîte f (gén en métal); (of gas) bombe f

cannabis ['kænəbɪs] n (drug) cannabis m

canned ['kænd] adj (food) en boîte, en conserve; (inf: music) enregistré(e); (BRIT inf: drunk) bourré(e); (US inf: worker) mis(e) à la porte

cannon ['kænən] (pl **cannon** or
cannons) n (gun) canon m
cannot ['kænɔt] = **can not**
canoe [kə'nu:] n pirogue f; (Sport)
canoë m; **canoeing** n (sport) canoë m
canon ['kænən] n (clergyman)
chanoine m; (standard) canon m
can-opener [-'əupnəʳ] n ouvre-
boîte m
can't [kɑ:nt] = **can not**
canteen [kæn'ti:n] n (eating place)
cantine f; (BRIT: of cutlery) ménagère f
canter ['kæntəʳ] vi aller au petit
galop
canvas ['kænvəs] n toile f
canvass ['kænvəs] vi (Pol): **to ~ for**
faire campagne pour ▷ vt sonder
canyon ['kænjən] n cañon m, gorge
(profonde)
cap [kæp] n casquette f; (for
swimming) bonnet m de bain; (of pen)
capuchon m; (of bottle) capsule f;
(BRIT: contraceptive: also: **Dutch ~**)
diaphragme m ▷ vt (outdo) surpasser;
(put limit on) plafonner
capability [keɪpə'bɪlɪtɪ] n aptitude
f, capacité f
capable ['keɪpəbl] adj capable
capacity [kə'pæsɪtɪ] n (of container)
capacité f, contenance f; (ability)
aptitude f
cape [keɪp] n (garment) cape f; (Geo)
cap m
caper ['keɪpəʳ] n (Culin: gen pl) câpre f;
(prank) farce f
capital ['kæpɪtl] n (also: **~ city**)
capitale f; (money) capital m; (also:
~ letter) majuscule f; **capitalism**
n capitalisme m; **capitalist** adj, n
capitaliste m/f; **capital punishment**
n peine capitale
Capitol ['kæpɪtl] n: **the ~** le Capitole
Capricorn ['kæprɪkɔ:n] n le
Capricorne
capsize [kæp'saɪz] vt faire chavirer
▷ vi chavirer
capsule ['kæpsju:l] n capsule f
captain ['kæptɪn] n capitaine m

caption ['kæpʃən] n légende f
captivity [kæp'tɪvɪtɪ] n captivité f
capture ['kæptʃəʳ] vt (prisoner, animal)
capturer; (town) prendre; (attention)
capter; (Comput) saisir ▷ n capture f;
(of data) saisie f de données
car [kɑ:ʳ] n voiture f, auto f; (US Rail)
wagon m, voiture
caramel ['kærəməl] n caramel m
carat ['kærət] n carat m
caravan ['kærəvæn] n caravane f;
caravan site n (BRIT) camping m
pour caravanes
carbohydrate [kɑ:bəu'haɪdreɪt]
n hydrate m de carbone; (food)
féculent m
carbon ['kɑ:bən] n carbone m;
carbon dioxide [-daɪ'ɔksaɪd] n gaz
m carbonique, dioxyde m de carbone;
carbon footprint n empreinte
f carbone; **carbon monoxide**
[-mɔ'nɔksaɪd] n oxyde m de carbone;
carbon-neutral adj neutre en carbone
car boot sale n voir article **"car
boot sale"**

  ● **CAR BOOT SALE**
  ●
  ● Type de brocante très populaire, où
  ● chacun vide sa cave ou son grenier.
  ● Les articles sont présentés dans
  ● des coffres de voitures et la vente
  ● a souvent lieu sur un parking ou
  ● dans un champ. Les brocanteurs
  ● d'un jour doivent s'acquitter d'une
  ● petite contribution pour participer
  ● à la vente.

---

carburettor, (US) **carburetor**
[kɑ:bju'rɛtəʳ] n carburateur m
card [kɑ:d] n carte f; (material) carton
m; **cardboard** n carton m; **card
game** n jeu m de cartes
cardigan ['kɑ:dɪgən] n cardigan m
cardinal ['kɑ:dɪnl] adj cardinal(e);
(importance) capital(e) ▷ n cardinal m
cardphone ['kɑ:dfəun] n téléphone
m à carte (magnétique)

care [kɛəʳ] n soin m, attention f; (worry) souci m ▷ vi: **to ~ about** (feel interest for) se soucier de, s'intéresser à; (person: love) être attaché(e) à; **in sb's ~** à la garde de qn, confié à qn; **~ of** (on letter) chez; **to take ~ (to do)** faire attention (à faire); **to take ~ of** vt s'occuper de; **I don't ~** ça m'est bien égal, peu m'importe; **I couldn't ~ less** cela m'est complètement égal, je m'en fiche complètement; **care for** vt fus s'occuper de; (like) aimer

career [kə'rɪəʳ] n carrière f ▷ vi (also: ~ **along**) aller à toute allure

care: carefree adj sans souci, insouciant(e); **careful** adj soigneux(-euse); (cautious) prudent(e); **(be) careful!** (fais) attention!; **carefully** adv avec soin, soigneusement; prudemment; **caregiver** n (US) (professional) travailleur social; (unpaid) personne qui s'occupe d'un proche qui est malade; **careless** adj négligent(e); (heedless) insouciant(e); **carelessness** n manque m de soin, négligence f; insouciance f; **carer** ['kɛərəʳ] n (professional) travailleur social; (unpaid) personne qui s'occupe d'un proche qui est malade; **caretaker** n gardien(ne), concierge m/f

car-ferry ['kɑːfɛrɪ] n (on sea) ferry(-boat) m; (on river) bac m

cargo ['kɑːgəʊ] (pl cargoes) n cargaison f, chargement m

car hire n (BRIT) location f de voitures

Caribbean [kærɪ'biːən] adj, n: **the ~ (Sea)** la mer des Antilles or des Caraïbes

caring ['kɛərɪŋ] adj (person) bienveillant(e); (society, organization) humanitaire

carnation [kɑː'neɪʃən] n œillet m

carnival ['kɑːnɪvl] n (public celebration) carnaval m; (US: funfair) fête foraine

carol ['kærəl] n: **(Christmas) ~** chant m de Noël

carousel [kærə'sɛl] n (for luggage) carrousel m; (US) manège m

car park (BRIT) n parking m, parc m de stationnement

carpenter ['kɑːpɪntəʳ] n charpentier m; (joiner) menuisier m

carpet ['kɑːpɪt] n tapis m ▷ vt recouvrir (d'un tapis); **fitted ~** (BRIT) moquette f

car rental n (US) location f de voitures

carriage ['kærɪdʒ] n (BRIT Rail) wagon m; (horse-drawn) voiture f; (of goods) transport m (: cost) port m; **carriageway** n (BRIT: part of road) chaussée f

carrier ['kærɪəʳ] n transporteur m, camionneur m; (company) entreprise f de transport; (Med) porteur(-euse); **carrier bag** n (BRIT) sac m en papier or en plastique

carrot ['kærət] n carotte f

carry ['kærɪ] vt (subj: person) porter; (: vehicle) transporter; (involve: responsibilities etc) comporter, impliquer; (Med: disease) être porteur de ▷ vi (sound) porter; **to get carried away** (fig) s'emballer, s'enthousiasmer; **carry on** vi (continue) continuer ▷ vt (conduct: business) diriger; (: conversation) entretenir; (continue: business, conversation) continuer; **to ~ on with sth/doing** continuer qch/à faire; **carry out** vt (orders) exécuter; (investigation) effectuer

cart [kɑːt] n charrette f ▷ vt (inf) transporter

carton ['kɑːtən] n (box) carton m; (of yogurt) pot m (en carton)

cartoon [kɑː'tuːn] n (Press) dessin m (humoristique); (satirical) caricature f; (comic strip) bande dessinée; (Cine) dessin animé

cartridge ['kɑːtrɪdʒ] n (for gun, pen) cartouche f

carve [kɑːv] vt (meat: also: ~ **up**) découper; (wood, stone) tailler, sculpter; **carving** n (in wood etc) sculpture f

car wash n station f de lavage (de voitures)

case [keɪs] n cas m; (Law) affaire f, procès m; (box) caisse f, boîte f; (for glasses) étui m; (BRIT: also: **suit~**) valise f; **in ~ of** en cas de; **in ~ he** au cas où il; **just in ~** à tout hasard; **in any ~** en tout cas, de toute façon

cash [kæʃ] n argent m; (Comm) (argent m) liquide m ▷ vt encaisser; **to pay (in) ~** payer (en argent) comptant or en espèces; **~ with order/on delivery** (Comm) payable or paiement à la commande/livraison; **I haven't got any ~** je n'ai pas de liquide; **cashback** n (discount) remise f; (at supermarket etc) retrait m (à la caisse); **cash card** n carte f de retrait; **cash desk** n (BRIT) caisse f; **cash dispenser** n distributeur m automatique de billets

cashew [kæˈʃuː] n (also: **~ nut**) noix f de cajou

cashier [kæˈʃɪəʳ] n caissier(-ère)

cashmere [ˈkæʃmɪəʳ] n cachemire m

cash point n distributeur m automatique de billets

cash register n caisse enregistreuse

casino [kəˈsiːnəu] n casino m

casket [ˈkɑːskɪt] n coffret m; (US: coffin) cercueil m

casserole [ˈkæsərəul] n (pot) cocotte f; (food) ragoût m (en cocotte)

cassette [kæˈsɛt] n cassette f; **cassette player** n lecteur m de cassettes

cast [kɑːst] (vb: pt, pp **cast**) vt (throw) jeter; (shadow: lit) projeter; (: fig) jeter; (glance) jeter ▷ n (Theat) distribution f; (also: **plaster ~**) plâtre m; **to ~ sb as Hamlet** attribuer à qn le rôle d'Hamlet; **to ~ one's vote** voter, exprimer son suffrage; **to ~ doubt on** jeter un doute sur; **cast off** vi (Naut) larguer les amarres; (Knitting) arrêter les mailles

castanets [kæstəˈnɛts] npl castagnettes fpl

caster sugar [ˈkɑːstə-] n (BRIT) sucre m semoule

cast-iron [ˈkɑːstaɪən] adj (lit) de or en fonte; (fig: will) de fer; (alibi) en béton

castle [ˈkɑːsl] n château m; (fortress) château-fort m; (Chess) tour f

casual [ˈkæʒjul] adj (by chance) de hasard, fait(e) au hasard, fortuit(e); (irregular: work etc) temporaire; (unconcerned) désinvolte; **~ wear** vêtements mpl sport inv

casualty [ˈkæʒjultɪ] n accidenté(e), blessé(e); (dead) victime f, mort(e); (BRIT Med: department) urgences fpl

cat [kæt] n chat m

Catalan [ˈkætəlæn] adj catalan(e)

catalogue, (US) **catalog** [ˈkætəlɔg] n catalogue m ▷ vt cataloguer

catalytic converter [kætəˈlɪtɪkkənˈvəːtəʳ] n pot m catalytique

cataract [ˈkætərækt] n (also Med) cataracte f

catarrh [kəˈtɑːʳ] n rhume m chronique, catarrhe f

catastrophe [kəˈtæstrəfɪ] n catastrophe f

catch [kætʃ] (pt, pp **caught**) vt attraper; (person: by surprise) prendre, surprendre; (understand) saisir; (get entangled) accrocher ▷ vi (fire) prendre; (get entangled) s'accrocher ▷ n (fish etc) prise f; (hidden problem) attrape f; (Tech) loquet m; cliquet m; **to ~ sb's attention** or **eye** attirer l'attention de qn; **to ~ fire** prendre feu; **to ~ sight of** apercevoir; **catch up** vi (with work) se rattraper, combler son retard ▷ vt (also: **~ up with**) rattraper; **catching** [ˈkætʃɪŋ] adj (Med) contagieux(-euse)

category [ˈkætɪgərɪ] n catégorie f

cater [ˈkeɪtəʳ] vi: **to ~ for** (BRIT: needs) satisfaire, pourvoir à; (readers, consumers) s'adresser à, pourvoir aux besoins de; (Comm: parties etc) préparer des repas pour

caterpillar ['kætəpɪləʳ] n chenille f
cathedral [kə'θi:drəl] n cathédrale f
Catholic ['kæθəlɪk] (Rel) adj
  catholique ▷ n catholique m/f
cattle ['kætl] npl bétail m, bestiaux
  mpl
catwalk ['kætwɔ:k] n passerelle f; (for
  models) podium m (de défilé de mode)
caught [kɔ:t] pt, pp of **catch**
cauliflower ['kɔlɪflauəʳ] n chou-
  fleur m
cause [kɔ:z] n cause f ▷ vt causer
caution ['kɔ:ʃən] n prudence f;
  (warning) avertissement m ▷ vt
  avertir, donner un avertissement à;
  cautious adj prudent(e)
cave [keɪv] n caverne f, grotte f; **cave
  in** vi (roof etc) s'effondrer
caviar(e) ['kævɪɑ:ʳ] n caviar m
cavity ['kævɪtɪ] n cavité f; (Med) carie f
cc abbr (= cubic centimetre) cm³; (on
  letter etc = carbon copy) cc
CCTV n abbr = **closed-circuit
  television**
CD n abbr (= compact disc) CD m; **CD
  burner** n graveur m de CD; **CD
  player** n platine f laser; **CD-ROM**
  [si:di:'rɔm] n abbr (= compact disc
  read-only memory) CD-ROM m inv; **CD
  writer** n graveur m de CD
cease [si:s] vt, vi cesser; **ceasefire** n
  cessez-le-feu m
cedar ['si:dəʳ] n cèdre m
ceilidh ['keɪlɪ] n bal m folklorique
  écossais or irlandais
ceiling ['si:lɪŋ] n (also fig) plafond m
celebrate ['sɛlɪbreɪt] vt, vi célébrer;
  celebration [sɛlɪ'breɪʃən] n
  célébration f
celebrity [sɪ'lɛbrɪtɪ] n célébrité f
celery ['sɛlərɪ] n céleri m (en
  branches)
cell [sɛl] n (gen) cellule f; (Elec) élément
  m (de pile)
cellar ['sɛləʳ] n cave f
cello ['tʃɛləu] n violoncelle m
Cellophane® ['sɛləfeɪn] n
  cellophane® f

cellphone ['sɛlfəun] n (téléphone m)
  portable m, mobile m
Celsius ['sɛlsɪəs] adj Celsius inv
Celtic ['kɛltɪk, 'sɛltɪk] adj celte,
  celtique
cement [sə'mɛnt] n ciment m
cemetery ['sɛmɪtrɪ] n cimetière m
censor ['sɛnsəʳ] n censeur m ▷ vt
  censurer; **censorship** n censure f
census ['sɛnsəs] n recensement m
cent [sɛnt] n (unit of dollar, euro) cent
  m (= un centième du dollar, de l'euro); see
  also **per cent**
centenary [sɛn'ti:nərɪ], (US)
centennial [sɛn'tɛnɪəl] n
  centenaire m
center ['sɛntəʳ] (US) = **centre**
centi... ['sɛntɪ]: **centigrade** adj
  centigrade; **centimetre**, (US)
  centimeter n centimètre m;
  centipede ['sɛntɪpi:d] n mille-
  pattes m inv
central ['sɛntrəl] adj central(e);
  Central America n Amérique
  centrale; **central heating** n
  chauffage central; **central
  reservation** n (BRIT Aut) terre-plein
  central
centre, (US) **center** ['sɛntəʳ] n centre
  m ▷ vt centrer; **centre-forward** n
  (Sport) avant-centre m; **centre-half** n
  (Sport) demi-centre m
century ['sɛntjurɪ] n siècle m; **in the
  twentieth ~** au vingtième siècle
CEO n abbr (US) = **chief executive
  officer**
ceramic [sɪ'ræmɪk] adj céramique
cereal ['si:rɪəl] n céréale f
ceremony ['sɛrɪmənɪ] n cérémonie f;
  to stand on ~ faire des façons
certain ['sə:tən] adj certain(e);
  to make ~ of s'assurer de; **for ~**
  certainement, sûrement; **certainly**
  adv certainement; **certainty** n
  certitude f
certificate [sə'tɪfɪkɪt] n certificat m
certify ['sə:tɪfaɪ] vt certifier; (award
  diploma to) conférer un diplôme etc

à; (*declare insane*) déclarer malade
mental(e)
cf. *abbr* (= *compare*) cf., voir
CFC *n abbr* (= *chlorofluorocarbon*) CFC *m*
chain [tʃeɪn] *n* (*gen*) chaîne *f* ▷ *vt*
(*also*: **~ up**) enchaîner, attacher (avec
une chaîne); **chain-smoke** *vi* fumer
cigarette sur cigarette
chair [tʃɛəʳ] *n* chaise *f*; (*armchair*)
fauteuil *m*; (*of university*) chaire *f*; (*of
meeting*) présidence *f* ▷ *vt* (*meeting*)
présider; **chairlift** *n* télésiège *m*;
chairman (*irreg*) *n* président *m*;
chairperson (*irreg*) *n* président(e);
chairwoman (*irreg*) *n* présidente *f*
chalet ['ʃæleɪ] *n* chalet *m*
chalk [tʃɔːk] *n* craie *f*
challenge ['tʃælɪndʒ] *n* défi *m* ▷ *vt*
défier; (*statement, right*) mettre
en question, contester; **to ~ sb
to do** mettre qn au défi de faire;
challenging *adj* (*task, career*) qui
représente un défi *or* une gageure;
(*tone, look*) de défi, provocateur(-trice)
chamber ['tʃeɪmbəʳ] *n* chambre
f; (*BRIT Law*: *gen pl*) cabinet *m*; **~ of
commerce** chambre de commerce;
chambermaid *n* femme *f* de
chambre
champagne [ʃæm'peɪn] *n*
champagne *m*
champion ['tʃæmpɪən] *n* (*also of
cause*) champion(ne); **championship**
n championnat *m*
chance [tʃɑːns] *n* (*luck*) hasard *m*;
(*opportunity*) occasion *f*, possibilité *f*;
(*hope, likelihood*) chance *f*; (*risk*) risque
m ▷ *vt* (*risk*) risquer ▷ *adj* fortuit(e),
de hasard; **to take a ~** prendre
un risque; **by ~** par hasard; **to ~ it**
risquer le coup, essayer
chancellor ['tʃɑːnsələʳ] *n* chancelier
m; **Chancellor of the Exchequer**
[-ɪks'tʃekəʳ] (*BRIT*) *n* chancelier *m* de
l'Échiquier
chandelier [ʃændə'lɪəʳ] *n* lustre *m*
change [tʃeɪndʒ] *vt* (*alter, replace*:
Comm: *money*) changer; (*switch,

substitute*: *hands, trains, clothes,
one's name etc*) changer de ▷ *vi*
(*gen*) changer; (*change clothes*) se
changer; (*be transformed*): **to ~ into**
se changer *or* transformer en ▷ *n*
changement *m*; (*money*) monnaie *f*;
to ~ gear (*Aut*) changer de vitesse;
to ~ one's mind changer d'avis;
a ~ of clothes des vêtements de
rechange; **for a ~** pour changer; **do
you have ~ for £10?** vous avez de la
monnaie de 10 livres?; **where can
I ~ some money?** où est-ce que je
peux changer de l'argent?; **keep
the ~!** gardez la monnaie!; **change
over** *vi* (*swap*) échanger; (*change:
drivers etc*) changer; (*change sides*:
players etc) changer de côté; **to ~ over
from sth to sth** passer de qch à qch;
changeable *adj* (*weather*) variable;
change machine *n* distributeur *m* de
monnaie; **changing room** *n* (*BRIT*:
in shop) salon *m* d'essayage (: *Sport*)
vestiaire *m*
channel ['tʃænl] *n* (*TV*) chaîne
f; (*waveband, groove, fig*: *medium*)
canal *m*; (*of river, sea*) chenal *m* ▷ *vt*
canaliser; **the (English) C~** la
Manche; **Channel Islands** *npl*; **the
Channel Islands** les îles *fpl* Anglo-
Normandes; **Channel Tunnel** *n*:
the Channel Tunnel le tunnel sous
la Manche
chant [tʃɑːnt] *n* chant *m*; (*Rel*)
psalmodie *f* ▷ *vt* chanter, scander
chaos ['keɪɔs] *n* chaos *m*
chaotic [keɪ'ɔtɪk] *adj* chaotique
chap [tʃæp] *n* (*BRIT inf*: *man*) type *m*
chapel ['tʃæpl] *n* chapelle *f*
chapped [tʃæpt] *adj* (*skin, lips*)
gercé(e)
chapter ['tʃæptəʳ] *n* chapitre *m*
character ['kærɪktəʳ] *n* caractère *m*;
(*in novel, film*) personnage *m*; (*eccentric
person*) numéro *m*, phénomène *m*;
characteristic ['kærɪktə'rɪstɪk] *adj*,
n caractéristique (*f*); **characterize**
['kærɪktəraɪz] *vt* caractériser

charcoal ['tʃɑːkəʊl] n charbon m de bois; (Art) charbon

charge [tʃɑːdʒ] n (accusation) accusation f; (Law) inculpation f; (cost) prix (demandé) ▷ vt (gun, battery, Mil: enemy) charger; (customer, sum) faire payer ▷ vi foncer; **charges** npl (costs) frais mpl; **to reverse the ~s** (BRIT Tel) téléphoner en PCV; **to take ~ of** se charger de; **to be in ~ of** être responsable de, s'occuper de; **to ~ sb (with)** (Law) inculper qn (de); **charge card** n carte f de client (émise par un grand magasin); **charger** n (also: **battery charger**) chargeur m

charismatic [kærɪz'mætɪk] adj charismatique

charity ['tʃærɪtɪ] n charité f; (organization) institution f charitable or de bienfaisance, œuvre f (de charité); **charity shop** n (BRIT) boutique vendant des articles d'occasion au profit d'une organisation caritative

charm [tʃɑːm] n charme m; (on bracelet) breloque f ▷ vt charmer, enchanter; **charming** adj charmant(e)

chart [tʃɑːt] n tableau m, diagramme m; graphique m; (map) carte marine ▷ vt dresser or établir la carte de; (sales, progress) établir la courbe de; **charts** npl (Mus) hit-parade m; **to be in the ~s** (record, pop group) figurer au hit-parade

charter ['tʃɑːtər] vt (plane) affréter ▷ n (document) charte f; **chartered accountant** n (BRIT) expert-comptable m; **charter flight** n charter m

chase [tʃeɪs] vt poursuivre, pourchasser; (also: ~ away) chasser ▷ n poursuite f, chasse f

chat [tʃæt] vi (also: have a ~) bavarder, causer; (on Internet) chatter ▷ n conversation f; (on Internet) chat m; **chat up** vt (BRIT inf: girl) baratiner; **chat room** n (Internet) salon m de discussion; **chat show** n (BRIT) talk-show m

chatter ['tʃætər] vi (person) bavarder, papoter ▷ n bavardage m, papotage m; **my teeth are ~ing** je claque des dents

chauffeur ['ʃəʊfər] n chauffeur m (de maître)

chauvinist ['ʃəʊvɪnɪst] n (also: **male ~**) phallocrate m, macho m; (nationalist) chauvin(e)

cheap [tʃiːp] adj bon marché inv, pas cher (chère); (reduced: ticket) à prix réduit; (: fare) réduit(e); (joke) facile, d'un goût douteux; (poor quality) à bon marché, de qualité médiocre ▷ adv à bon marché, pour pas cher; **can you recommend a ~ hotel/restaurant, please?** pourriez-vous m'indiquer un hôtel/restaurant bon marché?; **cheap day return** n billet m d'aller et retour réduit (valable pour la journée); **cheaply** adv à bon marché, à bon compte

cheat [tʃiːt] vi tricher; (in exam) copier ▷ vt tromper, duper; (rob): **to ~ sb out of sth** escroquer qch à qn ▷ n tricheur(-euse) m/f; escroc m; **cheat on** vt fus tromper

Chechnya [tʃɪtʃˈnjɑː] n Tchétchénie f

check [tʃɛk] vt vérifier; (passport, ticket) contrôler; (halt) enrayer; (restrain) maîtriser ▷ vi (official etc) se renseigner ▷ n vérification f; contrôle m; (curb) frein m; (BRIT: bill) addition f; (US) = **cheque**; (pattern: gen pl) carreaux mpl; **to ~ with sb** demander à qn; **check in** vi (in hotel) remplir sa fiche (d'hôtel); (at airport) se présenter à l'enregistrement ▷ vt (luggage) (faire) enregistrer; **check off** vt (tick off) cocher; **check out** vi (in hotel) régler sa note ▷ vt (investigate: story) vérifier; **check up** vi: **to ~ up (on sth)** vérifier (qch); **to ~ up on sb** se renseigner sur le compte de qn; **checkbook** n (US) = **chequebook**; **checked** adj (pattern, cloth) à carreaux; **checkers** n (US) jeu m de dames; **check-in** n (at airport: also:

check-in desk) enregistrement *m*;
checking account *n* (*us*) compte
courant; **checklist** *n* liste *f* de
contrôle; **checkmate** *n* échec et
mat *m*; **checkout** *n* (*in supermarket*)
caisse *f*; **checkpoint** *n* contrôle
m; **checkroom** (*us*) consigne *f*;
checkup *n* (*Med*) examen médical,
check-up *m*

cheddar ['tʃedə^r] *n* (*also*: **~ cheese**)
cheddar *m*

cheek [tʃi:k] *n* joue *f*; (*impudence*)
toupet *m*, culot *m*; **what a ~!** quel
toupet!; **cheekbone** *n* pommette *f*;
cheeky *adj* effronté(e), culotté(e)

cheer [tʃɪə^r] *vt* acclamer, applaudir;
(*gladden*) réjouir, réconforter ▷ *vi*
applaudir ▷ *n* (*gen pl*) acclamations
fpl, applaudissements *mpl*; bravos
mpl, hourras *mpl*; **~s!** à la vôtre!;
cheer up *vi* se dérider, reprendre
courage ▷ *vt* remonter le moral à
or de, dérider, égayer; **cheerful** *adj*
gai(e), joyeux(-euse)

cheerio [tʃɪərɪ'əu] *excl* (*BRIT*) salut!,
au revoir!

cheerleader ['tʃɪəli:də^r] *n membre
d'un groupe de majorettes qui chantent
et dansent pour soutenir leur équipe
pendant les matchs de football américain*

cheese [tʃi:z] *n* fromage *m*;
cheeseburger *n* cheeseburger *m*;
cheesecake *n* tarte *f* au fromage

chef [ʃef] *n* chef (cuisinier)

chemical ['kemɪkl] *adj* chimique ▷ *n*
produit *m* chimique

chemist ['kemɪst] *n* (*BRIT*:
pharmacist) pharmacien(ne);
(*scientist*) chimiste *m/f*; **chemistry** *n*
chimie *f*; **chemist's (shop)** *n* (*BRIT*)
pharmacie *f*

cheque, (*us*) **check** [tʃek] *n* chèque
m; **chequebook,** (*us*) **checkbook** *n*
chéquier *m*, carnet *m* de chèques;
cheque card *n* (*BRIT*) carte *f*
(d'identité) bancaire

cherry ['tʃerɪ] *n* cerise *f*; (*also*: **~ tree**)
cerisier *m*

chess [tʃes] *n* échecs *mpl*

chest [tʃest] *n* poitrine *f*; (*box*) coffre
m, caisse *f*

chestnut ['tʃesnʌt] *n* châtaigne *f*;
(*also*: **~ tree**) châtaignier *m*

chest of drawers *n* commode *f*

chew [tʃu:] *vt* mâcher; **chewing gum**
n chewing-gum *m*

chic [ʃi:k] *adj* chic *inv*, élégant(e)

chick [tʃɪk] *n* poussin *m*; (*inf*) fille *f*

chicken ['tʃɪkɪn] *n* poulet *m*; (*inf*:
coward) poule mouillée; **chicken out**
vi (*inf*) se dégonfler; **chickenpox** *n*
varicelle *f*

chickpea ['tʃɪkpi:] *n* pois *m* chiche

chief [tʃi:f] *n* chef *m* ▷ *adj*
principal(e); **chief executive**,
(*us*) **chief executive officer** *n*
directeur(-trice) général(e); **chiefly**
adv principalement, surtout

child (*pl* **children**) [tʃaɪld,
'tʃɪldrən] *n* enfant *m/f*; **child
abuse** *n* maltraitance *f* d'enfants;
(*sexual*) abus *mpl* sexuels sur des
enfants; **child benefit** *n* (*BRIT*) ≈
allocations familiales; **childbirth** *n*
accouchement *m*; **childcare** *n* (*for
working parents*) garde *f* des enfants
(*pour les parents qui travaillent*);
childhood *n* enfance *f*; **childish** *adj*
puéril(e), enfantin(e); **child minder**
n (*BRIT*) garde *f* d'enfants; **children**
['tʃɪldrən] *npl of* **child**

Chile ['tʃɪlɪ] *n* Chili *m*

chill [tʃɪl] *n* (*of water*) froid *m*; (*of air*)
fraîcheur *f*; (*Med*) refroidissement
m, coup *m* de froid ▷ *vt* (*person*) faire
frissonner; (*Culin*) mettre au frais,
rafraîchir; **chill out** *vi* (*inf*: *esp us*)
se relaxer

chil(l)i ['tʃɪlɪ] *n* piment *m* (rouge)

chilly ['tʃɪlɪ] *adj* froid(e), glacé(e);
(*sensitive to cold*) frileux(-euse)

chimney ['tʃɪmnɪ] *n* cheminée *f*

chimpanzee [tʃɪmpæn'zi:] *n*
chimpanzé *m*

chin [tʃɪn] *n* menton *m*

China ['tʃaɪnə] *n* Chine *f*

china ['tʃaɪnə] n (material) porcelaine f; (crockery) (vaisselle f en) porcelaine
Chinese [tʃaɪ'niːz] adj chinois(e) ▷ n (pl inv) Chinois(e); (Ling) chinois m
chip [tʃɪp] n (gen pl: Culin: BRIT) frite f; (: US: also: **potato ~**) chip m; (of wood) copeau m; (of glass, stone) éclat m; (also: **micro~**) puce f; (in gambling) fiche f ▷ vt (cup, plate) ébrécher; **chip shop** n (BRIT) friterie f

● **CHIP SHOP**
●
● Un chip shop, que l'on appelle
● également un "fish-and-chip shop",
● est un magasin où l'on vend des
● plats à emporter. Les chip shops sont
● d'ailleurs à l'origine des "takeaways".
● On y achète en particulier du
● poisson frit et des frites, mais
● on y trouve également des plats
● traditionnels britanniques ("steak
● pies", saucisses, etc). Tous les plats
● étaient à l'origine emballés dans du
● papier journal. Dans certains de ces
● magasins, on peut s'asseoir pour
● consommer sur place.

chiropodist [kɪ'rɔpədɪst] n (BRIT) pédicure m/f
chisel ['tʃɪzl] n ciseau m
chives [tʃaɪvz] npl ciboulette f, civette f
chlorine ['klɔːriːn] n chlore m
choc-ice ['tʃɔkaɪs] n (BRIT) esquimau® m
chocolate ['tʃɔklɪt] n chocolat m
choice [tʃɔɪs] n choix m ▷ adj de choix
choir ['kwaɪə[r]] n chœur m, chorale f
choke [tʃəuk] vi étouffer ▷ vt étrangler; étouffer; (block) boucher, obstruer ▷ n (Aut) starter m
cholesterol [kə'lɛstərɔl] n cholestérol m
chook [tʃuk] n (AUST, NZ inf) poule f
choose (pt chose, pp chosen) [tʃuːz, tʃəuz, 'tʃəuzn] vt choisir; **to ~ to do** décider de faire, juger bon de faire

chop [tʃɔp] vt (wood) couper (à la hache); (Culin: also: **~ up**) couper (fin), émincer, hacher (en morceaux) ▷ n (Culin) côtelette f; **chop down** vt (tree) abattre; **chop off** vt trancher; **chopsticks** ['tʃɔpstɪks] npl baguettes fpl
chord [kɔːd] n (Mus) accord m
chore [tʃɔː[r]] n travail m de routine; **household ~s** travaux mpl du ménage
chorus ['kɔːrəs] n chœur m; (repeated part of song, also fig) refrain m
chose [tʃəuz] pt of **choose**
chosen ['tʃəuzn] pp of **choose**
Christ [kraɪst] n Christ m
christen ['krɪsn] vt baptiser; **christening** n baptême m
Christian ['krɪstɪən] adj, n chrétien(ne); **Christianity** [krɪstɪ'ænɪtɪ] n christianisme m; **Christian name** n prénom m
Christmas ['krɪsməs] n Noël m or f; **happy** or **merry ~!** joyeux Noël!; **Christmas card** n carte f de Noël; **Christmas carol** n chant m de Noël; **Christmas Day** n le jour de Noël; **Christmas Eve** n la veille de Noël; la nuit de Noël; **Christmas pudding** n (esp BRIT) Christmas m pudding; **Christmas tree** n arbre m de Noël
chrome [krəum] n chrome m
chronic ['krɔnɪk] adj chronique
chrysanthemum [krɪ'sænθəməm] n chrysanthème m
chubby ['tʃʌbɪ] adj potelé(e), rondelet(te)
chuck [tʃʌk] vt (inf) lancer, jeter; (job) lâcher; **chuck out** vt (inf: person) flanquer dehors or à la porte; (: rubbish etc) jeter
chuckle ['tʃʌkl] vi glousser
chum [tʃʌm] n copain (copine)
chunk [tʃʌŋk] n gros morceau
church [tʃəːtʃ] n église f; **churchyard** n cimetière m
churn [tʃəːn] n (for butter) baratte f; (also: **milk ~**) (grand) bidon à lait

chute [ʃuːt] n goulotte f; (also: **rubbish ~**) vide-ordures m inv; (BRIT: children's slide) toboggan m
chutney ['tʃʌtnɪ] n chutney m
CIA n abbr (= Central Intelligence Agency) CIA f
CID n abbr (= Criminal Investigation Department) ≈ P.J. f
cider ['saɪdəʳ] n cidre m
cigar [sɪ'gɑːʳ] n cigare m
cigarette [sɪgə'rɛt] n cigarette f; **cigarette lighter** n briquet m
cinema ['sɪnəmə] n cinéma m
cinnamon ['sɪnəmən] n cannelle f
circle ['səːkl] n cercle m; (in cinema) balcon m ▷ vi faire or décrire des cercles ▷ vt (surround) entourer, encercler; (move round) faire le tour de, tourner autour de
circuit ['səːkɪt] n circuit m; (lap) tour m
circular ['səːkjuləʳ] adj circulaire ▷ n circulaire f; (as advertisement) prospectus m
circulate ['səːkjuleɪt] vi circuler ▷ vt faire circuler; **circulation** [səːkju'leɪʃən] n circulation f; (of newspaper) tirage m
circumstances ['səːkəmstənsɪz] npl circonstances fpl; (financial condition) moyens mpl, situation financière
circus ['səːkəs] n cirque m
cite [saɪt] vt citer
citizen ['sɪtɪzn] n (Pol) citoyen(ne); (resident): **the ~s of this town** les habitants de cette ville; **citizenship** n citoyenneté f; (BRIT Scol) ≈ éducation f civique
citrus fruits ['sɪtrəs-] npl agrumes mpl
city ['sɪtɪ] n (grande) ville f; **the C~** la Cité de Londres (centre des affaires); **city centre** n centre ville m; **city technology college** n (BRIT) établissement m d'enseignement technologique (situé dans un quartier défavorisé)

civic ['sɪvɪk] adj civique; (authorities) municipal(e)
civil ['sɪvɪl] adj civil(e); (polite) poli(e), civil(e); **civilian** [sɪ'vɪlɪən] adj, n civil(e)
civilization [sɪvɪlaɪ'zeɪʃən] n civilisation f
civilized ['sɪvɪlaɪzd] adj civilisé(e); (fig) où règnent les bonnes manières
civil: civil law n code civil; (study) droit civil; **civil rights** npl droits mpl civiques; **civil servant** n fonctionnaire m/f; **Civil Service** n fonction publique, administration f; **civil war** n guerre civile
CJD n abbr (= Creutzfeldt-Jakob disease) MCJ f
claim [kleɪm] vt (rights etc) revendiquer; (compensation) réclamer; (assert) déclarer, prétendre ▷ vi (for insurance) faire une déclaration de sinistre ▷ n revendication f; prétention f; (right) droit m; **(insurance) ~** demande f d'indemnisation, déclaration f de sinistre; **claim form** n (gen) formulaire m de demande
clam [klæm] n palourde f
clamp [klæmp] n crampon m; (on workbench) valet m; (on car) sabot m de Denver ▷ vt attacher; (car) mettre un sabot à; **clamp down on** vt fus sévir contre, prendre des mesures draconiennes à l'égard de
clan [klæn] n clan m
clap [klæp] vi applaudir
claret ['klærət] n (vin m de) bordeaux m (rouge)
clarify ['klærɪfaɪ] vt clarifier
clarinet [klærɪ'nɛt] n clarinette f
clarity ['klærɪtɪ] n clarté f
clash [klæʃ] n (sound) choc m, fracas m; (with police) affrontement m; (fig) conflit m ▷ vi se heurter; être or entrer en conflit; (colours) jurer; (dates, events) tomber en même temps
clasp [klɑːsp] n (of necklace, bag) fermoir m ▷ vt serrer, étreindre

class [klɑ:s] n (gen) classe f; (group, category) catégorie f ▷ vt classer, classifier

classic ['klæsɪk] adj classique ▷ n (author, work) classique m; **classical** adj classique

classification [klæsɪfɪ'keɪʃən] n classification f

classify ['klæsɪfaɪ] vt classifier, classer

classmate ['klɑ:smeɪt] n camarade m/f de classe

classroom ['klɑ:srum] n (salle f de) classe f; **classroom assistant** n assistant(e) d'éducation

classy ['klɑ:sɪ] (inf) adj classe (inf)

clatter ['klætə'] n cliquetis m ▷ vi cliqueter

clause [klɔ:z] n clause f; (Ling) proposition f

claustrophobic [klɔ:strə'fəubɪk] adj (person) claustrophobe; (place) où l'on se sent claustrophobe

claw [klɔ:] n griffe f; (of bird of prey) serre f; (of lobster) pince f

clay [kleɪ] n argile f

clean [kli:n] adj propre; (clear, smooth) net(te); (record, reputation) sans tache; (joke, story) correct(e) ▷ vt nettoyer; **clean up** vt nettoyer; (fig) remettre de l'ordre dans; **cleaner** n (person) nettoyeur(-euse), femme f de ménage; (product) détachant m; **cleaner's** n (also: **dry cleaner's**) teinturier m; **cleaning** n nettoyage m

cleanser ['klɛnzə'] n (for face) démaquillant m

clear [klɪə'] adj clair(e); (glass, plastic) transparent(e); (road, way) libre, dégagé(e); (profit, majority) net(te); (conscience) tranquille; (skin) frais (fraîche); (sky) dégagé(e) ▷ vt (road) dégager, déblayer; (table) débarrasser; (room etc: of people) faire évacuer; (cheque) compenser; (Law: suspect) innocenter; (obstacle) franchir or sauter sans heurter ▷ vi (weather) s'éclaircir; (fog) se dissiper

▷ adv: ~ **of** à distance de, à l'écart de; **to ~ the table** débarrasser la table, desservir; **clear away** vt (things, clothes etc) enlever, retirer; **to ~ away the dishes** débarrasser la table; **clear up** vt ranger, mettre en ordre; (mystery) éclaircir, résoudre; **clearance** n (removal) déblayage m; (permission) autorisation f; **clear-cut** adj précis(e), nettement défini(e); **clearing** n (in forest) clairière f; **clearly** adv clairement; (obviously) de toute évidence; **clearway** n (BRIT) route f à stationnement interdit

clench [klɛntʃ] vt serrer

clergy ['klə:dʒɪ] n clergé m

clerk [klɑ:k, US klə:rk] n (BRIT) employé(e) de bureau; (US: salesman/ woman) vendeur(-euse)

clever ['klɛvə'] adj (intelligent) intelligent(e); (skilful) habile, adroit(e); (device, arrangement) ingénieux(-euse), astucieux(-euse)

cliché ['kli:ʃeɪ] n cliché m

click [klɪk] n (Comput) clic m ▷ vi (Comput) cliquer ▷ vt: **to ~ one's tongue** faire claquer sa langue; **to ~ one's heels** claquer des talons; **to ~ on an icon** cliquer sur une icône

client ['klaɪənt] n client(e)

cliff [klɪf] n falaise f

climate ['klaɪmɪt] n climat m; **climate change** n changement m climatique

climax ['klaɪmæks] n apogée m, point culminant; (sexual) orgasme m

climb [klaɪm] vi grimper, monter; (plane) prendre de l'altitude ▷ vt (stairs) monter; (mountain) escalader; (tree) grimper à ▷ n montée f, escalade f; **to ~ over a wall** passer par dessus un mur; **climb down** vi (re)descendre; (BRIT fig) rabattre de ses prétentions; **climber** n (also: **rock climber**) grimpeur(-euse), varappeur(-euse); (plant) plante grimpante; **climbing** n (also: **rock climbing**) escalade f, varappe f

clinch [klɪntʃ] vt (deal) conclure, sceller

cling (pt, pp **clung**) [klɪŋ, klʌŋ] vi: **to ~ (to)** se cramponner (à), s'accrocher (à); (clothes) coller (à); **clingfilm** n film m alimentaire

clinic ['klɪnɪk] n clinique f; centre médical

clip [klɪp] n (for hair) barrette f; (also: **paper ~**) trombone m; (TV, Cine) clip m ⊳ vt (also: **~ together**: papers) attacher; (hair, nails) couper; (hedge) tailler; **clipping** n (from newspaper) coupure f de journal

cloak [kləʊk] n grande cape ⊳ vt (fig) masquer, cacher; **cloakroom** n (for coats etc) vestiaire m; (BRIT: W.C.) toilettes fpl

clock [klɒk] n (large) horloge f; (small) pendule f; **clock in, clock on** (BRIT) vi (with card) pointer (en arrivant); (start work) commencer à travailler; **clock off, clock out** (BRIT) vi (with card) pointer (en partant); (leave work) quitter le travail; **clockwise** adv dans le sens des aiguilles d'une montre; **clockwork** n rouages mpl, mécanisme m; (of clock) mouvement m (d'horlogerie) ⊳ adj (toy, train) mécanique

clog [klɒg] n sabot m ⊳ vt boucher, encrasser ⊳ vi (also: **~ up**) se boucher, s'encrasser

clone [kləʊn] n clone m ⊳ vt cloner

close[1] [kləʊs] adj (contact, link, watch) étroit(e); (examination) attentif(-ive), minutieux(-euse); (contest) très serré(e); (weather) lourd(e), étouffant(e); (near): **~ (to)** près (de), proche (de) ⊳ adv près, à proximité; **~ to** prep près de; **~ by, ~ at hand** adj, adv tout(e) près; **a ~ friend** un ami intime; **to have a ~ shave** (fig) l'échapper belle

close[2] [kləʊz] vt fermer ⊳ vi (shop etc) fermer; (lid, door etc) se fermer; (end) se terminer, se conclure ⊳ n (end) conclusion f; **what time do you ~?** à quelle heure fermez-vous?; **close**

down vi fermer (définitivement); **closed** adj (shop etc) fermé(e)

closely ['kləʊslɪ] adv (examine, watch) de près

closet ['klɒzɪt] n (cupboard) placard m, réduit m

close-up ['kləʊsʌp] n gros plan

closing time n heure f de fermeture

closure ['kləʊʒər] n fermeture f

clot [klɒt] n (of blood, milk) caillot m; (inf: person) ballot m ⊳ vi (external bleeding) se coaguler

cloth [klɒθ] n (material) tissu m, étoffe f; (BRIT: also: **tea ~**) torchon m; lavette f; (also: **table~**) nappe f

clothes [kləʊðz] npl vêtements mpl, habits mpl; **clothes line** n corde f (à linge); **clothes peg**, (US) **clothes pin** n pince f à linge

clothing ['kləʊðɪŋ] n = **clothes**

cloud [klaʊd] n (also Comput) nuage m; **cloud computing** n (Comput) informatique f en nuage; **cloud over** vi se couvrir; (fig) s'assombrir; **cloudy** adj nuageux(-euse), couvert(e); (liquid) trouble

clove [kləʊv] n clou m de girofle; **a ~ of garlic** une gousse d'ail

clown [klaʊn] n clown m ⊳ vi (also: **~ about, ~ around**) faire le clown

club [klʌb] n (society) club m; (weapon) massue f, matraque f; (also: **golf ~**) club ⊳ vt matraquer ⊳ vi: **to ~ together** s'associer; **clubs** npl (Cards) trèfle m; **club class** n (Aviat) classe f club

clue [kluː] n indice m; (in crosswords) définition f; **I haven't a ~** je n'en ai pas la moindre idée

clump [klʌmp] n: **~ of trees** bouquet m d'arbres

clumsy ['klʌmzɪ] adj (person) gauche, maladroit(e); (object) malcommode, peu maniable

clung [klʌŋ] pt, pp of **cling**

cluster ['klʌstər] n (petit) groupe; (of flowers) grappe f ⊳ vi se rassembler

clutch [klʌtʃ] n (Aut) embrayage m; (grasp): **~es** étreinte f, prise f ⊳ vt (*grasp*) agripper; (*hold tightly*) serrer fort; (*hold on to*) se cramponner à

cm *abbr* (= *centimetre*) cm

Co. *abbr* = **company, county**

c/o *abbr* (= *care of*) c/o, aux bons soins de

coach [kəutʃ] *n* (*bus*) autocar *m*; (*horse-drawn*) diligence *f*; (*of train*) voiture *f*, wagon *m*; (*Sport: trainer*) entraîneur(-euse); (*school: tutor*) répétiteur(-trice) ▷ *vt* (*Sport*) entraîner; (*student*) donner des leçons particulières à; **coach station** (*BRIT*) *n* gare routière; **coach trip** *n* excursion *f* en car

coal [kəul] *n* charbon *m*

coalition [kəuə'lɪʃən] *n* coalition *f*

coarse [kɔ:s] *adj* grossier(-ère), rude; (*vulgar*) vulgaire

coast [kəust] *n* côte *f* ▷ *vi* (*car, cycle*) descendre en roue libre; **coastal** *adj* côtier(-ère); **coastguard** *n* garde-côte *m*; **coastline** *n* côte *f*, littoral *m*

coat [kəut] *n* manteau *m*; (*of animal*) pelage *m*, poil *m*; (*of paint*) couche *f* ▷ *vt* couvrir, enduire; **coat hanger** *n* cintre *m*; **coating** *n* couche *f*, enduit *m*

coax [kəuks] *vt* persuader par des cajoleries

cob [kɔb] *n see* **corn**

cobbled ['kɔbld] *adj* pavé(e)

cobweb ['kɔbwɛb] *n* toile *f* d'araignée

cocaine [kə'keɪn] *n* cocaïne *f*

cock [kɔk] *n* (*rooster*) coq *m*; (*male bird*) mâle *m* ▷ *vt* (*gun*) armer; **cockerel** *n* jeune coq *m*

cockney ['kɔknɪ] *n* cockney *m/f* (*habitant des quartiers populaires de l'East End de Londres*), ≈ faubourien(ne)

cockpit ['kɔkpɪt] *n* (*in aircraft*) poste *m* de pilotage, cockpit *m*

cockroach ['kɔkrəutʃ] *n* cafard *m*, cancrelat *m*

cocktail ['kɔkteɪl] *n* cocktail *m*

cocoa ['kəukəu] *n* cacao *m*

coconut ['kəukənʌt] *n* noix *f* de coco

cod [kɔd] *n* morue fraîche, cabillaud *m*

C.O.D. *abbr* = **cash on delivery**

code [kəud] *n* code *m*; (*Tel: area code*) indicatif *m*

coeducational ['kəuɛdju'keɪʃənl] *adj* mixte

coffee ['kɔfɪ] *n* café *m*; **coffee bar** *n* (*BRIT*) café *m*; **coffee bean** *n* grain *m* de café; **coffee break** *n* pause-café *f*; **coffee maker** *n* cafetière *f*; **coffeepot** *n* cafetière *f*; **coffee shop** *n* café *m*; **coffee table** *n* (petite) table basse

coffin ['kɔfɪn] *n* cercueil *m*

cog [kɔg] *n* (*wheel*) roue dentée; (*tooth*) dent *f* (d'engrenage)

cognac ['kɔnjæk] *n* cognac *m*

coherent [kəu'hɪərənt] *adj* cohérent(e)

coil [kɔɪl] *n* rouleau *m*, bobine *f*; (*contraceptive*) stérilet *m* ▷ *vt* enrouler

coin [kɔɪn] *n* pièce *f* (de monnaie) ▷ *vt* (*word*) inventer

coincide [kəuɪn'saɪd] *vi* coïncider; **coincidence** [kəu'ɪnsɪdəns] *n* coïncidence *f*

Coke® [kəuk] *n* coca *m*

coke [kəuk] *n* (*coal*) coke *m*

colander ['kɔləndər] *n* passoire *f* (à légumes)

cold [kəuld] *adj* froid(e) ▷ *n* froid *m*; (*Med*) rhume *m*; **it's** ~ il fait froid; **to be** ~ (*person*) avoir froid; **to catch a** ~ s'enrhumer, attraper un rhume; **in** ~ **blood** de sang-froid; **cold sore** *n* bouton *m* de fièvre

coleslaw ['kəulslɔ:] *n* sorte de salade de chou cru

colic ['kɔlɪk] *n* colique(s) *f(pl)*

collaborate [kə'læbəreɪt] *vi* collaborer

collapse [kə'læps] *vi* s'effondrer, s'écrouler; (*Med*) avoir un malaise ▷ *n* effondrement *m*, écroulement *m*; (*of government*) chute *f*

collar ['kɔlər] *n* (*of coat, shirt*) col *m*; (*for dog*) collier *m*; **collarbone** *n* clavicule *f*

colleague ['kɔli:g] *n* collègue *m/f*

collect [kəˈlɛkt] vt rassembler; (pick up) ramasser; (as a hobby) collectionner; (BRIT: call for) (passer) prendre; (mail) faire la levée de, ramasser; (money owed) encaisser; (donations, subscriptions) recueillir ▷ vi (people) se rassembler; (dust, dirt) s'amasser; **to call ~** (US Tel) téléphoner en PCV; **collection** [kəˈlɛkʃən] n collection f; (of mail) levée f; (for money) collecte f, quête f; **collective** [kəˈlɛktɪv] adj collectif(-ive); **collector** n collectionneur m

college [ˈkɒlɪdʒ] n collège m; (of technology, agriculture etc) institut m

collide [kəˈlaɪd] vi: **to ~ (with)** entrer en collision (avec)

collision [kəˈlɪʒən] n collision f, heurt m

cologne [kəˈləun] n (also: **eau de ~**) eau f de cologne

colon [ˈkəulən] n (sign) deux-points mpl; (Med) côlon m

colonel [ˈkəːnl] n colonel m

colonial [kəˈləunɪəl] adj colonial(e)

colony [ˈkɒlənɪ] n colonie f

colour, (US) **color** [ˈkʌlər] n couleur f ▷ vt colorer; (dye) teindre; (paint) peindre; (with crayons) colorier; (news) fausser, exagérer ▷ vi (blush) rougir; **I'd like a different ~** je le voudrais dans un autre coloris; **colour in** vt colorier; **colour-blind**, (US) **color-blind** adj daltonien(ne); **coloured**, (US) **colored** adj coloré(e); (photo) en couleur; **colour film**, (US) **color film** n (for camera) pellicule f (en) couleur; **colourful**, (US) **colorful** adj coloré(e), vif (vive); (personality) pittoresque, haut(e) en couleurs; **colouring**, (US) **coloring** n colorant m; (complexion) teint m; **colour television**, (US) **color television** n télévision f (en) couleur

column [ˈkɒləm] n colonne f; (fashion column, sports column etc) rubrique f

coma [ˈkəumə] n coma m

comb [kəum] n peigne m ▷ vt (hair) peigner; (area) ratisser, passer au peigne fin

combat [ˈkɒmbæt] n combat m ▷ vt combattre, lutter contre

combination [kɒmbɪˈneɪʃən] n (gen) combinaison f

combine [kəmˈbaɪn] vt combiner ▷ vi s'associer; (Chem) se combiner ▷ n [ˈkɒmbaɪn] (Econ) trust m; (also: **~ harvester**) moissonneuse-batteuse(-lieuse) f; **to ~ sth with sth** (one quality with another) joindre ou allier qch à qch

 KEYWORD

come (pt came, pp come) [kʌm, keɪm] vi **1** (movement towards) venir; **to come running** arriver en courant; **he's come here to work** il est venu ici pour travailler; **come with me** suivez-moi

2 (arrive) arriver; **to come home** rentrer (chez soi or à la maison); **we've just come from Paris** nous arrivons de Paris

3 (reach): **to come to** (decision etc) parvenir à, arriver à; **the bill came to £40** la note s'est élevée à 40 livres

4 (occur): **an idea came to me** il m'est venu une idée

5 (be, become): **to come loose/undone** se défaire/desserrer; **I've come to like him** j'ai fini par bien l'aimer

come across vt fus rencontrer par hasard, tomber sur

come along vi (BRIT: pupil, work) faire des progrès, avancer

come back vi revenir

come down vi descendre; (prices) baisser; (buildings) s'écrouler; (: be demolished) être démoli(e)

come from vt fus (source) venir de; (place) venir de, être originaire de

come in vi entrer; (train) arriver;

(*fashion*) entrer en vogue; (*on deal etc*) participer

come off vi (*button*) se détacher; (*attempt*) réussir

come on vi (*lights, electricity*) s'allumer; (*central heating*) se mettre en marche; (*pupil, work, project*) faire des progrès, avancer; **come on!** viens!; allons!, allez!

come out vi sortir; (*sun*) se montrer; (*book*) paraître; (*stain*) s'enlever; (*strike*) cesser le travail, se mettre en grève

come round vi (*after faint, operation*) revenir à soi, reprendre connaissance

come to vi revenir à soi

come up vi monter; (*sun*) se lever; (*problem*) se poser; (*event*) survenir; (*in conversation*) être soulevé

come up with vt fus (*money*) fournir; **he came up with an idea** il a eu une idée, il a proposé quelque chose

comeback ['kʌmbæk] n (*Theat*) rentrée f

comedian [kə'miːdiən] n (*comic*) comique m; (*Theat*) comédien m

comedy ['kɔmɪdɪ] n comédie f; (*humour*) comique m

comet ['kɔmɪt] n comète f

comfort ['kʌmfət] n confort m, bien-être m; (*solace*) consolation f, réconfort m ▷ vt consoler, réconforter; **comfortable** adj confortable; (*person*) à l'aise; (*financially*) aisé(e); (*patient*) dont l'état est stationnaire; **comfort station** n (us) toilettes fpl

comic ['kɔmɪk] adj (*also:* **~al**) comique ▷ n (*person*) comique m; (BRIT: *magazine: for children*) magazine m de bandes dessinées or de BD; (: *for adults*) illustré m; **comic book** n (US: *for children*) magazine m de bandes dessinées or de BD; (: *for adults*) illustré m; **comic strip** n bande dessinée

comma ['kɔmə] n virgule f

command [kə'mɑːnd] n ordre m, commandement m; (*Mil: authority*) commandement; (*mastery*) maîtrise f ▷ vt (*troops*) commander; **to ~ sb to do** donner l'ordre or commander à qn de faire; **commander** n (*Mil*) commandant m

commemorate [kə'mɛməreɪt] vt commémorer

commence [kə'mɛns] vt, vi commencer

commend [kə'mɛnd] vt louer; (*recommend*) recommander

comment ['kɔmɛnt] n commentaire m ▷ vi: **to ~ on** faire des remarques sur; **"no ~"** "je n'ai rien à déclarer"; **commentary** ['kɔməntərɪ] n commentaire m; (*Sport*) reportage m (en direct); **commentator** ['kɔmənteɪtər] n commentateur m; (*Sport*) reporter m

commerce ['kɔmə:s] n commerce m

commercial [kə'mə:ʃəl] adj commercial(e) ▷ n (*Radio, TV*) annonce f publicitaire, spot m (publicitaire); **commercial break** n (*Radio, TV*) spot m (publicitaire)

commission [kə'mɪʃən] n (*committee, fee*) commission f ▷ vt (*work of art*) commander, charger un artiste de l'exécution de; **out of ~** (*machine*) hors service; **commissioner** n (*Police*) préfet m (de police)

commit [kə'mɪt] vt (*act*) commettre; (*resources*) consacrer; (*to sb's care*) confier (à); **to ~ o.s. (to do)** s'engager (à faire); **to ~ suicide** se suicider; **commitment** n engagement m; (*obligation*) responsabilité(s) f(pl)

committee [kə'mɪtɪ] n comité m; commission f

commodity [kə'mɔdɪtɪ] n produit m, marchandise f, article m

common ['kɔmən] adj (*gen*) commun(e); (*usual*) courant(e) ▷ n terrain communal; **commonly** adv communément, généralement; couramment; **commonplace** adj banal(e), ordinaire; **Commons**

npl (BRIT *Pol*): **the (House of) Commons** la chambre des Communes; **common sense** *n* bon sens; **Commonwealth** *n*: **the Commonwealth** le Commonwealth

communal ['kɔmjuːnl] *adj* (*life*) communautaire; (*for common use*) commun(e)

commune *n* ['kɔmjuːn] (*group*) communauté *f* ▷ *vi* [kə'mjuːn]: **to ~ with** (*nature*) communier avec

communicate [kə'mjuːnɪkeɪt] *vt* communiquer, transmettre ▷ *vi*: **to ~ (with)** communiquer (avec)

communication [kəmjuːnɪ'keɪʃən] *n* communication *f*

communion [kə'mjuːnɪən] *n* (*also*: **Holy C~**) communion *f*

communism ['kɔmjunɪzəm] *n* communisme *m*; **communist** *adj*, *n* communiste *m/f*

community [kə'mjuːnɪtɪ] *n* communauté *f*; **community centre**, (*us*) **community center** *n* foyer socio-éducatif, centre *m* de loisirs; **community service** *n* ≈ travail *m* d'intérêt général, TIG *m*

commute [kə'mjuːt] *vi* faire le trajet journalier (*de son domicile à un lieu de travail assez éloigné*) ▷ *vt* (*Law*) commuer; **commuter** *n* banlieusard(e) (*qui fait un trajet journalier pour se rendre à son travail*)

compact *adj* [kəm'pækt] compact(e) ▷ *n* ['kɔmpækt] (*also*: **powder ~**) poudrier *m*; **compact disc** *n* disque compact; **compact disc player** *n* lecteur *m* de disques compacts

companion [kəm'pænjən] *n* compagnon (compagne)

company ['kʌmpənɪ] *n* compagnie *f*; **to keep sb ~** tenir compagnie à qn; **company car** *n* voiture *f* de fonction; **company director** *n* administrateur(-trice)

comparable ['kɔmpərəbl] *adj* comparable

comparative [kəm'pærətɪv] *adj* (*study*) comparatif(-ive); (*relative*) relatif(-ive); **comparatively** *adv* (*relatively*) relativement

compare [kəm'pɛəʳ] *vt*: **to ~ sth/sb with** *or* **to** comparer qch/qn avec *or* à ▷ *vi*: **to ~ (with)** se comparer (à); être comparable (à); **comparison** [kəm'pærɪsn] *n* comparaison *f*

compartment [kəm'pɑːtmənt] *n* (*also Rail*) compartiment *m*; **a non-smoking ~** un compartiment non-fumeurs

compass ['kʌmpəs] *n* boussole *f*; **compasses** *npl* (*Math*) compas *m*

compassion [kəm'pæʃən] *n* compassion *f*, humanité *f*

compatible [kəm'pætɪbl] *adj* compatible

compel [kəm'pɛl] *vt* contraindre, obliger; **compelling** *adj* (*fig*: *argument*) irrésistible

compensate ['kɔmpənseɪt] *vt* indemniser, dédommager ▷ *vi*: **to ~ for** compenser; **compensation** [kɔmpən'seɪʃən] *n* compensation *f*; (*money*) dédommagement *m*, indemnité *f*

compete [kəm'piːt] *vi* (*take part*) concourir; (*vie*): **to ~ (with)** rivaliser (avec), faire concurrence (à)

competent ['kɔmpɪtənt] *adj* compétent(e), capable

competition [kɔmpɪ'tɪʃən] *n* (*contest*) compétition *f*, concours *m*; (*Econ*) concurrence *f*

competitive [kəm'pɛtɪtɪv] *adj* (*Econ*) concurrentiel(le); (*sports*) de compétition; (*person*) qui a l'esprit de compétition

competitor [kəm'pɛtɪtəʳ] *n* concurrent(e)

complacent [kəm'pleɪsnt] *adj* (*trop*) content(e) de soi

complain [kəm'pleɪn] *vi*: **to ~ (about)** se plaindre (de); (*in shop etc*) réclamer (au sujet de); **complaint** *n*

plainte f; (in shop etc) réclamation f;
(Med) affection f

complement ['komplɪmənt] n
complément m; (esp of ship's crew
etc) effectif complet ▷ vt (enhance)
compléter; **complementary**
[komplɪ'mɛntərɪ] adj complémentaire

complete [kəm'pliːt] adj
complet(-ète); (finished) achevé(e)
▷ vt achever, parachever; (set,
group) compléter; (a form) remplir;
completely adv complètement;
completion [kəm'pliːʃən] n
achèvement m; (of contract)
exécution f

complex ['komplɛks] adj complexe
▷ n (Psych, buildings etc) complexe m

complexion [kəm'plɛkʃən] n (of
face) teint m

compliance [kəm'plaɪəns] n
(submission) docilité f; (agreement):
~ **with** le fait de se conformer
à; **in** ~ **with** en conformité avec,
conformément à

complicate ['komplɪkeɪt] vt
compliquer; **complicated** adj
compliqué(e); **complication**
[komplɪ'keɪʃən] n complication f

compliment n ['komplɪmənt]
compliment m ▷ vt ['komplɪmɛnt]
complimenter; **complimentary**
[komplɪ'mɛntərɪ] adj flatteur(-euse);
(free) à titre gracieux

comply [kəm'plaɪ] vi: **to ~ with** se
soumettre à, se conformer à

component [kəm'pəunənt] adj
composant(e), constituant(e) ▷ n
composant m, élément m

compose [kəm'pəuz] vt composer;
(form): **to be ~d of** se composer de;
to ~ o.s. se calmer, se maîtriser;
composer n (Mus) compositeur m;
composition [kompə'zɪʃən] n
composition f

composure [kəm'pəuʒəʳ] n calme m,
maîtrise f de soi

compound ['kompaund] n (Chem,
Ling) composé m; (enclosure) enclos m,

enceinte f ▷ adj composé(e); (fracture)
compliqué(e)

comprehension [komprɪ'hɛnʃən] n
compréhension f

comprehensive [komprɪ'hɛnsɪv]
adj (très) complet(-ète); ~ **policy**
(Insurance) assurance f tous risques;
comprehensive (school) n (BRIT)
école secondaire non sélective avec
libre circulation d'une section à l'autre,
≈ CES m

> Be careful not to translate
> comprehensive by the French word
> compréhensif.

compress vt [kəm'prɛs] comprimer;
(text, information) condenser ▷ n
['komprɛs] (Med) compresse f

comprise [kəm'praɪz] vt (also: **be
~d of**) comprendre; (constitute)
constituer, représenter

compromise ['komprəmaɪz] n
compromis m ▷ vt compromettre ▷ vi
transiger, accepter un compromis

compulsive [kəm'pʌlsɪv] adj
(Psych) compulsif(-ive); (book, film etc)
captivant(e)

compulsory [kəm'pʌlsərɪ] adj
obligatoire

computer [kəm'pjuːtəʳ] n ordinateur
m; **computer game** n jeu m vidéo;
computer-generated adj de
synthèse; **computerize** vt (data)
traiter par ordinateur; (system,
office) informatiser; **computer
programmer** n programmeur(-euse);
computer programming n
programmation f; **computer science**
n informatique f; **computer studies**
npl informatique f; **computing**
[kəm'pjuːtɪŋ] n informatique f

con [kon] vt duper; (cheat) escroquer
▷ n escroquerie f

conceal [kən'siːl] vt cacher,
dissimuler

concede [kən'siːd] vt concéder
▷ vi céder

conceited [kən'siːtɪd] adj
vaniteux(-euse), suffisant(e)

conceive [kən'siːv] *vt, vi* concevoir

concentrate ['kɔnsəntreɪt] *vi* se concentrer ▷ *vt* concentrer

concentration [kɔnsən'treɪʃən] *n* concentration *f*

concept ['kɔnsɛpt] *n* concept *m*

concern [kən'səːn] *n* affaire *f*; (*Comm*) entreprise *f*, firme *f*; (*anxiety*) inquiétude *f*, souci *m* ▷ *vt* (*worry*) inquiéter; (*involve*) concerner; (*relate to*) se rapporter à; **to be ~ed (about)** s'inquiéter (de), être inquiet(-ète) (au sujet de); **concerning** *prep* en ce qui concerne, à propos de

concert ['kɔnsət] *n* concert *m*; **concert hall** *n* salle *f* de concert

concerto [kən'tʃəːtəu] *n* concerto *m*

concession [kən'sɛʃən] *n* (*compromise*) concession *f*; (*reduced price*) réduction *f*; **tax ~** dégrèvement fiscal; **"~s"** tarif réduit

concise [kən'saɪs] *adj* concis(e)

conclude [kən'kluːd] *vt* conclure; **conclusion** [kən'kluːʒən] *n* conclusion *f*

concrete ['kɔŋkriːt] *n* béton *m* ▷ *adj* concret(-ète); (*Constr*) en béton

concussion [kən'kʌʃən] *n* (*Med*) commotion *f* (cérébrale)

condemn [kən'dɛm] *vt* condamner

condensation [kɔndɛn'seɪʃən] *n* condensation *f*

condense [kən'dɛns] *vi* se condenser ▷ *vt* condenser

condition [kən'dɪʃən] *n* condition *f*; (*disease*) maladie *f* ▷ *vt* déterminer, conditionner; **on ~ that** à condition que + *sub*, à condition de; **conditional** [kən'dɪʃənl] *adj* conditionnel(le); **conditioner** *n* (*for hair*) baume démêlant; (*for fabrics*) assouplissant *m*

condo ['kɔndəu] *n* (*US inf*) = **condominium**

condom ['kɔndəm] *n* préservatif *m*

condominium [kɔndə'mɪnɪəm] *n* (*US: building*) immeuble *m* (en copropriété); (: *rooms*) appartement *m* (dans un immeuble en copropriété)

condone [kən'dəun] *vt* fermer les yeux sur, approuver (tacitement)

conduct *n* ['kɔndʌkt] conduite *f* ▷ *vt* [kən'dʌkt] conduire; (*manage*) mener, diriger; (*Mus*) diriger; **to ~ o.s.** se conduire, se comporter; **conductor** *n* (*of orchestra*) chef *m* d'orchestre; (*on bus*) receveur *m*; (*US: on train*) chef *m* de train; (*Elec*) conducteur *m*

cone [kəun] *n* cône *m*; (*for ice-cream*) cornet *m*; (*Bot*) pomme *f* de pin, cône

confectionery [kən'fɛkʃənrɪ] *n* (*sweets*) confiserie *f*

confer [kən'fəːʳ] *vt*: **to ~ sth on** conférer qch à ▷ *vi* conférer, s'entretenir

conference ['kɔnfərns] *n* conférence *f*

confess [kən'fɛs] *vt* confesser, avouer ▷ *vi* (*admit sth*) avouer; (*Rel*) se confesser; **confession** [kən'fɛʃən] *n* confession *f*

confide [kən'faɪd] *vi*: **to ~ in** s'ouvrir à, se confier à

confidence ['kɔnfɪdns] *n* confiance *f*; (*also*: **self-~**) assurance *f*, confiance en soi; (*secret*) confidence *f*; **in ~** (*speak, write*) en confidence, confidentiellement; **confident** *adj* (*self-assured*) sûr(e) de soi; (*sure*) sûr; **confidential** [kɔnfɪ'dɛnʃəl] *adj* confidentiel(le)

confine [kən'faɪn] *vt* limiter, borner; (*shut up*) confiner, enfermer; **confined** *adj* (*space*) restreint(e), réduit(e)

confirm [kən'fəːm] *vt* (*report, Rel*) confirmer; (*appointment*) ratifier; **confirmation** [kɔnfə'meɪʃən] *n* confirmation *f*; ratification *f*

confiscate ['kɔnfɪskeɪt] *vt* confisquer

conflict *n* ['kɔnflɪkt] conflit *m*, lutte *f* ▷ *vi* [kən'flɪkt] (*opinions*) s'opposer, se heurter

conform [kən'fɔːm] *vi*: **to ~ (to)** se conformer (à)

confront [kən'frʌnt] *vt* (*two people*) confronter; (*enemy, danger*) affronter, faire face à; (*problem*) faire face à; **confrontation** [kɔnfrən'teɪʃən] *n* confrontation *f*

confuse [kən'fjuːz] *vt* (*person*) troubler; (*situation*) embrouiller; (*one thing with another*) confondre; **confused** *adj* (*person*) dérouté(e), désorienté(e); (*situation*) embrouillé(e); **confusing** *adj* peu clair(e), déroutant(e); **confusion** [kən'fjuːʒən] *n* confusion *f*

congestion [kən'dʒɛstʃən] *n* (*Med*) congestion *f*; (*fig: traffic*) encombrement *m*

congratulate [kən'grætjuleɪt] *vt*: **to ~ sb (on)** féliciter qn (de); **congratulations** [kəngrætju'leɪʃənz] *npl*; **congratulations (on)** félicitations *fpl* (pour) ▷ *excl*: **congratulations!** (toutes mes) félicitations!

congregation [kɔngrɪ'geɪʃən] *n* assemblée *f* (des fidèles)

congress ['kɔngrɛs] *n* congrès *m*; (*Pol*): **C~** Congrès *m*; **congressman** (*irreg*) *n* membre *m* du Congrès; **congresswoman** (*irreg*) *n* membre *m* du Congrès

conifer ['kɔnɪfər] *n* conifère *m*

conjugate ['kɔndʒugeɪt] *vt* conjuguer

conjugation [kɔndʒə'geɪʃən] *n* conjugaison *f*

conjunction [kən'dʒʌŋkʃən] *n* conjonction *f*; **in ~ with** (conjointement) avec

conjure ['kʌndʒər] *vi* faire des tours de passe-passe

connect [kə'nɛkt] *vt* joindre, relier; (*Elec*) connecter; (*Tel: caller*) mettre en connexion; (: *subscriber*) brancher; (*fig*) établir un rapport entre, faire un rapprochement entre ▷ *vi* (*train*): **to ~ with** assurer la correspondance avec; **to be ~ed with** avoir un rapport avec; (*have dealings with*) avoir des rapports avec, être en relation avec; **connecting flight** (vol *m* de) correspondance *f*; **connection** [kə'nɛkʃən] *n* relation *f*, lien *m*; (*Elec*) connexion *f*; (*Tel*) communication *f*; (*train etc*) correspondance *f*

conquer ['kɔŋkər] *vt* conquérir; (*feelings*) vaincre, surmonter

conquest ['kɔŋkwɛst] *n* conquête *f*

cons [kɔnz] *npl see* **convenience; pro**

conscience ['kɔnʃəns] *n* conscience *f*

conscientious [kɔnʃɪ'ɛnʃəs] *adj* consciencieux(-euse)

conscious ['kɔnʃəs] *adj* conscient(e); (*deliberate*: insult, error) délibéré(e); **consciousness** *n* conscience *f*; (*Med*) connaissance *f*

consecutive [kən'sɛkjutɪv] *adj* consécutif(-ive); **on three ~ occasions** trois fois de suite

consensus [kən'sɛnsəs] *n* consensus *m*

consent [kən'sɛnt] *n* consentement *m* ▷ *vi*: **to ~ (to)** consentir (à)

consequence ['kɔnsɪkwəns] *n* suites *fpl*, conséquence *f*; (*significance*) importance *f*

consequently ['kɔnsɪkwəntlɪ] *adv* par conséquent, donc

conservation [kɔnsə'veɪʃən] *n* préservation *f*, protection *f*; (*also*: **nature ~**) défense *f* de l'environnement

Conservative [kən'sə:vətɪv] *adj*, *n* (*BRIT Pol*) conservateur(-trice)

conservative *adj* conservateur(-trice); (*cautious*) prudent(e)

conservatory [kən'sə:vətrɪ] *n* (*room*) jardin *m* d'hiver; (*Mus*) conservatoire *m*

consider [kən'sɪdər] *vt* (*study*) considérer, réfléchir à; (*take into account*) penser à, prendre en considération; (*regard, judge*) considérer, estimer; **to ~ doing sth** envisager de faire qch; **considerable** *adj* considérable; **considerably** *adv* nettement; **considerate** *adj*

prévenant(e), plein(e) d'égards;
consideration [kənsɪdə'reɪʃən] n
considération f; (*reward*) rétribution
f, rémunération f; **considering**
prep: **considering (that)** étant
donné (que)
consignment [kən'saɪnmənt] n
arrivage m, envoi m
consist [kən'sɪst] vi: **to ~ of** consister
en, se composer de
consistency [kən'sɪstənsɪ] n
(*thickness*) consistance f; (*fig*)
cohérence f
consistent [kən'sɪstənt] adj logique,
cohérent(e)
consolation [kɔnsə'leɪʃən] n
consolation f
console¹ [kən'səul] vt consoler
console² ['kɔnsəul] n console f
consonant ['kɔnsənənt] n
consonne f
conspicuous [kən'spɪkjuəs] adj
voyant(e), qui attire l'attention
conspiracy [kən'spɪrəsɪ] n
conspiration f, complot m
constable ['kʌnstəbl] n (*BRIT*) ≈
agent m de police, gendarme m; **chief
~** ≈ préfet m de police
constant ['kɔnstənt] adj
constant(e); incessant(e);
constantly adv constamment,
sans cesse
constipated ['kɔnstɪpeɪtɪd]
adj constipé(e); **constipation**
[kɔnstɪ'peɪʃən] n constipation f
constituency [kən'stɪtjuənsɪ] n
(*Pol: area*) circonscription électorale;
(: *electors*) électorat m
constitute ['kɔnstɪtjuːt] vt
constituer
constitution [kɔnstɪ'tjuːʃən] n
constitution f
constraint [kən'streɪnt] n
contrainte f
construct [kən'strʌkt] vt construire;
construction [kən'strʌkʃən] n
construction f; **constructive** adj
constructif(-ive)

consul ['kɔnsl] n consul m;
consulate ['kɔnsjulɪt] n consulat m
consult [kən'sʌlt] vt consulter;
consultant n (*Med*) médecin
consultant; (*other specialist*)
consultant m, (expert-)conseil m;
consultation [kɔnsəl'teɪʃən] n
consultation f; **consulting room** n
(*BRIT*) cabinet m de consultation
consume [kən'sjuːlt] vt
consommer; (*subj: flames, hatred,
desire*) consumer; **consumer** n
consommateur(-trice)
consumption [kən'sʌmpʃən] n
consommation f
cont. abbr (= continued) suite
contact ['kɔntækt] n contact m;
(*person*) connaissance f, relation f ▷ vt
se mettre en contact or en rapport
avec; **~ number** numéro m de
téléphone; **contact lenses** npl verres
mpl de contact
contagious [kən'teɪdʒəs] adj
contagieux(-euse)
contain [kən'teɪn] vt contenir;
to ~ o.s. se contenir, se maîtriser;
container n récipient m; (*for shipping
etc*) conteneur m
contaminate [kən'tæmɪneɪt] vt
contaminer
cont'd abbr (= continued) suite
contemplate ['kɔntəmpleɪt] vt
contempler; (*consider*) envisager
contemporary [kən'tɛmpərərɪ] adj
contemporain(e); (*design, wallpaper*)
moderne ▷ n contemporain(e)
contempt [kən'tɛmpt] n mépris m,
dédain m; **~ of court** (*Law*) outrage m
à l'autorité de la justice
contend [kən'tɛnd] vt: **to ~ that**
soutenir or prétendre que ▷ vi: **to
~ with** (*compete*) rivaliser avec;
(*struggle*) lutter avec
content [kən'tɛnt] adj content(e),
satisfait(e) ▷ vt contenter, satisfaire
▷ n ['kɔntɛnt] contenu m; (*of fat,
moisture*) teneur f; **contents** npl (*of
container etc*) contenu m; **(table of)**

~s table f des matières; **contented** adj content(e), satisfait(e)

contest n ['kɒntɛst] combat m, lutte f; (competition) concours m ▷ vt [kən'tɛst] contester, discuter; (compete for) disputer; (Law) attaquer; **contestant** [kən'tɛstənt] n concurrent(e); (in fight) adversaire m/f

context ['kɒntɛkst] n contexte m

continent ['kɒntɪnənt] n continent m; **the C~** (BRIT) l'Europe continentale; **continental** [kɒntɪ'nɛntl] adj continental(e); **continental breakfast** n café (or thé) complet; **continental quilt** n (BRIT) couette f

continual [kən'tɪnjuəl] adj continuel(le); **continually** adv continuellement, sans cesse

continue [kən'tɪnju:] vi continuer ▷ vt continuer; (start again) reprendre

continuity [kɒntɪ'nju:ɪtɪ] n continuité f; (TV) enchaînement m

continuous [kən'tɪnjuəs] adj continu(e), permanent(e); (Ling) progressif(-ive); **continuous assessment** (BRIT) n contrôle continu; **continuously** adv (repeatedly) continuellement; (uninterruptedly) sans interruption

contour ['kɒntuər] n contour m, profil m; (also: **~ line**) courbe f de niveau

contraception [kɒntrə'sɛpʃən] n contraception f

contraceptive [kɒntrə'sɛptɪv] adj contraceptif(-ive), anticonceptionnel(le) ▷ n contraceptif m

contract n ['kɒntrækt] contrat m ▷ vi [kən'trækt] (become smaller) se contracter, se resserrer ▷ vt contracter; (Comm): **to ~ to do sth** s'engager (par contrat) à faire qch; **contractor** n entrepreneur m

contradict [kɒntrə'dɪkt] vt contredire; **contradiction** [kɒntrə'dɪkʃən] n contradiction f

contrary¹ ['kɒntrərɪ] adj contraire, opposé(e) ▷ n contraire m; **on the ~** au contraire; **unless you hear to the ~** sauf avis contraire

contrary² [kən'trɛərɪ] adj (perverse) contrariant(e), entêté(e)

contrast n ['kɒntrɑ:st] contraste m ▷ vt [kən'trɑ:st] mettre en contraste, contraster; **in ~ to** or **with** contrairement à, par opposition à

contribute [kən'trɪbju:t] vi contribuer ▷ vt: **to ~ £10/an article to** donner 10 livres/un article à; **to ~ to** (gen) contribuer à; (newspaper) collaborer à; (discussion) prendre part à; **contribution** [kɒntrɪ'bju:ʃən] n contribution f; (BRIT: for social security) cotisation f; (to publication) article m; **contributor** n (to newspaper) collaborateur(-trice); (of money, goods) donateur(-trice)

control [kən'trəul] vt (process, machinery) commander; (temper) maîtriser; (disease) enrayer ▷ n maîtrise f; (power) autorité f; **controls** npl (of machine etc) commandes fpl; (on radio) boutons mpl de réglage; **to be in ~ of** être maître de, maîtriser; (in charge of) être responsable de; **everything is under ~** j'ai (or il a etc) la situation en main; **the car went out of ~** j'ai (or il a etc) perdu le contrôle du véhicule; **control tower** n (Aviat) tour f de contrôle

controversial [kɒntrə'və:ʃl] adj discutable, controversé(e)

controversy ['kɒntrəvə:sɪ] n controverse f, polémique f

convenience [kən'vi:nɪəns] n commodité f; **at your ~** quand or comme cela vous convient; **all modern ~s, all mod cons** (BRIT) avec tout le confort moderne, tout confort

convenient [kən'vi:nɪənt] adj commode

convent ['kɒnvənt] n couvent m

convention [kən'vɛnʃən] n
convention f; (custom) usage m;
conventional adj conventionnel(le)

conversation [kɔnvə'seɪʃən] n
conversation f

conversely [kɔn'vəːslɪ] adv
inversement, réciproquement

conversion [kən'vəːʃən] n
conversion f; (BRIT: of house)
transformation f, aménagement m;
(Rugby) transformation f

convert vt [kən'vəːt] (Rel, Comm)
convertir; (alter) transformer; (house)
aménager ▷ n ['kɔnvəːt] converti(e);
convertible adj convertible ▷ n
(voiture f) décapotable f

convey [kən'veɪ] vt transporter;
(thanks) transmettre; (idea)
communiquer; **conveyor belt** n
convoyeur m tapis roulant

convict vt [kən'vɪkt] déclarer (or
reconnaître) coupable ▷ n ['kɔnvɪkt]
forçat m, convict m; **conviction**
[kən'vɪkʃən] n (Law) condamnation f;
(belief) conviction f

convince [kən'vɪns] vt convaincre,
persuader; **convinced** adj:
convinced of/that convaincu(e) de/
que; **convincing** adj persuasif(-ive),
convaincant(e)

convoy ['kɔnvɔɪ] n convoi m

cook [kuk] vt (faire) cuire ▷ vi
cuire; (person) faire la cuisine ▷ n
cuisinier(-ière); **cookbook** n livre
m de cuisine; **cooker** n cuisinière f;
cookery n cuisine f; **cookery book**
n (BRIT) = **cookbook**; **cookie** n (US)
biscuit m, petit gâteau sec; **cooking**
n cuisine f

cool [kuːl] adj frais (fraîche); (not
afraid) calme; (unfriendly) froid(e);
(inf: trendy) cool inv (inf); (: great)
super inv (inf) ▷ vt, vi rafraîchir,
refroidir; **cool down** vi refroidir; (fig:
person, situation) se calmer; **cool off**
vi (become calmer) se calmer; (: lose
enthusiasm) perdre son enthousiasme

cop [kɔp] n (inf) flic m

cope [kəup] vi s'en sortir, tenir le
coup; **to ~ with** (problem) faire face à

copper ['kɔpə'] n cuivre m; (BRIT inf:
policeman) flic m

copy ['kɔpɪ] n copie f; (book etc)
exemplaire m ▷ vt copier; (imitate)
imiter; **copyright** n droit m d'auteur,
copyright m

coral ['kɔrəl] n corail m

cord [kɔːd] n corde f; (fabric)
velours côtelé; (Elec) cordon m
(d'alimentation), fil m (électrique);
cords npl (trousers) pantalon m de
velours côtelé; **cordless** adj sans fil

corduroy ['kɔːdərɔɪ] n velours côtelé

core [kɔː'] n (of fruit) trognon m,
cœur m; (fig: of problem etc) cœur ▷ vt
enlever le trognon or le cœur de

coriander [kɔrɪ'ændə'] n coriandre f

cork [kɔːk] n (material) liège m; (of
bottle) bouchon m; **corkscrew** n
tire-bouchon m

corn [kɔːn] n (BRIT: wheat) blé m; (US:
maize) maïs m; (on foot) cor m; **~ on the
cob** (Culin) épi m de maïs au naturel

corned beef ['kɔːnd-] n corned-
beef m

corner ['kɔːnə'] n coin m; (in road)
tournant m, virage m; (Football)
corner m ▷ vt (trap: prey) acculer; (fig)
coincer; (Comm: market) accaparer
▷ vi prendre un virage; **corner shop**
(BRIT) n magasin m du coin

cornflakes ['kɔːnfleɪks] npl
cornflakes mpl

cornflour ['kɔːnflauə'] n (BRIT) farine
f de maïs, maïzena® f

cornstarch ['kɔːnstɑːtʃ] n (US) farine
f de maïs, maïzena® f

Cornwall ['kɔːnwəl] n Cornouailles f

coronary ['kɔrənərɪ] n:
~ (thrombosis) infarctus m (du
myocarde), thrombose f coronaire

coronation [kɔrə'neɪʃən] n
couronnement m

coroner ['kɔrənə'] n coroner m,
officier de police judiciaire chargé de
déterminer les causes d'un décès

corporal ['kɔːpərl] n caporal m, brigadier m ▷ adj: **~ punishment** châtiment corporel

corporate ['kɔːpərɪt] adj (action, ownership) en commun; (Comm) de la société

corporation [kɔːpəˈreɪʃən] n (of town) municipalité f, conseil municipal; (Comm) société f

corps (pl **corps**) [kɔːʳ, kɔːz] n corps m; **the diplomatic ~** le corps diplomatique; **the press ~** la presse

corpse [kɔːps] n cadavre m

correct [kəˈrɛkt] adj (accurate) correct(e), exact(e); (proper) correct, convenable ▷ vt corriger; **correction** [kəˈrɛkʃən] n correction f

correspond [kɔrɪsˈpɔnd] vi correspondre; **to ~ to sth** (be equivalent to) correspondre à qch; **correspondence** n correspondance f; **correspondent** n correspondant(e); **corresponding** adj correspondant(e)

corridor ['kɔrɪdɔːʳ] n couloir m, corridor m

corrode [kəˈrəud] vt corroder, ronger ▷ vi se corroder

corrupt [kəˈrʌpt] adj corrompu(e); (Comput) altéré(e) ▷ vt corrompre; (Comput) altérer; **corruption** n corruption f; (Comput) altération f (de données)

Corsica ['kɔːsɪkə] n Corse f

cosmetic [kɔzˈmɛtɪk] n produit m de beauté, cosmétique m ▷ adj (fig: reforms) symbolique, superficiel(le); **cosmetic surgery** n chirurgie f esthétique

cosmopolitan [kɔzməˈpɔlɪtn] adj cosmopolite

cost [kɔst] (pt, pp **cost**) n coût m ▷ vi coûter ▷ vt établir le prix de revient de; **costs** npl (Comm) frais mpl; (Law) dépens mpl; **how much does it ~?** combien ça coûte?; **to ~ sb time/effort** demander du temps/un effort à qn; **it ~ him his life/job** ça lui

a coûté la vie/son emploi; **at all ~s** coûte que coûte, à tout prix

co-star ['kəustɑːʳ] n partenaire m/f

costly ['kɔstlɪ] adj coûteux(-euse)

cost of living n coût m de la vie

costume ['kɔstjuːm] n costume m; (BRIT: also: **swimming ~**) maillot m (de bain)

cosy, (US) **cozy** ['kəuzɪ] adj (room, bed) douillet(te); **to be ~** (person) être bien (au chaud)

cot [kɔt] n (BRIT: child's) lit m d'enfant, petit lit; (US: campbed) lit de camp

cottage ['kɔtɪdʒ] n petite maison (à la campagne), cottage m; **cottage cheese** n fromage blanc (maigre)

cotton ['kɔtn] n coton m; (thread) fil m (de coton); **cotton on** vi (inf): **to ~ on (to sth)** piger (qch); **cotton bud** (BRIT) n coton-tige® m; **cotton candy** (US) n barbe f à papa; **cotton wool** n (BRIT) ouate f, coton m hydrophile

couch [kautʃ] n canapé m; divan m

cough [kɔf] vi tousser ▷ n toux f; **I've got a ~** j'ai la toux; **cough mixture, cough syrup** n sirop m pour la toux

could [kud] pt of **can²**; **couldn't** = **could not**

council ['kaunsl] n conseil m; **city** or **town ~** conseil municipal; **council estate** n (BRIT) (quartier m or zone f de) logements loués à/par la municipalité; **council house** n (BRIT) maison f (à loyer modéré) louée par la municipalité; **councillor**, (US) **councilor** n conseiller(-ère); **council tax** n (BRIT) impôts locaux

counsel ['kaunsl] n conseil m; (lawyer) avocat(e) ▷ vt: **to ~ (sb to do sth)** conseiller (à qn de faire qch); **counselling**, (US) **counseling** n (Psych) aide psychosociale; **counsellor**, (US) **counselor** n conseiller(-ère); (US Law) avocat m

count [kaunt] vt, vi compter ▷ n compte m; (nobleman) comte m; **count in** vt (inf): **to ~ sb in on sth**

inclure qn dans qch; **count on** vt fus compter sur; **countdown** n compte m à rebours

counter ['kauntər] n comptoir m; (in post office, bank) guichet m; (in game) jeton m ▷ vt aller à l'encontre de, opposer ▷ adv: ~ **to** à l'encontre de; contrairement à; **counterclockwise** (us) adv en sens inverse des aiguilles d'une montre

counterfeit ['kauntəfɪt] n faux m, contrefaçon f ▷ vt contrefaire ▷ adj faux (fausse)

counterpart ['kauntəpɑːt] n (of person) homologue m/f

countess ['kauntɪs] n comtesse f

countless ['kauntlɪs] adj innombrable

country ['kʌntrɪ] n pays m; (native land) patrie f; (as opposed to town) campagne f; (region) région f, pays; **country and western (music)** n musique f country; **country house** n manoir m, (petit) château; **countryside** n campagne f

county ['kauntɪ] n comté m

coup (pl **coups**) [kuː, kuːz] n (achievement) beau coup; (also: ~ **d'état**) coup d'État

couple ['kʌpl] n couple m; **a ~ of** (two) deux; (a few) deux ou trois

coupon ['kuːpɒn] n (voucher) bon m de réduction; (detachable form) coupon m détachable, coupon-réponse m

courage ['kʌrɪdʒ] n courage m; **courageous** [kə'reɪdʒəs] adj courageux(-euse)

courgette [kuə'ʒɛt] n (BRIT) courgette f

courier ['kurɪər] n messager m, courrier m; (for tourists) accompagnateur(-trice)

course [kɔːs] n cours m; (of ship) route f; (for golf) terrain m; (part of meal) plat m; **of ~** adv bien sûr; **(no,) of ~ not!** bien sûr que non!, évidemment que non!; **~ of treatment** (Med) traitement m

court [kɔːt] n cour f; (Law) tribunal m; (Tennis) court m ▷ vt (woman) courtiser, faire la cour à; **to take to ~** actionner or poursuivre en justice

courtesy ['kəːtəsɪ] n courtoisie f, politesse f; **(by) ~ of** avec l'aimable autorisation de; **courtesy bus, courtesy coach** n navette gratuite

court: court-house ['kɔːthaus] n (us) palais m de justice; **courtroom** ['kɔːtrum] n salle f de tribunal; **courtyard** ['kɔːtjɑːd] n cour f

cousin ['kʌzn] n cousin(e); **first ~** cousin(e) germain(e)

cover ['kʌvər] vt couvrir; (Press: report on) faire un reportage sur; (feelings, mistake) cacher; (include) englober; (discuss) traiter ▷ n (of book, Comm) couverture f; (of pan) couvercle m; (over furniture) housse f; (shelter) abri m; **covers** npl (on bed) couvertures; **to take ~** se mettre à l'abri; **under ~** à l'abri; **under ~ of darkness** à la faveur de la nuit; **under separate ~** (Comm) sous pli séparé; **cover up** vi: **to ~ up for sb** (fig) couvrir qn; **coverage** n (in media) reportage m; **cover charge** n couvert m (supplément à payer); **cover-up** n tentative f pour étouffer une affaire

cow [kau] n vache f ▷ vt effrayer, intimider

coward ['kauəd] n lâche m/f; **cowardly** adj lâche

cowboy ['kaubɔɪ] n cow-boy m

cozy ['kəuzɪ] adj (us) = **cosy**

crab [kræb] n crabe m

crack [kræk] n (split) fente f, fissure f; (in cup, bone) fêlure f; (in wall) lézarde f; (noise) craquement m, coup (sec); (Drugs) crack m ▷ vt fendre, fissurer; fêler; lézarder; (whip) faire claquer; (nut) casser; (problem) résoudre; (code) déchiffrer ▷ cpd (athlete) de première classe, d'élite; **crack down on** vt fus (crime) sévir contre, réprimer; **cracked** adj (cup, *bone*) fêlé(e); (*broken*) cassé(e); (*wall*) lézardé(e); (*surface*) craquelé(e); (*inf*) toqué(e), timbré(e); **cracker** n (*also*: **Christmas cracker**) pétard m; (*biscuit*) biscuit (salé), craquelin m

crackle ['krækl] vi crépiter, grésiller

cradle ['kreɪdl] n berceau m

craft [krɑːft] n métier (artisanal); (*cunning*) ruse f, astuce f; (*boat*: pl inv) embarcation f, barque f; (*plane*: pl inv) appareil m; **craftsman** (*irreg*) n artisan m ouvrier (qualifié); **craftsmanship** n métier m, habileté f

cram [kræm] vt: **to ~ sth with** (*fill*) bourrer qch de; **to ~ sth into** (*put*) fourrer qch dans ▷ vi (*for exams*) bachoter

cramp [kræmp] n crampe f; **I've got ~ in my leg** j'ai une crampe à la jambe; **cramped** adj à l'étroit, très serré(e)

cranberry ['krænbəri] n canneberge f

crane [kreɪn] n grue f

crap [kræp] n (*inf*: *nonsense*) conneries fpl (!); (: *excrement*) merde f (!)

crash [kræʃ] n (*noise*) fracas m; (*of car, plane*) collision f; (*of business*) faillite f ▷ vt (*plane*) écraser ▷ vi (*plane*) s'écraser; (*two cars*) se percuter, s'emboutir; (*business*) s'effondrer; **to ~ into** se jeter or se fracasser contre; **crash course** n cours intensif; **crash helmet** n casque (protecteur)

crate [kreɪt] n cageot m; (*for bottles*) caisse f

crave [kreɪv] vt, vi: **to ~ (for)** avoir une envie irrésistible de

crawl [krɔːl] vi ramper; (*vehicle*) avancer au pas ▷ n (*Swimming*) crawl m

crayfish ['kreɪfɪʃ] n (pl inv: *freshwater*) écrevisse f; (: *saltwater*) langoustine f

crayon ['kreɪən] n crayon m (de couleur)

craze [kreɪz] n engouement m

crazy ['kreɪzɪ] adj fou (folle); **to be ~ about sb/sth** (*inf*) être fou de qn/qch

creak [kriːk] vi (*hinge*) grincer; (*floor, shoes*) craquer

cream [kriːm] n crème f ▷ adj (*colour*) crème inv; **cream cheese** n fromage m à la crème, fromage blanc; **creamy** adj crémeux(-euse)

crease [kriːs] n pli m ▷ vt froisser, chiffonner ▷ vi se froisser, se chiffonner

create [kriːˈeɪt] vt créer; **creation** [kriːˈeɪʃən] n création f; **creative** adj créatif(-ive); **creator** n créateur(-trice)

creature ['kriːtʃər] n créature f

crèche [krɛʃ] n garderie f, crèche f

credentials [krɪˈdɛnʃlz] npl (*references*) références fpl; (*identity papers*) pièce f d'identité

credibility [krɛdɪˈbɪlɪtɪ] n crédibilité f

credible ['krɛdɪbl] adj digne de foi, crédible

credit ['krɛdɪt] n crédit m; (*recognition*) honneur m; (*Scol*) unité f de valeur ▷ vt (*Comm*) créditer; (*believe*: also: **give ~ to**) ajouter foi à, croire; **credits** npl (*Cine*) générique m; **to be in ~** (*person, bank account*) être créditeur(-trice); **to ~ sb with** (*fig*) prêter or attribuer à qn; **credit card** n carte f de crédit; **do you take credit cards?** acceptez-vous les cartes de crédit?; **credit crunch** n crise f du crédit

creek [kriːk] n (*inlet*) crique f, anse f; (*us*: *stream*) ruisseau m, petit cours d'eau

creep (pt, pp **crept**) [kriːp, krɛpt] vi ramper

cremate [krɪˈmeɪt] vt incinérer

crematorium (pl **crematoria**) [krɛməˈtɔːrɪəm, -ˈtɔːrɪə] n four m crématoire

crept [krɛpt] pt, pp of **creep**

crescent ['krɛsnt] n croissant m; (*street*) rue f (en arc de cercle)

cress [krɛs] n cresson m

crest [krɛst] n crête f; (*of coat of arms*) timbre m

crew [kru:] n équipage m; (Cine)
équipe f (de tournage); **crew-neck**
n col ras

crib [krɪb] n lit m d'enfant; (for baby)
berceau m ▷ vt (inf) copier

cricket ['krɪkɪt] n (insect) grillon
m, cri-cri m inv; (game) cricket m;
cricketer n joueur m de cricket

crime [kraɪm] n crime m; **criminal**
['krɪmɪnl] adj, n criminel(le)

crimson ['krɪmzn] adj cramoisi(e)

cringe [krɪndʒ] vi avoir un
mouvement de recul

cripple ['krɪpl] n (offensive)
boiteux(-euse), infirme m/f ▷ vt
(person) estropier, paralyser; (ship,
plane) immobiliser; (production,
exports) paralyser

crisis (pl **crises**) ['kraɪsɪs, -si:z] n crise f

crisp [krɪsp] adj croquant(e);
(weather) vif (vive); (manner etc)
brusque; **crisps** (BRIT) npl (pommes
fpl) chips fpl; **crispy** adj croustillant(e)

criterion (pl **criteria**) [kraɪ'tɪərɪən,
-'tɪərɪə] n critère m

critic ['krɪtɪk] n critique m/f; **critical**
adj critique; **criticism** ['krɪtɪsɪzəm]
n critique f; **criticize** ['krɪtɪsaɪz] vt
critiquer

Croat ['krəuæt] adj, n = **Croatian**

Croatia [krəu'eɪʃə] n Croatie f;
Croatian adj croate ▷ n Croate m/f;
(Ling) croate m

crockery ['krɔkərɪ] n vaisselle f

crocodile ['krɔkədaɪl] n crocodile m

crocus ['krəukəs] n crocus m

croissant ['krwasã] n croissant m

crook [kruk] n (inf) escroc m; (of
shepherd) houlette f; **crooked**
['krukɪd] adj courbé(e), tordu(e);
(action) malhonnête

crop [krɔp] n (produce) culture f;
(amount produced) récolte f; (riding
crop) cravache f ▷ vt (hair) tondre;
crop up vi surgir, se présenter,
survenir

cross [krɔs] n croix f; (Biol) croisement
m ▷ vt (street etc) traverser; (arms,

legs, Biol) croiser; (cheque) barrer
▷ adj en colère, fâché(e); **cross off,
cross out** vt barrer, rayer; **cross
over** vi traverser; **cross-Channel
ferry** ['krɔs'tʃænl-] n ferry m qui fait
la traversée de la Manche; **cross-
country (race)** n cross(-country) m;
crossing n (sea passage) traversée f;
(also: **pedestrian crossing**) passage
clouté; **how long does the crossing
take?** combien de temps dure la
traversée?; **crossing guard** n (US)
contractuel qui fait traverser la rue aux
enfants; **crossroads** n carrefour m;
crosswalk n (US) passage clouté;
crossword n mots mpl croisés

crotch [krɔtʃ] n (of garment)
entrejambe m; (Anat) entrecuisse m

crouch [krautʃ] vi s'accroupir; (hide)
se tapir; (before springing) se ramasser

crouton ['kru:tɔn] n croûton m

crow [krəu] n (bird) corneille f; (of
cock) chant m du coq, cocorico m ▷ vi
(cock) chanter

crowd [kraud] n foule f ▷ vt bourrer,
remplir ▷ vi affluer, s'attrouper,
s'entasser; **crowded** adj bondé(e)

crown [kraun] n couronne f; (of head)
sommet m de la tête; (of hill) sommet
m ▷ vt (also tooth) couronner; **crown
jewels** npl joyaux mpl de la Couronne

crucial ['kru:ʃl] adj crucial(e),
décisif(-ive)

crucifix ['kru:sɪfɪks] n crucifix m

crude [kru:d] adj (materials)
brut(e); non raffiné(e); (basic)
rudimentaire, sommaire; (vulgar)
cru(e), grossier(-ière) ▷ n (also: ~ oil)
(pétrole m) brut m

cruel ['kruəl] adj cruel(le); **cruelty**
n cruauté f

cruise [kru:z] n croisière f ▷ vi (ship)
croiser; (car) rouler; (aircraft) voler

crumb [krʌm] n miette f

crumble ['krʌmbl] vt émietter ▷ vi
(plaster etc) s'effriter; (land, earth)
s'ébouler; (building) s'écrouler,
crouler; (fig) s'effondrer

crumpet ['krʌmpɪt] n petite crêpe (épaisse)

crumple ['krʌmpl] vt froisser, friper

crunch [krʌntʃ] vt croquer; (underfoot) faire craquer, écraser; faire crisser ▷ n (fig) instant m or moment m critique, moment de vérité; **crunchy** adj croquant(e), croustillant(e)

crush [krʌʃ] n (crowd) foule f, cohue f; (love): **to have a ~ on sb** avoir le béguin pour qn; (drink): **lemon ~** citron pressé ▷ vt écraser; (crumple) froisser; (grind, break up: garlic, ice) piler; (: grapes) presser; (hopes) anéantir

crust [krʌst] n croûte f; **crusty** adj (bread) croustillant(e); (inf: person) revêche, bourru(e)

crutch [krʌtʃ] n béquille f; (of garment) entrejambe m; (Anat) entrecuisse m

cry [kraɪ] vi pleurer; (shout: also: ~ **out**) crier ▷ n cri m; **cry out** vi (call out, shout) pousser un cri ▷ vt crier

crystal ['krɪstl] n cristal m

cub [kʌb] n petit m (d'un animal); (also: ~ **scout**) louveteau m

Cuba ['kju:bə] n Cuba m

cube [kju:b] n cube m ▷ vt (Math) élever au cube

cubicle ['kju:bɪkl] n (in hospital) box m; (at pool) cabine f

cuckoo ['kuku:] n coucou m

cucumber ['kju:kʌmbər] n concombre m

cuddle ['kʌdl] vt câliner, caresser ▷ vi se blottir l'un contre l'autre

cue [kju:] n queue f de billard; (Theat etc) signal m

cuff [kʌf] n (BRIT: of shirt, coat etc) poignet m, manchette f; (US: on trousers) revers m; (blow) gifle f; **off the ~** adv à l'improviste; **cufflinks** n boutons m de manchette

cuisine [kwɪ'zi:n] n cuisine f

cul-de-sac ['kʌldəsæk] n cul-de-sac m, impasse f

cull [kʌl] vt sélectionner ▷ n (of animals) abattage sélectif

culminate ['kʌlmɪneɪt] vi: **to ~ in** finir or se terminer par; (lead to) mener à

culprit ['kʌlprɪt] n coupable m/f

cult [kʌlt] n culte m

cultivate ['kʌltɪveɪt] vt cultiver

cultural ['kʌltʃərəl] adj culturel(le)

culture ['kʌltʃər] n culture f

cumin ['kʌmɪn] n (spice) cumin m

cunning ['kʌnɪŋ] n ruse f, astuce f ▷ adj rusé(e), malin(-igne); (clever: device, idea) astucieux(-euse)

cup [kʌp] n tasse f; (prize, event) coupe f; (of bra) bonnet m

cupboard ['kʌbəd] n placard m

cup final n (BRIT Football) finale f de la coupe

curator [kjuə'reɪtər] n conservateur m (d'un musée etc)

curb [kə:b] vt refréner, mettre un frein à ▷ n (fig) frein m; (US) bord m du trottoir

curdle ['kə:dl] vi (se) cailler

cure [kjuər] vt guérir; (Culin: salt) saler; (: smoke) fumer; (: dry) sécher ▷ n remède m

curfew ['kə:fju:] n couvre-feu m

curiosity [kjuərɪ'ɔsɪtɪ] n curiosité f

curious ['kjuərɪəs] adj curieux(-euse); **I'm ~ about him** il m'intrigue

curl [kə:l] n boucle f (de cheveux) ▷ vt, vi boucler; (tightly) friser, **curl up** vi s'enrouler; (person) se pelotonner; **curler** n bigoudi m, rouleau m; **curly** adj bouclé(e); (tightly curled) frisé(e)

currant ['kʌrnt] n raisin m de Corinthe, raisin sec; (fruit) groseille f

currency ['kʌrnsɪ] n monnaie f; **to gain ~** (fig) s'accréditer

current ['kʌrnt] n courant m ▷ adj (common) courant(e); (tendency, price, event) actuel(le); **current account** n (BRIT) compte courant; **current affairs** npl (questions fpl d') actualité f; **currently** adv actuellement

curriculum (*pl* **curriculums** *or* **curricula**) [kə'rɪkjuləm, -lə] *n* programme *m* d'études; **curriculum vitae** [-'viːtaɪ] *n* curriculum vitae (CV) *m*

curry ['kʌrɪ] *n* curry *m* ▷ *vt*: **to ~ favour with** chercher à gagner la faveur *or* à s'attirer les bonnes grâces de; **curry powder** *n* poudre *f* de curry

curse [kəːs] *vi* jurer, blasphémer ▷ *vt* maudire ▷ *n* (*spell*) malédiction *f*; (*problem, scourge*) fléau *m*; (*swearword*) juron *m*

cursor ['kəːsə'] *n* (*Comput*) curseur *m*

curt [kəːt] *adj* brusque, sec (sèche)

curtain ['kəːtn] *n* rideau *m*

curve [kəːv] *n* courbe *f*; (*in the road*) tournant *m*, virage *m* ▷ *vi* se courber; (*road*) faire une courbe; **curved** *adj* courbe

cushion ['kuʃən] *n* coussin *m* ▷ *vt* (*fall, shock*) amortir

custard ['kʌstəd] *n* (*for pouring*) crème anglaise

custody ['kʌstədɪ] *n* (*of child*) garde *f*; (*for offenders*): **to take sb into ~** placer qn en détention préventive

custom ['kʌstəm] *n* coutume *f*, usage *m*; (*Comm*) clientèle *f*

customer ['kʌstəmə'] *n* client(e)

customized ['kʌstəmaɪzd] *adj* personnalisé(e); (*car etc*) construit(e) sur commande

customs ['kʌstəmz] *npl* douane *f*; **customs officer** *n* douanier *m*

cut [kʌt] (*pt, pp* **cut**) *vt* couper; (*meat*) découper; (*reduce*) réduire ▷ *vi* couper ▷ *n* (*gen*) coupure *f*; (*of clothes*) coupe *f*; (*in salary etc*) réduction *f*; (*of meat*) morceau *m*; **to ~ a tooth** percer une dent; **to ~ one's finger** se couper le doigt; **to get one's hair ~** se faire couper les cheveux; **I've ~ myself** je me suis coupé; **cut back** *vt* (*plants*) tailler; (*production, expenditure*) réduire; **cut down** *vt* (*tree*) abattre; (*reduce*) réduire; **cut off** *vt* couper; (*fig*) isoler; **cut out** *vt* (*picture etc*)

découper; (*remove*) supprimer; **cut up** *vt* découper; **cutback** *n* réduction *f*

cute [kjuːt] *adj* mignon(ne), adorable

cutlery ['kʌtlərɪ] *n* couverts *mpl*

cutlet ['kʌtlɪt] *n* côtelette *f*

cut-price ['kʌt'praɪs], (*us*) **cut-rate** ['kʌt'reɪt] *adj* au rabais, à prix réduit

cutting ['kʌtɪŋ] *adj* (*fig*) cinglant(e) ▷ *n* (BRIT: *from newspaper*) coupure *f* (de journal); (*from plant*) bouture *f*

CV *n abbr* = **curriculum vitae**

cyberbullying ['saɪbəbuliɪŋ] *n* harcèlement *m* virtuel

cyberspace ['saɪbəspeɪs] *n* cyberespace *m*

cycle ['saɪkl] *n* cycle *m*; (*bicycle*) bicyclette *f*, vélo *m* ▷ *vi* faire de la bicyclette; **cycle hire** *n* location *f* de vélos; **cycle lane**, **cycle path** *n* piste *f* cyclable; **cycling** *n* cyclisme *m*; **cyclist** *n* cycliste *m/f*

cyclone ['saɪkləun] *n* cyclone *m*

cylinder ['sɪlɪndə'] *n* cylindre *m*

cymbals ['sɪmblz] *npl* cymbales *fpl*

cynical ['sɪnɪkl] *adj* cynique

Cypriot ['sɪprɪət] *adj* cypriote, chypriote ▷ *n* Cypriote *m/f*, Chypriote *m/f*

Cyprus ['saɪprəs] *n* Chypre *f*

cyst [sɪst] *n* kyste *m*; **cystitis** [sɪs'taɪtɪs] *n* cystite *f*

czar [zɑː'] *n* tsar *m*

Czech [tʃɛk] *adj* tchèque ▷ *n* Tchèque *m/f*; (*Ling*) tchèque *m*; **Czech Republic** *n*: **the Czech Republic** la République tchèque

d

D [diː] n (Mus) ré m

dab [dæb] vt (eyes, wound) tamponner; (paint, cream) appliquer (par petites touches or rapidement)

dad, daddy [dæd, 'dædɪ] n papa m

daffodil ['dæfədɪl] n jonquille f

daft [dɑːft] adj (inf) idiot(e), stupide

dagger ['dægə'] n poignard m

daily ['deɪlɪ] adj quotidien(ne), journalier(-ière) ▷ adv tous les jours

dairy ['dɛərɪ] n (shop) crémerie f, laiterie f; (on farm) laiterie f; **dairy produce** n produits laitiers

daisy ['deɪzɪ] n pâquerette f

dam [dæm] n (wall) barrage m; (water) réservoir m, lac m de retenue ▷ vt endiguer

damage ['dæmɪdʒ] n dégâts mpl, dommages mpl; (fig) tort m ▷ vt endommager, abîmer; (fig) faire du tort à; **damages** npl (Law) dommages-intérêts mpl

damn [dæm] vt condamner; (curse) maudire ▷ n (inf): **I don't give a ~** je m'en fous ▷ adj (inf: also: **~ed**): **this ~ ...** ce sacré or foutu ...; **~ (it)!** zut!

damp [dæmp] adj humide ▷ n humidité f ▷ vt (also: **~en**: cloth, rag) humecter; (: enthusiasm etc) refroidir

dance [dɑːns] n danse f; (ball) bal m ▷ vi danser; **dance floor** n piste f de danse; **dancer** n danseur(-euse); **dancing** n danse f

dandelion ['dændɪlaɪən] n pissenlit m

dandruff ['dændrəf] n pellicules fpl

D & T n abbr (BRIT Scol) = **design and technology**

Dane [deɪn] n Danois(e)

danger ['deɪndʒə'] n danger m; **~!** (on sign) danger!; **in ~** en danger; **he was in ~ of falling** il risquait de tomber; **dangerous** adj dangereux(-euse)

dangle ['dæŋgl] vt balancer ▷ vi pendre, se balancer

Danish ['deɪnɪʃ] adj danois(e) ▷ n (Ling) danois m

dare [dɛə'] vt: **to ~ sb to do** défier qn or mettre qn au défi de faire ▷ vi: **to ~ (to) do sth** oser faire qch; **I ~ say he'll turn up** il est probable qu'il viendra; **daring** adj hardi(e), audacieux(-euse) ▷ n audace f, hardiesse f

dark [dɑːk] adj (night, room) obscur(e), sombre; (colour, complexion) foncé(e), sombre ▷ n: **in the ~** dans le noir; **to be in the ~ about** (fig) ignorer tout de; **after ~** après la tombée de la nuit; **darken** vt obscurcir, assombrir ▷ vi s'obscurcir, s'assombrir; **darkness** n obscurité f; **darkroom** n chambre noire

darling ['dɑːlɪŋ] adj, n chéri(e)

dart [dɑːt] n fléchette f; (in sewing) pince f ▷ vi: **to ~ towards** se précipiter or s'élancer vers; **dartboard** n cible f (de jeu de fléchettes); **darts** n jeu m de fléchettes

dash [dæʃ] n (sign) tiret m; (small quantity) goutte f, larme f ▷ vt (throw) jeter *or* lancer violemment; (*hopes*) anéantir ▷ *vi*: **to ~ towards** se précipiter *or* se ruer vers

dashboard ['dæʃbɔːd] *n* (*Aut*) tableau *m* de bord

data ['deɪtə] *npl* données *fpl*; **database** *n* base *f* de données; **data processing** *n* traitement *m* des données

date [deɪt] *n* date *f*; (*with sb*) rendez-vous *m*; (*fruit*) datte *f* ▷ *vt* dater; (*person*) sortir avec; **~ of birth** date de naissance; **to ~** *adv* à ce jour; **out of ~** périmé(e); **up to ~** à la page, mis(e) à jour, moderne; **dated** *adj* démodé(e)

daughter ['dɔːtər] *n* fille *f*; **daughter-in-law** *n* belle-fille *f*, bru *f*

daunting ['dɔːntɪŋ] *adj* décourageant(e), intimidant(e)

dawn [dɔːn] *n* aube *f*, aurore *f* ▷ *vi* (*day*) se lever, poindre; **it ~ed on him that …** il lui vint à l'esprit que …

day [deɪ] *n* jour *m*; (*as duration*) journée *f*; (*period of time, age*) époque *f*, temps *m*; **the ~ before** la veille, le jour précédent; **the ~ after, the following ~** le lendemain, le jour suivant; **the ~ before yesterday** avant-hier; **the ~ after tomorrow** après-demain; **by ~** de jour; **day-care centre** ['deɪkɛə-] *n* (*for elderly etc*) centre *m* d'accueil de jour; (*for children*) garderie *f*; **daydream** *vi* rêver (tout éveillé); **daylight** *n* (*lumière f du*) jour *m*; **day return** *n* (*BRIT*) billet *m* d'aller-retour (*valable pour la journée*); **daytime** *n* jour *m*, journée *f*; **day-to-day** *adj* (*routine, expenses*) journalier(-ière); **day trip** *n* excursion *f* (d'une journée)

dazed [deɪzd] *adj* abruti(e)

dazzle ['dæzl] *vt* éblouir, aveugler; **dazzling** *adj* (*light*) aveuglant(e), éblouissant(e); (*fig*) éblouissant(e)

DC *abbr* (*Elec*) = **direct current**

dead [dɛd] *adj* mort(e); (*numb*) engourdi(e), insensible; (*battery*) à plat ▷ *adv* (*completely*) absolument,

complètement; (*exactly*) juste; **he was shot ~** il a été tué d'un coup de revolver; **~ tired** éreinté(e), complètement fourbu(e); **to stop ~** s'arrêter pile *or* net; **the line is ~** (*Tel*) la ligne est coupée; **dead end** *n* impasse *f*; **deadline** *n* date *f* or heure *f* limite; **deadly** *adj* mortel(le); (*weapon*) meurtrier(-ière); **Dead Sea** *n*: **the Dead Sea** la mer Morte

deaf [dɛf] *adj* sourd(e); **deafen** *vt* rendre sourd(e); **deafening** *adj* assourdissant(e)

deal [diːl] *n* affaire *f*, marché *m* ▷ *vt* (*pt, pp* **dealt**) (*blow*) porter; (*cards*) donner, distribuer; **a great ~ of** beaucoup de; **deal with** *vt fus* (*handle*) s'occuper *or* se charger de; (*be about*) traiter de; **dealer** *n* (*Comm*) marchand *m*; (*Cards*) donneur *m*; **dealings** *npl* (*in goods, shares*) opérations *fpl*, transactions *fpl*; (*relations*) relations *fpl*, rapports *mpl*

dealt [dɛlt] *pt, pp of* **deal**

dean [diːn] *n* (*Rel, BRIT Scol*) doyen *m*; (*US Scol*) conseiller principal (conseillère principale) d'éducation

dear [dɪər] *adj* cher (chère); (*expensive*) cher, coûteux(-euse) ▷ *n*: **my ~** mon cher (ma chère) ▷ *excl*: **~ me!** mon Dieu!; **D~ Sir/Madam** (*in letter*) Monsieur/Madame; **D~ Mr/Mrs X** Cher Monsieur/Chère Madame X; **dearly** *adv* (*love*) tendrement; (*pay*) cher

death [dɛθ] *n* mort *f*; (*Admin*) décès *m*; **death penalty** *n* peine *f* de mort; **death sentence** *n* condamnation *f* à mort

debate [dɪ'beɪt] *n* discussion *f*, débat *m* ▷ *vt* discuter, débattre

debit ['dɛbɪt] *n* débit *m* ▷ *vt*: **to ~ a sum to sb** *or* **to sb's account** porter une somme au débit de qn, débiter qn d'une somme; **debit card** *n* carte *f* de paiement

debris ['dɛbriː] *n* débris *mpl*, décombres *mpl*

debt [dɛt] n dette f; **to be in ~** avoir des dettes, être endetté(e)

debug [diːˈbʌg] vt (Comput) déboguer

debut [ˈdeɪbjuː] n début(s) m(pl)

Dec. abbr (= December) déc

decade [ˈdɛkeɪd] n décennie f, décade f

decaffeinated [dɪˈkæfɪneɪtɪd] adj décaféiné(e)

decay [dɪˈkeɪ] n (of food, wood etc) décomposition f, pourriture f; (of building) délabrement m; (also: **tooth ~**) carie f (dentaire) ▷ vi (rot) se décomposer, pourrir; (teeth) se carier

deceased [dɪˈsiːst] n: **the ~** le (la) défunt(e)

deceit [dɪˈsiːt] n tromperie f, supercherie f; **deceive** [dɪˈsiːv] vt tromper

December [dɪˈsɛmbəʳ] n décembre m

decency [ˈdiːsənsɪ] n décence f

decent [ˈdiːsənt] adj (proper) décent(e), convenable

deception [dɪˈsɛpʃən] n tromperie f

deceptive [dɪˈsɛptɪv] adj trompeur(-euse)

decide [dɪˈsaɪd] vt (subj: person) décider; (question, argument) trancher, régler ▷ vi se décider, décider; **to ~ to do/that** décider de faire/que; **to ~ on** décider, se décider pour

decimal [ˈdɛsɪməl] adj décimal(e) ▷ n décimale f

decision [dɪˈsɪʒən] n décision f

decisive [dɪˈsaɪsɪv] adj décisif(-ive); (manner, person) décidé(e), catégorique

deck [dɛk] n (Naut) pont m; (of cards) jeu m; (record deck) platine f; (of bus): **top ~** impériale f; **deckchair** n chaise longue

declaration [dɛkləˈreɪʃən] n déclaration f

declare [dɪˈklɛəʳ] vt déclarer

decline [dɪˈklaɪn] n (decay) déclin m; (lessening) baisse f ▷ vt refuser, décliner ▷ vi décliner; (business) baisser

decorate [ˈdɛkəreɪt] vt (adorn, give a medal to) décorer; (paint and paper) peindre et tapisser; **decoration** [dɛkəˈreɪʃən] n (medal etc, adornment) décoration f; **decorator** n peintre m en bâtiment

decrease n [ˈdiːkriːs] diminution f ▷ vt, vi [diːˈkriːs] diminuer

decree [dɪˈkriː] n (Pol, Rel) décret m; (Law) arrêt m, jugement m

dedicate [ˈdɛdɪkeɪt] vt consacrer; (book etc) dédier; **dedicated** adj (person) dévoué(e); (Comput) spécialisé(e), dédié(e); **dedicated word processor** station f de traitement de texte; **dedication** [dɛdɪˈkeɪʃən] n (devotion) dévouement m; (in book) dédicace f

deduce [dɪˈdjuːs] vt déduire, conclure

deduct [dɪˈdʌkt] vt: **to ~ sth (from)** déduire qch (de), retrancher qch (de); **deduction** [dɪˈdʌkʃən] n (deducting, deducing) déduction f; (from wage etc) prélèvement m, retenue f

deed [diːd] n action f, acte m; (Law) acte notarié, contrat m

deem [diːm] vt (formal) juger, estimer

deep [diːp] adj profond(e); (voice) grave ▷ adv: **spectators stood 20 ~** il y avait 20 rangs de spectateurs; **4 metres ~** de 4 mètres de profondeur; **how ~ is the water?** l'eau à quelle profondeur?; **deep-fry** vt faire frire (dans une friteuse); **deeply** adv profondément; (regret, interested) vivement

deer [dɪəʳ] n (pl inv): **(red) ~** cerf m; **(fallow) ~** daim m; **(roe) ~** chevreuil m

default [dɪˈfɔːlt] n (Comput: also: **~ value**) valeur f par défaut; **by ~** (Law) par défaut, par contumace; (Sport) par forfait

defeat [dɪˈfiːt] n défaite f ▷ vt (team, opponents) battre

defect n [ˈdiːfɛkt] défaut m ▷ vi [dɪˈfɛkt]: **to ~ to the enemy/the West** passer à l'ennemi/l'Ouest;

defective [dɪˈfɛktɪv] *adj* défectueux(-euse)

defence, *(us)* **defense** [dɪˈfɛns] *n* défense *f*

defend [dɪˈfɛnd] *vt* défendre; **defendant** *n* défendeur(-deresse); *(in criminal case)* accusé(e), prévenu(e); **defender** *n* défenseur *m*

defense [dɪˈfɛns] *n* *(us)* = **defence**

defensive [dɪˈfɛnsɪv] *adj* défensif(-ive) ▷ *n*: **on the ~** sur la défensive

defer [dɪˈfəːʳ] *vt* *(postpone)* différer, ajourner

defiance [dɪˈfaɪəns] *n* défi *m*; **in ~ of** au mépris de; **defiant** [dɪˈfaɪənt] *adj* provocant(e), de défi; *(person)* rebelle, intraitable

deficiency [dɪˈfɪʃənsɪ] *n* *(lack)* insuffisance *f*; *(: Med)* carence *f*; *(flaw)* faiblesse *f*; **deficient** [dɪˈfɪʃənt] *adj* *(inadequate)* insuffisant(e); **to be deficient in** manquer de

deficit [ˈdɛfɪsɪt] *n* déficit *m*

define [dɪˈfaɪn] *vt* définir

definite [ˈdɛfɪnɪt] *adj* *(fixed)* défini(e), (bien) déterminé(e); *(clear, obvious)* net(te), manifeste; *(certain)* sûr(e); **he was ~ about it** il a été catégorique; **definitely** *adv* sans aucun doute

definition [dɛfɪˈnɪʃən] *n* définition *f*; *(clearness)* netteté *f*

deflate [diːˈfleɪt] *vt* dégonfler

deflect [dɪˈflɛkt] *vt* détourner, faire dévier

defraud [dɪˈfrɔːd] *vt*: **to ~ sb of sth** escroquer qch à qn

defriend [diːˈfrɛnd] *vt* *(Internet)* supprimer de sa liste d'amis

defrost [diːˈfrɔst] *vt* *(fridge)* dégivrer; *(frozen food)* décongeler

defuse [diːˈfjuːz] *vt* désamorcer

defy [dɪˈfaɪ] *vt* défier; *(efforts etc)* résister à; **it defies description** cela défie toute description

degree [dɪˈgriː] *n* degré *m*; *(Scol)* diplôme *m* (universitaire); **a (first) ~ in maths** (BRIT) une licence en maths; **by ~s** *(gradually)* par degrés;

to some ~ jusqu'à un certain point, dans une certaine mesure

dehydrated [diːhaɪˈdreɪtɪd] *adj* déshydraté(e); *(milk, eggs)* en poudre

de-icer [ˈdiːˈaɪsəʳ] *n* dégivreur *m*

delay [dɪˈleɪ] *vt* retarder; *(payment)* différer ▷ *vi* s'attarder ▷ *n* délai *m*, retard *m*; **to be ~ed** être en retard

delegate *n* [ˈdɛlɪgɪt] délégué(e) ▷ *vt* [ˈdɛlɪgeɪt] déléguer

delete [dɪˈliːt] *vt* rayer, supprimer; *(Comput)* effacer

deli [ˈdɛlɪ] *n* épicerie fine

deliberate *adj* [dɪˈlɪbərɪt] *(intentional)* délibéré(e); *(slow)* mesuré(e) ▷ *vi* [dɪˈlɪbəreɪt] délibérer, réfléchir; **deliberately** *adv* *(on purpose)* exprès, délibérément

delicacy [ˈdɛlɪkəsɪ] *n* délicatesse *f*; *(choice food)* mets *m* or délicat, friandise *f*

delicate [ˈdɛlɪkɪt] *adj* délicat(e)

delicatessen [dɛlɪkəˈtɛsn] *n* épicerie fine

delicious [dɪˈlɪʃəs] *adj* délicieux(-euse)

delight [dɪˈlaɪt] *n* (grande) joie, grand plaisir ▷ *vt* enchanter; **she's a ~ to work with** c'est un plaisir de travailler avec elle; **to take ~ in** prendre grand plaisir à; **delighted** *adj*: **delighted (at** or **with sth)** ravi(e) (de qch); **to be delighted to do sth/that** être enchanté(e) or ravi(e) de faire qch/ que; **delightful** *adj* *(person)* adorable; *(meal, evening)* merveilleux(-euse)

delinquent [dɪˈlɪŋkwənt] *adj*, *n* délinquant(e)

deliver [dɪˈlɪvəʳ] *vt* *(mail)* distribuer; *(goods)* livrer; *(message)* remettre; *(speech)* prononcer; *(Med: baby)* mettre au monde; **delivery** *n* *(of mail)* distribution *f*; *(of goods)* livraison *f*; *(of speaker)* élocution *f*; *(Med)* accouchement *m*; **to take delivery of** prendre livraison de

delusion [dɪˈluːʒən] *n* illusion *f*

de luxe [dəˈlʌks] *adj* de luxe

delve [dɛlv] *vi*: **to ~ into** fouiller dans

demand [dɪ'mɑːnd] vt réclamer, exiger ▷ n exigence f; (claim) revendication f; (Econ) demande f; **in ~** demandé(e), recherché(e); **on ~** sur demande; **demanding** adj (person) exigeant(e); (work) astreignant(e)

Be careful not to translate to demand by the French word demander.

demise [dɪ'maɪz] n décès m

demo ['dɛməʊ] n abbr (inf: = demonstration) (protest) manif f; (Comput) démonstration f

democracy [dɪ'mɔkrəsɪ] n démocratie f; **democrat** ['dɛməkræt] n démocrate m/f; **democratic** [dɛmə'krætɪk] adj démocratique

demolish [dɪ'mɔlɪʃ] vt démolir

demolition [dɛmə'lɪʃən] n démolition f

demon ['diːmən] n démon m

demonstrate ['dɛmənstreɪt] vt démontrer, prouver; (show) faire une démonstration de ▷ vi: **to ~ (for/against)** manifester (en faveur de/contre); **demonstration** [dɛmən'streɪʃən] n démonstration f; (Pol etc) manifestation f; **demonstrator** n (Pol etc) manifestant(e)

demote [dɪ'məʊt] vt rétrograder

den [dɛn] n (of lion) tanière f; (room) repaire m

denial [dɪ'naɪəl] n (of accusation) démenti m; (of rights, guilt, truth) dénégation f

denim ['dɛnɪm] n jean m; **denims** npl (blue-)jeans mpl

Denmark ['dɛnmɑːk] n Danemark m

denomination [dɪnɔmɪ'neɪʃən] n (money) valeur f; (Rel) confession f

denounce [dɪ'naʊns] vt dénoncer

dense [dɛns] adj dense; (inf: stupid) obtus(e)

density ['dɛnsɪtɪ] n densité f

dent [dɛnt] n bosse f ▷ vt (also: **make a ~ in**) cabosser

dental ['dɛntl] adj dentaire; **dental floss** [-flɔs] n fil m dentaire; **dental surgery** n cabinet m de dentiste

dentist ['dɛntɪst] n dentiste m/f

dentures ['dɛntʃəz] npl dentier msg

deny [dɪ'naɪ] vt nier; (refuse) refuser

deodorant [diː'əʊdərənt] n déodorant m

depart [dɪ'pɑːt] vi partir; **to ~ from** (fig: differ from) s'écarter de

department [dɪ'pɑːtmənt] n (Comm) rayon m; (Scol) section f; (Pol) ministère m, département m; **department store** n grand magasin

departure [dɪ'pɑːtʃəʳ] n départ m; **a new ~** une nouvelle voie; **departure lounge** n salle f de départ

depend [dɪ'pɛnd] vi: **to ~ (up)on** dépendre de; (rely on) compter sur; **it ~s** cela dépend; **~ing on the result ...** selon le résultat ...; **dependant** n personne f à charge; **dependent** adj: **to be dependent (on)** dépendre (de) ▷ n = **dependant**

depict [dɪ'pɪkt] vt (in picture) représenter; (in words) (dé)peindre, décrire

deport [dɪ'pɔːt] vt déporter, expulser

deposit [dɪ'pɔzɪt] n (Chem, Comm, Geo) dépôt m; (of ore, oil) gisement m; (part payment) arrhes fpl, acompte m; (on bottle etc) consigne f; (for hired goods etc) cautionnement m, garantie f ▷ vt déposer; **deposit account** n compte m sur livret

depot ['dɛpəʊ] n dépôt m; (us Rail) gare f

depreciate [dɪ'priːʃɪeɪt] vi se déprécier, se dévaloriser

depress [dɪ'prɛs] vt déprimer; (press down) appuyer sur, abaisser; (wages etc) faire baisser; **depressed** adj (person) déprimé(e); (area) en déclin, touché(e) par le sous-emploi; **depressing** adj déprimant(e); **depression** [dɪ'prɛʃən] n dépression f

deprive [dɪ'praɪv] vt: **to ~ sb of** priver qn de; **deprived** adj déshérité(e)

d

dept. *abbr* (= *department*) dép, dépt

depth [dɛpθ] *n* profondeur *f*; **to be in the ~s of despair** être au plus profond du désespoir; **to be out of one's ~** (BRIT: *swimmer*) ne plus avoir pied; (*fig*) être dépassé(e), nager

deputy ['dɛpjutɪ] *n* (*second in command*) adjoint(e); (*Pol*) député *m*; (*US: also:* **~ sheriff**) shérif adjoint ▷ *adj:* **~ head** (*Scol*) directeur(-trice) adjoint(e), sous-directeur(-trice)

derail [dɪ'reɪl] *vt:* **to be ~ed** dérailler

derelict ['dɛrɪlɪkt] *adj* abandonné(e), à l'abandon

derive [dɪ'raɪv] *vt:* **to ~ sth from** tirer qch de; trouver qch dans ▷ *vi:* **to ~ from** provenir de, dériver de

descend [dɪ'sɛnd] *vt, vi* descendre; **to ~ from** descendre de, être issu(e) de; **to ~ to** s'abaisser à; **descendant** *n* descendant(e); **descent** *n* descente *f*; (*origin*) origine *f*

describe [dɪs'kraɪb] *vt* décrire; **description** [dɪs'krɪpʃən] *n* description *f*; (*sort*) sorte *f*, espèce *f*

desert *n* ['dɛzət] désert *m* ▷ *vt* [dɪ'zəːt] déserter, abandonner ▷ *vi* (*Mil*) déserter; **deserted** [dɪ'zəːtɪd] *adj* désert(e)

deserve [dɪ'zəːv] *vt* mériter

design [dɪ'zaɪn] *n* (*sketch*) plan *m*, dessin *m*; (*layout, shape*) conception *f*, ligne *f*; (*pattern*) dessin, motif(s) *m(pl)*; (*of dress, car*) modèle *m*; (*art*) design *m*, stylisme *m*; (*intention*) dessein *m* ▷ *vt* dessiner; (*plan*) concevoir; **design and technology** *n* (BRIT *Scol*) technologie *f*

designate *vt* ['dɛzɪɡneɪt] désigner ▷ *adj* ['dɛzɪɡnɪt] désigné(e)

designer [dɪ'zaɪnə*] *n* (*Archit, Art*) dessinateur(-trice); (*Industry*) concepteur *m*, designer *m*; (*Fashion*) styliste *m/f*

desirable [dɪ'zaɪərəbl] *adj* (*property, location, purchase*) attrayant(e)

desire [dɪ'zaɪə*] *n* désir *m* ▷ *vt* désirer, vouloir

desk [dɛsk] *n* (*in office*) bureau *m*; (*for pupil*) pupitre *m*; (BRIT: *in shop, restaurant*) caisse *f*; (*in hotel, at airport*) réception *f*; **desktop** ['dɛsktɔp] *n* bureau *m*; **desktop publishing** *n* publication assistée par ordinateur, PAO *f*

despair [dɪs'pɛə*] *n* désespoir *m* ▷ *vi:* **to ~ of** désespérer de

despatch [dɪs'pætʃ] *n, vt* = **dispatch**

desperate ['dɛspərɪt] *adj* désespéré(e); (*fugitive*) prêt(e) à tout; **to be ~ for sth/to do sth** avoir désespérément besoin de qch/de faire qch; **desperately** *adv* désespérément; (*very*) terriblement, extrêmement; **desperation** [dɛspə'reɪʃən] *n* désespoir *m*; **in (sheer) desperation** en désespoir de cause

despise [dɪs'paɪz] *vt* mépriser

despite [dɪs'paɪt] *prep* malgré, en dépit de

dessert [dɪ'zəːt] *n* dessert *m*; **dessertspoon** *n* cuiller *f* à dessert

destination [dɛstɪ'neɪʃən] *n* destination *f*

destined ['dɛstɪnd] *adj:* **~ for London** à destination de Londres

destiny ['dɛstɪnɪ] *n* destinée *f*, destin *m*

destroy [dɪs'trɔɪ] *vt* détruire; (*injured horse*) abattre; (*dog*) faire piquer

destruction [dɪs'trʌkʃən] *n* destruction *f*

destructive [dɪs'trʌktɪv] *adj* destructeur(-trice)

detach [dɪ'tætʃ] *vt* détacher; **detached** *adj* (*attitude*) détaché(e); **detached house** *n* pavillon *m*, maison(nette) (individuelle)

detail ['diːteɪl] *n* détail *m* ▷ *vt* raconter en détail, énumérer; **in ~** en détail; **detailed** *adj* détaillé(e)

detain [dɪ'teɪn] *vt* retenir; (*in captivity*) détenir

detect [dɪ'tɛkt] *vt* déceler, percevoir; (*Med, Police*) dépister; (*Mil, Radar, Tech*) détecter; **detection** [dɪ'tɛkʃən] *n* découverte f; **detective** n policier m; **private detective** détective privé; **detective story** n roman policier

detention [dɪ'tɛnʃən] n détention f; (Scol) retenue f, consigne f

deter [dɪ'tə:'] vt dissuader

detergent [dɪ'tə:dʒənt] n détersif m, détergent m

deteriorate [dɪ'tɪərɪəreɪt] vi se détériorer, se dégrader

determination [dɪtə:mɪ'neɪʃən] n détermination f

determine [dɪ'tə:mɪn] vt déterminer; **to ~ to do** résoudre de faire, se déterminer à faire; **determined** adj (person) déterminé(e), décidé(e); **determined to do** bien décidé à faire

deterrent [dɪ'tɛrənt] n effet m de dissuasion; force f de dissuasion

detest [dɪ'tɛst] vt détester, avoir horreur de

detour ['di:tuə'] n détour m; (us Aut: diversion) déviation f

detox ['di:tɔks] n détox f

detract [dɪ'trækt] vt: **to ~ from** (quality, pleasure) diminuer; (reputation) porter atteinte à

detrimental [dɛtrɪ'mɛntl] adj: **~ to** préjudiciable or nuisible à

devastating ['dɛvəsteɪtɪŋ] adj dévastateur(-trice); (news) accablant(e)

develop [dɪ'vɛləp] vt (gen) développer; (disease) commencer à souffrir de; (resources) mettre en valeur, exploiter; (land) aménager ▷ vi se développer; (situation, disease: evolve) évoluer; (facts, symptoms: appear) se manifester, se produire; **can you ~ this film?** pouvez-vous développer cette pellicule?; **developing country** n pays m en voie de développement; **development** n développement m; (of land) exploitation f; (new fact, event) rebondissement m, fait(s) nouveau(x)

device [dɪ'vaɪs] n (apparatus) appareil m, dispositif m

devil ['dɛvl] n diable m; démon m

devious ['di:vɪəs] adj (person) sournois(e), dissimulé(e)

devise [dɪ'vaɪz] vt imaginer, concevoir

devote [dɪ'vəut] vt: **to ~ sth to** consacrer qch à; **devoted** adj dévoué(e); **to be devoted to** être dévoué(e) or très attaché(e) à; (book etc) être consacré(e) à; **devotion** n dévouement m, attachement m; (Rel) dévotion f, piété f

devour [dɪ'vauə'] vt dévorer

devout [dɪ'vaut] adj pieux(-euse)

dew [dju:] n rosée f

diabetes [daɪə'bi:ti:z] n diabète m

diabetic [daɪə'bɛtɪk] n diabétique m/f ▷ adj (person) diabétique

diagnose [daɪəg'nəuz] vt diagnostiquer

diagnosis (pl **diagnoses**) [daɪəg'nəusɪs, -si:z] n diagnostic m

diagonal [daɪ'ægənl] adj diagonal(e) ▷ n diagonale f

diagram ['daɪəgræm] n diagramme m, schéma m

dial ['daɪəl] n cadran m ▷ vt (number) faire, composer

dialect ['daɪəlɛkt] n dialecte m

dialling code ['daɪəlɪŋ-], (us) **dial code** n indicatif m (téléphonique); **what's the ~ for Paris?** quel est l'indicatif de Paris?

dialling tone ['daɪəlɪŋ-], (us) **dial tone** n tonalité f

dialogue, (us) **dialog** ['daɪəlɔg] n dialogue m

diameter [daɪ'æmɪtə'] n diamètre m

diamond ['daɪəmənd] n diamant m; (shape) losange m; **diamonds** npl (Cards) carreau m

diaper ['daɪəpə'] n (us) couche f

diarrhoea, (us) **diarrhea** [daɪə'ri:ə] n diarrhée f

diary ['daɪərɪ] n (daily account) journal m; (book) agenda m

dice [daɪs] n (pl inv) dé m ▷ vt (Culin) couper en dés or en cubes

d

dictate vt [dɪk'teɪt] dicter; **dictation** [dɪk'teɪʃən] n dictée f

dictator [dɪk'teɪtəʳ] n dictateur m

dictionary ['dɪkʃənrɪ] n dictionnaire m

did [dɪd] pt of **do**

didn't [dɪdnt] = **did not**

die [daɪ] vi mourir; **to be dying for sth** avoir une envie folle de qch; **to be dying to do sth** mourir d'envie de faire qch; **die down** vi se calmer, s'apaiser; **die out** vi disparaître, s'éteindre

diesel ['diːzl] n (vehicle) diesel m; (also: ~ **oil**) carburant m diesel, gas-oil m

diet ['daɪət] n alimentation f; (restricted food) régime m ▷ vi (also: **be on a ~**) suivre un régime

differ ['dɪfəʳ] vi: **to ~ from sth** (be different) être différent(e) de qch, différer de qch; **to ~ from sb over sth** ne pas être d'accord avec qn au sujet de qch; **difference** n différence f; (quarrel) différend m, désaccord m; **different** adj différent(e); **differentiate** [dɪfə'renʃɪeɪt] vi: **to differentiate between** faire une différence entre; **differently** adv différemment

difficult ['dɪfɪkəlt] adj difficile; **difficulty** n difficulté f

dig [dɪg] vt (pt, pp **dug**) (hole) creuser; (garden) bêcher ▷ n (prod) coup m de coude; (fig: remark) coup de griffe or de patte; (Archaeology) fouille f; **to ~ one's nails into** enfoncer ses ongles dans; **dig up** vt déterrer

digest vt [daɪ'dʒest] digérer ▷ n ['daɪdʒest] sommaire m, résumé m; **digestion** [dɪ'dʒestʃən] n digestion f

digit ['dɪdʒɪt] n (number) chiffre m (de 0 à 9); (finger) doigt m; **digital** adj (system, recording, radio) numérique, digital(e); (watch) à affichage numérique or digital; **digital camera** n appareil m photo numérique; **digital TV** n télévision f numérique

dignified ['dɪgnɪfaɪd] adj digne

dignity ['dɪgnɪtɪ] n dignité f

digs [dɪgz] npl (BRIT inf) piaule f, chambre meublée

dilemma [daɪ'lemə] n dilemme m

dill [dɪl] n aneth m

dilute [daɪ'luːt] vt diluer

dim [dɪm] adj (light, eyesight) faible; (memory, outline) vague, indécis(e); (room) sombre; (inf: stupid) borné(e), obtus(e) ▷ vt (light) réduire, baisser; (us Aut) mettre en code, baisser

dime [daɪm] n (us) pièce f de 10 cents

dimension [daɪ'menʃən] n dimension f

diminish [dɪ'mɪnɪʃ] vt, vi diminuer

din [dɪn] n vacarme m

dine [daɪn] vi dîner; **diner** n (person) dîneur(-euse); (us: eating place) petit restaurant

dinghy ['dɪŋgɪ] n youyou m; (inflatable) canot m pneumatique; (also: **sailing ~**) voilier m, dériveur m

dingy ['dɪndʒɪ] adj miteux(-euse), minable

dining car ['daɪnɪŋ-] n (BRIT) voiture-restaurant f, wagon-restaurant m

dining room ['daɪnɪŋ-] n salle f à manger

dining table ['daɪnɪŋ-] n table f de (la) salle à manger

dinkum ['dɪŋkʌm] adj (AUST, NZ inf) vrai(e); **fair ~** vrai(e)

dinner ['dɪnəʳ] n (evening meal) dîner m; (lunch) déjeuner m; (public) banquet m; **dinner jacket** n smoking m; **dinner party** n dîner m; **dinner time** n (evening) heure f du dîner; (midday) heure du déjeuner

dinosaur ['daɪnəsɔːʳ] n dinosaure m

dip [dɪp] n (slope) déclivité f; (in sea) baignade f, bain m; (Culin) ≈ sauce f ▷ vt tremper, plonger; (BRIT Aut: lights) mettre en code, baisser ▷ vi plonger

diploma [dɪ'pləumə] n diplôme m

diplomacy [dɪ'pləuməsɪ] n diplomatie f

diplomat ['dɪpləmæt] n diplomate m; **diplomatic** [dɪplə'mætɪk] adj diplomatique

dipstick ['dɪpstɪk] n (BRIT Aut) jauge f de niveau d'huile

dire [daɪəʳ] adj (poverty) extrême; (awful) affreux(-euse)

direct [daɪ'rɛkt] adj direct(e) ▷ vt (tell way) diriger, orienter; (letter, remark) adresser; (Cine, TV) réaliser; (Theat) mettre en scène; (order) to ~ sb to do sth ordonner à qn de faire qch ▷ adv directement; **can you ~ me to ...?** pouvez-vous m'indiquer le chemin de ...?; **direct debit** n (BRIT Banking) prélèvement m automatique

direction [dɪ'rɛkʃən] n direction f; **directions** npl (to a place) indications fpl; **~s for use** mode m d'emploi; **sense of ~** sens m de l'orientation

directly [dɪ'rɛktlɪ] adv (in straight line) directement, tout droit; (at once) tout de suite, immédiatement

director [dɪ'rɛktəʳ] n directeur m; (Theat) metteur m en scène; (Cine, TV) réalisateur(-trice)

directory [dɪ'rɛktərɪ] n annuaire m; (Comput) répertoire m; **directory enquiries**, (US) **directory assistance** n (Tel: service) renseignements mpl

dirt [də:t] n saleté f; (mud) boue f; **dirty** adj sale; (joke) cochon(ne) ▷ vt salir

disability [dɪsə'bɪlɪtɪ] n invalidité f, infirmité f

disabled [dɪs'eɪbld] adj handicapé(e); (maimed) mutilé(e)

disadvantage [dɪsəd'vɑ:ntɪdʒ] n désavantage m, inconvénient m

disagree [dɪsə'gri:] vi (differ) ne pas concorder; (be against, think otherwise): **to ~ (with)** ne pas être d'accord (avec); **disagreeable** adj désagréable; **disagreement** n désaccord m, différend m

disappear [dɪsə'pɪəʳ] vi disparaître; **disappearance** n disparition f

disappoint [dɪsə'pɔɪnt] vt décevoir; **disappointed** adj déçu(e); **disappointing** adj décevant(e); **disappointment** n déception f

disapproval [dɪsə'pru:vəl] n désapprobation f

disapprove [dɪsə'pru:v] vi: **to ~ of** désapprouver

disarm [dɪs'ɑ:m] vt désarmer; **disarmament** [dɪs'ɑ:məmənt] n désarmement m

disaster [dɪ'zɑ:stəʳ] n catastrophe f, désastre m; **disastrous** adj désastreux(-euse)

disbelief ['dɪsbə'li:f] n incrédulité f

disc [dɪsk] n disque m; (Comput) = **disk**

discard [dɪs'kɑ:d] vt (old things) se débarrasser de; (fig) écarter, renoncer à

discharge vt [dɪs'tʃɑ:dʒ] (duties) s'acquitter de; (waste etc) déverser; décharger; (patient) renvoyer (chez lui); (employee, soldier) congédier, licencier ▷ n ['dɪstʃɑ:dʒ] (Elec, Med) émission f; (dismissal) renvoi m licenciement m

discipline ['dɪsɪplɪn] n discipline f ▷ vt discipliner; (punish) punir

disc jockey n disque-jockey m (DJ)

disclose [dɪs'kləʊz] vt révéler, divulguer

disco ['dɪskəʊ] n abbr discothèque f

discoloured, (US) **discolored** [dɪs'kʌləd] adj décoloré(e), jauni(e)

discomfort [dɪs'kʌmfət] n malaise m, gêne f; (lack of comfort) manque m de confort

disconnect [dɪskə'nɛkt] vt (Elec, Radio) débrancher; (gas, water) couper

discontent [dɪskən'tɛnt] n mécontentement m

discontinue [dɪskən'tɪnju:] vt cesser, interrompre; **"~d"** (Comm) "fin de série"

discount n ['dɪskaunt] remise f, rabais m ▷ vt [dɪs'kaunt] (report etc) ne pas tenir compte de

discourage [dɪs'kʌrɪdʒ] *vt*
décourager

discover [dɪs'kʌvə'] *vt* découvrir;
discovery *n* découverte *f*

discredit [dɪs'krɛdɪt] *vt* (*idea*) mettre
en doute; (*person*) discréditer

discreet [dɪ'skri:t] *adj* discret(-ète)

discrepancy [dɪ'skrɛpənsɪ] *n*
divergence *f*, contradiction *f*

discretion [dɪ'skrɛʃən] *n* discrétion *f*;
at the ~ of à la discrétion de

discriminate [dɪ'skrɪmɪneɪt] *vi*: **to
~ between** établir une distinction
entre, faire la différence entre; **to ~
against** pratiquer une discrimination
contre; **discrimination**
[dɪskrɪmɪ'neɪʃən] *n* discrimination *f*;
(*judgment*) discernement *m*

discuss [dɪ'skʌs] *vt* discuter de;
(*debate*) discuter; **discussion**
[dɪ'skʌʃən] *n* discussion *f*

disease [dɪ'zi:z] *n* maladie *f*

disembark [dɪsɪm'bɑ:k] *vt*, *vi*
débarquer

disgrace [dɪs'greɪs] *n* honte *f*;
(*disfavour*) disgrâce *f* ▷ *vt* déshonorer,
couvrir de honte; **disgraceful** *adj*
scandaleux(-euse), honteux(-euse)

disgruntled [dɪs'grʌntld] *adj*
mécontent(e)

disguise [dɪs'gaɪz] *n* déguisement *m*
▷ *vt* déguiser; **in ~** déguisé(e)

disgust [dɪs'gʌst] *n* dégoût *m*,
aversion *f* ▷ *vt* dégoûter, écœurer

disgusted [dɪs'gʌstɪd] *adj*
dégoûté(e), écœuré(e)

disgusting [dɪs'gʌstɪŋ] *adj*
dégoûtant(e)

dish [dɪʃ] *n* plat *m*; **to do** or **wash the
~es** faire la vaisselle; **dishcloth** *n*
(*for drying*) torchon *m*; (*for washing*)
lavette *f*

dishonest [dɪs'ɔnɪst] *adj*
malhonnête

dishtowel ['dɪʃtauəl] *n* (*US*) torchon
m (à vaisselle)

dishwasher ['dɪʃwɔʃə'] *n* lave-
vaisselle *m*

disillusion [dɪsɪ'lu:ʒən] *vt*
désabuser, désenchanter

disinfectant [dɪsɪn'fɛktənt] *n*
désinfectant *m*

disintegrate [dɪs'ɪntɪgreɪt] *vi* se
désintégrer

disk [dɪsk] *n* (*Comput*) disquette *f*;
single-/double-sided ~ disquette
une face/double face; **disk drive** *n*
lecteur *m* de disquette; **diskette** *n*
(*Comput*) disquette *f*

dislike [dɪs'laɪk] *n* aversion *f*,
antipathie *f* ▷ *vt* ne pas aimer

dislocate ['dɪsləkeɪt] *vt* disloquer,
déboîter

disloyal [dɪs'lɔɪəl] *adj* déloyal(e)

dismal ['dɪzml] *adj* (*gloomy*) lugubre,
maussade; (*very bad*) lamentable

dismantle [dɪs'mæntl] *vt* démonter

dismay [dɪs'meɪ] *n* consternation *f*
▷ *vt* consterner

dismiss [dɪs'mɪs] *vt* congédier,
renvoyer; (*idea*) écarter; (*Law*) rejeter;
dismissal *n* renvoi *m*

disobedient [dɪsə'bi:dɪənt] *adj*
désobéissant(e), indiscipliné(e)

disobey [dɪsə'beɪ] *vt* désobéir à

disorder [dɪs'ɔ:də'] *n* désordre
m; (*rioting*) désordres *mpl*; (*Med*)
troubles *mpl*

disorganized [dɪs'ɔ:gənaɪzd] *adj*
désorganisé(e)

disown [dɪs'əun] *vt* renier

dispatch [dɪs'pætʃ] *vt* expédier,
envoyer ▷ *n* envoi *m*, expédition *f*;
(*Mil, Press*) dépêche *f*

dispel [dɪs'pɛl] *vt* dissiper, chasser

dispense [dɪs'pɛns] *vt* (*medicine*)
préparer (et vendre); **dispense with**
vt fus se passer de; **dispenser** *n*
(*device*) distributeur *m*

disperse [dɪs'pə:s] *vt* disperser ▷ *vi*
se disperser

display [dɪs'pleɪ] *n* (*of goods*) étalage
m; affichage *m*; (*Comput: information*)
visualisation *f*; (: *device*) visuel *m*; (*of
feeling*) manifestation *f* ▷ *vt* montrer;
(*goods*) mettre à l'étalage, exposer;

(*results, departure times*) afficher; (*pej*) faire étalage de

displease [dɪs'pliːz] *vt* mécontenter, contrarier

disposable [dɪs'pəuzəbl] *adj* (*pack etc*) jetable; (*income*) disponible

disposal [dɪs'pəuzl] *n* (*of rubbish*) évacuation *f*, destruction *f*; (*of property etc: by selling*) vente *f*; (: *by giving away*) cession *f*; **at one's ~** à sa disposition

dispose [dɪs'pəuz] *vi*: **to ~ of** (*unwanted goods*) se débarrasser de, se défaire de; (*problem*) expédier; **disposition** [dɪspə'zɪʃən] *n* disposition *f*; (*temperament*) naturel *m*

disproportionate [dɪsprə'pɔːʃənət] *adj* disproportionné(e)

dispute [dɪs'pjuːt] *n* discussion *f*; (*also*: **industrial ~**) conflit *m* ▷ *vt* (*question*) contester; (*matter*) discuter

disqualify [dɪs'kwɔlɪfaɪ] *vt* (*Sport*) disqualifier; **to ~ sb for sth/from doing** rendre qn inapte à qch/à faire

disregard [dɪsrɪ'gɑːd] *vt* ne pas tenir compte de

disrupt [dɪs'rʌpt] *vt* (*plans, meeting, lesson*) perturber, déranger; **disruption** [dɪs'rʌpʃən] *n* perturbation *f*, dérangement *m*

dissatisfaction [dɪssætɪs'fækʃən] *n* mécontentement *m*, insatisfaction *f*

dissatisfied [dɪs'sætɪsfaɪd] *adj*: **~ (with)** insatisfait(e) (de)

dissect [dɪ'sɛkt] *vt* disséquer

dissent [dɪ'sɛnt] *n* dissentiment *m*, différence *f* d'opinion

dissertation [dɪsə'teɪʃən] *n* (*Scol*) mémoire *m*

dissolve [dɪ'zɔlv] *vt* dissoudre ▷ *vi* se dissoudre, fondre; **to ~ in(to) tears** fondre en larmes

distance [dɪstns] *n* distance *f*; **in the ~** au loin

distant [dɪstnt] *adj* lointain(e), éloigné(e); (*manner*) distant(e), froid(e)

distil, (*US*) **distill** [dɪs'tɪl] *vt* distiller; **distillery** *n* distillerie *f*

distinct [dɪs'tɪŋkt] *adj* distinct(e); (*clear*) marqué(e); **as ~ from** par opposition à; **distinction** [dɪs'tɪŋkʃən] *n* distinction *f*; (*in exam*) mention *f* très bien; **distinctive** *adj* distinctif(-ive)

distinguish [dɪs'tɪŋgwɪʃ] *vt* distinguer; **to ~ o.s.** se distinguer; **distinguished** *adj* (*eminent, refined*) distingué(e)

distort [dɪs'tɔːt] *vt* déformer

distract [dɪs'trækt] *vt* distraire, déranger; **distracted** *adj* (*not concentrating*) distrait(e); (*worried*) affolé(e); **distraction** [dɪs'trækʃən] *n* distraction *f*

distraught [dɪs'trɔːt] *adj* éperdu(e)

distress [dɪs'trɛs] *n* détresse *f* ▷ *vt* affliger; **distressing** *adj* douloureux(-euse), pénible

distribute [dɪs'trɪbjuːt] *vt* distribuer; **distribution** [dɪstrɪ'bjuːʃən] *n* distribution *f*; **distributor** *n* (*gen, Tech*) distributeur *m*; (*Comm*) concessionnaire *m/f*

district ['dɪstrɪkt] *n* (*of country*) région *f*; (*of town*) quartier *m*; (*Admin*) district *m*; **district attorney** *n* (*US*) ≈ procureur *m* de la République

distrust [dɪs'trʌst] *n* méfiance *f*, doute *m* ▷ *vt* se méfier de

disturb [dɪs'təːb] *vt* troubler; (*inconvenience*) déranger; **disturbance** *n* dérangement *m*; (*political etc*) troubles *mpl*; **disturbed** *adj* (*worried, upset*) agité(e), troublé(e); **to be emotionally disturbed** avoir des problèmes affectifs; **disturbing** *adj* troublant(e), inquiétant(e)

ditch [dɪtʃ] *n* fossé *m*; (*for irrigation*) rigole *f* ▷ *vt* (*inf*) abandonner; (*person*) plaquer

ditto ['dɪtəu] *adv* idem

dive [daɪv] *n* plongeon *m*; (*of submarine*) plongée *f* ▷ *vi* plonger; **to ~ into** (*bag etc*) plonger la main dans; (*place*) se précipiter dans; **diver** *n* plongeur *m*

d

diverse [daɪ'vəːs] *adj* divers(e)
diversion [daɪ'vəːʃən] *n* (*BRIT
Aut*) déviation *f*; (*distraction, Mil*)
diversion *f*
diversity [daɪ'vəːsɪtɪ] *n* diversité
f, variété *f*
divert [daɪ'vəːt] *vt* (*BRIT: traffic*)
dévier; (*plane*) dérouter; (*train, river*)
détourner
divide [dɪ'vaɪd] *vt* diviser; (*separate*)
séparer ▷ *vi* se diviser; **divided
highway** (*US*) *n* route *f* à quatre voies
divine [dɪ'vaɪn] *adj* divin(e)
diving ['daɪvɪŋ] *n* plongée (sous-
marine); **diving board** *n* plongeoir *m*
division [dɪ'vɪʒən] *n* division *f*;
(*separation*) séparation *f*; (*Comm*)
service *m*
divorce [dɪ'vɔːs] *n* divorce *m* ▷ *vt*
divorcer d'avec; **divorced** *adj*
divorcé(e); **divorcee** [dɪvɔː'siː] *n*
divorcé(e)
DIY *adj, n abbr* (*BRIT*) = **do-it-yourself**
dizzy ['dɪzɪ] *adj*: **I feel ~** la tête me
tourne, j'ai la tête qui tourne
DJ *n abbr* = **disc jockey**
DNA *n abbr* (= *deoxyribonucleic acid*)
ADN *m*

 KEYWORD

do [duː] *n* (*inf: party etc*) soirée *f*, fête *f*
▷ *aux vb* (*pt* **did**, *pp* **done**) **1** (*in negative
constructions*) non traduit; **I don't
understand** je ne comprends pas
2 (*to form questions*) non traduit;
didn't you know? vous ne le saviez
pas?; **what do you think?** qu'en
pensez-vous?
3 (*for emphasis, in polite expressions*):
**people do make mistakes
sometimes** on peut toujours se
tromper; **she does seem rather
late** je trouve qu'elle est bien en
retard; **do sit down/help yourself**
asseyez-vous/servez-vous je vous
en prie; **do take care!** faites bien
attention à vous!

4 (*used to avoid repeating vb*): **she
swims better than I do** elle nage
mieux que moi; **do you agree?**
— yes, I do/no I don't vous êtes
d'accord? — oui/non; **she lives
in Glasgow — so do I** elle habite
Glasgow — moi aussi; **he didn't like
it and neither did we** il n'a pas aimé
ça, et nous non plus; **who broke
it? — I did** qui l'a cassé? — c'est moi;
he asked me to help him and I did
il m'a demandé de l'aider, et c'est ce
que j'ai fait
5 (*in question tags*): **you like him,
don't you?** vous l'aimez bien, n'est-ce
pas?; **I don't know him, do I?** je ne
crois pas le connaître
▷ *vt* (*pt* **did**, *pp* **done**) **1** (*gen: carry out,
perform etc*) faire; (*visit: city, museum*)
faire, visiter; **what are you doing
tonight?** qu'est-ce que vous faites
ce soir?; **what do you do?** (*job*)
que faites-vous dans la vie?; **what
can I do for you?** que puis-je faire
pour vous?; **to do the cooking/
washing-up** faire la cuisine/la
vaisselle; **to do one's teeth/hair/
nails** se brosser les dents/se coiffer/
se faire les ongles
2 (*Aut etc: distance*) faire; (*: speed*) faire
du; **we've done 200 km already**
nous avons déjà fait 200 km; **the
car was doing 100** la voiture faisait
du 100 (à l'heure); **he can do 100 in
that car** il peut faire du 100 (à l'heure)
dans cette voiture-là
▷ *vi* (*pt* **did**, *pp* **done**) **1** (*act, behave*)
faire; **do as I do** faites comme moi
2 (*get on, fare*) marcher; **the firm
is doing well** l'entreprise marche
bien; **he's doing well/badly at
school** ça marche bien/mal pour lui
à l'école; **how do you do?** comment
allez-vous?; (*on being introduced*)
enchanté(e)!
3 (*suit*) aller; **will it do?** est-ce que
ça ira?
4 (*be sufficient*) suffire, aller; **will £10**

do? est-ce que 10 livres suffiront?; **that'll do** ça suffit, ça ira; **that'll do!** (in annoyance) ça va or suffit comme ça!; **to make do (with)** se contenter (de)

do up vt (laces, dress) attacher; (buttons) boutonner; (zip) fermer; (renovate: room) refaire; (: house) remettre à neuf

do with vt fus (need): **I could do with a drink/some help** quelque chose à boire/un peu d'aide ne serait pas de refus; **it could do with a wash** ça ne lui ferait pas de mal d'être lavé; (be connected with): **that has nothing to do with you** cela ne vous concerne pas; **I won't have anything to do with it** je ne veux pas m'en mêler

do without vi s'en passer; **if you're late for tea then you'll do without** si vous êtes en retard pour le dîner il faudra vous en passer ▷ vt fus se passer de; **I can do without a car** je peux me passer de voiture

dock [dɔk] n dock m; (wharf) quai m; (Law) banc m des accusés ▷ vi se mettre à quai; (Space) s'arrimer; **docks** npl (Naut) docks

doctor ['dɔktə'] n médecin m, docteur m; (PhD etc) docteur ▷ vt (drink) frelater; **call a ~!** appelez un docteur or un médecin!; **Doctor of Philosophy** n (degree) doctorat m; (person) titulaire m/f d'un doctorat

document ['dɔkjumənt] n document m; **documentary** [dɔkju'mɛntəri] adj, n documentaire (m); **documentation** [dɔkjumən'teɪʃən] n documentation f

dodge [dɔdʒ] n truc m; combine f ▷ vt esquiver, éviter

dodgy ['dɔdʒi] adj (BRIT inf: uncertain) douteux(-euse); (: shady) louche

does [dʌz] vb see **do**

doesn't ['dʌznt] = **does not**

dog [dɔg] n chien(ne) ▷ vt (follow closely) suivre de près; (fig: memory etc) poursuivre, harceler; **doggy bag** ['dɔgi-] n petit sac pour emporter les restes

do-it-yourself ['du:ɪtjɔː'sɛlf] n bricolage m

dole [dəul] n (BRIT: payment) allocation f de chômage; **on the ~** au chômage

doll [dɔl] n poupée f

dollar ['dɔlə'] n dollar m

dolphin ['dɔlfɪn] n dauphin m

dome [dəum] n dôme m

domestic [də'mɛstɪk] adj (duty, happiness) familial(e); (policy, affairs, flight) intérieur(e); (animal) domestique

dominant ['dɔmɪnənt] adj dominant(e)

dominate ['dɔmɪneɪt] vt dominer

domino ['dɔmɪnəu] (pl **dominoes**) n domino m; **dominoes** n (game) dominos mpl

donate [də'neɪt] vt faire don de, donner; **donation** [də'neɪʃən] n donation f, don m

done [dʌn] pp of **do**

dongle ['dɔngl] n (Comput) dongle m

donkey ['dɔŋkɪ] n âne m

donor ['dəunə'] n (of blood etc) donneur(-euse); (to charity) donateur(-trice); **donor card** n carte f de don d'organes

don't [dəunt] = **do not**

donut ['dəunʌt] (US) n = **doughnut**

doodle ['du:dl] vi gribouiller

doom [du:m] n (fate) destin m ▷ vt: **to be ~ed to failure** être voué(e) à l'échec

door [dɔː'] n porte f; (Rail, car) portière f; **doorbell** n sonnette f; **door handle** n poignée f de porte; (of car) poignée de portière; **doorknob** n poignée f or bouton m de porte; **doorstep** n pas m de (la) porte, seuil m; **doorway** n (embrasure f de) porte f

dope [dəup] n (inf: drug) drogue f; (: person) andouille f ▷ vt (horse etc) doper

dormitory ['dɔ:mɪtrɪ] *n* (BRIT) dortoir *m*; (US: *hall of residence*) résidence *f* universitaire

DOS [dɔs] *n abbr* (= *disk operating system*) DOS *m*

dosage ['dəusɪdʒ] *n* dose *f*; dosage *m*; (*on label*) posologie *f*

dose [dəus] *n* dose *f*

dot [dɔt] *n* point *m*; (*on material*) pois *m* ▷ *vt*: **~ted with** parsemé(e) de; **on the ~** à l'heure tapante; **dotcom** *n* point com *m*, pointcom *m*; **dotted line** ['dɔtɪd-] *n* ligne pointillée; **to sign on the dotted line** signer à l'endroit indiqué *or* sur la ligne pointillée

double ['dʌbl] *adj* double ▷ *adv* (*twice*): **to cost ~ (sth)** coûter le double (de qch) *or* deux fois plus (que qch) ▷ *n* double *m*; (*Cine*) doublure *f* ▷ *vt* doubler; (*fold*) plier en deux ▷ *vi* doubler; **on the ~, at the ~** au pas de course; **double back** *vi* (*person*) revenir sur ses pas; **double bass** *n* contrebasse *f*; **double bed** *n* grand lit; **double-check** *vt*, *vi* revérifier; **double-click** *vi* (*Comput*) double-cliquer; **double-cross** *vt* doubler, trahir; **double-decker** *n* autobus *m* à impériale; **double glazing** (BRIT) double vitrage *m*; **double room** *n* chambre *f* pour deux; **doubles** *n* (*Tennis*) double *m*; **double yellow lines** *npl* (BRIT Aut) double bande jaune marquant l'interdiction de stationner

doubt [daut] *n* doute *m* ▷ *vt* douter de; **no ~** sans doute; **to ~ that** douter que + *sub*; **doubtful** *adj* douteux(-euse); (*person*) incertain(e); **doubtless** *adv* sans doute, sûrement

dough [dəu] *n* pâte *f*; **doughnut**, (US) **donut** *n* beignet *m*

dove [dʌv] *n* colombe *f*

Dover ['dəuvər] *n* Douvres

down [daun] *n* (*fluff*) duvet *m* ▷ *adv* en bas, vers le bas; (*on the ground*) par terre ▷ *prep* en bas de; (*along*) le long de ▷ *vt* (*inf: drink*) siffler; **to walk ~**

a hill descendre une colline; **to run ~ the street** descendre la rue en courant; **~ with X!** à bas X!; **down-and-out** *n* (*tramp*) clochard(e); **downfall** *n* chute *f*; ruine *f*; **downhill** *adv*: **to go downhill** descendre; (*business*) péricliter

Downing Street ['daunɪŋ-] *n* (BRIT): **10 ~** = résidence du Premier ministre

● **DOWNING STREET**
●
● Downing Street est une rue de
● Westminster (à Londres) où se
● trouvent la résidence officielle
● du Premier ministre et celle du
● ministre des Finances. Le nom
● Downing Street est souvent utilisé
● pour désigner le gouvernement
● britannique.

down: download *vt* (*Comput*) télécharger; **downloadable** *adj* (*Comput*) téléchargeable; **downright** *adj* (*lie etc*) effronté(e); (*refusal*) catégorique

Down's syndrome [daunz-] *n* trisomie *f*

down: downstairs *adv* (*on or to ground floor*) au rez-de-chaussée; (*on or to floor below*) à l'étage inférieur; **down-to-earth** *adj* terre à terre *inv*; **downtown** *adv* en ville; **down under** *adv* en Australie *or* Nouvelle Zélande; **downward** ['daunwəd] *adj*, *adv* vers le bas; **downwards** ['daunwədz] *adv* vers le bas

doz. *abbr* = **dozen**

doze [dəuz] *vi* sommeiller

dozen ['dʌzn] *n* douzaine *f*; **a ~ books** une douzaine de livres; **~s of** des centaines de

Dr. *abbr* (= *doctor*) Dr; (*in street names*); = **drive**

drab [dræb] *adj* terne, morne

draft [drɑ:ft] *n* (*of letter, school work*) brouillon *m*; (*of literary work*) ébauche *f*; (*Comm*) traite *f*; (*US Mil: call-up*) conscription f ▷ vt faire le brouillon de; (*Mil: send*) détacher; *see also* **draught**

drag [dræg] vt traîner; (*river*) draguer ▷ vi traîner ▷ n (*inf*) casse-pieds m/f; (: *women's clothing*): **in ~** (en) travesti; **to ~ and drop** (*Comput*) glisser-poser

dragonfly ['drægənflaɪ] n libellule f

drain [dreɪn] n égout m; (*on resources*) saignée f ▷ vt (*land, marshes*) assécher; (*vegetables*) égoutter; (*reservoir etc*) vider ▷ vi (*water*) s'écouler; **drainage** n (*system*) système m d'égouts; (*act*) drainage m; **drainpipe** n tuyau m d'écoulement

drama ['drɑːmə] n (*art*) théâtre m, art m dramatique; (*play*) pièce f; (*event*) drame m; **dramatic** [drə'mætɪk] adj (*Theat*) dramatique; (*impressive*) spectaculaire

drank [dræŋk] pt of **drink**

drape [dreɪp] vt draper; **drapes** npl (*us*) rideaux mpl

drastic ['dræstɪk] adj (*measures*) d'urgence, énergique; (*change*) radical(e)

draught, (*us*) **draft** [drɑːft] n courant m d'air; **on ~** (*beer*) à la pression; **draught beer** n bière f (à la) pression; **draughts** n (*BRIT: game*) (jeu m de) dames fpl

draw [drɔː] (*vb: pt* **drew**, *pp* **drawn**) vt tirer; (*picture*) dessiner; (*attract*) attirer; (*line, circle*) tracer; (*money*) retirer; (*wages*) toucher ▷ vi (*Sport*) faire match nul ▷ n match nul; (*lottery*) loterie f; (*picking of ticket*) tirage m au sort; **draw out** vi (*lengthen*) s'allonger ▷ vt (*money*) retirer; **draw up** vi (*stop*) s'arrêter ▷ vt (*document*) établir, dresser; (*plan*) formuler, dessiner; (*chair*) approcher; **drawback** n inconvénient m, désavantage m

drawer [drɔːʳ] n tiroir m

drawing ['drɔːɪŋ] n dessin m; **drawing pin** n (*BRIT*) punaise f; **drawing room** n salon m

drawn [drɔːn] pp of **draw**

dread [drɛd] n épouvante f, effroi m ▷ vt redouter, appréhender; **dreadful** adj épouvantable, affreux(-euse)

dream [driːm] n rêve m ▷ vt, vi (*pt* **dreamed**, *pp* **dreamt**) rêver; **dreamer** n rêveur(-euse)

dreamt [drɛmt] pt, pp of **dream**

dreary ['drɪərɪ] adj triste; monotone

drench [drɛntʃ] vt tremper

dress [drɛs] n robe f; (*clothing*) habillement m, tenue f ▷ vt habiller; (*wound*) panser ▷ vi: **to get ~ed** s'habiller; **dress up** vi s'habiller; (*in fancy dress*) se déguiser; **dress circle** n (*BRIT*) premier balcon; **dresser** n (*furniture*) vaisselier m (: *us*) coiffeuse f, commode f; **dressing** n (*Med*) pansement m; (*Culin*) sauce f, assaisonnement m; **dressing gown** n (*BRIT*) robe f de chambre; **dressing room** n (*Theat*) loge f; (*Sport*) vestiaire m; **dressing table** n coiffeuse f; **dressmaker** n couturière f

drew [druː] pt of **draw**

dribble ['drɪbl] vi (*baby*) baver ▷ vt (*ball*) dribbler

dried [draɪd] adj (*fruit, beans*) sec (sèche); (*eggs, milk*) en poudre

drier ['draɪəʳ] n = **dryer**

drift [drɪft] n (*of current etc*) force f; direction f; (*of snow*) rafale f; coulée f (*on ground*) congère f; (*general meaning*) sens général ▷ vi (*boat*) aller à la dérive, dériver; (*sand, snow*) s'amonceler, s'entasser

drill [drɪl] n perceuse f; (*bit*) foret m; (*of dentist*) roulette f, fraise f; (*Mil*) exercice m ▷ vt percer; (*troops*) entraîner ▷ vi (*for oil*) faire un or des forage(s)

drink [drɪŋk] n boisson f; (*alcoholic*) verre m ▷ vt, vi (*pt* **drank**, *pp* **drunk**) boire; **to have a ~** boire quelque chose, boire un verre; **a ~ of water** un verre d'eau; **would you like a ~?** tu veux boire quelque chose?; **drink-driving** n conduite f en état d'ivresse;

drinker n buveur(-euse); **drinking water** n eau f potable

drip [drɪp] n (drop) goutte f; (Med: device) goutte-à-goutte m inv; (: liquid) perfusion f ▷ vi tomber goutte à goutte; (tap) goutter

drive [draɪv] (pt **drove**, pp **driven**) n promenade f or trajet m en voiture; (also: **~way**) allée f; (energy) dynamisme m, énergie f; (push) effort (concerté) campagne f; (Comput: also: **disk ~**) lecteur m de disquette ▷ vt conduire; (nail) enfoncer; (push) chasser, pousser; (Tech: motor) actionner; entraîner ▷ vi (be at the wheel) conduire; (travel by car) aller en voiture; **left-/right-hand ~** (Aut) conduite f à gauche/droite; **to ~ sb mad** rendre qn fou (folle); **drive-in** adj, n (esp US) drive-in m

driven ['drɪvn] pp of **drive**

driver ['draɪvə'] n conducteur(-trice); (of taxi, bus) chauffeur m; **driver's license** n (US) permis m de conduire

driveway ['draɪvweɪ] n allée f

driving ['draɪvɪŋ] n conduite f; **driving instructor** n moniteur m d'auto-école; **driving lesson** n leçon f de conduite; **driving licence** n (BRIT) permis m de conduire; **driving test** n examen m du permis de conduire

drizzle ['drɪzl] n bruine f, crachin m

droop [druːp] vi (flower) commencer à se faner; (shoulders, head) tomber

drop [drɔp] n (of liquid) goutte f; (fall) baisse f; (also: **parachute ~**) saut m ▷ vt laisser tomber; (voice, eyes, price) baisser; (passenger) déposer ▷ vi tomber; **drop in** vi (inf: visit): **to ~ in (on)** faire un saut (chez), passer (chez); **drop off** vi (sleep) s'assoupir ▷ vt (passenger) déposer; **drop out** vi (withdraw) se retirer; (student etc) abandonner, décrocher

drought [draut] n sécheresse f

drove [drəuv] pt of **drive**

drown [draun] vt noyer ▷ vi se noyer

drowsy ['drauzɪ] adj somnolent(e)

drug [drʌg] n médicament m; (narcotic) drogue f ▷ vt droguer; **to be on ~s** se droguer; **drug addict** n toxicomane m/f; **drug dealer** n revendeur(-euse) de drogue; **druggist** n (US) pharmacien(ne)-droguiste; **drugstore** n (US) pharmacie-droguerie f, drugstore m

drum [drʌm] n tambour m; (for oil, petrol) bidon m; **drums** npl (Mus) batterie f; **drummer** n (joueur m de) tambour m

drunk [drʌŋk] pp of **drink** ▷ adj ivre, soûl(e) ▷ n (also: **~ard**) ivrogne m/f; **to get ~** se soûler; **drunken** adj ivre, soûl(e); (rage, stupor) ivrogne, d'ivrogne

dry [draɪ] adj sec (sèche); (day) sans pluie ▷ vt sécher; (clothes) faire sécher ▷ vi sécher; **dry off** vi, vt sécher; **dry up** vi (river, supplies) se tarir; **dry-cleaner's** n teinturerie f; **dry-cleaning** n (process) nettoyage m à sec; **dryer** n (tumble-dryer) sèche-linge m inv; (for hair) sèche-cheveux m inv

DSS n abbr (BRIT) = **Department of Social Security**

DTP n abbr (= desktop publishing) PAO f

dual ['djuəl] adj double; **dual carriageway** n (BRIT) route f à quatre voies

dubious ['djuːbɪəs] adj hésitant(e), incertain(e); (reputation, company) douteux(-euse)

duck [dʌk] n canard m ▷ vi se baisser vivement, baisser subitement la tête

due [djuː] adj (money, payment) dû (due); (expected) attendu(e); (fitting) qui convient ▷ adv: **~ north** droit vers le nord; **~ to** (because of) en raison de; (caused by) dû à; **the train is ~ at 8 a.m.** le train est attendu à 8 h; **she is ~ back tomorrow** elle doit rentrer demain; **he is ~ £10** on lui doit 10 livres; **to give sb his or her ~** être juste envers qn

duel ['djuəl] *n* duel *m*

duet [djuːˈɛt] *n* duo *m*

dug [dʌg] *pt, pp of* **dig**

duke [djuːk] *n* duc *m*

dull [dʌl] *adj (boring)* ennuyeux(-euse); *(not bright)* morne, terne; *(sound, pain)* sourd(e); *(weather, day)* gris(e), maussade ⊳ *vt (pain, grief)* atténuer; *(mind, senses)* engourdir

dumb [dʌm] *adj* muet(te); *(stupid)* bête

dummy ['dʌmɪ] *n (tailor's model)* mannequin *m*; *(mock-up)* factice *m*, maquette *f*; *(BRIT: for baby)* tétine *f* ⊳ *adj* faux (fausse), factice

dump [dʌmp] *n (also:* **rubbish ~**) décharge (publique); *(inf: place)* trou *m* ⊳ *vt (put down)* déposer; déverser; *(get rid of)* se débarrasser de; *(Comput)* lister

dumpling ['dʌmplɪŋ] *n* boulette *f* (de pâte)

dune [djuːn] *n* dune *f*

dungarees [dʌŋgəˈriːz] *npl* bleu(s) *m(pl)*; *(for child, woman)* salopette *f*

dungeon ['dʌndʒən] *n* cachot *m*

duplex ['djuːplɛks] *n (us: also:* **~ apartment**) duplex *m*

duplicate *n* ['djuːplɪkət] double *m* ⊳ *vt* ['djuːplɪkeɪt] faire un double de; *(on machine)* polycopier; **in ~** en deux exemplaires, en double

durable ['djuərəbl] *adj* durable; *(clothes, metal)* résistant(e), solide

duration [djuəˈreɪʃən] *n* durée *f*

during ['djuərɪŋ] *prep* pendant, au cours de

dusk [dʌsk] *n* crépuscule *m*

dust [dʌst] *n* poussière *f* ⊳ *vt (furniture)* essuyer, épousseter; *(cake etc)*: **to ~ with** saupoudrer de; **dustbin** *n (BRIT)* poubelle *f*; **duster** *n* chiffon *m*; **dustman** *(irreg)* *n (BRIT)* boueux *m*, éboueur *m*; **dustpan** *n* pelle *f* à poussière; **dusty** *adj* poussiéreux(-euse)

Dutch [dʌtʃ] *adj* hollandais(e), néerlandais(e) ⊳ *n (Ling)* hollandais *m*, néerlandais *m* ⊳ *adv*: **to go ~** *or* **dutch** *(inf)* partager les frais; **the Dutch** *npl* les Hollandais, les Néerlandais; **Dutchman** *(irreg)* *n* Hollandais *m*; **Dutchwoman** *(irreg)* *n* Hollandaise *f*

duty ['djuːtɪ] *n* devoir *m*; *(tax)* droit *m*, taxe *f*; **on ~** de service; *(at night etc)* de garde; **off ~** libre, pas de service *or* de garde; **duty-free** *adj* exempté(e) de douane, hors-taxe

duvet ['duːveɪ] *n (BRIT)* couette *f*

DVD *n abbr (= digital versatile or video disc)* DVD *m*; **DVD burner** *n* graveur *m* de DVD; **DVD player** *n* lecteur *m* de DVD; **DVD writer** *n* graveur *m* de DVD

dwarf *(pl* **dwarves**) [dwɔːf, dwɔːvz] *n (offensive)* nain(e) ⊳ *vt* écraser

dwell *(pt, pp* **dwelt**) [dwɛl, dwɛlt] *vi* demeurer; **dwell on** *vt fus* s'étendre sur

dwelt [dwɛlt] *pt, pp of* **dwell**

dwindle ['dwɪndl] *vi* diminuer, décroître

dye [daɪ] *n* teinture *f* ⊳ *vt* teindre

dying ['daɪɪŋ] *adj* mourant(e), agonisant(e)

dynamic [daɪˈnæmɪk] *adj* dynamique

dynamite ['daɪnəmaɪt] *n* dynamite *f*

dyslexia [dɪsˈlɛksɪə] *n* dyslexie *f*

dyslexic [dɪsˈlɛksɪk] *adj, n* dyslexique *m/f*

E [i:] n (*Mus*) mi m

each [i:tʃ] *adj* chaque ▷ *pron* chacun(e); **~ other** l'un l'autre; **they hate ~ other** ils se détestent (mutuellement); **they have 2 books ~** ils ont 2 livres chacun; **they cost £5 ~** ils coûtent 5 livres (la) pièce

eager ['i:gəʳ] *adj* (*person, buyer*) empressé(e); (*keen: pupil, worker*) enthousiaste; **to be ~ to do sth** (*impatient*) brûler de faire qch; (*keen*) désirer vivement faire qch; **to be ~ for** (*event*) désirer vivement; (*vengeance, affection, information*) être avide de

eagle ['i:gl] n aigle m

ear [ɪəʳ] n oreille f; (*of corn*) épi m; **earache** n mal m aux oreilles; **eardrum** n tympan m

earl [ə:l] n comte m

earlier ['ə:lɪəʳ] *adj* (*date etc*) plus rapproché(e); (*edition etc*) plus

ancien(ne), antérieur(e) ▷ *adv* plus tôt

early ['ə:lɪ] *adv* tôt, de bonne heure; (*ahead of time*) en avance; (*near the beginning*) au début ▷ *adj* précoce, qui se manifeste (*or* se fait) tôt *or* de bonne heure; (*Christians, settlers*) premier(-ière); (*reply*) rapide; (*death*) prématuré(e); (*work*) de jeunesse; **to have an ~ night/start** se coucher/ partir tôt *or* de bonne heure; **in the ~** *or* **~ in the spring/19th century** au début *or* commencement du printemps/19ème siècle; **early retirement** n retraite anticipée

earmark ['ɪəma:k] *vt*: **to ~ sth for** réserver *or* destiner qch à

earn [ə:n] *vt* gagner; (*Comm: yield*) rapporter; **to ~ one's living** gagner sa vie

earnest ['ə:nɪst] *adj* sérieux(-euse) ▷ *n*: **in ~** *adv* sérieusement, pour de bon

earnings ['ə:nɪŋz] *npl* salaire m; gains *mpl*; (*of company etc*) profits *mpl*, bénéfices *mpl*

ear: earphones *npl* écouteurs *mpl*; **earplugs** *npl* boules *fpl* Quiès®; (*to keep out water*) protège-tympans *mpl*; **earring** n boucle f d'oreille

earth [ə:θ] n (*gen, also* ʙʀɪᴛ *Elec*) terre f ▷ *vt* (ʙʀɪᴛ *Elec*) relier à la terre; **earthquake** n tremblement m de terre, séisme m

ease [i:z] n facilité f, aisance f; (*comfort*) bien-être m ▷ *vt* (*soothe: mind*) tranquilliser; (*reduce: pain, problem*) réduire; (: *tension*) atténuer; (*loosen*) relâcher, détendre; (*help pass*): **to ~ sth in/out** faire pénétrer/sortir qch délicatement *or* avec douceur, faciliter la pénétration/la sortie de qch; **at ~** à l'aise; (*Mil*) au repos

easily ['i:zɪlɪ] *adv* facilement; (*by far*) de loin

east [i:st] n est m ▷ *adj* (*wind*) d'est; (*side*) est *inv* ▷ *adv* à l'est, vers l'est; **the E~** l'Orient m; (*Pol*) les pays *mpl* de

l'Est; **eastbound** adj en direction de l'est; (carriageway) est inv
Easter ['iːstəʳ] n Pâques fpl; **Easter egg** n œuf m de Pâques
eastern ['iːstən] adj de l'est, oriental(e)
Easter Sunday n le dimanche de Pâques
easy ['iːzɪ] adj facile; (manner) aisé(e) ▷ adv: **to take it** or **things ~** (rest) ne pas se fatiguer; (not worry) ne pas (trop) s'en faire; **easy-going** adj accommodant(e), facile à vivre
eat (pt **ate**, pp **eaten**) [iːt, eɪt, 'iːtn] vt, vi manger; **can we have something to ~?** est-ce qu'on peut manger quelque chose?; **eat out** vi manger au restaurant
eavesdrop ['iːvzdrɔp] vi: **to ~ (on)** écouter de façon indiscrète
e-bike ['iːbaɪk] n VAE m
e-book ['iːbuk] n livre m électronique
e-business ['iːbɪznɪs] n (company) entreprise f électronique; (commerce) commerce m électronique
eccentric [ɪk'sɛntrɪk] adj, n excentrique m/f
echo ['ɛkəu] (pl **echoes**) n écho m ▷ vt répéter ▷ vi résonner; faire écho
e-cigarette ['iːsɪgəret] n cigarette f électronique
eclipse [ɪ'klɪps] n éclipse f
eco-friendly [iːkəu'frɛndlɪ] adj non nuisible à l'environnement
ecological [iːkə'lɔdʒɪkəl] adj écologique
ecology [ɪ'kɔlədʒɪ] n écologie f
e-commerce ['iːkɔməːs] n commerce m électronique
economic [iːkə'nɔmɪk] adj économique; (profitable) rentable; **economical** adj économique; (person) économe; **economics** n (Scol) économie f politique ▷ npl (of project etc) côté m or aspect m économique
economist [ɪ'kɔnəmɪst] n économiste m/f

economize [ɪ'kɔnəmaɪz] vi économiser, faire des économies
economy [ɪ'kɔnəmɪ] n économie f; **economy class** n (Aviat) classe f touriste; **economy class syndrome** n syndrome m de la classe économique
ecstasy ['ɛkstəsɪ] n extase f; (Drugs) ecstasy m; **ecstatic** [ɛks'tætɪk] adj extatique, en extase
eczema ['ɛksɪmə] n eczéma m
edge [ɛdʒ] n bord m; (of knife etc) tranchant m, fil m ▷ vt border; **on ~** (fig) crispé(e), tendu(e)
edgy ['ɛdʒɪ] adj crispé(e), tendu(e)
edible ['ɛdɪbl] adj comestible; (meal) mangeable
Edinburgh ['ɛdɪnbərə] n Édimbourg; voir article **"Edinburgh Festival"**

● **EDINBURGH FESTIVAL**
●
● Le Festival d'Édimbourg, qui se tient
● chaque année durant trois semaines
● au mois d'août, est l'un des grands
● festivals européens. Il est réputé
● pour son programme officiel mais
● aussi pour son "off" (the
● Fringe) qui propose des spectacles
● aussi bien traditionnels que
● résolument d'avant-garde. Pendant
● la durée du Festival se tient par
● ailleurs, sur l'esplanade du château,
● un grand spectacle de musique
● militaire, le "Military Tattoo".

edit ['ɛdɪt] vt (text, book) éditer; (report) préparer; (film) monter; (magazine) diriger; (newspaper) être le rédacteur or la rédactrice en chef de; **edition** [ɪ'dɪʃən] n édition f; **editor** n (of newspaper) rédacteur(-trice), rédacteur(-trice) en chef; (of sb's work) éditeur(-trice); (also: **film editor**) monteur(-euse); **political/foreign editor** rédacteur politique/au service étranger; **editorial** [ɛdɪ'tɔːrɪəl] adj de la rédaction ▷ n éditorial m

educate ['ɛdjukeɪt] vt (teach)
instruire; (bring up) éduquer;
educated ['ɛdjukeɪtɪd] adj (person)
cultivé(e)

education [ɛdju'keɪʃən] n éducation
f; (studies) études fpl; (teaching)
enseignement m, instruction f;
educational adj pédagogique;
(institution) scolaire; (game, toy)
éducatif(-ive)

eel [i:l] n anguille f

eerie ['ɪərɪ] adj inquiétant(e),
spectral(e), surnaturel(le)

effect [ɪ'fɛkt] n effet m ▷ vt effectuer;
effects npl (property) effets, affaires
fpl; **to take ~** (Law) entrer en
vigueur, prendre effet; (drug) agir,
faire son effet; **in ~** en fait; **effective**
adj efficace; (actual) véritable;
effectively adv efficacement; (in
reality) effectivement, en fait

efficiency [ɪ'fɪʃənsɪ] n efficacité f; (of
machine, car) rendement m

efficient [ɪ'fɪʃənt] adj efficace;
(machine, car) d'un bon rendement;
efficiently adv efficacement

effort ['ɛfət] n effort m; **effortless**
adj sans effort, aisé(e); (achievement)
facile

e.g. adv abbr (= exempli gratia) par
exemple, p. ex.

egg [ɛg] n œuf m; **hard-boiled/soft-
boiled ~** œuf dur/à la coque; **eggcup**
n coquetier m; **egg plant** (US) n
aubergine f; **eggshell** n coquille f
d'œuf; **egg white** n blanc m d'œuf;
egg yolk n jaune m d'œuf

ego ['i:gəʊ] n (self-esteem) amour-
propre m; (Psych) moi m

Egypt ['i:dʒɪpt] n Égypte f; **Egyptian**
[ɪ'dʒɪpʃən] adj égyptien(ne) ▷ n
Égyptien(ne)

Eiffel Tower ['aɪfəl-] n tour f Eiffel

eight [eɪt] num huit; **eighteen**
num dix-huit; **eighteenth** num
dix-huitième; **eighth** num huitième;
eightieth ['eɪtɪɪθ] num quatre-
vingtième

eighty ['eɪtɪ] num quatre-vingt(s)

Eire ['ɛərə] n République f d'Irlande

either ['aɪðər] adj l'un ou l'autre; (both,
each) chaque ▷ pron: **~ (of them)** l'un
ou l'autre ▷ adv non plus ▷ conj: **~
good or bad** soit bon soit mauvais;
on ~ side de chaque côté; **I don't
like ~** je n'aime ni l'un ni l'autre; **no,
I don't ~** moi non plus; **which bike
do you want? — ~ will do** quel vélo
voulez-vous? — n'importe lequel;
answer with ~ yes or no répondez
par oui ou par non

eject [ɪ'dʒɛkt] vt (tenant etc) expulser;
(object) éjecter

elaborate adj [ɪ'læbərɪt]
compliqué(e), recherché(e),
minutieux(-euse) ▷ vt [ɪ'læbəreɪt]
élaborer ▷ vi entrer dans les détails

elastic [ɪ'læstɪk] adj, n élastique (m);
elastic band n (BRIT) élastique m

elbow ['ɛlbəʊ] n coude m

elder ['ɛldər] adj aîné(e) ▷ n (tree)
sureau m; **one's ~s** ses aînés; **elderly**
adj âgé(e); **~ people** les personnes
âgées

eldest ['ɛldɪst] adj, n: **the ~ (child)**
l'aîné(e) (des enfants)

elect [ɪ'lɛkt] vt élire; (choose): **to
~ to do** choisir de faire ▷ adj: **the
president ~** le président désigné;
election n élection f; **electoral** adj
électoral(e); **electorate** n électorat m

electric [ɪ'lɛktrɪk] adj électrique;
electrical adj électrique; **electric
blanket** n couverture chauffante;
electric fire n (BRIT) radiateur m
électrique; **electrician** [ɪlɛk'trɪʃən] n
électricien m; **electricity** [ɪlɛk'trɪsɪtɪ]
n électricité f; **electric shock** n choc
m or décharge f électrique; **electrify**
[ɪ'lɛktrɪfaɪ] vt (Rail) électrifier;
(audience) électriser

electronic [ɪlɛk'trɒnɪk] adj
électronique; **electronic mail** n
courrier m électronique; **electronics**
n électronique f

elegance ['ɛlɪgəns] n élégance f

elegant ['ɛlɪgənt] *adj* élégant(e)

element ['ɛlɪmənt] *n* (*gen*) élément *m*; (*of heater, kettle etc*) résistance *f*

elementary [ɛlɪ'mɛntərɪ] *adj* élémentaire; (*school, education*) primaire; **elementary school** *n* (*US*) école *f* primaire

elephant ['ɛlɪfənt] *n* éléphant *m*

elevate ['ɛlɪveɪt] *vt* élever

elevator ['ɛlɪveɪtə^r] *n* (*in warehouse etc*) élévateur *m*, monte-charge *m inv*; (*US: lift*) ascenseur *m*

eleven [ɪ'lɛvn] *num* onze; **eleventh** *num* onzième

eligible ['ɛlɪdʒəbl] *adj* éligible; (*for membership*) admissible; **an ~ young man** un beau parti; **to be ~ for sth** remplir les conditions requises pour qch

eliminate [ɪ'lɪmɪneɪt] *vt* éliminer

elm [ɛlm] *n* orme *m*

eloquent ['ɛləkwənt] *adj* éloquent(e)

else [ɛls] *adv*: **something ~** quelque chose d'autre, autre chose; **somewhere ~** ailleurs, autre part; **everywhere ~** partout ailleurs; **everyone ~** tous les autres; **nothing ~** rien d'autre; **where ~?** à quel autre endroit?; **little ~** pas grand-chose d'autre; **elsewhere** *adv* ailleurs, autre part

elusive [ɪ'luːsɪv] *adj* insaisissable

email ['iːmeɪl] *n abbr* (= *electronic mail*) (e-)mail *m*, courriel *m* ▷ *vt*: **to ~ sb** envoyer un (e-)mail *or* un courriel à qn; **email account** *n* compte *m* (e-)mail; **email address** *n* adresse *f* (e-)mail *or* électronique

embankment [ɪm'bæŋkmənt] *n* (*of road, railway*) remblai *m*, talus *m*; (*of river*) berge *f*, quai *m*; (*dyke*) digue *f*

embargo [ɪm'bɑːgəu] (*pl* **embargoes**) *n* (*Comm, Naut*) embargo *m*; (*prohibition*) interdiction *f*

embark [ɪm'bɑːk] *vi* embarquer ▷ *vt* embarquer; **to ~ on** (*journey etc*) commencer, entreprendre; (*fig*) se lancer *or* s'embarquer dans

embarrass [ɪm'bærəs] *vt* embarrasser, gêner; **embarrassed** *adj* gêné(e); **embarrassing** *adj* gênant(e), embarrassant(e); **embarrassment** *n* embarras *m*, gêne *f*; (*embarrassing thing, person*) source *f* d'embarras

embassy ['ɛmbəsɪ] *n* ambassade *f*

embrace [ɪm'breɪs] *vt* embrasser, étreindre; (*include*) embrasser ▷ *vi* s'embrasser, s'étreindre ▷ *n* étreinte *f*

embroider [ɪm'brɔɪdə^r] *vt* broder; **embroidery** *n* broderie *f*

embryo ['ɛmbrɪəu] *n* (*also fig*) embryon *m*

emerald ['ɛmərəld] *n* émeraude *f*

emerge [ɪ'məːdʒ] *vi* apparaître; (*from room, car*) surgir; (*from sleep, imprisonment*) sortir

emergency [ɪ'məːdʒənsɪ] *n* (*crisis*) cas *m* d'urgence; (*Med*) urgence *f*; **in an ~** en cas d'urgence; **state of ~** état *m* d'urgence; **emergency brake** (*US*) *n* frein *m* à main; **emergency exit** *n* sortie *f* de secours; **emergency landing** *n* atterrissage forcé; **emergency room** *n* (*US Med*) urgences *fpl*; **emergency services** *npl*: **the emergency services** (*fire, police, ambulance*) les services *mpl* d'urgence

emigrate ['ɛmɪgreɪt] *vi* émigrer; **emigration** [ɛmɪ'greɪʃən] *n* émigration *f*

eminent ['ɛmɪnənt] *adj* éminent(e)

emissions [ɪ'mɪʃənz] *npl* émissions *fpl*

emit [ɪ'mɪt] *vt* émettre

emoticon [ɪ'məutɪkən] *n* (*Comput*) émoticone *n*

emotion [ɪ'məuʃən] *n* sentiment *m*; **emotional** *adj* (*person*) émotif(-ive), très sensible; (*needs*) affectif(-ive); (*scene*) émouvant(e); (*tone, speech*) qui fait appel aux sentiments

emperor ['ɛmpərə^r] *n* empereur *m*

emphasis (*pl* **emphases**) ['ɛmfəsɪs, -siːz] *n* accent *m*; **to lay** *or* **place**

~ on sth (*fig*) mettre l'accent sur, insister sur

emphasize ['ɛmfəsaɪz] *vt* (*syllable, word, point*) appuyer *or* insister sur; (*feature*) souligner, accentuer

empire ['ɛmpaɪəʳ] *n* empire *m*

employ [ɪm'plɔɪ] *vt* employer; **employee** [ɪmplɔɪ'i:] *n* employé(e); **employer** *n* employeur(-euse); **employment** *n* emploi *m*; **employment agency** *n* agence *for* bureau *m* de placement

empower [ɪm'pauəʳ] *vt*: **to ~ sb to do** autoriser *or* habiliter qn à faire

empress ['ɛmprɪs] *n* impératrice *f*

emptiness ['ɛmptɪnɪs] *n* vide *m*; (*of area*) aspect *m* désertique

empty ['ɛmptɪ] *adj* vide; (*street, area*) désert(e); (*threat, promise*) en l'air, vain(e) ▷ *vt* vider ▷ *vi* se vider; (*liquid*) s'écouler; **empty-handed** *adj* les mains vides

EMU *n abbr* (= *European Monetary Union*) UME *f*

emulsion [ɪ'mʌlʃən] *n* émulsion *f*; (*also*: **~ paint**) peinture mate

enable [ɪ'neɪbl] *vt*: **to ~ sb to do** permettre à qn de faire

enamel [ɪ'næməl] *n* émail *m*; (*also*: **~ paint**) (*peinture f*) laque *f*

enchanting [ɪn'tʃɑ:ntɪŋ] *adj* ravissant(e), enchanteur(-eresse)

encl. *abbr* (*on letters etc* = *enclosed*) ci-joint(e); (: = *enclosure*) PJ *f*

enclose [ɪn'kləuz] *vt* (*land*) clôturer; (*space, object*) entourer; (*letter etc*): **to ~ (with)** joindre (à); **please find ~d** veuillez trouver ci-joint

enclosure [ɪn'kləuʒəʳ] *n* enceinte *f*

encore [ɔŋ'kɔːʳ] *excl, n* bis (*m*)

encounter [ɪn'kauntəʳ] *n* rencontre *f* ▷ *vt* rencontrer

encourage [ɪn'kʌrɪdʒ] *vt* encourager

encouraging [ɪn'kʌrɪdʒɪŋ] *adj* encourageant(e)

encyclop(a)edia [ɛnsaɪkləu'piːdɪə] *n* encyclopédie *f*

end [ɛnd] *n* fin *f*; (*of table, street, rope etc*) bout *m*, extrémité *f* ▷ *vt* terminer; (*also*: **bring to an ~, put an ~ to**) mettre fin à ▷ *vi* se terminer, finir; **in the ~** finalement; **on ~** (*object*) debout, dressé(e); **to stand on ~** (*hair*) se dresser sur la tête; **for hours on ~** pendant des heures (et des heures); **end up** *vi*: **to ~ up in** (*condition*) finir *or* se terminer par; (*place*) finir *or* aboutir à

endanger [ɪn'deɪndʒəʳ] *vt* mettre en danger; **an ~ed species** une espèce en voie de disparition

endearing [ɪn'dɪərɪŋ] *adj* attachant(e)

endeavour, (*US*) **endeavor** [ɪn'dɛvəʳ] *n* effort *m*; (*attempt*) tentative *f* ▷ *vt*: **to ~ to do** tenter *or* s'efforcer de faire

ending ['ɛndɪŋ] *n* dénouement *m*, conclusion *f*; (*Ling*) terminaison *f*

endless ['ɛndlɪs] *adj* sans fin, interminable

endorse [ɪn'dɔ:s] *vt* (*cheque*) endosser; (*approve*) appuyer, approuver, sanctionner; **endorsement** *n* (*approval*) appui *m*, aval *m*; (*BRIT: on driving licence*) contravention *f* (*portée au permis de conduire*)

endurance [ɪn'djuərəns] *n* endurance *f*

endure [ɪn'djuəʳ] *vt* (*bear*) supporter, endurer ▷ *vi* (*last*) durer

enemy ['ɛnəmɪ] *adj, n* ennemi(e)

energetic [ɛnə'dʒɛtɪk] *adj* énergique; (*activity*) très actif(-ive), qui fait se dépenser (*physiquement*)

energy ['ɛnədʒɪ] *n* énergie *f*

enforce [ɪn'fɔːs] *vt* (*law*) appliquer, faire respecter

engaged [ɪn'geɪdʒd] *adj* (*BRIT: busy, in use*) occupé(e); (*betrothed*) fiancé(e); **to get ~** se fiancer; **the line's ~** la ligne est occupée; **engaged tone** *n* (*BRIT Tel*) tonalité *f* occupé *inv*

engagement [ɪnˈɡeɪdʒmənt] n (undertaking) obligation f, engagement m; (appointment) rendez-vous m inv; (to marry) fiançailles fpl; **engagement ring** n bague f de fiançailles

engaging [ɪnˈɡeɪdʒɪŋ] adj engageant(e), attirant(e)

engine [ˈendʒɪn] n (Aut) moteur m; (Rail) locomotive f

⬛ Be careful not to translate engine by the French word engin.

engineer [endʒɪˈnɪəʳ] n ingénieur m; (BRIT: repairer) dépanneur m; (Navy, US Rail) mécanicien m; **engineering** n engineering m, ingénierie f; (of bridges, ships) génie m; (of machine) mécanique f

England [ˈɪŋɡlənd] n Angleterre f

English [ˈɪŋɡlɪʃ] adj anglais(e) ▷ n (Ling) anglais m; **the ~** npl les Anglais; **English Channel** n: **the English Channel** la Manche; **Englishman** (irreg) n Anglais m; **Englishwoman** (irreg) n Anglaise f

engrave [ɪnˈɡreɪv] vt graver

engraving [ɪnˈɡreɪvɪŋ] n gravure f

enhance [ɪnˈhɑːns] vt rehausser, mettre en valeur

enjoy [ɪnˈdʒɔɪ] vt aimer, prendre plaisir à; (have benefit of: health, fortune) jouir de; (: success) connaître; **to ~ o.s.** s'amuser; **enjoyable** adj agréable; **enjoyment** n plaisir m

enlarge [ɪnˈlɑːdʒ] vt accroître; (Phot) agrandir ▷ vi: **to ~ on** (subject) s'étendre sur; **enlargement** n (Phot) agrandissement m

enlist [ɪnˈlɪst] vt recruter; (support) s'assurer ▷ vi s'engager

enormous [ɪˈnɔːməs] adj énorme

enough [ɪˈnʌf] adj: **~ time/ books** assez or suffisamment de temps/livres ▷ adv: **big ~** assez or suffisamment grand ▷ pron: **have you got ~?** (en) avez-vous assez?; **~ to eat** assez à manger; **that's ~, thanks** cela suffit or c'est assez,

merci; **I've had ~ of him** j'en ai assez de lui; **he has not worked ~** il n'a pas assez or suffisamment travaillé, il n'a pas travaillé assez or suffisamment; **... which, funnily or oddly or strangely ~ ...** qui, chose curieuse, ...

enquire [ɪnˈkwaɪəʳ] vt, vi = **inquire**

enquiry [ɪnˈkwaɪərɪ] n = **inquiry**

enrage [ɪnˈreɪdʒ] vt mettre en fureur or en rage, rendre furieux(-euse)

enrich [ɪnˈrɪtʃ] vt enrichir

enrol, (US) **enroll** [ɪnˈrəul] vt inscrire ▷ vi s'inscrire; **enrolment**, (US) **enrollment** n inscription f

en route [ɔnˈruːt] adv en route, en chemin

en suite [ˈɔnswiːt] adj: **with ~ bathroom** avec salle de bains en attenante

ensure [ɪnˈʃuəʳ] vt assurer, garantir

entail [ɪnˈteɪl] vt entraîner, nécessiter

enter [ˈentəʳ] vt (room) entrer dans, pénétrer dans; (club, army) entrer à; (competition) s'inscrire à or pour; (sb for a competition) (faire) inscrire; (write down) inscrire, noter; (Comput) entrer, introduire ▷ vi entrer

enterprise [ˈentəpraɪz] n (company, undertaking) entreprise f; (initiative) (esprit m d')initiative f; **free ~** libre entreprise; **private ~** entreprise privée; **enterprising** adj entreprenant(e), dynamique; (scheme) audacieux(-euse)

entertain [entəˈteɪn] vt amuser, distraire; (invite) recevoir (à dîner); (idea, plan) envisager; **entertainer** n artiste m/f de variétés; **entertaining** adj amusant(e), distrayant(e); **entertainment** n (amusement) distraction f, divertissement m, amusement m; (show) spectacle m

enthusiasm [ɪnˈθuːzɪæzəm] n enthousiasme m

enthusiast [ɪnˈθuːzɪæst] n enthousiaste m/f; **enthusiastic** [ɪnθuːzɪˈæstɪk] adj enthousiaste;

to be enthusiastic about être enthousiasmé(e) par

entire [ɪn'taɪər] adj (tout) entier(-ère); **entirely** adv entièrement

entitle [ɪn'taɪtl] vt: **to ~ sb to sth** donner droit à qch à qn; **entitled** adj (book) intitulé(e); **to be entitled to do** avoir le droit de faire

entrance n ['ɛntrns] entrée f ▷ vt [ɪn'trɑːns] enchanter, ravir; **where's the ~?** où est l'entrée?; **to gain ~ to** (university etc) être admis à; **entrance examination** n examen m d'entrée or d'admission; **entrance fee** n (to museum etc) prix m d'entrée; (to join club etc) droit m d'inscription; **entrance ramp** n (us Aut) bretelle f d'accès; **entrant** n (in race etc) participant(e), concurrent(e); (BRIT: in exam) candidat(e)

entrepreneur ['ɔntrəprə'nəːr] n entrepreneur m

entrust [ɪn'trʌst] vt: **to ~ sth to** confier qch à

entry ['ɛntri] n entrée f; (in register, diary) inscription f; **"no ~"** "défense d'entrer", "entrée interdite"; (Aut) "sens interdit"; **entry phone** n (BRIT) interphone m (à l'entrée d'un immeuble)

envelope ['ɛnvələup] n enveloppe f

envious ['ɛnviəs] adj envieux(-euse)

environment [ɪn'vaɪərnmənt] n (social, moral) milieu m; (natural world): **the ~** l'environnement m; **environmental** [ɪnvaɪərn'mɛntl] adj (of surroundings) du milieu; (issue, disaster) écologique; **environmentally** [ɪnvaɪərn'mɛntli] adv: **environmentally sound/ friendly** qui ne nuit pas à l'environnement

envisage [ɪn'vɪzɪdʒ] vt (foresee) prévoir

envoy ['ɛnvɔɪ] n envoyé(e); (diplomat) ministre m plénipotentiaire

envy ['ɛnvɪ] n envie f ▷ vt envier; **to ~ sb sth** envier qch à qn

epic ['ɛpɪk] n épopée f ▷ adj épique

epidemic [ɛpɪ'dɛmɪk] n épidémie f

epilepsy ['ɛpɪlɛpsɪ] n épilepsie f; **epileptic** adj, n épileptique m/f; **epileptic fit** n crise f d'épilepsie

episode ['ɛpɪsəud] n épisode m

equal ['iːkwl] adj égal(e) ▷ vt égaler; **~ to** (task) à la hauteur de; **equality** [iː'kwɔlɪtɪ] n égalité f; **equalize** vt, vi (Sport) égaliser; **equally** adv également; (share) en parts égales; (treat) de la même façon; (pay) autant; (just as) tout aussi

equation [ɪ'kweɪʃən] n (Math) équation f

equator [ɪ'kweɪtər] n équateur m

equip [ɪ'kwɪp] vt équiper; **to ~ sb/ sth with** équiper or munir qn/ qch de; **equipment** n équipement m; (electrical etc) appareillage m, installation f

equivalent [ɪ'kwɪvəlnt] adj équivalent(e) ▷ n équivalent m; **to be ~ to** équivaloir à, être équivalent(e) à

ER abbr (BRIT: = Elizabeth Regina) la reine Élisabeth; (us Med: = emergency room) urgences fpl

era ['ɪərə] n ère f, époque f

erase [ɪ'reɪz] vt effacer; **eraser** n gomme f

e-reader ['iːriːdər] n liseuse f

erect [ɪ'rɛkt] adj droit(e) ▷ vt construire; (monument) ériger, élever; (tent etc) dresser; **erection** [ɪ'rɛkʃən] n (Physiol) érection f; (of building) construction f

ERM n abbr (= Exchange Rate Mechanism) mécanisme m des taux de change

erode [ɪ'rəud] vt éroder; (metal) ronger

erosion [ɪ'rəuʒən] n érosion f

erotic [ɪ'rɔtɪk] adj érotique

errand ['ɛrnd] n course f, commission f

erratic [ɪ'rætɪk] adj irrégulier(-ière), inconstant(e)

error ['ɛrər] n erreur f

erupt [ɪ'rʌpt] vi entrer en éruption; (fig) éclater; **eruption** [ɪ'rʌpʃən] n éruption f; (of anger, violence) explosion f

escalate ['ɛskəleɪt] vi s'intensifier; (costs) monter en flèche

escalator ['ɛskəleɪtər] n escalier roulant

escape [ɪ'skeɪp] n évasion f, fuite f; (of gas etc) fuite ▷ vi s'échapper, fuir; (from jail) s'évader; (fig) s'en tirer; (leak) s'échapper ▷ vt échapper à; **to ~ from** (person) échapper à; (place) s'échapper de; (fig) fuir; **his name ~s me** son nom m'échappe

escort vt [ɪ'skɔːt] escorter ▷ n ['ɛskɔːt] (Mil) escorte f

especially [ɪ'spɛʃlɪ] adv (particularly) particulièrement; (above all) surtout

espionage ['ɛspɪənɑːʒ] n espionnage m

essay ['ɛseɪ] n (Scol) dissertation f; (Literature) essai m

essence ['ɛsns] n essence f; (Culin) extrait m

essential [ɪ'sɛnʃl] adj essentiel(le); (basic) fondamental(e); **essentials** npl éléments essentiels; **essentially** adv essentiellement

establish [ɪ'stæblɪʃ] vt établir; (business) fonder, créer; (one's power etc) asseoir, affermir; **establishment** n établissement m; (founding) création f; (institution) établissement; **the Establishment** les pouvoirs établis; l'ordre établi

estate [ɪ'steɪt] n (land) domaine m, propriété f; (Law) biens mpl, succession f; (BRIT: also: **housing ~**) lotissement m; **estate agent** n (BRIT) agent immobilier; **estate car** n (BRIT) break m

estimate n ['ɛstɪmət] estimation f; (Comm) devis m ▷ vt ['ɛstɪmeɪt] estimer

etc abbr (= et cetera) etc

eternal [ɪ'təːnl] adj éternel(le)

eternity [ɪ'təːnɪtɪ] n éternité f

ethical ['ɛθɪkl] adj moral(e); **ethics** ['ɛθɪks] n éthique f ▷ npl moralité f

Ethiopia [iːθɪ'əupɪə] n Éthiopie f

ethnic ['ɛθnɪk] adj ethnique; (clothes, food) folklorique, exotique, propre aux minorités ethniques non-occidentales; **ethnic minority** n minorité f ethnique

e-ticket ['iːtɪkɪt] n billet m électronique

etiquette ['ɛtɪkɛt] n convenances fpl, étiquette f

EU n abbr (= European Union) UE f

euro ['juərəu] n (currency) euro m

Europe ['juərəp] n Europe f; **European** [juərə'piːən] adj européen(ne) ▷ n Européen(ne); **European Community** n Communauté européenne; **European Union** n Union européenne

Eurostar® ['juərəustɑːr] n Eurostar® m

evacuate [ɪ'vækjueɪt] vt évacuer

evade [ɪ'veɪd] vt échapper à; (question etc) éluder; (duties) se dérober à

evaluate [ɪ'væljueɪt] vt évaluer

evaporate [ɪ'væpəreɪt] vi s'évaporer; (fig: hopes, fear) s'envoler; (anger) se dissiper

eve [iːv] n: **on the ~ of** à la veille de

even ['iːvn] adj (level, smooth) régulier(-ière); (equal) égal(e); (number) pair(e) ▷ adv même; **~ if** même si + indic; **~ though** alors même que + cond; **~ more** encore plus; **~ faster** encore plus vite; **~ so** quand même; **not ~** pas même; **~ he was there** même lui était là; **~ on Sundays** même le dimanche; **to get ~ with sb** prendre sa revanche sur qn

evening ['iːvnɪŋ] n soir m; (as duration, event) soirée f; **in the ~** le soir; **evening class** n cours m du soir; **evening dress** n (man's) tenue f de soirée, smoking m; (woman's) robe f de soirée

event [ɪ'vɛnt] n événement m; (Sport)
épreuve f; **in the ~ of** en cas de;
eventful adj mouvementé(e)
eventual [ɪ'vɛntʃuəl] adj final(e)

> Be careful not to translate
> eventual by the French word
> éventuel.

eventually [ɪ'vɛntʃuəlɪ] adv
finalement

> Be careful not to translate
> eventually by the French word
> éventuellement.

ever ['ɛvəʳ] adv jamais; (at all times)
toujours; **why ~ not?** mais enfin,
pourquoi pas?; **the best ~** le meilleur
qu'on ait jamais vu; **have you ~ seen
it?** l'as-tu déjà vu?, as-tu eu l'occasion
or t'est-il arrivé de le voir?; **~ since** (as
adv) depuis; (as conj) depuis que; **~ so
pretty** si joli; **evergreen** n arbre m à
feuilles persistantes

🔘 **KEYWORD**

every ['ɛvrɪ] adj **1** (each) chaque;
every one of them tous (sans
exception); **every shop in town
was closed** tous les magasins en ville
étaient fermés
2 (all possible) tous (toutes) les; **I
gave you every assistance** j'ai fait
tout mon possible pour vous aider; **I
have every confidence in him** j'ai
entièrement or pleinement confiance
en lui; **we wish you every success**
nous vous souhaitons beaucoup
de succès
3 (showing recurrence) tous les; **every
day** tous les jours, chaque jour;
every other car une voiture sur
deux; **every other/third day** tous
les deux/trois jours; **every now and
then** de temps en temps; **everybody**
pron = **everyone**; **everyday** adj
(expression) courant(e), d'usage
courant; (use) courant; (clothes, life)
de tous les jours; (occurrence, problem)
quotidien(ne); **everyone** pron tout

le monde, tous pl; **everything** pron
tout; **everywhere** adv partout;
everywhere you go you meet ... où
qu'on aille on rencontre ...

evict [ɪ'vɪkt] vt expulser
evidence ['ɛvɪdns] n (proof)
preuve(s) f(pl); (of witness)
témoignage m; (sign): **to show ~
of** donner des signes de; **to give ~**
témoigner, déposer
evident ['ɛvɪdnt] adj évident(e);
evidently adv de toute évidence;
(apparently) apparemment
evil ['iːvl] adj mauvais(e) ▷ n mal m
evoke [ɪ'vəuk] vt évoquer
evolution [iːvə'luːʃən] n évolution f
evolve [ɪ'vɔlv] vt élaborer ▷ vi
évoluer, se transformer
ewe [juː] n brebis f
ex [ɛks] n (inf): **my ex** mon ex
ex- [ɛks] prefix ex-
exact [ɪg'zækt] adj exact(e) ▷ vt: **to
~ sth (from)** (signature, confession)
extorquer qch (à); (apology) exiger qch
(de); **exactly** adv exactement
exaggerate [ɪg'zædʒəreɪt]
vt, vi exagérer; **exaggeration**
[ɪgzædʒə'reɪʃən] n exagération f
exam [ɪg'zæm] n abbr (Scol)
= **examination**
examination [ɪgzæmɪ'neɪʃən] n
(Scol, Med) examen m; **to take** or **sit
an ~** (BRIT) passer un examen
examine [ɪg'zæmɪn] vt (gen)
examiner; (Scol, Law: person)
interroger; **examiner** n
examinateur(-trice)
example [ɪg'zɑːmpl] n exemple m;
for ~ par exemple
exasperated [ɪg'zɑːspəreɪtɪd] adj
exaspéré(e)
excavate ['ɛkskəveɪt] vt (site)
fouiller, excaver; (object) mettre
au jour
exceed [ɪk'siːd] vt dépasser; (one's
powers) outrepasser; **exceedingly**
adv extrêmement

excel [ɪk'sɛl] vi exceller ▷ vt surpasser; **to ~ o.s.** se surpasser

excellence ['ɛksələns] n excellence f

excellent ['ɛksələnt] adj excellent(e)

except [ɪk'sɛpt] prep (also: **~ for, ~ing**) sauf, excepté, à l'exception de ▷ vt excepter; **~ if/when** sauf si/quand; **~ that** excepté que, si ce n'est que; **exception** [ɪk'sɛpʃən] n exception f; **to take exception to** s'offusquer de; **exceptional** [ɪk'sɛpʃənl] adj exceptionnel(le); **exceptionally** [ɪk'sɛpʃənəlɪ] adv exceptionnellement

excerpt ['ɛksə:pt] n extrait m

excess [ɪk'sɛs] n excès m; **excess baggage** n excédent m de bagages; **excessive** adj excessif(-ive)

exchange [ɪks'tʃeɪndʒ] n échange m; (also: **telephone ~**) central m ▷ vt: **to ~ (for)** échanger (contre); **could I ~ this, please?** est-ce que je peux échanger ceci, s'il vous plaît?; **exchange rate** n taux m de change

excite [ɪk'saɪt] vt exciter; **excited** adj (tout) excité(e); **to get excited** s'exciter; **excitement** n excitation f; **exciting** adj passionnant(e)

exclaim [ɪk'skleɪm] vi s'exclamer; **exclamation** [ɛksklə'meɪʃən] n exclamation f; **exclamation mark**, (US) **exclamation point** n point m d'exclamation

exclude [ɪk'sklu:d] vt exclure

excluding [ɪk'sklu:dɪŋ] prep: **~ VAT** la TVA non comprise

exclusion [ɪk'sklu:ʒən] n exclusion f

exclusive [ɪk'sklu:sɪv] adj exclusif(-ive); (club, district) sélect(e); (item of news) en exclusivité; **~ of VAT** TVA non comprise; **exclusively** adv exclusivement

excruciating [ɪk'skru:ʃɪeɪtɪŋ] adj (pain) atroce, déchirant(e); (embarrassing) pénible

excursion [ɪk'skə:ʃən] n excursion f

excuse n [ɪk'skju:s] excuse f ▷ vt [ɪk'skju:z] (forgive) excuser; **to ~ sb from** (activity) dispenser qn de; **~ me!** excusez-moi!, pardon!; **now if you will ~ me, ...** maintenant, si vous (le) permettez ...

ex-directory ['ɛksdɪ'rɛktərɪ] adj (BRIT) sur la liste rouge

execute ['ɛksɪkju:t] vt exécuter; **execution** [ɛksɪ'kju:ʃən] n exécution f

executive [ɪg'zɛkjutɪv] n (person) cadre m; (managing group) bureau m; (Pol) exécutif m ▷ adj exécutif(-ive); (position, job) de cadre

exempt [ɪg'zɛmpt] adj: **~ from** exempté(e) or dispensé(e) de ▷ vt: **to ~ sb from** exempter or dispenser qn de

exercise ['ɛksəsaɪz] n exercice m ▷ vt exercer; (patience etc) faire preuve de; (dog) promener ▷ vi (also: **to take ~**) prendre de l'exercice; **exercise book** n cahier m

exert [ɪg'zə:t] vt exercer, employer; **to ~ o.s.** se dépenser; **exertion** [ɪg'zə:ʃən] n effort m

exhale [ɛks'heɪl] vt exhaler ▷ vi expirer

exhaust [ɪg'zɔ:st] n (also: **~ fumes**) gaz mpl d'échappement; (also: **~ pipe**) tuyau m d'échappement ▷ vt épuiser; **exhausted** adj épuisé(e); **exhaustion** [ɪg'zɔ:stʃən] n épuisement m; **nervous exhaustion** fatigue nerveuse

exhibit [ɪg'zɪbɪt] n (Art) objet exposé, pièce exposée, (Law) pièce à conviction ▷ vt (Art) exposer; (courage, skill) faire preuve de; **exhibition** [ɛksɪ'bɪʃən] n exposition f

exhilarating [ɪg'zɪləreɪtɪŋ] adj grisant(e), stimulant(e)

exile ['ɛksaɪl] n exil m; (person) exilé(e) ▷ vt exiler

exist [ɪg'zɪst] vi exister; **existence** n existence f; **existing** adj actuel(le)

exit ['ɛksɪt] n sortie f ▷ vi (Comput, Theat) sortir; **where's the ~?** où est la sortie?; **exit ramp** n (US Aut) bretelle f d'accès

exotic [ɪgˈzɒtɪk] adj exotique
expand [ɪkˈspænd] vt (area) agrandir; (quantity) accroître ▷ vi (trade, etc) se développer, s'accroître; (gas, metal) se dilater
expansion [ɪkˈspænʃən] n (territorial, economic) expansion f; (of trade, influence etc) développement m; (of production) accroissement m; (of population) croissance f; (of gas, metal) expansion, dilatation f
expect [ɪkˈspɛkt] vt (anticipate) s'attendre à, s'attendre à ce que + sub; (count on) compter sur, escompter; (require) demander, exiger; (suppose) supposer; (await: also baby) attendre ▷ vi: **to be ~ing** (pregnant woman) être enceinte; **expectation** [ɛkspɛkˈteɪʃən] n (hope) attente f, espérance(s) f(pl); (belief) attente f
expedition [ɛkspəˈdɪʃən] n expédition f
expel [ɪkˈspɛl] vt chasser, expulser; (Scol) renvoyer, exclure
expenditure [ɪkˈspɛndɪtʃəʳ] n (act of spending) dépense f; (money spent) dépenses fpl
expense [ɪkˈspɛns] n (high cost) coût m; (spending) dépense f, frais mpl; **expenses** npl frais mpl; dépenses; **at the ~ of** (fig) aux dépens de; **expense account** n (note f de) frais mpl
expensive [ɪkˈspɛnsɪv] adj cher (chère), coûteux(-euse); **it's too ~** ça coûte trop cher
experience [ɪkˈspɪərɪəns] n expérience f ▷ vt connaître; (feeling) éprouver; **experienced** adj expérimenté(e)
experiment [ɪkˈspɛrɪmənt] n expérience f ▷ vi faire une expérience; **experimental** [ɪkspɛrɪˈmɛntl] adj expérimental(e)
expert [ˈɛkspəːt] adj expert(e) ▷ n expert m; **expertise** [ɛkspəːˈtiːz] n (grande) compétence
expire [ɪkˈspaɪəʳ] vi expirer; **expiry** n expiration f; **expiry date** n date

f d'expiration; (on label) à utiliser avant...
explain [ɪkˈspleɪn] vt expliquer; **explanation** [ɛkspləˈneɪʃən] n explication f
explicit [ɪkˈsplɪsɪt] adj explicite; (definite) formel(le)
explode [ɪkˈspləʊd] vi exploser
exploit n [ˈɛksplɔɪt] exploit m ▷ vt [ɪkˈsplɔɪt] exploiter; **exploitation** [ɛksplɔɪˈteɪʃən] n exploitation f
explore [ɪkˈsplɔːʳ] vt explorer; (possibilities) étudier, examiner; **explorer** n explorateur(-trice)
explosion [ɪkˈspləʊʒən] n explosion f; **explosive** [ɪkˈspləʊsɪv] adj explosif(-ive) ▷ n explosif m
export vt [ɛkˈspɔːt] exporter ▷ n [ˈɛkspɔːt] exportation f ▷ cpd [ˈɛkspɔːt] d'exportation; **exporter** n exportateur m
expose [ɪkˈspəʊz] vt exposer; (unmask) démasquer, dévoiler; **exposed** adj (land, house) exposé(e); **exposure** [ɪkˈspəʊʒəʳ] n exposition f; (publicity) couverture f; (Phot: speed) (temps m de) pose f; (: shot) pose; **to die of exposure** (Med) mourir de froid
express [ɪkˈsprɛs] adj (definite) formel(le), exprès(-esse); (BRIT: letter etc) exprès inv ▷ n (train) rapide m ▷ vt exprimer; **expression** [ɪkˈsprɛʃən] n expression f; **expressway** n (us) voie f express (à plusieurs files)
exquisite [ɛkˈskwɪzɪt] adj exquis(e)
extend [ɪkˈstɛnd] vt (visit, street) prolonger; remettre; (building) agrandir; (offer) présenter, offrir; (hand, arm) tendre ▷ vi (land) s'étendre; **extension** n (of visit, street) prolongation f; (building) annexe f, (telephone: in offices) poste m; (: in private house) téléphone m supplémentaire; **extension cable, extension lead** n (Elec) rallonge f; **extensive** adj étendu(e), vaste; (damage, alterations) considérable; (inquiries) approfondi(e)

extent [ɪkˈstɛnt] n étendue f; **to some ~** dans une certaine mesure; **to the ~ of ...** au point de ...; **to what ~?** dans quelle mesure?, jusqu'à quel point?; **to such an ~ that ...** à tel point que ...

exterior [ɛkˈstɪərɪəʳ] adj extérieur(e) ▷ n extérieur m

external [ɛkˈstəːnl] adj externe

extinct [ɪkˈstɪŋkt] adj (volcano) éteint(e); (species) disparu(e); **extinction** n extinction f

extinguish [ɪkˈstɪŋgwɪʃ] vt éteindre

extra [ˈɛkstrə] adj supplémentaire, de plus ▷ adv (in addition) en plus ▷ n supplément m; (perk) à-coté m; (Cine, Theat) figurant(e)

extract vt [ɪkˈstrækt] extraire; (tooth) arracher; (money, promise) soutirer ▷ n [ˈɛkstrækt] extrait m

extradite [ˈɛkstrədaɪt] vt extrader

extraordinary [ɪkˈstrɔːdnrɪ] adj extraordinaire

extravagance [ɪkˈstrævəgəns] n (excessive spending) prodigalités fpl; (thing bought) folie f, dépense excessive; **extravagant** adj extravagant(e); (in spending: person) prodigue, dépensier(-ière); (: tastes) dispendieux(-euse)

extreme [ɪkˈstriːm] adj, n extrême (m); **extremely** adv extrêmement

extremist [ɪkˈstriːmɪst] adj, n extrémiste m/f

extrovert [ˈɛkstrəvəːt] n extraverti(e)

eye [aɪ] n œil m; (of needle) trou m, chas m ▷ vt examiner; **to keep an ~ on** surveiller; **eyeball** n globe m oculaire; **eyebrow** n sourcil m; **eye drops** npl gouttes fpl pour les yeux; **eyelash** n cil m; **eyelid** n paupière f; **eyeliner** n eye-liner m; **eye shadow** n ombre f à paupières; **eyesight** n vue f; **eye witness** n témoin m oculaire

f

F [ɛf] n (Mus) fa m

fabric [ˈfæbrɪk] n tissu m

fabulous [ˈfæbjuləs] adj fabuleux(-euse); (inf: super) formidable, sensationnel(le)

face [feɪs] n visage m, figure f; (expression) air m; (of clock) cadran m; (of cliff) paroi f; (of mountain) face f; (of building) façade f ▷ vt faire face à; (facts etc) accepter; **~ down** (person) à plat ventre; (card) face en dessous; **to lose/save ~** perdre/sauver la face; **to pull a ~** faire une grimace; **in the ~ of** (difficulties etc) face à, devant; **on the ~ of it** à première vue; **~ to ~** face à face; **face up to** vt fus faire face à, affronter; **face cloth** n (BRIT) gant m de toilette; **face pack** n (BRIT) masque m (de beauté)

facial [ˈfeɪʃl] adj facial(e) ▷ n soin complet du visage

facilitate [fəˈsɪlɪteɪt] vt faciliter

facilities [fəˈsɪlɪtɪz] *npl* installations *fpl*, équipement *m*; **credit ~** facilités de paiement

fact [fækt] *n* fait *m*; **in ~** en fait

faction [ˈfækʃən] *n* faction *f*

factor [ˈfæktər] *n* facteur *m*; (of sun cream) indice *m* (de protection); **I'd like a ~ 15 suntan lotion** je voudrais une crème solaire d'indice 15

factory [ˈfæktərɪ] *n* usine *f*, fabrique *f*

factual [ˈfæktjuəl] *adj* basé(e) sur les faits

faculty [ˈfækltɪ] *n* faculté *f*; (US: teaching staff) corps enseignant

fad [fæd] *n* (personal) manie *f*; (craze) engouement *m*

fade [feɪd] *vi* se décolorer, passer; (light, sound) s'affaiblir; (flower) se faner; **fade away** *vi* (sound) s'affaiblir

fag [fæg] *n* (BRIT inf: cigarette) clope *f*

Fahrenheit [ˈfɑːrənhaɪt] *n* Fahrenheit *m inv*

fail [feɪl] *vt* (exam) échouer à; (candidate) recaler; (subj: courage, memory) faire défaut à ▷ *vi* échouer; (eyesight, health, light: also: **be ~ing**) baisser, s'affaiblir; (brakes) lâcher; **to ~ to do sth** (neglect) négliger de or ne pas faire qch; (be unable) ne pas arriver or parvenir à faire qch; **without ~** à coup sûr; sans faute; **failing** *n* défaut *m* ▷ *prep* faute de; **failing that** à défaut, sinon; **failure** [ˈfeɪljər] *n* échec *m*; (person) raté(e); (mechanical etc) défaillance *f*

faint [feɪnt] *adj* faible; (recollection) vague; (mark) à peine visible ▷ *n* évanouissement *m* ▷ *vi* s'évanouir; **to feel ~** défaillir; **faintest** *adj*: **I haven't the faintest idea** je n'en ai pas la moindre idée; **faintly** *adv* faiblement; (vaguely) vaguement

fair [fɛər] *adj* équitable, juste; (hair) blond(e); (skin, complexion) pâle, blanc (blanche); (weather) beau (belle); (good enough) assez bon(ne); (sizeable) considérable ▷ *adv*: **to play ~** jouer franc jeu ▷ *n* foire *f*; (BRIT: funfair) fête

(foraine); **fairground** *n* champ *m* de foire; **fair-haired** *adj* (person) aux cheveux clairs, blond(e); **fairly** *adv* (justly) équitablement; (quite) assez; **fair trade** *n* commerce *m* équitable; **fairway** *n* (Golf) fairway *m*

fairy [ˈfɛərɪ] *n* fée *f*; **fairy tale** *n* conte *m* de fées

faith [feɪθ] *n* foi *f*; (trust) confiance *f*; (sect) culte *m*, religion *f*; **faithful** *adj* fidèle; **faithfully** *adv* fidèlement; **yours faithfully** (BRIT: in letters) veuillez agréer l'expression de mes salutations les plus distinguées

fake [feɪk] *n* (painting etc) faux *m*; (person) imposteur *m* ▷ *adj* faux (fausse) ▷ *vt* (emotions) simuler; (painting) faire un faux de

falcon [ˈfɔːlkən] *n* faucon *m*

fall [fɔːl] *n* chute *f*; (decrease) baisse *f*; (US: autumn) automne *m* ▷ *vi* (pt **fell**, pp **fallen**) tomber; (price, temperature, dollar) baisser; **falls** *npl* (waterfall) chute *f* d'eau, cascade *f*; **to ~ flat** *vi* (on one's face) tomber de tout son long, s'étaler; (joke) tomber à plat; (plan) échouer; **fall apart** *vi* (object) tomber en morceaux; **fall down** *vi* (person) tomber; (building) s'effondrer, s'écrouler; **fall for** *vt fus* (trick) se laisser prendre à; (person) tomber amoureux(-euse) de; **fall off** *vi* tomber; (diminish) baisser, diminuer; **fall out** *vi* (friends etc) se brouiller; (hair, teeth) tomber; **fall over** *vi* tomber (par terre); **fall through** *vi* (plan, project) tomber à l'eau

fallen [ˈfɔːlən] *pp of* **fall**

fallout [ˈfɔːlaut] *n* retombées (radioactives)

false [fɔːls] *adj* faux (fausse); **under ~ pretences** sous un faux prétexte; **false alarm** *n* fausse alerte; **false teeth** *npl* (BRIT) fausses dents, dentier *m*

fame [feɪm] *n* renommée *f*, renom *m*

familiar [fəˈmɪlɪər] *adj* familier(-ière); **to be ~ with sth** connaître qch;

familiarize [fə'mɪlɪəraɪz] vt: **to
familiarize o.s. with** se familiariser
avec
family ['fæmɪlɪ] n famille f; **family
doctor** n médecin m de famille;
family planning n planning familial
famine ['fæmɪn] n famine f
famous ['feɪməs] adj célèbre
fan [fæn] n (folding) éventail m;
(Elec) ventilateur m; (person) fan m,
admirateur(-trice); (Sport) supporter
m/f ▷ vt éventer; (fire, quarrel) attiser
fanatic [fə'nætɪk] n fanatique m/f
fan belt n courroie f de ventilateur
fan club n fan-club m
fancy ['fænsɪ] n (whim) fantaisie f,
envie f; (imagination) imagination
f ▷ adj (luxury) de luxe; (elaborate:
jewellery, packaging) fantaisie inv
▷ vt (feel like, want) avoir envie de;
(imagine) imaginer; **to take a ~ to** se
prendre d'affection pour; s'enticher
de; **he fancies her** elle lui plaît;
fancy dress n déguisement m,
travesti m
fan heater n (BRIT) radiateur
soufflant
fantasize ['fæntəsaɪz] vi fantasmer
fantastic [fæn'tæstɪk] adj
fantastique
fantasy ['fæntəsɪ] n imagination f,
fantaisie f; (unreality) fantasme m
fanzine ['fænzi:n] n fanzine m
FAQ n abbr (= frequently asked question)
FAQ f inv, faq f inv
far [fɑːʳ] adj (distant) lointain(e),
éloigné(e) ▷ adv loin; **the ~ side/
end** l'autre côté/bout; **it's not ~
(from here)** ce n'est pas loin (d'ici);
~ away, ~ off au loin, dans le lointain;
~ better beaucoup mieux; **~ from**
loin de; **by ~** de loin, de beaucoup;
go as ~ as the bridge allez jusqu'au
pont; **as ~ as I know** pour autant que
je sache; **how ~ is it to ...?** combien
y a-t-il jusqu'à ...?; **how ~ have you
got with your work?** où en êtes-
vous dans votre travail?

farce [fɑːs] n farce f
fare [fɛəʳ] n (on trains, buses) prix m du
billet; (in taxi) prix de la course; (food)
table f, chère f; **half ~** demi-tarif;
full ~ plein tarif
Far East n: **the ~** l'Extrême-Orient m
farewell [fɛə'wɛl] excl, n adieu m
farm [fɑːm] n ferme f ▷ vt cultiver;
farmer n fermier(-ière); **farmhouse**
n (maison f de) ferme f; **farming** n
agriculture f; (of animals) élevage m;
farmyard n cour f de ferme
far-reaching ['fɑː'riːtʃɪŋ] adj d'une
grande portée
fart [fɑːt] (inf!) vi péter
farther ['fɑːðəʳ] adv plus loin ▷ adj
plus éloigné(e), plus lointain(e)
farthest ['fɑːðɪst] superlative of **far**
fascinate ['fæsɪneɪt] vt fasciner,
captiver
fascinating ['fæsɪneɪtɪŋ] adj
fascinant(e)
fascination [fæsɪ'neɪʃən] n
fascination f
fascist ['fæʃɪst] adj, n fasciste m/f
fashion ['fæʃən] n mode f; (manner)
façon f, manière f ▷ vt façonner;
in ~ à la mode; **out of ~** démodé(e);
fashionable adj à la mode; **fashion
show** n défilé m de mannequins or
de mode
fast [fɑːst] adj rapide; (clock): **to be
~** avancer; (dye, colour) grand or bon
teint inv ▷ adv vite, rapidement;
(stuck, held) solidement ▷ n jeûne m
▷ vi jeûner; **~ asleep** profondément
endormi
fasten ['fɑːsn] vt attacher, fixer;
(coat) attacher, fermer ▷ vi se fermer,
s'attacher
fast food n fast food m, restauration
f rapide
fat [fæt] adj gros(se) ▷ n graisse f; (on
meat) gras m; (for cooking) matière
grasse
fatal ['feɪtl] adj (mistake) fatal(e);
(injury) mortel(le); **fatality** [fə'tælɪtɪ]
n (road death etc) victime f, décès m;

fatally adv fatalement; (injured) mortellement

fate [feɪt] n destin m; (of person) sort m

father ['fɑːðəʳ] n père m; **Father Christmas** n le Père Noël; **father-in-law** n beau-père m

fatigue [fə'tiːg] n fatigue f

fattening ['fætnɪŋ] adj (food) qui fait grossir

fatty ['fætɪ] adj (food) gras(se) ▷ n (inf) gros (grosse)

faucet ['fɔːsɪt] n (US) robinet m

fault [fɔːlt] n faute f; (defect) défaut m; (Geo) faille f ▷ vt trouver des défauts à, prendre en défaut; **it's my ~** c'est de ma faute; **to find ~ with** trouver à redire or à critiquer à; **at ~** fautif(-ive), coupable; **faulty** adj défectueux(-euse)

fauna ['fɔːnə] n faune f

favour, (US) **favor** ['feɪvəʳ] n faveur f; (help) service m ▷ vt (proposition) être en faveur de; (pupil etc) favoriser; (team, horse) donner gagnant; **to do sb a ~** rendre un service à qn; **in ~ of** en faveur de; **to find ~ with sb** trouver grâce aux yeux de qn; **favourable**, (US) **favorable** adj favorable; **favourite**, (US) **favorite** ['feɪvrɪt] adj, n favori(te)

fawn [fɔːn] n (deer) faon m ▷ adj (also: **~-coloured**) fauve ▷ vi: **to ~ (up)on** flatter servilement

fax [fæks] n (document) télécopie f; (machine) télécopieur m ▷ vt envoyer par télécopie

FBI n abbr (US: = Federal Bureau of Investigation) FBI m

fear [fɪəʳ] n crainte f, peur f ▷ vt craindre; **for ~ of** de peur que + sub or de + infinitive; **fearful** adj craintif(-ive); (sight, noise) affreux(-euse), épouvantable; **fearless** adj intrépide

feasible ['fiːzəbl] adj faisable, réalisable

feast [fiːst] n festin m, banquet m; (Rel: also: **~ day**) fête f ▷ vi festoyer

feat [fiːt] n exploit m, prouesse f

feather ['fɛðəʳ] n plume f

feature ['fiːtʃəʳ] n caractéristique f; (article) chronique f, rubrique f ▷ vt (film) avoir pour vedette(s) ▷ vi figurer (en bonne place); **features** npl (of face) traits mpl; **a (special) ~ on sth/sb** un reportage sur qch/qn; **feature film** n long métrage

Feb. abbr (= February) fév

February ['fɛbruərɪ] n février m

fed [fɛd] pt, pp of **feed**

federal ['fɛdərəl] adj fédéral(e)

federation [fɛdə'reɪʃən] n fédération f

fed up adj: **to be ~ (with)** en avoir marre or plein le dos (de)

fee [fiː] n rémunération f; (of doctor, lawyer) honoraires mpl; (of school, college etc) frais mpl de scolarité; (for examination) droits mpl

feeble ['fiːbl] adj faible; (attempt, excuse) pauvre; (joke) piteux(-euse)

feed [fiːd] n (of animal) nourriture f, pâture f; (on printer) mécanisme m d'alimentation ▷ vt (pt, pp **fed**) (person) nourrir; (BRIT: baby: breastfeed) allaiter; (: with bottle) donner le biberon à; (horse etc) donner à manger à; (machine) alimenter; (data etc): **to ~ sth into** enregistrer qch dans; **feedback** n (Elec) effet m Larsen; (from person) réactions fpl

feel [fiːl] n (sensation) sensation f; (impression) impression f ▷ vt (pt, pp **felt**) (touch) toucher; (explore) tâter, palper; (cold, pain) sentir; (grief, anger) ressentir, éprouver; (think, believe): **to ~ (that)** trouver que; **to ~ hungry/cold** avoir faim/froid; **to ~ lonely/better** se sentir seul/mieux; **I don't ~ well** je ne me sens pas bien; **it ~s soft** c'est doux au toucher; **to ~ like** (want) avoir envie de; **feeling** n (physical) sensation f; (emotion, impression) sentiment m; **to hurt sb's feelings** froisser qn

feet [fiːt] npl of **foot**

fell [fɛl] pt of **fall** ▷ vt (tree) abattre

fellow ['fɛləu] n type m; (comrade)
compagnon m; (of learned
society) membre m ▷ cpd: **their
~ prisoners/students** leurs
camarades prisonniers/étudiants;
fellow citizen n concitoyen(ne);
fellow countryman (irreg) n
compatriote m; **fellow men** npl
semblables mpl; **fellowship** n
(society) association f; (comradeship)
amitié f, camaraderie f; (Scol) sorte de
bourse universitaire

felony ['fɛlənɪ] n crime m, forfait m

felt [fɛlt] pt, pp of **feel** ▷ n feutre m;
felt-tip n (also: **felt-tip pen**) stylo-
feutre m

female ['fi:meɪl] n (Zool) femelle f;
(pej: woman) bonne femme ▷ adj (Biol)
femelle; (sex, character) féminin(e);
(vote etc) des femmes

feminine ['fɛmɪnɪn] adj féminin(e)

feminist ['fɛmɪnɪst] n féministe m/f

fence [fɛns] n barrière f ▷ vi faire de
l'escrime; **fencing** n (sport) escrime m

fend [fɛnd] vi: **to ~ for o.s.** se
débrouiller (tout seul); **fend off** vt
(attack etc) parer; (questions) éluder

fender ['fɛndə^r] n garde-feu m inv; (on
boat) défense f; (us: of car) aile f

fennel ['fɛnl] n fenouil m

ferment vi [fə'mɛnt] fermenter
▷ n ['fə:mɛnt] (fig) agitation f,
effervescence f

fern [fə:n] n fougère f

ferocious [fə'rəuʃəs] adj féroce

ferret ['fɛrɪt] n furet m

ferry ['fɛrɪ] n (small) bac m; (large:
also: **~boat**) ferry(-boat) m) m ▷ vt
transporter

fertile ['fə:taɪl] adj fertile; (Biol)
fécond(e); **fertilize** ['fə:tɪlaɪz] vt
fertiliser; (Biol) féconder; **fertilizer**
n engrais m

festival ['fɛstɪvəl] n (Rel) fête f; (Art,
Mus) festival m

festive ['fɛstɪv] adj de fête; **the
~ season** (BRIT: Christmas) la période
des fêtes

fetch [fɛtʃ] vt aller chercher; (BRIT: sell
for) rapporter

fête [feɪt] n fête f, kermesse f

fetus ['fi:təs] n (US) = **foetus**

feud [fju:d] n querelle f, dispute f

fever ['fi:və^r] n fièvre f; **feverish** adj
fiévreux(-euse), fébrile

few [fju:] adj (not many) peu de ▷ pron
peu; **a ~** (as adj) quelques; (as pron)
quelques-uns(-unes); **quite a ~ ...**
adj un certain nombre de ..., pas mal
de ...; **in the past ~ days** ces derniers
jours; **fewer** adj moins de; **fewest** adj
le moins nombreux

fiancé [fɪ'ɑ̃:ŋseɪ] n fiancé m; **fiancée**
n fiancée f

fiasco [fɪ'æskəu] n fiasco m

fib [fɪb] n bobard m

fibre, (US) **fiber** ['faɪbə^r] n fibre f;
fibreglass, (US) **Fiberglass®** n fibre
f de verre

fickle ['fɪkl] adj inconstant(e), volage,
capricieux(-euse)

fiction ['fɪkʃən] n romans mpl,
littérature f romanesque; (invention)
fiction f; **fictional** adj fictif(-ive)

fiddle ['fɪdl] n (Mus) violon m;
(cheating) combine f; escroquerie
f ▷ vt (BRIT: accounts) falsifier,
maquiller; **fiddle with** vt fus tripoter

fidelity [fɪ'dɛlɪtɪ] n fidélité f

fidget ['fɪdʒɪt] vi se trémousser,
remuer

field [fi:ld] n champ m; (fig) domaine
m, champ; (Sport: ground) terrain m;
field marshal n maréchal m

fierce [fɪəs] adj (look, animal) féroce,
sauvage; (wind, attack, person)
(très) violent(e); (fighting, enemy)
acharné(e)

fifteen [fɪf'ti:n] num quinze;
fifteenth num quinzième

fifth [fɪfθ] num cinquième

fiftieth ['fɪftɪɪθ] num cinquantième

fifty ['fɪftɪ] num cinquante; **fifty-fifty**
adv moitié-moitié ▷ adj: **to have a
fifty-fifty chance (of success)** avoir
une chance sur deux (de réussir)

fig | 400

fig [fɪg] *n* figue *f*

fight [faɪt] (*pt, pp* **fought**) *n* (*between persons*) bagarre *f*; (*argument*) dispute *f*; (*Mil*) combat *m*; (*against cancer etc*) lutte *f* ▷ *vt* se battre contre; (*cancer, alcoholism, emotion*) combattre, lutter contre; (*election*) se présenter à ▷ *vi* se battre; (*argue*) se disputer; (*fig*): **to ~ (for/against)** lutter (pour/contre); **fight back** *vi* rendre les coups; (*after illness*) reprendre le dessus ▷ *vt* (*tears*) réprimer; **fight off** *vt* repousser; (*disease, sleep, urge*) lutter contre; **fighting** *n* combats *mpl*; (*brawls*) bagarres *fpl*

figure ['fɪgə'] *n* (*Drawing, Geom*) figure *f*; (*number*) chiffre *m*; (*body, outline*) silhouette *f*; (*person's shape*) ligne *f*, formes *fpl*; (*person*) personnage *m* ▷ *vt* (*us: think*) supposer ▷ *vi* (*appear*) figurer; (*us: make sense*) s'expliquer; **figure out** *vt* (*understand*) arriver à comprendre; (*plan*) calculer

file [faɪl] *n* (*tool*) lime *f*; (*dossier*) dossier *m*; (*folder*) dossier, chemise *f* (: *binder*) classeur *m*; (*Comput*) fichier *m*; (*row*) file *f* ▷ *vt* (*nails, wood*) limer; (*papers*) classer; (*Law: claim*) faire enregistrer; déposer; **filing cabinet** *n* classeur *m* (*meuble*)

Filipino [fɪlɪ'piːnəu] *adj* philippin(e) ▷ *n* (*person*) Philippin(e)

fill [fɪl] *vt* remplir; (*vacancy*) pourvoir à » **to eat one's ~** manger à sa faim; **to ~ with** remplir de; **fill in** *vt* (*hole*) boucher; (*form*) remplir; **fill out** *vt* (*form, receipt*) remplir; **fill up** *vt* remplir ▷ *vi* (*Aut*) faire le plein

fillet ['fɪlɪt] *n* filet *m*; **fillet steak** *n* filet *m* de bœuf, tournedos *m*

filling ['fɪlɪŋ] *n* (*Culin*) garniture *f*, farce *f*; (*for tooth*) plombage *m*; **filling station** *n* station-service *f*, station *f* d'essence

film [fɪlm] *n* film *m*; (*Phot*) pellicule *f*, film; (*of powder, liquid*) couche *f*, pellicule ▷ *vt* (*scene*) filmer ▷ *vi* tourner; **I'd like a 36-exposure ~** je voudrais une pellicule de 36 poses; **film star** *n* vedette *f* de cinéma

filter ['fɪltə'] *n* filtre *m* ▷ *vt* filtrer; **filter lane** *n* (BRIT Aut: *at traffic lights*) voie *f* de dégagement; (: *on motorway*) voie *f* de sortie

filth [fɪlθ] *n* saleté *f*; **filthy** *adj* sale, dégoûtant(e); (*language*) ordurier(-ière), grossier(-ière)

fin [fɪn] *n* (*of fish*) nageoire *f*; (*of shark*) aileron *m*; (*of diver*) palme *f*

final ['faɪnl] *adj* final(e), dernier(-ière); (*decision, answer*) définitif(-ive) ▷ *n* (BRIT Sport) finale *f*; **finals** *npl* (US) (*Scol*) examens *mpl* de dernière année; (*Sport*) finale *f*; **finale** [fɪ'nɑːlɪ] *n* finale *m*; **finalist** *n* (*Sport*) finaliste *m/f*; **finalize** *vt* mettre au point; **finally** *adv* (*eventually*) enfin, finalement; (*lastly*) en dernier lieu

finance [faɪ'næns] *n* finance *f* ▷ *vt* financer; **finances** *npl* finances *fpl*; **financial** [faɪ'nænʃəl] *adj* financier(-ière); **financial year** *n* année *f* budgétaire

find [faɪnd] *vt* (*pt, pp* **found**) trouver; (*lost object*) retrouver ▷ *n* trouvaille *f*, découverte *f*; **to ~ sb guilty** (Law) déclarer qn coupable; **find out** *vt* se renseigner sur; (*truth, secret*) découvrir; (*person*) démasquer ▷ *vi*: **to ~ out about** (*make enquiries*) se renseigner sur; (*by chance*) apprendre; **findings** *npl* (Law) conclusions *fpl*, verdict *m*; (*of report*) constatations *fpl*

fine [faɪn] *adj* (*weather*) beau (belle); (*excellent*) excellent(e); (*thin, subtle, not coarse*) fin(e); (*acceptable*) bien *inv* ▷ *adv* (*well*) très bien; (*small*) fin, finement ▷ *n* (Law) amende *f*; contravention *f* ▷ *vt* (Law) condamner à une amende; donner une contravention à; **he's ~** il va bien; **the weather is ~** il fait beau; **fine arts** *npl* beaux-arts *mpl*

finger ['fɪŋgə'] *n* doigt *m* ▷ *vt* palper, toucher; **index ~** index *m*; **fingernail** *n* ongle *m* (de la main); **fingerprint** *n* empreinte digitale; **fingertip** n bout m du doigt

finish ['fɪnɪʃ] n fin f; (Sport) arrivée f; (polish etc) finition f ▷ vt finir, terminer ▷ vi finir, se terminer; **to ~ doing sth** finir de faire qch; **to ~ third** arriver or terminer troisième; **when does the show ~?** quand est-ce que le spectacle se termine?; **finish off** vt finir, terminer; (kill) achever; **finish up** vi, vt finir

Finland ['fɪnlənd] n Finlande f; **Finn** n Finnois(e), Finlandais(e); **Finnish** adj finnois(e), finlandais(e) ▷ n (Ling) finnois m

fir [fəːʳ] n sapin m

fire ['faɪəʳ] n feu m; (accidental) incendie m; (heater) radiateur m ▷ vt (discharge): **to ~ a gun** tirer un coup de feu; (fig: interest) enflammer, animer; (inf: dismiss) mettre à la porte, renvoyer ▷ vi (shoot) tirer, faire feu; **~!** au feu!; **on ~** en feu; **to set ~ to sth, set sth on ~** mettre le feu à qch; **fire alarm** n avertisseur m d'incendie; **firearm** n arme f à feu; **fire brigade** n (régiment m de sapeurs-)pompiers mpl; **fire engine** n (BRIT) pompe f à incendie; **fire escape** n escalier m de secours; **fire exit** n issue f or sortie f de secours; **fire extinguisher** n extincteur m; **fireman** (irreg) n pompier m; **fireplace** n cheminée f; **fire station** n caserne f de pompiers; **fire truck** n (US) = **fire engine**; **firewall** n (Internet) pare-feu m; **firewood** n bois m de chauffage; **fireworks** npl (display) feu(x) m(pl) d'artifice

firm [fəːm] adj ferme ▷ n compagnie f, firme f; **firmly** adv fermement

first [fəːst] adj premier(-ière) ▷ adv (before other people) le premier, la première; (before other things) en premier, d'abord; (when listing reasons etc) en premier lieu, premièrement; (in the beginning) au début ▷ n (person: in race)

premier(-ière); (BRIT Scol) mention f très bien; (Aut) première f; **the ~ of January** le premier janvier; **at ~** au commencement, au début; **~ of all** tout d'abord, pour commencer; **first aid** n premiers secours or soins; **first-aid kit** n trousse f à pharmacie; **first-class** adj (ticket etc) de première classe; (excellent) excellent(e), exceptionnel(le); (post) en tarif prioritaire; **first-hand** adj de première main; **first lady** n (US) femme f du président; **firstly** adv premièrement, en premier lieu; **first name** n prénom m; **first-rate** adj excellent(e)

fiscal ['fɪskl] adj fiscal(e); **fiscal year** n exercice financier

fish [fɪʃ] n (pl inv) poisson m ▷ vt, vi pêcher; **~ and chips** poisson frit et frites; **fisherman** (irreg) n pêcheur m; **fish fingers** npl (BRIT) bâtonnets mpl de poisson (congelés); **fishing** n pêche f; **to go fishing** aller à la pêche; **fishing boat** n barque f de pêche; **fishing line** n ligne f (de pêche); **fishmonger** n (BRIT) marchand m de poisson; **fishmonger's (shop)** n (BRIT) poissonnerie f; **fish sticks** npl (US) = **fish fingers**; **fishy** adj (inf) suspect(e), louche

fist [fɪst] n poing m

fit [fɪt] adj (Med, Sport) en (bonne) forme; (proper) convenable; approprié(e) ▷ vt (subj: clothes) aller à; (put in, attach) installer, poser; (equip) équiper, garnir, munir; (suit) convenir à ▷ vi (clothes) aller; (parts) s'adapter; (in space, gap) entrer, s'adapter ▷ n (Med) accès m, crise f; (of anger) accès; (of hysterics, jealousy) crise; **~ to** (ready to) en état de; **~ for** (worthy) digne de; (capable) apte à; **to keep ~** se maintenir en forme; **this dress is a tight/good ~** cette robe est un peu juste/(me) va très bien; **a ~ of coughing** une quinte de toux; **by ~s and starts** par à-coups;

fit in vi (add up) cadrer; (integrate) s'intégrer; (to new situation) s'adapter; **fitness** n (Med) forme f physique; **fitted** adj (jacket, shirt) ajusté(e); **fitted carpet** n moquette f; **fitted kitchen** n (BRIT) cuisine équipée; **fitted sheet** n drap-housse m; **fitting** adj approprié(e) ▷ n (of dress) essayage m; (of piece of equipment) pose f, installation f; **fitting room** n (in shop) cabine f d'essayage; **fittings** npl installations fpl

five [faɪv] num cinq; **fiver** n (inf: US) billet de cinq dollars; (: BRIT) billet m de cinq livres

fix [fɪks] vt (date, amount etc) fixer; (sort out) arranger; (mend) réparer; (make ready: meal, drink) préparer ▷ n: **to be in a ~** être dans le pétrin; **fix up** vt (meeting) arranger; **to ~ sb up with sth** faire avoir qch à qn; **fixed** adj (prices etc) fixe; **fixture** n installation f (fixe); (Sport) rencontre f (au programme)

fizzy ['fɪzɪ] adj pétillant(e), gazeux(-euse)

flag [flæg] n drapeau m; (also: **~stone**) dalle f ▷ vi faiblir; fléchir; **flag down** vt héler, faire signe (de s'arrêter) à; **flagpole** n mât m

flair [fleəʳ] n flair m

flak [flæk] n (Mil) tir antiaérien; (inf: criticism) critiques fpl

flake [fleɪk] n (of rust, paint) écaille f; (of snow, soap powder) flocon m ▷ vi (also: **~ off**) s'écailler

flamboyant [flæm'bɔɪənt] adj flamboyant(e), éclatant(e); (person) haut(e) en couleur

flame [fleɪm] n flamme f

flamingo [flə'mɪŋgəu] n flamant m (rose)

flammable ['flæməbl] adj inflammable

flan [flæn] n (BRIT) tarte f

flank [flæŋk] n flanc m ▷ vt flanquer

flannel ['flænl] n (BRIT: also: **face ~**) gant m de toilette; (fabric) flanelle f

flap [flæp] n (of pocket, envelope) rabat m ▷ vt (wings) battre (de) ▷ vi (sail, flag) claquer

flare [fleəʳ] n (signal) signal lumineux; (Mil) fusée éclairante; (in skirt etc) évasement m; **flares** npl (trousers) pantalon m à pattes d'éléphant; **flare up** vi s'embraser; (fig: person) se mettre en colère, s'emporter; (: revolt) éclater

flash [flæʃ] n éclair m; (also: **news ~**) flash m (d'information); (Phot) flash m ▷ vt (switch on) allumer (brièvement); (direct): **to ~ sth at** braquer qch sur; (send: message) câbler; (smile) lancer ▷ vi briller; jeter des éclairs; (light on ambulance etc) clignoter; **a ~ of lightning** un éclair; **in a ~** en un clin d'œil; **to ~ one's headlights** faire un appel de phares; **he ~ed by** or **past** il passa (devant nous) comme un éclair; **flashback** n flashback m, retour m en arrière; **flashbulb** n ampoule f de flash; **flashlight** n lampe f de poche

flask [flɑːsk] n flacon m, bouteille f; (also: **vacuum ~**) bouteille f thermos®

flat [flæt] adj plat(e); (tyre) dégonflé(e), à plat; (beer) éventé(e); (battery) à plat; (denial) catégorique; (Mus) bémol inv (: voice) faux (fausse) ▷ n (BRIT: apartment) appartement m; (Aut) crevaison f, pneu crevé; (Mus) bémol m; **~ out** (work) sans relâche; (race) à fond; **flatten** vt (also: **flatten out**) aplatir; (crop) coucher; (house, city) raser

flatter ['flætəʳ] vt flatter; **flattering** adj flatteur(-euse); (clothes) seyant(e)

flaunt [flɔːnt] vt faire étalage de

flavour, (US) **flavor** ['fleɪvəʳ] n goût m, saveur f; (of ice cream etc) parfum m ▷ vt parfumer, aromatiser; **vanilla-~ed** à l'arôme de vanille, vanillé(e); **what ~s do you have?** quels parfums avez-vous?; **flavouring**, (US) **flavoring** n arôme m (synthétique)

flaw [flɔ:] n défaut m; **flawless** adj sans défaut

flea [fli:] n puce f; **flea market** n marché m aux puces

fled [flɛd] pt, pp of **flee**

flee (pt, pp **fled**) [fli:, flɛd] vt fuir, s'enfuir de ▷ vi fuir, s'enfuir

fleece [fli:s] n (of sheep) toison f; (top) (laine f) polaire f ▷ vt (inf) voler, filouter

fleet [fli:t] n flotte f; (of lorries, cars etc) parc m; convoi m

fleeting ['fli:tɪŋ] adj fugace, fugitif(-ive); (visit) très bref (brève)

Flemish ['flɛmɪʃ] adj flamand(e) ▷ n (Ling) flamand m; **the ~** npl les Flamands

flesh [flɛʃ] n chair f

flew [flu:] pt of **fly**

flex [flɛks] n fil m or câble m électrique (souple) ▷ vt (knee) fléchir; (muscles) bander; **flexibility** n flexibilité f; **flexible** adj flexible; (person, schedule) souple; **flexitime**, (us) **flextime** n horaire m variable or à la carte

flick [flɪk] n petit coup; (with finger) chiquenaude f ▷ vt donner un petit coup à; (switch) appuyer sur; **flick through** vt fus feuilleter

flicker ['flɪkər] vi (light, flame) vaciller

flies [flaɪz] npl of **fly**

flight [flaɪt] n vol m; (escape) fuite f; (also: ~ **of steps**) escalier m; **flight attendant** n steward m, hôtesse f de l'air

flimsy ['flɪmzɪ] adj peu solide; (clothes) trop léger(-ère); (excuse) pauvre, mince

flinch [flɪntʃ] vi tressaillir; **to ~ from** se dérober à, reculer devant

fling [flɪŋ] vt (pt, pp **flung**) jeter, lancer

flint [flɪnt] n silex m; (in lighter) pierre f (à briquet)

flip [flɪp] vt (throw) donner une chiquenaude à; (switch) appuyer sur; (us: pancake) faire sauter; **to ~ sth over** retourner qch

flip-flops ['flɪpflɔps] npl (esp BRIT) tongs fpl

flipper ['flɪpər] n (of animal) nageoire f; (for swimmer) palme f

flirt [flə:t] vi flirter ▷ n flirteur(-euse)

float [fləut] n flotteur m; (in procession) char m; (sum of money) réserve f ▷ vi flotter

flock [flɔk] n (of sheep) troupeau m; (of birds) vol m; (of people) foule f

flood [flʌd] n inondation f; (of letters, refugees etc) flot m ▷ vt inonder ▷ vi (place) être inondé; (people): **to ~ into** envahir; **flooding** n inondation f; **floodlight** n projecteur m

floor [flɔ:r] n sol m; (storey) étage m; (of sea, valley) fond m ▷ vt (knock down) terrasser; (baffle) désorienter; **ground ~**, (us) **first ~** rez-de-chaussée m; **first ~**, (us) **second ~** premier étage; **what ~ is it on?** c'est à quel étage?; **floorboard** n planche f (du plancher); **flooring** n sol m; (wooden) plancher m; (covering) revêtement m de sol; **floor show** n spectacle m de variétés

flop [flɔp] n fiasco m ▷ vi (fail) faire fiasco; (fall) s'affaler, s'effondrer; **floppy** adj lâche, flottant(e) ▷ n (Comput: also: **floppy disk**) disquette f

flora ['flɔːrə] n flore f

floral ['flɔːrl] adj floral(e); (dress) à fleurs

florist ['flɔrɪst] n fleuriste m/f; **florist's (shop)** n magasin m or boutique f de fleuriste

flotation [fləu'teɪʃən] n (of shares) émission f; (of company) lancement m (en Bourse)

flour ['flauər] n farine f

flourish ['flʌrɪʃ] vi prospérer ▷ n (gesture) moulinet m

flow [fləu] n (of water, traffic etc) écoulement m; (tide, influx) flux m; (of blood, Elec) circulation f; (of river) courant m ▷ vi couler; (traffic) s'écouler; (robes, hair) flotter

flower ['flaʊə'] n fleur f ▷ vi fleurir;
flower bed n plate-bande f;
flowerpot n pot m (à fleurs)
flown [fləʊn] pp of **fly**
fl. oz. abbr = **fluid ounce**
flu [fluː] n grippe f
fluctuate ['flʌktjʊeɪt] vi varier,
fluctuer
fluent ['fluːənt] adj (speech, style)
coulant(e), aisé(e); **he speaks ~
French, he's ~ in French** il parle le
français couramment
fluff [flʌf] n duvet m; (on jacket, carpet)
peluche f; **fluffy** adj duveteux(-euse);
(toy) en peluche
fluid ['fluːɪd] n fluide m; (in diet)
liquide m ▷ adj fluide; **fluid ounce** n
(BRIT) = 0.028 l; 0.05 pints
fluke [fluːk] n coup m de veine
flung [flʌŋ] pt, pp of **fling**
fluorescent [fluə'rɛsnt] adj
fluorescent(e)
fluoride ['fluəraɪd] n fluor m
flurry ['flʌrɪ] n (of snow) rafale f,
bourrasque f; **a ~ of activity** un
affairement soudain
flush [flʌʃ] n (on face) rougeur f; (fig:
of youth etc) éclat m ▷ vt nettoyer à
grande eau ▷ vi rougir ▷ adj (level):
~ with au ras de, de niveau avec; **to ~
the toilet** tirer la chasse (d'eau)
flute [fluːt] n flûte f
flutter ['flʌtə'] n (of panic, excitement)
agitation f; (of wings) battement m
▷ vi (bird) battre des ailes, voleter
fly [flaɪ] (pt **flew**, pp **flown**) n (insect)
mouche f; (on trousers: also: **flies**)
braguette f ▷ vt (plane) piloter;
(passengers, cargo) transporter (par
avion); (distance) parcourir ▷ vi voler;
(passengers) aller en avion; (escape)
s'enfuir, fuir; (flag) se déployer; **fly
away, fly off** vi s'envoler; **fly-drive**
n formule f avion plus voiture; **flying**
n (activity) aviation f; (action) vol
m ▷ adj: **flying visit** visite f éclair
inv; **with flying colours** haut la
main; **flying saucer** n soucoupe

volante; **flyover** n (BRIT: overpass)
pont routier
FM abbr (Radio: = frequency modulation)
FM
foal [fəʊl] n poulain m
foam [fəʊm] n écume f; (on beer)
mousse f; (also: **~ rubber**) caoutchouc
m mousse ▷ vi (liquid) écumer; (soapy
water) mousser
focus ['fəʊkəs] n (pl **focuses**) foyer
m; (of interest) centre m ▷ vt (field
glasses etc) mettre au point ▷ vi: **to
~ (on)** (with camera) régler la mise au
point (sur); (with eyes) fixer son regard
(sur); (fig: concentrate) se concentrer
(sur); **out of/in ~** (picture) flou(e)/
net(te); (camera) pas au point/
au point
foetus, (US) **fetus** ['fiːtəs] n fœtus m
fog [fɔg] n brouillard m; **foggy** adj:
it's foggy il y a du brouillard; **fog
lamp**, (US) **fog light** n (Aut) phare m
anti-brouillard
foil [fɔɪl] vt déjouer, contrecarrer ▷ n
feuille f de métal; (kitchen foil) papier
m d'alu(minium); **to act as a ~ to**
(fig) servir de repoussoir à
fold [fəʊld] n (bend, crease) pli m; (Agr)
parc m à moutons; (fig) bercail m ▷ vt
plier; **to ~ one's arms** croiser les
bras; **fold up** vi (map etc) se plier, se
replier; (business) fermer boutique
▷ vt (map etc) plier, replier; **folder** n
(for papers) chemise f (: binder) classeur
m; (Comput) dossier m; **folding** adj
(chair, bed) pliant(e)
foliage ['fəʊlɪɪdʒ] n feuillage m
folk [fəʊk] npl gens mpl ▷ cpd
folklorique; **folks** npl (inf: parents)
famille f, parents mpl; **folklore**
['fəʊklɔː'] n folklore m; **folk music** n
musique f folklorique; (contemporary)
musique folk, folk m; **folk song** n
chanson f folklorique; (contemporary)
chanson folk inv
follow ['fɔləʊ] vt suivre; (on Twitter)
s'abonner aux tweets de ▷ vi suivre;
(result) s'ensuivre; **to ~ suit** (fig) faire

de même; **follow up** vt (letter, offer) donner suite à; (case) suivre; **follower** n disciple m/f, partisan(e); **following** adj suivant(e) ▷ n partisans mpl, disciples mpl; **follow-up** n suite f; (on file, case) suivi m

fond [fɔnd] adj (memory, look) tendre, affectueux(-euse); (hopes, dreams) un peu fou (folle); **to be ~ of** aimer beaucoup

food [fuːd] n nourriture f; **food mixer** n mixeur m; **food poisoning** n intoxication f alimentaire; **food processor** n robot m de cuisine; **food stamp** n (us) bon m de nourriture (pour indigents)

fool [fuːl] n idiot(e); (Culin) mousse f de fruits ▷ vt berner, duper; **fool about, fool around** vi (pej: waste time) traînailler, glandouiller; (: behave foolishly) faire l'idiot or l'imbécile; **foolish** adj idiot(e), stupide; (rash) imprudent(e); **foolproof** adj (plan etc) infaillible

foot (pl **feet**) [fut, fiːt] n pied m; (of animal) patte f; (measure) pied (= 30.48 cm; 12 inches) ▷ vt (bill) payer; **on ~** à pied; **footage** n (Cine: length) ≈ métrage m; (: material) séquences fpl; **foot-and-mouth (disease)** [futənd'mauθ-] n fièvre aphteuse; **football** n (ball) ballon m (de football); (sport: BRIT) football m; (: US) football américain; **footballer** n (BRIT) = **football player**, **football match** n (BRIT) match m de foot(ball); **football player** n footballeur(-euse), joueur(-euse) de football; (US) joueur(-euse) de football américain; **footbridge** n passerelle f; **foothills** npl contreforts mpl; **foothold** n prise f (de pied); **footing** n (fig) position f; **to lose one's footing** perdre pied; **footnote** n note f (en bas de page); **footpath** n sentier m; **footprint** n trace f (de pied); **footstep** n pas m; **footwear** n chaussures fpl

for [fɔːʳ] prep **1** (indicating destination, intention, purpose) pour; **the train for London** le train pour (or à destination de) Londres; **he left for Rome** il est parti pour Rome; **he went for the paper** il est allé chercher le journal; **is this for me?** c'est pour moi?; **it's time for lunch** c'est l'heure du déjeuner; **what's it for?** ça sert à quoi?; **what for?** (why?) pourquoi?; (to what end?) pour quoi faire?, à quoi bon?; **for sale** à vendre; **to pray for peace** prier pour la paix

2 (on behalf of, representing) pour; **the MP for Hove** le député de Hove; **to work for sb/sth** travailler pour qn/ qch; **I'll ask him for you** je vais lui demander pour toi; **G for George** G comme Georges

3 (because of) pour; **for this reason** pour cette raison; **for fear of being criticized** de peur d'être critiqué

4 (with regard to) pour; **it's cold for July** il fait froid pour juillet; **a gift for languages** un don pour les langues

5 (in exchange for): **I sold it for £5** je l'ai vendu 5 livres; **to pay 50 pence for a ticket** payer un billet 50 pence

6 (in favour of) pour; **are you for or against us?** êtes-vous pour ou contre nous?; **I'm all for it** je suis tout à fait pour; **vote for X** votez pour X

7 (referring to distance) pendant, sur; **there are roadworks for 5 km** il y a des travaux sur or pendant 5 km; **we walked for miles** nous avons marché pendant des kilomètres

8 (referring to time) pendant; depuis; pour; **he was away for 2 years** il a été absent pendant 2 ans; **she will be away for a month** elle sera absente (pendant) un mois; **it hasn't rained for 3 weeks** ça fait 3 semaines qu'il ne pleut pas, il ne pleut pas depuis 3 semaines; **I have known her for years** je la connais

depuis des années; **can you do it for
tomorrow?** est-ce que tu peux le faire
pour demain?
9 (*with infinitive clauses*): **it is not for
me to decide** ce n'est pas à moi de
décider; **it would be best for you
to leave** le mieux serait que vous
partiez; **there is still time for you
to do it** vous avez encore le temps
de le faire; **for this to be possible ...**
pour que cela soit possible ..
10 (*in spite of*): **for all that** malgré
cela, néanmoins; **for all his work/
efforts** malgré tout son travail/tous
ses efforts; **for all his complaints,
he's very fond of her** il a beau se
plaindre, il l'aime beaucoup
▶ *conj* (*since, as: formal*) car

forbid (*pt* **forbad** *or* **forbade**, *pp*
forbidden) [fə'bɪd, -'bæd, -'bɪdn]
vt défendre, interdire; **to ~ sb to do**
défendre *or* interdire à qn de faire;
forbidden *adj* défendu(e)
force [fɔːs] *n* force *f* ▶ *vt* forcer; (*push*)
pousser (de force); **to ~ o.s. to do** se
forcer à faire; **in ~** (*rule, law, prices*) en
vigueur; (*in large numbers*) en force;
forced *adj* forcé(e); **forceful** *adj*
énergique
ford [fɔːd] *n* gué *m*
fore [fɔːʳ] *n*: **to the ~** en évidence;
forearm *n* avant-bras *m inv*;
forecast *n* prévision *f*; (*also:*
weather forecast) prévisions *fpl*
météorologiques, météo *f* ▶ *vt*
(*irreg: like* **cast**) prévoir; **forecourt**
n (*of garage*) devant *m*; **forefinger**
n index *m*; **forefront** *n*: **in the
forefront of** au premier rang *or* plan
de; **foreground** *n* premier plan;
forehead ['fɒrɪd] *n* front *m*
foreign ['fɒrɪn] *adj* étranger(-
ère); (*trade*) extérieur(e); (*travel*)
à l'étranger; **foreign currency** *n*
devises étrangères; **foreigner** *n*
étranger(-ère); **foreign exchange** *n*
(*system*) change *m*; (*money*) devises

fpl; **Foreign Office** *n* (BRIT) ministère
m des Affaires étrangères; **Foreign
Secretary** *n* (BRIT) ministre *m* des
Affaires étrangères
fore: foreman (*irreg*) *n* (*in construction*)
contremaître *m*; **foremost** *adj* le (la)
plus en vue, premier(-ière) ▷ *adv*:
first and foremost avant tout, tout
d'abord; **forename** *n* prénom *m*
forensic [fə'rɛnsɪk] *adj*: **~ medicine**
médecine légale
foresee (*pt* **foresaw**, *pp* **foreseen**)
[fɔː'siː, -'sɔː, -'siːn] *vt* prévoir;
foreseeable *adj* prévisible
foreseen [fɔː'siːn] *pp of* **foresee**
forest ['fɒrɪst] *n* forêt *f*; **forestry** *n*
sylviculture *f*
forever [fə'rɛvəʳ] *adv* pour toujours;
(*fig: endlessly*) continuellement
foreword ['fɔːwəːd] *n* avant-propos
m inv
forfeit ['fɔːfɪt] *vt* perdre
forgave [fə'geɪv] *pt of* **forgive**
forge [fɔːdʒ] *n* forge *f* ▶ *vt* (*signature*)
contrefaire; (*wrought iron*) forger; **to
~ money** (BRIT) fabriquer de la fausse
monnaie; **forger** *n* faussaire *m*;
forgery *n* faux *m*, contrefaçon *f*
forget (*pt* **forgot**, *pp* **forgotten**)
[fə'gɛt, -'gɔt, -'gɔtn] *vt*, *vi* oublier;
I've forgotten my key/passport
j'ai oublié ma clé/mon passeport;
forgetful *adj* distrait(e), étourdi(e)
forgive (*pt* **forgave**, *pp* **forgiven**)
[fə'gɪv, -'geɪv, -'gɪvn] *vt* pardonner;
to ~ sb for sth/for doing sth
pardonner qch à qn/à qn de faire qch
forgot [fə'gɔt] *pt of* **forget**
forgotten [fə'gɔtn] *pp of* **forget**
fork [fɔːk] *n* (*for eating*) fourchette
f; (*for gardening*) fourche *f*; (*of roads*)
bifurcation *f* ▷ *vi* (*road*) bifurquer
forlorn [fə'lɔːn] *adj* (*deserted*)
abandonné(e); (*hope, attempt*)
désespéré(e)
form [fɔːm] *n* forme *f*; (*Scol*) classe
f; (*questionnaire*) formulaire *m* ▷ *vt*
former; (*habit*) contracter; **to ~ part**

of sth faire partie de qch; **on top ~** en pleine forme

formal ['fɔːməl] adj (offer, receipt) en bonne et due forme; (person) cérémonieux(-euse); (occasion, dinner) officiel(le); (garden) à la française; (clothes) de soirée; **formality** [fɔːˈmælɪtɪ] n formalité f

format ['fɔːmæt] n format m ▷ vt (Comput) formater

formation [fɔːˈmeɪʃən] n formation f

former ['fɔːmə'] adj ancien(ne); (before n) précédent(e); **the ~ ... the latter** le premier ... le second, celui-là ... celui-ci; **formerly** adv autrefois

formidable ['fɔːmɪdəbl] adj redoutable

formula ['fɔːmjulə] n formule f

fort [fɔːt] n fort m

forthcoming [fɔːθ'kʌmɪŋ] adj qui va paraître or avoir lieu prochainement; (character) ouvert(e), communicatif(-ive); (available) disponible

fortieth ['fɔːtɪɪθ] num quarantième

fortify ['fɔːtɪfaɪ] vt (city) fortifier; (person) remonter

fortnight ['fɔːtnaɪt] n (BRIT) quinzaine f, quinze jours mpl; **fortnightly** adj bimensuel(le) ▷ adv tous les quinze jours

fortress ['fɔːtrɪs] n forteresse f

fortunate ['fɔːtʃənɪt] adj heureux(-euse); (person) chanceux(-euse); **it is ~ that** c'est une chance que, il est heureux que; **fortunately** adv heureusement, par bonheur

fortune ['fɔːtʃən] n chance f; (wealth) fortune f; **fortune-teller** n diseuse f de bonne aventure

forty ['fɔːtɪ] num quarante

forum ['fɔːrəm] n forum m, tribune f

forward ['fɔːwəd] adj (movement, position) en avant, vers l'avant; (not shy) effronté(e); (in time) en avance ▷ adv (also: **~s**) en avant ▷ n (Sport) avant m ▷ vt (letter) faire suivre; (parcel, goods) expédier; (fig) promouvoir, favoriser; **to move ~**

avancer; **forwarding address** n adresse f de réexpédition; **forward slash** n barre f oblique

fossick ['fɔsɪk] vi (AUST, NZ inf) chercher; **to ~ around for** fouiner (inf) pour trouver

fossil ['fɔsl] adj, n fossile m

foster ['fɔstə'] vt (encourage) encourager, favoriser; (child) élever (sans adopter); **foster child** n enfant élevé dans une famille d'accueil

fought [fɔːt] pt, pp of **fight**

foul [faul] adj (weather, smell, food) infect(e); (language) ordurier(-ière) ▷ n (Football) faute f ▷ vt (dirty) salir, encrasser; **he's got a ~ temper** il a un caractère de chien; **foul play** n (Law) acte criminel

found [faund] pt, pp of **find** ▷ vt (establish) fonder; **foundation** [faun'deɪʃən] n (act) fondation f; (base) fondement m; (also: **foundation cream**) fond m de teint; **foundations** npl (of building) fondations fpl

founder ['faundə'] n fondateur m ▷ vi couler, sombrer

fountain ['fauntɪn] n fontaine f; **fountain pen** n stylo m (à encre)

four [fɔː'] num quatre; **on all ~s** à quatre pattes; **four-letter word** n obscénité f, gros mot; **four-poster** n (also: **four-poster bed**) lit m à baldaquin; **fourteen** num quatorze; **fourteenth** num quatorzième; **fourth** num quatrième ▷ n (Aut: also: **fourth gear**) quatrième f; **four-wheel drive** n (Aut: car) voiture f à quatre roues motrices

fowl [faul] n volaille f

fox [fɔks] n renard m ▷ vt mystifier

foyer ['fɔɪeɪ] n (in hotel) vestibule m; (Theat) foyer m

fracking ['frækɪŋ] n fracturation f hydraulique

fraction ['frækʃən] n fraction f

fracture ['fræktʃə'] n fracture f ▷ vt fracturer

fragile ['frædʒaɪl] adj fragile
fragment ['frægmənt] n fragment m
fragrance ['freɪɡrəns] n parfum m
frail [freɪl] adj fragile, délicat(e);
(person) frêle
frame [freɪm] n (of building)
charpente f; (of human, animal)
charpente f, ossature f; (of
picture) cadre m; (of door, window)
encadrement m, chambranle m;
(of spectacles: also: ~s) monture f
▷ vt (picture) encadrer; ~ of mind
disposition f d'esprit; **framework** n
structure f
France [frɑːns] n la France
franchise ['fræntʃaɪz] n (Pol) droit m
de vote; (Comm) franchise f
frank [fræŋk] adj franc (franche)
▷ vt (letter) affranchir; **frankly** adv
franchement
frantic ['fræntɪk] adj (hectic)
frénétique; (distraught) hors de soi
fraud [frɔːd] n supercherie f, fraude f,
tromperie f; (person) imposteur m
fraught [frɔːt] adj (tense: person)
très tendu(e); (: situation) pénible;
~ **with** (difficulties etc) chargé(e) de,
plein(e) de
fray [freɪ] vt effilocher ▷ vi s'effilocher
freak [friːk] n (eccentric person)
phénomène m; (unusual event) hasard
m extraordinaire; (pej: fanatic):
health food ~ fana m/f or obsédé(e)
de l'alimentation saine ▷ adj (storm)
exceptionnel(le); (accident) bizarre
freckle ['frɛkl] n tache f de rousseur
free [friː] adj libre; (gratis) gratuit(e)
▷ vt (prisoner etc) libérer; (jammed
object or person) dégager; **is this seat
~?** la place est libre?; ~ **(of charge)**
gratuitement; **freedom** n liberté f;
Freefone® n numéro vert;
free gift n prime f; **free kick** n (Sport) coup
franc; **freelance** adj (journalist etc)
indépendant(e), free-lance inv ▷ adv
en free-lance; **freely** adv librement;
(liberally) libéralement; **Freepost®** n
(BRIT) port payé; **free-range** adj (egg)

de ferme; (chicken) fermier; **freeway**
n (US) autoroute f; **free will** n libre
arbitre m; **of one's own free will** de
son plein gré
freeze [friːz] (pt froze, pp frozen)
vi geler ▷ vt geler; (food) congeler;
(prices, salaries) bloquer, geler ▷ n
gel m; (of prices, salaries) blocage m;
freezer n congélateur m; **freezing**
adj: **freezing (cold)** (room etc)
glacial(e); (person, hands) gelé(e),
glacé(e) ▷ n: **3 degrees below
freezing** 3 degrés au-dessous de
zéro; **it's freezing** il fait un froid
glacial; **freezing point** n point m de
congélation
freight [freɪt] n (goods) fret m,
cargaison f; (money charged) fret, prix
m du transport; **freight train** n (US)
train m de marchandises
French [frɛntʃ] adj français(e)
▷ n (Ling) français m; **the** ~ npl les
Français; **what's the ~ (word) for
...?** comment dit-on ... en français?;
French bean n (BRIT) haricot vert;
French bread n pain m français;
French dressing n (Culin) vinaigrette
f; **French fried potatoes, French
fries** (US) npl (pommes de terre
fpl) frites fpl; **Frenchman** (irreg)
n Français m; **French stick** n ≈
baguette f; **French window** n porte-
fenêtre f; **Frenchwoman** (irreg) n
Française f
frenzy ['frɛnzɪ] n frénésie f
frequency ['friːkwənsɪ] n
fréquence f
frequent adj ['friːkwənt] fréquent(e)
▷ vt [frɪ'kwɛnt] fréquenter;
frequently ['friːkwəntlɪ] adv
fréquemment
fresh [frɛʃ] adj frais (fraîche);
(new) nouveau (nouvelle); (cheeky)
familier(-ière), culotté(e); **freshen** vi
(wind, air) fraîchir; **freshen up** vi faire
un brin de toilette; **fresher** n (BRIT
University: inf) bizuth m, étudiant(e)
de première année; **freshly** adv

nouvellement, récemment;
freshman (*irreg*) *n* (*US*) = **fresher**;
freshwater *adj* (*fish*) d'eau douce
fret [frɛt] *vi* s'agiter, se tracasser
friction ['frɪkʃən] *n* friction *f*,
frottement *m*
Friday ['fraɪdɪ] *n* vendredi *m*
fridge [frɪdʒ] *n* (*BRIT*) frigo *m*,
frigidaire® *m*
fried [fraɪd] *adj* frit(e); **~ egg** œuf *m*
sur le plat
friend [frɛnd] *n* ami(e) ▷ *vt* (*Internet*)
ajouter comme ami(e); **friendly**
adj amical(e); (*kind*) sympathique,
gentil(le); (*place*) accueillant(e); (*Pol*:
country) ami(e) ▷ *n* (*also*: **friendly
match**) match amical; **friendship**
n amitié *f*
fries [fraɪz] (*esp US*) *npl* = **chips**
frigate ['frɪgɪt] *n* frégate *f*
fright [fraɪt] *n* peur *f*, effroi *m*; **to
give sb a ~** faire peur à qn; **to take
~** prendre peur, s'effrayer; **frighten**
vt effrayer, faire peur à; **frightened**
adj: **to be frightened (of)** avoir peur
(de); **frightening** *adj* effrayant(e);
frightful *adj* affreux(-euse)
frill [frɪl] *n* (*of dress*) volant *m*; (*of shirt*)
jabot *m*
fringe [frɪndʒ] *n* (*BRIT*: *of hair*) frange
f; (*edge*: *of forest etc*) bordure *f*
Frisbee® ['frɪzbɪ] *n* Frisbee® *m*
fritter ['frɪtər] *n* beignet *m*
frivolous ['frɪvələs] *adj* frivole
fro [frəu] *adv see* **to**
frock [frɔk] *n* robe *f*
frog [frɔg] *n* grenouille *f*; **frogman**
(*irreg*) *n* homme-grenouille *m*

KEYWORD

from [frɔm] *prep* **1** (*indicating starting
place, origin etc*) de; **where do you
come from?, where are you from?**
d'où venez-vous?; **where has he
come from?** d'où arrive-t-il?; **from
London to Paris** de Londres à Paris;
to escape from sb/sth échapper

à qn/qch; **a letter/telephone call
from my sister** une lettre/un appel
de ma sœur; **to drink from the
bottle** boire à (même) la bouteille;
tell him from me that ... dites-lui de
ma part que ...
2 (*indicating time*) (à partir) de; **from
one o'clock to** or **until** or **till two**
d'une heure à deux heures; **from
January (on)** à partir de janvier
3 (*indicating distance*) de; **the hotel
is one kilometre from the beach**
l'hôtel est à un kilomètre de la plage
4 (*indicating price, number etc*) de;
prices range from £10 to £50 les prix
varient entre 10 livres et 50 livres; **the
interest rate was increased from
9% to 10%** le taux d'intérêt est passé
de 9% à 10%
5 (*indicating difference*) de; **he can't
tell red from green** il ne peut pas
distinguer le rouge du vert; **to be
different from sb/sth** être différent
de qn/qch
6 (*because of, on the basis of*): **from
what he says** d'après ce qu'il dit;
weak from hunger affaibli par
la faim

front [frʌnt] *n* (*of house, dress*)
devant *m*; (*of coach, train*) avant *m*;
(*promenade*: *also*: **sea ~**) bord *m* de
mer; (*Mil, Pol, Meteorology*) front
m; (*fig*: *appearances*) contenance *f*,
façade *f* ▷ *adj* de devant; (*seat, wheel*)
avant *inv* ▷ *vi*: **in ~ (of)** devant;
front door *n* porte *f* d'entrée; (*of car*)
portière *f* avant; **frontier** ['frʌntɪər]
n frontière *f*; **front page** *n* première
page; **front-wheel drive** *n* traction
f avant
frost [frɔst] *n* gel *m*, gelée *f*; (*also*:
hoar~) givre *m*; **frostbite** *n* gelures
fpl; **frosting** *n* (*esp US*: *on cake*)
glaçage *m*; **frosty** *adj* (*window*)
couvert(e) de givre; (*weather, welcome*)
glacial(e)
froth [frɔθ] *n* mousse *f*; écume *f*

frown [fraun] n froncement m de
sourcils ▷ vi froncer les sourcils

froze [frəuz] pt of **freeze**

frozen ['frəuzn] pp of **freeze** ▷ adj
(food) congelé(e); (person, also assets)
gelé(e)

fruit [fru:t] n (pl inv) fruit m; **fruit
juice** n jus m de fruit; **fruit machine**
n (BRIT) machine f à sous; **fruit salad**
n salade f de fruits

frustrate [frʌs'treɪt] vt frustrer;
frustrated adj frustré(e)

fry (pt, pp **fried**) [fraɪ, -d] vt (faire) frire
▷ n: **small ~** le menu fretin; **frying
pan** n poêle f (à frire)

ft. abbr = **foot; feet**

fudge [fʌdʒ] n (Culin) sorte de confiserie
à base de sucre, de beurre et de lait

fuel [fjuəl] n (for heating) combustible
m; (for engine) carburant m; **fuel
tank** n (in vehicle) réservoir m de or
à carburant

fulfil, (US) **fulfill** [ful'fɪl] vt (function,
condition) remplir; (order) exécuter;
(wish, desire) satisfaire, réaliser

full [ful] adj plein(e); (details, hotel, bus)
complet(-ète); (busy: day) chargé(e);
(skirt) ample, large ▷ adv: **to know ~
well that** savoir fort bien que; **I'm ~
(up)** j'ai bien mangé; **~ employment/
fare** plein emploi/tarif; **a ~ two
hours** deux bonnes heures; **at ~
speed** à toute vitesse; **in ~** (reproduce,
quote, pay) intégralement; (write name
etc) en toutes lettres; **full-length** adj
(portrait) en pied; (coat) long(ue); **full-
length film** long métrage; **full moon**
n pleine lune; **full-scale** adj (model)
grandeur nature inv; (search, retreat)
complet(-ète), total(e); **full stop** n
point m; **full-time** adj, adv (work) à
plein temps; **fully** adv entièrement,
complètement

fumble ['fʌmbl] vi fouiller, tâtonner;
fumble with vt fus tripoter

fume [fju:m] vi (rage) rager; **fumes**
[fju:mz] npl vapeurs fpl, émanations
fpl, gaz mpl

fun [fʌn] n amusement m,
divertissement m; **to have ~**
s'amuser; **for ~** pour rire; **to make ~
of** se moquer de

function ['fʌŋkʃən] n fonction f;
(reception, dinner) cérémonie f, soirée
officielle ▷ vi fonctionner

fund [fʌnd] n caisse f, fonds m;
(source, store) source f, mine f; **funds**
npl (money) fonds mpl

fundamental [fʌndə'mɛntl] adj
fondamental(e)

funeral ['fju:nərəl] n enterrement
m, obsèques fpl (more formal occasion);
funeral director n entrepreneur
m des pompes funèbres; **funeral
parlour** n (BRIT) dépôt m mortuaire

funfair ['fʌnfɛəʳ] n (BRIT) fête
(foraine)

fungus (pl **fungi**) ['fʌŋgəs, -gaɪ] n
champignon m; (mould) moisissure f

funnel ['fʌnl] n entonnoir m; (of ship)
cheminée f

funny ['fʌnɪ] adj amusant(e), drôle;
(strange) curieux(-euse), bizarre

fur [fəːʳ] n fourrure f; (BRIT: in kettle
etc) (dépôt m de) tartre m; **fur coat** n
manteau m de fourrure

furious ['fjuərɪəs] adj furieux(-euse);
(effort) acharné(e)

furnish ['fəːnɪʃ] vt meubler; (supply)
fournir; **furnishings** npl mobilier m,
articles mpl d'ameublement

furniture ['fəːnɪtʃəʳ] n meubles mpl,
mobilier m; **piece of ~** meuble m

furry ['fəːrɪ] adj (animal) à fourrure;
(toy) en peluche

further ['fəːðəʳ] adj supplémentaire,
autre; nouveau (nouvelle) ▷ adv
plus loin; (more) davantage;
(moreover) de plus ▷ vt faire avancer
or progresser, promouvoir; **further
education** n enseignement m
postscolaire (recyclage, formation
professionnelle); **furthermore** adv de
plus, en outre

furthest ['fəːðɪst] superlative of **far**

fury ['fjuərɪ] n fureur f

fuse, (US) **fuze** [fjuːz] n fusible m; (for bomb etc) amorce f, détonateur m ▷ vt, vi (metal) fondre; (BRIT Elec): **to ~ the lights** faire sauter les fusibles or les plombs; **fuse box** n boîte f à fusibles

fusion ['fjuːʒən] n fusion f

fuss [fʌs] n (anxiety, excitement) chichis mpl, façons fpl; (commotion) tapage m; (complaining, trouble) histoire(s) f(pl); **to make a ~** faire des façons (or des histoires); **to make a ~ of sb** dorloter qn; **fussy** adj (person) tatillon(ne), difficile, chichiteux(-euse); (dress, style) tarabiscoté(e)

future ['fjuːtʃəʳ] adj futur(e) ▷ n avenir m; (Ling) futur m; **futures** npl (Comm) opérations fpl à terme; **in (the) ~** à l'avenir

fuze [fjuːz] n, vt, vi (US) = **fuse**

fuzzy ['fʌzɪ] adj (Phot) flou(e); (hair) crépu(e)

FYI abbr = **for your information**

G [dʒiː] n (Mus) sol m

g. abbr (= gram) g

gadget ['gædʒɪt] n gadget m

Gaelic ['geɪlɪk] adj, n (Ling) gaélique (m)

gag [gæg] n (on mouth) bâillon m; (joke) gag m ▷ vt (prisoner etc) bâillonner

gain [geɪn] n (improvement) gain m; (profit) gain, profit m ▷ vt gagner ▷ vi (watch) avancer; **to ~ from/by** gagner de/à; **to ~ on sb** (catch up) rattraper qn; **to ~ 3lbs (in weight)** prendre 3 livres; **to ~ ground** gagner du terrain

gal. abbr = **gallon**

gala ['gɑːlə] n gala m

galaxy ['gæləksɪ] n galaxie f

gale [geɪl] n coup m de vent

gall bladder ['gɔːl-] n vésicule f biliaire

gallery ['gælərɪ] n (also: **art ~**) musée m; (private) galerie; (in theatre) dernier balcon

gallon ['gæln] n gallon m (Brit = 4.543 l; US = 3.785 l)

gallop ['gæləp] n galop m ▷ vi galoper

gallstone ['gɔːlstəun] n calcul m (biliaire)

gamble ['gæmbl] n pari m, risque calculé ▷ vt, vi jouer; **to ~ on** (fig) miser sur; **gambler** n joueur m; **gambling** n jeu m

game [geɪm] n jeu m; (event) match m; (of tennis, chess, cards) partie f; (Hunting) gibier m ▷ adj (willing): **to be ~ (for)** être prêt(e) (à or pour); **games** npl (Scol) sport m; (sport event) jeux m; **big ~** gros gibier; **games console** ['geɪmz-] n console f de jeux vidéo; **game show** n jeu télévisé

gammon ['gæmən] n (bacon) quartier m de lard fumé; (ham) jambon fumé or salé

gang [gæŋ] n bande f; (of workmen) équipe f

gangster ['gæŋstə'] n gangster m

gap [gæp] n trou m; (in time) intervalle m; (difference): **~ (between)** écart m (entre)

gape [geɪp] vi (person) être or rester bouche bée; (hole, shirt) être ouvert(e)

gap year n année que certains étudiants prennent pour voyager ou pour travailler avant d'entrer à l'université

garage ['gærɑːʒ] n garage m; **garage sale** n vide-grenier m

garbage ['gɑːbɪdʒ] n (US: rubbish) ordures fpl, détritus mpl; (inf: nonsense) âneries fpl; **garbage can** n (US) poubelle f, boîte f à ordures; **garbage collector** n (US) éboueur m

garden ['gɑːdn] n jardin m; **gardens** npl (public) jardin public; (private) parc m; **garden centre** (BRIT) n pépinière f, jardinerie f; **gardener** n jardinier m; **gardening** n jardinage m

garlic ['gɑːlɪk] n ail m

garment ['gɑːmənt] n vêtement m

garnish ['gɑːnɪʃ] (Culin) vt garnir ▷ n décoration f

gas [gæs] n gaz m; (US: gasoline) essence f ▷ vt asphyxier; **I can**

smell ~ ça sent le gaz; **gas cooker** n (BRIT) cuisinière f à gaz; **gas cylinder** n bouteille f de gaz; **gas fire** n (BRIT) radiateur m à gaz

gasket ['gæskɪt] n (Aut) joint m de culasse

gasoline ['gæsəliːn] n (US) essence f

gasp [gɑːsp] n halètement m; (of shock etc): **she gave a small ~ of pain** la douleur lui coupa le souffle ▷ vi haleter; (fig) avoir le souffle coupé

gas: gas pedal n (US) accélérateur m; **gas station** n (US) station-service f; **gas tank** n (US Aut) réservoir m d'essence

gastric band ['gæstrɪk-] n anneau m gastrique

gate [geɪt] n (of garden) portail m; (of field, at level crossing) barrière f; (of building, town, at airport) porte f

gateau (pl **gateaux**) ['gætəu, -z] n gros gâteau à la crème

gatecrash ['geɪtkræʃ] vt s'introduire sans invitation dans

gateway ['geɪtweɪ] n porte f

gather ['gæðə'] vt (flowers, fruit) cueillir; (pick up) ramasser; (assemble: objects) rassembler; (: people) réunir; (: information) recueillir; (understand) comprendre; (Sewing) froncer ▷ vi (assemble) se rassembler; **to ~ speed** prendre de la vitesse; **gathering** n rassemblement m

gauge [geɪdʒ] n (instrument) jauge f ▷ vt jauger; (fig) juger de

gave [geɪv] pt of **give**

gay [geɪ] adj (homosexual) homosexuel(le); (colour) gai, vif (vive)

gaze [geɪz] n regard m fixe ▷ vi: **to ~ at** fixer du regard

GB abbr = **Great Britain**

GCSE n abbr (BRIT: = General Certificate of Secondary Education) examen passé à l'âge de 16 ans sanctionnant les connaissances de l'élève

gear [gɪə'] n matériel m, équipement m; (Tech) engrenage m; (Aut) vitesse

f ▷ vt (fig: adapt) adapter; **top** or
(US) **high/low ~** quatrième (or
cinquième)/première vitesse; **in ~** en
prise; **gear up** vi: **to ~ up (to do)** se
préparer (à faire); **gear box** n boîte
f de vitesse; **gear lever** n levier m de
vitesse; **gear shift** (US), **gear stick**
(BRIT) n = **gear lever**

geese [gi:s] npl of **goose**

gel [dʒɛl] n gelée f

gem [dʒɛm] n pierre précieuse

Gemini ['dʒɛmɪnaɪ] n les Gémeaux
mpl

gender ['dʒɛndə^r] n genre m; (person's
sex) sexe m

gene [dʒi:n] n (Biol) gène m

general ['dʒɛnərl] n général m
▷ adj général(e); **in ~** en général;
general anaesthetic, (US)
general anesthetic n anesthésie
générale; **general election** n
élection(s) législative(s); **generalize**
vi généraliser; **generally** adv
généralement; **general practitioner**
n généraliste m/f; **general store** n
épicerie f

generate ['dʒɛnəreɪt] vt engendrer;
(electricity) produire

generation [dʒɛnə'reɪʃən] n
génération f; (of electricity etc)
production f

generator ['dʒɛnəreɪtə^r] n
générateur m

generosity [dʒɛnə'rɔsɪtɪ] n
générosité f

generous ['dʒɛnərəs] adj
généreux(-euse); (copious)
copieux(-euse)

genetic [dʒɪ'nɛtɪk] adj génétique;
~ engineering ingénierie m
génétique; **~ fingerprinting** système
m d'empreinte génétique; **genetically
modified** adj (food etc) génétiquement
modifié(e); **genetics** n génétique f

Geneva [dʒɪ'ni:və] n Genève

genitals ['dʒɛnɪtlz] npl organes
génitaux

genius ['dʒi:nɪəs] n génie m

genome ['dʒi:nəum] n génome m

gent [dʒɛnt] n abbr (BRIT inf)
= **gentleman**

gentle ['dʒɛntl] adj doux (douce);
(breeze, touch) léger(-ère)

gentleman ['dʒɛntlmən] (irreg)
n monsieur m; (well-bred man)
gentleman m

gently ['dʒɛntlɪ] adv doucement

gents [dʒɛnts] n W.-C. mpl (pour
hommes)

genuine ['dʒɛnjuɪn] adj véritable,
authentique; (person, emotion)
sincère; **genuinely** adv sincèrement,
vraiment

geographic(al) [dʒɪə'græfɪk(l)-] adj
géographique

geography [dʒɪ'ɔgrəfɪ] n
géographie f

geology [dʒɪ'ɔlədʒɪ] n géologie f

geometry [dʒɪ'ɔmɛtrɪ] n géométrie f

geranium [dʒɪ'reɪnɪəm] n
géranium m

geriatric [dʒɛrɪ'ætrɪk] adj
gériatrique ▷ n patient(e) gériatrique

germ [dʒə:m] n (Med) microbe m

German ['dʒə:mən] adj allemand(e)
▷ n Allemand(e); (Ling) allemand m;
German measles n rubéole f

Germany ['dʒə:mənɪ] n Allemagne f

gesture ['dʒɛstjə^r] n geste m

KEYWORD

get [gɛt] (pt, pp **got**, (US) pp **gotten**)
vi **1** (become, be) devenir; **to get old/
tired** devenir vieux/fatigué, vieillir/se
fatiguer; **to get drunk** s'enivrer; **to
get dirty** se salir; **to get married** se
marier; **when do I get paid?** quand
est-ce que je serai payé?; **it's getting
late** il se fait tard

2 (go): **to get to/from** aller à/de;
to get home rentrer chez soi; **how
did you get here?** comment es-tu
arrivé ici?

3 (begin) commencer or se mettre
à; **to get to know sb** apprendre à

connaître qn; **I'm getting to like him** je commence à l'apprécier; **let's get going** or **started** allons-y

4 (*modal aux vb*): **you've got to do it** il faut que vous le fassiez; **I've got to tell the police** je dois le dire à la police

▶ *vt* **1**: **to get sth done** (*do*) faire qch; (*have done*) faire faire qch; **to get sb/sb ready** préparer qch/qn; **to get one's hair cut** se faire couper les cheveux; **to get the car going** or **to go** (*faire*) démarrer la voiture; **to get sb to do sth** faire faire qch à qn

2 (*obtain: money, permission, results*) obtenir, avoir; (*buy*) acheter; (*find: job, flat*) trouver; (*fetch: person, doctor, object*) aller chercher; **to get sth for sb** procurer qch à qn; **get me Mr Jones, please** (*on phone*) passez-moi Mr Jones, s'il vous plaît; **can I get you a drink?** est-ce que je peux vous servir à boire?

3 (*receive: present, letter*) recevoir, avoir; (*acquire: reputation*) avoir; (*: prize*) obtenir; **what did you get for your birthday?** qu'est-ce que tu as eu pour ton anniversaire?; **how much did you get for the painting?** combien avez-vous vendu le tableau?

4 (*catch*) prendre, saisir, attraper; (*hit: target etc*) atteindre; **to get sb by the arm/throat** prendre or saisir or attraper qn par le bras/à la gorge; **get him!** arrête-le!; **the bullet got him in the leg** il a pris la balle dans la jambe

5 (*take, move*): **to get sth to sb** faire parvenir qch à qn; **do you think we'll get it through the door?** on arrivera à le faire passer par la porte?

6 (*catch, take: plane, bus etc*) prendre; **where do I get the train for Birmingham?** où prend-on le train pour Birmingham?

7 (*understand*) comprendre, saisir; (*hear*) entendre; **I've got it!** j'ai compris!; **I don't get your meaning** je ne vois or comprends pas ce que vous voulez dire; **I didn't get your name** je n'ai pas entendu votre nom

8 (*have, possess*): **to have got** avoir; **how many have you got?** vous en avez combien?

9 (*illness*) avoir; **I've got a cold** j'ai le rhume; **she got pneumonia and died** elle a fait une pneumonie et elle en est morte

get away *vi* partir, s'en aller; (*escape*) s'échapper

get away with *vt fus* (*punishment*) en être quitte pour; (*crime etc*) se faire pardonner

get back *vi* (*return*) rentrer ▶ *vt* récupérer, recouvrer; **when do we get back?** quand serons-nous de retour?

get in *vi* entrer; (*arrive home*) rentrer; (*train*) arriver

get into *vt fus* entrer dans; (*car, train etc*) monter dans; (*clothes*) mettre, enfiler, endosser; **to get into bed/a rage** se mettre au lit/en colère

get off *vi* (*from train etc*) descendre; (*depart: person, car*) s'en aller ▶ *vt* (*remove: clothes, stain*) enlever ▶ *vt fus* (*train, bus*) descendre de; **where do I get off?** où est-ce que je dois descendre?

get on *vi* (*at exam etc*) se débrouiller; (*agree*): **to get on (with)** s'entendre (avec); **how are you getting on?** comment ça va? ▶ *vt fus* monter dans; (*horse*) monter sur

get out *vi* sortir; (*of vehicle*) descendre ▶ *vt* sortir

get out of *vt fus* sortir de; (*duty etc*) échapper à, se soustraire à

get over *vt fus* (*illness*) se remettre de

get through *vi* (*Tel*) avoir la communication; **to get through to sb** atteindre qn

get up *vi* (*rise*) se lever ▶ *vt fus* monter

getaway [ˈgɛtəweɪ] *n* fuite *f*

Ghana ['gɑːnə] n Ghana m

ghastly ['gɑːstlɪ] adj atroce, horrible

ghetto ['gɛtəu] n ghetto m

ghost [gəust] n fantôme m, revenant m

giant ['dʒaɪənt] n géant(e) ▷ adj géant(e), énorme

gift [gɪft] n cadeau m; (donation, talent) don m; **gifted** adj doué(e); **gift shop**, (US) **gift store** n boutique f de cadeaux; **gift token**, **gift voucher** n chèque-cadeau m

gig [gɪg] n (inf: concert) concert m

gigabyte ['dʒɪgəbaɪt] n gigaoctet m

gigantic [dʒaɪ'gæntɪk] adj gigantesque

giggle ['gɪgl] vi pouffer, ricaner sottement

gills [gɪlz] npl (of fish) ouïes fpl, branchies fpl

gilt [gɪlt] n dorure f ▷ adj doré(e)

gimmick ['gɪmɪk] n truc m

gin [dʒɪn] n gin m

ginger ['dʒɪndʒə'] n gingembre m

gipsy ['dʒɪpsɪ] n = **gypsy**

giraffe [dʒɪ'rɑːf] n girafe f

girl [gəːl] n fille f, fillette f; (young unmarried woman) jeune fille; (daughter) fille; **an English ~** une jeune Anglaise; **girl band** n girls band m; **girlfriend** n (of girl) amie f; (of boy) petite amie; **Girl Guide** n (BRIT) éclaireuse f; (Roman Catholic) guide f; **Girl Scout** n (US) = **Girl Guide**

gist [dʒɪst] n essentiel m

give [gɪv] (pt **gave**, pp **given**) vt donner ▷ vi (break) céder; (stretch: fabric) se prêter; **to ~ sb sth**, **~ sth to sb** donner qch à qn; (gift) offrir qch à qn; (message) transmettre qch à qn; **to ~ sb a call/kiss** appeler/ embrasser qn; **to ~ a cry/sigh** pousser un cri/un soupir; **give away** vt donner; (give free) faire cadeau de; (betray) donner, trahir; (disclose) révéler; **give back** vt rendre; **give in** vi céder ▷ vt donner; **give out** vt (food etc) distribuer; **give up** vi

renoncer ▷ vt renoncer à; **to ~ up smoking** arrêter de fumer; **to ~ o.s. up** se rendre

given ['gɪvn] pp of **give** ▷ adj (fixed: time, amount) donné(e), déterminé(e) ▷ conj: **~ the circumstances ...** étant donné les circonstances ...; vu les circonstances ...; **~ that ...** étant donné que ...

glacier ['glæsɪə'] n glacier m

glad [glæd] adj content(e); **gladly** ['glædlɪ] adv volontiers

glamorous ['glæmərəs] adj (person) séduisant(e); (job) prestigieux(-euse)

glamour, (US) **glamor** ['glæmə'] n éclat m, prestige m

glance [glɑːns] n coup m d'œil ▷ vi: **to ~ at** jeter un coup d'œil à

gland [glænd] n glande f

glare [glɛə'] n (of anger) regard furieux; (of light) lumière éblouissante; (of publicity) feux mpl ▷ vi briller d'un éclat aveuglant; **to ~ at** lancer un regard or des regards furieux à; **glaring** adj (mistake) criant(e), qui saute aux yeux

glass [glɑːs] n verre m; **glasses** npl (spectacles) lunettes fpl

glaze [gleɪz] vt (door) vitrer; (pottery) vernir ▷ n vernis m

gleam [gliːm] vi luire, briller

glen [glɛn] n vallée f

glide [glaɪd] vi glisser; (Aviat, bird) planer; **glider** n (Aviat) planeur m

glimmer ['glɪmə'] n lueur f

glimpse [glɪmps] n vision passagère, aperçu m ▷ vt entrevoir, apercevoir

glint [glɪnt] vi étinceler

glisten ['glɪsn] vi briller, luire

glitter ['glɪtə'] vi scintiller, briller

global ['gləubl] adj (world-wide) mondial(e); (overall) global(e); **globalization** n mondialisation f; **global warming** n réchauffement m de la planète

globe [gləub] n globe m

gloom [gluːm] n obscurité f; (sadness) tristesse f, mélancolie f; **gloomy**

adj (*person*) morose; (*place, outlook*) sombre

glorious ['glɔːrɪəs] *adj* glorieux(-euse); (*beautiful*) splendide

glory ['glɔːrɪ] *n* gloire *f*; splendeur *f*

gloss [glɔs] *n* (*shine*) brillant *m*, vernis *m*; (*also:* ~ **paint**) peinture brillante

glossary ['glɔsərɪ] *n* glossaire *m*, lexique *m*

glossy ['glɔsɪ] *adj* brillant(e), luisant(e) ▷ *n* (*also:* ~ **magazine**) revue *f* de luxe

glove [glʌv] *n* gant *m*; **glove compartment** *n* (*Aut*) boîte *f* à gants, vide-poches *m inv*

glow [gləu] *vi* rougeoyer; (*face*) rayonner; (*eyes*) briller

glucose ['gluːkəus] *n* glucose *m*

glue [gluː] *n* colle *f* ▷ *vt* coller

GM *abbr* (= *genetically modified*) génétiquement modifié(e)

gm *abbr* (= *gram*) g

GM crop *n* culture *f* OGM

GMO *n abbr* (= *genetically modified organism*) OGM *m*

GMT *abbr* (= *Greenwich Mean Time*) GMT

gnaw [nɔː] *vt* ronger

go [gəu] (*pt* **went**, *pp* **gone**) *vi* aller; (*depart*) partir, s'en aller; (*work*) marcher; (*break*) céder; (*time*) passer; (*be sold*): **to go for £10** se vendre 10 livres; (*become*): **to go pale/mouldy** pâlir/moisir ▷ *n* (*pl* **goes**): **to have a go (at)** essayer (de faire); **to be on the go** être en mouvement; **whose go is it?** à qui est-ce de jouer?; **he's going to do it** il va le faire, il est sur le point de le faire; **to go for a walk** aller se promener; **to go dancing/shopping** aller danser/ faire les courses; **to go and see sb, go to see sb** aller voir qn; **how did it go?** comment est-ce que ça s'est passé?; **to go round the back/by the shop** passer par derrière/devant le magasin; **... to go** (*us: food*) ... à emporter; **go ahead** *vi* (*take place*) avoir lieu; (*get going*) y aller; **go away**

vi partir, s'en aller; **go back** *vi* rentrer; revenir; (*go again*) retourner; **go by** *vi* (*years, time*) passer, s'écouler ▷ *vt fus* s'en tenir à; (*believe*) en croire; **go down** *vi* descendre; (*number, price, amount*) baisser; (*ship*) couler; (*sun*) se coucher ▷ *vt fus* descendre; **go for** *vt fus* (*fetch*) aller chercher; (*like*) aimer; (*attack*) s'en prendre à; attaquer; **go in** *vi* entrer; **go into** *vt fus* entrer dans; (*investigate*) étudier, examiner; (*embark on*) se lancer dans; **go off** *vi* partir, s'en aller; (*food*) se gâter; (*milk*) tourner; (*bomb*) sauter; (*alarm clock*) sonner; (*alarm*) se déclencher; (*lights etc*) s'éteindre; (*event*) se dérouler ▷ *vt fus* ne plus aimer; **the gun went off** le coup est parti; **go on** *vi* continuer; (*happen*) se passer; (*lights*) s'allumer ▷ *vt fus*: **to go on doing** continuer à faire; **go out** *vi* sortir; (*fire, light*) s'éteindre; (*tide*) descendre; **to go out with sb** sortir avec qn; **go over** *vi, vt fus* (*check*) revoir, vérifier; **go past** *vt fus*: **to go past sth** passer devant qch; **go round** *vi* (*circulate: news, rumour*) circuler; (*revolve*) tourner; (*suffice*) suffire (pour tout le monde); (*visit*): **to go round to sb's** passer chez qn; aller chez qn; (*make a detour*): **to go round (by)** faire un détour (par); **go through** *vt fus* (*town etc*) traverser; (*search through*) fouiller; (*suffer*) subir; **go up** *vi* monter; (*price*) augmenter ▷ *vt fus* gravir; **go with** *vt fus* aller avec; **go without** *vt fus* se passer de

go-ahead ['gəuəhed] *adj* dynamique, entreprenant(e) ▷ *n* feu vert

goal [gəul] *n* but *m*; **goalkeeper** *n* gardien *m* de but; **goal-post** *n* poteau *m* de but

goat [gəut] *n* chèvre *f*

gobble ['gɔbl] *vt* (*also:* ~ **down**, ~ **up**) engloutir

god [gɔd] *n* dieu *m*; **God** Dieu; **godchild** *n* filleul(e); **goddaughter**

n filleule *f*; **goddess** *n* déesse *f*; **godfather** *n* parrain *m*; **godmother** *n* marraine *f*; **godson** *n* filleul *m*

goggles ['gɔglz] *npl* (*for skiing etc*) lunettes (protectrices); (*for swimming*) lunettes de piscine

going ['gəuɪŋ] *n* (*conditions*) état *m* du terrain ▷ *adj*: **the ~ rate** le tarif (en vigueur)

gold [gəuld] *n* or *m* ▷ *adj* en or; (*reserves*) d'or; **golden** *adj* (*made of gold*) en or; (*gold in colour*) doré(e); **goldfish** *n* poisson *m* rouge; **goldmine** *n* mine *f* d'or; **gold-plated** *adj* plaqué(e) or *inv*

golf [gɔlf] *n* golf *m*; **golf ball** *n* balle *f* de golf; (*on typewriter*) boule *f*; **golf club** *n* club *m* de golf; (*stick*) club *m*, crosse *f* de golf; **golf course** *n* terrain *m* de golf; **golfer** *n* joueur(-euse) de golf

gone [gɔn] *pp of* **go**

gong [gɔŋ] *n* gong *m*

good [gud] *adj* bon(ne); (*kind*) gentil(le); (*child*) sage; (*weather*) beau ▷ *n* bien *m*; **goods** *npl* marchandise *f*, articles *mpl*; **~!** bon!, très bien!; **to be ~ at** être bon en; **to be ~ for** être bon pour; **it's no ~ complaining** cela ne sert à rien de se plaindre; **to make ~** (*deficit*) combler; (*losses*) compenser; **for ~** (*for ever*) pour de bon, une fois pour toutes; **would you be ~ enough to …?** auriez-vous la bonté or l'amabilité de …?; **is this any ~?** (*will it do?*) est-ce que ceci fera l'affaire?, est-ce que cela peut vous rendre service?; (*what's it like?*) qu'est-ce que ça vaut?; **a ~ deal (of)** beaucoup (de); **a ~ many** beaucoup (de); **~ morning/afternoon!** bonjour!; **~ evening!** bonsoir!; **~ night!** bonsoir!; (*on going to bed*) bonne nuit!; **goodbye** *excl* au revoir!; **to say goodbye to sb** dire au revoir à qn; **Good Friday** *n* Vendredi saint; **good-looking** *adj* beau (belle), bien *inv*; **good-natured** *adj* (*person*)

qui a un bon naturel; **goodness** *n* (*of person*) bonté *f*; **for goodness sake!** je vous en prie!; **goodness gracious!** mon Dieu!; **goods train** *n* (BRIT) train *m* de marchandises; **goodwill** *n* bonne volonté

google ['gugl] *vi* faire une recheche Google® ▷ *vt* googler

goose (*pl* **geese**) [guːs, giːs] *n* oie *f*

gooseberry ['guzbərı] *n* groseille *f* à maquereau; **to play ~** (BRIT) tenir la chandelle

goose bumps, goose pimples *npl* chair *f* de poule

gorge [gɔːdʒ] *n* gorge *f* ▷ *vt*: **to ~ o.s. (on)** se gorger (de)

gorgeous ['gɔːdʒəs] *adj* splendide, superbe

gorilla [gə'rılə] *n* gorille *m*

gosh [gɔʃ] (*inf*) *excl* mince alors!

gospel ['gɔspl] *n* évangile *m*

gossip ['gɔsɪp] *n* (*chat*) bavardages *mpl*; (*malicious*) commérage *m*, cancans *mpl*; (*person*) commère *f* ▷ *vi* bavarder; cancaner, faire des commérages; **gossip column** *n* (*Press*) échos *mpl*

got [gɔt] *pt*, *pp of* **get**

gotten ['gɔtn] (US) *pp of* **get**

gourmet ['guəmeı] *n* gourmet *m*, gastronome *m/f*

govern ['gʌvən] *vt* gouverner; (*influence*) déterminer; **government** *n* gouvernement *m*; (BRIT: *ministers*) ministère *m*; **governor** *n* (*of colony, state, bank*) gouverneur *m*; (*of school, hospital etc*) administrateur(-trice); (BRIT: *of prison*) directeur(-trice)

gown [gaun] *n* robe *f*; (*of teacher*, BRIT: *of judge*) toge *f*

GP *n abbr* (*Med*) = **general practitioner**

GPS *n abbr* (= *global positioning system*) GPS *m*

grab [græb] *vt* saisir, empoigner ▷ *vi*: **to ~ at** essayer de saisir

grace [greıs] *n* grâce *f* ▷ *vt* (*honour*) honorer; (*adorn*) orner; **5 days'**

~ un répit de 5 jours; **graceful** adj gracieux(-euse), élégant(e); **gracious** ['greɪʃəs] adj bienveillant(e)

grade [greɪd] n (Comm: quality) qualité f; (: size) calibre m; (: type) catégorie f; (in hierarchy) grade m, échelon m; (Scol) note f; (us: school class) classe f; (: gradient) pente f ▷ vt classer; (by size) calibrer; **grade crossing** n (us) passage m à niveau; **grade school** n (us) école f primaire

gradient ['greɪdɪənt] n inclinaison f, pente f

gradual ['grædjuəl] adj graduel(le), progressif(-ive); **gradually** adv peu à peu, graduellement

graduate n ['grædjuɪt] diplômé(e) d'université; (us: of high school) diplômé(e) de fin d'études ▷ vi ['grædjueɪt] obtenir un diplôme d'université (or de fin d'études); **graduation** [grædju'eɪʃən] n cérémonie f de remise des diplômes

graffiti [grə'fiːtɪ] npl graffiti mpl

graft [grɑːft] n (Agr, Med) greffe f; (bribery) corruption f ▷ vt greffer; **hard ~** (BRIT inf) boulot acharné

grain [greɪn] n (single piece) grain m; (no pl: cereals) céréales fpl; (us: corn) blé m

gram [græm] n gramme m

grammar ['græmə'] n grammaire f; **grammar school** n (BRIT) ≈ lycée m

gramme [græm] n = **gram**

gran [græn] n (inf) (BRIT) mamie f (inf), mémé f (inf)

grand [grænd] adj magnifique, splendide; (gesture etc) noble; **grandad** n (inf) = **granddad**; **grandchild** (pl **grandchildren**) n petit-fils m, petite-fille f; **grandchildren** npl petits-enfants; **granddad** n (inf) papy m (inf), papi m (inf), pépé m (inf); **granddaughter** n petite-fille f; **grandfather** n grand-père m; **grandma** n (inf) = **gran**; **grandmother** n grand-mère f; **grandpa** n (inf) = **granddad**;

grandparents npl grands-parents mpl; **grand piano** n piano m à queue; **Grand Prix** ['grɑ̃:'priː] n (Aut) grand prix automobile; **grandson** n petit-fils m

granite ['grænɪt] n granit m

granny ['grænɪ] n (inf) = **gran**

grant [grɑːnt] vt accorder; (a request) accéder à; (admit) concéder ▷ n (Scol) bourse f; (Admin) subside m, subvention f; **to take sth for ~ed** considérer qch comme acquis; **to take sb for ~ed** considérer qn comme faisant partie du décor

grape [greɪp] n raisin m

grapefruit ['greɪpfruːt] n pamplemousse m

graph [grɑːf] n graphique m, courbe f; **graphic** ['græfɪk] adj graphique; (vivid) vivant(e); **graphics** n (art) arts mpl graphiques; (process) graphisme m ▷ npl (drawings) illustrations fpl

grasp [grɑːsp] vt saisir ▷ n (grip) prise f; (fig) compréhension f, connaissance f

grass [grɑːs] n herbe f; (lawn) gazon m; **grasshopper** n sauterelle f

grate [greɪt] n grille f de cheminée ▷ vi grincer ▷ vt (Culin) râper

grateful ['greɪtful] adj reconnaissant(e)

grater ['greɪtə'] n râpe f

gratitude ['grætɪtjuːd] n gratitude f

grave [greɪv] n tombe f ▷ adj grave, sérieux(-euse)

gravel ['grævl] n gravier m

gravestone ['greɪvstəun] n pierre tombale

graveyard ['greɪvjɑːd] n cimetière m

gravity ['grævɪtɪ] n (Physics) gravité f; pesanteur f; (seriousness) gravité

gravy ['greɪvɪ] n jus m (de viande), sauce f (au jus de viande)

gray [greɪ] adj (us) = **grey**

graze [greɪz] vi paître, brouter ▷ vt (touch lightly) frôler, effleurer; (scrape) écorcher ▷ n écorchure f

grease [griːs] n (fat) graisse f;
(lubricant) lubrifiant m ▷ vt graisser;
lubrifier; **greasy** adj gras(se),
graisseux(-euse); (hands, clothes)
graisseux

great [greɪt] adj grand(e); (heat,
pain etc) très fort(e), intense; (inf)
formidable; **Great Britain** n Grande-
Bretagne f; **great-grandfather**
n arrière-grand-père m; **great-
grandmother** n arrière-grand-mère
f; **greatly** adv très, grandement; (with
verbs) beaucoup

Greece [griːs] n Grèce f

greed [griːd] n (also: **~iness**)
avidité f; (for food) gourmandise
f; **greedy** adj avide; (for food)
gourmand(e)

Greek [griːk] adj grec (grecque) ▷ n
Grec (Grecque); (Ling) grec m

green [griːn] adj vert(e);
(inexperienced) (bien) jeune, naïf(-ïve);
(ecological: product etc) écologique
▷ n (colour) vert m; (on golf course)
green m; (stretch of grass) pelouse
f; **greens** npl (vegetables) légumes
verts; **green card** n (Aut) carte
verte; (us: work permit) permis m de
travail; **greengage** n reine-claude f;
greengrocer n (Brit) marchand m
de fruits et légumes; **greengrocer's
(shop)** n magasin m de fruits et
légumes; **greenhouse** n serre f; **the
greenhouse effect** l'effet m de serre

Greenland ['griːnlənd] n
Groenland m

green salad n salade verte

green tax n écotaxe f

greet [griːt] vt accueillir; **greeting** n
salutation f; **Christmas/birthday
greetings** souhaits mpl de Noël/de
bon anniversaire; **greeting(s) card** n
carte f de vœux

grew [gruː] pt of **grow**

grey, (us) **gray** [greɪ] adj gris(e);
(dismal) sombre; **grey-haired**, (us)
gray-haired adj aux cheveux gris;
greyhound n lévrier m

grid [grɪd] n grille f; (Elec) réseau
m; **gridlock** n (traffic jam)
embouteillage m

grief [griːf] n chagrin m, douleur f

grievance ['griːvəns] n doléance f,
grief m; (cause for complaint) grief

grieve [griːv] vi avoir du chagrin;
se désoler ▷ vt faire de la peine à,
affliger; **to ~ for sb** pleurer qn

grill [grɪl] n (on cooker) gril m; (also:
mixed ~) grillade(s) f(pl) ▷ vt (Culin)
griller; (inf: question) cuisiner

grille [grɪl] n grillage m; (Aut)
calandre f

grim [grɪm] adj sinistre, lugubre;
(serious, stern) sévère

grime [graɪm] n crasse f

grin [grɪn] n large sourire m ▷ vi
sourire

grind [graɪnd] (pt, pp **ground**) vt
écraser; (coffee, pepper etc) moudre;
(us: meat) hacher ▷ n (work) corvée f

grip [grɪp] n (handclasp) poigne f;
(control) prise f; (handle) poignée
f; (holdall) sac m de voyage ▷ vt
saisir, empoigner; (viewer, reader)
captiver; **to come to ~s with** se
colleter avec, en venir aux prises
avec; **to ~ the road** (Aut) adhérer à
la route; **gripping** adj prenant(e),
palpitant(e)

grit [grɪt] n gravillon m; (courage) cran
m ▷ vt (road) sabler; **to ~ one's teeth**
serrer les dents

grits [grɪts] npl (us) gruau m de maïs

groan [grəun] n (of pain)
gémissement m ▷ vi gémir

grocer ['grəusə^r] n épicier m;
groceries npl provisions fpl; **grocer's
(shop), grocery** n épicerie f

groin [grɔɪn] n aine f

groom [gruːm] n (for horses)
palefrenier m; (also: **bride~**) marié m
▷ vt (horse) panser; (fig): **to ~ sb for**
former qn pour

groove [gruːv] n sillon m, rainure f

grope [grəup] vi tâtonner; **to ~ for**
chercher à tâtons

gross [grəus] *adj* grossier(-ière); (*Comm*) brut(e); **grossly** *adv* (*greatly*) très, grandement

grotesque [grə'tɛsk] *adj* grotesque

ground [graund] *pt, pp of* **grind** ▷ *n* sol *m*, terre *f*; (*land*) terrain *m*, terres *fpl*; (*Sport*) terrain; (*reason: gen pl*) raison *f*; (*us: also:* **~ wire**) terre *f* ▷ *vt* (*plane*) empêcher de décoller, retenir au sol; (*us Elec*) équiper d'une prise de terre; **grounds** *npl* (*gardens etc*) parc *m*, domaine *m*; (*of coffee*) marc *m*; **on the ~, to the ~** par terre; **to gain/lose ~** gagner/perdre du terrain; **ground floor** *n* (*BRIT*) rez-de-chaussée *m*; **groundsheet** *n* (*BRIT*) tapis *m* de sol; **groundwork** *n* préparation *f*

group [gru:p] *n* groupe *m* ▷ *vt* (*also:* **~ together**) grouper ▷ *vi* (*also:* **~ together**) se grouper

grouse [graus] *n* (*pl inv: bird*) grouse *f* (*sorte de coq de bruyère*) ▷ *vi* (*complain*) rouspéter, râler

grovel ['grɔvl] *vi* (*fig*): **to ~ (before)** ramper (devant)

grow (*pt* **grew**, *pp* **grown**) [grəu, gru:, grəun] *vi* (*plant*) pousser, croître; (*person*) grandir; (*increase*) augmenter, se développer; (*become*) devenir; **to ~ rich/weak** s'enrichir/s'affaiblir ▷ *vt* cultiver, faire pousser; (*hair, beard*) laisser pousser; **grow on** *vt fus*: **that painting is ~ing on me** je finirai par aimer ce tableau; **grow up** *vi* grandir

growl [graul] *vi* grogner

grown [grəun] *pp of* **grow**; **grown-up** *n* adulte *m/f*, grande personne *f*

growth [grəuθ] *n* croissance *f*, développement *m*; (*what has grown*) pousse *f*, poussée *f*; (*Med*) grosseur *f*, tumeur *f*

grub [grʌb] *n* larve *f*; (*inf: food*) bouffe *f*

grubby ['grʌbɪ] *adj* crasseux(-euse)

grudge [grʌdʒ] *n* rancune *f* ▷ *vt*: **to ~ sb sth** (*in giving*) donner qch à qn à contre-cœur; (*resent*) reprocher qch à qn; **to bear sb a ~ (for)** garder rancune or en vouloir à qn (de)

gruelling, (*us*) **grueling** ['gruəlɪŋ] *adj* exténuant(e)

gruesome ['gru:səm] *adj* horrible

grumble ['grʌmbl] *vi* rouspéter, ronchonner

grumpy ['grʌmpɪ] *adj* grincheux(-euse)

grunt [grʌnt] *vi* grogner

guarantee [gærən'ti:] *n* garantie *f* ▷ *vt* garantir

guard [gɑ:d] *n* garde *f*; (*one man*) garde *m*; (*BRIT Rail*) chef *m* de train; (*safety device: on machine*) dispositif *m* de sûreté; (*also:* **fire~**) garde-feu *inv* ▷ *vt* garder, surveiller; (*protect*): **to ~ sb/sth (against** or **from)** protéger qn/qch (contre); **to be on one's ~** (*fig*) être sur ses gardes; **guardian** *n* gardien(ne); (*of minor*) tuteur(-trice)

guerrilla [gə'rɪlə] *n* guérillero *m*

guess [gɛs] *vi* deviner ▷ *vt* deviner; (*estimate*) évaluer; (*us*) croire, penser ▷ *n* supposition *f*, hypothèse *f*; **to take** or **have a ~** essayer de deviner

guest [gɛst] *n* invité(e); (*in hotel*) client(e); **guest house** *n* pension *f*; **guest room** *n* chambre *f* d'amis

guidance ['gaɪdəns] *n* (*advice*) conseils *mpl*

guide [gaɪd] *n* (*person*) guide *m/f*; (*book*) guide *m*; (*also:* **Girl G~**) éclaireuse *f*; (*Roman Catholic*) guide *f* ▷ *vt* guider; **is there an English-speaking ~?** est-ce que l'un des guides parle anglais?; **guidebook** *n* guide *m*; **guide dog** *n* chien *m* d'aveugle; **guided tour** *n* visite guidée; **what time does the guided tour start?** la visite guidée commence à quelle heure?; **guidelines** *npl* (*advice*) instructions générales, conseils *mpl*

guild [gɪld] *n* (*Hist*) corporation *f*; (*sharing interests*) cercle *m*, association *f*

guilt [gɪlt] n culpabilité f; **guilty** adj
coupable
guinea pig ['gɪnɪ-] n cobaye m
guitar [gɪ'tɑːʳ] n guitare f; **guitarist** n
guitariste m/f
gulf [gʌlf] n golfe m; (abyss) gouffre m
gull [gʌl] n mouette f
gulp [gʌlp] vi avaler sa salive; (from
emotion) avoir la gorge serrée,
s'étrangler ▷ vt (also: ~ **down**) avaler
gum [gʌm] n (Anat) gencive f; (glue)
colle f; (also: **chewing-~**) chewing-
gum m ▷ vt coller
gun [gʌn] n (small) revolver m,
pistolet m; (rifle) fusil m, carabine
f; (cannon) canon m; **gunfire** n
fusillade f; **gunman** (irreg) n bandit
armé; **gunpoint** n: **at gunpoint**
sous la menace du pistolet (or fusil);
gunpowder n poudre f à canon;
gunshot n coup m de feu
gush [gʌʃ] vi jaillir; (fig) se répandre
en effusions
gust [gʌst] n (of wind) rafale f
gut [gʌt] n intestin m, boyau m; **guts**
npl (inf: Anat) boyaux mpl; (: courage)
cran m
gutter ['gʌtəʳ] n (of roof) gouttière f;
(in street) caniveau m
guy [gaɪ] n (inf: man) type m; (also:
~**rope**) corde f; (figure) effigie de Guy
Fawkes
Guy Fawkes' Night [gaɪ'fɔːks-] n
voir article **"Guy Fawkes' Night"**

gym [dʒɪm] n (also: ~**nasium**)
gymnase m; (also: ~**nastics**) gym f;
gymnasium n gymnase m; **gymnast**
n gymnaste m/f; **gymnastics** n,
npl gymnastique f; **gym shoes** npl
chaussures fpl de gym(nastique)
gynaecologist, (US) **gynecologist**
[gaɪnɪ'kɒlədʒɪst] n gynécologue m/f
gypsy ['dʒɪpsɪ] n gitan(e),
bohémien(ne)

hair [hɛəʳ] n cheveux mpl; (on body) poils mpl; (of animal) pelage m; (single hair: on head) cheveu m; (: on body, of animal) poil m; **to do one's ~** se coiffer; **hairband** n (elasticated) bandeau m; (plastic) serre-tête m; **hairbrush** n brosse f à cheveux; **haircut** n coupe f (de cheveux); **hairdo** n coiffure f; **hairdresser** n coiffeur(-euse); **hairdresser's** n salon m de coiffure, coiffeur m; **hair dryer** n sèche-cheveux m, séchoir m; **hair gel** n gel m pour cheveux; **hair spray** n laque f (pour les cheveux); **hairstyle** n coiffure f; **hairy** adj poilu(e), chevelu(e); (inf: frightening) effrayant(e)

haka ['hɑːkə] n (NZ) haka m

hake [heɪk] (pl **hake** or **hakes**) n colin m, merlu m

half [hɑːf] n (pl **halves**) moitié f; (of beer: also: **~ pint**) ≈ demi m; (Rail, bus: also: **~ fare**) demi-tarif m; (Sport: of match) mi-temps f ▷ adj demi(e) ▷ adv (à) moitié, à demi; **~ an hour** une demi-heure; **~ a dozen** une demi-douzaine; **~ a pound** une demi-livre, ≈ 250 g; **two and a ~** deux et demi; **to cut sth in ~** couper qch en deux; **half board** n (BRIT: in hotel) demi-pension f; **half-brother** n demi-frère m; **half day** n demi-journée f; **half fare** n demi-tarif m; **half-hearted** adj tiède, sans enthousiasme; **half-hour** n demi-heure f; **half-price** adj à moitié prix ▷ adv (also: **at half-price**) à moitié prix; **half term** n (BRIT Scol) vacances fpl (de demi-trimestre); **half-time** n mi-temps f; **halfway** adv à mi-chemin; **halfway through sth** au milieu de qch

hall [hɔːl] n salle f; (entrance way: big) hall m; (: small) entrée f; (US: corridor) couloir m; (mansion) château m, manoir m

hallmark ['hɔːlmɑːk] n poinçon m; (fig) marque f

hallo [hə'ləʊ] excl = **hello**

haberdashery [hæbə'dæʃərɪ] n (BRIT) mercerie f

habit ['hæbɪt] n habitude f; (costume: Rel) habit m

habitat ['hæbɪtæt] n habitat m

hack [hæk] vt hacher, tailler ▷ n (pej: writer) nègre m; **hacker** n (Comput) pirate m (informatique)

had [hæd] pt, pp of **have**

haddock ['hædək] (pl **haddock** or **haddocks**) n églefin m; **smoked ~** haddock m

hadn't ['hædnt] = **had not**

haemorrhage, (US) **hemorrhage** ['hɛmərɪdʒ] n hémorragie f

haemorrhoids, (US) **hemorrhoids** ['hɛmərɔɪdz] npl hémorroïdes fpl

haggle ['hægl] vi marchander

Hague [heɪg] n: **The ~** La Haye

hail [heɪl] n grêle f ▷ vt (call) héler; (greet) acclamer ▷ vi grêler; **hailstone** n grêlon m

hall of residence n (BRIT) pavillon m
or résidence f universitaire

Hallowe'en, Halloween
['hæləʊ'iːn] n veille f de la Toussaint

hallucination [həluːsɪ'neɪʃən] n
hallucination f

hallway ['hɔːlweɪ] n (entrance)
vestibule m; (corridor) couloir m

halo ['heɪləʊ] n (of saint etc) auréole f

halt [hɔːlt] n halte f, arrêt m ▷ vt faire
arrêter; (progress etc) interrompre ▷ vi
faire halte, s'arrêter

halve [hɑːv] vt (apple etc) partager or
diviser en deux; (reduce by half) réduire
de moitié

halves [hɑːvz] npl of **half**

ham [hæm] n jambon m

hamburger ['hæmbɜːgəʳ] n
hamburger m

hamlet ['hæmlɪt] n hameau m

hammer ['hæməʳ] n marteau m
▷ vt (nail) enfoncer; (fig) éreinter,
démolir ▷ vi (at door) frapper à
coups redoublés; **to ~ a point
home to sb** faire rentrer qch dans
la tête de qn

hammock ['hæmək] n hamac m

hamper ['hæmpəʳ] vt gêner ▷ n
panier m (d'osier)

hamster ['hæmstəʳ] n hamster m

hamstring ['hæmstrɪŋ] n (Anat)
tendon m du jarret

hand [hænd] n main f; (of clock)
aiguille f; (handwriting) écriture f; (at
cards) jeu m; (worker) ouvrier(-ière)

▷ vt passer, donner; **to give sb a ~**
donner un coup de main à qn; **at ~**
à portée de la main; **in ~** (situation)
en main; (work) en cours; **to be on ~**
(person) être disponible; (emergency
services) se tenir prêt(e) (à intervenir);
to ~ (information etc) sous la main,
à portée de la main; **on the one ~
..., on the other ~** d'une part ...,
d'autre part; **hand down** vt passer;
(tradition, heirloom) transmettre; (US:
sentence, verdict) prononcer; **hand in**
vt remettre; **hand out** vt distribuer;
hand over vt remettre; (powers
etc) transmettre; **handbag** n sac m
à main; **hand baggage** n = **hand
luggage**; **handbook** n manuel
m; **handbrake** n frein m à main;
handcuffs npl menottes fpl; **handful**
n poignée f

handicap ['hændɪkæp] n handicap
m ▷ vt handicaper

handkerchief ['hæŋkətʃɪf] n
mouchoir m

handle ['hændl] n (of door etc)
poignée f; (of cup etc) anse f; (of knife
etc) manche m; (of saucepan) queue f;
(for winding) manivelle f ▷ vt toucher,
manier; (deal with) s'occuper de;
(treat: people) prendre; **"~ with care"**
"fragile"; **to fly off the ~** s'énerver;
handlebar(s) n(pl) guidon m

hand: hand luggage n bagages mpl
à main; **handmade** adj fait(e) à la
main; **handout** n (money) aide f, don
m; (leaflet) prospectus m; (at lecture)
polycopié m; **hands-free** adj mains
libres inv ▷ n (also: **hands-free kit**) kit
m mains libres inv

handsome ['hænsəm] adj beau
(belle); (profit) considérable

handwriting ['hændraɪtɪŋ] n
écriture f

handy ['hændɪ] adj (person)
adroit(e); (close at hand) sous la main;
(convenient) pratique

hang (pt, pp **hung**) [hæŋ, hʌŋ] vt
accrocher; (criminal) pendre ▷ vi

pendre; (*hair, drapery*) tomber ▷ *n*: **to get the ~ of (doing) sth** (*inf*) attraper le coup pour faire qch; **hang about, hang around** *vi* traîner; **hang down** *vi* pendre; **hang on** *vi* (*wait*) attendre; **hang out** *vt* (*washing*) étendre (dehors) ▷ *vi* (*inf: live*) habiter, percher; (: *spend time*) traîner; **hang round** *vi* = **hang about**; **hang up** *vi* (*Tel*) raccrocher ▷ *vt* (*coat, painting etc*) accrocher, suspendre

hanger ['hæŋə^r] *n* cintre *m*, portemanteau *m*

hang-gliding ['hæŋglaɪdɪŋ] *n* vol *m* libre *or* sur aile delta

hangover ['hæŋəʊvə^r] *n* (*after drinking*) gueule *f* de bois

hankie, hanky ['hæŋkɪ] *n abbr* = **handkerchief**

happen ['hæpən] *vi* arriver, se passer, se produire; **what's ~ing?** que se passe-t-il?; **she ~ed to be free** il s'est trouvé (*or* se trouvait) qu'elle était libre; **as it ~s** justement

happily ['hæpɪlɪ] *adv* heureusement; (*cheerfully*) joyeusement

happiness ['hæpɪnɪs] *n* bonheur *m*

happy ['hæpɪ] *adj* heureux(-euse); **~ with** (*arrangements etc*) satisfait(e) de; **to be ~ to do** faire volontiers; **~ birthday!** bon anniversaire!

harass ['hærəs] *vt* accabler, tourmenter; **harassment** *n* tracasseries *fpl*

harbour, (*US*) **harbor** ['hɑ:bə^r] *n* port *m* ▷ *vt* héberger, abriter; (*hopes, suspicions*) entretenir

hard [hɑ:d] *adj* (*question, problem*) difficile; (*facts, evidence*) concret(-ète) ▷ *adv* (*work*) dur; (*think, try*) sérieusement; **to look ~ at** regarder fixement; (*thing*) regarder de près; **no ~ feelings!** sans rancune!; **to be ~ of hearing** être dur(e) d'oreille; **to be ~ done by** être traité(e) injustement; **hardback** *n* livre relié; **hardboard** *n* Isorel® *m*; **hard disk** *n* (*Comput*) disque dur;

harden *vt* durcir; (*fig*) endurcir ▷ *vi* (*substance*) durcir

hardly ['hɑ:dlɪ] *adv* (*scarcely*) à peine; (*harshly*) durement; **~ anywhere/ ever** presque nulle part/jamais

hard: hardship *n* (*difficulties*) épreuves *fpl*; (*deprivation*) privations *fpl*; **hard shoulder** *n* (BRIT *Aut*) accotement stabilisé; **hard-up** *adj* (*inf*) fauché(e); **hardware** *n* quincaillerie *f*; (*Comput, Mil*) matériel *m*; **hardware shop**, (*US*) **hardware store** *n* quincaillerie *f*; **hard-working** *adj* travailleur(-euse)

hardy ['hɑ:dɪ] *adj* robuste; (*plant*) résistant(e) au gel

hare [hɛə^r] *n* lièvre *m*

harm [hɑ:m] *n* mal *m*; (*wrong*) tort *m* ▷ *vt* (*person*) faire du mal *or* du tort à; (*thing*) endommager; **out of ~'s way** à l'abri du danger, en lieu sûr; **harmful** *adj* nuisible; **harmless** *adj* inoffensif(-ive)

harmony ['hɑ:mənɪ] *n* harmonie *f*

harness ['hɑ:nɪs] *n* harnais *m* ▷ *vt* (*horse*) harnacher; (*resources*) exploiter

harp [hɑ:p] *n* harpe *f* ▷ *vi*: **to ~ on about** revenir toujours sur

harsh [hɑ:ʃ] *adj* (*hard*) dur(e); (*severe*) sévère; (*unpleasant: sound*) discordant(e); (: *light*) cru(e)

harvest ['hɑ:vɪst] *n* (*of corn*) moisson *f*; (*of fruit*) récolte *f*; (*of grapes*) vendange *f* ▷ *vt* moissonner; récolter; vendanger

has [hæz] *vb see* **have**

hashtag ['hæʃtæg] *n* (*on Twitter*) mot-dièse *m*, hashtag *m*

hasn't ['hæznt] = **has not**

hassle ['hæsl] *n* (*inf: fuss*) histoire(s) *f(pl)*

haste [heɪst] *n* hâte *f*, précipitation *f*; **hasten** ['heɪsn] *vt* hâter, accélérer ▷ *vi* se hâter, s'empresser; **hastily** *adv* à la hâte; (*leave*) précipitamment; **hasty** *adj* (*decision, action*) hâtif(-ive); (*departure, escape*) précipité(e)

hat [hæt] *n* chapeau *m*

hatch [hætʃ] *n* (*Naut: also:* **~way**) écoutille *f*; (*BRIT: also:* **service ~**) passe-plats *m inv* ▷ *vi* éclore

hatchback ['hætʃbæk] *n* (*Aut*) modèle *m* avec hayon arrière

hate [heɪt] *vt* haïr, détester ▷ *n* haine *f*; **hatred** ['heɪtrɪd] *n* haine *f*

haul [hɔːl] *vt* traîner, tirer ▷ *n* (*of fish*) prise *f*; (*of stolen goods etc*) butin *m*

haunt [hɔːnt] *vt* (*subj: ghost, fear*) hanter; (: *person*) fréquenter ▷ *n* repaire *m*; **haunted** *adj* (*castle etc*) hanté(e); (*look*) égaré(e), hagard(e)

KEYWORD

have [hæv] (*pt, pp* **had**) *aux vb*
1 (*gen*) avoir; être; **to have eaten/ slept** avoir mangé/dormi; **to have arrived/gone** être arrivé(e)/allé(e); **having finished** *or* **when he had finished, he left** quand il a eu fini, il est parti; **we'd already eaten** nous avions déjà mangé
2 (*in tag questions*): **you've done it, haven't you?** vous l'avez fait, n'est-ce pas?
3 (*in short answers and questions*): **no I haven't!/yes we have!** mais non!/ mais si!; **so I have!** ah oui!, oui c'est vrai!; **I've been there before, have you?** j'y suis déjà allé, et vous?
▶ *modal aux vb* (*be obliged*): **to have (got) to do sth** devoir faire qch, être obligé(e) de faire qch; **she has (got) to do it** elle doit le faire, il faut qu'elle le fasse; **you haven't to tell her** vous n'êtes pas obligé de le lui dire; (*must not*) ne le lui dites surtout pas; **do you have to book?** il faut réserver?
▶ *vt* **1** (*possess*) avoir; **he has (got) blue eyes/dark hair** il a les yeux bleus/les cheveux bruns
2 (*referring to meals etc*): **to have breakfast** prendre le petit déjeuner; **to have dinner/lunch** dîner/ déjeuner; **to have a drink** prendre

un verre; **to have a cigarette** fumer une cigarette
3 (*receive*) avoir, recevoir; (*obtain*) avoir; **may I have your address?** puis-je avoir votre adresse?; **you can have it for £5** vous pouvez l'avoir pour 5 livres; **I must have it for tomorrow** il me le faut pour demain; **to have a baby** avoir un bébé
4 (*maintain, allow*): **I won't have it!** ça ne se passera pas comme ça!; **we can't have that** nous ne tolérerons pas ça
5 (*by sb else*): **to have sth done** faire faire qch; **to have one's hair cut** se faire couper les cheveux; **to have sb do sth** faire faire qch à qn
6 (*experience, suffer*) avoir; **to have a cold/flu** avoir un rhume/la grippe; **to have an operation** se faire opérer; **she had her bag stolen** elle s'est fait voler son sac
7 (*+noun*): **to have a swim/walk** nager/se promener; **to have a bath/shower** prendre un bain/une douche; **let's have a look** regardons; **to have a meeting** se réunir; **to have a party** organiser une fête; **let me have a try** laissez-moi essayer

haven ['heɪvn] *n* port *m*; (*fig*) havre *m*

haven't ['hævnt] = **have not**

havoc ['hævək] *n* ravages *mpl*

Hawaii [hə'waɪɪ] *n* (*îles fpl*) Hawaï *m*

hawk [hɔːk] *n* faucon *m*

hawthorn ['hɔːθɔːn] *n* aubépine *f*

hay [heɪ] *n* foin *m*; **hay fever** *n* rhume *m* des foins; **haystack** *n* meule *f* de foin

hazard ['hæzəd] *n* (*risk*) danger *m*, risque *m* ▷ *vt* risquer, hasarder; **hazardous** *adj* hasardeux(-euse), risqué(e); **hazard warning lights** *npl* (*Aut*) feux *mpl* de détresse

haze [heɪz] *n* brume *f*

hazel ['heɪzl] *n* (*tree*) noisetier *m* ▷ *adj* (*eyes*) noisette *inv*; **hazelnut** *n* noisette *f*

h

hazy ['heɪzɪ] adj brumeux(-euse); (idea) vague

he [hiː] pron il; **it is he who ...** c'est lui qui ...; **here he is** le voici

head [hɛd] n tête f; (leader) chef m; (of school) directeur(-trice); (of secondary school) proviseur m ▷ vt (list) être en tête de; (group, company) être à la tête de; **~s or tails** pile ou face; **~ first** la tête la première; **~ over heels in love** follement or éperdument amoureux(-euse); **to ~ the ball** faire une tête; **head for** vt fus se diriger vers; (disaster) aller à; **head off** vt (threat, danger) détourner; **headache** n mal m de tête; **to have a headache** avoir mal à la tête; **heading** n titre m; (subject title) rubrique f; **headlamp** (BRIT) n = **headlight**; **headlight** n phare m; **headline** n titre m; **head office** n siège m, bureau m central; **headphones** npl casque m (à écouteurs); **headquarters** npl (of business) bureau or siège central; (Mil) quartier général; **headroom** n (in car) hauteur f de plafond; (under bridge) hauteur limite; **headscarf** n foulard m; **headset** n = **headphones**; **headteacher** n directeur(-trice); (of secondary school) proviseur m; **head waiter** n maître m d'hôtel

heal [hiːl] vt, vi guérir

health [hɛlθ] n santé f; **health care** n services médicaux; **health centre** n (BRIT) centre m de santé; **health food** n aliment(s) naturel(s); **Health Service** n: **the Health Service** (BRIT) ≈ la Sécurité Sociale; **healthy** adj (person) en bonne santé; (climate, food, attitude etc) sain(e)

heap [hiːp] n tas m ▷ vt (also: ~ up) entasser, amonceler; **she ~ed her plate with cakes** elle a chargé son assiette de gâteaux; **~s (of)** (inf: lots) des tas (de)

hear (pt, pp heard) [hɪər, həːd] vt entendre; (news) apprendre ▷ vi entendre; **to ~ about** entendre parler de; (have news of) avoir des nouvelles de; **to ~ from sb** recevoir des nouvelles de qn

heard [həːd] pt, pp of **hear**

hearing ['hɪərɪŋ] n (sense) ouïe f; (of witnesses) audition f; (of a case) audience f; **hearing aid** n appareil m acoustique

hearse [həːs] n corbillard m

heart [hɑːt] n cœur m; **hearts** npl (Cards) cœur; **at ~** au fond; **by ~** (learn, know) par cœur; **to lose/ take ~** perdre/prendre courage; **heart attack** n crise f cardiaque; **heartbeat** n battement m de cœur; **heartbroken** adj: **to be heartbroken** avoir beaucoup de chagrin; **heartburn** n brûlures fpl d'estomac; **heart disease** n maladie f cardiaque

hearth [hɑːθ] n foyer m, cheminée f

heartless ['hɑːtlɪs] adj (person) sans cœur, insensible; (treatment) cruel(le)

hearty ['hɑːtɪ] adj chaleureux(-euse); (appetite) solide; (dislike) cordial(e); (meal) copieux(-euse)

heat [hiːt] n chaleur f; (Sport: also: qualifying ~) éliminatoire f ▷ vt chauffer; **heat up** vi (liquid) chauffer; (room) se réchauffer ▷ vt réchauffer; **heated** adj chauffé(e); (fig) passionné(e), échauffé(e), excité(e); **heater** n appareil m de chauffage; radiateur m; (in car) chauffage m; (water heater) chauffe-eau m

heather ['hɛðər] n bruyère f

heating ['hiːtɪŋ] n chauffage m

heatwave ['hiːtweɪv] n vague f de chaleur

heaven ['hɛvn] n ciel m, paradis m; (fig) paradis; **heavenly** adj céleste, divin(e)

heavily ['hɛvɪlɪ] adv lourdement; (drink, smoke) beaucoup; (sleep, sigh) profondément

heavy ['hɛvɪ] adj lourd(e); (work, rain, user, eater) gros(se); (drinker, smoker) grand(e); (schedule, week) chargé(e)

Hebrew ['hi:bru:] *adj* hébraïque ▷ *n* (*Ling*) hébreu *m*

Hebrides ['hɛbrɪdi:z] *npl*; **the ~** les Hébrides *fpl*

hectare ['hɛktɑːʳ] *n* (BRIT) hectare *m*

hectic ['hɛktɪk] *adj* (*schedule*) très chargé(e); (*day*) mouvementé(e); (*lifestyle*) trépidant(e)

he'd [hi:d] = **he would**; **he had**

hedge [hɛdʒ] *n* haie *f* ▷ *vi* se dérober ▷ *vt*: **to ~ one's bets** (*fig*) se couvrir

hedgehog ['hɛdʒhɔg] *n* hérisson *m*

heed [hi:d] *vt* (*also*: **take ~ of**) tenir compte de, prendre garde à

heel [hi:l] *n* talon *m* ▷ *vt* retalonner

hefty ['hɛftɪ] *adj* (*person*) costaud(e); (*parcel*) lourd(e); (*piece, price*) gros(se)

height [haɪt] *n* (*of person*) taille *f*, grandeur *f*; (*of object*) hauteur *f*; (*of plane, mountain*) altitude *f*; (*high ground*) hauteur, éminence *f*; (*fig*: *of glory, fame, power*) sommet *m*; (*: of luxury, stupidity*) comble *m*; **at the ~ of summer** au cœur de l'été; **heighten** *vt* hausser, surélever; (*fig*) augmenter

heir [ɛəʳ] *n* héritier *m*; **heiress** *n* héritière *f*

held [hɛld] *pt*, *pp of* **hold**

helicopter ['hɛlɪkɔptəʳ] *n* hélicoptère *m*

hell [hɛl] *n* enfer *m*; **oh ~!** (*inf*) merde!

he'll [hi:l] = **he will**; **he shall**

hello [hə'ləu] *excl* bonjour!; (*to attract attention*) hé!; (*surprise*) tiens!

helmet ['hɛlmɪt] *n* casque *m*

help [hɛlp] *n* aide *f*; (*cleaner etc*) femme *f* de ménage ▷ *vt*, *vi* aider; **~!** au secours!; **~ yourself** servez-vous; **can you ~ me?** pouvez-vous m'aider?; **can I ~ you?** (*in shop*) vous désirez?; **he can't ~ it** il n'y peut rien; **help out** *vi* aider ▷ *vt*: **to ~ sb out** aider qn; **helper** *n* aide *m/f*, assistant(e); **helpful** *adj* serviable, obligeant(e); (*useful*) utile; **helping** *n* portion *f*; **helpless** *adj* impuissant(e); (*baby*) sans défense; **helpline** *n* service *m*

d'assistance téléphonique; (*free*) ≈ numéro vert

hem [hɛm] *n* ourlet *m* ▷ *vt* ourler

hemisphere ['hɛmɪsfɪəʳ] *n* hémisphère *m*

hemorrhage ['hɛmərɪdʒ] *n* (US) = **haemorrhage**

hemorrhoids ['hɛmərɔɪdz] *npl* (US) = **haemorrhoids**

hen [hɛn] *n* poule *f*; (*female bird*) femelle *f*

hence [hɛns] *adv* (*therefore*) d'où, de là; **2 years ~** d'ici 2 ans

hen night, hen party *n* soirée *f* entre filles (*avant le mariage de l'une d'elles*)

hepatitis [hɛpə'taɪtɪs] *n* hépatite *f*

her [həːʳ] *pron* (*direct*) la, l' + *vowel or h mute*; (*indirect*) lui; (*stressed, after prep*) elle ▷ *adj* son (sa), ses *pl*; *see also* **me**, **my**

herb [hə:b] *n* herbe *f*; **herbal** *adj* à base de plantes; **herbal tea** *n* tisane *f*

herd [hə:d] *n* troupeau *m*

here [hɪəʳ] *adv* ici; (*time*) alors ▷ *excl* tiens!, tenez!; **~!** (*present*) présent!; **~ is, ~ are** voici; **~ he/she is** le (la) voici

hereditary [hɪ'rɛdɪtrɪ] *adj* héréditaire

heritage ['hɛrɪtɪdʒ] *n* héritage *m*, patrimoine *m*

hernia ['hə:nɪə] *n* hernie *f*

hero ['hɪərəu] (*pl* **heroes**) *n* héros *m*; **heroic** [hɪ'rəuɪk] *adj* héroïque

heroin ['hɛrəuɪn] *n* héroïne *f* (*drogue*)

heroine ['hɛrəuɪn] *n* héroïne *f* (*femme*)

heron ['hɛrən] *n* héron *m*

herring ['hɛrɪŋ] *n* hareng *m*

hers [hə:z] *pron* le sien(ne), les siens (siennes); *see also* **mine¹**

herself [hə:'sɛlf] *pron* (*reflexive*) se; (*emphatic*) elle-même; (*after prep*) elle; *see also* **oneself**

he's [hi:z] = **he is**; **he has**

hesitant ['hɛzɪtənt] *adj* hésitant(e), indécis(e)

hesitate ['hɛzɪteɪt] vi: **to ~ (about/to do)** hésiter (sur/à faire); **hesitation** [hɛzɪ'teɪʃən] n hésitation f

heterosexual ['hɛtərəu'sɛksjuəl] adj, n hétérosexuel(le)

hexagon ['hɛksəgən] n hexagone m

hey [heɪ] excl hé!

heyday ['heɪdeɪ] n: **the ~ of** l'âge m d'or de, les beaux jours de

HGV n abbr = **heavy goods vehicle**

hi [haɪ] excl salut!; (to attract attention) hé!

hibernate ['haɪbəneɪt] vi hiberner

hiccough, hiccup ['hɪkʌp] vi hoqueter ▷ n: **to have (the) ~s** avoir le hoquet

hid [hɪd] pt of **hide**

hidden ['hɪdn] pp of **hide** ▷ adj: **~ agenda** intentions non déclarées

hide [haɪd] (pt **hid**, pp **hidden**) n (skin) peau f ▷ vt cacher ▷ vi: **to ~ (from sb)** se cacher (de qn)

hideous ['hɪdɪəs] adj hideux(-euse), atroce

hiding ['haɪdɪŋ] n (beating) correction f, volée f de coups; **to be in ~** (concealed) se tenir caché(e)

hi-fi ['haɪfaɪ] adj, n abbr (= high fidelity) hi-fi f inv

high [haɪ] adj haut(e); (speed, respect, number) grand(e); (price) élevé(e); (wind) fort(e), violent(e); (voice) aigu(ë) ▷ adv haut, en haut; **20 m ~** haut(e) de 20 m; **~ in the air** haut dans le ciel; **highchair** n (child's) chaise haute; **high-class** adj (neighbourhood, hotel) chic inv, de grand standing; **higher education** n études supérieures; **high heels** npl talons hauts, hauts talons; **high jump** n (Sport) saut m en hauteur; **highlands** ['haɪləndz] npl région montagneuse; **the Highlands** (in Scotland) les Highlands mpl; **highlight** n (fig: of event) point culminant ▷ vt (emphasize) faire ressortir, souligner; **highlights** npl (in hair) reflets mpl; **highlighter** n (pen) surligneur (lumineux); **highly** adv extrêmement, très; (unlikely) fort; (recommended, skilled, qualified) hautement; **to speak highly of** dire beaucoup de bien de; **highness** n: **His/Her Highness** son Altesse f; **high-rise** n (also: **high-rise block, high-rise building**) tour f (d'habitation); **high school** n lycée m; (US) établissement m d'enseignement supérieur; **high season** n (BRIT) haute saison; **high street** n (BRIT) grand-rue f; **high-tech** (inf) adj de pointe; **highway** n (BRIT) route f; (US) route nationale; **Highway Code** n (BRIT) code m de la route

hijack ['haɪdʒæk] vt détourner (par la force); **hijacker** n auteur m d'un détournement d'avion, pirate m de l'air

hike [haɪk] vi faire des excursions à pied ▷ n excursion f à pied, randonnée f; **hiker** n promeneur(-euse), excursionniste m/f; **hiking** n excursions fpl à pied, randonnée f

hilarious [hɪ'lɛərɪəs] adj (behaviour, event) désopilant(e)

hill [hɪl] n colline f; (fairly high) montagne f; (on road) côte f; **hillside** n (flanc m de) coteau m; **hill walking** n randonnée f de basse montagne; **hilly** adj vallonné(e), montagneux(-euse)

him [hɪm] pron (direct) le, l' + vowel or h mute; (stressed, indirect, after prep) lui; see also **me**; **himself** pron (reflexive) se; (emphatic) lui-même; (after prep) lui; see also **oneself**

hind [haɪnd] adj de derrière

hinder ['hɪndəʳ] vt gêner; (delay) retarder

hindsight ['haɪndsaɪt] n: **with (the benefit of) ~** avec du recul, rétrospectivement

Hindu ['hɪnduː] n Hindou(e); **Hinduism** n (Rel) hindouisme m

hinge [hɪndʒ] n charnière f ▷ vi (fig):
to ~ on dépendre de

hint [hɪnt] n allusion f; (advice) conseil
m; (clue) indication f ▷ vt: **to ~ that**
insinuer que ▷ vi: **to ~ at** faire une
allusion à

hip [hɪp] n hanche f

hippie, hippy ['hɪpɪ] n hippie m/f

hippo ['hɪpəu] (pl **hippos**) n
hippopotame m

hippopotamus (pl
hippopotamuses or **hippopotami**)
[hɪpə'pɔtəməs, hɪpə'pɔtəmaɪ] n
hippopotame m

hippy ['hɪpɪ] n = **hippie**

hire ['haɪəʳ] vt (BRIT: car, equipment)
louer; (worker) embaucher, engager
▷ n location f; **for ~** à louer; (taxi)
libre; **I'd like to ~ a car** je voudrais
louer une voiture; **hire(d) car** n
(BRIT) voiture f de location; **hire
purchase** n (BRIT) achat m (or vente f)
à tempérament or crédit

his [hɪz] pron le sien(ne), les siens
(siennes) ▷ adj son (sa), ses pl;
mine¹; **my**

Hispanic [hɪs'pænɪk] adj (in US)
hispano-américain(e) ▷ n Hispano-
Américain(e)

hiss [hɪs] vi siffler

historian [hɪ'stɔːrɪən] n
historien(ne)

historic(al) [hɪ'stɔrɪk(l)] adj
historique

history ['hɪstərɪ] n histoire f

hit [hɪt] vt (pt, pp **hit**) frapper; (reach:
target) atteindre, toucher; (collide
with: car) entrer en collision avec,
heurter; (fig: affect) toucher ▷ n coup
m; (success) succès m; (song) tube m;
(to website) visite f; (on search engine)
résultat m de recherche; **to ~ it off
with sb** bien s'entendre avec qn; **hit
back** vi: **to ~ back at sb** prendre sa
revanche sur qn

hitch [hɪtʃ] vt (fasten) accrocher,
attacher; (also: **~ up**) remonter d'une
saccade ▷ vi faire de l'autostop ▷ n

(difficulty) anicroche f, contretemps
m; **to ~ a lift** faire du stop; **hitch-hike**
vi faire de l'auto-stop; **hitch-hiker** n
auto-stoppeur(-euse); **hitch-hiking**
n auto-stop m, stop m (inf)

hi-tech ['haɪtɛk] adj de pointe

hitman ['hɪtmæn] (irreg) n (inf) tueur
m à gages

HIV n abbr (= human immunodeficiency
virus) HIV m, VIH m; **~-negative**
séronégatif(-ive); **~-positive**
séropositif(-ive)

hive [haɪv] n ruche f

hoard [hɔːd] n (of food) provisions
fpl, réserves fpl; (of money) trésor m
▷ vt amasser

hoarse [hɔːs] adj enroué(e)

hoax [həuks] n canular m

hob [hɔb] n plaque chauffante

hobble ['hɔbl] vi boitiller

hobby ['hɔbɪ] n passe-temps favori

hobo ['həubəu] n (US) vagabond m

hockey ['hɔkɪ] n hockey m; **hockey
stick** n crosse f de hockey

hog [hɔg] n porc (châtré) ▷ vt (fig)
accaparer; **to go the whole ~** aller
jusqu'au bout

Hogmanay [hɔgmə'neɪ] n réveillon
m du jour de l'An, Saint-Sylvestre f

● **HOGMANAY**

● La Saint-Sylvestre ou "New Year's
● Eve" se nomme Hogmanay en
● Écosse. En cette occasion, la
● famille et les amis se réunissent
● pour entendre sonner les douze
● coups de minuit et pour fêter le
● "first-footing", une coutume qui
● veut qu'on se rende chez ses amis et
● voisins en apportant quelque chose
● à boire (du whisky en général) et
● un morceau de charbon en gage de
● prospérité pour la nouvelle année.

hoist [hɔɪst] n palan m ▷ vt hisser

hold [həuld] (pt, pp **held**) vt tenir;
(contain) contenir; (meeting)

tenir; (*keep back*) retenir; (*believe*) considérer; (*possess*) avoir ▷ *vi* (*withstand pressure*) tenir (bon); (*be valid*) valoir; (*on telephone*) attendre ▷ *n* prise *f*; (*find*) influence *f*; (*Naut*) cale *f*; **to catch** *or* **get (a) ~ of** saisir; **to get ~ of** (*find*) trouver; **~ the line!** (*Tel*) ne quittez pas!; **to ~ one's own** (*fig*) (bien) se défendre; **hold back** *vt* retenir; (*secret*) cacher; **hold on** *vi* tenir bon; (*wait*) attendre; **~ on!** (*Tel*) ne quittez pas!; **to ~ on to sth** (*grasp*) se cramponner à qch; (*keep*) conserver *or* garder qch; **hold out** *vt* offrir ▷ *vi* (*resist*): **to ~ out (against)** résister (devant), tenir bon (devant); **hold up** *vt* (*raise*) lever; (*support*) soutenir; (*delay*) retarder (: *traffic*) ralentir; (*rob*) braquer; **holdall** *n* (*BRIT*) fourre-tout *m inv*; **holder** *n* (*container*) support *m*; (*of ticket, record*) détenteur(-trice); (*of office, title, passport etc*) titulaire *m/f*
hole [həʊl] *n* trou *m*
holiday ['hɔlɪdɪ] *n* (*BRIT*: *vacation*) vacances *fpl*; (*day off*) jour *m* de congé; (*public*) jour férié; **to be on ~** être en vacances; **I'm here on ~** je suis ici en vacances; **holiday camp** *n* (*also*: **holiday centre**) camp *m* de vacances; **holiday job** *n* (*BRIT*) boulot *m* (*inf*) de vacances; **holiday-maker** *n* (*BRIT*) vacancier(-ière); **holiday resort** *n* centre *m* de villégiature *or* de vacances
Holland ['hɔlənd] *n* Hollande *f*
hollow ['hɔləʊ] *adj* creux(-euse); (*fig*) faux (fausse) ▷ *n* creux *m*; (*in land*) dépression *f* (de terrain), cuvette *f* ▷ *vt*: **to ~ out** creuser, évider
holly ['hɔlɪ] *n* houx *m*
holocaust ['hɔləkɔ:st] *n* holocauste *m*
holy ['həʊlɪ] *adj* saint(e); (*bread, water*) bénit(e); (*ground*) sacré(e)
home [həʊm] *n* foyer *m*, maison *f*; (*country*) pays natal, patrie *f*; (*institution*) maison ▷ *adj* de famille; (*Econ, Pol*) national(e), intérieur(e);

(*Sport: team*) qui reçoit; (: *match, win*) sur leur (*or* notre) terrain ▷ *adv* chez soi, à la maison; au pays natal; (*right in: nail etc*) à fond; **at ~** chez soi, à la maison; **to go** (*or* **come**) **~** rentrer (chez soi), rentrer à la maison (*or* au pays); **make yourself at ~** faites comme chez vous; **home address** *n* domicile permanent; **homeland** *n* patrie *f*; **homeless** *adj* sans foyer, sans abri; **homely** *adj* (*plain*) simple, sans prétention; (*welcoming*) accueillant(e); **home-made** *adj* fait(e) à la maison; **home match** *n* match *m* à domicile; **Home Office** *n* (*BRIT*) ministère *m* de l'Intérieur; **home owner** *n* propriétaire occupant; **home page** *n* (*Comput*) page *f* d'accueil; **Home Secretary** *n* (*BRIT*) ministre *m* de l'Intérieur; **homesick** *adj*: **to be homesick** avoir le mal du pays; (*missing one's family*) s'ennuyer de sa famille; **home town** *n* ville natale; **homework** *n* devoirs *mpl*
homicide ['hɔmɪsaɪd] *n* (*US*) homicide *m*
homoeopathic, (*US*) **homeopathic** [həʊmɪəʊ'pæθɪk] *adj* (*medicine*) homéopathique; (*doctor*) homéopathe
homoeopathy, (*US*) **homeopathy** [həʊmɪ'ɔpəθɪ] *n* homéopathie *f*
homosexual [hɔməʊ'sɛksjuəl] *adj*, *n* homosexuel(le)
honest ['ɔnɪst] *adj* honnête; (*sincere*) franc (franche); **honestly** *adv* honnêtement; franchement; **honesty** *n* honnêteté *f*
honey ['hʌnɪ] *n* miel *m*; **honeymoon** *n* lune *f* de miel, voyage *m* de noces; **we're on honeymoon** nous sommes en voyage de noces; **honeysuckle** *n* chèvrefeuille *m*
Hong Kong ['hɔŋ'kɔŋ] *n* Hong Kong
honorary ['ɔnərərɪ] *adj* honoraire; (*duty, title*) honorifique; **~ degree** diplôme *m* honoris causa

honour, (US) **honor** ['ɔnər] vt
honorer ▷ n honneur m; **to
graduate with ~s** obtenir sa licence
avec mention; **honourable**, (US)
honorable adj honorable; **honours
degree** n (Scol) ≈ licence f avec
mention

hood [hud] n capuchon m; (of cooker)
hotte f; (BRIT Aut) capote f; (US Aut)
capot m; **hoodie** ['hudɪ] n (top)
sweat m à capuche

hoof (pl **hoofs** or **hooves**) [huːf,
huːvz] n sabot m

hook [huk] n crochet m; (on dress)
agrafe f; (for fishing) hameçon m ▷ vt
accrocher; **off the ~** (Tel) décroché

hooligan ['huːlɪɡən] n voyou m

hoop [huːp] n cerceau m

hoot [huːt] vi (BRIT Aut) klaxonner;
(siren) mugir; (owl) hululer

Hoover® ['huːvər] (BRIT) n aspirateur
m ▷ vt: **to hoover** (room) passer
l'aspirateur dans; (carpet) passer
l'aspirateur sur

hooves [huːvz] npl of **hoof**

hop [hɔp] vi sauter; (on one foot)
sauter à cloche-pied; (bird) sautiller

hope [həup] vt, vi espérer ▷ n
espoir m; **I ~ so** je l'espère; **I ~
not** j'espère que non; **hopeful**
adj (person) plein(e) d'espoir;
(situation) prometteur(-euse),
encourageant(e); **hopefully** adv
(expectantly) avec espoir, avec
optimisme; (one hopes) avec un
peu de chance; **hopeless** adj
désespéré(e); (useless) nul(le)

hops [hɔps] npl houblon m

horizon [hə'raɪzn] n horizon
m; **horizontal** [hɔrɪ'zɔntl] adj
horizontal(e)

hormone ['hɔːməun] n hormone f

horn [hɔːn] n corne f; (Mus) cor m;
(Aut) klaxon m

horoscope ['hɔrəskəup] n
horoscope m

horrendous [hə'rɛndəs] adj
horrible, affreux(-euse)

horrible ['hɔrɪbl] adj horrible,
affreux(-euse)

horrid ['hɔrɪd] adj (person) détestable;
(weather, place, smell) épouvantable

horrific [hɔ'rɪfɪk] adj horrible

horrifying ['hɔrɪfaɪɪŋ] adj
horrifiant(e)

horror ['hɔrər] n horreur f; **horror
film** n film m d'épouvante

hors d'œuvre [ɔ'dəːvrə] n hors
d'œuvre m

horse [hɔːs] n cheval m; **horseback:
on horseback** adj, adv à cheval;
horse chestnut n (nut) marron m
(d'Inde); (tree) marronnier m (d'Inde);
horsepower n puissance f (en
chevaux); (unit) cheval-vapeur m
(CV); **horse-racing** n courses fpl de
chevaux; **horseradish** n raifort m;
horse riding n (BRIT) équitation f

hose [həuz] n tuyau m; (also: **garden
~**) tuyau d'arrosage; **hosepipe** n
tuyau m; (in garden) tuyau d'arrosage

hospital ['hɔspɪtl] n hôpital m; **in ~** à
l'hôpital; **where's the nearest ~?** où
est l'hôpital le plus proche?

hospitality [hɔspɪ'tælɪtɪ] n
hospitalité f

host [həust] n hôte m; (TV, Radio)
présentateur(-trice); (large number): **a
~ of** une foule de; (Rel) hostie f

hostage ['hɔstɪdʒ] n otage m

hostel ['hɔstl] n foyer m; (also: **youth
~**) auberge f de jeunesse

hostess ['həustɪs] n hôtesse f; (BRIT:
also: **air ~**) hôtesse de l'air; (TV, Radio)
présentatrice f

hostile ['hɔstaɪl] adj hostile

hostility [hɔ'stɪlɪtɪ] n hostilité f

hot [hɔt] adj chaud(e); (as opposed
to only warm) très chaud; (spicy)
fort(e); (fig: contest) acharné(e);
(topic) brûlant(e); (temper) violent(e),
passionné(e); **to be ~** (person) avoir
chaud; (thing) être (très) chaud; **it's ~**
(weather) il fait chaud; **hot dog** n
hot-dog m

hotel [həu'tɛl] n hôtel m

hotspot ['hɔtspɔt] n (Comput: also: **wireless ~**) borne f wifi, hotspot m

hot-water bottle [hɔt'wɔːtə-] n bouillotte f

hound [haund] vt poursuivre avec acharnement ▷ n chien courant

hour ['auə^r] n heure f; **hourly** adj toutes les heures; (rate) horaire

house n [haus] maison f; (Pol) chambre f; (Theat) salle f; auditoire m ▷ vt [hauz] (person) loger, héberger; **on the ~** (fig) aux frais de la maison; **household** n (Admin etc) ménage m; (people) famille f, maisonnée f; **householder** n propriétaire m/f; (head of house) chef m de famille; **housekeeper** n gouvernante f; **housekeeping** n (work) ménage m; **housewife** (irreg) n ménagère f; femme f au foyer; **house wine** n cuvée f maison or du patron; **housework** n (travaux mpl du) ménage m

housing ['hauzɪŋ] n logement m; **housing development**, **housing estate** (BRIT) n (blocks of flats) cité f; (houses) lotissement m

hover ['hɔvə^r] vi planer; **hovercraft** n aéroglisseur m, hovercraft m

how [hau] adv comment; **~ are you?** comment allez-vous?; **~ do you do?** bonjour; (on being introduced) enchanté(e); **~ long have you been here?** depuis combien de temps êtes-vous là?; **~ lovely/awful!** que or comme c'est joli/affreux!; **~ much time/many people?** combien de temps/gens?; **~ much does it cost?** ça coûte combien?; **~ old are you?** quel âge avez-vous?; **~ tall is he?** combien mesure-t-il?; **~ is school?** ça va à l'école?; **~ was the film?** comment était le film?

however [hau'ɛvə^r] conj pourtant, cependant ▷ adv: **~ I do it** de quelque manière que je m'y prenne; **~ cold it is** même s'il fait très froid; **~ did you do it?** comment y êtes-vous donc arrivé?

howl [haul] n hurlement m ▷ vi hurler; (wind) mugir

H.P. n abbr (BRIT) = **hire purchase**

h.p. abbr (Aut) = **horsepower**

HQ n abbr (= headquarters) QG m

hr abbr (= hour) h

hrs abbr (= hours) h

HTML n abbr (= hypertext markup language) HTML m

hubcap ['hʌbkæp] n (Aut) enjoliveur m

huddle ['hʌdl] vi: **to ~ together** se blottir les uns contre les autres

huff [hʌf] n: **in a ~** fâché(e)

hug [hʌg] vt serrer dans ses bras; (shore, kerb) serrer ▷ n: **to give sb a ~** serrer qn dans ses bras

huge [hjuːdʒ] adj énorme, immense

hull [hʌl] n (of ship) coque f

hum [hʌm] vt (tune) fredonner ▷ vi fredonner; (insect) bourdonner; (plane, tool) vrombir

human ['hjuːmən] adj humain(e) ▷ n (also: **~ being**) être humain

humane [hjuː'meɪn] adj humain(e), humanitaire

humanitarian [hjuːmænɪ'tɛərɪən] adj humanitaire

humanity [hjuː'mænɪtɪ] n humanité f

human rights npl droits mpl de l'homme

humble ['hʌmbl] adj humble, modeste

humid ['hjuːmɪd] adj humide; **humidity** [hjuː'mɪdɪtɪ] n humidité f

humiliate [hjuː'mɪlɪeɪt] vt humilier

humiliating [hjuː'mɪlɪeɪtɪŋ] adj humiliant(e)

humiliation [hjuːmɪlɪ'eɪʃən] n humiliation f

hummus ['huməs] n houm(m)ous m

humorous ['hjuːmərəs] adj humoristique

humour, (US) **humor** ['hjuːmə^r] n humour m; (mood) humeur f ▷ vt (person) faire plaisir à; se prêter aux caprices de

hump [hʌmp] n bosse f
hunch [hʌntʃ] n (premonition) intuition f
hundred ['hʌndrəd] num cent; ~s of des centaines de; **hundredth** ['hʌndrədɪdθ] num centième
hung [hʌŋ] pt, pp of hang
Hungarian [hʌŋ'gɛərɪən] adj hongrois(e) ▷ n Hongrois(e); (Ling) hongrois m
Hungary ['hʌŋgərɪ] n Hongrie f
hunger ['hʌŋgə'] n faim f ▷ vi: **to ~ for** avoir faim de, désirer ardemment
hungry ['hʌŋgrɪ] adj affamé(e); **to be ~** avoir faim; **~ for** (fig) avide de
hunt [hʌnt] vt (seek) chercher; (Sport) chasser ▷ vi (search): **to ~ for** chercher (partout); (Sport) chasser ▷ n (Sport) chasse f; **hunter** n chasseur m; **hunting** n chasse f
hurdle ['hə:dl] n (Sport) haie f; (fig) obstacle m
hurl [hə:l] vt lancer (avec violence); (abuse, insults) lancer
hurrah, hurray [hu'rɑ:, hu'reɪ] excl hourra!
hurricane ['hʌrɪkən] n ouragan m
hurry ['hʌrɪ] n hâte f, précipitation f ▷ vi se presser, se dépêcher ▷ vt (person) faire presser, faire se dépêcher; (work) presser; **to be in a ~** être pressé(e); **to do sth in a ~** faire qch en vitesse; **hurry up** vi se dépêcher
hurt [hə:t] (pt, pp hurt) vt (cause pain to) faire mal à; (injure, fig) blesser ▷ vi faire mal ▷ adj blessé(e); **my arm ~s** j'ai mal au bras; **to ~ o.s.** se faire mal
husband ['hʌzbənd] n mari m
hush [hʌʃ] n calme m, silence m ▷ vt faire taire; **~!** chut!
husky ['hʌskɪ] adj (voice) rauque ▷ n chien m esquimau or de traîneau
hut [hʌt] n hutte f; (shed) cabane f
hyacinth ['haɪəsɪnθ] n jacinthe f
hydrofoil ['haɪdrəfɔɪl] n hydrofoil m
hydrogen ['haɪdrədʒən] n hydrogène m

hygiene ['haɪdʒi:n] n hygiène f; **hygienic** [haɪ'dʒi:nɪk] adj hygiénique
hymn [hɪm] n hymne m; cantique m
hype [haɪp] n (inf) matraquage m publicitaire or médiatique
hyperlink ['haɪpəlɪŋk] n hyperlien m
hypermarket ['haɪpəmɑ:kɪt] (BRIT) n hypermarché m
hyphen ['haɪfn] n trait m d'union
hypnotize ['hɪpnətaɪz] vt hypnotiser
hypocrite ['hɪpəkrɪt] n hypocrite m/f
hypocritical [hɪpə'krɪtɪkl] adj hypocrite
hypothesis (pl hypotheses) [haɪ'pɒθɪsɪs, -si:z] n hypothèse f
hysterical [hɪ'stɛrɪkl] adj hystérique; (funny) hilarant(e)
hysterics [hɪ'stɛrɪks] npl; **to be in/ have ~** (anger, panic) avoir une crise de nerfs; (laughter) attraper un fou rire

h

I [aɪ] *pron* je; (*before vowel*) j'; (*stressed*) moi

ice [aɪs] *n* glace *f*; (*on road*) verglas *m* ▷ *vt* (*cake*) glacer ▷ *vi* (*also:* **~ over**) geler; (*also:* **~ up**) se givrer; **iceberg** *n* iceberg *m*; **ice cream** *n* glace *f*; **ice cube** *n* glaçon *m*; **ice hockey** *n* hockey *m* sur glace

Iceland ['aɪslənd] *n* Islande *f*; **Icelander** *n* Islandais(e); **Icelandic** [aɪs'lændɪk] *adj* islandais(e) ▷ *n* (*Ling*) islandais *m*

ice: ice lolly *n* (*BRIT*) esquimau *m*; **ice rink** *n* patinoire *f*; **ice skating** *n* patinage *m* (sur glace)

icing ['aɪsɪŋ] *n* (*Culin*) glaçage *m*; **icing sugar** *n* (*BRIT*) sucre *m* glace

icon ['aɪkɔn] *n* icône *f*

ICT *n abbr* (*BRIT Scol*: = *information and communications technology*) TIC *fpl*

icy ['aɪsɪ] *adj* glacé(e); (*road*) verglacé(e); (*weather, temperature*) glacial(e)

I'd [aɪd] = **I would; I had**

ID card *n* carte *f* d'identité

idea [aɪ'dɪə] *n* idée *f*

ideal [aɪ'dɪəl] *n* idéal *m* ▷ *adj* idéal(e); **ideally** [aɪ'dɪəlɪ] *adv* (*preferably*) dans l'idéal; (*perfectly*): **he is ideally suited to the job** il est parfait pour ce poste

identical [aɪ'dɛntɪkl] *adj* identique

identification [aɪdɛntɪfɪ'keɪʃən] *n* identification *f*; **means of ~** pièce *f* d'identité

identify [aɪ'dɛntɪfaɪ] *vt* identifier

identity [aɪ'dɛntɪtɪ] *n* identité *f*; **identity card** *n* carte *f* d'identité; **identity theft** *n* usurpation *f* d'identité

ideology [aɪdɪ'ɔlədʒɪ] *n* idéologie *f*

idiom ['ɪdɪəm] *n* (*phrase*) expression *f* idiomatique; (*style*) style *m*

idiot ['ɪdɪət] *n* idiot(e), imbécile *m/f*

idle ['aɪdl] *adj* (*doing nothing*) sans occupation, désœuvré(e); (*lazy*) oisif(-ive), paresseux(-euse); (*unemployed*) au chômage; (*machinery*) au repos; (*question, pleasures*) vain(e), futile ▷ *vi* (*engine*) tourner au ralenti

idol ['aɪdl] *n* idole *f*

idyllic [ɪ'dɪlɪk] *adj* idyllique

i.e. *abbr* (= *id est: that is*) c. à d., c'est-à-dire

if [ɪf] *conj* si; **if necessary** si nécessaire, le cas échéant; **if so** si c'est le cas; **if not** sinon; **if only I could!** si seulement je pouvais!; *see also* **as; even**

ignite [ɪg'naɪt] *vt* mettre le feu à, enflammer ▷ *vi* s'enflammer

ignition [ɪg'nɪʃən] *n* (*Aut*) allumage *m*; **to switch on/off the ~** mettre/couper le contact

ignorance ['ɪgnərəns] *n* ignorance *f*

ignorant ['ɪgnərənt] *adj* ignorant(e); **to be ~ of** (*subject*) ne rien connaître en; (*events*) ne pas être au courant de

ignore [ɪg'nɔːʳ] *vt* ne tenir aucun compte de; (*mistake*) ne pas relever;

(person: pretend to not see) faire semblant de ne pas reconnaître; (: pay no attention to) ignorer

ill [ɪl] adj (sick) malade; (bad) mauvais(e) ▷ n mal m ▷ adv: **to speak/think ~ of sb** dire/penser du mal de qn; **to be taken ~** tomber malade

I'll [aɪl] = **I will; I shall**

illegal [ɪ'li:gl] adj illégal(e)

illegible [ɪ'lɛdʒɪbl] adj illisible

illegitimate [ɪlɪ'dʒɪtɪmət] adj illégitime

ill health n mauvaise santé

illiterate [ɪ'lɪtərət] adj illettré(e)

illness ['ɪlnɪs] n maladie f

illuminate [ɪ'lu:mɪneɪt] vt (room, street) éclairer; (for special effect) illuminer

illusion [ɪ'lu:ʒən] n illusion f

illustrate ['ɪləstreɪt] vt illustrer

illustration [ɪlə'streɪʃən] n illustration f

I'm [aɪm] = **I am**

image ['ɪmɪdʒ] n image f; (public face) image de marque

imaginary [ɪ'mædʒɪnərɪ] adj imaginaire

imagination [ɪmædʒɪ'neɪʃən] n imagination f

imaginative [ɪ'mædʒɪnətɪv] adj imaginatif(-ive); (person) plein(e) d'imagination

imagine [ɪ'mædʒɪn] vt s'imaginer; (suppose) imaginer, supposer

imam [ɪ'mɑ:m] n imam m

imbalance [ɪm'bæləns] n déséquilibre m

imitate ['ɪmɪteɪt] vt imiter; **imitation** [ɪmɪ'teɪʃən] n imitation f

immaculate [ɪ'mækjulət] adj impeccable; (Rel) immaculé(e)

immature [ɪmə'tjuər] adj (fruit) qui n'est pas mûr(e); (person) qui manque de maturité

immediate [ɪ'mi:dɪət] adj immédiat(e); **immediately** adv (at once) immédiatement; **immediately next to** juste à côté de

immense [ɪ'mɛns] adj immense, énorme

immerse [ɪ'mə:s] vt immerger, plonger; **to be ~d in** (fig) être plongé dans

immigrant ['ɪmɪgrənt] n immigrant(e); (already established) immigré(e); **immigration** [ɪmɪ'greɪʃən] n immigration f

imminent ['ɪmɪnənt] adj imminent(e)

immoral [ɪ'mɔrl] adj immoral(e)

immortal [ɪ'mɔ:tl] adj, n immortel(le)

immune [ɪ'mju:n] adj: **~ (to)** immunisé(e) (contre); **immune system** n système m immunitaire

immunize ['ɪmjunaɪz] vt immuniser

impact ['ɪmpækt] n choc m, impact m; (fig) impact

impair [ɪm'pɛər] vt détériorer, diminuer

impartial [ɪm'pɑ:ʃl] adj impartial(e)

impatience [ɪm'peɪʃəns] n impatience f

impatient [ɪm'peɪʃənt] adj impatient(e); **to get** or **grow ~** s'impatienter

impeccable [ɪm'pɛkəbl] adj impeccable, parfait(e)

impending [ɪm'pɛndɪŋ] adj imminent(e)

imperative [ɪm'pɛrətɪv] adj (need) urgent(e), pressant(e); (tone) impérieux(-euse) ▷ n (Ling) impératif m

imperfect [ɪm'pə:fɪkt] adj imparfait(e); (goods etc) défectueux(-euse) ▷ n (Ling: also: **~ tense**) imparfait m

imperial [ɪm'pɪərɪəl] adj impérial(e); (BRIT: measure) légal(e)

impersonal [ɪm'pə:sənl] adj impersonnel(le)

impersonate [ɪm'pə:səneɪt] vt se faire passer pour; (Theat) imiter

impetus ['ɪmpətəs] n impulsion f; (of runner) élan m

implant [ɪm'plɑːnt] vt (Med)
implanter; (fig: idea, principle)
inculquer

implement n ['ɪmplɪmənt] outil m,
instrument m; (for cooking) ustensile
m ▷ vt ['ɪmplɪment] exécuter

implicate ['ɪmplɪkeɪt] vt impliquer,
compromettre

implication [ɪmplɪ'keɪʃən] n
implication f; **by ~** indirectement

implicit [ɪm'plɪsɪt] adj implicite;
(complete) absolu(e), sans réserve

imply [ɪm'plaɪ] vt (hint) suggérer,
laisser entendre; (mean) indiquer,
supposer

impolite [ɪmpə'laɪt] adj impoli(e)

import vt [ɪm'pɔːt] importer ▷ n
['ɪmpɔːt] (Comm) importation f;
(meaning) portée f, signification f

importance [ɪm'pɔːtns] n
importance f

important [ɪm'pɔːtnt] adj
important(e); **it's not ~** c'est sans
importance, ce n'est pas important

importer [ɪm'pɔːtər] n
importateur(-trice)

impose [ɪm'pəuz] vt imposer ▷ vi:
to ~ on sb abuser de la gentillesse
de qn; **imposing** adj imposant(e),
impressionnant(e)

impossible [ɪm'pɔsɪbl] adj
impossible

impotent ['ɪmpətnt] adj
impuissant(e)

impoverished [ɪm'pɔvərɪʃt] adj
pauvre, appauvri(e)

impractical [ɪm'præktɪkl] adj pas
pratique; (person) qui manque d'esprit
pratique

impress [ɪm'prɛs] vt impressionner,
faire impression sur; (mark) imprimer,
marquer; **to ~ sth on sb** faire bien
comprendre qch à qn

impression [ɪm'prɛʃən] n
impression f; (of stamp, seal)
empreinte f; (imitation) imitation
f; **to be under the ~ that** avoir
l'impression que

impressive [ɪm'prɛsɪv] adj
impressionnant(e)

imprison [ɪm'prɪzn] vt emprisonner,
mettre en prison; **imprisonment**
n emprisonnement m; (period):
**to sentence sb to 10 years'
imprisonment** condamner qn à 10
ans de prison

improbable [ɪm'prɔbəbl] adj
improbable; (excuse) peu plausible

improper [ɪm'prɔpər] adj (unsuitable)
déplacé(e), de mauvais goût;
(indecent) indécent(e); (dishonest)
malhonnête

improve [ɪm'pruːv] vt améliorer
▷ vi s'améliorer; (pupil etc) faire
des progrès; **improvement** n
amélioration f; (of pupil etc)
progrès m

improvise ['ɪmprəvaɪz] vt, vi
improviser

impulse ['ɪmpʌls] n impulsion f;
on ~ impulsivement, sur un coup
de tête; **impulsive** [ɪm'pʌlsɪv] adj
impulsif(-ive)

 KEYWORD

in [ɪn] prep **1** (indicating place, position)
dans; **in the house/the fridge** dans
la maison/le frigo; **in the garden**
dans le or au jardin; **in town** en ville;
in the country à la campagne; **in
school** à l'école; **in here/there** ici/là

2 (with place names, of town, region,
country): **in London** à Londres; **in
England** en Angleterre; **in Japan**
au Japon; **in the United States** aux
États-Unis

3 (indicating time: during): **in spring**
au printemps; **in summer** en été;
in May/2005 en mai/2005; **in the
afternoon** (dans) l'après-midi; **at 4
o'clock in the afternoon** à 4 heures
de l'après-midi

4 (indicating time: in the space of) en;
(: future) dans; **I did it in 3 hours/
days** je l'ai fait en 3 heures/jours; **I'll**

see you in 2 weeks or **in 2 weeks'
time** je te verrai dans 2 semaines
5 (indicating manner etc) à; **in a loud/
soft voice** à voix haute/basse; **in
pencil** au crayon; **in writing** par
écrit; **in French** en français; **the boy
in the blue shirt** le garçon à or avec la
chemise bleue
6 (indicating circumstances): **in
the sun** au soleil; **in the shade** à
l'ombre; **in the rain** sous la pluie; **a
change in policy** un changement
de politique
7 (indicating mood, state): **in tears** en
larmes; **in anger** sous le coup de la
colère; **in despair** au désespoir; **in
good condition** en bon état; **to live
in luxury** vivre dans le luxe
8 (with ratios, numbers): **1 in 10
households, 1 household in 10** 1
ménage sur 10; **20 pence in the
pound** 20 pence par livre sterling;
they lined up in twos ils se mirent
en rangs (deux) par deux; **in
hundreds** par centaines
9 (referring to people, works) chez; **the
disease is common in children**
c'est une maladie courante chez les
enfants; **in (the works of) Dickens**
chez Dickens, dans (l'œuvre de)
Dickens
10 (indicating profession etc) dans;
to be in teaching être dans
l'enseignement
11 (after superlative) de; **the best
pupil in the class** le meilleur élève
de la classe
12 (with present participle): **in saying
this** en disant ceci
▶ adv: **to be in** (person: at home,
work) être là; (train, ship, plane) être
arrivé(e); (in fashion) être à la mode;
to ask sb in inviter qn à qn à entrer; **to
run/limp** etc **in** entrer en courant/
boitant etc
▶ n: **the ins and outs (of)** (of
proposal, situation etc) les tenants et
aboutissants (de)

inability [ɪnə'bɪlɪtɪ] n incapacité f;
~ to pay incapacité de payer
inaccurate [ɪn'ækjurət] adj
inexact(e); (person) qui manque de
précision
inadequate [ɪn'ædɪkwət] adj
insuffisant(e), inadéquat(e)
inadvertently [ɪnəd'vɜːtntlɪ] adv
par mégarde
inappropriate [ɪnə'prəuprɪət] adj
inopportun(e), mal à propos; (word,
expression) impropre
inaugurate [ɪ'nɔːgjureɪt] vt
inaugurer; (president, official) investir
de ses fonctions
Inc. abbr = **incorporated**
incapable [ɪn'keɪpəbl] adj: **~ (of)**
incapable (de)
incense n ['ɪnsɛns] encens m ▷ vt
[ɪn'sɛns] (anger) mettre en colère
incentive [ɪn'sɛntɪv] n
encouragement m, raison f de se
donner de la peine
inch [ɪntʃ] n pouce m (= 25 mm; 12 in a
foot); **within an ~ of** à deux doigts de;
he wouldn't give an ~ (fig) il n'a pas
voulu céder d'un pouce
incidence ['ɪnsɪdns] n (of crime,
disease) fréquence f
incident ['ɪnsɪdnt] n incident m
incidentally [ɪnsɪ'dɛntəlɪ] adv (by
the way) à propos
inclination [ɪnklɪ'neɪʃən] n
inclination f; (desire) envie f
incline n ['ɪnklaɪn] pente f, plan
incliné ▷ vt [ɪn'klaɪn] incliner ▷ vi
(surface) s'incliner; **to be ~d to do**
(have a tendency to do) avoir tendance
à faire
include [ɪn'kluːd] vt inclure,
comprendre; **service is/is not
~d** le service est compris/n'est pas
compris; **including** prep y compris;
inclusion n inclusion f; **inclusive** adj
inclus(e), compris(e); **inclusive of
tax** taxes comprises
income ['ɪnkʌm] n revenu m; (from
property etc) rentes fpl; **income**

support n (BRIT) ≈ revenu m
minimum d'insertion, RMI m;
income tax n impôt m sur le revenu
incoming ['ɪnkʌmɪŋ] adj (passengers,
mail) à l'arrivée; (government, tenant)
nouveau (nouvelle)
incompatible [ɪnkəm'pætɪbl] adj
incompatible
incompetence [ɪn'kɔmpɪtns] n
incompétence f, incapacité f
incompetent [ɪn'kɔmpɪtnt] adj
incompétent(e), incapable
incomplete [ɪnkəm'pliːt] adj
incomplet(-ète)
inconsistent [ɪnkən'sɪstnt] adj
qui manque de constance; (work)
irrégulier(-ière); (statement) peu
cohérent(e); ~ **with** en contradiction
avec
inconvenience [ɪnkən'viːnjəns]
n inconvénient m; (trouble)
dérangement m ▷ vt déranger
inconvenient [ɪnkən'viːnjənt]
adj malcommode; (time, place) mal
choisi(e), qui ne convient pas; (visitor)
importun(e)
incorporate [ɪn'kɔːpəreɪt] vt
incorporer; (contain) contenir
incorporated [ɪn'kɔːpəreɪtɪd] adj:
~ **company** ≈ société f anonyme
incorrect [ɪnkə'rɛkt] adj
incorrect(e); (opinion, statement)
inexact(e)
increase n ['ɪnkriːs] augmentation
f ▷ vi, vt [ɪn'kriːs] augmenter;
increasingly adv de plus en plus
incredible [ɪn'krɛdɪbl] adj
incroyable; **incredibly** adv
incroyablement
incur [ɪn'kəː'] vt (expenses) encourir;
(anger, risk) s'exposer à; (debt)
contracter; (loss) subir
indecent [ɪn'diːsnt] adj indécent(e),
inconvenant(e)
indeed [ɪn'diːd] adv (confirming,
agreeing) en effet, effectivement; (for
emphasis) vraiment; (furthermore)
d'ailleurs; **yes ~!** certainement!

indefinitely [ɪn'dɛfɪnɪtlɪ] adv (wait)
indéfiniment
independence [ɪndɪ'pɛndns] n
indépendance f; **Independence Day**
n (US) fête de l'Indépendance américaine

- **INDEPENDENCE DAY**
-
- L'*Independence Day* est la fête
- nationale aux États-Unis, le 4
- juillet. Il commémore l'adoption de
- la déclaration d'Indépendance, en
- 1776, écrite par Thomas Jefferson
- et proclamant la séparation des 13
- colonies américaines de la Grande-
- Bretagne.

independent [ɪndɪ'pɛndnt]
adj indépendant(e); (radio) libre;
independent school n (BRIT) école
privée
index ['ɪndɛks] n (pl indexes)
(in book) index m; (in library etc)
catalogue m; (pl **indices**) (ratio, sign)
indice m
India ['ɪndɪə] n Inde f; **Indian**
adj indien(ne) ▷ n Indien(ne);
(American) Indian Indien(ne)
(d'Amérique)
indicate ['ɪndɪkeɪt] vt indiquer ▷ vi
(BRIT Aut): **to ~ left/right** mettre
son clignotant à gauche/à droite;
indication [ɪndɪ'keɪʃən] n indication
f, signe m; **indicative** [ɪn'dɪkətɪv]
adj: **to be indicative of sth** être
symptomatique de qch ▷ n (Ling)
indicatif m; **indicator** n (sign)
indicateur m; (Aut) clignotant m
indices ['ɪndɪsiːz] npl of **index**
indict [ɪn'daɪt] vt accuser;
indictment n accusation f
indifference [ɪn'dɪfrəns] n
indifférence f
indifferent [ɪn'dɪfrənt] adj
indifférent(e); (poor) médiocre,
quelconque
indigenous [ɪn'dɪdʒɪnəs] adj
indigène

indigestion [ɪndɪ'dʒɛstʃən] n
indigestion f, mauvaise digestion

indignant [ɪn'dɪgnənt] adj: ~ **(at
sth/with sb)** indigné(e) (de qch/
contre qn)

indirect [ɪndɪ'rɛkt] adj indirect(e)

indispensable [ɪndɪ'spɛnsəbl] adj
indispensable

individual [ɪndɪ'vɪdjuəl] n individu
m ▷ adj individuel(le); (characteristic)
particulier(-ière), original(e);
individually adv individuellement

Indonesia [ɪndə'niːzɪə] n Indonésie f

indoor ['ɪndɔːʳ] adj d'intérieur; (plant)
d'appartement; (swimming pool)
couvert(e); (sport, games) pratiqué(e)
en salle; **indoors** [ɪn'dɔːz] adv à
l'intérieur

induce [ɪn'djuːs] vt (persuade)
persuader; (bring about) provoquer;
(labour) déclencher

indulge [ɪn'dʌldʒ] vt (whim) céder à,
satisfaire; (child) gâter ▷ vi: **to ~ in
sth** (luxury) s'offrir qch, se permettre
qch; (fantasies etc) se livrer à qch;
indulgent adj indulgent(e)

industrial [ɪn'dʌstrɪəl] adj
industriel(le); (injury) du travail;
(dispute) ouvrier(-ière); **industrial
estate** n (BRIT) zone industrielle;
industrialist n industriel m;
industrial park n (US) zone
industrielle

industry ['ɪndəstrɪ] n industrie f;
(diligence) zèle m, application f

inefficient [ɪnɪ'fɪʃənt] adj inefficace

inequality [ɪnɪ'kwɔlɪtɪ] n inégalité f

inevitable [ɪn'ɛvɪtəbl] adj inévitable;
inevitably adv inévitablement,
fatalement

inexpensive [ɪnɪk'spɛnsɪv] adj bon
marché inv

inexperienced [ɪnɪk'spɪərɪənst] adj
inexpérimenté(e)

inexplicable [ɪnɪk'splɪkəbl] adj
inexplicable

infamous ['ɪnfəməs] adj infâme,
abominable

infant ['ɪnfənt] n (baby) nourrisson m;
(young child) petit(e) enfant

infantry ['ɪnfəntrɪ] n infanterie f

infant school n (BRIT) classes fpl
préparatoires (entre 5 et 7 ans)

infect [ɪn'fɛkt] vt (wound) infecter;
(person, blood) contaminer; **infection**
[ɪn'fɛkʃən] n infection f; (contagion)
contagion f; **infectious** [ɪn'fɛkʃəs]
adj infectieux(-euse); (also fig)
contagieux(-euse)

infer [ɪn'fəːʳ] vt: **to ~ (from)** conclure
(de), déduire (de)

inferior [ɪn'fɪərɪəʳ] adj inférieur(e);
(goods) de qualité inférieure ▷ n
inférieur(e); (in rank) subalterne m/f

infertile [ɪn'fəːtaɪl] adj stérile

infertility [ɪnfə'tɪlɪtɪ] n infertilité
f, stérilité f

infested [ɪn'fɛstɪd] adj: ~ **(with)**
infesté(e) (de)

infinite ['ɪnfɪnɪt] adj infini(e); (time,
money) illimité(e); **infinitely** adv
infiniment

infirmary [ɪn'fəːmərɪ] n hôpital m;
(in school, factory) infirmerie f

inflamed [ɪn'fleɪmd] adj
enflammé(e)

inflammation [ɪnflə'meɪʃən] n
inflammation f

inflatable [ɪn'fleɪtəbl] adj gonflable

inflate [ɪn'fleɪt] vt (tyre, balloon)
gonfler; (fig: exaggerate) grossir;
(: increase) gonfler; **Inflation**
[ɪn'fleɪʃən] n (Econ) inflation f

inflexible [ɪn'flɛksɪbl] adj inflexible,
rigide

inflict [ɪn'flɪkt] vt: **to ~ on** infliger à

influence ['ɪnfluəns] n influence
f ▷ vt influencer; **under the ~ of
alcohol** en état d'ébriété; **influential**
[ɪnflu'ɛnʃl] adj influent(e)

influenza [ɪnflu'ɛnzə] n grippe f

influx ['ɪnflʌks] n afflux m

info ['ɪnfəu] (inf) n (= information)
renseignements mpl

inform [ɪn'fɔːm] vt: **to ~ sb (of)**
informer or avertir qn (de) ▷ vi: **to**

~ on sb dénoncer qn, informer contre qn

informal [ɪn'fɔːml] adj (person, manner, party) simple; (visit, discussion) dénué(e) de formalités; (announcement, invitation) non officiel(le); (colloquial) familier(-ère)

information [ɪnfə'meɪʃən] n information(s) f(pl); renseignements mpl; (knowledge) connaissances fpl; **a piece of ~** un renseignement; **information office** n bureau m de renseignements; **information technology** n informatique f

informative [ɪn'fɔːmətɪv] adj instructif(-ive)

infra-red [ɪnfrə'rɛd] adj infrarouge

infrastructure ['ɪnfrəstrʌktʃəʳ] n infrastructure f

infrequent [ɪn'friːkwənt] adj peu fréquent(e), rare

infuriate [ɪn'fjuərɪeɪt] vt mettre en fureur

infuriating [ɪn'fjuərɪeɪtɪŋ] adj exaspérant(e)

ingenious [ɪn'dʒiːnjəs] adj ingénieux(-euse)

ingredient [ɪn'griːdɪənt] n ingrédient m; (fig) élément m

inhabit [ɪn'hæbɪt] vt habiter; **inhabitant** n habitant(e)

inhale [ɪn'heɪl] vt inhaler; (perfume) respirer; (smoke) avaler ▷ vi (breathe in) aspirer; (in smoking) avaler la fumée; **inhaler** n inhalateur m

inherent [ɪn'hɪərənt] adj: **~ (in or to)** inhérent(e) (à)

inherit [ɪn'hɛrɪt] vt hériter (de); **inheritance** n héritage m

inhibit [ɪn'hɪbɪt] vt (Psych) inhiber; (growth) freiner; **inhibition** [ɪnhɪ'bɪʃən] n inhibition f

initial [ɪ'nɪʃl] adj initial(e) ▷ n initiale f ▷ vt parafer; **initials** npl initiales fpl; (as signature) parafe m; **initially** adv initialement, au début

initiate [ɪ'nɪʃɪeɪt] vt (start) entreprendre; amorcer; (enterprise)

lancer; (person) initier; **to ~ proceedings against sb** (Law) intenter une action à qn, engager des poursuites contre qn

initiative [ɪ'nɪʃətɪv] n initiative f

inject [ɪn'dʒɛkt] vt injecter; (person): **to ~ sb with sth** faire une piqûre de qch à qn; **injection** [ɪn'dʒɛkʃən] n injection f, piqûre f

injure [ɪn'dʒəʳ] vt blesser; (damage: reputation etc) compromettre; **to ~ o.s.** se blesser; **injured** adj (person, leg etc) blessé(e); **injury** n blessure f; (wrong) tort m

injustice [ɪn'dʒʌstɪs] n injustice f

ink [ɪŋk] n encre f; **ink-jet printer** ['ɪŋkdʒɛt-] n imprimante f à jet d'encre

inland adj ['ɪnlənd] intérieur(e) ▷ adv [ɪn'lænd] à l'intérieur, dans les terres; **Inland Revenue** n (BRIT) fisc m

in-laws ['ɪnlɔːz] npl beaux-parents mpl; belle famille

inmate ['ɪnmeɪt] n (in prison) détenu(e); (in asylum) interné(e)

inn [ɪn] n auberge f

inner ['ɪnəʳ] adj intérieur(e); **inner-city** adj (schools, problems) de quartiers déshérités

inning ['ɪnɪŋ] n (US Baseball) tour m de batte; **innings** npl (Cricket) tour de batte

innocence ['ɪnəsns] n innocence f

innocent ['ɪnəsnt] adj innocent(e)

innovation [ɪnəu'veɪʃən] n innovation f

innovative ['ɪnəu'veɪtɪv] adj novateur(-trice); (product) innovant(e)

in-patient ['ɪnpeɪʃənt] n malade hospitalisé(e)

input ['ɪnput] n (contribution) contribution f; (resources) ressources fpl; (Comput) entrée f (de données) (: data) données fpl ▷ vt (Comput) introduire, entrer

inquest ['ɪnkwɛst] n enquête (criminelle); (coroner's) enquête judiciaire

inquire [ɪn'kwaɪəʳ] vi demander ▷ vt demander; **to ~ about** s'informer de, se renseigner sur; **to ~ when/where/whether** demander quand/où/si; **inquiry** n demande f de renseignements; (Law) enquête f, investigation f; **"inquiries"** "renseignements"

ins. abbr = **inches**

insane [ɪn'seɪn] adj fou (folle); (Med) aliéné(e)

insanity [ɪn'sænɪtɪ] n folie f; (Med) aliénation (mentale)

insect ['ɪnsɛkt] n insecte m; **insect repellent** n crème f anti-insectes

insecure [ɪnsɪ'kjuəʳ] adj (person) anxieux(-euse); (job) précaire; (building etc) peu sûr(e)

insecurity [ɪnsɪ'kjuərɪtɪ] n insécurité f

insensitive [ɪn'sɛnsɪtɪv] adj insensible

insert vt [ɪn'sə:t] insérer ▷ n ['ɪnsə:t] insertion f

inside ['ɪn'saɪd] n intérieur m ▷ adj intérieur(e) ▷ adv à l'intérieur, dedans ▷ prep à l'intérieur de; (of time): **~ 10 minutes** en moins de 10 minutes; **to go ~** rentrer; **inside lane** n (Aut: in Britain) voie f de gauche; (: in US, Europe) voie f de droite; **inside out** adv à l'envers; (know) à fond; **to turn sth inside out** retourner qch

insight ['ɪnsaɪt] n perspicacité f, (glimpse, idea) aperçu m

insignificant [ɪnsɪɡ'nɪfɪknt] adj insignifiant(e)

insincere [ɪnsɪn'sɪəʳ] adj hypocrite

insist [ɪn'sɪst] vi insister; **to ~ on doing** insister pour faire; **to ~ on sth** exiger qch; **to ~ that** insister pour que + sub; (claim) maintenir or soutenir que; **insistent** adj insistant(e), pressant(e); (noise, action) ininterrompu(e)

insomnia [ɪn'sɔmnɪə] n insomnie f

inspect [ɪn'spɛkt] vt inspecter; (BRIT: ticket) contrôler; **inspection** [ɪn'spɛkʃən] n inspection f; (BRIT: of tickets) contrôle m; (BRIT: inspector n inspecteur(-trice); (BRIT: on buses, trains) contrôleur(-euse)

inspiration [ɪnspə'reɪʃən] n inspiration f; **inspire** [ɪn'spaɪəʳ] vt inspirer; **inspiring** adj inspirant(e)

instability [ɪnstə'bɪlɪtɪ] n instabilité f

install, (US) **instal** [ɪn'stɔ:l] vt installer; **installation** [ɪnstə'leɪʃən] n installation f

instalment, (US) **installment** [ɪn'stɔ:lmənt] n (payment) acompte m, versement partiel; (of TV serial etc) épisode m; **in ~s** (pay) à tempérament; (receive) en plusieurs fois

instance ['ɪnstəns] n exemple m; **for ~** par exemple; **in the first ~** tout d'abord, en premier lieu

instant ['ɪnstənt] n instant m ▷ adj immédiat(e), urgent(e); (coffee, food) instantané(e), en poudre; **instantly** adv immédiatement, tout de suite; **instant messaging** n messagerie f instantanée

instead [ɪn'stɛd] adv au lieu de cela; **~ of** au lieu de; **~ of sb** à la place de qn

instinct ['ɪnstɪŋkt] n instinct m; **instinctive** adj instinctif(-ive)

institute ['ɪnstɪtju:t] n institut m ▷ vt instituer, établir; (inquiry) ouvrir; (proceedings) entamer

institution [ɪnstɪ'tju:ʃən] n institution f; (school) établissement m (scolaire); (for care) établissement (psychiatrique etc)

instruct [ɪn'strʌkt] vt: **to ~ sb in sth** enseigner qch à qn; **to ~ sb to do** charger qn or ordonner à qn de faire; **instruction** [ɪn'strʌkʃən] n instruction f; **instructions** npl (orders) directives fpl; **instructions for use** mode m d'emploi; **instructor** n professeur m; (for skiing, driving) moniteur m

instrument ['ɪnstrumənt] n instrument m; **instrumental**

[ɪnstru'mentl] adj (Mus)
instrumental(e); **to be**
instrumental in sth/in doing sth
contribuer à qch/à faire qch
insufficient [ɪnsə'fɪʃənt] adj
insuffisant(e)
insulate ['ɪnsjuleɪt] vt isoler; (against
sound) insonoriser; **insulation**
[ɪnsju'leɪʃən] n isolation f; (against
sound) insonorisation f
insulin ['ɪnsjulɪn] n insuline f
insult n ['ɪnsʌlt] insulte f, affront
m ▷ vt [ɪn'sʌlt] insulter, faire un
affront à; **insulting** adj insultant(e),
injurieux(-euse)
insurance [ɪn'ʃuərəns] n assurance
f; **fire/life ~** assurance-incendie/-
vie; **insurance company** n
compagnie for société f d'assurances;
insurance policy n police f
d'assurance
insure [ɪn'ʃuər] vt assurer; **to ~ (o.s.)**
against (fig) parer à
intact [ɪn'tækt] adj intact(e)
intake ['ɪnteɪk] n (Tech) admission
f; (consumption) consommation f;
(BRIT Scol): **an ~ of 200 a year** 200
admissions par an
integral ['ɪntɪgrəl] adj (whole)
intégral(e); (part) intégrant(e)
integrate ['ɪntɪgreɪt] vt intégrer ▷ vi
s'intégrer
integrity [ɪn'tegrɪtɪ] n intégrité f
intellect ['ɪntəlekt] n intelligence
f; **intellectual** [ɪntə'lektjuəl] adj, n
intellectuel(le)
intelligence [ɪn'telɪdʒəns] n
intelligence f; (Mil) informations fpl,
renseignements mpl
intelligent [ɪn'telɪdʒənt] adj
intelligent(e)
intend [ɪn'tend] vt (gift etc): **to ~ sth**
for destiner qch à; **to ~ to do** avoir
l'intention de faire
intense [ɪn'tens] adj intense; (person)
véhément(e)
intensify [ɪn'tensɪfaɪ] vt intensifier
intensity [ɪn'tensɪtɪ] n intensité f

intensive [ɪn'tensɪv] adj
intensif(-ive); **intensive care** n:
to be in intensive care être en
réanimation; **intensive care unit** n
service m de réanimation
intent [ɪn'tent] n intention f ▷ adj
attentif(-ive), absorbé(e); **to all ~s**
and purposes en fait, pratiquement;
to be ~ on doing sth être (bien)
décidé à faire qch
intention [ɪn'tenʃən] n intention
f; **intentional** adj intentionnel(le),
délibéré(e)
interact [ɪntər'ækt] vi avoir
une action réciproque; (people)
communiquer; **interaction**
[ɪntər'ækʃən] n interaction f;
interactive adj (Comput) interactif,
conversationnel(le)
intercept [ɪntə'sept] vt intercepter;
(person) arrêter au passage
interchange n ['ɪntətʃeɪndʒ]
(exchange) échange m; (on motorway)
échangeur m
intercourse ['ɪntəkɔːs] n: **sexual ~**
rapports sexuels
interest ['ɪntrɪst] n intérêt m; (Comm:
stake, share) participation f, intérêts
mpl ▷ vt intéresser; **interested** adj
intéressé(e); **to be interested in sth**
s'intéresser à qch; **I'm interested**
in going ça m'intéresse d'y aller;
interesting adj intéressant(e);
interest rate n taux m d'intérêt
interface ['ɪntəfeɪs] n (Comput)
interface f
interfere [ɪntə'fɪər] vi: **to ~ in**
(quarrel) s'immiscer dans; (other
people's business) se mêler de; **to ~**
with (object) tripoter, toucher à;
(plans) contrecarrer; (duty) être en
conflit avec; **interference** n (gen)
ingérence f; (Radio, TV) parasites mpl
interim ['ɪntərɪm] adj provisoire;
(post) intérimaire ▷ n: **in the ~** dans
l'intérim
interior [ɪn'tɪərɪər] n intérieur m ▷ adj
intérieur(e); (minister, department)

de l'intérieur; **interior design** n
architecture f d'intérieur
intermediate [ɪntə'miːdɪət] adj
intermédiaire; (Scol: course, level)
moyen(ne)
intermission [ɪntə'mɪʃən] n pause f;
(Theat, Cine) entracte m
intern vt [ɪn'təːn] interner ▷ n
['ɪntəːn] (US) interne m/f
internal [ɪn'təːnl] adj interne; (dispute,
reform etc) intérieur(e); **Internal
Revenue Service** n (US) fisc m
international [ɪntə'næʃənl] adj
international(e) ▷ n (BRIT Sport)
international m
Internet [ɪntə'nɛt] n: **the ~** l'Internet
m; **Internet café** n cybercafé m;
Internet Service Provider n
fournisseur m d'accès à Internet;
Internet user n internaute m/f
interpret [ɪn'təːprɪt] vt
interpréter ▷ vi servir d'interprète;
interpretation [ɪntəːprɪ'teɪʃən]
n interprétation f; **interpreter** n
interprète m/f; **could you act as an
interpreter for us?** pourriez-vous
nous servir d'interprète?
interrogate [ɪn'tɛrəugeɪt] vt
interroger; (suspect etc) soumettre
à un interrogatoire; **interrogation**
[ɪntɛrəu'geɪʃən] n interrogation f; (by
police) interrogatoire m
interrogative [ɪntə'rɔgətɪv] adj
interrogateur(-trice) ▷ n (Ling)
interrogatif m
interrupt [ɪntə'rʌpt] vt, vi
interrompre; **interruption**
[ɪntə'rʌpʃən] n interruption f
intersection [ɪntə'sɛkʃən] n (of
roads) croisement m
interstate ['ɪntəsteɪt] (US) n
autoroute f (qui relie plusieurs États)
interval ['ɪntəvl] n intervalle m;
(BRIT: Theat) entracte m; (: Sport)
mi-temps f; **at ~s** par intervalles
intervene [ɪntə'viːn] vi (time)
s'écouler (entre-temps); (event)
survenir; (person) intervenir

interview ['ɪntəvjuː] n (Radio, TV)
interview f; (for job) entrevue f ▷ vt
interviewer, avoir une entrevue
avec; **interviewer** n (Radio, TV)
interviewer m
intimate adj ['ɪntɪmət] intime;
(friendship) profond(e); (knowledge)
approfondi(e) ▷ vt ['ɪntɪmeɪt]
suggérer, laisser entendre; (announce)
faire savoir
intimidate [ɪn'tɪmɪdeɪt] vt intimider
intimidating [ɪn'tɪmɪdeɪtɪŋ] adj
intimidant(e)
into ['ɪntu] prep dans; **~ pieces/
French** en morceaux/français
intolerant [ɪn'tɔlrnt] adj: **~ (of)**
intolérant(e) (de)
intranet [ɪn'trənɛt] n intranet m
intransitive [ɪn'trænsɪtɪv] adj
intransitif(-ive)
intricate ['ɪntrɪkət] adj complexe,
compliqué(e)
intrigue [ɪn'triːg] n intrigue f ▷ vt
intriguer; **intriguing** adj fascinant(e)
introduce [ɪntrə'djuːs] vt introduire;
(TV show etc) présenter; **to ~ sb
(to sb)** présenter qn (à qn); **to ~
sb to** (pastime, technique) initier qn
à; **introduction** [ɪntrə'dʌkʃən]
n introduction f; (of person)
présentation f; (to new experience)
initiation f; **introductory**
[ɪntrə'dʌktərɪ] adj préliminaire,
introductif(-ive)
intrude [ɪn'truːd] vi (person) être
importun(e); **to ~ on** or **into**
(conversation etc) s'immiscer dans;
intruder n intrus(e)
intuition [ɪntjuː'ɪʃən] n intuition f
inundate ['ɪnʌndeɪt] vt: **to ~ with**
inonder de
invade [ɪn'veɪd] vt envahir
invalid n ['ɪnvəlɪd] malade m/f;
(with disability) invalide m/f ▷ adj
[ɪn'vælɪd] (not valid) invalide, non
valide
invaluable [ɪn'væljuəbl] adj
inestimable, inappréciable

i

invariably [ɪn'vɛərɪəblɪ] *adv*
invariablement; **she is ~ late** elle est
toujours en retard

invasion [ɪn'veɪʒən] *n* invasion *f*

invent [ɪn'vɛnt] *vt* inventer;
invention [ɪn'vɛnʃən] *n* invention *f*;
inventor *n* inventeur(-trice)

inventory ['ɪnvəntrɪ] *n* inventaire *m*

inverted commas [ɪn'və:tɪd-] *npl*
(BRIT) guillemets *mpl*

invest [ɪn'vɛst] *vt* investir ▷ *vi*: **to ~ in**
placer de l'argent *or* investir dans; *(fig:
acquire)* s'offrir, faire l'acquisition de

investigate [ɪn'vɛstɪgeɪt] *vt* étudier,
examiner; *(crime)* faire une enquête
sur; **investigation** [ɪnvɛstɪ'geɪʃən] *n*
(of crime) enquête *f*, investigation *f*

investigator [ɪn'vɛstɪgeɪtə'] *n*
investigateur(-trice); **private ~**
détective privé

investment [ɪn'vɛstmənt] *n*
investissement *m*, placement *m*

investor [ɪn'vɛstə'] *n* épargnant(e);
(shareholder) actionnaire *m/f*

invisible [ɪn'vɪzɪbl] *adj* invisible

invitation [ɪnvɪ'teɪʃən] *n*
invitation *f*

invite [ɪn'vaɪt] *vt* inviter; *(opinions
etc)* demander; **inviting** *adj*
engageant(e), attrayant(e)

invoice ['ɪnvɔɪs] *n* facture *f* ▷ *vt*
facturer

involve [ɪn'vɔlv] *vt* *(entail)* impliquer;
(concern) concerner; *(require)*
nécessiter; **to ~ sb in** *(theft etc)*
impliquer qn dans; *(activity, meeting)*
faire participer qn à; **involved** *adj*
(complicated) complexe; **to be
involved in** *(take part)* participer à;
involvement *n* *(personal role)* rôle
m; *(participation)* participation *f*;
(enthusiasm) enthousiasme *m*

inward ['ɪnwəd] *adj* *(movement)*
vers l'intérieur; *(thought, feeling)*
profond(e), intime ▷ *adv* = **inwards**;
inwards *adv* vers l'intérieur

iPod® ['aɪpɔd] *n* iPod® *m*

IQ *n abbr* (= *intelligence quotient*) Q.I. *m*

IRA *n abbr* (= *Irish Republican Army*) IRA *f*

Iran [ɪ'rɑ:n] *n* Iran *m*; **Iranian**
[ɪ'reɪnɪən] *adj* iranien(ne) ▷ *n*
Iranien(ne)

Iraq [ɪ'rɑ:k] *n* Irak *m*; **Iraqi** *adj*
irakien(ne) ▷ *n* Irakien(ne)

Ireland ['aɪələnd] *n* Irlande *f*

iris, irises ['aɪrɪs, -ɪz] *n* iris *m*

Irish ['aɪrɪʃ] *adj* irlandais(e) ▷ *npl*;
the ~ les Irlandais; **Irishman** *(irreg)*
n Irlandais *m*; **Irishwoman** *(irreg)* *n*
Irlandaise *f*

iron ['aɪən] *n* fer *m*; *(for clothes)* fer *m* à
repasser ▷ *adj* de *or* en fer ▷ *vt* *(clothes)*
repasser

ironic(al) [aɪ'rɔnɪk(l)] *adj* ironique;
ironically *adv* ironiquement

ironing ['aɪənɪŋ] *n* *(activity)*
repassage *m*; *(clothes: ironed)* linge
repassé; *(: to be ironed)* linge à
repasser; **ironing board** *n* planche
f à repasser

irony ['aɪrənɪ] *n* ironie *f*

irrational [ɪ'ræʃənl] *adj*
irrationnel(le); *(person)* qui n'est pas
rationnel

irregular [ɪ'rɛgjulə'] *adj*
irrégulier(-ière); *(surface)* inégal(e);
(action, event) peu orthodoxe

irrelevant [ɪ'rɛləvənt] *adj* sans
rapport, hors de propos

irresistible [ɪrɪ'zɪstɪbl] *adj*
irrésistible

irresponsible [ɪrɪ'spɔnsɪbl] *adj* *(act)*
irréfléchi(e); *(person)* qui n'a pas le
sens des responsabilités

irrigation [ɪrɪ'geɪʃən] *n* irrigation *f*

irritable ['ɪrɪtəbl] *adj* irritable

irritate ['ɪrɪteɪt] *vt* irriter; **irritating**
adj irritant(e); **irritation** [ɪrɪ'teɪʃən]
n irritation *f*

IRS *n abbr* (US) = **Internal Revenue
Service**

is [ɪz] *vb see* **be**

ISDN *n abbr* (= *Integrated Services Digital
Network*) RNIS *m*

Islam ['ɪzlɑ:m] *n* Islam *m*; **Islamic**
[ɪz'lɑ:mɪk] *adj* islamique

island ['aɪlənd] n île f; (also: **traffic ~**) refuge m (pour piétons); **islander** n habitant(e) d'une île, insulaire m/f

isle [aɪl] n île f

isn't ['ɪznt] = **is not**

isolated ['aɪsəleɪtɪd] adj isolé(e)

isolation [aɪsə'leɪʃən] n isolement m

ISP n abbr = **Internet Service Provider**

Israel ['ɪzreɪl] n Israël m; **Israeli** [ɪz'reɪlɪ] adj israélien(ne) ▷ n Israélien(ne)

issue ['ɪʃuː] n question f, problème m; (of banknotes) émission f; (of newspaper) numéro m; (of book) publication f, parution f ▷ vt (rations, equipment) distribuer; (orders) donner; (statement) publier, faire; (certificate, passport) délivrer; (banknotes, cheques, stamps) émettre, mettre en circulation; **at ~** en jeu, en cause; **to take ~ with sb (over sth)** exprimer son désaccord avec qn (sur qch)

IT n abbr = **information technology**

KEYWORD

it [ɪt] pron **1** (specific: subject) il (elle); (: direct object) le (la, l'); (: indirect object) lui; **it's on the table** c'est or il (or elle) est sur la table; **I can't find it** je n'arrive pas à le trouver; **give it to me** donne-le-moi

2 (after prep): **about/from/of it** en; **I spoke to him about it** je lui en ai parlé; **what did you learn from it?** qu'est-ce que vous en avez retiré?; **I'm proud of it** j'en suis fier; **in/to it** y; **put the book in it** mettez-y le livre; **he agreed to it** il y a consenti; **did you go to it?** (party, concert etc) est-ce que vous y êtes allé(s)?

3 (impersonal) il; ce, cela, ça; **it's Friday tomorrow** demain, c'est vendredi or nous sommes vendredi; **it's 6 o'clock** il est 6 heures; **how far is it? — it's 10 miles** c'est loin? — c'est à 10 miles; **who is it? — it's me** qui est-ce? — c'est moi; **it's raining** il pleut

Italian [ɪ'tæljən] adj italien(ne) ▷ n Italien(ne); (Ling) italien m

italics [ɪ'tælɪks] npl italique m

Italy ['ɪtəlɪ] n Italie f

itch [ɪtʃ] n démangeaison f ▷ vi (person) éprouver des démangeaisons; (part of body) démanger; **I'm ~ing to do** l'envie me démange de faire; **itchy** adj: **my back is itchy** j'ai le dos qui me démange

it'd ['ɪtd] = **it would; it had**

item ['aɪtəm] n (gen) article m; (on agenda) question f, point m; (also: **news ~**) nouvelle f

itinerary [aɪ'tɪnərərɪ] n itinéraire m

it'll ['ɪtl] = **it will; it shall**

its [ɪts] adj son (sa), ses pl

it's [ɪts] = **it is; it has**

itself [ɪt'sɛlf] pron (reflexive) se; (emphatic) lui-même (elle-même)

ITV n abbr (BRIT: = Independent Television) chaîne de télévision commerciale

I've [aɪv] = **I have**

ivory ['aɪvərɪ] n ivoire m

ivy ['aɪvɪ] n lierre m

i

J

jab [dʒæb] vt: **to ~ sth into** enfoncer or planter qch dans ▷ n (Med: inf) piqûre f

jack [dʒæk] n (Aut) cric m; (Cards) valet m

jacket ['dʒækɪt] n veste f, veston m; (of book) couverture f, jaquette f; **jacket potato** n pomme f de terre en robe des champs

jackpot ['dʒækpɒt] n gros lot

Jacuzzi® [dʒə'kuːzɪ] n jacuzzi® m

jagged ['dʒægɪd] adj dentelé(e)

jail [dʒeɪl] n prison f ▷ vt emprisonner, mettre en prison; **jail sentence** n peine f de prison

jam [dʒæm] n confiture f; (also: **traffic ~**) embouteillage m ▷ vt (passage etc) encombrer, obstruer; (mechanism, drawer etc) bloquer, coincer; (Radio) brouiller ▷ vi (mechanism, sliding part) se coincer, se bloquer; (gun) s'enrayer; **to be in a ~** (inf) être dans le pétrin; **to ~ sth into** (stuff) entasser or comprimer qch dans; (thrust) enfoncer qch dans

Jamaica [dʒə'meɪkə] n Jamaïque f

jammed [dʒæmd] adj (window etc) coincé(e)

janitor ['dʒænɪtər] n (caretaker) concierge m

January ['dʒænjuərɪ] n janvier m

Japan [dʒə'pæn] n Japon m; **Japanese** [dʒæpə'niːz] adj japonais(e) ▷ n (pl inv) Japonais(e); (Ling) japonais m

jar [dʒɑːr] n (stone, earthenware) pot m; (glass) bocal m ▷ vi (sound) produire un son grinçant or discordant; (colours etc) détonner, jurer

jargon ['dʒɑːgən] n jargon m

javelin ['dʒævlɪn] n javelot m

jaw [dʒɔː] n mâchoire f

jazz [dʒæz] n jazz m

jealous ['dʒɛləs] adj jaloux(-ouse); **jealousy** n jalousie f

jeans [dʒiːnz] npl jean m

Jello® ['dʒɛləu] (US) n gelée f

jelly ['dʒɛlɪ] n (dessert) gelée f; (US: jam) confiture f; **jellyfish** n méduse f

jeopardize ['dʒɛpədaɪz] vt mettre en danger or péril

jerk [dʒəːk] n secousse f, saccade f; (of muscle) spasme m; (inf) pauvre type m ▷ vt (shake) donner une secousse à; (pull) tirer brusquement ▷ vi (vehicles) cahoter

jersey ['dʒəːzɪ] n tricot m; (fabric) jersey m

Jesus ['dʒiːzəs] n Jésus

jet [dʒɛt] n (of gas, liquid) jet m; (Aviat) avion m à réaction, jet m; **jet lag** n décalage m horaire; **jet-ski** vi faire du jet-ski or scooter des mers

jetty ['dʒɛtɪ] n jetée f, digue f

Jew [dʒuː] n Juif m

jewel ['dʒuːəl] n bijou m, joyau m; (in watch) rubis m; **jeweller**, (US) **jeweler** n bijoutier(-ière), joaillier m; **jeweller's (shop)** n (BRIT) bijouterie f, joaillerie f; **jewellery**, (US) **jewelry** n bijoux mpl

Jewish ['dʒuːɪʃ] adj juif (juive)

jigsaw ['dʒɪgsɔ:] n (also: ~ puzzle) puzzle m

job [dʒɔb] n (chore, task) travail m, tâche f; (employment) emploi m, poste m, place f; **it's a good ~ that ...** c'est heureux or c'est une chance que ... + sub; **just the ~!** (c'est) juste or exactement ce qu'il faut!; **job centre** (BRIT) n ≈ ANPE f, ≈ Agence nationale pour l'emploi; **jobless** adj sans travail, au chômage

jockey ['dʒɔkɪ] n jockey m ▷ vi: **to ~ for position** manœuvrer pour être bien placé

jog [dʒɔg] vt secouer ▷ vi (Sport) faire du jogging; **to ~ sb's memory** rafraîchir la mémoire de qn; **jogging** n jogging m

join [dʒɔɪn] vt (put together) unir, assembler; (become member of) s'inscrire à; (meet) rejoindre, retrouver; (queue) se joindre à ▷ vi (roads, rivers) se rejoindre, se rencontrer ▷ n raccord m; **join in** vi se mettre de la partie ▷ vt fus se mêler à; **join up** vi (meet) se rejoindre; (Mil) s'engager

joiner ['dʒɔɪnəʳ] (BRIT) n menuisier m

joint [dʒɔɪnt] n (Tech) jointure f; joint m; (Anat) articulation f, jointure; (BRIT Culin) rôti m; (inf: place) boîte f; (of cannabis) joint ▷ adj commun(e); (committee) mixte, paritaire; (winner) ex aequo; **joint account** n compte joint; **jointly** adv ensemble, en commun

joke [dʒəuk] n plaisanterie f; (also: practical ~) farce f ▷ vi plaisanter; **to play a ~ on** jouer un tour à, faire une farce à; **joker** n (Cards) joker m

jolly ['dʒɔlɪ] adj gai(e), enjoué(e); (enjoyable) amusant(e), plaisant(e) ▷ adv (BRIT inf) rudement, drôlement

jolt [dʒəult] n cahot m, secousse f; (shock) choc m ▷ vt cahoter, secouer

Jordan ['dʒɔ:dən] n (country) Jordanie f

journal ['dʒə:nl] n journal m; **journalism** n journalisme m; **journalist** n journaliste m/f

journey ['dʒə:nɪ] n voyage m; (distance covered) trajet m; **the ~ takes two hours** le trajet dure deux heures; **how was your ~?** votre voyage s'est bien passé?

joy [dʒɔɪ] n joie f; **joyrider** n voleur(-euse) de voiture (qui fait une virée dans le véhicule volé); **joy stick** n (Aviat) manche m à balai; (Comput) manche à balai, manette f (de jeu)

Jr abbr = **junior**

judge [dʒʌdʒ] n juge m ▷ vt juger; (estimate: weight, size etc) apprécier; (consider) estimer

judo ['dʒu:dəu] n judo m

jug [dʒʌg] n pot m, cruche f

juggle ['dʒʌgl] vi jongler; **juggler** n jongleur m

juice [dʒu:s] n jus m; **juicy** adj juteux(-euse)

July [dʒu:'laɪ] n juillet m

jumble ['dʒʌmbl] n fouillis m ▷ vt (also: ~ up, ~ together) mélanger, brouiller; **jumble sale** n (BRIT) vente f de charité

- ● **JUMBLE SALE**
- ●
- ● Les jumble sales ont lieu dans les
- ● églises, salles des fêtes ou halls
- ● d'écoles, et l'on y vend des articles
- ● de toutes sortes, en général bon
- ● marché et surtout d'occasion, pour
- ● collecter des fonds pour une œuvre
- ● de charité, une école (par exemple,
- ● pour acheter des ordinateurs), ou
- ● encore une église (pour réparer
- ● un toit etc).

jumbo ['dʒʌmbəu] adj (also: ~ jet) (avion) gros porteur (à réaction)

jump [dʒʌmp] vi sauter, bondir; (with fear etc) sursauter; (increase) monter en flèche ▷ vt sauter, franchir ▷ n saut m, bond m; (with fear etc) sursaut m; (fence) obstacle m; **to ~ the queue** (BRIT) passer avant son tour

jumper ['dʒʌmpəʳ] n (BRIT: pullover) pull-over m; (US: pinafore dress) robe-chasuble f

jump leads, (US) **jumper cables** npl câbles mpl de démarrage

Jun. abbr = **June**; **junior**

junction ['dʒʌŋkʃən] n (BRIT: of roads) carrefour m; (of rails) embranchement m

June [dʒu:n] n juin m

jungle ['dʒʌŋgl] n jungle f

junior ['dʒu:nɪəʳ] adj, n: **he's ~ to me (by two years), he's my ~ (by two years)** il est mon cadet (de deux ans), il est plus jeune que moi (de deux ans); **he's ~ to me** (seniority) il est en dessous de moi (dans la hiérarchie), j'ai plus d'ancienneté que lui; **junior high school** n (US) ≈ collège m d'enseignement secondaire; see also **high school**; **junior school** n (BRIT) école f primaire

junk [dʒʌŋk] n (rubbish) camelote f; (cheap goods) bric-à-brac m inv; **junk food** n snacks vite prêts (sans valeur nutritive)

junkie ['dʒʌŋkɪ] n (inf) junkie m, drogué(e)

junk mail n prospectus mpl; (Comput) messages mpl publicitaires

Jupiter ['dʒu:pɪtəʳ] n (planet) Jupiter f

jurisdiction [dʒuərɪs'dɪkʃən] n juridiction f; **it falls** or **comes within/outside our ~** cela est/n'est pas de notre compétence or ressort

jury ['dʒuərɪ] n jury m

just [dʒʌst] adj juste ▷ adv: **he's ~ done it/left** il vient de le faire/partir; **~ right/two o'clock** exactement or juste ce qu'il faut/deux heures; **we were ~ going** nous partions; **I was ~ about to phone** j'allais téléphoner; **~ as he was leaving** au moment or à l'instant précis où il partait; **~ before/enough/here** juste avant/assez/là; **it's ~ me/a mistake** ce n'est que moi/(rien) qu'une erreur; **~ missed/caught** manqué/attrapé de justesse; **~ listen to this!** écoutez un peu ça!; **she's ~ as clever as you** elle est tout aussi intelligente que vous; **it's ~ as well that you ...** heureusement que vous ...; **~ a minute!, ~ one moment!** un instant (s'il vous plaît)!

justice ['dʒʌstɪs] n justice f; (US: judge) juge m de la Cour suprême

justification [dʒʌstɪfɪ'keɪʃən] n justification f

justify ['dʒʌstɪfaɪ] vt justifier

jut [dʒʌt] vi (also: ~ **out**) dépasser, faire saillie

juvenile ['dʒu:vənaɪl] adj juvénile; (court, books) pour enfants ▷ n adolescent(e)

K

K, k [keɪ] *abbr* (= *one thousand*) K
kangaroo [kæŋɡə'ruː] *n* kangourou *m*
karaoke [kɑːrə'əʊkɪ] *n* karaoké *m*
karate [kə'rɑːtɪ] *n* karaté *m*
kebab [kə'bæb] *n* kebab *m*
keel [kiːl] *n* quille *f*; **on an even ~**
(*fig*) à flot
keen [kiːn] *adj* (*eager*) plein(e)
d'enthousiasme; (*interest, desire,
competition*) vif (vive); (*eye, intelligence*)
pénétrant(e); (*edge*) effilé(e); **to be ~ to
do** *or* **on doing sth** désirer vivement
faire qch, tenir beaucoup à faire qch; **to
be ~ on sth/sb** aimer beaucoup qch/qn
keep [kiːp] (*pt, pp* **kept**) *vt* (*retain,
preserve*) garder; (*hold back*) retenir;
(*shop, accounts, promise, diary*) tenir;
(*support*) entretenir; (*chickens, bees,
pigs etc*) élever ▷ *vi* (*food*) se conserver;
(*remain: in a certain state or place*)
rester ▷ *n* (*of castle*) donjon *m*; (*food
etc*) **enough for his ~** assez pour
(assurer) sa subsistance; **to ~ doing

sth (*continue*) continuer à faire qch;
(*repeatedly*) ne pas arrêter de faire
qch; **to ~ sb from doing/sth from
happening** empêcher qn de faire *or*
que qn (ne) fasse/que qch (n')arrive;
to ~ sb happy/a place tidy faire
que qn soit content/qu'un endroit
reste propre; **to ~ sth to o.s.** garder
qch pour soi, tenir qch secret; **to
~ sth from sb** cacher qch à qn; **to
~ time** (*clock*) être à l'heure, ne pas
retarder; **for ~s** (*inf*) pour de bon,
pour toujours; **keep away** *vt*: **to ~
sth/sb away from sb** tenir qch/qn
éloigné de qn ▷ *vi*: **to ~ away (from)**
ne pas s'approcher (de); **keep back** *vt*
(*crowds, tears, money*) retenir; (*conceal:
information*): **to ~ sth back from sb**
cacher qch à qn ▷ *vi* rester en arrière;
keep off *vt* (*dog, person*) éloigner ▷ *vi*:
if the rain ~s off s'il ne pleut pas; **~
your hands off!** pas touche! (*inf*);
"~ off the grass" "pelouse interdite";
keep on *vi* continuer; **to ~ on doing**
continuer à faire; **don't ~ on about
it!** arrête (d'en parler)!; **keep out** *vt*
empêcher d'entrer ▷ *vi* (*stay out*) rester
en dehors; **"~ out"** "défense d'entrer";
keep up *vi* (*fig: in comprehension*)
suivre ▷ *vt* continuer, maintenir; **to ~
up with sb** (*in work etc*) se maintenir
au même niveau que qn; (*in race etc*)
aller aussi vite que qn; **keeper** *n*
gardien(ne); **keep-fit** *n* gymnastique *f*
(d'entretien); **keeping** *n* (*care*) garde *f*;
in keeping with en harmonie avec
kennel ['kɛnl] *n* niche *f*; **kennels** *npl*
(*for boarding*) chenil *m*
Kenya ['kɛnjə] *n* Kenya *m*
kept [kɛpt] *pt, pp of* **keep**
kerb [kəːb] *n* (BRIT) bordure *f* du trottoir
kerosene ['kɛrəsiːn] *n* kérosène *m*
ketchup ['kɛtʃəp] *n* ketchup *m*
kettle ['kɛtl] *n* bouilloire *f*
key [kiː] *n* (*gen, Mus*) clé *f*; (*of piano,
typewriter*) touche *f*; (*on map*) légende
f ▷ *adj* (*factor, role, area*) clé *inv* ▷ *vt*
(*also*: **~ in**) (*text*) saisir; **can I have my**

~? je peux avoir ma clé?; **a ~ issue** un problème fondamental; **keyboard** n clavier m; **keyhole** n trou m de la serrure; **keypad** n pavé m numérique; (of smartphone) clavier m; **keyring** n porte-clés m

kg abbr (= kilogram) K

khaki ['kɑːkɪ] adj, n kaki m

kick [kɪk] vt donner un coup de pied à ▷ vi (horse) ruer ▷ n coup m de pied; (inf: thrill): **he does it for ~s** il le fait parce que ça l'excite, il le fait pour le plaisir; **to ~ the habit** (inf) arrêter; **kick off** vi (Sport) donner le coup d'envoi; **kick-off** n (Sport) coup m d'envoi

kid [kɪd] n (inf: child) gamin(e), gosse m/f; (animal, leather) chevreau m ▷ vi (inf) plaisanter, blaguer

kidnap ['kɪdnæp] vt enlever, kidnapper; **kidnapping** n enlèvement m

kidney ['kɪdnɪ] n (Anat) rein m; (Culin) rognon m; **kidney bean** n haricot m rouge

kill [kɪl] vt tuer ▷ n mise f à mort; **to ~ time** tuer le temps; **killer** n tueur(-euse); (murderer) meurtrier(-ière); **killing** n meurtre m; (of group of people) tuerie f, massacre m; (inf): **to make a killing** se remplir les poches, réussir un beau coup

kiln [kɪln] n four m

kilo ['kiːləu] n kilo m; **kilobyte** n (Comput) kilo-octet m; **kilogram(me)** n kilogramme m; **kilometre**, (us) **kilometer** ['kɪləmiːtəʳ] n kilomètre m; **kilowatt** n kilowatt m

kilt [kɪlt] n kilt m

kin [kɪn] n see **next-of-kin**

kind [kaɪnd] adj gentil(le), aimable ▷ n sorte f, espèce f; (species) genre m; **to be two of a ~** se ressembler; **in ~** (Comm) en nature; **~ of** (inf: rather) plutôt; **a ~ of** une sorte de; **what ~ of ...?** quelle sorte de ...?

kindergarten ['kɪndəgɑːtn] n jardin m d'enfants

kindly ['kaɪndlɪ] adj bienveillant(e), plein(e) de gentillesse ▷ adv avec bonté; **will you ~ ...** auriez-vous la bonté or l'obligeance de ...

kindness ['kaɪndnɪs] n (quality) bonté f, gentillesse f

king [kɪŋ] n roi m; **kingdom** n royaume m; **kingfisher** n martin-pêcheur m; **king-size(d) bed** n grand lit (de 1,95 m de large)

kiosk ['kiːɔsk] n kiosque m; (BRIT: also: **telephone ~**) cabine f (téléphonique)

kipper ['kɪpəʳ] n hareng fumé et salé

kiss [kɪs] n baiser m ▷ vt embrasser; **to ~ (each other)** s'embrasser; **kiss of life** (BRIT) bouche à bouche m

kit [kɪt] n équipement, matériel m; (set of tools etc) trousse f; (for assembly) kit m

kitchen ['kɪtʃɪn] n cuisine f

kite [kaɪt] n (toy) cerf-volant m

kitten ['kɪtn] n petit chat, chaton m

kitty ['kɪtɪ] n (money) cagnotte f

kiwi ['kiːwiː] n (also: **~ fruit**) kiwi m

km abbr (= kilometre) km

km/h abbr (= kilometres per hour) km/h

knack [næk] n: **to have the ~ (of doing)** avoir le coup (pour faire)

knee [niː] n genou m; **kneecap** n rotule f

kneel (pt, pp **knelt**) [niːl, nɛlt] vi (also: **~ down**) s'agenouiller

knelt [nɛlt] pt, pp of **kneel**

knew [njuː] pt of **know**

knickers ['nɪkəz] npl (BRIT) culotte f (de femme)

knife (pl **knives**) [naɪf, naɪvz] n couteau m ▷ vt poignarder, frapper d'un coup de couteau

knight [naɪt] n chevalier m; (Chess) cavalier m

knit [nɪt] vt tricoter ▷ vi tricoter; (broken bones) se ressouder; **to ~ one's brows** froncer les sourcils; **knitting** n tricot m; **knitting needle** n aiguille f à tricoter; **knitwear** n tricots mpl, lainages mpl

knives [naɪvz] npl of **knife**

knob [nɔb] n bouton m; (BRIT): **a ~ of butter** une noix de beurre

knock [nɔk] vt frapper; (bump into) heurter; (inf: fig) dénigrer ▷ vi (at door

etc): **to ~ at/on** frapper à/sur ▷ *n*
coup *m*; **knock down** *vt* renverser;
(*price*) réduire; **knock off** *vi* (*inf: finish*)
s'arrêter (de travailler) ▷ *vt* (*vase,
object*) faire tomber; (*inf: steal*) piquer;
(*fig: from price etc*): **to ~ off £10** faire
une remise de 10 livres; **knock out** *vt*
assommer; (*Boxing*) mettre k.-o.; (*in
competition*) éliminer; **knock over**
vt (*object*) faire tomber; (*pedestrian*)
renverser; **knockout** *n* (*Boxing*)
knock-out *m*, K.-O. *m*; **knockout
competition** (BRIT) compétition *f*
avec épreuves éliminatoires
knot [nɔt] *n* (*gen*) nœud *m* ▷ *vt* nouer
know [nəu] (*pt* knew, *pp* known) *vt*
savoir; (*person, place*) connaître; **to
~ that** savoir que; **to ~ how to do**
savoir faire; **to ~ how to swim** savoir
nager; **to ~ about/of sth** (*event*) être
au courant de qch; (*subject*) connaître
qch; **I don't ~** je ne sais pas; **do you
~ where I can …?** savez-vous où je
peux …?; **know-all** *n* (BRIT *pej*) je-sais-
tout *m/f*; **know-how** *n* savoir-faire *m*,
technique *f*, compétence *f*; **knowing**
adj (*look etc*) entendu(e); **knowingly**
adv (*on purpose*) sciemment; (*smile,
look*) d'un air entendu; **know-it-all** *n*
(US) = **know-all**
knowledge ['nɔlɪdʒ] *n* connaissance
f; (*learning*) connaissances, savoir
m; **without my ~** à mon insu;
knowledgeable *adj* bien informé(e)
known [nəun] *pp* of **know** ▷ *adj* (*thief,
facts*) notoire; (*expert*) célèbre
knuckle ['nʌkl] *n* articulation *f* (des
phalanges), jointure *f*
koala [kəu'ɑːlə] *n* (*also:* ~ **bear**)
koala *m*
Koran [kɔ'rɑːn] *n* Coran *m*
Korea [kə'rɪə] *n* Corée *f*; **Korean** *adj*
coréen(ne) ▷ *n* Coréen(ne)
kosher ['kəuʃə**r**] *adj* kascher *inv*
Kosovar, Kosovan ['kɔsəvɑː**r**,
'kɔsəvən] *adj* kosovar(e)
Kosovo ['kɔsəvəu] *n* Kosovo *m*
Kuwait [ku'weɪt] *n* Koweït *m*

L *abbr* (BRIT Aut: = *learner*) *signale un
conducteur débutant*
l. *abbr* (= *litre*) l
lab [læb] *n abbr* (= *laboratory*) labo *m*
label ['leɪbl] *n* étiquette *f*; (*brand: of
record*) marque *f* ▷ *vt* étiqueter
labor *etc* ['leɪbə**r**] (US) *n* = **labour**
laboratory [lə'bɔrətərɪ] *n*
laboratoire *m*
Labor Day *n* (US, CANADA) fête *f* du
travail (*le premier lundi de septembre*)

● **LABOR DAY**

● *Labor Day* aux États-Unis et au
● Canada est fixée au premier lundi
● de septembre. Instituée par le
● Congrès en 1894 après avoir été
● réclamée par les mouvements
● ouvriers pendant douze ans, elle
● a perdu une grande partie de son
● caractère politique pour devenir
● un jour férié assez ordinaire et

● l'occasion de partir pour un long
● week-end avant la rentrée des
● classes.

labor union n (US) syndicat m
Labour ['leɪbəʳ] n (BRIT Pol: also:
the ~ Party) le parti travailliste, les
travaillistes mpl
labour, (US) **labor** ['leɪbəʳ] n (work)
travail m; (workforce) main-d'œuvre f
▷ vi: **to ~ (at)** travailler dur (à), peiner
(sur) ▷ vt: **to ~ a point** insister sur un
point; **in ~** (Med) en travail; **labourer**,
(US) **laborer** n manœuvre m; **farm
labourer** ouvrier m agricole
lace [leɪs] n dentelle f; (of shoe etc)
lacet m ▷ vt (shoe: also: ~ **up**) lacer
lack [læk] n manque m ▷ vt manquer
de; **through** or **for ~ of** faute de, par
manque de; **to be ~ing** manquer,
faire défaut; **to be ~ing in** manquer
de
lacquer ['lækəʳ] n laque f
lacy ['leɪsɪ] adj (made of lace) en
dentelle; (like lace) comme de la
dentelle
lad [læd] n garçon m, gars m
ladder ['lædəʳ] n échelle f; (BRIT:
in tights) maille filée ▷ vt, vi (BRIT:
tights) filer
ladle ['leɪdl] n louche f
lady ['leɪdɪ] n dame f; **"ladies and
gentlemen ..."** "Mesdames (et)
Messieurs ..."; **young ~** jeune fille f;
(married) jeune femme f; **the ladies'
(room)** les toilettes fpl des dames;
ladybird, (US) **ladybug** n coccinelle f
lag [læg] n retard m ▷ vi (also: ~
behind) rester en arrière, traîner;
(fig) rester à la traîne ▷ vt (pipes)
calorifuger
lager ['lɑːgəʳ] n bière blonde
lagoon [lə'guːn] n lagune f
laid [leɪd] pt, pp of **lay**; **laid back** adj
(inf) relaxe, décontracté(e)
lain [leɪn] pp of **lie**
lake [leɪk] n lac m
lamb [læm] n agneau m

lame [leɪm] adj (also fig)
boiteux(-euse)
lament [lə'mɛnt] n lamentation f
▷ vt pleurer, se lamenter sur
lamp [læmp] n lampe f; **lamppost**
n (BRIT) réverbère m; **lampshade** n
abat-jour m inv
land [lænd] n (as opposed to sea) terre
f (ferme); (country) pays m; (soil)
terre; (piece of land) terrain m; (estate)
terre(s), domaine(s) m(pl) ▷ vi (from
ship) débarquer; (Aviat) atterrir; (fig:
fall) (re)tomber ▷ vt (passengers,
goods) débarquer; (obtain) décrocher;
to ~ sb with sth (inf) coller qch à qn;
landing n (from ship) débarquement
m; (Aviat) atterrissage m; (of staircase)
palier m; **landing card** n carte f
de débarquement; **landlady** n
propriétaire f, logeuse f; (of pub)
patronne f; **landline** n ligne f fixe;
landlord n propriétaire m, logeur
m; (of pub etc) patron m; **landmark**
n (point m de) repère m; **to be a
landmark** (fig) faire date or époque;
landowner n propriétaire foncier
or terrien; **landscape** n paysage
m; **landslide** n (Geo) glissement m
(de terrain); (fig: Pol) raz-de-marée
(électoral)
lane [leɪn] n (in country) chemin m;
(Aut: of road) voie f; (: line of traffic) file
f; (in race) couloir m
language ['læŋgwɪdʒ] n langue f;
(way one speaks) langage m; **what ~s
do you speak?** quelles langues parlez-
vous?; **bad ~** grossièretés fpl, langage
grossier; **language laboratory** n
laboratoire m de langues; **language
school** n école f de langue
lantern ['læntn] n lanterne f
lap [læp] n (of track) tour m (de piste);
(of body): **in** or **on one's ~** sur les
genoux ▷ vt (also: ~ **up**) laper ▷ vi
(waves) clapoter
lapel [lə'pɛl] n revers m
lapse [læps] n défaillance f; (in
behaviour) écart m (de conduite)

▷ vi (Law) cesser d'être en vigueur; (contract) expirer; **to ~ into bad habits** prendre de mauvaises habitudes; **~ of time** laps m de temps, intervalle m

laptop (computer) ['læptɔp-] n (ordinateur m) portable m

lard [lɑːd] n saindoux m

larder ['lɑːdəʳ] n garde-manger m inv

large [lɑːdʒ] adj grand(e); (person, animal) gros (grosse); **at ~ (free)** en liberté; (generally) en général; pour la plupart; see also **by; largely** adv en grande partie; (principally) surtout; **large-scale** adj (map, drawing etc) à grande échelle; (fig) important(e)

lark [lɑːk] n (bird) alouette f; (joke) blague f, farce f

larrikin ['lærikɪn] n (AUST, NZ inf) fripon m (inf)

laryngitis [lærɪn'dʒaɪtɪs] n laryngite f

lasagne [lə'zænjə] n lasagne f

laser ['leɪzəʳ] n laser m; **laser printer** n imprimante f laser

lash [læʃ] n coup m de fouet; (also: **eye~**) cil m ▷ vt fouetter; (tie) attacher; **lash out** vi: **to ~ out (at** or **against sb/sth)** attaquer violemment (qn/qch)

lass [læs] (BRIT) n (jeune) fille f

last [lɑːst] adj dernier(-ière) ▷ adv en dernier; (most recently) la dernière fois; (finally) finalement ▷ vi durer; **~ week** la semaine dernière; **~ night** (evening) hier soir; (night) la nuit dernière; **at ~** enfin; **~ but one** avant-dernier(-ière); **lastly** adv en dernier lieu, pour finir; **last-minute** adj de dernière minute

latch [lætʃ] n loquet m; **latch onto** vt fus (cling to: person, group) s'accrocher à; (: idea) se mettre en tête

late [leɪt] adj (not on time) en retard; (far on in day etc) tardif(-ive); (: edition, delivery) dernier(-ière); (dead) défunt(e) ▷ adv tard; (behind time, schedule) en retard; **to be 10 minutes ~** avoir 10 minutes de retard; **sorry I'm ~** désolé d'être en retard; **it's too ~** il est trop tard; **of ~** dernièrement; **in ~ May** vers la fin (du mois) de mai, fin mai; **the ~ Mr X** feu M. X; **latecomer** n retardataire m/f; **lately** adv récemment; **later** adj (date etc) ultérieur(e); (version etc) plus récent(e) ▷ adv plus tard; **latest** ['leɪtɪst] adj tout(e) dernier(-ière); **at the latest** au plus tard

lather ['lɑːðəʳ] n mousse f (de savon) ▷ vt savonner

Latin ['lætɪn] n latin m ▷ adj latin(e); **Latin America** n Amérique latine; **Latin American** adj latino-américain(e), d'Amérique latine ▷ n Latino-Américain(e)

latitude ['lætɪtjuːd] n (also fig) latitude f

latter ['lætəʳ] adj deuxième, dernier(-ière) ▷ n: **the ~** ce dernier, celui-ci

laugh [lɑːf] n rire m ▷ vi rire; **(to do sth) for a ~** (faire qch) pour rire; **laugh at** vt fus se moquer de; (joke) rire de; **laughter** n rire m; (of several people) rires mpl

launch [lɔːntʃ] n lancement m; (also: **motor ~**) vedette f ▷ vt (ship, rocket, plan) lancer; **launch into** vt fus se lancer dans

launder ['lɔːndəʳ] vt laver; (fig: money) blanchir

Launderette® [lɔːn'drɛt], (US) **Laundromat®** ['lɔːndrəmæt] n laverie f (automatique)

laundry ['lɔːndrɪ] n (clothes) linge m; (business) blanchisserie f; (room) buanderie f; **to do the ~** faire la lessive

lava ['lɑːvə] n lave f

lavatory ['lævətərɪ] n toilettes fpl

lavender ['lævəndəʳ] n lavande f

lavish ['lævɪʃ] adj (amount) copieux(-euse); (person: giving freely): **~ with** prodigue de ▷ vt: **to ~ sth on sb** prodiguer qch à qn; (money) dépenser qch sans compter pour qn

law [lɔː] n loi f; (science) droit m; **lawful** adj légal(e), permis(e); **lawless** adj (action) illégal(e); (place) sans loi

lawn [lɔːn] n pelouse f; **lawnmower** n tondeuse f à gazon

lawsuit ['lɔːsuːt] n procès m

lawyer ['lɔːjəʳ] n (consultant, with company) juriste m; (for sales, wills etc) ≈ notaire m; (partner, in court) ≈ avocat m

lax [læks] adj relâché(e)

laxative ['læksətɪv] n laxatif m

lay [leɪ] pt of **lie** ▷ adj laïque; (not expert) profane ▷ vt (pt, pp **laid**) poser, mettre; (eggs) pondre; (trap) tendre; (plans) élaborer; **to ~ the table** mettre la table; **lay down** vt poser; (rules etc) établir; **to ~ down the law** (fig) faire la loi; **lay off** vt (workers) licencier; **lay on** vt (provide: meal etc) fournir; **lay out** vt (design) dessiner, concevoir; (display) disposer; (spend) dépenser; **lay-by** n (BRIT) aire f de stationnement (sur le bas-côté)

layer ['leɪəʳ] n couche f

layman ['leɪmən] (irreg) n (Rel) laïque m; (non-expert) profane m

layout ['leɪaʊt] n disposition f, plan m, agencement m; (Press) mise f en page

lazy ['leɪzɪ] adj paresseux(-euse)

lb. abbr (weight) = **pound**

lead¹ (pt, pp **led**) [liːd, lɛd] n (front position) tête f; (distance, time ahead) avance f; (clue) piste f; (Elec) fil m; (for dog) laisse f; (Theat) rôle principal ▷ vt (guide) mener, conduire; (be leader of) être à la tête de ▷ vi (Sport) mener, être en tête; **to ~ to** (road, pipe) mener à, conduire à; (result in) conduire à, aboutir à; **to be in the ~** (Sport) (in race) mener, être en tête; (in match) mener (à la marque); **to ~ sb to do sth** amener qn à faire qch; **to ~ the way** montrer le chemin; **lead up to** vt conduire à; (in conversation) en venir à

lead² [lɛd] n (metal) plomb m; (in pencil) mine f

leader ['liːdəʳ] n (of team) chef m; (of party etc) dirigeant(e), leader m; (Sport: in league) leader; (: in race) coureur m de tête; **leadership** n (position) direction f; **under the leadership of ...** sous la direction de ...; **qualities of leadership** qualités fpl de chef or de meneur

lead-free ['lɛdfriː] adj sans plomb

leading ['liːdɪŋ] adj de premier plan; (main) principal(e); (in race) de tête

lead singer [liːd-] n (in pop group) (chanteur m) vedette f

leaf (pl **leaves**) [liːf, liːvz] n feuille f; (of table) rallonge f; **to turn over a new ~** (fig) changer de conduite or d'existence; **leaf through** vt (book) feuilleter

leaflet ['liːflɪt] n prospectus m, brochure f; (Pol, Rel) tract m

league [liːg] n ligue f; (Football) championnat m; **to be in ~ with** avoir partie liée avec, être de mèche avec

leak [liːk] n (lit, fig) fuite f ▷ vi (pipe, liquid etc) fuir; (shoes) prendre l'eau; (ship) faire eau ▷ vt (liquid) répandre; (information) divulguer

lean (pt, pp **leaned** or **leant**) [liːn, lɛnt] adj maigre ▷ vt: **to ~ sth on** appuyer qch sur ▷ vi (slope) pencher; (rest): **to ~ against** s'appuyer contre; être appuyé(e) contre; **to ~ on** s'appuyer sur; **lean forward** vi se pencher en avant; **lean over** vi se pencher; **leaning** n: **leaning (towards)** penchant m (pour)

leant [lɛnt] pt, pp of **lean**

leap (pt, pp **leaped** or **leapt**) [liːp, lɛpt] n bond m, saut m ▷ vi bondir, sauter

leapt [lɛpt] pt, pp of **leap**

leap year n année f bissextile

learn (pt, pp **learned** or **learnt**) [ləːn, ləːnt] vt, vi apprendre; **to ~ (how) to do sth** apprendre à faire qch; **to ~ about sth** (Scol) étudier qch; (hear, read) apprendre qch; **learner** n débutant(e); (BRIT: also: **learner**

driver) (conducteur(-trice)) débutant(e); **learning** n savoir m

learnt [lə:nt] pp of **learn**

lease [li:s] n bail m ▷ vt louer à bail

leash [li:ʃ] n laisse f

least [li:st] adj: **the ~** (+ noun) le (la) plus petit(e), le (la) moindre; (smallest amount of) le moins de ▷ pron: **(the) ~** le moins ▷ adv (+ verb) le moins; (+ adj): **the ~** le (la) moins; **the ~ money** le moins d'argent, **the ~ expensive** le (la) moins cher (chère) **the ~ possible effort** le moins d'effort possible; **at ~** au moins; (or rather) du moins; **you could at ~ have written** tu aurais au moins pu écrire; **not in the ~** pas le moins du monde

leather ['lɛðəʳ] n cuir m

leave (pt, pp **left**) [li:v, lɛft] vt laisser; (go away from) quitter; (forget) oublier ▷ vi partir, s'en aller ▷ n (time off) congé m; (Mil, also consent) permission f; **what time does the train/bus ~?** le train/le bus part à quelle heure?; **to ~ sth to sb** (money etc) laisser qch à qn; **to be left** rester; **there's some milk left over** il reste du lait; **~ it to me!** laissez-moi faire!, je m'en occupe!; **on ~** en permission; **leave behind** vt (also fig) laisser; (forget) laisser, oublier; **leave out** vt oublier, omettre

leaves [li:vz] npl of **leaf**

Lebanon ['lɛbənən] n Liban m

lecture ['lɛktʃəʳ] n conférence f; (Scol) cours (magistral) ▷ vi donner des cours; enseigner ▷ vt (scold) sermonner, réprimander; **to give a ~ (on)** faire une conférence (sur), faire un cours (sur); **lecture hall** n amphithéâtre m; **lecturer** n (speaker) conférencier(-ière); (BRIT: at university) professeur m (d'université), prof m/f de fac (inf); **lecture theatre** n = **lecture hall**

Be careful not to translate lecture by the French word lecture.

led [lɛd] pt, pp of **lead¹**

ledge [lɛdʒ] n (of window, on wall) rebord m; (of mountain) saillie f, corniche f

leek [li:k] n poireau m

left [lɛft] pt, pp of **leave** ▷ adj gauche ▷ adv à gauche ▷ n gauche f; **there are two ~** il en reste deux; **on the ~, to the ~** à gauche; **the L-** (Pol) la gauche; **left-hand** adj: **the left-hand side** la gauche, le côté gauche; **left-hand drive** n (vehicle) véhicule m avec la conduite à gauche; **left-handed** adj gaucher(-ère); (scissors etc) pour gauchers; **left-luggage locker** n (BRIT) (casier m à) consigne f automatique; **left-luggage (office)** n (BRIT) consigne f; **left-overs** npl restes mpl; **left-wing** adj (Pol) de gauche

leg [lɛg] n jambe f; (of animal) patte f; (of furniture) pied m; (Culin: of chicken) cuisse f; (of journey) étape f; **1st/2nd ~** (Sport) match m aller/retour; **~ of lamb** (Culin) gigot m d'agneau

legacy ['lɛgəsɪ] n (also fig) héritage m, legs m

legal ['li:gl] adj (permitted by law) légal(e); (relating to law) juridique; **legal holiday** (US) n jour férié; **legalize** vt légaliser; **legally** adv légalement

legend ['lɛdʒənd] n légende f; **legendary** ['lɛdʒəndərɪ] adj légendaire

leggings ['lɛgɪŋz] npl caleçon m

legible ['lɛdʒəbl] adj lisible

legislation [lɛdʒɪs'leɪʃən] n législation f

legislative ['lɛdʒɪslətɪv] adj législatif(-ive)

legitimate [lɪ'dʒɪtɪmət] adj légitime

leisure ['lɛʒəʳ] n (free time) temps libre, loisirs mpl; **at ~** (tout) à loisir; **at your ~** (later) à tête reposée; **leisure centre** n (BRIT) centre m de loisirs; **leisurely** adj tranquille, fait(e) sans se presser

lemon ['lɛmən] n citron m;
lemonade n (fizzy) limonade f;
lemon tea n thé m au citron
lend (pt, pp **lent**) [lɛnd, lɛnt] vt: **to ~
sth (to sb)** prêter qch (à qn); **could
you ~ me some money?** pourriez-
vous me prêter de l'argent?
length [lɛŋθ] n longueur f; (section:
of road, pipe etc) morceau m, bout m;
~ of time durée f; **it is 2 metres in
~** cela fait 2 mètres de long; **at ~** (at last)
enfin, à la fin; (lengthily) longuement;
lengthen vt allonger, prolonger ▷ vi
s'allonger; **lengthways** adv dans le
sens de la longueur, en long; **lengthy**
adj (très) long (longue)
lens [lɛnz] n lentille f; (of spectacles)
verre m; (of camera) objectif m
Lent [lɛnt] n carême m
lent [lɛnt] pt, pp of **lend**
lentil ['lɛntl] n lentille f
Leo ['liːəʊ] n le Lion
leopard ['lɛpəd] n léopard m
leotard ['liːətɑːd] n justaucorps m
leprosy ['lɛprəsɪ] n lèpre f
lesbian ['lɛzbɪən] n lesbienne f ▷ adj
lesbien(ne)
less [lɛs] adj moins de ▷ pron, adv
moins ▷ prep: **~ tax/10% discount**
avant impôt/10% de remise;
~ than that/you moins que cela/
vous; **~ than half** moins de la moitié;
~ than ever moins que jamais; **~ and
~** de moins en moins; **the ~ he works
...** moins il travaille ...; **lessen** vi
diminuer, s'amoindrir, s'atténuer ▷ vt
diminuer, réduire, atténuer; **lesser**
['lɛsə'] adj moindre; **to a lesser
extent** or **degree** à un degré moindre
lesson ['lɛsn] n leçon f; **to teach sb a
~** (fig) donner une bonne leçon à qn
let (pt, pp **let**) [lɛt] vt laisser; (BRIT:
lease) louer; **to ~ sb do sth** laisser
qn faire qch; **to ~ sb know sth**
faire savoir qch à qn, prévenir qn de
qch; **to ~ go** lâcher prise; **the ~ him come** qu'il vienne;
~ go of sth, to ~ sth go lâcher qch; **~'s go**
allons-y; **~ him come** qu'il vienne;

"to ~" (BRIT) "à louer"; **let down** vt
(lower) baisser; (BRIT: tyre) dégonfler;
(disappoint) décevoir; **let in** vt laisser
entrer; (visitor etc) faire entrer; **let
off** vt (allow to leave) laisser partir;
(not punish) ne pas punir; (firework etc)
faire partir; (bomb) faire exploser; **let
out** vt laisser sortir; (scream) laisser
échapper; (BRIT: rent out) louer
lethal ['liːθl] adj mortel(le), fatal(e);
(weapon) meurtrier(-ère)
letter ['lɛtə'] n lettre f; **letterbox** n
(BRIT) boîte f aux or à lettres
lettuce ['lɛtɪs] n laitue f, salade f
leukaemia, (US) **leukemia**
[luːˈkiːmɪə] n leucémie f
level ['lɛvl] adj (flat) plat(e), plan(e),
uni(e); (horizontal) horizontal(e) ▷ n
niveau m ▷ vt niveler, aplanir; **A ~s**
npl (BRIT) ≈ baccalauréat m; **to be ~
with** être au même niveau que; **to
draw ~ with** (runner, car) arriver à la
hauteur de, rattraper; **on the ~** (fig:
honest) régulier(-ière); **level crossing**
n (BRIT) passage m à niveau
lever ['liːvə'] n levier m; **leverage** n
(influence): **leverage (on** or **with)**
prise f (sur)
levy ['lɛvɪ] n taxe f, impôt m ▷ vt (tax)
lever; (fine) infliger
liability [laɪəˈbɪlətɪ] n responsabilité
f; (handicap) handicap m
liable ['laɪəbl] adj (subject): **~ to**
sujet(te) à, passible de; (responsible):
~ (for) responsable (de); (likely): **~ to
do** susceptible de faire
liaise [liːˈeɪz] vi: **to ~ with** assurer la
liaison avec
liar ['laɪə'] n menteur(-euse)
libel ['laɪbl] n diffamation f;
(document) écrit m diffamatoire ▷ vt
diffamer
liberal ['lɪbərl] adj libéral(e);
(generous): **~ with** prodigue de,
généreux(-euse) avec ▷ n: **L ~** (Pol)
libéral(e); **Liberal Democrat** n (BRIT)
libéral(e)-démocrate m/f
liberate ['lɪbəreɪt] vt libérer

liberation [lɪbə'reɪʃən] n libération f
liberty ['lɪbətɪ] n liberté f; **to be at
~** (criminal) être en liberté; **at ~ to
do** libre de faire; **to take the ~ of**
prendre la liberté de, se permettre de
Libra ['liːbrə] n la Balance
librarian [laɪ'brɛərɪən] n
bibliothécaire m/f
library ['laɪbrərɪ] n bibliothèque f
▮ Be careful not to translate library
by the French word librairie.
Libya ['lɪbɪə] n Libye f
lice [laɪs] npl of **louse**
licence, (US) **license** ['laɪsns] n
autorisation f, permis m; (Comm)
licence f; (Radio, TV) redevance f;
driving ~, (US) **driver's license**
permis m (de conduire)
license ['laɪsns] n (US) = **licence**;
licensed adj (for alcohol) patenté(e)
pour la vente des spiritueux, qui a une
patente de débit de boissons; (car)
muni(e) de la vignette; **license plate**
n (US Aut) plaque f minéralogique;
licensing hours (BRIT) npl heures fpl
d'ouvertures (des pubs)
lick [lɪk] vt lécher; (inf: defeat) écraser,
flanquer une piquette or raclée à; **to ~
one's lips** (fig) se frotter les mains
lid [lɪd] n couvercle m; (eyelid)
paupière f
lie [laɪ] n mensonge m ▷ vi (pt, pp **lied**)
(tell lies) mentir; (pt, **lay**, pp **lain**)
(rest) être étendu(e) or allongé(e)
or couché(e) (: object: be situated) se
trouver, être; **to ~ low** (fig) se cacher,
rester caché(e); **to tell ~s** mentir; **lie
about, lie around** vi (things) traîner;
(BRIT: person) traînasser, flemmarder;
lie down vi se coucher, s'étendre
Liechtenstein ['lɪktənstaɪn] n
Liechtenstein m
lie-in ['laɪɪn] n (BRIT): **to have a ~**
faire la grasse matinée
lieutenant [lɛf'tɛnənt, US
luː'tɛnənt] n lieutenant m
life (pl **lives**) [laɪf, laɪvz] n vie f;
to come to ~ (fig) s'animer; **life**

assurance n (BRIT) = **life insurance**;
lifeboat n canot m or chaloupe f de
sauvetage; **lifeguard** n surveillant
m de baignade; **life insurance**
n assurance-vie f; **life jacket** n
gilet m or ceinture f de sauvetage;
lifelike adj qui semble vrai(e) or
vivant(e), ressemblant(e); (painting)
réaliste; **life preserver** n (US) gilet
m or ceinture f de sauvetage; **life
sentence** n condamnation f à vie or
à perpétuité; **lifestyle** n style m de
vie; **lifetime** n: **in his lifetime** de
son vivant
lift [lɪft] vt soulever, lever; (end)
supprimer, lever ▷ vi (fog) se lever ▷ n
(BRIT: elevator) ascenseur m; **to give
sb a ~** (BRIT) emmener or prendre
qn en voiture; **can you give me
a ~ to the station?** pouvez-vous
m'emmener à la gare?; **lift up** vt
soulever; **lift-off** n décollage m
light [laɪt] n lumière f; (lamp) lampe
f; (Aut: rear light) feu m; (: headlamp)
phare m; (for cigarette etc): **have you
got a ~?** avez-vous du feu? ▷ vt (pt,
pp **lit**) (candle, cigarette, fire) allumer;
(room) éclairer ▷ adj (room, colour)
clair(e); (not heavy, also fig) léger(-ère);
(not strenuous) peu fatigant(e); **lights**
npl (traffic lights) feux mpl; **to come to
~** être dévoilé(e) or découvert(e); **in
the ~ of** à la lumière de; étant donné;
light up vi s'allumer; (face) s'éclairer;
(smoke) allumer une cigarette or
une pipe etc ▷ vt (illuminate) éclairer,
illuminer; **light bulb** n ampoule f;
lighten vt (light up) éclairer; (make
lighter) éclaircir; (make less heavy)
alléger; **lighter** n (also: **cigarette
lighter**) briquet m; **light-hearted**
adj gai(e), joyeux(-euse), enjoué(e);
lighthouse n phare m; **lighting** n
éclairage m; (in theatre) éclairages;
lightly adv légèrement; **to get off
lightly** s'en tirer à bon compte
lightning ['laɪtnɪŋ] n foudre f; (flash)
éclair m

lightweight ['laɪtweɪt] *adj (suit)* léger(-ère) ▷ *n (Boxing)* poids léger

like [laɪk] *vt* aimer (bien) ▷ *prep* comme ▷ *adj* semblable, pareil(le) ▷ *n*: **the ~** *(pej)* (d')autres du même genre *or* acabit; **his ~s and dislikes** ses goûts *mpl or* préférences *fpl*; **I would ~, I'd ~** je voudrais, j'aimerais; **would you ~ a coffee?** voulez-vous du café?; **to be/look ~ sb/sth** ressembler à qn/qch; **what's he ~?** comment est-il?; **what does it look ~?** de quoi est-ce que ça a l'air?; **what does it taste ~?** quel goût est-ce que ça a?; **that's just ~ him** c'est bien de lui, ça lui ressemble; **do it ~ this** fais-le comme ceci; **it's nothing ~ ...** ce n'est pas du tout comme ...; **likeable** *adj* sympathique, agréable

likelihood ['laɪklɪhud] *n* probabilité *f*

likely ['laɪklɪ] *adj (result, outcome)* probable; *(excuse)* plausible; **he's ~ to leave** il va sûrement partir, il risque fort de partir; **not ~!** *(inf)* pas de danger!

likewise ['laɪkwaɪz] *adv* de même, pareillement

liking ['laɪkɪŋ] *n (for person)* affection *f*; *(for thing)* penchant *m*, goût *m*; **to be to sb's ~** être au goût de qn, plaire à qn

lilac ['laɪlək] *n* lilas *m*

Lilo® ['laɪləu] *n* matelas *m* pneumatique

lily ['lɪlɪ] *n* lis *m*; **~ of the valley** muguet *m*

limb [lɪm] *n* membre *m*

limbo ['lɪmbəu] *n*: **to be in ~** *(fig)* être tombé(e) dans l'oubli

lime [laɪm] *n (tree)* tilleul *m*; *(fruit)* citron vert, lime *f*; *(Geo)* chaux *f*

limelight ['laɪmlaɪt] *n*: **in the ~** *(fig)* en vedette, au premier plan

limestone ['laɪmstəun] *n* pierre f à chaux; *(Geo)* calcaire *m*

limit ['lɪmɪt] *n* limite *f* ▷ *vt* limiter; **limited** *adj* limité(e), restreint(e);

to be limited to se limiter à, ne concerner que

limousine ['lɪməziːn] *n* limousine *f*

limp [lɪmp] *n*: **to have a ~** boiter ▷ *vi* boiter ▷ *adj* mou (molle)

line [laɪn] *n (gen)* ligne *f*; *(stroke)* trait *m*; *(wrinkle)* ride *f*; *(rope)* corde *f*; *(wire)* fil *m*; *(of poem)* vers *m*; *(row, series)* rangée *f*; *(of people)* file *f*, queue *f*; *(railway track)* voie *f*; *(Comm: series of goods)* article(s) *m(pl)*, ligne de produits; *(work)* métier *m* ▷ *vt (subj: trees, crowd)* border; **to ~ (with)** *(clothes)* doubler (de); *(box)* garnir *or* tapisser (de); **to stand in ~** *(us)* faire la queue; **in his ~ of business** dans sa partie, dans son rayon; **to be in ~ for sth** *(fig)* être en lice pour qch; **in ~ with** en accord avec, en conformité avec; **in a ~** aligné(e); **line up** *vi* s'aligner, se mettre en rang(s); *(in queue)* faire la queue ▷ *vt* aligner; *(event)* prévoir; *(find)* trouver; **to have sb/sth ~d up** avoir qn/qch en vue *or* de prévu(e)

linear ['lɪnɪər] *adj* linéaire

linen ['lɪnɪn] *n* linge *m* (de corps *or* de maison); *(cloth)* lin *m*

liner ['laɪnər] *n (ship)* paquebot *m* de ligne; *(for bin)* sac-poubelle *m*

line-up ['laɪnʌp] *n (us: queue)* file *f*; *(also:* **police ~)** parade *f* d'identification; *(Sport)* (composition *f* de l')équipe *f*

linger ['lɪŋgər] *vi* s'attarder; traîner; *(smell, tradition)* persister

lingerie ['lænʒəriː] *n* lingerie *f*

linguist ['lɪŋgwɪst] *n* linguiste *m/f*; **to be a good ~** être doué(e) pour les langues; **linguistic** *adj* linguistique

lining ['laɪnɪŋ] *n* doublure *f*; *(of brakes)* garniture *f*

link [lɪŋk] *n (connection)* lien *m*, rapport *m*; *(Internet)* lien; *(of a chain)* maillon *m* ▷ *vt* relier, lier, unir; **links** *npl (Golf)* terrain *m* de golf *m*; **link up** *vt* relier ▷ *vi (people)* se rejoindre; *(companies etc)* s'associer

lion ['laɪən] n lion m; **lioness** n lionne f

lip [lɪp] n lèvre f; (of cup etc) rebord m;
lip-read vi (irreg: like **read**) lire sur les
lèvres; **lip salve** [-sælv] n pommade
f pour les lèvres, pommade rosat;
lipstick n rouge m à lèvres

liqueur [lɪˈkjuəʳ] n liqueur f

liquid ['lɪkwɪd] n liquide m ▷ adj
liquide; **liquidizer** ['lɪkwɪdaɪzəʳ] n
(BRIT Culin) mixer m

liquor ['lɪkəʳ] n spiritueux m, alcool m;
liquor store (US) n magasin m de vins
et spiritueux

Lisbon ['lɪzbən] n Lisbonne

lisp [lɪsp] n zézaiement m ▷ vi
zézayer

list [lɪst] n liste f ▷ vt (write down)
inscrire; (make list of) faire la liste de;
(enumerate) énumérer

listen ['lɪsn] vi écouter; **to ~ to**
écouter; **listener** n auditeur(-trice)

lit [lɪt] pt, pp of **light**

liter ['liːtəʳ] n (US) = **litre**

literacy ['lɪtərəsɪ] n degré m
d'alphabétisation, fait m de savoir lire
et écrire; (BRIT Scol) enseignement m
de la lecture et de l'écriture

literal ['lɪtərl] adj littéral(e); **literally**
adv littéralement; (really) réellement

literary ['lɪtərərɪ] adj littéraire

literate ['lɪtərət] adj qui sait lire et
écrire; (educated) instruit(e)

literature ['lɪtrɪtʃəʳ] n littérature
f; (brochures etc) copie f publicitaire,
prospectus mpl

litre, (US) **liter** ['liːtəʳ] n litre m

litter ['lɪtəʳ] n (rubbish) détritus mpl;
(dirtier) ordures fpl; (young animals)
portée f; **litter bin** n (BRIT) poubelle f

little ['lɪtl] adj (small) petit(e); (not
much): **~ milk** peu de lait ▷ adv peu;
a ~ un peu (de); **a ~ milk** un peu de
lait; **a ~ bit** un peu; **as ~ as possible**
le moins possible; **~ by ~** petit à petit,
peu à peu; **little finger** n auriculaire
m, petit doigt

live¹ [laɪv] adj (animal) vivant(e), en
vie; (wire) sous tension; (broadcast)
(transmis(e)) en direct; (unexploded)
non explosé(e)

live² [lɪv] vi vivre; (reside) vivre,
habiter; **to ~ in London** habiter
(à) Londres; **where do you ~?** où
habitez-vous?; **live together** vi vivre
ensemble, cohabiter; **live up to** vt fus
se montrer à la hauteur de

livelihood ['laɪvlɪhud] n moyens mpl
d'existence

lively ['laɪvlɪ] adj vif (vive), plein(e)
d'entrain; (place, book) vivant(e)

liven up ['laɪvn-] vt (room etc) égayer;
(discussion, evening) animer ▷ vi
s'animer

liver ['lɪvəʳ] n foie m

lives [laɪvz] npl of **life**

livestock ['laɪvstɔk] n cheptel m,
bétail m

living ['lɪvɪŋ] adj vivant(e), en vie ▷ n:
to earn or **make a ~** gagner sa vie;
living room n salle f de séjour

lizard ['lɪzəd] n lézard m

load [ləud] n (weight) poids m; (thing
carried) chargement m, charge f; (Elec,
Tech) charge ▷ vt charger; (also: **~ up**)
to ~ (with) (lorry, ship) charger (de);
(gun, camera) charger (avec); **a ~ of,
~s of** (fig) un or des tas de, des masses
de; **to talk a ~ of rubbish** (inf) dire
des bêtises; **loaded** adj (dice) pipé(e);
(question) insidieux(-euse); (inf: rich)
bourré(e) de fric

loaf (pl **loaves**) [ləuf, ləuvz] n pain m,
miche f ▷ vi (also: **~ about, ~ around**)
fainéanter, traîner

loan [ləun] n prêt m ▷ vt prêter; **on ~**
prêté(e), en prêt

loathe [ləuð] vt détester, avoir en
horreur

loaves [ləuvz] npl of **loaf**

lobby ['lɔbɪ] n hall m, entrée f; (Pol)
groupe m de pression, lobby m ▷ vt
faire pression sur

lobster ['lɔbstəʳ] n homard m

local ['ləukl] adj local(e) ▷ n (BRIT:
pub) pub m or café m du coin; **the
locals** npl les gens mpl du pays or du

coin; **local anaesthetic**, (US) **local anesthetic** n anesthésie locale; **local authority** n collectivité locale, municipalité f; **local government** n administration locale or municipale; **locally** ['ləukəlɪ] adv localement; dans les environs or la région

locate [ləu'keɪt] vt (find) trouver, repérer; (situate) situer; **to be ~d in** être situé à or en

location [ləu'keɪʃən] n emplacement m; **on ~** (Cine) en extérieur

> Be careful not to translate location by the French word location.

loch [lɔx] n lac m, loch m

lock [lɔk] n (of door, box) serrure f; (of canal) écluse f; (of hair) mèche f, boucle f ▷ vt (with key) fermer à clé ▷ vi (door etc) fermer à clé; (wheels) se bloquer; **lock in** vt enfermer; **lock out** vt enfermer dehors; (on purpose) mettre à la porte; **lock up** vt (person) enfermer; (house) fermer à clé ▷ vi tout fermer (à clé)

locker ['lɔkə'] n casier m; (in station) consigne f automatique; **locker-room** ['lɔkə'ru:m] (US) n (Sport) vestiaire m

locksmith ['lɔksmɪθ] n serrurier m

locomotive [ləukə'məutɪv] n locomotive f

locum ['ləukəm] n (Med) suppléant(e) de médecin etc

lodge [lɔdʒ] n pavillon m (de gardien); (also: **hunting ~**) pavillon de chasse ▷ vi (person): **to ~ with** être logé(e) chez, être en pension chez; (bullet) se loger ▷ vt (appeal etc) présenter; déposer; **to ~ a complaint** porter plainte; **lodger** n locataire m/f; (with room and meals) pensionnaire m/f

lodging ['lɔdʒɪŋ] n logement m

loft [lɔft] n grenier m; (apartment) grenier aménagé (en appartement) (gén dans ancien entrepôt ou fabrique)

log [lɔg] n (of wood) bûche f; (Naut) livre m or journal m de bord; (of car) ≈

carte grise ▷ vt enregistrer; **log in, log on** vi (Comput) ouvrir une session, entrer dans le système; **log off, log out** vi (Comput) clore une session, sortir du système

logic ['lɔdʒɪk] n logique f; **logical** adj logique

login ['lɔgɪn] n (Comput) identifiant m

Loire [lwa:] n: **the (River) ~** la Loire

lollipop ['lɔlɪpɔp] n sucette f; **lollipop man/lady** (irreg) (BRIT) n contractuel(le) qui fait traverser la rue aux enfants

lolly ['lɔlɪ] n (inf: ice) esquimau m; (: lollipop) sucette f

London ['lʌndən] n Londres; **Londoner** n Londonien(ne)

lone [ləun] adj solitaire

loneliness ['ləunlɪnɪs] n solitude f, isolement m

lonely ['ləunlɪ] adj seul(e); (childhood etc) solitaire; (place) solitaire, isolé(e)

long [lɔŋ] adj long (longue) ▷ adv longtemps ▷ vi: **to ~ for sth/to do sth** avoir très envie de qch/de faire qch, attendre qch avec impatience/ attendre avec impatience de faire qch; **how ~ is this river/course?** quelle est la longueur de ce fleuve/ la durée de ce cours?; **6 metres ~** (long) de 6 mètres; **6 months ~** qui dure 6 mois, de 6 mois; **all night ~** toute la nuit; **he no ~er comes** il ne vient plus; **I can't stand it any ~er** je ne peux plus le supporter; **~ before** longtemps avant; **before ~** (+ future) avant peu, dans peu de temps; (+ past) peu de temps après; **don't be ~!** fais vite!, dépêche-toi!; **I shan't be ~** je n'en ai pas pour longtemps; **at ~ last** enfin; **so** or **as ~ as** à condition que + sub; **long-distance** adj (race) de fond; (call) interurbain(e); **long-haul** adj (flight) long-courrier; **longing** n désir m, envie f; (nostalgia) nostalgie f ▷ adj plein(e) d'envie or de nostalgie

longitude ['lɔŋgɪtjuːd] n longitude f

long: long jump n saut m en longueur; **long-life** adj (batteries etc) longue durée inv; (milk) longue conservation; **long-sighted** adj (BRIT) presbyte; (fig) prévoyant(e); **long-standing** adj de longue date; **long-term** adj à long terme

loo [lu:] n (BRIT inf) w.-c. mpl, petit coin

look [luk] vi regarder; (seem) sembler, paraître, avoir l'air; (building etc): **to ~ south/on to the sea** donner au sud/sur la mer ▷ n regard m; (appearance) air m, allure f, aspect m; **looks** npl (good looks) physique m, beauté f; **to ~ like** ressembler à; **to have a ~** regarder; **to have a ~ at sth** jeter un coup d'œil à qch; **~ (here)!** (annoyance) écoutez!; **look after** vt fus s'occuper de; (luggage etc: watch over) garder, surveiller; **look around** vi regarder autour de soi; **look at** vt fus regarder; (problem etc) examiner; **look back** vi: **to ~ back at sth/sb** se retourner pour regarder qch/qn; **to ~ back on** (event, period) évoquer, repenser à; **look down on** vt fus (fig) regarder de haut, dédaigner; **look for** vt fus chercher; **we're ~ing for a hotel/restaurant** nous cherchons un hôtel/restaurant; **look forward to** vt fus attendre avec impatience; **~ing forward to hearing from you** (in letter) dans l'attente de vous lire; **look into** vt fus (matter, possibility) examiner, étudier; **look out** vi (beware): **to ~ out (for)** prendre garde (à), faire attention (à); **~ out!** attention!; **look out for** vt fus (seek) être à la recherche de; (try to spot) guetter; **look round** vt fus (house, shop) faire le tour de ▷ vi (turn) regarder derrière soi, se retourner; **look through** vt fus (papers, book) examiner (: briefly) parcourir; **look up** vi lever les yeux; (improve) s'améliorer ▷ vt (word) chercher; **look up to** vt fus avoir du respect pour; **lookout** n (tower etc) poste m de guet; (person)

guetteur m; **to be on the lookout (for)** guetter

loom [lu:m] vi (also: ~ **up**) surgir; (event) paraître imminent(e); (threaten) menacer

loony ['lu:nɪ] adj, n (inf) timbré(e), cinglé(e) m/f

loop [lu:p] n boucle f ▷ vt: **to ~ sth round sth** passer qch autour de qch; **loophole** n (fig) porte f de sortie; échappatoire f

loose [lu:s] adj (knot, screw) desserré(e); (clothes) vague, ample, lâche; (hair) dénoué(e), épars(e); (not firmly fixed) pas solide; (morals, discipline) relâché(e); (translation) approximatif(-ive) ▷ n: **to be on the ~** être en liberté; **~ connection** (Elec) mauvais contact; **to be at a ~ end** or (us) **at ~ ends** (fig) ne pas trop savoir quoi faire; **loosely** adv sans serrer; (imprecisely) approximativement; **loosen** vt desserrer, relâcher, défaire

loot [lu:t] n butin m ▷ vt piller

lop-sided ['lɔp'saɪdɪd] adj de travers, asymétrique

lord [lɔ:d] n seigneur m; **L~ Smith** lord Smith; **the L~** (Rel) le Seigneur; **my L~** (to noble) Monsieur le comte/le baron; (to judge) Monsieur le juge; (to bishop) Monseigneur; **good L~!** mon Dieu!; **Lords** npl (BRIT Pol): **the (House of) Lords** la Chambre des Lords

lorry ['lɔrɪ] n (BRIT) camion m; **lorry driver** n (BRIT) camionneur m, routier m

lose (pt, pp **lost**) [lu:z, lɔst] vt perdre ▷ vi perdre; **I've lost my wallet/passport** j'ai perdu mon portefeuille/passeport; **to ~ (time)** (clock) retarder; **lose out** vi être perdant(e); **loser** n perdant(e)

loss [lɔs] n perte f; **to make a ~** enregistrer une perte; **to be at a ~** être perplexe or embarrassé(e)

lost [lɔst] pt, pp of **lose** ▷ adj perdu(e); **to get ~** vi se perdre;

I'm ~ je me suis perdu; **~ and found property** n (US) objets trouvés; **~ and found** n (US) (bureau m des) objets trouvés; **lost property** n (BRIT) objets trouvés; **lost property office** or **department** (bureau m des) objets trouvés

lot [lɔt] n (at auctions, set) lot m; (destiny) sort m, destinée f; **the ~** (everything) le tout; (everyone) tous mpl, toutes fpl; **a ~** beaucoup; **a ~ of** beaucoup de; **~s of** des tas de; **to draw ~s (for sth)** tirer (qch) au sort

lotion ['ləʊʃən] n lotion f

lottery ['lɔtərɪ] n loterie f

loud [laʊd] adj bruyant(e), sonore; (voice) fort(e); (condemnation etc) vigoureux(-euse); (gaudy) voyant(e), tapageur(-euse) ▷ adv (speak etc) fort; **out ~** tout haut; **loudly** adv fort, bruyamment; **loudspeaker** n haut-parleur m

lounge [laʊndʒ] n salon m; (of airport) salle f; (BRIT: also: **~ bar**) (salle de) café m or bar m ▷ vi (also: **~ about, ~ around**) se prélasser, paresser

louse (pl **lice**) [laʊs, laɪs] n pou m

lousy ['laʊzɪ] (inf) adj (bad quality) infect(e), moche; **I feel ~** je suis mal fichu(e)

love [lʌv] n amour m ▷ vt aimer; (caringly, kindly) aimer beaucoup; **I ~ chocolate** j'adore le chocolat; **to ~ to do** aimer beaucoup or adorer faire; **"15 ~"** (Tennis) "15 à rien or zéro"; **to be/fall in ~ with** être/ tomber amoureux(-euse) de; **to make ~** faire l'amour; **~ from Anne, ~, Anne** affectueusement, Anne; **I ~ you** je t'aime; **love affair** n liaison (amoureuse); **love life** n vie sentimentale

lovely ['lʌvlɪ] adj (pretty) ravissant(e); (friend, wife) charmant(e); (holiday, surprise) très agréable, merveilleux(-euse)

lover ['lʌvər] n amant m; (person in love) amoureux(-euse); (amateur): **a ~**
of un(e) ami(e) de, un(e) amoureux(- euse) de

loving ['lʌvɪŋ] adj affectueux(-euse), tendre, aimant(e)

low [ləʊ] adj bas (basse); (quality) mauvais(e), inférieur(e) ▷ adv bas ▷ n (Meteorology) dépression f; **to feel ~** se sentir déprimé(e); **he's very ~** (ill) il est bien bas or très affaibli; **to turn (down) ~** vt baisser; **to be ~ on** (supplies etc) être à court de; **to reach a new** or **an all-time ~** tomber au niveau le plus bas; **low- alcohol** adj à faible teneur en alcool, peu alcoolisé(e); **low-calorie** adj hypocalorique

lower ['ləʊər] adj inférieur(e) ▷ vt baisser; (resistance) diminuer; **to ~ o.s. to** s'abaisser à

low-fat ['ləʊ'fæt] adj maigre

loyal ['lɔɪəl] adj loyal(e), fidèle; **loyalty** n loyauté f, fidélité f; **loyalty card** n carte f de fidélité

L-plates ['ɛlpleɪts] npl (BRIT) plaques fpl (obligatoires) d'apprenti conducteur

Lt abbr (= lieutenant) Lt.

Ltd abbr (Comm: = limited) ≈ SA

luck [lʌk] n chance f; **bad ~** malchance f, malheur m; **good ~!** bonne chance!; **bad** or **hard** or **tough ~!** pas de chance!; **luckily** adv heureusement, par bonheur; **lucky** adj (person) qui a de la chance; (coincidence) heureux(-euse); (number etc) qui porte bonheur

lucrative ['lu:krətɪv] adj lucratif(-ive), rentable, qui rapporte

ludicrous ['lu:dɪkrəs] adj ridicule, absurde

luggage ['lʌgɪdʒ] n bagages mpl; **our ~ hasn't arrived** nos bagages ne sont pas arrivés; **could you send someone to collect our ~?** pourriez- vous envoyer quelqu'un chercher nos bagages?; **luggage rack** n (in train) porte-bagages m inv; (on car) galerie f

lukewarm ['lu:kwɔ:m] adj tiède

lull [lʌl] *n* accalmie *f*; (*in conversation*) pause *f* ▷ *vt*: **to ~ sb to sleep** bercer qn pour qu'il s'endorme; **to be ~ed into a false sense of security** s'endormir dans une fausse sécurité

lullaby ['lʌləbaɪ] *n* berceuse *f*

lumber ['lʌmbəʳ] *n* (*wood*) bois *m* de charpente; (*junk*) bric-à-brac *m inv* ▷ *vt* (*BRIT inf*): **to ~ sb with sth/sb** coller *or* refiler qch/qn à qn

luminous ['lu:mɪnəs] *adj* lumineux(-euse)

lump [lʌmp] *n* morceau *m*; (*in sauce*) grumeau *m*; (*swelling*) grosseur *f* ▷ *vt* (*also*: **~ together**) réunir, mettre en tas; **lump sum** *n* somme globale *or* forfaitaire; **lumpy** *adj* (*sauce*) qui a des grumeaux; (*bed*) défoncé(e), peu confortable

lunatic ['lu:nətɪk] *n* fou (folle), dément(e) ▷ *adj* fou (folle), dément(e)

lunch [lʌntʃ] *n* déjeuner *m* ▷ *vi* déjeuner; **lunch break, lunch hour** *n* pause *f* de midi, heure *f* du déjeuner; **lunchtime** *n*: **it's lunchtime** c'est l'heure du déjeuner

lung [lʌŋ] *n* poumon *m*

lure [luəʳ] *n* (*attraction*) attrait *m*, charme *m*; (*in hunting*) appât *m*, leurre *m* ▷ *vt* attirer *or* persuader par la ruse

lurk [lə:k] *vi* se tapir, se cacher

lush [lʌʃ] *adj* luxuriant(e)

lust [lʌst] *n* (*sexual*) désir (sexuel); (*Rel*) luxure *f*; (*fig*): **~ for** soif *f* de

Luxembourg ['lʌksəmbə:g] *n* Luxembourg *m*

luxurious [lʌɡ'zjuərɪəs] *adj* luxueux(-euse)

luxury ['lʌkʃərɪ] *n* luxe *m* ▷ *cpd* de luxe

Lycra® ['laɪkrə] *n* Lycra® *m*

lying ['laɪɪŋ] *n* mensonge(s) *m(pl)* ▷ *adj* (*statement, story*) mensonger(-ère), faux (fausse); (*person*) menteur(-euse)

Lyons ['ljɔ̃] *n* Lyon *m*

lyrics ['lɪrɪks] *npl* (*of song*) paroles *fpl*

m. *abbr* (= *metre*) m; (= *million*) M; (= *mile*) mi

ma [mɑ:] (*inf*) *n* maman *f*

M.A. *n abbr* (*Scol*) = **Master of Arts**

mac [mæk] *n* (*BRIT*) imper(méable *m*) *m*

macaroni [mækə'rəʊnɪ] *n* macaronis *mpl*

Macedonia [mæsɪ'dəʊnɪə] *n* Macédoine *f*; **Macedonian** [mæsɪ'dəʊnɪən] *adj* macédonien(ne) ▷ *n* Macédonien(ne); (*Ling*) macédonien *m*

machine [mə'ʃi:n] *n* machine *f* ▷ *vt* (*dress etc*) coudre à la machine; (*Tech*) usiner; **machine gun** *n* mitrailleuse *f*; **machinery** *n* machinerie *f*, machines *fpl*; (*fig*) mécanisme(s) *m(pl)*; **machine washable** *adj* (*garment*) lavable en machine

macho ['mætʃəʊ] *adj* macho *inv*

mackerel ['mækrl] *n* (*pl inv*) maquereau *m*

mackintosh ['mækɪntɔʃ] *n* (*BRIT*) imperméable *m*

mad [mæd] *adj* fou (folle); (*foolish*) insensé(e); (*angry*) furieux(-euse); **to be ~ (keen) about** or **on sth** (*inf*) être follement passionné de qch, être fou de qch

Madagascar [mædə'gæskə^r] *n* Madagascar *m*

madam ['mædəm] *n* madame *f*

mad cow disease *n* maladie *f* des vaches folles

made [meɪd] *pt, pp of* **make**; **made-to-measure** *adj* (*BRIT*) fait(e) sur mesure; **made-up** ['meɪdʌp] *adj* (*story*) inventé(e), fabriqué(e)

madly ['mædlɪ] *adv* follement; **~ in love** éperdument amoureux(-euse)

madman ['mædmən] (*irreg*) *n* fou *m*, aliéné *m*

madness ['mædnɪs] *n* folie *f*

Madrid [mə'drɪd] *n* Madrid

Mafia ['mæfɪə] *n* maf(f)ia *f*

mag [mæg] *n abbr* (*BRIT inf*: = *magazine*) magazine *m*

magazine [mægə'zi:n] *n* (*Press*) magazine *m*, revue *f*; (*Radio, TV*) magazine

maggot ['mægət] *n* ver *m*, asticot *m*

magic ['mædʒɪk] *n* magie *f* ▷ *adj* magique; **magical** *adj* magique; (*experience, evening*) merveilleux(-euse); **magician** [mə'dʒɪʃən] *n* magicien(ne)

magistrate ['mædʒɪstreɪt] *n* magistrat *m*; juge *m*

magnet ['mægnɪt] *n* aimant *m*; **magnetic** [mæg'nɛtɪk] *adj* magnétique

magnificent [mæg'nɪfɪsnt] *adj* superbe, magnifique; (*splendid*: *robe, building*) somptueux(-euse), magnifique

magnify ['mægnɪfaɪ] *vt* grossir; (*sound*) amplifier; **magnifying glass** *n* loupe *f*

magpie ['mægpaɪ] *n* pie *f*

mahogany [mə'hɔgənɪ] *n* acajou *m*

maid [meɪd] *n* bonne *f*; (*in hotel*) femme *f* de chambre; **old ~** (*pej*) vieille fille

maiden name *n* nom *m* de jeune fille

mail [meɪl] *n* poste *f*; (*letters*) courrier *m* ▷ *vt* envoyer (par la poste); **by ~** par la poste; **mailbox** *n* (*US, also Comput*) boîte *f* aux lettres; **mailing list** *n* liste *f* d'adresses; **mailman** (*irreg*) *n* (*US*) facteur *m*; **mail-order** *n* vente *f* or achat *m* par correspondance

main [meɪn] *adj* principal(e) ▷ *n* (*pipe*) conduite principale, canalisation *f*; **the ~s** (*Elec*) le secteur; **the ~ thing** l'essentiel *m*; **in the ~** dans l'ensemble; **main course** *n* (*Culin*) plat *m* de résistance; **mainland** *n* continent *m*; **mainly** *adv* principalement, surtout; **main road** *n* grand axe, route nationale; **mainstream** *n* (*fig*) courant principal; **main street** *n* rue *f* principale

maintain [meɪn'teɪn] *vt* entretenir; (*continue*) maintenir, préserver; (*affirm*) soutenir; **maintenance** ['meɪntənəns] *n* entretien *m*; (*Law*: *alimony*) pension *f* alimentaire

maisonette [meɪzə'nɛt] *n* (*BRIT*) appartement *m* en duplex

maize [meɪz] *n* (*BRIT*) maïs *m*

majesty ['mædʒɪstɪ] *n* majesté *f*; (*title*): **Your M~** Votre Majesté

major ['meɪdʒə^r] *n* (*Mil*) commandant *m* ▷ *adj* (*important*) important(e); (*most important*) principal(e); (*Mus*) majeur(e) ▷ *vi* (*US Scol*): **to ~ (in)** se spécialiser (en)

Majorca [mə'jɔ:kə] *n* Majorque *f*

majority [mə'dʒɔrɪtɪ] *n* majorité *f*

make [meɪk] *vt* (*pt, pp* **made**) faire; (*manufacture*) faire, fabriquer; (*earn*) gagner; (*decision*) prendre; (*friend*) se faire; (*speech*) faire, prononcer; (*cause to be*): **to ~ sb sad** *etc* rendre qn triste *etc*; (*force*): **to ~ sb do sth** obliger qn à faire qch, faire faire qch à qn; (*equal*): **2 and 2 ~ 4** 2 et 2 font 4 ▷ *n* (*manufacture*) fabrication *f*; (*brand*) marque *f*; **to ~ the bed** faire le lit; **to ~ a fool of sb** (*ridicule*) ridiculiser qn; (*trick*) avoir or duper qn; **to ~ a profit** faire un or des bénéfice(s); **to ~ a loss** essuyer une perte; **to ~ it** (in time etc) y arriver; (succeed) réussir; **what time do you ~ it?** quelle heure avez-vous?; **I ~ it £249** d'après mes calculs ça fait 249 livres; **to be made of** être en; **to ~ do with** se contenter de; se débrouiller avec; **make off** vi filer; **make out** vt (write out: cheque) faire; (decipher) déchiffrer; (understand) comprendre; (see) distinguer; (claim, imply) prétendre, vouloir faire croire; **make up** vt (invent) inventer, imaginer; (constitute) constituer; (parcel, bed) faire ▷ vi se réconcilier; (with cosmetics) se maquiller, se farder; **to be made up of** se composer de; **make up for** vt fus compenser; (lost time) rattraper; **makeover** ['meɪkəʊvəʳ] n (by beautician) soins mpl de maquillage; (change of image) changement m d'image; **maker** n fabricant m; (of film, programme) réalisateur(-trice); **makeshift** adj provisoire, improvisé(e); **make-up** n maquillage m

making ['meɪkɪŋ] n (fig): **in the ~** en formation or gestation; **to have the ~s of** (actor, athlete) avoir l'étoffe de

malaria [mə'lɛərɪə] n malaria f, paludisme m

Malaysia [mə'leɪzɪə] n Malaisie f

male [meɪl] n (Biol, Elec) mâle m ▷ adj (sex, attitude) masculin(e); (animal) mâle; (child etc) du sexe masculin

malicious [mə'lɪʃəs] adj méchant(e), malveillant(e)

Be careful not to translate malicious by the French word malicieux.

malignant [mə'lɪgnənt] adj (Med) malin(-igne)

mall [mɔːl] n (also: **shopping ~**) centre commercial

mallet ['mælɪt] n maillet m

malnutrition [mælnjuː'trɪʃən] n malnutrition f

malpractice [mæl'præktɪs] n faute professionnelle; négligence f

malt [mɔːlt] n malt m ▷ cpd (whisky) pur malt

Malta ['mɔːltə] n Malte f; **Maltese** [mɔːl'tiːz] adj maltais(e) ▷ n (pl inv) Maltais(e)

mammal ['mæml] n mammifère m

mammoth ['mæməθ] n mammouth m ▷ adj géant(e), monstre

man (pl **men**) [mæn, mɛn] n homme m; (Sport) joueur m; (Chess) pièce f ▷ vt (Naut: ship) garnir d'hommes; (machine) assurer le fonctionnement de; (Mil: gun) servir; (: post) être de service à; **an old ~** un vieillard; **~ and wife** mari et femme

manage ['mænɪdʒ] vi se débrouiller; (succeed) y arriver, réussir ▷ vt (business) gérer; (team, operation) diriger; (control: ship) manier, manœuvrer; (: person) savoir s'y prendre avec; **to ~ to do** se débrouiller pour faire; (succeed) réussir à faire; **manageable** adj maniable; (task etc) faisable; (number) raisonnable; **management** n (running) administration f, direction f; (people in charge: of business, firm) dirigeants mpl, cadres mpl; (: of hotel, shop, theatre) direction; **manager** n (of business) directeur m; (of institution etc) administrateur m; (of department, unit) responsable m/f, chef m; (of hotel etc) gérant m; (Sport) manager m; (of artist) impresario m; **manageress** n directrice f; (of hotel etc) gérante f; **managerial** [mænɪ'dʒɪərɪəl] adj directorial(e); (skills) de cadre, de gestion; **managing director** n directeur général

mandarin ['mændərɪn] n (also: **~ orange**) mandarine f

mandate ['mændeɪt] n mandat m

mandatory ['mændətərɪ] adj obligatoire

mane [meɪn] n crinière f

maneuver [mə'nu:vəʳ] (US) n
= **manoeuvre**

mangetout ['mɔnʒ'tu:] n mangetout m inv

mango ['mæŋgəu] (pl **mangoes**) n
mangue f

man: **manhole** n trou m d'homme;
manhood n (age) âge m d'homme;
(manliness) virilité f

mania ['meɪnɪə] n manie f; **maniac**
['meɪnɪæk] n maniaque m/f; (fig)
fou (folle)

manic ['mænɪk] adj maniaque

manicure ['mænɪkjuəʳ] n manucure f

manifest ['mænɪfɛst] vt manifester
▷ adj manifeste, évident(e)

manifesto [mænɪ'fɛstəu] n (Pol)
manifeste m

manipulate [mə'nɪpjuleɪt] vt
manipuler; (system, situation)
exploiter

man: **mankind** [mæn'kaɪnd] n
humanité f, genre humain; **manly** adj
viril(e); **man-made** adj artificiel(le);
(fibre) synthétique

manner ['mænəʳ] n manière f,
façon f; (behaviour) attitude f,
comportement m; **manners** npl;
(good) ~s (bonnes) manières; **bad ~s**
mauvaises manières; **all ~ of** toutes
sortes de

manoeuvre, (US) **maneuver**
[mə'nu:vəʳ] vt (move) manœuvrer;
(manipulate: person) manipuler;
(: situation) exploiter ▷ n manœuvre f

manpower ['mænpauəʳ] n main-
d'œuvre f

mansion ['mænʃən] n château m,
manoir m

manslaughter ['mænslɔ:təʳ] n
homicide m involontaire

mantelpiece ['mæntlpi:s] n
cheminée f

manual ['mænjuəl] adj manuel(le)
▷ n manuel m

manufacture [mænju'fæktʃəʳ]
vt fabriquer ▷ n fabrication f;
manufacturer n fabricant m

manure [mə'njuəʳ] n fumier m;
(artificial) engrais m

manuscript ['mænjuskrɪpt] n
manuscrit m

many ['mɛnɪ] adj beaucoup de, de
nombreux(-euses) ▷ pron beaucoup,
un grand nombre; **a great ~** un grand
nombre (de); **~ a ...** bien des ..., plus
d'un(e) ...

map [mæp] n carte f; (of town) plan
m; **can you show it to me on the
~?** pouvez-vous me l'indiquer sur la
carte?; **map out** vt tracer; (fig: task)
planifier

maple ['meɪpl] n érable m

mar [mɑ:ʳ] vt gâcher, gâter

marathon ['mærəθən] n
marathon m

marble ['mɑ:bl] n marbre m; (toy)
bille f

March [mɑ:tʃ] n mars m

march [mɑ:tʃ] vi marcher au pas;
(demonstrators) défiler ▷ n marche f;
(demonstration) manifestation f

mare [mɛəʳ] n jument f

margarine [mɑ:dʒə'ri:n] n
margarine f

margin ['mɑ:dʒɪn] n marge f;
marginal adj marginal(e); **marginal
seat** (Pol) siège disputé; **marginally**
adv très légèrement, sensiblement

marigold ['mærɪgəuld] n souci m

marijuana [mærɪ'wɑ:nə] n
marijuana f

marina [mə'ri:nə] n marina f

marinade n [mærɪ'neɪd] marinade f

marinate ['mærɪneɪt] vt (faire)
mariner

marine [mə'ri:n] adj marin(e) ▷ n
fusilier marin; (US) marine m

marital ['mærɪtl] adj matrimonial(e);
marital status n situation f de
famille

maritime ['mærɪtaɪm] adj maritime

marjoram ['mɑ:dʒərəm] n
marjolaine f

mark [mɑ:k] n marque f; (of skid
etc) trace f; (BRIT Scol) note f; (oven

temperature): **(gas) ~ 4** thermostat m 4 ▷ *vt* (*also* Sport: *player*) marquer; (*stain*) tacher; (BRIT *Scol*) corriger, noter; **to ~ time** marquer le pas; **marked** *adj* (*obvious*) marqué(e), net(te); **marker** *n* (*sign*) jalon m; (*bookmark*) signet m

market ['mɑ:kɪt] *n* marché m ▷ *vt* (*Comm*) commercialiser; **marketing** *n* marketing m; **marketplace** *n* place *f* du marché; (*Comm*) marché m; **market research** *n* étude *f* de marché

marmalade ['mɑ:məleɪd] *n* confiture *f* d'oranges

maroon [mə'ru:n] *vt*: **to be ~ed** être abandonné(e); (*fig*) être bloqué(e) ▷ *adj* (*colour*) bordeaux *inv*

marquee [mɑ:'ki:] *n* chapiteau m

marriage ['mærɪdʒ] *n* mariage m; **marriage certificate** *n* extrait m d'acte de mariage

married ['mærɪd] *adj* marié(e); (*life, love*) conjugal(e)

marrow ['mærəu] *n* (*of bone*) moelle *f*; (*vegetable*) courge *f*

marry ['mærɪ] *vt* épouser, se marier avec; (*subj: father, priest etc*) marier ▷ *vi* (*also*: **get married**) se marier

Mars [mɑ:z] *n* (*planet*) Mars *f*

Marseilles [mɑ:'seɪ] *n* Marseille *f*

marsh [mɑ:ʃ] *n* marais m, marécage m

marshal ['mɑ:ʃl] *n* maréchal m; (US: *fire, police*) ≈ capitaine m; (*for demonstration, meeting*) membre m du service d'ordre ▷ *vt* rassembler

martyr ['mɑ:tə'] *n* martyr(e)

marvel ['mɑ:vl] *n* merveille *f* ▷ *vi*: **to ~ (at)** s'émerveiller (de); **marvellous**, (US) **marvelous** *adj* merveilleux(-euse)

Marxism ['mɑ:ksɪzəm] *n* marxisme m

Marxist ['mɑ:ksɪst] *adj*, *n* marxiste (m/f)

marzipan ['mɑ:zɪpæn] *n* pâte *f* d'amandes

mascara [mæs'kɑ:rə] *n* mascara m

mascot ['mæskət] *n* mascotte *f*

masculine ['mæskjulɪn] *adj* masculin(e) ▷ *n* masculin m

mash [mæʃ] *vt* (*Culin*) faire une purée de; **mashed potato(es)** *n(pl)* purée *f* de pommes de terre

mask [mɑ:sk] *n* masque m ▷ *vt* masquer

mason ['meɪsn] *n* (*also*: **stone~**) maçon m; (*also*: **free~**) franc-maçon m; **masonry** *n* maçonnerie *f*

mass [mæs] *n* multitude *f*, masse *f*; (*Physics*) masse *f*; (*Rel*) messe *f* ▷ *cpd* (*communication*) de masse; (*unemployment*) massif(-ive) ▷ *vi* masser; **masses** *npl*; **the ~es** les masses; **~es of** (*inf*) des tas de

massacre ['mæsəkə'] *n* massacre m

massage ['mæsɑ:ʒ] *n* massage m ▷ *vt* masser

massive ['mæsɪv] *adj* énorme, massif(-ive)

mass media *npl* mass-media *mpl*

mass-produce ['mæsprə'dju:s] *vt* fabriquer en série

mast [mɑ:st] *n* mât m; (*Radio, TV*) pylône m

master ['mɑ:stə'] *n* maître m; (*in secondary school*) professeur m; (*in primary school*) instituteur m; (*title for boys*): **M~ X** Monsieur X ▷ *vt* maîtriser; (*learn*) apprendre à fond; **M~ of Arts/Science (MA/MSc)** *n* ≈ titulaire m/f d'une maîtrise (en lettres/science); **M~ of Arts/Science degree (MA/MSc)** *n* ≈ maîtrise *f*; **mastermind** *n* esprit supérieur ▷ *vt* diriger, être le cerveau de; **masterpiece** *n* chef-d'œuvre m

masturbate ['mæstəbeɪt] *vi* se masturber

mat [mæt] *n* petit tapis; (*also*: **door~**) paillasson m; (*also*: **table~**) set m de table ▷ *adj* = **matt**

match [mætʃ] *n* allumette *f*; (*game*) match m, partie *f*; (*fig*) égal(e) ▷ *vt* (*also*: **~ up**) assortir; (*go well with*) aller bien avec, s'assortir à; (*equal*) égaler, valoir ▷ *vi* être assorti(e); **to be a good ~** être bien assorti(e); **matchbox** *n* boîte *f* d'allumettes; **matching** *adj* assorti(e)

mate [meɪt] *n* (*inf*) copain (copine); (*animal*) partenaire *m/f*, mâle (femelle); (*in merchant navy*) second *m* ▷ *vi* s'accoupler

material [mə'tɪərɪəl] *n* (*substance*) matière *f*, matériau *m*; (*cloth*) tissu *m*, étoffe *f*; (*information, data*) données *fpl* ▷ *adj* matériel(le); (*relevant: evidence*) pertinent(e); **materials** *npl* (*equipment*) matériaux *mpl*

materialize [mə'tɪərɪəlaɪz] *vi* se matérialiser, se réaliser

maternal [mə'tə:nl] *adj* maternel(le)

maternity [mə'tə:nɪtɪ] *n* maternité *f*; **maternity hospital** *n* maternité *f*; **maternity leave** *n* congé *m* de maternité

math [mæθ] *n* (*us*: = *mathematics*) maths *fpl*

mathematical [mæθə'mætɪkl] *adj* mathématique

mathematician [mæθəmə'tɪʃən] *n* mathématicien(ne)

mathematics [mæθə'mætɪks] *n* mathématiques *fpl*

maths [mæθs] *n abbr* (*BRIT*: = *mathematics*) maths *fpl*

matinée ['mætɪneɪ] *n* matinée *f*

matron ['meɪtrən] *n* (*in hospital*) infirmière-chef *f*; (*in school*) infirmière *f*

matt [mæt] *adj* mat(e)

matter ['mætəʳ] *n* question *f*; (*Physics*) matière *f*, substance *f*; (*Med: pus*) pus *m* ▷ *vi* importer; **matters** *npl* (*affairs, situation*) la situation; **it doesn't ~** cela n'a pas d'importance; (*I don't mind*) cela ne fait rien; **what's the ~?** qu'est-ce qu'il y a?, qu'est-ce qui ne va pas?; **no ~ what** quoi qu'il arrive; **as a ~ of course** tout naturellement; **as a ~ of fact** en fait; **reading ~** (*BRIT*) de quoi lire, de la lecture

mattress ['mætrɪs] *n* matelas *m*

mature [mə'tjuəʳ] *adj* mûr(e); (*cheese*) fait(e); (*wine*) arrivé(e) à maturité ▷ *vi* mûrir; (*cheese, wine*) se faire; **mature student** *n* étudiant(e) plus âgé(e) que la moyenne; **maturity** *n* maturité *f*

maul [mɔ:l] *vt* lacérer

mauve [məuv] *adj* mauve

max *abbr* = **maximum**

maximize ['mæksɪmaɪz] *vt* (*profits etc, chances*) maximiser

maximum (*pl* **maxima**) ['mæksɪməm, -mə] *adj* maximum ▷ *n* maximum *m*

May [meɪ] *n* mai *m*

may [meɪ] (*conditional* **might**) *vi* (*indicating possibility*): **he ~ come** il se peut qu'il vienne; (*be allowed to*): **~ I smoke?** puis-je fumer?; (*wishes*): **~ God bless you!** (que) Dieu vous bénisse!; **you ~ as well go** vous feriez aussi bien d'y aller

maybe ['meɪbi:] *adv* peut-être; **~ he'll ...** peut-être qu'il ...

May Day *n* le Premier mai

mayhem ['meɪhɛm] *n* grabuge *m*

mayonnaise [meɪə'neɪz] *n* mayonnaise *f*

mayor [mɛəʳ] *n* maire *m*; **mayoress** *n* (*female mayor*) maire *m*; (*wife of mayor*) épouse *f* du maire

maze [meɪz] *n* labyrinthe *m*, dédale *m*

MD *n abbr* (*Comm*) = **managing director**

me [mi:] *pron* me, m' + *vowel or h mute*; (*stressed, after prep*) moi; **it's me** c'est moi; **he heard me** il m'a entendu; **give me a book** donnez-moi un livre; **it's for me** c'est pour moi

meadow ['mɛdəu] *n* prairie *f*, pré *m*

meagre, (*us*) **meager** ['mi:gəʳ] *adj* maigre

meal [mi:l] *n* repas *m*; (*flour*) farine *f*; **mealtime** *n* heure *f* du repas

mean [mi:n] *adj* (*with money*) avare, radin(e); (*unkind*) mesquin(e), méchant(e); (*shabby*) misérable;

(*average*) moyen(ne) ▷ vt (*pt, pp*
meant) (*signify*) signifier, vouloir dire;
(*refer to*) faire allusion à, parler de;
(*intend*): **to ~ to do** avoir l'intention de
faire ▷ n moyenne f; **means** npl (*way,
money*) moyens mpl; **to be ~t for** être
destiné(e) à; **do you ~ it?** vous êtes
sérieux?; **what do you ~?** que voulez-
vous dire?; **by ~s of** (*instrument*) au
moyen de; **by all ~s** je vous en prie

meaning ['mi:nɪŋ] n signification
f, sens m; **meaningful** adj
significatif(-ive); (*relationship*)
valable; **meaningless** adj dénué(e)
de sens

meant [mɛnt] pt, pp of **mean**

meantime ['mi:ntaɪm] adv (*also:* **in
the ~**) pendant ce temps

meanwhile ['mi:nwaɪl] adv
= **meantime**

measles ['mi:zlz] n rougeole f

measure ['mɛʒəʳ] vt, vi mesurer ▷ n
mesure f; (*ruler*) règle (graduée)

measurements ['mɛʒəməntz] npl
mesures fpl; **chest/hip ~** tour m de
poitrine/hanches

meat [mi:t] n viande f; **I don't eat ~**
je ne mange pas de viande; **cold ~s**
(*BRIT*) viandes froides; **meatball** n
boulette f de viande

Mecca ['mɛkə] n la Mecque

mechanic [mɪ'kænɪk] n mécanicien
m; **can you send a ~?** pouvez-vous
nous envoyer un mécanicien?;
mechanical adj mécanique

mechanism ['mɛkənɪzəm] n
mécanisme m

medal ['mɛdl] n médaille f;
medallist, (*US*) **medalist** n (*Sport*)
médaillé(e)

meddle ['mɛdl] vi: **to ~ in** se mêler
de, s'occuper de; **to ~ with** toucher à

media ['mi:dɪə] npl media mpl ▷ npl
of **medium**

mediaeval [mɛdɪ'i:vl] adj
= **medieval**

mediate ['mi:dɪeɪt] vi servir
d'intermédiaire

medical ['mɛdɪkl] adj médical(e)
▷ n (*also:* **~ examination**) visite
médicale; (*private*) examen médical;
medical certificate n certificat
médical

medicated ['mɛdɪkeɪtɪd] adj
traitant(e), médicamenteux(-euse)

medication [mɛdɪ'keɪʃən] n (*drugs
etc*) médication f

medicine ['mɛdsɪn] n médecine f;
(*drug*) médicament m

medieval [mɛdɪ'i:vl] adj médiéval(e)

mediocre [mi:dɪ'əʊkəʳ] adj médiocre

meditate ['mɛdɪteɪt] vi: **to ~ (on)**
méditer (sur)

meditation [mɛdɪ'teɪʃən] n
méditation f

Mediterranean [mɛdɪtə'reɪnɪən]
adj méditerranéen(ne); **the ~ (Sea)** la
(mer) Méditerranée

medium ['mi:dɪəm] adj moyen(ne)
▷ n (pl **media**) (*means*) moyen m;
(*person*) médium m; **the happy ~**
le juste milieu; **medium-sized** adj
de taille moyenne; **medium wave**
n (*Radio*) ondes moyennes, petites
ondes

meek [mi:k] adj doux (douce),
humble

meet (pt, pp **met**) [mi:t, mɛt]
vt rencontrer; (*by arrangement*)
retrouver, rejoindre; (*for the first time*)
faire la connaissance de; (*go and
fetch*): **I'll ~ you at the station** j'irai te
chercher à la gare; (*opponent, danger,
problem*) faire face à; (*requirements*)
satisfaire à, répondre à ▷ vi (*friends*) se
rencontrer; se retrouver; (*in session*)
se réunir; (*join: lines, roads*) se joindre;
nice ~ing you ravi d'avoir fait votre
connaissance; **meet up** vi: **to ~ up
with sb** rencontrer qn; **meet with** vt
fus (*difficulty*) rencontrer; **to ~ with
success** être couronné(e) de succès;
meeting n (*of group of people*) réunion
f; (*between individuals*) rendez-vous m;
she's at or **in a meeting** (*Comm*) elle
est en réunion; **meeting place** n lieu

m de (la) réunion; (*for appointment*) lieu de rendez-vous

megabyte ['mɛgəbaɪt] *n* (*Comput*) méga-octet *m*

megaphone ['mɛgəfəun] *n* porte-voix *m inv*

megapixel ['mɛgəpɪksl] *n* mégapixel *m*

melancholy ['mɛlənkəlɪ] *n* mélancolie *f* ▷ *adj* mélancolique

melody ['mɛlədɪ] *n* mélodie *f*

melon ['mɛlən] *n* melon *m*

melt [mɛlt] *vi* fondre ▷ *vt* faire fondre

member ['mɛmbəʳ] *n* membre *m*; **M~ of the European Parliament** eurodéputé *m*; **M~ of Parliament** (*BRIT*) député *m*; **membership** *n* (*becoming a member*) adhésion *f*; admission *f*; (*members*) membres *mpl*, adhérents *mpl*; **membership card** *n* carte *f* de membre

memento [mə'mɛntəu] *n* souvenir *m*

memo ['mɛməu] *n* note *f* (de service)

memorable ['mɛmərəbl] *adj* mémorable

memorandum (*pl* **memoranda**) [mɛmə'rændəm, -də] *n* note *f* (de service)

memorial [mɪ'mɔːrɪəl] *n* mémorial *m* ▷ *adj* commémoratif(-ive)

memorize ['mɛməraɪz] *vt* apprendre *or* retenir par cœur

memory ['mɛmərɪ] *n* (*also Comput*) mémoire *f*; (*recollection*) souvenir *m*; **in ~ of** à la mémoire de; **memory card** *n* (*for digital camera*) carte *f* mémoire; **memory stick** *n* (*Comput: flash pen*) clé *f* USB; (*: card*) carte *f* mémoire

men [mɛn] *npl of* **man**

menace ['mɛnɪs] *n* menace *f*; (*inf: nuisance*) peste *f*, plaie *f* ▷ *vt* menacer

mend [mɛnd] *vt* réparer; (*darn*) raccommoder, repriser ▷ *n*: **on the ~** en voie de guérison; **to ~ one's ways** s'amender

meningitis [mɛnɪn'dʒaɪtɪs] *n* méningite *f*

menopause ['mɛnəupɔːz] *n* ménopause *f*

men's room (*US*) *n*: **the ~** les toilettes *fpl* pour hommes

menstruation [mɛnstru'eɪʃən] *n* menstruation *f*

menswear ['mɛnzwɛəʳ] *n* vêtements *mpl* d'hommes

mental ['mɛntl] *adj* mental(e); **mental hospital** *n* (*pej*) hôpital *m* psychiatrique; **mentality** [mɛn'tælɪtɪ] *n* mentalité *f*; **mentally** *adv*: **mentally ill people** les malades mentaux

menthol ['mɛnθɔl] *n* menthol *m*

mention ['mɛnʃən] *n* mention *f* ▷ *vt* mentionner, faire mention de; **don't ~ it!** je vous en prie, il n'y a pas de quoi!

menu ['mɛnjuː] *n* (*set menu, Comput*) menu *m*; (*list of dishes*) carte *f*

MEP *n abbr* = **Member of the European Parliament**

mercenary ['məːsɪnərɪ] *adj* (*person*) intéressé(e), mercenaire ▷ *n* mercenaire *m*

merchandise ['məːtʃəndaɪz] *n* marchandises *fpl*

merchant ['məːtʃənt] *n* négociant *m*, marchand *m*; **merchant bank** *n* (*BRIT*) banque *f* d'affaires; **merchant navy**, (*US*) **merchant marine** *n* marine marchande

merciless ['məːsɪlɪs] *adj* impitoyable, sans pitié

mercury ['məːkjurɪ] *n* mercure *m*

mercy ['məːsɪ] *n* pitié *f*, merci *f*; (*Rel*) miséricorde *f*; **at the ~ of** à la merci de

mere [mɪəʳ] *adj* simple; (*chance*) pur(e); **a ~ two hours** seulement deux heures; **merely** *adv* simplement, purement

merge [məːdʒ] *vt* unir; (*Comput*) fusionner, interclasser ▷ *vi* (*colours, shapes, sounds*) se mêler; (*roads*) se joindre; (*Comm*) fusionner; **merger** n (*Comm*) fusion f

meringue [məˈræŋ] n meringue f

merit [ˈmɛrɪt] n mérite m, valeur f ▷ vt mériter

mermaid [ˈməːmeɪd] n sirène f

merry [ˈmɛrɪ] adj gai(e); **M-Christmas!** joyeux Noël; **merry-go-round** n manège m

mesh [mɛʃ] n mailles fpl

mess [mɛs] n désordre m, fouillis m, pagaille f; (*muddle: of life*) gâchis m; (: *of economy*) pagaille f; (*dirt*) saleté f; (*Mil*) mess m, cantine f; **to be (in) a ~** être en désordre; **to be/get o.s. in a ~** (*fig*) être/se mettre dans le pétrin; **mess about, mess around** (*inf*) vi perdre son temps; **mess up** vt (*inf: dirty*) salir; (*spoil*) gâcher; **mess with** (*inf*) vt fus (*challenge, confront*) se frotter à; (*interfere with*) toucher à

message [ˈmɛsɪdʒ] n message m; **can I leave a ~?** est-ce que je peux laisser un message?; **are there any ~s for me?** est-ce que j'ai des messages?

messenger [ˈmɛsɪndʒəʳ] n messager m

Messrs, Messrs. [ˈmɛsəz] abbr (*on letters: = messieurs*) MM

messy [ˈmɛsɪ] adj (*dirty*) sale; (*untidy*) en désordre

met [mɛt] pt, pp of **meet**

metabolism [mɛˈtæbəlɪzəm] n métabolisme m

metal [ˈmɛtl] n métal m ▷ cpd en métal; **metallic** [mɛˈtælɪk] adj métallique

metaphor [ˈmɛtəfəʳ] n métaphore f

meteor [ˈmiːtɪəʳ] n météore m; **meteorite** [ˈmiːtɪəraɪt] n météorite m/f

meteorology [miːtɪəˈrɔlədʒɪ] n météorologie f

meter [ˈmiːtəʳ] n (*instrument*) compteur m; (*also*: **parking ~**) parc(o)mètre m; (*us: unit*) = **metre** ▷ vt (*us Post*) affranchir à la machine

method [ˈmɛθəd] n méthode f; **methodical** [mɪˈθɔdɪkl] adj méthodique

methylated spirit [ˈmɛθɪleɪtɪd-] n (*BRIT*) alcool m à brûler

meticulous [mɛˈtɪkjuləs] adj méticuleux(-euse)

metre, (*us*) **meter** [ˈmiːtəʳ] n mètre m

metric [ˈmɛtrɪk] adj métrique

metro [ˈmɛtrəu] n métro m

metropolitan [mɛtrəˈpɔlɪtən] adj métropolitain(e); **the M~ Police** (*BRIT*) la police londonienne

Mexican [ˈmɛksɪkən] adj mexicain(e) ▷ n Mexicain(e)

Mexico [ˈmɛksɪkəu] n Mexique m

mg abbr (= milligram) mg

mice [maɪs] npl of **mouse**

micro... [maɪkrəu] prefix micro...; **microchip** n (*Elec*) puce f; **microphone** n microphone m; **microscope** n microscope m

mid [mɪd] adj: **~ May** la mi-mai; **~ afternoon** le milieu de l'après-midi; **in ~ air** en plein ciel; **he's in his ~ thirties** il a dans les trente-cinq ans; **midday** n midi m

middle [ˈmɪdl] n milieu m; (*waist*) ceinture f, taille f ▷ adj du milieu; (*average*) moyen(ne); **in the ~ of the night** au milieu de la nuit; **middle-aged** adj d'un certain âge, ni vieux ni jeune; **Middle Ages** npl: **the Middle Ages** le moyen âge; **middle class(es)** n(pl): **the middle class(es)** ≈ les classes moyennes; **middle-class** adj bourgeois(e); **Middle East** n: **the Middle East** le Proche-Orient, le Moyen-Orient; **middle name** n second prénom; **middle school** n (*us*) école pour les enfants de 12 à 14 ans ≈ collège m; (*BRIT*) école pour les enfants de 8 à 14 ans

midge [mɪdʒ] n moucheron m

midget [ˈmɪdʒɪt] n (*offensive*) nain(e)

midnight [ˈmɪdnaɪt] n minuit m

midst [mɪdst] n: **in the ~ of** au milieu de

m

midsummer [mɪd'sʌmə^r] n milieu m de l'été

midway [mɪd'weɪ] adj, adv: **~ (between)** à mi-chemin (entre); **~ through ...** au milieu de ..., en plein(e) ...

midweek [mɪd'wiːk] adv au milieu de la semaine, en pleine semaine

midwife (pl **midwives**) ['mɪdwaɪf, -vz] n sage-femme f

midwinter [mɪd'wɪntə^r] n milieu m de l'hiver

might [maɪt] vb see **may** ▷ n puissance f, force f; **mighty** adj puissant(e)

migraine ['miːgreɪn] n migraine f

migrant ['maɪgrənt] n (bird, animal) migrateur m; (person) migrant(e) ▷ adj migrateur(-trice); (worker) saisonnier(-ière)

migrate [maɪ'greɪt] vi migrer

migration [maɪ'greɪʃən] n migration f

mike [maɪk] n abbr (= microphone) micro m

mild [maɪld] adj doux (douce); (reproach, infection) léger(-ère); (illness) bénin(-igne); (interest) modéré(e); (taste) peu relevé(e); **mildly** ['maɪldlɪ] adv doucement; légèrement; **to put it mildly** (inf) c'est le moins qu'on puisse dire

mile [maɪl] n mil(l)e m (= 1609 m); **mileage** n distance f en milles, ≈ kilométrage m; **mileometer** [maɪ'lɔmɪtə^r] n compteur m kilométrique; **milestone** n borne f; (fig) jalon m

military ['mɪlɪtərɪ] adj militaire

militia [mɪ'lɪʃə] n milice f

milk [mɪlk] n lait m ▷ vt (cow) traire; (fig: person) dépouiller, plumer; (: situation) exploiter à fond; **milk chocolate** n chocolat m au lait; **milkman** (irreg) n laitier m; **milky** adj (drink) au lait; (colour) laiteux(-euse)

mill [mɪl] n moulin m; (factory) usine f, fabrique f; (spinning mill) filature f;

(flour mill) minoterie f ▷ vt moudre, broyer ▷ vi (also: **~ about**) grouiller

millennium (pl **millenniums** or **millennia**) [mɪ'lɛnɪəm, -'lɛnɪə] n millénaire m

milli... ['mɪlɪ] prefix milli...; **milligram(me)** n milligramme m; **millilitre**, (US) **milliliter** n millilitre m; **millimetre**, (US) **millimeter** n millimètre m

million ['mɪljən] n million m; **a ~ pounds** un million de livres sterling; **millionaire** [mɪljə'nɛə^r] n millionnaire m; **millionth** [mɪljə'nθ] num millionième

milometer [maɪ'lɔmɪtə^r] n = **mileometer**

mime [maɪm] n mime m ▷ vt, vi mimer

mimic ['mɪmɪk] n imitateur(-trice) ▷ vt, vi imiter, contrefaire

min. abbr (= minute(s)) mn.; (= minimum) min.

mince [mɪns] vt hacher ▷ n (BRIT Culin) viande hachée, hachis m; **mincemeat** n hachis de fruits secs utilisés en pâtisserie; (US) viande hachée, hachis m; **mince pie** n sorte de tarte aux fruits secs

mind [maɪnd] n esprit m ▷ vt (attend to, look after) s'occuper de; (be careful) faire attention à; (object to): **I don't ~ the noise** je ne crains pas le bruit, le bruit ne me dérange pas; **it is on my ~** cela me préoccupe; **to change one's ~** changer d'avis; **to my ~** à mon avis, selon moi; **to bear sth in ~** tenir compte de qch; **to have sb/sth in ~** avoir qn/qch en tête; **to make up one's ~** se décider; **do you ~ if ...?** est-ce que cela vous gêne si ...?; **I don't ~** cela ne me dérange pas; (don't care) ça m'est égal; **~ you, ...** remarquez, ...; **never ~** peu importe, ça ne fait rien; (don't worry) ne vous en faites pas; **"~ the step"** "attention à la marche"; **mindless** adj irréfléchi(e); (violence, crime) insensé(e); (boring: job) idiot(e)

mine¹ [maɪn] *pron* le (la) mien(ne), les miens (miennes); **a friend of ~** un de mes amis, un ami à moi; **this book is ~** ce livre est à moi

mine² [maɪn] *n* mine *f* ▷ *vt* (*coal*) extraire; (*ship, beach*) miner; **minefield** *n* champ *m* de mines; **miner** *n* mineur *m*

mineral ['mɪnərəl] *adj* minéral(e) ▷ *n* minéral *m*; **mineral water** *n* eau minérale

mingle ['mɪŋgl] *vi*: **to ~ with** se mêler à

miniature ['mɪnətʃər] *adj* (en) miniature ▷ *n* miniature *f*

minibar ['mɪnɪbɑːr] *n* minibar *m*

minibus ['mɪnɪbʌs] *n* minibus *m*

minicab ['mɪnɪkæb] *n* (BRIT) taxi *m* indépendant

minimal ['mɪnɪml] *adj* minimal(e)

minimize ['mɪnɪmaɪz] *vt* (*reduce*) réduire au minimum; (*play down*) minimiser

minimum ['mɪnɪməm] *n* (*pl* **minima**) minimum *m* ▷ *adj* minimum

mining ['maɪnɪŋ] *n* exploitation minière

miniskirt ['mɪnɪskəːt] *n* mini-jupe *f*

minister ['mɪnɪstər] *n* (BRIT Pol) ministre *m*; (Rel) pasteur *m*

ministry ['mɪnɪstrɪ] *n* (BRIT Pol) ministère *m*; (Rel): **to go into the ~** devenir pasteur

minor ['maɪnər] *adj* petit(e), de peu d'importance; (Mus, poet, problem) mineur(e) ▷ *n* (Law) mineur(e)

minority [maɪ'nɔrɪtɪ] *n* minorité *f*

mint [mɪnt] *n* (*plant*) menthe *f*; (*sweet*) bonbon *m* à la menthe ▷ *vt* (*coins*) battre; **the (Royal) M~, the (US) M~** ≈ l'hôtel *m* de la Monnaie; **in ~ condition** à l'état de neuf

minus ['maɪnəs] *n* (*also*: **~ sign**) signe *m* moins ▷ *prep* moins; **12 ~ 6 equals 6** 12 moins 6 égal 6; **~ 24°C** moins 24°C

minute¹ ['mɪnɪt] *n* minute *f*; **minutes** *npl* (*of meeting*) procès-verbal *m*, compte rendu; **wait a ~!**

(attendez) un instant!; **at the last ~** à la dernière minute

minute² [maɪ'njuːt] *adj* minuscule; (*detailed*) minutieux(-euse); **in ~ detail** par le menu

miracle ['mɪrəkl] *n* miracle *m*

miraculous [mɪ'rækjuləs] *adj* miraculeux(-euse)

mirage ['mɪrɑːʒ] *n* mirage *m*

mirror ['mɪrər] *n* miroir *m*, glace *f*; (*in car*) rétroviseur *m*

misbehave [mɪsbɪ'heɪv] *vi* mal se conduire

misc. *abbr* = **miscellaneous**

miscarriage ['mɪskærɪdʒ] *n* (Med) fausse couche; **~ of justice** erreur *f* judiciaire

miscellaneous [mɪsɪ'leɪnɪəs] *adj* (*items, expenses*) divers(es); (*selection*) varié(e)

mischief ['mɪstʃɪf] *n* (*naughtiness*) sottises *fpl*; (*playfulness*) espièglerie *f*; (*harm*) mal *m*, dommage *m*; (*maliciousness*) méchanceté *f*; **mischievous** ['mɪstʃɪvəs] *adj* (*playful, naughty*) coquin(e), espiègle

misconception [mɪskən'sɛpʃən] *n* idée fausse

misconduct [mɪs'kɔndʌkt] *n* inconduite *f*; **professional ~** faute professionnelle

miser ['maɪzər] *n* avare *m/f*

miserable ['mɪzərəbl] *adj* (*person, expression*) malheureux(-euse); (*conditions*) misérable; (*weather*) maussade; (*offer, donation*) minable; (*failure*) pitoyable

misery ['mɪzərɪ] *n* (*unhappiness*) tristesse *f*; (*pain*) souffrances *fpl*; (*wretchedness*) misère *f*

misfortune [mɪs'fɔːtʃən] *n* malchance *f*, malheur *m*

misgiving [mɪs'gɪvɪŋ] *n* (*apprehension*) craintes *fpl*; **to have ~s about sth** avoir des doutes quant à qch

misguided [mɪs'gaɪdɪd] *adj* malavisé(e)

m

mishap ['mɪʃæp] n mésaventure f
misinterpret [mɪsɪn'tə:prɪt] vt mal
interpréter
misjudge [mɪs'dʒʌdʒ] vt méjuger, se
méprendre sur le compte de
mislay [mɪs'leɪ] vt (irreg: like **lay**)
égarer
mislead [mɪs'li:d] vt (irreg: like **lead¹**)
induire en erreur; **misleading** adj
trompeur(-euse)
misplace [mɪs'pleɪs] vt égarer; **to be
~d** (trust etc) être mal placé(e)
misprint ['mɪsprɪnt] n faute f
d'impression
misrepresent [mɪsrɛprɪ'zɛnt] vt
présenter sous un faux jour
Miss [mɪs] n Mademoiselle
miss [mɪs] vt (fail to get, attend, see)
manquer, rater; (regret the absence
of): **I ~ him/it** il/cela me manque ▷ vi
manquer ▷ n (shot) coup manqué; **we
~ed our train** nous avons raté notre
train; **you can't ~ it** vous ne pouvez
pas vous tromper; **miss out** vt (BRIT)
oublier; **miss out on** vt fus (fun, party)
rater, manquer; (chance, bargain)
laisser passer
missile ['mɪsaɪl] n (Aviat) missile m;
(object thrown) projectile m
missing ['mɪsɪŋ] adj manquant(e);
(after escape, disaster: person)
disparu(e); **to go ~** disparaître; **~ in
action** (Mil) porté(e) disparu(e)
mission ['mɪʃən] n mission f; **on
a ~ to sb** en mission auprès de qn;
missionary n missionnaire m/f
misspell ['mɪs'spɛl] vt (irreg: like
spell) mal orthographier
mist [mɪst] n brume f ▷ vi (also: **~
over**, **~ up**) devenir brumeux(-euse);
(BRIT: windows) s'embuer
mistake [mɪs'teɪk] n erreur f, faute
f ▷ vt (irreg: like **take**) (meaning)
mal comprendre; (intentions)
se méprendre sur; **to ~ for**
prendre pour, par erreur, par
inadvertance; **to make a ~** (in
writing) faire une faute; (in calculating
etc) faire une erreur; **there must be
some ~** il doit y avoir une erreur, se
tromper; **mistaken** pp of **mistake**
▷ adj (idea etc) erroné(e); **to be
mistaken** faire erreur, se tromper
mister ['mɪstər] n (inf) Monsieur
m; see **Mr**
mistletoe ['mɪsltəu] n gui m
mistook [mɪs'tuk] pt of **mistake**
mistress ['mɪstrɪs] n maîtresse f;
(BRIT: in primary school) institutrice f;
(: in secondary school) professeur m
mistrust [mɪs'trʌst] vt se méfier de
misty ['mɪstɪ] adj brumeux(-euse);
(glasses, window) embué(e)
misunderstand [mɪsʌndə'stænd]
vt, vi (irreg: like **understand**) mal
comprendre; **misunderstanding** n
méprise f, malentendu m; **there's
been a misunderstanding** il y a eu
un malentendu
misunderstood [mɪsʌndə'stud] pt,
pp of **misunderstand** ▷ adj (person)
incompris(e)
misuse n [mɪs'ju:s] mauvais emploi;
(of power) abus m ▷ vt [mɪs'ju:z] mal
employer; abuser de
mitt(en) ['mɪt(n)] n moufle f;
(fingerless) mitaine f
mix [mɪks] vt mélanger; (sauce,
drink etc) préparer ▷ vi se mélanger;
(socialize): **he doesn't ~ well** il est
peu sociable ▷ n mélange m; **to ~ sth
with sth** mélanger qch à qch; **cake
~** préparation f pour gâteau; **mix up**
vt mélanger; (confuse) confondre; **to
be ~ed up in sth** être mêlé(e) à qch
or impliqué(e) dans qch; **mixed** adj
(feelings, reactions) contradictoire;
(school, marriage) mixte; **mixed grill**
n (BRIT) assortiment m de grillades;
mixed salad n salade f de crudités;
mixed-up adj (person) désorienté(e),
embrouillé(e); **mixer** n (for food)
batteur m, mixeur m; (drink) boisson
gazeuse (servant à couper un alcool);
(person): **he is a good mixer** il est
très sociable; **mixture** n assortiment

m, mélange *m*; (*Med*) préparation *f*;
mix-up *n*: **there was a mix-up** il y a eu confusion

ml *abbr* (= millilitre(s)) ml

mm *abbr* (= millimetre) mm

moan [məun] *n* gémissement *m* ▷ *vi* gémir; (*inf: complain*): **to ~ (about)** se plaindre (de)

moat [məut] *n* fossé *m*, douves *fpl*

mob [mɔb] *n* foule *f*; (*disorderly*) cohue *f* ▷ *vt* assaillir

mobile ['məubaɪl] *adj* mobile ▷ *n* (*Art*) mobile *m*; (*BRIT inf: phone*) (téléphone *m*) portable *m*, mobile *m*; **mobile home** *n* caravane *f*; **mobile phone** *n* (téléphone *m*) portable *m*, mobile *m*

mobility [məu'bɪlɪtɪ] *n* mobilité *f*

mobilize ['məubɪlaɪz] *vt*, *vi* mobiliser

mock [mɔk] *vt* ridiculiser; (*laugh at*) se moquer de ▷ *adj* faux (fausse); **mocks** *npl* (*BRIT Scol*) examens blancs; **mockery** *n* moquerie *f*, raillerie *f*

mod cons ['mɔd'kɔnz] *npl abbr* (*BRIT*) = **modern conveniences**; *see* **convenience**

mode [məud] *n* mode *m*; (*of transport*) moyen *m*

model ['mɔdl] *n* modèle *m*; (*person: for fashion*) mannequin *m*; (*: for artist*) modèle ▷ *vt* (*with clay etc*) modeler ▷ *vi* travailler comme mannequin ▷ *adj* (*railway: toy*) modèle réduit *inv*; (*child, factory*) modèle; **to ~ clothes** présenter des vêtements; **to ~ o.s. on** imiter

modem ['məudɛm] *n* modem *m*

moderate ['mɔdərət] *adj* modéré(e); (*amount, change*) peu important(e) ▷ *vi* ['mɔdəreɪt] se modérer, se calmer ▷ *vt* ['mɔdəreɪt] modérer

moderation [mɔdə'reɪʃən] *n* modération *f*, mesure *f*; **in ~** à dose raisonnable, pris(e) *or* pratiqué(e) modérément

modern ['mɔdən] *adj* moderne; **modernize** *vt* moderniser; **modern languages** *npl* langues vivantes

modest ['mɔdɪst] *adj* modeste; **modesty** *n* modestie *f*

modification [mɔdɪfɪ'keɪʃən] *n* modification *f*

modify ['mɔdɪfaɪ] *vt* modifier

module ['mɔdjuːl] *n* module *m*

mohair ['məuhɛəʳ] *n* mohair *m*

Mohammed [mə'hæmɛd] *n* Mahomet *m*

moist [mɔɪst] *adj* humide, moite; **moisture** ['mɔɪstʃəʳ] *n* humidité *f*; (*on glass*) buée *f*; **moisturizer** ['mɔɪstʃəraɪzəʳ] *n* crème hydratante

mold *etc* [məuld] (*US*) = **mould**

mole [məul] *n* (*animal, spy*) taupe *f*; (*spot*) grain *m* de beauté

molecule ['mɔlɪkjuːl] *n* molécule *f*

molest [məu'lɛst] *vt* (*assault sexually*) attenter à la pudeur de

molten ['məultən] *adj* fondu(e); (*rock*) en fusion

mom [mɔm] *n* (*US*) = **mum**

moment ['məumənt] *n* moment *m*, instant *m*; **at the ~** en ce moment; **momentarily** *adv* momentanément; (*US: soon*) bientôt; **momentary** *adj* momentané(e), passager(-ère); **momentous** [məu'mɛntəs] *adj* important(e), capital(e)

momentum [məu'mɛntəm] *n* élan *m*, vitesse acquise; (*fig*) dynamique *f*; **to gather ~** prendre de la vitesse; (*fig*) gagner du terrain

mommy ['mɔmɪ] *n* (*US: mother*) maman *f*

Monaco ['mɔnəkəu] *n* Monaco *f*

monarch ['mɔnək] *n* monarque *m*; **monarchy** *n* monarchie *f*

monastery ['mɔnəstərɪ] *n* monastère *m*

Monday ['mʌndɪ] *n* lundi *m*

monetary ['mʌnɪtərɪ] *adj* monétaire

money ['mʌnɪ] *n* argent *m*; **to make ~** (*person*) gagner de l'argent; (*business*) rapporter; **money belt** *n* ceinture-portefeuille *f*; **money order** *n* mandat *m*

mongrel ['mʌŋɡrəl] *n* (*dog*) bâtard *m*

monitor ['mɒnɪtə'] n (TV, Comput)
écran m, moniteur m ▷ vt contrôler;
(foreign station) être à l'écoute de;
(progress) suivre de près

monk [mʌŋk] n moine m

monkey ['mʌŋkɪ] n singe m

monologue ['mɒnəlɒg] n
monologue m

monopoly [mə'nɒpəlɪ] n monopole m

monosodium glutamate
[mɒnə'səʊdɪəm 'gluːtəmeɪt] n
glutamate m de sodium

monotonous [mə'nɒtənəs] adj
monotone

monsoon [mɒn'suːn] n mousson f

monster ['mɒnstə'] n monstre m

month [mʌnθ] n mois m; **monthly**
adj mensuel(le) ▷ adv mensuellement

Montreal [mɒntrɪ'ɔːl] n Montréal m

monument ['mɒnjumənt] n
monument m

mood [muːd] n humeur f, disposition
f; **to be in a good/bad ~** être de
bonne/mauvaise humeur; **moody**
adj (variable) d'humeur changeante,
lunatique; (sullen) morose, maussade

moon [muːn] n lune f; **moonlight** n
clair m de lune

moor [muə'] n lande f ▷ vt (ship)
amarrer ▷ vi mouiller

moose [muːs] n (pl inv) élan m

mop [mɒp] n balai m à laver; (for
dishes) lavette f à vaisselle ▷ vt
éponger, essuyer; **~ of hair** tignasse
f; **mop up** vt éponger

mope [məʊp] vi avoir le cafard, se
morfondre

moped ['məʊpɛd] n cyclomoteur m

moral ['mɒrl] adj moral(e) ▷ n morale
f; **morals** npl moralité f

morale [mɒ'rɑːl] n moral m

morality [mə'rælɪtɪ] n moralité f

morbid ['mɔːbɪd] adj morbide

KEYWORD

more [mɔː'] adj **1** (greater in number
etc) plus (de), davantage (de); **more**
people/work (than)** plus de gens/
de travail (que)

2 (additional) encore (de); **do you want
(some) more tea?** voulez-vous encore
du thé?; **is there any more wine?**
reste-t-il du vin?; **I have no** or **I don't
have any more money** je n'ai plus
d'argent; **it'll take a few more weeks**
ça prendra encore quelques semaines

▷ pron plus, davantage; **more than
10** plus de 10; **it cost more than
we expected** cela a coûté plus que
prévu; **I want more** j'en veux plus or
davantage; **is there any more?** est-
ce qu'il en reste?; **there's no more**
il n'y en a plus; **a little more** un peu
plus; **many/much more** beaucoup
plus, bien davantage

▷ adv plus; **more dangerous/easily
(than)** plus dangereux/facilement
(que); **more and more expensive** de
plus en plus cher; **more or less** plus
ou moins; **more than ever** plus que
jamais; **once more** encore une fois,
une fois de plus

moreover [mɔː'rəʊvə'] adv de plus

morgue [mɔːg] n morgue f

morning ['mɔːnɪŋ] n matin m; (as
duration) matinée f ▷ cpd matinal(e);
(paper) du matin; **in the ~** le matin;
7 o'clock in the ~ 7 heures du matin;
morning sickness n nausées
matinales

Moroccan [mə'rɒkən] adj
marocain(e) ▷ n Marocain(e)

Morocco [mə'rɒkəʊ] n Maroc m

moron ['mɔːrɒn] n (offensive) idiot(e),
minus m/f

morphine ['mɔːfiːn] n morphine f

morris dancing ['mɒrɪs-] n (BRIT)
danses folkloriques anglaises

● **MORRIS DANCING**
●
● Le morris dancing est une
● danse folklorique anglaise
● traditionnellement réservée aux

hommes. Habillés tout en blanc
et portant des clochettes, ils
exécutent différentes figures avec
des mouchoirs et de longs bâtons.
Cette danse est très populaire dans
les fêtes de village.

Morse [mɔːs] n (also: ~ **code**) morse m
mortal ['mɔːtl] adj, n mortel(le)
mortar ['mɔːtər] n mortier m
mortgage ['mɔːgɪdʒ] n hypothèque
f; (loan) prêt m (or crédit m)
hypothécaire ▷ vt hypothéquer
mortician [mɔːˈtɪʃən] n (US)
entrepreneur m de pompes funèbres
mortified ['mɔːtɪfaɪd] adj mort(e)
de honte
mortuary ['mɔːtjuərɪ] n morgue f
mosaic [məuˈzeɪɪk] n mosaïque f
Moscow ['mɔskəu] n Moscou
Moslem ['mɔzləm] adj, n = **Muslim**
mosque [mɔsk] n mosquée f
mosquito [mɔsˈkiːtəu] (pl
mosquitoes) n moustique m
moss [mɔs] n mousse f
most [məust] adj (majority of) la
plupart de; (greatest amount of) le plus
de ▷ pron la plupart ▷ adv le plus;
(very) très, extrêmement; **the** ~ le
plus; ~ **fish** la plupart des poissons;
the ~ **beautiful woman in the
world** la plus belle femme du monde;
~ **of** (with plural) la plupart de; (with
singular) la plus grande partie de; ~ **of
them** la plupart d'entre eux; ~ **of
the time** la plupart du temps; **I saw**
~ (a lot but not all) j'en ai vu la plupart;
(more than anyone else) c'est moi qui
en ai vu le plus; **at the (very)** ~ au
plus; **to make the** ~ **of** profiter au
maximum de; **mostly** adv (chiefly)
surtout, principalement; (usually)
généralement
MOT n abbr (BRIT: = Ministry of
Transport): **the** ~ **(test)** visite
technique (annuelle) obligatoire des
véhicules à moteur
motel [məuˈtɛl] n motel m

moth [mɔθ] n papillon m de nuit; (in
clothes) mite f
mother ['mʌðər] n mère f ▷ vt
(pamper, protect) dorloter;
motherhood n maternité f; **mother-
in-law** n belle-mère f; **mother-of-
pearl** n nacre f; **Mother's Day** n fête
f des Mères; **mother-to-be** n future
maman; **mother tongue** n langue
maternelle
motif [məuˈtiːf] n motif m
motion ['məuʃən] n mouvement m;
(gesture) geste m; (at meeting) motion
f ▷ vt, vi: **to** ~ **(to) sb to do** faire
signe à qn de faire; **motionless** adj
immobile, sans mouvement; **motion
picture** n film m
motivate ['məutɪveɪt] vt motiver
motivation [məutɪˈveɪʃən] n
motivation f
motive ['məutɪv] n motif m, mobile m
motor ['məutər] n moteur m; (BRIT
inf: vehicle) auto f; **motorbike** n moto
f; **motorboat** n bateau m à moteur;
motorcar n (BRIT) automobile f;
motorcycle n moto f; **motorcyclist**
n motocycliste m/f; **motoring** (BRIT)
n tourisme m automobile; **motorist**
n automobiliste m/f; **motor racing** n
(BRIT) course f automobile;
motorway n (BRIT) autoroute f
motto ['mɔtəu] (pl **mottoes**) n
devise f
mould, (US) **mold** [məuld] n moule
m; (mildew) moisissure f ▷ vt mouler,
modeler; (fig) façonner; **mouldy**, (US)
moldy adj moisi(e); (smell) de moisi
mound [maund] n monticule m,
tertre m
mount [maunt] n (hill) mont m,
montagne f; (horse) monture f;
(for picture) carton m de montage
▷ vt monter; (horse) monter à;
(bike) monter sur; (picture) monter
sur carton ▷ vi (inflation, tension)
augmenter; **mount up** vi s'élever,
monter; (bills, problems, savings)
s'accumuler

m

mountain ['mauntɪn] n
montagne f ▷ cpd de (la) montagne;
mountain bike n VTT m, vélo
m tout terrain; **mountaineer** n
alpiniste m/f; **mountaineering** n
alpinisme m; **mountainous** adj
montagneux(-euse); **mountain
range** n chaîne f de montagnes

mourn [mɔ:n] vt pleurer ▷ vi: **to
~ for sb** pleurer qn; **to ~ for sth**
se lamenter sur qch; **mourner** n
parent(e) or ami(e) du défunt;
personne f en deuil or venue rendre
hommage au défunt; **mourning** n
deuil m; **in mourning** en deuil

mouse (pl **mice**) [maus, maɪs] n
(also Comput) souris f; **mouse mat** n
(Comput) tapis m de souris

moussaka [mu'sɑːkə] n moussaka f

mousse [mu:s] n mousse f

moustache, (US) **mustache**
[məs'tɑːʃ] n moustache(s) f(pl)

mouth (pl **mouths**) [mauθ, mauðz]
n bouche f; (of dog, cat) gueule f; (of
river) embouchure f; (of hole, cave)
ouverture f; **mouthful** n bouchée
f; **mouth organ** n harmonica m;
mouthpiece n (of musical instrument)
bec m, embouchure f; (spokesperson)
porte-parole m inv; **mouthwash** n
eau f dentifrice

move [mu:v] n (movement)
mouvement m; (in game) coup m
(: turn to play) tour m; (change of
house) déménagement m; (change
of job) changement m d'emploi ▷ vt
déplacer, bouger; (emotionally)
émouvoir; (Pol: resolution etc)
proposer ▷ vi (gen) bouger, remuer;
(traffic) circuler; (also: ~ house)
déménager; (in game) jouer; **can you
~ your car, please?** pouvez-vous
déplacer votre voiture, s'il vous
plaît?; **to ~ sb to do sth** pousser
or inciter qn à faire qch; **to get a ~
on** se dépêcher, se remuer; **move
back** vi revenir, retourner; **move
in** vi (to a house) emménager; (police,

soldiers) intervenir; **move off** vi
s'éloigner, s'en aller; **move on** vi
se remettre en route; **move out** vi
(of house) déménager; **move over**
vi se pousser, se déplacer; **move
up** vi avancer; (employee) avoir de
l'avancement; (pupil) passer dans
la classe supérieure; **movement** n
mouvement m

movie ['mu:vɪ] n film m; **movies** npl;
the ~s le cinéma; **movie theater** (US)
n cinéma m

moving ['mu:vɪŋ] adj en
mouvement; (touching)
émouvant(e)

mow (pt **mowed**, pp **mowed** or
mown) [məu, -d, -n] vt faucher;
(lawn) tondre; **mower** n (also:
lawnmower) tondeuse f à gazon

mown [məun] pp of **mow**

Mozambique [məuzəm'bi:k] n
Mozambique m

MP n abbr (BRIT) = **Member of
Parliament**

MP3 n mp3 m; **MP3 player** n baladeur
m numérique, lecteur m mp3

mpg n abbr = **miles per gallon**
(30 mpg = 9,4 l. aux 100 km)

m.p.h. abbr = **miles per hour** (60 mph
= 96 km/h)

Mr, (US) **Mr.** ['mɪstə^r] n: **~ X** Monsieur
X, M. X

Mrs, (US) **Mrs.** ['mɪsɪz] n: **~ X**
Madame X, Mme X

Ms, (US) **Ms.** [mɪz] n (Miss or Mrs): **~ X**
Madame X, Mme X

MSP n abbr (= Member of the Scottish
Parliament) député m au Parlement
écossais

Mt abbr (Geo: = mount) Mt

much [mʌtʃ] adj beaucoup de ▷ adv,
n, pron beaucoup; **we don't have
~ time** nous n'avons pas beaucoup
de temps; **how ~ is it?** combien
est-ce que ça coûte?; **it's not ~** ce
n'est pas beaucoup; **too ~** trop (de);
so ~ tant (de); **I like it very/so ~**
j'aime beaucoup/tellement ça; **as ~**

as autant de; **that's ~ better** c'est beaucoup mieux

muck [mʌk] n (mud) boue f; (dirt) ordures fpl; **muck up** vt (inf: ruin) gâcher, esquinter; (dirty) salir; (exam, interview) se planter à; **mucky** adj (dirty) boueux(-euse), sale

mucus ['mju:kəs] n mucus m

mud [mʌd] n boue f

muddle ['mʌdl] n (mess) pagaille f, fouillis m; (mix-up) confusion f ▷ vt (also: ~ up) brouiller, embrouiller; **to get in a ~** (while explaining etc) s'embrouiller

muddy ['mʌdɪ] adj boueux(-euse)

mudguard ['mʌdgɑ:d] n garde-boue m inv

muesli ['mju:zlɪ] n muesli m

muffin ['mʌfɪn] n (roll) petit pain rond et plat; (cake) petit gâteau au chocolat ou aux fruits

muffled ['mʌfld] adj étouffé(e), voilé(e)

muffler ['mʌflər] n (scarf) cache-nez m inv; (us Aut) silencieux m

mug [mʌg] n (cup) tasse f (sans soucoupe); (: for beer) chope f; (inf: face) bouille f; (: fool) poire f ▷ vt (assault) agresser; **mugger** ['mʌgər] n agresseur m; **mugging** n agression f

muggy ['mʌgɪ] adj lourd(e), moite

mule [mju:l] n mule f

multicoloured, (us) **multicolored** ['mʌltɪkʌləd] adj multicolore

multimedia ['mʌltɪ'mi:dɪə] adj multimédia inv

multinational [mʌltɪ'næʃənl] n multinationale f ▷ adj multinational(e)

multiple ['mʌltɪpl] adj multiple ▷ n multiple m; **multiple choice (test)** n QCM m, questionnaire m à choix multiple; **multiple sclerosis** [-sklɪ'rəʊsɪs] n sclérose f en plaques

multiplex (cinema) ['mʌltɪpleks-] n (cinéma m) multisalles m

multiplication [mʌltɪplɪ'keɪʃən] n multiplication f

multiply ['mʌltɪplaɪ] vt multiplier ▷ vi se multiplier

multistorey ['mʌltɪ'stɔ:rɪ] adj (BRIT: building) à étages; (: car park) à étages or niveaux multiples

mum [mʌm] n (BRIT) maman f ▷ adj: **to keep ~** ne pas souffler mot

mumble ['mʌmbl] vt, vi marmotter, marmonner

mummy ['mʌmɪ] n (BRIT: mother) maman f; (embalmed) momie f

mumps [mʌmps] n oreillons mpl

munch [mʌntʃ] vt, vi mâcher

municipal [mju:'nɪsɪpl] adj municipal(e)

mural ['mjuərl] n peinture murale

murder ['mə:dər] n meurtre m, assassinat m ▷ vt assassiner; **murderer** n meurtrier m, assassin m

murky ['mə:kɪ] adj sombre, ténébreux(-euse); (water) trouble

murmur ['mə:mər] n murmure m ▷ vt, vi murmurer

muscle ['mʌsl] n muscle m; (fig) force f; **muscular** ['mʌskjulər] adj musculaire; (person, arm) musclé(e)

museum [mju:'zɪəm] n musée m

mushroom ['mʌʃrum] n champignon m ▷ vi (fig) pousser comme un (or des) champignon(s)

music ['mju:zɪk] n musique f; **musical** adj musical(e); (person) musicien(ne) ▷ n (show) comédie musicale; **musical instrument** n instrument m de musique; **musician** [mju:'zɪʃən] n musicien(ne)

Muslim ['mʌzlɪm] adj, n musulman(e)

muslin ['mʌzlɪn] n mousseline f

mussel ['mʌsl] n moule f

must [mʌst] aux vb (obligation): **I ~ do it** je dois le faire, il faut que je le fasse; (probability): **he ~ be there by now** il doit y être maintenant, il y est probablement maintenant; (suggestion, invitation): **you ~ come and see me** il faut que vous veniez me voir ▷ n nécessité f, impératif m;

it's a ~ c'est indispensable; **I ~ have
made a mistake** j'ai dû me tromper
mustache ['mʌstæʃ] *n* (*us*)
= **moustache**
mustard ['mʌstəd] *n* moutarde *f*
mustn't ['mʌsnt] = **must not**
mutilate ['mju:tɪleɪt] *vt* mutiler
mutiny ['mju:tɪnɪ] *n* mutinerie *f* ▷ *vi*
se mutiner
mutter ['mʌtər] *vt*, *vi* marmonner,
marmotter
mutton ['mʌtn] *n* mouton *m*
mutual ['mju:tʃuəl] *adj* mutuel(le),
réciproque; (*benefit*, *interest*)
commun(e)
muzzle ['mʌzl] *n* museau *m*;
(*protective device*) muselière *f*; (*of gun*)
gueule *f* ▷ *vt* museler
my [maɪ] *adj* mon (ma), mes *pl*; **my
house/car/gloves** ma maison/ma
voiture/mes gants; **I've washed my
hair/cut my finger** je me suis lavé
les cheveux/coupé le doigt; **is this
my pen or yours?** c'est mon stylo ou
c'est le vôtre?
myself [maɪ'sɛlf] *pron* (*reflexive*) me;
(*emphatic*) moi-même; (*after prep*)
moi; *see also* **oneself**
mysterious [mɪs'tɪərɪəs] *adj*
mystérieux(-euse)
mystery ['mɪstərɪ] *n* mystère *m*
mystical ['mɪstɪkl] *adj* mystique
mystify ['mɪstɪfaɪ] *vt* (*deliberately*)
mystifier; (*puzzle*) ébahir
myth [mɪθ] *n* mythe *m*; **mythology**
[mɪ'θɔlədʒɪ] *n* mythologie *f*

n/a *abbr* (= *not applicable*) n.a.
nag [næg] *vt* (*scold*) être toujours
après, reprendre sans arrêt
nail [neɪl] *n* (*human*) ongle *m*; (*metal*)
clou *m* ▷ *vt* clouer; **to ~ sth to sth**
clouer qch à qch; **to ~ sb down to a
date/price** contraindre qn à accepter
or donner une date/un prix; **nailbrush**
n brosse *f* à ongles; **nailfile** *n* lime *f* à
ongles; **nail polish** *n* vernis *m* à ongles;
nail polish remover *n* dissolvant *m*;
nail scissors *npl* ciseaux *mpl* à ongles;
nail varnish *n* (*BRIT*) = **nail polish**
naïve [naɪ'iːv] *adj* naïf(-ïve)
naked ['neɪkɪd] *adj* nu(e)
name [neɪm] *n* nom *m*; (*reputation*)
réputation *f* ▷ *vt* nommer; (*identify*:
accomplice etc) citer; (*price*, *date*) fixer,
donner; **by ~** par son nom; de nom;
in the ~ of au nom de; **what's your
~?** comment vous appelez-vous?, quel
est votre nom?; **namely** *adv* à savoir
nanny ['nænɪ] *n* bonne *f* d'enfants

nap [næp] n (sleep) (petit) somme
napkin ['næpkɪn] n serviette f (de table)
nappy ['næpɪ] n (BRIT) couche f
narcotics [nɑː'kɔtɪkz] npl (illegal drugs) stupéfiants mpl
narrative ['nærətɪv] n récit m ▷ adj narratif(-ive)
narrator [nə'reɪtər] n narrateur(-trice)
narrow ['nærəu] adj étroit(e); (fig) restreint(e), limité(e) ▷ vi (road) devenir plus étroit, se rétrécir; (gap, difference) se réduire; **to have a ~ escape** l'échapper belle; **narrow down** vt restreindre; **narrowly** adv: **he narrowly missed injury/the tree** il a failli se blesser/rentrer dans l'arbre; **he only narrowly missed the target** il a manqué la cible de peu or de justesse; **narrow-minded** adj à l'esprit étroit, borné(e); (attitude) borné(e)
nasal ['neɪzl] adj nasal(e)
nasty ['nɑːstɪ] adj (person: malicious) méchant(e); (: rude) très désagréable; (smell) dégoûtant(e); (wound, situation) mauvais(e), vilain(e)
nation ['neɪʃən] n nation f
national ['næʃənl] adj national(e) ▷ n (abroad) ressortissant(e); (when home) national(e); **national anthem** n hymne national; **national dress** n costume national; **National Health Service** n (BRIT) service national de santé, ≈ Sécurité Sociale; **National Insurance** n (BRIT) ≈ Sécurité Sociale; **nationalist** adj, n nationaliste m/f; **nationality** [næʃə'nælɪtɪ] n nationalité f; **nationalize** vt nationaliser; **national park** n parc national; **National Trust** n (BRIT) ≈ Caisse f nationale des monuments historiques et des sites

● **NATIONAL TRUST**
●
● Le National Trust est un organisme
● indépendant, à but non lucratif,
● dont la mission est de protéger et,
● de mettre en valeur les monuments
● et les sites britanniques en raison
● de leur intérêt historique ou de leur
● beauté naturelle.

nationwide ['neɪʃənwaɪd] adj s'étendant à l'ensemble du pays; (problem) à l'échelle du pays entier
native ['neɪtɪv] n habitant(e) du pays, autochtone m/f ▷ adj du pays, indigène; (country) natal(e); (language) maternel(le); (ability) inné(e); **Native American** n Indien(ne) d'Amérique ▷ adj amérindien(ne); **native speaker** n locuteur natif
NATO ['neɪtəu] n abbr (= North Atlantic Treaty Organization) OTAN f
natural ['nætʃrəl] adj naturel(le); **natural gas** n gaz naturel; **natural history** n histoire naturelle; **naturally** adv naturellement; **natural resources** npl ressources naturelles
nature ['neɪtʃər] n nature f; **by ~** par tempérament, de nature; **nature reserve** n (BRIT) réserve naturelle
naughty ['nɔːtɪ] adj (child) vilain(e), pas sage
nausea ['nɔːsɪə] n nausée f
naval ['neɪvl] adj naval(e)
navel ['neɪvl] n nombril m
navigate ['nævɪgeɪt] vt (steer) diriger, piloter ▷ vi naviguer; (Aut) indiquer la route à suivre; **navigation** [nævɪ'geɪʃən] n navigation f
navy ['neɪvɪ] n marine f
navy-blue ['neɪvɪ'bluː] adj bleu marine inv
Nazi ['nɑːtsɪ] n Nazi(e)
NB abbr (= nota bene) NB
near [nɪər] adj proche ▷ adv près ▷ prep (also: ~ **to**) près de ▷ vt approcher de; **in the ~ future** dans un proche avenir; **nearby** [nɪə'baɪ] adj proche ▷ adv tout près, à proximité; **nearly** adv presque; **I nearly fell** j'ai failli tomber; **it's not**

n

nearly big enough ce n'est vraiment pas assez grand, c'est loin d'être assez grand; **near-sighted** adj myope

neat [ni:t] adj (person, work) soigné(e); (room etc) bien tenu(e) or rangé(e); (solution, plan) habile; (spirits) pur(e); **neatly** adv avec soin or ordre; (skilfully) habilement

necessarily ['nɛsɪsərɪlɪ] adv nécessairement; **not ~** pas nécessairement or forcément

necessary ['nɛsɪsrɪ] adj nécessaire; **if ~** si besoin est, le cas échéant

necessity [nɪ'sɛsɪtɪ] n nécessité f; chose nécessaire or essentielle

neck [nɛk] n cou m; (of horse, garment) encolure f; (of bottle) goulot m; **~ and ~** à égalité; **necklace** ['nɛklɪs] n collier m; **necktie** ['nɛktaɪ] n (esp US) cravate f

nectarine ['nɛktərɪn] n brugnon m, nectarine f

need [ni:d] n besoin m ⊳ vt avoir besoin de; **to ~ to do** devoir faire; avoir besoin de faire; **you don't ~ to go** vous n'avez pas besoin or vous n'êtes pas obligé de partir; **a signature is ~ed** il faut une signature; **there's no ~ to do ....** il n'y a pas lieu de faire ..., il n'est pas nécessaire de faire ...

needle ['ni:dl] n aiguille f ⊳ vt (inf) asticoter, tourmenter

needless ['ni:dlɪs] adj inutile; **~ to say, ...** inutile de dire que ...

needlework ['ni:dlwə:k] n (activity) travaux mpl d'aiguille; (object) ouvrage m

needn't ['ni:dnt] = need not

needy ['ni:dɪ] adj nécessiteux(-euse)

negative ['nɛgətɪv] n (Phot, Elec) négatif m; (Ling) terme m de négation ⊳ adj négatif(-ive)

neglect [nɪ'glɛkt] vt négliger; (garden) ne pas entretenir; (duty) manquer à ⊳ n (of person, duty, garden) le fait de négliger; **(state of) ~** abandon m; **to ~ to do sth** négliger

or omettre de faire qch; **to ~ one's appearance** se négliger

negotiate [nɪ'gəʊʃɪeɪt] vi négocier ⊳ vt négocier; (obstacle) franchir, négocier; **to ~ with sb for sth** négocier avec qn en vue d'obtenir qch

negotiation [nɪgəʊʃɪ'eɪʃən] n négociation f, pourparlers mpl

negotiator [nɪ'gəʊʃɪeɪtər] n négociateur(-trice)

neighbour, (us) **neighbor** ['neɪbər] n voisin(e); **neighbourhood**, (us) **neighborhood** n (place) quartier m; (people) voisinage m; **neighbouring**, (us) **neighboring** adj voisin(e), avoisinant(e)

neither ['naɪðər] adj, pron aucun(e) (des deux), ni l'un(e) ni l'autre ⊳ conj: **~ do I** moi non plus ⊳ adv: **~ good nor bad** ni bon ni mauvais; **~ of them** ni l'un ni l'autre

neon ['ni:ɔn] n néon m

Nepal [nɪ'pɔ:l] n Népal m

nephew ['nɛvju:] n neveu m

nerve [nə:v] n nerf m; (bravery) sang-froid m, courage m; (cheek) aplomb m, toupet m; **nerves** npl (nervousness) nervosité f; **he gets on my ~s** il m'énerve

nervous ['nə:vəs] adj nerveux(-euse); (anxious) inquiet(-ète), plein(e) d'appréhension; (timid) intimidé(e); **nervous breakdown** n dépression nerveuse

nest [nɛst] n nid m ⊳ vi (se) nicher, faire son nid

Net [nɛt] n (Comput): **the ~** (Internet) le Net

net [nɛt] n filet m; (fabric) tulle f ⊳ adj net(te) ⊳ vt (fish etc) prendre au filet; **netball** n netball m

Netherlands ['nɛðələndz] npl; **the ~** les Pays-Bas mpl

nett [nɛt] adj = net

nettle ['nɛtl] n ortie f

network ['nɛtwə:k] n réseau m; **there's no ~ coverage here** (Tel) il n'y a pas de réseau ici

neurotic [njuə'rɔtɪk] adj névrosé(e)
neuter ['nju:tə'] adj neutre ▷ vt (cat etc) châtrer, couper
neutral ['nju:trəl] adj neutre ▷ n (Aut) point mort
never ['nɛvə'] adv (ne ...) jamais; **I ~ went** je n'y suis pas allé; **I've ~ been to Spain** je ne suis jamais allé en Espagne; **~ again** plus jamais; **~ in my life** jamais de ma vie; see also **mind**; **never-ending** adj interminable; **nevertheless** [nɛvəðə'lɛs] adv néanmoins, malgré tout
new [nju:] adj nouveau (nouvelle); (brand new) neuf (neuve); **New Age** n New Age m; **newborn** adj nouveau-né(e); **newcomer** ['nju:kʌmə'] n nouveau venu (nouvelle venue); **newly** adv nouvellement, récemment
news [nju:z] n nouvelle(s) f(pl); (Radio, TV) informations fpl, actualités fpl; **a piece of ~** une nouvelle; **news agency** n agence f de presse; **newsagent** n (BRIT) marchand m de journaux; **newscaster** n (Radio, TV) présentateur(-trice); **newsletter** n bulletin m; **newspaper** n journal m; **newsreader** n = **newscaster**
newt [nju:t] n triton m
New Year n Nouvel An; **Happy ~!** Bonne Année!; **New Year's Day** n le jour de l'An; **New Year's Eve** n la Saint-Sylvestre
New York [-'jɔ:k] n New York
New Zealand [-'zi:lənd] n Nouvelle-Zélande f; **New Zealander** n Néo-Zélandais(e)
next [nɛkst] adj (in time) prochain(e); (seat, room) voisin(e), d'à côté; (meeting, bus stop) suivant(e) ▷ adv la fois suivante; la prochaine fois; (afterwards) ensuite; **~ to** prep à côté de; **~ to nothing** presque rien; **~ time** adv la prochaine fois; **the ~ day** le lendemain, le jour suivant or d'après; **~ year** l'année prochaine; **~ please!** (at doctor's etc) au suivant!;

the week after ~ dans deux semaines; **next door** adv à côté ▷ adj (neighbour) d'à côté; **next-of-kin** n parent m le plus proche
NHS n abbr (BRIT) = **National Health Service**
nibble ['nɪbl] vt grignoter
nice [naɪs] adj (holiday, trip, taste) agréable; (flat, picture) joli(e); (person) gentil(le); (distinction, point) subtil(e); **nicely** adv agréablement; joliment; gentiment; subtilement
niche [ni:ʃ] n (Archit) niche f
nick [nɪk] n (indentation) encoche f; (wound) entaille f; (BRIT inf): **in good ~** en bon état ▷ vt (cut): **to ~ o.s.** se couper; (BRIT inf: steal) faucher, piquer; **in the ~ of time** juste à temps
nickel ['nɪkl] n nickel m; (US) pièce f de 5 cents
nickname ['nɪkneɪm] n surnom m ▷ vt surnommer
nicotine ['nɪkəti:n] n nicotine f
niece [ni:s] n nièce f
Nigeria [naɪ'dʒɪərɪə] n Nigéria m/f
night [naɪt] n nuit f; (evening) soir m; **at ~** la nuit; **by ~** de nuit; **last ~** (evening) hier soir; (night-time) la nuit dernière; **night club** n boîte f de nuit; **nightdress** n chemise f de nuit; **nightie** ['naɪtɪ] n chemise f de nuit; **nightlife** n vie f nocturne; **nightly** adj (news) du soir; (by night) nocturne ▷ adv (every evening) tous les soirs; (every night) toutes les nuits; **nightmare** n cauchemar m; **night school** n cours mpl du soir; **night shift** n équipe f de nuit; **night-time** n nuit f
nil [nɪl] n (BRIT Sport) zéro m
nine [naɪn] num neuf; **nineteen** num dix-neuf; **nineteenth** [naɪn'ti:nθ] num dix-neuvième; **ninetieth** ['naɪntɪɪθ] num quatre-vingt-dixième; **ninety** num quatre-vingt-dix
ninth [naɪnθ] num neuvième
nip [nɪp] vt pincer ▷ vi (BRIT inf): **to ~ out/down/up** sortir/descendre/monter en vitesse

n

nipple ['nɪpl] n (Anat) mamelon m, bout m du sein

nitrogen ['naɪtrədʒən] n azote m

 KEYWORD

no [nəu] adv (opposite of "yes") non; **are you coming? — no (I'm not)** est-ce que vous venez? — non; **would you like some more? — no thank you** vous en voulez encore? — non merci
▸ adj (not any) (ne ...) pas de, (ne ...) aucun(e); **I have no money/ books** je n'ai pas d'argent/de livres; **no student would have done it** aucun étudiant ne l'aurait fait; **"no smoking"** "défense de fumer"; **"no dogs"** "les chiens ne sont pas admis"
▸ n (pl **noes**) non m

nobility [nəu'bɪlɪtɪ] n noblesse f

noble ['nəubl] adj noble

nobody ['nəubədɪ] pron (ne ...) personne

nod [nɔd] vi faire un signe de (la) tête (affirmatif ou amical); (sleep) somnoler ▸ vt: **to ~ one's head** faire un signe de (la) tête; (in agreement) faire signe que oui ▸ n signe m de (la) tête; **nod off** vi s'assoupir

noise [nɔɪz] n bruit m; **I can't sleep for the ~** je n'arrive pas à dormir à cause du bruit; **noisy** adj bruyant(e)

nominal ['nɔmɪnl] adj (rent, fee) symbolique; (value) nominal(e)

nominate ['nɔmɪneɪt] vt (propose) proposer; (appoint) nommer; **nomination** [nɔmɪ'neɪʃən] n nomination f; **nominee** [nɔmɪ'niː] n candidat agréé; personne nommée

none [nʌn] pron aucun(e); **~ of you** aucun d'entre vous, personne parmi vous; **I have ~ left** je n'en ai plus; **he's ~ the worse for it** il ne s'en porte pas plus mal

nonetheless ['nʌnðə'les] adv néanmoins

non-fiction [nɔn'fɪkʃən] n littérature f non romanesque

nonsense ['nɔnsəns] n absurdités fpl, idioties fpl; **~!** ne dites pas d'idioties!

non: **non-smoker** n non-fumeur m; **non-smoking** adj non-fumeur; **non-stick** adj qui n'attache pas

noodles ['nuːdlz] npl nouilles fpl

noon [nuːn] n midi m

no-one ['nəuwʌn] pron = **nobody**

nor [nɔːʳ] conj = **neither** ▸ adv see **neither**

norm [nɔːm] n norme f

normal ['nɔːml] adj normal(e); **normally** adv normalement

Normandy ['nɔːməndɪ] n Normandie f

north [nɔːθ] n nord m ▸ adj nord inv; (wind) du nord ▸ adv au or vers le nord; **North Africa** n Afrique f du Nord; **North African** adj nord-africain(e), d'Afrique du Nord ▸ n Nord-Africain(e); **North America** n Amérique f du Nord; **North American** n Nord-Américain(e) ▸ adj nord-américain(e), d'Amérique du Nord; **northbound** ['nɔːθbaund] adj (traffic) en direction du nord; (carriageway) nord inv; **north-east** n nord-est m; **northern** ['nɔːðən] adj du nord, septentrional(e); **Northern Ireland** n Irlande f du Nord; **North Korea** n Corée f du Nord; **North Pole** n: **the North Pole** le pôle Nord; **North Sea** n: **the North Sea** la mer du Nord; **north-west** n nord-ouest m

Norway ['nɔːweɪ] n Norvège f; **Norwegian** [nɔː'wiːdʒən] adj norvégien(ne) ▸ n Norvégien(ne); (Ling) norvégien m

nose [nəuz] n nez m; (of dog, cat) museau m; (fig) flair m; **nose about, nose around** vi fouiner or fureter (partout); **nosebleed** n saignement m de nez; **nosey** adj (inf) curieux(-euse)

nostalgia [nɔs'tældʒɪə] n nostalgie f

nostalgic [nɔs'tældʒɪk] adj nostalgique

nostril ['nɔstrɪl] n narine f; (of horse) naseau m

nosy ['nəuzɪ] (inf) adj = **nosey**

not [nɔt] adv (ne …) pas; **he is ~** or **isn't here** il n'est pas ici; **you must ~** or **mustn't do that** tu ne dois pas faire ça; **I hope ~** j'espère que non; **~ at all** pas du tout; (after thanks) de rien; **it's too late, isn't it?** c'est trop tard, n'est-ce pas?; **~ yet/now** pas encore/maintenant; see also **only**

notable ['nəutəbl] adj notable; **notably** adv (particularly) en particulier; (markedly) spécialement

notch [nɔtʃ] n encoche f

note [nəut] n note f; (letter) mot m; (banknote) billet m ▷ vt (also: **~ down**) noter; (notice) constater; **notebook** n carnet m; (for shorthand etc) bloc-notes m; **noted** ['nəutɪd] adj réputé(e); **notepad** n bloc-notes m; **notepaper** n papier m à lettres

nothing ['nʌθɪŋ] n rien m; **he does ~** il ne fait rien; **~ new** rien de nouveau; **for ~** (free) pour rien, gratuitement; (in vain) pour rien; **~ at all** rien du tout; **~ much** pas grand-chose

notice ['nəutɪs] n (announcement, warning) avis m ▷ vt remarquer, s'apercevoir de; **advance ~** préavis m; **at short ~** dans un délai très court; **until further ~** jusqu'à nouvel ordre; **to give ~, hand in one's ~** (employee) donner sa démission, démissionner; **to take ~ of** prêter attention à; **to bring sth to sb's ~** porter qch à la connaissance de qn; **noticeable** adj visible

notice board n (BRIT) panneau m d'affichage

notify ['nəutɪfaɪ] vt: **to ~ sb of sth** avertir qn de qch

notion ['nəuʃən] n idée f; (concept) notion f; **notions** npl (US: haberdashery) mercerie f

notorious [nəu'tɔːrɪəs] adj notoire (souvent en mal)

notwithstanding [nɔtwɪθ'stændɪŋ] adv néanmoins ▷ prep en dépit de

nought [nɔːt] n zéro m

noun [naun] n nom m

nourish ['nʌrɪʃ] vt nourrir; **nourishment** n nourriture f

Nov. abbr (= November) nov

novel ['nɔvl] n roman m ▷ adj nouveau (nouvelle), original(e); **novelist** n romancier m; **novelty** n nouveauté f

November [nəu'vɛmbə^r] n novembre m

novice ['nɔvɪs] n novice m/f

now [nau] adv maintenant ▷ conj: **~ (that)** maintenant (que); **right ~** tout de suite; **by ~** à l'heure qu'il est; **that's the fashion just ~** c'est la mode en ce moment or maintenant; **~ and then, ~ and again** de temps en temps; **from ~ on** dorénavant; **nowadays** ['nauədeɪz] adv de nos jours

nowhere ['nəuwɛə^r] adv (ne …) nulle part

nozzle ['nɔzl] n (of hose) jet m, lance f; (of vacuum cleaner) suceur m

nr abbr (BRIT) = **near**

nuclear ['njuːklɪə^r] adj nucléaire

nucleus (pl **nuclei**) ['njuːklɪəs, 'njuːklɪaɪ] n noyau m

nude [njuːd] adj nu(e) ▷ n (Art) nu m; **in the ~** (tout(e)) nu(e)

nudge [nʌdʒ] vt donner un (petit) coup de coude à

nudist ['njuːdɪst] n nudiste m/f

nudity ['njuːdɪtɪ] n nudité f

nuisance ['njuːsns] n: **it's a ~** c'est (très) ennuyeux or gênant; **he's a ~** il est assommant or casse-pieds; **what a ~!** quelle barbe!

numb [nʌm] adj engourdi(e); (with fear) paralysé(e)

number ['nʌmbə^r] n nombre m; (numeral) chiffre m; (of house, car, telephone, newspaper) numéro m ▷ vt numéroter; (amount to) compter;

a ~ of un certain nombre de; **they were seven in ~** ils étaient (au nombre de) sept; **to be ~ed among** compter parmi; **number plate** n (BRIT Aut) plaque f minéralogique or d'immatriculation; **Number Ten** n (BRIT: 10 Downing Street) résidence du Premier ministre

numerical [njuːˈmɛrɪkl] adj numérique

numerous [ˈnjuːmərəs] adj nombreux(-euse)

nun [nʌn] n religieuse f, sœur f

nurse [nəːs] n infirmière f; (also: **~maid**) bonne f d'enfants ▷ vt (patient, cold) soigner

nursery [ˈnəːsərɪ] n (room) nursery f; (institution) crèche f, garderie f; (for plants) pépinière f; **nursery rhyme** n comptine f, chansonnette f pour enfants; **nursery school** n école maternelle; **nursery slope** n (BRIT Ski) piste f pour débutants

nursing [ˈnəːsɪŋ] n (profession) profession f d'infirmière; (care) soins mpl; **nursing home** n clinique f; (for convalescence) maison f de convalescence or de repos; (for old people) maison de retraite

nurture [ˈnəːtʃəʳ] vt élever

nut [nʌt] n (of metal) écrou m; (fruit: walnut) noix f; (: hazelnut) noisette f; (: peanut) cacahuète f (terme générique en anglais)

nutmeg [ˈnʌtmɛg] n (noix f) muscade f

nutrient [ˈnjuːtrɪənt] n substance nutritive

nutrition [njuːˈtrɪʃən] n nutrition f, alimentation f

nutritious [njuːˈtrɪʃəs] adj nutritif(-ive), nourrissant(e)

nuts [nʌts] (inf) adj dingue

NVQ n abbr (BRIT) = **National Vocational Qualification**

nylon [ˈnaɪlɔn] n nylon m ▷ adj de or en nylon

O

oak [əuk] n chêne m ▷ cpd de or en (bois de) chêne

O.A.P. n abbr (BRIT) = **old age pensioner**

oar [ɔːʳ] n aviron m, rame f

oasis (pl **oases**) [əuˈeɪsɪs, əuˈeɪsiːz] n oasis f

oath [əuθ] n serment m; (swear word) juron m; **on** (BRIT) or **under ~** sous serment; assermenté(e)

oatmeal [ˈəutmiːl] n flocons mpl d'avoine

oats [əuts] n avoine f

obedience [əˈbiːdɪəns] n obéissance f

obedient [əˈbiːdɪənt] adj obéissant(e)

obese [əuˈbiːs] adj obèse

obesity [əuˈbiːsɪtɪ] n obésité f

obey [əˈbeɪ] vt obéir à; (instructions, regulations) se conformer à ▷ vi obéir

obituary [əˈbɪtjuərɪ] n nécrologie f

object n [ˈɔbdʒɪkt] objet m; (purpose) but m, objet; (Ling) complément *m* d'objet ▷ *vi* [əb'dʒɛkt]: **to ~ to** (*attitude*) désapprouver; (*proposal*) protester contre, élever une objection contre; **I ~!** je proteste!; **he ~ed that …** il a fait valoir *or* a objecté que …; **money is no ~** l'argent n'est pas un problème; **objection** [əb'dʒɛkʃən] *n* objection *f*; **if you have no objection** si vous n'y voyez pas d'inconvénient; **objective** *n* objectif *m* ▷ *adj* objectif(-ive)

obligation [ɔblɪ'geɪʃən] *n* obligation *f*, devoir *m*; (*debt*) dette *f* (de reconnaissance)

obligatory [ə'blɪgətərɪ] *adj* obligatoire

oblige [ə'blaɪdʒ] *vt* (*force*): **to ~ sb to do** obliger *or* forcer qn à faire; (*do a favour*) rendre service à, obliger; **to be ~d to sb for sth** être obligé(e) à qn de qch

oblique [ə'bliːk] *adj* oblique; (*allusion*) indirect(e)

obliterate [ə'blɪtəreɪt] *vt* effacer

oblivious [ə'blɪvɪəs] *adj*: **~ of** oublieux(-euse) de

oblong ['ɔblɔŋ] *adj* oblong(ue) ▷ *n* rectangle *m*

obnoxious [əb'nɔkʃəs] *adj* odieux(-euse); (*smell*) nauséabond(e)

oboe ['əubəu] *n* hautbois *m*

obscene [əb'siːn] *adj* obscène

obscure [əb'skjuəʳ] *adj* obscur(e) ▷ *vt* obscurcir; (*hide: sun*) cacher

observant [əb'zɜːvnt] *adj* observateur(-trice)

observation [ɔbzə'veɪʃən] *n* observation *f*; (*by police etc*) surveillance *f*

observatory [əb'zɜːvətrɪ] *n* observatoire *m*

observe [əb'zɜːv] *vt* observer; (*remark*) faire observer *or* remarquer; **observer** *n* observateur(-trice)

obsess [əb'sɛs] *vt* obséder; **obsession** [əb'sɛʃən] *n* obsession *f*; **obsessive** *adj* obsédant(e)

obsolete ['ɔbsəliːt] *adj* dépassé(e), périmé(e)

obstacle ['ɔbstəkl] *n* obstacle *m*

obstinate ['ɔbstɪnɪt] *adj* obstiné(e); (*pain, cold*) persistant(e)

obstruct [əb'strʌkt] *vt* (*block*) boucher, obstruer; (*hinder*) entraver; **obstruction** [əb'strʌkʃən] *n* obstruction *f*; (*to plan, progress*) obstacle *m*

obtain [əb'teɪn] *vt* obtenir

obvious ['ɔbvɪəs] *adj* évident(e), manifeste; **obviously** *adv* manifestement; **obviously!** bien sûr!; **obviously not!** évidemment pas!, bien sûr que non!

occasion [ə'keɪʒən] *n* occasion *f*; (*event*) événement *m*; **occasional** *adj* pris(e) (*or* fait(e) *etc*) de temps en temps; (*worker, spending*) occasionnel(le); **occasionally** *adv* de temps en temps, quelquefois

occult [ɔ'kʌlt] *adj* occulte ▷ *n*: **the ~** le surnaturel

occupant ['ɔkjupənt] *n* occupant *m*

occupation [ɔkju'peɪʃən] *n* occupation *f*; (*job*) métier *m*, profession *f*

occupy ['ɔkjupaɪ] *vt* occuper; **to ~ o.s. with** *or* **by doing** s'occuper à faire

occur [ə'kɜːʳ] *vi* se produire; (*difficulty, opportunity*) se présenter; (*phenomenon, error*) se rencontrer; **to ~ to sb** venir à l'esprit de qn; **occurrence** [ə'kʌrəns] *n* (*existence*) présence *f*, existence *f*; (*event*) cas *m*, fait *m*

ocean ['əuʃən] *n* océan *m*

o'clock [ə'klɔk] *adv*: **it is 5 ~** il est 5 heures

Oct. *abbr* (= *October*) oct

October [ɔk'təubəʳ] *n* octobre *m*

octopus ['ɔktəpəs] *n* pieuvre *f*

odd [ɔd] *adj* (*strange*) bizarre, curieux(-euse); (*number*) impair(e); (*not of a set*) dépareillé(e); **60-~** 60 et quelques; **at ~ times** de temps en temps; **the ~ one out** l'exception *f*; **oddly** *adv* bizarrement,

o

curieusement; **odds** npl (in betting) cote f; **it makes no odds** cela n'a pas d'importance; **odds and ends** de petites choses; **at odds** en désaccord

odometer [ɔ'dɔmɪtəʳ] n (us) odomètre m

odour, (us) **odor** ['əudəʳ] n odeur f

KEYWORD

of [ɔv, əv] prep **1** (gen) de; **a friend of ours** un de nos amis; **a boy of 10** un garçon de 10 ans; **that was kind of you** c'était gentil de votre part **2** (expressing quantity, amount, dates etc) de; **a kilo of flour** un kilo de farine; **how much of this do you need?** combien vous en faut-il?; **there were three of them** (people) ils étaient 3; (objects) il y en avait 3; **three of us went** 3 d'entre nous y sont allé(e)s; **the 5th of July** le 5 juillet; **a quarter of 4** (us) 4 heures moins le quart **3** (from, out of) en, de; **a statue of marble** une statue de or en marbre; **made of wood** (fait) en bois

off [ɔf] adj, adv (engine) coupé(e); (light, TV) éteint(e); (tap) fermé(e); (BRIT: food) mauvais(e), avancé(e); (: milk) tourné(e); (absent) absent(e); (cancelled) annulé(e); (removed): **the lid was ~** le couvercle était retiré or n'était pas mis; (away): **to run/ drive ~** partir en courant/en voiture ▷ prep de; **to be ~** (to leave) partir, s'en aller; **to be ~ sick** être absent pour cause de maladie; **a day ~** un jour de congé; **to have an ~ day** n'être pas en forme; **he had his coat ~** il avait enlevé son manteau; **10% ~** (Comm) 10% de rabais; **5 km ~ (the road)** à 5 km (de la route); **~ the coast** au large de la côte; **it's a long way ~** c'est loin (d'ici); **I'm ~ meat** je ne mange plus de viande; je n'aime plus la viande; **on**

the ~ chance à tout hasard; **~ and on, on and ~** de temps à autre

offence, (us) **offense** [ə'fɛns] n (crime) délit m, infraction f; **to take ~ at** se vexer de, s'offenser de

offend [ə'fɛnd] vt (person) offenser, blesser; **offender** n délinquant(e); (against regulations) contrevenant(e)

offense [ə'fɛns] n (us) = **offence**

offensive [ə'fɛnsɪv] adj offensant(e), choquant(e); (smell etc) très déplaisant(e); (weapon) offensif(-ive) ▷ n (Mil) offensive f

offer ['ɔfəʳ] n offre f, proposition f ▷ vt offrir, proposer; **"on ~"** (Comm) "en promotion"

offhand [ɔf'hænd] adj désinvolte ▷ adv spontanément

office ['ɔfɪs] n (place) bureau m; (position) charge f, fonction f; **doctor's ~** (us) cabinet (médical); **to take ~** entrer en fonctions; **office block**, (us) **office building** n immeuble m de bureaux; **office hours** npl heures fpl de bureau; (us Med) heures de consultation

officer ['ɔfɪsəʳ] n (Mil etc) officier m; (also: **police ~**) agent m (de police); (of organization) membre m du bureau directeur

office worker n employé(e) de bureau

official [ə'fɪʃl] adj (authorized) officiel(le) ▷ n officiel m; (civil servant) fonctionnaire m/f; (of railways, post office, town hall) employé(e)

off: off-licence n (BRIT: shop) débit m de vins et de spiritueux; **off-line** adj (Comput) (en mode) autonome (: switched off) non connecté(e); **off-peak** adj aux heures creuses; (electricity, ticket) au tarif heures creuses; **off-putting** adj (BRIT) (remark) rébarbatif(-ive); (person) rebutant(e), peu engageant(e); **off-season** adj, adv hors-saison inv

offset ['ɔfsɛt] vt (irreg: like **set**) (counteract) contrebalancer, compenser

offshore [ɔfˈʃɔːʳ] *adj* (*breeze*) de terre; (*island*) proche du littoral; (*fishing*) côtier(-ière)

offside [ˈɔfˈsaɪd] *adj* (*Sport*) hors jeu; (*Aut: in Britain*) de droite; (*: in US, Europe*) de gauche

offspring [ˈɔfsprɪŋ] *n* progéniture *f*

often [ˈɔfn] *adv* souvent; **how ~ do you go?** vous y allez tous les combien?; **every so ~** de temps en temps, de temps à autre

oh [əu] *excl* ô!, oh!, ah!

oil [ɔɪl] *n* huile *f*; (*petroleum*) pétrole *m*; (*for central heating*) mazout *m* ▷ *vt* (*machine*) graisser; **oil filter** *n* (*Aut*) filtre *m* à huile; **oil painting** *n* peinture *f* à l'huile; **oil refinery** *n* raffinerie *f* de pétrole; **oil rig** *n* derrick *m*; (*at sea*) plate-forme pétrolière; **oil slick** *n* nappe *f* de mazout; **oil tanker** *n* (*ship*) pétrolier *m*; (*truck*) camion-citerne *m*; **oil well** *n* puits *m* de pétrole; **oily** *adj* huileux(-euse); (*food*) gras(se)

ointment [ˈɔɪntmənt] *n* onguent *m*

O.K., okay [ˈəuˈkeɪ] (*inf*) *excl* d'accord! ▷ *vt* approuver, donner son accord à ▷ *adj* (*not bad*) pas mal; **is it ~?, are you ~?** ça va?

old [əuld] *adj* vieux (vieille); (*person*) vieux, âgé(e); (*former*) ancien(ne), vieux; **how ~ are you?** quel âge avez-vous?; **he's 10 years ~** il a 10 ans, il est âgé de 10 ans; **~er brother/sister** frère/sœur aîné(e); **old age** *n* vieillesse *f*; **old-age pensioner** *n* (BRIT) retraité(e); **old-fashioned** *adj* démodé(e); (*person*) vieux jeu *inv*; **old people's home** *n* (*esp* BRIT) maison *f* de retraite

olive [ˈɔlɪv] *n* (*fruit*) olive *f*; (*tree*) olivier *m* ▷ *adj* (*also*: **~-green**) (vert) olive *inv*; **olive oil** *n* huile *f* d'olive

Olympic [əuˈlɪmpɪk] *adj* olympique; **the ~ Games, the ~s** les Jeux *mpl* olympiques

omelet(te) [ˈɔmlɪt] *n* omelette *f*

omen [ˈəumən] *n* présage *m*

ominous [ˈɔmɪnəs] *adj* menaçant(e), inquiétant(e); (*event*) de mauvais augure

omit [əuˈmɪt] *vt* omettre

 KEYWORD

on [ɔn] *prep* **1** (*indicating position*) sur; **on the table** sur la table; **on the wall** sur le *or* au mur; **on the left** à gauche

2 (*indicating means, method, condition etc*): **on foot** à pied; **on the train/plane** (*be*) dans le train/l'avion; (*go*) en train/avion; **on the telephone/radio/television** au téléphone/à la radio/à la télévision; **to be on drugs** se droguer; **on holiday**, (*US*) **on vacation** en vacances

3 (*referring to time*): **on Friday** vendredi; **on Fridays** le vendredi; **on June 20th** le 20 juin; **a week on Friday** vendredi en huit; **on arrival** à l'arrivée; **on seeing this** en voyant cela

4 (*about, concerning*) sur, de; **a book on Balzac/physics** un livre sur Balzac/de physique

▶ *adv* **1** (*referring to dress*): **to have one's coat on** avoir (mis) son manteau; **to put one's coat on** mettre son manteau; **what's she got on?** qu'est-ce qu'elle porte?

2 (*referring to covering*): **screw the lid on tightly** vissez bien le couvercle

3 (*further, continuously*): **to walk** *etc* **on** continuer à marcher *etc*; **from that day on** depuis ce jour

▶ *adj* **1** (*in operation: machine*) en marche; (*: radio, TV, light*) allumé(e); (*: tap, gas*) ouvert(e); (*: brakes*) mis(e); **is the meeting still on?** (*not cancelled*) est-ce que la réunion a bien lieu?; **when is this film on?** quand passe ce film?

2 (*inf*): **that's not on!** (*not acceptable*) cela ne se fait pas!; (*not possible*) pas question!

o

once [wʌns] *adv* une fois; (*formerly*)
autrefois ▷ *conj* une fois que + *sub*;
~ he had left/it was done une fois
qu'il fut parti/ que ce fut terminé;
at ~ tout de suite, immédiatement;
(*simultaneously*) à la fois; **all at ~**
tout d'un coup; **~ a week** une fois par
semaine; **~ more** encore une fois;
~ and for all une fois pour toutes;
~ upon a time there was ... il y avait
une fois ..., il était une fois ...

oncoming ['ɒnkʌmɪŋ] *adj* (*traffic*)
venant en sens inverse

KEYWORD

one [wʌn] *num* un(e); **one hundred
and fifty** cent cinquante; **one by
one** un(e) à *or* par un(e); **one day**
un jour
▶ *adj* 1 (*sole*) seul(e), unique; **the
one book which** l'unique *or* le seul
livre qui; **the one man who** le seul
(homme) qui
2 (*same*) même; **they came in the
one car** ils sont venus dans la même
voiture
▶ *pron* 1: **this one** celui-ci (celle-ci);
that one celui-là (celle-là); **I've
already got one/a red one** j'en ai
déjà un(e)/un(e) rouge; **which one
do you want?** lequel voulez-vous?
2: **one another** l'un(e) l'autre; **to
look at one another** se regarder
3 (*impersonal*) on; **one never knows**
on ne sait jamais; **to cut one's finger**
se couper le doigt; **one needs to eat**
il faut manger

one-off [wʌn'ɔf] *n* (BRIT *inf*)
exemplaire *m* unique

oneself [wʌn'sɛlf] *pron* se; (*after prep,
also emphatic*) soi-même; **to hurt ~**
se faire mal; **to keep sth for ~** garder
qch pour soi; **to talk to ~** se parler à
soi-même; **by ~** tout seul

one: one-shot [wʌn'ʃɔt] (US) *n*
= **one-off**; **one-sided** *adj* (*argument,
decision*) unilatéral(e); **one-to-one**
adj (*relationship*) univoque; **one-way**
adj (*street, traffic*) à sens unique

ongoing ['ɒngəʊɪŋ] *adj* en cours;
(*relationship*) suivi(e)

onion ['ʌnjən] *n* oignon *m*

on-line ['ɒnlaɪn] *adj* (Comput) en ligne
(: *switched on*) connecté(e)

onlooker ['ɒnlʊkə^r] *n*
spectateur(-trice)

only ['əʊnlɪ] *adv* seulement ▷ *adj*
seul(e), unique ▷ *conj* seulement,
mais; **an ~ child** un enfant unique;
not ~ ... but also non seulement
... mais aussi; **I ~ took one** j'en ai
seulement pris un, je n'en ai pris qu'un

on-screen [ɒn'skriːn] *adj* à l'écran

onset ['ɒnsɛt] *n* début *m*; (*of winter, old
age*) approche *f*

onto ['ɒntu] *prep* sur

onward(s) ['ɒnwəd(z)] *adv* (*move*) en
avant; **from that time ~** à partir de
ce moment

oops [ʊps] *excl* houp!

ooze [uːz] *vi* suinter

opaque [əʊ'peɪk] *adj* opaque

open ['əʊpn] *adj* ouvert(e); (*car*)
découvert(e); (*road, view*) dégagé(e);
(*meeting*) public(-ique); (*admiration*)
manifeste ▷ *vt* ouvrir ▷ *vi* (*flower,
eyes, door, debate*) s'ouvrir; (*shop,
bank, museum*) ouvrir; (*book etc:
commence*) commencer, débuter;
is it ~ to public? est-ce ouvert au
public?; **what time do you ~?** à
quelle heure ouvrez-vous?; **in the ~
(air)** en plein air; **open up** *vt* ouvrir;
(*blocked road*) dégager ▷ *vi* s'ouvrir;
open-air *adj* en plein air; **opening** *n*
ouverture *f*; (*opportunity*) occasion
f; (*work*) débouché *m*; (*job*) poste
vacant; **opening hours** *npl* heures
fpl d'ouverture; **open learning** *n*
enseignement universitaire à la carte,
notamment par correspondance;
(*distance learning*) télé-enseignement
m; **openly** *adv* ouvertement;
open-minded *adj* à l'esprit ouvert;

open-necked adj à col ouvert;
open-plan adj sans cloisons; **Open
University** n (BRIT) cours universitaires
par correspondance

● **OPEN UNIVERSITY**
●
●
● L'*Open University* a été fondée en
● 1969. L'enseignement comprend
● des cours (certaines plages horaires
● sont réservées à cet effet à la
● télévision et à la radio), des devoirs
● qui sont envoyés par l'étudiant
● à son directeur ou sa directrice
● d'études, et un séjour obligatoire en
● université d'été. Il faut préparer un
● certain nombre d'unités de valeur
● pendant une période de temps
● déterminée et obtenir la moyenne
● à un certain nombre d'entre elles
● pour recevoir le diplôme visé.

opera ['ɔpərə] n opéra m; **opera
house** n opéra m; **opera singer** n
chanteur(-euse) d'opéra
operate ['ɔpəreɪt] vt (machine)
faire marcher, faire fonctionner ▷ vi
fonctionner; **to ~ on sb (for)** (Med)
opérer qn (de)
operating room n (US Med) salle f
d'opération
operating theatre n (BRIT Med)
salle f d'opération
operation [ɔpə'reɪʃən] n opération
f; (of machine) fonctionnement m; **to
have an ~ (for)** se faire opérer (de);
to be in ~ (machine) être en service;
(system) être en vigueur; **operational**
adj opérationnel(le); (ready for use) en
état de marche
operative ['ɔpərətɪv] adj (measure) en
vigueur ▷ n (in factory) ouvrier(-ière)
operator ['ɔpəreɪtəʳ] n (of
machine) opérateur(-trice); (Tel)
téléphoniste m/f
opinion [ə'pɪnjən] n opinion f, avis
m; **in my ~** à mon avis; **opinion poll** n
sondage m d'opinion

opponent [ə'pəunənt] n adversaire
m/f
opportunity [ɔpə'tjuːnɪtɪ] n
occasion f; **to take the ~ to do** or **of
doing** profiter de l'occasion pour faire
oppose [ə'pəuz] vt s'opposer à; **to be
~d to sth** être opposé(e) à qch; **as ~d
to** par opposition à
opposite ['ɔpəzɪt] adj opposé(e);
(house etc) d'en face ▷ adv en face
▷ prep en face de ▷ n opposé m,
contraire m; (of word) contraire
opposition [ɔpə'zɪʃən] n opposition f
oppress [ə'pres] vt opprimer
opt [ɔpt] vi: **to ~ for** opter pour; **to ~
to do** choisir de faire; **opt out** vi: **to ~
out of** choisir de ne pas participer à or
de ne pas faire
optician [ɔp'tɪʃən] n opticien(ne)
optimism ['ɔptɪmɪzəm] n
optimisme m
optimist ['ɔptɪmɪst] n optimiste
m/f; **optimistic** [ɔptɪ'mɪstɪk] adj
optimiste
optimum ['ɔptɪməm] adj optimum
option ['ɔpʃən] n choix m, option f;
(Scol) matière f à option; **optional** adj
facultatif(-ive)
or [ɔːʳ] conj ou; (with negative): **he
hasn't seen or heard anything** il
n'a rien vu ni entendu; **or else** sinon;
ou bien
oral ['ɔːrəl] adj oral(e) ▷ n oral m
orange ['ɔrɪndʒ] n (fruit) orange f
▷ adj orange inv; **orange juice** n jus
m d'orange
orbit ['ɔːbɪt] n orbite f ▷ vt graviter
autour de
orchard ['ɔːtʃəd] n verger m
orchestra ['ɔːkɪstrə] n orchestre m;
(US: seating) (fauteuils mpl d')orchestre
orchid ['ɔːkɪd] n orchidée f
ordeal [ɔː'diːl] n épreuve f
order ['ɔːdəʳ] n ordre m; (Comm)
commande f ▷ vt ordonner;
(Comm) commander; **in ~** en ordre;
(document) en règle; **out of ~**
(not in correct order) en désordre;

o

(*machine*) hors service; (*telephone*) en dérangement; **a machine in working ~** une machine en état de marche; **in ~ to do/that** pour faire/que + *sub*; **could I ~ now, please?** je peux commander, s'il vous plaît?; **to be on ~** être en commande; **to ~ sb to do** ordonner à qn de faire; **order form** *n* bon *m* de commande; **orderly** *n* (*Mil*) ordonnance *f*; (*Med*) garçon *m* de salle ▷ *adj* (*room*) en ordre; (*mind*) méthodique; (*person*) qui a de l'ordre

ordinary ['ɔːdnrɪ] *adj* ordinaire, normal(e); (*pej*) ordinaire, quelconque; **out of the ~** exceptionnel(le)

ore [ɔːʳ] *n* minerai *m*

oregano [ɒrɪ'gɑːnəʊ] *n* origan *m*

organ ['ɔːɡən] *n* organe *m*; (*Mus*) orgue *m*, orgues *fpl*; **organic** [ɔː'ɡænɪk] *adj* organique; (*crops etc*) biologique, naturel(le); **organism** *n* organisme *m*

organization [ɔːɡənaɪ'zeɪʃən] *n* organisation *f*

organize ['ɔːɡənaɪz] *vt* organiser; **organized** ['ɔːɡənaɪzd] *adj* (*planned*) organisé(e); (*efficient*) bien organisé; **organizer** *n* organisateur(-trice)

orgasm ['ɔːɡæzəm] *n* orgasme *m*

orgy ['ɔːdʒɪ] *n* orgie *f*

oriental [ɔːrɪ'ɛntl] *adj* oriental(e)

orientation [ɔːrɪɛn'teɪʃən] *n* (*attitudes*) tendance *f*; (*in job*) orientation *f*; (*of building*) orientation, exposition *f*

origin ['ɒrɪdʒɪn] *n* origine *f*

original [ə'rɪdʒɪnl] *adj* original(e); (*earliest*) originel(le) ▷ *n* original *m*; **originally** *adv* (*at first*) à l'origine

originate [ə'rɪdʒɪneɪt] *vi*: **to ~ from** être originaire de; (*suggestion*) provenir de; **to ~ in** (*custom*) prendre naissance dans, avoir son origine dans

Orkney ['ɔːknɪ] *n* (*also*: **the ~s, the ~ Islands**) les Orcades *fpl*

ornament ['ɔːnəmənt] *n* ornement *m*; (*trinket*) bibelot *m*; **ornamental** [ɔːnə'mɛntl] *adj* décoratif(-ive); (*garden*) d'agrément

ornate [ɔː'neɪt] *adj* très orné(e)

orphan ['ɔːfn] *n* orphelin(e)

orthodox ['ɔːθədɒks] *adj* orthodoxe

orthopaedic, (*us*) **orthopedic** [ɔːθə'piːdɪk] *adj* orthopédique

osteopath ['ɒstɪəpæθ] *n* ostéopathe *m/f*

ostrich ['ɒstrɪtʃ] *n* autruche *f*

other ['ʌðəʳ] *adj* autre ▷ *pron*: **the ~ (one)** l'autre; **~s** (*other people*) d'autres ▷ *adv*: **~ than** autrement que; à part; **the ~ day** l'autre jour; **otherwise** *adv*, *conj* autrement

Ottawa ['ɒtəwə] *n* Ottawa

otter ['ɒtəʳ] *n* loutre *f*

ouch [autʃ] *excl* aïe!

ought [ɔːt] *aux vb*: **I ~ to do it** je devrais le faire, il faudrait que je le fasse; **this ~ to have been corrected** cela aurait dû être corrigé; **he ~ to win** (*probability*) il devrait gagner

ounce [auns] *n* once *f* (*28.35g; 16 in a pound*)

our ['auəʳ] *adj* notre, nos *pl*; *see also* **my**; **ours** *pron* le (la) nôtre, les nôtres; *see also* **mine¹**; **ourselves** *pl pron* (*reflexive, after preposition*) nous; (*emphatic*) nous-mêmes; *see also* **oneself**

oust [aust] *vt* évincer

out [aut] *adv* dehors; (*published, not at home etc*) sorti(e); (*light, fire*) éteint(e); (*absent*) il est sorti; **to be ~ in one's calculations** s'être trompé dans ses calculs; **to run/back etc ~** sortir en courant/en reculant etc; **~ loud** *adv* à haute voix; **~ of** *prep* (*outside*) en dehors de; (*because of: anger etc*) par; (*from among*): **10 ~ of 10** 10 sur 10; (*without*): **~ of petrol** sans essence, à court d'essence; **~ of order** (*machine*) en panne; (*Tel: line*) en dérangement; **outback** n (in Australia) intérieur m; **outbound** adj: **outbound (from/for)** en partance (de/pour); **outbreak** n (of violence) éruption f, explosion f; (of disease) de nombreux cas; **the outbreak of war south of the border** la guerre qui s'est déclarée au sud de la frontière; **outburst** n explosion f, accès m; **outcast** n exilé(e); (socially) paria m, **outcome** n issue f, résultat m; **outcry** n tollé (général); **outdated** adj démodé(e); **outdoor** adj de or en plein air; **outdoors** adv dehors; au grand air

outer ['autə^r] adj extérieur(e); **outer space** n espace m cosmique

outfit ['autfɪt] n (clothes) tenue f

out: outgoing adj (president, tenant) sortant(e); (character) ouvert(e), extraverti(e); **outgoings** npl (BRIT: expenses) dépenses fpl; **outhouse** n appentis m, remise f

outing ['autɪŋ] n sortie f; excursion f

out: outlaw n hors-la-loi m inv ▷ vt (person) mettre hors la loi; (practice) proscrire; **outlay** n dépenses fpl; (investment) mise f de fonds; **outlet** n (for liquid etc) issue f, sortie f; (for emotion) exutoire m; (also: **retail outlet**) point m de vente; (US Elec) prise f de courant; **outline** n (shape) contour m; (summary) esquisse f, grandes lignes ▷ vt (fig: theory, plan) exposer à grands traits; **outlook** n perspective f; (point of view) attitude f; **outnumber** vt surpasser en nombre; **out-of-date** adj (passport, ticket) périmé(e); (theory, idea) dépassé(e); (custom) désuet(-ète); (clothes) démodé(e); **out-of-doors** adv = **outdoors**; **out-of-the-way** adj loin de tout; **out-of-town** adj (shopping centre etc) en périphérie; **outpatient** n malade m/f en consultation externe; **outpost** n avant-poste m; **output** n rendement m, production f; (Comput) sortie f ▷ vt (Comput) sortir

outrage ['autreɪdʒ] n (anger) indignation f; (violent act) atrocité f, acte m de violence; (scandal) scandale m ▷ vt outrager; **outrageous** [aut'reɪdʒəs] adj atroce; (scandalous) scandaleux(-euse)

outright adv [aut'raɪt] complètement; (deny, refuse) catégoriquement; (ask) carrément; (kill) sur le coup ▷ adj ['autraɪt] complet(-ète); catégorique

outset ['autset] n début m

outside [aut'saɪd] n extérieur m ▷ adj extérieur(e) ▷ adv (au) dehors, à l'extérieur ▷ prep hors de, à l'extérieur de; (in front of) devant; **at the ~** (fig) au plus or maximum; **outside lane** n (Aut: in Britain) voie f de droite; (: in US, Europe) voie de gauche; **outside line** n (Tel) ligne extérieure; **outsider** n (stranger) étranger(-ère)

out: outsize adj énorme; (clothes) grande taille inv; **outskirts** npl faubourgs mpl; **outspoken** adj très franc (franche); **outstanding** adj remarquable, exceptionnel(le); (unfinished: work, business) en suspens, en souffrance; (debt) impayé(e); (problem) non réglé(e)

outward ['autwəd] adj (sign, appearances) extérieur(e); (journey) (d')aller; **outwards** adv (esp BRIT) = **outward**

outweigh [aut'weɪ] vt l'emporter sur

oval ['əuvl] adj, n ovale m

ovary ['əuvərɪ] n ovaire m

oven ['ʌvn] n four m; **oven glove** n gant m de cuisine; **ovenproof** adj allant au four; **oven-ready** adj prêt(e) à cuire

over ['əuvə^r] adv (par-)dessus ▷ adj (finished) fini(e), terminé(e); (too much) en plus ▷ prep sur; par-dessus; (above) au-dessus de; (on the other side of) de l'autre côté de; (more than) plus de; (during) pendant; (about, concerning): **they fell out ~ money/ her** ils se sont brouillés pour des

questions d'argent/à cause d'elle;
~ here ici; **~ there** là-bas; **all ~**
(*everywhere*) partout; **~ and ~** (*again*)
à plusieurs reprises; **~ and above**
en plus de; **to ask sb ~** inviter qn (à
passer); **to fall ~** tomber; **to turn
sth ~** retourner qch
overall ['əʊvərɔːl] *adj* (*length*)
total(e); (*study, impression*)
d'ensemble ▷ *n* (BRIT) blouse *f* ▷ *adv*
[əʊvər'ɔːl] dans l'ensemble, en
général; **overalls** *npl* (*boiler suit*) bleus
mpl (de travail)
overboard ['əʊvəbɔːd] *adv* (Naut)
par-dessus bord
overcame [əʊvə'keɪm] *pt of*
overcome
overcast ['əʊvəkɑːst] *adj* couvert(e)
overcharge [əʊvə'tʃɑːdʒ] *vt*: **to ~ sb
for sth** faire payer qch trop cher à qn
overcoat ['əʊvəkəʊt] *n* pardessus *m*
overcome [əʊvə'kʌm] *vt* (*irreg:
like* **come**) (*defeat*) triompher
de; (*difficulty*) surmonter ▷ *adj*
(*emotionally*) bouleversé(e); **~ with
grief** accablé(e) de douleur
over: overcrowded *adj* bondé(e);
(*city, country*) surpeuplé(e); **overdo**
vt (*irreg: like* **do**) exagérer; (*overcook*)
trop cuire; **to overdo it, to overdo
things** (*work too hard*) en faire
trop, se surmener; **overdone**
[əʊvə'dʌn] *adj* (*vegetables, steak*)
trop cuit(e); **overdose** *n* dose
excessive; **overdraft** *n* découvert
m; **overdrawn** *adj* (*account*) à
découvert; **overdue** *adj* en retard;
(*bill*) impayé(e); (*change*) qui tarde;
overestimate *vt* surestimer
overflow *vi* [əʊvə'fləʊ] déborder
▷ *n* ['əʊvəfləʊ] (*also:* **~ pipe**) tuyau *m*
d'écoulement, trop-plein *m*
overgrown [əʊvə'grəʊn] *adj* (*garden*)
envahi(e) par la végétation
overhaul *vt* [əʊvə'hɔːl] réviser ▷ *n*
['əʊvəhɔːl] révision *f*
overhead *adv* [əʊvə'hɛd] au-dessus
▷ *adj* ['əʊvəhɛd] aérien(ne); (*lighting*)

vertical(e) ▷ *n* ['əʊvəhɛd] (US)
= **overheads; overhead projector**
n rétroprojecteur *m*; **overheads** *npl*
(BRIT) frais généraux
over: overhear *vt* (*irreg: like* **hear**)
entendre (par hasard); **overheat**
vi (*engine*) chauffer; **overland** *adj*,
adv par voie de terre; **overlap** *vi* se
chevaucher; **overleaf** *adv* au verso;
overload *vt* surcharger; **overlook** *vt*
(*have view of*) donner sur; (*miss*) oublier,
négliger; (*forgive*) fermer les yeux sur
overnight *adv* [əʊvə'naɪt] (*happen*)
durant la nuit; (*fig*) soudain ▷ *adj*
['əʊvənaɪt] d'une (*or* de) nuit;
soudain(e); **to stay ~** (**with sb**)
passer la nuit (chez qn); **overnight
bag** *n* nécessaire *m* de voyage
overpass ['əʊvəpɑːs] *n* (US: *for cars*)
pont autoroutier; (*for pedestrians*)
passerelle *f*, pont *m*
overpower [əʊvə'paʊə'] *vt* vaincre;
(*fig*) accabler; **overpowering** *adj*
irrésistible; (*heat, stench*) suffocant(e)
over: overreact [əʊvəri:'ækt] *vi*
réagir de façon excessive; **overrule**
vt (*decision*) annuler; (*claim*) rejeter;
(*person*) rejeter l'avis de; **overrun**
vt (*irreg: like* **run**) (*Mil: country etc*)
occuper; (*time limit etc*) dépasser ▷ *vi*
dépasser le temps imparti
overseas [əʊvə'si:z] *adv* outre-mer;
(*abroad*) à l'étranger ▷ *adj* (*trade*)
extérieur(e); (*visitor*) étranger(-ère)
oversee [əʊvə'si:] *vt* (*irreg: like* **see**)
surveiller
overshadow [əʊvə'ʃædəʊ] *vt* (*fig*)
éclipser
oversight ['əʊvəsaɪt] *n* omission
f, oubli *m*
oversleep [əʊvə'sli:p] *vi* (*irreg: like*
sleep) se réveiller (trop) tard
overspend [əʊvə'spɛnd] *vi* (*irreg: like*
spend) dépenser de trop
overt [əʊ'və:t] *adj* non dissimulé(e)
overtake [əʊvə'teɪk] *vt* (*irreg: like*
take) dépasser; (BRIT Aut) dépasser,
doubler

over: overthrow vt (irreg: like **throw**) (government) renverser; **overtime** n heures fpl supplémentaires; **overturn** vt renverser; (decision, plan) annuler ▷ vi se retourner; **overweight** adj (person) trop gros(se); **overwhelm** vt (subj: emotion) accabler, submerger; (enemy, opponent) écraser; **overwhelming** adj (victory, defeat) écrasant(e); (desire) irrésistible

owe [əu] vt devoir; **to ~ sb sth, to ~ sth to sb** devoir qch à qn; **how much do I ~ you?** combien est-ce que je vous dois?; **owing to** prep à cause de, en raison de

owl [aul] n hibou m

own [əun] vt posséder ▷ adj propre; **a room of my ~** une chambre à moi, ma propre chambre; **to get one's ~ back** prendre sa revanche; **on one's ~** tout(e) seul(e); **own up** vi avouer; **owner** n propriétaire m/f; **ownership** n possession f

ox (pl **oxen**) [ɔks, 'ɔksn] n bœuf m

Oxbridge ['ɔksbrɪdʒ] n (BRIT) les universités d'Oxford et de Cambridge

oxen ['ɔksən] npl of **ox**

oxygen ['ɔksɪdʒən] n oxygène m

oyster ['ɔɪstər] n huître f

oz. abbr = **ounce; ounces**

ozone ['əuzəun] n ozone m; **ozone friendly** adj qui n'attaque pas or qui préserve la couche d'ozone; **ozone layer** n couche f d'ozone

p

p abbr (BRIT) = **penny; pence**

P.A. n abbr = **personal assistant; public address system**

p.a. abbr = **per annum**

pace [peɪs] n pas m; (speed) allure f; vitesse f ▷ vi: **to ~ up and down** faire les cent pas; **to keep ~ with** aller à la même vitesse que; (events) se tenir au courant de; **pacemaker** n (Med) stimulateur m cardiaque; (Sport: also: **pacesetter**) meneur(-euse) de train

Pacific [pə'sɪfɪk] n: **the ~ (Ocean)** le Pacifique, l'océan m Pacifique

pacifier ['pæsɪfaɪər] n (US: dummy) tétine f

pack [pæk] n paquet m; (of hounds) meute f; (of thieves, wolves etc) bande f; (of cards) jeu m; (US: of cigarettes) paquet; (back pack) sac m à dos ▷ vt (goods) empaqueter, emballer; (in suitcase etc) emballer; (box) remplir; (cram) entasser ▷ vi: **to ~ (one's bags)** faire ses bagages; **pack in** (BRIT *inf*) *vi* (*machine*) tomber en panne ▷ *vt* (*boyfriend*) plaquer; **~ it in!** laisse tomber!; **pack off** *vt*: **to ~ sb off to** expédier qn à; **pack up** *vi* (BRIT *inf*: *machine*) tomber en panne; (*person*) se tirer ▷ *vt* (*belongings*) ranger; (*goods*, *presents*) empaqueter, emballer

package ['pækɪdʒ] *n* paquet *m*; (*also*: **~ deal**) (*agreement*) marché global; (*purchase*) forfait *m*; (*Comput*) progiciel *m* ▷ *vt* (*goods*) conditionner; **package holiday** *n* (BRIT) vacances organisées; **package tour** *n* voyage organisé

packaging ['pækɪdʒɪŋ] *n* (*wrapping materials*) emballage *m*

packed [pækt] *adj* (*crowded*) bondé(e); **packed lunch** (BRIT) *n* repas froid

packet ['pækɪt] *n* paquet *m*

packing ['pækɪŋ] *n* emballage *m*

pact [pækt] *n* pacte *m*, traité *m*

pad [pæd] *n* bloc-notes *m*) *m*; (*to prevent friction*) tampon *m* ▷ *vt* rembourrer; **padded** *adj* (*jacket*) matelassé(e); (*bra*) rembourré(e)

paddle ['pædl] *n* (*oar*) pagaie *f*; (*us: for table tennis*) raquette *f* de ping-pong ▷ *vi* (*with feet*) barboter, faire trempette ▷ *vt*: **to ~ a canoe** etc pagayer; **paddling pool** *n* petit bassin

paddock ['pædək] *n* enclos *m*; (*Racing*) paddock *m*

padlock ['pædlɔk] *n* cadenas *m*

paedophile, (*us*) **pedophile** ['piːdəʊfaɪl] *n* pédophile *m*

page [peɪdʒ] *n* (*of book*) page *f*; (*also*: **~ boy**) groom *m*, chasseur *m*; (*at wedding*) garçon *m* d'honneur ▷ *vt* (*in hotel etc*) (faire) appeler

pager ['peɪdʒəʳ] *n* bip *m* (*inf*), Alphapage® *m*

paid [peɪd] *pt*, *pp of* **pay** ▷ *adj* (*work*, *official*) rémunéré(e); (*holiday*) payé(e); **to put ~ to** (BRIT) mettre fin à, mettre par terre

pain [peɪn] *n* douleur *f*; (*inf*: *nuisance*) plaie *f*; **to be in ~** souffrir, avoir

mal; **to take ~s to do** se donner du mal pour faire; **painful** *adj* douloureux(-euse); (*difficult*) difficile, pénible; **painkiller** *n* calmant *m*, analgésique *m*; **painstaking** ['peɪnzteɪkɪŋ] *adj* (*person*) soigneux(-euse); (*work*) soigné(e)

paint [peɪnt] *n* peinture *f* ▷ *vt* peindre; **to ~ the door blue** peindre la porte en bleu; **paintbrush** *n* pinceau *m*; **painter** *n* peintre *m*; **painting** *n* peinture *f*; (*picture*) tableau *m*

pair [pɛəʳ] *n* (*of shoes, gloves etc*) paire *f*; (*of people*) couple *m*; **~ of scissors** (paire de) ciseaux *mpl*; **~ of trousers** pantalon *m*

pajamas [pə'dʒɑːməz] *npl* (*us*) pyjama *m*

Pakistan [pɑːkɪ'stɑːn] *n* Pakistan *m*; **Pakistani** *adj* pakistanais(e) ▷ *n* Pakistanais(e)

pal [pæl] *n* (*inf*) copain (copine)

palace ['pæləs] *n* palais *m*

pale [peɪl] *adj* pâle; **~ blue** *adj* bleu pâle *inv*

Palestine ['pælɪstaɪn] *n* Palestine *f*; **Palestinian** [pælɪs'tɪnɪən] *adj* palestinien(ne) ▷ *n* Palestinien(ne)

palm [pɑːm] *n* (*Anat*) paume *f*; (*also*: **~ tree**) palmier *m* ▷ *vt*: **to ~ sth off on sb** (*inf*) refiler qch à qn

pamper ['pæmpəʳ] *vt* gâter, dorloter

pamphlet ['pæmflət] *n* brochure *f*

pan [pæn] *n* (*also*: **sauce~**) casserole *f*; (*also*: **frying ~**) poêle *f*

pancake ['pænkeɪk] *n* crêpe *f*

panda ['pændə] *n* panda *m*

pandemic [pæn'dɛmɪk] *n* pandémie *f*

pane [peɪn] *n* carreau *m* (de fenêtre), vitre *f*

panel ['pænl] *n* (*of wood, cloth etc*) panneau *m*; (*Radio*, *TV*) panel *m*, invités *mpl*; (*for interview, exams*) jury *m*

panhandler ['pænhændləʳ] *n* (*us inf*) mendiant(e)

panic ['pænɪk] *n* panique *f*, affolement *m* ▷ *vi* s'affoler, paniquer

panorama [pænə'rɑ:mə] n
panorama m

pansy ['pænzı] n (Bot) pensée f

pant [pænt] vi haleter

panther ['pænθəʳ] n panthère f

panties ['pæntɪz] npl slip m, culotte f

pantomime ['pæntəmaɪm] n (BRIT)
spectacle m de Noël

● **PANTOMIME**

● Une pantomime (à ne pas confondre
● avec le mot tel qu'on l'utilise
● en français), que l'on appelle
● également de façon familière
● "panto", est un genre de farce où le
● personnage principal est souvent
● un jeune garçon et où il y a toujours
● une "dame", c'est-à-dire une vieille
● femme jouée par un homme, et
● un méchant. La plupart du temps,
● l'histoire est basée sur un conte de
● fées comme Cendrillon ou Le Chat
● botté, et le public est encouragé
● à participer en prévenant le héros
● d'un danger imminent. Ce genre
● de spectacle, qui s'adresse surtout
● aux enfants, vise également un
● public d'adultes au travers des
● nombreuses plaisanteries faisant
● allusion à des faits d'actualité.

pants [pænts] npl (BRIT: woman's)
culotte f, slip m; (: man's) slip, caleçon
m; (US: trousers) pantalon m

pantyhose ['pæntɪhəuz] npl (US)
collant m

paper ['peɪpəʳ] n papier m; (also:
wall~) papier peint; (also: **news~**)
journal m; (academic essay) article
m; (exam) épreuve écrite ▷ adj en or
de papier ▷ vt tapisser (de papier
peint); **papers** npl (also: **identity ~s**)
papiers mpl (d'identité); **paperback**
n livre broché or non relié; (small) livre
m de poche; **paper bag** n sac m en
papier; **paper clip** n trombone m;
paper shop n (BRIT) marchand m de

journaux; **paperwork** n papiers mpl;
(pej) paperasserie f

paprika ['pæprɪkə] n paprika m

par [pɑːʳ] n pair m; (Golf) normale f du
parcours; **on a ~ with** à égalité avec,
au même niveau que

paracetamol [pærə'si:təmɔl] n
(BRIT) paracétamol m

parachute ['pærəʃu:t] n
parachute m

parade [pə'reɪd] n défilé m ▷ vt (fig)
faire étalage de ▷ vi défiler

paradise ['pærədaɪs] n paradis m

paradox ['pærədɔks] n paradoxe m

paraffin ['pærəfɪn] n (BRIT): **~ (oil)**
pétrole (lampant)

paragraph ['pærəgrɑːf] n
paragraphe m

parallel ['pærəlɛl] adj: **~ (with or to)**
parallèle (à); (fig) analogue (à) ▷ n
(line) parallèle f; (fig, Geo) parallèle m

paralysed ['pærəlaɪzd] adj
paralysé(e)

paralysis (pl **paralyses**) [pə'rælɪsɪs,
-si:z] n paralysie f

paramedic [pærə'mɛdɪk] n
auxiliaire m/f médical(e)

paranoid ['pærənɔɪd] adj (Psych)
paranoïaque; (neurotic) paranoïde

parasite ['pærəsaɪt] n parasite m

parcel ['pɑːsl] n paquet m, colis m ▷ vt
(also: **~ up**) empaqueter

pardon ['pɑːdn] n pardon m; (Law)
grâce f ▷ vt pardonner à; (Law)
gracier; **~!** pardon!; **~ me!** (after
burping etc) excusez-moi!; **I beg your
~!** (I'm sorry) pardon!, je suis désolé!; **(I
beg your) ~?**, (US) **~ me?** (what did you
say?) pardon?

parent ['pɛərənt] n (father) père
m; (mother) mère f; **parents** npl
parents mpl; **parental** [pə'rɛntl] adj
parental(e), des parents

Paris ['pærɪs] n Paris

parish ['pærɪʃ] n paroisse f; (BRIT: civil)
≈ commune f

Parisian [pə'rɪzɪən] adj parisien(ne),
de Paris ▷ n Parisien(ne)

P

park [pɑːk] n parc m, jardin public
▷ vt garer ▷ vi se garer; **can I ~ here?**
est-ce que je peux me garer ici?

parking ['pɑːkɪŋ] n stationnement
m; **"no ~"** "stationnement interdit";
parking lot n (US) parking m, parc m
de stationnement; **parking meter**
n parc(o)mètre m; **parking ticket**
n P.-V. m

▮ Be careful not to translate *parking*
by the French word *parking*.

parkway ['pɑːkweɪ] n (US) route f
express (*en site vert ou aménagé*)

parliament ['pɑːləmənt] n
parlement m; **parliamentary**
[pɑːlə'mɛntərɪ] adj parlementaire

Parmesan [pɑːmɪ'zæn] n (also:
~ cheese) Parmesan m

parole [pə'rəʊl] n: **on ~** en liberté
conditionnelle

parrot ['pærət] n perroquet m

parsley ['pɑːslɪ] n persil m

parsnip ['pɑːsnɪp] n panais m

parson ['pɑːsn] n ecclésiastique m;
(*Church of England*) pasteur m

part [pɑːt] n partie f, (*of machine*)
pièce f, (*Theat*) rôle m; (*of serial*)
épisode m; (*US: in hair*) raie f ▷ adv
= **partly** ▷ vt séparer ▷ vi (*people*) se
séparer; (*crowd*) s'ouvrir; **to take ~ in**
participer à, prendre part à; **to take
sb's ~** prendre le parti de qn, prendre
parti pour qn; **for my ~** en ce qui me
concerne; **for the most ~** en grande
partie; dans la plupart des cas; **in ~**
en partie; **to take sth in good/bad
~** prendre qch du bon/mauvais côté;
part with vt fus (*person*) se séparer
de; (*possessions*) se défaire de

partial ['pɑːʃl] adj (*incomplete*)
partiel(le); **to be ~ to** aimer, avoir un
faible pour

participant [pɑː'tɪsɪpənt] n (*in
competition, campaign*) participant(e)

participate [pɑː'tɪsɪpeɪt] vi: **to ~
(in)** participer (à), prendre part (à)

particle ['pɑːtɪkl] n particule f; (*of
dust*) grain m

particular [pə'tɪkjulər] adj (*specific*)
particulier(-ière); (*special*) particulier,
spécial(e); (*fussy*) difficile, exigeant(e);
(*careful*) méticuleux(-euse); **in ~** en
particulier, surtout; **particularly** adv
particulièrement; (*in particular*) en
particulier; **particulars** npl détails
mpl; (*information*) renseignements mpl

parting ['pɑːtɪŋ] n séparation f; (BRIT:
in hair) raie f

partition [pɑː'tɪʃən] n (*Pol*) partition
f, division f; (*wall*) cloison f

partly ['pɑːtlɪ] adv en partie,
partiellement

partner ['pɑːtnər] n (*Comm*)
associé(e); (*Sport*) partenaire m/f;
(*spouse*) conjoint(e); (*lover*) ami(e); (*at
dance*) cavalier(-ière); **partnership** n
association f

partridge ['pɑːtrɪdʒ] n perdrix f

part-time ['pɑːt'taɪm] adj, adv à
mi-temps, à temps partiel

party ['pɑːtɪ] n (*Pol*) parti m;
(*celebration*) fête f; (: *formal*) réception
f; (: *in evening*) soirée f; (*group*) groupe
m; (*Law*) partie f

pass [pɑːs] vt (*time, object*) passer;
(*place*) passer devant; (*friend*)
croiser; (*exam*) être reçu(e) à, réussir;
(*overtake*) dépasser; (*approve*)
approuver, accepter ▷ vi passer;
(*Scol*) être reçu(e) or admis(e), réussir
▷ n (*permit*) laissez-passer m inv;
(*membership card*) carte f d'accès
or d'abonnement; (*in mountains*)
col m; (*Sport*) passe f; (*Scol: also:* **~
mark**); **to get a ~** être reçu(e) (sans
mention); **to ~ sth** passer qch
à qn; **could you ~ the salt/oil,
please?** pouvez-vous me passer le
sel/l'huile, s'il vous plaît?; **to make
a ~ at sb** (*inf*) faire des avances à qn;
pass away vi mourir; **pass by** vi
passer ▷ vt (*ignore*) négliger; **pass on**
vt (*hand on*): **to ~ on (to)** transmettre
(à); **pass out** vi s'évanouir; **pass over**
vt (*ignore*) passer sous silence; **pass
up** vt (*opportunity*) laisser passer;

passable adj (road) praticable; (work) acceptable

> Be careful not to translate to pass an exam by the French expression passer un examen.

passage ['pæsɪdʒ] n (also: **~way**) couloir m; (gen, in book) passage m; (by boat) traversée f

passenger ['pæsɪndʒəʳ] n passager(-ère)

passer-by [pɑːsəˈbaɪ] n passant(e)

passing place n (Aut) aire f de croisement

passion ['pæʃən] n passion f; **passionate** adj passionné(e); **passion fruit** n fruit m de la passion

passive ['pæsɪv] adj (also: Ling) passif(-ive)

passport ['pɑːspɔːt] n passeport m; **passport control** n contrôle m des passeports; **passport office** n bureau m de délivrance des passeports

password ['pɑːswɜːd] n mot m de passe

past [pɑːst] prep (in front of) devant; (further than) au delà de, plus loin que; après; (later than) après ▷ adv: **to run ~** passer en courant ▷ adj passé(e); (president etc) ancien(ne) ▷ n passé m; **he's ~ forty** il a dépassé la quarantaine, il a plus de or passé quarante ans; **ten/quarter ~ eight** (BRIT) huit heures dix/un or et quart; **for the ~ few/3 days** depuis quelques/3 jours; ces derniers/3 jours

pasta ['pæstə] n pâtes fpl

paste [peɪst] n pâte f; (Culin: meat) pâté m (à tartiner); (: tomato) purée f, concentré m; (glue) colle f (de pâte) ▷ vt coller

pastel ['pæstl] adj pastel inv ▷ n (Art: pencil) (crayon m) pastel m; (: drawing) (dessin m au) pastel; (colour) ton m pastel inv

pasteurized ['pæstəraɪzd] adj pasteurisé(e)

pastime ['pɑːstaɪm] n passe-temps m inv, distraction f

pastor ['pɑːstəʳ] n pasteur m

pastry ['peɪstrɪ] n pâte f; (cake) pâtisserie f

pasture ['pɑːstʃəʳ] n pâturage m

pasty¹ n ['pæstɪ] petit pâté (en croûte)

pasty² ['peɪstɪ] adj (complexion) terreux(-euse)

pat [pæt] vt donner une petite tape à; (dog) caresser

patch [pætʃ] n (of material) pièce f; (eye patch) cache m; (spot) tache f; (of land) parcelle f; (on tyre) rustine f ▷ vt (clothes) rapiécer; **a bad ~** (BRIT) une période difficile; **patchy** adj inégal(e); (incomplete) fragmentaire

pâté ['pæteɪ] n pâté m, terrine f

patent ['peɪtnt, US 'pætnt] n brevet m (d'invention) ▷ vt faire breveter ▷ adj patent(e), manifeste

paternal [pəˈtɜːnl] adj paternel(le)

paternity leave [pəˈtɜːnɪtɪ-] n congé m de paternité

path [pɑːθ] n chemin m, sentier m; (in garden) allée f; (of missile) trajectoire f

pathetic [pəˈθɛtɪk] adj (pitiful) pitoyable; (very bad) lamentable, minable

pathway ['pɑːθweɪ] n chemin m, sentier m; (in garden) allée f

patience ['peɪʃns] n patience f; (BRIT Cards) réussite f

patient ['peɪʃnt] n malade m/f; (of dentist etc) patient(e) ▷ adj patient(e)

patio ['pætɪəu] n patio m

patriotic [pætrɪˈɔtɪk] adj patriotique; (person) patriote

patrol [pəˈtrəul] n patrouille f ▷ vt patrouiller dans; **patrol car** n voiture f de police

patron ['peɪtrən] n (in shop) client(e); (of charity) patron(ne); **~ of the arts** mécène m

patronizing ['pætrənaɪzɪŋ] adj condescendant(e)

P

pattern ['pætən] n (Sewing) patron m; (design) motif m; **patterned** adj à motifs

pause [pɔːz] n pause f, arrêt m ▷ vi faire une pause, s'arrêter

pave [peɪv] vt paver, daller; **to ~ the way for** ouvrir la voie à

pavement ['peɪvmənt] n (BRIT) trottoir m; (US) chaussée f

pavilion [pə'vɪlɪən] n pavillon m; (Sport) stand m

paving ['peɪvɪŋ] n (material) pavé m

paw [pɔː] n patte f

pawn [pɔːn] n (Chess, also fig) pion m ▷ vt mettre en gage; **pawnbroker** n prêteur m sur gages

pay [peɪ] (pt, pp **paid**) n salaire m; (of manual worker) paie f ▷ vt payer ▷ vi payer; (be profitable) être rentable; **can I ~ by credit card?** est-ce que je peux payer par carte de crédit?; **to ~ attention (to)** prêter attention (à); **to ~ sb a visit** rendre visite à qn; **to ~ one's respects to sb** présenter ses respects à qn; **pay back** vt rembourser; **pay for** vt fus payer; **pay in** vt verser; **pay off** vt (debts) régler, acquitter; (person) rembourser ▷ vi (scheme, decision) se révéler payant(e); **pay out** vt (money) payer, sortir de sa poche; **pay up** vt (amount) payer; **payable** adj payable; **to make a cheque payable to sb** établir un chèque à l'ordre de qn; **pay-as-you-go** adj (mobile phone) à carte prépayée; **payday** n jour m de paie; **pay envelope** n (US) paie f; **payment** n paiement m; (of bill) règlement m; (of deposit, cheque) versement m; **monthly payment** mensualité f; **payout** n (from insurance) dédommagement m; (in competition) prix m; **pay packet** n (BRIT) paie f; **pay phone** n cabine f téléphonique, téléphone public; **pay raise** n (US) = **pay rise**; **pay rise** n (BRIT) augmentation f (de salaire); **payroll** n registre m du personnel;

pay slip n (BRIT) bulletin m de paie, feuille f de paie; **pay television** n chaînes fpl payantes; **paywall** n (Comput) mur m (payant)

PC n abbr = **personal computer**; (BRIT) = **police constable** ▷ adj abbr = **politically correct**

p.c. abbr = **per cent**

pcm n abbr (= per calendar month) par mois

PDA n abbr (= personal digital assistant) agenda m électronique

PE n abbr (= physical education) EPS f

pea [piː] n (petit) pois

peace [piːs] n paix f; (calm) calme m, tranquillité f; **peaceful** adj paisible, calme

peach [piːtʃ] n pêche f

peacock ['piːkɔk] n paon m

peak [piːk] n (mountain) pic m, cime f; (of cap) visière f; (fig: highest level) maximum m; (: of career, fame) apogée m; **peak hours** npl heures fpl d'affluence or de pointe

peanut ['piːnʌt] n arachide f, cacahuète f; **peanut butter** n beurre m de cacahuète

pear [pɛə^r] n poire f

pearl [pəːl] n perle f

peasant ['pɛznt] n paysan(ne)

peat [piːt] n tourbe f

pebble ['pɛbl] n galet m, caillou m

peck [pɛk] vt (also: ~ at) donner un coup de bec à; (food) picorer ▷ n coup m de bec; (kiss) bécot m; **peckish** adj (BRIT inf): **I feel peckish** je mangerais bien quelque chose, j'ai la dent

peculiar [pɪ'kjuːlɪə^r] adj (odd) étrange, bizarre, curieux(-euse); (particular) particulier(-ière); **~ to** particulier à

pedal ['pɛdl] n pédale f ▷ vi pédaler

pedestal ['pɛdəstl] n piédestal m

pedestrian [pɪ'dɛstrɪən] n piéton m; **pedestrian crossing** n (BRIT) passage clouté; **pedestrianized** adj: **a pedestrianized street** une rue piétonne; **pedestrian precinct**,

(US) **pedestrian zone** n (BRIT) zone piétonne
pedigree ['pɛdɪgri:] n ascendance f; (of animal) pedigree m ▷ cpd (animal) de race
pedophile ['pi:dəʊfaɪl] (US) n = **paedophile**
pee [pi:] vi (inf) faire pipi, pisser
peek [pi:k] vi jeter un coup d'œil (furtif)
peel [pi:l] n pelure f, épluchure f; (of orange, lemon) écorce f ▷ vt peler, éplucher ▷ vi (paint etc) s'écailler; (wallpaper) se décoller; (skin) peler
peep [pi:p] n (look) coup d'œil furtif; (sound) pépiement m ▷ vi jeter un coup d'œil (furtif)
peer [pɪəʳ] vi: **to ~ at** regarder attentivement, scruter ▷ n (noble) pair m; (equal) pair, égal(e)
peg [pɛg] n (for coat etc) patère f; (BRIT: also: **clothes ~**) pince f à linge
pelican ['pɛlɪkən] n pélican m; **pelican crossing** n (BRIT Aut) feu m à commande manuelle
pelt [pɛlt] vt: **to ~ sb (with)** bombarder qn (de) ▷ vi (rain) tomber à seaux; (inf: run) courir à toutes jambes ▷ n peau f
pelvis ['pɛlvɪs] n bassin m
pen [pɛn] n (for writing) stylo m; (for sheep) parc m
penalty ['pɛnltɪ] n pénalité f; sanction f; (fine) amende f; (Sport) pénalisation f; (Football) penalty m; (Rugby) pénalité f
pence [pɛns] npl of **penny**
pencil ['pɛnsl] n crayon m; **pencil in** vt noter provisoirement; **pencil case** n trousse f (d'écolier); **pencil sharpener** n taille-crayon(s) m inv
pendant ['pɛndnt] n pendentif m
pending ['pɛndɪŋ] prep en attendant ▷ adj en suspens
penetrate ['pɛnɪtreɪt] vt pénétrer dans; (enemy territory) entrer en
pen friend n (BRIT) correspondant(e)
penguin ['pɛŋgwɪn] n pingouin m

penicillin [pɛnɪ'sɪlɪn] n pénicilline f
peninsula [pə'nɪnsjʊlə] n péninsule f
penis ['pi:nɪs] n pénis m, verge f
penitentiary [pɛnɪ'tɛnʃərɪ] n (US) prison f
penknife ['pɛnnaɪf] n canif m
penniless ['pɛnɪlɪs] adj sans le sou
penny (pl **pennies** or **pence**) ['pɛnɪ, 'pɛnɪz, pɛns] n (BRIT) penny m; (US) cent m
pen pal n correspondant(e)
pension ['pɛnʃən] n (from company) retraite f; **pensioner** n (BRIT) retraité(e)
pentagon ['pɛntəgən] n: **the P~** (US Pol) le Pentagone
penthouse ['pɛnthaʊs] n appartement m (de luxe) en attique
penultimate [pɪ'nʌltɪmət] adj pénultième, avant-dernier(-ière)
people ['pi:pl] npl gens mpl; personnes fpl; (inhabitants) population f; (Pol) peuple m ▷ n (nation, race) peuple m; **several ~ came** plusieurs personnes sont venues; **~ say that ...** on dit or les gens disent que ...
pepper ['pɛpəʳ] n poivre m; (vegetable) poivron m ▷ vt (Culin) poivrer; **peppermint** n (sweet) pastille f de menthe
per [pəːʳ] prep par; **~ hour** (miles etc) à l'heure; (fee) (de) l'heure; **~ kilo** etc le kilo etc; **~ day/person** par jour/ personne; **~ annum** per an
perceive [pə'siːv] vt percevoir; (notice) remarquer, s'apercevoir de
per cent adv pour cent
percentage [pə'sɛntɪdʒ] n pourcentage m
perception [pə'sɛpʃən] n perception f; (insight) sensibilité f
perch [pəːtʃ] n (fish) perche f; (for bird) perchoir m ▷ vi (se) percher
percussion [pə'kʌʃən] n percussion f
perennial [pə'rɛnɪəl] n (Bot) (plante f) vivace f, plante pluriannuelle

p

perfect ['pə:fɪkt] *adj* parfait(e)
▷ *n (also:* ~ **tense**) parfait *m* ▷ *vt*
[pə'fɛkt] *(technique, skill, work of art)*
parfaire; *(method, plan)* mettre au
point; **perfection** [pə'fɛkʃən] *n*
perfection *f*; **perfectly** ['pə:fɪktlɪ]
adv parfaitement

perform [pə'fɔ:m] *vt (carry out)*
exécuter; *(concert etc)* jouer,
donner ▷ *vi (actor, musician)* jouer;
performance *n* représentation
f, spectacle *m*; *(of an artist)*
interprétation *f*; *(Sport: of car,
engine)* performance *f*; *(of company,
economy)* résultats *mpl*; **performer** *n*
artiste *m/f*

perfume ['pə:fju:m] *n* parfum *m*

perhaps [pə'hæps] *adv* peut-être

perimeter [pə'rɪmɪtə'] *n*
périmètre *m*

period ['pɪərɪəd] *n* période *f*; *(Hist)*
époque *f*; *(Scol)* cours *m*; *(full stop)*
point *m*; *(Med)* règles *fpl* ▷ *adj*
(costume, furniture) d'époque;
periodical [pɪərɪ'ɔdɪkl] *n* périodique
m; **periodically** *adv* périodiquement

perish ['pɛrɪʃ] *vi* périr, mourir; *(decay)*
se détériorer

perjury ['pə:dʒərɪ] *n (Law: in court)*
faux témoignage; *(breach of oath)*
parjure *m*

perk [pə:k] *n (inf)* avantage *m*,
à-côté *m*

perm [pə:m] *n (for hair)* permanente *f*

permanent ['pə:mənənt] *adj*
permanent(e); **permanently**
adv de façon permanente; *(move
abroad)* définitivement; *(open, closed)*
en permanence; *(tired, unhappy)*
constamment

permission [pə'mɪʃən] *n* permission
f, autorisation *f*

permit *n* ['pə:mɪt] permis *m*

perplex [pə'plɛks] *vt (person)* rendre
perplexe

persecute ['pə:sɪkju:t] *vt* persécuter

persecution [pə:sɪ'kju:ʃən] *n*
persécution *f*

persevere [pə:sɪ'vɪə'] *vi* persévérer

Persian ['pə:ʃən] *adj* persan(e); **the ~
Gulf** le golfe Persique

persist [pə'sɪst] *vi*: **to ~ (in doing)**
persister (à faire), s'obstiner (à faire);
persistent *adj* persistant(e), tenace

person ['pə:sn] *n* personne *f*; **in
~** en personne; **personal** *adj*
personnel(le); **personal assistant** *n*
secrétaire personnel(le); **personal
computer** *n* ordinateur individuel,
PC *m*; **personality** [pə:sə'nælɪtɪ]
n personnalité *f*; **personally** *adv*
personnellement; **to take sth
personally** se sentir visé(e) par
qch; **personal organizer** *n* agenda
(personnel); *(electronic)* agenda
électronique; **personal stereo** *n*
Walkman® *m*, baladeur *m*

personnel [pə:sə'nɛl] *n* personnel *m*

perspective [pə'spɛktɪv] *n*
perspective *f*

perspiration [pə:spɪ'reɪʃən] *n*
transpiration *f*

persuade [pə'sweɪd] *vt*: **to ~ sb to
do sth** persuader qn de faire qch,
amener *or* décider qn à faire qch

persuasion [pə'sweɪʒən] *n*
persuasion *f*; *(creed)* conviction *f*

persuasive [pə'sweɪsɪv] *adj*
persuasif(-ive)

perverse [pə'və:s] *adj* pervers(e);
(contrary) entêté(e), contrariant(e)

pervert *n* ['pə:və:t] perverti(e) ▷ *vt*
[pə'və:t] pervertir; *(words)* déformer

pessimism ['pɛsɪmɪzəm] *n*
pessimisme *m*

pessimist ['pɛsɪmɪst] *n* pessimiste
m/f; **pessimistic** [pɛsɪ'mɪstɪk] *adj*
pessimiste

pest [pɛst] *n* animal *m (or* insecte *m)*
nuisible; *(fig)* fléau *m*

pester ['pɛstə'] *vt* importuner,
harceler

pesticide ['pɛstɪsaɪd] *n* pesticide *m*

pet [pɛt] *n* animal familier ▷ *cpd
(favourite)* favori(e) ▷ *vt (stroke)*
caresser, câliner; **teacher's ~**

chouchou *m* du professeur; **~ hate** bête noire

petal ['pɛtl] *n* pétale *m*

petite [pə'ti:t] *adj* menu(e)

petition [pə'tɪʃən] *n* pétition *f*

petrified ['pɛtrɪfaɪd] *adj* (*fig*) mort(e) de peur

petrol ['pɛtrəl] *n* (BRIT) essence *f*; **I've run out of ~** je suis en panne d'essence

> Be careful not to translate *petrol* by the French word *pétrole*.

petroleum [pə'trəuliəm] *n* pétrole *m*

petrol: petrol pump *n* (BRIT: *in car*, *at garage*) pompe *f* à essence; **petrol station** *n* (BRIT) station-service *f*; **petrol tank** *n* (BRIT) réservoir *m* d'essence

petticoat ['pɛtɪkəut] *n* jupon *m*

petty ['pɛtɪ] *adj* (*mean*) mesquin(e); (*unimportant*) insignifiant(e), sans importance

pew [pju:] *n* banc *m* (d'église)

pewter ['pju:tə'] *n* étain *m*

phantom ['fæntəm] *n* fantôme *m*

pharmacist ['fɑ:məsɪst] *n* pharmacien(ne)

pharmacy ['fɑ:məsɪ] *n* pharmacie *f*

phase [feɪz] *n* phase *f*, période *f*; **phase in** *vt* introduire progressivement; **phase out** *vt* supprimer progressivement

Ph.D. *abbr* = **Doctor of Philosophy**

pheasant ['fɛznt] *n* faisan *m*

phenomena [fə'nɔmɪnə] *npl of* **phenomenon**

phenomenal [fɪ'nɔmɪnl] *adj* phénoménal(e)

phenomenon (*pl* **phenomena**) [fə'nɔmɪnən, -nə] *n* phénomène *m*

Philippines ['fɪlɪpi:nz] *npl* (*also*: **Philippine Islands**): **the ~** les Philippines *fpl*

philosopher [fɪ'lɔsəfə'] *n* philosophe *m*

philosophical [fɪlə'sɔfɪkl] *adj* philosophique

philosophy [fɪ'lɔsəfɪ] *n* philosophie *f*

phlegm [flɛm] *n* flegme *m*

phobia ['fəubjə] *n* phobie *f*

phone [fəun] *n* téléphone *m* ▷ *vt* téléphoner à ▷ *vi* téléphoner; **to be on the ~** avoir le téléphone; (*be calling*) être au téléphone; **phone back** *vt*, *vi* rappeler; **phone up** *vt* téléphoner à ▷ *vi* téléphoner; **phone book** *n* annuaire *m*; **phone box**, (US) **phone booth** *n* cabine *f* téléphonique; **phone call** *n* coup *m* de fil *or* de téléphone; **phonecard** *n* télécarte *f*; **phone number** *n* numéro *m* de téléphone

phonetics [fə'nɛtɪks] *n* phonétique *f*

phoney ['fəunɪ] *adj* faux (fausse), factice; (*person*) pas franc (franche)

photo ['fəutəu] *n* photo *f*; **photo album** *n* album *m* de photos; **photocopier** *n* copieur *m*; **photocopy** *n* photocopie *f* ▷ *vt* photocopier

photograph ['fəutəgræf] *n* photographie *f* ▷ *vt* photographier; **photographer** [fə'tɔgrəfə'] *n* photographe *m/f*, **photography** [fə'tɔgrəfɪ] *n* photographie *f*

phrase [freɪz] *n* expression *f*; (*Ling*) locution *f* ▷ *vt* exprimer; **phrase book** *n* recueil *m* d'expressions (pour touristes)

physical ['fɪzɪkl] *adj* physique; **physical education** *n* éducation *f* physique; **physically** *adv* physiquement

physician [fɪ'zɪʃən] *n* médecin *m*

physicist ['fɪzɪsɪst] *n* physicien(ne)

physics ['fɪzɪks] *n* physique *f*

physiotherapist [fɪzɪəu'θɛrəpɪst] *n* kinésithérapeute *m/f*

physiotherapy [fɪzɪəu'θɛrəpɪ] *n* kinésithérapie *f*

physique [fɪ'zi:k] *n* (*appearance*) physique *m*; (*health etc*) constitution *f*

pianist ['pi:ənɪst] *n* pianiste *m/f*

piano [pɪ'ænəu] *n* piano *m*

pick [pɪk] *n* (*tool: also*: **~-axe**) pic *m*, pioche *f* ▷ *vt* choisir; (*gather*) cueillir;

p

(*remove*) prendre; (*lock*) forcer; **take your ~** faites votre choix; **the ~ of** le meilleur(e) de; **to ~ one's nose** se mettre les doigts dans le nez; **to ~ one's teeth** se curer les dents; **to ~ a quarrel with sb** chercher noise à qn; **pick on** vt fus (*person*) harceler; **pick out** vt choisir; (*distinguish*) distinguer; **pick up** vi (*improve*) remonter, s'améliorer ▷ vt ramasser; (*collect*) passer prendre; (*Aut: give lift to*) prendre; (*learn*) apprendre; (*Radio*) capter; **to ~ up speed** prendre de la vitesse; **to ~ o.s. up** se relever

pickle ['pɪkl] n (*also*: **~s**) (*as condiment*) pickles mpl ▷ vt conserver dans du vinaigre or dans de la saumure; **in a ~** (*fig*) dans le pétrin

pickpocket ['pɪkpɔkɪt] n pickpocket m

pick-up ['pɪkʌp] n (*also*: **~ truck**) pick-up m inv

picnic ['pɪknɪk] n pique-nique m ▷ vi pique-niquer; **picnic area** n aire f de pique-nique

picture ['pɪktʃəʳ] n (*also TV*) image f; (*painting*) peinture f, tableau m; (*photograph*) photo(graphie) f; (*drawing*) dessin m; (*film*) film m; (*fig: description*) description f ▷ vt (*imagine*) se représenter; **pictures** npl; **the ~s** (*BRIT*) le cinéma; **to take a ~ of sb/sth** prendre qn/qch en photo; **would you take a ~ of us, please?** pourriez-vous nous prendre en photo, s'il vous plaît?; **picture frame** n cadre m; **picture messaging** n picture messaging m, messagerie f d'images

picturesque [pɪktʃə'rɛsk] adj pittoresque

pie [paɪ] n tourte f; (*of fruit*) tarte f; (*of meat*) pâté m en croûte

piece [piːs] n morceau m; (*item*): **a ~ of furniture/advice** un meuble/conseil ▷ vt: **to ~ together** rassembler; **to take to ~s** démonter

pie chart n graphique m à secteurs, camembert m

pier [pɪəʳ] n jetée f

pierce [pɪəs] vt percer, transpercer; **pierced** adj (*ears*) percé(e)

pig [pɪg] n cochon m, porc m; (*pej: unkind person*) mufle m; (: *greedy person*) goinfre m

pigeon ['pɪdʒən] n pigeon m

piggy bank ['pɪgɪ-] n tirelire f

pigsty ['pɪgstaɪ] n porcherie f

pigtail ['pɪgteɪl] n natte f, tresse f

pike [paɪk] n (*fish*) brochet m

pilchard ['pɪltʃəd] n pilchard m (*sorte de sardine*)

pile [paɪl] n (*pillar, of books*) pile f; (*heap*) tas m; (*of carpet*) épaisseur f; **pile up** vi (*accumulate*) s'entasser, s'accumuler ▷ vt (*put in heap*) empiler, entasser; (*accumulate*) accumuler; **piles** npl hémorroïdes fpl; **pile-up** n (*Aut*) télescopage m, collision f en série

pilgrim ['pɪlgrɪm] n pèlerin m; *voir article* **"Pilgrim Fathers"**

● PILGRIM FATHERS

Les *Pilgrim Fathers* ("Pères pèlerins") sont un groupe de puritains qui quittèrent l'Angleterre en 1620 pour fuir les persécutions religieuses. Ayant traversé l'Atlantique à bord du "Mayflower", ils fondèrent New Plymouth en Nouvelle-Angleterre, dans ce qui est aujourd'hui le Massachusetts. Ces Pères pèlerins sont considérés comme les fondateurs des États-Unis, et l'on commémore chaque année, le jour de "Thanksgiving", la réussite de leur première récolte.

pilgrimage ['pɪlgrɪmɪdʒ] n pèlerinage m

pill [pɪl] n pilule f; **the ~** la pilule

pillar ['pɪləʳ] n pilier m

pillow ['pɪləu] n oreiller m; **pillowcase, pillowslip** n taie f d'oreiller

pilot ['paɪlət] *n* pilote *m* ▷ *cpd* (*scheme etc*) pilote, expérimental(e) ▷ *vt* piloter; **pilot light** *n* veilleuse *f*

pimple ['pɪmpl] *n* bouton *m*

PIN *n abbr* (= *personal identification number*) code *m* confidentiel

pin [pɪn] *n* épingle *f*; (*Tech*) cheville *f* ▷ *vt* épingler; **~s and needles** fourmis *fpl*; **to ~ sb down** (*fig*) coincer qn; **to ~ sth on sb** (*fig*) mettre qch sur le dos de qn

pinafore ['pɪnəfɔːʳ] *n* tablier *m*

pinch [pɪntʃ] *n* pincement *m*; (*of salt etc*) pincée *f* ▷ *vt* pincer; (*inf: steal*) piquer, chiper ▷ *vi* (*shoe*) serrer; **at a ~** à la rigueur

pine [paɪn] *n* (*also:* **~ tree**) pin *m* ▷ *vi*: **to ~ for** aspirer à, désirer ardemment

pineapple ['paɪnæpl] *n* ananas *m*

ping [pɪŋ] *n* (*noise*) tintement *m*; **ping-pong®** *n* ping-pong® *m*

pink [pɪŋk] *adj* rose ▷ *n* (*colour*) rose *m*

pinpoint ['pɪnpɔɪnt] *vt* indiquer (avec précision)

pint [paɪnt] *n* pinte *f* (*Brit* = 0,57 l; *US* = 0,47 l), (*BRIT inf*) ≈ demi *m*, ≈ pot *m*

pioneer [paɪə'nɪəʳ] *n* pionnier *m*

pious ['paɪəs] *adj* pieux(-euse)

pip [pɪp] *n* (*seed*) pépin *m*; **pips** *npl*; **the ~s** (*BRIT: time signal on radio*) le top

pipe [paɪp] *n* tuyau *m*, conduite *f*; (*for smoking*) pipe *f* ▷ *vt* amener par tuyau; **pipeline** *n* (*for gas*) gazoduc *m*, pipeline *m*; (*for oil*) oléoduc *m*, pipeline; **piper** *n* (*flautist*) joueur(-euse) de pipeau; (*of bagpipes*) joueur(-euse) de cornemuse

pirate ['paɪərət] *n* pirate *m* ▷ *vt* (*CD, video, book*) pirater

Pisces ['paɪsiːz] *n* les Poissons *mpl*

piss [pɪs] *vi* (*inf!*) pisser (!); **pissed** *adj* (*infl: BRIT: drunk*) bourré(e); (: *US: angry*) furieux(-euse)

pistol ['pɪstl] *n* pistolet *m*

piston ['pɪstən] *n* piston *m*

pit [pɪt] *n* trou *m*, fosse *f*; (*also:* **coal ~**) puits *m* de mine; (*also:* **orchestra ~**) fosse d'orchestre; (*US: fruit stone*)

noyau *m* ▷ *vt*: **to ~ o.s.** *or* **one's wits against** se mesurer à

pitch [pɪtʃ] *n* (*BRIT Sport*) terrain *m*; (*Mus*) ton *m*; (*fig: degree*) degré *m*; (*tar*) poix *f* ▷ *vt* (*throw*) lancer; (*tent*) dresser ▷ *vi* (*fall*): **to ~ into/off** tomber dans/de; **pitch-black** *adj* noir(e) comme poix

pitfall ['pɪtfɔːl] *n* piège *m*

pith [pɪθ] *n* (*of orange etc*) intérieur *m* de l'écorce

pitiful ['pɪtɪful] *adj* (*touching*) pitoyable; (*contemptible*) lamentable

pity ['pɪtɪ] *n* pitié *f* ▷ *vt* plaindre; **what a ~!** quel dommage!

pizza ['piːtsə] *n* pizza *f*

placard ['plækɑːd] *n* affiche *f*; (*in march*) pancarte *f*

place [pleɪs] *n* endroit *m*, lieu *m*; (*proper position, job, rank, seat*) place *f*; (*home*): **at/to his ~** chez lui ▷ *vt* (*position*) placer, mettre; (*identify*) situer; reconnaître; **to take ~** avoir lieu; **to change ~s with sb** changer de place avec qn; **out of ~** (*not suitable*) déplacé(e), inopportun(e); **in the first ~** d'abord, en premier; **place mat** *n* set *m* de table; (*in linen etc*) napperon *m*; **placement** *n* (*during studies*) stage *m*

placid ['plæsɪd] *adj* placide

plague [pleɪg] *n* (*Med*) peste *f* ▷ *vt* (*fig*) tourmenter

plaice [pleɪs] *n* (*pl inv*) carrelet *m*

plain [pleɪn] *adj* (*in one colour*) uni(e); (*clear*) clair(e), évident(e); (*simple*) simple; (*not handsome*) quelconque, ordinaire ▷ *adv* franchement, carrément ▷ *n* plaine *f*; **plain chocolate** *n* chocolat *m* à croquer; **plainly** *adv* clairement; (*frankly*) carrément, sans détours

plaintiff ['pleɪntɪf] *n* plaignant(e)

plait [plæt] *n* tresse *f*, natte *f*

plan [plæn] *n* plan *m*; (*scheme*) projet *m* ▷ *vt* (*think in advance*) projeter; (*prepare*) organiser ▷ *vi* faire des projets; **to ~ to do** projeter de faire

p

plane [pleɪn] n (Aviat) avion m; (also:
~ tree) platane m; (tool) rabot m; (Art,
Math etc) plan m; (fig) niveau m, plan
▷ vt (with tool) raboter
planet ['plænɪt] n planète f
plank [plæŋk] n planche f
planning ['plænɪŋ] n planification f;
family ~ planning familial
plant [plɑ:nt] n plante f; (machinery)
matériel m; (factory) usine f ▷ vt
planter; (bomb) déposer, poser;
(microphone, evidence) cacher
plantation [plæn'teɪʃən] n
plantation f
plaque [plæk] n plaque f
plaster ['plɑ:stər] n plâtre m; (also:
~ of Paris) plâtre à mouler; (BRIT: also:
sticking ~) pansement adhésif ▷ vt
plâtrer; (cover): **to ~ with** couvrir de;
plaster cast n (Med) plâtre m; (model,
statue) moule m
plastic ['plæstɪk] n plastique m ▷ adj
(made of plastic) en plastique; **plastic
bag** n sac m en plastique; **plastic
surgery** n chirurgie f esthétique
plate [pleɪt] n (dish) assiette f; (sheet of
metal, on door, Phot) plaque f; (in book)
gravure f; (dental) dentier m
plateau (pl plateaus or plateaux)
['plætəʊ, -z] n plateau m
platform ['plætfɔ:m] n (at meeting)
tribune f; (stage) estrade f; (Rail) quai
m; (Pol) plateforme f
platinum ['plætɪnəm] n platine m
platoon [plə'tu:n] n peloton m
platter ['plætər] n plat m
plausible ['plɔ:zɪbl] adj plausible;
(person) convaincant(e)
play [pleɪ] n jeu m; (Theat) pièce f (de
théâtre) ▷ vt (game) jouer à; (team,
opponent) jouer contre; (instrument)
jouer de; (part, piece of music, note)
jouer; (CD etc) passer ▷ vi jouer; **to ~
safe** ne prendre aucun risque; **play
back** vt repasser, réécouter; **play
up** vi (cause trouble) faire des siennes;
player n joueur(-euse); (Mus)
musicien(ne); **playful** adj enjoué(e);

playground n cour f de récréation;
(in park) aire f de jeux; **playgroup** n
garderie f; **playing card** n carte f à
jouer; **playing field** n terrain m de
sport; **playschool** n = **playgroup**;
playtime n (Scol) récréation f;
playwright n dramaturge m
plc abbr (BRIT: = public limited company)
≈ SARL f
plea [pli:] n (request) appel m; (Law)
défense f
plead [pli:d] vt plaider; (give as
excuse) invoquer ▷ vi (Law) plaider;
(beg): **to ~ with sb (for sth)** implorer
qn (d'accorder qch); **to ~ guilty/
not guilty** plaider coupable/non
coupable
pleasant ['plɛznt] adj agréable
please [pli:z] excl s'il te (or vous)
plaît ▷ vt plaire à ▷ vi (think fit): **do
as you ~** faites comme il vous plaira;
~ yourself! (inf) (faites) comme
vous voulez!; **pleased** adj: **pleased
(with)** content(e) (de); **pleased to
meet you** enchanté (de faire votre
connaissance)
pleasure ['plɛʒər] n plaisir m; **"it's a
~"** "je vous en prie"
pleat [pli:t] n pli m
pledge [plɛdʒ] n (promise) promesse f
▷ vt promettre
plentiful ['plɛntɪful] adj
abondant(e), copieux(-euse)
plenty ['plɛntɪ] n: **~ of** beaucoup de;
(sufficient) (bien) assez de
pliers ['plaɪəz] npl pinces fpl
plight [plaɪt] n situation f critique
plod [plɒd] vi avancer péniblement;
(fig) peiner
plonk [plɒŋk] (inf) n (BRIT: wine)
pinard m, piquette f ▷ vt: **to ~ sth
down** poser brusquement qch
plot [plɒt] n complot m, conspiration
f; (of story, play) intrigue f; (of land) lot
m de terrain, lopin m ▷ vt (mark out)
tracer point par point; (Naut) pointer;
(make graph of) faire le graphique de;
(conspire) comploter ▷ vi comploter

plough, (US) **plow** [plau] n charrue f ▷ vt (earth) labourer; **to ~ money into** investir dans

ploy [plɔɪ] n stratagème m

pls abbr (= please) SVP m

pluck [plʌk] vt (fruit) cueillir; (musical instrument) pincer; (bird) plumer; **to ~ one's eyebrows** s'épiler les sourcils; **to ~ up courage** prendre son courage à deux mains

plug [plʌg] n (stopper) bouchon m, bonde f; (Elec) prise f de courant; (Aut: also: **spark(ing) ~**) bougie f ▷ vt (hole) boucher; (inf: advertise) faire du battage pour, matraquer; **plug in** vt (Elec) brancher; **plughole** n (BRIT) trou m (d'écoulement)

plum [plʌm] n (fruit) prune f

plumber ['plʌmə'] n plombier m

plumbing ['plʌmɪŋ] n (trade) plomberie f; (piping) tuyauterie f

plummet ['plʌmɪt] vi (person, object) plonger; (sales, prices) dégringoler

plump [plʌmp] adj rondelet(te), dodu(e), bien en chair; **plump for** vt fus (inf: choose) se décider pour

plunge [plʌndʒ] n plongeon m; (fig) chute f ▷ vt plonger ▷ vi (fall) tomber, dégringoler; (dive) plonger; **to take the ~** se jeter à l'eau

pluperfect [pluː'pəːfɪkt] n (Ling) plus-que-parfait m

plural ['pluərl] adj pluriel(le) ▷ n pluriel m

plus [plʌs] n (also: **~ sign**) signe m plus; (advantage) atout m ▷ prep plus; **ten/twenty ~** plus de dix/vingt

ply [plaɪ] n (of wool) fil m ▷ vt (a trade) exercer ▷ vi (ship) faire la navette; **to ~ sb with drink** donner continuellement à boire à qn; **plywood** n contreplaqué m

P.M. n abbr (BRIT) = **prime minister**

p.m. adv abbr (= post meridiem) de l'après-midi

PMS n abbr (= premenstrual syndrome) syndrome prémenstruel

PMT n abbr (= premenstrual tension) syndrome prémenstruel

pneumatic drill [njuː'mætɪk-] n marteau-piqueur m

pneumonia [njuː'məunɪə] n pneumonie f

poach [pəutʃ] vt (cook) pocher; (steal) pêcher (or chasser) sans permis ▷ vi braconner; **poached** adj (egg) poché(e)

P.O. Box n abbr = **post office box**

pocket ['pɔkɪt] n poche f ▷ vt empocher; **to be (£5) out of ~** (BRIT) en être de sa poche (pour 5 livres); **pocketbook** n (US: wallet) portefeuille m; **pocket money** n argent m de poche

pod [pɔd] n cosse f

podcast ['pɔdkɑːst] n podcast m ▷ vi podcaster

podiatrist [pɔ'diːətrɪst] n (US) pédicure m/f

poem ['pəuɪm] n poème m

poet ['pəuɪt] n poète m; **poetic** [pəu'ɛtɪk] adj poétique; **poetry** n poésie f

poignant ['pɔɪnjənt] adj poignant(e)

P

point [pɔɪnt] n point m; (tip) pointe f; (in time) moment m; (in space) endroit m; (subject, idea) point, sujet m; (purpose) but m; (also: **decimal ~**): **2 ~ 3 (2.3)** 2 virgule 3 (2,3); (BRIT Elec: also: **power ~**) prise f (de courant) ▷ vt (show) indiquer; (gun etc) **to ~ sth at** braquer or diriger qch sur ▷ vi: **to ~ at** montrer du doigt; **points** npl (Rail) aiguillage m; **to make a ~ of doing sth** ne pas manquer de faire qch; **to get/miss the ~** comprendre/ne pas comprendre; **to come to the ~** en venir au fait; **there's no ~ (in doing)** cela ne sert à rien (de faire); **to be on the ~ of doing sth** être sur le point de faire qch; **point out** vt (mention) faire remarquer, souligner; **point-blank** adv (fig) catégoriquement; (also: **at point-blank range**) à bout portant; **pointed** adj (shape) pointu(e); (*remark*) plein(e) de sous-entendus; **pointer** n (*needle*) aiguille f; (*clue*) indication f; (*advice*) tuyau m; **pointless** adj inutile, vain(e); **point of view** n point m de vue

poison ['pɔɪzn] n poison m ▷ vt empoisonner; **poisonous** adj (*snake*) venimeux(-euse); (*substance, plant*) vénéneux(-euse); (*fumes*) toxique

poke [pəuk] vt (*jab with finger, stick etc*) piquer; pousser du doigt; (*put*): **to ~ sth in(to)** fourrer or enfoncer qch dans; **poke about** vi fureter; **poke out** vi (*stick out*) sortir

poker ['pəukəʳ] n tisonnier m; (*Cards*) poker m

Poland ['pəulənd] n Pologne f

polar ['pəuləʳ] adj polaire; **polar bear** n ours blanc

Pole [pəul] n Polonais(e)

pole [pəul] n (*of wood*) mât m, perche f; (*Elec*) poteau m; (*Geo*) pôle m; **pole bean** n (*US*) haricot m (à rames); **pole vault** n saut m à la perche

police [pə'li:s] npl police f ▷ vt maintenir l'ordre dans; **police car** n voiture f de police; **police constable** n (*BRIT*) agent m de police; **police force** n police f, forces fpl de l'ordre; **policeman** (*irreg*) n agent m de police, policier m; **police officer** n agent m de police; **police station** n commissariat m de police; **policewoman** (*irreg*) n femme-agent f

policy ['pɔlɪsɪ] n politique f; (*also:* **insurance ~**) police f (d'assurance)

polio ['pəulɪəu] n polio f

Polish ['pəulɪʃ] adj polonais(e) ▷ n (*Ling*) polonais m

polish ['pɔlɪʃ] n (*for shoes*) cirage m; (*for floor*) cire f, encaustique f; (*for nails*) vernis m; (*shine*) éclat m, poli m; (*fig: refinement*) raffinement m ▷ vt (*put polish on: shoes, wood*) cirer; (*make shiny*) astiquer, faire briller; **polish off** vt (*food*) liquider; **polished** adj (*fig*) raffiné(e)

polite [pə'laɪt] adj poli(e); **politeness** n politesse f

political [pə'lɪtɪkl] adj politique; **politically** adv politiquement; **politically correct** politiquement correct(e)

politician [pɔlɪ'tɪʃən] n homme/femme politique, politicien(ne)

politics ['pɔlɪtɪks] n politique f

poll [pəul] n scrutin m, vote m; (*also:* **opinion ~**) sondage m (d'opinion) ▷ vt (*votes*) obtenir

pollen ['pɔlən] n pollen m

polling station n (*BRIT*) bureau m de vote

pollute [pə'lu:t] vt polluer

pollution [pə'lu:ʃən] n pollution f

polo ['pəuləu] n polo m; **polo-neck** adj à col roulé ▷ n (*sweater*) pull m à col roulé; **polo shirt** n polo m

polyester [pɔlɪ'estəʳ] n polyester m

polystyrene [pɔlɪ'staɪri:n] n polystyrène m

polythene ['pɔlɪθi:n] n (*BRIT*) polyéthylène m; **polythene bag** n sac m en plastique

pomegranate ['pɔmɪgrænɪt] n grenade f

pompous ['pɔmpəs] adj pompeux(-euse)

pond [pɔnd] n étang m; (*stagnant*) mare f

ponder ['pɔndəʳ] vt considérer, peser

pony ['pəunɪ] n poney m; **ponytail** n queue f de cheval; **pony trekking** n (*BRIT*) randonnée f équestre or à cheval

poodle ['pu:dl] n caniche m

pool [pu:l] n (*of rain*) flaque f; (*pond*) mare f; (*artificial*) bassin m; (*also:* **swimming ~**) piscine f; (*sth shared*) fonds commun; (*billiards*) poule f ▷ vt mettre en commun; **pools** npl (*football*) ≈ loto sportif

poor [puəʳ] adj pauvre; (*mediocre*) médiocre, faible, mauvais(e) ▷ npl: **the ~** les pauvres mpl; **poorly** adv (*badly*) mal, médiocrement ▷ *adj* souffrant(e), malade

pop [pɔp] *n* (*noise*) bruit sec; (*Mus*) musique *f* pop; (*inf: drink*) soda *m*; (*us inf: father*) papa *m* ▷ *vt* (*put*) fourrer, mettre (rapidement) ▷ *vi* éclater; (*cork*) sauter; **pop in** *vi* entrer en passant; **pop out** *vi* sortir; **popcorn** *n* pop-corn *m*

pope [pəʊp] *n* pape *m*

poplar ['pɔplər] *n* peuplier *m*

popper ['pɔpər] *n* (*BRIT*) bouton-pression *m*

poppy ['pɔpɪ] *n* (*wild*) coquelicot *m*; (*cultivated*) pavot *m*

Popsicle® ['pɔpsɪkl] *n* (*us*) esquimau *m* (*glace*)

pop star *n* pop star *f*

popular ['pɔpjʊlər] *adj* populaire; (*fashionable*) à la mode; **popularity** [pɔpjʊ'lærɪtɪ] *n* popularité *f*

population [pɔpjʊ'leɪʃən] *n* population *f*

pop-up *adj* (*Comput: menu, window*) pop up *inv* ▷ *n* pop up *m inv*, fenêtre *f* pop up

porcelain ['pɔːslɪn] *n* porcelaine *f*

porch [pɔːtʃ] *n* porche *m*; (*us*) véranda *f*

pore [pɔːr] *n* pore *m* ▷ *vi*: **to ~ over** s'absorber dans, être plongé(e) dans

pork [pɔːk] *n* porc *m*; **pork chop** *n* côte *f* de porc; **pork pie** *n* pâté *m* de porc en croûte

porn [pɔːn] *adj* (*inf*) porno ▷ *n* (*inf*) porno *m*; **pornographic** [pɔːnə'græfɪk] *adj* pornographique; **pornography** [pɔː'nɔgrəfɪ] *n* pornographie *f*

porridge ['pɔrɪdʒ] *n* porridge *m*

port [pɔːt] *n* (*harbour*) port *m*; (*Naut: left side*) bâbord *m*; (*wine*) porto *m*; (*Comput*) port *m*, accès *m*; **~ of call** (port d')escale *f*

portable ['pɔːtəbl] *adj* portatif(-ive)

porter ['pɔːtər] *n* (*for luggage*) porteur *m*; (*doorkeeper*) gardien(ne); portier *m*

portfolio [pɔːt'fəʊlɪəʊ] *n* portefeuille *m*; (*of artist*) portfolio *m*

portion ['pɔːʃən] *n* portion *f*, part *f*

portrait ['pɔːtreɪt] *n* portrait *m*

portray [pɔː'treɪ] *vt* faire le portrait de; (*in writing*) dépeindre, représenter; (*subj: actor*) jouer

Portugal ['pɔːtjʊgl] *n* Portugal *m*

Portuguese [pɔːtjʊ'giːz] *adj* portugais(e) ▷ *n* (*pl inv*) Portugais(e); (*Ling*) portugais *m*

pose [pəʊz] *n* pose *f* ▷ *vi* poser; (*pretend*): **to ~ as** se faire passer pour ▷ *vt* poser; (*problem*) créer

posh [pɔʃ] *adj* (*inf*) chic *inv*

position [pə'zɪʃən] *n* position *f*; (*job, situation*) situation *f* ▷ *vt* mettre en place *or* en position

positive ['pɔzɪtɪv] *adj* positif(-ive); (*certain*) sûr(e), certain(e); (*definite*) formel(le), catégorique; **positively** *adv* (*affirmatively, enthusiastically*) de façon positive; (*inf: really*) carrément

possess [pə'zɛs] *vt* posséder; **possession** [pə'zɛʃən] *n* possession *f*; **possessions** *npl* (*belongings*) affaires *fpl*; **possessive** *adj* possessif(-ive)

possibility [pɔsɪ'bɪlɪtɪ] *n* possibilité *f*; (*event*) éventualité *f*

possible ['pɔsɪbl] *adj* possible; **as big as ~** aussi gros que possible; **possibly** *adv* (*perhaps*) peut-être; **I cannot possibly come** il m'est impossible de venir

post [pəʊst] *n* (*BRIT: mail*) poste *f*; (*: letters, delivery*) courrier *m*; (*job, situation*) poste *m*; (*pole*) poteau *m*; (*Internet*) post *m* ▷ *vt* (*Internet*) poster; (*BRIT: send by post*) poster; (*appoint*): **to ~ to** affecter à; **where can I ~ these cards?** où est-ce que je peux poster ces cartes postales?; **postage** *n* tarifs *mpl* d'affranchissement; **postal** *adj* postal(e); **postal order** *n* mandat(-poste *m*) *m*; **postbox** *n* (*BRIT*) boîte *f* aux lettres (*publique*); **postcard** *n* carte postale; **postcode** *n* (*BRIT*) code postal

P

poster ['pəustə^r] n affiche f
postgraduate ['pəust'grædjuət] n
≈ étudiant(e) de troisième cycle
postman ['pəustmən] (irreg) (BRIT)
n facteur m
postmark ['pəustma:k] n cachet m
(de la poste)
post-mortem [pəust'mɔ:təm] n
autopsie f
post office n (building) poste f;
(organization): **the Post Office** les
postes fpl
postpone [pəs'pəun] vt remettre (à
plus tard), reculer
posture ['pɒstʃə^r] n posture f; (fig)
attitude f
postwoman [pəust'wumən] (irreg)
(BRIT) n factrice f
pot [pɒt] n (for cooking) marmite f,
casserole f; (teapot) théière f; (for
coffee) cafetière f; (for plants, jam) pot
m; (inf: marijuana) herbe f ▷ vt (plant)
mettre en pot; **to go to ~** (inf) aller
à vau-l'eau
potato [pə'teɪtəu] (pl **potatoes**) n
pomme f de terre; **potato peeler** n
épluche-légumes m
potent ['pəutnt] adj puissant(e);
(drink) fort(e), très alcoolisé(e);
(man) viril
potential [pə'tɛnʃl] adj potentiel(le)
▷ n potentiel m
pothole ['pɒthəul] n (in road) nid m
de poule; (BRIT: underground) gouffre
m, caverne f
pot plant n plante f d'appartement
potter ['pɒtə^r] n potier m ▷ vi (BRIT):
to ~ around or **about** bricoler;
pottery n poterie f
potty ['pɒtɪ] n (child's) pot m
pouch [pautʃ] n (Zool) poche f; (for
tobacco) blague f; (for money) bourse f
poultry ['pəultrɪ] n volaille f
pounce [pauns] vi: **to ~ (on)** bondir
(sur), fondre (sur)
pound [paund] n livre f (weight =
453g, 16 ounces; money = 100 pence);
(for dogs, cars) fourrière f ▷ vt (beat)

bourrer de coups, marteler; (crush)
piler, pulvériser ▷ vi (heart) battre
violemment, taper; **pound sterling**
n livre f sterling
pour [pɔ:^r] vt verser ▷ vi couler à flots;
(rain) pleuvoir à verse; **to ~ sb a drink**
verser or servir à boire à qn; **pour in** vi
(people) affluer, se précipiter; (news,
letters) arriver en masse; **pour out**
vi (people) sortir en masse ▷ vt vider;
(fig) déverser; (serve: a drink) verser;
pouring adj: **pouring rain** pluie
torrentielle
pout [paut] vi faire la moue
poverty ['pɒvətɪ] n pauvreté f, misère f
powder ['paudə^r] n poudre f ▷ vt
poudrer; **powdered milk** n lait m
en poudre
power ['pauə^r] n (strength, nation)
puissance f, force f; (ability, Pol: of
party, leader) pouvoir m; (of speech,
thought) faculté f; (Elec) courant
m; **to be in ~** être au pouvoir;
power cut n (BRIT) coupure f de
courant; **power failure** n panne f de
courant; **powerful** adj puissant(e);
(performance etc) très fort(e);
powerless adj impuissant(e); **power
point** n (BRIT) prise f de courant;
power station n centrale f électrique
p.p. abbr (= per procurationem: by
proxy) p.p.
PR n abbr = **public relations**
practical ['præktɪkl] adj pratique;
practical joke n farce f; **practically**
adv (almost) pratiquement
practice ['præktɪs] n pratique f; (of
profession) exercice m; (at football etc)
entraînement m; (business) cabinet m
▷ vt, vi (US) = **practise**; **in ~** (in reality)
en pratique; **out of ~** rouillé(e)
practise, (US) **practice** ['præktɪs]
vt (work at: piano, backhand etc)
s'exercer à, travailler; (train for: sport)
s'entraîner à; (a sport, religion, method)
pratiquer; (profession) exercer ▷ vi
s'exercer, travailler; (train) s'entraîner;
(lawyer, doctor) exercer; **practising**,

(US) **practicing** adj (Christian etc) pratiquant(e); (lawyer) en exercice

practitioner [præk'tɪʃənər] n praticien(ne)

pragmatic [præg'mætɪk] adj pragmatique

prairie ['prɛərɪ] n savane f

praise [preɪz] n éloge(s) m(pl), louange(s) f(pl) ⊳ vt louer, faire l'éloge de

pram [præm] n (BRIT) landau m, voiture f d'enfant

prank [præŋk] n farce f

prawn [prɔːn] n crevette f (rose); **prawn cocktail** n cocktail m de crevettes

pray [preɪ] vi prier; **prayer** [preər] n prière f

preach [priːtʃ] vi prêcher; **preacher** n prédicateur m; (US: clergyman) pasteur m

precarious [prɪ'kɛərɪəs] adj précaire

precaution [prɪ'kɔːʃən] n précaution f

precede [prɪ'siːd] vt, vi précéder; **precedent** ['prɛsɪdənt] n précédent m; **preceding** [prɪ'siːdɪŋ] adj qui précède (or précédait)

precinct ['priːsɪŋkt] n (US: district) circonscription f, arrondissement m; **pedestrian ~** (BRIT) zone piétonnière; **shopping ~** (BRIT) centre commercial

precious ['prɛʃəs] adj précieux(-euse)

precise [prɪ'saɪs] adj précis(e); **precisely** adv précisément

precision [prɪ'sɪʒən] n précision f

predator ['prɛdətər] n prédateur m, rapace m

predecessor ['priːdɪsɛsər] n prédécesseur m

predicament [prɪ'dɪkəmənt] n situation f difficile

predict [prɪ'dɪkt] vt prédire; **predictable** adj prévisible; **prediction** [prɪ'dɪkʃən] n prédiction f

predominantly [prɪ'dɔmɪnəntlɪ] adv en majeure partie; (especially) surtout

preface ['prɛfəs] n préface f

prefect ['priːfɛkt] n (BRIT: in school) élève chargé de certaines fonctions de discipline

prefer [prɪ'fəːr] vt préférer; **preferable** ['prɛfrəbl] adj préférable; **preferably** ['prɛfrəblɪ] adv de préférence; **preference** ['prɛfrəns] n préférence f

prefix ['priːfɪks] n préfixe m

pregnancy ['prɛgnənsɪ] n grossesse f

pregnant ['prɛgnənt] adj enceinte; (animal) pleine

prehistoric ['priːhɪs'tɔrɪk] adj préhistorique

prejudice ['prɛdʒudɪs] n préjugé m; **prejudiced** adj (person) plein(e) de préjugés; (in a matter) partial(e)

preliminary [prɪ'lɪmɪnərɪ] adj préliminaire

prelude ['prɛljuːd] n prélude m

premature ['prɛmətʃuər] adj prématuré(e)

premier ['prɛmɪər] adj premier(-ière), principal(e) ⊳ n (Pol: Prime Minister) premier ministre; (Pol: President) chef m de l'État

premiere ['prɛmɪɛər] n première f

Premier League n première division

premises ['prɛmɪsɪz] npl locaux mpl; **on the ~** sur les lieux; sur place

premium ['priːmɪəm] n prime f; **to be at a ~** (fig: housing etc) être très demandé(e), être rarissime

premonition [prɛmə'nɪʃən] n prémonition f

preoccupied [priː'ɔkjupaɪd] adj préoccupé(e)

prepaid [priː'peɪd] adj payé(e) d'avance

preparation [prɛpə'reɪʃən] n préparation f; **preparations** npl (for trip, war) préparatifs mpl

preparatory school n (BRIT) école primaire privée; (US) lycée privé

prepare [prɪ'pɛər] vt préparer ⊳ vi: **to ~ for** se préparer à

P

prepared [prɪ'pɛəd] *adj*: ~ **for** préparé(e) à; ~ **to** prêt(e) à
preposition [prɛpə'zɪʃən] *n* préposition *f*
prep school *n* = **preparatory school**
prerequisite [priːˈrɛkwɪzɪt] *n* condition *f* préalable
preschool ['priːˈskuːl] *adj* préscolaire; (*child*) d'âge préscolaire
prescribe [prɪ'skraɪb] *vt* prescrire
prescription [prɪ'skrɪpʃən] *n* (*Med*) ordonnance *f* (: *medicine*) médicament *m* (obtenu sur ordonnance); **could you write me a ~?** pouvez-vous me faire une ordonnance?
presence ['prɛzns] *n* présence *f*; **in sb's ~** en présence de qn; ~ **of mind** présence d'esprit
present ['prɛznt] *adj* présent(e); (*current*) présent, actuel(le) ▷ *n* cadeau *m*; (*actuality*) présent *m* ▷ *vt* [prɪ'zɛnt] présenter; (*prize, medal*) remettre; (*give*): **to ~ sb with sth** offrir qch à qn; **at ~** en ce moment; **to give sb a ~** offrir un cadeau à qn; **presentable** [prɪ'zɛntəbl] *adj* présentable;
presentation [prɛzn'teɪʃən] *n* présentation *f*; (*ceremony*) remise *f* du cadeau (*or* de la médaille *etc*); **present-day** *adj* contemporain(e), actuel(le); **presenter** [prɪ'zɛntər] *n* (*BRIT Radio, TV*) présentateur(-trice); **presently** *adv* (*soon*) tout à l'heure, bientôt; (*with verb in past*) peu après; (*at present*) en ce moment
preservation [prɛzə'veɪʃən] *n* préservation *f*, conservation *f*
preservative [prɪ'zə:vətɪv] *n* agent *m* de conservation
preserve [prɪ'zə:v] *vt* (*keep safe*) préserver, protéger; (*maintain*) conserver, garder; (*food*) mettre en conserve ▷ *n* (*for game, fish*) réserve *f*; (*often pl: jam*) confiture *f*
preside [prɪ'zaɪd] *vi* présider
president ['prɛzɪdənt] *n* président(e); **presidential** [prɛzɪ'dɛnʃl] *adj* présidentiel(le)

press [prɛs] *n* (*tool, machine, newspapers*) presse *f*; (*for wine*) pressoir *m* ▷ *vt* (*push*) appuyer sur; (*squeeze*) presser, serrer; (*clothes: iron*) repasser; (*insist*): **to ~ sth on sb** presser qn d'accepter qch; (*urge, entreat*): **to ~ sb to do** *or* **into doing sth** pousser qn à faire qch ▷ *vi* appuyer; **we are ~ed for time** le temps nous manque; **to ~ for sth** faire pression pour obtenir qch; **press conference** *n* conférence *f* de presse; **pressing** *adj* urgent(e), pressant(e); **press stud** *n* (*BRIT*) bouton-pression *m*; **press-up** *n* (*BRIT*) traction *f*
pressure ['prɛʃər] *n* pression *f*; (*stress*) tension *f*; **to put ~ on sb (to do sth)** faire pression sur qn (pour qu'il fasse qch); **pressure cooker** *n* cocotte-minute® *f*; **pressure group** *n* groupe *m* de pression
prestige [prɛs'tiːʒ] *n* prestige *m*
prestigious [prɛs'tɪdʒəs] *adj* prestigieux(-euse)
presumably [prɪ'zjuːməblɪ] *adv* vraisemblablement
presume [prɪ'zjuːm] *vt* présumer, supposer
pretence, (*US*) **pretense** [prɪ'tɛns] *n* (*claim*) prétention *f*; **under false ~s** sous des prétextes fallacieux
pretend [prɪ'tɛnd] *vt* (*feign*) feindre, simuler ▷ *vi* (*feign*) faire semblant
pretense [prɪ'tɛns] *n* (*US*) = **pretence**
pretentious [prɪ'tɛnʃəs] *adj* prétentieux(-euse)
pretext ['priːtɛkst] *n* prétexte *m*
pretty ['prɪtɪ] *adj* joli(e) ▷ *adv* assez
prevail [prɪ'veɪl] *vi* (*win*) l'emporter, prévaloir; (*be usual*) avoir cours; **prevailing** *adj* (*widespread*) courant(e), répandu(e); (*wind*) dominant(e)
prevalent ['prɛvələnt] *adj* répandu(e), courant(e)
prevent [prɪ'vɛnt] *vt*: **to ~ (from doing)** empêcher (de faire); **prevention** [prɪ'vɛnʃən]

n prévention *f*; **preventive** *adj* préventif(-ive)

preview ['pri:vju:] *n* (*of film*) avant-première *f*

previous ['pri:vɪəs] *adj* (*last*) précédent(e); (*earlier*) antérieur(e); **previously** *adv* précédemment, auparavant

prey [preɪ] *n* proie *f* ▷ *vi*: **to ~ on** s'attaquer à; **it was ~ing on his mind** ça le rongeait or minait

price [praɪs] *n* prix *m* ▷ *vt* (*goods*) fixer le prix de; **priceless** *adj* sans prix, inestimable; **price list** *n* tarif *m*

prick [prɪk] *n* (*sting*) piqûre *f* ▷ *vt* piquer; **to ~ up one's ears** dresser or tendre l'oreille

prickly ['prɪklɪ] *adj* piquant(e), épineux(-euse); (*fig: person*) irritable

pride [praɪd] *n* fierté *f*; (*pej*) orgueil *m* ▷ *vt*: **to ~ o.s. on** se flatter de; s'enorgueillir de

priest [pri:st] *n* prêtre *m*

primarily ['praɪmərɪlɪ] *adv* principalement, essentiellement

primary ['praɪmərɪ] *adj* primaire; (*first in importance*) premier(-ière), primordial(e) ▷ *n* (*US: election*) (élection *f*) primaire *f*; **primary school** *n* (*BRIT*) école *f* primaire

prime [praɪm] *adj* primordial(e), fondamental(e); (*excellent*) excellent(e) ▷ *vt* (*fig*) mettre au courant ▷ *n*: **in the ~ of life** dans la fleur de l'âge; **Prime Minister** *n* Premier ministre

primitive ['prɪmɪtɪv] *adj* primitif(-ive)

primrose ['prɪmrəuz] *n* primevère *f*

prince [prɪns] *n* prince *m*

princess [prɪn'sɛs] *n* princesse *f*

principal ['prɪnsɪpl] *adj* principal(e) ▷ *n* (*head teacher*) directeur *m*, principal *m*; **principally** *adv* principalement

principle ['prɪnsɪpl] *n* principe *m*; **in ~** en principe; **on ~** par principe

print [prɪnt] *n* (*mark*) empreinte *f*; (*letters*) caractères *mpl*; (*fabric*) imprimé *m*; (*Art*) gravure *f*, estampe *f*; (*Phot*) épreuve *f* ▷ *vt* imprimer; (*publish*) publier; (*write in capitals*) écrire en majuscules; **out of ~** épuisé(e); **print out** *vt* (*Comput*) imprimer; **printer** *n* (*machine*) imprimante *f*; (*person*) imprimeur *m*; **printout** *n* (*Comput*) sortie *f* imprimante

prior ['praɪə*ʳ*] *adj* antérieur(e), précédent(e); (*more important*) prioritaire ▷ *adv*: **~ to doing** avant de faire

priority [praɪ'ɔrɪtɪ] *n* priorité *f*; **to have** or **take ~ over sth/sb** avoir la priorité sur qch/qn

prison ['prɪzn] *n* prison *f* ▷ *cpd* pénitentiaire; **prisoner** *n* prisonnier(-ière); **prisoner of war** *n* prisonnier(-ière) de guerre

pristine ['prɪsti:n] *adj* virginal(e)

privacy ['prɪvəsɪ] *n* intimité *f*, solitude *f*

private ['praɪvɪt] *adj* (*not public*) privé(e); (*personal*) personnel(le); (*house, car, lesson*) particulier(-ière); (*quiet: place*) tranquille ▷ *n* soldat *m* de deuxième classe; **"~"** (*on envelope*) "personnelle"; (*on door*) "privé"; **in ~** en privé; **privately** *adv* en privé; (*within oneself*) intérieurement; **private property** *n* propriété privée; **private school** *n* école privée

privatize ['praɪvɪtaɪz] *vt* privatiser

privilege ['prɪvɪlɪdʒ] *n* privilège *m*

prize [praɪz] *n* prix *m* ▷ *adj* (*example, idiot*) parfait(e); (*bull, novel*) primé(e) ▷ *vt* priser, faire grand cas de; **prize-giving** *n* distribution *f* des prix; **prizewinner** *n* gagnant(e)

pro [prəu] *n* (*inf: Sport*) professionnel(le) ▷ *prep* pro; **pros** *npl*; **the ~s and cons** le pour et le contre

probability [prɔbə'bɪlɪtɪ] *n* probabilité *f*; **in all ~** très probablement

probable ['prɔbəbl] *adj* probable

probably ['prɔbəblɪ] *adv* probablement

P

probation [prə'beɪʃən] n: **on ~**
(employee) à l'essai; (Law) en liberté
surveillée
probe [prəub] n (Med, Space) sonde
f; (enquiry) enquête f, investigation f
▷ vt sonder, explorer
problem ['prɔbləm] n problème m
procedure [prə'si:dʒəʳ] n (Admin,
Law) procédure f; (method) marche f à
suivre, façon f de procéder
proceed [prə'si:d] vi (go forward)
avancer; (act) procéder; (continue):
to ~ (with) continuer, poursuivre;
to ~ to do se mettre à faire;
proceedings npl (measures) mesures
fpl; (Law: against sb) poursuites fpl;
(meeting) réunion f, séance f; (records)
compte rendu; actes mpl; **proceeds**
['prəusi:dz] npl produit m, recette f
process ['prəusɛs] n processus m;
(method) procédé m ▷ vt traiter
procession [prə'sɛʃən] n défilé
m, cortège m; **funeral ~** (on foot)
cortège funèbre; (in cars) convoi m
mortuaire
proclaim [prə'kleɪm] vt déclarer,
proclamer
prod [prɔd] vt pousser
produce n ['prɔdju:s] (Agr) produits
mpl ▷ vt [prə'dju:s] produire; (show)
présenter; (cause) provoquer, causer;
(Theat) monter, mettre en scène;
(TV: programme) réaliser; (: play, film)
mettre en scène; (Radio: programme)
réaliser; (: play) mettre en ondes;
producer n (Theat) metteur m en
scène; (Agr, Comm, Cine) producteur
m; (TV: of programme) réalisateur
m; (: of play, film) metteur en scène;
(Radio: of programme) réalisateur; (: of
play) metteur en ondes
product ['prɔdʌkt] n produit
m; **production** [prə'dʌkʃən] n
production f; (Theat) mise f en
scène; **productive** [prə'dʌktɪv]
adj productif(-ive); **productivity**
[prɔdʌk'tɪvɪtɪ] n productivité f
Prof. [prɔf] abbr (= professor) Prof

profession [prə'fɛʃən] n profession
f; **professional** n professionnel(le)
▷ adj professionnel(le); (work) de
professionnel
professor [prə'fɛsəʳ] n professeur
m (titulaire d'une chaire); (us: teacher)
professeur m
profile ['prəufaɪl] n profil m
profit ['prɔfɪt] n (from trading)
bénéfice m; (advantage) profit m
▷ vi: **to ~ (by or from)** profiter (de);
profitable adj lucratif(-ive), rentable
profound [prə'faund] adj profond(e)
programme, (us) **program**
['prəugræm] n (Comput)
programme m; (Radio, TV) émission
f ▷ vt programmer; **programmer**
n programmeur(-euse);
programming, (us) **programing** n
programmation f
progress n ['prəugrɛs] progrès m(pl)
▷ vi [prə'grɛs] progresser, avancer; **in
~** en cours; **progressive** [prə'grɛsɪv]
adj progressif(-ive); (person)
progressiste
prohibit [prə'hɪbɪt] vt interdire,
défendre
project n ['prɔdʒɛkt] (plan) projet
m, plan m; (venture) opération f,
entreprise f; (Scol: research) étude f,
dossier m ▷ vt [prə'dʒɛkt] projeter
▷ vi [prə'dʒɛkt] (stick out) faire saillie,
s'avancer; **projection** [prə'dʒɛkʃən]
n projection f; (overhang) saillie
f; **projector** [prə'dʒɛktəʳ] n
projecteur m
prolific [prə'lɪfɪk] adj prolifique
prolong [prə'lɔŋ] vt prolonger
prom [prɔm] n abbr = **promenade**;
(us: ball) bal m d'étudiants; **the P~s**
série de concerts de musique classique

● **PROM**
●
●
● En Grande-Bretagne, un promenade
● concert ou prom est un concert de
● musique classique, ainsi appelé
● car, à l'origine, le public restait

debout et se promenait au lieu de rester assis. De nos jours, une partie du public reste debout, mais il y a également des places assises (plus chères). Les *Proms* les plus connus sont les Proms londoniens. La dernière séance (the "Last Night of the Proms") est un grand événement médiatique où se jouent des airs traditionnels et patriotiques. Aux États-Unis et au Canada, le *prom* ou *promenade* est un bal organisé par le lycée.

promenade [prɔmə'nɑːd] *n* (*by sea*) esplanade *f*, promenade *f*

prominent ['prɔmɪnənt] *adj* (*standing out*) proéminent(e); (*important*) important(e)

promiscuous [prə'mɪskjuəs] *adj* (*sexually*) de mœurs légères

promise ['prɔmɪs] *n* promesse *f* ▷ *vt, vi* promettre; **promising** *adj* prometteur(-euse)

promote [prə'məut] *vt* promouvoir; (*new product*) lancer; **promotion** [prə'məuʃən] *n* promotion *f*

prompt [prɔmpt] *adj* rapide ▷ *n* (*Comput*) message *m* (de guidage) ▷ *vt* (*cause*) entraîner, provoquer; (*Theat*) souffler (son rôle *or* ses répliques) à; **at 8 o'clock ~** à 8 heures précises; **to ~ sb to do** inciter *or* pousser qn à faire; **promptly** *adv* (*quickly*) rapidement, sans délai; (*on time*) ponctuellement

prone [prəun] *adj* (*lying*) couché(e) (face contre terre); (*liable*): **~ to** enclin(e) à

prong [prɔŋ] *n* (*of fork*) dent *f*

pronoun ['prəunaun] *n* pronom *m*

pronounce [prə'nauns] *vt* prononcer; **how do you ~ it?** comment est-ce que ça se prononce?

pronunciation [prənʌnsɪ'eɪʃən] *n* prononciation *f*

proof [pruːf] *n* preuve *f* ▷ *adj*: **~ against** à l'épreuve de

prop [prɔp] *n* support *m*, étai *m*; (*fig*) soutien *m* ▷ *vt* (*also*: **~ up**) étayer, soutenir; **props** *npl* accessoires *mpl*

propaganda [prɔpə'gændə] *n* propagande *f*

propeller [prə'pɛləʳ] *n* hélice *f*

proper ['prɔpəʳ] *adj* (*suited, right*) approprié(e), bon (bonne); (*seemly*) correct(e), convenable; (*authentic*) vrai(e), véritable; (*referring to place*): **the village ~** le village proprement dit; **properly** *adv* correctement, convenablement; **proper noun** *n* nom *m* propre

property ['prɔpətɪ] *n* (*possessions*) biens *mpl*; (*house etc*) propriété *f*; (*land*) terres *fpl*, domaine *m*

prophecy ['prɔfɪsɪ] *n* prophétie *f*

prophet ['prɔfɪt] *n* prophète *m*

proportion [prə'pɔːʃən] *n* proportion *f*; (*share*) part *f*; partie *f*; **proportions** *npl* (*size*) dimensions *fpl*; **proportional, proportionate** *adj* proportionnel(le)

proposal [prə'pəuzl] *n* proposition *f*, offre *f*; (*plan*) projet *m*; (*of marriage*) demande *f* en mariage

propose [prə'pəuz] *vt* proposer, suggérer ▷ *vi* faire sa demande en mariage; **to ~ to do** avoir l'intention de faire

proposition [prɔpə'zɪʃən] *n* proposition *f*

proprietor [prə'praɪətəʳ] *n* propriétaire *m/f*

prose [prəuz] *n* prose *f*; (*Scol: translation*) thème *m*

prosecute ['prɔsɪkjuːt] *vt* poursuivre; **prosecution** [prɔsɪ'kjuːʃən] *n* poursuites *fpl* judiciaires; (*accusing side: in criminal case*) accusation *f*; (: *in civil case*) la partie plaignante; **prosecutor** *n* (*lawyer*) procureur *m*; (*also*: **public prosecutor**) ministère public; (*us: plaintiff*) plaignant(e)

prospect *n* ['prɔspɛkt] perspective *f*; (*hope*) espoir *m*, chances *fpl* ▷ *vt, vi*

P

[prə'spɛkt] prospecter; **prospects** npl (for work etc) possibilités fpl d'avenir, débouchés mpl; **prospective** [prə'spɛktɪv] adj (possible) éventuel(le); (future) futur(e)

prospectus [prə'spɛktəs] n prospectus m

prosper ['prɔspər] vi prospérer; **prosperity** [prɔ'spɛrɪtɪ] n prospérité f; **prosperous** adj prospère

prostitute ['prɔstɪtjuːt] n prostituée f; **male ~** prostitué m

protect [prə'tɛkt] vt protéger; **protection** [prə'tɛkʃən] n protection f; **protective** adj protecteur(-trice); (clothing) de protection

protein ['prəutiːn] n protéine f

protest n ['prəutɛst] protestation f ▷ vi [prə'tɛst]: **to ~ against/about** protester contre/à propos de; **to ~ (that)** protester que

Protestant ['prɔtɪstənt] adj, n protestant(e)

protester, protestor [prə'tɛstər] n (in demonstration) manifestant(e)

protractor [prə'træktər] n (Geom) rapporteur m

proud [praud] adj fier(-ère); (pej) orgueilleux(-euse)

prove [pruːv] vt prouver, démontrer ▷ vi: **to ~ correct** etc s'avérer juste etc; **to ~ o.s.** montrer ce dont on est capable

proverb ['prɔvəːb] n proverbe m

provide [prə'vaɪd] vt fournir; **to ~ sb with sth** fournir qch à qn; **provide for** vt fus (person) subvenir aux besoins de; (future event) prévoir; **provided** conj: **provided (that)** à condition que + sub; **providing** [prə'vaɪdɪŋ] conj à condition que + sub

province ['prɔvɪns] n province f; (fig) domaine m; **provincial** [prə'vɪnʃəl] adj provincial(e)

provision [prə'vɪʒən] n (supplying) fourniture f; approvisionnement m; (stipulation) disposition f; **provisions**

npl (food) provisions fpl; **provisional** adj provisoire

provocative [prə'vɔkətɪv] adj provocateur(-trice), provocant(e)

provoke [prə'vəuk] vt provoquer

prowl [praul] vi (also: **~ about, ~ around**) rôder

proximity [prɔk'sɪmɪtɪ] n proximité f

proxy ['prɔksɪ] n: **by ~** par procuration

prudent ['pruːdnt] adj prudent(e)

prune [pruːn] n pruneau m ▷ vt élaguer

pry [praɪ] vi: **to ~ into** fourrer son nez dans

PS n abbr (= postscript) PS m

pseudonym ['sjuːdənɪm] n pseudonyme m

PSHE n abbr (BRIT Scol: = personal, social and health education) cours d'éducation personnelle, sanitaire et sociale préparant à la vie adulte

psychiatric [saɪkɪ'ætrɪk] adj psychiatrique

psychiatrist [saɪ'kaɪətrɪst] n psychiatre m/f

psychic ['saɪkɪk] adj (also: **~al**) (méta)psychique; (person) doué(e) de télépathie or d'un sixième sens

psychoanalysis (pl **psychoanalyses**) [saɪkəuə'nælɪsɪs, -siːz] n psychanalyse f

psychological [saɪkə'lɔdʒɪkl] adj psychologique

psychologist [saɪ'kɔlədʒɪst] n psychologue m/f

psychology [saɪ'kɔlədʒɪ] n psychologie f

psychotherapy [saɪkəu'θɛrəpɪ] n psychothérapie f

pt abbr = **pint; pints; point; points**

PTO abbr (= please turn over) TSVP

PTV abbr (US) = **pay television**

pub [pʌb] n abbr (= public house) pub m

puberty ['pjuːbətɪ] n puberté f

public ['pʌblɪk] adj public(-ique) ▷ n public m; **in ~** en public; **to make ~** rendre public

publication [pʌblɪ'keɪʃən] n
publication f
public: public company n société
f anonyme; **public convenience** n
(BRIT) toilettes fpl; **public holiday**
n (BRIT) jour férié; **public house** n
(BRIT) pub m
publicity [pʌb'lɪsɪtɪ] n publicité f
publicize ['pʌblɪsaɪz] vt (make
known) faire connaître, rendre
public; (advertise) faire de la publicité
pour
public: public limited company n
≈ société f anonyme (SA) (cotée en
Bourse); **publicly** adv publiquement,
en public; **public opinion** n opinion
publique; **public relations** n or npl
relations publiques (RP); **public
school** n (BRIT) école privée; (US)
école publique; **public transport**,
(US) **public transportation** n
transports mpl en commun
publish ['pʌblɪʃ] vt publier; **publisher**
n éditeur m; **publishing** n (industry)
édition f
pub lunch n repas m de bistrot
pudding ['pudɪŋ] n (BRIT: dessert)
dessert m, entremets m; (sweet dish)
pudding m, gâteau m
puddle ['pʌdl] n flaque f d'eau
puff [pʌf] n bouffée f ▷ vt (also: ~
out: sails, cheeks) gonfler ▷ vi (pant)
haleter; **puff pastry**, (US) **puff paste**
n pâte feuilletée
pull [pul] n (tug): **to give sth a ~** tirer
sur qch ▷ vt tirer; (trigger) presser;
(strain: muscle, tendon) se claquer
▷ vi tirer; **to ~ to pieces** mettre en
morceaux; **to ~ one's punches**
(also fig) ménager son adversaire;
to ~ one's weight y mettre du sien;
to ~ o.s. together se ressaisir; **to
~ sb's leg** (fig) faire marcher qn;
pull apart vt (break) mettre en
pièces, démantibuler; **pull away** vi
(vehicle: move off) partir; (draw back)
s'éloigner; **pull back** vt (lever etc)
tirer sur; (curtains) ouvrir ▷ vi (refrain)

s'abstenir; (Mil: withdraw) se retirer;
pull down vt baisser, abaisser;
(house) démolir; **pull in** vi (Aut) se
ranger; (Rail) entrer en gare; **pull off**
vt enlever, ôter; (deal etc) conclure;
pull out vi démarrer, partir; (Aut:
come out of line) déboîter ▷ vt (from
bag, pocket) sortir; (remove) arracher;
pull over vi (Aut) se ranger; **pull up** vi
(stop) s'arrêter ▷ vt remonter; (uproot)
déraciner, arracher
pulley ['pulɪ] n poulie f
pullover ['puləuvər] n pull-over m,
tricot m
pulp [pʌlp] n (of fruit) pulpe f; (for
paper) pâte f à papier
pulpit ['pulpɪt] n chaire f
pulse [pʌls] n (of blood) pouls m; (of
heart) battement m; **pulses** npl (Culin)
légumineuses fpl
puma ['pjuːmə] n puma m
pump [pʌmp] n pompe f; (shoe)
escarpin m ▷ vt pomper; **pump up**
vt gonfler
pumpkin ['pʌmpkɪn] n potiron m,
citrouille f
pun [pʌn] n jeu m de mots,
calembour m
punch [pʌntʃ] n (blow) coup m de
poing; (tool) poinçon m; (drink) punch
m ▷ vt (make a hole in) poinçonner,
perforer; (hit): **to ~ sb/sth** donner un
coup de poing à qn/sur qch; **punch-
up** n (BRIT inf) bagarre f
punctual ['pʌŋktjuəl] adj
ponctuel(le)
punctuation [pʌŋktju'eɪʃən] n
ponctuation f
puncture ['pʌŋktʃər] n (BRIT)
crevaison f ▷ vt crever
punish ['pʌnɪʃ] vt punir; **punishment**
n punition f, châtiment m
punk [pʌŋk] n (person: also: ~ **rocker**)
punk m/f; (music: also: ~ **rock**) le
punk; (US inf: hoodlum) voyou m
pup [pʌp] n chiot m
pupil ['pjuːpl] n élève m/f; (of eye)
pupille f

P

puppet ['pʌpɪt] n marionnette f, pantin m
puppy ['pʌpɪ] n chiot m, petit chien
purchase ['pəːtʃɪs] n achat m ▷ vt acheter
pure [pjuəʳ] adj pur(e); **purely** adv purement
purify ['pjuərɪfaɪ] vt purifier, épurer
purity ['pjuərɪtɪ] n pureté f
purple ['pəːpl] adj violet(te); (face) cramoisi(e)
purpose ['pəːpəs] n intention f, but m; **on ~** exprès
purr [pəːʳ] vi ronronner
purse [pəːs] n (BRIT: for money) porte-monnaie m inv; (US: handbag) sac m (à main) ▷ vt serrer, pincer
pursue [pə'sjuː] vt poursuivre
pursuit [pə'sjuːt] n poursuite f; (occupation) occupation f, activité f
pus [pʌs] n pus m
push [puʃ] n poussée f ▷ vt pousser; (button) appuyer sur; (fig: product) mettre en avant, faire de la publicité pour ▷ vi pousser; **to ~ for** (better pay, conditions) réclamer; **push in** vi s'introduire de force; **push off** vi (inf) filer, ficher le camp; **push on** vi (continue) continuer; **push over** vt renverser; **push through** vt (in crowd) se frayer un chemin; **pushchair** n (BRIT) poussette f; **pusher** n (also: **drug pusher**) revendeur(-euse) (de drogue), ravitailleur(-euse) (en drogue); **push-up** n (US) traction f
pussy(-cat) ['pusɪ-] n (inf) minet m
put (pt, pp **put**) [put] vt mettre; (place) poser, placer; (say) dire, exprimer; (a question) poser; (case, view) exposer, présenter; (estimate) estimer; **put aside** vt mettre de côté; **put away** vt (store) ranger; **put back** vt (replace) remettre, replacer; (postpone) remettre; **put by** vt (money) mettre de côté, économiser; **put down** vt (parcel etc) poser, déposer; (in writing) mettre par écrit, inscrire; (suppress: revolt etc) réprimer, écraser; (attribute)

attribuer; (animal) abattre; (cat, dog) faire piquer; **put forward** vt (ideas) avancer, proposer; **put in** vt (complaint) soumettre; (time, effort) consacrer; **put off** vt (postpone) remettre à plus tard, ajourner; (discourage) dissuader; **put on** vt (clothes, lipstick, CD) mettre; (light etc) allumer; (play etc) monter; (weight) prendre; (assume: accent, manner) prendre; **put out** vt (take outside) mettre dehors; (one's hand) tendre; (light etc) éteindre; (person: inconvenience) déranger, gêner; **put through** vt (Tel: caller) mettre en communication; (: call) passer; (plan) faire accepter; **put together** vt mettre ensemble; (assemble: furniture) monter, assembler; (: meal) préparer; **put up** vt (raise) lever, relever, remonter; (hang) accrocher; (build) construire, ériger; (increase) augmenter; (accommodate) loger; **put up with** vt fus supporter
putt [pʌt] n putt m; **putting green** n green m
puzzle ['pʌzl] n énigme f, mystère m; (game) jeu m, casse-tête m; (jigsaw) puzzle m; (also: **crossword ~**) mots croisés ▷ vt intriguer, rendre perplexe ▷ vi: **to ~ over** chercher à comprendre; **puzzled** adj perplexe; **puzzling** adj déconcertant(e), inexplicable
pyjamas [pɪ'dʒɑːməz] npl (BRIT) pyjama m
pylon ['paɪlən] n pylône m
pyramid ['pɪrəmɪd] n pyramide f
Pyrenees [pɪrə'niːz] npl Pyrénées fpl

q

quack [kwæk] n (of duck) coin-coin m inv; (pej: doctor) charlatan m

quadruple [kwɔ'druːpl] vt, vi quadrupler

quail [kweɪl] n (Zool) caille f ▷ vi: **to ~ at** or **before** reculer devant

quaint [kweɪnt] adj bizarre; (old-fashioned) désuet(-ète); (picturesque) au charme vieillot, pittoresque

quake [kweɪk] vi trembler ▷ n abbr = **earthquake**

qualification [kwɔlɪfɪ'keɪʃən] n (often pl: degree etc) diplôme m; (training) qualification(s) f(pl); (ability) compétence(s) f(pl); (limitation) réserve f, restriction f

qualified ['kwɔlɪfaɪd] adj (trained) qualifié(e); (professionally) diplômé(e); (fit, competent) compétent(e), qualifié(e); (limited) conditionnel(le)

qualify ['kwɔlɪfaɪ] vt qualifier; (modify) atténuer, nuancer ▷ vi: **to ~ (as)** obtenir son diplôme (de); **to ~ (for)** remplir les conditions requises (pour); (Sport) se qualifier (pour)

quality ['kwɔlɪtɪ] n qualité f

qualm [kwɑːm] n doute m; scrupule m

quantify ['kwɔntɪfaɪ] vt quantifier

quantity ['kwɔntɪtɪ] n quantité f

quarantine ['kwɔrntiːn] n quarantaine f

quarrel ['kwɔrl] n querelle f, dispute f ▷ vi se disputer, se quereller

quarry ['kwɔrɪ] n (for stone) carrière f; (animal) proie f, gibier m

quart [kwɔːt] n ≈ litre m

quarter ['kwɔːtər] n quart m; (of year) trimestre m; (district) quartier m; (US, CANADA: 25 cents) (pièce f de) vingt-cinq cents mpl ▷ vt partager en quartiers or en quatre; (Mil) caserner, cantonner; **quarters** npl logement m; (Mil) quartiers mpl, cantonnement m; **a ~ of an hour** un quart d'heure; **quarter final** n quart m de finale; **quarterly** adj trimestriel(le) ▷ adv tous les trois mois

quartet(te) [kwɔː'tɛt] n quatuor m; (jazz players) quartette m

quartz [kwɔːts] n quartz m

quay [kiː] n (also: ~side) quai m

queasy ['kwiːzɪ] adj: **to feel ~** avoir mal au cœur

Quebec [kwɪ'bɛk] n (city) Québec; (province) Québec m

queen [kwiːn] n (gen) reine f; (Cards etc) dame f

queer [kwɪər] adj étrange, curieux(-euse); (suspicious) louche ▷ n (offensive) homosexuel m

quench [kwɛntʃ] vt: **to ~ one's thirst** se désaltérer

query ['kwɪərɪ] n question f ▷ vt (disagree with, dispute) mettre en doute, questionner

quest [kwɛst] n recherche f, quête f

question ['kwɛstʃən] n question f ▷ vt (person) interroger; (plan, idea) mettre en question or en doute; **beyond ~** sans aucun doute; **out of the ~** hors de

question; **questionable** *adj* discutable; **question mark** *n* point *m* d'interrogation; **questionnaire** [kwɛstʃə'nɛər] *n* questionnaire *m*

queue [kju:] (BRIT) *n* queue *f*, file *f* ▷ *vi* (*also*: **~ up**) faire la queue

quiche [ki:ʃ] *n* quiche *f*

quick [kwɪk] *adj* rapide; (*mind*) vif (vive); (*agile*) agile, vif (vive) ▷ *n*: **cut to the ~** (*fig*) touché(e) au vif; **be ~!** dépêche-toi!; **quickly** *adv* (*fast*) vite, rapidement; (*immediately*) tout de suite

quid [kwɪd] *n* (*pl inv*: BRIT *inf*) livre *f*

quiet ['kwaɪət] *adj* tranquille, calme; (*voice*) bas(se); (*ceremony, colour*) discret(-ète) ▷ *n* tranquillité *f*, calme *m*; (*silence*) silence *m*; **quietly** *adv* tranquillement; (*silently*) silencieusement; (*discreetly*) discrètement

quilt [kwɪlt] *n* édredon *m*; (*continental quilt*) couette *f*

quirky ['kwɜ:kɪ] *adj* singulier(-ère)

quit [kwɪt] (*pt, pp* **quit** *or* **quitted**) *vt* quitter ▷ *vi* (*give up*) abandonner, renoncer; (*resign*) démissionner

quite [kwaɪt] *adv* (*rather*) assez, plutôt; (*entirely*) complètement, tout à fait; **~ a few of them** un assez grand nombre d'entre eux; **that's not ~ right** ce n'est pas tout à fait juste; **~ (so)!** exactement!

quits [kwɪts] *adj*: **~ (with)** quitte (envers); **let's call it ~** restons-en là

quiver ['kwɪvər] *vi* trembler, frémir

quiz [kwɪz] *n* (*on TV*) jeu-concours *m* (télévisé); (*in magazine etc*) test *m* de connaissances ▷ *vt* interroger

quota ['kwəʊtə] *n* quota *m*

quotation [kwəʊ'teɪʃən] *n* citation *f*; (*estimate*) devis *m*; **quotation marks** *npl* guillemets *mpl*

quote [kwəʊt] *n* citation *f*; (*estimate*) devis *m* ▷ *vt* (*sentence, author*) citer; (*price*) donner, soumettre ▷ *vi*: **to ~ from** citer; **quotes** *npl* (*inverted commas*) guillemets *mpl*

rabbi ['ræbaɪ] *n* rabbin *m*

rabbit ['ræbɪt] *n* lapin *m*

rabies ['reɪbi:z] *n* rage *f*

RAC *n abbr* (BRIT: = *Royal Automobile Club*) ≈ ACF *m*

rac(c)oon [rə'ku:n] *n* raton *m* laveur

race [reɪs] *n* (*species*) race *f*; (*competition, rush*) course *f* ▷ *vt* (*person*) faire la course avec ▷ *vi* (*compete*) faire la course, courir; (*pulse*) battre très vite; **race car** *n* (US) = **racing car**; **racecourse** *n* champ *m* de courses; **racehorse** *n* cheval *m* de course; **racetrack** *n* piste *f*

racial ['reɪʃl] *adj* racial(e)

racing ['reɪsɪŋ] *n* courses *fpl*; **racing car** *n* (BRIT) voiture *f* de course; **racing driver** *n* (BRIT) pilote *m* de course

racism ['reɪsɪzəm] *n* racisme *m*; **racist** ['reɪsɪst] *adj*, *n* raciste *m/f*

rack [ræk] *n* (*for guns, tools*) râtelier *m*; (*for clothes*) portant *m*; (*for bottles*) casier m; (also: **luggage ~**) filet m à bagages; (also: **roof ~**) galerie f; (also: **dish ~**) égouttoir m ▷ vt tourmenter; **to ~ one's brains** se creuser la cervelle

racket ['rækɪt] n (for tennis) raquette f; (noise) tapage m, vacarme m; (swindle) escroquerie f

racquet ['rækɪt] n raquette f

radar ['reɪdɑːʳ] n radar m

radiation [reɪdɪ'eɪʃən] n rayonnement m; (radioactive) radiation f

radiator ['reɪdɪeɪtəʳ] n radiateur m

radical ['rædɪkl] adj radical(e)

radio ['reɪdɪəu] n radio f ▷ vt (person) appeler par radio; **on the ~** à la radio; **radioactive** adj radioactif(-ive); **radio station** n station f de radio

radish ['rædɪʃ] n radis m

RAF n abbr (BRIT) = **Royal Air Force**

raffle ['ræfl] n tombola f

raft [rɑːft] n (craft: also: **life ~**) radeau m; (logs) train m de flottage

rag [ræg] n chiffon m; (pej: newspaper) feuille f, torchon m; (for charity) attractions organisées par les étudiants au profit d'œuvres de charité; **rags** npl haillons mpl

rage [reɪdʒ] n (fury) rage f, fureur f ▷ vi (person) être fou (folle) de rage; (storm) faire rage, être déchaîné(e); **it's all the ~** cela fait fureur

ragged ['rægɪd] adj (edge) inégal(e), qui accroche; (clothes) en loques; (appearance) déguenillé(e)

raid [reɪd] n (Mil) raid m; (criminal) hold-up m inv; (by police) descente f, rafle f ▷ vt faire un raid sur or un hold-up dans or une descente dans

rail [reɪl] n (on stair) rampe f; (on bridge, balcony) balustrade f; (of ship) bastingage m; (for train) rail m; **railcard** n (BRIT) carte f de chemin de fer; **railing(s)** n(pl) grille f; **railway**, (US) **railroad** n chemin m de fer; (track) voie f ferrée; **railway line** n (BRIT) ligne f de chemin de fer; (track)

voie ferrée; **railway station** n (BRIT) gare f

rain [reɪn] n pluie f ▷ vi pleuvoir; **in the ~** sous la pluie; **it's ~ing** il pleut; **rainbow** n arc-en-ciel m; **raincoat** n imperméable m; **raindrop** n goutte f de pluie; **rainfall** n chute f de pluie; (measurement) hauteur f des précipitations; **rainforest** n forêt tropicale; **rainy** adj pluvieux(-euse)

raise [reɪz] n augmentation f ▷ vt (lift) lever; hausser; (increase) augmenter; (morale) remonter; (standards) améliorer; (a protest, doubt) provoquer, causer; (a question) soulever; (cattle, family) élever; (crop) faire pousser; (army, funds) rassembler; (loan) obtenir; **to ~ one's voice** élever la voix

raisin ['reɪzn] n raisin sec

rake [reɪk] n (tool) râteau m; (person) débauché m ▷ vt (garden) ratisser

rally ['rælɪ] n (Pol etc) meeting m, rassemblement m; (Aut) rallye m; (Tennis) échange m ▷ vt rassembler, rallier; (support) gagner ▷ vi (sick person) aller mieux; (Stock Exchange) reprendre

RAM [ræm] n abbr (Comput: = random access memory) mémoire vive

ram [ræm] n bélier m ▷ vt (push) enfoncer; (crash into: vehicle) emboutir; (: lamppost etc) percuter

Ramadan [ræmə'dæn] n Ramadan m

ramble ['ræmbl] n randonnée f ▷ vi (walk) se promener, faire une randonnée; (pej: also: **~ on**) discourir, pérorer; **rambler** n promeneur(-euse), randonneur(-euse); **rambling** adj (speech) décousu(e); (house) plein(e) de coins et de recoins; (Bot) grimpant(e)

ramp [ræmp] n (incline) rampe f; (Aut) dénivellation f; (in garage) pont m; **on/off ~** (US Aut) bretelle f d'accès

rampage ['ræmpeɪdʒ] n: **to be on the ~** se déchaîner

r

ran [ræn] *pt of* **run**

ranch [rɑːntʃ] *n* ranch *m*

random ['rændəm] *adj* fait(e) or établi(e) au hasard; (*Comput, Math*) aléatoire ▷ *n*: **at ~** au hasard

rang [ræŋ] *pt of* **ring**

range [reɪndʒ] *n* (*of mountains*) chaîne *f*; (*of missile, voice*) portée *f*; (*of products*) choix *m*, gamme *f*; (*also*: **shooting ~**) champ *m* de tir; (*also*: **kitchen ~**) fourneau *m* (de cuisine) ▷ *vt* (*place*) mettre en rang, placer ▷ *vi*: **to ~ over** couvrir; **to ~ from ... to** aller de ... à

ranger ['reɪndʒəʳ] *n* garde *m* forestier

rank [ræŋk] *n* rang *m*; (*Mil*) grade *m*; (*BRIT: also*: **taxi ~**) station *f* de taxis ▷ *vi*: **to ~ among** compter or se classer parmi ▷ *adj* (*smell*) nauséabond(e); **the ~ and file** (*fig*) la masse, la base

ransom ['rænsəm] *n* rançon *f*; **to hold sb to ~** (*fig*) exercer un chantage sur qn

rant [rænt] *vi* fulminer

rap [ræp] *n* (*music*) rap *m* ▷ *vt* (*door*) frapper sur or à; (*table etc*) taper sur

rape [reɪp] *n* viol *m*; (*Bot*) colza *m* ▷ *vt* violer

rapid ['ræpɪd] *adj* rapide; **rapidly** *adv* rapidement; **rapids** *npl* (*Geo*) rapides *mpl*

rapist ['reɪpɪst] *n* auteur *m* d'un viol

rapport [ræ'pɔːʳ] *n* entente *f*

rare [rɛəʳ] *adj* rare; (*Culin: steak*) saignant(e); **rarely** *adv* rarement

rash [ræʃ] *adj* imprudent(e), irréfléchi(e) ▷ *n* (*Med*) rougeur *f*, éruption *f*; (*of events*) série *f* (noire)

rasher ['ræʃəʳ] *n* fine tranche (de lard)

raspberry ['rɑːzbərɪ] *n* framboise *f*

rat [ræt] *n* rat *m*

rate [reɪt] *n* (*ratio*) taux *m*, pourcentage *m*; (*speed*) vitesse *f*, rythme *m*; (*price*) tarif *m* ▷ *vt* (*price*) évaluer, estimer; (*people*) classer; **rates** *npl* (*BRIT: property tax*) impôts

locaux; **to ~ sb/sth as** considérer qn/qch comme

rather ['rɑːðəʳ] *adv* (*somewhat*) assez, plutôt; (*to some extent*) un peu; **it's ~ expensive** c'est assez cher; (*too much*) c'est un peu cher; **there's ~ a lot** il y en a beaucoup; **I would** or **I'd ~ go** j'aimerais mieux or je préférerais partir; **or ~** (*more accurately*) ou plutôt

rating ['reɪtɪŋ] *n* (*assessment*) évaluation *f*; (*score*) classement *m*; (*Finance*) cote *f*; **ratings** *npl* (*Radio*) indice(s) *m(pl)* d'écoute; (*TV*) Audimat® *m*

ratio ['reɪʃɪəu] *n* proportion *f*; **in the ~ of 100 to 1** dans la proportion de 100 contre 1

ration ['ræʃən] *n* ration *f* ▷ *vt* rationner; **rations** *npl* (*food*) vivres *mpl*

rational ['ræʃənl] *adj* raisonnable, sensé(e); (*solution, reasoning*) logique; (*Med: person*) lucide

rat race *n* foire *f* d'empoigne

rattle ['rætl] *n* (*of door, window*) battement *m*; (*of coins, chain*) cliquetis *m*; (*of train, engine*) bruit *m* de ferraille; (*for baby*) hochet *m* ▷ *vi* cliqueter; (*car, bus*): **to ~ along** rouler en faisant un bruit de ferraille ▷ *vt* agiter (bruyamment); (*inf: disconcert*) décontenancer

rave [reɪv] *vi* (*in anger*) s'emporter; (*with enthusiasm*) s'extasier; (*Med*) délirer ▷ *n* (*inf: party*) rave *f*, soirée *f* techno

raven ['reɪvən] *n* grand corbeau

ravine [rə'viːn] *n* ravin *m*

raw [rɔː] *adj* (*uncooked*) cru(e); (*not processed*) brut(e); (*sore*) à vif, irrité(e); (*inexperienced*) inexpérimenté(e); **~ materials** matières premières

ray [reɪ] *n* rayon *m*; **~ of hope** lueur *f* d'espoir

razor ['reɪzəʳ] *n* rasoir *m*; **razor blade** *n* lame *f* de rasoir

Rd *abbr* = **road**

RE n abbr (BRIT: = religious education) instruction religieuse

re [ri:] prep concernant

reach [ri:tʃ] n portée f, atteinte f; (of river etc) étendue f ▷ vt atteindre, arriver à; (conclusion, decision) parvenir à ▷ vi s'étendre; **out of/ within ~** (object) hors de/à portée; **reach out** vt tendre ▷ vi: **to ~ out (for)** allonger le bras (pour prendre)

react [ri:ˈækt] vi réagir; **reaction** [ri:ˈækʃən] n réaction f; **reactor** [ri:ˈæktər] n réacteur m

read (pt, pp read) [ri:d, red] vi lire ▷ vt lire; (understand) comprendre, interpréter; (study) étudier; (meter) relever; (subj: instrument etc) indiquer, marquer; **read out** vt lire à haute voix; **reader** n lecteur(-trice)

readily [ˈredɪlɪ] adv volontiers, avec empressement; (easily) facilement

reading [ˈri:dɪŋ] n lecture f; (understanding) interprétation f; (on instrument) indications fpl

ready [ˈredɪ] adj prêt(e); (willing) prêt, disposé(e); (available) disponible ▷ n: **at the ~** (Mil) prêt à faire feu; **when will my photos be ~?** quand est-ce que mes photos seront prêtes?; **to get ~** (as vi) se préparer; (as vt) préparer; **ready-cooked** adj précuit(e); **ready-made** adj tout(e) faite(e)

real [rɪəl] adj (world, life) réel(le); (genuine) véritable; (proper) vrai(e) ▷ adv (us inf: very) vraiment; **real ale** n bière traditionnelle; **real estate** n biens fonciers or immobiliers; **realistic** [rɪəˈlɪstɪk] adj réaliste; **reality** [ri:ˈælɪtɪ] n réalité f; **reality TV** n téléréalité f

realization [rɪəlaɪˈzeɪʃən] n (awareness) prise f de conscience; (fulfilment, also: of asset) réalisation f

realize [ˈrɪəlaɪz] vt (understand) se rendre compte de, prendre conscience de; (a project, Comm: asset) réaliser

really [ˈrɪəlɪ] adv vraiment; **~?** vraiment?, c'est vrai?

realm [relm] n royaume m; (fig) domaine m

realtor [ˈrɪəltɔːr] n (us) agent immobilier

reappear [ri:əˈpɪər] vi réapparaître, reparaître

rear [rɪər] adj de derrière, arrière inv; (Aut: wheel etc) arrière ▷ n arrière m ▷ vt (cattle, family) élever ▷ vi (also: ~ up: animal) se cabrer

rearrange [ri:əˈreɪndʒ] vt réarranger

rear: rear-view mirror n (Aut) rétroviseur m; **rear-wheel drive** n (Aut) traction f arrière

reason [ˈri:zn] n raison f ▷ vi: **to ~ with sb** raisonner qn, faire entendre raison à qn; **it stands to ~ that** il va sans dire que; **reasonable** adj raisonnable; (not bad) acceptable; **reasonably** adv (behave) raisonnablement; (fairly) assez; **reasoning** n raisonnement m

reassurance [ri:əˈʃuərəns] n (factual) assurance f, garantie f; (emotional) réconfort m

reassure [ri:əˈʃuər] vt rassurer

rebate [ˈri:beɪt] n (on tax etc) dégrèvement m

rebel n [ˈrebl] rebelle m/f ▷ vi [rɪˈbel] se rebeller, se révolter; **rebellion** [rɪˈbeljən] n rébellion f, révolte f; **rebellious** [rɪˈbeljəs] adj rebelle

rebuild [ri:ˈbɪld] vt (irreg: like build) reconstruire

recall vt [rɪˈkɔ:l] rappeler; (remember) se rappeler, se souvenir de ▷ n [ˈri:kɔl] rappel m; (ability to remember) mémoire f

receipt [rɪˈsi:t] n (document) reçu m; (for parcel etc) accusé m de réception; (act of receiving) réception f; **receipts** npl (Comm) recettes fpl; **can I have a ~, please?** je peux avoir un reçu, s'il vous plaît?

receive [rɪˈsi:v] vt recevoir; (guest) recevoir, accueillir; **receiver** n (Tel)

r

récepteur m, combiné m; (Radio) récepteur; (of stolen goods) receleur m; (for bankruptcies) administrateur m judiciaire

recent ['riːsnt] adj récent(e);
recently adv récemment

reception [rɪ'sɛpʃən] n réception f; (welcome) accueil m, réception;
reception desk n réception f;
receptionist n réceptionniste m/f

recession [rɪ'sɛʃən] n (Econ) récession f

recharge [riː'tʃɑːdʒ] vt (battery) recharger

recipe ['rɛsɪpɪ] n recette f

recipient [rɪ'sɪpɪənt] n (of payment) bénéficiaire m/f; (of letter) destinataire m/f

recital [rɪ'saɪtl] n récital m

recite [rɪ'saɪt] vt (poem) réciter

reckless ['rɛkləs] adj (driver etc) imprudent(e); (spender etc) insouciant(e)

reckon ['rɛkən] vt (count) calculer, compter; (consider) considérer, estimer; (think): **I ~ (that)** ... je pense (que) ..., j'estime (que) ...

reclaim [rɪ'kleɪm] vt (land: from sea) assécher; (demand back) réclamer (le remboursement or la restitution de); (waste materials) récupérer

recline [rɪ'klaɪn] vi être allongé(e) or étendu(e)

recognition [rɛkəg'nɪʃən] n reconnaissance f; **transformed beyond ~** méconnaissable

recognize ['rɛkəgnaɪz] vt: **to ~ (by/ as)** reconnaître (à/comme étant)

recollection [rɛkə'lɛkʃən] n souvenir m

recommend [rɛkə'mɛnd] vt recommander; **can you ~ a good restaurant?** pouvez-vous me conseiller un bon restaurant?;
recommendation [rɛkəmɛn'deɪʃən] n recommandation f

reconcile ['rɛkənsaɪl] vt (two people) réconcilier; (two facts) concilier, accorder; **to ~ o.s. to** se résigner à

reconsider [riːkən'sɪdər] vt reconsidérer

reconstruct [riːkən'strʌkt] vt (building) reconstruire; (crime, system) reconstituer

record n ['rɛkɔːd] rapport m, récit m; (of meeting etc) procès-verbal m; (register) registre m; (file) dossier m; (Comput) article m; (also: **police ~**) casier m judiciaire; (Mus: disc) disque m; (Sport) record m ▷ adj ['rɛkɔːd] record inv ▷ vt [rɪ'kɔːd] (set down) noter; (Mus: song etc) enregistrer; **public ~s** archives fpl; **in ~ time** dans un temps record; **recorded delivery** n (BRIT Post): **to send sth recorded delivery** ≈ envoyer qch en recommandé; **recorder** n (Mus) flûte f à bec; **recording** n (Mus) enregistrement m; **record player** n tourne-disque m

recount [rɪ'kaunt] vt raconter

recover [rɪ'kʌvər] vt récupérer ▷ vi (from illness) se rétablir; (from shock) se remettre; **recovery** n récupération f; rétablissement m; (Econ) redressement m

recreate [riːkrɪ'eɪt] vt recréer

recreation [rɛkrɪ'eɪʃən] n (leisure) récréation f, détente f; **recreational drug** n drogue récréative; **recreational vehicle** n (US) camping-car m

recruit [rɪ'kruːt] n recrue f ▷ vt recruter; **recruitment** n recrutement m

rectangle ['rɛktæŋgl] n rectangle m; **rectangular** [rɛk'tæŋgjulər] adj rectangulaire

rectify ['rɛktɪfaɪ] vt (error) rectifier, corriger

rector ['rɛktər] n (Rel) pasteur m

recur [rɪ'kəːr] vi se reproduire; (idea, opportunity) se retrouver; (symptoms) réapparaître; **recurring** adj (problem) périodique, fréquent(e); (Math) périodique

recyclable [riː'saɪkləbl] adj recyclable

recycle [ri:ˈsaɪkl] *vt, vi* recycler
recycling [ri:ˈsaɪklɪŋ] *n* recyclage *m*
red [rɛd] *n* rouge *m*; (*Pol: pej*) rouge
m/f ▷ *adj* rouge; (*hair*) roux (rousse);
in the ~ (*account*) à découvert;
(*business*) en déficit; **Red Cross**
n Croix-Rouge *f*; **redcurrant** *n*
groseille *f* (rouge)
redeem [rɪˈdiːm] *vt* (*debt*)
rembourser; (*sth in pawn*) dégager;
(*fig, also Rel*) racheter
red: red-haired *adj* roux (rousse);
redhead *n* roux (rousse); **red-hot** *adj*
chauffé(e) au rouge, brûlant(e); **red
light** *n*: **to go through a red light**
(*Aut*) brûler un feu rouge; **red-light
district** *n* quartier mal famé
red meat *n* viande *f* rouge
reduce [rɪˈdjuːs] *vt* réduire; (*lower*)
abaisser; **"~ speed now"** (*Aut*)
"ralentir"; **to ~ sb to tears** faire
pleurer qn; **reduced** *adj* réduit(e);
"greatly reduced prices" "gros
rabais"; **at a reduced price** (*goods*)
au rabais; (*ticket etc*) à prix réduit;
reduction [rɪˈdʌkʃən] *n* réduction
f; (*of price*) baisse *f*; (*discount*) rabais
m; réduction; **is there a reduction
for children/students?** y a-t-il
une réduction pour les enfants/les
étudiants?
redundancy [rɪˈdʌndənsɪ] *n* (BRIT)
licenciement *m*, mise *f* au chômage
redundant [rɪˈdʌndnt] *adj* (BRIT:
worker) licencié(e), mis(e) au
chômage; (*detail, object*) superflu(e);
to be made ~ (*worker*) être licencié,
être mis au chômage
reed [riːd] *n* (Bot) roseau *m*
reef [riːf] *n* (at sea) récif *m*, écueil *m*
reel [riːl] *n* bobine *f*; (*Fishing*) moulinet
m; (*Cine*) bande *f*; (*dance*) quadrille
écossais *m* ▷ *vi* (*sway*) chanceler
ref [rɛf] *n abbr* (inf: = referee) arbitre *m*
refectory [rɪˈfɛktərɪ] *n* réfectoire *m*
refer [rɪˈfəːʳ] *vt*: **to ~ sb to** (*inquirer,
patient*) adresser qn à; (*reader: to text*)
renvoyer qn à ▷ *vi*: **to ~ to** (*allude to*)

parler de, faire allusion à; (*consult*) se
reporter à; (*apply to*) s'appliquer à
referee [rɛfəˈriː] *n* arbitre *m*; (BRIT:
for job application) répondant(e) ▷ *vt*
arbitrer
reference [ˈrɛfrəns] *n* référence *f*,
renvoi *m*; (*mention*) allusion *f*, mention
f; (*for job application: letter*) références;
lettre *f* de recommandation; **with ~
to** en ce qui concerne; (*Comm: in letter*)
me référant à; **reference number** *n*
(*Comm*) numéro *m* de référence
refill *vt* [riːˈfɪl] remplir à nouveau;
(*pen, lighter etc*) recharger ▷ *n* [ˈriːfɪl]
(*for pen etc*) recharge *f*
refine [rɪˈfaɪn] *vt* (*sugar, oil*) raffiner;
(*taste*) affiner; (*idea, theory*) peaufiner;
refined *adj* (*person, taste*) raffiné(e);
refinery *n* raffinerie *f*
reflect [rɪˈflɛkt] *vt* (*light, image*)
réfléchir, refléter ▷ *vi* (*think*) réfléchir,
méditer; **it ~s badly on him** cela le
discrédite; **it ~s well on him** c'est
tout à son honneur; **reflection**
[rɪˈflɛkʃən] *n* réflexion *f*; (*image*) reflet
m; **on reflection** réflexion faite
reflex [ˈriːflɛks] *adj, n* réflexe (*m*)
reform [rɪˈfɔːm] *n* réforme *f* ▷ *vt*
réformer
refrain [rɪˈfreɪn] *vi*: **to ~ from doing**
s'abstenir de faire ▷ *n* refrain *m*
refresh [rɪˈfrɛʃ] *vt* rafraîchir;
(*subj: food, sleep etc*) redonner
des forces à; **refreshing** *adj*
(*drink*) rafraîchissant(e); (*sleep*)
réparateur(-trice); **refreshments** *npl*
rafraîchissements *mpl*
refrigerator [rɪˈfrɪdʒəreɪtəʳ] *n*
réfrigérateur *m*, frigidaire *m*
refuel [riːˈfjuəl] *vi* se ravitailler en
carburant
refuge [ˈrɛfjuːdʒ] *n* refuge *m*; **to
take ~ in** se réfugier dans; **refugee**
[rɛfjuˈdʒiː] *n* réfugié(e)
refund *n* [ˈriːfʌnd] remboursement *m*
▷ *vt* [rɪˈfʌnd] rembourser
refurbish [riːˈfəːbɪʃ] *vt* remettre
à neuf

r

refusal [rɪˈfjuːzəl] *n* refus *m*; **to have first ~ on sth** avoir droit de préemption sur qch

refuse¹ [ˈrɛfjuːs] *n* ordures *fpl*, détritus *mpl*

refuse² [rɪˈfjuːz] *vt, vi* refuser; **to ~ to do sth** refuser de faire qch

regain [rɪˈɡeɪn] *vt* (*lost ground*) regagner; (*strength*) retrouver

regard [rɪˈɡɑːd] *n* respect *m*, estime *f*, considération *f* ▷ *vt* considérer; **to give one's ~s to** faire ses amitiés à; **"with kindest ~s"** "bien amicalement"; **as ~s, with ~ to** en ce qui concerne; **regarding** *prep* en ce qui concerne; **regardless** *adv* quand même; **regardless of** sans se soucier de

regenerate [rɪˈdʒɛnəreɪt] *vt* régénérer ▷ *vi* se régénérer

reggae [ˈrɛɡeɪ] *n* reggae *m*

regiment [ˈrɛdʒɪmənt] *n* régiment *m*

region [ˈriːdʒən] *n* région *f*; **in the ~ of** (*fig*) aux alentours de; **regional** *adj* régional(e)

register [ˈrɛdʒɪstər] *n* registre *m*; (*also:* **electoral ~**) liste électorale ▷ *vt* enregistrer, inscrire; (*birth*) déclarer; (*vehicle*) immatriculer; (*letter*) envoyer en recommandé; (*subj: instrument*) marquer ▷ *vi* s'inscrire; (*at hotel*) signer le registre; (*make impression*) être (bien) compris(e); **registered** *adj* (BRIT: *letter*) recommandé(e); **registered trademark** *n* marque déposée

registrar [ˈrɛdʒɪstrɑːʳ] *n* officier *m* de l'état civil

registration [rɛdʒɪsˈtreɪʃən] *n* (*act*) enregistrement *m*; (*of student*) inscription *f*; (BRIT Aut: *also:* **~ number**) numéro *m* d'immatriculation

registry office [ˈrɛdʒɪstrɪ-] *n* (BRIT) bureau *m* de l'état civil; **to get married in a ~** ≈ se marier à la mairie

regret [rɪˈɡrɛt] *n* regret *m* ▷ *vt* regretter; **regrettable** *adj* regrettable, fâcheux(-euse)

regular [ˈrɛɡjuləʳ] *adj* régulier(-ière); (*usual*) habituel(le), normal(e); (*soldier*) de métier; (*Comm: size*) ordinaire ▷ *n* (*client etc*) habitué(e); **regularly** *adv* régulièrement

regulate [ˈrɛɡjuleɪt] *vt* régler; **regulation** [rɛɡjuˈleɪʃən] *n* (*rule*) règlement *m*; (*adjustment*) réglage *m*

rehabilitation [ˈriːəbɪlɪˈteɪʃən] *n* (*of offender*) réhabilitation *f*; (*of addict*) réadaptation *f*

rehearsal [rɪˈhəːsəl] *n* répétition *f*

rehearse [rɪˈhəːs] *vt* répéter

reign [reɪn] *n* règne *m* ▷ *vi* régner

reimburse [riːɪmˈbəːs] *vt* rembourser

rein [reɪn] *n* (*for horse*) rêne *f*

reincarnation [riːɪnkɑːˈneɪʃən] *n* réincarnation *f*

reindeer [ˈreɪndɪəʳ] *n* (*pl inv*) renne *m*

reinforce [riːɪnˈfɔːs] *vt* renforcer; **reinforcements** *npl* (Mil) renfort(s) *m(pl)*

reinstate [riːɪnˈsteɪt] *vt* rétablir, réintégrer

reject *n* [ˈriːdʒɛkt] (*Comm*) article *m* de rebut ▷ *vt* [rɪˈdʒɛkt] refuser; (*idea*) rejeter; **rejection** [rɪˈdʒɛkʃən] *n* rejet *m*, refus *m*

rejoice [rɪˈdʒɔɪs] *vi*: **to ~ (at *or* over)** se réjouir de

relate [rɪˈleɪt] *vt* (*tell*) raconter; (*connect*) établir un rapport entre ▷ *vi*: **to ~ to** (*connect*) se rapporter à; **to ~ to sb** (*interact*) entretenir des rapports avec qn; **related** *adj* apparenté(e); **related to** (*subject*) lié(e) à; **relating to** *prep* concernant

relation [rɪˈleɪʃən] *n* (*person*) parent(e); (*link*) rapport *m*, lien *m*; **relations** *npl* (*relatives*) famille *f*; **relationship** *n* rapport *m*, lien *m*; (*personal ties*) relations *fpl*, rapports; (*also:* **family relationship**) lien de parenté; (*affair*) liaison *f*

relative ['rɛlətɪv] n parent(e) ▷ adj relatif(-ive); (respective) respectif(-ive); **relatively** adv relativement

relax [rɪ'læks] vi (muscle) se relâcher; (person: unwind) se détendre ▷ vt relâcher; (mind, person) détendre; **relaxation** [riːlæk'seɪʃən] n relâchement m; (of mind) détente f; (recreation) détente, délassement m; **relaxed** adj relâché(e); détendu(e); **relaxing** adj délassant(e)

relay ['riːleɪ] n (Sport) course f de relais ▷ vt (message) retransmettre, relayer

release [rɪ'liːs] n (from prison, obligation) libération f; (of gas etc) émission f; (of film etc) sortie f; (new recording) disque m ▷ vt (prisoner) libérer; (book, film) sortir; (report, news) rendre public, publier; (gas etc) émettre, dégager; (free: from wreckage etc) dégager; (Tech: catch, spring etc) déclencher; (let go: person, animal) relâcher; (: hand, object) lâcher; (: grip, brake) desserrer

relegate ['rɛləgeɪt] vt reléguer; (BRIT Sport): **to be ~d** descendre dans une division inférieure

relent [rɪ'lɛnt] vi se laisser fléchir; **relentless** adj implacable; (non-stop) continuel(le)

relevant ['rɛləvənt] adj (question) pertinent(e); (corresponding) approprié(e); (fact) significatif(-ive); (information) utile

reliable [rɪ'laɪəbl] adj (person, firm) sérieux(-euse), fiable; (method, machine) fiable; (news, information) sûr(e)

relic ['rɛlɪk] n (Rel) relique f; (of the past) vestige m

relief [rɪ'liːf] n (from pain, anxiety) soulagement m; (help, supplies) secours m(pl); (Art, Geo) relief m

relieve [rɪ'liːv] vt (pain, patient) soulager; (fear, worry) dissiper; (bring help) secourir; (take over from: gen) relayer; (: guard) relever; **to ~ sb of sth** débarrasser qn de qch; **to ~ o.s.**

(euphemism) se soulager, faire ses besoins; **relieved** adj soulagé(e)

religion [rɪ'lɪdʒən] n religion f

religious [rɪ'lɪdʒəs] adj religieux(-euse); (book) de piété; **religious education** n instruction religieuse

relish ['rɛlɪʃ] n (Culin) condiment m; (enjoyment) délectation f ▷ vt (food etc) savourer; **to ~ doing** se délecter à faire

relocate [riːləu'keɪt] vt (business) transférer ▷ vi se transférer, s'installer or s'établir ailleurs

reluctance [rɪ'lʌktəns] n répugnance f

reluctant [rɪ'lʌktənt] adj peu disposé(e), qui hésite; **reluctantly** adv à contrecœur, sans enthousiasme

rely on [rɪ'laɪ-] vt fus (be dependent on) dépendre de; (trust) compter sur

remain [rɪ'meɪn] vi rester; **remainder** n reste m; (Comm) fin f de série; **remaining** adj qui reste; **remains** npl restes mpl

remand [rɪ'mɑːnd] n: **on ~** en détention préventive ▷ vt: **to be ~ed in custody** être placé(e) en détention préventive

remark [rɪ'mɑːk] n remarque f, observation f ▷ vt (faire) remarquer, dire; **remarkable** adj remarquable

remarry [riː'mærɪ] vi se remarier

remedy ['rɛmədɪ] n: **~ (for)** remède m (contre or à) ▷ vt remédier à

remember [rɪ'mɛmbəʳ] vt se rappeler, se souvenir de; (send greetings): **~ me to him** saluez-le de ma part; **Remembrance Day** [rɪ'mɛmbrəns-] n (BRIT) ≈ (le jour de) l'Armistice m, ≈ le 11 novembre

- **REMEMBRANCE DAY**

- *Remembrance Day* ou *Remembrance Sunday* est le dimanche le plus proche du 11 novembre, jour où la Première Guerre mondiale a officiellement pris fin. Il rend hommage aux victimes des deux guerres mondiales. À cette occasion, on observe deux minutes de silence à 11h, heure de la signature de l'armistice avec l'Allemagne en 1918; certaines membres de la famille royale et du gouvernement déposent des gerbes de coquelicots au cénotaphe de Whitehall, et des couronnes sont placées sur les monuments aux morts dans toute la Grande-Bretagne; par ailleurs, les gens portent des coquelicots artificiels fabriqués et vendus par des membres de la légion britannique blessés au combat, au profit des blessés de guerre et de leur famille.

remind [rɪ'maɪnd] vt: **to ~ sb of sth** rappeler qch à qn; **to ~ sb to do** penser à qn à faire, rappeler à qn qu'il doit faire; **reminder** n (Comm: letter) rappel m; (note etc) pense-bête m; (souvenir) souvenir m

reminiscent [rɛmɪ'nɪsnt] adj: **~ of** qui rappelle, qui fait penser à

remnant ['rɛmnənt] n reste m, restant m; (of cloth) coupon m

remorse [rɪ'mɔ:s] n remords m

remote [rɪ'məʊt] adj éloigné(e), lointain(e); (person) distant(e); (possibility) vague; **remote control** n télécommande f; **remotely** adv au loin; (slightly) très vaguement

removal [rɪ'mu:vəl] n (taking away) enlèvement m; suppression f; (BRIT: from house) déménagement m; (from office: dismissal) renvoi m; (of stain) nettoyage m; (Med) ablation f; **removal man** (irreg) n (BRIT) déménageur m; **removal van** n (BRIT) camion m de déménagement

remove [rɪ'mu:v] vt enlever, retirer; (employee) renvoyer; (stain) faire partir; (abuse) supprimer; (doubt) chasser

Renaissance [rɪ'neɪsɑ̃s] n: **the ~** la Renaissance

rename [ri:'neɪm] vt rebaptiser

render ['rɛndə*] vt rendre

rendezvous ['rɔndɪvu:] n rendez-vous m inv

renew [rɪ'nju:] vt renouveler; (negotiations) reprendre; (acquaintance) renouer; **renewable** adj (energy) renouvelable

renovate ['rɛnəveɪt] vt rénover; (work of art) restaurer

renowned [rɪ'naʊnd] adj renommé(e)

rent [rɛnt] n loyer m ▷ vt louer; **rental** n (for television, car) (prix m de) location f

reorganize [ri:'ɔ:gənaɪz] vt réorganiser

rep [rɛp] n abbr (Comm) = **representative**

repair [rɪ'pɛə*] n réparation f ▷ vt réparer; **in good/bad ~** en bon/mauvais état; **where can I get this ~ed?** où est-ce que je peux faire réparer ceci?; **repair kit** n trousse f de réparations

repay [ri:'peɪ] vt (irreg: like pay) (money, creditor) rembourser; (sb's efforts) récompenser; **repayment** n remboursement m

repeat [rɪ'pi:t] n (Radio, TV) reprise f ▷ vt répéter; (promise, attack, also Comm: order) renouveler; (Scol: a class) redoubler ▷ vi répéter; **can you ~ that, please?** pouvez-vous répéter, s'il vous plaît?; **repeatedly** adv souvent, à plusieurs reprises; **repeat prescription** n (BRIT): **I'd like a repeat prescription** je voudrais renouveler mon ordonnance

repellent [rɪ'pɛlənt] adj repoussant(e) ▷ n: **insect ~** insectifuge m

repercussions [ri:pə'kʌʃənz] npl répercussions fpl

repetition [rɛpɪ'tɪʃən] n répétition f

repetitive [rɪ'pɛtɪtɪv] adj (movement, work) répétitif(-ive); (speech) plein(e) de redites

replace [rɪ'pleɪs] vt (put back) remettre, replacer; (take the place of) remplacer; **replacement** n (substitution) remplacement m; (person) remplaçant(e)

replay ['riːpleɪ] n (of match) match rejoué; (of tape, film) répétition f

replica ['rɛplɪkə] n réplique f, copie exacte

reply [rɪ'plaɪ] n réponse f ▷ vi répondre

report [rɪ'pɔːt] n rapport m; (Press etc) reportage m; (BRIT: also: **school ~**) bulletin m (scolaire); (of gun) détonation f ▷ vt rapporter, faire un compte rendu de; (Press etc) faire un reportage sur; (notify: accident) signaler; (: culprit) dénoncer ▷ vi (make a report) faire un rapport; **I'd like to ~ a theft** je voudrais signaler un vol; **to ~ (to sb)** (present o.s.) se présenter (chez qn); **report card** n (US, SCOTTISH) bulletin m (scolaire); **reportedly** adv: **she is reportedly living in Spain** elle habiterait en Espagne; **he reportedly told them to ...** il leur aurait dit de ...; **reporter** n reporter m

represent [rɛprɪ'zɛnt] vt représenter; (view, belief) présenter, expliquer; (describe): **to ~ sth as** présenter or décrire qch comme; **representation** [rɛprɪzɛn'teɪʃən] n représentation f; **representative** n représentant(e); (US Pol) député m ▷ adj représentatif(-ive), caractéristique

repress [rɪ'prɛs] vt réprimer; **repression** [rɪ'prɛʃən] n répression f

reprimand ['rɛprɪmɑːnd] n réprimande f ▷ vt réprimander

reproduce [riːprə'djuːs] vt reproduire ▷ vi se reproduire; **reproduction** [riːprə'dʌkʃən] n reproduction f

reptile ['rɛptaɪl] n reptile m

republic [rɪ'pʌblɪk] n république f; **republican** adj, n républicain(e)

reputable ['rɛpjutəbl] adj de bonne réputation; (occupation) honorable

reputation [rɛpju'teɪʃən] n réputation f

request [rɪ'kwɛst] n demande f; (formal) requête f ▷ vt: **to ~ (of or from sb)** demander (à qn); **request stop** n (BRIT: for bus) arrêt facultatif

require [rɪ'kwaɪər] vt (need: subj: person) avoir besoin de; (: thing, situation) nécessiter, demander; (want) exiger; (order): **to ~ sb to do sth/sth of sb** exiger que qn fasse qch/qch de qn; **requirement** n (need) exigence f; besoin m; (condition) condition f (requise)

resat [riː'sæt] pt, pp of **resit**

rescue ['rɛskjuː] n (from accident) sauvetage m; (help) secours mpl ▷ vt sauver

research [rɪ'səːtʃ] n recherche(s) f(pl) ▷ vt faire des recherches sur

resemblance [rɪ'zɛmbləns] n ressemblance f

resemble [rɪ'zɛmbl] vt ressembler à

resent [rɪ'zɛnt] vt être contrarié(e) par; **resentful** adj irrité(e), plein(e) de ressentiment; **resentment** n ressentiment m

reservation [rɛzə'veɪʃən] n (booking) réservation f; **to make a ~ (in an hotel/a restaurant/on a plane)** réserver or retenir une chambre/une table/une place; **reservation desk** n (US: in hotel) réception f

reserve [rɪ'zəːv] n réserve f; (Sport) remplaçant(e) ▷ vt (seats etc) réserver, retenir; **reserved** adj réservé(e)

reservoir ['rɛzəvwɑːr] n réservoir m

reshuffle ['riːʃʌfl] n: **Cabinet ~** (Pol) remaniement ministériel

residence ['rɛzɪdəns] n résidence f; **residence permit** n (BRIT) permis m de séjour

r

resident ['rɛzɪdənt] n (of country) résident(e); (of area, house) habitant(e); (in hotel) pensionnaire ▷ adj résidant(e); **residential** [rɛzɪ'dɛnʃəl] adj de résidence; (area) résidentiel(le); (course) avec hébergement sur place

residue ['rɛzɪdjuː] n reste m; (Chem, Physics) résidu m

resign [rɪ'zaɪn] vt (one's post) se démettre de ▷ vi démissionner; **to ~ o.s. to** (endure) se résigner à; **resignation** [rɛzɪg'neɪʃən] n (from post) démission f; (state of mind) résignation f

resin ['rɛzɪn] n résine f

resist [rɪ'zɪst] vt résister à; **resistance** n résistance f

resit vt ['riː'sɪt] (irreg: like **sit**) (BRIT: exam) repasser ▷ n ['riːsɪt] deuxième session f (d'un examen)

resolution [rɛzə'luːʃən] n résolution f

resolve [rɪ'zɔlv] n résolution f ▷ vt (problem) résoudre; (decide): **to ~ to do** résoudre or décider de faire

resort [rɪ'zɔːt] n (seaside town) station f balnéaire; (for skiing) station de ski; (recourse) recours m ▷ vi: **to ~ to** avoir recours à; **in the last ~** en dernier ressort

resource [rɪ'sɔːs] n ressource f; **resourceful** adj ingénieux(-euse), débrouillard(e)

respect [rɪs'pɛkt] n respect m ▷ vt respecter; **respectable** adj respectable; (quite good: result etc) honorable; **respectful** adj respectueux(-euse); **respective** adj respectif(-ive); **respectively** adv respectivement

respite ['rɛspaɪt] n répit m

respond [rɪs'pɔnd] vi répondre; (react) réagir; **response** [rɪs'pɔns] n réponse f; (reaction) réaction f

responsibility [rɪspɔnsɪ'bɪlɪtɪ] n responsabilité f

responsible [rɪs'pɔnsɪbl] adj (liable): **~ (for)** responsable (de); (person) digne de confiance; (job) qui comporte des responsabilités; **responsibly** adv avec sérieux

responsive [rɪs'pɔnsɪv] adj (student, audience) réceptif(-ive); (brakes, steering) sensible

rest [rɛst] n repos m; (stop) arrêt m, pause f; (Mus) silence m; (support) support m, appui m; (remainder) reste m, restant m ▷ vi se reposer; (be supported): **to ~ on** appuyer or reposer sur ▷ vt (lean): **to ~ sth on/against** appuyer qch sur/contre; **the ~ of them** les autres

restaurant ['rɛstərɔŋ] n restaurant m; **restaurant car** n (BRIT Rail) wagon-restaurant m

restless ['rɛstlɪs] adj agité(e)

restoration [rɛstə'reɪʃən] n (of building) restauration f; (of stolen goods) restitution f

restore [rɪ'stɔːʳ] vt (building) restaurer; (sth stolen) restituer; (peace, health) rétablir; **to ~ to** (former state) ramener à

restrain [rɪs'treɪn] vt (feeling) contenir; (person): **to ~ (from doing)** retenir (de faire); **restraint** n (restriction) contrainte f; (moderation) retenue f; (of style) sobriété f

restrict [rɪs'trɪkt] vt restreindre, limiter; **restriction** [rɪs'trɪkʃən] n restriction f, limitation f

rest room n (US) toilettes fpl

restructure [riː'strʌktʃəʳ] vt restructurer

result [rɪ'zʌlt] n résultat m ▷ vi: **to ~ in** aboutir à, se terminer par; **as a ~ of** à la suite de

resume [rɪ'zjuːm] vt (work, journey) reprendre ▷ vi (work etc) reprendre

résumé ['reɪzjuːmeɪ] n (summary) résumé m; (US: curriculum vitae) curriculum vitae m inv

resuscitate [rɪ'sʌsɪteɪt] vt (Med) réanimer

retail ['riːteɪl] adj de or au détail ▷ adv au détail; **retailer** n détaillant(e)

retain [rɪ'teɪn] vt (keep) garder, conserver

retaliation [rɪtælɪ'eɪʃən] n représailles fpl, vengeance f

retire [rɪ'taɪəʳ] vi (give up work) prendre sa retraite; (withdraw) se retirer, partir; (go to bed) (aller) se coucher; **retired** adj (person) retraité(e); **retirement** n retraite f

retort [rɪ'tɔ:t] vi riposter

retreat [rɪ'tri:t] n retraite f ▷ vi battre en retraite

retrieve [rɪ'tri:v] vt (sth lost) récupérer; (situation, honour) sauver; (error, loss) réparer; (Comput) rechercher

retrospect ['rɛtrəspɛkt] n: **in ~** rétrospectivement, après coup; **retrospective** [rɛtrə'spɛktɪv] adj rétrospectif(-ive); (law) rétroactif(-ive) ▷ n (Art) rétrospective f

return [rɪ'tə:n] n (going or coming back) retour m; (of sth stolen etc) restitution f; (Finance: from land, shares) rapport m ▷ cpd (journey) de retour; (BRIT: ticket) aller et retour; (match) retour ▷ vi (person etc: come back) revenir; (: go back) retourner ▷ vt rendre; (bring back) rapporter; (send back) renvoyer; (put back) remettre; (Pol: candidate) élire; **returns** npl (Comm) recettes fpl; (Finance) bénéfices mpl; **many happy ~s (of the day)!** bon anniversaire!; **by ~ (of post)** par retour (du courrier); **in ~ (for)** en échange (de); **a ~ (ticket) for ...** un billet aller et retour pour ...; **return ticket** n (esp BRIT) billet m aller-retour

retweet [ri:'twi:t] vt (on Twitter) retweeter

reunion [ri:'ju:nɪən] n réunion f

reunite [ri:ju:'naɪt] vt réunir

revamp [ri:'væmp] vt (house) retaper; (firm) réorganiser

reveal [rɪ'vi:l] vt (make known) révéler; (display) laisser voir; **revealing** adj révélateur(-trice); (dress) au décolleté généreux or suggestif

revel ['rɛvl] vi: **to ~ in sth/in doing** se délecter de qch/à faire

revelation [rɛvə'leɪʃən] n révélation f

revenge [rɪ'vɛndʒ] n vengeance f; (in game etc) revanche f ▷ vt venger; **to take ~ (on)** se venger (sur)

revenue ['rɛvənju:] n revenu m

Reverend ['rɛvərənd] adj: **the ~ John Smith** (Anglican) le révérend John Smith; (Catholic) l'abbé (John) Smith; (Protestant) le pasteur (John) Smith

reversal [rɪ'və:sl] n (of opinion) revirement m; (of order) renversement m; (of direction) changement m

reverse [rɪ'və:s] n contraire m, opposé m; (back) dos m, envers m; (of paper) verso m; (of coin) revers m; (Aut: also: **~ gear**) marche f arrière ▷ adj (order, direction) opposé(e), inverse ▷ vt (order, position) changer, inverser; (direction, policy) changer complètement de; (decision) annuler; (roles) renverser ▷ vi (BRIT Aut) faire marche arrière; **reversing lights** npl (BRIT Aut) feux mpl de marche arrière or de recul

revert [rɪ'və:t] vi: **to ~ to** revenir à, retourner à

review [rɪ'vju:] n revue f; (of book, film) critique f; (of situation, policy) examen m, bilan m; (US: examination) examen ▷ vt passer en revue; faire la critique de; examiner

revise [rɪ'vaɪz] vt réviser, modifier; (manuscript) revoir, corriger ▷ vi (study) réviser; **revision** [rɪ'vɪʒən] n révision f

revival [rɪ'vaɪvəl] n reprise f; (recovery) rétablissement m; (of faith) renouveau m

revive [rɪ'vaɪv] vt (person) ranimer; (custom) rétablir; (economy) relancer; (hope, courage) raviver, faire renaître; (play, fashion) reprendre ▷ vi (person) reprendre connaissance (: from ill health) se rétablir; (hope etc) renaître; (activity) reprendre

r

revolt [rɪ'vəult] n révolte f ▷ vi
se révolter, se rebeller ▷ vt
révolter, dégoûter; **revolting** adj
dégoûtant(e)

revolution [rɛvə'lu:ʃən] n révolution
f; (of wheel etc) tour m, révolution;
revolutionary adj, n révolutionnaire
(m/f)

revolve [rɪ'vɔlv] vi tourner

revolver [rɪ'vɔlvə'] n revolver m

reward [rɪ'wɔ:d] n récompense f
▷ vt: **to ~ (for)** récompenser (de);
rewarding adj (fig) qui (en) vaut la
peine, gratifiant(e)

rewind [ri:'waɪnd] vt (irreg: like
wind²) (tape) réembobiner

rewritable [ri:'raɪtəbl] adj (CD, DVD)
réinscriptible

rewrite [ri:'raɪt] (irreg: like **write**)
vt récrire

rheumatism ['ru:mətɪzəm] n
rhumatisme m

Rhine [raɪn] n: **the (River) ~** le Rhin

rhinoceros [raɪ'nɔsərəs] n
rhinocéros m

rhubarb ['ru:bɑ:b] n rhubarbe f

rhyme [raɪm] n rime f; (verse) vers mpl

rhythm ['rɪðm] n rythme m

rib [rɪb] n (Anat) côte f

ribbon ['rɪbən] n ruban m; **in ~s** (torn)
en lambeaux

rice [raɪs] n riz m; **rice pudding** n
riz m au lait

rich [rɪtʃ] adj riche; (gift, clothes)
somptueux(-euse); **to be ~ in sth**
être riche en qch

rid [rɪd] (pt, pp **rid**) vt: **to ~ sb of**
débarrasser qn de; **to get ~ of** se
débarrasser de

ridden ['rɪdn] pp of **ride**

riddle ['rɪdl] n (puzzle) énigme f ▷ vt:
to be ~d with être criblé(e) de; (fig)
être en proie à

ride [raɪd] (pt **rode**, pp **ridden**) n
promenade f, tour m; (distance
covered) trajet m ▷ vi (as sport)
monter (à cheval), faire du cheval;
(go somewhere: on horse, bicycle) aller

(à cheval or bicyclette etc); (travel: on
bicycle, motor cycle, bus) rouler ▷ vt (a
horse) monter; (distance) parcourir,
faire; **to ~ a horse/bicycle** monter à
cheval/à bicyclette; **to take sb for a
~** (fig) faire marcher qn; (cheat) rouler
qn; **rider** n cavalier(-ière); (in race)
jockey m; (on bicycle) cycliste m/f; (on
motorcycle) motocycliste m/f

ridge [rɪdʒ] n (of hill) faîte m; (of roof,
mountain) arête f; (on object) strie f

ridicule ['rɪdɪkju:l] n ridicule m;
dérision f ▷ vt ridiculiser, tourner en
dérision; **ridiculous** [rɪ'dɪkjuləs]
adj ridicule

riding ['raɪdɪŋ] n équitation f;
riding school n manège m, école f
d'équitation

rife [raɪf] adj répandu(e); **~ with**
abondant(e) en

rifle ['raɪfl] n fusil m (à canon rayé)
▷ vt vider, dévaliser

rift [rɪft] n fente f, fissure f; (fig:
disagreement) désaccord m

rig [rɪg] n (also: **oil ~**: on land) derrick
m; (: at sea) plate-forme pétrolière
▷ vt (election etc) truquer

right [raɪt] adj (true) juste, exact(e);
(correct) bon (bonne); (suitable)
approprié(e), convenable; (just)
juste, équitable; (morally good) bien
inv; (not left) droit(e) ▷ n (moral good)
bien m; (title, claim) droit m; (not left)
droite f ▷ adv (answer) correctement;
(treat) bien, comme il faut; (not on
the left) à droite ▷ vt redresser ▷ excl
bon!; **do you have the ~ time?**
avez-vous l'heure juste or exacte?; **to
be ~** (person) avoir raison; (answer)
être juste or correct(e); **by ~s** en
toute justice; **on the ~** à droite; **to
be in the ~** avoir raison; **~ in the
middle** en plein milieu; **~ away**
immédiatement; **right angle** n
(Math) angle droit; **rightful** adj (heir)
légitime; **right-hand** adj: **the right-
hand side** la droite; **right-hand
drive** n conduite f à droite; (vehicle)

véhicule *m* avec la conduite à droite;
right-handed *adj* (*person*) droitier(-
ière); **rightly** *adv* bien, correctement;
(*with reason*) à juste titre; **right
of way** *n* (*on path etc*) droit *m* de
passage; (*Aut*) priorité *f*; **right-wing**
adj (*Pol*) de droite

rigid ['rɪdʒɪd] *adj* rigide; (*principle,
control*) strict(e)

rigorous ['rɪgərəs] *adj*
rigoureux(-euse)

rim [rɪm] *n* bord *m*; (*of spectacles*)
monture *f*; (*of wheel*) jante *f*

rind [raɪnd] *n* (*of bacon*) couenne *f*; (*of
lemon etc*) écorce *f*, zeste *m*; (*of cheese*)
croûte *f*

ring [rɪŋ] *n* anneau *m*; (*on finger*)
bague *f*; (*also*: **wedding ~**) alliance *f*;
(*of people, objects*) cercle *m*; (*of spies*)
réseau *m*; (*of smoke etc*) rond *m*; (*arena*)
piste *f*, arène *f*; (*for boxing*) ring *m*;
(*sound of bell*) sonnerie *f* ▷ *vi* (*pt* **rang**,
pp **rung**) (*telephone, bell*) sonner;
(*person: by telephone*) téléphoner;
(*ears*) bourdonner; (*also*: **~ out**:
voice, words) retentir ▷ *vt* (*also*: **~ up**:
téléphoner à, appeler; **to ~ the bell**
sonner; **to give sb a ~** (*Tel*) passer
un coup de téléphone *or* de fil à qn;
ring back *vt, vi* (*BRIT Tel*) rappeler;
ring off *vi* (*BRIT Tel*) raccrocher; **ring
up** *vt* (*BRIT Tel*) téléphoner à, appeler;
ringing tone *n* (*BRIT Tel*) tonalité *f*
d'appel; **ringleader** *n* (*of gang*) chef
m, meneur *m*; **ring road** *n* (*BRIT*)
rocade *f*; (*motorway*) périphérique *m*;
ringtone *n* (*on mobile*) sonnerie *f* (*de
téléphone portable*)

rink [rɪŋk] *n* (*also*: **ice ~**) patinoire *f*

rinse [rɪns] *n* rinçage *m* ▷ *vt* rincer

riot ['raɪət] *n* émeute *f*, bagarres
fpl ▷ *vi* (*demonstrators*) manifester
avec violence; (*population*) se
soulever, se révolter; **to run ~** se
déchaîner

rip [rɪp] *n* déchirure *f* ▷ *vt* déchirer
▷ *vi* se déchirer; **rip off** *vt* (*inf: cheat*)
arnaquer; **rip up** *vt* déchirer

ripe [raɪp] *adj* (*fruit*) mûr(e); (*cheese*)
fait(e)

rip-off ['rɪpɔf] *n* (*inf*): **it's a ~!** c'est du
vol manifeste!, c'est de l'arnaque!

ripple ['rɪpl] *n* ride *f*, ondulation *f*; (*of
applause, laughter*) cascade *f* ▷ *vi* se
rider, onduler

rise [raɪz] *n* (*slope*) côte *f*, pente *f*;
(*hill*) élévation *f*; (*increase: in wages:
BRIT*) augmentation *f*; (: *in prices,
temperature*) hausse *f*, augmentation;
(*fig: to power etc*) ascension *f* ▷ *vi*
(*pt* **rose**, *pp* **risen**) s'élever, monter;
(*prices, numbers*) augmenter, monter;
(*waters, river*) monter; (*sun, wind,
person: from chair, bed*) se lever; (*also:
~ up: tower, building*) s'élever; (: *rebel*)
se révolter; se rebeller; (*in rank*)
s'élever; **to give ~ to** donner lieu à;
to ~ to the occasion se montrer à
la hauteur; **risen** ['rɪzn] *pp of* **rise**;
rising *adj* (*increasing: number, prices*)
en hausse; (*tide*) montant(e); (*sun,
moon*) levant(e)

risk [rɪsk] *n* risque *m* ▷ *vt* risquer; **to
take** *or* **run the ~ of doing** courir le
risque de faire; **at ~** en danger; **at
one's own ~** à ses risques et périls;
risky *adj* risqué(e)

rite [raɪt] *n* rite *m*; **the last ~s** les
derniers sacrements

ritual ['rɪtjuəl] *adj* rituel(le) ▷ *n*
rituel *m*

rival ['raɪvl] *n* rival(e); (*in business*)
concurrent(e) ▷ *adj* rival(e); qui fait
concurrence ▷ *vt* (*match*) égaler;
rivalry *n* rivalité *f*; (*in business*)
concurrence *f*

river ['rɪvəʳ] *n* rivière *f*; (*major: also fig*)
fleuve *m* ▷ *cpd* (*port, traffic*) fluvial(e);
up/down ~ en amont/aval;
riverbank *n* rive *f*, berge *f*

rivet ['rɪvɪt] *n* rivet *m* ▷ *vt* (*fig*) river,
fixer

Riviera [rɪvɪ'ɛərə] *n*: **the (French) ~**
la Côte d'Azur

road [rəud] *n* route *f*; (*in town*) rue *f*;
(*fig*) chemin, voie *f* ▷ *cpd* (*accident*)

de la route; **major/minor ~**
route principale or à priorité/voie
secondaire; **which ~ do I take for
...?** quelle route dois-je prendre pour
aller à ...?; **roadblock** n barrage
routier; **road map** n carte routière;
road rage n comportement très agressif
de certains usagers de la route; **road
safety** n sécurité routière; **roadside**
n bord m de la route, bas-côté m; **road
sign** n panneau m de signalisation;
road tax n (BRIT Aut) taxe f sur les
automobiles; **roadworks** npl travaux
mpl (de réfection des routes)
roam [rəʊm] vi errer, vagabonder
roar [rɔːʳ] n rugissement m; (of crowd)
hurlements mpl; (of vehicle, thunder,
storm) grondement m ▷ vi rugir;
hurler; gronder; **to ~ with laughter**
rire à gorge déployée
roast [rəʊst] n rôti m ▷ vt (meat)
(faire) rôtir; (coffee) griller, torréfier;
roast beef n rôti m de bœuf, rosbif m
rob [rɒb] vt (person) voler; (bank)
dévaliser; **to ~ sb of sth** voler or
dérober qch à qn; (fig: deprive) priver
qn de qch; **robber** n bandit m, voleur
m; **robbery** n vol m
robe [rəʊb] n (for ceremony etc) robe
f; (also: **bath~**) peignoir m; (us: rug)
couverture f ▷ vt revêtir (d'une robe)
robin ['rɒbɪn] n rouge-gorge m
robot ['rəʊbɒt] n robot m
robust [rəʊ'bʌst] adj robuste;
(material, appetite) solide
rock [rɒk] n (substance) roche f, roc m;
(boulder) rocher m, roche; (us: small
stone) caillou m; (BRIT: sweet) ≈ sucre
m d'orge ▷ vt (swing gently: cradle)
balancer; (: child) bercer; (shake)
ébranler, secouer ▷ vi se balancer,
être ébranlé(e) or secoué(e); **on the
~s** (drink) avec des glaçons; (marriage
etc) en train de craquer; **rock and roll**
n rock (and roll) m, rock'n'roll m; **rock
climbing** n varappe f
rocket ['rɒkɪt] n fusée f; (Mil) fusée,
roquette f; (Culin) roquette

rocking chair ['rɒkɪŋ-] n fauteuil
m à bascule
rocky ['rɒkɪ] adj (hill) rocheux(-euse);
(path) rocailleux(-euse)
rod [rɒd] n (metallic) tringle f; (Tech)
tige f; (wooden) baguette f; (also:
fishing ~) canne f à pêche
rode [rəʊd] pt of **ride**
rodent ['rəʊdnt] n rongeur m
rogue [rəʊg] n coquin(e)
role [rəʊl] n rôle m; **role-model** n
modèle m à émuler
roll [rəʊl] n rouleau m; (of banknotes)
liasse f; (also: **bread ~**) petit pain;
(register) liste f; (sound: of drums etc)
roulement m ▷ vt rouler; (also: **~ up**)
(string) enrouler; (also: **~ out**: pastry)
étendre au rouleau, abaisser ▷ vi
rouler; **roll over** vi se retourner; **roll
up** vi (inf: arrive) arriver, s'amener ▷ vt
(carpet, cloth, map) rouler; (sleeves)
retrousser; **roller** n rouleau m;
(wheel) roulette f; (for road) rouleau
compresseur; (for hair) bigoudi m;
roller coaster n montagnes fpl
russes; **roller skates** npl patins mpl à
roulettes; **roller-skating** n patin m à
roulettes; **to go roller-skating** faire
du patin à roulettes; **rolling pin** n
rouleau m à pâtisserie
ROM [rɒm] n abbr (Comput: = read-only
memory) mémoire morte, ROM f
Roman ['rəʊmən] adj romain(e) ▷ n
Romain(e); **Roman Catholic** adj, n
catholique (m/f)
romance [rə'mæns] n (love affair)
idylle f; (charm) poésie f; (novel) roman
m à l'eau de rose
Romania [rəʊ'meɪnɪə] n = **Rumania**
Roman numeral n chiffre romain
romantic [rə'mæntɪk] adj
romantique; (novel, attachment)
sentimental(e)
Rome [rəʊm] n Rome
roof [ruːf] n toit m; (of tunnel, cave)
plafond m ▷ vt couvrir (d'un toit); **the
~ of the mouth** la voûte du palais;
roof rack n (Aut) galerie f

rook [ruk] n (bird) freux m; (Chess) tour f

room [ru:m] n (in house) pièce f; (also: **bed~**) chambre f (à coucher); (in school etc) salle f; (space) place f; **roommate** n camarade m/f de chambre; **room service** n service m des chambres (dans un hôtel); **roomy** adj spacieux(-euse); (garment) ample

rooster ['ru:stə'] n coq m

root [ru:t] n (Bot, Math) racine f; (fig: of problem) origine f, fond m ▷ vi (plant) s'enraciner

rope [rəup] n corde f; (Naut) cordage m ▷ vt (tie up or together) attacher; (climbers: also: **~ together**) encorder; (area: also: **~ off**) interdire l'accès de; (: divide off) séparer; **to know the ~s** (fig) être au courant, connaître les ficelles

rort [rɔ:t] n (AUST, NZ inf) arnaque f (inf) ▷ vt escroquer

rose [rəuz] pt of **rise** ▷ n rose f; (also: **~bush**) rosier m

rosé ['rəuzeɪ] n rosé m

rosemary ['rəuzmərɪ] n romarin m

rosy ['rəuzɪ] adj rose; **a ~ future** un bel avenir

rot [rɒt] n (decay) pourriture f; (fig: pej: nonsense) idioties fpl, balivernes fpl ▷ vt, vi pourrir

rota ['rəutə] n liste f, tableau m de service

rotate [rəu'teɪt] vt (revolve) faire tourner; (change round: crops) alterner; (: jobs) faire à tour de rôle ▷ vi (revolve) tourner

rotten ['rɒtn] adj (decayed) pourri(e); (dishonest) corrompu(e); (inf: bad) mauvais(e), moche; **to feel ~ (ill)** être mal fichu(e)

rough [rʌf] adj (cloth, skin) rêche, rugueux(-euse); (terrain) accidenté(e); (path) rocailleux(-euse); (voice) rauque, rude; (person, manner: coarse) rude, fruste; (: violent) brutal(e); (district, weather) mauvais(e); (sea) houleux(-euse); (plan) ébauché(e);

(guess) approximatif(-ive) ▷ n (Golf) rough m ▷ vt: **to ~ it** vivre à la dure; **to sleep ~** (BRIT) coucher à la dure; **roughly** adv (handle) rudement, brutalement; (speak) avec brusquerie; (make) grossièrement; (approximately) à peu près, en gros

roulette [ru:'let] n roulette f

round [raund] adj rond(e) ▷ n rond m, cercle m; (BRIT: of toast) tranche f; (duty: of policeman, milkman etc) tournée f; (: of doctor) visites fpl; (game: of cards, in competition) partie f; (Boxing) round m; (of talks) série f ▷ vt (corner) tourner ▷ prep autour de ▷ adv: **right ~, all ~** tout autour; **~ of ammunition** cartouche f; **~ of applause** applaudissements mpl; **~ of drinks** tournée f; **the long way ~** (par) le chemin le plus long; **all (the) year ~** toute l'année; **it's just ~ the corner** (fig) c'est tout près; **to go ~ to sb's (house)** aller chez qn; **go ~ the back** passez par derrière; **enough to go ~** assez pour tout le monde; **she arrived ~ (about) noon** (BRIT) elle est arrivée vers midi; **~ the clock** 24 heures sur 24; **round off** vt (speech etc) terminer; **round up** vt rassembler; (criminals) effectuer une rafle de; (prices) arrondir (au chiffre supérieur); **roundabout** n (BRIT: Aut) rond-point m (à sens giratoire); (: at fair) manège m (de chevaux de bois) ▷ adj (route, means) détourné(e); **round trip** n (voyage m) aller et retour m; **roundup** n rassemblement m; (of criminals) rafle f

rouse [rauz] vt (wake up) réveiller; (stir up) susciter, provoquer; (interest) éveiller; (suspicions) susciter, éveiller

route [ru:t] n itinéraire m; (of bus) parcours m; (of trade, shipping) route f

router n (Comput) routeur m

routine [ru:'ti:n] adj (work) ordinaire, courant(e); (procedure) d'usage ▷ n (habits) habitudes fpl; (pej) train-train m; (Theat) numéro m

r

row¹ [rəu] n (line) rangée f; (of people, seats, Knitting) rang m; (behind one another: of cars, people) file f ▷ vi (in boat) ramer; (as sport) faire de l'aviron ▷ vt (boat) faire aller à la rame or à l'aviron; **in a ~** (fig) d'affilée

row² [rau] n (noise) vacarme m; (dispute) dispute f, querelle f; (scolding) réprimande f, savon m ▷ vi (also: **to have a ~**) se disputer, se quereller

rowboat ['rəubəut] n (US) canot m (à rames)

rowing ['rəuɪŋ] n canotage m; (as sport) aviron m; **rowing boat** n (BRIT) canot m (à rames)

royal ['rɔɪəl] adj royal(e); **royalty** n (royal persons) (membres mpl de la) famille royale; (payment: to author) droits mpl d'auteur; (: to inventor) royalties fpl

rpm abbr (= revolutions per minute) t/mn (= tours/minute)

R.S.V.P. abbr (= répondez s'il vous plaît) RSVP

Rt. Hon. abbr (BRIT: = Right Honourable) titre donné aux députés de la Chambre des communes

rub [rʌb] n: **to give sth a ~** donner un coup de chiffon or de torchon à qch ▷ vt frotter; (person) frictionner; (hands) se frotter; **to ~ sb up** (BRIT) or **to ~ sb** (US) **the wrong way** prendre qn à rebrousse-poil; **rub in** vt (ointment) faire pénétrer; **rub off** vi partir; **rub out** vt effacer

rubber ['rʌbəʳ] n caoutchouc m; (BRIT: eraser) gomme f (à effacer); **rubber band** n élastique m; **rubber gloves** npl gants mpl en caoutchouc

rubbish ['rʌbɪʃ] n (from household) ordures fpl; (fig: pej) choses fpl sans valeur; camelote f; (nonsense) bêtises fpl, idioties fpl; **rubbish bin** n (BRIT) boîte f à ordures, poubelle f; **rubbish dump** n (BRIT: in town) décharge publique, dépotoir m

rubble ['rʌbl] n décombres mpl; (smaller) gravats mpl; (Constr) blocage m

ruby ['ruːbɪ] n rubis m

rucksack ['rʌksæk] n sac m à dos

rudder ['rʌdəʳ] n gouvernail m

rude [ruːd] adj (impolite: person) impoli(e); (: word, manners) grossier(-ière); (shocking) indécent(e), inconvenant(e)

ruffle ['rʌfl] vt (hair) ébouriffer; (clothes) chiffonner; (fig: person): **to get ~d** s'énerver

rug [rʌg] n petit tapis; (BRIT: blanket) couverture f

rugby ['rʌgbɪ] n (also: **~ football**) rugby m

rugged ['rʌgɪd] adj (landscape) accidenté(e); (features, character) rude

ruin ['ruːɪn] n ruine f ▷ vt ruiner; (spoil: clothes) abîmer; (: event) gâcher; **ruins** npl (of building) ruine(s)

rule [ruːl] n règle f; (regulation) règlement m; (government) autorité f, gouvernement m ▷ vt (country) gouverner; (person) dominer; (decide) décider ▷ vi commander; **as a ~** normalement, en règle générale; **rule out** vt exclure; **ruler** n (sovereign) souverain(e); (leader) chef m (d'État); (for measuring) règle f; **ruling** adj (party) au pouvoir; (class) dirigeant(e) ▷ n (Law) décision f

rum [rʌm] n rhum m

Rumania [ruːˈmeɪnɪə] n Roumanie f; **Rumanian** adj roumain(e) ▷ n Roumain(e); (Ling) roumain m

rumble ['rʌmbl] n grondement m; (of stomach, pipe) gargouillement m ▷ vi gronder; (stomach, pipe) gargouiller

rumour, (US) **rumor** ['ruːməʳ] n rumeur f, bruit m (qui court) ▷ vt: **it is ~ed that** le bruit court que

rump steak n romsteck m

run [rʌn] (pt **ran**, pp **run**) n (race) course f; (outing) tour m or promenade f (en voiture); (distance travelled) parcours m, trajet m; (series) suite f, série f; (Theat) série de représentations; (Ski) piste f; (Cricket, Baseball) point m; (in tights, stockings) maille filée, échelle f ▷ vt (business) diriger; (competition, course) organiser; (hotel, house) tenir; (race) participer à; (Comput: program) exécuter; (to pass: hand, finger): **to ~ sth over** promener or passer qch sur; (water, bath) faire couler; (Press: feature) publier ▷ vi courir; (pass: road etc) passer; (work: machine, factory) marcher; (bus, train) circuler; (continue: play) se jouer, être à l'affiche; (: contract) être valide or en vigueur; (flow: river, bath, nose) couler; (colours, washing) déteindre; (in election) être candidat, se présenter; **at a ~** au pas de course; **to go for a ~** aller courir or faire un peu de course à pied; (in car) faire un tour or une promenade (en voiture); **there was a ~ on** (meat, tickets) les gens se sont rués sur; **in the long ~** à la longue; **on the ~** en fuite; **I'll ~ you to the station** je vais vous emmener or conduire à la gare; **to ~ a risk** courir un risque; **run after** vt fus (to catch up) courir après; (chase) poursuivre; **run away** vi s'enfuir; **run down** vt (Aut: knock over) renverser; (BRIT: reduce: production) réduire progressivement; (: factory/shop) réduire progressivement la production/ l'activité de; (criticize) critiquer, dénigrer; **to be ~ down** (tired) être fatigué(e) or à plat; **run into** vt fus (meet: person) rencontrer par hasard; (: trouble) se heurter à; (collide with) heurter; **run off** vi s'enfuir ▷ vt (water) laisser s'écouler; (copies) tirer; **run out** vi (person) sortir en courant; (liquid) couler; (lease) expirer; (money) être épuisé(e); **run out of** vt fus se trouver à court de; **run over** vt (Aut) écraser ▷ vt fus (revise) revoir, reprendre; **run through** vt fus (recap) reprendre, revoir; (play) répéter; **run up** vi: **to ~ up against** (difficulties) se heurter

à; **runaway** adj (horse) emballé(e); (truck) fou (folle); (person) fugitif(-ive); (child) fugueur(-euse)

rung [rʌŋ] pp of **ring** ▷ n (of ladder) barreau m

runner ['rʌnəʳ] n (in race: person) coureur(-euse); (: horse) partant m; (on sledge) patin m; (for drawer etc) coulisseau m; **runner bean** n (BRIT) haricot m (à rames); **runner-up** n second(e)

running ['rʌnɪŋ] n (in race etc) course f; (of business, organization) direction f, gestion f ▷ adj (water) courant(e); (commentary) suivi(e); **6 days ~** 6 jours de suite; **to be in/out of the ~ for sth** être/ne pas être sur les rangs pour qch

runny ['rʌnɪ] adj qui coule

run-up ['rʌnʌp] n (BRIT): **~ to sth** période f précédant qch

runway ['rʌnweɪ] n (Aviat) piste f (d'envol or d'atterrissage)

rupture ['rʌptʃəʳ] n (Med) hernie f

rural ['ruərl] adj rural(e)

rush [rʌʃ] n (of crowd, Comm: sudden demand) ruée f; (hurry) hâte f; (of anger, joy) accès m; (current) flot m; (Bot) jonc m ▷ vt (hurry) transporter or envoyer d'urgence ▷ vi se précipiter; **to ~ sth off** (do quickly) faire qch à la hâte; **rush hour** n heures fpl de pointe or d'affluence

Russia ['rʌʃə] n Russie f; **Russian** adj russe ▷ n Russe m/f; (Ling) russe m

rust [rʌst] n rouille f ▷ vi rouiller

rusty ['rʌstɪ] adj rouillé(e)

ruthless ['ruːθlɪs] adj sans pitié, impitoyable

RV n abbr (US) = **recreational vehicle**

rye [raɪ] n seigle m

S

Sabbath ['sæbəθ] n (Jewish) sabbat m; (Christian) dimanche m

sabotage ['sæbətɑːʒ] n sabotage m ▷ vt saboter

saccharin(e) ['sækərɪn] n saccharine f

sachet ['sæʃeɪ] n sachet m

sack [sæk] n (bag) sac m ▷ vt (dismiss) renvoyer, mettre à la porte; (plunder) piller, mettre à sac; **to get the ~** être renvoyé(e) or mis(e) à la porte

sacred ['seɪkrɪd] adj sacré(e)

sacrifice ['sækrɪfaɪs] n sacrifice m ▷ vt sacrifier

sad [sæd] adj (unhappy) triste; (deplorable) triste, fâcheux(-euse); (inf: pathetic: thing) triste, lamentable; (: person) minable

saddle ['sædl] n selle f ▷ vt (horse) seller; **to be ~d with sth** (inf) avoir qch sur les bras

sadistic [sə'dɪstɪk] adj sadique

sadly ['sædlɪ] adv tristement; (unfortunately) malheureusement; (seriously) fort

sadness ['sædnɪs] n tristesse f

s.a.e. n abbr (BRIT: = stamped addressed envelope) enveloppe affranchie pour la réponse

safari [sə'fɑːrɪ] n safari m

safe [seɪf] adj (out of danger) hors de danger, en sécurité; (not dangerous) sans danger; (cautious) prudent(e); (sure: bet) assuré(e) ▷ n coffre-fort m; **~ and sound** sain(e) et sauf; **(just) to be on the ~ side** pour plus de sûreté, par précaution; **safely** adv (assume, say) sans risque d'erreur; (drive, arrive) sans accident; **safe sex** n rapports sexuels protégés

safety ['seɪftɪ] n sécurité f; **safety belt** n ceinture f de sécurité; **safety pin** n épingle f de sûreté or de nourrice

saffron ['sæfrən] n safran m

sag [sæg] vi s'affaisser, fléchir; (hem, breasts) pendre

sage [seɪdʒ] n (herb) sauge f; (person) sage m

Sagittarius [sædʒɪ'tɛərɪəs] n le Sagittaire

Sahara [sə'hɑːrə] n: **the ~ (Desert)** le (désert du) Sahara m

said [sɛd] pt, pp of **say**

sail [seɪl] n (on boat) voile f; (trip): **to go for a ~** faire un tour en bateau ▷ vt (boat) manœuvrer, piloter ▷ vi (travel: ship) avancer, naviguer; (set off) partir, prendre la mer; (Sport) faire de la voile; **they ~ed into Le Havre** ils sont entrés dans le port du Havre; **sailboat** n (US) bateau m à voiles, voilier m; **sailing** n (Sport) voile f; **to go sailing** faire de la voile; **sailing boat** n bateau m à voiles, voilier m; **sailor** n marin m, matelot m

saint [seɪnt] n saint(e)

sake [seɪk] n: **for the ~ of** (out of concern for) pour (l'amour de), dans l'intérêt de; (*out of consideration for*) par égard pour

salad ['sæləd] *n* salade *f*; **salad cream** *n* (BRIT) (sorte *f* de) mayonnaise *f*; **salad dressing** *n* vinaigrette *f*

salami [sə'lɑːmɪ] *n* salami *m*

salary ['sælərɪ] *n* salaire *m*, traitement *m*

sale [seɪl] *n* vente *f*; (*at reduced prices*) soldes *mpl*; **sales** *npl* (*total amount sold*) chiffre *m* de ventes; **"for ~"** "à vendre"; **on ~** en vente; **sales assistant**, (US) **sales clerk** *n* vendeur(-euse); **salesman** (*irreg*) *n* (*in shop*) vendeur *m*; **salesperson** (*irreg*) *n* (*in shop*) vendeur(-euse); **sales rep** *n* (*Comm*) représentant(e) *m/f*; **saleswoman** (*irreg*) *n* (*in shop*) vendeuse *f*

saline ['seɪlaɪn] *adj* salin(e)

saliva [sə'laɪvə] *n* salive *f*

salmon ['sæmən] *n* (*pl inv*) saumon *m*

salon ['sælɔn] *n* salon *m*

saloon [sə'luːn] *n* (US) bar *m*; (BRIT Aut) berline *f*; (*ship's lounge*) salon *m*

salt [sɔːlt] *n* sel *m* ▷ *vt* saler; **saltwater** *adj* (*fish etc*) (d'eau) de mer; **salty** *adj* salé(e)

salute [sə'luːt] *n* salut *m*; (*of guns*) salve *f* ▷ *vt* saluer

salvage ['sælvɪdʒ] *n* (*saving*) sauvetage *m*; (*things saved*) biens sauvés *or* récupérés ▷ *vt* sauver, récupérer

Salvation Army [sæl'veɪʃən-] *n* Armée *f* du Salut

same [seɪm] *adj* même ▷ *pron*: **the ~** le (la) même, les mêmes; **the ~ book as** le même livre que; **at the ~ time** en même temps; (*yet*) néanmoins; **all** *or* **just the ~** tout de même, quand même; **to do the ~** faire de même, en faire autant; **to do the ~ as sb** faire comme qn; **and the ~ to you!** et à vous de même!; (*after insult*) toi-même!

sample ['sɑːmpl] *n* échantillon *m*; (*Med*) prélèvement *m* ▷ *vt* (*food, wine*) goûter

sanction ['sæŋkʃən] *n* approbation *f*, sanction *f* ▷ *vt* cautionner, sanctionner; **sanctions** *npl* (*Pol*) sanctions

sanctuary ['sæŋktjuərɪ] *n* (*holy place*) sanctuaire *m*; (*refuge*) asile *m*; (*for wildlife*) réserve *f*

sand [sænd] *n* sable *m* ▷ *vt* (*also:* **~ down**: *wood etc*) poncer

sandal ['sændl] *n* sandale *f*

sand: sandbox *n* (US: *for children*) tas *m* de sable; **sand castle** *n* château *m* de sable; **sand dune** *n* dune *f* de sable; **sandpaper** *n* papier *m* de verre; **sandpit** *n* (BRIT: *for children*) tas *m* de sable; **sands** *npl* plage *f* (de sable); **sandstone** ['sændstəun] *n* grès *m*

sandwich ['sændwɪtʃ] *n* sandwich *m* ▷ *vt* (*also:* **~ in**) intercaler; **~ed between** pris en sandwich entre; **cheese/ham ~** sandwich au fromage/jambon

sandy ['sændɪ] *adj* sablonneux(-euse); (*colour*) sable *inv*, blond roux *inv*

sane [seɪn] *adj* (*person*) sain(e) d'esprit; (*outlook*) sensé(e), sain(e)

sang [sæŋ] *pt of* **sing**

sanitary towel, (US) **sanitary napkin** ['sænɪtərɪ-] *n* serviette *f* hygiénique

sanity ['sænɪtɪ] *n* santé mentale; (*common sense*) bon sens

sank [sæŋk] *pt of* **sink**

Santa Claus [sæntə'klɔːz] *n* le Père Noël

sap [sæp] *n* (*of plants*) sève *f* ▷ *vt* (*strength*) saper, miner

sapphire ['sæfaɪəʳ] *n* saphir *m*

sarcasm ['sɑːkæzm] *n* sarcasme *m*, raillerie *f*

sarcastic [sɑː'kæstɪk] *adj* sarcastique

sardine [sɑː'diːn] *n* sardine *f*

S

SASE n abbr (US: = self-addressed stamped envelope) enveloppe affranchie pour la réponse

sat [sæt] pt, pp of **sit**

Sat. abbr (= Saturday) sa

satchel ['sætʃl] n cartable m

satellite ['sætəlaɪt] n satellite m; **satellite dish** n antenne f parabolique; **satellite navigation system** n système m de navigation par satellite; **satellite television** n télévision f par satellite

satin ['sætɪn] n satin m ▷ adj en or de satin, satiné(e)

satire ['sætaɪə'] n satire f

satisfaction [sætɪs'fækʃən] n satisfaction f

satisfactory [sætɪs'fæktərɪ] adj satisfaisant(e)

satisfied ['sætɪsfaɪd] adj satisfait(e); **to be ~ with sth** être satisfait de qch

satisfy ['sætɪsfaɪ] vt satisfaire, contenter; (convince) convaincre, persuader

Saturday ['sætədɪ] n samedi m

sauce [sɔːs] n sauce f; **saucepan** n casserole f

saucer ['sɔːsə'] n soucoupe f

Saudi Arabia ['saudɪ-] n Arabie f Saoudite

sauna ['sɔːnə] n sauna m

sausage ['sɔsɪdʒ] n saucisse f; (salami etc) saucisson m; **sausage roll** n friand m

sautéed ['səuteɪd] adj sauté(e)

savage ['sævɪdʒ] adj (cruel, fierce) brutal(e), féroce; (primitive) primitif(-ive), sauvage ▷ n sauvage m/f ▷ vt attaquer férocement

save [seɪv] vt (person, belongings) sauver; (money) mettre de côté, économiser; (time) (faire) gagner; (keep) garder; (Comput) sauvegarder; (Sport: stop) arrêter; (avoid: trouble) éviter ▷ vi (also: ~ up) mettre de l'argent de côté ▷ n (Sport) arrêt m (du ballon) ▷ prep sauf, à l'exception de

saving ['seɪvɪŋ] n économie f; **savings** npl économies fpl

savings account n compte m d'épargne

savings and loan association (US) n ≈ société f de crédit immobilier

savoury, (US) **savory** ['seɪvərɪ] adj savoureux(-euse); (dish: not sweet) salé(e)

saw [sɔː] pt of **see** ▷ n (tool) scie f ▷ vt (pt **sawed**, pp **sawed** or **sawn**) scier; **sawdust** n sciure f

sawn [sɔːn] pp of **saw**

saxophone ['sæksəfəun] n saxophone m

say [seɪ] vt (pt, pp **said**) dire ▷ n: **to have one's ~** dire ce qu'on a à dire; **to have a ~** avoir voix au chapitre; **could you ~ that again?** pourriez-vous répéter ce que vous venez de dire?; **to ~ yes/no** dire oui/non; **my watch ~s 3 o'clock** ma montre indique 3 heures, il est 3 heures à ma montre; **that is to ~** c'est-à-dire; **that goes without ~ing** cela va sans dire, cela va de soi; **saying** n dicton m, proverbe m

scab [skæb] n croûte f; (pej) jaune m

scaffolding ['skæfəldɪŋ] n échafaudage m

scald [skɔːld] n brûlure f ▷ vt ébouillanter

scale [skeɪl] n (of fish) écaille f; (Mus) gamme f; (of ruler, thermometer etc) graduation f, échelle (graduée); (of salaries, fees etc) barème m; (of map, also size, extent) échelle ▷ vt (mountain) escalader; **scales** npl balance f; (larger) bascule f; (also: **bathroom ~s**) pèse-personne m inv; **~ of charges** tableau m des tarifs; **on a large ~** sur une grande échelle, en grand

scallion ['skæljən] n (US: salad onion) ciboule f

scallop ['skɔləp] n coquille f Saint-Jacques; (Sewing) feston m

scalp [skælp] n cuir chevelu ▷ vt scalper

scalpel ['skælpl] n scalpel m

scam [skæm] n (inf) arnaque f

scampi ['skæmpɪ] npl langoustines (frites), scampi mpl

scan [skæn] vt (examine) scruter, examiner; (glance at quickly) parcourir; (TV, Radar) balayer ▷ n (Med) scanographie f

scandal ['skændl] n scandale m; (gossip) ragots mpl

Scandinavia [skændɪˈneɪvɪə] n Scandinavie f; **Scandinavian** adj scandinave ▷ n Scandinave m/f

scanner ['skænəʳ] n (Radar, Med) scanner m, scanographe m; (Comput) scanner

scapegoat ['skeɪpgəʊt] n bouc m émissaire

scar [skɑːʳ] n cicatrice f ▷ vt laisser une cicatrice or une marque à

scarce [skɛəs] adj rare, peu abondant(e); **to make o.s. ~** (inf) se sauver; **scarcely** adv à peine, presque pas

scare [skɛəʳ] n peur f, panique f ▷ vt effrayer, faire peur à; **to ~ sb stiff** faire une peur bleue à qn; **bomb ~** alerte f à la bombe; **scarecrow** n épouvantail m; **scared** adj: **to be scared** avoir peur

scarf (pl **scarves**) [skɑːf, skɑːvz] n (long) écharpe f; (square) foulard m

scarlet ['skɑːlɪt] adj écarlate

scarves [skɑːvz] npl of **scarf**

scary ['skɛərɪ] adj (inf) effrayant(e); (film) qui fait peur

scatter ['skætəʳ] vt éparpiller, répandre; (crowd) disperser ▷ vi se disperser

scenario [sɪˈnɑːrɪəʊ] n scénario m

scene [siːn] n (Theat, fig etc) scène f; (of crime, accident) lieu(x) m(pl), endroit m; (sight, view) spectacle m, vue f; **scenery** n (Theat) décor(s) m(pl); (landscape) paysage m; **scenic** adj offrant de beaux paysages or panoramas

scent [sɛnt] n parfum m, odeur f; (fig: track) piste f

sceptical, (US) **skeptical** ['skɛptɪkl] adj sceptique

schedule ['ʃɛdjuːl, US 'skɛdjuːl] n programme m, plan m; (of trains) horaire m; (of prices etc) barème m, tarif m ▷ vt prévoir; **on ~** à l'heure (prévue); à la date prévue; **to be ahead of/behind ~** avoir de l'avance/du retard; **scheduled flight** n vol régulier

scheme [skiːm] n plan m, projet m; (plot) complot m, combine f; (arrangement) arrangement m, classification f; (pension scheme etc) régime m ▷ vt, vi comploter, manigancer

schizophrenic [skɪtsəˈfrɛnɪk] adj schizophrène

scholar ['skɒləʳ] n érudit(e); (pupil) boursier(-ère); **scholarship** n érudition f; (grant) bourse f (d'études)

school [skuːl] n (gen) école f; (secondary school) collège m; lycée m; (in university) faculté f; (US: university) université f ▷ cpd scolaire; **schoolbook** n livre m scolaire or de classe; **schoolboy** n écolier m; (at secondary school) collégien m; lycéen m; **schoolchildren** npl écoliers mpl; (at secondary school) collégiens mpl; lycéens mpl; **schoolgirl** n écolière f; (at secondary school) collégienne f; lycéenne f; **schooling** n instruction f, études fpl; **schoolteacher** n (primary) instituteur(-trice); (secondary) professeur m

science ['saɪəns] n science f; **science fiction** n science-fiction f; **scientific** [saɪənˈtɪfɪk] adj scientifique; **scientist** n scientifique m/f; (eminent) savant m

sci-fi ['saɪfaɪ] n abbr (inf: = science fiction) SF f

scissors ['sɪzəz] npl ciseaux mpl; **a pair of ~** une paire de ciseaux

scold [skəʊld] vt gronder

scone [skɒn] n sorte de petit pain rond au lait

scoop [sku:p] n pelle f (à main); (for ice cream) boule f à glace; (Press) reportage exclusif or à sensation

scooter ['sku:tə'] n (motor cycle) scooter m; (toy) trottinette f

scope [skəup] n (capacity: of plan, undertaking) portée f, envergure f; (: of person) compétence f, capacités fpl; (opportunity) possibilités fpl

scorching ['skɔ:tʃɪŋ] adj torride, brûlant(e)

score [skɔ:'] n score m, décompte m des points; (Mus) partition f ▷ vt (goal, point) marquer; (success) remporter; (cut: leather, wood, card) entailler, inciser ▷ vi marquer des points; (Football) marquer un but; (keep score) compter les points; **on that ~** sur ce chapitre, à cet égard; **a ~ of** (twenty) vingt; **~s of** (fig) des tas de; **to ~ 6 out of 10** obtenir 6 sur 10; **score out** vt rayer, barrer, biffer; **scoreboard** n tableau m; **scorer** n (Football) auteur m du but; buteur m; (keeping score) marqueur m

scorn [skɔ:n] n mépris m, dédain m

Scorpio ['skɔ:pɪəu] n le Scorpion

scorpion ['skɔ:pɪən] n scorpion m

Scot [skɔt] n Écossais(e)

Scotch [skɔtʃ] n whisky m, scotch m

Scotch tape® (us) n scotch® m, ruban adhésif

Scotland ['skɔtlənd] n Écosse f

Scots [skɔts] adj écossais(e); **Scotsman** (irreg) n Écossais m; **Scotswoman** (irreg) n Écossaise f; **Scottish** ['skɔtɪʃ] adj écossais(e); **the Scottish Parliament** le Parlement écossais

scout [skaut] n (Mil) éclaireur m; (also: **boy ~**) scout m; **girl ~** (us) guide f

scowl [skaul] vi se renfrogner; **to ~ at** regarder de travers

scramble ['skræmbl] n (rush) bousculade f, ruée f ▷ vi grimper/ descendre tant bien que mal; **to ~ for** se bousculer or se disputer pour

(avoir); **to go scrambling** (Sport) faire du trial; **scrambled eggs** npl œufs brouillés

scrap [skræp] n bout m, morceau m; (fight) bagarre f; (also: **~ iron**) ferraille f ▷ vt jeter, mettre au rebut; (fig) abandonner, laisser tomber ▷ vi se bagarrer; **scraps** npl (waste) déchets mpl; **scrapbook** n album m

scrape [skreip] vt, vi gratter, racler ▷ n: **to get into a ~** s'attirer des ennuis; **scrape through** vi (exam etc) réussir de justesse

scrap paper n papier m brouillon

scratch [skrætʃ] n égratignure f, rayure f; (on paint) éraflure f; (from claw) coup m de griffe ▷ vt (rub) (se) gratter; (paint etc) érafler; (with claw, nail) griffer ▷ vi (se) gratter; **to start from ~** partir de zéro; **to be up to ~** être à la hauteur; **scratch card** n carte f à gratter

scream [skri:m] n cri perçant, hurlement m ▷ vi crier, hurler

screen [skri:n] n écran m; (in room) paravent m; (fig) écran, rideau m ▷ vt masquer, cacher; (from the wind etc) abriter, protéger; (film) projeter; (candidates etc) filtrer; **screening** n (of film) projection f; (Med) test m (or tests) de dépistage; **screenplay** n scénario m; **screen saver** n (Comput) économiseur m d'écran; **screenshot** n (Comput) capture f d'écran

screw [skru:] n vis f ▷ vt (also: **~ in**) visser; **screw up** vt (paper etc) froisser; **to ~ up one's eyes** se plisser les yeux; **screwdriver** n tournevis m

scribble ['skrɪbl] n gribouillage m ▷ vt gribouiller, griffonner

script [skrɪpt] n (Cine etc) scénario m, texte m; (writing) (écriture f) script m

scroll [skrəul] n rouleau m ▷ vt (Comput) faire défiler (sur l'écran)

scrub [skrʌb] n (land) broussailles fpl ▷ vt (floor) nettoyer à la brosse; (pan) récurer; (washing) frotter

scruffy ['skrʌfɪ] adj débraillé(e)

scrum(mage) ['skrʌm(ɪdʒ)] n mêlée f

scrutiny ['skru:tɪnɪ] n examen minutieux

scuba diving ['sku:bə-] n plongée sous-marine

sculptor ['skʌlptər] n sculpteur m

sculpture ['skʌlptər] n sculpture f

scum [skʌm] n écume f, mousse f; (pej: people) rebut m, lie f

scurry ['skʌrɪ] vi filer à toute allure; **to ~ off** détaler, se sauver

sea [si:] n mer f ▷ cpd marin(e), de (la) mer, maritime; **by** or **beside the ~** (holiday, town) au bord de la mer; **by ~** par mer, en bateau; **out to ~** au large; **(out) at ~** en mer; **to be all at ~** (fig) nager complètement; **seafood** n fruits mpl de mer; **sea front** n bord m de mer; **seagull** n mouette f

seal [si:l] n (animal) phoque m; (stamp) sceau m, cachet m ▷ vt sceller; (envelope) coller (: with seal) cacheter; **seal off** vt (forbid entry to) interdire l'accès de

sea level n niveau m de la mer

seam [si:m] n couture f; (of coal) veine f, filon m

search [sə:tʃ] n (for person, thing, Comput) recherche(s) f(pl); (of drawer, pockets) fouille f; (Law: at sb's home) perquisition f ▷ vt fouiller; (examine) examiner minutieusement; scruter ▷ vi: **to ~ for** chercher; **in ~ of** à la recherche de; **search engine** n (Comput) moteur m de recherche; **search party** n expédition f de secours

sea: seashore n rivage m, plage f, bord m de (la) mer; **seasick** adj: **to be seasick** avoir le mal de mer; **seaside** n bord m de mer; **seaside resort** n station f balnéaire

season ['si:zn] n saison f ▷ vt assaisonner, relever; **to be in/out of ~** être/ne pas être de saison; **seasonal** adj saisonnier(-ière); **seasoning** n assaisonnement

m; **season ticket** n carte f d'abonnement

seat [si:t] n siège m; (in bus, train: place) place f; (buttocks) postérieur m; (of trousers) fond m ▷ vt faire asseoir, placer; (have room for) avoir des places assises pour, pouvoir accueillir; **to be ~ed** être assis; **seat belt** n ceinture f de sécurité; **seating** n sièges fpl, places assises

sea: sea water n eau f de mer; **seaweed** n algues fpl

sec. abbr (= second) sec

secluded [sɪ'klu:dɪd] adj retiré(e), à l'écart

second ['sɛkənd] num deuxième, second(e) ▷ adv (in race etc) en seconde position ▷ n (unit of time) seconde f; (Aut: also: ~ **gear**) seconde; (Comm: imperfect) article m de second choix; (BRIT Scol) ≈ licence f avec mention ▷ vt (motion) appuyer; **seconds** npl (inf: food) rab m (inf); **secondary** adj secondaire; **secondary school** n (age 11 to 15) collège m; (age 15 to 18) lycée m; **second-class** adj de deuxième classe; (Rail) de seconde (classe); (Post) au tarif réduit; (pej) de qualité inférieure ▷ adv (Rail) en seconde; (Post) au tarif réduit; **secondhand** adj d'occasion; (information) de seconde main; **secondly** adv deuxièmement; **second-rate** adj de deuxième ordre, de qualité inférieure; **second thoughts** npl; **to have second thoughts** changer d'avis; **on second thoughts** or (US) **thought** à la réflexion

secrecy ['si:krəsɪ] n secret m

secret ['si:krɪt] adj secret(-ète) ▷ n secret m; **in ~** adv en secret, secrètement, en cachette

secretary ['sɛkrətrɪ] n secrétaire m/f; **S~ of State (for)** (Pol) ministre m (de)

secretive ['si:krətɪv] adj réservé(e); (pej) cachottier(-ière), dissimulé(e)

secret service n services secrets

sect [sɛkt] n secte f

section ['sɛkʃən] n section f; (Comm) rayon m; (of document) section, article m, paragraphe m; (cut) coupe f

sector ['sɛktəʳ] n secteur m

secular ['sɛkjuləʳ] adj laïque

secure [sɪ'kjuəʳ] adj (free from anxiety) sans inquiétude, sécurisé(e); (firmly fixed) solide, bien attaché(e) (or fermé(e) etc); (in safe place) en lieu sûr, en sûreté ▷ vt (fix) fixer, attacher; (get) obtenir, se procurer

security [sɪ'kjuərɪtɪ] n sécurité f, mesures fpl de sécurité; (for loan) caution f, garantie f; **securities** npl (Stock Exchange) valeurs fpl, titres mpl; **security guard** n garde chargé de la sécurité; (transporting money) convoyeur m de fonds

sedan [sə'dæn] n (us Aut) berline f

sedate [sɪ'deɪt] adj calme; posé(e) ▷ vt donner des sédatifs à

sedative ['sɛdɪtɪv] n calmant m, sédatif m

seduce [sɪ'dju:s] vt séduire; **seductive** [sɪ'dʌktɪv] adj séduisant(e); (smile) séducteur(-trice); (fig: offer) alléchant(e)

see [si:] (pt **saw**, pp **seen**) vt (gen) voir; (accompany): **to ~ sb to the door** reconduire or raccompagner qn jusqu'à la porte ▷ vi voir; **to ~ that** (ensure) veiller à ce que + sub, faire en sorte que + sub, s'assurer que; **~ you soon/later/tomorrow!** à bientôt/plus tard/demain!; **see off** vt accompagner (à l'aéroport etc); **see out** vt (take to door) raccompagner à la porte; **see through** vt mener à bonne fin ▷ vt fus voir clair dans; **see to** vt fus s'occuper de, se charger de

seed [si:d] n graine f; (fig) germe m; (Tennis etc) tête f de série; **to go to ~** (plant) monter en graine; (fig) se laisser aller

seeing ['si:ɪŋ] conj: **~ (that)** vu que, étant donné que

seek [si:k] (pt, pp **sought**) vt chercher, rechercher

seem [si:m] vi sembler, paraître; **there ~s to be ...** il semble qu'il y a ..., on dirait qu'il y a ...; **seemingly** adv apparemment

seen [si:n] pp of **see**

seesaw ['si:sɔ:] n (jeu m de) bascule f

segment ['sɛgmənt] n segment m; (of orange) quartier m

segregate ['sɛgrɪgeɪt] vt séparer, isoler

Seine [seɪn] n: **the (River) ~** la Seine

seize [si:z] vt (grasp) saisir, attraper; (take possession of) s'emparer de; (opportunity) saisir

seizure ['si:ʒəʳ] n (Med) crise f, attaque f; (of power) prise f

seldom ['sɛldəm] adv rarement

select [sɪ'lɛkt] adj choisi(e), d'élite; (hotel, restaurant, club) chic inv, sélect inv ▷ vt sélectionner, choisir; **selection** n sélection f, choix m; **selective** adj sélectif(-ive); (school) à recrutement sélectif

self (pl **selves**) [sɛlf, sɛlvz] n: **the ~** le moi inv ▷ prefix auto-; **self-assured** adj sûr(e) de soi, plein(e) d'assurance; **self-catering** adj (BRIT: flat) avec cuisine, où l'on peut faire sa cuisine; (: holiday) en appartement (or chalet etc) loué; **self-centred**, (US) **self-centered** adj égocentrique; **self-confidence** n confiance f en soi; **self-confident** adj sûr(e) de soi, plein(e) d'assurance; **self-conscious** adj timide, qui manque d'assurance; **self-contained** adj (BRIT: flat) avec entrée particulière, indépendant(e); **self-control** n maîtrise f de soi; **self-defence**, (US) **self-defense** n autodéfense f; (Law) légitime défense f; **self-drive** adj (BRIT): **self-drive car** voiture f de location; **self-employed** adj qui travaille à son compte; **self-esteem** n amour-propre m; **self-harm** vi s'automutiler; **self-indulgent** adj qui ne se refuse rien; **self-interest** n intérêt personnel;

selfish adj égoïste; **self-pity** n apitoiement m sur soi-même; **self-raising** [sɛlf'reɪzɪŋ], (US) **self-rising** [sɛlf'raɪzɪŋ] adj: **self-raising flour** farine f pour gâteaux (avec levure incorporée); **self-respect** n respect m de soi, amour-propre m; **self-service** adj, n libre-service (m), self-service (m)

selfie [sɛlfɪ] n selfie m

sell (pt, pp **sold**) [sɛl, səuld] vt vendre ▷ vi se vendre; **to ~ at** or **for 10 euros** se vendre 10 euros; **sell off** vt liquider; **sell out** vi: **to ~ out (of sth)** (use up stock) vendre tout son stock (de qch); **sell-by date** n date f limite de vente; **seller** n vendeur(-euse), marchand(e)

Sellotape® [sɛləutɛɪp] n (BRIT) scotch® m

selves [sɛlvz] npl of **self**

semester [sɪ'mɛstə'] n (esp US) semestre m

semi... [sɛmɪ] prefix semi-, demi-; à demi, à moitié; **semicircle** n demi-cercle m; **semidetached (house)** n (BRIT) maison jumelée or jumelle; **semi-final** n demi-finale f

seminar [sɛmɪnɑː'] n séminaire m

semi-skimmed [sɛmɪ'skɪmd] adj demi-écrémé(e)

senate [sɛnɪt] n sénat m; (US): **the S~** le Sénat; **senator** n sénateur m

send (pt, pp **sent**) [sɛnd, sɛnt] vt envoyer; **send back** vt renvoyer; **send for** vt fus (by post) se faire envoyer, commander par correspondance; **send in** vt (report, application, resignation) remettre; **send off** vt (goods) envoyer, expédier; (BRIT Sport: player) expulser or renvoyer du terrain; **send on** vt (BRIT: letter) faire suivre; (luggage etc: in advance) (faire) expédier à l'avance; **send out** vt (invitation) envoyer (par la poste); (emit: light, heat, signal) émettre; **send up** vt (person, price) faire monter; (BRIT: parody) mettre en boîte, parodier; **sender** n expéditeur(-trice); **send-off** n: **a good send-off** des adieux chaleureux

senile [si:naɪl] adj sénile

senior [si:nɪə'] adj (high-ranking) de haut niveau; (of higher rank): **to be ~ to sb** être le supérieur de qn; **senior citizen** n personne f du troisième âge; **senior high school** n (US) ≈ lycée m

sensation [sɛn'seɪʃən] n sensation f; **sensational** adj qui fait sensation; (marvellous) sensationnel(le)

sense [sɛns] n sens m; (feeling) sentiment m; (meaning) sens, signification f; (wisdom) bon sens ▷ vt sentir, pressentir; **it makes ~** c'est logique; **senseless** adj insensé(e), stupide; (unconscious) sans connaissance; **sense of humour**, (US) **sense of humor** n sens m de l'humour

sensible [sɛnsɪbl] adj sensé(e), raisonnable; (shoes etc) pratique

Be careful not to translate sensible by the French word sensible.

sensitive [sɛnsɪtɪv] adj: **~ (to)** sensible (à)

sensual [sɛnsjuəl] adj sensuel(le)

sensuous [sɛnsjuəs] adj voluptueux(-euse), sensuel(le)

sent [sɛnt] pt, pp of **send**

sentence [sɛntns] n (Ling) phrase f; (Law: judgment) condamnation f, sentence f; (: punishment) peine f ▷ vt: **to ~ sb to death/to 5 years** condamner qn à mort/à 5 ans

sentiment [sɛntɪmənt] n sentiment m; (opinion) opinion f, avis m; **sentimental** [sɛntɪ'mɛntl] adj sentimental(e)

separate adj [sɛprɪt] séparé(e); (organization) indépendant(e); (day, occasion, issue) différent(e) ▷ vt [sɛpəreɪt] séparer; (distinguish) distinguer ▷ vi [sɛpəreɪt] se séparer; **separately** adv séparément; **separates** npl (clothes) coordonnés mpl; **separation** [sɛpə'reɪʃən] n séparation f

S

September [sɛp'tɛmbəʳ] n
septembre m
septic ['sɛptɪk] adj (wound) infecté(e);
septic tank n fosse f septique
sequel ['si:kwl] n conséquence f;
séquelles fpl; (of story) suite f
sequence ['si:kwəns] n ordre m,
suite f; (in film) séquence f; (dance)
numéro m
sequin ['si:kwɪn] n paillette f
Serb [sə:b] adj, n = **Serbian**
Serbia ['sə:bɪə] n Serbie f
Serbian ['sə:bɪən] adj serbe ▷ n Serbe
m/f; (Ling) serbe m
sergeant ['sɑ:dʒənt] n sergent m;
(Police) brigadier m
serial ['sɪərɪəl] n feuilleton m; **serial
killer** n meurtrier m tuant en série;
serial number n numéro m de série
series ['sɪərɪz] n série f; (Publishing)
collection f
serious ['sɪərɪəs] adj sérieux(-euse);
(accident etc) grave; **seriously** adv
sérieusement; (hurt) gravement
sermon ['sə:mən] n sermon m
servant ['sə:vənt] n domestique m/f;
(fig) serviteur (servante)
serve [sə:v] vt (employer etc) servir,
être au service de; (purpose) servir
à; (customer, food, meal) servir; (subj:
train) desservir; (apprenticeship) faire,
accomplir; (prison term) faire; purger
▷ vi (Tennis) servir; (be useful): **to ~
as/for/to do** servir de/à/à faire ▷ n
(Tennis) service m; **it ~s him right**
c'est bien fait pour lui; **server** n
(Comput) serveur m
service ['sə:vɪs] n (gen) service m;
(Aut) révision f; (Rel) office m ▷ vt
(car etc) réviser; **services** npl (Econ:
tertiary sector) (secteur m) tertiaire
m, secteur des services; (Brit: on
motorway) station-service f; (Mil): **the
S~s** npl les forces armées; **to be of ~
to sb, to do sb a ~** rendre service à
qn; **~ included/not included** service
compris/non compris; **service area**
n (on motorway) aire f de services;

service charge n (Brit) service m;
serviceman (irreg) n militaire m;
service station n station-service f
serviette [sə:vɪ'ɛt] n (Brit) serviette
f (de table)
session ['sɛʃən] n (sitting) séance f;
to be in ~ siéger, être en session or
en séance
set [sɛt] (pt, pp set) n série f,
assortiment m; (of tools etc) jeu m;
(Radio, TV) poste m; (Tennis) set m;
(group of people) cercle m, milieu m;
(Cine) plateau m; (Theat: stage) scène
f; (: scenery) décor m; (Math) ensemble
m; (Hairdressing) mise f en plis ▷ adj
(fixed) fixe, déterminé(e); (ready)
prêt(e) ▷ vt (place) mettre, poser,
placer; (fix, establish) fixer; (: record)
établir; (assign: task, homework)
donner; (exam) composer; (adjust)
régler; (decide: rules etc) fixer, choisir
▷ vi (sun) se coucher; (jam, jelly,
concrete) prendre; (bone) se ressouder;
to be ~ on doing être résolu(e)
à faire; **to ~ to music** mettre en
musique; **to ~ on fire** mettre le feu
à; **to ~ free** libérer; **to ~ sth going**
déclencher qch; **to ~ sail** partir,
prendre la mer; **set aside** vt mettre
de côté; (time) garder; **set down** vt
(subj: bus, train) déposer; **set in** vi
(infection, bad weather) s'installer;
(complications) survenir, surgir; **set
off** vi se mettre en route, partir ▷ vt
(bomb) faire exploser; (cause to start)
déclencher; (show up well) mettre en
valeur, faire valoir; **set out** vi: **to ~
out (from)** partir (de) ▷ vt (arrange)
disposer; (state) présenter, exposer;
to ~ out to do entreprendre de
faire; avoir pour but or intention de
faire; **set up** vt (organization) fonder,
créer; **setback** n (hitch) revers m,
contretemps m; **set menu** n menu m
settee [sɛ'ti:] n canapé m
setting ['sɛtɪŋ] n cadre m; (of jewel)
monture f; (position: of controls)
réglage m

settle ['sɛtl] vt (argument, matter, account) régler; (problem) résoudre; (Med: calm) calmer ▷ vi (bird, dust etc) se poser; **to ~ for sth** accepter qch, se contenter de qch; **to ~ on sth** opter or se décider pour qch; **settle down** vi (get comfortable) s'installer; (become calmer) se calmer; se ranger; **settle in** vi s'installer; **settle up** vi: **to ~ up with sb** régler (ce que l'on doit à) qn; **settlement** n (payment) règlement m; (agreement) accord m; (village etc) village m, hameau m

setup ['sɛtʌp] n (arrangement) manière f dont les choses sont organisées; (situation) situation f, allure f des choses

seven ['sɛvn] num sept; **seventeen** num dix-sept; **seventeenth** [sɛvn'tiːnθ] num dix-septième; **seventh** num septième; **seventieth** ['sɛvntɪɪθ] num soixante-dixième; **seventy** num soixante-dix

sever ['sɛvəʳ] vt couper, trancher; (relations) rompre

several ['sɛvərl] adj, pron plusieurs pl; **~ of us** plusieurs d'entre nous

severe [sɪ'vɪəʳ] adj (stern) sévère, strict(e); (serious) grave, sérieux(-euse); (plain) sévère, austère

sew (pt sewed, pp sewn) [səu, səud, səun] vt, vi coudre

sewage ['suːɪdʒ] n vidange(s) f(pl)

sewer ['suːəʳ] n égout m

sewing ['səuɪŋ] n couture f; (item(s)) ouvrage m; **sewing machine** n machine f à coudre

sewn [səun] pp of **sew**

sex [sɛks] n sexe m; **to have ~ with** avoir des rapports (sexuels) avec; **sexism** ['sɛksɪzəm] n sexisme m; **sexist** adj sexiste; **sexual** ['sɛksjuəl] adj sexuel(le); **sexual intercourse** n rapports sexuels; **sexuality** [sɛksju'ælɪtɪ] n sexualité f; **sexy** adj sexy inv

shabby ['ʃæbɪ] adj miteux(-euse); (behaviour) mesquin(e), méprisable

shack [ʃæk] n cabane f, hutte f

shade [ʃeɪd] n ombre f; (for lamp) abat-jour m inv; (of colour) nuance f, ton m; (US: window shade) store m; (small quantity): **a ~ of** un soupçon de ▷ vt abriter du soleil, ombrager; **shades** npl (US: sunglasses) lunettes fpl de soleil; **in the ~** à l'ombre; **a ~ smaller** un tout petit peu plus petit

shadow ['ʃædəu] n ombre f ▷ vt (follow) filer; **shadow cabinet** n (BRIT Pol) cabinet parallèle formé par le parti qui n'est pas au pouvoir

shady ['ʃeɪdɪ] adj ombragé(e); (fig: dishonest) louche, véreux(-euse)

shaft [ʃɑːft] n (of arrow, spear) hampe f; (Aut, Tech) arbre m; (of mine) puits m; (of lift) cage f; (of light) rayon m, trait m

shake [ʃeɪk] (pt shook, pp shaken) vt secouer; (bottle, cocktail) agiter; (house, confidence) ébranler ▷ vi trembler; **to ~ one's head** (in refusal etc) dire or faire non de la tête; (in dismay) secouer la tête; **to ~ hands with sb** serrer la main à qn; **shake off** vt secouer; (pursuer) se débarrasser de; **shake up** vt secouer; **shaky** adj (hand, voice) tremblant(e); (building) branlant(e), peu solide

shall [ʃæl] aux vb: **I ~ go** j'irai; **~ I open the door?** j'ouvre la porte?; **I'll open the coffee, ~ I?** je vais chercher le café, d'accord?

shallow ['ʃæləu] adj peu profond(e); (fig) superficiel(le), qui manque de profondeur

sham [ʃæm] n frime f

shambles ['ʃæmblz] n confusion f, pagaïe f, fouillis m

shame [ʃeɪm] n honte f ▷ vt faire honte à; **it is a ~ (that/to do)** c'est dommage (que + sub/de faire); **what a ~!** quel dommage!; **shameful** adj honteux(-euse), scandaleux(-euse); **shameless** adj éhonté(e), effronté(e)

shampoo [ʃæm'puː] n shampooing m ▷ vt faire un shampooing à

shandy ['ʃændɪ] n bière panachée

shan't [ʃɑːnt] = **shall not**

shape [ʃeɪp] n forme f ▷ vt façonner, modeler; (sb's ideas, character) former; (sb's life) déterminer ▷ vi (also: ~ **up**: events) prendre tournure; (: person) faire des progrès, s'en sortir; **to take** ~ prendre forme or tournure

share [ʃɛəʳ] n part f; (Comm) action f ▷ vt partager; (have in common) avoir en commun; **to ~ out (among** or **between)** partager (entre); **shareholder** n (BRIT) actionnaire m/f

shark [ʃɑːk] n requin m

sharp [ʃɑːp] adj (razor, knife) tranchant(e), bien aiguisé(e); (point, voice) aigu(ë); (nose, chin) pointu(e); (outline, increase) net(te); (cold, pain) vif (vive); (taste) piquant(e), âcre; (Mus) dièse; (person: quick-witted) vif (vive), éveillé(e); (: unscrupulous) malhonnête ▷ n (Mus) dièse m ▷ adv: **at 2 o'clock** ~ à 2 heures pile or tapantes; **sharpen** vt aiguiser; (pencil) tailler; (fig) aviver; **sharpener** n (also: **pencil sharpener**) taille-crayon(s) m inv; **sharply** adv (turn, stop) brusquement; (stand out) nettement; (criticize, retort) sèchement, vertement

shatter [ˈʃætəʳ] vt briser; (fig: upset) bouleverser; (: ruin) briser, ruiner ▷ vi voler en éclats, se briser; **shattered** adj (overwhelmed, grief-stricken) bouleversé(e); (inf: exhausted) éreinté(e)

shave [ʃeɪv] vt raser ▷ vi se raser ▷ n: **to have a** ~ se raser; **shaver** n (also: **electric shaver**) rasoir m électrique

shaving cream n crème f à raser

shaving foam n mousse f à raser

shavings [ˈʃeɪvɪŋz] npl (of wood etc) copeaux mpl

shawl [ʃɔːl] n châle m

she [ʃiː] pron elle

sheath [ʃiːθ] n gaine f, fourreau m, étui m; (contraceptive) préservatif m

shed [ʃɛd] n remise f, resserre f ▷ vt (pt, pp **shed**) (leaves, fur etc) perdre;

(tears) verser, répandre; (workers) congédier

she'd [ʃiːd] = **she had; she would**

sheep [ʃiːp] n (pl inv) mouton m; **sheepdog** n chien m de berger; **sheepskin** n peau f de mouton

sheer [ʃɪəʳ] adj (utter) pur(e), pur et simple; (steep) à pic, abrupt(e); (almost transparent) extrêmement fin(e) ▷ adv à pic, abruptement

sheet [ʃiːt] n (on bed) drap m; (of paper) feuille f; (of glass, metal etc) feuille, plaque f

sheik(h) [ʃeɪk] n cheik m

shelf (pl **shelves**) [ʃɛlf, ʃɛlvz] n étagère f, rayon m

shell [ʃɛl] n (on beach) coquillage m; (of egg, nut etc) coquille f; (explosive) obus m; (of building) carcasse f ▷ vt (peas) écosser; (Mil) bombarder (d'obus)

she'll [ʃiːl] = **she will; she shall**

shellfish [ˈʃɛlfɪʃ] n (pl inv: crab etc) crustacé m; (: scallop etc) coquillage m ▷ npl (as food) fruits mpl de mer

shelter [ˈʃɛltəʳ] n abri m, refuge m ▷ vt abriter, protéger; (give lodging to) donner asile à ▷ vi s'abriter, se mettre à l'abri; **sheltered** adj (life) retiré(e), à l'abri des soucis; (spot) abrité(e)

shelves [ʃɛlvz] npl of **shelf**

shelving [ˈʃɛlvɪŋ] n (shelves) rayonnage(s) m(pl)

shepherd [ˈʃɛpəd] n berger m ▷ vt (guide) guider, escorter; **shepherd's pie** n ≈ hachis m Parmentier

sheriff [ˈʃɛrɪf] (US) n shérif m

sherry [ˈʃɛrɪ] n xérès m, sherry m

she's [ʃiːz] = **she is; she has**

Shetland [ˈʃɛtlənd] n (also: **the ~s, the ~ Isles** or **Islands**) les îles fpl Shetland

shield [ʃiːld] n bouclier m; (protection) écran m de protection ▷ vt: **to ~ (from)** protéger (de or contre)

shift [ʃɪft] n (change) changement m; (work period) période f de travail; (of workers) équipe f, poste m ▷ vt

déplacer, changer de place; (*remove*)
enlever ▷ *vi* changer de place, bouger

shin [ʃɪn] *n* tibia *m*

shine [ʃaɪn] *n* éclat *m*, brillant *m*
▷ *vi* (*pt, pp* **shone**) briller ▷ *vt* (*pt, pp*
shined) (*polish*) faire briller *or* reluire;
to ~ sth on sth (*torch*) braquer qch
sur qch

shingles ['ʃɪŋglz] *n* (*Med*) zona *m*

shiny ['ʃaɪnɪ] *adj* brillant(e)

ship [ʃɪp] *n* bateau *m*; (*large*) navire
m ▷ *vt* transporter (par mer); (*send*)
expédier (par mer); **shipment** *n*
cargaison *f*; **shipping** *n* (*ships*) navires
mpl; (*traffic*) navigation *f*; (*the industry*)
industrie navale; (*transport*) transport
m; **shipwreck** *n* épave *f*; (*event*)
naufrage *m* ▷ *vt*: **to be shipwrecked**
faire naufrage; **shipyard** *n* chantier
naval

shirt [ʃəːt] *n* chemise *f*; (*woman's*)
chemisier *m*; **in ~ sleeves** en bras
de chemise

shit [ʃɪt] *excl* (*inf!*) merde (!)

shiver ['ʃɪvəʳ] *n* frisson *m* ▷ *vi*
frissonner

shock [ʃɔk] *n* choc *m*; (*Elec*) secousse *f*,
décharge *f*; (*Med*) commotion *f*, choc
▷ *vt* (*scandalize*) choquer, scandaliser;
(*upset*) bouleverser; **shocking**
adj (*outrageous*) choquant(e),
scandaleux(-euse); (*awful*)
épouvantable

shoe [ʃuː] *n* chaussure *f*, soulier *m*;
(*also*: **horse~**) fer *m* à cheval ▷ *vt* (*pt,
pp* **shod**) (*horse*) ferrer; **shoelace** *n*
lacet *m* (de soulier); **shoe polish** *n*
cirage *m*; **shoeshop** *n* magasin *m* de
chaussures

shone [ʃɔn] *pt, pp of* **shine**

shonky ['ʃɒŋkɪ] *adj* (*AUST, NZ inf*:
untrustworthy) louche

shook [ʃuk] *pt of* **shake**

shoot [ʃuːt] (*pt, pp* **shot**) *n* (*on branch,
seedling*) pousse *f* ▷ *vt* (*game: hunt*)
chasser; (: *aim at*) tirer; (: *kill*) abattre;
(*person*) blesser/tuer d'un coup de
fusil (*or* de revolver); (*execute*) fusiller;

(*arrow*) tirer; (*gun*) tirer un coup de;
(*Cine*) tourner ▷ *vi* (*with gun, bow*): **to
~ (at)** tirer (sur); (*Football*) shooter,
tirer; **shoot down** *vt* (*plane*) abattre;
shoot up *vi* (*fig: prices etc*) monter en
flèche; **shooting** *n* (*shots*) coups *mpl*
de feu; (*attack*) fusillade *f*; (*murder*)
homicide *m* (à l'aide d'une arme à feu);
(*Hunting*) chasse *f*

shop [ʃɔp] *n* magasin *m*; (*workshop*)
atelier *m* ▷ *vi* (*also*: **go ~ping**) faire ses
courses *or* ses achats; **shop assistant**
n (*BRIT*) vendeur(-euse); **shopkeeper**
n marchand(e), commerçant(e);
shoplifting *n* vol *m* à l'étalage;
shopping *n* (*goods*) achats *mpl*,
provisions *fpl*; **shopping bag** *n* sac
m (à provisions); **shopping centre**,
(*US*) **shopping center** *n* centre
commercial; **shopping mall** *n* centre
commercial; **shopping trolley** *n*
(*BRIT*) Caddie® *m*; **shop window** *n*
vitrine *f*

shore [ʃɔːʳ] *n* (*of sea, lake*) rivage *m*, rive
f ▷ *vt*: **to ~ (up)** étayer; **on ~** à terre

short [ʃɔːt] *adj* (*not long*) court(e);
(*soon finished*) court, bref (brève);
(*person, step*) petit(e); (*curt*) brusque,
sec (sèche); (*insufficient*) insuffisant(e)
▷ *n* (*also*: **~ film**) court métrage; (*Elec*)
court-circuit *m*; **to be ~ of sth** être
à court de *or* manquer de qch; **in ~**
bref; en bref; **~ of doing** à moins de
faire; **everything ~ of** tout sauf;
it is ~ for c'est l'abréviation *or* le
diminutif de; **to cut ~** (*speech, visit*)
abréger, écourter; **to fall ~ of** ne
pas être à la hauteur de; **to run ~ of**
arriver à court de, venir à manquer
de; **to stop ~** s'arrêter net; **to stop
~ of** ne pas aller jusqu'à; **shortage** *n*
manque *m*, pénurie *f*; **shortbread**
n ≈ sablé *m*; **shortcoming** *n* défaut
m; **short(crust) pastry** *n* (*BRIT*)
pâte brisée; **shortcut** *n* raccourci
m; **shorten** *vt* raccourcir; (*text,
visit*) abréger; **shortfall** *n* déficit *m*;
shorthand *n* (*BRIT*) sténo(graphie)

S

f; **shortlist** n (BRIT: for job) liste f des candidats sélectionnés; **short-lived** adj de courte durée; **shortly** adv bientôt, sous peu; **shorts** npl; **(a pair of) shorts** un short; **short-sighted** adj (BRIT) myope; (fig) qui manque de clairvoyance; **short-sleeved** adj à manches courtes; **short story** n nouvelle f; **short-tempered** adj qui s'emporte facilement; **short-term** adj (effect) à court terme

shot [ʃɔt] pt, pp of **shoot** ▷ n coup m (de feu); (try) coup, essai m; (injection) piqûre f; (Phot) photo f; **to be a good/poor ~** (person) tirer bien/mal; **like a ~** comme une flèche; (very readily) sans hésiter; **shotgun** n fusil m de chasse

should [ʃud] aux vb: **I ~ go now** je devrais partir maintenant; **he ~ be there now** il devrait être arrivé maintenant; **I ~ go if I were you** si j'étais vous j'irais; **I ~ like to** volontiers, j'aimerais bien

shoulder ['ʃəuldər] n épaule f ▷ vt (fig) endosser, se charger de; **shoulder blade** n omoplate f

shouldn't ['ʃudnt] = **should not**

shout [ʃaut] n cri m ▷ vt crier ▷ vi crier, pousser des cris

shove [ʃʌv] vt pousser; (inf: put): **to ~ sth in** fourrer or ficher qch dans ▷ n poussée f

shovel ['ʃʌvl] n pelle f ▷ vt pelleter, enlever (or enfourner) à la pelle

show [ʃəu] (pt **showed**, pp **shown**) n (of emotion) manifestation f, démonstration f; (semblance) semblant m, apparence f; (exhibition) exposition f, salon m; (Theat, TV) spectacle m; (Cine) séance f ▷ vt montrer; (film) passer; (courage etc) faire preuve de, manifester; (exhibit) exposer ▷ vi se voir, être visible; **can you ~ me where it is, please?** pouvez-vous me montrer où c'est?; **to be on ~** être exposé(e); **it's just for ~** c'est juste pour l'effet; **show in**

vt faire entrer; **show off** vi (pej) crâner ▷ vt (display) faire valoir, étalage de; **show out** vt reconduire à la porte; **show up** vi (stand out) ressortir; (inf: turn up) se montrer ▷ vt (unmask) démasquer, dénoncer; (flaw) faire ressortir; **show business** n le monde du spectacle

shower ['ʃauər] n (for washing) douche f; (rain) averse f; (of stones etc) pluie f, grêle f; (US: party) réunion organisée pour la remise de cadeaux ▷ vi prendre une douche, se doucher ▷ vt: **to ~ sb with** (gifts etc) combler qn de; **to have** or **take a ~** prendre une douche, se doucher; **shower cap** n bonnet m de douche; **shower gel** n gel m douche

showing ['ʃəuɪŋ] n (of film) projection f

show jumping [-dʒʌmpɪŋ] n concours m hippique

shown [ʃəun] pp of **show**

show: show-off n (inf: person) crâneur(-euse), m'as-tu-vu(e); **showroom** n magasin m or salle f d'exposition

shrank [ʃræŋk] pt of **shrink**

shred [ʃrɛd] n (gen pl) lambeau m, petit morceau; (fig: of truth, evidence) parcelle f ▷ vt mettre en lambeaux, déchirer; (documents) détruire; (Culin: grate) râper; (: lettuce etc) couper en lanières

shrewd [ʃruːd] adj astucieux(-euse), perspicace; (business person) habile

shriek [ʃriːk] n cri perçant or aigu, hurlement m ▷ vt, vi hurler, crier

shrimp [ʃrɪmp] n crevette grise

shrine [ʃraɪn] n (place) lieu m de pèlerinage

shrink (pt **shrank**, pp **shrunk**) [ʃrɪŋk, ʃræŋk, ʃrʌŋk] vi rétrécir; (fig) diminuer; (also: **~ away**) reculer ▷ vt (wool) (faire) rétrécir ▷ n (inf, pej) psychanalyste m/f; **to ~ from (doing) sth** reculer devant (la pensée de faire) qch

shrivel ['ʃrɪvl], **shrivel up** vt ratatiner, flétrir ▷ vi se ratatiner, se flétrir

shroud [ʃraʊd] n linceul m ▷ vt: **~ed in mystery** enveloppé(e) de mystère

Shrove Tuesday ['ʃrəʊv-] n (le) Mardi gras

shrub [ʃrʌb] n arbuste m

shrug [ʃrʌg] n haussement m d'épaules ▷ vt, vi: **to ~ (one's shoulders)** hausser les épaules; **shrug off** vt faire fi de

shrunk [ʃrʌŋk] pp of **shrink**

shudder ['ʃʌdər] n frisson m, frémissement m ▷ vi frissonner, frémir

shuffle ['ʃʌfl] vt (cards) battre; **to ~ (one's feet)** traîner les pieds

shun [ʃʌn] vt éviter, fuir

shut (pt, pp **shut**) [ʃʌt] vt fermer ▷ vi (se) fermer; **shut down** vt fermer définitivement ▷ vi fermer définitivement; **shut up** vi (inf: keep quiet) se taire ▷ vt (close) fermer; (silence) faire taire; **shutter** n volet m; (Phot) obturateur m

shuttle ['ʃʌtl] n navette f; (also: **~ service**) (service m de) navette f; **shuttlecock** n volant m (de badminton)

shy [ʃaɪ] adj timide

siblings ['sɪblɪŋz] npl (formal) frères et sœurs mpl (de mêmes parents)

Sicily ['sɪsɪlɪ] n Sicile f

sick [sɪk] adj (ill) malade; (BRIT: humour) noir(e), macabre; (vomiting): **to be ~** vomir; **to feel ~** avoir envie de vomir, avoir mal au cœur; **to be ~ of** (fig) en avoir assez de; **sickening** adj (fig) écœurant(e), révoltant(e), répugnant(e); **sick leave** n congé m de maladie; **sickly** adj maladif(-ive), souffreteux(-euse); (causing nausea) écœurant(e); **sickness** n maladie f; (vomiting) vomissement(s) m(pl)

side [saɪd] n côté m; (of lake, road) bord m; (of mountain) versant m; (fig: aspect) côté, aspect m; (team: Sport) équipe

f; (TV: channel) chaîne f ▷ adj (door, entrance) latéral(e) ▷ vi: **to ~ with sb** prendre le parti de qn, se ranger du côté de qn; **by the ~ of** au bord de; **~ by ~** côte à côte; **to rock from ~ to ~** se balancer; **to take ~s (with)** prendre parti (pour); **sideboard** n buffet m; **sideboards**, (US) **sideburns** npl (whiskers) pattes fpl; **side effect** n effet m secondaire; **sidelight** n (Aut) veilleuse f; **sideline** n (Sport) (ligne f de) touche f; (fig) activité f secondaire; **side order** n garniture f; **side road** n petite route, route transversale; **side street** n rue transversale; **sidetrack** vt (fig) faire dévier de son sujet; **sidewalk** n (US) trottoir m; **sideways** adv de côté

siege [siːdʒ] n siège m

sieve [sɪv] n tamis m, passoire f ▷ vt tamiser, passer (au tamis)

sift [sɪft] vt passer au tamis or au crible; (fig) passer au crible

sigh [saɪ] n soupir m ▷ vi soupirer, pousser un soupir

sight [saɪt] n (faculty) vue f; (spectacle) spectacle m ▷ vt apercevoir; **in ~** visible; (fig) en vue; **out of ~** hors de vue; **sightseeing** n tourisme m; **to go sightseeing** faire du tourisme

sign [saɪn] n (gen) signe m; (with hand etc) signe, geste m; (notice) panneau m, écriteau m; (also: **road ~**) panneau de signalisation ▷ vt signer; **where do I ~?** où dois-je signer?; **sign for** vt fus (item) signer le reçu pour; **sign in** vi signer le registre (en arrivant); **sign on** vi (BRIT: as unemployed) s'inscrire au chômage; (enrol) s'inscrire ▷ vt (employee) embaucher; **sign over** vt: **to ~ sth over to sb** céder qch par écrit à qn; **sign up** vi (Mil) s'engager; (for course) s'inscrire

signal ['sɪgnl] n signal m ▷ vi (Aut) mettre son clignotant ▷ vt (person) faire signe à; (message) communiquer par signaux

signature ['sɪgnətʃər] n signature f

S

significance [sɪgˈnɪfɪkəns] n
signification f; importance f

significant [sɪgˈnɪfɪkənt] adj
significatif(-ive); (important)
important(e), considérable

signify [ˈsɪgnɪfaɪ] vt signifier

sign language n langage m par
signes

signpost [ˈsaɪnpəust] n poteau
indicateur

Sikh [siːk] adj, n Sikh m/f

silence [ˈsaɪlns] n silence m ▷ vt faire
taire, réduire au silence

silent [ˈsaɪlnt] adj silencieux(-euse);
(film) muet(te); **to keep** or **remain ~**
garder le silence, ne rien dire

silhouette [sɪluːˈɛt] n silhouette f

silicon chip [ˈsɪlɪkən-] n puce f
électronique

silk [sɪlk] n soie f ▷ cpd de or en soie

silly [ˈsɪlɪ] adj stupide, sot(te), bête

silver [ˈsɪlvəʳ] n argent m; (money)
monnaie f(en pièces d'argent); (also:
~ware) argenterie f ▷ adj (made
of silver) d'argent, en argent; (in
colour) argenté(e); **silver-plated** adj
plaqué(e) argent

SIM card [ˈsɪm-] abbr (Tel) carte
f SIM

similar [ˈsɪmɪləʳ] adj: **~ (to)**
semblable (à); **similarity**
[sɪmɪˈlærɪtɪ] n ressemblance f,
similarité f; **similarly** adv de la même
façon, de même

simmer [ˈsɪməʳ] vi cuire à feu doux,
mijoter

simple [ˈsɪmpl] adj simple;
simplicity [sɪmˈplɪsɪtɪ] n simplicité
f; **simplify** [ˈsɪmplɪfaɪ] vt simplifier;
simply adv simplement; (without
fuss) avec simplicité; (absolutely)
absolument

simulate [ˈsɪmjuleɪt] vt simuler,
feindre

simultaneous [sɪməlˈteɪnɪəs] adj
simultané(e); **simultaneously** adv
simultanément

sin [sɪn] n péché m ▷ vi pécher

since [sɪns] adv, prep depuis ▷ conj
(time) depuis que; (because) puisque,
étant donné que, comme; **~ then,
ever ~** depuis ce moment-là

sincere [sɪnˈsɪəʳ] adj sincère;
sincerely adv sincèrement; **yours
sincerely** (at end of letter) veuillez
agréer, Monsieur (or Madame)
l'expression de mes sentiments
distingués or les meilleurs

sing (pt **sang**, pp **sung**) [sɪŋ, sæŋ, sʌŋ]
vt, vi chanter

Singapore [sɪŋgəˈpɔːʳ] n
Singapour m

singer [ˈsɪŋəʳ] n chanteur(-euse)

singing [ˈsɪŋɪŋ] n (of person, bird)
chant m

single [ˈsɪŋgl] adj seul(e), unique;
(unmarried) célibataire; (not double)
simple ▷ n (BRIT: also: **~ ticket**) aller m
(simple); (record) 45 tours m; **singles**
npl (Tennis) simple m; **every ~ day**
chaque jour sans exception; **single
out** vt choisir; (distinguish) distinguer;
single bed n lit m d'une personne or à
une place; **single file** n: **in single file**
en file indienne; **single-handed** adv
tout(e) seul(e), sans (aucune) aide;
single-minded adj résolu(e), tenace;
single parent n parent unique (or
célibataire); **single-parent family**
famille monoparentale; **single
room** n chambre f à un lit or pour une
personne

singular [ˈsɪŋgjuləʳ] adj
singulier(-ière); (odd) singulier,
étrange; (outstanding) remarquable;
(Ling) (au) singulier, du singulier ▷ n
(Ling) singulier m

sinister [ˈsɪnɪstəʳ] adj sinistre

sink [sɪŋk] (pt **sank**, pp **sunk**) n
évier m; (washbasin) lavabo m ▷ vt
(ship) (faire) couler, faire sombrer;
(foundations) creuser ▷ vi couler,
sombrer; (ground etc) s'affaisser; **to ~
into sth** (chair) s'enfoncer dans qch;
sink in vi (explanation) rentrer (inf),
être compris

sinus ['saɪnəs] n (Anat) sinus m inv

sip [sɪp] n petite gorgée ▷ vt boire à petites gorgées

sir [səʳ] n monsieur m; **S~ John Smith** sir John Smith; **yes ~** oui Monsieur

siren ['saɪərn] n sirène f

sirloin ['sə:lɔɪn] n (also: **~ steak**) aloyau m

sister ['sɪstəʳ] n sœur f; (nun) religieuse f, (bonne) sœur; (BRIT: nurse) infirmière f en chef; **sister-in-law** n belle-sœur f

sit (pt, pp **sat**) [sɪt, sæt] vi s'asseoir; (be sitting) être assis(e); (assembly) être en séance, siéger; (for painter) poser ▷ vt (exam) passer, se présenter à; **sit back** vi (in seat) bien s'installer, se carrer; **sit down** vi s'asseoir; **sit on** vt fus (jury, committee) faire partie de; **sit up** vi s'asseoir; (straight) se redresser; (not go to bed) rester debout, ne pas se coucher

sitcom ['sɪtkɔm] n abbr (TV: = situation comedy) sitcom f, comédie f de situation

site [saɪt] n emplacement m, site m; (also: **building ~**) chantier m; (Internet) site m web ▷ vt placer

sitting ['sɪtɪŋ] n (of assembly etc) séance f; (in canteen) service m; **sitting room** n salon m

situated ['sɪtjueɪtɪd] adj situé(e)

situation [sɪtju'eɪʃən] n situation f; **"~s vacant/wanted"** (BRIT) "offres/demandes d'emploi"

six [sɪks] num six; **sixteen** num seize; **sixteenth** [sɪks'tiːnθ] num seizième; **sixth** ['sɪksθ] num sixième; **sixth form** n (BRIT) ≈ classes fpl de première et de terminale; **sixth-form college** n lycée n'ayant que des classes de première et de terminale; **sixtieth** ['sɪkstɪɪθ] num soixantième; **sixty** num soixante

size [saɪz] n dimensions fpl; (of person) taille f; (of clothing) taille f; (of shoes) pointure f; (of problem) ampleur f; (glue) colle f; **sizeable** adj assez grand(e); (amount, problem, majority) assez important(e)

sizzle ['sɪzl] vi grésiller

skate [skeɪt] n patin m; (fish: pl inv) raie f ▷ vi patiner; **skateboard** n skateboard m, planche f à roulettes; **skateboarding** n skateboard m; **skater** n patineur(-euse); **skating** n patinage m; **skating rink** n patinoire f

skeleton ['skɛlɪtn] n squelette m; (outline) schéma m

skeptical ['skɛptɪkl] (US) adj = **sceptical**

sketch [skɛtʃ] n (drawing) croquis m, esquisse f; (outline plan) aperçu m; (Theat) sketch m, saynète f ▷ vt esquisser, faire un croquis or une esquisse de; (plan etc) esquisser

skewer ['skjuːəʳ] n brochette f

ski [skiː] n ski m ▷ vi skier, faire du ski; **ski boot** n chaussure f de ski

skid [skɪd] n dérapage m ▷ vi déraper

ski: skier n skieur(-euse); **skiing** n ski m; **to go skiing** (aller) faire du ski

skilful, (US) **skillful** ['skɪlful] adj habile, adroit(e)

ski lift n remonte-pente m inv

skill [skɪl] n (ability) habileté f, adresse f, talent m; (requiring training) compétences fpl; **skilled** adj habile, adroit(e); (worker) qualifié(e)

skim [skɪm] vt (soup) écumer; (glide over) raser, effleurer ▷ vi: **to ~ through** (fig) parcourir; **skimmed milk**, (US) **skim milk** n lait écrémé

skin [skɪn] n peau f ▷ vt (fruit etc) éplucher; (animal) écorcher; **skinhead** n skinhead m; **skinny** adj maigre, maigrichon(ne)

skip [skɪp] n petit bond or saut; (BRIT: container) benne f ▷ vi gambader, sautiller; (with rope) sauter à la corde ▷ vt (pass over) sauter

ski: ski pass n forfait-skieur(s) m; **ski pole** n bâton m de ski

skipper ['skɪpəʳ] n (Naut, Sport) capitaine m; (in race) skipper m

s

skipping rope ['skɪpɪŋ-], (US) **skip rope** n corde f à sauter

skirt [skə:t] n jupe f ▷ vt longer, contourner

skirting board ['skə:tɪŋ-] n (BRIT) plinthe f

ski slope n piste f de ski

ski suit n combinaison f de ski

skull [skʌl] n crâne m

skunk [skʌŋk] n mouffette f

sky [skaɪ] n ciel m; **skyscraper** n gratte-ciel m inv

slab [slæb] n (of stone) dalle f; (of meat, cheese) tranche épaisse

slack [slæk] adj (loose) lâche, desserré(e); (slow) stagnant(e); (careless) négligent(e), peu sérieux(-euse) or conscencieux(-euse); **slacks** npl pantalon m

slain [sleɪn] pp of **slay**

slam [slæm] vt (door) (faire) claquer; (throw) jeter violemment, flanquer; (inf: criticize) éreinter, démolir ▷ vi claquer

slander ['slɑ:ndər] n calomnie f; (Law) diffamation f

slang [slæŋ] n argot m

slant [slɑ:nt] n inclinaison f; (fig) angle m, point m de vue

slap [slæp] n claque f, gifle f; (on the back) tape f ▷ vt donner une claque or une gifle (or une tape) à ▷ adv (directly) tout droit, en plein; **to ~ on** (paint) appliquer rapidement

slash [slæʃ] vt entailler, taillader; (fig: prices) casser

slate [sleɪt] n ardoise f ▷ vt (fig: criticize) éreinter, démolir

slaughter ['slɔ:tər] n carnage m, massacre m; (of animals) abattage m ▷ vt (animal) abattre; (people) massacrer; **slaughterhouse** n abattoir m

Slav [slɑ:v] adj slave

slave [sleɪv] n esclave m/f ▷ vi (also: ~ **away**) trimer, travailler comme un forçat; **slavery** n esclavage m

slay (pt **slew**, pp **slain**) [sleɪ, slu:, sleɪn] vt (literary) tuer

sleazy ['sli:zɪ] adj miteux(-euse), minable

sled [slɛd] (US) n = **sledge**

sledge [slɛdʒ] n luge f

sleek [sli:k] adj (hair, fur) brillant(e), luisant(e); (car, boat) aux lignes pures or élégantes

sleep [sli:p] n sommeil m ▷ vi (pt, pp **slept**) dormir; **to go to ~** s'endormir; **sleep in** vi (oversleep) se réveiller trop tard; (on purpose) faire la grasse matinée; **sleep together** vi (have sex) coucher ensemble; **sleeper** n (person) dormeur(-euse); (BRIT Rail: on track) traverse f; (: train) train-couchettes m; (: berth) couchette f; **sleeping bag** ['sli:pɪŋ-] n sac m de couchage; **sleeping car** n wagon-lits m, voiture-lits f; **sleeping pill** n somnifère m; **sleepover** n nuit f chez un copain or une copine; **we're having a sleepover at Jo's** nous allons passer la nuit chez Jo; **sleepwalk** vi marcher en dormant; **sleepy** adj (fig) endormi(e)

sleet [sli:t] n neige fondue

sleeve [sli:v] n manche f; (of record) pochette f; **sleeveless** adj (garment) sans manches

sleigh [sleɪ] n traîneau m

slender ['slɛndər] adj svelte, mince; (fig) faible, ténu(e)

slept [slɛpt] pt, pp of **sleep**

slew [slu:] pt of **slay**

slice [slaɪs] n tranche f; (round) rondelle f; (utensil) spatule f; (also: **fish ~**) pelle f à poisson ▷ vt couper en tranches (or en rondelles)

slick [slɪk] adj (skilful) bien ficelé(e); (salesperson) qui a du bagout ▷ n (also: **oil ~**) nappe f de pétrole, marée noire

slide (pt, pp **slid**) [slaɪd, slɪd] n (in playground) toboggan m; (Phot) diapositive f; (BRIT: also: **hair ~**) barrette f; (in prices) chute f, baisse f

▷ vt (faire) glisser ▷ vi glisser; **sliding** adj (door) coulissant(e)

slight [slaɪt] adj (slim) mince, menu(e); (frail) frêle; (trivial) faible, insignifiant(e); (small) petit(e), léger(-ère) before n ▷ n offense f, affront m ▷ vt (offend) blesser, offenser; **not in the ~est** pas le moins du monde, pas du tout; **slightly** adv légèrement, un peu

slim [slɪm] adj mince ▷ vi maigrir; (diet) suivre un régime amaigrissant; **slimming** n amaigrissement m ▷ adj (diet, pills) amaigrissant(e), pour maigrir; (food) qui ne fait pas grossir

slimy ['slaɪmɪ] adj visqueux(-euse), gluant(e)

sling [slɪŋ] n (Med) écharpe f; (for baby) porte-bébé m; (weapon) fronde f, lance-pierre m ▷ vt (pt, pp **slung**) lancer, jeter

slip [slɪp] n faux pas; (mistake) erreur f, bévue f; (underskirt) combinaison f; (of paper) petite feuille, fiche f ▷ vt (slide) glisser ▷ vi (slide) glisser; (decline) baisser; (move smoothly): **to ~ into/out of** se glisser or se faufiler dans/hors de; **to ~ sth on/off** enfiler/enlever qch; **to give sb the ~** fausser compagnie à qn; **a ~ of the tongue** un lapsus; **slip up** vi faire une erreur, gaffer

slipped disc [slɪpt-] n déplacement m de vertèbre

slipper ['slɪpəʳ] n pantoufle f

slippery ['slɪpərɪ] adj glissant(e)

slip road n (BRIT: to motorway) bretelle f d'accès

slit [slɪt] n fente f; (cut) incision f ▷ vt (pt, pp **slit**) fendre; couper, inciser

slog [slɔg] n (BRIT: effort) gros effort; (work) tâche fastidieuse ▷ vi travailler très dur

slogan ['sləʊgən] n slogan m

slope [sləʊp] n pente f, côte f; (side of mountain) versant m; (slant) inclinaison f ▷ vi: **to ~ down** être or descendre en pente; **to ~ up** monter;

sloping adj en pente, incliné(e); (handwriting) penché(e)

sloppy ['slɔpɪ] adj (work) peu soigné(e), bâclé(e); (appearance) négligé(e), débraillé(e)

slot [slɔt] n fente f ▷ vt: **to ~ sth into** encastrer or insérer qch dans; **slot machine** n (BRIT: vending machine) distributeur m (automatique), machine f à sous; (for gambling) appareil m or machine à sous

Slovakia [sləʊ'vækɪə] n Slovaquie f

Slovene [sləʊ'viːn] adj slovène ▷ n Slovène m/f; (Ling) slovène m

Slovenia [sləʊ'viːnɪə] n Slovénie f; **Slovenian** adj, n = **Slovene**

slow [sləʊ] adj lent(e); (watch): **to be ~** retarder ▷ adv lentement ▷ vt, vi ralentir; **"~"** (road sign) "ralentir"; **slow down** vi ralentir; **slowly** adv lentement; **slow motion** n: **in slow motion** au ralenti

slug [slʌg] n limace f; (bullet) balle f; **sluggish** adj (person) mou (molle), lent(e); (stream, engine, trading) lent(e)

slum [slʌm] n (house) taudis m; **slums** npl (area) quartiers mpl pauvres

slump [slʌmp] n baisse soudaine, effondrement m; (Econ) crise f ▷ vi s'effondrer, s'affaisser

slung [slʌŋ] pt, pp of **sling**

slur [sləːʳ] n (smear): **~ (on)** atteinte f (à); insinuation f (contre) ▷ vt mal articuler

slush [slʌʃ] n neige fondue

sly [slaɪ] adj (person) rusé(e); (smile, expression, remark) sournois(e)

smack [smæk] n (slap) tape f; (on face) gifle f ▷ vt donner une tape à; (on face) gifler; (on bottom) donner la fessée à ▷ vi: **to ~ of** avoir des relents de, sentir

small [smɔːl] adj petit(e); **small ads** npl (BRIT) petites annonces; **small change** n petite or menue monnaie

smart [smɑːt] adj élégant(e), chic inv; (clever) intelligent(e); (quick) vif (vive), prompt(e) ▷ vi faire mal, brûler;

S

smart card n carte f à puce; **smart phone** n smartphone m

smash [smæʃ] n (also: **~-up**) collision f, accident m; (Mus) succès foudroyant ▷ vt casser, briser, fracasser; (opponent) écraser; (Sport: record) pulvériser ▷ vi se briser, se fracasser; s'écraser; **smashing** adj (inf) formidable

smear [smɪəʳ] n (stain) tache f; (mark) trace f; (Med) frottis m ▷ vt enduire; (make dirty) salir; **smear test** n (BRIT Med) frottis m

smell [smɛl] (pt, pp **smelt** or **smelled**) n odeur f; (sense) odorat m ▷ vt sentir ▷ vi (pej) sentir mauvais; **smelly** adj qui sent mauvais, malodorant(e)

smelt [smɛlt] pt, pp of **smell**

smile [smaɪl] n sourire m ▷ vi sourire

smirk [smə:k] n petit sourire suffisant or affecté

smog [smɔg] n brouillard mêlé de fumée

smoke [sməuk] n fumée f ▷ vt, vi fumer; **do you mind if I ~?** ça ne vous dérange pas que je fume?; **smoke alarm** n détecteur m de fumée; **smoked** adj (bacon, glass) fumé(e); **smoker** n (person) fumeur(-euse); (Rail) wagon m fumeurs; **smoking** n: **"no smoking"** (sign) "défense de fumer"; **smoky** adj enfumé(e); (taste) fumé(e)

smooth [smu:ð] adj lisse; (sauce) onctueux(-euse); (flavour, whisky) moelleux(-euse); (movement) régulier(-ière), sans à-coups or heurts; (flight) sans secousses; (pej: person) doucereux(-euse), mielleux(-euse) ▷ vt (also: **~ out**) lisser, défroisser; (creases, difficulties) faire disparaître

smother ['smʌðəʳ] vt étouffer

SMS n abbr (= short message service) SMS m; **SMS message** n (message m) SMS m

smudge [smʌdʒ] n tache f, bavure f ▷ vt salir, maculer

smug [smʌg] adj suffisant(e), content(e) de soi

smuggle ['smʌgl] vt passer en contrebande or en fraude; **smuggling** n contrebande f

snack [snæk] n casse-croûte m inv; **snack bar** n snack(-bar) m

snag [snæg] n inconvénient m, difficulté f

snail [sneɪl] n escargot m

snake [sneɪk] n serpent m

snap [snæp] n (sound) claquement m, bruit sec; (photograph) photo f, instantané m ▷ adj subit(e), fait(e) sans réflechir ▷ vt (fingers) faire claquer; (break) casser net ▷ vi se casser net or avec un bruit sec; (speak sharply) parler d'un ton brusque; **to ~ open/shut** s'ouvrir/se refermer brusquement; **snap at** vt fus (subj: dog) essayer de mordre; **snap up** vt sauter sur, saisir; **snapshot** n photo f, instantané m

snarl [snɑ:l] vi gronder

snatch [snætʃ] n ▷ vt saisir (d'un geste vif); (steal) voler; **to ~ some sleep** arriver à dormir un peu

sneak [sni:k] (US: pt, pp **snuck**) vi: **to ~ in/out** entrer/sortir furtivement or à la dérobée ▷ n (inf: pej: informer) faux jeton; **to ~ up on sb** s'approcher de qn sans faire de bruit; **sneakers** npl tennis mpl, baskets fpl

sneer [snɪəʳ] vi ricaner; **to ~ at sb/sth** se moquer de qn/qch avec mépris

sneeze [sni:z] vi éternuer

sniff [snɪf] vi renifler ▷ vt renifler, flairer; (glue, drug) sniffer, respirer

snigger ['snɪgəʳ] vi ricaner

snip [snɪp] n (cut) entaille f; (BRIT inf: bargain) (bonne) occasion or affaire f ▷ vt couper

sniper ['snaɪpəʳ] n tireur embusqué

snob [snɔb] n snob m/f

snooker ['snu:kəʳ] n sorte de jeu de billard

snoop [snu:p] vi: **to ~ about** fureter

snooze [snuːz] *n* petit somme ▷ *vi*
faire un petit somme
snore [snɔːʳ] *vi* ronfler ▷ *n*
ronflement *m*
snorkel ['snɔːkl] *n* (*of swimmer*)
tuba *m*
snort [snɔːt] *n* grognement *m* ▷ *vi*
grogner; (*horse*) renâcler
snow [snəu] *n* neige *f* ▷ *vi* neiger;
snowball *n* boule *f* de neige;
snowdrift *n* congère *f*; **snowman**
(*irreg*) *n* bonhomme *m* de neige;
snowplough, (*US*) **snowplow** *n*
chasse-neige *m inv*; **snowstorm** *n*
tempête *f* de neige
snub [snʌb] *vt* repousser, snober ▷ *n*
rebuffade *f*
snuck [snʌk] (*US*) *pt*, *pp* of **sneak**
snug [snʌg] *adj* douillet(te),
confortable; (*person*) bien au chaud

 KEYWORD

so [səu] *adv* **1** (*thus, likewise*) ainsi,
de cette façon; **if so** si oui; **so do** *or*
have I moi aussi; **it's 5 o'clock — so**
it is! il est 5 heures — en effet! *or* c'est
vrai!; **I hope/think so** je l'espère/
le crois; **so far** jusqu'ici, jusqu'à
maintenant; (*in past*) jusque-là
2 (*in comparisons etc: to such a degree*)
si, tellement; **so big (that)** si *or*
tellement grand (que); **she's not so**
clever as her brother elle n'est pas
aussi intelligente que son frère
3: **so much** *adj*, *adv* tant (de); **I've**
got so much work j'ai tant de travail;
I love you so much je vous aime
tant; **so many** tant (de)
4 (*phrases*): **10 or so** à peu près *or*
environ 10; **so long!** (*inf: goodbye*) au
revoir!, à un de ces jours!; **so (what)?**
(*inf*) (bon) et alors?, et après?
▷ *conj* **1** (*expressing purpose*): **so as to**
do pour faire, afin de faire; **so (that)**
pour que *or* afin que + *sub*
2 (*expressing result*) donc, par
conséquent; **so that** si bien que; **so**

that's the reason! c'est donc (pour)
ça!; **so you see, I could have gone**
alors tu vois, j'aurais pu y aller

soak [səuk] *vt* faire *or* laisser tremper;
(*drench*) tremper ▷ *vi* tremper; **soak**
up *vt* absorber; **soaking** *adj* (*also*:
soaking wet) trempé(e)
so-and-so ['səuənsəu] *n* (*somebody*)
un(e) tel(le)
soap [səup] *n* savon *m*; **soap opera**
n feuilleton télévisé (*quotidienneté*
réaliste ou embellie); **soap powder** *n*
lessive *f*, détergent *m*
soar [sɔːʳ] *vi* monter (en flèche),
s'élancer; (*building*) s'élancer
sob [sɔb] *n* sanglot *m* ▷ *vi* sangloter
sober ['səubəʳ] *adj* qui n'est pas (*or*
plus) ivre; (*serious*) sérieux(-euse),
sensé(e); (*colour, style*) sobre,
discret(-ète); **sober up** *vi* se dégriser
so-called ['səu'kɔːld] *adj* soi-disant
inv
soccer ['sɔkəʳ] *n* football *m*
sociable ['səuʃəbl] *adj* sociable
social ['səuʃl] *adj* social(e);
(*sociable*) sociable ▷ *n* (petite)
fête; **socialism** *n* socialisme *m*;
socialist *adj*, *n* socialiste (*m/f*);
socialize *vi*: **to socialize with**
(*meet often*) fréquenter; (*get to know*)
lier connaissance *or* parler avec;
social life *n* vie sociale; **socially**
adv socialement, en société; **social**
media *npl* médias *mpl* sociaux; **social**
networking *n* réseaux *mpl* sociaux;
social networking site *n* site *m* de
réseautage; **social security** *n* aide
sociale; **social services** *npl* services
sociaux; **social work** *n* assistance
sociale; **social worker** *n* assistant(e)
sociale(e)
society [sə'saiəti] *n* société *f*; (*club*)
société, association *f*; (*also*: **high ~**)
(haute) société, grand monde
sociology [səusi'ɔlədʒi] *n*
sociologie *f*
sock [sɔk] *n* chaussette *f*

S

socket ['sɔkɪt] n cavité f; (Elec: also: **wall ~**) prise f de courant

soda ['səudə] n (Chem) soude f; (also: **~ water**) eau f de Seltz; (us: also: **~ pop**) soda m

sodium ['səudɪəm] n sodium m

sofa ['səufə] n sofa m, canapé m; **sofa bed** n canapé-lit m

soft [sɔft] adj (not rough) doux (douce); (not hard) doux, mou (molle); (not loud) doux, léger(-ère); (kind) doux, gentil(le); **soft drink** n boisson non alcoolisée; **soft drugs** npl drogues douces; **soften** ['sɔfn] vt (r)amollir; (fig) adoucir ▷ vi se ramollir; (fig) s'adoucir; **softly** adv doucement; (touch) légèrement; (kiss) tendrement; **software** n (Comput) logiciel m, software m

soggy ['sɔgɪ] adj (clothes) trempé(e); (ground) détrempé(e)

soil [sɔɪl] n (earth) sol m, terre f ▷ vt salir; (fig) souiller

solar ['səulə'] adj solaire; **solar power** n énergie f solaire; **solar system** n système m solaire

sold [səuld] pt, pp of **sell**

soldier ['səuldʒə'] n soldat m, militaire m

sold out adj (Comm) épuisé(e)

sole [səul] n (of foot) plante f; (of shoe) semelle f; (fish: pl inv) sole f ▷ adj seul(e), unique; **solely** adv seulement, uniquement

solemn ['sɔləm] adj solennel(le); (person) sérieux(-euse), grave

solicitor [sə'lɪsɪtə'] n (BRIT: for wills etc) ≈ notaire m; (: in court) ≈ avocat m

solid ['sɔlɪd] adj (not liquid) solide; (not hollow: mass) compact(e); (: metal, rock, wood) massif(-ive) ▷ n solide m

solitary ['sɔlɪtərɪ] adj solitaire

solitude ['sɔlɪtjuːd] n solitude f

solo ['səuləu] n solo m ▷ adv (fly) en solitaire; **soloist** n soliste m/f

soluble ['sɔljubl] adj soluble

solution [sə'luːʃən] n solution f

solve [sɔlv] vt résoudre

solvent ['sɔlvənt] adj (Comm) solvable n (Chem) (dis)solvant m

sombre, (us) **somber** ['sɔmbə'] adj sombre, morne

 KEYWORD

some [sʌm] adj **1** (a certain amount or number of): **some tea/water/ice cream** du thé/de l'eau/de la glace; **some children/apples** des enfants/pommes; **I've got some money but not much** j'ai de l'argent mais pas beaucoup

2 (certain: in contrasts): **some people say that ...** il y a des gens qui disent que ...; **some films were excellent, but most were mediocre** certains films étaient excellents, mais la plupart étaient médiocres

3 (unspecified): **some woman was asking for you** il y avait une dame qui vous demandait; **he was asking for some book (or other)** il demandait un livre quelconque; **some day** un de ces jours; **some day next week** un jour la semaine prochaine

▶ pron **1** (a certain number) quelques-un(e)s, certain(e)s; **I've got some** (books etc) j'en ai (quelques-uns); **some (of them) have been sold** certains ont été vendus

2 (a certain amount) un peu; **I've got some** (money, milk) j'en ai (un peu); **would you like some?** est-ce que vous en voulez?, en voulez-vous?; **could I have some of that cheese?** pourrais-je avoir un peu de ce fromage?; **I've read some of the book** j'ai lu une partie du livre

▶ adv: **some 10 people** quelque 10 personnes, 10 personnes environ; **somebody** ['sʌmbədɪ] pron = **someone**; **somehow** adv d'une façon ou d'une autre; (for some reason) pour une raison ou une autre; **someone** pron quelqu'un; **someplace** adv (us) = **somewhere**;

something pron quelque chose m; **something interesting** quelque chose d'intéressant; **something to do** quelque chose à faire; **sometime** adv (in future) un de ces jours, un jour ou l'autre; (in past): **sometime last month** au cours du mois dernier; **sometimes** adv quelquefois, parfois; **somewhat** adv quelque peu, un peu; **somewhere** adv quelque part; **somewhere else** ailleurs, autre part

son [sʌn] n fils m
song [sɔŋ] n chanson f; (of bird) chant m
son-in-law ['sʌnɪnlɔ:] n gendre m, beau-fils m
soon [su:n] adv bientôt; (early) tôt; ~ **afterwards** peu après; see also **as**; **sooner** adv (time) plus tôt; (preference): **I would sooner do that** j'aimerais autant or je préférerais faire ça; **sooner or later** tôt ou tard
soothe [su:ð] vt calmer, apaiser
sophisticated [sə'fɪstɪkeɪtɪd] adj raffiné(e), sophistiqué(e); (machinery) hautement perfectionné(e), très complexe
sophomore ['sɔfəmɔ:ʳ] n (us) étudiant(e) de seconde année
soprano [sə'prɑ:nəu] n (singer) soprano m/f
sorbet ['sɔ:beɪ] n sorbet m
sordid ['sɔ:dɪd] adj sordide
sore [sɔ:ʳ] adj (painful) douloureux(-euse), sensible ▷ n plaie f
sorrow ['sɔrəu] n peine f, chagrin m
sorry ['sɔrɪ] adj désolé(e); (condition, excuse, tale) triste, déplorable; ~! pardon!, excusez-moi!; ~? pardon?; **to feel ~ for sb** plaindre qn
sort [sɔ:t] n genre m, espèce f, sorte f; (make: of coffee, car etc) marque f ▷ vt (also: ~ **out**: select which to keep) trier; (classify) classer; (tidy) ranger; **sort out** vt (problem) résoudre, régler
SOS n SOS m

so-so ['səusəu] adv comme ci comme ça
sought [sɔ:t] pt, pp of **seek**
soul [səul] n âme f
sound [saund] adj (healthy) en bonne santé, sain(e); (safe, not damaged) solide, en bon état; (reliable, not superficial) sérieux(-euse), solide; (sensible) sensé(e) ▷ adv: ~ **asleep** profondément endormi(e) ▷ n (noise, volume) son m; (louder) bruit m; (Geo) détroit m, bras m de mer ▷ vt (alarm) sonner ▷ vi sonner, retentir; (fig: seem) sembler (être); **to ~ like** ressembler à; **sound bite** n phrase toute faite (pour être citée dans les médias); **soundtrack** n (of film) bande f sonore
soup [su:p] n soupe f, potage m
sour ['sauəʳ] adj aigre; **it's ~ grapes** c'est du dépit
source [sɔ:s] n source f
south [sauθ] n sud m ▷ adj sud inv; (wind) du sud ▷ adv au sud, vers le sud; **South Africa** n Afrique f du Sud; **South African** adj sud-africain(e) ▷ n Sud-Africain(e); **South America** n Amérique f du Sud; **South American** adj sud-américain(e) ▷ n Sud-Américain(e); **southbound** adj en direction du sud; (carriageway) sud inv; **south-east** n sud-est m; **southern** ['sʌðən] adj (du) sud; méridional(e); **South Korea** n Corée f du Sud; **South of France** n: **the South of France** le Sud de la France, le Midi; **South Pole** n: **the South Pole** le Pôle Sud; **southward(s)** adv vers le sud; **south-west** n sud-ouest m
souvenir [su:və'nɪəʳ] n souvenir m (objet)
sovereign ['sɔvrɪn] adj, n souverain(e)
sow¹ (pt **sowed**, pp **sown**) [səu, səud, səun] vt semer
sow² n [sau] truie f
soya ['sɔɪə], (us) **soy** [sɔɪ] n: ~ **bean** graine f de soja; ~ **sauce** sauce f au soja

S

spa [spɑː] n (town) station thermale; (US: also: **health ~**) établissement m de cure de rajeunissement

space [speɪs] n (gen) espace m; (room) place f; espace; (length of time) laps m de temps ▷ cpd spatial(e) ▷ vt (also: **~ out**) espacer; **spacecraft** n engin or vaisseau spatial; **spaceship** n = **spacecraft**

spacious ['speɪʃəs] adj spacieux(-euse), grand(e)

spade [speɪd] n (tool) bêche f, pelle f; (child's) pelle; **spades** npl (Cards) pique m

spaghetti [spə'gɛtɪ] n spaghetti mpl

Spain [speɪn] n Espagne f

spam [spæm] n (Comput) pourriel m

span [spæn] n (of bird, plane) envergure f; (of arch) portée f; (in time) espace m de temps, durée f ▷ vt enjamber, franchir; (fig) couvrir, embrasser

Spaniard ['spænjəd] n Espagnol(e)

Spanish ['spænɪʃ] adj espagnol(e), d'Espagne ▷ n (Ling) espagnol m; **the Spanish** npl les Espagnols

spank [spæŋk] vt donner une fessée à

spanner ['spænər] n (BRIT) clé f (de mécanicien)

spare [spɛər] adj de réserve, de rechange; (surplus) de or en trop, de reste ▷ n (part) pièce f de rechange, pièce détachée ▷ vt (do without) se passer de; (afford to give) donner, accorder, passer; (not hurt) épargner; **to ~** (surplus) en surplus, de trop; **spare part** n pièce f de rechange, pièce détachée; **spare room** n chambre f d'ami; **spare time** n moments mpl de loisir; **spare tyre**, (US) **spare tire** n (Aut) pneu m de rechange; **spare wheel** n (Aut) roue f de secours

spark [spɑːk] n étincelle f

sparkle ['spɑːkl] n scintillement m, étincellement m, éclat m ▷ vi étinceler, scintiller

sparkling ['spɑːklɪŋ] adj (wine) mousseux(-euse), pétillant(e); (water) pétillant(e), gazeux(-euse)

spark plug n bougie f

sparrow ['spærəu] n moineau m

sparse [spɑːs] adj clairsemé(e)

spasm ['spæzəm] n (Med) spasme m

spat [spæt] pt, pp of **spit**

spate [speɪt] n (fig): **~ of** avalanche f or torrent m de

spatula ['spætjulə] n spatule f

speak (pt **spoke**, pp **spoken**) [spiːk, spəuk, 'spəukn] vt (language) parler; (truth) dire ▷ vi parler; (make a speech) prendre la parole; **to ~ to sb/of or about sth** parler à qn/de qch; **I don't ~ French** je ne parle pas français; **do you ~ English?** parlez-vous anglais?; **can I ~ to ...?** est-ce que je peux parler à ...?; **speaker** n (in public) orateur m; (also: **loudspeaker**) haut-parleur m; (for stereo etc) baffle m, enceinte f; (Pol): **the Speaker** (BRIT) le président de la Chambre des communes or des représentants; (US) le président de la Chambre

spear [spɪər] n lance f ▷ vt transpercer

special ['spɛʃl] adj spécial(e); **special delivery** n (Post): **by special delivery** en express; **special effects** npl (Cine) effets spéciaux; **specialist** n spécialiste m/f; **speciality** [spɛʃɪ'ælɪtɪ] n (BRIT) spécialité f; **specialize** vi: **to specialize (in)** se spécialiser (dans); **specially** adv spécialement, particulièrement; **special needs** npl (BRIT) difficultés fpl d'apprentissage scolaire; **special offer** n (Comm) réclame f; **special school** n (BRIT) établissement m d'enseignement spécialisé; **specialty** n (US) = **speciality**

species ['spiːʃiːz] n (pl inv) espèce f

specific [spə'sɪfɪk] adj (not vague) précis(e), explicite; (particular) particulier(-ière); **specifically** adv explicitement, précisément;

(*intend, ask, design*) expressément, spécialement

specify ['spɛsɪfaɪ] *vt* spécifier, préciser

specimen ['spɛsɪmən] *n* spécimen *m*, échantillon *m*; (*Med: of blood*) prélèvement *m*; (: *of urine*) échantillon *m*

speck [spɛk] *n* petite tache, petit point; (*particle*) grain *m*

spectacle ['spɛktəkl] *n* spectacle *m*; **spectacles** *npl* (BRIT) lunettes *fpl*; **spectacular** [spɛk'tækjulə^r] *adj* spectaculaire

spectator [spɛk'teɪtə^r] *n* spectateur(-trice)

spectrum (*pl* **spectra**) ['spɛktrəm, -rə] *n* spectre *m*; (*fig*) gamme *f*

speculate ['spɛkjuleɪt] *vi* spéculer; (*ponder*): **to ~ about** s'interroger sur

sped [spɛd] *pt, pp of* **speed**

speech [spiːtʃ] *n* (*faculty*) parole *f*; (*talk*) discours *m*, allocution *f*; (*manner of speaking*) façon *f* de parler, langage *m*; (*enunciation*) élocution *f*; **speechless** *adj* muet(te)

speed [spiːd] *n* vitesse *f*; (*promptness*) rapidité *f* ▷ *vi* (*pt, pp* **sped**) (*Aut: exceed speed limit*) faire un excès de vitesse; **at full** *or* **top ~** à toute vitesse *or* allure; **speed up** (*pt, pp* **speeded up**) *vi* aller plus vite, accélérer ▷ *vt* accélérer; **speedboat** *n* vedette *f*, hors-bord *m inv*; **speed camera** *n* (*Aut*) radar *m* (*automatique*); **speeding** *n* (*Aut*) excès *m* de vitesse; **speed limit** *n* limitation *f* de vitesse, vitesse maximale permise; **speedometer** [spɪ'dɔmɪtə^r] *n* compteur *m* (de vitesse); **speedy** *adj* rapide, prompt(e)

spell [spɛl] *n* (*also*: **magic ~**) sortilège *m*, charme *m*; (*period of time*) (*courte*) période ▷ *vt* (*pt, pp* **spelled** *or* **spelt**) (*in writing*) écrire, orthographier; (*aloud*) épeler; (*fig*) signifier; **to cast a ~ on sb** jeter un sort à qn; **he can't ~** il fait

des fautes d'orthographe; **spell out** *vt* (*explain*): **to ~ sth out for sb** expliquer qch clairement à qn; **spellchecker** ['spɛltʃɛkə^r] *n* (*Comput*) correcteur *m or* vérificateur *m* orthographique; **spelling** *n* orthographe *f*

spelt [spɛlt] *pt, pp of* **spell**

spend (*pt, pp* **spent**) [spɛnd, spɛnt] *vt* (*money*) dépenser; (*time, life*) passer; (*devote*) consacrer; **spending** *n*: **government spending** les dépenses publiques

spent [spɛnt] *pt, pp of* **spend** ▷ *adj* (*cartridge, bullets*) vide

sperm [spəːm] *n* spermatozoïde *m*; (*semen*) sperme *m*

sphere [sfɪə^r] *n* sphère *f*; (*fig*) sphère, domaine *m*

spice [spaɪs] *n* épice *f* ▷ *vt* épicer

spicy ['spaɪsɪ] *adj* épicé(e), relevé(e); (*fig*) piquant(e)

spider ['spaɪdə^r] *n* araignée *f*

spike [spaɪk] *n* pointe *f*; (*Bot*) épi *m*

spill (*pt, pp* **spilt** *or* **spilled**) [spɪl, -t, -d] *vt* renverser; répandre ▷ *vi* se répandre; **spill over** *vi* déborder

spilt [spɪlt] *pt, pp of* **spill**

spin [spɪn] (*pt, pp* **spun**) *n* (*revolution of wheel*) tour *m*; (*Aviat*) (*chute f en*) vrille *f*; (*trip in car*) petit tour, balade *f*; (*on ball*) effet *m* ▷ *vt* (*wool etc*) filer; (*wheel*) faire tourner ▷ *vi* (*turn*) tourner, tournoyer

spinach ['spɪnɪtʃ] *n* épinards *mpl*

spinal ['spaɪnl] *adj* vertébral(e), spinal(e); **spinal cord** *n* moelle épinière

spin doctor *n* (*inf*) personne employée pour présenter un parti politique sous un jour favorable

spin-dryer [spɪn'draɪə^r] *n* (BRIT) essoreuse *f*

spine [spaɪn] *n* colonne vertébrale; (*thorn*) épine *f*, piquant *m*

spiral ['spaɪərl] *n* spirale *f* ▷ *vi* (*fig: prices etc*) monter en flèche

spire ['spaɪə^r] *n* flèche *f*, aiguille *f*

S

spirit ['spɪrɪt] n (soul) esprit m, âme f; (ghost) esprit, revenant m; (mood) esprit, état m d'esprit; (courage) courage m, énergie f; **spirits** npl (drink) spiritueux mpl, alcool m; **in good ~s** de bonne humeur

spiritual ['spɪrɪtjuəl] adj spirituel(le); (religious) religieux(-euse)

spit [spɪt] n (for roasting) broche f; (spittle) crachat m; (saliva) salive f ▷ vi (pt, pp **spat**) cracher; (sound) crépiter; (rain) crachiner

spite [spaɪt] n rancune f, dépit m ▷ vt contrarier, vexer; **in ~ of** en dépit de, malgré; **spiteful** adj malveillant(e), rancunier(-ière)

splash [splæʃ] n (sound) plouf m; (of colour) tache f ▷ vt éclabousser ▷ vi (also: **~ about**) barboter, patauger; **splash out** vi (BRIT) faire une folie

splendid ['splɛndɪd] adj splendide, superbe, magnifique

splinter ['splɪntəʳ] n (wood) écharde f; (metal) éclat m ▷ vi (wood) se fendre; (glass) se briser

split [splɪt] (pt, pp **split**) n fente f, déchirure f; (fig: Pol) scission f ▷ vt fendre, déchirer; (party) diviser; (work, profits) partager, répartir ▷ vi (break) se fendre, se briser; (divide) se diviser; **split up** vi (couple) se séparer, rompre; (meeting) se disperser

spoil (pt, pp **spoiled** or **spoilt**) [spɔɪl, -d, -t] vt (damage) abîmer; (mar) gâcher; (child) gâter

spoilt [spɔɪlt] pt, pp of **spoil** ▷ adj (child) gâté(e); (ballot paper) nul(le)

spoke [spəʊk] pt of **speak** ▷ n rayon m

spoken ['spəʊkn] pp of **speak**

spokesman ['spəʊksmən] (irreg) n porte-parole m inv

spokesperson ['spəʊkspə:sn] (irreg) n porte-parole m inv

spokeswoman ['spəʊkswumən] (irreg) n porte-parole m inv

sponge [spʌndʒ] n éponge f; (Culin: also: **~ cake**) ≈ biscuit m de Savoie ▷ vt

éponger ▷ vi: **to ~ off** or **on** vivre aux crochets de; **sponge bag** n (BRIT) trousse f de toilette

sponsor ['spɒnsəʳ] n (Radio, TV, Sport) sponsor m; (for application) parrain m, marraine f; (BRIT: for fund-raising event) donateur(-trice) ▷ vt sponsoriser; parrainer; faire un don à; **sponsorship** n sponsoring m; parrainage m; dons mpl

spontaneous [spɒn'teɪnɪəs] adj spontané(e)

spooky ['spu:kɪ] adj (inf) qui donne la chair de poule

spoon [spu:n] n cuiller f; **spoonful** n cuillerée f

sport [spɔ:t] n sport m; (person) chic type m/chic fille f ▷ vt (wear) arborer; **sport jacket** n (US) = **sports jacket**; **sports car** n voiture f de sport; **sports centre** (BRIT) n centre sportif; **sports jacket** (BRIT) veste f de sport; **sportsman** (irreg) n sportif m; **sports utility vehicle** n véhicule m de loisirs (de type SUV); **sportswear** n vêtements mpl de sport; **sportswoman** (irreg) n sportive f; **sporty** adj sportif(-ive)

spot [spɒt] n tache f; (dot: on pattern) pois m; (pimple) bouton m; (place) endroit m, coin m ▷ vt (notice) apercevoir, repérer; **on the ~** sur place, sur les lieux; (immediately) sur le champ; **spotless** adj immaculé(e); **spotlight** n projecteur m; (Aut) phare m auxiliaire

spouse [spauz] n époux (épouse)

sprain [spreɪn] n entorse f, foulure f ▷ vt: **to ~ one's ankle** se fouler or se tordre la cheville

sprang [spræŋ] pt of **spring**

sprawl [sprɔ:l] vi s'étaler

spray [spreɪ] n jet m (en fines gouttelettes); (from sea) embruns mpl; (aerosol) vaporisateur m, bombe f; (for garden) pulvérisateur m; (of flowers) petit bouquet ▷ vt vaporiser, pulvériser; (crops) traiter

spread [sprɛd] (*pt, pp* **spread**) *n* (*distribution*) répartition *f*; (*Culin*) pâte *f* à tartiner; (*inf: meal*) festin *m* ▷ *vt* (*paste, contents*) étendre, étaler; (*rumour, disease*) répandre, propager; (*wealth*) répartir ▷ *vi* s'étendre; se répandre; se propager; (*stain*) s'étaler; **spread out** *vi* (*people*) se disperser; **spreadsheet** *n* (*Comput*) tableur *m*

spree [spri:] *n*: **to go on a ~** faire la fête

spring [sprɪŋ] (*pt* **sprang**, *pp* **sprung**) *n* (*season*) printemps *m*; (*leap*) bond *m*, saut *m*; (*coiled metal*) ressort *m*; (*of water*) source *f* ▷ *vi* bondir, sauter; **spring up** *vi* (*problem*) se présenter, surgir; (*plant, buildings*) surgir de terre; **spring onion** *n* (BRIT) ciboule *f*, cive *f*

sprinkle ['sprɪŋkl] *vt*: **to ~ water** *etc* **on, ~ with water** *etc* asperger d'eau *etc*; **to ~ sugar** *etc* **on, ~ with sugar** *etc* saupoudrer de sucre *etc*

sprint [sprɪnt] *n* sprint *m* ▷ *vi* courir à toute vitesse; (*Sport*) sprinter

sprung [sprʌŋ] *pp of* **spring**

spun [spʌn] *pt, pp of* **spin**

spur [spə:ʳ] *n* éperon *m*; (*fig*) aiguillon *m* ▷ *vt* (*also:* **~ on**) éperonner aiguillonner; **on the ~ of the moment** sous l'impulsion du moment

spurt [spə:t] *n* jet *m*; (*of blood*) jaillissement *m*; (*of energy*) regain *m*, sursaut *m* ▷ *vi* jaillir, gicler

spy [spaɪ] *n* espion(ne) *m* ▷ *vi*: **to ~ on** espionner, épier ▷ *vt* (*see*) apercevoir

Sq. *abbr* (*in address*) = **square**

sq. *abbr* (*Math etc*) = **square**

squabble ['skwɔbl] *vi* se chamailler

squad [skwɔd] *n* (*Mil, Police*) escouade *f*, groupe *m*; (*Football*) contingent *m*

squadron ['skwɔdrn] *n* (*Mil*) escadron *m*; (*Aviat, Naut*) escadrille *f*

squander ['skwɔndəʳ] *vt* gaspiller, dilapider

square [skwɛəʳ] *n* carré *m*; (*in town*) place *f* ▷ *adj* carré(e) ▷ *vt* (*arrange*)

régler; arranger; (*Math*) élever au carré; (*reconcile*) concilier; **all ~** quitte; à égalité; **a ~ meal** un repas convenable; **2 metres ~** (de) 2 mètres sur 2; **1 ~ metre** 1 mètre carré; **square root** *n* racine carrée

squash [skwɔʃ] *n* (BRIT *Sport*) squash *m*; (US: *vegetable*) courge *f*; (*drink*): **lemon/orange ~** citronnade *f*/ orangeade *f* ▷ *vt* écraser

squat [skwɔt] *adj* petit(e) et épais(se), ramassé(e) ▷ *vi* (*also*: **~ down**) s'accroupir; **squatter** *n* squatter *m*

squeak [skwi:k] *vi* (*hinge, wheel*) grincer; (*mouse*) pousser un petit cri

squeal [skwi:l] *vi* pousser un *or* des cri(s) aigu(s) *or* perçant(s); (*brakes*) grincer

squeeze [skwi:z] *n* pression *f* ▷ *vt* presser; (*hand, arm*) serrer

squid [skwɪd] *n* calmar *m*

squint [skwɪnt] *vi* loucher

squirm [skwə:m] *vi* se tortiller

squirrel ['skwɪrəl] *n* écureuil *m*

squirt [skwə:t] *vi* jaillir, gicler ▷ *vt* faire gicler

Sr *abbr* = **senior**

Sri Lanka [srɪ'læŋkə] *n* Sri Lanka *m*

St *abbr* = **saint**; **street**

stab [stæb] *n* (*with knife etc*) coup *m* (de couteau *etc*); (*of pain*) lancée *f*; (*inf: try*): **to have a ~ at (doing) sth** s'essayer à (faire) qch ▷ *vt* poignarder

stability [stə'bɪlɪtɪ] *n* stabilité *f*

stable ['steɪbl] *n* écurie *f* ▷ *adj* stable

stack [stæk] *n* tas *m*, pile *f* ▷ *vt* empiler, entasser

stadium ['steɪdɪəm] *n* stade *m*

staff [stɑ:f] *n* (*work force*) personnel *m*; (BRIT *Scol: also*: **teaching ~**) professeurs *mpl*, enseignants *mpl*, personnel enseignant ▷ *vt* pourvoir en personnel

stag [stæg] *n* cerf *m*

stage [steɪdʒ] *n* scène *f*; (*platform*) estrade *f*; (*point*) étape *f*, stade *m*; (*profession*): **the ~** le théâtre ▷ *vt* (*play*) monter, mettre en scène; (*demonstration*) organiser; **in ~s** par étapes, par degrés

> Be careful not to translate *stage* by the French word *stage*.

stagger ['stægə^r] *vi* chanceler, tituber ▷ *vt* (*person: amaze*) stupéfier; (*hours, holidays*) étaler, échelonner; **staggering** *adj* (*amazing*) stupéfiant(e), renversant(e)

stagnant ['stægnənt] *adj* stagnant(e)

stag night, stag party *n* enterrement *m* de vie de garçon

stain [steɪn] *n* tache *f*; (*colouring*) colorant *m* ▷ *vt* tacher; (*wood*) teindre; **stained glass** *n* (*decorative*) verre coloré; (*in church*) vitraux *mpl*; **stainless steel** *n* inox *m*, acier *m* inoxydable

staircase ['stɛəkeɪs] *n* = **stairway**

stairs [stɛəz] *npl* escalier *m*

stairway ['stɛəweɪ] *n* escalier *m*

stake [steɪk] *n* pieu *m*, poteau *m*; (*Comm: interest*) intérêts *mpl*; (*Betting*) enjeu *m* ▷ *vt* risquer, jouer; (*also:* **~ out:** *area*) marquer, délimiter; **to be at ~** être en jeu

stale [steɪl] *adj* (*bread*) rassis(e); (*food*) pas frais (fraîche); (*beer*) éventé(e); (*smell*) de renfermé; (*air*) confiné(e)

stalk [stɔːk] *n* tige *f* ▷ *vt* traquer

stall [stɔːl] *n* (*in street, market etc*) éventaire *m*, étal *m*; (*in stable*) stalle *f* ▷ *vt* (*Aut*) caler; (*fig: delay*) retarder ▷ *vi* (*Aut*) caler; (*fig*) essayer de gagner du temps; **stalls** *npl* (*BRIT: in cinema, theatre*) orchestre *m*

stamina ['stæmɪnə] *n* vigueur *f*, endurance *f*

stammer ['stæmə^r] *n* bégaiement *m* ▷ *vi* bégayer

stamp [stæmp] *n* timbre *m*; (*also:* **rubber ~**) tampon *m*; (*mark: also fig*) empreinte *f*; (*on document*) cachet *m* ▷ *vi* (*also:* **~ one's foot**) taper du pied ▷ *vt* (*letter*) timbrer; (*with rubber stamp*) tamponner; **stamp out** *vt*

(*fire*) piétiner; (*crime*) éradiquer; (*opposition*) éliminer; **stamped addressed envelope** *n* (*BRIT*) enveloppe affranchie pour la réponse

stampede [stæm'piːd] *n* ruée *f*; (*of cattle*) débandade *f*

stance [stæns] *n* position *f*

stand [stænd] (*pt, pp* **stood**) *n* (*position*) position *f*; (*for taxis*) station *f* (de taxis); (*Comm*) étalage *m*, stand *m*; (*Sport: also:* **~s**) tribune *f*; (*also:* **music ~**) pupitre *m* ▷ *vi* être *or* se tenir (debout); (*rise*) se lever, se mettre debout; (*be placed*) se trouver; (*remain: offer etc*) rester valable ▷ *vt* (*place*) mettre, poser; (*tolerate, withstand*) supporter; (*treat, invite*) offrir, payer; **to make a ~** prendre position; **to ~ for parliament** (*BRIT*) se présenter aux élections (*comme candidat à la députation*); **I can't ~ him** je ne peux pas le voir; **stand back** *vi* (*move back*) reculer, s'écarter; **stand by** *vi* (*be ready*) se tenir prêt(e) ▷ *vt fus* (*opinion*) s'en tenir à; (*person*) ne pas abandonner, soutenir; **stand down** *vi* (*withdraw*) se retirer; **stand for** *vt fus* (*signify*) représenter, signifier; (*tolerate*) supporter, tolérer; **stand in for** *vt fus* remplacer; **stand out** *vi* (*be prominent*) ressortir; **stand up** *vi* (*rise*) se lever, se mettre debout; **stand up for** *vt fus* défendre; **stand up to** *vt fus* tenir tête à, résister à

standard ['stændəd] *n* (*norm*) norme *f*, étalon *m*; (*level*) niveau *m* (voulu); (*criterion*) critère *m*; (*flag*) étendard *m* ▷ *adj* (*size etc*) ordinaire, normal(e); (*model, feature*) standard *inv*; (*practice*) courant(e); (*text*) de base; **standards** *npl* (*morals*) morale *f*, principes *mpl*; **standard of living** *n* niveau *m* de vie

stand-by ticket *n* (*Aviat*) billet *m* stand-by

standing ['stændɪŋ] *adj* debout *inv*; (*permanent*) permanent(e) ▷ *n* réputation *f*, rang *m*, standing *m*; **of many years' ~** qui dure *or* existe depuis longtemps; **standing order** n (BRIT: at bank) virement m automatique, prélèvement m bancaire

stand: standpoint n point m de vue; **standstill** n: **at a standstill** à l'arrêt; (fig) au point mort; **to come to a standstill** s'immobiliser, s'arrêter

stank [stæŋk] pt of **stink**

staple ['steɪpl] n (for papers) agrafe f ▷ adj (food, crop, industry etc) de base principal(e) ▷ vt agrafer

star [stɑː^r] n étoile f; (celebrity) vedette f ▷ vt (Cine) avoir pour vedette; **stars** npl; **the ~s** (Astrology) l'horoscope m

starboard ['stɑːbəd] n tribord m

starch [stɑːtʃ] n amidon m; (in food) fécule f

stardom ['stɑːdəm] n célébrité f

stare [steə^r] n regard m fixe ▷ vi: **to ~ at** regarder fixement

stark [stɑːk] adj (bleak) désolé(e), morne ▷ adv: **~ naked** complètement nu(e)

start [stɑːt] n commencement m, début m; (of race) départ m; (sudden movement) sursaut m; (advantage) avance f, avantage m ▷ vt commencer; (cause: fight) déclencher; (rumour) donner naissance à; (fashion) lancer; (found: business, newspaper) lancer, créer; (engine) mettre en marche ▷ vi (begin) commencer; (begin journey) partir, se mettre en route; (jump) sursauter; **when does the film ~?** à quelle heure est-ce que le film commence?; **to ~ doing** or **to do sth** se mettre à faire qch; **start off** vi commencer; (leave) partir; **start out** vi (begin) commencer; (set out) partir; **start up** vi commencer; (car) démarrer ▷ vt (fight) déclencher; (business) créer; (car) mettre en marche; **starter** n (Aut) démarreur m; (Sport: official) starter m; (BRIT Culin) entrée f; **starting point** n point m de départ

startle ['stɑːtl] vt faire sursauter; donner un choc à; **startling** adj surprenant(e), saisissant(e)

starvation [stɑːˈveɪʃən] n faim f, famine f

starve [stɑːv] vi mourir de faim ▷ vt laisser mourir de faim

state [steɪt] n état m; (Pol) État m ▷ vt (declare) déclarer, affirmer; (specify) indiquer, spécifier; **States** npl; **the S~s** les États-Unis; **to be in a ~** être dans tous ses états; **stately home** ['steɪtlɪ-] n manoir m or château m (ouvert au public); **statement** n déclaration f; (Law) déposition f; **state school** n école publique; **statesman** (irreg) n homme m d'État

static ['stætɪk] n (Radio) parasites mpl; (also: **~ electricity**) électricité f statique ▷ adj statique

station ['steɪʃən] n gare f; (also: **police ~**) poste m or commissariat m (de police) ▷ vt placer, poster

stationary ['steɪʃnərɪ] adj à l'arrêt, immobile

stationer's (shop) n (BRIT) papeterie f

stationery ['steɪʃnərɪ] n papier m à lettres, petit matériel de bureau

station wagon n (US) break m

statistic [stəˈtɪstɪk] n statistique f; **statistics** n (science) statistique f

statue ['stætjuː] n statue f

stature ['stætʃə^r] n stature f; (fig) envergure f

status ['steɪtəs] n position f, situation f; (prestige) prestige m; (Admin, official position) statut m; **status quo** [-ˈkwəu] n: **the status quo** le statu quo

statutory ['stætjutrɪ] adj statutaire, prévu(e) par un article de loi

staunch [stɔːntʃ] adj sûr(e), loyal(e)

stay [steɪ] n (period of time) séjour m ▷ vi rester; (reside) loger; (spend some time) séjourner; **to ~ put** ne pas bouger; **to ~ the night** passer la nuit; **stay away** vi (from person, building)

S

ne pas s'approcher; (*from event*) ne pas venir; **stay behind** *vi* rester en arrière; **stay in** *vi* (*at home*) rester à la maison; **stay on** *vi* rester; **stay out** *vi* (*of house*) ne pas rentrer; (*strikers*) rester en grève; **stay up** *vi* (*at night*) ne pas se coucher

steadily ['stɛdɪlɪ] *adv* (*regularly*) progressivement; (*firmly*) fermement; (*walk*) d'un pas ferme; (*fixedly: look*) sans détourner les yeux

steady ['stɛdɪ] *adj* stable, solide, ferme; (*regular*) constant(e), régulier(-ière); (*person*) calme, pondéré(e) ▷ *vt* assurer, stabiliser; (*nerves*) calmer; **a ~ boyfriend** un petit ami

steak [steɪk] *n* (*meat*) bifteck *m*, steak *m*; (*fish, pork*) tranche *f*

steal (*pt* **stole**, *pp* **stolen**) [stiːl, stəʊl, 'stəʊln] *vt, vi* voler; (*move*) se faufiler, se déplacer furtivement; **my wallet has been stolen** on m'a volé mon portefeuille

steam [stiːm] *n* vapeur *f* ▷ *vt* (*Culin*) cuire à la vapeur ▷ *vi* fumer; **steam up** *vi* (*window*) se couvrir de buée; **to get ~ed up about sth** (*fig: inf*) s'exciter à propos de qch; **steamy** *adj* humide; (*window*) embué(e); (*sexy*) torride

steel [stiːl] *n* acier *m* ▷ *cpd* d'acier

steep [stiːp] *adj* raide, escarpé(e); (*price*) très élevé(e), excessif(-ive) ▷ *vt* (*faire*) tremper

steeple ['stiːpl] *n* clocher *m*

steer [stɪə*] *vt* diriger; (*boat*) gouverner; (*lead: person*) guider, conduire ▷ *vi* tenir le gouvernail; **steering** *n* (*Aut*) conduite *f*; **steering wheel** *n* volant *m*

stem [stɛm] *n* (*of plant*) tige *f*; (*of glass*) pied *m* ▷ *vt* contenir, endiguer; (*attack, spread of disease*) juguler

step [stɛp] *n* pas *m*; (*stair*) marche *f*; (*action*) mesure *f*, disposition *f* ▷ *vi*: **to ~ forward/back** faire un pas en avant/arrière, avancer/reculer; **steps** *npl* (*BRIT*) = **stepladder**; **to**

be in/out of ~ (with) (*fig*) aller dans le sens (de)/être déphasé(e) (par rapport à); **step down** *vi* (*fig*) se retirer, se désister; **step in** *vi* (*fig*) intervenir; **step up** *vt* (*production, sales*) augmenter; (*campaign, efforts*) intensifier; **stepbrother** *n* demi-frère *m*; **stepchild** (*pl* **stepchildren**) *n* beau-fils *m*, belle-fille *f*; **stepdaughter** *n* belle-fille *f*; **stepfather** *n* beau-père *m*; **stepladder** *n* (*BRIT*) escabeau *m*; **stepmother** *n* belle-mère *f*; **stepsister** *n* demi-sœur *f*; **stepson** *n* beau-fils *m*

stereo ['stɛrɪəʊ] *n* (*sound*) stéréo *f*; (*hi-fi*) chaîne *f* stéréo ▷ *adj* (*also*: **~phonic**) stéréo(phonique)

stereotype ['stɪərɪətaɪp] *n* stéréotype *m* ▷ *vt* stéréotyper

sterile ['stɛraɪl] *adj* stérile; **sterilize** ['stɛrɪlaɪz] *vt* stériliser

sterling ['stəːlɪŋ] *adj* (*silver*) de bon aloi, fin(e) ▷ *n* (*currency*) livre *f* sterling *inv*

stern [stəːn] *adj* sévère ▷ *n* (*Naut*) arrière *m*, poupe *f*

steroid ['stɪərɔɪd] *n* stéroïde *m*

stew [stjuː] *n* ragoût *m* ▷ *vt, vi* cuire à la casserole

steward ['stjuːəd] *n* (*Aviat, Naut, Rail*) steward *m*; **stewardess** *n* hôtesse *f*

stick [stɪk] (*pt, pp* **stuck**) *n* bâton *m*; (*for walking*) canne *f*; (*of chalk etc*) morceau *m* ▷ *vt* (*glue*) coller; (*thrust*): **to ~ sth into** piquer *or* planter *or* enfoncer qch dans; (*inf: put*) mettre, fourrer; (: *tolerate*) supporter ▷ *vi* (*adhere*) tenir, coller; (*remain*) rester; (*get jammed: door, lift*) se bloquer; **stick out** *vi* dépasser, sortir; **stick up** *vi* dépasser, sortir; **stick up for** *vt fus* défendre; **sticker** *n* auto-collant *m*; **sticking plaster** *n* sparadrap *m*, pansement adhésif; **stick insect** *n* phasme *m*; **stick shift** *n* (*US Aut*) levier *m* de vitesses

sticky ['stɪkɪ] *adj* poisseux(-euse);
(*label*) adhésif(-ive); (*fig: situation*)
délicat(e)

stiff [stɪf] *adj* (*gen*) raide, rigide;
(*door, brush*) dur(e); (*difficult*) difficile,
ardu(e); (*cold*) froid(e), distant(e);
(*strong, high*) fort(e), élevé(e) ▷ *adv*:
to be bored/scared/frozen ~
s'ennuyer à mourir/être mort(e) de
peur/froid

stifling ['staɪflɪŋ] *adj* (*heat*)
suffocant(e)

stigma ['stɪgmə] *n* stigmate *m*

stiletto [stɪ'letəu] *n* (*BRIT: also:*
~ heel) talon *m* aiguille

still [stɪl] *adj* immobile ▷ *adv* (*up to
this time*) encore, toujours; (*even*)
encore; (*nonetheless*) quand même,
tout de même

stimulate ['stɪmjuleɪt] *vt* stimuler

stimulus (*pl* **stimuli**) ['stɪmjuləs,
'stɪmjulaɪ] *n* stimulant *m*; (*Biol,
Psych*) stimulus *m*

sting [stɪŋ] *n* piqûre *f*; (*organ*) dard *m*
▷ *vt, vi* (*pt, pp* **stung**) piquer

stink [stɪŋk] *n* puanteur *f* ▷ *vi* (*pt*
stank, *pp* **stunk**) puer, empester

stir [stəː^r] *n* agitation *f*, sensation
f ▷ *vt* remuer ▷ *vi* remuer, bouger;
stir up *vt* (*trouble*) fomenter,
provoquer; **stir-fry** *vt* faire sauter
▷ *n*: **vegetable stir-fry** légumes
sautés à la poêle

stitch [stɪtʃ] *n* (*Sewing*) point *m*;
(*Knitting*) maille *f*; (*Med*) point de
suture; (*pain*) point de côté ▷ *vt*
coudre, piquer; (*Med*) suturer

stock [stɔk] *n* réserve *f*, provision
f; (*Comm*) stock *m*; (*Agr*) cheptel *m*,
bétail *m*; (*Culin*) bouillon *m*; (*Finance*)
valeurs *fpl*, titres *mpl*; (*descent,
origin*) souche *f* ▷ *adj* (*fig: reply etc*)
classique ▷ *vt* (*have in stock*) avoir,
vendre; **in ~** en stock, en magasin;
out of ~ épuisé(e); **to take ~** (*fig*)
faire le point; **~s and shares** valeurs
(mobilières), titres; **stockbroker**
['stɔkbrəukə^r] *n* agent *m* de

change; **stock cube** *n* (*BRIT Culin*)
bouillon-cube *m*; **stock exchange** *n*
Bourse *f* (des valeurs); **stockholder**
['stɔkhəuldə^r] *n* (*US*) actionnaire *m/f*

stocking ['stɔkɪŋ] *n* bas *m*

stock market *n* Bourse *f*, marché
financier

stole [stəul] *pt of* **steal** ▷ *n* étole *f*

stolen ['stəuln] *pp of* **steal**

stomach ['stʌmək] *n* estomac *m*;
(*abdomen*) ventre *m* ▷ *vt* supporter,
digérer; **stomachache** *n* mal *m* à
l'estomac *or* au ventre

stone [stəun] *n* pierre *f*; (*pebble*)
caillou *m*, galet *m*; (*in fruit*) noyau *m*;
(*Med*) calcul *m*; (*BRIT: weight*) = 6.348
kg; 14 pounds ▷ *cpd* de *or* en pierre ▷ *vt*
(*person*) lancer des pierres sur, lapider;
(*fruit*) dénoyauter

stood [stud] *pt, pp of* **stand**

stool [stuːl] *n* tabouret *m*

stoop [stuːp] *vi* (*also:* **have a ~**) être
voûté(e); (*also:* **~ down**: *bend*) se
baisser, se courber

stop [stɔp] *n* arrêt *m*; (*in punctuation*)
point *m* ▷ *vt* arrêter; (*break off*)
interrompre; (*also:* **put a ~ to**)
mettre fin à; (*prevent*) empêcher
▷ *vi* s'arrêter; (*rain, noise etc*) cesser,
s'arrêter; **to ~ doing sth** cesser *or*
arrêter de faire qch; **to ~ sb (from)
doing sth** empêcher qn de faire qch;
~ it! arrête!; **stop by** *vi* s'arrêter (au
passage); **stop off** *vi* faire une courte
halte; **stopover** *n* halte *f*; (*Aviat*)
escale *f*; **stoppage** *n* (*strike*) arrêt *m*
de travail; (*obstruction*) obstruction *f*

storage ['stɔːrɪdʒ] *n*
emmagasinage *m*

store [stɔː^r] *n* (*stock*) provision *f*,
réserve *f*; (*depot*) entrepôt *m*; (*BRIT:
large shop*) grand magasin; (*US:
shop*) magasin *m* ▷ *vt* emmagasiner;
(*information*) enregistrer; **stores** *npl*
(*food*) provisions; **who knows what
is in ~ for us?** qui sait ce que l'avenir
nous réserve *or* ce qui nous attend?;
storekeeper *n* (*US*) commerçant(e)

S

storey, (US) **story** ['stɔːrɪ] n étage m

storm [stɔːm] n tempête f; (thunderstorm) orage m ▷ vi (fig) fulminer ▷ vt prendre d'assaut; **stormy** adj orageux(-euse)

story ['stɔːrɪ] n histoire f; (Press: article) article m; (US) = **storey**

stout [staut] adj (strong) solide; (fat) gros(se), corpulent(e) ▷ n bière brune

stove [stəuv] n (for cooking) fourneau m (: small) réchaud m; (for heating) poêle m

straight [streɪt] adj droit(e); (hair) raide; (frank) honnête, franc (franche); (simple) simple ▷ adv (tout) droit; (drink) sec, sans eau; **to put** or **get ~** mettre en ordre, mettre de l'ordre dans; (fig) mettre au clair; **~ away, ~ off** (at once) tout de suite; **straighten** vt ajuster; (bed) arranger; **straighten out** vt (fig) débrouiller; **straighten up** vi (stand up) se redresser; **straightforward** adj simple; (frank) honnête, direct(e)

strain [streɪn] n (Tech) tension f; pression f; (physical) effort m; (mental) tension (nerveuse); (Med) entorse f; (breed: of plants) variété f; (: of animals) race f ▷ vt (fig: resources etc) mettre à rude épreuve, grever; (hurt: back etc) se faire mal à; (vegetables) égoutter; **strains** npl (Mus) accords mpl, accents mpl; **strained** adj (muscle) froissé(e); (laugh etc) forcé(e), contraint(e); (relations) tendu(e); **strainer** n passoire f

strait [streɪt] n (Geo) détroit m; **straits** npl; **to be in dire ~s** (fig) avoir de sérieux ennuis

strand [strænd] n (of thread) fil m, brin m; (of rope) toron m; (of hair) mèche f ▷ vt (boat) échouer; **stranded** adj en rade, en plan

strange [streɪndʒ] adj (not known) inconnu(e); (odd) étrange, bizarre; **strangely** adv étrangement, bizarrement; see also

enough; **stranger** n (unknown) inconnu(e); (from somewhere else) étranger(-ère)

strangle ['stræŋgl] vt étrangler

strap [stræp] n lanière f, courroie f, sangle f; (of slip, dress) bretelle f

strategic [strə'tiːdʒɪk] adj stratégique

strategy ['strætɪdʒɪ] n stratégie f

straw [strɔː] n paille f; **that's the last ~!** ça c'est le comble!

strawberry ['strɔːbərɪ] n fraise f

stray [streɪ] adj (animal) perdu(e), errant(e); (scattered) isolé(e) ▷ vi s'égarer; **~ bullet** balle perdue

streak [striːk] n bande f, filet m; (in hair) raie f ▷ vt zébrer, strier

stream [striːm] n (brook) ruisseau m; (current) courant m, flot m; (of people) défilé ininterrompu, flot ▷ vt (Scol) répartir par niveau ▷ vi ruisseler; **to ~ in/out** entrer/sortir à flots

street [striːt] n rue f; **streetcar** n (US) tramway m; **street light** n réverbère m; **street map, street plan** n plan m des rues

strength [streŋθ] n force f; (of girder, knot etc) solidité f; **strengthen** vt renforcer; (muscle) fortifier; (building, Econ) consolider

strenuous ['strenjuəs] adj vigoureux(-euse), énergique; (tiring) ardu(e), fatigant(e)

stress [stres] n (force, pressure) pression f; (mental strain) tension (nerveuse), stress m; (accent) accent m; (emphasis) insistance f ▷ vt insister sur, souligner; (syllable) accentuer; **stressed** adj (tense) stressé(e); (syllable) accentué(e); **stressful** adj (job) stressant(e)

stretch [stretʃ] n (of sand etc) étendue f ▷ vi s'étirer; (extend): **to ~ to** or **as far as** s'étendre jusqu'à ▷ vt tendre, étirer; (fig) pousser (au maximum); **at a ~** d'affilée; **stretch out** vi s'étendre ▷ vt (arm etc) allonger, tendre; (to spread) étendre

stretcher ['strɛtʃər] n brancard m, civière f

strict [strɪkt] adj strict(e); **strictly** adv strictement

stridden ['strɪdn] pp of **stride**

stride [straɪd] n grand pas, enjambée f ▷ vi (pt **strode**, pp **stridden**) marcher à grands pas

strike [straɪk] (pt, pp **struck**) n grève f; (of oil etc) découverte f; (attack) raid m ▷ vt (hit) frapper; (oil etc) trouver, découvrir; (make: agreement, deal) conclure ▷ vi faire grève; (attack) attaquer; (clock) sonner; **to go on** or **come out on strike** se mettre en grève, faire grève; **to ~ a match** frotter une allumette; **striker** n gréviste m/f; (Sport) buteur m; **striking** adj frappant(e), saisissant(e); (attractive) éblouissant(e)

string [strɪŋ] n ficelle f, fil m; (row: of beads) rang m; (Mus) corde f ▷ vt (pt, pp **strung**): **to ~ out** échelonner; **to ~ together** enchaîner; **the strings** npl (Mus) les instruments mpl à cordes; **to pull ~s** (fig) faire jouer le piston

strip [strɪp] n bande f; (Sport) tenue f ▷ vt (undress) déshabiller; (paint) décaper; (fig) dégarnir, dépouiller; (also: ~ **down**) (machine) démonter ▷ vi se déshabiller; **strip off** vt (paint etc) décaper ▷ vi (person) se déshabiller

stripe [straɪp] n raie f, rayure f; (Mil) galon m; **striped** adj rayé(e), à rayures

stripper ['strɪpər] n strip-teaseuse f

strip-search ['strɪpsəːtʃ] vt: **to ~ sb** fouiller qn (en le faisant se déshabiller)

strive (pt **strove**, pp **striven**) [straɪv, strəuv, 'strɪvn] vi: **to ~ to do/for sth** s'efforcer de faire/d'obtenir qch

strode [strəud] pt of **stride**

stroke [strəuk] n coup m; (Med) attaque f; (Swimming: style) (sorte f de) nage f ▷ vt caresser; **at a ~** d'un (seul) coup

stroll [strəul] n petite promenade ▷ vi flâner, se promener nonchalamment; **stroller** n (us: for child) poussette f

strong [strɔŋ] adj (gen) fort(e); (healthy) vigoureux(-euse); (heart, nerves) solide; **they are 50 ~** ils sont au nombre de 50; **stronghold** n forteresse f, fort m; (fig) bastion m; **strongly** adv fortement, avec force; vigoureusement, solidement

strove [strəuv] pt of **strive**

struck [strʌk] pt, pp of **strike**

structure ['strʌktʃər] n structure f; (building) construction f

struggle ['strʌgl] n lutte f ▷ vi lutter, se battre

strung [strʌŋ] pt, pp of **string**

stub [stʌb] n (of cigarette) bout m, mégot m; (of ticket etc) talon m ▷ vt: **to ~ one's toe (on sth)** se heurter le doigt de pied (contre qch); **stub out** vt écraser

stubble ['stʌbl] n chaume m; (on chin) barbe f de plusieurs jours

stubborn ['stʌbən] adj têtu(e), obstiné(e), opiniâtre

stuck [stʌk] pt, pp of **stick** ▷ adj (jammed) bloqué(e), coincé(e)

stud [stʌd] n (on boots etc) clou m; (collar stud) bouton m de col; (earring) petite boucle d'oreille; (of horses: also: ~ **farm**) écurie f, haras m; (also: ~ **horse**) étalon m ▷ vt (fig): **~ded with** parsemé(e) or criblé(e) de

student ['stjuːdənt] n étudiant(e) ▷ adj (life) estudiantin(e), étudiant(e), d'étudiant; (residence, restaurant) universitaire; (loan, movement) étudiant; **student driver** n (us) (conducteur(-trice)) débutant(e); **students' union** n (BRIT: association) ≈ union f des étudiants; (: building) ≈ foyer m des étudiants

studio ['stjuːdɪəu] n studio m, atelier m; (TV etc) studio; **studio flat**, (us) **studio apartment** n studio m

S

study ['stʌdɪ] n étude f; (room) bureau m ▷ vt étudier; (examine) examiner ▷ vi étudier, faire ses études

stuff [stʌf] n (gen) chose(s) f(pl), truc m; (belongings) affaires fpl, trucs; (substance) substance f ▷ vt rembourrer; (Culin) farcir; (inf: push) fourrer; **stuffing** n bourre f, rembourrage m; (Culin) farce f; **stuffy** adj (room) mal ventilé(e) or aéré(e); (ideas) vieux jeu inv

stumble ['stʌmbl] vi trébucher; **to ~ across** or **on** (fig) tomber sur

stump [stʌmp] n souche f; (of limb) moignon m ▷ vt: **to be ~ed** sécher, ne pas savoir que répondre

stun [stʌn] vt (blow) étourdir; (news) abasourdir, stupéfier

stung [stʌŋ] pt, pp of **sting**

stunk [stʌŋk] pp of **stink**

stunned [stʌnd] adj assommé(e); (fig) sidéré(e)

stunning ['stʌnɪŋ] adj (beautiful) étourdissant(e); (news etc) stupéfiant(e)

stunt [stʌnt] n (in film) cascade f, acrobatie f; (publicity) truc m publicitaire ▷ vt retarder, arrêter

stupid ['stjuːpɪd] adj stupide, bête; **stupidity** [stjuːˈpɪdɪtɪ] n stupidité f, bêtise f

sturdy ['stəːdɪ] adj (person, plant) robuste, vigoureux(-euse); (object) solide

stutter ['stʌtər] n bégaiement m ▷ vi bégayer

style [staɪl] n style m; (distinction) allure f, cachet m, style; (design) modèle m; **stylish** adj élégant(e), chic inv; **stylist** n (hair stylist) coiffeur(-euse)

sub... [sʌb] prefix sub..., sous-; **subconscious** adj subconscient(e)

subdued [səbˈdjuːd] adj (light) tamisé(e); (person) qui a perdu de son entrain

subject n ['sʌbdʒɪkt] sujet m; (Scol) matière f ▷ vt [səbˈdʒɛkt]: **to ~ to** soumettre à; **to be ~ to** (law) être soumis(e) à; **subjective** [səbˈdʒɛktɪv] adj subjectif(-ive); **subject matter** n (content) contenu m

subjunctive [səbˈdʒʌŋktɪv] n subjonctif m

submarine [sʌbməˈriːn] n sous-marin m

submission [səbˈmɪʃən] n soumission f

submit [səbˈmɪt] vt soumettre ▷ vi se soumettre

subordinate [səˈbɔːdɪnət] adj (junior) subalterne; (Grammar) subordonné(e) ▷ n subordonné(e)

subscribe [səbˈskraɪb] vi cotiser; **to ~ to** (opinion, fund) souscrire à; (newspaper) s'abonner à; être abonné(e) à

subscription [səbˈskrɪpʃən] n (to magazine etc) abonnement m

subsequent ['sʌbsɪkwənt] adj ultérieur(e), suivant(e); **subsequently** adv par la suite

subside [səbˈsaɪd] vi (land) s'affaisser; (flood) baisser; (wind, feelings) tomber

subsidiary [səbˈsɪdɪərɪ] adj subsidiaire; accessoire; (BRIT Scol: subject) complémentaire ▷ n filiale f

subsidize ['sʌbsɪdaɪz] vt subventionner

subsidy ['sʌbsɪdɪ] n subvention f

substance ['sʌbstəns] n substance f

substantial [səbˈstænʃl] adj substantiel(le); (fig) important(e)

substitute ['sʌbstɪtjuːt] n (person) remplaçant(e); (thing) succédané m ▷ vt: **to ~ sth/sb for** substituer qch/qn à, remplacer par qch/qn; **substitution** n substitution f

subtitles ['sʌbtaɪtlz] npl (Cine) sous-titres mpl

subtle ['sʌtl] adj subtil(e)

subtract [səbˈtrækt] vt soustraire, retrancher

suburb ['sʌbəːb] n faubourg m; **the ~s** la banlieue; **suburban** [səˈbəːbən] adj de banlieue, suburbain(e)

subway ['sʌbweɪ] n (BRIT: underpass) passage souterrain; (US: railway) métro m

succeed [sək'siːd] vi réussir ▷ vt succéder à; **to ~ in doing** réussir à faire

success [sək'sɛs] n succès m; réussite f; **successful** adj (business) prospère, qui réussit; (attempt) couronné(e) de succès; **to be successful (in doing)** réussir (à faire); **successfully** adv avec succès

succession [sək'sɛʃən] n succession f

successive [sək'sɛsɪv] adj successif(-ive)

successor [sək'sɛsər] n successeur m

succumb [sə'kʌm] vi succomber

such [sʌtʃ] adj tel (telle); (of that kind): **~ a book** un livre de ce genre or pareil, un tel livre; (so much): **~ courage** un tel courage ▷ adv si; **~ a long trip** un si long voyage; **~ a lot of** tellement or tant de; **~ as** (like) tel (telle) que, comme; **as ~** adv en tant que tel (telle), à proprement parler; **such-and-such** adj tel ou tel (telle ou telle)

suck [sʌk] vt sucer; (breast, bottle) téter

Sudan [su'dɑːn] n Soudan m

sudden ['sʌdn] adj soudain(e), subit(e); **all of a ~** soudain, tout à coup; **suddenly** adv brusquement, tout à coup, soudain

sudoku [su'dəuku:] n sudoku m

sue [su:] vt poursuivre en justice, intenter un procès à

suede [sweɪd] n daim m, cuir suédé

suffer ['sʌfər] vt souffrir, subir; (bear) tolérer, supporter, subir ▷ vi souffrir; **to ~ from** (illness) souffrir de, avoir; **suffering** n souffrance(s) f(pl)

suffice [sə'faɪs] vi suffire

sufficient [sə'fɪʃənt] adj suffisant(e)

suffocate ['sʌfəkeɪt] vi suffoquer; étouffer

sugar ['ʃugər] n sucre m ▷ vt sucrer

suggest [sə'dʒɛst] vt suggérer, proposer; (indicate) sembler indiquer; **suggestion** n suggestion f

suicide ['suɪsaɪd] n suicide m; **~ bombing** attentat m suicide; see also **commit**; **suicide bomber** n kamikaze m/f

suit [su:t] n (man's) costume m, complet m; (woman's) tailleur m, ensemble m; (Cards) couleur f; (lawsuit) procès m ▷ vt (subj: clothes, hairstyle) aller à; (be convenient for) convenir à; (adapt): **to ~ sth to** adapter or approprier qch à; **well ~ed** (couple) faits l'un pour l'autre, très bien assortis; **suitable** adj qui convient; approprié(e), adéquat(e); **suitcase** n valise f

suite [swi:t] n (of rooms, also Mus) suite f; (furniture): **bedroom/dining room ~** (ensemble m de) chambre f à coucher/salle f à manger; **a three-piece ~** un salon (canapé et deux fauteuils)

sulfur ['sʌlfər] (US) n = **sulphur**

sulk [sʌlk] vi bouder

sulphur, (US) **sulfur** ['sʌlfər] n soufre m

sultana [sʌl'tɑːnə] n (fruit) raisin (sec) de Smyrne

sum [sʌm] n somme f; (Scol etc) calcul m; **sum up** vt résumer ▷ vi résumer

summarize ['sʌməraɪz] vt résumer

summary ['sʌmərɪ] n résumé m

summer ['sʌmər] n été m ▷ cpd d'été, estival(e); **in (the) ~** en été, pendant l'été; **summer holidays** npl grandes vacances; **summertime** n (season) été m

summit ['sʌmɪt] n sommet m; (also: **~ conference**) (conférence f au) sommet m

summon ['sʌmən] vt appeler, convoquer; **to ~ a witness** citer or assigner un témoin

sun [sʌn] n soleil m

Sun. abbr (= Sunday) dim

sun: sunbathe vi prendre un bain de soleil; **sunbed** n lit pliant; (with sun lamp) lit à ultra-violets; **sunblock** n écran m total; **sunburn** n coup m de

S

soleil; **sunburned, sunburnt** *adj*
bronzé(e), hâlé(e); (*painfully*) brûlé(e)
par le soleil
Sunday ['sʌndɪ] *n* dimanche *m*
sunflower ['sʌnflauə'] *n*
tournesol *m*
sung [sʌŋ] *pp of* **sing**
sunglasses ['sʌnglɑːsɪz] *npl* lunettes
fpl de soleil
sunk [sʌŋk] *pp of* **sink**
sun: sunlight *n* (lumière *f* du) soleil
m; **sun lounger** *n* chaise longue;
sunny *adj* ensoleillé(e); **it is sunny** il
fait (du) soleil, il y a du soleil; **sunrise**
n lever *m* du soleil; **sun roof** *n* (*Aut*)
toit ouvrant; **sunscreen** *n* crème *f*
solaire; **sunset** *n* coucher *m* du soleil;
sunshade *n* (*over table*) parasol *m*;
sunshine *n* (lumière *f* du) soleil *m*;
sunstroke *n* insolation *f*, coup *m* de
soleil; **suntan** *n* bronzage *m*; **suntan
lotion** *n* lotion *f* or lait *m* solaire;
suntan oil *n* huile *f* solaire
super ['suːpə'] *adj* (*inf*) formidable
superb [suː'pəːb] *adj* superbe,
magnifique
superficial [suːpə'fɪʃəl] *adj*
superficiel(le)
superintendent
[suːpərɪn'tɛndənt] *n* directeur(-
trice); (*Police*) ≈ commissaire *m*
superior [su'pɪərɪə'] *adj* supérieur(e);
(*smug*) condescendant(e),
méprisant(e) ▷ *n* supérieur(e)
superlative [su'pəːlətɪv] *n* (*Ling*)
superlatif *m*
supermarket ['suːpəmɑːkɪt] *n*
supermarché *m*
supernatural [suːpə'nætʃərəl] *adj*
surnaturel(le) ▷ *n*: **the ~** le surnaturel
superpower ['suːpəpauə'] *n* (*Pol*)
superpuissance *f*
superstition [suːpə'stɪʃən] *n*
superstition *f*
superstitious [suːpə'stɪʃəs] *adj*
superstitieux(-euse)
superstore ['suːpəstɔː'] *n* (*BRIT*)
hypermarché *m*, grande surface

supervise ['suːpəvaɪz] *vt* (*children
etc*) surveiller; (*organization, work*)
diriger; **supervision** [suːpə'vɪʒən] *n*
surveillance *f*; (*monitoring*) contrôle *m*;
(*management*) direction *f*; **supervisor**
n surveillant(e); (*in shop*) chef *m*
de rayon
supper ['sʌpə'] *n* dîner *m*; (*late*)
souper *m*
supple ['sʌpl] *adj* souple
supplement *n* ['sʌplɪmənt]
supplément *m* ▷ *vt* [sʌplɪ'mɛnt]
ajouter à, compléter
supplier [sə'plaɪə'] *n* fournisseur *m*
supply [sə'plaɪ] *vt* (*provide*) fournir;
(*equip*): **to ~ (with)** approvisionner
or ravitailler (en); fournir (en) ▷ *n*
provision *f*, réserve *f*; (*supplying*)
approvisionnement *m*; **supplies** *npl*
(*food*) vivres *mpl*; (*Mil*) subsistances *fpl*
support [sə'pɔːt] *n* (*moral, financial
etc*) soutien *m*, appui *m*; (*Tech*)
support *m*, soutien ▷ *vt* soutenir,
supporter; (*financially*) subvenir aux
besoins de; (*uphold*) être pour, être
partisan de, appuyer; (*Sport: team*)
être pour; **supporter** *n* (*Pol etc*)
partisan(e); (*Sport*) supporter *m*
suppose [sə'pəuz] *vt, vi* supposer;
imaginer; **to be ~d to do/be** être
censé(e) faire/être; **supposedly**
[sə'pəuzɪdlɪ] *adv* soi-disant;
supposing *conj* si, à supposer que
+ *sub*
suppress [sə'prɛs] *vt* (*revolt,
feeling*) réprimer; (*information*) faire
disparaître; (*scandal, yawn*) étouffer
supreme [su'priːm] *adj* suprême
surcharge ['səːtʃɑːdʒ] *n* surcharge *f*
sure [ʃuə'] *adj* (*gen*) sûr(e); (*definite,
convinced*) sûr, certain(e); **~!** (*of course*)
bien sûr!; **~ enough** effectivement;
to make ~ of sth/that s'assurer de
qch/que, vérifier qch/que; **surely** *adv*
sûrement; certainement
surf [səːf] *n* (*waves*) ressac *m* ▷ *vt*: **to
~ the Net** surfer sur Internet, surfer
sur le Net

surface ['sə:fɪs] n surface f ▷ vt (road) poser un revêtement sur ▷ vi remonter à la surface; (fig) faire surface; **by ~ mail** par voie de terre; (by sea) par voie maritime

surfboard ['sə:fbɔ:d] n planche f de surf

surfer ['sə:fə'] n (in sea) surfeur(-euse); **web** or **Net ~** internaute m/f

surfing ['sə:fɪŋ] n (in sea) surf m

surge [sə:dʒ] n (of emotion) vague f ▷ vi déferler

surgeon ['sə:dʒən] n chirurgien m

surgery ['sə:dʒərɪ] n chirurgie f; (BRIT: room) cabinet m (de consultation); (also: **~ hours**) heures fpl de consultation

surname ['sə:neɪm] n nom m de famille

surpass [sə:'pɑ:s] vt surpasser, dépasser

surplus ['sə:pləs] n surplus m, excédent m ▷ adj en surplus, de trop; (Comm) excédentaire

surprise [sə'praɪz] n (gen) surprise f; (astonishment) étonnement m ▷ vt surprendre, étonner; **surprised** adj (look, smile) surpris(e), étonné(e); **to be surprised** être surpris; **surprising** adj surprenant(e), étonnant(e); **surprisingly** adv (easy, helpful) étonnamment, étrangement; **(somewhat) surprisingly, he agreed** curieusement, il a accepté

surrender [sə'rɛndə'] n reddition f, capitulation f ▷ vi se rendre, capituler

surround [sə'raund] vt entourer; (Mil etc) encercler; **surrounding** adj environnant(e); **surroundings** npl environs mpl, alentours mpl

surveillance [sə:'veɪləns] n surveillance f

survey n ['sə:veɪ] enquête f, étude f; (in house buying etc) inspection f, (rapport m d')expertise f; (of land) levé m ▷ vt [sə:'veɪ] (situation) passer en revue; (examine carefully) inspecter; (building) expertiser; (land) faire le levé de; (look at) embrasser du regard;

surveyor n (of building) expert m; (of land) (arpenteur m) géomètre m

survival [sə'vaɪvl] n survie f

survive [sə'vaɪv] vi survivre; (custom etc) subsister ▷ vt (accident etc) survivre à, réchapper de; (person) survivre à; **survivor** n survivant(e)

suspect adj, n ['sʌspɛkt] suspect(e) ▷ vt [səs'pɛkt] soupçonner, suspecter

suspend [səs'pɛnd] vt suspendre; **suspended sentence** n (Law) condamnation f avec sursis; **suspenders** npl (BRIT) jarretelles fpl; (US) bretelles fpl

suspense [səs'pɛns] n attente f, incertitude f; (in film etc) suspense m; **to keep sb in ~** tenir qn en suspens, laisser qn dans l'incertitude

suspension [səs'pɛnʃən] n (gen, Aut) suspension f; (of driving licence) retrait m provisoire; **suspension bridge** n pont suspendu

suspicion [səs'pɪʃən] n soupçon(s) m(pl); **suspicious** adj (suspecting) soupçonneux(-euse), méfiant(e); (causing suspicion) suspect(e)

sustain [səs'teɪn] vt soutenir; (subj: food) nourrir, donner des forces à; (damage) subir; (injury) recevoir

SUV n abbr (esp US: = sports utility vehicle) SUV m, véhicule m de loisirs

swallow ['swɔləu] n (bird) hirondelle f ▷ vt avaler; (fig: story) gober

swam [swæm] pt of **swim**

swamp [swɔmp] n marais m, marécage m ▷ vt submerger

swan [swɔn] n cygne m

swap [swɔp] n échange m, troc m ▷ vt: **to ~ (for)** échanger (contre), troquer (contre)

swarm [swɔ:m] n essaim m ▷ vi (bees) essaimer; (people) grouiller; **to be ~ing with** grouiller de

sway [sweɪ] vi se balancer, osciller ▷ vt (influence) influencer

swear [swɛəʳ] (*pt* **swore**, *pp* **sworn**) *vt*, *vi* jurer; **swear in** *vt* assermenter; **swearword** *n* gros mot, juron *m*

sweat [swɛt] *n* sueur *f*, transpiration *f* ▷ *vi* suer

sweater ['swɛtəʳ] *n* tricot *m*, pull *m*

sweatshirt ['swɛtʃəːt] *n* sweat-shirt *m*

sweaty ['swɛtɪ] *adj* en sueur, moite *or* mouillé(e) de sueur

Swede [swiːd] *n* Suédois(e)

swede [swiːd] *n* (BRIT) rutabaga *m*

Sweden ['swiːdn] *n* Suède *f*; **Swedish** ['swiːdɪʃ] *adj* suédois(e) ▷ *n* (Ling) suédois *m*

sweep [swiːp] (*pt*, *pp* **swept**) *n* (*curve*) grande courbe; (*also*: **chimney ~**) ramoneur *m* ▷ *vt* balayer; (*subj*: *current*) emporter

sweet [swiːt] *n* (BRIT: *pudding*) dessert *m*; (*candy*) bonbon *m* ▷ *adj* doux (douce); (*not savoury*) sucré(e); (*kind*) gentil(le); (*baby*) mignon(ne); **sweetcorn** *n* maïs doux; **sweetener** ['swiːtnəʳ] *n* (Culin) édulcorant *m*; **sweetheart** *n* amoureux(-euse); **sweetshop** *n* (BRIT) confiserie *f*

swell [swɛl] (*pt* **swelled**, *pp* **swollen** *or* **swelled**) *n* (*of sea*) houle *f* ▷ *adj* (US *inf*: *excellent*) chouette ▷ *vt* (*increase*) grossir, augmenter ▷ *vi* (*increase*) grossir, augmenter; (*sound*) s'enfler; (Med: *also*: **~ up**) enfler; **swelling** *n* (Med) enflure *f* (: *lump*) grosseur *f*

swept [swɛpt] *pt*, *pp* of **sweep**

swerve [swəːv] *vi* (*to avoid obstacle*) faire une embardée *or* un écart; (*off the road*) dévier

swift [swɪft] *n* (*bird*) martinet *m* ▷ *adj* rapide, prompt(e)

swim [swɪm] (*pt* **swam**, *pp* **swum**) *n*: **to go for a ~** aller nager *or* se baigner ▷ *vi* nager; (Sport) faire de la natation; (*fig*: *head*, *room*) tourner ▷ *vt* traverser (à la nage); **to ~ a length** nager une longueur; **swimmer** *n* nageur(-euse); **swimming** *n* nage *f*, natation *f*; **swimming costume** *n*

(BRIT) maillot *m* (de bain); **swimming pool** *n* piscine *f*; **swimming trunks** *npl* maillot *m* de bain; **swimsuit** *n* maillot *m* (de bain)

swine flu ['swaɪn-] *n* grippe *f* A

swing [swɪŋ] (*pt*, *pp* **swung**) *n* (*in playground*) balançoire *f*; (*movement*) balancement *m*, oscillations *fpl*; (*change in opinion etc*) revirement *m* ▷ *vt* balancer, faire osciller; (*also*: **~ round**) tourner, faire virer ▷ *vi* se balancer, osciller; (*also*: **~ round**) virer, tourner; **to be in full ~** battre son plein

swipe card ['swaɪp-] *n* carte *f* magnétique

swirl [swəːl] *vi* tourbillonner, tournoyer

Swiss [swɪs] *adj* suisse ▷ *n* (*pl inv*) Suisse(-esse)

switch [swɪtʃ] *n* (*for light, radio etc*) bouton *m*; (*change*) changement *m*, revirement *m* ▷ *vt* (*change*) changer; **switch off** *vt* éteindre; (*engine, machine*) arrêter; **could you ~ off the light?** pouvez-vous éteindre la lumière?; **switch on** *vt* allumer; (*engine, machine*) mettre en marche; **switchboard** *n* (Tel) standard *m*

Switzerland ['swɪtsələnd] *n* Suisse *f*

swivel ['swɪvl] *vi* (*also*: **~ round**) pivoter, tourner

swollen ['swəulən] *pp of* **swell**

swoop [swuːp] *n* (*by police etc*) rafle *f*, descente *f* ▷ *vi* (*bird*: *also*: **~ down**) descendre en piqué, piquer

swop [swɔp] *n*, *vt* = **swap**

sword [sɔːd] *n* épée *f*; **swordfish** *n* espadon *m*

swore [swɔːʳ] *pt of* **swear**

sworn [swɔːn] *pp of* **swear** ▷ *adj* (*statement, evidence*) donné(e) sous serment; (*enemy*) juré(e)

swum [swʌm] *pp of* **swim**

swung [swʌŋ] *pt*, *pp of* **swing**

syllable ['sɪləbl] *n* syllabe *f*

syllabus ['sɪləbəs] *n* programme *m*

symbol ['sɪmbl] n symbole m;
  symbolic(al) [sɪm'bɔlɪk(l)] adj
  symbolique
symmetrical [sɪ'mɛtrɪkl] adj
  symétrique
symmetry ['sɪmɪtrɪ] n symétrie f
sympathetic [sɪmpə'θɛtɪk] adj
  (showing pity) compatissant(e);
  (understanding) bienveillant(e),
  compréhensif(-ive); **~ towards** bien
  disposé(e) envers

> Be careful not to translate
> sympathetic by the French word
> sympathique.

sympathize ['sɪmpəθaɪz] vi: **to
  ~ with sb** plaindre qn; (in grief)
  s'associer à la douleur de qn; **to ~
  with sth** comprendre qch
sympathy ['sɪmpəθɪ] n (pity)
  compassion f
symphony ['sɪmfənɪ] n symphonie f
symptom ['sɪmptəm] n symptôme
  m; indice m
synagogue ['sɪnəgɔg] n synagogue f
syndicate ['sɪndɪkɪt] n syndicat
  m, coopérative f; (Press) agence f
  de presse
syndrome ['sɪndrəum] n
  syndrome m
synonym ['sɪnənɪm] n synonyme m
synthetic [sɪn'θɛtɪk] adj synthétique
Syria ['sɪrɪə] n Syrie f
syringe [sɪ'rɪndʒ] n seringue f
syrup ['sɪrəp] n sirop m; (BRIT: also:
  golden ~) mélasse raffinée
system ['sɪstəm] n système m;
  (Anat) organisme m; **systematic**
  [sɪstə'mætɪk] adj systématique;
  méthodique; **systems analyst** n
  analyste-programmeur m/f

ta [tɑː] excl (BRIT inf) merci!
tab [tæb] n (label) étiquette f; (on
  drinks can etc) languette f; **to keep ~s
  on** (fig) surveiller
table ['teɪbl] n table f ▷ vt (BRIT:
  motion etc) présenter; **to lay** or
  set the ~ mettre le couvert or la
  table; **tablecloth** n nappe f; **table
  d'hôte** [tɑːbl'dəut] adj (meal)
  à prix fixe; **table lamp** n lampe
  décorative or de table; **tablemat** n
  (for plate) napperon m, set m; (for
  hot dish) dessous-de-plat m inv; **table-
  spoon** n cuiller f de service;
  (also: **tablespoonful**: as measurement)
  cuillerée f à soupe
tablet ['tæblɪt] n (Med) comprimé m;
  (Comput) tablette f (tactile); (of stone)
  plaque f
table tennis n ping-pong m
tabloid ['tæblɔɪd] n (newspaper)
  quotidien m populaire
taboo [tə'buː] adj, n tabou (m)

t

tack [tæk] n (nail) petit clou; (fig) direction f ▷ vt (nail) clouer; (sew) bâtir ▷ vi (Naut) tirer un or des bord(s); **to ~ sth on to (the end of) sth** (of letter, book) rajouter qch à la fin de qch

tackle ['tækl] n matériel m, équipement m; (for lifting) appareil m de levage; (Football, Rugby) plaquage m ▷ vt (difficulty, animal, burglar) s'attaquer à; (person: challenge) s'expliquer avec; (Football, Rugby) plaquer

tacky ['tækɪ] adj collant(e); (paint) pas sec (sèche); (pej: poor-quality) minable; (: showing bad taste) ringard(e)

tact [tækt] n tact m; **tactful** adj plein(e) de tact

tactics ['tæktɪks] npl tactique f

tactless ['tæktlɪs] adj qui manque de tact

tadpole ['tædpəʊl] n têtard m

taffy ['tæfɪ] n (us) (bonbon m au) caramel m

tag [tæg] n étiquette f

tail [teɪl] n queue f; (of shirt) pan m ▷ vt (follow) suivre, filer; **tails** npl (suit) habit m; see also **head**

tailor ['teɪlər] n tailleur m (artisan)

Taiwan ['taɪwɑːn] n Taïwan (no article); **Taiwanese** [taɪwə'niːz] adj taïwanais(e) ▷ n inv Taïwanais(e)

take [teɪk] (pt **took**, pp **taken**) vt prendre; (gain: prize) remporter; (require: effort, courage) demander; (tolerate) accepter, supporter; (hold: passengers etc) contenir; (accompany) emmener, accompagner; (bring, carry) apporter, emporter; (exam) passer, se présenter à; **to ~ sth from** (drawer etc) prendre qch dans; (person) prendre qch à; **I ~ it that** je suppose que; **to be ~n ill** tomber malade; **it won't ~ long** ça ne prendra pas longtemps; **I was quite ~n with her/it** elle/cela m'a beaucoup plu; **take after** vt fus ressembler à; **take apart** vt démonter; **take away** vt

(carry off) emporter; (remove) enlever; (subtract) soustraire; **take back** vt (return) rendre, rapporter; (one's words) retirer; **take down** vt (building) démolir; (letter etc) prendre, écrire; **take in** vt (deceive) tromper, rouler; (understand) comprendre, saisir; (include) couvrir, inclure; (lodger) prendre; (dress, waistband) reprendre; **take off** vi (Aviat) décoller ▷ vt (remove) enlever; **take on** vt (work) accepter, se charger de; (employee) prendre, embaucher; (opponent) accepter de se battre contre; **take out** vt sortir; (remove) enlever; (invite) sortir avec; **to ~ sth out of** (out of drawer etc) prendre qch dans; **to ~ sb out to a restaurant** emmener qn au restaurant; **take over** vt (business) reprendre ▷ vi: **to ~ over from sb** prendre la relève de qn; **take up** vt (one's story) reprendre; (dress) raccourcir; (occupy: time, space) prendre, occuper; (engage in: hobby etc) se mettre à; (accept: offer, challenge) accepter; **takeaway** (BRIT) adj (food) à emporter ▷ n (shop, restaurant) ≈ magasin m qui vend des plats à emporter; **taken** pp of take; **takeoff** n (Aviat) décollage m; **takeout** adj, n (us) = **takeaway**; **takeover** n (Comm) rachat m; **takings** npl (Comm) recette f

talc [tælk] n (also: **~um powder**) talc m

tale [teɪl] n (story) conte m, histoire f; (account) récit m; **to tell ~s** (fig) rapporter

talent ['tælnt] n talent m, don m; **talented** adj doué(e), plein(e) de talent

talk [tɔːk] n (a speech) causerie f, exposé m; (conversation) discussion f; (interview) entretien m; (gossip) racontars mpl (pej) ▷ vi parler; (chatter) bavarder; **talks** npl (Pol etc) entretiens mpl; **to ~ about** parler de; **to ~ sb out of/into doing** persuader

qn de ne pas faire/de faire; **to ~ shop**
parler métier or affaires; **talk over** vt
discuter (de); **talk show** n (TV, Radio)
émission-débat f

tall [tɔ:l] adj (person) grand(e);
(building, tree) haut(e); **to be 6 feet ~**
≈ mesurer 1 mètre 80

tambourine [tæmbə'ri:n] n
tambourin m

tame [teɪm] adj apprivoisé(e); (fig:
story, style) insipide

tamper ['tæmpə'] vi: **to ~ with**
toucher à (en cachette ou sans
permission)

tampon ['tæmpən] n tampon m
hygiénique or périodique

tan [tæn] n (also: **sun~**) bronzage m
▷ vt, vi bronzer, brunir ▷ adj (colour)
marron clair inv

tandem ['tændəm] n tandem m

tangerine [tændʒə'ri:n] n
mandarine f

tangle ['tæŋgl] n enchevêtrement m;
to get in(to) a ~ s'emmêler

tank [tæŋk] n réservoir m; (for fish)
aquarium m; (Mil) char m d'assaut,
tank m

tanker ['tæŋkə'] n (ship) pétrolier m,
tanker m; (truck) camion-citerne m

tanned [tænd] adj bronzé(e)

tantrum ['tæntrəm] n accès m
de colère

Tanzania [tænzə'nɪə] n Tanzanie f

tap [tæp] n (on sink etc) robinet m;
(gentle blow) petite tape ▷ vt frapper
or taper légèrement; (resources)
exploiter, utiliser; (telephone)
mettre sur écoute; **on ~** (fig:
resources) disponible; **tap dancing** n
claquettes fpl

tape [teɪp] n (for tying) ruban m; (also:
magnetic ~) bande f (magnétique);
(cassette) cassette f; (sticky) Scotch®
m ▷ vt (record) enregistrer (au
magnétoscope or sur cassette);
(stick) coller avec du Scotch®; **tape
measure** n mètre m à ruban; **tape
recorder** n magnétophone m

tapestry ['tæpɪstrɪ] n tapisserie f

tar [tɑ:] n goudron m

target ['tɑ:gɪt] n cible f; (fig: objective)
objectif m

tariff ['tærɪf] n (Comm) tarif m; (taxes)
tarif douanier

tarmac ['tɑ:mæk] n (BRIT: on road)
macadam m; (Aviat) aire f d'envol

tarpaulin [tɑ:'pɔ:lɪn] n bâche
goudronnée

tarragon ['tærəgən] n estragon m

tart [tɑ:t] n (Culin) tarte f; (BRIT inf: pej:
prostitute) poule f ▷ adj (flavour) âpre,
aigrelet(te)

tartan ['tɑ:tn] n tartan m ▷ adj
écossais(e)

tartar(e) sauce ['tɑ:tə-] n sauce
f tartare

task [tɑ:sk] n tâche f; **to take to ~**
prendre à partie

taste [teɪst] n goût m; (fig: glimpse,
idea) idée f, aperçu m ▷ vt goûter ▷ vi:
to ~ of (fish etc) avoir le or un goût de;
you can ~ the garlic (in it) on sent
bien l'ail; **to have a ~ of sth** goûter (à)
qch; **can I have a ~?** je peux goûter?;
to be in good/bad or poor ~ être de
bon/mauvais goût; **tasteful** adj de
bon goût; **tasteless** adj (food) insipide;
(remark) de mauvais goût; **tasty** adj
savoureux(-euse), délicieux(-euse)

tatters ['tætəz] npl: **in ~** (also:
tattered) en lambeaux

tattoo [tə'tu:] n tatouage m;
(spectacle) parade f militaire ▷ vt
tatouer

taught [tɔ:t] pt, pp of **teach**

taunt [tɔ:nt] n raillerie f ▷ vt railler

Taurus ['tɔ:rəs] n le Taureau

taut [tɔ:t] adj tendu(e)

tax [tæks] n (on goods etc) taxe f; (on
income) impôts mpl, contributions fpl
▷ vt taxer; imposer; (fig: patience etc)
mettre à l'épreuve; **tax disc** n (BRIT
Aut) vignette f (automobile); **tax-free**
adj exempt(e) d'impôts

taxi ['tæksɪ] n taxi m ▷ vi (Aviat) rouler
(lentement) au sol; **taxi driver** n

chauffeur *m* de taxi; **taxi rank**, (*us*)
taxi stand *n* station *f* de taxis
tax payer [-peɪəʳ] *n* contribuable *m/f*
tax return *n* déclaration *f* d'impôts
or de revenus
TB *n abbr* = **tuberculosis**
tbc *abbr* = **to be confirmed**
tea [tiː] *n* thé *m*; (*BRIT*: *snack: for
children*) goûter *m*; **high ~** (*BRIT*)
collation combinant goûter et dîner; **tea
bag** *n* sachet *m* de thé; **tea break** *n*
(*BRIT*) pause-thé *f*
teach (*pt, pp* **taught**) [tiːtʃ, tɔːt] *vt*:
to ~ sb sth, to ~ sth to sb apprendre
qch à qn; (*in school etc*) enseigner
qch à qn ▷ *vi* enseigner; **teacher** *n*
(*in secondary school*) professeur *m*; (*in
primary school*) instituteur(-trice);
teaching *n* enseignement
m; **teaching assistant** *n*
aide-éducateur(-trice)
tea: teacup *n* tasse *f* à thé; **tea leaves**
npl feuilles *fpl* de thé
team [tiːm] *n* équipe *f*; (*of animals*)
attelage *m*; **team up** *vi*: **to ~ up
(with)** faire équipe (avec)
teapot ['tiːpɔt] *n* théière *f*
tear¹ ['tɪəʳ] *n* larme *f*; **in ~s** en larmes
tear² [tɛəʳ] (*pt* **tore**, *pp* **torn**) *n*
déchirure *f* ▷ *vt* déchirer ▷ *vi* se
déchirer; **tear apart** *vt* (*also fig*)
déchirer; **tear down** *vt* (*building,
statue*) démolir; (*poster, flag*)
arracher; **tear off** *vt* (*sheet of paper
etc*) arracher; (*one's clothes*) enlever
à toute vitesse; **tear up** *vt* (*sheet
of paper etc*) déchirer, mettre en
morceaux *or* pièces
tearful ['tɪəful] *adj* larmoyant(e)
tear gas ['tɪə-] *n* gaz *m* lacrymogène
tearoom ['tiːruːm] *n* salon *m* de thé
tease [tiːz] *vt* taquiner; (*unkindly*)
tourmenter
tea: teaspoon *n* petite cuiller; (*also:*
teaspoonful: *as measurement*) ≈
cuillerée *f* à café; **teatime** *n* l'heure *f*
du thé; **tea towel** *n* (*BRIT*) torchon *m*
(à vaisselle)

technical ['tɛknɪkl] *adj* technique
technician [tɛk'nɪʃən] *n*
technicien(ne)
technique [tɛk'niːk] *n* technique *f*
technology [tɛk'nɔlədʒɪ] *n*
technologie *f*
teddy (bear) ['tɛdɪ-] *n* ours *m* (en
peluche)
tedious ['tiːdɪəs] *adj*
fastidieux(-euse)
tee [tiː] *n* (*Golf*) tee *m*
teen [tiːn] *adj* = **teenage** ▷ *n* (*us*)
= **teenager**
teenage ['tiːneɪdʒ] *adj* (*fashions etc*)
pour jeunes, pour adolescents; (*child*)
qui est adolescent(e); **teenager** *n*
adolescent(e)
teens [tiːnz] *npl*: **to be in one's ~**
être adolescent(e)
teeth [tiːθ] *npl of* **tooth**
teetotal ['tiː'təutl] *adj* (*person*) qui ne
boit jamais d'alcool
telecommunications
['tɛlɪkəmjuːnɪ'keɪʃənz] *n*
télécommunications *fpl*
telegram ['tɛlɪgræm] *n*
télégramme *m*
telegraph pole ['tɛlɪgrɑːf-] *n*
poteau *m* télégraphique
telephone ['tɛlɪfəun] *n* téléphone
m ▷ *vt* (*person*) téléphoner à;
(*message*) téléphoner; **to be on
the ~** (*be speaking*) être au téléphone;
telephone book *n* = **telephone
directory**; **telephone box**, (*us*)
telephone booth *n* cabine *f*
téléphonique; **telephone call** *n*
appel *m* téléphonique; **telephone
directory** *n* annuaire *m* (du
téléphone); **telephone number** *n*
numéro *m* de téléphone
telesales ['tɛlɪseɪlz] *npl* télévente *f*
telescope ['tɛlɪskəup] *n* télescope *m*
televise ['tɛlɪvaɪz] *vt* téléviser
television ['tɛlɪvɪʒən] *n* télévision *f*;
on ~ à la télévision; **television
programme** *n* (*BRIT*) émission *f* de
télévision

tell (pt, pp **told**) [tɛl, təuld] vt dire; (relate: story) raconter; (distinguish): **to ~ sth from** distinguer qch de ▷ vi (talk): **to ~ of** parler de; (have effect) se faire sentir, se voir; **to ~ sb to do** dire à qn de faire; **to ~ the time** (know how to) savoir lire l'heure; **tell off** vt réprimander, gronder; **teller** n (in bank) caissier(-ière)

telly ['tɛlɪ] n abbr (BRIT inf: = television) télé f

temp [tɛmp] n (BRIT: = temporary worker) intérimaire m/f ▷ vi travailler comme intérimaire

temper ['tɛmpəʳ] n (nature) caractère m; (mood) humeur f; (fit of anger) colère f ▷ vt (moderate) tempérer, adoucir; **to be in a ~** être en colère; **to lose one's ~** se mettre en colère

temperament ['tɛmprəmənt] n (nature) tempérament m; **temperamental** [tɛmprə'mɛntl] adj capricieux(-euse)

temperature ['tɛmprətʃəʳ] n température f; **to have** or **run a ~** avoir de la fièvre

temple ['tɛmpl] n (building) temple m; (Anat) tempe f

temporary ['tɛmpərərɪ] adj temporaire, provisoire; (job, worker) temporaire

tempt [tɛmpt] vt tenter; **to ~ sb into doing** induire qn à faire; **temptation** n tentation f; **tempting** adj tentant(e); (food) appétissant(e)

ten [tɛn] num dix

tenant ['tɛnənt] n locataire m/f

tend [tɛnd] vt s'occuper de ▷ vi: **to ~ to do** avoir tendance à faire; **tendency** ['tɛndənsɪ] n tendance f

tender ['tɛndəʳ] adj tendre; (delicate) délicat(e); (sore) sensible ▷ n (Comm: offer) soumission f; (money): **legal ~** cours légal ▷ vt offrir

tendon ['tɛndən] n tendon m

tenner ['tɛnəʳ] n (BRIT inf) billet m de dix livres

tennis ['tɛnɪs] n tennis m; **tennis ball** n balle f de tennis; **tennis court** n (court m de) tennis m; **tennis match** n match m de tennis; **tennis player** n joueur(-euse) de tennis; **tennis racket** n raquette f de tennis

tenor ['tɛnəʳ] n (Mus) ténor m

tenpin bowling ['tɛnpɪn-] n (BRIT) bowling m (à 10 quilles)

tense [tɛns] adj tendu(e) ▷ n (Ling) temps m

tension ['tɛnʃən] n tension f

tent [tɛnt] n tente f

tentative ['tɛntətɪv] adj timide, hésitant(e); (conclusion) provisoire

tenth [tɛnθ] num dixième

tent: tent peg n piquet m de tente; **tent pole** n montant m de tente

tepid ['tɛpɪd] adj tiède

term [tə:m] n terme m; (Scol) trimestre m ▷ vt appeler; **terms** npl (conditions) conditions fpl; (Comm) tarif m; **in the short/long ~** à court/ long terme; **to come to ~s with** (problem) faire face à; **to be on good ~s with** bien s'entendre avec, être en bons termes avec

terminal ['tə:mɪnl] adj (disease) dans sa phase terminale; (patient) incurable ▷ n (Elec) borne f; (for oil, ore etc: also Comput) terminal m; (also: **air ~**) aérogare f; (BRIT: also: **coach ~**) gare routière

terminate ['tə:mɪneɪt] vt mettre fin à; (pregnancy) interrompre

termini ['tə:mɪnaɪ] npl of **terminus**

terminology [tə:mɪ'nɔlədʒɪ] n terminologie f

terminus (pl **termini**) ['tə:mɪnəs, 'tə:mɪnaɪ] n terminus m inv

terrace ['tɛrəs] n terrasse f; (BRIT: row of houses) rangée f de maisons (attenantes les unes aux autres); **the ~s** (BRIT Sport) les gradins mpl; **terraced** adj (garden) en terrasses; (in a row: house) attenant(e) aux maisons voisines

terrain [tɛ'reɪn] n terrain m (sol)

terrestrial [tɪˈrestrɪəl] *adj* terrestre

terrible [ˈterɪbl] *adj* terrible, atroce; (*weather, work*) affreux(-euse), épouvantable; **terribly** *adv* terriblement; (*very badly*) affreusement mal

terrier [ˈterɪəʳ] *n* terrier *m* (*chien*)

terrific [təˈrɪfɪk] *adj* (*very great*) fantastique, incroyable, terrible; (*wonderful*) formidable, sensationnel(le)

terrified [ˈterɪfaɪd] *adj* terrifié(e); **to be ~ of sth** avoir très peur de qch

terrify [ˈterɪfaɪ] *vt* terrifier; **terrifying** *adj* terrifiant(e)

territorial [terɪˈtɔːrɪəl] *adj* territorial(e)

territory [ˈterɪtəri] *n* territoire *m*

terror [ˈterəʳ] *n* terreur *f*; **terrorism** *n* terrorisme *m*; **terrorist** *n* terroriste *m/f*; **terrorist attack** *n* attentat *m* terroriste

test [test] *n* (*trial, check*) essai *m*; (*of courage etc*) épreuve *f*; (*Med*) examen *m*; (*Chem*) analyse *f*; (*Scol*) interrogation *f* de contrôle; (*also*: **driving ~**) (examen du) permis *m* de conduire ▷ *vt* essayer; mettre à l'épreuve; examiner; analyser; faire subir une interrogation à

testicle [ˈtestɪkl] *n* testicule *m*

testify [ˈtestɪfaɪ] *vi* (*Law*) témoigner, déposer; **to ~ to sth** (*Law*) attester qch

testimony [ˈtestɪməni] *n* (*Law*) témoignage *m*, déposition *f*

test: test match *n* (*Cricket, Rugby*) match international; **test tube** *n* éprouvette *f*

tetanus [ˈtetənəs] *n* tétanos *m*

text [tekst] *n* texte *m*; (*on mobile phone*) SMS *m inv*, texto® *m* ▷ *vt* (*inf*) envoyer un SMS *or* texto® à; **textbook** *n* manuel *m*

textile [ˈtekstaɪl] *n* textile *m*

text message *n* SMS *m inv*, texto® *m*

text messaging [-ˈmesɪdʒɪŋ] *n* messagerie textuelle

texture [ˈtekstʃəʳ] *n* texture *f*; (*of skin, paper etc*) grain *m*

Thai [taɪ] *adj* thaïlandais(e) ▷ *n* Thaïlandais(e)

Thailand [ˈtaɪlænd] *n* Thaïlande *f*

Thames [temz] *n*: **the (River) ~** la Tamise

than [ðæn, ðən] *conj* que; (*with numerals*): **more ~ 10/once** plus de 10/d'une fois; **I have more/less ~ you** j'en ai plus/moins que toi; **she has more apples ~ pears** elle a plus de pommes que de poires; **it is better to phone ~ to write** il vaut mieux téléphoner (plutôt) qu'écrire; **she is older ~ you think** elle est plus âgée que tu le crois

thank [θæŋk] *vt* remercier, dire merci à; **thanks** *npl* remerciements *mpl*; **~s!** merci!; **~ you (very much)** merci (beaucoup); **~ God** Dieu merci; **~s to** *prep* grâce à; **thankfully** *adv* (*fortunately*) heureusement; **Thanksgiving (Day)** *n* jour *m* d'action de grâce

---

● **THANKSGIVING (DAY)**
●
● *Thanksgiving (Day)* est un jour de
● congé aux États-Unis, le quatrième
● jeudi du mois de novembre,
● commémorant la bonne récolte
● que les Pèlerins venus de
● Grande-Bretagne ont eue en 1621;
● traditionnellement, c'était un jour
● où l'on remerciait Dieu et où l'on
● organisait un grand festin. Une
● fête semblable, mais qui n'a aucun
● rapport avec les Pères Pèlerins, a
● lieu au Canada le deuxième lundi
● d'octobre.

 KEYWORD

that [ðæt] *adj* (*demonstrative*) ce, cet + *vowel or h mute*, cette *f*; **that man/woman/book** cet homme/ cette femme/ce livre; (*not this*) cet

homme-là/cette femme-là/ce livre-là; **that one** celui-là (celle-là)
▶ *pron* **1** (*demonstrative*) ce; (: *not this one*) cela, ça; (: *that one*) celui (celle); **who's that?** qui est-ce?; **what's that?** qu'est-ce que c'est?; **is that you?** c'est toi?; **I prefer this to that** je préfère ceci à cela *or* ça; **that's what he said** c'est *or* voilà ce qu'il a dit; **will you eat all that?** tu vas manger tout ça?; **that is (to say)** c'est-à-dire, à savoir
2 (*relative: subject*) qui; (: *object*) que; (: *after prep*) lequel (laquelle), lesquels (lesquelles) *pl*; **the book that I read** le livre que j'ai lu; **the books that are in the library** les livres qui sont dans la bibliothèque; **all that I have** tout ce que j'ai; **the box that I put it in** la boîte dans laquelle je l'ai mis; **the people that I spoke to** les gens auxquels *or* à qui j'ai parlé
3 (*relative, of time*) où; **the day that he came** le jour où il est venu
▶ *conj* que; **he thought that I was ill** il pensait que j'étais malade
▶ *adv* (*demonstrative*): **I don't like it that much** ça ne me plaît pas tant que ça; **I didn't know it was that bad** je ne savais pas que c'était si *or* aussi mauvais; **it's about that high** c'est à peu près de cette hauteur

thatched [θætʃt] *adj* (*roof*) de chaume; **~ cottage** chaumière *f*
thaw [θɔ:] *n* dégel *m* ▷ *vi* (*ice*) fondre; (*food*) dégeler ▷ *vt* (*food*) (faire) dégeler

KEYWORD

the [ðiː, ðə] *def art* **1** (*gen*) le, la *f*, l' + *vowel or h mute*, les *pl* (NB: à + le(s) = **au(x)**; de + le = **du**; de + les = **des**); **the boy/girl/ink** le garçon/la fille/l'encre; **the children** les enfants; **the history of the world** l'histoire du monde; **give it to the postman** donne-le au facteur; **to**

play the piano/flute jouer du piano/de la flûte
2 (+ *adj to form n*) le, la *f*, l' + *vowel or h mute*, les *pl*; **the rich and the poor** les riches et les pauvres; **to attempt the impossible** tenter l'impossible
3 (*in titles*): **Elizabeth the First** Elisabeth première; **Peter the Great** Pierre le Grand
4 (*in comparisons*): **the more he works, the more he earns** plus il travaille, plus il gagne de l'argent

theatre, (*us*) **theater** [ˈθɪətəʳ] *n* théâtre *m*; (*Med: also:* **operating ~**) salle *f* d'opération
theft [θɛft] *n* vol *m* (*larcin*)
their [ðɛəʳ] *adj* leur, leurs *pl*; *see also* **my**; **theirs** *pron* le (la) leur, les leurs; *see also* **mine¹**
them [ðɛm, ðəm] *pron* (*direct*) les; (*indirect*) leur; (*stressed, after prep*) eux (elles); **give me a few of ~** donnez m'en quelques uns (*or* quelques unes); *see also* **me**
theme [θiːm] *n* thème *m*; **theme park** *n* parc *m* à thème
themselves [ðəmˈsɛlvz] *pl pron* (*reflexive*) se; (*emphatic, after prep*) eux-mêmes (elles-mêmes); **between ~** entre eux (elles); *see also* **oneself**
then [ðɛn] *adv* (*at that time*) alors, à ce moment-là; (*next*) puis, ensuite; (*and also*) et puis ▷ *conj* (*therefore*) alors, dans ce cas ▷ *adj*: **the ~ president** le président d'alors *or* de l'époque; **by ~** (*past*) à ce moment-là; (*future*) d'ici là; **from ~ on** dès lors; **until ~** jusqu'à ce moment-là, jusque-là
theology [θɪˈɔlədʒɪ] *n* théologie *f*
theory [ˈθɪərɪ] *n* théorie *f*
therapist [ˈθɛrəpɪst] *n* thérapeute *m/f*
therapy [ˈθɛrəpɪ] *n* thérapie *f*

KEYWORD

there [ðɛəʳ] *adv* **1**: **there is, there are** il y a; **there are 3 of them**

(people, things) il y en a 3; **there is no-one here/no bread left** il n'y a personne/il n'y a plus de pain; **there has been an accident** il y a eu un accident

2 *(referring to place)* là, là-bas; **it's there** c'est là(-bas); **in/on/up/down there** là-dedans/là-dessus/là-haut/en bas; **he went there on Friday** il y est allé vendredi; **I want that book there** je veux ce livre-là; **there he is!** le voilà!

3: **there, there!** *(esp to child)* allons, allons!

there: **thereabouts** *adv (place)* par là, près de là; *(amount)* environ, à peu près; **thereafter** *adv* par la suite; **thereby** *adv* ainsi; **therefore** *adv* donc, par conséquent

there's ['ðɛəz] = **there is**; **there has**

thermal ['θə:ml] *adj* thermique; **~ underwear** sous-vêtements *mpl* en Thermolactyl®

thermometer [θə'mɒmɪtəʳ] *n* thermomètre *m*

thermostat ['θə:məustæt] *n* thermostat *m*

these [ði:z] *pl pron* ceux-ci (celles-ci) ▷ *pl adj* ces; *(not those)*: **~ books** ces livres-ci

thesis *(pl* **theses**) ['θi:sɪs, 'θi:si:z] *n* thèse *f*

they [ðeɪ] *pl pron* ils (elles); *(stressed)* eux (elles); **~ say that ...** *(it is said that)* on dit que ...; **they'd** = **they had**; **they would**; **they'll** = **they shall**; **they will**; **they're** = **they are**; **they've** = **they have**

thick [θɪk] *adj* épais(se); *(stupid)* bête, borné(e) ▷ *n*: **in the ~ of** au beau milieu de, en plein cœur de; **it's 20 cm ~** ça a 20 cm d'épaisseur; **thicken** *vi* s'épaissir ▷ *vt (sauce etc)* épaissir; **thickness** *n* épaisseur *f*

thief *(pl* **thieves**) [θi:f, θi:vz] *n* voleur(-euse)

thigh [θaɪ] *n* cuisse *f*

thin [θɪn] *adj* mince; *(skinny)* maigre; *(soup)* peu épais(se); *(hair, crowd)* clairsemé(e) ▷ *vt (also:* **~ down**: *sauce, paint)* délayer

thing [θɪŋ] *n* chose *f*; *(object)* objet *m*; *(contraption)* truc *m*; **things** *npl (belongings)* affaires *fpl*; **the ~ is ...** c'est que ...; **the best ~ would be to** le mieux serait de; **how are ~s?** comment ça va?; **to have a ~ about** *(be obsessed by)* être obsédé(e) par; *(hate)* détester; **poor ~!** le *(or* la) pauvre!

think *(pt, pp* **thought**) [θɪŋk, θɔ:t] *vi* penser, réfléchir ▷ *vt* penser, croire; *(imagine)* s'imaginer; **what did you ~ of them?** qu'avez-vous pensé d'eux?; **to ~ about sth/sb** penser à qch/qn; **I'll ~ about it** je vais y réfléchir; **to ~ of doing** avoir l'idée de faire; **I ~ so/not** je crois *or* pense que oui/non; **to ~ well of** avoir une haute opinion de; **think over** *vt* bien réfléchir à; **think up** *vt* inventer, trouver

third [θə:d] *num* troisième ▷ *n (fraction)* tiers *m*; *(Aut)* troisième *(vitesse)* f; *(BRIT Scol: degree)* ≈ licence *f* avec mention passable; **thirdly** *adv* troisièmement; **third party insurance** *n (BRIT)* assurance *f* au tiers; **Third World** *n*: **the Third World** le Tiers-Monde

thirst [θə:st] *n* soif *f*; **thirsty** *adj* qui a soif, assoiffé(e); *(work)* qui donne soif; **to be thirsty** avoir soif

thirteen [θə:'ti:n] *num* treize; **thirteenth** [θə:'ti:nθ] *num* treizième

thirtieth ['θə:tɪɪθ] *num* trentième

thirty ['θə:tɪ] *num* trente

KEYWORD

this [ðɪs] *adj (demonstrative)* ce, cet + *vowel or h mute*, cette *f*; **this man/woman/book** cet homme/ cette femme/ce livre; *(not that)* cet homme-ci/cette femme-ci/ce livre-ci; **this one** celui-ci (celle-ci)

▶ *pron* (*demonstrative*) ce (: *not that one*) celui-ci (celle-ci), ceci; **who's this?** qui est-ce?; **what's this?** qu'est-ce que c'est?; **I prefer this to that** je préfère ceci à cela; **this is where I live** c'est ici que j'habite; **this is what he said** voici ce qu'il a dit; **this is Mr Brown** (*in introductions*) je vous présente Mr Brown; (*in photo*) c'est Mr Brown; (*on telephone*) ici Mr Brown
▶ *adv* (*demonstrative*): **it was about this big** c'était à peu près de cette grandeur *or* grand comme ça; **I didn't know it was this bad** je ne savais pas que c'était si *or* aussi mauvais

thistle ['θɪsl] *n* chardon *m*
thorn [θɔːn] *n* épine *f*
thorough ['θʌrə] *adj* (*search*) minutieux(-euse); (*knowledge, research*) approfondi(e); (*work, person*) consciencieux(-euse); (*cleaning*) à fond; **thoroughly** *adv* (*search*) minutieusement; (*study*) en profondeur; (*clean*) à fond; (*very*) tout à fait
those [ðəʊz] *pl pron* ceux-là (celles-là) ▶ *pl adj* ces; (*not these*): **~ books** ces livres-là
though [ðəʊ] *conj* bien que + *sub*, quoique + *sub* ▶ *adv* pourtant
thought [θɔːt] *pt, pp of* **think** ▶ *n* pensée *f*; (*idea*) idée *f*; (*opinion*) avis *m*; **thoughtful** *adj* (*deep in thought*) pensif(-ive); (*serious*) réfléchi(e); (*considerate*) prévenant(e); **thoughtless** *adj* qui manque de considération
thousand ['θaʊzənd] *num* mille; **one ~** mille; **two ~** deux mille; **~s of** des milliers de; **thousandth** *num* millième
thrash [θræʃ] *vt* rouer de coups; (*inf: defeat*) donner une raclée à (*inf*)
thread [θrɛd] *n* fil *m*; (*of screw*) pas *m*, filetage *m* ▶ *vt* (*needle*) enfiler
threat [θrɛt] *n* menace *f*; **threaten** *vi* (*storm*) menacer ▶ *vt*: **to threaten**

sb with sth/to do menacer qn de qch/de faire; **threatening** *adj* menaçant(e)
three [θriː] *num* trois; **three-dimensional** *adj* à trois dimensions; **three-piece suite** *n* salon *m* (canapé et deux fauteuils); **three-quarters** *npl* trois-quarts *mpl*; **three-quarters full** aux trois-quarts plein
threshold ['θrɛʃhəʊld] *n* seuil *m*
threw [θruː] *pt of* **throw**
thrill [θrɪl] *n* (*excitement*) émotion *f*, sensation forte; (*shudder*) frisson *m* ▶ *vt* (*audience*) électriser; **thrilled** *adj*: **thrilled (with)** ravi(e) de; **thriller** *n* film *m* (*or* roman *m or* pièce *f*) à suspense; **thrilling** *adj* (*book, play etc*) saisissant(e); (*news, discovery*) excitant(e)
thriving ['θraɪvɪŋ] *adj* (*business, community*) prospère
throat [θrəʊt] *n* gorge *f*; **to have a sore ~** avoir mal à la gorge
throb [θrɒb] *vi* (*heart*) palpiter; (*engine*) vibrer; **my head is ~bing** j'ai des élancements dans la tête
throne [θrəʊn] *n* trône *m*
through [θruː] *prep* à travers; (*time*) pendant, durant; (*by means of*) par, par l'intermédiaire de; (*owing to*) à cause de ▶ *adj* (*ticket, train, passage*) direct(e) ▶ *adv* à travers; **(from) Monday ~ Friday** (*US*) de lundi à vendredi; **to put sb ~ to sb** (*Tel*) passer qn à qn; **to be ~** (*BRIT Tel*) avoir la communication; (*esp US: have finished*) avoir fini; **"no ~ traffic"** (*US*) "passage interdit"; **"no ~ road"** (*BRIT*) "impasse"; **throughout** *prep* (*place*) partout dans; (*time*) durant tout(e) le ▶ *adv* partout
throw [θrəʊ] *n* jet *m*; (*Sport*) lancer *m* ▶ *vt* (*pt* **threw**, *pp* **thrown**) lancer, jeter; (*Sport*) lancer; (*rider*) désarçonner; (*fig*) décontenancer; **to ~ a party** donner une réception; **throw away** *vt* jeter; (*money*) gaspiller; **throw in** *vt* (*Sport*: *ball*)

t

remettre en jeu; (*include*) ajouter; **throw off** vt se débarrasser de; **throw out** vt jeter; (*reject*) rejeter; (*person*) mettre à la porte; **throw up** vi vomir

thrown [θrəʊn] pp of **throw**

thru [θru:] (*US*) prep = **through**

thrush [θrʌʃ] n (*Zool*) grive f

thrust [θrʌst] vt (pt, pp **thrust**) pousser brusquement; (*push in*) enfoncer

thud [θʌd] n bruit sourd

thug [θʌg] n voyou m

thumb [θʌm] n (*Anat*) pouce m ▷ vt: **to ~ a lift** faire de l'auto-stop, arrêter une voiture; **thumbtack** n (*US*) punaise f (*clou*)

thump [θʌmp] n grand coup; (*sound*) bruit sourd ▷ vt cogner sur ▷ vi cogner, frapper

thunder ['θʌndər] n tonnerre m ▷ vi tonner; (*train etc*): **to ~ past** passer dans un grondement or un bruit de tonnerre; **thunderstorm** n orage m

Thursday ['θə:zdɪ] n jeudi m

thus [ðʌs] adv ainsi

thwart [θwɔ:t] vt contrecarrer

thyme [taɪm] n thym m

Tibet [tɪ'bɛt] n Tibet m

tick [tɪk] n (*sound: of clock*) tic-tac m; (*mark*) coche f; (*Zool*) tique f ▷ vi faire tic-tac ▷ vt (*item on list*) cocher; **in a ~** (*BRIT inf*) dans un instant; **tick off** vt (*item on list*) cocher; (*person*) réprimander, attraper

ticket ['tɪkɪt] n billet m; (*for bus, tube*) ticket m; (*in shop, on goods*) étiquette f; (*for library*) carte f; (*also:* **parking ~**) contravention f, p.-v. m; **ticket barrier** n (*BRIT Rail*) portillon m automatique; **ticket collector** n contrôleur(-euse); **ticket inspector** n contrôleur(-euse); **ticket machine** n billetterie f automatique; **ticket office** n guichet m, bureau m de vente des billets

tickle ['tɪkl] vi chatouiller ▷ vt chatouiller; **ticklish** adj (*person*)

chatouilleux(-euse); (*problem*) épineux(-euse)

tide [taɪd] n marée f; (*fig: of events*) cours m

tidy ['taɪdɪ] adj (*room*) bien rangé(e); (*dress, work*) net (nette), soigné(e); (*person*) ordonné(e), qui a de l'ordre ▷ vt (*also:* **~ up**) ranger

tie [taɪ] n (*string etc*) cordon m; (*BRIT: also:* **neck~**) cravate f; (*fig: link*) lien m; (*Sport: draw*) égalité f de points match nul ▷ vt (*parcel*) attacher; (*ribbon*) nouer ▷ vi (*Sport*) faire match nul; finir à égalité de points; **to ~ sth in a bow** faire un nœud à or avec qch; **to ~ a knot in sth** faire un nœud à qch; **tie down** vt: **to ~ sb down to** (*fig*) contraindre qn à accepter; **to feel ~d down** (*by relationship*) se sentir coincé(e); **tie up** vt (*parcel*) ficeler; (*dog, boat*) attacher; (*prisoner*) ligoter; (*arrangements*) conclure; **to be ~d up** (*busy*) être pris(e) or occupé(e)

tier [tɪər] n gradin m; (*of cake*) étage m

tiger ['taɪgər] n tigre m

tight [taɪt] adj (*rope*) tendu(e), raide; (*clothes*) étroit(e), très juste; (*budget, programme, bend*) serré(e); (*control*) strict(e), sévère; (*inf: drunk*) ivre, rond(e) ▷ adv (*squeeze*) très fort; (*shut*) à bloc, hermétiquement; **hold ~!** accrochez-vous bien!; **tighten** vt (*rope*) tendre; (*screw*) resserrer; (*control*) renforcer ▷ vi se tendre; se resserrer; **tightly** adv (*grasp*) bien, très fort; **tights** npl (*BRIT*) collant m

tile [taɪl] n (*on roof*) tuile f; (*on wall or floor*) carreau m

till [tɪl] n caisse (enregistreuse) ▷ prep, conj = **until**

tilt [tɪlt] vt pencher, incliner ▷ vi pencher, être incliné(e)

timber ['tɪmbər] n (*material*) bois m de construction

time [taɪm] n temps m; (*epoch: often pl*) époque f, temps m; (*by clock*) heure f; (*moment*) moment m; (*occasion, also Math*) fois f; (*Mus*) mesure f ▷ vt (*race*) chronométrer; (*programme*) minuter; (*visit*) fixer; (*remark etc*) choisir le moment de; **a long ~** un long moment, longtemps; **four at a ~** quatre à la fois; **for the ~ being** pour le moment; **from ~ to ~** de temps en temps; **at ~s** parfois; **in ~** (*soon enough*) à temps; (*after some time*) avec le temps, à la longue; (*Mus*) en mesure; **in a week's ~** dans une semaine; **in no ~** en un rien de temps; **any ~** n'importe quand; **on ~** à l'heure; **5 ~s 5** 5 fois 5; **what ~ is it?** quelle heure est-il?; **what ~ is the museum/shop open?** à quelle heure ouvre le musée/magasin?; **to have a good ~** bien s'amuser; **time limit** n limite f de temps, délai m; **timely** adj opportun(e); **timer** n (*in kitchen*) compte-minutes m inv; (*Tech*) minuteur m; **time-share** n maison f/appartement m en multipropriété; **timetable** n (*Rail*) (indicateur m) horaire m; (*Scol*) emploi m du temps; **time zone** n fuseau m horaire

timid ['tɪmɪd] adj timide; (*easily scared*) peureux(-euse)

timing ['taɪmɪŋ] n (*Sport*) chronométrage m; **the ~ of his resignation** le moment choisi pour sa démission

tin [tɪn] n étain m; (*also:* **~ plate**) fer-blanc m; (*BRIT: can*) boîte f (de conserve); (*for baking*) moule m (à gâteau); (*for storage*) boîte f; **tinfoil** n papier m d'étain *or* d'aluminium

tingle ['tɪŋɡl] vi picoter; (*person*) avoir des picotements

tinker ['tɪŋkər]: **tinker with** vt fus bricoler, rafistoler

tinned [tɪnd] adj (*BRIT: food*) en boîte, en conserve

tin opener [-'əupnər] n (*BRIT*) ouvre-boîte(s) m

tinsel ['tɪnsl] n guirlandes fpl de Noël (*argentées*)

tint [tɪnt] n teinte f; (*for hair*) shampooing colorant; **tinted** adj (*hair*) teint(e); (*spectacles, glass*) teinté(e)

tiny ['taɪnɪ] adj minuscule

tip [tɪp] n (*end*) bout m; (*gratuity*) pourboire m; (*BRIT: for rubbish*) décharge f; (*advice*) tuyau m ▷ vt (*waiter*) donner un pourboire à; (*tilt*) incliner; (*overturn: also:* **~ over**) renverser; (*empty: also:* **~ out**) déverser; **how much should I ~?** combien de pourboire est-ce qu'il faut laisser?; **tip off** vt prévenir, avertir

tiptoe ['tɪptəu] n: **on ~** sur la pointe des pieds

tire ['taɪər] n (*US*) = **tyre** ▷ vt fatiguer ▷ vi se fatiguer; **tired** adj fatigué(e); **to be tired of** en avoir assez de, être las (lasse) de; **tire pressure** (*US*) n = **tyre pressure**; **tiring** adj fatigant(e)

tissue ['tɪʃuː] n tissu m; (*paper handkerchief*) mouchoir m en papier, kleenex® m; **tissue paper** n papier m de soie

tit [tɪt] n (*bird*) mésange f; **to give ~ for tat** rendre coup pour coup

title ['taɪtl] n titre m

T-junction ['tiː'dʒʌŋkʃən] n croisement m en T

TM n abbr = **trademark**

 KEYWORD

to [tuː, tə] prep (*with noun/pronoun*) **1** (*direction*) à; (*: towards*) vers; envers; **to go to France/Portugal/London/school** aller en France/au Portugal/à Londres/à l'école; **to go to Claude's/the doctor's** aller chez Claude/le docteur; **the road to Edinburgh** la route d'Édimbourg **2** (*as far as*) (jusqu')à; **to count to 10** compter jusqu'à 10; **from 40 to 50 people** de 40 à 50 personnes **3** (*with expressions of time*): **a quarter to 5** 5 heures moins le quart; **it's twenty to 3** il est 3 heures moins vingt

t

4 (*for, of*) de; **the key to the front door** la clé de la porte d'entrée; **a letter to his wife** une lettre (adressée) à sa femme
5 (*expressing indirect object*) à; **to give sth to sb** donner qch à qn; **to talk to sb** parler à qn; **to be a danger to sb** être dangereux(-euse) pour qn
6 (*in relation to*) à; **3 goals to 2** 3 (buts) à 2; **30 miles to the gallon** ≈ 9,4 litres aux cent (km)
7 (*purpose; result*): **to come to sb's aid** venir au secours de qn, porter secours à qn; **to sentence sb to death** condamner qn à mort; **to my surprise** à ma grande surprise
▶ *prep* (*with vb*) **1** (*simple infinitive*): **to go/eat** aller/manger
2 (*following another vb*): **to want/ try/start to do** vouloir/essayer de/ commencer à faire
3 (*with vb omitted*): **I don't want to** je ne veux pas
4 (*purpose, result*) pour; **I did it to help you** je l'ai fait pour vous aider
5 (*equivalent to relative clause*): **I have things to do** j'ai des choses à faire; **the main thing is to try** l'important est d'essayer
6 (*after adjective etc*): **ready to go** prêt(e) à partir; **too old/young to ...** trop vieux/jeune pour ...
▶ *adv*: **push/pull the door to** tirez/ poussez la porte

toad [təud] *n* crapaud *m*; **toadstool** *n* champignon (vénéneux)
toast [təust] *n* (*Culin*) pain grillé, toast *m*; (*drink, speech*) toast ▷ *vt* (*Culin*) faire griller; (*drink to*) porter un toast à; **toaster** *n* grille-pain *m inv*
tobacco [tə'bækəu] *n* tabac *m*
toboggan [tə'bɔgən] *n* toboggan *m*; (*child's*) luge *f*
today [tə'deɪ] *adv, n* (*also fig*) aujourd'hui (*m*)
toddler [ˈtɔdlə^r] *n* enfant *m/f* qui commence à marcher, bambin *m*

toe [təu] *n* doigt *m* de pied, orteil *m*; (*of shoe*) bout *m* ▷ *vt*: **to ~ the line** (*fig*) obéir, se conformer; **toenail** *n* ongle *m* de l'orteil
toffee [ˈtɔfɪ] *n* caramel *m*
together [təˈgɛðə^r] *adv* ensemble; (*at same time*) en même temps; **~ with** *prep* avec
toilet [ˈtɔɪlət] *n* (*BRIT: lavatory*) toilettes *fpl*, cabinets *mpl*; **to go to the ~** aller aux toilettes; **where's the ~?** où sont les toilettes?; **toilet bag** *n* (*BRIT*) nécessaire *m* de toilette; **toilet paper** *n* papier *m* hygiénique; **toiletries** *npl* articles *mpl* de toilette; **toilet roll** *n* rouleau *m* de papier hygiénique
token [ˈtəukən] *n* (*sign*) marque *f*, témoignage *m*; (*metal disc*) jeton *m* ▷ *adj* (*fee, strike*) symbolique; **book/ record ~** (*BRIT*) chèque-livre/ -disque *m*
Tokyo [ˈtəukjəu] *n* Tokyo
told [təuld] *pt, pp of* **tell**
tolerant [ˈtɔlərnt] *adj*: **~ (of)** tolérant(e) (à l'égard de)
tolerate [ˈtɔləreɪt] *vt* supporter
toll [təul] *n* (*tax, charge*) péage *m* ▷ *vi* (*bell*) sonner; **the accident ~ on the roads** le nombre des victimes de la route; **toll call** *n* (*us Tel*) appel *m* (à) longue distance; **toll-free** *adj* (*us*) gratuit(e) ▷ *adv* gratuitement
tomato [təˈmɑːtəu] (*pl* **tomatoes**) *n* tomate *f*; **tomato sauce** *n* sauce *f* tomate
tomb [tuːm] *n* tombe *f*; **tombstone** *n* pierre tombale
tomorrow [təˈmɔrəu] *adv, n* (*also fig*) demain (*m*); **the day after ~** après-demain; **a week ~** demain en huit; **~ morning** demain matin
ton [tʌn] *n* tonne *f* (*Brit*: = 1016 kg; *US* = 907 kg; *metric* = 1000 kg); **~s of** (*inf*) des tas de
tone [təun] *n* ton *m*; (*of radio, BRIT Tel*) tonalité *f* ▷ *vi* (*also*: **~ in**) s'harmoniser; **tone down** *vt* (*colour, criticism*) adoucir

tongs [tɒŋz] npl pinces fpl; (for coal) pincettes fpl; (for hair) fer m à friser

tongue [tʌŋ] n langue f; **~ in cheek** adv ironiquement

tonic ['tɒnɪk] n (Med) tonique m; (also: **~ water**) Schweppes® m

tonight [tə'naɪt] adv, n cette nuit; (this evening) ce soir

tonne [tʌn] n (BRIT: metric ton) tonne f

tonsil ['tɒnsl] n amygdale f; **tonsillitis** [tɒnsɪ'laɪtɪs] n: **to have tonsillitis** avoir une angine or une amygdalite

too [tuː] adv (excessively) trop; (also) aussi; **~ much** (as adv) trop; (as adj) trop de; **~ many** adj trop de

took [tʊk] pt of **take**

tool [tuːl] n outil m; **tool box** n boîte f à outils; **tool kit** n trousse f à outils

tooth (pl **teeth**) [tuːθ, tiːθ] n (Anat, Tech) dent f; **to brush one's teeth** se laver les dents; **toothache** n mal m de dents; **to have toothache** avoir mal aux dents; **toothbrush** n brosse f à dents; **toothpaste** n (pâte f) dentifrice m; **toothpick** n cure-dent m

top [tɒp] n (of mountain, head) sommet m; (of page, ladder) haut m; (of box, cupboard, table) dessus m; (lid: of box, jar) couvercle m; (: of bottle) bouchon m; (toy) toupie f; (Dress: blouse etc) haut m; (: of pyjamas) veste f ▷ adj du haut; (in rank) premier(-ière); (best) meilleur(e) ▷ vt (exceed) dépasser; (be first in) être en tête de; **from ~ to bottom** de fond en comble; **on ~ of** sur; (in addition to) en plus de; **over the ~** (inf) (behaviour etc) qui dépasse les limites; **top up**, (us) **top off** vt (bottle) remplir; (salary) compléter; **to ~ up one's mobile (phone)** recharger son compte; **top floor** n dernier étage; **top hat** n haut-de-forme m

topic ['tɒpɪk] n sujet m, thème m; **topical** adj d'actualité

topless ['tɒplɪs] adj (bather etc) aux seins nus

topping ['tɒpɪŋ] n (Culin) couche de crème, fromage etc qui recouvre un plat

topple ['tɒpl] vt renverser, faire tomber ▷ vi basculer; tomber

top-up ['tɒpʌp] n (for mobile phone) recharge f, minutes fpl; **top-up card** n (for mobile phone) recharge f

torch [tɔːtʃ] n torche f; (BRIT: electric) lampe f de poche

tore [tɔːʳ] pt of **tear²**

torment n ['tɔːmɛnt] tourment m ▷ vt [tɔː'mɛnt] tourmenter; (fig: annoy) agacer

torn [tɔːn] pp of **tear²**

tornado [tɔː'neɪdəʊ] (pl **tornadoes**) n tornade f

torpedo [tɔː'piːdəʊ] (pl **torpedoes**) n torpille f

torrent ['tɒrnt] n torrent m; **torrential** [tɔ'rɛnʃl] adj torrentiel(le)

tortoise ['tɔːtəs] n tortue f

torture ['tɔːtʃəʳ] n torture f ▷ vt torturer

Tory ['tɔːrɪ] adj, n (BRIT Pol) tory m/f, conservateur(-trice)

toss [tɒs] vt lancer, jeter; (BRIT: pancake) faire sauter; (head) rejeter en arrière ▷ vi: **to ~ up for sth** (BRIT) jouer qch à pile ou face; **to ~ a coin** jouer à pile ou face; **to ~ and turn** (in bed) se tourner et se retourner

total ['təʊtl] adj total(e) ▷ n total m ▷ vt (add up) faire le total de, additionner; (amount to) s'élever à

totalitarian [təʊtælɪ'tɛərɪən] adj totalitaire

totally ['təʊtəlɪ] adv totalement

t

touch [tʌtʃ] n contact m, toucher m; (sense, skill: of pianist etc) toucher ▷ vt (gen) toucher; (tamper with) toucher à; **a ~ of** (fig) un petit peu de; une touche de; **to get in ~ with** prendre contact avec; **to lose ~** (friends) se perdre de vue; **touch down** vi (Aviat) atterrir; (on sea) amerrir; **touchdown** n (Aviat) atterrissage m; (on sea) amerrissage m; (us Football) essai m; **touched** adj (moved) touché(e); **touching**

adj touchant(e), attendrissant(e);
touchline *n* (Sport) (ligne *f* de) touche
f; **touch-sensitive** *adj* (keypad) à
effleurement; (screen) tactile

tough [tʌf] *adj* dur(e); (resistant)
résistant(e), solide; (meat) dur,
coriace; (firm) inflexible; (task,
problem, situation) difficile

tour ['tuə'] *n* voyage *m*; (also:
package ~) voyage organisé; (of
town, museum) tour *m*, visite *f*; (by
band) tournée *f* ▷ *vt* visiter; **tour
guide** *n* (person) guide *m/f*

tourism ['tuərɪzm] *n* tourisme *m*

tourist ['tuərɪst] *n* touriste *m/f* ▷ *cpd*
touristique; **tourist office** *n* syndicat
m d'initiative

tournament ['tuənəmənt] *n*
tournoi *m*

tour operator *n* (BRIT) organisateur
m de voyages, tour-opérateur *m*

tow [təu] *vt* remorquer; (caravan,
trailer) tracter; **"on ~"**, (US) **"in ~"**
(Aut) "véhicule en remorque"; **tow
away** *vt* (subj: police) emmener à
la fourrière; (: breakdown service)
remorquer

toward(s) [tə'wɔ:d(z)] *prep* vers;
(of attitude) envers, à l'égard de; (of
purpose) pour

towel ['tauəl] *n* serviette *f* (de
toilette); **towelling** *n* (fabric) tissu-
éponge *m*

tower ['tauə'] *n* tour *f*; **tower block** *n*
(BRIT) tour *f* (d'habitation)

town [taun] *n* ville *f*; **to go to ~** aller
en ville; (fig) y mettre le paquet;
town centre *n* (BRIT) centre *m* de
la ville, centre-ville *m*; **town hall** *n*
≈ mairie *f*

tow truck *n* (US) dépanneuse *f*

toxic ['tɔksɪk] *adj* toxique

toy [tɔɪ] *n* jouet *m*; **toy with** *vt fus*
jouer avec; (idea) caresser; **toyshop** *n*
magasin *m* de jouets

trace [treɪs] *n* trace *f* ▷ *vt* (draw)
tracer, dessiner; (follow) suivre la
trace de; (locate) retrouver

tracing paper ['treɪsɪŋ-] *n* papier-
calque *m*

track [træk] *n* (mark) trace *f*; (path:
gen) chemin *m*, piste *f*; (: of bullet etc)
trajectoire *f*; (: of suspect, animal)
piste; (Rail) voie ferrée, rails *mpl*;
(Comput, Sport) piste; (on CD) piste;
(on record) plage *f* ▷ *vt* suivre la trace or
la piste de; **to keep ~ of** suivre; **track
down** *vt* (prey) trouver et capturer;
(sth lost) finir par retrouver; **tracksuit**
n survêtement *m*

tractor ['træktə'] *n* tracteur *m*

trade [treɪd] *n* commerce *m*; (skill,
job) métier *m* ▷ *vi* faire du commerce
▷ *vt* (exchange): **to ~ sth (for sth)**
échanger qch (contre qch); **to ~
with/in** faire du commerce avec/
le commerce de; **trade in** *vt* (old
car etc) faire reprendre; **trademark**
n marque *f* de fabrique; **trader** *n*
commerçant(e), négociant(e);
tradesman (irreg) *n* (shopkeeper)
commerçant *m*; **trade union** *n*
syndicat *m*

trading ['treɪdɪŋ] *n* affaires *fpl*,
commerce *m*

tradition [trə'dɪʃən] *n* tradition *f*;
traditional *adj* traditionnel(le)

traffic ['træfɪk] *n* trafic *m*; (cars)
circulation *f* ▷ *vi*: **to ~ in** (pej: liquor,
drugs) faire le trafic de; **traffic circle**
n (US) rond-point *m*; **traffic island** *n*
refuge *m* (pour piétons); **traffic jam**
n embouteillage *m*; **traffic lights** *npl*
feux *mpl* (de signalisation); **traffic
warden** *n* contractuel(le)

tragedy ['trædʒədɪ] *n* tragédie *f*

tragic ['trædʒɪk] *adj* tragique

trail [treɪl] *n* (tracks) trace *f*, piste
f; (path) chemin *m*, piste; (of smoke
etc) traînée *f* ▷ *vt* (drag) traîner, tirer;
(follow) suivre ▷ *vi* traîner; (in game,
contest) être en retard; **trailer** *n* (Aut)
remorque *f*; (US: caravan) caravane *f*;
(Cine) bande-annonce *f*

train [treɪn] *n* train *m*; (in underground)
rame *f*; (of dress) traîne *f*; (BRIT: series):

~ of events série *f* d'événements ▷ *vt* (*apprentice, doctor etc*) former; (*Sport*) entraîner; (*dog*) dresser; (*memory*) exercer; (*point: gun etc*): **to ~ sth on** braquer qch sur ▷ *vi* recevoir sa formation; (*Sport*) s'entraîner; **one's ~ of thought** le fil de sa pensée; **what time does the ~ from Paris get in?** à quelle heure arrive le train de Paris?; **is this the ~ for ...?** c'est bien le train pour ...?; **trainee** [treɪ'ni:] *n* stagiaire *m/f*; (*in trade*) apprenti(e); **trainer** *n* (*Sport*) entraîneur(-euse); (*of dogs etc*) dresseur(-euse); **trainers** *npl* (*shoes*) chaussures *fpl* de sport; **training** *n* formation *f*; (*Sport*) entraînement *m*; (*of dog etc*) dressage *m*; **in training** (*Sport*) à l'entraînement; (*fit*) en forme; **training course** *n* cours *m* de formation professionnelle; **training shoes** *npl* chaussures *fpl* de sport

trait [treɪt] *n* trait *m* (de caractère)

traitor ['treɪtə'] *n* traître *m*

tram [træm] *n* (BRIT: *also*: **~car**) tram(way) *m*

tramp [træmp] *n* (*person*) vagabond(e), clochard(e); (*inf, pej: woman*): **to be a ~** être coureuse

trample ['træmpl] *vt*: **to ~ (underfoot)** piétiner

trampoline ['træmpəliːn] *n* trampoline *m*

tranquil ['træŋkwɪl] *adj* tranquille; **tranquilizer**, (us) **tranquilizer** *n* (*Med*) tranquillisant *m*

transaction [træn'zækʃən] *n* transaction *f*

transatlantic ['trænzət'læntɪk] *adj* transatlantique

transcript ['trænskrɪpt] *n* transcription *f* (*texte*)

transfer *n* ['trænsfə'] (*gen, also Sport*) transfert *m*; (*Pol: of power*) passation *f*; (*of money*) virement *m*; (*picture, design*) décalcomanie *f*; (: *stick-on*) autocollant *m* ▷ *vt* [træns'fə:'] transférer; passer; virer; **to ~ the**

charges (BRIT Tel) téléphoner en P.C.V.

transform [træns'fɔ:m] *vt* transformer; **transformation** *n* transformation *f*

transfusion [træns'fju:ʒən] *n* transfusion *f*

transit ['trænzɪt] *n*: **in ~** en transit

transition [træn'zɪʃən] *n* transition *f*

transitive ['trænzɪtɪv] *adj* (*Ling*) transitif(-ive)

translate [trænz'leɪt] *vt*: **to ~ (from/into)** traduire (du/en); **can you ~ this for me?** pouvez-vous me traduire ceci?; **translation** [trænz'leɪʃən] *n* traduction *f*; (*Scol: as opposed to prose*) version *f*; **translator** *n* traducteur(-trice)

transmission [trænz'mɪʃən] *n* transmission *f*

transmit [trænz'mɪt] *vt* transmettre; (*Radio, TV*) émettre; **transmitter** *n* émetteur *m*

transparent [træns'pærnt] *adj* transparent(e)

transplant ['trænsplɑ:nt] *n* (*Med*) transplantation *f*

transport *n* ['trænspɔ:t] transport *m* ▷ *vt* [træns'pɔ:t] transporter; **transportation** [trænspɔ:'teɪʃən] *n* (*moyen m de*) transport *m*

transvestite [trænz'vɛstaɪt] *n* travesti(e)

trap [træp] *n* (*snare, trick*) piège *m*; (*carriage*) cabriolet *m* ▷ *vt* prendre au piège; (*confine*) coincer

trash [træʃ] *n* (*inf, pej: goods*) camelote *f*; (: *nonsense*) sottises *fpl*; (US: *rubbish*) ordures *fpl*; **trash can** *n* (US) poubelle *f*

trauma ['trɔ:mə] *n* traumatisme *m*; **traumatic** [trɔ:'mætɪk] *adj* traumatisant(e)

travel ['trævl] *n* voyage(s) *m(pl)* ▷ *vi* voyager; (*news, sound*) se propager ▷ *vt* (*distance*) parcourir; **travel agency** *n* agence *f* de voyages; **travel agent** *n* agent *m* de voyages; **travel insurance**

n assurance-voyage *f*; **traveller**, (*us*) **traveler** *n* voyageur(-euse); **traveller's cheque**, (*us*) **traveler's check** *n* chèque *m* de voyage; **travelling**, (*us*) **traveling** *n* voyage(s) *m(pl)*; **travel-sick** *adj*: **to get travel-sick** avoir le mal de la route (*or* de mer *or* de l'air); **travel sickness** *n* mal *m* de la route (*or* de mer *or* de l'air)

tray [treɪ] *n* (*for carrying*) plateau *m*; (*on desk*) corbeille *f*

treacherous ['trɛtʃərəs] *adj* traître(sse); (*ground, tide*) dont il faut se méfier

treacle ['triːkl] *n* mélasse *f*

tread [trɛd] *n* (*step*) pas *m*; (*sound*) bruit *m* de pas; (*of tyre*) chape *f*, bande *f* de roulement ▷ *vi* (*pt* **trod**, *pp* **trodden**) marcher; **tread on** *vt fus* marcher sur

treasure ['trɛʒəʳ] *n* trésor *m* ▷ *vt* (*value*) tenir beaucoup à; **treasurer** *n* trésorier(-ière)

treasury ['trɛʒərɪ] *n*: **the T~**, (*us*) **the T~ Department** ≈ le ministère des Finances

treat [triːt] *n* petit cadeau, petite surprise ▷ *vt* traiter; **to ~ sb to sth** offrir qch à qn; **treatment** *n* traitement *m*

treaty ['triːtɪ] *n* traité *m*

treble ['trɛbl] *adj* triple ▷ *vt, vi* tripler

tree [triː] *n* arbre *m*

trek [trɛk] *n* (*long walk*) randonnée *f*; (*tiring walk*) longue marche, trotte *f*

tremble ['trɛmbl] *vi* trembler

tremendous [trɪ'mɛndəs] *adj* (*enormous*) énorme; (*excellent*) formidable, fantastique

trench [trɛntʃ] *n* tranchée *f*

trend [trɛnd] *n* (*tendency*) tendance *f*; (*of events*) cours *m*; (*fashion*) mode *f*; **trendy** *adj* (*idea, person*) dans le vent; (*clothes*) dernier cri *inv*

trespass ['trɛspəs] *vi*: **to ~ on** s'introduire sans permission dans; **"no ~ing"** "propriété privée", "défense d'entrer"

trial ['traɪəl] *n* (*Law*) procès *m*, jugement *m*; (*test: of machine etc*) essai *m*; **trials** *npl* (*unpleasant experiences*) épreuves *fpl*; **trial period** *n* période *f* d'essai

triangle ['traɪæŋgl] *n* (*Math, Mus*) triangle *m*

triangular [traɪ'æŋgjuləʳ] *adj* triangulaire

tribe [traɪb] *n* tribu *f*

tribunal [traɪ'bjuːnl] *n* tribunal *m*

tribute ['trɪbjuːt] *n* tribut *m*, hommage *m*; **to pay ~ to** rendre hommage à

trick [trɪk] *n* (*magic*) tour *m*; (*joke, prank*) tour, farce *f*; (*skill, knack*) astuce *f*; (*Cards*) levée *f* ▷ *vt* attraper, rouler; **to play a ~ on sb** jouer un tour à qn; **that should do the ~** (*inf*) ça devrait faire l'affaire

trickle ['trɪkl] *n* (*of water etc*) filet *m* ▷ *vi* couler en un filet *or* goutte à goutte

tricky ['trɪkɪ] *adj* difficile, délicat(e)

tricycle ['traɪsɪkl] *n* tricycle *m*

trifle ['traɪfl] *n* bagatelle *f*; (*Culin*) ≈ diplomate *m* ▷ *adv*: **a ~ long** un peu long

trigger ['trɪgəʳ] *n* (*of gun*) gâchette *f*

trim [trɪm] *adj* (*house, garden*) bien tenu(e); (*figure*) svelte ▷ *n* (*haircut etc*) légère coupe; (*on car*) garnitures *fpl* ▷ *vt* (*cut*) couper légèrement; (*Naut: a sail*) gréer; (*decorate*): **to ~ (with)** décorer (de)

trio ['triːəu] *n* trio *m*

trip [trɪp] *n* voyage *m*; (*excursion*) excursion *f*; (*stumble*) faux pas ▷ *vi* faire un faux pas, trébucher; **trip up** *vi* trébucher ▷ *vt* faire un croc-en-jambe à

triple ['trɪpl] *adj* triple

triplets ['trɪplɪts] *npl* triplés(-ées)

tripod ['traɪpɔd] *n* trépied *m*

triumph ['traɪʌmf] *n* triomphe *m* ▷ *vi*: **to ~ (over)** triompher (de); **triumphant** [traɪ'ʌmfənt] *adj* triomphant(e)

trivial ['trɪvɪəl] adj insignifiant(e); (commonplace) banal(e)

trod [trɒd] pt of **tread**

trodden ['trɒdn] pp of **tread**

troll [trɒl] n (Comput) troll m, trolleur(-euse) m/f

trolley ['trɒlɪ] n chariot m

trombone [trɒm'bəun] n trombone m

troop [tru:p] n bande f, groupe m; **troops** npl (Mil) troupes fpl (: men) hommes mpl, soldats mpl

trophy ['trəufɪ] n trophée m

tropical ['trɒpɪkl] adj tropical(e)

trot [trɒt] n trot m ▷ vi trotter; **on the ~** (BRIT fig) d'affilée

trouble ['trʌbl] n difficulté(s) f(pl), problème(s) m(pl); (worry) ennuis mpl, soucis mpl; (bother, effort) peine f; (Pol) conflit(s) m(pl), troubles mpl; (Med): **stomach** etc ~ troubles gastriques etc ▷ vt (disturb) déranger, gêner; (worry) inquiéter ▷ vi: **to ~ to do** prendre la peine de faire; **troubles** npl (Pol etc) troubles; (personal) ennuis, soucis; **to be in ~** avoir des ennuis; (ship, climber etc) être en difficulté; **to have ~ doing sth** avoir du mal à faire qch; **it's no ~!** je vous en prie!; **the ~ is ...** le problème, c'est que ...; **what's the ~?** qu'est-ce qui ne va pas?; **troubled** adj (person) inquiet(-ète); (times, life) agité(e); **troublemaker** n élément perturbateur, fauteur m de troubles; **troublesome** adj (child) fatigant(e), difficile; (cough) gênant(e)

trough [trɒf] n (also: **drinking ~**) abreuvoir m; (also: **feeding ~**) auge f; (depression) creux m

trousers ['trauzəz] npl pantalon m; **short ~** (BRIT) culottes courtes

trout [traut] n (pl inv) truite f

truant ['truənt] n: **to play ~** (BRIT) faire l'école buissonnière

truce [tru:s] n trêve f

truck [trʌk] n camion m; (Rail) wagon m à plate-forme; **truck driver** n camionneur m

true [tru:] adj vrai(e); (accurate) exact(e); (genuine) vrai, véritable; (faithful) fidèle; **to come ~** se réaliser

truly ['tru:lɪ] adv vraiment, réellement; (truthfully) sans mentir; **yours ~** (in letter) je vous prie d'agréer, Monsieur (or Madame etc), l'expression de mes sentiments respectueux

trumpet ['trʌmpɪt] n trompette f

trunk [trʌŋk] n (of tree, person) tronc m; (of elephant) trompe f; (case) malle f; (US Aut) coffre m; **trunks** npl (also: **swimming ~s**) maillot m or slip m de bain

trust [trʌst] n confiance f; (responsibility): **to place sth in sb's ~** confier la responsabilité de qch à qn; (Law) fidéicommis m ▷ vt (rely on) avoir confiance en; (entrust): **to ~ sth to sb** confier qch à qn; (hope): **to ~ (that)** espérer (que); **to take sth on ~** accepter qch les yeux fermés; **trusted** adj en qui l'on a confiance; **trustworthy** adj digne de confiance

truth [tru:θ, tru:ðz] n vérité f; **truthful** adj (person) qui dit la vérité; (answer) sincère

try [traɪ] n essai m, tentative f; (Rugby) essai m ▷ vt (attempt) essayer, tenter; (test: sth new: also: ~ **out**) essayer, tester; (Law: person) juger; (strain) éprouver ▷ vi essayer; **to ~ to do** essayer de faire; (seek) chercher à faire; **try on** vt (clothes) essayer; **trying** adj pénible

T-shirt ['ti:ʃə:t] n tee-shirt m

tub [tʌb] n cuve f; (for washing clothes) baquet m; (bath) baignoire f

tube [tju:b] n tube m; (BRIT: underground) métro m; (for tyre) chambre f à air

tuberculosis [tjubə:kju'ləusɪs] n tuberculose f

tube station n (BRIT) station f de métro

tuck [tʌk] vt (put) mettre; **tuck away** vt cacher, ranger; (money) mettre de

côté; (*building*): **to be ~ed away** être
caché(e); **tuck in** *vt* rentrer; (*child*)
border ▷ *vi* (*eat*) manger de bon
appétit; attaquer le repas
tucker ['tʌkə'] *n* (AUST, NZ *inf*) bouffe
f (*inf*)
tuck shop *n* (BRIT Scol) boutique *f* à
provisions
Tuesday ['tju:zdɪ] *n* mardi *m*
tug [tʌg] *n* (*ship*) remorqueur *m* ▷ *vt*
tirer (sur)
tuition [tju:'ɪʃən] *n* (BRIT:
lessons) leçons *fpl*; (: *private*) cours
particuliers; (US: *fees*) frais *mpl* de
scolarité
tulip ['tju:lɪp] *n* tulipe *f*
tumble ['tʌmbl] *n* (*fall*) chute *f*,
culbute *f* ▷ *vi* tomber, dégringoler;
to ~ to sth (*inf*) réaliser qch; **tumble
dryer** *n* (BRIT) séchoir *m* (à linge) à
air chaud
tumbler ['tʌmblə'] *n* verre (droit),
gobelet *m*
tummy ['tʌmɪ] *n* (*inf*) ventre *m*
tumour, (US) **tumor** ['tju:mə'] *n*
tumeur *f*
tuna ['tju:nə] *n* (*pl inv*: *also*: ~ **fish**)
thon *m*
tune [tju:n] *n* (*melody*) air *m* ▷ *vt*
(*Mus*) accorder; (*Radio, TV, Aut*)
régler, mettre au point; **to be in/
out of ~** (*instrument*) être accordé/
désaccordé; (*singer*) chanter juste/
faux; **tune in** *vi* (*Radio, TV*); **to ~ in
(to)** se mettre à l'écoute (de); **tune up**
vi (*musician*) accorder son instrument
tunic ['tju:nɪk] *n* tunique *f*
Tunis ['tju:nɪs] *n* Tunis
Tunisia [tju:'nɪzɪə] *n* Tunisie *f*
Tunisian [tju:'nɪzɪən] *adj*
tunisien(ne) ▷ *n* Tunisien(ne)
tunnel ['tʌnl] *n* tunnel *m*; (*in mine*)
galerie *f* ▷ *vi* creuser un tunnel (*or*
une galerie)
turbulence ['tə:bjuləns] *n* (*Aviat*)
turbulence *f*
turf [tə:f] *n* gazon *m*; (*clod*) motte *f* (de
gazon) ▷ *vt* gazonner

Turk [tə:k] *n* Turc (Turque)
Turkey ['tə:kɪ] *n* Turquie *f*
turkey ['tə:kɪ] *n* dindon *m*, dinde *f*
Turkish ['tə:kɪʃ] *adj* turc (turque) ▷ *n*
(*Ling*) turc *m*
turmoil ['tə:mɔɪl] *n* trouble *m*,
bouleversement *m*
turn [tə:n] *n* tour *m*; (*in road*) tournant
m; (*tendency*: *of mind, events*) tournure
f; (*performance*) numéro *m*; (*Med*) crise
f, attaque *f* ▷ *vt* tourner; (*collar, steak*)
retourner; (*age*) atteindre; (*change*): **to
~ sth into** changer qch en ▷ *vi* (*object,
wind, milk*) tourner; (*person: look back*)
se (re)tourner; (*reverse direction*) faire
demi-tour; (*become*) devenir; **to ~
into** se changer en, se transformer
en; **a good ~** un service; **it gave me
quite a ~** ça m'a fait un coup; **"no
left ~"** (*Aut*) "défense de tourner à
gauche"; **~ left/right at the next
junction** tournez à gauche/droite
au prochain carrefour; **it's your ~**
c'est (à) votre tour; **in ~** à son tour;
à tour de rôle; **to take ~s** se relayer;
turn around *vi* (*person*) se retourner
▷ *vt* (*object*) tourner; **turn away** *vi* se
détourner, tourner la tête ▷ *vt* (*reject:
person*) renvoyer; (: *business*) refuser;
turn back *vi* revenir, faire demi-tour;
turn down *vt* (*refuse*) rejeter, refuser;
(*reduce*) baisser; (*fold*) rabattre; **turn
in** *vi* (*inf: go to bed*) aller se coucher
▷ *vt* (*fold*) rentrer; **turn off** *vi* (*from
road*) tourner ▷ *vt* (*light, radio etc*)
éteindre; (*tap*) fermer; (*engine*) arrêter;
I can't ~ the heating off je n'arrive
pas à éteindre le chauffage; **turn
on** *vt* (*light, radio etc*) allumer; (*tap*)
ouvrir; (*engine*) mettre en marche; **I
can't ~ the heating on** je n'arrive pas
à allumer le chauffage; **turn out** *vt*
(*light, gas*) éteindre; (*produce*) produire
▷ *vi* (*voters, troops*) se présenter; **to
~ out to be ...** s'avérer ..., se révéler
...; **turn over** *vi* (*person*) se retourner
▷ *vt* (*object*) retourner; (*page*) tourner;
turn round *vi* faire demi-tour;

(*rotate*) tourner; **turn to** vt fus: **to ~ to sb** s'adresser à qn; **turn up** vi (*person*) arriver, se pointer (*inf*); (*lost object*) être retrouvé(e) ▷ vt (*collar*) remonter; (*radio, heater*) mettre plus fort; **turning** n (*in road*) tournant m; **turning point** n (*fig*) tournant m, moment décisif

turnip ['tə:nɪp] n navet m

turn: turnout n (*of voters*) taux m de participation; **turnover** n (*Comm: amount of money*) chiffre m d'affaires; (: *of goods*) roulement m; (*of staff*) renouvellement m, changement m; **turnstile** n tourniquet m (*d'entrée*); **turn-up** n (BRIT: *on trousers*) revers m

turquoise ['tə:kwɔɪz] n (*stone*) turquoise f ▷ adj turquoise inv

turtle ['tə:tl] n tortue marine; **turtleneck (sweater)** n pullover m à col montant

tusk [tʌsk] n défense f (*d'éléphant*)

tutor ['tju:təʳ] n (BRIT Scol: *in college*) directeur(-trice) d'études; (*private teacher*) précepteur(-trice); **tutorial** [tju:'tɔ:rɪəl] n (Scol) (séance f de) travaux mpl pratiques

tuxedo [tʌk'si:dəu] n (US) smoking m

TV [ti:'vi:] n abbr (= *television*) télé f, TV f

tweed [twi:d] n tweed m

tweet [twi:t] (*on Twitter*) n tweet m ▷ vt, vi tweeter

tweezers ['twi:zəz] npl pince f à épiler

twelfth [twɛlfθ] num douzième

twelve [twɛlv] num douze; **at ~ (o'clock)** à midi; (*midnight*) à minuit

twentieth ['twɛntɪɪθ] num vingtième

twenty ['twɛntɪ] num vingt; **in ~ fourteen** en deux mille quatorze

twice [twaɪs] adv deux fois; **~ as much** deux fois plus

twig [twɪg] n brindille f ▷ vt, vi (*inf*) piger

twilight ['twaɪlaɪt] n crépuscule m

twin [twɪn] adj, n jumeau(-elle) ▷ vt jumeler; **twin-bedded room** n

= **twin room**; **twin beds** npl lits mpl jumeaux

twinkle ['twɪŋkl] vi scintiller; (*eyes*) pétiller

twin room n chambre f à deux lits

twist [twɪst] n torsion f, tour m; (*in wire, flex*) tortillon m; (*bend: in road*) tournant m; (*in story*) coup m de théâtre ▷ vt tordre; (*weave*) entortiller; (*roll around*) enrouler; (*fig*) déformer ▷ vi (*road, river*) serpenter; **to ~ one's ankle/wrist** (*Med*) se tordre la cheville/le poignet

twit [twɪt] n (*inf*) crétin(e)

twitch [twɪtʃ] n (*pull*) coup sec, saccade f; (*nervous*) tic m ▷ vi se convulser; avoir un tic

two [tu:] num deux; **to put ~ and ~ together** (*fig*) faire le rapprochement

type [taɪp] n (*category*) genre m, espèce f; (*model*) modèle m; (*example*) type m; (*Typ*) type, caractère m ▷ vt (*letter etc*) taper (à la machine); **typewriter** n machine f à écrire

typhoid ['taɪfɔɪd] n typhoïde f

typhoon [taɪ'fu:n] n typhon m

typical ['tɪpɪkl] adj typique, caractéristique; **typically** ['tɪpɪklɪ] adv (*as usual*) comme d'habitude; (*characteristically*) typiquement

typing ['taɪpɪŋ] n dactylo(graphie) f

typist ['taɪpɪst] n dactylo m/f

tyre, (US) **tire** ['taɪəʳ] n pneu m; **tyre pressure** n (BRIT) pression f (de gonflage)

t

U

UFO ['juːfəu] *n abbr* (= *unidentified flying object*) ovni *m*

Uganda [juːˈgændə] *n* Ouganda *m*

ugly ['ʌglɪ] *adj* laid(e), vilain(e); (*fig*) répugnant(e)

UHT *adj abbr* (= *ultra-heat treated*): **~ milk** lait *m* UHT *or* longue conservation

UK *n abbr* = **United Kingdom**

ulcer ['ʌlsə^r] *n* ulcère *m*; **mouth ~** aphte *f*

ultimate ['ʌltɪmət] *adj* ultime, final(e); (*authority*) suprême; **ultimately** *adv* (*at last*) en fin de compte; (*fundamentally*) finalement; (*eventually*) par la suite

ultimatum (*pl* **ultimatums** *or* **ultimata**) [ʌltɪˈmeɪtəm, -tə] *n* ultimatum *m*

ultrasound ['ʌltrəsaund] *n* (*Med*) ultrason *m*

ultraviolet ['ʌltrəˈvaɪəlɪt] *adj* ultraviolet(te)

umbrella [ʌmˈbrɛlə] *n* parapluie *m*; (*for sun*) parasol *m*

umpire ['ʌmpaɪə^r] *n* arbitre *m*; (*Tennis*) juge *m* de chaise

UN *n abbr* = **United Nations**

unable [ʌnˈeɪbl] *adj*: **to be ~ to** ne (pas) pouvoir, être dans l'impossibilité de; (*not capable*) être incapable de

unacceptable [ʌnəkˈsɛptəbl] *adj* (*behaviour*) inadmissible; (*price, proposal*) inacceptable

unanimous [juːˈnænɪməs] *adj* unanime

unarmed [ʌnˈɑːmd] *adj* (*person*) non armé(e); (*combat*) sans armes

unattended [ʌnəˈtɛndɪd] *adj* (*car, child, luggage*) sans surveillance

unattractive [ʌnəˈtræktɪv] *adj* peu attrayant(e); (*character*) peu sympathique

unavailable [ʌnəˈveɪləbl] *adj* (*article, room, book*) (qui n'est) pas disponible; (*person*) (qui n'est) pas libre

unavoidable [ʌnəˈvɔɪdəbl] *adj* inévitable

unaware [ʌnəˈwɛə^r] *adj*: **to be ~ of** ignorer, ne pas savoir, être inconscient(e) de; **unawares** *adv* à l'improviste, au dépourvu

unbearable [ʌnˈbɛərəbl] *adj* insupportable

unbeatable [ʌnˈbiːtəbl] *adj* imbattable

unbelievable [ʌnbɪˈliːvəbl] *adj* incroyable

unborn [ʌnˈbɔːn] *adj* à naître

unbutton [ʌnˈbʌtn] *vt* déboutonner

uncalled-for [ʌnˈkɔːldfɔː^r] *adj* déplacé(e), injustifié(e)

uncanny [ʌnˈkænɪ] *adj* étrange, troublant(e)

uncertain [ʌnˈsəːtn] *adj* incertain(e); (*hesitant*) hésitant(e); **uncertainty** *n* incertitude *f*, doutes *mpl*

unchanged [ʌnˈtʃeɪndʒd] *adj* inchangé(e)

uncle ['ʌŋkl] *n* oncle *m*

unclear [ʌnˈklɪər] adj (qui n'est) pas clair(e) or évident(e); **I'm still ~ about what I'm supposed to do** je ne sais pas encore exactement ce que je dois faire

uncomfortable [ʌnˈkʌmfətəbl] adj inconfortable, peu confortable; (uneasy) mal à l'aise, gêné(e); (situation) désagréable

uncommon [ʌnˈkɔmən] adj rare, singulier(-ière), peu commun(e)

unconditional [ʌnkənˈdɪʃənl] adj sans conditions

unconscious [ʌnˈkɔnʃəs] adj sans connaissance, évanoui(e); (unaware) **~ (of)** inconscient(e) (de) ▷ n: **the ~** l'inconscient m

uncontrollable [ʌnkənˈtrəʊləbl] adj (child, dog) indiscipliné(e); (temper, laughter) irrépressible

unconventional [ʌnkənˈvɛnʃənl] adj peu conventionnel(le)

uncover [ʌnˈkʌvər] vt découvrir

undecided [ʌndɪˈsaɪdɪd] adj indécis(e), irrésolu(e)

undeniable [ʌndɪˈnaɪəbl] adj indéniable, incontestable

under [ˈʌndər] prep sous; (less than) (de) moins de; au-dessous de; (according to) selon, en vertu de ▷ adv au-dessous; en dessous; **~ there** là-dessous; **~ the circumstances** étant donné les circonstances; **~ repair** (en cours de) réparation; **undercover** adj secret(-ète), clandestin(e); **underdone** adj (Culin) saignant(e); (: pej) pas assez cuit(e); **underestimate** vt sous-estimer, mésestimer; **undergo** vt (irreg: like **go**) subir; (treatment) suivre; **undergraduate** n étudiant(e) (qui prépare la licence); **underground** adj souterrain(e); (fig) clandestin(e) ▷ n (BRIT: railway) métro m; (Pol) clandestinité f; **undergrowth** n broussailles fpl, sous-bois m; **underline** vt souligner; **undermine** vt saper, miner; **underneath**

[ʌndəˈniːθ] adv (en) dessous ▷ prep sous, au-dessous de; **underpants** npl caleçon m, slip m; **underpass** n (BRIT: for pedestrians) passage souterrain; (: for cars) passage inférieur; **underprivileged** adj défavorisé(e); **underscore** vt souligner; **undershirt** n (US) tricot m de corps; **underskirt** n (BRIT) jupon m

understand [ʌndəˈstænd] vt, vi (irreg: like **stand**) comprendre; **I don't ~** je ne comprends pas; **understandable** adj compréhensible; **understanding** adj compréhensif(-ive) ▷ n compréhension f; (agreement) accord m

understatement [ˈʌndəsteɪtmənt] n: **that's an ~** c'est (bien) peu dire, le terme est faible

understood [ʌndəˈstʊd] pt, pp of **understand** ▷ adj entendu(e); (implied) sous-entendu(e)

undertake [ʌndəˈteɪk] vt (irreg: like **take**) (job, task) entreprendre; (duty) se charger de; **to ~ to do sth** s'engager à faire qch

undertaker [ˈʌndəteɪkər] n (BRIT) entrepreneur m des pompes funèbres, croque-mort m

undertaking [ˈʌndəteɪkɪŋ] n entreprise f; (promise) promesse f

under: underwater adv sous l'eau ▷ adj sous-marin(e); **underway** adj: **to be underway** (meeting, investigation) être en cours; **underwear** n sous-vêtements mpl; (women's only) dessous mpl; **underwent** pt of **undergo**; **underworld** n (of crime) milieu m, pègre f

undesirable [ʌndɪˈzaɪərəbl] adj peu souhaitable; (person, effect) indésirable

undisputed [ˈʌndɪsˈpjuːtɪd] adj incontesté(e)

undo [ʌnˈduː] vt (irreg: like **do**) défaire

undone |

undone [ʌn'dʌn] *pp of* **undo** ▷ *adj*: **to come ~** se défaire

undoubtedly [ʌn'dautɪdlɪ] *adv* sans aucun doute

undress [ʌn'drɛs] *vi* se déshabiller

unearth [ʌn'ə:θ] *vt* déterrer; *(fig)* dénicher

uneasy [ʌn'i:zɪ] *adj* mal à l'aise, gêné(e); *(worried)* inquiet(-ète); *(feeling)* désagréable; *(peace, truce)* fragile

unemployed [ʌnɪm'plɔɪd] *adj* sans travail, au chômage ▷ *n*: **the ~** les chômeurs *mpl*

unemployment [ʌnɪm'plɔɪmənt] *n* chômage *m*; **unemployment benefit**, *(us)* **unemployment compensation** *n* allocation *f* de chômage

unequal [ʌn'i:kwəl] *adj* inégal(e)

uneven [ʌn'i:vn] *adj* inégal(e); *(quality, work)* irrégulier(-ière)

unexpected [ʌnɪk'spɛktɪd] *adj* inattendu(e), imprévu(e); **unexpectedly** *adv (succeed)* contre toute attente; *(arrive)* à l'improviste

unfair [ʌn'fɛəʳ] *adj*: **~ (to)** injuste (envers)

unfaithful [ʌn'feɪθful] *adj* infidèle

unfamiliar [ʌnfə'mɪlɪəʳ] *adj* étrange, inconnu(e); **to be ~ with sth** mal connaître qch

unfashionable [ʌn'fæʃnəbl] *adj (clothes)* démodé(e); *(place)* peu chic *inv*

unfasten [ʌn'fɑ:sn] *vt* défaire; *(belt, necklace)* détacher; *(open)* ouvrir

unfavourable, *(us)* **unfavorable** [ʌn'feɪvrəbl] *adj* défavorable

unfinished [ʌn'fɪnɪʃt] *adj* inachevé(e)

unfit [ʌn'fɪt] *adj (physically: ill)* en mauvaise santé; *(: out of condition)* pas en forme; *(incompetent)*: **~ (for)** impropre (à); *(work, service)* inapte (à)

unfold [ʌn'fəuld] *vt* déplier ▷ *vi* se dérouler

unforgettable [ʌnfə'gɛtəbl] *adj* inoubliable

unfortunate [ʌn'fɔ:tʃnət] *adj* malheureux(-euse); *(event, remark)* malencontreux(-euse); **unfortunately** *adv* malheureusement

unfriend [ʌn'frɛnd] *vt (Internet)* supprimer de sa liste d'amis

unfriendly [ʌn'frɛndlɪ] *adj* peu aimable, froid(e)

unfurnished [ʌn'fə:nɪʃt] *adj* non meublé(e)

unhappiness [ʌn'hæpɪnɪs] *n* tristesse *f*, peine *f*

unhappy [ʌn'hæpɪ] *adj* triste, malheureux(-euse); *(unfortunate: remark etc)* malheureux(-euse); *(not pleased)*: **~ with** mécontent(e) de, peu satisfait(e) de

unhealthy [ʌn'hɛlθɪ] *adj (gen)* malsain(e); *(person)* maladif(-ive)

unheard-of [ʌn'hə:dɔv] *adj* inouï(e), sans précédent

unhelpful [ʌn'hɛlpful] *adj (person)* peu serviable; *(advice)* peu utile

unhurt [ʌn'hə:t] *adj* indemne, sain(e) et sauf

unidentified [ʌnaɪ'dɛntɪfaɪd] *adj* non identifié(e); *see also* **UFO**

uniform ['ju:nɪfɔ:m] *n* uniforme *m* ▷ *adj* uniforme

unify ['ju:nɪfaɪ] *vt* unifier

unimportant [ʌnɪm'pɔ:tənt] *adj* sans importance

uninhabited [ʌnɪn'hæbɪtɪd] *adj* inhabité(e)

unintentional [ʌnɪn'tɛnʃənəl] *adj* involontaire

union ['ju:njən] *n* union *f*; *(also:* **trade ~)** syndicat *m* ▷ *cpd* de syndicat, syndical(e); **Union Jack** *n* drapeau du Royaume-Uni

unique [ju:'ni:k] *adj* unique

unisex ['ju:nɪsɛks] *adj* unisexe

unit ['ju:nɪt] *n* unité *f*; *(section: of furniture etc)* élément *m*, bloc *m*; *(team, squad)* groupe *m*, service *m*; **kitchen ~** élément de cuisine

unite [ju:'naɪt] *vt* unir ▷ *vi* s'unir; **united** *adj* uni(e); *(country, party)*

unifié(e); (*efforts*) conjugué(e);
United Kingdom n Royaume-Uni
m; **United Nations (Organization)**
n (Organisation f des) Nations unies;
United States (of America) n
États-Unis mpl

unity ['ju:nɪtɪ] n unité f

universal [ju:nɪ'vɜːsl] adj
universel(le)

universe ['ju:nɪvɜːs] n univers m

university [ju:nɪ'vɜːsɪtɪ] n
université f ▷ cpd (*student, professor*)
d'université; (*education, year, degree*)
universitaire

unjust [ʌn'dʒʌst] adj injuste

unkind [ʌn'kaɪnd] adj peu gentil(le),
méchant(e)

unknown [ʌn'nəun] adj inconnu(e)

unlawful [ʌn'lɔːful] adj illégal(e)

unleaded [ʌn'lɛdɪd] n (*also*: **~ petrol**)
essence f sans plomb

unleash [ʌn'liːʃ] vt (*fig*) déchaîner,
déclencher

unless [ʌn'lɛs] conj: **~ he leaves** à
moins qu'il (ne) parte; **~ otherwise
stated** sauf indication contraire

unlike [ʌn'laɪk] adj dissemblable,
différent(e) ▷ prep à la différence de,
contrairement à

unlikely [ʌn'laɪklɪ] adj (*result,
event*) improbable; (*explanation*)
invraisemblable

unlimited [ʌn'lɪmɪtɪd] adj illimité(e)

unlisted ['ʌn'lɪstɪd] adj (*US Tel*) sur
la liste rouge

unload [ʌn'ləud] vt décharger

unlock [ʌn'lɔk] vt ouvrir

unlucky [ʌn'lʌkɪ] adj (*person*)
malchanceux(-euse); (*object, number*)
qui porte malheur; **to be ~** (*person*) ne
pas avoir de chance

unmarried [ʌn'mærɪd] adj
célibataire

unmistak(e)able [ʌnmɪs'teɪkəbl]
adj indubitable; qu'on ne peut pas ne
pas reconnaître

unnatural [ʌn'nætʃrəl] adj non
naturel(le); (*perversion*) contre nature

unnecessary [ʌn'nɛsəsərɪ] adj
inutile, superflu(e)

UNO ['ju:nəu] n abbr = **United
Nations Organization**

unofficial [ʌnə'fɪʃl] adj (*news*)
officieux(-euse), non officiel(le);
(*strike*) ≈ sauvage

unpack [ʌn'pæk] vi défaire sa valise
▷ vt (*suitcase*) défaire; (*belongings*)
déballer

unpaid [ʌn'peɪd] adj (*bill*) impayé(e);
(*holiday*) non-payé(e), sans salaire;
(*work*) non rétribué(e)

unpleasant [ʌn'plɛznt] adj
déplaisant(e), désagréable

unplug [ʌn'plʌg] vt débrancher

unpopular [ʌn'pɔpjulə^r] adj
impopulaire

unprecedented [ʌn'prɛsɪdɛntɪd]
adj sans précédent

unpredictable [ʌnprɪ'dɪktəbl] adj
imprévisible

unprotected ['ʌnprə'tɛktɪd] adj
(*sex*) non protégé(e)

unqualified [ʌn'kwɔlɪfaɪd] adj
(*teacher*) non diplômé(e), sans titres;
(*success*) sans réserve, total(e);
(*disaster*) total(e)

unravel [ʌn'rævl] vt démêler

unreal [ʌn'rɪəl] adj irréel(le);
(*extraordinary*) incroyable

unrealistic ['ʌnrɪə'lɪstɪk] adj (*idea*)
irréaliste; (*estimate*) peu réaliste

unreasonable [ʌn'riːznəbl] adj qui
n'est pas raisonnable

unrelated [ʌnrɪ'leɪtɪd] adj sans
rapport; (*people*) sans lien de parenté

unreliable [ʌnrɪ'laɪəbl] adj sur qui
(or quoi) on ne peut pas compter,
peu fiable

unrest [ʌn'rɛst] n agitation f,
troubles mpl

unroll [ʌn'rəul] vt dérouler

unruly [ʌn'ruːlɪ] adj indiscipliné(e)

unsafe [ʌn'seɪf] adj (*in danger*) en
danger; (*journey, car*) dangereux(-euse)

unsatisfactory ['ʌnsætɪs'fæktərɪ]
adj peu satisfaisant(e)

u

unscrew [ʌn'skruː] vt dévisser

unsettled [ʌn'sɛtld] adj (restless) perturbé(e); (unpredictable) instable; incertain(e); (not finalized) non résolu(e)

unsettling [ʌn'sɛtlɪŋ] adj qui a un effet perturbateur

unsightly [ʌn'saɪtlɪ] adj disgracieux(-euse), laid(e)

unskilled [ʌn'skɪld] adj: ~ worker manœuvre m

unspoiled ['ʌn'spɔɪld], **unspoilt** ['ʌn'spɔɪlt] adj (place) non dégradé(e)

unstable [ʌn'steɪbl] adj instable

unsteady [ʌn'stɛdɪ] adj mal assuré(e), chancelant(e), instable

unsuccessful [ʌnsək'sɛsful] adj (attempt) infructueux(-euse); (writer, proposal) qui n'a pas de succès; **to be ~** (in attempting sth) ne pas réussir; ne pas avoir de succès; (application) ne pas être retenu(e)

unsuitable [ʌn'suːtəbl] adj qui ne convient pas, peu approprié(e); (time) inopportun(e)

unsure [ʌn'ʃuəʳ] adj pas sûr(e); **to be ~ of o.s.** ne pas être sûr de soi, manquer de confiance en soi

untidy [ʌn'taɪdɪ] adj (room) en désordre; (appearance, person) débraillé(e); (person: in character) sans ordre, désordonné(e); (work) peu soigné(e)

untie [ʌn'taɪ] vt (knot, parcel) défaire; (prisoner, dog) détacher

until [ən'tɪl] prep jusqu'à; (after negative) avant ▷ conj jusqu'à ce que + sub; (in past, after negative) avant que + sub; **~ he comes** jusqu'à ce qu'il vienne, jusqu'à son arrivée; **~ now** jusqu'à présent, jusqu'ici; **~ then** jusque-là

untrue [ʌn'truː] adj (statement) faux (fausse)

unused¹ [ʌn'juːzd] adj (new) neuf (neuve)

unused² [ʌn'juːst] adj: **to be ~ to sth/to doing sth** ne pas avoir l'habitude de qch/de faire qch

unusual [ʌn'juːʒuəl] adj insolite, exceptionnel(le), rare; **unusually** adv exceptionnellement, particulièrement

unveil [ʌn'veɪl] vt dévoiler

unwanted [ʌn'wɔntɪd] adj (child, pregnancy) non désiré(e); (clothes etc) à donner

unwell [ʌn'wɛl] adj souffrant(e); **to feel ~** ne pas se sentir bien

unwilling [ʌn'wɪlɪŋ] adj: **to be ~ to do** ne pas vouloir faire

unwind [ʌn'waɪnd] vt (irreg: like **wind²**) dérouler ▷ vi (relax) se détendre

unwise [ʌn'waɪz] adj imprudent(e), peu judicieux(-euse)

unwittingly [ʌn'wɪtɪŋlɪ] adv involontairement

unwrap [ʌn'ræp] vt défaire; ouvrir

unzip [ʌn'zɪp] vt ouvrir (la fermeture éclair de); (Comput) dézipper

⭕ **KEYWORD**

up [ʌp] prep: **he went up the stairs/the hill** il a monté l'escalier/la colline; **the cat was up a tree** le chat était dans un arbre; **they live further up the street** ils habitent plus haut dans la rue; **go up that road and turn left** remontez la rue et tournez à gauche

▶ adv **1** en haut; en l'air; (upwards, higher): **up in the sky/the mountains** (là-haut) dans le ciel/les montagnes; **put it a bit higher up** mettez-le un peu plus haut; **to stand up** (get up) se lever, se mettre debout; (be standing) être debout; **up there** là-haut; **up above** au-dessus

2: **to be up** (out of bed) être levé(e); (prices) avoir augmenté or monté; (finished): **when the year was up** à la fin de l'année

3: **up to** (as far as) jusqu'à; **up to now** jusqu'à présent

4: **to be up to** (depending on): **it's up**

to you c'est à vous de décider; (*equal to*): **he's not up to it** (*job, task etc*) il n'en est pas capable; (*inf: be doing*): **what is he up to?** qu'est-ce qu'il peut bien faire?

▸ *n*: **ups and downs** hauts et bas *mpl*

up-and-coming [ʌpənd'kʌmɪŋ] *adj* plein(e) d'avenir *or* de promesses

upbringing ['ʌpbrɪŋɪŋ] *n* éducation *f*

update [ʌp'deɪt] *vt* mettre à jour

upfront [ʌp'frʌnt] *adj* (*open*) franc (franche) ▸ *adv* (*pay*) d'avance; **to be ~ about sth** ne rien cacher de qch

upgrade [ʌp'greɪd] *vt* (*person*) promouvoir; (*job*) revaloriser; (*property, equipment*) moderniser

upheaval [ʌp'hi:vl] *n* bouleversement *m*; (*in room*) branle-bas *m*; (*event*) crise *f*

uphill [ʌp'hɪl] *adj* qui monte; (*fig: task*) difficile, pénible ▸ *adv* (*face, look*) en amont, vers l'amont; **to go ~** monter

upholstery [ʌp'həʊlstərɪ] *n* rembourrage *m*; (*cover*) tissu *m* d'ameublement; (*of car*) garniture *f*

upload ['ʌpləʊd] *vt* (*Comput*) télécharger

upmarket [ʌp'mɑːkɪt] *adj* (*product*) haut de gamme *inv*; (*area*) chic *inv*

upon [ə'pɒn] *prep* sur

upper ['ʌpəʳ] *adj* supérieur(e); du dessus ▸ *n* (*of shoe*) empeigne *f*; **upper-class** *adj* de la haute société, aristocratique; (*district*) élégant(e), huppé(e); (*accent, attitude*) caractéristique des classes supérieures

upright ['ʌpraɪt] *adj* droit(e); (*fig*) droit, honnête

uprising ['ʌpraɪzɪŋ] *n* soulèvement *m*, insurrection *f*

uproar ['ʌprɔːʳ] *n* tumulte *m*, vacarme *m*; (*protests*) protestations *fpl*

upset *n* ['ʌpset] dérangement *m* ▸ *vt* [ʌp'set] (*irreg: like* **set**) (*glass etc*) renverser; (*plan*) déranger;

(*person: offend*) contrarier; (*: grieve*) faire de la peine à; bouleverser ▸ *adj* [ʌp'set] contrarié(e); peiné(e); **to have a stomach ~** (*BRIT*) avoir une indigestion

upside down ['ʌpsaɪd-] *adv* à l'envers; **to turn sth ~** (*fig: place*) mettre sens dessus dessous

upstairs [ʌp'stɛəz] *adv* en haut ▸ *adj* (*room*) du dessus, d'en haut ▸ *n*: **the ~** l'étage *m*

up-to-date ['ʌptə'deɪt] *adj* moderne; (*information*) très récent(e)

upward ['ʌpwəd] *adj* ascendant(e); vers le haut ▸ *adv* = **upwards**

upwards *adv* vers le haut; (*more than*): **~ of** plus de

uranium [juə'reɪnɪəm] *n* uranium *m*

Uranus [juə'reɪnəs] *n* Uranus *f*

urban ['əːbən] *adj* urbain(e)

urge [əːdʒ] *n* besoin (impératif), envie (pressante) ▸ *vt* (*person*): **to ~ sb to do** exhorter qn à faire, pousser qn à faire, recommander vivement à qn de faire

urgency ['əːdʒənsɪ] *n* urgence *f*; (*of tone*) insistance *f*

urgent ['əːdʒənt] *adj* urgent(e); (*plea, tone*) pressant(e)

urinal ['juərɪnl] *n* (*BRIT*: *place*) urinoir *m*

urinate ['juərɪneɪt] *vi* uriner

urine ['juərɪn] *n* urine *f*

URL *abbr* (= *uniform resource locator*) URL *f*

US *n abbr* = **United States**

us [ʌs] *pron* nous; *see also* **me**

USA *n abbr* = **United States of America**

USB stick *n* clé *f* USB

use *n* [juːs] emploi *m*, utilisation *f*; (*usefulness*) utilité *f* ▸ *vt* [juːz] se servir de, utiliser, employer; **in ~** en usage; **out of ~** hors d'usage; **to be of ~** servir, être utile; **it's no ~** ça ne sert à rien; **to have the ~ of** avoir l'usage de; **she ~d to do it** elle le faisait (autrefois), elle avait

coutume de le faire; **to be ~d to**
avoir l'habitude de, être habitué(e)
à; **use up** *vt* finir, épuiser; (*food*)
consommer; **used** [ju:zd] *adj* (*car*)
d'occasion; **useful** *adj* utile; **useless**
adj inutile; (*inf: person*) nul(le); **user**
n utilisateur(-trice), usager *m*;
user-friendly *adj* convivial(e), facile
d'emploi; **username** *n* (*Comput*) nom
m d'utilisateur
usual ['ju:ʒuəl] *adj* habituel(le); **as
~** comme d'habitude; **usually** *adv*
d'habitude, d'ordinaire
ute [ju:t] *n* (*AUST, NZ*) pick-up *m inv*
utensil [ju:'tɛnsl] *n* ustensile *m*;
kitchen ~s batterie *f* de cuisine
utility [ju:'tɪlɪtɪ] *n* utilité *f*; (*also*:
public ~) service public
utilize ['ju:tɪlaɪz] *vt* utiliser; (*make
good use of*) exploiter
utmost ['ʌtməust] *adj* extrême, le
plus grand(e) ▷ *n*: **to do one's ~** faire
tout son possible
utter ['ʌtəʳ] *adj* total(e), complet(-ète)
▷ *vt* prononcer, proférer; (*sounds*)
émettre; **utterly** *adv* complètement,
totalement
U-turn ['ju:'tə:n] *n* demi-tour *m*; (*fig*)
volte-face *f inv*

v. *abbr* = **verse**; (= *vide*) v.; (= *versus*)
vs; (= *volt*) V
vacancy ['veɪkənsɪ] *n* (*job*) poste
vacant; (*room*) chambre *f* disponible;
"no vacancies" "complet"
vacant ['veɪkənt] *adj* (*post*) vacant(e);
(*seat etc*) libre, disponible; (*expression*)
distrait(e)
vacate [və'keɪt] *vt* quitter
vacation [və'keɪʃən] *n* (*esp US*)
vacances *fpl*; **on ~** en vacances;
vacationer, vacationist (*US*) *n*
vacancier(-ière)
vaccination [væksɪ'neɪʃən] *n*
vaccination *f*
vaccine ['væksi:n] *n* vaccin *m*
vacuum ['vækjum] *n* vide *m*;
vacuum cleaner *n* aspirateur *m*
vagina [və'dʒaɪnə] *n* vagin *m*
vague [veɪg] *adj* vague, imprécis(e);
(*blurred: photo, memory*) flou(e)
vain [veɪn] *adj* (*useless*) vain(e);
(*conceited*) vaniteux(-euse); **in ~**
en vain

Valentine's Day ['væləntaɪnz-] n
Saint-Valentin f
valid ['vælɪd] adj (document) valide,
valable; (excuse) valable
valley ['vælɪ] n vallée f
valuable ['væljuəbl] adj (jewel)
de grande valeur; (time, help)
précieux(-euse); **valuables** npl objets
mpl de valeur
value ['vælju:] n valeur f ▷ vt (fix
price) évaluer, expertiser; (appreciate)
apprécier; **values** npl (principles)
valeurs fpl
valve [vælv] n (in machine) soupape f;
(on tyre) valve f; (Med) valve, valvule f
vampire ['væmpaɪə'] n vampire m
van [væn] n (Aut) camionnette f
vandal ['vændl] n vandale m/f;
vandalism n vandalisme m;
vandalize vt saccager
vanilla [və'nɪlə] n vanille f
vanish ['vænɪʃ] vi disparaître
vanity ['vænɪtɪ] n vanité f
vapour, (US) **vapor** ['veɪpə'] n
vapeur f; (on window) buée f
variable ['veərɪəbl] adj variable;
(mood) changeant(e)
variant ['veərɪənt] n variante f
variation [veərɪ'eɪʃən] n variation f;
(in opinion) changement m
varied ['veərɪd] adj varié(e), divers(e)
variety [və'raɪətɪ] n variété f;
(quantity) nombre m, quantité f
various ['veərɪəs] adj divers(e),
différent(e); (several) divers, plusieurs
varnish ['vɑ:nɪʃ] n vernis m ▷ vt vernir
vary ['veərɪ] vt, vi varier, changer
vase [vɑ:z] n vase m
Vaseline® ['væsɪli:n] n vaseline f
vast [vɑ:st] adj vaste, immense;
(amount, success) énorme
VAT [væt] n abbr (BRIT: = value added
tax) TVA f
vault [vɔ:lt] n (of roof) voûte f; (tomb)
caveau m; (in bank) salle f des coffres;
chambre forte ▷ vt (also: ~ over)
sauter (d'un bond)
VCR n abbr = **video cassette recorder**

VDU n abbr = **visual display unit**
veal [vi:l] n veau m
veer [vɪə'] vi tourner; (car, ship) virer
vegan ['vi:gən] n végétalien(ne)
vegetable ['vedʒtəbl] n légume m
▷ adj végétal(e)
vegetarian [vedʒɪ'teərɪən] adj,
n végétarien(ne); **do you have
any ~ dishes?** avez-vous des plats
végétariens?
vegetation [vedʒɪ'teɪʃən] n
végétation f
vehicle ['vi:ɪkl] n véhicule m
veil [veɪl] n voile m
vein [veɪn] n veine f; (on leaf) nervure f
Velcro® ['velkrəu] n velcro® m
velvet ['velvɪt] n velours m
vending machine ['vendɪŋ-] n
distributeur m automatique
vendor ['vendə'] n vendeur(-euse);
street ~ marchand ambulant
Venetian blind [vɪ'ni:ʃən-] n store
vénitien
vengeance ['vendʒəns] n
vengeance f; **with a ~** (fig) vraiment,
pour de bon
venison ['venɪsn] n venaison f
venom ['venəm] n venin m
vent [vent] n conduit m d'aération;
(in dress, jacket) fente f ▷ vt (fig: one's
feelings) donner libre cours à
ventilation [ventɪ'leɪʃən] n
ventilation f, aération f
venture ['ventʃə'] n entreprise f ▷ vt
risquer, hasarder ▷ vi s'aventurer, se
risquer; **a business ~** une entreprise
commerciale
venue ['venju:] n lieu m
Venus ['vi:nəs] n (planet) Vénus f
verb [və:b] n verbe m; **verbal** adj
verbal(e)
verdict ['və:dɪkt] n verdict m
verge [və:dʒ] n bord m; **"soft ~s"**
(BRIT) "accotements non stabilisés";
on the ~ of doing sur le point de faire
verify ['verɪfaɪ] vt vérifier
versatile ['və:sətaɪl] adj
polyvalent(e)

V

verse [vəːs] n vers mpl; (stanza) strophe f; (in Bible) verset m
version ['vəːʃən] n version f
versus ['vəːsəs] prep contre
vertical ['vəːtɪkl] adj vertical(e)
very ['vɛrɪ] adv très ▷ adj: **the ~ book which** le livre même que; **the ~ last** le tout dernier; **at the ~ least** au moins; **~ much** beaucoup
vessel ['vɛsl] n (Anat, Naut) vaisseau m; (container) récipient m; see also **blood vessel**
vest [vɛst] n (BRIT: underwear) tricot m de corps; (US: waistcoat) gilet m
vet [vɛt] n abbr (BRIT: = veterinary surgeon) vétérinaire m/f; (US: = veteran) ancien(ne) combattant(e) ▷ vt examiner minutieusement
veteran ['vɛtərn] n vétéran m; (also: **war ~**) ancien combattant
veterinary surgeon ['vɛtrɪnərɪ-] (BRIT) n vétérinaire m/f
veto ['viːtəu] n (pl vetoes) veto m ▷ vt opposer son veto à
via ['vaɪə] prep par, via
viable ['vaɪəbl] adj viable
vibrate [vaɪ'breɪt] vi: **to ~ (with)** vibrer (de)
vibration [vaɪ'breɪʃən] n vibration f
vicar ['vɪkəʳ] n pasteur m (de l'Église anglicane)
vice [vaɪs] n (evil) vice m; (Tech) étau m; **vice-chairman** (irreg) n vice-président(e)
vice versa ['vaɪsɪ'vəːsə] adv vice versa
vicinity [vɪ'sɪnɪtɪ] n environs mpl, alentours mpl
vicious ['vɪʃəs] adj (remark) cruel(le), méchant(e); (blow) brutal(e); (dog) méchant(e), dangereux(-euse); **a ~ circle** un cercle vicieux
victim ['vɪktɪm] n victime f
victor ['vɪktəʳ] n vainqueur m
Victorian [vɪk'tɔːrɪən] adj victorien(ne)
victorious [vɪk'tɔːrɪəs] adj victorieux(-euse)

victory ['vɪktərɪ] n victoire f
video ['vɪdɪəu] n (video film) vidéo f; (also: **~ cassette**) vidéocassette f; (also: **~ cassette recorder**) magnétoscope m ▷ vt (with recorder) enregistrer; (with camera) filmer; **video camera** n caméra f vidéo inv; **video game** n jeu m vidéo inv; **videophone** n vidéophone m; **video recorder** n magnétoscope m; **video shop** n vidéoclub m; **video tape** n bande f vidéo inv; (cassette) vidéocassette f
vie [vaɪ] vi: **to ~ with** lutter avec, rivaliser avec
Vienna [vɪ'ɛnə] n Vienne
Vietnam, Viet Nam ['vjɛt'næm] n Viêt-nam or Vietnam m; **Vietnamese** [vjɛtnə'miːz] adj vietnamien(ne) ▷ n (pl inv) Vietnamien(ne)
view [vjuː] n vue f; (opinion) avis m, vue ▷ vt voir, regarder; (situation) considérer; (house) visiter; **on ~** (in museum etc) exposé(e); **in full ~ of sb** sous les yeux de qn; **in my ~** à mon avis; **in ~ of the fact that** étant donné que; **viewer** n (TV) téléspectateur(-trice); **viewpoint** n point m de vue
vigilant ['vɪdʒɪlənt] adj vigilant(e)
vigorous ['vɪgərəs] adj vigoureux(-euse)
vile [vaɪl] adj (action) vil(e); (smell, food) abominable; (temper) massacrant(e)
villa ['vɪlə] n villa f
village ['vɪlɪdʒ] n village m; **villager** n villageois(e)
villain ['vɪlən] n (scoundrel) scélérat m; (BRIT: criminal) bandit m; (in novel etc) traître m
vinaigrette [vɪneɪ'grɛt] n vinaigrette f
vine [vaɪn] n vigne f
vinegar ['vɪnɪgəʳ] n vinaigre m
vineyard ['vɪnjɑːd] n vignoble m
vintage ['vɪntɪdʒ] n (year) année f, millésime m ▷ cpd (car) d'époque; (wine) de grand cru

vinyl ['vaɪnl] n vinyle m
viola [vɪ'əʊlə] n alto m
violate ['vaɪəleɪt] vt violer
violation [vaɪə'leɪʃən] n violation f;
in ~ of (rule, law) en infraction à, en
violation de
violence ['vaɪələns] n violence f
violent ['vaɪələnt] adj violent(e)
violet ['vaɪələt] adj (colour) violet(te)
▷ n (plant) violette f
violin [vaɪə'lɪn] n violon m
VIP n abbr (= very important person)
VIP m
viral ['vaɪərəl] adj (also Comput)
viral(e)
virgin ['vɜːdʒɪn] n vierge f
Virgo ['vɜːgəʊ] n la Vierge
virtual ['vɜːtjuəl] adj (Comput,
Physics) virtuel(le); (in effect): **it's a
~ impossibility** c'est quasiment
impossible; **virtually** adv (almost)
pratiquement; **virtual reality** n
(Comput) réalité virtuelle
virtue ['vɜːtjuː] n vertu f; (advantage)
mérite m, avantage m; **by ~ of** en
vertu or raison de
virus ['vaɪərəs] n virus m
visa ['viːzə] n visa m
vise [vaɪs] n (US Tech) = **vice**
visibility [vɪzɪ'bɪlɪtɪ] n visibilité f
visible ['vɪzəbl] adj visible
vision ['vɪʒən] n (sight) vue f, vision f;
(foresight, in dream) vision
visit ['vɪzɪt] n visite f; (stay) séjour m
▷ vt (person: us: also: **~ with**) rendre
visite à; (place) visiter; **visiting
hours** npl heures fpl de visite; **visitor**
n visiteur(-euse); (to one's house)
invité(e); **visitor centre**, (US) **visitor
center** n hall m or centre m d'accueil
visual ['vɪzjuəl] adj visuel(le);
visualize vt se représenter
vital ['vaɪtl] adj vital(e); **of ~
importance (to sb/sth)** d'une
importance capitale (pour qn/qch)
vitality [vaɪ'tælɪtɪ] n vitalité f
vitamin ['vɪtəmɪn] n vitamine f

vivid ['vɪvɪd] adj (account) frappant(e),
vivant(e); (light, imagination) vif (vive)
V-neck ['viːnɛk] n décolleté m en V
vocabulary [vəu'kæbjulərɪ] n
vocabulaire m
vocal ['vəukl] adj vocal(e); (articulate)
qui n'hésite pas à s'exprimer, qui sait
faire entendre ses opinions
vocational [vəu'keɪʃənl] adj
professionnel(le)
vodka ['vɔdkə] n vodka f
vogue [vəug] n: **to be in ~** être en
vogue or à la mode
voice [vɔɪs] n voix f ▷ vt (opinion)
exprimer, formuler; **voice mail** n
(system) messagerie f vocale, boîte f
vocale; (device) répondeur m
void [vɔɪd] n vide m ▷ adj (invalid)
nul(le); (empty): **~ of** vide de,
dépourvu(e) de
volatile ['vɔlətaɪl] adj volatil(e);
(fig: person) versatile; (: situation)
explosif(-ive)
volcano [vɔl'keɪnəu] (pl **volcanoes**)
n volcan m
volleyball ['vɔlɪbɔːl] n volley(-ball) m
volt [vəult] n volt m; **voltage** n
tension f, voltage m
volume ['vɔljuːm] n volume m; (of
tank) capacité f
voluntarily ['vɔləntrɪlɪ] adv
volontairement
voluntary ['vɔləntərɪ] adj
volontaire; (unpaid) bénévole
volunteer [vɔlən'tɪər] n volontaire
m/f ▷ vt (information) donner
spontanément ▷ vi (Mil) s'engager
comme volontaire; **to ~ to do** se
proposer pour faire
vomit ['vɔmɪt] n vomissure f ▷ vt,
vi vomir
vote [vəut] n vote m, suffrage m;
(votes cast) voix f, vote; (franchise)
droit m de vote ▷ vt (chairman) élire;
(propose): **to ~ that** proposer que +
sub ▷ vi voter; **~ of thanks**
discours m de remerciement;

V

voter n électeur(-trice); **voting** n scrutin m, vote m

voucher ['vautʃəʳ] n (for meal, petrol, gift) bon m

vow [vau] n vœu m, serment m ▷ vi jurer

vowel ['vauəl] n voyelle f

voyage ['vɔɪɪdʒ] n voyage m par mer, traversée f

vulgar ['vʌlgəʳ] adj vulgaire

vulnerable ['vʌlnərəbl] adj vulnérable

vulture ['vʌltʃəʳ] n vautour m

W

waddle ['wɔdl] vi se dandiner

wade [weɪd] vi: **to ~ through** marcher dans, patauger dans; (fig: book) venir à bout de

wafer ['weɪfəʳ] n (Culin) gaufrette f

waffle ['wɔfl] n (Culin) gaufre f ▷ vi parler pour ne rien dire; faire du remplissage

wag [wæg] vt agiter, remuer ▷ vi remuer

wage [weɪdʒ] n (also: ~s) salaire m, paye f ▷ vt: **to ~ war** faire la guerre

wag(g)on ['wægən] n (horse-drawn) chariot m; (BRIT Rail) wagon m (de marchandises)

wail [weɪl] n gémissement m; (of siren) hurlement m ▷ vi gémir; (siren) hurler

waist [weɪst] n taille f, ceinture f; **waistcoat** n (BRIT) gilet m

wait [weɪt] n attente f ▷ vi attendre; **to ~ for sb/sth** attendre qn/qch; **to keep sb ~ing** faire attendre qn; **~ for me, please** attendez-moi, s'il vous plaît; **I can't ~ to ...** (fig) je meurs d'envie de ...; **to lie in ~ for** guetter; **wait on** vt fus servir; **waiter** n garçon m (de café), serveur m; **waiting list** n liste f d'attente; **waiting room** n salle f d'attente; **waitress** ['weɪtrɪs] n serveuse f

waive [weɪv] vt renoncer à, abandonner

wake [weɪk] (pt **woke** or **waked**, pp **woken** or **waked**) vt (also: **~ up**) réveiller ▷ vi (also: **~ up**) se réveiller ▷ n (for dead person) veillée f mortuaire; (Naut) sillage m

Wales [weɪlz] n pays m de Galles; **the Prince of ~** le prince de Galles

walk [wɔːk] n promenade f; (short) petit tour; (gait) démarche f; (path) chemin m; (in park etc) allée f ▷ vi marcher; (for pleasure, exercise) se promener ▷ vt (distance) faire à pied; (dog) promener; **10 minutes' ~ from** à 10 minutes de marche de; **to go for a ~** se promener; faire un tour; **from all ~s of life** de toutes conditions sociales; **walk out** vi (go out) sortir; (as protest) partir (en signe de protestation); (strike) se mettre en grève; **to ~ out on sb** quitter qn; **walker** n (person) marcheur(-euse); **walkie-talkie** ['wɔːkɪ'tɔːkɪ] n talkie-walkie m; **walking** n marche f à pied; **walking shoes** npl chaussures fpl de marche; **walking stick** n canne f; **Walkman®** n Walkman® m; **walkway** n promenade f, cheminement piéton

wall [wɔːl] n mur m; (of tunnel, cave) paroi f

wallet ['wɔlɪt] n portefeuille m; **I can't find my ~** je ne retrouve plus mon portefeuille

wallpaper ['wɔːlpeɪpəʳ] n papier peint ▷ vt tapisser

walnut ['wɔːlnʌt] n noix f; (tree, wood) noyer m

walrus ['wɔːlrəs] (pl **walrus** or **walruses**) n morse m

waltz [wɔːlts] n valse f ▷ vi valser

wand [wɔnd] n (also: **magic ~**) baguette f (magique)

wander ['wɔndəʳ] vi (person) errer, aller sans but; (thoughts) vagabonder ▷ vt errer dans

want [wɔnt] vt vouloir; (need) avoir besoin de ▷ n: **for ~ of** par manque de, faute de; **to ~ to do** vouloir faire; **to ~ sb to do** vouloir que qn fasse; **wanted** adj (criminal) recherché(e) par la police

war [wɔːʳ] n guerre f; **to make ~ (on)** faire la guerre (à)

ward [wɔːd] n (in hospital) salle f; (Pol) section électorale; (Law: child: also: **~ of court**) pupille m/f

warden ['wɔːdn] n (BRIT: of institution) directeur(-trice); (of park, game reserve) gardien(ne); (BRIT: also: **traffic ~**) contractuel(le)

wardrobe ['wɔːdrəub] n (cupboard) armoire f; (clothes) garde-robe f

warehouse ['wɛəhaus] n entrepôt m

warfare ['wɔːfɛəʳ] n guerre f

warhead ['wɔːhɛd] n (Mil) ogive f

warm [wɔːm] adj chaud(e); (person, thanks, welcome, applause) chaleureux(-euse); **it's ~** il fait chaud; **I'm ~** j'ai chaud; **warm up** vi (person, room) se réchauffer; (athlete, discussion) s'échauffer ▷ vt (food) (faire) réchauffer; (water) (faire) chauffer; (engine) faire chauffer; **warmly** adv (dress) chaudement; (thank, welcome) chaleureusement; **warmth** n chaleur f

warn [wɔːn] vt avertir, prévenir; **to ~ sb (not) to do** conseiller à qn de (ne pas) faire; **warning** n avertissement m; (notice) avis m; **warning light** n avertisseur lumineux

warrant ['wɔrnt] n (guarantee) garantie f; (Law: to arrest) mandat m d'arrêt; (: to search) mandat de perquisition ▷ vt (justify, merit) justifier

warranty ['wɔrəntɪ] n garantie f

W

warrior ['wɔrɪəʳ] n guerrier(-ière)
Warsaw ['wɔːsɔː] n Varsovie
warship ['wɔːʃɪp] n navire m de
guerre
wart [wɔːt] n verrue f
wartime ['wɔːtaɪm] n: **in ~** en temps
de guerre
wary ['wɛərɪ] adj prudent(e)
was [wɒz] pt of **be**
wash [wɒʃ] vt laver ▷ vi se laver; (sea):
to ~ over/against sth inonder/
baigner qch ▷ n (clothes) lessive f;
(washing programme) lavage m; (of
ship) sillage m; **to have a ~** se laver,
faire sa toilette; **wash up** vi (BRIT)
faire la vaisselle; (US: have a wash) se
débarbouiller; **washbasin** n lavabo
m; **washer** n (Tech) rondelle f, joint
m; **washing** n (BRIT: linen etc: dirty)
linge m; (: clean) lessive f; **washing
line** n (BRIT) corde f à linge; **washing
machine** n machine f à laver;
washing powder n (BRIT) lessive f
(en poudre)
Washington ['wɒʃɪŋtən] n
Washington m
wash: washing-up n (BRIT) vaisselle
f; **washing-up liquid** n (BRIT) produit
m pour la vaisselle; **washroom** n (US)
toilettes fpl
wasn't ['wɒznt] = **was not**
wasp [wɒsp] n guêpe f
waste [weɪst] n gaspillage m; (of time)
perte f; (rubbish) déchets mpl; (also:
household ~) ordures fpl ▷ adj (land,
ground: in city) à l'abandon; (leftover): **~
material** déchets ▷ vt gaspiller; (time,
opportunity) perdre; **waste ground** n
(BRIT) terrain m vague; **wastepaper
basket** n corbeille f à papier
watch [wɒtʃ] n montre f; (act of
watching) surveillance f; (guard: Mil)
sentinelle f; (: Naut) homme m de
quart; (Naut: spell of duty) quart m ▷ vt
(look at) observer (: match, programme)
regarder; (spy on, guard) surveiller;
(be careful of) faire attention à ▷ vi
regarder; (keep guard) monter la
garde; **to keep ~** faire le guet; **watch
out** vi faire attention; **watchdog** n
chien m de garde; (fig) gardien(ne);
watch strap n bracelet m de montre
water ['wɔːtəʳ] n eau f ▷ vt (plant,
garden) arroser ▷ vi (eyes) larmoyer; **in
British ~s** dans les eaux territoriales
Britanniques; **to make sb's mouth
~** mettre l'eau à la bouche de qn;
water down vt (milk etc) couper
avec de l'eau; (fig: story) édulcorer;
watercolour, (US) **watercolor** n
aquarelle f; **watercress** n cresson
m (de fontaine); **waterfall** n chute
f d'eau; **watering can** n arrosoir
m; **watermelon** n pastèque f;
waterproof adj imperméable;
water-skiing n ski m nautique
watt [wɒt] n watt m
wave [weɪv] n vague f; (of hand) geste
m, signe m; (Radio) onde f; (in hair)
ondulation f; (fig) vague ▷ vi faire
signe de la main; (flag) flotter au vent;
(grass) ondoyer ▷ vt (handkerchief)
agiter; (stick) brandir; **wavelength** n
longueur f d'ondes
waver ['weɪvəʳ] vi vaciller; (voice)
trembler; (person) hésiter
wavy ['weɪvɪ] adj (hair, surface)
ondulé(e); (line) onduleux(-euse)
wax [wæks] n cire f; (for skis) fart m
▷ vt cirer; (car) lustrer; (skis) farter ▷ vi
(moon) croître
way [weɪ] n chemin m, voie f;
(distance) distance f; (direction)
chemin, direction f; (manner) façon f,
manière f; (habit) habitude f, façon;
which ~? — this ~/that ~ par où
or de quel côté? — par ici/par là; **to
lose one's ~** perdre son chemin; **on
the ~ (to)** en route (pour); **to be on
one's ~** être en route; **to be in the ~**
bloquer le passage; (fig) gêner; **it's
a long ~ away** c'est loin d'ici; **to go
out of one's ~ to do** (fig) se donner
beaucoup de mal pour faire; **to be
under ~** (work, project) être en cours;
in a ~ dans un sens; **by the ~** à

propos; **"~ in"** (BRIT) "entrée"; **"~ out"** (BRIT) "sortie"; **the ~ back** le chemin du retour; **"give ~"** (BRIT Aut) "cédez la priorité"; **no ~!** (inf) pas question!

W.C. n abbr (BRIT: = water closet) w.-c. mpl, waters mpl

we [wiː] pl pron nous

weak [wiːk] adj faible; (health) fragile; (beam etc) peu solide; (tea, coffee) léger(-ère); **weaken** vi faiblir ▷ vt affaiblir; **weakness** n faiblesse f; (fault) point m faible

wealth [wɛlθ] n (money, resources) richesse(s) f(pl); (of details) profusion f; **wealthy** adj riche

weapon ['wɛpən] n arme f; **~s of mass destruction** armes fpl de destruction massive

wear [wɛəʳ] (pt **wore**, pp **worn**) n (use) usage m; (deterioration through use) usure f ▷ vt (clothes) porter; (put on) mettre; (damage: through use) user ▷ vi (last) faire de l'usage; (rub etc through) s'user; **sports/baby~** vêtements mpl de sport/pour bébés; **evening ~** tenue f de soirée; **wear off** vi disparaître; **wear out** vt user; (person, strength) épuiser

weary ['wɪərɪ] adj (tired) épuisé(e); (dispirited) las (lasse), abattu(e) ▷ vi: **to ~ of** se lasser de

weasel ['wiːzl] n (Zool) belette f

weather ['wɛðəʳ] n temps m ▷ vt (storm: lit, fig) essuyer; (crisis) survivre à; **under the ~** (fig: ill) mal fichu(e); **weather forecast** n prévisions fpl météorologiques, météo f

weave (pt **wove**, pp **woven**) [wiːv, wəʊv, 'wəʊvn] vt (cloth) tisser; (basket) tresser

web [wɛb] n (of spider) toile f; (on duck's foot) palmure f; (fig) tissu m; (Comput): **the (World-Wide) W~** le Web; **web address** n adresse f Web; **webcam** n webcam f; **webinar** ['wɛbɪnɑːʳ] n (Comput) séminaire m en ligne; **web page** n (Comput) page f Web; **website** n (Comput) site m Web

wed [wɛd] (pt, pp **wedded**) vt épouser ▷ vi se marier

we'd [wiːd] = **we had**; **we would**

wedding ['wɛdɪŋ] n mariage m; **wedding anniversary** n anniversaire m de mariage; **silver/golden wedding anniversary** noces fpl d'argent/d'or; **wedding day** n jour m du mariage; **wedding dress** n robe f de mariée; **wedding ring** n alliance f

wedge [wɛdʒ] n (of wood etc) coin m; (under door etc) cale f; (of cake) part f ▷ vt (fix) caler; (push) enfoncer, coincer

Wednesday ['wɛdnzdɪ] n mercredi m

wee [wiː] adj (SCOTTISH) petit(e); tout(e) petit(e)

weed [wiːd] n mauvaise herbe ▷ vt désherber; **weedkiller** n désherbant m

week [wiːk] n semaine f; **a ~ today/on Tuesday** aujourd'hui/mardi en huit; **weekday** n jour m de semaine; (Comm) jour ouvrable; **weekend** n week-end m; **weekly** adv une fois par semaine, chaque semaine ▷ adj, n hebdomadaire (m)

weep [wiːp] (pt, pp **wept**) vi (person) pleurer

weigh [weɪ] vt, vi peser; **to ~ anchor** lever l'ancre; **weigh up** vt examiner

weight [weɪt] n poids m; **to put on/lose ~** grossir/maigrir; **weightlifting** n haltérophilie f

weir [wɪəʳ] n barrage m

weird [wɪəd] adj bizarre; (eerie) surnaturel(le)

welcome ['wɛlkəm] adj bienvenu(e) ▷ n accueil m ▷ vt accueillir; (also: **bid ~**) souhaiter la bienvenue à; (be glad of) se réjouir de; **you're ~!** (after thanks) de rien, il n'y a pas de quoi

weld [wɛld] vt souder

welfare ['wɛlfɛəʳ] n (wellbeing) bien-être m; (social aid) assistance sociale; **welfare state** n État-providence m

well [wɛl] n puits m ▷ adv bien ▷ adj: **to be ~** aller bien ▷ excl eh bien!; (relief also) bon!; (resignation) enfin!; **~ done!** bravo!; **get ~ soon!** remets-toi

W

vite!; **to do ~** bien réussir; (business) prospérer; **as ~** (in addition) aussi, également; **as ~ as** aussi bien que or de; en plus de

we'll [wi:l] = **we will; we shall**

well: well-behaved adj sage, obéissant(e); **well-built** adj (person) bien bâti(e); **well-dressed** adj bien habillé(e), bien vêtu(e); **well-groomed** ['-'gru:md] adj très soigné(e)

wellies ['wɛlɪz] npl (BRIT inf) = **wellingtons**

wellingtons ['wɛlɪŋtənz] npl (also: **wellington boots**) bottes fpl en caoutchouc

well: well-known adj (person) bien connu(e); **well-off** adj aisé(e), assez riche; **well-paid** [wel'peɪd] adj bien payé(e)

Welsh [wɛlʃ] adj gallois(e) ▷ n (Ling) gallois m; **the Welsh** npl (people) les Gallois; **Welshman** (irreg) n Gallois m; **Welshwoman** (irreg) n Galloise f

went [wɛnt] pt of **go**

wept [wɛpt] pt, pp of **weep**

were [wəːʳ] pt of **be**

we're [wɪəʳ] = **we are**

weren't [wəːnt] = **were not**

west [wɛst] n ouest m ▷ adj (wind) d'ouest; (side) ouest inv ▷ adv s or vers l'ouest; **the W~** l'Occident m, l'Ouest m; **westbound** ['wɛstbaund] adj en direction de l'ouest; (carriageway) ouest inv; **western** adj occidental(e), de or à l'ouest ▷ n (Cine) western m; **West Indian** adj antillais(e) ▷ n Antillais(e); **West Indies** [-'ɪndɪz] npl Antilles fpl

wet [wɛt] adj mouillé(e); (damp) humide; (soaked: also: **~ through**) trempé(e); (rainy) pluvieux(-euse); **to get ~** se mouiller; **"~ paint"** "attention peinture fraîche"; **wetsuit** n combinaison f de plongée

we've [wi:v] = **we have**

whack [wæk] vt donner un grand coup à

whale [weɪl] n (Zool) baleine f

wharf (pl **wharves**) [wɔːf, wɔːvz] n quai m

 KEYWORD

what [wɔt] adj **1** (in questions) quel(le); **what size is he?** quelle taille fait-il?; **what colour is it?** de quelle couleur est-ce?; **what books do you need?** quels livres vous faut-il?

2 (in exclamations): **what a mess!** quel désordre!; **what a fool I am!** que je suis bête!

▶ pron **1** (interrogative) que; de/à/en etc quoi; **what are you doing?** que faites-vous?, qu'est-ce que vous faites?; **what is happening?** qu'est-ce qui se passe?, que se passe-t-il?; **what are you talking about?** de quoi parlez-vous?; **what are you thinking about?** à quoi pensez-vous?; **what is it called?** comment est-ce que ça s'appelle?; **what about me?** et moi?; **what about doing …?** et si on faisait …?

2 (relative: subject) ce qui; (: direct object) ce que; (: indirect object) ce à quoi, ce dont; **I saw what you did/ was on the table** j'ai vu ce que vous avez fait/ce qui était sur la table; **tell me what you remember** dites-moi ce dont vous vous souvenez; **what I want is a cup of tea** ce que je veux, c'est une tasse de thé

▶ excl (disbelieving) quoi!, comment!

whatever [wɔt'ɛvəʳ] adj: **take ~ book you prefer** prenez le livre que vous préférez, peu importe lequel; **~ book you take** quel que soit le livre que vous preniez ▷ pron: **do ~ is necessary** faites (tout) ce qui est nécessaire; **~ happens** quoi qu'il arrive; **no reason ~ or whatsoever** pas la moindre raison; **nothing ~ or whatsoever** rien du tout

whatsoever [wɔtsəu'ɛvəʳ] *adj see* **whatever**

wheat [wi:t] *n* blé *m*, froment *m*

wheel [wi:l] *n* roue *f*; (*Aut: also*: **steering ~**) volant *m*; (*Naut*) gouvernail *m* ▷ *vt* (*pram etc*) pousser, rouler ▷ *vi* (*birds*) tournoyer; (*also*: **~ round**: *person*) se retourner, faire volte-face; **wheelbarrow** *n* brouette *f*; **wheelchair** *n* fauteuil roulant; **wheel clamp** *n* (*Aut*) sabot *m* (de Denver)

wheeze [wi:z] *vi* respirer bruyamment

 KEYWORD

when [wen] *adv* quand; **when did he go?** quand est-ce qu'il est parti?
▷ *conj* **1** (*at, during, after the time that*) quand, lorsque; **she was reading when I came in** elle lisait quand *or* lorsque je suis entré
2 (*on, at which*): **on the day when I met him** le jour où je l'ai rencontré
3 (*whereas*) alors que; **I thought I was wrong when in fact I was right** j'ai cru que j'avais tort alors qu'en fait j'avais raison

whenever [wɛn'ɛvəʳ] *adv* quand donc ▷ *conj* quand; (*every time that*) chaque fois que

where [wɛəʳ] *adv, conj* où; **this is ~** c'est là que; **whereabouts** *adv* où donc ▷ *n*: **nobody knows his whereabouts** personne ne sait où il se trouve; **whereas** *conj* alors que; **whereby** *adv* (*formal*) par lequel (*or* laquelle *etc*); **wherever** *adv* où donc ▷ *conj* où que + *sub*; **sit wherever you like** asseyez-vous (là) où vous voulez

whether ['wɛðəʳ] *conj* si; **I don't know ~ to accept or not** je ne sais pas si je dois accepter ou non; **it's doubtful ~** il est peu probable que + *sub*; **~ you go or not** que vous y alliez ou non

 KEYWORD

which [wɪtʃ] *adj* **1** (*interrogative, direct, indirect*) quel(le); **which picture do you want?** quel tableau voulez-vous?; **which one?** lequel (laquelle)?
2: **in which case** auquel cas; **we got there at 8pm, by which time the cinema was full** quand nous sommes arrivés à 20h, le cinéma était complet
▷ *pron* **1** (*interrogative*) lequel (laquelle), lesquels (lesquelles) *pl*; **I don't mind which** peu importe lequel; **which (of these) are yours?** lesquels sont à vous?; **tell me which you want** dites-moi lesquels *or* ceux que vous voulez
2 (*relative: subject*) qui; (: *object*) que; sur/vers *etc* lequel (laquelle) (*NB: à* + *lequel* = **auquel**; *de* + *lequel* = **duquel**); **the apple you ate/which is on the table** la pomme que vous avez mangée/qui est sur la table; **the chair on which you are sitting** la chaise sur laquelle vous êtes assis; **the book of which you spoke** le livre dont vous avez parlé; **he said he knew, which is true/I was afraid of** il a dit qu'il le savait, ce qui est vrai/ce que je craignais; **after which** après quoi

whichever [wɪtʃ'ɛvəʳ] *adj*: **take ~ book you prefer** prenez le livre que vous préférez, peu importe lequel; **~ book you take** quel que soit le livre que vous preniez

while [waɪl] *n* moment *m* ▷ *conj* pendant que; (*as long as*) tant que; (*as, whereas*) alors que; (*though*) bien que + *sub*, quoique + *sub*; **for a ~** pendant quelque temps; **in a ~** dans un moment

whilst [waɪlst] *conj* = **while**

whim [wɪm] *n* caprice *m*

whine [waɪn] *n* gémissement *m*; (*of engine, siren*) plainte stridente ▷ *vi*

W

gémir, geindre, pleurnicher; (dog,
engine, siren) gémir
whip [wɪp] n fouet m; (for riding)
cravache f; (Pol: person) chef m de file
(assurant la discipline dans son groupe
parlementaire) ▷ vt fouetter; (snatch)
enlever (or sortir) brusquement;
whipped cream n crème fouettée
whirl [wəːl] vi tourbillonner; (dancers)
tournoyer ▷ vt faire tourbillonner;
faire tournoyer
whisk [wɪsk] n (Culin) fouet m ▷ vt
(eggs) fouetter, battre; **to ~ sb away**
or **off** emmener qn rapidement
whiskers ['wɪskəz] npl (of animal)
moustaches fpl; (of man) favoris mpl
whisky, (IRISH, US) **whiskey** ['wɪskɪ]
n whisky m
whisper ['wɪspər] n chuchotement m
▷ vt, vi chuchoter
whistle ['wɪsl] n (sound) sifflement
m; (object) sifflet m ▷ vi siffler ▷ vt
siffler, siffloter
white [waɪt] adj blanc (blanche); (with
fear) blême ▷ n blanc m; (person) blanc
(blanche); **White House** n (US): **the
White House** la Maison-Blanche;
whitewash n (paint) lait m de chaux
▷ vt blanchir à la chaux; (fig) blanchir
whiting ['waɪtɪŋ] n (pl inv: fish)
merlan m
Whitsun ['wɪtsn] n la Pentecôte
whittle ['wɪtl] vt: **to ~ away, to ~
down** (costs) réduire, rogner
whizz [wɪz] vi aller (or passer) à toute
vitesse
who [huː] pron qui
whoever [huːˈɛvər] pron: **~ finds it**
celui (celle) qui le trouve (, qui que
ce soit), quiconque le trouve; **ask ~
you like** demandez à qui vous voulez;
~ he marries qui que ce soit or quelle
que soit la personne qu'il épouse;
~ told you that? qui a bien pu vous
dire ça?, qui donc vous a dit ça?
whole [həul] adj (complete) entier(-
ière), tout(e); (not broken) intact(e),
complet(-ète) ▷ n (entire unit) tout

m; (all): **the ~ of** la totalité de,
tout(e) le; **the ~ of the town** la ville
tout entière; **on the ~, as a ~** dans
l'ensemble; **wholefood(s)** n(pl)
aliments complets; **wholeheartedly**
[həulˈhɑːtɪdlɪ] adv sans réserve;
to agree wholeheartedly être
entièrement d'accord; **wholemeal**
adj (BRIT: flour, bread) complet(-ète);
wholesale n (vente f en) gros m
▷ adj (price) de gros; (destruction)
systématique; **wholewheat**
adj = **wholemeal**; **wholly** adv
entièrement, tout à fait

 KEYWORD

whom [huːm] pron **1** (interrogative)
qui; **whom did you see?** qui avez-
vous vu?; **to whom did you give it?**
à qui l'avez-vous donné?
2 (relative) que à /de etc qui; **the man
whom I saw/to whom I spoke**
l'homme que j'ai vu/à qui j'ai parlé

whore [hɔːr] n (inf: pej) putain f

 KEYWORD

whose [huːz] adj **1** (possessive,
interrogative): **whose book is this?,
whose is this book?** à qui est ce
livre?; **whose pencil have you
taken?** à qui est le crayon que vous
avez pris?, c'est le crayon de qui que
vous avez pris?; **whose daughter
are you?** de qui êtes-vous la fille?
2 (possessive, relative): **the man
whose son you rescued** l'homme
dont or de qui vous avez sauvé le fils;
**the girl whose sister you were
speaking to** la fille à la sœur de qui or
de laquelle vous parliez; **the woman
whose car was stolen** la femme
dont la voiture a été volée
▷ pron à qui; **whose is this?** à qui
est ceci?; **I know whose it is** je sais
à qui c'est

away) couper le souffle à; **the ~(s)** (*Mus*) les instruments *mpl* à vent

wind² [*pt, pp* **wound**] [waɪnd, waʊnd] *vt* enrouler; (*wrap*) envelopper; (*clock, toy*) remonter ▷ *vi* (*road, river*) serpenter; **wind down** *vt* (*car window*) baisser; (*fig: production, business*) réduire progressivement; **wind up** *vt* (*clock*) remonter; (*debate*) terminer, clôturer

windfall ['wɪndfɔːl] *n* coup *m* de chance

wind farm *n* ferme *f* éolienne

winding ['waɪndɪŋ] *adj* (*road*) sinueux(-euse); (*staircase*) tournant(e)

windmill ['wɪndmɪl] *n* moulin *m* à vent

window ['wɪndəu] *n* fenêtre *f*; (*in car, train: also*: **~pane**) vitre *f*; (*in shop etc*) vitrine *f*; **window box** *n* jardinière *f*; **window cleaner** *n* (*person*) laveur(-euse) de vitres; **window pane** *n* vitre *f*, carreau *m*; **window seat** *n* (*on plane*) place *f* côté hublot; **windowsill** *n* (*inside*) appui *m* de la fenêtre; (*outside*) rebord *m* de la fenêtre

windscreen ['wɪndskriːn] *n* pare-brise *m inv*; **windscreen wiper** *n* essuie-glace *m inv*

windshield ['wɪndʃiːld] (*us*) *n* = **windscreen**

windsurfing ['wɪndsəːfɪŋ] *n* planche *f* à voile

wind turbine [-təːbaɪn] *n* éolienne *f*

windy ['wɪndɪ] *adj* (*day*) de vent, venteux(-euse); (*place, weather*) venteux; **it's ~** il y a du vent

wine [waɪn] *n* vin *m*; **wine bar** *n* bar *m* à vin; **wine glass** *n* verre *m* à vin; **wine list** *n* carte *f* des vins; **wine tasting** *n* dégustation *f* (de vins)

wing [wɪŋ] *n* aile *f*; **wings** *npl* (*Theat*) coulisses *fpl*; **wing mirror** *n* (*BRIT*) rétroviseur latéral

wink [wɪŋk] *n* clin *m* d'œil ▷ *vi* faire un clin d'œil; (*blink*) cligner des yeux

winner ['wɪnər] *n* gagnant(e)

winning ['wɪnɪŋ] *adj* (*team*) gagnant(e); (*goal*) décisif(-ive); (*charming*) charmeur(-euse)

winter ['wɪntər] *n* hiver *m* ▷ *vi* hiverner; **in ~** en hiver; **winter sports** *npl* sports *mpl* d'hiver; **wintertime** *n* hiver *m*

wipe [waɪp] *n*: **to give sth a ~** donner un coup de torchon/de chiffon/d'éponge à qch ▷ *vt* essuyer; (*erase: tape*) effacer; **to ~ one's nose** se moucher; **wipe out** *vt* (*debt*) éteindre, amortir; (*memory*) effacer; (*destroy*) anéantir; **wipe up** *vt* essuyer

wire ['waɪər] *n* fil *m* (de fer); (*Elec*) fil électrique; (*Tel*) télégramme *m* ▷ *vt* (*house*) faire l'installation électrique de; (*also*: **~ up**) brancher; (*person: send telegram to*) télégraphier à

wireless ['waɪəlɪs] *adj* sans fil; **wireless technology** *n* technologie *f* sans fil

wiring ['waɪərɪŋ] *n* (*Elec*) installation *f* électrique

wisdom ['wɪzdəm] *n* sagesse *f*; (*of action*) prudence *f*; **wisdom tooth** *n* dent *f* de sagesse

wise [waɪz] *adj* sage, prudent(e); (*remark*) judicieux(-euse)

wish [wɪʃ] *n* (*desire*) désir *m*; (*specific desire*) souhait *m*, vœu *m* ▷ *vt* souhaiter, désirer, vouloir; **best ~es** (*on birthday etc*) meilleurs vœux; **with best ~es** (*in letter*) bien amicalement; **to ~ sb goodbye** dire au revoir à qn; **he ~ed me well** il m'a souhaité bonne chance; **to ~ to do/sb to do** désirer *or* vouloir faire/que qn fasse; **to ~ for** souhaiter

wistful ['wɪstful] *adj* mélancolique

wit [wɪt] *n* (*also*: **~s**: *intelligence*) intelligence *f*, esprit *m*; (*presence of mind*) présence *f* d'esprit; (*wittiness*) esprit; (*person*) homme/femme d'esprit

witch [wɪtʃ] *n* sorcière *f*

KEYWORD

with [wɪð, wɪθ] *prep* **1** (*in the company of*) avec; (: *at the home of*) chez; **we stayed with friends** nous avons logé chez des amis; **I'll be with you in a minute** je suis à vous dans un instant **2** (*descriptive*): **a room with a view** une chambre avec vue; **the man with the grey hat/blue eyes** l'homme au chapeau gris/aux yeux bleus **3** (*indicating manner, means, cause*): **with tears in her eyes** les larmes aux yeux; **to walk with a stick** marcher avec une canne; **red with anger** rouge de colère; **to shake with fear** trembler de peur; **to fill sth with water** remplir qch d'eau **4** (*in phrases*): **I'm with you** (*I understand*) je vous suis; **to be with it** (*inf: up-to-date*) être dans le vent

withdraw [wɪθ'drɔː] *vt* (*irreg: like draw*) retirer ▷ *vi* se retirer; **withdrawal** *n* retrait *m*; (*Med*) état *m* de manque; **withdrawn** *pp of* **withdraw** ▷ *adj* (*person*) renfermé(e) **withdrew** [wɪθ'druː] *pt of* **withdraw** **wither** ['wɪðər] *vi* se faner **withhold** [wɪθ'həuld] *vt* (*irreg: like hold*) (*money*) retenir; (*decision*) remettre; **to ~ (from)** (*permission*) refuser (à); (*information*) cacher (à) **within** [wɪð'ɪn] *prep* à l'intérieur de ▷ *adv* à l'intérieur; **~ his reach** à sa portée; **~ sight of** en vue de; **~ a mile of** à moins d'un mille de; **~ the week** avant la fin de la semaine **without** [wɪð'aut] *prep* sans; **~ a coat** sans manteau; **~ speaking** sans parler; **to go** *or* **do ~ sth** se passer de qch **withstand** [wɪθ'stænd] *vt* (*irreg: like stand*) résister à **witness** ['wɪtnɪs] *n* (*person*) témoin *m* ▷ *vt* (*event*) être témoin de; (*document*)

attester l'authenticité de; **to bear ~ to sth** témoigner de qch **witty** ['wɪtɪ] *adj* spirituel(le), plein(e) d'esprit **wives** [waɪvz] *npl of* **wife** **wizard** ['wɪzəd] *n* magicien *m* **wk** *abbr* = **week** **wobble** ['wɔbl] *vi* trembler; (*chair*) branler **woe** [wəu] *n* malheur *m* **woke** [wəuk] *pt of* **wake** **woken** ['wəukn] *pp of* **wake** **wolf** (*pl* **wolves**) [wulf, wulvz] *n* loup *m* **woman** (*pl* **women**) ['wumən, 'wɪmɪn] *n* femme *f* ▷ *cpd*: **~ doctor** femme *f* médecin; **~ teacher** professeur *m* femme **womb** [wuːm] *n* (*Anat*) utérus *m* **women** ['wɪmɪn] *npl of* **woman** **won** [wʌn] *pt, pp of* **win** **wonder** ['wʌndər] *n* merveille *f*, miracle *m*; (*feeling*) émerveillement *m* ▷ *vi*: **to ~ whether/why** se demander si/pourquoi; **to ~ at** (*surprise*) s'étonner de; (*admiration*) s'émerveiller de; **to ~ about** songer à; **it's no ~ that** il n'est pas étonnant que + *sub*; **wonderful** *adj* merveilleux(-euse) **won't** [wəunt] = **will not** **wood** [wud] *n* (*timber, forest*) bois *m*; **wooden** *adj* en bois; (*fig: actor*) raide; (: *performance*) qui manque de naturel; **woodwind** *n*: **the woodwind** les bois *mpl*; **woodwork** *n* menuiserie *f* **wool** [wul] *n* laine *f*; **to pull the ~ over sb's eyes** (*fig*) en faire accroire à qn; **woollen**, (*us*) **woolen** *adj* or en laine; **woolly**, (*us*) **wooly** *adj* laineux(-euse); (*fig: ideas*) confus(e) **word** [wəːd] *n* mot *m*; (*spoken*) parole *f*; (*promise*) parole; (*news*) nouvelles *fpl* ▷ *vt* rédiger, formuler; **in other ~s** en d'autres termes; **to have a ~ with sb** toucher un mot à qn; **to break/keep one's ~** manquer à sa parole/tenir (sa) parole;

W

wording n termes mpl, langage m; (of document) libellé m; **word processing** n traitement m de texte; **word processor** n machine f de traitement de texte

wore [wɔːʳ] pt of **wear**

work [wəːk] n travail m; (Art, Literature) œuvre f ▷ vi travailler; (mechanism) marcher, fonctionner; (plan etc) marcher; (medicine) agir ▷ vt (clay, wood etc) travailler; (mine etc) exploiter; (machine) faire marcher or fonctionner; (miracles etc) faire; **works** n (BRIT: factory) usine f; **how does this ~?** comment est-ce que ça marche?; **the TV isn't ~ing** la télévision est en panne or ne marche pas; **to be out of ~** être au chômage or sans emploi; **to ~ loose** se défaire, se desserrer; **work out** vi (plans etc) marcher; (Sport) s'entraîner ▷ vt (problem) résoudre; (plan) élaborer; **it ~s out at £100** ça fait 100 livres; **worker** n travailleur(-euse), ouvrier(-ière); **work experience** n stage m; **workforce** n main-d'œuvre f; **working class** n classe ouvrière ▷ adj: **working-class** ouvrier(-ière), de la classe ouvrière; **working week** n semaine f de travail; **workman** (irreg) n ouvrier m; **work of art** n œuvre f d'art; **workout** n (Sport) séance f d'entraînement; **work permit** n permis m de travail; **workplace** n lieu m de travail; **worksheet** n (Scol) feuille f d'exercices; **workshop** n atelier m; **work station** n poste m de travail; **work surface** n plan m de travail; **worktop** n plan m de travail

world [wəːld] n monde m ▷ cpd (champion) du monde; (power, war) mondial(e); **to think the ~ of sb** (fig) ne jurer que par qn; **World Cup** n: **the World Cup** (Football) la Coupe du monde; **world-wide** adj universel(le); **World-Wide Web** n: **the World-Wide Web** le Web

worm [wəːm] n (also: **earth~**) ver m

worn [wɔːn] pp of **wear** ▷ adj usé(e); **worn-out** adj (object) complètement usé(e); (person) épuisé(e)

worried ['wʌrɪd] adj inquiet(-ète); **to be ~ about sth** être inquiet au sujet de qch

worry ['wʌrɪ] n souci m ▷ vt inquiéter ▷ vi s'inquiéter, se faire du souci; **worrying** adj inquiétant(e)

worse [wəːs] adj pire, plus mauvais(e) ▷ adv plus mal ▷ n pire m; **to get ~** (condition, situation) empirer, se dégrader; **a change for the ~** une détérioration; **worsen** vt, vi empirer; **worse off** adj moins à l'aise financièrement; (fig): **you'll be worse off this way** ça ira moins bien de cette façon

worship ['wəːʃɪp] n culte m ▷ vt (God) rendre un culte à; (person) adorer

worst [wəːst] adj le (la) pire, le (la) plus mauvais(e) ▷ adv le plus mal ▷ n pire m; **at ~** au pis aller

worth [wəːθ] n valeur f ▷ adj: **to be ~** valoir; **it's ~ it** cela en vaut la peine, ça vaut la peine; **it is ~ one's while (to do)** ça vaut le coup (inf) (de faire); **worthless** adj qui ne vaut rien; **worthwhile** adj (activity) qui en vaut la peine; (cause) louable

worthy ['wəːðɪ] adj (person) digne; (motive) louable; **~ of** digne de

 KEYWORD

would [wʊd] aux vb **1** (conditional tense): **if you asked him he would do it** si vous le lui demandiez, il le ferait; **if you had asked him he would have done it** si vous le lui aviez demandé, il l'aurait fait

2 (in offers, invitations, requests): **would you like a biscuit?** voulez-vous un biscuit?; **would you close the door please?** voulez-vous fermer la porte, s'il vous plaît?

3 (in indirect speech): **I said I would do**

yellow ['jɛləu] *adj*, *n* jaune (*m*);
Yellow Pages® *npl* (*Tel*) pages *fpl*
jaunes

yes [jɛs] *adv* oui; (*answering negative question*) si ▷ *n* oui *m*; **to say ~ (to)**
dire oui (à)

yesterday ['jɛstədɪ] *adv*, *n* hier (*m*);
~ morning/evening hier matin/soir;
all day ~ toute la journée d'hier

yet [jɛt] *adv* encore; (*in questions*) déjà
▷ *conj* pourtant, néanmoins; **it is not finished ~** ce n'est pas encore fini *or*
toujours pas fini; **have you eaten ~?**
vous avez déjà mangé?; **the best ~**
le meilleur jusqu'ici *or* jusque-là; **as ~**
jusqu'ici, encore

yew [ju:] *n* if *m*

Yiddish ['jɪdɪʃ] *n* yiddish *m*

yield [ji:ld] *n* production *f*, rendement
m; (*Finance*) rapport *m* ▷ *vt* produire,
rendre, rapporter; (*surrender*) céder
▷ *vi* céder; (*us Aut*) céder la priorité

yob(bo) ['jɔb(əu)] *n* (*BRIT inf*)
loubar(d) *m*

yoga ['jəugə] *n* yoga *m*

yog(h)urt ['jɔgət] *n* yaourt *m*

yolk [jəuk] *n* jaune *m* (d'œuf)

○ KEYWORD

you [ju:] *pron* **1** (*subject*) tu; (: *polite form*) vous; (: *plural*) vous; **you are very kind** vous êtes très gentil; **you French enjoy your food** vous autres
Français, vous aimez bien manger;
you and I will go toi et moi *or* vous
et moi, nous irons; **there you are!**
vous voilà!

2 (*object: direct, indirect*) te, t' + *vowel*;
vous; **I know you** je te *or* vous
connais; **I gave it to you** je te l'ai
donné, je vous l'ai donné

3 (*stressed*) toi; vous; **I told you to do it** c'est à toi *or* vous que j'ai dit de le faire

4 (*after prep, in comparisons*) toi; vous;
it's for you c'est pour toi *or* vous;
she's younger than you elle est plus
jeune que toi *or* vous

5 (*impersonal: one*) on; **fresh air doe.**
you good l'air frais fait du bien; **you**
never know on ne sait jamais; **you**
can't do that! ça ne se fait pas!

you'd [ju:d] = **you had**; **you would**

you'll [ju:l] = **you will**; **you shall**

young [jʌŋ] *adj* jeune ▷ *npl* (*of animal*)
petits *mpl*; **the ~** (*people*) les jeunes, la
jeunesse; **my ~er brother** mon frère
cadet; **youngster** *n* jeune *m/f*; (*child*)
enfant *m/f*

your [jɔːʳ] *adj* ton (ta), tes *pl*; (*polite form, pl*) votre, vos *pl*; *see also* **my**

you're [juəʳ] = **you are**

yours [jɔːz] *pron* le (la) tien(ne), les
tiens (tiennes); (*polite form, pl*) le (la)
vôtre, les vôtres; vos *pl*; **is it ~?** c'est à toi (*or*
à vous)?; **a friend of ~** un(e) de tes
(*or* de vos) amis; *see also* **faithfully;**
mine¹; sincerely

yourself [jɔː'sɛlf] *pron* (*reflexive*) te;
(: *polite form*) vous; (*after prep*) toi;
vous; (*emphatic*) toi-même; vous-
même; *see also* **oneself; yourselves**
pl pron vous; (*emphatic*) vous-mêmes;
see also **oneself**

youth [ju:θ] *n* jeunesse *f*; (*young man*)
jeune homme *m*; **youth club** *n* centre
m de jeunes; **youthful** *adj* jeune;
(*enthusiasm etc*) juvénile; **youth**
hostel *n* auberge *f* de jeunesse

you've [ju:v] = **you have**

Yugoslav ['ju:gəuslɑːv] *adj* (*Hist*)
yougoslave ▷ *n* Yougoslave *m/f*

Yugoslavia [ju:gəu'slɑːvɪə] *n* (*Hist*)
Yougoslavie *f*

Z

zoology [zuːˈɒlədʒɪ] n zoologie f
zoom [zuːm] vi: **to ~ past** passer en trombe; **zoom lens** n zoom m
zucchini [zuːˈkiːnɪ] n (US) courgette f

zeal [ziːl] n (revolutionary etc) ferveur f; (keenness) ardeur f, zèle m
zebra [ˈziːbrə] n zèbre m; **zebra crossing** n (BRIT) passage clouté or pour piétons
zero [ˈzɪərəʊ] n zéro m
zest [zɛst] n entrain m, élan m; (of lemon etc) zeste m
zigzag [ˈzɪgzæg] n zigzag m ▷ vi zigzaguer, faire des zigzags
Zimbabwe [zɪmˈbɑːbwɪ] n Zimbabwe m
zinc [zɪŋk] n zinc m
zip [zɪp] n (also: **~ fastener**) fermeture f éclair® or à glissière ▷ vt (file) zipper; (also: **~ up**) fermer (avec une fermeture éclair®); **zip code** n (US) code postal; **zip file** n (Comput) fichier m zip inv; **zipper** n (US) = **zip**
zit [zɪt] (inf) n bouton m
zodiac [ˈzəʊdɪæk] n zodiaque m
zone [zəʊn] n zone f
zoo [zuː] n zoo m